GIVE ME LIBERTY!

BRIEF FOURTH EDITION

OKLAHOMA STATE UNIVERSITY

NORTON CUSTOM

W. W. NORTON & COMPANY, INC.

NEW YORK • LONDON

W. W. Norton & Company has been independent since its founding in 1923, when William Warder Norton and Mary D. Herter Norton first published lectures delivered at the People's Institute, the adult education division of New York City's Cooper Union. The Nortons soon expanded their program beyond the Institute, publishing books by celebrated academics from America and abroad. By mid-century, the two major pillars of Norton's publishing program—trade books and college texts—were firmly established. In the 1950s, the Norton family transferred control of the company to its employees, and today—with a staff of four hundred and a comparable number of trade, college, and professional titles published each year—W. W. Norton & Company stands as the largest and oldest publishing house owned wholly by its employees.

Materials are included from the following:

Give Me Liberty, Brief Fourth Edition (Eric Foner)
Copyright © 2014, 2012 by Eric Foner
The Norton Mix: History
Copyright © 2013 by W. W. Norton & Company, Inc.

Editor: Katie Hannah
Managing editor, College: Marian Johnson
Project editor: Hannah Bachman
Editorial assistant: Laura Dragonette
Production Manager: Diana Spiegle
Design Director: Rubina Yeh

ISBN: 978-0-393-27682-4

W. W. Norton & Company, Inc., 500 Fifth Avenue, New York, NY 10110
www.wwnorton.com
W. W. Norton & Company, Ltd., Castle House, 75/76 Wells Street, London W1T3QT

1 2 3 4 5 6 7 8 9 0

CONTENTS

READINGS FROM THE *NORTON MIX: HISTORY*

GIVE ME LIBERTY!

Brief Fourth Edition

GIVE ME LIBERTY!

AN AMERICAN HISTORY

★

Brief Fourth Edition

ERIC FONER

W · W · NORTON & COMPANY

NEW YORK · LONDON

For my mother, Liza Foner (1909–2005), an accomplished artist who lived through most of the twentieth century and into the twenty-first

W. W. Norton & Company has been independent since its founding in 1923, when William Warder Norton and Mary D. Herter Norton first published lectures delivered at the People's Institute, the adult education division of New York City's Cooper Union. The firm soon expanded its program beyond the Institute, publishing books by celebrated academics from America and abroad. By mid-century, the two major pillars of Norton's publishing program—trade books and college texts—were firmly established. In the 1950s, the Norton family transferred control of the company to its employees, and today—with a staff of 400 and a comparable number of trade, college, and professional titles published each year—W. W. Norton & Company stands as the largest and oldest publishing house owned wholly by its employees.

Editor: Steve Forman
Associate Editor: Justin Cahill
Editorial Assistant: Penelope Lin
Managing Editor, College: Marian Johnson
Managing Editor, College Digital Media: Kim Yi
Project Editor: Diane Cipollone
Copy Editor: Elizabeth Dubrulle
Marketing Manager: Sarah England
Media Editors: Steve Hoge, Tacy Quinn
Assistant Editor, Media: Stefani Wallace
Production Manager: Sean Mintus
Art Director: Rubina Yeh
Designer: Chin-Yee Lai
Photo Editor: Stephanie Romeo
Photo Research: Donna Ranieri
Permissions Manager: Megan Jackson
Permissions Clearing: Bethany Salminen
Composition and Layout: Jouve
Manufacturing: Transcontinental

Library of Congress Cataloging-in-Publication Data has been applied for.

ISBN 978-0-393-92032-1

W. W. Norton & Company, Inc., 500 Fifth Avenue, New York, NY 10110-0017
wwnorton.com

W. W. Norton & Company Ltd., Castle House, 75/76 Wells Street, London W1T 3QT
1 2 3 4 5 6 7 8 9 0

Contents

15. "WHAT IS FREEDOM?": RECONSTRUCTION, 1865–1877 ... 441

APPENDIX

MAPS

TABLES AND FIGURES

PREFACE

Since it originally appeared late in 2004, *Give Me Liberty! An American History* has gone through three editions and been adopted for use in survey courses at close to one thousand two- and four-year colleges in the United States, as well as a good number overseas. Of course, I am extremely gratified by this response. The book offers students a clear narrative of American history from the earliest days of European exploration and conquest of the New World to the first decade of the twenty-first century. Its central theme is the changing contours of American freedom.

The comments I have received from instructors and students encourage me to think that *Give Me Liberty!* has worked well in the classroom. These comments have also included many valuable suggestions, ranging from corrections of typographical and factual errors to thoughts about subjects that need more extensive treatment. In preparing new editions of the book I have tried to take these suggestions into account, as well as incorporating the insights of recent historical scholarship.

Since the original edition was written, I have frequently been asked to produce a more succinct version of the textbook, which now runs to some 1,200 pages. This Brief Edition is a response to these requests. The text of the current volume is about one-third shorter than the full version. The result, I believe, is a book more suited to use in one-semester survey courses, classes where the instructor wishes to supplement the text with additional readings, and in other situations where a briefer volume is desirable.

Since some publishers have been known to assign the task of reduction in cases like this to editors rather than the actual author, I wish to emphasize that I did all the cutting and necessary rewriting for this Brief Edition myself. My guiding principle was to preserve the coverage, structure, and emphases of the regular edition and to compress the book by eliminating details of secondary importance, streamlining the narrative of events, and avoiding unnecessary repetition. While the book is significantly shorter, no subject treated in the full edition has been eliminated entirely and nothing essential, I believe, has been sacrificed. The sequence of chapters and subjects remains the same, and the freedom theme is present and operative throughout.

In abridging the textbook I have retained the original interpretive framework as well as the new emphases added when the second and third editions of the book were published. The second edition incorporated new material about the history of Native Americans, an area of American history that has been the subject of significant new scholarship in the past few years. It also devoted greater attention to the history of immigration and the controversies surrounding it—issues of considerable relevance to American social and political life today.

The most significant change in the third edition reflected my desire to place American history more fully in a global context. In the past few years, scholars writing about the American past have sought to delineate the influences of the United States on the rest of the world as well as the global developments that have helped to shape the course of events here at home. They have also devoted greater attention to transnational processes—the expansion of empires, international labor migrations, the rise and fall of slavery, the globalization of economic enterprise—that cannot be understood solely within the confines of one country's national boundaries. Without seeking in any way to homogenize the history of individual nations or neglect the domestic forces that have shaped American development, this edition retains this emphasis.

The most significant changes in this Fourth Edition reflect my desire to integrate more fully into the narrative the history of American religion. Today, this is a thriving subfield of American historical writing, partly because of the increased prominence in our own time of debates over the relations between government and religion and over the definition of religious liberty—issues that are deeply rooted in the American experience. The Brief Edition also employs a bright new design for the text and its various elements. The popular Voices of Freedom feature—a pair of excerpts from primary source documents in each chapter that illuminate divergent interpretations of freedom—is present here. So too are the useful chapter opening focus questions, which appear in the running heads of the relevant text pages as well. There are chapter opening chronologies and end-of-chapter review pages with questions and key terms. As a new feature in the Brief Edition there are marginal glosses in the text pages that are meant to highlight key points and indicate the chapter structure for students. They are also useful means for review. The Brief Edition features more than 400 illustrations and over 100 captioned maps in easy to read four-color renditions. The Further Readings sections appear in the Appendix along with the Glossary and the collection of key documents. The Brief Edition is fully supported by the same array of print and electronic supplements that support the other editions of *Give Me Liberty!* These materials have been revised to match the content of the Brief Edition.

Americans have always had a divided attitude toward history. On the one hand, they tend to be remarkably future-oriented, dismissing events of even the recent past as "ancient history" and sometimes seeing history as a burden to be overcome, a prison from which to escape. On the other hand, like many other peoples, Americans have always looked to history for a sense of personal or group identity and of national cohesiveness. This is why so many Americans devote time and energy to tracing their family trees and why they visit historical museums and National Park Service historical sites in ever-increasing numbers. My hope is that this book will help to convince readers with all degrees of interest that history does matter to them.

The novelist and essayist James Baldwin once observed that history "does not refer merely, or even principally, to the past. On the contrary, the great force of history comes from the fact that we carry it within us, . . . [that] history is literally present in all that we do." As Baldwin recognized, the power of history is evident in our own world. Especially in a political democracy like the United States, whose government is designed to rest on the consent of informed citizens, knowledge of the past is essential—not only for those of us whose profession is the teaching and writing of history, but for everyone. History, to be sure, does not offer simple lessons or immediate answers to current questions. Knowing the history of immigration to the United States, and all of the tensions, turmoil, and aspirations associated with it, for example, does not tell us what current immigration policy ought to be. But without that knowledge, we have no way of understanding which approaches have worked and which have not—essential information for the formulation of future public policy.

History, it has been said, is what the present chooses to remember about the past. Rather than a fixed collection of facts, or a group of interpretations that cannot be challenged, our understanding of history is constantly changing. There is nothing unusual in the fact that each generation rewrites history to meet its own needs, or that scholars disagree among themselves on basic questions like the causes of the Civil War or the reasons for the Great Depression. Precisely because each generation asks different questions of the past, each generation formulates different answers. The past thirty years have witnessed a remarkable expansion of the scope of historical study. The experiences of groups neglected by earlier scholars, including women, African-Americans, working people, and others, have received unprecedented attention from historians. New subfields—social history, cultural history, and family history among them—have taken their place alongside traditional political and diplomatic history.

Give Me Liberty! draws on this voluminous historical literature to present an up-to-date and inclusive account of the American past, paying due attention to the experience of diverse groups of Americans while in no way neglecting the events and processes Americans have experienced in common. It devotes serious attention to political, social, cultural, and economic history, and to their interconnections. The narrative brings together major events and prominent leaders with the many groups of ordinary people who make up American society. *Give Me Liberty!* has a rich cast of characters, from Thomas Jefferson to campaigners for woman suffrage, from Franklin D. Roosevelt to former slaves seeking to breathe meaning into emancipation during and after the Civil War.

The unifying theme of freedom that runs through the text gives shape to the narrative and integrates the numerous strands that make up the American experience. This approach builds on that of my earlier book, *The Story of American Freedom* (1998), although *Give Me Liberty!* places events and personalities in the foreground and is more geared to the structure of the introductory survey course.

Freedom, and battles to define its meaning, has long been central to my own scholarship and undergraduate teaching, which focuses on the nineteenth century and especially the era of Civil War and Reconstruction (1850–1877). This was a time when the future of slavery tore the nation apart and emancipation produced a national debate over what rights the former slaves, and all Americans, should enjoy as free citizens. I have found that attention to clashing definitions of freedom and the struggles of different groups to achieve freedom as they understood it offers a way of making sense of the bitter battles and vast transformations of that pivotal era. I believe that the same is true for American history as a whole.

No idea is more fundamental to Americans' sense of themselves as individuals and as a nation than freedom. The central term in our political language, freedom—or liberty, with which it is almost always used interchangeably—is deeply embedded in the record of our history and the language of everyday life. The Declaration of Independence lists liberty among mankind's inalienable rights; the Constitution announces its purpose as securing liberty's blessings. The United States fought the Civil War to bring about a new birth of freedom, World War II for the Four Freedoms, and the Cold War to defend the Free World. Americans' love of liberty has been represented by liberty poles, liberty caps, and statues of liberty, and acted out by burning stamps and burning draft cards, by running away from slavery, and by demonstrating for the right to vote. "Every man in the street, white, black, red or yellow," wrote the educator and statesman Ralph Bunche in 1940, "knows that this is 'the land of the free' . . . 'the cradle of liberty.'"

The very universality of the idea of freedom, however, can be misleading. Freedom is not a fixed, timeless category with a single unchanging definition. Indeed, the history of the United States is, in part, a story of debates, disagreements, and struggles over freedom. Crises like the American Revolution, the Civil War, and the Cold War have permanently transformed the idea of freedom. So too have demands by various groups of Americans to enjoy greater freedom. The meaning of freedom has been constructed not only in congressional debates and political treatises, but on plantations and picket lines, in parlors and even bedrooms.

Over the course of our history, American freedom has been both a reality and a mythic ideal—a living truth for millions of Americans, a cruel mockery for others. For some, freedom has been what some scholars call a "habit of the heart," an ideal so taken for granted that it is lived out but rarely analyzed. For others, freedom is not a birthright but a distant goal that has inspired great sacrifice.

Give Me Liberty! draws attention to three dimensions of freedom that have been critical in American history: (1) the meanings of freedom; (2) the social conditions that make freedom possible; and (3) the boundaries of freedom that determine who is entitled to enjoy freedom and who is not. All have changed over time.

In the era of the American Revolution, for example, freedom was primarily a set of rights enjoyed in public activity—including the right of a community to be governed by laws to which its representatives had consented and of individuals to engage in religious worship without governmental interference. In the nineteenth century, freedom came to be closely identified with each person's opportunity to develop to the fullest his or her innate talents. In the twentieth, the "ability to choose," in both public and private life, became perhaps the dominant understanding of freedom. This development was encouraged by the explosive growth of the consumer marketplace which offered Americans an unprecedented array of goods with which to satisfy their needs and desires. During the 1960s, a crucial chapter in the history of American freedom, the idea of personal freedom was extended into virtually every realm, from attire and "lifestyle" to relations between the sexes. Thus, over time, more and more areas of life have been drawn into Americans' debates about the meaning of freedom.

A second important dimension of freedom focuses on the social conditions necessary to allow freedom to flourish. What kinds of economic institutions and relationships best encourage individual freedom? In the colonial era and for more than a century after independence, the answer centered on economic autonomy, enshrined in the glorification of the independent small producer—the farmer, skilled craftsman, or shopkeeper—who did not have to depend on another person for his livelihood. As the industrial economy matured, new conceptions of economic freedom came to the fore: "liberty of contract" in the Gilded Age, "industrial freedom" (a say in corporate decision making) in the Progressive era, economic security during the New Deal, and, more recently, the ability to enjoy mass consumption within a market economy.

The boundaries of freedom, the third dimension of this theme, have inspired some of the most intense struggles in American history. Although founded on the premise that liberty is an entitlement of all humanity, the United States for much of its history deprived many of its own people of freedom. Non-whites have rarely enjoyed the same access to freedom as white Americans. The belief in equal opportunity as the birthright of all Americans has coexisted with persistent efforts to limit freedom by race, gender, class, and in other ways.

Less obvious, perhaps, is the fact that one person's freedom has frequently been linked to another's servitude. In the colonial era and nineteenth century, expanding freedom for many Americans rested on the lack of freedom—slavery, indentured servitude, the subordinate position of women—for others. By the same token, it has been through battles at the boundaries—the efforts of racial minorities, women, and others to secure greater freedom—that the meaning and experience of freedom have been deepened and the concept extended into new realms.

Time and again in American history, freedom has been transformed by the demands of excluded groups for inclusion. The idea of freedom as a universal birthright owes much to abolitionists who sought to extend the blessings of liberty to blacks and to immigrant groups who insisted on full recognition as American citizens. The principle of equal protection of the law without regard to race, which became a central element of American freedom, arose from the antislavery struggle and Civil War and was reinvigorated by the civil rights revolution of the 1960s, which called itself the "freedom movement." The battle for the right of free speech by labor radicals and birth control advocates in the first part of the twentieth century helped to make civil liberties an essential element of freedom for all Americans.

Freedom is the oldest of clichés and the most modern of aspirations. At various times in our history, it has served as the rallying cry of the powerless and as a justification of the status quo. Freedom helps to bind our culture together and exposes the contradictions between what America claims to be and what it sometimes has been. American history is not a narrative of continual progress toward greater and greater freedom. As the abolitionist Thomas Wentworth Higginson noted after the Civil War, "revolutions may go backward." While freedom can be achieved, it may also be taken away. This happened, for example, when the equal rights granted to former slaves immediately after the Civil War were essentially nullified during the era of segregation. As was said in the eighteenth century, the price of freedom is eternal vigilance.

In the early twenty-first century, freedom continues to play a central role in our political and social life and thought. It is invoked by individuals and groups of all kinds, from critics of economic globalization to those who seek to export American freedom overseas. As with the longer version of the book, I hope that this Brief Edition of *Give Me Liberty!* will offer beginning students a clear account of the course of American history, and of its central theme, freedom, which today remains as varied, contentious, and ever-changing as America itself.

ACKNOWLEDGMENTS

All works of history are, to a considerable extent, collaborative books, in that every writer builds on the research and writing of previous scholars. This is especially true of a textbook that covers the entire American experience, over more than five centuries. My greatest debt is to the innumerable historians on whose work I have drawn in preparing this volume. The Suggested Reading list in the Appendix offers only a brief introduction to the vast body of historical scholarship that has influenced and informed this book. More specifically, however, I wish to thank the following scholars, who generously read portions of this work and offered valuable comments, criticisms, and suggestions:

Wayne Ackerson, Salisbury University
Mary E. Adams, City College of San Francisco
Jeff Adler, University of Florida
David Anderson, Louisiana Tech University
John Barr, Lone Star College, Kingwood
Lauren Braun-Strumfels, Raritan Valley Community College
James Broussard, Lebanon Valley College
Michael Bryan, Greenville Technical College
Stephanie Cole, The University of Texas at Arlington
Ashley Cruseturner, McLennan Community College
Jim Dudlo, Brookhaven College
Beverly Gage, Yale University
Monica Gisolfi, University of North Carolina, Wilmington
Adam Goudsouzian, University of Memphis
Mike Green, Community College of Southern Nevada
Vanessa Gunther, California State University, Fullerton
David E. Hamilton, University of Kentucky
Brian Harding, Mott Community College
Sandra Harvey, Lone Star College–Cy Fair
April Holm, University of Mississippi
David Hsiung, Juniata College
James Karmel, Harford Community College
Kelly Knight, Penn State University
Marianne Leeper, Trinity Valley Community College
Jeffrey K. Lucas, University of North Carolina at Pembroke
Tina Margolis, Westchester Community College
Kent McGaughy, HCC Northwest College
James Mills, University of Texas, Brownsville
Gil Montemayor, McLennan Community College
Jonathan Noyalas, Lord Fairfax Community College
Robert M. O'Brien, Lone Star College–Cy Fair

Joseph Palermo, California State University, Sacramento

Ann Plane, University of California, Santa Barbara

Nancy Marie Robertson, Indiana University–Purdue University
  Indianapolis

Esther Robinson, Lone Star College–Cy Fair

Richard Samuelson, California State University, San Bernadino

Diane Sager, Maple Woods Community College

John Shaw, Portland Community College

Mark Spencer, Brock University

David Stebenne, Ohio State University

Judith Stein, City College, City University of New York

George Stevens, Duchess Community College

Robert Tinkler, California State University, Chico

Elaine Thompson, Louisiana Tech University

David Weiman, Barnard College

William Young, Maple Woods Community College

I am particularly grateful to my colleagues in the Columbia University Department of History: Pablo Piccato, for his advice on Latin American history; Evan Haefeli and Ellen Baker, who read and made many suggestions for improvements in their areas of expertise (colonial America and the history of the West, respectively); and Sarah Phillips, who offered advice on treating the history of the environment.

I am also deeply indebted to the graduate students at Columbia University's Department of History who helped with this project. Theresa Ventura offered invaluable assistance in gathering material for the new sections placing American history in a global context. April Holm provided similar assistance for new coverage in this edition of the history of American religion and debates over religious freedom. James Delbourgo conducted research for the chapters on the colonial era. Beverly Gage did the same for the twentieth century. Daniel Freund provided all-round research assistance. Victoria Cain did a superb job of locating images. I also want to thank my colleagues Elizabeth Blackmar and Alan Brinkley for offering advice and encouragement throughout the writing of this book.

Many thanks to Joshua Brown, director of the American Social History Project, whose website, History Matters, lists innumerable online resources for the study of American history. Nancy Robertson at IUIPUI did a superb job revising and enhancing the in-book pedagogy. Monica Gisolfi (University of North Carolina, Wilmington) and Robert Tinkler (California State University, Chico) did excellent work on the Instructor's Manual and Test Bank. Kathleen Thomas (University of Wisconsin, Stout) helped greatly in the revisions of the companion media packages.

At W. W. Norton & Company, Steve Forman was an ideal editor—patient, encouraging, and always ready to offer sage advice. I would also like to thank Steve's assistants, Justin Cahill and Penelope Lin, for their indispensable and always cheerful help on all aspects of the project; Ellen Lohman and Debbie Nichols for their careful copyediting and proof reading work. Stephanie Romeo and Donna Ranieri for their resourceful attention to the illustrations program; Hope Miller Goodell and Chin-Yee Lai for their refinements of the book design; Mike Fodera and Debra Morton-Hoyt for splendid work on the covers for the Fourth Edition; Kim Yi for keeping the many threads of the project aligned and then tying them together; Sean Mintus for his efficiency and care in book production; Steve Hoge for orchestrating the rich media package that accompanies the textbook; Jessica Brannon-Wranosky, Texas A&M University–Commerce, our digital media author for the terrific new web quizzes and outlines; Volker Janssen, California State University, Fullerton, for the helpful new online reading exercises; Nicole Netherton, Steve Dunn, and Mike Wright for their alert reads of the U.S. survey market and their hard work in helping establish *Give Me Liberty!* within it; and Drake McFeely, Roby Harrington, and Julia Reidhead for maintaining Norton as an independent, employee-owned publisher dedicated to excellence in its work.

Many students may have heard stories of how publishing companies alter the language and content of textbooks in an attempt to maximize sales and avoid alienating any potential reader. In this case, I can honestly say that W. W. Norton allowed me a free hand in writing the book and, apart from the usual editorial corrections, did not try to influence its content at all. For this I thank them, while I accept full responsibility for the interpretations presented and for any errors the book may contain. Since no book of this length can be entirely free of mistakes, I welcome readers to send me corrections at ef17@columbia.edu.

My greatest debt, as always, is to my family—my wife, Lynn Garafola, for her good-natured support while I was preoccupied by a project that consumed more than its fair share of my time and energy, and my daughter, Daria, who while a ninth and tenth grader read every chapter as it was written and offered invaluable suggestions about improving the book's clarity, logic, and grammar.

Eric Foner
New York City
July 2013

CHAPTER 1

A NEW WORLD

★

France Bringing the Faith to the Indians of New France. European nations justified colonization with the argument that they were bringing Christianity—without which freedom was impossible—to Native Americans. In this painting from the 1670s, an Indian kneels before a female representation of France. Both hold a painting of the Trinity.

FOCUS
QUESTIONS

- *What were the major patterns of Native American life in North America before Europeans arrived?*

- *How did Indian and European ideas of freedom differ on the eve of contact?*

- *What impelled European explorers to look west across the Atlantic?*

- *What happened when the peoples of the Americas came in contact with Europeans?*

- *What were the chief features of the Spanish empire in America?*

- *What were the chief features of the French and Dutch empires in North America?*

T he discovery of America," the British writer Adam Smith announced in his celebrated work *The Wealth of Nations* (1776), was one of "the two greatest and most important events recorded in the history of mankind." Historians no longer use the word "discovery" to describe the European exploration, conquest, and colonization of a hemisphere already home to millions of people. But there can be no doubt that when Christopher Columbus made landfall in the West Indian islands in 1492, he set in motion some of the most pivotal developments in human history. Immense changes soon followed in both the Old and New Worlds; the consequences of these changes are still with us today.

The peoples of the American continents and Europe, previously unaware of each other's existence, were thrown into continuous interaction. Crops new to each hemisphere crossed the Atlantic, reshaping diets and transforming the natural environment. Because of their long isolation, the inhabitants of North and South America had developed no immunity to the germs that also accompanied the colonizers. As a result, they suffered a series of devastating epidemics, the greatest population catastrophe in human history. Within a decade of Columbus's voyage, a fourth continent—Africa—found itself drawn into the new Atlantic system of trade and population movement. In Africa, Europeans found a supply of unfree labor that enabled them to exploit the fertile lands of the Western Hemisphere. Indeed, of approximately 10 million men, women, and children who crossed from the Old World to the New between 1492 and 1820, the vast majority, about 7.7 million, were African slaves.

From the vantage point of 1776, the year the United States declared itself an independent nation, it seemed to Adam Smith that the "discovery" of America had produced both great "benefits" and great "misfortunes." To the nations of western Europe, the development of American colonies brought an era of "splendor and glory." Smith also noted, however, that to the "natives" of the Americas the years since 1492 had been ones of "dreadful misfortunes" and "every sort of injustice." And for millions of Africans, the settlement of America meant a descent into the abyss of slavery.

Long before Columbus sailed, Europeans had dreamed of a land of abundance, riches, and ease beyond the western horizon. Europeans envisioned America as a religious refuge, a society of equals, a source of power and glory. They searched the New World for golden cities and fountains of eternal youth. Some of these dreams would indeed be fulfilled. To many European settlers, America offered a far greater chance to own land and worship as they pleased than existed in Europe, with its rigid, unequal social order and official churches. Yet the New World also became the site of many forms of unfree labor, including indentured servitude, forced labor, and one of the most brutal and unjust systems, plantation slavery. The conquest and settlement of the Western Hemisphere opened new chapters in the long histories of both freedom and slavery.

THE FIRST AMERICANS

The Settling of the Americas

The residents of the Americas were no more a single group than Europeans or Africans. They spoke hundreds of different languages and lived in numerous kinds of societies. Most, however, were descended from bands of hunters and fishers who had crossed the Bering Strait via a land bridge at various times between 15,000 and 60,000 years ago—the exact dates are hotly debated by archaeologists.

The New World was new to Europeans but an ancient homeland to those who already lived there. The hemisphere had witnessed many changes during its human history. First, the early inhabitants and their descendants spread across the two continents, reaching the tip of South America perhaps 11,000 years ago. As the climate warmed, they faced a food crisis as the immense animals they hunted, including woolly mammoths and giant bison, became extinct. Around 9,000 years ago, at the same time that agriculture was being developed in the Near East, it also emerged in modern-day Mexico and the Andes, and then spread to other parts of the Americas, making settled civilizations possible.

Emergence of agriculture

Indian Societies of the Americas

North and South America were hardly an empty wilderness when Europeans arrived. The hemisphere contained cities, roads, irrigation systems, extensive trade networks, and large structures such as the pyramid-temples whose beauty still inspires wonder. With a population close to 250,000, **Tenochtitlán**, the capital of the Aztec empire in what is now Mexico, was one of the world's largest cities. Farther south lay the Inca kingdom, centered in modern-day Peru. Its population of perhaps 12 million was linked by a complex system of roads and bridges that extended 2,000 miles along the Andes mountain chain.

Roads, trade networks, and irrigation systems

Indian civilizations in North America had not developed the scale, grandeur, or centralized organization of the Aztec and Inca societies to their south.

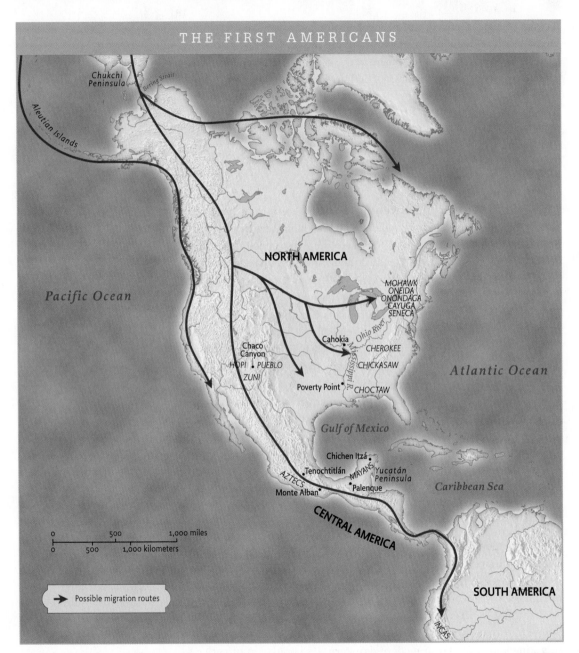

A map illustrating the probable routes by which the first Americans settled the Western Hemisphere at various times between 15,000 and 60,000 years ago.

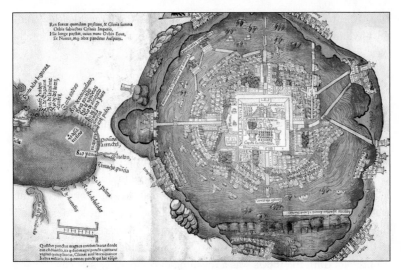

Map of the Aztec capital Tenochtitlán and the Gulf of Mexico, probably produced by a Spanish conquistador and published in 1524 in an edition of the letters of Hernán Cortés. The map shows the city's complex system of canals, bridges, and dams, with the Great Temple at the center. Gardens and a zoo are also visible.

North American Indians lacked the technologies Europeans had mastered, such as metal tools and machines, gunpowder, and the scientific knowledge necessary for long-distance navigation. No society north of Mexico had achieved literacy (although some made maps on bark and animal hides). Their "backwardness" became a central justification for European conquest. But, over time, Indian societies had perfected techniques of farming, hunting, and fishing, developed structures of political power and religious belief, and engaged in far-reaching networks of trade and communication.

Justification for conquest

Mound Builders of the Mississippi River Valley

Remarkable physical remains still exist from some of the early civilizations in North America. Around 3,500 years ago, before Egyptians built the pyramids, Native Americans constructed a large community centered on a series of giant semicircular mounds on a bluff overlooking the Mississippi River in present-day Louisiana. Known today as Poverty Point, it was a commercial and governmental center whose residents established trade routes throughout the Mississippi and Ohio River valleys.

More than a thousand years before Columbus sailed, Indians of the Ohio River valley, called "mound builders" by eighteenth-century settlers who encountered the large earthen burial mounds they created, had traded across half the continent. After their decline, another culture flourished in the Mississippi River valley, centered on the city of **Cahokia** near present-day St. Louis, a fortified community with between 10,000 and

"Mound builders"

30,000 inhabitants in the year 1200. It stood as the largest settled community in what is now the United States until surpassed in population by New York and Philadelphia around 1800.

Western Indians

Village life and trade

In the arid northeastern area of present-day Arizona, the Hopi and Zuni and their ancestors engaged in settled village life for over 3,000 years. During the peak of the region's culture, between the years 900 and 1200, these peoples built great planned towns with large multiple-family dwellings in local canyons, constructed dams and canals to gather and distribute water, and conducted trade with groups as far away as central Mexico and the Mississippi River valley. The largest of their structures, Pueblo Bonita, in Chaco Canyon, New Mexico, stood five stories high and had over 600 rooms. Not until the 1880s was a dwelling of comparable size constructed in the United States.

After the decline of these communities, probably because of drought, survivors moved to the south and east, where they established villages and perfected the techniques of desert farming. These were the people Spanish explorers called the Pueblo Indians (because they lived in small villages, or *pueblos*, when the Spanish first encountered them in the sixteenth century). On the Pacific coast, another densely populated region, hundreds of distinct groups resided in independent villages and lived primarily by fishing, hunting sea mammals, and gathering wild plants and nuts.

A modern aerial photograph of the ruins of Pueblo Bonita, in Chaco Canyon in present-day New Mexico. The rectangular structures are the foundations of dwellings, and the circular ones are *kivas,* or places of religious worship.

Indians of Eastern North America

In eastern North America, hundreds of tribes inhabited towns and villages scattered from the Gulf of Mexico to present-day Canada. They lived on corn, squash, and beans, supplemented by fishing and hunting deer, turkeys, and other animals. Indian trade routes crisscrossed the eastern part of the continent. Tribes frequently warred with one another to obtain goods, seize captives, or take revenge for the killing of relatives. They conducted diplomacy and made peace. Little in the way of centralized authority existed until, in the fifteenth century, various leagues or confederations emerged in an effort to bring order to local regions. In the Southeast, the Choctaw, Cherokee, and Chickasaw each united dozens of towns in loose alliances. In present-day New York and Pennsylvania, five **Iroquois** peoples—the Mohawk, Oneida, Cayuga, Seneca, and Onondaga—formed a Great League of Peace, bringing a period of stability to the area.

The most striking feature of Native American society at the time Europeans arrived was its sheer diversity. Each group had its own political system and set of religious beliefs, and North America was home to literally hundreds of mutually unintelligible languages. Indians did not think of themselves as a single unified people, an idea invented by Europeans and only many years later adopted by Indians themselves. Indian identity centered on the immediate social group—a tribe, village, chiefdom, or confederacy. When Europeans first arrived, many Indians saw them as simply one group among many. The sharp dichotomy between Indians and "white" persons did not emerge until later in the colonial era.

Diversity of Native American society

Native American Religion

Nonetheless, the diverse Indian societies of North America did share certain common characteristics. Their lives were steeped in religious ceremonies often directly related to farming and hunting. Spiritual power, they

The Village of Secoton, by John White, an English artist who spent a year on the Outer Banks of North Carolina in 1585–1586 as part of an expedition sponsored by Sir Walter Raleigh. A central street links houses surrounded by fields of corn. In the lower part, dancing Indians take part in a religious ceremony.

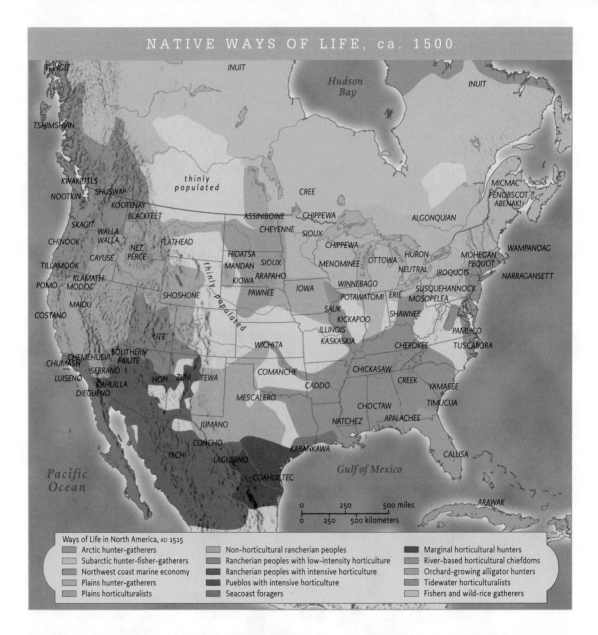

NATIVE WAYS OF LIFE, ca. 1500

TLINGIT
INUIT
Hudson Bay
INUIT
TSHIMSHIAN
KWAKIUTLS
NOOTKIN SHUSWAP
KOOTENAY
BLACKFEET
SKAGIT
WALLA
CHINOOK WALLA
NEZ FLATHEAD
CAYUSE PERCE
TILLAMOOK
KLAMATH
POMO MODOC
MAIDU
COSTANO
SHOSHONE
UTE
CHEMEHUEVI SOUTHERN
CHUMASH PAIUTE
SERRANO
LUISENO
CAHUILLA HOPI ZUNI TEWA
DIEGUENO
JUMANO
CONCHO
YACHI LAGUERNO
COAHUILTEC
thinly populated
CREE
ASSINIBOINE CHIPPEWA
CHEYENNE
SIOUX
CHIPPEWA
HIDATSA
MANDAN SIOUX
KIOWA ARAPAHO
PAWNEE IOWA
thinly populated
WICHITA
COMANCHE
CADDO
MESCALERO
KABANKAWA
Gulf of Mexico
ALGONQUIAN
L. Superior
MENOMINEE OTTAWA HURON
L. Michigan L. Ontario
NEUTRAL
WINNEBAGO IROQUOIS
POTAWATOMI ERIE
SAUK L. Erie
KICKAPOO SHAWNEE
ILLINOIS
KASKASKIA
MOSOPELEA
SUSQUEHANNOCK
CHEROKEE
CHICKASAW CREEK
CHOCTAW
NATCHEZ APALACHEE
MICMAC
PENOBSCOT
ABENAKI
WAMPANOAG
MOHEGAN
PEQUOT
NARRAGANSETT
PAMLICO
TUSCARORA
YAMASEE
TIMUCUA
CALUSA
ARAWAK

Pacific Ocean

0 250 500 miles
0 250 500 kilometers

Ways of Life in North America, AD 1515

- Arctic hunter-gatherers
- Subarctic hunter-fisher-gatherers
- Northwest coast marine economy
- Plains hunter-gatherers
- Plains horticulturalists
- Non-horticultural rancherian peoples
- Rancherian peoples with low-intensity horticulture
- Rancherian peoples with intensive horticulture
- Pueblos with intensive horticulture
- Seacoast foragers
- Marginal horticultural hunters
- River-based horticultural chiefdoms
- Orchard-growing alligator hunters
- Tidewater horticulturalists
- Fishers and wild-rice gatherers

The native population of North America at the time of first contact with Europeans consisted of numerous tribes with their own languages, religious beliefs, and economic and social structures. This map suggests the numerous ways of life existing at the time.

believed, suffused the world, and sacred spirits could be found in all kinds of living and inanimate things—animals, plants, trees, water, and wind. Through religious ceremonies, they aimed to harness the aid of powerful supernatural forces to serve human interests. Indian villages also held elaborate religious rites, participation in which helped to define the boundaries of community membership. In all Indian societies, those who seemed to possess special abilities to invoke supernatural powers—shamans, medicine men, and other religious leaders—held positions of respect and authority.

Indian religious rituals

In some respects, Indian religion was not that different from popular spiritual beliefs in Europe. Most Indians held that a single Creator stood atop the spiritual hierarchy. Nonetheless, nearly all Europeans arriving in the New World quickly concluded that Indians were in dire need of being converted to a true, Christian faith.

Land and Property

Equally alien in European eyes were Indian attitudes toward property. Generally, village leaders assigned plots of land to individual families to use for a season or more, and tribes claimed specific areas for hunting. Unclaimed land remained free for anyone to use. Families "owned" the right to use land, but they did not own the land itself. Indians saw land as a common resource, not an economic commodity. There was no market in real estate before the coming of Europeans.

Land as a common resource

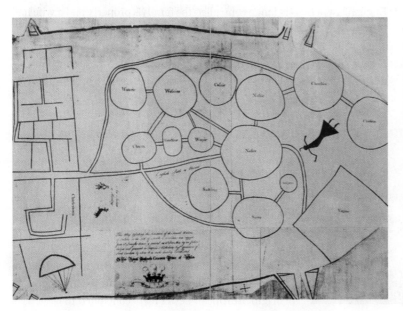

A Catawba map illustrates the differences between Indian and European conceptions of landed property. The map depicts not possession of a specific territory, but trade and diplomatic connections between various native groups and with the colony of Virginia, represented by the rectangle on the lower right. The map, inscribed on deerskin, was originally presented by Indian chiefs to Governor Francis Nicholson of South Carolina in 1721. This copy, the only version that survives, was made by the governor for the authorities in London. It added English labels that conveyed what the Indians had related orally with the gift.

Nor were Indians devoted to the accumulation of wealth and material goods. Especially east of the Mississippi River, where villages moved every few years when soil or game became depleted, acquiring numerous possessions made little sense. However, status certainly mattered in Indian societies. Tribal leaders tended to come from a small number of families, and chiefs lived more splendidly than average members of society. But their reputation often rested on their willingness to share goods with others rather than hoarding them for themselves.

Gift giving

Generosity was among the most valued social qualities, and gift giving was essential to Indian society. Trade, for example, meant more than a commercial transaction—it was accompanied by elaborate ceremonies of gift exchange that bound different groups in webs of mutual obligation. "There are no beggars among them," reported the English colonial leader Roger Williams of New England's Indians.

Gender Relations

Matrilineal societies

The system of gender relations in most Indian societies also differed markedly from that of Europe. Membership in a family defined women's lives, but they openly engaged in premarital sexual relations and could even choose to divorce their husbands. Most, although not all, Indian societies were matrilineal—that is, centered on clans or kinship groups in which children became members of the mother's family, not the father's. Under English law, a married man controlled the family's property and a wife had no independent legal identity. In contrast, Indian women owned dwellings and tools, and a husband generally moved to live with the family of his wife. Because men were frequently away on the hunt, women took responsibility not only for household duties but for most agricultural work as well.

Indian women planting crops while men break the sod. An engraving by Theodor de Bry, based on a painting by Jacques Le Moyne de Morgues. Morgues was part of an expedition of French Huguenots to Florida in 1564; he escaped when the Spanish destroyed the outpost in the following year.

European Views of the Indians

Europeans tended to view Indians in extreme terms. They were regarded either as "noble savages," gentle, friendly, and superior in some ways to Europeans, or as uncivilized and brutal savages. Over time, however, negative images of Indians came to overshadow positive ones. Early European descriptions of North American Indians as barbaric centered on three areas—religion, land use, and gender relations. Whatever their country of origin, European newcomers concluded that Indians lacked genuine religion, or in fact worshiped the devil. Whereas the Indians saw nature as a world of spirits and souls, the Europeans viewed it as a collection of potential commodities, a source of economic opportunity.

Europeans invoked the Indians' distinctive pattern of land use and ideas about property to answer the awkward question raised by a British minister at an early stage of England's colonization: "By what right or warrant can we enter into the land of these Savages, take away their rightful inheritance from them, and plant ourselves in their places?" While the Spanish claimed title to land in America by right of conquest and papal authority, the English, French, and Dutch came to rely on the idea that Indians had not actually "used" the land and thus had no claim to it. Despite the Indians' highly developed agriculture and well-established towns, Europeans frequently described them as nomads without settled communities.

In the Indians' gender division of labor and matrilineal family structures, Europeans saw weak men and mistreated women. Hunting and fishing, the primary occupations of Indian men, were considered leisure activities in much of Europe, not "real" work. Because Indian women worked in the fields, Europeans often described them as lacking freedom. Europeans insisted that by subduing the Indians, they were actually bringing them freedom—the freedom of true religion, private property, and the liberation of both men and women from uncivilized and unchristian gender roles.

A seventeenth-century engraving by a French Jesuit priest illustrates many Europeans' view of Indian religion. A demon hovers over an Iroquois longhouse, suggesting that Indians worship the devil.

INDIAN FREEDOM, EUROPEAN FREEDOM

Indian Freedom

Although many Europeans initially saw Indians as embodying freedom, most colonizers quickly concluded that the notion of "freedom" was alien to Indian societies. European settlers reached this conclusion in part because Indians did not appear to live under established governments or fixed laws, followed their own—not European—definitions of authority, and lacked the kind of order and discipline common in European society. Indians also did not define freedom as individual autonomy or tie it to the ownership of property—two attributes important to Europeans.

What were the Indians' ideas of freedom? The modern notion of freedom as personal independence had little meaning in most Indian societies, but individuals were expected to think for themselves and did not always have to go along with collective decision making. Far more important

Freedom in the group

than individual autonomy were kinship ties, the ability to follow one's spiritual values, and the well-being and security of one's community. In Indian culture, group autonomy and self-determination, and the mutual obligations that came with a sense of belonging and connectedness, took precedence over individual freedom. Ironically, the coming of Europeans, armed with their own language of liberty, would make freedom a preoccupation of American Indians, as part and parcel of the very process by which they were reduced to dependence on the colonizers.

Christian Liberty

On the eve of colonization, Europeans held numerous ideas of freedom. Some were as old as the city-states of ancient Greece, others arose during the political struggles of the early modern era. Some laid the foundations for modern conceptions of freedom, others are quite unfamiliar today. Freedom was not a single idea but a collection of distinct rights and privileges, many enjoyed by only a small portion of the population.

Freedom as a spiritual condition

One conception common throughout Europe understood freedom less as a political or social status than as a moral or spiritual condition. Freedom meant abandoning the life of sin to embrace the teachings of Christ. **"Christian Liberty,"** however, had no connection to later ideas of religious toleration, a notion that scarcely existed anywhere on the eve of colonization. Every nation in Europe had an established church that decreed what forms of religious worship and belief were acceptable. Dissenters faced persecution by the state as well as condemnation by church authorities. Religious uniformity was thought to be essential to public order; the modern idea that a person's religious beliefs and practices are a matter of private choice, not legal obligation, was almost unknown.

Freedom and Authority

In its secular form, the equating of liberty with obedience to a higher authority suggested that freedom meant not anarchy but obedience to law. The identification of freedom with the rule of law did not, though, mean that all subjects of the crown enjoyed the same degree of freedom. Early modern European societies were extremely hierarchical, with marked gradations of social status ranging from the king and hereditary aristocracy down to the urban and rural poor. Inequality was built into virtually every social relationship.

Hierarchy in the family

Within families, men exercised authority over their wives and children. According to the widespread legal doctrine known as "coverture," when a woman married she surrendered her legal identity, which became "covered" by that of her husband. She could not own property or sign contracts in her own name, control her wages if she worked, write a separate will, or, except in the rarest of circumstances, go to court seeking a divorce. The husband had the exclusive right to his wife's "company," including domestic labor and sexual relations.

Everywhere in Europe, family life depended on male dominance and female submission. Indeed, political writers of the sixteenth century explicitly compared the king's authority over his subjects with the husband's over his family. Both were ordained by God.

Liberty and Liberties

In this hierarchical society, liberty came from knowing one's social place and fulfilling the duties appropriate to one's rank. Most men lacked the freedom that came with economic independence. Property qualifications and other restrictions limited the electorate to a minuscule part of the adult male population. The law required strict obedience of employees, and breaches of labor contracts carried criminal penalties.

Hierarchy in society

European ideas of freedom still bore the imprint of the Middle Ages, when "liberties" meant formal, specific privileges such as self-government, exemption from taxation, or the right to practice a particular trade, granted to individuals or groups by contract, royal decree, or purchase. Only those who enjoyed the "freedom of the city," for example, could engage in certain economic activities. Numerous modern civil liberties did not exist. The law decreed acceptable forms of religious worship. The government regularly suppressed publications it did not like, and criticism of authority could lead to imprisonment. Nonetheless, every European country that colonized the New World claimed to be spreading freedom—for its own population and for Native Americans.

THE EXPANSION OF EUROPE

It is fitting that the second epochal event that Adam Smith linked to Columbus's voyage of 1492 was the discovery by Portuguese navigators of a sea route from Europe to Asia around the southern tip of Africa. The European conquest of America began as an offshoot of the quest for a sea route to India, China, and the islands of the East Indies, the source of the silk, tea, spices, porcelain, and other luxury goods on which international trade in the early modern era centered. For centuries, this commerce had been conducted across land, from China and South Asia to the Middle East

Sea route to the East

and the Mediterranean region. Profit and piety—the desire to eliminate Islamic middlemen and win control of the lucrative trade for Christian western Europe—combined to inspire the quest for a direct route to Asia.

Chinese and Portuguese Navigation

Zheng He's voyages

At the beginning of the fifteenth century, one might have predicted that China would establish the world's first global empire. Between 1405 and 1433, Admiral Zheng He led seven large naval expeditions in the Indian Ocean. The first convoy consisted of 62 ships that were larger than those of any European nation, along with 225 support vessels and more than 25,000 men. On his sixth voyage, Zheng explored the coast of East Africa. Had his ships continued westward, they could easily have reached North and South America. But as a wealthy land-based empire, China did not feel the need for overseas expansion, and after 1433 the government ended support for long-distance maritime expeditions.

New techniques of sailing and navigation

It fell to Portugal, far removed from the overland route to Asia, to begin exploring the Atlantic. Taking advantage of new long-distance ships known as **caravels** and new navigational devices such as the compass and quadrant, the Portuguese showed that it was possible to sail down the coast of Africa and return to Portugal. No European sailor had seen the coast of Africa below the Sahara. But in that year, a Portuguese ship brought a sprig of rosemary from West Africa, proof that one could sail beyond the desert and return.

Little by little, Portuguese ships moved farther down the coast. In 1485, they reached Benin, an imposing city whose craftsmen produced bronze sculptures that still inspire admiration for their artistic beauty and superb casting techniques. The Portuguese established fortified trading posts on the western coast of Africa. The profits reaped by these Portuguese "factories"—so named because merchants were known as "factors"—inspired other European powers to follow in their footsteps.

Portuguese explorations

Portugal also began to colonize Madeira, the Azores, and the Canary and Cape Verde Islands, which lie in the Atlantic off the African coast. The Portuguese established plantations on the Atlantic islands, eventually replacing the native populations with thousands of slaves shipped from Africa—an ominous precedent for the New World.

Freedom and Slavery in Africa

Slavery in Africa long predated the coming of Europeans. Traditionally, African slaves tended to be criminals, debtors, and captives in war. They worked within the households of their owners and had well-defined rights, such as possessing property and marrying free persons. It was not uncom-

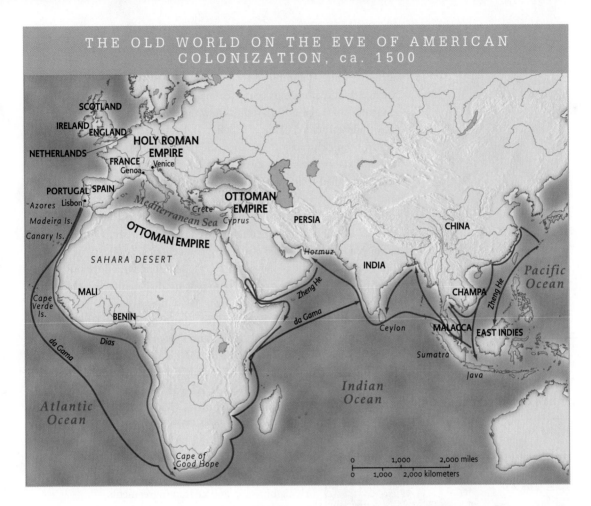

THE OLD WORLD ON THE EVE OF AMERICAN COLONIZATION, ca. 1500

mon for African slaves to acquire their freedom. Slavery was one of several forms of labor, not the basis of the economy as it would become in large parts of the New World. The coming of the Portuguese, soon followed by traders from other European nations, accelerated the buying and selling of slaves within Africa. At least 100,000 African slaves were transported to Spain and Portugal between 1450 and 1500.

Having reached West Africa, Portuguese mariners pushed their explorations ever southward along the coast. Bartholomeu Dias reached the Cape of Good Hope at the continent's southern tip in 1487. In 1498, Vasco da Gama sailed around it to India, demonstrating the feasibility of a sea route to the East. With a population of under 1 million, Portugal established a vast trading empire, with bases in India, southern China, and Indonesia. But six years before da Gama's voyage, Christopher Columbus had, he believed, discovered a new route to China and India by sailing west.

In the fifteenth century, the world known to Europeans was limited to Europe, parts of Africa, and Asia. Explorers from Portugal sought to find a sea route to the East in order to circumvent the Italian city-states and Middle Eastern rulers who controlled the overland trade.

THE EXPANSION OF EUROPE | 15

The Voyages of Columbus

A seasoned mariner and fearless explorer from Genoa, a major port in northern Italy, Columbus had for years sailed the Mediterranean and North Atlantic, studying ocean currents and wind patterns. Like nearly all navigators of the time, Columbus knew the earth was round. But he drastically underestimated its size. He believed that by sailing westward he could relatively quickly cross the Atlantic and reach Asia. No one in Europe knew that two giant continents lay 3,000 miles to the west. The Vikings, to be sure, had sailed from Greenland to Newfoundland around the year 1000 and established a settlement, Vinland. But this outpost was abandoned after a few years and had been forgotten, except in Norse legends.

Norse settlement

For Columbus, as for other figures of the time, religious and commercial motives reinforced one another. A devout Catholic, he drew on the Bible for his estimate of the size of the globe. Along with developing trade with the East, he hoped to convert Asians to Christianity and enlist them in a crusade to redeem Jerusalem from Muslim control.

Columbus sought financial support throughout Europe for the planned voyage. Eventually, King Ferdinand and Queen Isabella of Spain agreed to become sponsors. Their marriage in 1469 had united the warring kingdoms of Aragon and Castile. In 1492, they completed the ***reconquista***—the "reconquest" of Spain from the Moors, African Muslims who had occupied part of the Iberian Peninsula for centuries. With Spain's territory united, Ferdinand and Isabella—like the rulers of the Italian city-states—were anxious to circumvent the Muslim stranglehold on eastern trade. It is not surprising, then, that Columbus set sail with royal letters of introduction to Asian rulers, authorizing him to negotiate trade agreements.

Columbus's Landfall, an engraving from *La lettera dell'isole* (Letter from the Islands). This 1493 pamphlet reproduced, in the form of a poem, Columbus's first letter describing his voyage of the previous year. Under the watchful eye of King Ferdinand of Spain, Columbus and his men land on a Caribbean island, while local Indians flee.

CONTACT

Columbus in the New World

On October 12, 1492, after only thirty-three days of sailing from the Canary Islands, where he had stopped to resupply his three ships, Columbus and his expedition arrived at the Bahamas. Soon afterward, he encountered the far larger islands of Hispaniola (today the site of Haiti and the Dominican Republic) and Cuba. When one of his ships ran aground, he abandoned it and left thirty-eight men behind on Hispaniola. But he found room to bring ten inhabitants of the island back to Spain for conversion to Christianity.

In the following year, 1493, Columbus returned with seventeen ships and more than 1,000 men to explore the area and establish a Spanish outpost. Columbus's settlement on the island of Hispaniola, which he named La Isabella, failed, but in 1502 another Spanish explorer, Nicolás de Ovando, arrived with 2,500 men and established a permanent base, the first center of the Spanish empire in America. Columbus went to his grave believing that he had discovered a westward route to Asia. The explorations of another Italian, Amerigo Vespucci, along the coast of South America between 1499 and 1502 made plain that a continent entirely unknown to Europeans had been encountered. The New World would come to bear not Columbus's name but one based on Vespucci's—America. Vespucci also realized that the native inhabitants were distinct peoples, not residents of the East Indies as Columbus had believed, although the name "Indians," applied to them by Columbus, has endured to this day.

Hispaniola settlement

Vespucci

Exploration and Conquest

Thanks to Johannes Gutenberg's invention of the printing press in the 1430s, news of Columbus's achievement traveled quickly, at least among the educated minority in Europe. Other explorers were inspired to follow in his wake. John Cabot, a Genoese merchant who had settled in England, reached Newfoundland in 1497. Soon, scores of fishing boats from France, Spain, and England were active in the region. Pedro Cabral claimed Brazil for Portugal in 1500.

But the Spanish took the lead in exploration and conquest. Inspired by a search for wealth, national glory, and the desire to spread Catholicism, Spanish conquistadores, often accompanied by religious missionaries and carrying flags emblazoned with the sign of the cross, radiated outward from Hispaniola. In 1513, Vasco Núñez de Balboa trekked across the isthmus of Panama and became the first European to gaze upon the Pacific Ocean. Between 1519 and 1522, Ferdinand Magellan led the first expedition to sail around the world, encountering Pacific islands and peoples previously unknown to Europe.

Spain takes the lead

The first explorer to encounter a major American civilization was Hernán Cortés, who in 1519 arrived at Tenochtitlán, the nerve center of the Aztec empire, whose wealth and power rested on domination of numerous subordinate peoples nearby. The Aztecs were violent warriors who engaged in the ritual sacrifice of captives and others, sometimes thousands at a time. This practice thoroughly alienated their neighbors.

Cortés

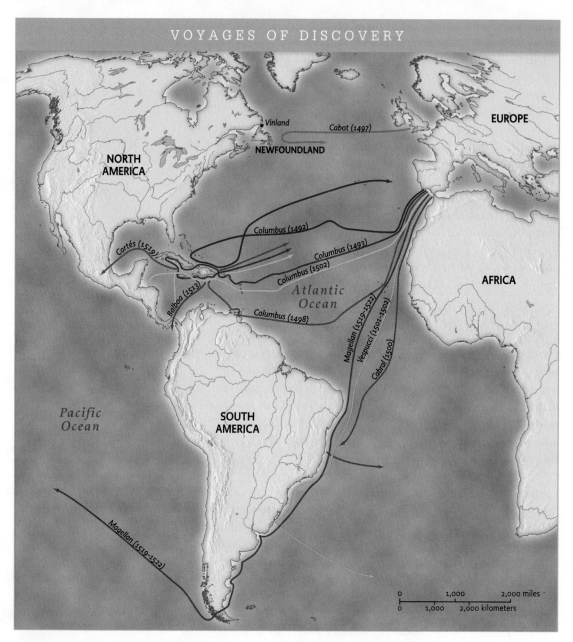

VOYAGES OF DISCOVERY

Vinland

Cabot (1497)

NEWFOUNDLAND

EUROPE

NORTH AMERICA

Cortés (1519)

Columbus (1492)

Columbus (1493)

Columbus (1502)

Balboa (1513)

Atlantic Ocean

Columbus (1498)

AFRICA

Magellan (1519-1522)

Vespucci (1501-1502)

Cabral (1500)

Pacific Ocean

SOUTH AMERICA

Magellan (1519-1522)

| 0 | 1,000 | 2,000 miles |
| 0 | 1,000 | 2,000 kilometers |

Christopher Columbus's first Atlantic crossing, in 1492, was soon followed by voyages of discovery by English, Portuguese, Spanish, and Italian explorers.

With only a few hundred European men, Cortés conquered the Aztec city, relying on superior military technology such as iron weapons and gunpowder, as well as shrewdness in enlisting the aid of some of the Aztecs' subject peoples, who supplied him with thousands of warriors. His most powerful ally, however, was disease—a smallpox epidemic that devastated Aztec society. A few years later, Francisco Pizarro conquered the great Inca kingdom centered in modern-day Peru. Pizarro's tactics were typical of the conquistadores. He captured the Incan king, demanded and received a ransom, and then killed the king anyway. Soon, treasure fleets carrying cargoes of gold and silver from the mines of Mexico and Peru were traversing the Atlantic to enrich the Spanish crown.

Engravings, from the *Florentine Codex*, of the forces of Cortés marching on Tenochtitlán and assaulting the city with cannon fire. The difference in military technology between the Spanish and Aztecs is evident. Indians who allied with Cortés had helped him build vessels and carry them in pieces over mountains to the city. The codex (a volume formed by stitching together manuscript pages) was prepared under the supervision of a Spanish missionary in sixteenth-century Mexico.

The Demographic Disaster

The transatlantic flow of goods and people is sometimes called the **Columbian Exchange**. Plants, animals, and cultures that had evolved independently on separate continents were now thrown together. Products introduced to Europe from the Americas included corn, tomatoes, potatoes, peanuts, and tobacco, while people from the Old World brought wheat, rice, sugarcane, horses, cattle, pigs, and sheep to the New. But Europeans also carried germs previously unknown in the Americas.

No one knows exactly how many people lived in the Americas at the time of Columbus's voyages—current estimates range between 50 and 90 million, most of whom lived in Central and South America. In 1492, the Indian population within what are now the borders of the United States was between 2 and 5 million. The Indian populations of the Americas suffered a catastrophic decline because of contact with Europeans and their wars, enslavement, and especially diseases like smallpox, influenza, and measles. Never having encountered these diseases, Indians had not developed antibodies to fight them. The result was devastating. The population of Mexico would fall by more than 90 percent in the sixteenth century, from perhaps 20 million to under 2 million. As for the area that now forms the United States, its Native American population fell continuously. It reached its lowest point around 1900, at only 250,000.

Decline of Indian populations

Overall, the death of perhaps 80 million people—close to one-fifth of humankind—in the first century and a half after contact with Europeans represents the greatest loss of life in human history. It was disease as much as military prowess and more advanced technology that enabled Europeans to conquer the Americas.

THE SPANISH EMPIRE

By the middle of the sixteenth century, Spain had established an immense empire that reached from Europe to the Americas and Asia. The Atlantic and Pacific oceans, once barriers separating different parts of the world, now became highways for the exchange of goods and the movement of people. Spanish galleons carried gold and silver from Mexico and Peru eastward to Spain and westward to Manila in the Philippines and on to China.

Extent of the empire

Stretching from the Andes Mountains of South America through present-day Mexico and the Caribbean and eventually into Florida and the southwestern United States, Spain's empire exceeded in size the Roman empire of the ancient world. Its center was Mexico City, a magnificent capital built on the ruins of the Aztec city of Tenochtitlán that boasted churches, hospitals, monasteries, government buildings, and the New World's first university. Unlike the English and French New World empires, Spanish

A late-seventeenth-century painting of the Plaza Mayor (main square) of Mexico City. The image includes a parade of over 1,000 persons, of different ethnic groups and occupations, dressed in their characteristic attire.

America was essentially an urban civilization. For centuries, its great cities, notably Mexico City, Quito, and Lima, far outshone any urban centers in North America and most of those in Europe.

Governing Spanish America

At least in theory, the government of Spanish America reflected the absolutism of the newly unified nation at home. Authority originated with the king and flowed downward through the Council of the Indies—the main body in Spain for colonial administration—and then to viceroys in Mexico and Peru and other local officials in America. The Catholic Church also played a significant role in the administration of Spanish colonies, frequently exerting its authority on matters of faith, morals, and treatment of the Indians.

Authority in Spanish America

Successive kings kept elected assemblies out of Spain's New World empire. Royal officials were generally appointees from Spain, rather than *criollos*, as persons born in the colonies of European ancestry were called. But as Spain's power declined in Europe beginning in the seventeenth century, the local elite came to enjoy more and more effective authority over colonial affairs.

Colonists and Indians in Spanish America

Despite the decline in the native population, Spanish America remained populous enough that, with the exception of the West Indies and a few cities, large-scale importations of African slaves were unnecessary. Instead, the Spanish forced tens of thousands of Indians to work in gold and silver mines, which supplied the empire's wealth, and on large-scale farms, or *haciendas*, controlled by Spanish landlords. In Spanish America, unlike other New World empires, Indians performed most of the labor.

Labor in Spanish America

The opportunity for social advancement drew numerous colonists from Spain—225,000 in the sixteenth century and a total of 750,000 in the three centuries of Spain's colonial rule. Eventually, a significant number came in families, but at first the large majority were young, single men, many of them laborers, craftsmen, and soldiers. Many also came as government officials, priests, professionals, and minor aristocrats, all ready to direct the manual work of Indians, since living without having to labor was a sign of noble status. The most successful of these colonists enjoyed lives of luxury similar to those of the upper classes at home.

Unlike in the later British empire, Indian inhabitants always outnumbered European colonists and their descendants in Spanish America, and large areas remained effectively under Indian control for many years.

Spanish authorities granted Indians certain rights within colonial society and looked forward to their eventual assimilation. Indeed, the success of the Spanish empire depended on the nature of the native societies on which it could build. In Florida, the Amazon, and Caribbean islands like Jamaica, which lacked major Indian cities and large native populations, Spanish rule remained tenuous.

The Spanish crown ordered wives of colonists to join them in America and demanded that single men marry. But with the population of Spanish women remaining low, the intermixing of the colonial and Indian peoples soon began. As early as 1514, the Spanish government formally approved of such marriages, partly as a way of bringing Christianity to the native population. By 1600, **mestizos** (persons of mixed origin) made up a large part of the urban population of Spanish America. Over time, Spanish America evolved into a hybrid culture, part Spanish, part Indian, and in some areas part African, but with a single official faith, language, and governmental system.

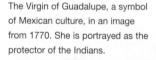

A hybrid culture

Justifications for Conquest

The Europeans who crossed the Atlantic in the wake of Columbus's voyage had immense confidence in the superiority of their own cultures to those they encountered in America. They expected these societies to abandon their own beliefs and traditions and embrace those of the newcomers. Failure to do so reinforced the conviction that these people were uncivilized "heathens" (non-Christians). In addition, Europeans brought with them a long history of using violence to subdue their foes and a missionary zeal to spread the benefits of their own civilization to others, while reaping the benefits of empire. Spain was no exception.

To further legitimize Spain's claim to rule the New World, a year after Columbus's first voyage Pope Alexander VI divided the non-Christian world between Spain and Portugal. The line was subsequently adjusted to give Portugal control of Brazil, with the remainder of the Western Hemisphere falling under Spanish authority. Its missionary purpose in colonization was already familiar because of the long holy war against Islam within Spain itself and Spain's 1492 order that all Muslims and Jews had to convert to Catholicism or leave the country. But missionary zeal was powerfully reinforced in the sixteenth century, when the Protestant Reformation divided the Catholic Church. In 1517, Martin Luther, a German priest, posted his Ninety-Five Theses, which accused the Church of worldliness and corruption. Luther wanted to cleanse the Church of abuses such as the sale of indulgences (official dispensations forgiving sins). He insisted that all

The Virgin of Guadalupe, a symbol of Mexican culture, in an image from 1770. She is portrayed as the protector of the Indians.

Spanish conquistadores murdering Indians at Cuzco, in Peru. The Dutch-born engraver Theodor de Bry and his sons illustrated ten volumes about New World exploration published between 1590 and 1618. A Protestant, de Bry created vivid images that helped to spread the Black Legend of Spain as a uniquely cruel colonizer.

believers should read the Bible for themselves, rather than relying on priests to interpret it for them. His call for reform led to the rise of new Protestant churches independent of Rome and plunged Europe into more than a century of religious and political strife.

Spain, the most powerful bastion of orthodox Catholicism, redoubled its efforts to convert the Indians to the "true faith." Spain insisted that the primary goal of colonization was to save the Indians from heathenism and prevent them from falling under the sway of Protestantism.

Converting Indians

Piety and Profit

To the Spanish colonizers, the large native populations of the Americas were not only souls to be saved but also a labor force to be organized to extract gold and silver for the mother country. The tension between these two outlooks would mark Spanish rule in America for three centuries. On the one hand, religious orders established missions throughout the empire, and over time millions of Indians were converted to Catholicism. On the other hand, Spanish rule, especially in its initial period, decimated the Indian population and subjected Indians to brutal labor conditions. The conquistadores and subsequent governors, who required conquered peoples to acknowledge the Catholic Church and provide gold and silver,

Tensions in the empire

saw no contradiction between serving God and enriching themselves. Others, however, did.

As early as 1537, Pope Paul III, who hoped to see Indians become devout subjects of Catholic monarchs, outlawed Indians' enslavement (an edict never extended to apply to Africans). Fifteen years later, the Dominican priest Bartolomé de Las Casas published an account of the decimation of the Indian population with the compelling title *A Very Brief Account of the Destruction of the Indies.*

Las Casas

Las Casas's writings denounced Spain for causing the death of millions of innocent people and for denying Indians their freedom. He narrated in shocking detail the "strange cruelties" carried out by "the Christians," including the burning alive of men, women, and children and the imposition of forced labor. "The entire human race is one," he proclaimed, and while he continued to believe that Spain had a right to rule in America, largely on religious grounds, he called for Indians to enjoy "all guarantees of liberty and justice" from the moment they became subjects of Spain. Las Casas also suggested, however, that importing slaves from Africa would help to protect the Indians from exploitation.

Reforming the Empire

Largely because of Las Casas's efforts, Spain in 1542 promulgated the New Laws, commanding that Indians no longer be enslaved. In 1550, Spain abolished the *encomienda* system, under which the first settlers had been granted authority over conquered Indian lands with the right to extract forced labor from the native inhabitants. In its place, the government established the *repartimiento* **system**, whereby residents of Indian villages remained legally free and entitled to wages, but were still required to perform a fixed amount of labor each year. The Indians were not slaves—they had access to land, were paid wages, and could not be bought and sold. But since the requirement that they work for the Spanish remained the essence of the system, it still allowed for many abuses by Spanish landlords and by priests who required Indians to toil on mission lands as part of the conversion process.

Over time, Spain's brutal treatment of Indians improved somewhat. But Las Casas's writings, translated almost immediately into several European languages, contributed to the spread of the **Black**

TABLE 1.1 Estimated Regional Populations: The Americas, ca. 1500	
North America	3,800,000
Mexico	17,200,000
Central America	5,625,000
Hispaniola	1,000,000
The Caribbean	3,000,000
The Andes	15,700,000
South America	8,620,000
Total	54,945,000

Legend—the image of Spain as a uniquely brutal and exploitative colonizer. This image would provide a potent justification for other European powers to challenge Spain's predominance in the New World.

Exploring North America

While the Spanish empire centered on Mexico, Peru, and the West Indies, the hope of finding a new kingdom of gold soon led Spanish explorers into territory that now forms part of the United States. Juan Ponce de León, who had conquered Puerto Rico, entered Florida in 1513 in search of slaves, wealth, and a fabled fountain of youth, only to be repelled by local Indians. In the late 1530s and 1540s, Juan Rodriguez Cabrillo explored the Pacific coast as far north as present-day Oregon, and expeditions led by Hernando de Soto, Cabeza de Vaca, Francisco Vásquez de Coronado, and others marched through the Gulf region and the Southwest, fruitlessly searching for another Mexico or Peru. These expeditions, really mobile communities with hundreds of adventurers, priests, potential settlers, slaves, and livestock, spread disease and devastation among Indian communities. De Soto's was particularly brutal. His men tortured, raped, and enslaved countless Indians and transmitted deadly diseases. When Europeans in the seventeenth century returned to colonize the area traversed by de Soto's party, little remained of the societies he had encountered.

De Soto

Spain in Florida and the Southwest

Nonetheless, these explorations established Spain's claim to a large part of what is now the American South and Southwest. The first region to be colonized within the present-day United States was Florida. Spain hoped to establish a military base there to combat pirates who threatened the treasure fleet that each year sailed from Havana for Europe loaded with gold and silver from Mexico and Peru. Spain also wanted to forestall French incursions in the area. In 1565, Philip II of Spain authorized the nobleman Pedro Menéndez de Avilés to lead a colonizing expedition to Florida. Menéndez destroyed a small outpost at Fort Caroline, which a group of Huguenots (French Protestants) had established in 1562 near present-day

Florida as military base

TABLE 1.2 Estimated Regional Populations: The World, ca. 1500	
India	110,000,000
China	103,000,000
Other Asia	55,400,000
Western Europe	57,200,000
The Americas	55,000,000
Russia and Eastern Europe	34,000,000
Sub-Saharan Africa	38,300,000
Japan	15,400,000
World Total	467,300,000

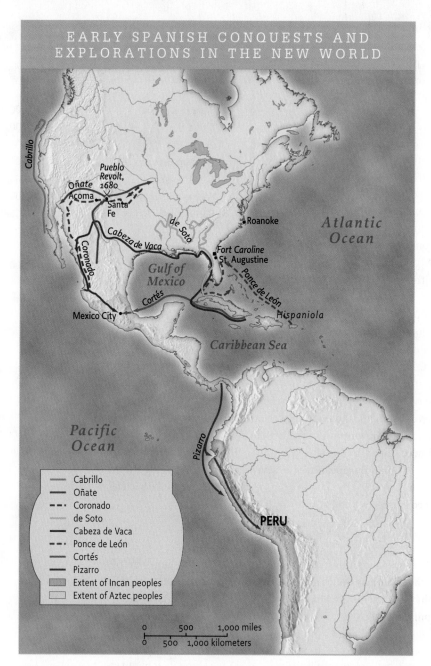

EARLY SPANISH CONQUESTS AND EXPLORATIONS IN THE NEW WORLD

Cabrillo

Pueblo Revolt, 1680

Oñate

Acoma

Santa Fe

de Soto

Cabeza de Vaca

Coronado

Roanoke

Atlantic Ocean

Fort Caroline

St. Augustine

Gulf of Mexico

Cortés

Ponce de León

Mexico City

Hispaniola

Caribbean Sea

Pacific Ocean

Pizarro

PERU

Legend:
- Cabrillo
- Oñate
- Coronado
- de Soto
- Cabeza de Vaca
- Ponce de León
- Cortés
- Pizarro
- Extent of Incan peoples
- Extent of Aztec peoples

0   500   1,000 miles

0   500   1,000 kilometers

By around 1600, New Spain had become a vast empire stretching from the modern-day American Southwest through Mexico, Central America, and into the former Inca kingdom in South America. This map shows early Spanish exploration, especially in the present-day United States, Mexico, and Peru.

Jacksonville. Menéndez and his men went on to establish Spanish forts on St. Simons Island, Georgia, and at St. Augustine, Florida. The latter remains the oldest site in the United States continuously inhabited by European settlers and their descendants. In general, though, Florida failed to attract settlers, remaining an isolated military settlement, in effect a fortified outpost of Cuba. As late as 1763, Spanish Florida had only 4,000 inhabitants of European descent.

Spain took even longer to begin the colonization of the American Southwest. It was not until 1598 that Juan de Oñate led a group of 400 soldiers, colonists, and missionaries north from Mexico to establish a permanent settlement. While searching for fabled deposits of precious metals, Oñate's nephew and fourteen soldiers were killed by inhabitants of Acoma, the "sky city" located on a high bluff in present-day New Mexico.

Juan de Oñate in New Mexico

Oñate decided to teach the local Indians a lesson. After a two-day siege, his forces scaled the seemingly impregnable heights and destroyed Acoma, killing more than 800 of its 1,500 or so inhabitants, including 300 women. Of the 600 Indians captured, the women and children were consigned to servitude in Spanish families, while adult men were punished by the cutting off of one foot. Oñate's message was plain—any Indians who resisted Spanish authority would be crushed. In 1606, however, Oñate was ordered home and punished for his treatment of New Mexico's Indians. In 1610, Spain established the capital of New Mexico at Santa Fe, the first permanent European settlement in the Southwest.

The Pueblo Revolt

In 1680, New Mexico's small and vulnerable colonist population numbered less than 3,000. Relations between the Pueblo Indians and colonial authorities had deteriorated throughout the seventeenth century, as governors, settlers, and missionaries sought to exploit the labor of an Indian population that declined from about 60,000 in 1600 to some 17,000 eighty years later. Franciscan friars worked relentlessly to convert Indians to Catholicism, often using intimidation and violence. As the Inquisition—the persecution of non-Catholics—became more and more intense in Spain, so did the friars' efforts to stamp out traditional religious ceremonies in New Mexico. At the same time, the Spanish assumed that the Indians could never unite against the colonizers. In August 1680, they were proven wrong.

Religious tensions

Little is known about the life of Popé, who became the main organizer of an uprising that aimed to drive the Spanish from the colony and restore the Indians' traditional autonomy. Under Popé's leadership, New Mexico's Indians joined in a coordinated uprising. Ironically, because

Popé

VOICES OF FREEDOM

From Bartolomé de Las Casas, *History of the Indies* (1528)

Las Casas was the Dominican priest who condemned the treatment of Indians in the Spanish empire. His widely disseminated *History of the Indies* helped to establish the Black Legend of Spanish cruelty.

The Indians [of Hispaniola] were totally deprived of their freedom and were put in the harshest, fiercest, most horrible servitude and captivity which no one who has not seen it can understand. Even beasts enjoy more freedom when they are allowed to graze in the fields. But our Spaniards gave no such opportunity to Indians and truly considered them perpetual slaves, since the Indians had not the free will to dispose of their persons but instead were disposed of according to Spanish greed and cruelty, not as men in captivity but as beasts tied to a rope to prevent free movement. When they were allowed to go home, they often found it deserted and had no other recourse than to go out into the woods to find food and to die. When they fell ill, which was very frequently because they are a delicate people unaccustomed to such work, the Spaniards did not believe them and pitilessly called them lazy dogs and kicked and beat them; and when illness was apparent they sent them home as useless. . . . They would go then, falling into the first stream and dying there in desperation; others would hold on longer but very few ever made it home. I sometimes came upon dead bodies on my way, and upon others who were gasping and moaning in their death agony, repeating "Hungry, hungry." And this was the freedom, the good treatment and the Christianity the Indians received.

About eight years passed under [Spanish rule] and this disorder had time to grow; no one gave it a thought and the multitude of people who originally lived on the island . . . was consumed at such a rate that in these eight years 90 per cent had perished. From here this sweeping plague went to San Juan, Jamaica, Cuba and the continent, spreading destruction over the whole hemisphere.

From "Declaration of Josephe"
(December 19, 1681)

Josephe was a Spanish-speaking Indian questioned by a royal attorney in Mexico City investigating the Pueblo Revolt. The revolt of the Indian population, in 1680, temporarily drove Spanish settlers from present-day New Mexico.

Asked what causes or motives the said Indian rebels had for renouncing the law of God and obedience to his Majesty, and for committing so many of crimes, [he answered] the causes they have were alleged ill treatment and injuries received from [Spanish authorities], because they beat them, took away what they had, and made them work without pay. Thus he replies.

Asked if he has learned if it has come to his notice during the time that he has been here the reason why the apostates burned the images, churches, and things pertaining to divine worship, making a mockery and a trophy of them, killing the priests and doing the other things they did, he said that he knows and had heard it generally stated that while they were besieging the villa the rebellious traitors burned the church and shouted in loud voices, "Now the God of the Spaniards, who was their father, is dead, and Santa Maria, who was their mother, and the saints, who were pieces of rotten wood," saying that only their own god lived. Thus they ordered all the temples and images, crosses and rosaries burned, and their function being over, they all went to bathe in the rivers, saying that they thereby washed away the water of baptism. For their churches, they placed on the four sides and in the center of the plaza some small circular enclosures of stone where they went to offer flour, feathers, and the seed of maguey [a local plant], maize, and tobacco, and performed other superstitious rites, giving the children to understand that they must all do this in the future. The captains and the chiefs ordered that the names of Jesus and Mary should nowhere be uttered. . . . He has seen many houses of idolatry which they have built, dancing the dance of the cachina [part of a traditional Indian religious ceremony], which this declarant has also danced. Thus he replies to the question.

QUESTIONS

1. *Why does Las Casas, after describing the ill treatment of Indians, write, "And this was the freedom, the good treatment and the Christianity the Indians received"?*

2. *What role did religion play in the Pueblo Revolt?*

3. *What ideas of freedom are apparent in the two documents?*

the Pueblos spoke six different languages, Spanish became the revolt's "lingua franca" (a common means of communication among persons of different linguistic backgrounds). Some 2,000 warriors destroyed isolated farms and missions, killing 400 colonists, including 21 Franciscan missionaries. Most of the Spanish survivors, accompanied by several hundred Christian Indians, made their way south out of New Mexico. Within a few weeks, a century of colonization in the area had been destroyed.

The **Pueblo Revolt** was the most complete victory for Native Americans over Europeans and the only wholesale expulsion of settlers in the history of North America. Cooperation among the Pueblo peoples, however, soon evaporated. By the end of the 1680s, warfare had broken out among several villages, even as Apache and Navajo raids continued. Popé died around 1690. In 1692, the Spanish launched an invasion that reconquered New Mexico. Some communities welcomed them back as a source of military protection. But Spain had learned a lesson. In the eighteenth century, colonial authorities adopted a more tolerant attitude toward traditional religious practices and made fewer demands on Indian labor.

St. Anthony and the Infant Jesus, painted on a tanned buffalo hide by a Franciscan priest in New Mexico in the early eighteenth century. This was not long after the Spanish reconquered the area, from which they had been driven by the Pueblo Revolt.

THE FRENCH AND DUTCH EMPIRES

If the Black Legend inspired a sense of superiority among Spain's European rivals, the precious metals that poured from the New World into the Spanish treasury aroused the desire to match Spain's success. The establishment of Spain's American empire transformed the balance of power in the world economy. The Atlantic replaced the overland route to Asia as the major axis of global trade. During the seventeenth century, the French, Dutch, and English established colonies in North America. England's mainland colonies, to be discussed in the next chapter, consisted of agricultural settlements with growing populations whose hunger for land produced incessant conflict with native peoples. New France and

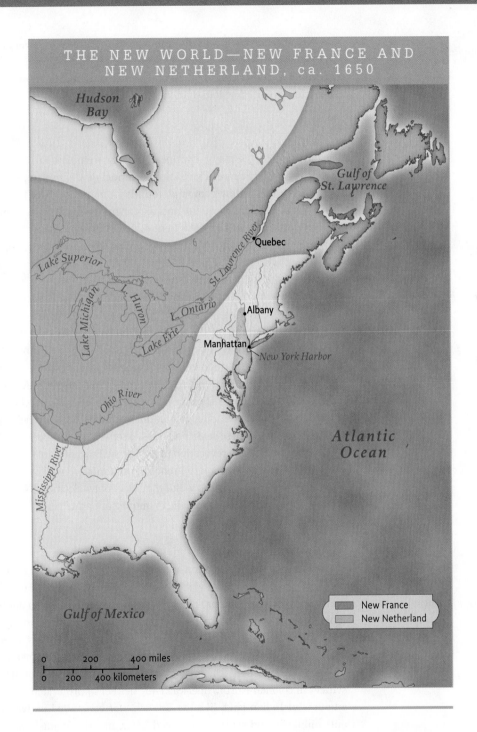

THE NEW WORLD—NEW FRANCE AND
NEW NETHERLAND, ca. 1650

Hudson
Bay

Gulf of
St. Lawrence

Lake Superior

St. Lawrence River

•Quebec

Lake Michigan

L. Huron

L. Ontario

Lake Erie

•Albany

Manhattan

New York Harbor

Ohio River

Atlantic
Ocean

Mississippi River

New France
New Netherland

Gulf of Mexico

0   200   400 miles
0   200   400 kilometers

New Netherland were primarily commercial ventures that never attracted large numbers of colonists. More dependent on Indians as trading partners and military allies, these French and Dutch settlements allowed Native Americans greater freedom than the English.

French Colonization

The first of Spain's major European rivals to embark on New World explorations was France. The explorer Samuel de Champlain, sponsored by a French fur-trading company, founded Quebec in 1608. In 1673, the Jesuit priest Jacques Marquette and the fur trader Louis Joliet located the Mississippi River, and by 1681 René-Robert Cavelier, Sieur de La Salle, had descended to the Gulf of Mexico, claiming the entire Mississippi River valley for France. New France eventually formed a giant arc along the St. Lawrence, Mississippi, and Ohio rivers.

Settlement in New France

By 1700, the number of white inhabitants of New France had risen to only 19,000. With a far larger population than England, France sent many fewer emigrants to the Western Hemisphere. The government at home feared that significant emigration would undermine France's role as a European great power and might compromise its effort to establish trade and good relations with the Indians. Unfavorable reports about America circulated widely in France. Canada was widely depicted as an icebox, a land of savage Indians, a dumping ground for criminals. Most French who left their homes during these years preferred to settle in the Netherlands, Spain, or the West Indies. The revocation in 1685 of the Edict of Nantes, which had extended religious toleration to French Protestants, led well over 100,000 Huguenots to flee their country. But they were not welcome in New France, which the crown desired to remain an outpost of Catholicism.

New France and the Indians

With its small white population and emphasis on the fur trade rather than agricultural settlement, the viability of New France depended on friendly relations with local Indians. The French prided themselves on adopting a more humane policy than their imperial rivals. "Only our nation," declared one French writer, "knows the secret of winning the Indians' affection." The French worked out a complex series of military, commercial, and diplomatic connections, the most enduring alliances between Indians and settlers in colonial North America. They neither appropriated substantial amounts of Indian land, like the English, nor conquered native inhabitants militarily and set them to forced labor, like the Spanish. Samuel de Champlain, the intrepid explorer who dominated the early history of New

Alliances with Indians

This engraving, which appears in Samuel de Champlain's 1613 account of his voyages, is the only likeness of the explorer from his own time. Champlain, wearing European armor and brandishing an arquebus (an advanced weapon of the period), stands at the center of this pitched battle between his Indian allies and the hostile Iroquois.

France, denied that Native Americans were intellectually or culturally inferior to Europeans. Although he occasionally engaged in wars with local Indians, he dreamed of creating a colony based on mutual respect between diverse peoples. The Jesuits, a missionary religious order, did seek, with some success, to convert Indians to Catholicism. But unlike Spanish missionaries in early New Mexico, they allowed Christian Indians to retain a high degree of independence and much of their traditional social structure, and they did not seek to suppress all traditional religious practices.

Jesuits

Like other colonists throughout North America, however, the French brought striking changes in Indian life. Contact with Europeans was inevitably followed by the spread of disease. Participation in the fur trade drew natives into the burgeoning Atlantic economy, introducing new goods and transforming hunting from a search for food into a quest for marketable commodities. Indians were soon swept into the rivalries among European empires.

As in the Spanish empire, New France witnessed considerable cultural exchange and intermixing between colonial and native populations. On the "middle ground" of the upper Great Lakes region in French America, Indians and whites encountered each other for many years on a basis of relative equality. And *métis*, or children of marriages between Indian women and French traders and officials, became guides, traders, and interpreters. Like the Spanish, the French seemed willing to accept Indians as part of colonial society. Indians who converted to Catholicism were promised full citizenship. In fact, however, it was far rarer for natives to adopt French ways than for French settlers to become attracted to the "free" life of the Indians. "It happens more commonly," one official complained, "that a Frenchman becomes savage than a savage becomes a Frenchman."

The middle ground

Movement between societies

The Dutch Empire

Henry Hudson

In 1609, Henry Hudson, an Englishman employed by the Dutch East India Company, sailed into New York Harbor searching for a northwest passage to Asia. Hudson and his crew became the first Europeans to sail up the river that now bears his name. Hudson did not find a route to Asia, but he did encounter abundant fur-bearing animals and Native Americans more than willing to trade furs for European goods. He claimed the area for the Netherlands, and his voyage planted the seeds of what would eventually become a great metropolis, New York City. In 1624, the Dutch West India Company, which had been awarded a monopoly of Dutch trade with America, settled colonists on Manhattan Island.

Dutch trade

These ventures formed one small part in the rise of the Dutch overseas empire. In the early seventeenth century, the Netherlands dominated international commerce, and Amsterdam was Europe's foremost shipping and banking center. The small nation had entered a golden age of rapidly accumulating wealth and stunning achievements in painting, philosophy, and the sciences. With a population of only 2 million, the Netherlands established a far-flung empire that reached from Indonesia to South Africa and the Caribbean and temporarily wrested control of Brazil from Portugal.

Dutch Freedom

The Dutch prided themselves on their devotion to liberty. Indeed, in the early seventeenth century they enjoyed two freedoms not recognized elsewhere in Europe—freedom of the press and of private religious practice. Amsterdam became a haven for persecuted Protestants from all over Europe and for Jews as well.

New Netherland

Despite the Dutch reputation for cherishing freedom, New Netherland was hardly governed democratically. New Amsterdam, the main population center, was essentially a fortified military outpost controlled by appointees of the West India Company. Although the governor called on prominent citizens for advice from time to time, neither an elected assembly nor a town council, the basic unit of government at home, was established.

In other ways, however, the colonists enjoyed more liberty than their counterparts elsewhere in North America. Even their slaves possessed rights. Some enjoyed "half-freedom"—they were required to pay an annual fee to the company and work for it when called upon, but they were given land to support their families. Settlers employed slaves on family farms or for household or craft labor, not on large plantations as in the West Indies.

Women in the Dutch settlement enjoyed far more independence than in other colonies. According to Dutch law, married women retained their

NIEUW AMSTERDAM
op 't Eylant Manhattans.

separate legal identity. They could go to court, borrow money, and own property. Men were used to sharing property with their wives.

A view of New Amsterdam from 1651 illustrates the tiny size of the outpost.

New Netherland attracted a remarkably diverse population. As early as the 1630s, at least eighteen languages were said to be spoken in New Amsterdam, whose residents included not only Dutch settlers but also Africans, Belgians, English, French, Germans, Irish, and Scandinavians.

The Dutch and Religious Toleration

The Dutch long prided themselves on being uniquely tolerant in religious matters compared to other European nations and their empires. It would be wrong, however, to attribute modern ideas of religious freedom to either the Dutch government and company at home or the rulers of New Netherland. Both Holland and New Netherland had an official religion, the Dutch Reformed Church, one of the Protestant national churches to emerge from the Reformation. The Dutch commitment to freedom of conscience extended to religious devotion exercised in private, not public worship in nonestablished churches.

When Jews, Quakers, Lutherans, and others demanded the right to practice their religion openly, Governor Petrus Stuyvesant adamantly refused, seeing such diversity as a threat to a godly, prosperous order. Twenty-three Jews arrived in New Amsterdam in 1654 from Brazil and the Caribbean. Referring to them as "members of a deceitful race," Stuyvesant ordered the newcomers to leave. But the company overruled him, noting that Jews at home had invested "a large amount of capital" in its shares.

Denial of religious freedom

Nonetheless, it is true that the Dutch dealt with religious pluralism in ways quite different from the practices common in other New World empires. Religious dissent was tolerated as long as it did not involve open and public worship. No one in New Netherland was forced to attend the official church, nor was anyone executed for holding the wrong religious beliefs (as would happen in Puritan New England).

Religious pluralism

Settling New Netherland

Sparse European settlement in New Netherland

During the seventeenth century, the Netherlands sent 1 million people overseas (many of them recent immigrants who were not in fact Dutch) to populate and govern their far-flung colonies. Very few, however, made North America their destination. By the mid-1660s, the European population of New Netherland numbered only 9,000. New Netherland remained a tiny backwater in the Dutch empire. So did an even smaller outpost near present-day Wilmington, Delaware, established in 1638 by a group of Dutch merchants. To circumvent the West India Company's trade monopoly, they claimed to be operating under the Swedish flag and called their settlement New Sweden. Only 300 settlers were living there when New Netherland seized the colony in 1655.

Features of European Settlement

The Dutch came to North America to trade, not to conquer. Mindful of the Black Legend of Spanish cruelty, the Dutch determined to treat the native inhabitants more humanely than the Spanish. Having won their own independence from Spain after the longest and bloodiest war of sixteenth-century Europe, many Dutch identified with American Indians as fellow victims of Spanish oppression.

The seal of New Netherland, adopted by the Dutch West India Company in 1630, suggests the centrality of the fur trade to the colony's prospects. Surrounding the beaver is *wampum*, a string of beads used by Indians in religious rituals and as currency.

From the beginning, Dutch authorities recognized Indian sovereignty over the land and forbade settlement in any area until it had been purchased. But they also required tribes to make payments to colonial authorities. Near the coast, where most newcomers settled, New Netherland was hardly free of conflict with the Indians. With the powerful Iroquois Confederacy of the upper Hudson Valley, however, the Dutch established friendly commercial and diplomatic relations.

Thus, before the planting of English colonies in North America, other European nations had established various kinds of settlements in the New World. Despite their differences, the Spanish, French, and Dutch empires shared certain features. All brought Christianity, new forms of technology and learning, new legal systems and family relations, and new forms of economic enterprise and wealth creation. They also brought savage warfare and widespread disease. These empires were aware of one another's existence. They studied and borrowed from one another, each lauding itself as superior to the others.

From the outset, dreams of freedom—for Indians, for settlers, for the entire world through the spread of Christianity—inspired and justified colonization. It would be no different when, at the beginning of the seventeenth century, England entered the struggle for empire in North America.

CHAPTER REVIEW AND ONLINE RESOURCES

REVIEW QUESTIONS

1. Describe why the "discovery" of America was one of the "most important events recorded in the history of mankind," according to Adam Smith.

2. Describe the different global economies that Europeans participated in or created during the European age of expansion.

3. One of the most striking features of Indian societies at the time of the encounter with Europeans was their diversity. Support this statement with several examples.

4. Compare and contrast European values and ways of life with those of the Indians. Consider addressing religion, views about ownership of land, gender relations, and notions of freedom.

5. What were the main factors fueling the European age of expansion?

6. Compare the different economic and political systems of Spain, Portugal, the Netherlands, and France in the age of expansion.

7. Compare the political, economic, and religious motivations behind the French and Dutch empires with those of New Spain.

8. How would European settlers explain their superiority to Native Americans and justify both the conquest of Native lands and terminating their freedom?

KEY TERMS

Tenochtitlán (p. 3)

Cahokia (p. 5)

Iroquois (p. 7)

"Christian Liberty" (p. 12)

caravels (p. 14)

reconquista (p. 16)

Columbian Exchange (p. 19)

mestizos (p. 22)

repartimiento system (p. 24)

Black Legend (p. 24)

Pueblo Revolt (p. 30)

métis (p. 33)

wwnorton.com /studyspace

VISIT STUDYSPACE FOR THESE RESOURCES AND MORE

- A chapter outline
- A diagnostic chapter quiz
- Interactive maps
- Map worksheets
- Multimedia documents

CHAPTER 2

BEGINNINGS OF ENGLISH AMERICA

★

1607–1660

The Armada Portrait of Queen Elizabeth I, by the artist George Gower, commemorates the defeat of the Spanish Armada in 1588 and appears to link it with English colonization of the New World. England's victorious navy is visible through the window, while the queen's hand rests on a globe, with her fingers pointing to the coast of North America.

On April 26, 1607, three small ships carrying colonists from England sailed into the mouth of Chesapeake Bay. After exploring the area for a little over two weeks, they chose a site sixty miles inland on the James River for their settlement, hoping to protect themselves from marauding Spanish warships. Here they established Jamestown (named for the king of England) as the capital of the colony of Virginia (named for his predecessor, Elizabeth I, the "virgin queen"). But despite these bows to royal authority, the voyage was sponsored not by the English government, which in 1607 was hard-pressed for funds, but by the **Virginia Company**, a private business organization whose shareholders included merchants, aristocrats, and members of Parliament, and to which the queen had given her blessing before her death in 1603.

When the three ships returned home, 104 settlers remained in Virginia. All were men, for the Virginia Company had more interest in searching for gold and in other ways exploiting the area's natural resources than in establishing a functioning society. Nevertheless, Jamestown became the first permanent English settlement in the area that is now the United States. The settlers were the first of tens of thousands of Europeans who crossed the Atlantic during the seventeenth century to live and work in North America. They led the way for new empires that mobilized labor and economic resources, reshaped societies throughout the Atlantic world, and shifted the balance of power at home from Spain and Portugal to the nations of northwestern Europe.

English North America in the seventeenth century was a place where entrepreneurs sought to make fortunes, religious minorities hoped to worship without governmental interference and to create societies based on biblical teachings, and aristocrats dreamed of re-creating a vanished world of feudalism. For ordinary men and women, emigration offered an escape from lives of deprivation and inequality. "No man," wrote John Smith, an early leader of Jamestown, "will go from [England] to have less freedom" in America. The settlers of English America came to enjoy greater rights than colonists of other empires, including the power to choose members of elected assemblies, protections of the common law such as the right to trial by jury, and access to land, the key to economic independence. In some colonies, though by no means all, colonists enjoyed considerably more religious freedom than existed in Europe.

Many degrees of freedom coexisted in seventeenth-century North America, from the slave, stripped completely of liberty, to the independent landowner, who enjoyed a full range of rights. The settlers' success, however, rested on depriving Native Americans of their land and, in some colonies, on importing large numbers of African slaves as laborers. Freedom and lack of freedom expanded together in seventeenth-century America.

FOCUS QUESTIONS

- *What were the main contours of English colonization in the seventeenth century?*

- *What challenges did the early English settlers face?*

- *How did Virginia and Maryland develop in their early years?*

- *What made the English settlement of New England distinctive?*

- *What were the main sources of discord in early New England?*

- *How did the English Civil War affect the colonies in America?*

ENGLAND AND THE NEW WORLD

Unifying the English Nation

As the case of Spain suggests, early empire building was, in large part, an extension of the consolidation of national power in Europe. But during the sixteenth century, England was a second-rate power racked by internal disunity. Henry VIII, crowned in 1509, launched the Reformation in England. When the Pope refused to annul his marriage to Catherine of Aragon, Henry severed the nation from the Catholic Church. In its place he established the Church of England, or Anglican Church, with himself at the head. Decades of religious strife followed, as did considerable persecution of Catholics under Henry's successor, Edward VI. In 1553, Edward's half sister Mary became queen. She temporarily restored Catholicism as the state religion and executed a number of Protestants. Mary's successor, Elizabeth I (reigned 1558–1603), restored the Anglican ascendancy and executed more than 100 Catholic priests.

Religious strife in England

England and Ireland

England's long struggle to conquer and pacify Ireland, which lasted well into the seventeenth century, absorbed money and energy that might have been directed toward the New World. In subduing Ireland, whose Catholic population was deemed a threat to the stability of Protestant rule in England, the government employed a variety of approaches, including military conquest, the slaughter of civilians, the seizure of land and introduction of English economic practices, and the dispatch of large numbers of settlers. Rather than seeking to absorb the Irish into English society, the English excluded the native population from a territory of settlement known as the Pale, where the colonists created their own social order.

Subduing Ireland

The methods used in Ireland anticipated policies England would undertake in America. Some sixteenth-century English writers directly compared the allegedly barbaric "wild Irish" with American Indians.

England and North America

Not until the reign of Elizabeth I did the English turn their attention to North America, although sailors and adventurers still showed more interest in raiding Spanish cities and treasure fleets in the Caribbean than establishing settlements. The government granted charters (grants of exclusive rights and privileges) to Sir Humphrey Gilbert and Sir Walter Raleigh, authorizing them to establish colonies in North America at their own expense.

With little or no support from the crown, both ventures failed. Gilbert, who had earned a reputation for brutality in the Irish wars by murdering civilians and burning their crops, established a short-lived settlement on Newfoundland in 1582. Three years later, Raleigh dispatched a fleet of five ships with some 100 colonists to set up a base on **Roanoke** Island, off the North Carolina coast. But the colonists, mostly young men under military leadership, abandoned the venture in 1586 and returned to England. A second group of 100 settlers, composed of families who hoped to establish a permanent colony, was dispatched that year. Their fate remains a mystery. When a ship bearing supplies arrived in 1590, the sailors found the colony abandoned. Raleigh, by now nearly bankrupt, lost his enthusiasm for colonization. To establish a successful colony, it seemed clear, would require more planning and economic resources than any individual could provide.

The failed Roanoke settlement

Motives for Colonization

As in the case of Spain, national glory, profit, and religious mission merged in early English thinking about the New World. The Reformation heightened the English government's sense of Catholic Spain as its mortal enemy (a belief reinforced in 1588 when a Spanish naval armada unsuccessfully attempted to invade the British Isles). By the late sixteenth century, anti-Catholicism had become deeply ingrained in English popular culture. Reports of the atrocities of Spanish rule were widely circulated. English translations of Bartolomé de Las Casas's writings appeared during Elizabeth's reign.

Religion and imperial purpose

Although atrocities were hardly confined to any one nation—as England's own conduct in Ireland demonstrated—the idea that the empire of Catholic Spain was uniquely murderous and tyrannical enabled the English to describe their own imperial ambitions in the language of freedom. In *A Discourse Concerning Western Planting*, written in 1584, the Protestant minister and scholar Richard Hakluyt listed twenty-three reasons that Queen Elizabeth I should support the establishment of colonies. Among them was the idea that English settlements would strike a blow against Spain's empire and therefore form part of a divine mission to rescue the New World and its inhabitants from the influence of Catholicism and tyranny.

Richard Hakluyt

An engraving by Theodor de Bry depicts colonists hunting and fishing in Virginia. Promotional images such as this emphasized the abundance of the New World and suggested that colonists could live familiar lives there.

But bringing freedom to Indians was hardly the only motivation Hakluyt and other writers advanced. National power and glory, they argued, could be achieved through colonization. England, a relatively minor power at the end of the sixteenth century, could come to rival great nations like Spain and France.

Yet another motivation was that colonists could enrich the mother country and themselves by providing English consumers with goods now supplied by foreigners and opening a new market for English products. Unlike early adventurers such as Raleigh, who thought of wealth in terms of deposits of gold, Hakluyt insisted that trade would be the basis of England's empire.

The Social Crisis

Equally important, America could be a refuge for England's "surplus" population, benefiting mother country and emigrants alike. The late sixteenth century was a time of social crisis in England, with economic growth unable to keep pace with the needs of a population that grew from 3 million in 1550 to about 4 million in 1600. In the sixteenth and seventeenth centuries, landlords sought profits by raising sheep for the expanding trade in wool and introducing more modern farming practices such as crop rotation. They evicted small farmers and fenced in "commons" previously open to all.

While many landlords, farmers, and town merchants benefited from the **enclosure movement**, as this process was called, thousands of persons were uprooted from the land. Many flooded into England's cities. Others, denounced by authorities as rogues, vagabonds, and vagrants, wandered the roads in search of work. "All our towns," wrote the Puritan leader John Winthrop in 1629, shortly before leaving England for Massachusetts, "complain of the burden of poor people and strive by all means to rid any such as they have." England, he added somberly, "grows weary of her inhabitants."

For years, the government struggled to deal with this social crisis, sometimes resorting to extreme measures, such as whipping or hanging the unemployed or forcing them to accept any job offered to them. Another solution was to encourage the unruly poor to leave for the New World.

From poverty to emigration

As colonists, they could become productive citizens, contributing to the nation's wealth.

Masterless Men

Although authorities saw wandering or unemployed "masterless men" as a danger to society, working for wages was itself widely associated with servility and loss of liberty. Only those who controlled their own labor could be regarded as truly free. Indeed, popular tales and ballads romanticized the very vagabonds, highwaymen, and even beggars denounced by the propertied and powerful, since despite their poverty they at least enjoyed freedom from wage work.

The image of the New World as a unique place of opportunity, where the English laboring classes could regain economic independence by acquiring land and where even criminals would enjoy a second chance, was deeply rooted from the earliest days of settlement. John Smith had scarcely landed in Virginia in 1607 when he wrote that in America "every man may be the master and owner of his own labor and land." The main lure for emigrants from England to the New World was not so much riches in gold and silver as the promise of independence that followed from owning land. Economic freedom and the possibility of passing it on to one's children attracted the largest number of English colonists.

The New World as a land of opportunity

THE COMING OF THE ENGLISH

English Emigrants

Seventeenth-century North America was an unstable and dangerous environment. Diseases decimated Indian and settler populations alike. Without sustained immigration, most settlements would have collapsed. With a population of between 4 million and 5 million, about half that of Spain and a quarter of that of France, England produced a far larger number of men, women, and children willing to brave the dangers of emigration to the New World. In large part, this was because economic conditions in England were so bad.

Between 1607 and 1700, more than half a million people left England. North America was not the destination of the majority of these emigrants. Approximately 180,000 settled in Ireland, and about the same number migrated to the West Indies, where the introduction of sugar cultivation promised riches for those who could obtain land. Nonetheless, the population of England's mainland colonies quickly outstripped that of their rivals. The Chesapeake area, where the tobacco-producing colonies of Virginia

A pamphlet published in 1609 promoting emigration to Virginia.

NOVA BRITANNIA.
OFFERING MOST
Excellent fruites by Planting in
VIRGINIA.

Exciting all such as be well affected
to further the same.

LONDON
Printed for SAMVEL MACHAM, and are to be sold at
his Shop in Pauls Church-yard, at the
Signe of the Bul-head.
1609.

and Maryland developed a constant demand for cheap labor, received about 120,000 settlers. New England attracted 21,000 emigrants, nearly all of them arriving before 1640. In the second part of the seventeenth century, the Middle Colonies (New York, New Jersey, and Pennsylvania) attracted about 23,000 settlers. Although the arrivals to New England and the Middle Colonies included many families, the majority of newcomers were young, single men from the bottom rungs of English society, who had little to lose by emigrating.

Demographics of colonists

Indentured Servants

Settlers who could pay for their own passage—government officials, clergymen, merchants, artisans, landowning farmers, and members of the lesser nobility—arrived in America as free persons. Most quickly acquired land. In the seventeenth century, however, nearly two-thirds of English settlers came as **indentured servants**, who voluntarily surrendered their freedom for a specified time (usually five to seven years) in exchange for passage to America.

Slavery and indentured servitude

Like slaves, servants could be bought and sold, could not marry without the permission of their owner, were subject to physical punishment, and saw their obligation to labor enforced by the courts. But, unlike slaves, servants could look forward to a release from bondage. Assuming they survived their period of labor, servants would receive a payment known as "freedom dues" and become free members of society.

Given the high death rate, many servants did not live to the end of their terms. Freedom dues were sometimes so meager that they did not enable recipients to acquire land. Many servants found the reality of life in the New World less appealing than they had anticipated. Employers constantly complained of servants running away, not working diligently, or being unruly, all manifestations of what one commentator called their "fondness for freedom."

Land and Liberty

Landownership as the basis of liberty

Access to land played many roles in seventeenth-century America. Land, English settlers believed, was the basis of liberty. Owning land gave men control over their own labor and, in most colonies, the right to vote. The promise of immediate access to land lured free settlers, and freedom dues that included land persuaded potential immigrants to sign contracts as indentured servants. Land in America also became a way for the king to reward relatives and allies. Each colony was launched with a huge grant of land from the crown, either to a company or to a private individual known as a proprietor. Some grants, if taken literally, stretched from the Atlantic Ocean to the Pacific.

Without labor, however, land would have little value. Since emigrants did not come to America intending to work the land of others (except temporarily in the case of indentured servants), the very abundance of "free" land eventually led many property owners to turn to slaves as a workforce.

Englishmen and Indians

Land in North America, of course, was already occupied. And the arrival of English settlers presented the native inhabitants of eastern North America with the greatest crisis in their history. Unlike the Spanish, English colonists were chiefly interested in displacing the Indians and settling on their land, not intermarrying with them, organizing their labor, or making them subjects of the crown. The English exchanged goods with the native population, and Indians often traveled through colonial settlements. Fur traders on the frontiers of settlement sometimes married Indian women, partly as a way of gaining access to native societies and the kin networks essential to economic relationships. Most English settlers, however, remained obstinately separate from their Indian neighbors. Moreover, the aim of converting Indians to Christianity foundered on Indian indifference to the religious disputes that racked Europe and the unavoidable reality that churches transplanted to English America had their hands full providing religious services for European colonists.

The English and Indian land

Failure of converting Indians

Despite their insistence that Indians had no real claim to the land since they did not cultivate or improve it, most colonial authorities acquired land by purchase, often in treaties forced upon Indians after they had suffered military defeat. To keep the peace, some colonial governments tried to prevent the private seizure or purchase of Indian lands, or they declared certain areas off-limits to settlers. But these measures were rarely enforced and ultimately proved ineffective. New settlers and freed servants sought land for themselves, and those who established families in America needed land for their children.

The seventeenth century was marked by recurrent warfare between colonists and Indians. These conflicts generated a strong feeling of superiority among the colonists and left them intent on maintaining the real and imagined boundaries separating the two peoples. Over time the English displaced the original inhabitants more thoroughly than any other European empire.

Recurrent warfare between colonists and Indians

The Transformation of Indian Life

Many eastern Indians initially welcomed the newcomers, or at least their goods, which they appreciated for their practical advantages. Items like woven cloth, metal kettles, iron axes, fishhooks, hoes, and guns were quickly integrated into Indian life. Indians also displayed a great desire for goods like colorful glass beads and copper ornaments that could be incorporated into their religious ceremonies.

Changes in Indian farming, hunting, and cooking practices

As Indians became integrated into the Atlantic economy, subtle changes took place in Indian life. European metal goods changed their farming, hunting, and cooking practices. Men devoted more time to hunting beaver for fur trading. Later observers would describe this trade as one in which Indians exchanged valuable commodities like furs and animal skins for worthless European trinkets. In fact, both Europeans and Indians gave up goods they had in abundance in exchange for items in short supply in their own society. But as the colonists achieved military superiority over the Indians, the profits of trade mostly flowed to colonial and European merchants. Growing connections with Europeans stimulated warfare among Indian tribes, and the overhunting of beaver and deer forced some groups to encroach on territory claimed by others. And newcomers from Europe brought epidemics that decimated Indian populations.

A drawing by the artist John White shows ten male and seven female Native Americans dancing around a circle of posts in a religious ritual. White was a careful observer of their clothing, body markings, and objects used in the ceremony.

As settlers fenced in more and more land and introduced new crops and livestock, the natural environment changed in ways that undermined traditional Indian agriculture and hunting. Pigs and cattle roamed freely, trampling Indian corn-fields and gardens. The need for wood to build and heat homes and export to England depleted forests on which Indians relied for hunting. The rapid expansion of the fur trade diminished the population of beaver and other animals. In short, Indians' lives were powerfully altered by the changes set in motion in 1607 when English colonists landed at Jamestown.

SETTLING THE CHESAPEAKE

The Jamestown Colony

The early history of Jamestown was, to say the least, not promising. The colony's leadership changed repeatedly, its inhabitants suffered an extraordinarily high death rate, and, with the Virginia Company seeking a quick profit, supplies from England proved inadequate. The first settlers were "a quarrelsome band of gentlemen and servants." They included few farmers and laborers and numerous sons of English gentry who preferred to prospect for gold rather than farm.

Disease and lack of food took a heavy toll. By the end of the first year, the original population of 104 had fallen by half. New arrivals (including the first two women, who landed in 1608) brought the numbers up to 400 in 1609, but by 1610, after a winter long remembered as the "starving time," only 65 settlers remained alive. At one point, the survivors abandoned Jamestown and sailed for England, only to be intercepted and persuaded to return to Virginia by ships carrying a new governor, 250 colonists, and supplies.

Only rigorous military discipline held the colony together. **John Smith** imposed a regime of forced labor on company lands. "He that will not work, shall not eat," Smith declared. Smith's autocratic mode of governing alienated many of the colonists. After being injured in an accidental

The only known contemporary portrait of a New England Indian, this 1681 painting by an unnamed artist was long thought to represent Ninigret II, a leader of the Narragansetts of Rhode Island. It has been more recently identified as David, an Indian who saved the life of John Winthrop II, a governor of colonial Connecticut. Apart from the wampum beads around his neck, everything the Indian wears is of English manufacture.

John Smith's iron rule

gunpowder explosion in 1609, he was forced to return to England. But his immediate successors continued his iron rule.

The Virginia Company slowly realized that for the colony to survive it would have to abandon the search for gold, grow its own food, and find a marketable commodity. It would also have to attract more settlers. With this end in view, it announced new policies in 1618. Instead of retaining all the land for itself, the company introduced the **headright system**, awarding fifty acres of land to any colonist who paid for his own or another's passage. Thus, anyone who brought in a sizable number of servants would immediately acquire a large estate. In place of the governor's militaristic regime, a "charter of grants and liberties" was issued, including the establishment of a **House of Burgesses**. When it convened in 1619, this became the first elected assembly in colonial America. Also in 1619, the first twenty blacks arrived in Virginia on a Dutch vessel. These events laid the foundation for a society that would one day be dominated economically and politically by slaveowning planters.

By 1650, English settlement in the Chesapeake had spread well beyond the initial colony at Jamestown, as tobacco planters sought fertile land near navigable waterways.

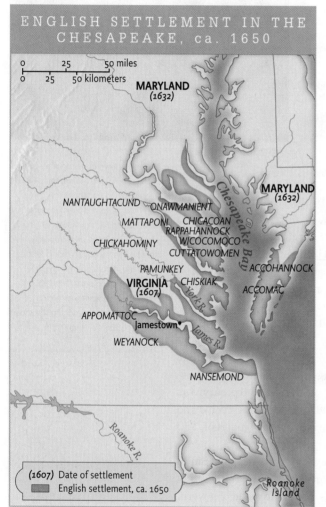

ENGLISH SETTLEMENT IN THE CHESAPEAKE, ca. 1650

0   25   50 miles
0   25   50 kilometers

MARYLAND (1632)

NANTAUGHTACUND   ONAWMANIENT
MATTAPONI   CHICACOAN
RAPPAHANNOCK
CHICKAHOMINY   WICOCOMOCO
CUTTATOWOMEN
PAMUNKEY   CHISKIAK   ACCOHANNOCK
VIRGINIA (1607)   ACCOMAC
APPOMATTOC
Jamestown
WEYANOCK

Chesapeake Bay
York R.
James R.

MARYLAND (1632)

NANSEMOND

Roanoke R.

(1607) Date of settlement
English settlement, ca. 1650

Roanoke Island

Powhatan and Pocahontas

When the English arrived at Jamestown, they landed in an area inhabited by some 15,000 to 25,000 Indians living in numerous small agricultural villages. Most acknowledged the rule of Wahunsonacock, a shrewd and forceful leader who had recently consolidated his authority over the region and collected tribute from some thirty subordinate tribes. Called Powhatan by the settlers after the Indian word for both his tribe and his title of paramount chief, he quickly realized the advantages of trade with the newcomers.

In the first two years of Jamestown's existence, relations with Indians were mostly peaceful and based on a fairly equal give-and-take. At one point, Smith was captured by the Indians and threatened with execution by Powhatan, only to be rescued by Pocahontas, reputedly the favorite among his many children by dozens of wives. The incident has come down in legend as an example of a rebellious, love-struck teenager defying her father. In fact, it was probably part of an elaborate ceremony designed by Powhatan to demonstrate his power over the colonists and incorporate them into his realm. Pocahontas subsequently became an intermediary between the two peoples, bringing food and messages to Jamestown. In 1614, she married the English colonist John Rolfe. Two years later, she accompanied her husband to England, where she caused a sensation in the court of James I as a symbol of Anglo-Indian harmony and missionary success. But she succumbed to disease in 1617. Her father died the following year.

The Uprising of 1622

Once it became clear that the English were interested in establishing a permanent and constantly expanding colony, not a trading post, conflict with local Indians was inevitable. In 1622, Powhatan's brother and successor, Opechancanough, led a brilliantly planned surprise attack that in a single day wiped out one-quarter of Virginia's settler population of 1,200. The surviving 900 colonists organized themselves into military bands, which then massacred scores of Indians and devastated their villages. By going to war, declared Governor Francis Wyatt, the Indians had forfeited any claim to the land. Virginia's policy, he continued, must now be nothing less than the "expulsion of the savages to gain the free range of the country."

The unsuccessful uprising of 1622 fundamentally shifted the balance of power in the colony. The settlers' supremacy was reinforced in 1644 when a last desperate rebellion led by Opechancanough, now said to be 100 years old, was crushed after causing the deaths of some 500 colonists. Virginia forced a treaty on the surviving coastal Indians, who now numbered less than 2,000, that acknowledged their subordination to the government at Jamestown and required them to move to tribal reservations to the west and not enter areas of European settlement without permission. Settlers spreading inland into the Virginia countryside continued to seize Indian lands.

The destruction caused by the **Uprising of 1622** was the last in a series of blows suffered by the Virginia Company. Two years later, it surrendered its charter and Virginia became the first royal colony, its governor now appointed by the crown. Investors had not turned a profit, and although the company had sent 6,000 settlers to Virginia, its white population

Powhatan, the most prominent Indian leader in the original area of English settlement in Virginia. This image, showing Powhatan and his court, was engraved on John Smith's map of Virginia and included in Smith's *General History of Virginia*, published in 1624.

The only portrait of Pocahontas made during her lifetime was engraved by Simon van de Passe in England in 1616. After converting to Christianity, Pocahontas took the name Rebecca.

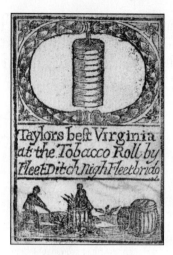

An advertisement for tobacco includes images of slaves handling barrels and tobacco plants.

Tobacco and social change in Virginia

numbered only 1,200 when the king assumed control. The government in London for years paid little attention to Virginia. Henceforth, the local elite, not a faraway company, controlled the colony's development. And that elite was growing rapidly in wealth and power thanks to the cultivation of a crop introduced from the West Indies by John Rolfe—tobacco.

A Tobacco Colony

King James I considered **tobacco** "harmful to the brain and dangerous to the lungs" and issued a spirited warning against its use. But increasing numbers of Europeans enjoyed smoking and believed the tobacco plant had medicinal benefits. Tobacco became Virginia's substitute for gold. It enriched an emerging class of tobacco planters, as well as members of the colonial government who assigned good land to themselves. The crown profited from customs duties (taxes on tobacco that entered or left the kingdom). The spread of tobacco farming produced a dispersed society with few towns and inspired a frenzied scramble for land. By the middle of the seventeenth century, a new influx of immigrants with ample financial resources—sons of merchants and English gentlemen—had taken advantage of the headright system and governmental connections to acquire large estates along navigable rivers. They established themselves as the colony's social and political elite.

The expansion of tobacco cultivation also led to an increased demand for field labor, met for most of the seventeenth century by young, male indentured servants. Despite harsh conditions of work in the tobacco fields, a persistently high death rate, and laws mandating punishments from whipping to an extension of service for those who ran away or were unruly, the abundance of land continued to attract migrants. Of the 120,000 English immigrants who entered the Chesapeake region during the seventeenth century, three-quarters came as servants. Virginia's white society increasingly came to resemble that of England, with a wealthy landed gentry at the top; a group of small farmers, mostly former indentured servants who had managed to acquire land, in the middle; and an army of poor laborers—servants and landless former indentured servants—at the bottom.

Women and the Family

Virginia, however, lacked one essential element of English society—stable family life. Given the demand for male servants to work in the tobacco fields, men in the Chesapeake outnumbered women for most

Processing tobacco was as labor intensive as caring for the plant in the fields. Here slaves and female indentured servants work with the crop after it has been harvested.

of the seventeenth century by four or five to one. The vast majority of women who emigrated to the region came as indentured servants. Since they usually had to complete their terms of service before marrying, they did not begin to form families until their mid-twenties. The high death rate, unequal ratio between the sexes, and late age of marriage retarded population growth and resulted in large numbers of single men, widows, and orphans.

In the colonies as in England, a married woman possessed certain rights before the law, including a claim to "**dower rights**" of one-third of her husband's property in the event that he died before she did. When the widow died, however, the property passed to the husband's male heirs. (English law was far less generous than in Spain, where a woman could hold independently any property inherited from her parents, and a man and wife owned jointly all the wealth accumulated during a marriage.)

Women's lives

Social conditions in the colonies, however, opened the door to roles women rarely assumed in England. A widow or one of the few women who never married could sometimes take advantage of her legal status as a femme sole (a woman alone, who enjoyed an independent legal identity denied to married women) to make contracts and conduct business. Margaret Brent, who emigrated to the Chesapeake in 1638, acquired land, managed her own plantation, and acted as a lawyer in court. But because most women came to Virginia as indentured servants, they could look forward only to a life of hard labor in the tobacco fields and early death.

The Maryland Experiment

The second Chesapeake colony, Maryland, followed a similar course of development. As in Virginia, tobacco came to dominate the economy and tobacco planters the society. But in other ways, Maryland's history was strikingly different.

Proprietary colony

Maryland was established in 1632 as a proprietary colony, that is, a grant of land and governmental authority to a single individual. This was Cecilius Calvert, the son of a recently deceased favorite of King Charles I. The charter granted him "full, free, and absolute power," including control of trade and the right to initiate all legislation, with an elected assembly confined to approving or disapproving his proposals. Although Calvert disliked representative institutions, the charter guaranteed to colonists "all privileges, franchises, and liberties" of Englishmen. While these were not spelled out, they undoubtedly included the idea of a government limited by the law. Here was a recipe for conflict, and Maryland had more than its share during the seventeenth century.

Religion in Maryland

Further aggravating instability in the colony was the fact that Calvert, a Catholic, envisioned Maryland as a refuge for his persecuted coreligionists in England, especially the younger sons of Catholic gentry who had few economic or political prospects in England. In Maryland, he hoped, Protestants and Catholics could live in a harmony unknown in Europe. Most appointed officials were Catholic, including relatives of the proprietor. But Protestants always formed a majority of the settlers. Most, as in Virginia, came as indentured servants.

Maryland as a refuge for persecuted Catholics

As in Virginia, the death rate remained very high. Almost 70 percent of male settlers in Maryland died before reaching the age of fifty, and half the children born in the colony did not live to adulthood. But at least initially, Maryland seems to have offered servants greater opportunity for landownership than Virginia. Unlike in the older colony, freedom dues in Maryland included fifty acres of land. As tobacco planters engrossed the best land later in the century, however, the prospects for landless men diminished.

THE NEW ENGLAND WAY

The Rise of Puritanism

As Virginia and Maryland evolved toward societies dominated by a small aristocracy ruling over numerous bound laborers, a very different social order emerged in seventeenth-century New England. The early history of that region is intimately connected to the religious movement known as **"Puritanism,"** which arose in England late in the sixteenth century. The term was initially coined by opponents to ridicule those not satisfied with the progress of the Protestant Reformation in England. Puritans differed among themselves on many issues. But all shared the conviction that the Church of England retained too many elements of Catholicism in its religious rituals and doctrines. Puritans saw elaborate church ceremonies, the rule that priests could not marry, and ornate church decorations as vestiges of "popery." Many rejected the Catholic structure of religious authority descending from a pope or king to archbishops, bishops, and priests. Only independent local congregations, they believed, should choose clergymen and determine modes of worship. These Puritans were called "Congregationalists." They believed that neither the church nor the nation was living up to its ideals.

Puritanism and the Protestant Reformation in England

Puritans considered religious belief a complex and demanding matter and urged believers to seek the truth by reading the Bible and listening to sermons by educated ministers, rather than devoting themselves to sacraments administered by priests and to what Puritans considered formulaic prayers. The sermon was the central rite of Puritan practice. In the course of a lifetime, according to one estimate, the average Puritan listened to some 7,000 sermons. In their religious beliefs, Puritans followed the ideas of the French-born Swiss theologian John Calvin. The world, Calvin taught, was divided between the elect and the damned, but no one knew who was destined to be saved, which had already been determined by God. Nevertheless, leading a good life and prospering economically might be indications of God's grace, whereas idleness and immoral behavior were sure signs of damnation.

The Bible and the sermon

John Calvin

Moral Liberty

Puritanism was characterized by a zeal that alienated many who held differing religious views. A minority of Puritans (such as those who settled in Plymouth Colony) became separatists, abandoning the Church of England entirely to form their own independent churches. Most,

A portrait of John Winthrop, first governor of the Massachusetts Bay Colony, painted in the 1640s.

however, hoped to purify the church from within. But in the 1620s and 1630s, as Charles I seemed to be moving toward a restoration of Catholic ceremonies and the Church of England dismissed Puritan ministers and censored their writings, many Puritans decided to emigrate. When Puritans emigrated to New England, they hoped to escape what they believed to be the religious and worldly corruptions of English society. They would establish a "city set upon a hill," a Bible Commonwealth whose influence would flow back across the Atlantic and rescue England from godlessness and social decay.

Like so many other emigrants to America, Puritans came in search of liberty, especially the right to worship and govern themselves in what they deemed a truly Christian manner. Freedom certainly did not mean unrestrained action, improper religious practices, or sinful behavior, of which, Puritans thought, there were far too many examples in England. In a 1645 speech to the Massachusetts legislature explaining the Puritan conception of freedom, **John Winthrop**, the colony's governor, distinguished sharply between two kinds of liberty. "Natural" liberty, or acting without restraint, suggested "a liberty to do evil." This was the false idea of freedom supposedly adopted by the Irish, Indians, and bad Christians generally. Genuine **"moral" liberty** meant "a liberty to that only which is good." It was quite compatible with severe restraints on speech, religion, and personal behavior. True freedom, Winthrop insisted, depended on "subjection to authority," both religious and secular; otherwise, anarchy was sure to follow. To Puritans, liberty meant that the elect had a right to establish churches and govern society, not that others could challenge their beliefs or authority.

Freedom and subjection to authority

The Pilgrims at Plymouth

The first Puritans to emigrate to America were a group of separatists known as the **Pilgrims**. They had already fled to the Netherlands in 1608. A decade later, fearing that their children were being corrupted by the surrounding culture, they decided to emigrate to Virginia. In September 1620, the *Mayflower*, carrying 150 settlers and crew (among them many non-Puritans), embarked from England. Blown off course, they landed not in Virginia but hundreds of miles to the north, on Cape Cod. Here the 102 who survived the journey established the colony of Plymouth. Before landing, the Pilgrim leaders drew up the **Mayflower Compact**, in which the adult men going ashore agreed to obey "just and equal laws" enacted by representatives of their own choosing. This was the first written frame of government in what is now the United States.

Plymouth colony

The Pilgrims arrived in an area whose native population had recently been decimated by smallpox. They established Plymouth on the site of an abandoned Indian village whose fields had been cleared before the epidemic and were ready for cultivation. Nonetheless, the settlers arrived six weeks before winter without food or farm animals. Half died during the first winter, and the remaining colonists survived only through the help of local Indians. In the autumn of 1621, the Pilgrims invited their Indian allies to a harvest feast celebrating their survival, the first Thanksgiving.

The Pilgrims hoped to establish a society based on the lives of the early Christian saints. Their government rested on the principle of consent, and voting was not restricted to church members. All land was held in common until 1627, when it was divided among the settlers. Plymouth survived as an independent colony until 1691, but it was soon overshadowed by Massachusetts Bay to its north.

Seal of the Massachusetts Bay Colony. The Indian's scanty attire suggests a lack of civilization. His statement "Come Over and Help Us," based on an incident in the Bible, illustrates the English conviction that they were liberating the native population, rather than exploiting them as other empires had.

The Great Migration

Chartered in 1629, the Massachusetts Bay Company was founded by a group of London merchants who hoped to further the Puritan cause and turn a profit through trade with the Indians. The first five ships sailed from England in 1629, and by 1642 some 21,000 Puritans had emigrated to Massachusetts, a flow of population long remembered as the **Great Migration**. After 1640, migration to New England virtually ceased, and in some years more colonists left the region than arrived. Nonetheless, the Great Migration established the basis for a stable and thriving society.

In many ways, the settling of New England was unique. Although servants represented about one-quarter of the Great Migration, most settlers arrived in Massachusetts in families. Compared with colonists in Virginia and Maryland, they were older and more prosperous, and the number of men and women more equally balanced. Because of the even sex ratio and New England's healthier climate, the population grew rapidly, doubling every twenty-seven years. By 1700 New England's white population of 91,000 outnumbered that of both the Chesapeake and the West Indies.

A migration of families

The Puritan Family

Whatever their differences with other Englishmen on religious matters, Puritans shared with the larger society a belief in male authority within the household as well as an adherence to the common-law tradition that severely limited married women's legal and economic rights. Male authority was especially vital in America because in a farming society

Male authority in the household

The Savage Family, a 1779 painting by the New England artist Edward Savage, depicts several generations of a typically numerous Puritan family.

without large numbers of slaves or servants, control over the labor of one's family was essential to a man's economic success.

Women and Puritan religion

To be sure, Puritans deemed women to be the spiritual equals of men, and women were allowed to become full church members. Although all ministers were men, the Puritan belief in the ability of believers to interpret the Bible opened the door for some women to claim positions of religious leadership. The ideal Puritan marriage was based on reciprocal affection and companionship, and divorce was legal. Yet within the household, the husband's authority was virtually absolute.

Family and society

The family was the foundation of strong communities, and unmarried adults seemed a danger to the social fabric. The typical New England woman married at twenty-two, a younger age than her English counterpart, and gave birth seven times. Because New England was a far healthier environment than the Chesapeake, more children survived infancy. Thus, much of a woman's adult life was devoted to bearing and rearing children.

Government and Society in Massachusetts

Since Puritans feared excessive individualism and lack of social unity, the leaders of Massachusetts organized the colony in self-governing towns. Groups of settlers received a land grant from the colony's government and then subdivided it, with residents awarded house lots in a central area and land on the outskirts for farming. Much land remained in commons, either for collective use or to be divided among later settlers or the sons of the town's founders. Each town had its own Congregational Church. Each, according to a law of 1647, was required to establish a school, since the ability to read the Bible was central to Puritan belief. To train an educated ministry, Harvard College was established in 1636 (nearly a century after the Royal University of Mexico, founded in 1551), and two years later the first printing press in English America was established in Cambridge.

The New England town

Wishing to rule the colony without outside interference and to prevent non-Puritans from influencing decision making, the eight shareholders of the Massachusetts Bay Company emigrated to America, taking the charter with them and transforming a commercial document into a form of government. In 1634, a group of deputies elected by freemen (landowning church members) was added to form a single ruling body, the General Court. Ten years later, company officers and elected deputies were divided into two legislative houses. Unlike Virginia, whose governors were appointed first by a faraway company and, after 1624, by the crown, or Maryland, where authority rested with a single proprietor, the freemen of Massachusetts elected their governor.

The Massachusetts Bay Charter

The principle of consent was central to Puritanism. Churches were formed by voluntary agreement among members, who elected the

An embroidered banner depicting the main building at Harvard, the first college established in the English colonies. It was probably made by a Massachusetts woman for a husband or son who attended Harvard.

minister. No important church decision was made without the agreement of the male members. Towns governed themselves, and local officials, delegates to the General Court, and the colonial governor were all elected. Puritans, however, were hardly believers in equality. Church membership, a status that carried great prestige and power, was a restrictive category. Anyone could worship at a church, but to be a full member required demonstrating that one had experienced divine grace and could be considered a "visible saint," usually by testifying about a conversion experience. Voting in colony-wide elections was limited to men who had been accepted as full church members. Puritan democracy was for those within the circle of church membership; those outside the boundary occupied a secondary place in the Bible Commonwealth.

Church membership

Church and State in Puritan Massachusetts

Seventeenth-century New England was a hierarchical society in which socially prominent families were assigned the best land and the most desirable seats in church. Ordinary settlers were addressed as "goodman" and "goodwife," while the better sort were called "gentleman" and "lady" or "master" and "mistress." When the General Court in 1641 issued a Body of Liberties outlining the rights and responsibilities of Massachusetts colonists, it adopted the traditional understanding of liberties as privileges that derived from one's place in the social order. Inequality was considered an expression of God's will, and while some liberties, such as freedom of speech and assembly, applied to all inhabitants, there were separate lists of rights for freemen, women, children, and servants. The Body of Liberties also allowed for slavery. The first African slave appears in the records of Massachusetts Bay in 1640.

The Body of Liberties

Massachusetts forbade ministers to hold office so as not to interfere with their spiritual responsibilities. But church and state were closely interconnected. The law required each town to establish a church and to levy a tax to support the minister. Massachusetts prescribed the death penalty for, among other things, worshiping "any god, but the lord god," practicing witchcraft, or committing blasphemy.

Like many others in the seventeenth century, Puritans believed that religious uniformity was essential to social order. Thus, the church and civil government were intimately interconnected. Puritans did not believe in religious toleration—there was one truth, and their faith embodied it. Religious liberty meant the liberty to practice this truth. But the desire to give autonomy to local congregations soon clashed with the desire for religious uniformity.

Religious uniformity

NEW ENGLANDERS DIVIDED

Modern ideas of individualism, privacy, and personal freedom would have struck Puritans as quite strange. They considered too much emphasis on the "self" dangerous to social harmony and community stability. In the closely knit towns of New England, residents carefully monitored one another's behavior and chastised or expelled those who violated communal norms. Towns banished individuals for such offenses as criticizing the church or government, complaining about the colony in letters home to England, or, in the case of one individual, Abigail Gifford, for being "a very burdensome woman." Tolerance of difference was not high on the list of Puritan values.

By the mid-seventeenth century, English settlement in New England had spread well inland and up and down the Atlantic coast.

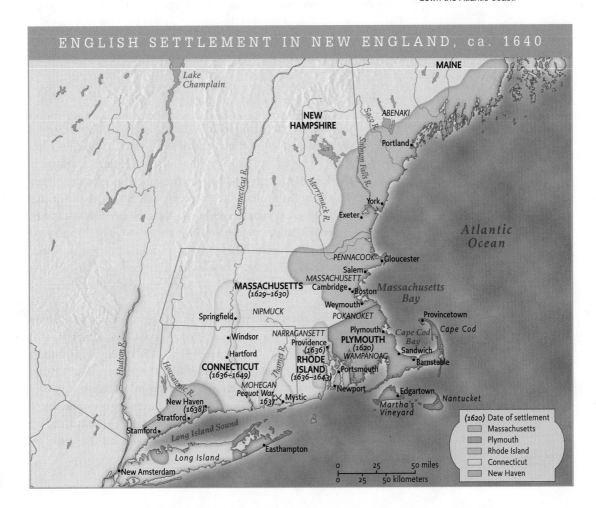

ENGLISH SETTLEMENT IN NEW ENGLAND, ca. 1640

Roger Williams

Roger Williams, New England's most prominent advocate of religious toleration.

Differences of opinion about how to organize a Bible Commonwealth, however, emerged almost from the founding of Massachusetts. With its emphasis on individual interpretation of the Bible, Puritanism contained the seeds of its own fragmentation. The first sustained criticism of the existing order came from the young minister Roger Williams, who arrived in Massachusetts in 1631 and soon began to insist that its congregations withdraw from the Church of England and that church and state be separated. Williams believed that any law-abiding citizen should be allowed to practice whatever form of religion he chose.

Williams aimed to strengthen religion, not weaken it. The embrace of government, he insisted, corrupted the purity of Christian faith and drew believers into endless religious wars like those that racked Europe. Furthermore, Williams rejected the conviction that Puritans were an elect people on a divine mission to spread the true faith. Williams denied that God had singled out any group as special favorites.

Rhode Island and Connecticut

Religious freedom in Rhode Island

Banished from Massachusetts in 1636, Williams and his followers moved south, where they established the colony of Rhode Island, which eventually received a charter from London. Rhode Island became a beacon of religious freedom. It had no established church, no religious qualifications for voting until the eighteenth century, and no requirement that citizens attend church. It became a haven for Dissenters (Protestants who belonged to denominations other than the established church) and Jews persecuted in other colonies. Rhode Island's frame of government was also more democratic. The assembly was elected twice a year, the governor annually, and town meetings were held more frequently than elsewhere in New England.

Religious disagreements in Massachusetts generated other colonies as well. In 1636, the minister Thomas Hooker established a settlement at Hartford. Its system of government, embodied in the Fundamental Orders of 1639, was modeled on that of Massachusetts—with the significant exception that men did not have to be church members to vote. Quite different was the colony of New Haven, founded in 1638 by emigrants who wanted an even closer connection between church and state. In 1662, Hartford and New Haven received a royal charter that united them as the colony of Connecticut.

Connecticut

The Trials of Anne Hutchinson

Another threat to the Puritan establishment both because of her gender and influential following was Anne Hutchinson. A midwife and the daughter of a clergyman, Hutchinson, wrote John Winthrop, was "a woman of a ready wit and bold spirit." Hutchinson began holding meetings in her home, where she led discussions of religious issues among men and women, including a number of prominent merchants and public officials. In Hutchinson's view, salvation was God's direct gift to the elect and could not be earned by good works, devotional practices, or other human effort. Most Puritans shared this belief. What set Hutchinson apart was her charge that nearly all the ministers in Massachusetts were guilty of faulty preaching for distinguishing "saints" from the damned on the basis of activities such as church attendance and moral behavior rather than an inner state of grace.

Hutchinson's criticisms of Puritan leaders

Critics denounced Hutchinson for Antinomianism (a term for putting one's own judgment or faith above both human law and the teachings of the church). In 1637, she was tried in civil court for sedition (expressing opinions dangerous to authority). An articulate woman, Hutchinson ably debated her university-educated accusers during her trial. But when she said God spoke to her directly rather than through ministers or the Bible, she violated Puritan doctrine and sealed her own fate. Such a claim, the colony's leaders felt, posed a threat to organized churches—and, indeed, to all authority. Hutchinson and a number of her followers were banished.

Hutchinson's trial

Anne Hutchinson lived in New England for only eight years, but she left her mark on the region's religious culture. As in the case of Roger Williams, her career showed how the Puritan belief in individual interpretation of the Bible could easily lead to criticism of the religious and political establishment. It would take many years before religious toleration—which violated the Puritans' understanding of "moral liberty" and social harmony—came to Massachusetts.

Significance of Anne Hutchinson

Puritans and Indians

Along with disruptive religious controversies, New England, like other colonies, had to deal with the difficult problem of relations with Indians. The native population of New England numbered perhaps 100,000 when the Puritans arrived. But because of recent epidemics, the migrants encountered fewer Indians near the coast than in other

VOICES OF FREEDOM

From "The Trial of Anne Hutchinson" (1637)

Anne Hutchinson began holding religious meetings in her home in Massachusetts in 1634. She attracted followers who believed that most ministers were not adhering strictly to Puritan theology. In 1637, she was placed on trial for sedition. In her defense, she claimed to be inspired by a revelation from God, a violation of Puritan beliefs. The examination of Hutchinson is a classic example of the clash between established power and individual conscience.

GOV. JOHN WINTHROP: Mrs. Hutchinson, you are called here as one of those that have troubled the peace of the commonwealth and the churches here; you are known to be a woman that hath had a great share in the promoting and divulging of those opinions that are the cause of this trouble, . . . and you have maintained a meeting and an assembly in your house that hath been condemned by the general assembly as a thing not tolerable nor comely on the sight of God nor fitting for your sex . . .

MRS. ANNE HUTCHINSON: That's matter of conscience, Sir.

GOV. JOHN WINTHROP: Your conscience you must keep, or it must be kept for you. . . . Your course is not to be suffered for. Besides we find such a course as this to be greatly prejudicial to the state. . . . And besides that it will not well stand with the commonwealth that families should be neglected for so many neighbors and dames and so much time spent. We see no rule of God for this. We see not that any should have authority to set up any other exercises besides what authority hath already set up . . .

MRS. ANNE HUTCHINSON: I bless the Lord, he hath let me see which was the clear ministry and which the wrong. . . . Now if you do condemn me for speaking what in my conscience I know to be truth I must commit myself unto the Lord.

MR. NOWEL (ASSISTANT TO THE COURT): How do you know that was the spirit?

MRS. ANNE HUTCHINSON: By an immediate revelation.

DEP. GOV. THOMAS DUDLEY: How! An immediate revelation. . . .

GOV. JOHN WINTHORP: Mrs. Hutchinson, the sentence of the court you hear is that your are banished from out of our jurisdiction as being a woman not fit for our society, and are to be imprisoned till the court shall send you away.

John Winthrop, governor of the Massachusetts Bay Colony, describes two very different definitions of liberty in this speech.

The great questions that have troubled the country, are about the authority of the magistrates and the liberty of the people. . . . Concerning liberty, I observe a great mistake in the country about that. There is a twofold liberty, natural (I mean as our nature is now corrupt) and civil or federal. The first is common to man with beasts and other creatures. By this, man, as he stands in relation to man simply, hath liberty to do what he lists; it is a liberty to do evil as well as to [do] good. This liberty is incompatible and inconsistent with authority, and cannot endure the least restraint of the most just authority. The exercise and maintaining of this liberty makes men grow more evil, and in time to be worse than brute beasts. . . . This is that great enemy of truth and peace, that wild beast, which all the ordinances of God are bent against, to restrain and subdue it.

The other kind of liberty I call civil or federal, it may also be termed moral. . . . This liberty is the proper end and object of authority, and cannot subsist without it; and it is a liberty to that only which is good, just, and honest. . . . This liberty is maintained and exercised in a way of subjection to authority; it is of the same kind of liberty wherewith Christ hath made us free. The woman's own choice makes . . . a man her husband; yet being so chosen, he is her lord, and she is to be subject to him, yet in a way of liberty, not of bondage; and a true wife accounts her subjection her honor and freedom, and would not think her condition safe and free, but in her subjection to her husband's authority. Such is the liberty of the church under the authority of Christ.

QUESTIONS

1. *To what extent does Hutchinson's being a woman play a part in the accusations against her?*

2. *Why does Winthrop consider "natural" liberty dangerous?*

3. *How do Hutchinson and Winthrop differ in their understanding of religious liberty?*

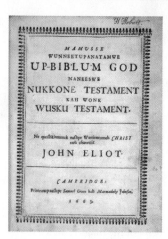

The title page of a translation of the Bible into the Massachusett language, published by John Eliot in 1663.

parts of eastern North America. In areas of European settlement, colonists quickly outnumbered the native population. Some settlers, notably Roger Williams, sought to treat the Indians with justice. Williams insisted that the king had no right to grant land already belonging to someone else. No town, said Williams, should be established before its site had been purchased. John Winthrop, on the other hand, believed uncultivated land could legitimately be taken. Although he recognized the benefits of buying land rather than simply seizing it, he insisted that such purchases require Indians to submit to English authority and pay tribute to the colonists.

To New England's leaders, the Indians represented both savagery and temptation. They enjoyed freedom but of the wrong kind—what Winthrop condemned as undisciplined "natural liberty." Puritans feared that Indian society might attract colonists who lacked the proper moral fiber. In 1642, the Connecticut General Court set a penalty of three years at hard labor for any colonist who abandoned "godly society" to live with the Indians. To counteract the attraction of Indian life, the leaders of New England also encouraged the publication of **"captivity" narratives** by those captured by Indians. The most popular was ***The Sovereignty and Goodness of God*** by Mary Rowlandson, who was seized with other settlers and held for three months until ransomed during an Indian war in the 1670s. Rowlandson acknowledged that she had been well treated and suffered "not the least abuse or unchastity," but her book's overriding theme was her determination to return to Christian society.

Puritans announced that they intended to bring Christian faith to the Indians, but they did nothing in the first two decades of settlement to accomplish this. They generally saw Indians as an obstacle to be pushed aside, rather than as potential converts.

The Pequot War

Conflict between Indians and New England colonists

Indians in New England lacked a paramount chief like Powhatan in Virginia. Coastal Indian tribes, their numbers severely reduced by disease, initially sought to forge alliances with the newcomers to enhance their own position against inland rivals. But as the white population expanded and new towns proliferated, conflict with the region's Indians became unavoidable. The turning point came in 1637 when a fur trader was killed by Pequots—a powerful tribe who controlled southern New England's fur trade and exacted tribute from other Indians. A force of Connecticut and Massachusetts soldiers, augmented by Narragansett allies, surrounded the main Pequot fortified village at Mystic and set it ablaze, killing those

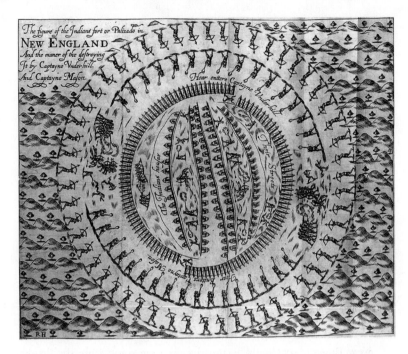

An engraving from John Underhill's *News from America*, published in London in 1638, shows the destruction of the Pequot village on the Mystic River in 1637. The colonial forces, firing guns, are aided by Indian allies with bows and arrows.

who tried to escape. Over 500 men, women, and children lost their lives in the massacre. By the end of the war a few months later, most of the Pequot had been exterminated or sold into Caribbean slavery. The treaty that restored peace decreed that their name be wiped from the historical record.

Massacre at Mystic

The colonists' ferocity shocked their Indian allies, who considered European military practices barbaric. Pilgrim leader William Bradford agreed: "It was a fearful sight to see them frying in the fire," he wrote of the raid on Mystic. But to most Puritans, the defeat of a "barbarous nation" by "the sword of the Lord" offered further proof that Indians were unworthy of sharing New England with the visible saints of the church.

The New England Economy

The leaders of the New England colonies prided themselves on the idea that religion was the primary motivation for emigration. But economic motives were hardly unimportant. One promotional pamphlet of the 1620s spoke of New England as a place "where religion and profit jump together."

Economic motivation for emigrants

Most Puritans came from the middle ranks of society and paid for their family's passage rather than indenturing themselves to labor. They sought in New England not only religious liberty but also economic advancement—if not riches, then at least a "competency," the economic independence that came with secure landownership or craft status.

Fish and timber exports

Lacking a marketable staple like sugar or tobacco, New Englanders turned to fishing and timber for exports. With very few slaves in seventeenth-century New England, most households relied on the labor of their own members, including women in the home and children in the fields. Sons remained unmarried into their mid-twenties, when they could expect to receive land from their fathers, from local authorities, or by moving to a new town.

A Growing Commercial Society

Per capita wealth in New England lagged far behind that of the Chesapeake, but it was much more equally distributed. A majority of New England families owned their own land, the foundation for a comfortable independence. Nonetheless, as in the Chesapeake, economic development produced some social inequalities. For example, on completing their terms, indentured servants rarely achieved full church membership or received grants of land. Most became disenfranchised wage earners.

New England gradually assumed a growing role within the British empire based on trade. As early as the 1640s, New England merchants shipped and marketed the staples of other colonies to markets in Europe and Africa. They engaged in a particularly profitable trade with the West Indies, whose growing slave plantations they supplied with fish, timber, and agricultural produce gathered at home. Especially in Boston, a powerful class of merchants arose who challenged some key Puritan policies, including the subordination of economic activity to the common good. As early as the 1630s, when the General Court established limits on prices and wages and gave a small group of merchants a monopoly on imports from Europe, others protested. Some left Boston to establish a new town at Portsmouth, in the region eventually chartered as the royal colony of New Hampshire. Others remained to fight, with increasing success, for the right to conduct business as they pleased. By the 1640s, Massachusetts had repealed many of its early economic regulations. Eventually, the Puritan experiment would evolve into a merchant-dominated colonial government.

Some Puritan leaders were understandably worried about their society's growing commercialization. By 1650, less than half the population of Boston had become full church members, which forced Puritan leaders to deal with the religious status of the third generation. Should they uphold the rigorous admission standards of the Congregational Church, thus limiting its size? Or should they make admission easier and remain con-

Mrs. Elizabeth Freake and Baby Mary. Painted by an anonymous artist in the 1670s, this portrait depicts the wife and daughter of John Freake, a prominent Boston merchant and lawyer. To illustrate the family's wealth, Mrs. Freake wears a triple strand of pearls, a garnet bracelet, and a gold ring, and her child wears a yellow silk dress.

nected to more people? The **Half-Way Covenant** of 1662 tried to address this problem by allowing for the baptism of and a kind of "half-way" membership for grandchildren of those who emigrated during the Great Migration. But church membership continued to stagnate.

By the 1660s and 1670s, ministers were regularly castigating the people for selfishness and a "great backsliding" from the colony's original purposes. These warnings, called "jeremiads" after the ancient Hebrew prophet Jeremiah, interpreted crop failures and disease as signs of divine disapproval and warned of further punishment to come if New Englanders did not mend their ways. Yet hard work and commercial success had always been central Puritan values. In this sense, the commercialization of New England was as much a fulfillment of the Puritan mission in America as a betrayal.

Jeremiads

RELIGION, POLITICS, AND FREEDOM

The Rights of Englishmen

Even as English emigrants began the settlement of colonies in North America, England itself became enmeshed in political and religious conflict, in which ideas of liberty played a central role. By 1600, the traditional definition of "liberties" as a set of privileges confined to one or another social group still persisted, but alongside it had arisen the idea that certain "rights of Englishmen" applied to all within the kingdom. This tradition rested on the Magna Carta (or Great Charter) of 1215. An agreement between King John and a group of barons, the Magna Carta listed a series of "liberties" granted by the king to "all the free men of our realm," a restricted group at the time, since many residents of England were serfs. The liberties mentioned in the Magna Carta included protection against arbitrary imprisonment and the seizure of one's property without due process of law.

The Magna Carta

Over time, the document came to be seen as embodying the idea of **"English freedom"**—that the king was subject to the rule of law, and that all persons should enjoy security of person and property. These rights were embodied in the common law, whose provisions, such as habeas corpus (a protection against being imprisoned without a legal charge), the right to face one's accuser, and trial by jury came to apply to all free subjects of the English crown. As serfdom slowly disappeared, the number of Englishmen considered "freeborn," and therefore entitled to these rights, expanded enormously.

Rights of "free borns"

The execution of Charles I in 1649, a central event of the English Civil War.

The English Civil War

At the beginning of the seventeenth century, when English emigrants began arriving in the New World, "freedom" still played only a minor role in England's political debates. But the political upheavals of that century elevated the notion of "English freedom" to a central place. The struggle for political supremacy between Parliament and the Stuart monarchs James I and Charles I culminated in the English Civil War of the 1640s.

The struggles of monarchy and Parliament

The leaders of the House of Commons (the elective body that, along with the hereditary aristocrats of the House of Lords, makes up the English Parliament) accused the Stuart kings of endangering liberty by imposing taxes without parliamentary consent, imprisoning political foes, and leading the nation back toward Catholicism. Civil war broke out in 1642, resulting in a victory for the forces of Parliament. In 1649, Charles I was beheaded, the monarchy abolished, and England declared "a Commonwealth and Free State"—a nation governed by the will of the people. Oliver Cromwell, the head of the victorious Parliamentary army, ruled for almost a decade after the execution of the king. In 1660, the monarchy was restored and Charles II assumed the throne. But by then, the breakdown of authority had stimulated intense discussions of liberty, authority, and what it meant to be a "freeborn Englishman."

England's Debate over Freedom

The Levellers and the Diggers

The idea of freedom suddenly took on new and expanded meanings between 1640 and 1660. The writer John Milton called for freedom of speech and of the press. New religious sects sprang up, demanding religious toleration for all Protestants as well as the end of public financing and special privileges for the Anglican Church. The Levellers, history's first democratic political movement, proposed a written constitution, the Agreement of the People, which began by proclaiming "at how high a rate we value our just freedom." Although "democracy" was still widely equated with anarchy, the document proposed to abolish the monarchy and House of Lords and to greatly expand the right to vote.

The Levellers offered a glimpse of the modern definition of freedom as a universal entitlement in a society based on equal rights, not a function of social class. Another new group, the Diggers, went even further, hoping to give freedom an economic underpinning through the common ownership of land. Previous discussion of freedom, declared Gerard Winstanley, the Diggers' leader, said that true freedom applied equally "to the poor as well as the rich"; all were entitled to "a comfortable livelihood in this their own land." Some of the ideas of liberty that flourished during the 1640s and 1650s would be carried to America by English emigrants.

Meeting of the General Council of the Army at Putney, scene of the debate in 1647 over liberty and democracy between Levellers and more-conservative army officers.

The Civil War and English America

The Civil War, accompanied by vigorous discussions of the rights of free-born Englishmen, inevitably reverberated in England's colonies, dividing them from one another and internally. Most New Englanders sided with Parliament in the Civil War of the 1640s. Some returned to England to join the Parliamentary army or take up pulpits to help create a godly common-wealth at home. But Puritan leaders were increasingly uncomfortable as the idea of religious toleration for Protestants gained favor in England.

Meanwhile, a number of followers of Anne Hutchinson became Quakers, one of the sects that sprang up in England during the Civil War. Quakers held that the spirit of God dwelled within every individual, not just the elect, and that this "inner light," rather than the Bible or teach-ings of the clergy, offered the surest guidance in spiritual matters. When Quakers appeared in Massachusetts, colonial officials had them whipped, fined, and banished. In 1659 and 1660, four Quakers who returned from exile were hanged. When Charles II, after the restoration of the monarchy in 1660, reaffirmed the Massachusetts charter, he ordered the colony to recognize the "liberty of conscience" of all Protestants.

The Quakers

In Maryland, the combination of the religious and political battles of the Civil War, homegrown conflict between Catholic and Protestant settlers, and anti-proprietary feeling produced a violent civil war within the colony, later recalled as the "plundering time." Indeed, Maryland in the 1640s verged on total anarchy, with a pro-Parliament force assaulting those loyal to Charles I.

After years of struggle between the Protestant planter class and the Catholic elite, Maryland in 1649 adopted an **Act Concerning Religion**, which institutionalized the principle of toleration that had prevailed from the colony's beginning. All Christians were guaranteed the "free exercise" of religion. Although the Act did not grant this right to non-Christians, it did, over time, bring some political stability to Maryland. The law was also a milestone in the history of religious freedom in colonial America.

Cromwell and the Empire

Oliver Cromwell, who ruled England from 1649 until his death in 1658, undertook an aggressive policy of colonial expansion, the promotion of Protestantism, and commercial empowerment in the British Isles and the Western Hemisphere. His army forcibly extended English control over Ireland, massacring civilians, banning the public practice of Catholicism, and seizing land owned by Catholics. In the Caribbean, England seized Jamaica, a valuable sugar island, from Spain.

By the middle of the seventeenth century, several English colonies existed along the Atlantic coast of North America. Established as part of an ad hoc process rather than arising under any coherent national plan, they differed enormously in economic, political, and social structure. The seeds had been planted, in the Chesapeake, for the development of plantation societies based on unfree labor, and in New England, for settlements centered on small towns and family farms. Throughout the colonies, many residents enjoyed freedoms they had not possessed at home, especially access to land and the right to worship as they desired. Others found themselves confined to unfree labor for many years or an entire lifetime.

The next century would be a time of crisis and consolidation as the population expanded, social conflicts intensified, and Britain moved to exert greater control over its flourishing North American colonies.

CHAPTER REVIEW AND ONLINE RESOURCES

REVIEW QUESTIONS

1. Compare and contrast settlement patterns, treatment of Indians, and religion of the Spanish and English in the Americas.

2. For English settlers, land was the basis of independence and liberty. Explain the reasoning behind that concept and how it differed from the Indians' conception of land.

3. Describe the factors promoting and limiting religious freedom in the New England and Chesapeake colonies.

4. Describe who chose to emigrate to North America from England in the seventeenth century and explain their reasons.

5. In what ways did the economy, government, and household structure differ in New England and the Chesapeake colonies?

6. The English believed that, unlike the Spanish, their motives for colonization were pure, and that the growth of empire and freedom would always go hand-in-hand. How did the expansion of the British empire affect the freedoms of Native Americans, the Irish, and even many English citizens?

7. Considering politics, social tensions, and debates over the meaning of liberty, how do the events and aftermath of the English Civil War demonstrate that the English colonies in North America were part of a larger Atlantic community?

8. How did the tobacco economy draw the Chesapeake colonies into the greater Atlantic World?

KEY TERMS

Virginia Company (p. 39)
Roanoke (p. 41)
A Discourse Concerning Western Planting (p. 41)
enclosure movement (p. 42)
indentured servant (p. 44)
John Smith (p. 47)
headright system (p. 48)
House of Burgesses (p. 48)
Uprising of 1622 (p. 49)
tobacco (p. 50)
dower rights (p. 51)
Puritanism (p. 53)
John Winthrop (p. 54)
Moral liberty (p. 54)
Pilgrims (p. 54)
Mayflower Compact (p. 54)
Great Migration (p. 55)
captivity narratives (p. 64)
The Sovereignty and Goodness of God (p. 64)
Pequot War (p. 64)
Half-Way Covenant (p. 67)
English freedom (p. 67)
Act Concerning Religion (p. 70)

wwnorton.com
/studyspace

VISIT STUDYSPACE FOR THESE RESOURCES AND MORE
- A chapter outline
- A diagnostic chapter quiz
- Interactive maps
- Map worksheets
- Multimedia documents

CHAPTER 3

CREATING ANGLO-AMERICA

★

1660–1750

The Residence of David Twining, a painting of a Pennsylvania farm as it appeared in the eighteenth century. Edward Hicks, who had lived there as a youth, painted the scene from memory in the 1840s. Hicks depicts a prosperous farm, largely self-sufficient but also producing for the market, typical of colonial eastern Pennsylvania. One of the farm workers is a slave.

In the last quarter of the seventeenth century, a series of crises rocked the European colonies of North America. Social and political tensions boiled over in sometimes ruthless conflicts between rich and poor, free and slave, settler and Indian, and members of different religious groups. At the same time, struggles within and between European empires echoed in the colonies.

The bloodiest and most bitter conflict occurred in southern New England, where in 1675 an Indian alliance launched attacks on farms and settlements that were encroaching on Indian lands. It was the most dramatic and violent warfare in the region in the entire seventeenth century.

New Englanders described the Wampanoag leader **Metacom** (known to the colonists as King Philip) as the uprising's mastermind, although in fact most tribes fought under their own leaders. By 1676, Indian forces had attacked nearly half of New England's ninety towns. Twelve in Massachusetts were destroyed. As refugees fled eastward, the line of settlement was pushed back almost to the Atlantic coast. Some 1,000 settlers, out of a population of 52,000, and 3,000 of New England's 20,000 Indians, perished in the fighting.

In mid-1676, the tide of battle turned and a ferocious counterattack broke the Indians' power once and for all. Although the uprising united numerous tribes, others remained loyal to the colonists. The role of the Iroquois in providing essential military aid to the colonists helped to solidify their developing alliance with the government of New York. Together, colonial and Indian forces inflicted devastating punishment on the rebels. Metacom was executed, Indian villages were destroyed, and captives were killed or sold into slavery in the West Indies. Both sides committed atrocities in this merciless conflict, but in its aftermath the image of Indians as bloodthirsty savages became firmly entrenched in the New England mind.

In the long run, **King Philip's War** produced a broadening of freedom for white New Englanders by expanding their access to land. But this freedom rested on the final dispossession of the region's Indians.

FOCUS QUESTIONS

- *How did the English empire in America expand in the mid-seventeenth century?*

- *How was slavery established in the Western Atlantic world?*

- *What major social and political crises rocked the colonies in the late seventeenth century?*

- *What were the directions of social and economic change in the eighteenth-century colonies?*

- *How did patterns of class and gender roles change in eighteenth-century America?*

GLOBAL COMPETITION AND THE EXPANSION OF ENGLAND'S EMPIRE

The Mercantilist System

By the middle of the seventeenth century, it was apparent that the colonies could be an important source of wealth for England. According to the prevailing theory known as "**mercantilism**," governments should regulate economic activity so as to promote national power. They should encourage manufacturing and commerce by special bounties, monopolies, and other measures. Above all, trade should be controlled so that more gold and silver flowed into countries than left them. That is, exports of goods, which generated revenue from abroad, should exceed imports, which required paying foreigners for their products. In the mercantilist outlook, the role

The role of colonies

of colonies was to serve the interests of the mother country by producing marketable raw materials and importing manufactured goods from home. "Foreign trade," declared an influential work written in 1664 by a London merchant, formed the basis of "England's treasure." Commerce, not territorial plunder, was the foundation of empire.

Parliament in 1651 passed the first **Navigation Act**, which aimed to wrest control of world trade from the Dutch, whose merchants profited from free trade with all parts of the world and all existing empires. Additional measures followed in 1660 and 1663. According to the Navigation laws,

Enumerated goods

certain "enumerated" goods—essentially the most valuable colonial products, such as tobacco and sugar—had to be transported in English ships and sold initially in English ports, although they could then be re-exported to foreign markets. Similarly, most European goods imported into the colonies had to be shipped through England, where customs duties were paid. This enabled English merchants, manufacturers, shipbuilders, and sailors to reap the benefits of colonial trade, and the government to enjoy added income from taxes. As members of the empire, American colonies would profit as well, since their ships were considered English. Indeed, the Navigation Acts stimulated the rise of New England's shipbuilding industry.

The Conquest of New Netherland

The restoration of the English monarchy when Charles II assumed the throne in 1660 sparked a new period of colonial expansion. The government chartered new trading ventures, notably the Royal African Company, which was given a monopoly of the slave trade. Within a generation, the number of English colonies in North America doubled.

First to come under English control was New Netherland, seized in 1664 during an Anglo-Dutch war that also saw England gain control of Dutch trading posts in Africa. King Charles II awarded the colony to his younger brother James, the duke of York, with "full and absolute power" to govern as he pleased. (Hence the colony's name became New York.) English rule transformed this minor military base into an important imperial outpost, a seaport trading with the Caribbean and Europe, and a launching pad for military operations against the French. New York's European population, around 9,000 when the English assumed control, rose to 20,000 by 1685.

English rule in New York

English rule expanded the freedom of some New Yorkers, while reducing that of others. The terms of surrender guaranteed that the English would respect the religious beliefs and property holdings of the colony's many ethnic communities. But English law ended the Dutch tradition by which married women conducted business in their own name and inherited some of the property acquired during marriage. There had been many female traders in New Amsterdam, but few remained by the end of the seventeenth century.

The English also introduced more restrictive attitudes toward blacks. In colonial New York City, as in New Amsterdam, those residents who enjoyed the status of "freeman," obtained by birth in the city or by an act of local authorities, enjoyed special privileges, including the right to work in various trades. But the English, in a reversal of Dutch practice, expelled free blacks from many skilled jobs.

English rule and blacks

Others benefited enormously from English rule. The duke of York and his appointed governors continued the Dutch practice of awarding immense land grants to favorites. By 1700, nearly 2 million acres of land were owned by only five New York families who intermarried regularly, exerted considerable political influence, and formed one of colonial America's most tightly knit landed elites.

New York and the Indians

Initially, English rule also strengthened the position of the Iroquois Confederacy of upstate New York. Sir Edmund Andros, who had been appointed governor of New York after fighting the French in the Caribbean, formed an alliance known as the **Covenant Chain**, in which the imperial ambitions of the English and Indians reinforced one another. The Five (later Six) Iroquois Nations assisted Andros in clearing parts of New York of rival tribes and helped the British in attacks on the French and

The Iroquois Nations

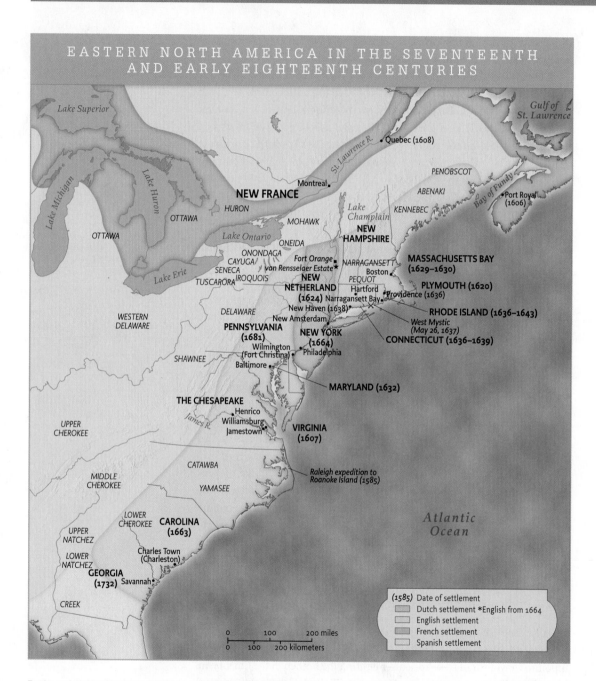

EASTERN NORTH AMERICA IN THE SEVENTEENTH AND EARLY EIGHTEENTH CENTURIES

Lake Superior

Gulf of St. Lawrence

Quebec (1608)

Lake Michigan

Lake Huron

Montreal

PENOBSCOT

NEW FRANCE

HURON

ABENAKI

Port Royal (1606)

Bay of Fundy

OTTAWA

KENNEBEC

Lake Ontario

Lake Champlain

NEW HAMPSHIRE

OTTAWA

MOHAWK

ONEIDA

ONONDAGA

Fort Orange

NARRAGANSETT

MASSACHUSETTS BAY (1629–1630)

CAYUGA

van Rensselaer Estate ★

Boston

SENECA

Lake Erie

NEW NETHERLAND (1624)

PEQUOT

PLYMOUTH (1620)

TUSCARORA

IROQUOIS

Hartford

Narragansett Bay

Providence (1636)

DELAWARE

New Haven (1638)

RHODE ISLAND (1636–1643)

WESTERN DELAWARE

New Amsterdam

West Mystic (May 26, 1637)

PENNSYLVANIA (1681)

NEW YORK (1664)

CONNECTICUT (1636–1639)

SHAWNEE

Wilmington (Fort Christina)

Philadelphia

Baltimore

MARYLAND (1632)

THE CHESAPEAKE

Henrico

UPPER CHEROKEE

James R.

Williamsburg

Jamestown

VIRGINIA (1607)

CATAWBA

MIDDLE CHEROKEE

YAMASEE

Raleigh expedition to Roanoke Island (1585)

Atlantic Ocean

LOWER CHEROKEE

CAROLINA (1663)

UPPER NATCHEZ

Charles Town (Charleston)

LOWER NATCHEZ

GEORGIA (1732)

Savannah

CREEK

(1585) Date of settlement
Dutch settlement *English from 1664
English settlement
French settlement
Spanish settlement

0   100   200 miles
0   100   200 kilometers

By the early eighteenth century, numerous English colonies populated eastern North America, while the French had established their own presence to the north and west.

their Indian allies. Andros, for his part, recognized the Iroquois claim to authority over Indian communities in the vast area stretching to the Ohio River. But beginning in the 1680s, Indians around the Great Lakes and Ohio Valley regrouped and with French aid attacked the Iroquois, pushing them to the east. By the end of the century, the Iroquois Nations adopted a policy of careful neutrality, seeking to play the European empires off one another while continuing to profit from the fur trade.

The Charter of Liberties

Many New York colonists, meanwhile, began to complain that they were being denied the "liberties of Englishmen," especially the right to consent to taxation. In 1683, the duke of York agreed to call an elected assembly, whose first act was to draft a Charter of Liberties and Privileges. The Charter required that elections be held every three years among male property owners and the freemen of New York City; it also reaffirmed traditional English rights such as trial by jury and security of property, as well as religious toleration for all Protestants.

English rights

The Founding of Carolina

For more than three decades after the establishment of Maryland in 1634, no new English settlement was planted in North America. Then, in 1663, Charles II awarded to eight proprietors the right to establish a colony

An engraving representing the Grand Council of the Iroquois Nations of the area of present-day upstate New York. From a book about American Indians published in Paris by a Jesuit missionary, who depicts the Indians in the attire of ancient Romans. Note the prevalence of wampum belts in the image, in the foreground and in the hand and at the feet of the central figure. Wampum was used to certify treaties and other transactions.

to the north of Florida, as a barrier to Spanish expansion. Not until 1670 did the first settlers arrive to found Carolina. In its early years, Carolina was the "colony of a colony," an offshoot of the tiny island of Barbados. In the mid-seventeenth century, Barbados was the Caribbean's richest plantation economy, but a shortage of available land led wealthy planters to seek opportunities in Carolina for their sons. At first, Carolinians armed friendly Indians, employing them on raids into Spanish Florida, and enslaved others, shipping them to other mainland colonies and the West Indies. Between 1670 and 1720, the number of Indian slaves exported from Charleston was larger than the number of African slaves imported. In 1715, the Yamasee and Creek rebelled, but the uprising was crushed, and most of the remaining Indians were enslaved or driven out of the colony into Spanish Florida.

The Fundamental Constitutions of Carolina, issued by the proprietors in 1669, proposed to establish a feudal society with a hereditary nobility, serfs, and slaves. Needing to attract settlers quickly, however, the proprietors also provided for an elected assembly and religious toleration—by now recognized as essential to enticing migrants to North America. They also instituted a generous headright system, offering 150 acres for each member of an arriving family (in the case of indentured servants, of course, the land went to the employer) and 100 acres to male servants who completed their terms.

The proprietors instituted a rigorous legal code that promised slave-owners "absolute power and authority" over their human property and included imported slaves in the headright system. This allowed any persons who settled in Carolina and brought with them slaves instantly to acquire large new landholdings. In its early days, however, the economy centered on cattle raising and trade with local Indians. Carolina grew slowly until planters discovered the staple—rice—that would make them the wealthiest elite in English North America and their colony an epicenter of mainland slavery.

The Holy Experiment

The last English colony to be established in the seventeenth century was Pennsylvania in 1681. The proprietor, William Penn, envisioned it as a place where those facing religious persecution in Europe could enjoy spiritual freedom, and colonists and Indians would coexist in harmony.

A devout member of the **Society of Friends, or Quakers**, Penn was particularly concerned with establishing a refuge for his coreligionists, who faced increasing persecution in England. He had already assisted a group of English Quakers in purchasing half of what became the colony of New Jersey from Lord John Berkeley, who had received a land grant from the duke of York. Penn was largely responsible for the frame of government announced in 1677, the West Jersey Concessions, which created an elected assembly with a broad suffrage and established religious liberty.

Like the Puritans, Penn considered his colony a "holy experiment," but of a different kind—"a free colony for all mankind that should go hither." He hoped that Pennsylvania could be governed according to Quaker principles, among them the equality of all persons (including women, blacks, and Indians) before God and the primacy of the individual conscience. To Quakers, liberty was a universal entitlement, not the possession of any single people—a position that would eventually make them the first group of whites to repudiate slavery. Penn also treated Indians with a consideration almost unique in the colonial experience, arranging to purchase land before reselling it to colonists and offering refuge to tribes driven out of other colonies by warfare. Since Quakers were pacifists who came to America unarmed and did not even organize a militia until the 1740s, peace with the native population was essential.

Religious freedom was Penn's most fundamental principle. His Charter of Liberty, approved by the assembly in 1682, offered "Christian liberty" to all who affirmed a belief in God and did not use their freedom to promote "licentiousness." There was no established church in Pennsylvania, and attendance at religious services was entirely voluntary, although Jews were barred from office by a required oath affirming belief in the divinity of Jesus Christ. At the same time, the Quakers upheld a strict code of personal morality. Penn's Frame of Government prohibited swearing, drunkenness, and adultery. Not religious uniformity but a virtuous citizenry would be the foundation of Penn's social order.

A Quaker Meeting, a painting by an unidentified British artist, dating from the late eighteenth or early nineteenth century. It illustrates the prominent place of women in Quaker gatherings.

Penn and religious liberty

Land in Pennsylvania

Given the power to determine the colony's form of government, Penn established an appointed council to originate legislation and an assembly elected by male taxpayers and "freemen" (owners of 100 acres of land for free immigrants and 50 acres for former indentured servants). These rules made a majority of the male population eligible to vote. Penn owned all the colony's land and sold it to settlers at low prices, which helped the colony prosper. Pennsylvania's religious toleration, healthy climate, and inexpensive land, along with Penn's aggressive efforts to publicize the colony's advantages, soon attracted immigrants from all over western Europe.

Freedoms in Pennsylvania

Ironically, the freedoms Pennsylvania offered to European immigrants contributed to the deterioration of freedom for others. The colony's successful efforts to attract settlers would eventually come into conflict with Penn's benevolent Indian policy. And the opening of Pennsylvania caused fewer indentured servants to choose Virginia and Maryland, a development that did much to shift those colonies toward reliance on slave labor.

ORIGINS OF AMERICAN SLAVERY

The turn to slavery

The incessant demand for workers spurred by the spread of tobacco cultivation eventually led Chesapeake planters to turn to the transatlantic trade in slaves. Compared with indentured servants, slaves offered planters many advantages. As Africans, they could not claim the protections of English common law. Slaves' terms of service never expired, and they therefore did not become a population of unruly landless men. Their children were slaves, and their skin color made it more difficult for them to escape into the surrounding society. African men, moreover, unlike their Native American counterparts, were accustomed to intensive agricultural labor, and they had encountered many diseases known in Europe and developed resistance to them, so were less likely to succumb to epidemics.

Englishmen and Africans

English views of alien peoples

The English had long viewed alien peoples with disdain, including the Irish, Native Americans, and Africans. They described these strangers in remarkably similar language as savage, pagan, and uncivilized, often comparing them to animals. "Race"—the idea that humanity is divided into well-defined groups associated with skin color—is a modern concept that had not fully developed in the seventeenth century. Nor had "racism"—an ideology based on the belief that some races are inherently superior to others and entitled to rule over them.

Nonetheless, anti-black stereotypes flourished in seventeenth-century England. Africans were seen as so alien—in color, religion, and social practices—that they were "enslavable" in a way that poor Englishmen were not. Most English also deemed Indians to be uncivilized. But the Indian population declined so rapidly, and it was so easy for Indians, familiar with the countryside, to run away, that Indian slavery never became viable in the Atlantic colonies.

Slavery in History

Slavery has existed for nearly the entire span of human history. It was central to the societies of ancient Greece and Rome. In the Mediterranean world, a slave trade in Slavic peoples survived into the fifteenth century. (The English word "slavery" derives from "Slav.") In West Africa, as noted in Chapter 1, slavery and a slave trade predated the coming of Europeans, and small-scale slavery existed among Native Americans. But slavery in nearly all these instances differed greatly from the institution that developed in the New World.

In the Americas, slavery was based on the plantation, an agricultural enterprise that brought together large numbers of workers under the control of a single owner. This imbalance magnified the possibility of slave resistance and made it necessary to police the system rigidly. Labor on slave plantations was far more demanding than the household slavery common in Africa, and the death rate among slaves much higher. In the New World, slavery would come to be associated with race, a concept that drew a permanent line between whites and blacks.

Plantation slavery

Slavery in the West Indies

A sense of Africans as alien and inferior made their enslavement by the English possible. But prejudice by itself did not create North American slavery. For this institution to take root, planters and government authorities had to be convinced that importing African slaves was the best way to solve their persistent shortage of labor. During the seventeenth century, the shipping of slaves from Africa to the New World became a major international business. By 1600, huge sugar plantations worked by slaves from Africa had made their appearance in Brazil, a colony of Portugal. In the seventeenth century, England, Holland, Denmark, and France joined Spain as owners of West Indian islands.

Sugar and slavery

With the Indian population having been wiped out by disease, and with the white indentured servants unwilling to do the back-breaking, monotonous work of sugar cultivation, the massive importation of slaves from Africa

Cutting Sugar Cane, an engraving from *Ten Views in Antigua*, published in 1823. Male and female slaves harvest and load the sugar crop while an overseer on horseback addresses a slave. During the eighteenth century, sugar was the chief crop produced by Western Hemisphere slaves.

began. On Barbados, for example, the slave population increased from 20,000 to more than 80,000 between 1660 and 1670. By the end of the seventeenth century, huge sugar plantations manned by hundreds of slaves dominated the West Indian economy, and on most of the islands the African population far outnumbered that of European origin.

Sugar was the first crop to be mass-marketed to consumers in Europe. Before its emergence, international trade consisted largely of precious metals like gold and silver, and luxury goods aimed at an elite market, like the spices and silks imported from Asia. Sugar was by far the most important product of the British, French, and Portuguese empires, and New World sugar plantations produced immense profits. Saint Domingue, today's Haiti, was the jewel of the French empire. In 1660, Barbados generated more trade than all the other English colonies combined.

Compared with its rapid introduction in Brazil and the West Indies, slavery developed slowly in North America. Slaves cost more than indentured servants, and the high death rate among tobacco workers made it economically unappealing to pay for a lifetime of labor. As late as 1680, there were only 4,500 blacks in the Chesapeake, a little over 5 percent of the region's population. The most important social distinction in the seventeenth-century Chesapeake was not between black and white but between the white plantation owners who dominated politics and society and everybody else—small farmers, indentured servants, and slaves.

Slavery and the Law

Centuries before the voyages of Columbus, Spain had enacted a series of laws granting slaves certain rights relating to marriage, the holding of property, and access to freedom. These laws were transferred to Spain's American empire. They were often violated but nonetheless gave slaves opportunities to claim rights under the law. The law of slavery in English North America would become far more repressive than in the Spanish empire, especially on the all-important question of whether avenues existed by which slaves could obtain freedom.

For much of the seventeenth century, however, the legal status of Chesapeake blacks remained ambiguous and the line between slavery

English and Spanish empires on slavery

and freedom more permeable than it would later become. The first Africans, twenty in all, arrived in Virginia in 1619. Although the first black arrivals were almost certainly treated as slaves, it appears that at least some managed to become free after serving a term of years. To be sure, racial distinctions were enacted into law from the outset. As early as the 1620s, the law barred blacks from serving in the Virginia militia. In 1643, a poll tax (a tax levied on individuals) was imposed on African but not white women. In both Virginia and Maryland, however, free blacks could sue and testify in court, and some even managed to acquire land and purchase white servants or African slaves. Blacks and whites labored side by side in the tobacco fields, sometimes ran away together, and established intimate relationships.

Rights of the free blacks

The Rise of Chesapeake Slavery

Not until the 1660s did the laws of Virginia and Maryland refer explicitly to slavery. As tobacco planting spread and the demand for labor increased, the condition of black and white servants diverged sharply. Authorities sought to improve the status of white servants, hoping to counteract the widespread impression in England that Virginia was a death trap. At the same time, access to freedom for blacks receded.

A Virginia law of 1662 provided that in the case of a child one of whose parents was free and one slave, the status of the offspring followed that of the mother. (This provision not only reversed the European practice of defining a child's status through the father but also made the sexual abuse of slave women profitable for slaveholders, since any children that resulted remained the owner's property.) In 1667, the Virginia House of Burgesses decreed that religious conversion did not release a slave from bondage. Thus, Christians could own other Christians as slaves. Authorities also defined all offspring of interracial relationships as illegitimate. By 1680, even though the black population was still small, notions of racial difference were well entrenched in the law. In British North America, unlike the Spanish empire, no distinctive mulatto, or mixed-race, class existed; the law treated everyone with African ancestry as black.

Legal changes in the 1660s

Black slavery

Bacon's Rebellion: Land and Labor in Virginia

Virginia's shift from white indentured servants to African slaves as the main plantation labor force was accelerated by one of the most dramatic confrontations of this era, **Bacon's Rebellion** of 1676. Governor William

Berkeley had for thirty years run a corrupt regime in alliance with an inner circle of the colony's wealthiest tobacco planters. He rewarded his followers with land grants and lucrative offices. But as tobacco farming spread inland, planters connected with the governor engrossed the best lands, leaving freed servants (a growing population, since Virginia's death rate was finally falling) with no options but to work as tenants or to move to the frontier. By the 1670s, poverty among whites had reached levels reminiscent of England. In addition, the right to vote, previously enjoyed by all adult men, was confined to landowners in 1670. Governor Berkeley maintained peaceful relations with Virginia's remaining native population. His refusal to allow white settlement in areas reserved for Indians angered many land-hungry colonists.

Social tension in Virginia

Long-simmering social tensions coupled with widespread resentment against the injustices of the Berkeley regime erupted in Bacon's Rebellion. In 1676, after a minor confrontation between Indians and colonists on Virginia's western frontier, settlers demanded that the governor authorize the extermination or removal of the colony's Indians, to open more land for whites. When Berkeley refused, a series of Indian massacres quickly grew into a full-fledged rebellion against Berkeley and his system of rule.

Sir William Berkeley, governor of colonial Virginia, 1641–1652 and 1660–1677, in a portrait by Sir Peter Lely. Berkeley's authoritarian rule helped to spark Bacon's Rebellion.

To some extent, Bacon's Rebellion was a conflict within the Virginia elite—between Berkeley's men and the backers of Nathaniel Bacon, a wealthy and ambitious planter who disdained Berkeley's cronies. But Bacon's call for the removal of all Indians from the colony, a reduction of taxes at a time of economic recession, and an end to rule by "grandees" rapidly gained support from small farmers, landless men, indentured servants, and even some Africans. The bulk of his army consisted of discontented men who had recently been servants.

Bacon promised freedom (including access to Indian lands) to all who joined his ranks. In 1676, Bacon gathered an armed force for an unauthorized and indiscriminate campaign against those he called the governor's "protected and darling Indians." He refused Berkeley's order to disband and marched on Jamestown, burning it to the ground. The governor fled, and Bacon became the ruler of Virginia. Only the arrival of a squadron of warships from England restored order.

The specter of a civil war among whites greatly frightened Virginia's ruling elite, who took dramatic steps to consolidate their power and improve their image after Bacon's death in October 1676. They restored property qualifications for voting, which Bacon had rescinded, and reduced taxes. They also adopted a more aggressive Indian policy, opening western areas to small farmers, many of whom prospered from a rise in tobacco prices after 1680. To avert the further rise of a rebellious population of landless former indentured servants, Virginia's authorities accelerated the shift to slaves (who would never become free) on the tobacco plantations.

Effects of Bacon's Rebellion

A Slave Society

Between 1680 and 1700, slave labor began to supplant indentured servitude on Chesapeake plantations. Bacon's Rebellion contributed to this development, but so did other factors. As the death rate began to fall, it became more economical to purchase a laborer for life. Moreover, the Royal Africa Company's monopoly on the English slave trade ended, thus opening the door to other traders and reducing the price of imported African slaves.

By 1700, blacks constituted more than 10 percent of Virginia's population. Fifty years later, they made up nearly half. Recognizing the growing importance of slavery, the House of Burgesses in 1705 enacted a new **slave code**. Slaves were property, completely subject to the will of their masters and, more generally, of the white community. They could be bought and sold, leased, fought over in court, and passed on to one's descendants. Henceforth, blacks and whites were tried in separate courts. No black, free or slave, could own arms, strike a white man, or employ a white servant. Virginia had changed from a "society with slaves," in which slavery was one system of labor among others, to a "slave society," where slavery stood at the center of the economic process.

Slave code of 1705

One sentiment shared by Europeans, Native Americans, and Africans was fear of enslavement. Throughout history, slaves have run away and in other ways resisted bondage. They did the same in the colonial Chesapeake. Colonial newspapers were filled with advertisements for runaway slaves. These notices described the appearance and skills of the fugitive and included such comments as "he has great notions of freedom." After the suppression of a slave conspiracy in 1709, Alexander Spotswood, the governor of Virginia, warned planters to be vigilant. The desire for freedom, he reminded them, can "call together all those who long to shake off the fetters of slavery."

Runaway slaves

COLONIES IN CRISIS

Uprisings

King Philip's War of 1675 and Bacon's Rebellion the following year coincided with disturbances in other colonies. In Maryland, where the proprietor, Lord Baltimore, in 1670 had suddenly restricted the right to vote to owners of fifty acres of land or a certain amount of personal property, a Protestant uprising unsuccessfully sought to oust his government and restore the suffrage for all freemen. In several colonies, increasing settlement on the frontier led to resistance by alarmed Indians. The Pueblo Revolt of 1680 (discussed in Chapter 1) indicated that the crisis of colonial authority was not confined to the British empire.

The Glorious Revolution

Parliamentary supremacy

Turmoil in England also reverberated in the colonies. In 1688, the long struggle for domination of English government between Parliament and the crown reached its culmination in the **Glorious Revolution**, which established parliamentary supremacy once and for all and secured the

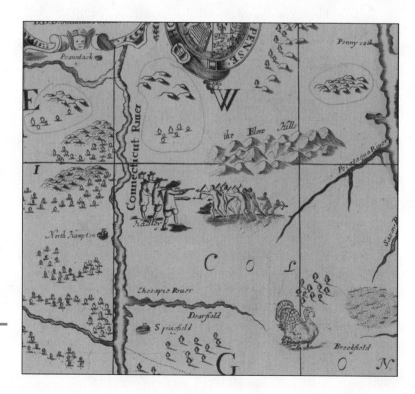

A scene from King Philip's War, included on a 1675 map of New England.

Protestant succession to the throne. Under Charles II, Parliament had asserted its authority in the formation of national policy. When Charles died in 1685, he was succeeded by his brother James II (formerly the duke of York), a practicing Catholic and a believer that kings ruled by divine right. In 1687, James decreed religious toleration for both Protestant Dissenters and Catholics. The following year, the birth of James's son raised the alarming prospect of a Catholic succession. A group of English aristocrats invited the Dutch nobleman William of Orange, the husband of James's Protestant daughter Mary, to assume the throne in the name of English liberties. As the landed elite and leaders of the Anglican Church rallied to William's cause, James II fled and the revolution was complete.

Unlike the broad social upheaval that marked the English Civil War of the 1640s, the Glorious Revolution was in effect a coup engineered by a small group of aristocrats in alliance with an ambitious Dutch prince. But the overthrow of James II entrenched more firmly than ever the notion that liberty was the birthright of all Englishmen and that the king was subject to the rule of law. To justify the ouster of James II, Parliament in 1689 enacted a **Bill of Rights**, which listed parliamentary powers such as control over taxation as well as rights of individuals, including trial by jury. In the following year, the Toleration Act allowed Protestant Dissenters (but not Catholics) to worship freely, although only Anglicans could hold public office.

Liberty as the birthright of all Englishmen

As always, British politics were mirrored in the American colonies. After the Glorious Revolution, Protestant domination was secured in most of the colonies, with the established churches of England (Anglican) and Scotland (Presbyterian) growing the fastest, while Catholics and Dissenters suffered various forms of discrimination. Throughout English America the Glorious Revolution powerfully reinforced among the colonists the sense of sharing a proud legacy of freedom and Protestantism with the mother country.

The Glorious Revolution in America

The Glorious Revolution exposed fault lines in colonial society and offered local elites an opportunity to regain authority that had recently been challenged. Until the mid-1670s, the North American colonies had essentially governed themselves, with little interference from England. Governor Berkeley ran Virginia as he saw fit; proprietors in New York, Maryland, and Carolina governed in any fashion they could persuade colonists to accept; and New England colonies elected their own officials and openly flouted trade regulations. In 1675, however, England established the

English authority and colonial autonomy

Lords of Trade to oversee colonial affairs. Three years later, the Lords questioned the Massachusetts government about its compliance with the Navigation Acts. They received the surprising reply that since the colony had no representatives in Parliament, the Acts did not apply to it unless the Massachusetts General Court approved.

In the 1680s, England moved to reduce colonial autonomy. Shortly before his death, Charles II revoked the Massachusetts charter, citing wholesale violations of the Navigation Acts. James II between 1686 and 1688 combined Connecticut, Plymouth, Massachusetts, New Hampshire, Rhode Island, New York, and East and West Jersey into a single super-colony, the **Dominion of New England**. It was ruled by the former New York governor Sir Edmund Andros, who did not have to answer to an elected assembly. These events reinforced the impression that James II was an enemy of freedom.

Rebellions in American colonies

In 1689, news of the overthrow of James II triggered rebellions in several American colonies. In April, the Boston militia seized and jailed Edmund Andros and other officials, whereupon the New England colonies reestablished the governments abolished when the Dominion of New England was created. In May, a rebel militia headed by Captain Jacob Leisler established a Committee of Safety and took control of New York. Two months later, Maryland's Protestant Association overthrew the government of the colony's Catholic proprietor, Lord Baltimore.

All of these new regimes claimed to have acted in the name of English liberties and looked to London for approval. But the degrees of success of these coups varied markedly. Concluding that Lord Baltimore had mismanaged the Maryland colony, William revoked his charter (although the proprietor retained his land and rents) and established a new, Protestant-dominated government. In 1715, after the Baltimore family had converted to Anglicanism, proprietary power was restored. But the events of 1689 transformed the ruling group in Maryland and put an end to the colony's unique history of religious toleration.

Turmoil in New York

The outcome in New York was far different. Although it was not his intention, Jacob Leisler's regime divided the colony along ethnic and economic lines. Members of the Dutch majority reclaimed local power after more than two decades of English rule, while bands of rebels ransacked the homes of wealthy New Yorkers. William refused to recognize Leisler's authority and dispatched a new governor, backed by troops. Many of Leisler's followers were imprisoned, and he himself was executed, a reflection of the hatred the rebellion had inspired. For generations, the rivalry between Leisler and anti-Leisler parties polarized New York politics.

The New England colonies, after deposing Edmund Andros, lobbied hard in London for the restoration of their original charters. Most were successful, but Massachusetts was not. In 1691, the crown issued a new charter that absorbed Plymouth into Massachusetts and transformed the political structure of the Bible Commonwealth. Town government remained intact, but henceforth property ownership, not church membership, would be the requirement to vote in elections for the General Court. The governor was now appointed in London rather than elected. Massachusetts became a royal colony, the majority of whose voters were no longer Puritan "saints." Moreover, it was required to abide by the **English Toleration Act** of 1690—that is, to allow all Protestants to worship freely.

Political change in Massachusetts

These events produced an atmosphere of considerable tension in Massachusetts, exacerbated by raids by French troops and their Indian allies on the northern New England frontier. The advent of religious toleration heightened anxieties among the Puritan clergy, who considered other Protestant denominations a form of heresy. Indeed, not a few Puritans thought they saw the hand of Satan in the events of 1690 and 1691.

The Salem Witch Trials

Belief in magic, astrology, and witchcraft was widespread in seventeenth-century Europe and America, existing alongside the religious beliefs sanctioned by the clergy and churches. Witches were individuals, usually women, who were accused of having entered into a pact with the devil to obtain supernatural powers, which they used to harm others or to interfere with natural processes. When a child was stillborn or crops failed, many believed that witchcraft was at work.

In Europe and the colonies, witchcraft was punishable by execution. It is estimated that between the years 1400 and 1800, more than 50,000 people were executed in Europe after being convicted of witchcraft. Witches were, from time to time, hanged in seventeenth-century New England. Most were women beyond childbearing age who were outspoken, economically independent, or estranged from their husbands, or who in other ways violated traditional gender norms.

Until 1692, the prosecution of witches had been sporadic. But in that year, a series of trials and executions took place in Salem that made its name to this day a byword for fanaticism and persecution. The crisis began when several young girls began to

An engraving from Ralph Gardiner's *England's Grievance Discovered*, published in 1655, depicts women hanged as witches in England. The letters identify local officials: A is the hangman, B the town crier, C the sheriff, and D a magistrate.

suffer fits and nightmares, attributed by their elders to witchcraft. Soon, three witches had been named, including Tituba, an Indian from the Caribbean who was a slave in the home of one of the girls. Since the only way to avoid prosecution was to confess and name others, accusations of witchcraft began to snowball. By the middle of 1692, hundreds of residents of Salem had come forward to accuse their neighbors. Although many of the accused confessed to save their lives, fourteen women and five men were hanged, protesting their innocence to the end.

Executions in Salem

As accusations and executions multiplied, it became clear that something was seriously wrong with the colony's system of justice. The governor of Massachusetts dissolved the Salem court and ordered the remaining prisoners released. The events in Salem discredited the tradition of prosecuting witches and encouraged prominent colonists to seek scientific explanations for natural events such as comets and illnesses, rather than attribute them to magic.

THE GROWTH OF COLONIAL AMERICA

As stability returned after the crises of the late seventeenth century, English North America experienced an era of remarkable growth. Between 1700 and 1770, crude backwoods settlements became bustling provincial capitals. The hazards of disease among colonists diminished, agricultural settlement pressed westward, and hundreds of thousands of newcomers arrived from the Old World. Thanks to a high birthrate and continuing immigration, the population of England's mainland colonies, 265,000 in 1700, grew nearly tenfold, to over 2.3 million seventy years later. (It is worth noting, however, that because of the decline suffered by the Indians, the North American population was considerably lower in 1770 than it had been in 1492.)

Population increase

A Diverse Population

Probably the most striking characteristic of colonial American society in the eighteenth century was its sheer diversity. In 1700, the colonies were essentially English outposts. In the eighteenth century, African and non-English European arrivals skyrocketed, while the number emigrating from England declined.

Surge in African and non-English arrivals

About 30 percent of European immigrants to the colonies during the eighteenth century continued to arrive as bound laborers who had

TABLE 3.1   Origins and Status of Migrants to British North American Colonies, 1700–1775

	TOTAL	SLAVES	INDENTURED SERVANTS	CONVICTS	FREE
Africa	278,400	278,400	—	—	—
Ireland	108,600	—	39,000	17,500	52,100
Germany	84,500	—	30,000	—	54,500
England/Wales	73,100	—	27,200	32,500	13,400
Scotland	35,300	—	7,400	2,200	25,700
Other	5,900	—	—	—	5,900
Total	585,800	278,400	103,600	52,200	151,600

temporarily sacrificed their freedom to make the voyage to the New World. But as the colonial economy prospered, poor indentured migrants were increasingly joined by professionals and skilled craftsmen—teachers, ministers, weavers, carpenters—whom England could ill afford to lose. This brought to an end official efforts to promote English emigration.

End of official English emigration efforts

Nevertheless, the government in London remained convinced that colonial development enhanced the nation's power and wealth. To bolster the Chesapeake labor force, nearly 50,000 convicts (a group not desired in Britain) were sent to work in the tobacco fields. Officials also actively encouraged Protestant immigration from the non-English (and less prosperous) parts of the British Isles and from the European continent, promising newcomers easy access to land and the right to worship freely.

Among eighteenth-century migrants from the British Isles, the 70,000 English newcomers were considerably outnumbered by 145,000 from Scotland and Ulster, the northern part of Ireland, where many Scots had settled as part of England's effort to subdue the island. Mostly Presbyterians, they added significantly to religious diversity in North America.

The German Migration

Germans the largest group of newcomers from Europe

Germans, 85,000 in all, formed the largest group of newcomers from the European continent. In the eighteenth century, Germany was divided into numerous small states, each with a ruling prince who determined the

VOICES OF FREEDOM

From Memorial against Non-English Immigration (December 1727)

Only a minority of emigrants from Europe to British North America in the eighteenth century came from the British Isles. Some English settlers, such as the authors of this petition from Pennsylvania to the authorities in London, found the growing diversity of the colonial population quite disturbing.

How careful every European state, that has Colonies in America, has been of preserving the advantages arising from them wholly to their own Nation and People, is obvious to all who will consider the policy & conduct of the Spanish, French & others in relation to theirs. . . .

About the year 1710 a Company of religious People called Menists [Mennonites] from the Palatinate of the Rhine, transported themselves into the Province of Pennsylvania from Holland in British shipping, and purchased Lands at low rates towards the River Susquehanna. The Terms & Reception they met with proved so encouraging, that they invited diverse of their relations and friends to follow them. In the succeeding years . . . several thousands were settled in that Province. . . . We are now assured by the same people that five or six thousand more are to follow them this next ensuing year. . . .

All these men young & old who arrived since the first, come generally very well armed. Many of them are Papists, & most of them appear inured to War & other hardships. They retire commonly back into the woods amongst or behind the remoter inhabitants, sometimes purchase land, but often sit down on any piece they find vacant that they judge convenient for them without asking questions. . . . Few of them apply now to be Naturalized, [and] they . . . generally . . . adhere to their own customs. The part of the country they principally settle in is that towards the French of Canada, whose interest, it may be apprehended, . . . (since several of them speak their language) [they] would as willingly favor as the English. . . . It is hoped therefore that nothing need be added to shew the present necessity of putting a stop to that augmentation of their strength. . . . A general provision against all Foreigners may be necessary.

From Letter by a Swiss-German Immigrant to Pennsylvania
(August 23, 1769)

Germans were among the most numerous immigrants to the eighteenth-century colonies. Many wrote letters to family members at home, relating their experiences and impressions.

Dearest Father, Brother, and Sister and Brother-in-law,

I have told you quite fully about the trip, and I will tell you what will not surprise you—that we have a free country. Of the sundry craftsmen, one may do whatever one wants. Nor does the land require payment of tithes [taxes to support a local landlord, typical in Europe]. . . . The land is very big from Canada to the east of us to Carolina in the south and to the Spanish border in the west. . . . One can settle wherever one wants without asking anyone when he buys or leases something. . . .

I have always enough to do and we have no shortage of food. Bread is plentiful. If I work for two days I earn more bread than in eight days [at home]. . . . Also I can buy many things so reasonably [for example] a pair of shoes for [roughly] seven Pennsylvania shillings. . . . I think that with God's help I will obtain land. I am not pushing for it until I am in a better position.

I would like for my brother to come . . . and it will then be even nicer in the country. . . . I assume that the land has been described to you sufficiently by various people and it is not surprising that the immigrant agents [demand payment]. For the journey is long and it costs much to stay away for one year. . . .

Johannes Hänner

QUESTIONS

1. *What do the petitioners find objectionable about non-English migrants to Pennsylvania?*

2. *What does Johannes Hänner have in mind when he calls America a "free country"?*

3. *How do these documents reflect different views of who should be entitled to the benefits of freedom in the American colonies?*

Among the most striking features of eighteenth-century colonial society was the racial and ethnic diversity of the population (except in New England). This resulted from increased immigration from the non-English parts of the British Isles and from mainland Europe, as well as the rapid expansion of the slave trade from Africa.

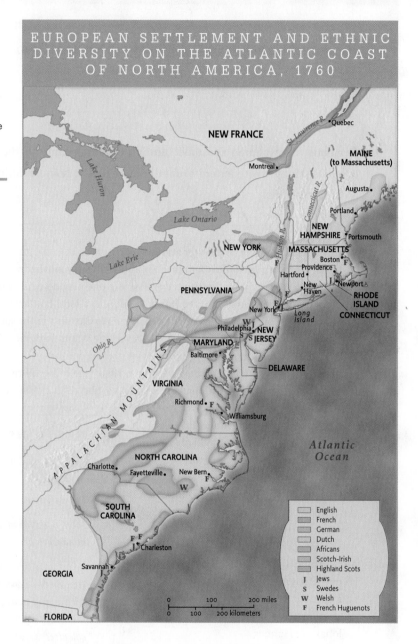

EUROPEAN SETTLEMENT AND ETHNIC DIVERSITY ON THE ATLANTIC COAST OF NORTH AMERICA, 1760

NEW FRANCE

Quebec

Montreal

MAINE (to Massachusetts)

Augusta

Portland

Lake Huron

Lake Ontario

Lake Erie

NEW HAMPSHIRE   Portsmouth

NEW YORK   MASSACHUSETTS
Boston
Providence
Hartford
New Haven   Newport
RHODE ISLAND
CONNECTICUT
Long Island

PENNSYLVANIA

New York

Philadelphia   NEW JERSEY

MARYLAND
Baltimore

Ohio R.

DELAWARE

VIRGINIA

Richmond

Williamsburg

Atlantic Ocean

APPALACHIAN MOUNTAINS

NORTH CAROLINA
Charlotte   Fayetteville   New Bern

SOUTH CAROLINA

Savannah   Charleston

GEORGIA

FLORIDA

	English
	French
	German
	Dutch
	Africans
	Scotch-Irish
	Highland Scots
J	Jews
S	Swedes
W	Welsh
F	French Huguenots

0   100   200 miles
0   100   200 kilometers

official religion. Those who found themselves worshiping the "wrong" religion—Lutherans in Catholic areas, Catholics in Lutheran areas, and everywhere, followers of small Protestant sects such as Mennonites, Moravians, and Dunkers—faced persecution. Many decided to emigrate.

Other migrants were motivated by persistent agricultural crises and the difficulty of acquiring land.

English and Dutch merchants created a well-organized system whereby "**redemptioners**" (as indentured families were called) received passage in exchange for a promise to work off their debt in America. Most settled in frontier areas—rural New York, western Pennsylvania, and the southern backcountry—where they formed tightly knit farming communities in which German for many years remained the dominant language.

German settlements

Religious Diversity

Eighteenth-century British America was not a "melting pot" of cultures. Ethnic groups tended to live and worship in relatively homogeneous communities. But outside of New England, which received few immigrants and retained its overwhelmingly English ethnic character, American society had a far more diverse population than Britain. Nowhere was this more evident than in the practice of religion.

Apart from New Jersey (formed from East and West Jersey in 1702), Rhode Island, and Pennsylvania, the colonies did not adhere to a modern separation of church and state. Nearly every colony levied taxes to pay the salaries of ministers of an established church, and most barred Catholics and Jews from voting and holding public office. But increasingly, de facto toleration among Protestant denominations flourished. By the mid-eighteenth century, dissenting Protestants in most colonies had gained the right to worship as they pleased and own their churches, although many places still barred them from holding public office and taxed them to support the official church. A visitor to Pennsylvania in 1750 described the colony's religious diversity: "We find there Lutherans, Reformed, Catholics, Quakers, Menonists or Anabaptists, Herrnhuters or Moravian Brethren, Pietists, Seventh Day Baptists, Dunkers, Presbyterians, . . . Jews, Mohammedans, Pagans."

William Penn's Treaty with the Indians. Penn's grandson, Thomas, the proprietor of Pennsylvania, commissioned this romanticized painting from the artist Benjamin West in 1771, by which time harmony between Indians and colonists had long since turned to hostility. In the nineteenth century, many reproductions of this image circulated, reminding Americans that Indians had once been central figures in their history.

Indian Life in Transition

The tide of newcomers, who equated liberty with secure possession of land, threatened to engulf the surviving Indian populations. By the eighteenth century, Indian societies that had existed for centuries had disappeared, the victims of disease and warfare, and the communities that remained were well integrated into the British imperial system. Indeed, Indian warriors did much of the fighting in the century's imperial wars. Few Indians chose to live among whites rather than in their own communities. But they had become well accustomed to using European products like knives, hatchets, needles, kettles, and firearms. Alcohol introduced by traders created social chaos in many Indian communities. One Cherokee told the governor of South Carolina in 1753, "The clothes we wear, we cannot make ourselves. . . . We use their ammunition with which we kill deer. . . . Every necessary thing we must have from the white people."

Indians and settlers

While traders saw in Indian villages potential profits and British officials saw allies against France and Spain, farmers and planters viewed Indians as little more than an obstruction to their desire for land. They expected Indians to give way to white settlers. In Pennsylvania, for example, the flood of German and Scotch-Irish settlers into the backcountry upset the relatively peaceful Indian-white relations constructed by William Penn. The infamous **Walking Purchase** of 1737 brought the fraudulent dealing so common in other colonies to Pennsylvania. The Lenni Lanape Indians agreed to cede a tract of land bounded by the distance a man could walk in thirty-six hours. To their amazement, Governor James Logan hired a team of swift runners, who marked out an area far in excess of what the Indians had anticipated. By 1760, when Pennsylvania's population, a mere 20,000 in 1700, had grown to 220,000, Indian-colonist relations, initially the most harmonious in British North America, had become poisoned by suspicion and hostility.

Regional Diversity

By the mid-eighteenth century, the different regions of the British colonies had developed distinct economic and social orders. Small farms tilled by family labor and geared primarily to production for local consumption predominated in New England and the new settlements of the **backcountry** (the area stretching from central Pennsylvania southward through the Shenandoah Valley of Virginia and into upland North and South

The backcountry

Carolina). The backcountry was the most rapidly growing region in North America. By the eve of the American Revolution, the region contained one-quarter of Virginia's population and half of South Carolina's. Most were farm families raising grain and livestock.

In the older portions of the Middle Colonies of New York, New Jersey, and Pennsylvania, farmers were more oriented to commerce than on the frontier. They grew grain both for their own use and for sale abroad and supplemented the work of family members by employing wage laborers, tenants, and in some instances slaves. With its fertile soil, favorable climate, initially peaceful Indian relations, generous governmental land distribution policy, and rivers that facilitated long-distance trading, Pennsylvania came to be known as "the best poor man's country." Ordinary colonists there enjoyed a standard of living unimaginable in Europe.

"The best poor man's country"

The Consumer Revolution

During the eighteenth century, Great Britain eclipsed the Dutch as the leading producer and trader of inexpensive consumer goods, including colonial products like coffee and tea, and such manufactured goods as linen, metalware, pins, ribbons, glassware, ceramics, and clothing. Trade integrated the British empire. As the American colonies were drawn more and more fully into the system of Atlantic commerce, they shared in the era's consumer revolution. In port cities and small inland towns, shops proliferated and American newspapers were filled with advertisements for British goods.

Inexpensive consumer goods

Consumerism in a modern sense—the mass production, advertising, and sale of consumer goods—did not exist in colonial America. Nonetheless, even modest farmers and artisans owned books, ceramic plates, metal cutlery, and items made of imported silk and cotton. Tea, once a luxury enjoyed only by the wealthy, became virtually a necessity of life.

This piece of china made in England and exported to New England celebrates the coronation of James II in 1685. It is an example of the growing colonial demand for English consumer goods.

Colonial Cities

Colonial cities like Boston, New York, Philadelphia, and Charleston were quite small by the standards of Europe or Spanish America. In 1700, when the population of Mexico City stood at 100,000, Boston had 6,000 residents and New York 4,500.

British North American cities were mainly gathering places for agricultural goods and for imported items to be distributed to the countryside. Nonetheless, the expansion of trade encouraged the rise of port cities, home to a growing population of colonial merchants and **artisans** (skilled craftsmen) as well as an increasing number of poor. In 1770, with some 30,000 inhabitants, Philadelphia was "the capital of the New World," at least its British component, and, after London and Liverpool, the empire's third busiest port. The financial, commercial, and cultural center of British America, Philadelphia founded its growth on economic integration with the rich agricultural region nearby. Philadelphia merchants organized the collection of farm goods, supplied rural storekeepers, and extended credit to consumers. They exported flour, bread, and meat to the West Indies and Europe.

The city was also home to a large population of furniture makers, jewelers, and silversmiths serving wealthier citizens, and hundreds of lesser artisans like weavers, blacksmiths, coopers, and construction workers. The typical artisan owned his own tools and labored in a small workshop, often his home, assisted by family members and young journeymen and apprentices learning the trade. The artisan's skill gave him a far greater degree of economic freedom than those dependent on others for a livelihood.

American craftsmen and the expanding consumer market

Despite the influx of British goods, American craftsmen benefited from the expanding consumer market. Most journeymen enjoyed a reasonable chance of rising to the status of master and establishing workshops of their own.

An Atlantic World

People, ideas, and goods flowed back and forth across the Atlantic, knitting together the empire and its diverse populations—British merchants and consumers, American colonists, African slaves, and surviving Indians—and creating webs of interdependence among the European empires. As trade expanded, the North American and West Indian colonies became the major overseas market for British manufactured goods. Although most colonial output was consumed at home, North Americans shipped

Trade in the Atlantic world

farm products to Britain, the West Indies, and with the exception of goods like tobacco "enumerated" under the Navigation Acts, outside the empire. Virtually the entire Chesapeake tobacco crop was marketed in Britain, with most of it then re-exported to Europe by British merchants. Most of the bread and flour exported from the colonies was destined for the West Indies. African slaves there grew sugar that could be distilled into rum, a product increasingly popular among both North American colonists and Indians, who obtained it by trading furs and deerskins that were then shipped to Europe. The mainland colonies carried on a flourishing trade in fish and grains with southern Europe. Ships built in New England made up one-third of the British empire's trading fleet.

Advantages of British empire

Membership in the empire had many advantages for the colonists. Most Americans did not complain about British regulation of their trade because commerce enriched the colonies as well as the mother country and lax enforcement of the Navigation Acts allowed smuggling to flourish. In a dangerous world, moreover, the Royal Navy protected American shipping.

And despite the many differences between life in England and its colonies, eighteenth-century English America drew closer to, and in some ways became more similar to, the mother country across the Atlantic.

SOCIAL CLASSES IN THE COLONIES

The Colonial Elite

Most free Americans benefited from economic growth, but as colonial society matured an elite emerged that, while neither as powerful or wealthy as the aristocracy of England, increasingly dominated politics and society. In New England and the Middle Colonies, expanding trade made possible the emergence of a powerful upper class of merchants, often linked by family or commercial ties to great trading firms in London. By 1750, the colonies of the Chesapeake and Lower South were dominated by slave plantations producing staple crops, especially tobacco and rice, for the world market. Here great planters accumulated enormous wealth. The colonial elite also included the rulers of proprietary colonies like Pennsylvania and Maryland.

Merchants, gentry, and planters

America had no titled aristocracy as in Britain. But throughout British America, men of prominence controlled colonial government. In Virginia, the upper class was so tightly knit and intermarried so often that the colony was said to be governed by a "**cousinocracy**." Nearly every Virginian of note achieved prominence through family connections. Thomas Jefferson's grandfather was a justice of the peace (an important local official), militia captain, and sheriff, and his father was a member of the House of Burgesses. George Washington's father, grandfather, and great-grandfather had been justices of the peace. The Virginia gentry used its control of provincial government to gain possession of large tracts of land as western areas opened for settlement.

A 1732 portrait of Daniel, Peter, and Andrew Oliver, sons of a wealthy Boston merchant. The prominent display of their delicate hands tells the viewer that they have never had to do manual labor.

The richest group of mainland colonists were South Carolina planters. Like their Virginia counterparts, South Carolina grandees lived a lavish lifestyle amid imported furniture, fine wines, silk clothing, and other items from England. Their wealth enabled them to spend much of their time enjoying the social life of Charleston, the only real urban center south of Philadelphia and the richest city in British North America.

Anglicization

For much of the eighteenth century, the American colonies had more regular trade and communications with Britain than among themselves. Rather than thinking of themselves as distinctively American, they became more and more English—a process historians call "Anglicization."

Wealthy Americans tried to model their lives on British etiquette and behavior. Somewhat resentful at living in provincial isolation—"at the end of the world," as one Virginia aristocrat put it—they sought to demonstrate their status and legitimacy by importing the latest London fashions and literature, sending their sons to Britain for education, and building homes equipped with fashionable furnishings modeled on the country estates and town houses of the English gentry.

Colonial elites and English identity

Throughout the colonies, elites emulated what they saw as England's balanced, stable social order. Liberty, in their eyes, meant, in part, the power to rule—the right of those blessed with wealth and prominence to dominate others. They viewed society as a hierarchical structure in which some men were endowed with greater talents than others and were destined to rule. Each place in the hierarchy carried with it different responsibilities, and one's status was revealed in dress, manners, and the splendor of one's home. On both sides of the Atlantic, elites viewed work as something reserved for common folk and slaves. Freedom from labor was the mark of the gentleman.

Poverty in the Colonies

At the other end of the social scale, poverty emerged as a visible feature of eighteenth-century colonial life. Although not considered by most colonists part of their society, the growing number of slaves lived in impoverished conditions. Among free Americans, poverty was hardly as widespread as in Britain, where in the early part of the century between one-quarter and one-half of the people regularly required public assistance. But as the colonial population expanded, access to land diminished rapidly, especially in long-settled areas, forcing many propertyless males to seek work in their region's cities or in other colonies.

Increase in poverty in eighteenth-century colonies

In colonial cities, the number of propertyless wage earners subsisting at the poverty line steadily increased. In Boston, one-third of the population in 1771 owned no property at all. In rural Augusta County, carved out of Virginia's Shenandoah River valley in 1738, land was quickly engrossed by planters and speculators. By the 1760s, two-thirds of the county's white men owned no land and had little prospect of obtaining it unless they migrated farther west. Taking the colonies as a whole, half of the wealth at mid-century was concentrated in the hands of the richest 10 percent of the population.

The richest 10 percent

Attitudes and policies toward poverty in colonial America mirrored British precedents. The better-off colonists generally viewed the poor as lazy, shiftless, and responsible for their own plight. To minimize the burden on taxpayers, poor persons were frequently set to labor in workhouses, where they produced goods that reimbursed authorities for part of their upkeep.

The Middle Ranks

The large majority of free Americans lived between the extremes of wealth and poverty. Along with racial and ethnic diversity, what distinguished the mainland colonies from Europe was the wide distribution of land and the economic autonomy of most ordinary free families. Altogether, perhaps two-thirds of the free male population were farmers who owned their own land.

Landownership and freedom

By the eighteenth century, colonial farm families viewed landownership almost as a right, the social precondition of freedom. They strongly resented efforts, whether by Native Americans, great landlords, or colonial governments, to limit their access to land. A dislike of personal dependence and an understanding of freedom as not relying on others for a livelihood sank deep roots in British North America.

This portrait of the Cheney family by an unknown late-eighteenth-century artist illustrates the high birthrate in colonial America and suggests how many years of a woman's life were spent bearing and raising children.

Women and the Household Economy

In the household economy of eighteenth-century America, the family was the center of economic life. The independence of the small farmer depended in considerable measure on the labor of dependent women and children. "He that hath an industrious family shall soon be rich," declared one colonial saying, and the high birthrate in part reflected the need for as many hands as possible on colonial farms.

As the population grew and the death rate declined, family life stabilized and more marriages became lifetime commitments. Free women were expected to devote their lives to being good wives and mothers. As colonial society became more structured, opportunities that had existed for women in the early period receded. In Connecticut, for example, the courts were informal and unorganized in the seventeenth century, and women often represented themselves. In the eighteenth century, it became necessary to hire a lawyer as one's spokesman in court. Women, barred from practicing as attorneys, disappeared from judicial proceedings. Because of the desperate need for labor in the seventeenth century, men and women both did various kinds of work. In the eighteenth century, the division of labor along gender lines solidified. Women's work was clearly defined, including cooking, cleaning, sewing, making butter, and assisting with agricultural chores. Even as the consumer revolution reduced the demands on many women by making available store-bought goods previously produced at home, women's work seemed to increase. Lower infant mortality meant more time spent in child care and domestic chores.

Division of labor along gender lines

North America at Mid-Century

By the mid-eighteenth century, the area that would become the United States was home to a remarkable diversity of peoples and different kinds of social organization, from Pueblo villages of the Southwest to tobacco plantations of the Chesapeake, towns and small farms of New England, and fur-trading outposts of the northern and western frontier. Elites tied to imperial centers of power dominated the political and economic life of nearly every colony. But large numbers of colonists enjoyed far greater opportunities for freedom—access to the vote, prospects of acquiring land, the right to worship as they pleased, and an escape from oppressive government—than existed in Europe. The colonies' economic growth contributed to a high birthrate, long life expectancy, and expanding demand for consumer goods.

Opportunities for freedom

Yet many others found themselves confined to the partial freedom of indentured servitude or to the complete absence of freedom in slavery. Both timeless longings for freedom and new and unprecedented forms of unfreedom had been essential to the North American colonies' remarkable development.

Freedom and unfreedom

CHAPTER REVIEW AND ONLINE RESOURCES

REVIEW QUESTIONS

1. Both the Puritans and William Penn viewed their colonies as "holy experiments." How did they differ?

2. The textbook states "Prejudice by itself did not create American slavery." Examine the economic forces, events, and laws that shaped the experiences of enslaved people.

3. How did English leaders understand the place and role of the American colonies in England's empire?

4. How did King Philip's War, Bacon's Rebellion, and the Salem witch trials illustrate a widespread crisis in British North America in the late seventeenth century?

5. The social structure of the eighteenth-century colonies was growing more open for some but not for others. Consider the statement with respect to: men and women; whites and blacks; and rich and poor.

6. By the end of the seventeenth century, commerce was the foundation of empire and the leading cause of competition between European empires. Explain how the North American colonies were directly linked to Atlantic commerce by laws and trade.

7. If you traveled from New England to the South, how would you describe the diversity you saw between the different colonies?

8. What impact did the family's being the center of economic life have on gender relations and the roles of women?

KEY TERMS

Metacom (p. 73)

King Philip's War (p. 73)

mercantilism (p. 74)

Navigation Acts (p. 74)

Covenant Chain (p. 75)

Society of Friends (Quakers) (p. 78)

sugar (p. 82)

Bacon's Rebellion (p. 83)

slave code of 1705 (p. 85)

Glorious Revolution (p. 86)

English Bill of Rights (p. 87)

Lords of Trade (p. 88)

Dominion of New England (p. 88)

English Toleration Act (p. 89)

Salem witch trials (p. 89)

redemptioners (p. 95)

Walking Purchase (p. 96)

backcountry (p. 96)

artisans (p. 97)

"cousinocracy" (p. 99)

wwnorton.com
/studyspace

VISIT STUDYSPACE FOR THESE
RESOURCES AND MORE
- A chapter outline
- A diagnostic chapter quiz
- Interactive maps
- Map worksheets
- Multimedia documents

CHAPTER 4

SLAVERY, FREEDOM, AND THE STRUGGLE FOR EMPIRE

★

TO 1763

The Old Plantation, a late-eighteenth-century watercolor, depicts slaves dancing in a plantation's slave quarters, perhaps at a wedding. The musical instruments and pottery are African in origin while much of the clothing is of European manufacture, indicating the mixing of African and white cultures among the era's slaves. The artist has recently been identified as John Rose, owner of a rice plantation near Beaufort, South Carolina.

Sometime in the mid-1750s, Olaudah Equiano, the eleven-year-old son of a West African village chief, was kidnapped by slave traders. He soon found himself on a ship headed for Barbados. Equiano was sold to a plantation owner in Virginia and then purchased by a British sea captain, who renamed him Gustavus Vassa. While still a slave, he enrolled in a school in England where he learned to read and write, and then enlisted in the Royal Navy. In 1763, however, Equiano was sold once again and returned to the Caribbean. Three years later, he was able to purchase his freedom and went on to experience shipwrecks, a colonizing venture in Central America, and even an expedition to the Arctic Circle.

Equiano eventually settled in London, and in 1789 he published *The Interesting Narrative of the Life of Olaudah Equiano, or Gustavus Vassa, the African*, which he described as a "history of neither a saint, a hero, nor a tyrant," but of a victim of slavery who through luck or fate ended up more fortunate than most of his people. He condemned the idea that Africans were inferior to Europeans and therefore deserved to be slaves. The book became the era's most widely read account by a slave of his own experiences. Equiano died in 1797.

Recent scholars have suggested that Equiano may have been born in the New World rather than Africa. In either case, while his life was no doubt unusual, it illuminates broad patterns of eighteenth-century American history. As noted in the previous chapter, this was a period of sustained development for British North America. Compared with England and Scotland—united to create Great Britain by the Act of Union of 1707—the colonies were growing much more rapidly.

Ideas, people, and goods flowed back and forth across the ocean. Even as the colonies' populations became more diverse, they were increasingly integrated into the British empire. Their laws and political institutions were extensions of those of Britain, their ideas about society and culture reflected British values, their economies were geared to serving the empire's needs.

Equiano's life also underscores the greatest irony in the history of the eighteenth century—the simultaneous expansion of freedom and slavery. This was the era when the idea of the "freeborn Englishman" became powerfully entrenched in the outlook of both colonists and Britons. More than any other principle, liberty was seen as what made the British empire distinct. Yet the eighteenth century was also the height of the Atlantic slave trade, a commerce increasingly dominated by British merchants and ships. Although concentrated in the Chesapeake

FOCUS QUESTIONS

- *How did African slavery differ regionally in eighteenth-century North America?*

- *What factors led to distinct African-American cultures in the eighteenth century?*

- *What were the meanings of British liberty in the eighteenth century?*

- *What concepts and institutions dominated colonial politics in the eighteenth century?*

- *How did the Great Awakening challenge the religious and social structure of British North America?*

- *How did the Spanish and French empires in America develop in the eighteenth century?*

- *What was the impact of the Seven Years' War on imperial and Indian–white relations?*

The frontispiece of Olaudah Equiano's account of his life, the best-known narrative by an eighteenth-century slave. The portrait of Equiano in European dress and holding a Bible challenges stereotypes of blacks as "savages" incapable of becoming civilized.

Triangular trade routes

and areas farther south, slavery existed in every colony of British North America. And unlike Equiano, very few slaves were fortunate enough to gain their freedom.

SLAVERY AND EMPIRE

Of the estimated 7.7 million Africans transported to the New World between 1492 and 1820, more than half arrived between 1700 and 1800. The **Atlantic slave trade** would later be condemned by statesmen and general opinion as a crime against humanity. But in the eighteenth century, it was a regularized business in which European merchants, African traders, and American planters engaged in complex bargaining over human lives, all with the expectation of securing a profit. The slave trade was a vital part of world commerce.

In the British empire of the eighteenth century, free laborers working for wages were atypical and slavery was the norm. The first mass consumer goods in international trade were produced by slaves—sugar, rice, coffee, and tobacco. The rising demand for these products fueled the rapid growth of the Atlantic slave trade.

Atlantic Trade

In the eighteenth century, the Caribbean remained the commercial focus of the British empire and the major producer of revenue for the crown. A series of triangular trading routes crisscrossed the Atlantic, carrying British manufactured goods to Africa and the colonies, colonial products including tobacco, indigo, sugar, and rice to Europe, and slaves from Africa to the New World. Most colonial vessels, however, went back and forth between cities like New York, Charleston, and Savannah, and to ports in the Caribbean. Merchants in New York, Massachusetts, and Rhode Island participated actively in the slave trade, shipping slaves from Africa to the Caribbean or southern colonies. The slave economies of the West Indies were the largest market for fish, grain, livestock, and lumber exported from New England and the Middle Colonies. In Britain itself, the profits from slavery and the slave trade stimulated the rise of ports like Liverpool and Bristol and the growth of banking, shipbuilding, and insurance. They also helped to finance the early industrial revolution.

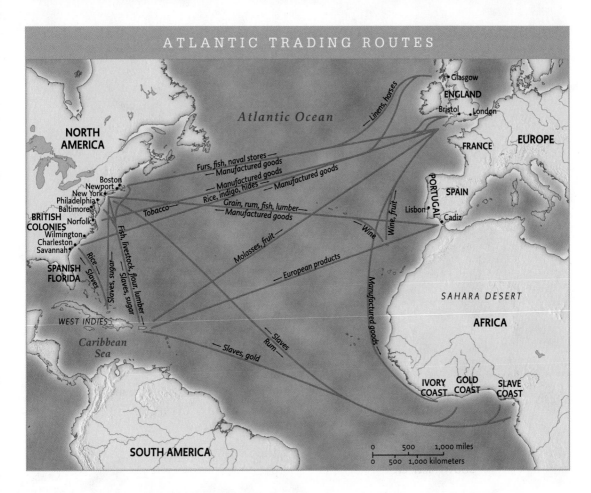

ATLANTIC TRADING ROUTES

A series of trading routes crisscrossed the Atlantic, bringing manufactured goods to Africa and Britain's American colonies, slaves to the New World, and colonial products to Europe.

With slavery so central to Atlantic commerce, it should not be surprising that for large numbers of free colonists and Europeans, freedom meant in part the power and right to enslave others. And as slavery became more and more entrenched, so too, as the Quaker abolitionist John Woolman commented in 1762, did "the idea of slavery being connected with the black color, and liberty with the white."

Africa and the Slave Trade

A few African societies, like Benin for a time, opted out of the Atlantic slave trade, hoping to avoid the disruptions it inevitably caused. But most African rulers took part, and they proved quite adept at playing

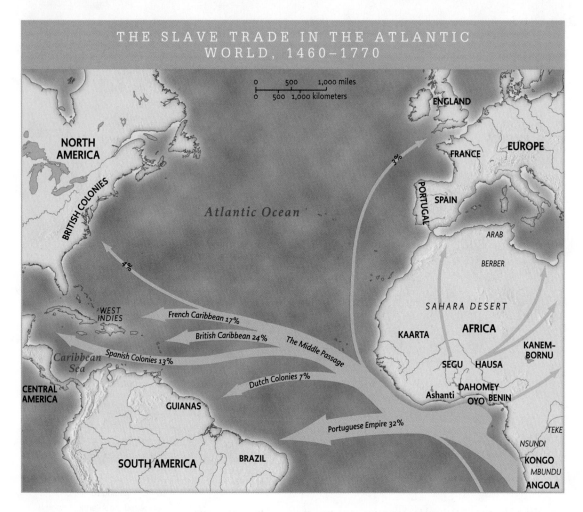

THE SLAVE TRADE IN THE ATLANTIC WORLD, 1460–1770

0   500   1,000 miles
0   500   1,000 kilometers

ENGLAND

NORTH AMERICA

EUROPE

FRANCE

BRITISH COLONIES

PORTUGAL

SPAIN

Atlantic Ocean

ARAB

3%

BERBER

4%

SAHARA DESERT

WEST INDIES

French Caribbean 17%

AFRICA

KAARTA

KANEM-BORNU

British Caribbean 24%

The Middle Passage

Spanish Colonies 13%

Caribbean Sea

SEGU   HASUA

Dutch Colonies 7%

DAHOMEY

CENTRAL AMERICA

Ashanti   OYO BENIN

GUIANAS

TEKE

Portuguese Empire 32%

NSUNDI

SOUTH AMERICA   BRAZIL

KONGO

MBUNDU

ANGOLA

The Atlantic slave trade expanded rapidly in the eighteenth century. The mainland colonies received only a tiny proportion of the Africans brought to the New World, most of whom were transported to Brazil and the West Indies.

the Europeans off against one another, collecting taxes from foreign merchants, and keeping the capture and sale of slaves under their own control. Few Europeans ventured inland from the coast. Traders remained in their "factories" and purchased slaves brought to them by African rulers and dealers.

From a minor institution, slavery grew to become more and more central to West African society, a source of wealth for African merchants and of power for newly emerging African kingdoms. The loss every year of tens of thousands of men and women in the prime of their lives to the slave trade weakened and distorted West Africa's society and economy.

Slavery's impact in West Africa

The Middle Passage

For slaves, the voyage across the Atlantic—known as the **Middle Passage** because it was the second, or middle, leg in the triangular trading routes linking Europe, Africa, and America—was a harrowing experience. Men, women, and children were crammed aboard vessels as tightly as possible to maximize profits. Equiano, who later described "the shrieks of the women and the groans of the dying," survived the Middle Passage, but many Africans did not. Diseases such as measles and smallpox spread rapidly, and about one slave in five perished before reaching the New World. Ship captains were known to throw the sick overboard in order to prevent the spread of epidemics.

Only a small proportion (less than 5 percent) of slaves carried to the New World were destined for mainland North America. The vast majority landed in Brazil or the West Indies, where the high death rate on the sugar plantations led to a constant demand for new slave imports. Overall, the area that was to become the United States imported between 400,000 and 600,000 slaves. By 1770, due to the natural reproduction of the slave population, around one-fifth of the estimated 2.3 million persons (not including Indians) living in the English colonies of North America were Africans and their descendants.

This image, made by a sailor in 1769 for the ship's owner, a merchant in Nantes, France, depicts the interior of a slave-trading vessel, the *Marie-Séraphique*. The cargo carried in barrels, generally guns, cloth, and metal goods, were to be traded for slaves. The third image from the left depicts the conditions under which slaves endured the Middle Passage across the Atlantic. The ship carried over 300 slaves. The broadside also included a calculation of the profit of the voyage.

Chesapeake Slavery

By the mid-eighteenth century, three distinct slave systems were well entrenched in Britain's mainland colonies: tobacco-based plantation slavery in the Chesapeake, rice-based plantation slavery in South Carolina and Georgia, and nonplantation slavery in New England and the Middle Colonies. The largest and oldest of these was the plantation system of the Chesapeake, where more than 270,000 slaves resided in 1770, nearly half of the region's population. Virginia and Maryland were as closely tied to Britain as any other colonies and their economies were models of mercantilist policy (described in Chapter 3).

As Virginia expanded westward, so did slavery. By the eve of the American Revolution, the center of gravity of slavery in the colony had

Tobacco-based plantation slavery

shifted from the Tidewater (the region along the coast) to the Piedmont farther inland. Most Chesapeake slaves, male and female, worked in the tobacco fields, but thousands labored as teamsters, as boatmen, and in skilled crafts. Numerous slave women became cooks, seamstresses, dairy maids, and personal servants. Slavery was common on small farms as well as plantations; nearly half of Virginia's white families owned at least one slave in 1770.

Slavery transformed Chesapeake society into an elaborate hierarchy of degrees of freedom. At the top stood large planters, below them numerous lesser planters and landowning yeomen, and at the bottom a large population of convicts, indentured servants, tenant farmers (who made up half the white households in 1770), and, of course, the slaves. Violence lay at the heart of the slave system. Even a planter like Landon Carter, who prided himself on his concern for the well-being of his slaves, noted casually in his diary, "they have been severely whipped day by day."

Race took on more and more importance as a line of social division. Whites increasingly considered free blacks dangerous and undesirable. Free blacks lost the right to employ white servants and to bear arms, were subjected to special taxes, and could be punished for striking a white person, regardless of the cause. In 1723, Virginia revoked the voting privileges of property-owning free blacks. Because Virginia law required that freed slaves be sent out of the colony, free blacks remained only a tiny part of the population—less than 4 percent in 1750.

The Rice Kingdom

As in early Virginia, frontier conditions allowed leeway to South Carolina's small population of African-born slaves, who farmed, tended livestock, and were initially allowed to serve in the militia to fight the Spanish and Indians. And as in Virginia, the introduction of a marketable staple crop, in this case rice, led directly to economic development, the large-scale importation of slaves, and a growing divide between white and black. In the 1740s, another staple, indigo (a crop used in producing blue dye), was developed. Like rice, indigo required large-scale cultivation and was grown by slaves.

Since rice production requires considerable capital investment to drain swamps and create irrigation systems, it is economically advantageous for rice plantations to be as large as possible. Thus, South Carolina planters owned far more land and slaves than their counterparts in Virginia. Moreover, since mosquitoes bearing malaria (a disease to which

Benjamin Latrobe's watercolor, *An Overseer Doing His Duty*, was sketched near Fredericksburg, Virginia, in 1798. The title is meant to be ironic: the well-dressed overseer relaxes while two female slaves work in the fields.

Africans had developed partial immunity) flourished in the watery rice fields, planters tended to leave plantations under the control of overseers and the slaves themselves.

In the Chesapeake, field slaves worked in groups under constant supervision. Under the "task" system that developed in eighteenth-century South Carolina, individual slaves were assigned daily jobs, the completion of which allowed them time for leisure or to cultivate crops of their own. In 1762, one rice district had a population of only 76 white males among 1,000 slaves. By 1770, the number of South Carolina slaves had reached 100,000, well over half the colony's population.

The task system

The Georgia Experiment

Rice cultivation also spread into Georgia. The colony was founded in 1733 by a group of philanthropists led by James Oglethorpe, a wealthy reformer who sought to improve conditions for imprisoned debtors and abolish slavery. Oglethorpe hoped to establish a haven where the "worthy poor" of England could enjoy economic opportunity. The government in London supported the creation of Georgia to protect South Carolina against the Spanish and their Indian allies in Florida.

James Oglethorpe

Initially, the proprietors banned liquor and slaves, leading to continual battles with settlers, who desired both. By the 1740s, Georgia offered the spectacle of colonists pleading for the "English liberty" of self-government so that they could enact laws introducing slavery. In 1751, the proprietors surrendered the colony to the crown. The colonists quickly won the right to an elected assembly, which met in Savannah. It repealed the ban on slavery (and liquor), as well as an early measure that had limited landholdings to 500 acres. Georgia became a miniature version of South Carolina. By 1770, as many as 15,000 slaves labored on its coastal rice plantations.

Social and political change in Georgia

Slavery in the North

Small farms in northern colonies

Unlike in the plantation regions, slavery was far less central to the economies of New England and the Middle Colonies, where small farms predominated. Slaves made up only a small percentage of these colonies' populations, and it was unusual for even rich families to own more than one slave. Nonetheless, slavery was not entirely marginal to northern colonial life. Slaves worked as farm hands, in artisan shops, as stevedores loading and unloading ships, and as personal servants. But with slaves so small a part of the population that they seemed to pose no threat to the white majority, laws were less harsh than in the South. In New England, where in 1770 the 17,000 slaves represented less than 3 percent of the region's population, slave marriages were recognized in law; the severe physical punishment of slaves was prohibited; and slaves could bring suits in court, testify against whites, and own property and pass it on to their children—rights unknown in the South.

Slavery had been present in New York from the earliest days of Dutch settlement. As New York City's role in the slave trade expanded, so did slavery in the city. In 1746, its 2,440 slaves amounted to one-fifth of New York City's total population. Most were domestic workers, but slaves worked in all sectors of the economy. In 1770, about 27,000 slaves lived in New York and New Jersey, 10 percent

TABLE 4.1 Slave Population as Percentage of Total Population of Original Thirteen Colonies, 1770

COLONY	SLAVE POPULATION	PERCENTAGE
New Hampshire	654	1%
Massachusetts	4,754	2
Connecticut	5,698	3
Rhode Island	3,761	6
New York	19,062	12
New Jersey	8,220	7
Pennsylvania	5,561	2
Delaware	1,836	5
Maryland	63,818	32
Virginia	187,600	42
North Carolina	69,600	35
South Carolina	75,168	61
Georgia	15,000	45

of their total population. Slavery was also a significant presence in Philadelphia, although the institution stagnated after 1750 as artisans and merchants relied increasingly on wage laborers, whose numbers were augmented by population growth and the completion of the terms of indentured servants.

SLAVE CULTURES AND SLAVE RESISTANCE

Becoming African-American

The nearly 300,000 Africans brought to the mainland colonies during the eighteenth century were not a single people. They came from different cultures, spoke different languages, and practiced many religions. Slavery threw together individuals who would never otherwise have encountered one another and who had never considered their color or residence on a single continent a source of identity or unity. Their bond was not kinship, language, or even "race," but slavery itself. The process of creating a cohesive culture took many years. But by the nineteenth century, slaves no longer identified themselves as Ibo, Ashanti, Yoruba, and so on, but as African-Americans. In music, art, folklore, language, and religion, their cultural expressions emerged as a synthesis of African traditions, European elements, and new conditions in America.

Diverse origins

African-American culture

For most of the eighteenth century, the majority of American slaves were African by birth. Advertisements seeking information about runaways often described them by African origin ("young Gambia Negro," "new Banbara Negro fellow") and spoke of their bearing on their bodies "country marks"—visible signs of ethnic identity in Africa. Indeed, during the eighteenth century, black life in the colonies was "re-Africanized" as the earlier Creoles (slaves born in the New World) came to be outnumbered by large-scale importations from Africa.

African Religion in Colonial America

No experience was more wrenching for African slaves in the colonies than the transition from traditional religions to Christianity. Although African religions varied as much as those on other continents, they shared some elements, especially belief in the presence of spiritual forces in nature and a close relationship between the sacred and secular worlds. In the religions of West Africa, the region from which most slaves brought to British North America originated, there was no hard and fast distinction between the secular and spiritual worlds. Nature was suffused with spirits and the dead could influence the living. It was customary, Equiano wrote, before eating, to set aside some food for the spirits of departed ancestors.

Although some slaves came to the colonies familiar with Christianity or Islam, the majority of North American slaves practiced traditional African religions (which many Europeans deemed superstition or even witchcraft) well into the eighteenth century. When they did adopt Christian practices, many slaves merged them with traditional beliefs, adding the Christian God to their own pantheon of lesser spirits, whom they continued to worship.

African-American Cultures

Distinctive cultures

By the mid-eighteenth century, the three slave systems in British North America had produced distinct African-American cultures. In the Chesapeake, because of a more healthful climate, the slave population began to reproduce itself by 1740. Because of the small size of most plantations and the large number of white yeoman farmers, slaves here were continuously exposed to white culture. They soon learned English, and many were swept up in the religious revivals known as the Great Awakening, discussed later in this chapter.

In South Carolina and Georgia, two very different black societies emerged. On the rice plantations, slaves lived in extremely harsh conditions and had a low birthrate throughout the eighteenth century, making

An advertisement seeking the return of a runaway slave from Port Royal, in the Sea Islands of South Carolina. "Mustee" was a term for a person of mixed European and African ancestry. From the *South Carolina Gazette*, June 11, 1747.

Run away on the 13th of *March* last, a Muſtee Fellow named *Cyrus*, who lately belonged to Meſſrs. *Mulryne* and *Williams* of *Port-Royal*. Whoever ſecures, or brings the ſaid Fellow to me, or to Mr. *David Brown* of *Charles-Town* Shipwright, ſhall have TWENTY POUNDS Reward, and the Charges allow'd by Law. And whoever gives me Information of his being employed by any Perſon, ſo that he may be convicted thereof, ſhall, upon ſuch Conviction, have THIRTY POUNDS current Money paid him, by   *David Linn*.

A bay ſtray Horſe, about 13 Hands and an half

rice production dependent on continued slave imports from Africa. The slaves seldom came into contact with whites. They constructed African-style houses, chose African names for their children, and spoke Gullah, a language that mixed various African roots and was unintelligible to most whites. In Charleston and Savannah, however, the experience of slaves who labored as servants or skilled workers was quite different. They assimilated more quickly into Euro-American culture, and sexual liaisons between white owners and slave women produced the beginning of a class of free mulattos.

Regional differences

In the northern colonies, where slaves represented a smaller part of the population, dispersed in small holdings among the white population, a distinctive African-American culture developed more slowly. Living in close proximity to whites, they enjoyed more mobility and access to the mainstream of life than their counterparts farther south. But they had fewer opportunities to create stable family life or a cohesive community.

Resistance to Slavery

The common threads that linked these regional African-American cultures were the experience of slavery and the desire for freedom. Throughout the eighteenth century, blacks risked their lives in efforts to resist enslavement. Colonial newspapers, especially in the southern colonies, were filled with advertisements for runaway slaves. In South Carolina and Georgia, they fled to Florida, to uninhabited coastal and river swamps, or to Charleston and Savannah, where they could pass for free. In the Chesapeake and Middle Colonies, fugitive slaves tended to be familiar with white culture and therefore, as one advertisement put it, could "pretend to be free."

Slaves' desire for freedom

What Edward Trelawny, the colonial governor of Jamaica, called "a dangerous spirit of liberty" was widespread among the New World's slaves. The eighteenth century's first slave uprising occurred in New York City in 1712, when a group of slaves set fire to houses on the outskirts of the city and killed the first nine whites who arrived on the scene. During the 1730s and 1740s, continuous warfare involving European empires and Indians opened the door to slave resistance. In 1731, a slave rebellion in Louisiana, where the French and the Natchez Indians were at war, temporarily halted efforts to introduce the plantation system in that region.

Slave rebellions

Slaves seized the opportunity for rebellion offered by the War of Jenkins' Ear, which pitted England against Spain. In September 1739, a group of South Carolina slaves, most of them recently arrived from Kongo where some, it appears, had been soldiers, seized a store containing numerous weapons at the town of Stono. Beating drums to attract followers, the armed band marched southward toward Florida, burning houses and barns, killing whites they encountered, and shouting "Liberty." The **Stono Rebellion** took the lives of more than two dozen whites and as many as 200 slaves. Some slaves managed to reach Florida, where in 1740 they were armed by the Spanish to help repel an attack on St. Augustine by a force from Georgia.

Panic in New York

In 1741, a panic (which some observers compared to the fear of witches in Salem in the 1690s) swept New York City. Rumors spread that slaves, with some white allies, planned to burn part of the city, seize weapons, and either turn New York over to Spain or murder the white population. More than 150 blacks and 20 whites were arrested, and 34 alleged conspirators, including 4 white persons, were executed. Historians still disagree as to how extensive the plot was or whether it existed at all. In eighteenth-century America, dreams of freedom knew no racial boundary.

AN EMPIRE OF FREEDOM

British Patriotism

Despite the centrality of slavery to its empire, eighteenth-century Great Britain prided itself on being the world's most advanced and freest nation.

British power

It was not only the era's greatest naval and commercial power but also the home of a complex governmental system, with a powerful Parliament representing the interests of a self-confident landed aristocracy and merchant class. For much of the eighteenth century, Britain found itself at war with France, which had replaced Spain as its major continental rival. This situation led to a large military, high taxes, and the creation of the Bank of England to help finance the conflicts. For both Britons and colonists, war helped to sharpen a sense of national identity against foreign foes.

British identity

British patriotic sentiment became more assertive as the eighteenth century progressed. Symbols of British identity proliferated: the songs "God Save the King" and "Rule Britannia," and even the modern rules of cricket, the national sport. Writers hailed commerce as a progressive, civilizing force, a way for different peoples to interact for mutual benefit without domination or military conflict. Especially in contrast to France, Britain saw itself as a realm of widespread prosperity, individual liberty, the rule of law, and the Protestant faith. Wealth, religion, and freedom went together.

The British Constitution

Central to this sense of British identity was the concept of liberty. Eighteenth-century Britons believed power and liberty to be natural antagonists. To mediate between them, advocates of British freedom celebrated the rule of law, the right to live under legislation to which one's representatives had consented, restraints on the arbitrary exercise of political authority, and rights such as trial by jury enshrined in the common law. In its "balanced constitution" and the principle that no man,

A 1770 engraving from the *Boston Gazette* by Paul Revere illustrates the association of British patriotism and liberty. Britannia sits with a liberty cap and her national shield, and releases a bird from a cage.

even the king, is above the law, Britons claimed to have devised the best means of preventing political tyranny. Until the 1770s, most colonists believed themselves to be part of the freest political system mankind had ever known.

These ideas sank deep roots not only within the "political nation"—those who voted, held office, and engaged in structured political debate—but also far more broadly in British and colonial society. Increasingly, the idea of liberty lost its traditional association with privileges derived from membership in a distinct social class and became more and more identified with a general right to resist arbitrary government. Ordinary persons thought nothing of taking to the streets to protest efforts by merchants to raise the cost of bread above the traditional "just price" or the Royal Navy's practice of "impressment"—kidnapping poor men on the streets for maritime service.

Power, liberty, and law

Republican Liberty

Liberty was central to two sets of political ideas that flourished in the Anglo-American world. One is termed by scholars **"republicanism,"** which celebrated active participation in public life by economically independent citizens as the essence of liberty. Republicans assumed that only property-owning citizens possessed **"virtue"**—defined in the eighteenth century not simply as a personal moral quality but as the willingness to subordinate self-interest to the pursuit of the public good.

Moral and economic ideas of liberty

In eighteenth-century Britain, this body of thought about freedom was most closely associated with a group of critics known as the "Country

Party" because much of their support arose from the landed gentry. They called for the election of men of "independence" who could not be controlled by the ministry, and they criticized the expanding national debt and the growing wealth of financial speculators. Britain, they claimed, was succumbing to luxury and political manipulation—in other words, a loss of virtue—thereby endangering the careful balance of its system of government and, indeed, liberty itself. In Britain, Country Party writings had little impact, but they were eagerly devoured in the American colonies, whose elites were attracted to the emphasis on the political role of the independent landowner and their warnings against the constant tendency of political power to infringe on liberty.

Liberal Freedom

The second set of eighteenth-century political ideas celebrating freedom came to be known as "**liberalism**" (although its meaning was quite different from what the word suggests today). Whereas republican liberty had a public and social quality, liberalism was essentially individual and private. The leading philosopher of liberalism was John Locke, whose *Two Treatises of Government*, written around 1680, had limited influence in his own lifetime but became extremely well known in the next century. Government, he wrote, was formed by a mutual agreement among equals (the parties being male heads of households, not all persons). In this "social contract," men surrendered a part of their right to govern themselves in order to enjoy the benefits of the rule of law. They retained, however, their natural rights, whose existence predated the establishment of political authority. Protecting the security of life, liberty, and property required shielding a realm of private life and personal concerns—including family relations, religious preferences, and economic activity—from interference by the state. During the eighteenth century, Lockean ideas—individual rights, the consent of the governed, the right of rebellion against unjust or oppressive government—would become familiar on both sides of the Atlantic.

Like other Britons, Locke spoke of liberty as a universal right yet seemed to exclude many persons from its full benefits. The free individual in liberal thought was essentially the propertied white man. Slaves, he wrote, "cannot be considered as any part of civil society." Nonetheless, by proclaiming that all individuals possess natural rights that no government may violate, Lockean liberalism opened the door to the poor, women, and even slaves to challenge limitations on their own freedom.

The title page of John Locke's *Two Treatises of Government*, which traced the origins of government to an original state of nature and insisted that political authorities must not abridge mankind's natural rights.

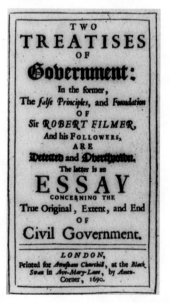

In the eighteenth century, republicanism and liberalism often rein-forced each other. Both political outlooks could inspire a commitment to constitutional government and restraints on despotic power. Both empha-sized the security of property as a foundation of freedom. Both traditions were transported to eighteenth-century America and would eventually help to divide the empire.

Relationship between republicanism and liberalism

THE PUBLIC SPHERE

Colonial politics for most of the eighteenth century was considerably less tempestuous than in the seventeenth, with its bitter struggles for power and frequent armed uprisings. Political stability in Britain coupled with the maturation of local elites in America made for more tranquil government.

The Right to Vote

In many respects, politics in eighteenth-century America had a more democratic quality than in Great Britain. Suffrage requirements varied from colony to colony, but as in Britain the linchpin of voting laws was the property qualification. Its purpose was to ensure that men who possessed an economic stake in society and the independence of judgment that went with it determined the policies of the government. Slaves, servants, ten-ants, adult sons living in the homes of their parents, the poor, and women all lacked a "will of their own" and were therefore ineligible to vote. The wide distribution of property in the colonies, however, meant that a far higher percentage of the population enjoyed voting rights than in the Old World. It is estimated that between 50 and 80 percent of adult white men could vote in eighteenth-century colonial America, as opposed to fewer than 5 percent in Britain at the time.

Property and the vote

Colonial politics, however, was hardly democratic in a modern sense. Voting was almost everywhere considered a male prerogative. In some colonies, Jews, Catholics, and Protestant Dissenters like Baptists and Quakers could not vote. Propertied free blacks, who enjoyed the franchise in Virginia, North Carolina, South Carolina, and Georgia in the early days of settlement, lost that right during the eighteenth century (although North Carolina restored it in the 1730s). In the northern colonies, although the law did not bar blacks from voting, local custom did. Native Americans were generally prohibited from voting.

Limits on voting

Political Cultures

Despite the broad electorate among white men, "the people" existed only on election day. Between elections, members of colonial assemblies remained out of touch with their constituents. Strongly competitive elections were the norm only in the Middle Colonies. Considerable power in colonial politics rested with those who held appointive, not elective, office. Governors and councils were appointed by the crown in the nine royal colonies and by the proprietors of Pennsylvania and Maryland. Moreover, laws passed by colonial assemblies could be vetoed by governors or in London. In New England, most town officers were elected, but local officials in other colonies were appointed by the governor or by powerful officials in London.

Property qualifications for officeholding were far higher than for voting. In South Carolina, for example, nearly every adult white male could meet the voting qualification of fifty acres of land or payment of twenty shillings in taxes, but to sit in the assembly one had to own 500 acres of land and ten slaves or town property worth £1,000. As a result, throughout the eighteenth century nearly all of South Carolina's legislators were planters or wealthy merchants.

In some colonies, an ingrained tradition of "deference"—the assumption among ordinary people that wealth, education, and social prominence carried a right to public office—sharply limited effective choice in elections. Virginia politics, for example, combined political democracy for white men with the tradition that voters should choose among candidates from the gentry. Aspirants for public office actively sought to ingratiate themselves with ordinary voters, distributing food and liquor freely at the courthouse where balloting took place. In Thomas Jefferson's first campaign for the House of Burgesses in 1768, his expenses included hiring two men "for

Appointive office

Qualifications for voting and office

Democracy and deference

This 1765 engraving depicting an election in Pennsylvania suggests the intensity of political debate in the Middle Colonies, as well as the social composition of the electorate. Those shown arguing outside the Old Court House in Philadelphia include physicians (with wigs and gold-topped canes), ministers, and lawyers. A line of men wait on the steps to vote.

bringing up rum" to the polling place. Even in New England, with its larger number of elective positions, town leaders were generally the largest property holders, and offices frequently passed down from generation to generation in the same family.

The Rise of the Assemblies

In the seventeenth century, the governor was the focal point of political authority, and colonial assemblies were weak bodies that met infrequently. But in the eighteenth, as economic development enhanced the power of American elites, the assemblies they dominated became more and more assertive. Their leaders insisted that assemblies possessed the same rights and powers in local affairs as the House of Commons enjoyed in Britain. The most successful governors were those who accommodated the rising power of the assemblies and used their appointive powers and control of land grants to win allies among assembly members.

Colonial governors

Many of the conflicts between governors and elected assemblies stemmed from the colonies' economic growth. To deal with the scarcity of gold and silver coins, the only legal form of currency, some colonies printed paper money, although this was strongly opposed by the governors, authorities in London, and British merchants who did not wish to be paid in what they considered worthless paper. Numerous battles also took place over land policy (sometimes involving divergent attitudes toward the remaining Indian population) and the level of rents charged to farmers on land owned by the crown or proprietors.

Conflicts between governors and assemblies

In their negotiations and conflicts with royal governors, leaders of the assemblies drew on the writings of the English Country Party, whose emphasis on the constant tension between liberty and political power and the dangers of executive influence over the legislature made sense of their own experience. Of the European settlements in North America, only the British colonies possessed any considerable degree of popular participation in government. This fact reinforced the assemblies' claim to embody the rights of Englishmen and the principle of popular consent to government.

Popular participation in British colonial government

Politics in Public

The language of liberty reverberated outside the relatively narrow world of elective and legislative politics. The "political nation" was dominated by the American gentry, whose members addressed each other in letters, speeches, newspaper articles, and pamphlets filled with Latin expressions and references to classical learning. But especially in colonial towns and cities, the eighteenth century witnessed a considerable expansion of the "public sphere"—the world of political organization and debate independent of the government, where an informed citizenry openly discussed questions that had previously been the preserve of officials.

In Boston, New York, and Philadelphia, clubs proliferated where literary, philosophical, scientific, and political issues were debated. Such groups were generally composed of men of property and commerce, but some drew ordinary citizens into discussions of public affairs. Colonial taverns and coffeehouses also became important sites not only for social conviviality but also for political debates. In Philadelphia, one clergyman commented, "the poorest laborer thinks himself entitled to deliver his sentiments in matters of religion or politics with as much freedom as the gentleman or scholar."

The Colonial Press

Neither the Spanish possessions of Florida and New Mexico nor New France possessed a printing press, although missionaries had established one in Mexico City in the 1530s. In British North America, however, the press expanded rapidly during the eighteenth century. So did the number of political broadsides and pamphlets published, especially at election time. By the eve of the American Revolution, some three-quarters of the free adult male population in the colonies (and more than one-third of the women) could read and write, and a majority of American families owned at least one book. Circulating libraries appeared in many colonial cities and towns, making possible a wider dissemination of knowledge at a time when books were still expensive. The first, the Library Company of Philadelphia, was established by Benjamin Franklin in 1731.

The first continuously published colonial newspaper, the *Boston News-Letter*, appeared in 1704. There were thirteen colonial newspapers by 1740 and twenty-five in 1765, mostly weeklies with small circulations—an average of 600 sales per issue. Probably the best-edited newspaper was the *Pennsylvania Gazette*, established in 1728 in Philadelphia and purchased the following year by Benjamin Franklin. At its peak, the *Gazette* attracted 2,000 subscribers. By the 1730s, political commentary was widespread in the American press.

Freedom of Expression and Its Limits

The public sphere thrived on the free exchange of ideas. But freedom of expression was not generally considered one of the ancient rights of

Englishmen. The phrase "freedom of speech" originated in Britain during the sixteenth century. A right of legislators, not ordinary citizens, it referred to the ability of members of Parliament to express their views without fear of reprisal, on the grounds that only in this way could they effectively represent the people. Outside of Parliament, free speech had no legal protection. A subject could be beheaded for accusing the king of failing to hold "true" religious beliefs, and language from swearing to criticism of the government exposed a person to criminal penalties.

As for **freedom of the press**, governments on both sides of the Atlantic viewed this as extremely dangerous. Until 1695, when a British law requiring the licensing of printed works before publication lapsed, no newspaper, book, or pamphlet could legally be printed without a government license. After 1695, the government could not censor newspapers, books, and pamphlets before they appeared in print, although it continued to try to manage the press by direct payments to publishers and individual journalists. Authors and publishers could still be prosecuted for "seditious libel"—a crime that included defaming government officials—or punished for contempt.

Elected assemblies, not governors, most frequently discouraged freedom of the press in colonial America. Dozens of publishers were hauled before assemblies and forced to apologize for comments regarding one or another member. Colonial newspapers vigorously defended freedom of the press as a central component of liberty, insisting that the citizenry had a right to monitor the workings of government and subject public officials to criticism. But since government printing contracts were crucial for economic success, few newspapers attacked colonial governments unless financially supported by an opposition faction.

Freedom of speech

The first page of the *New York Weekly Journal*, edited by John Peter Zenger, one of four issues ordered to be burned by local authorities.

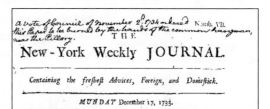

The Trial of Zenger

The most famous colonial court case involving freedom of the press demonstrated that popular sentiment opposed prosecutions for criticism of public officials. This was the 1735 trial of John Peter Zenger, a German-born printer who had emigrated to New York as a youth. Financed by wealthy opponents of Governor William Cosby, Zenger's newspaper, the *Weekly Journal*, lambasted the governor for corruption, influence peddling, and "tyranny." New York's council ordered four issues burned and had Zenger himself arrested and tried for seditious libel. Zenger's attorney, Andrew Hamilton, urged the jury to judge not the publisher but the governor. If they decided that Zenger's charges were correct, they must acquit him, and, Hamilton proclaimed, "every man who prefers freedom to a life of slavery will bless you."

Zenger was found not guilty. The case sent a warning to prosecutors that libel cases might be very difficult to win, especially in the superheated atmosphere of New York partisan politics. The outcome helped to promote the idea that the publication of truth should always be permitted, and it demonstrated that the idea of free expression was becoming ingrained in the popular imagination.

Freedom of expression

The American Enlightenment

During the eighteenth century, many educated Americans began to be influenced by the outlook of the European Enlightenment. This philosophical movement, which originated among French thinkers and soon spread to Britain, sought to apply the scientific method of careful investigation based on research and experiment to political and social life. Enlightenment ideas crisscrossed the Atlantic along with goods and people. Enlightenment thinkers insisted that every human institution, authority, and tradition be judged before the bar of reason. The self-educated Benjamin Franklin's wide range of activities—establishing a newspaper, debating club, and library; publishing the widely circulated *Poor Richard's Almanack*; and conducting experiments to demonstrate that lightning is a form of electricity—exemplified the Enlightenment spirit and made him probably the best-known American in the eighteenth-century world.

Enlightenment thinkers hoped that "reason," not religious enthusiasm, could govern human life. During the eighteenth century, many prominent Americans moved toward the position called Arminianism, which taught that reason alone was capable of establishing the essentials of religion. Others adopted Deism, a belief that God essentially withdrew after creating the world, leaving it to function according to scientific laws without divine intervention. Belief in miracles, in the revealed truth of the Bible, and in the innate sinfulness of mankind were viewed by Arminians, Deists, and others as outdated superstitions that should be abandoned in the modern age.

In the seventeenth century, the English scientist Isaac Newton had revealed the natural laws that governed the physical universe. Here, Deists believed, was the purest evidence of God's handiwork. Deists concluded that the best form of religious devotion was to study the workings

A 1762 portrait of Benjamin Franklin, done in London by the English artist Mason Chamberlain while Franklin was in the city as agent for the Pennsylvania Assembly. Franklin is depicted as a scientist making notes on his experiments, rather than a politician.

of nature, rather than to worship in organized churches or appeal to divine grace for salvation. By the late colonial era, a small but influential group of leading Americans, including Benjamin Franklin and Thomas Jefferson, could be classified as Deists.

Deists

THE GREAT AWAKENING

Like freedom of the press, religion was another realm where the actual experience of liberty outstripped its legal recognition. Religion remained central to eighteenth-century American life. Sermons, theological treatises, and copies of the Bible were by far the largest category of material produced by colonial printers.

Religious Revivals

Many ministers were concerned that westward expansion, commercial development, the growth of Enlightenment rationalism, and lack of individual engagement in church services were undermining religious devotion. These fears helped to inspire the revivals that swept through the colonies beginning in the 1730s. Known collectively as the **Great Awakening**, the revivals were less a coordinated movement than a series of local events united by a commitment to a "religion of the heart," a more emotional and personal Christianity than that offered by existing churches.

A more emotional and personal Christianity

The eighteenth century witnessed a revival of religious fundamentalism in many parts of the world, in part a response to the rationalism of the Enlightenment and a desire for greater religious purity. In the Middle East and Central Asia, where Islam was widespread, followers of a form of the religion known as Wahabbism called for a return to the practices of the religion's early days. Methodism and other forms of enthusiastic religion were flourishing in Europe. Like other intellectual currents of the time, the Great Awakening was a transatlantic movement.

During the 1720s and 1730s, the New Jersey Dutch Reformed clergyman Theodore Frelinghuysen, his Presbyterian neighbors William and Gilbert Tennent, and the Massachusetts Congregationalist minister Jonathan Edwards pioneered an intensely emotional style of preaching. Edwards's famous sermon *Sinners in the Hands of an Angry God* portrayed sinful man as a "loathsome insect" suspended over a bottomless pit of eternal fire by a

Jonathan Edwards

George Whitefield, the English evangelist who helped to spark the Great Awakening in the colonies. Painted around 1742 by John Wollaston, who had emigrated from England to the colonies, the work depicts Whitefield's powerful effect on male and female listeners. It also illustrates Whitefield's eye problem, which led critics to dub him "Dr. Squintum."

slender thread that might break at any moment. Only a "new birth"—immediately acknowledging one's sins and pleading for divine grace—could save men from eternal damnation.

The Preaching of Whitefield

More than any other individual, the English minister George Whitefield, who declared "the whole world his parish," sparked the Great Awakening. For two years after his arrival in America in 1739, Whitefield brought his highly emotional brand of preaching to colonies from Georgia to New England. God, Whitefield proclaimed, was merciful. Rather than being predestined for damnation, men and women could save themselves by repenting of their sins. Whitefield appealed to the passions of his listeners, powerfully sketching the boundless joy of salvation and the horrors of damnation.

Tens of thousands of colonists flocked to Whitefield's sermons, which were widely reported in the American press, making him a celebrity and helping to establish the revivals as the first major intercolonial event in North American history. In Whitefield's footsteps, a host of traveling preachers or "evangelists" (meaning, literally, bearers of good news) held revivalist meetings, often to the alarm of established ministers.

The Awakening's Impact

By the time they subsided in the 1760s, the revivals had changed the religious configuration of the colonies and enlarged the boundaries of liberty. Whitefield had inspired the emergence of numerous Dissenting churches. Congregations split into factions headed by Old Lights (traditionalists) and New Lights (revivalists), and new churches proliferated—Baptist, Methodist, Presbyterian, and others. Many of these new churches began to criticize the colonial practice of levying taxes to support an established church; they defended religious freedom as one of the natural rights government must not restrict.

Although the revivals were primarily a spiritual matter, the Great Awakening threw into question many forms of authority, and inspired criticism of aspects of colonial society. Revivalist preachers frequently criticized commercial society, insisting that believers should make salvation, not profit, "the one business of their lives." Preaching to the small farmers of the southern backcountry, Baptist and Methodist revivalists criticized the worldliness of wealthy planters and attacked as sinful activities such

Critique of commercial society

as gambling, horse racing, and lavish entertainments on the Sabbath. A few preachers explicitly condemned slavery. Especially in the Chesapeake, the revivals brought numerous slaves into the Christian fold, an important step in their acculturation as African-Americans.

The revivals encouraged many colonists to trust their own views rather than those of established elites. In listening to the sermons of self-educated preachers, forming Bible study groups, and engaging in intense religious discussions, ordinary colonists asserted the right to independent judgment. Although the revivalists' aim was spiritual salvation, the independent frame of mind they encouraged would have significant political consequences.

Independent judgement

IMPERIAL RIVALRIES

Spanish North America

The rapid growth of Britain's North American colonies took place at a time of increased jockeying for power among European empires. But the colonies of England's rivals, although covering immense territories, remained thinly populated and far weaker economically. The Spanish empire encompassed an area that stretched from the Pacific coast and New Mexico into the Great Plains and eastward through Texas and Florida. After 1763, it also included Louisiana, which Spain obtained from France. On paper a vast territorial empire, Spanish North America actually consisted of a few small and isolated urban clusters, most prominently St. Augustine in Florida, San Antonio in Texas, and Santa Fe and Albuquerque in New Mexico.

Extent of Spanish empire

New Mexico's population in 1765 was only 20,000, equally divided between Spanish settlers and Pueblo Indians. Spain began the colonization of Texas at the beginning of the eighteenth century, partly as a buffer to prevent French commercial influence, then spreading in the Mississippi Valley, from intruding into New Mexico. The Spanish established complexes consisting of religious missions and *presidios* (military outposts) at Los Adaes, La Bahía, and San Antonio. But the region attracted few settlers. Texas had only 1,200 Spanish colonists in 1760. Florida stagnated as well.

Colonization of Texas

The Spanish in California

On the Pacific coast, Russian fur traders in the eighteenth century established a series of forts and trading posts in Alaska. Spain, alarmed by

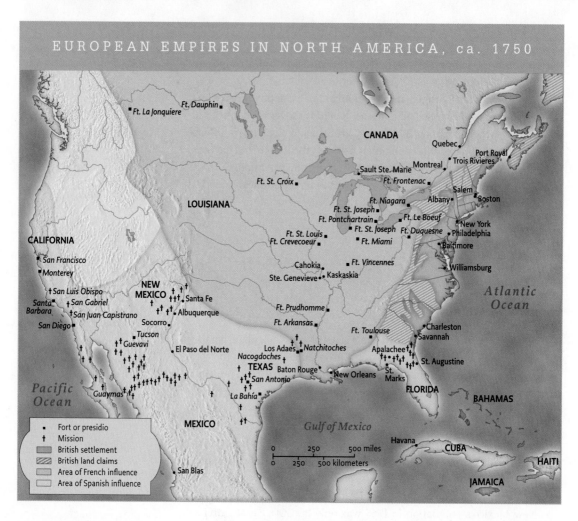

Three great empires—the British, French, and Spanish—competed for influence in North America for much of the eighteenth century.

what it saw as a danger to its American empire, ordered the colonization of California. A string of Spanish missions and *presidios* soon dotted the California coastline, from San Diego to Los Angeles, Santa Barbara, Monterey, San Francisco, and Sonoma. Born on the Spanish Mediterranean island of Mallorca, **Father Junípero Serra** became one of the most controversial figures in California's early history. He founded the first California mission, in San Diego, in 1769 and administered the mission network until his death in 1784. Serra was widely praised in Spain for converting thousands of Indians to Christianity. But forced labor and disease took a heavy toll among Indians who lived at the missions Serra directed.

Present-day California was a densely populated area, with a native population of perhaps 250,000 when Spanish settlement began. But as in other regions, the coming of soldiers and missionaries proved a disaster for the Indians. More than any other Spanish colony, California was a mission frontier. These outposts served simultaneously as religious institutions and centers of government and labor. Father Serra and other missionaries hoped to convert the natives to Christianity and settled farming. The missions also relied on forced Indian labor to grow grain, work in orchards and vineyards, and tend cattle. By 1821, when Mexico won its independence from Spain, California's native population had declined by more than one-third. But the area had not attracted Spanish settlers. When Spanish rule came to an end in 1821, *Californios* (California residents of Spanish descent) numbered only 3,200.

Spanish missions

The French Empire

A greater rival to British power in North America—as well as in Europe and the Caribbean—was France. During the eighteenth century, the population and economy of Canada expanded. At the same time, French traders pushed into the Mississippi River valley southward from the Great Lakes and northward from Mobile, founded in 1702, and New Orleans, established in 1718. In the St. Lawrence River valley of French Canada, prosperous farming communities developed. By 1750, the area had a population of about 55,000 colonists. Another 10,000 (about half Europeans, half African-American slaves) resided in Louisiana.

French expansion

Despite these gains, the population of French North America continued to be dwarfed by the British colonies. Prejudice against emigration to North America remained widespread in France because many there viewed the French colony as a place of cruel exile for criminals and social outcasts. Nonetheless, by claiming control of a large arc of territory and by establishing close trading and military relations with many Indian tribes, the French empire posed a real challenge to the British. French

French ties to Indian tribes

A sketch of New Orleans as it appeared in 1720.

forts and trading posts ringed the British colonies. The French were a presence on the New England and New York frontiers and in western Pennsylvania.

BATTLE FOR THE CONTINENT

The Middle Ground

The Ohio Valley

For much of the eighteenth century, the western frontier of British North America was the flashpoint of imperial rivalries. The Ohio Valley became caught up in a complex struggle for power involving the French, British, rival Indian communities, and settlers and land companies pursuing their own interests. On this "**middle ground**" between European empires and Indian sovereignty, villages sprang up where members of numerous tribes lived side by side, along with European traders and the occasional missionary.

By the mid-eighteenth century, Indians had learned that direct military confrontation with Europeans meant suicide, and that an alliance with a single European power exposed them to danger from others. The Indians of the Ohio Valley sought (with some success) to play the British and French empires off one another and to control the lucrative commerce with whites. The Iroquois were masters of balance-of-power diplomacy.

In 1750, few white settlers inhabited the Ohio Valley. But already, Scotch-Irish and German immigrants, Virginia planters, and land speculators were eyeing the region's fertile soil. In 1749, the government of

The Ohio Company

Virginia awarded an immense land grant—half a million acres—to the Ohio Company. The company's members included the colony's royal governor, Robert Dinwiddie, and the cream of Virginia society—Lees, Carters, and the young George Washington. The land grant sparked the French to bolster their presence in the region. It was the Ohio Company's demand for French recognition of its land claims that inaugurated the Seven Years' War (known in the colonies as the French and Indian War), the first of the century's imperial wars to begin in the colonies and the first to result in a decisive victory for one combatant. It permanently altered the global balance of power.

The Seven Years' War

The world's leading empire

Only in the eighteenth century, after numerous wars against its great rivals France and Spain, did Britain emerge as the world's leading empire and its center of trade and banking. By the 1750s, British possessions and trade reached around the globe. The existence of global empires implied that warfare among them would also be global.

What became a worldwide struggle for imperial domination, which eventually spread to Europe, West Africa, and Asia, began in 1754 with British efforts to dislodge the French from forts they had constructed in western Pennsylvania. In the previous year, George Washington, then only twenty-one years old, had been dispatched by the colony's governor on an unsuccessful mission to persuade French soldiers to abandon a fort they were building on lands claimed by the Ohio Company. In 1754, Washington returned to the area with two companies of soldiers. After an ill-considered attempt against a larger French and Indian force, resulting in the loss of one-third of his men, Washington was forced to surrender. Soon afterward, an expedition led by General Edward Braddock against Fort Duquesne (today's Pittsburgh) was ambushed by French and Indian forces, leaving Braddock and two-thirds of his 3,000 soldiers dead or wounded.

Benjamin Franklin produced this famous cartoon in 1754, calling on Britain's North American colonies to unite against the French.

For two years, the war went against the British. The southern back-country was ablaze with fighting among British forces, colonists, and Indians. Inhumanity flourished on all sides. Indians killed hundreds of colonists in western Pennsylvania and pushed the line of settlement all the way back to Carlisle, only 100 miles west of Philadelphia. In Nova Scotia, the British rounded up around 5,000 local French residents, called **Acadians**, confiscated their land, and expelled them from the region, selling their farms to settlers from New England. Some of those expelled eventually returned to France; others ended up as far away as Louisiana, where their descendants came to be known as Cajuns.

As the British government under Secretary of State William Pitt, who took office in 1757, raised huge sums of money and poured men and naval forces into the war, the tide of battle turned. By 1759, Britain—with colonial and Indian soldiers playing a major role—had captured the pivotal French outposts Forts Duquesne, Ticonderoga (north of Albany), and Louisbourg on Cape Breton Island, which guarded the mouth of the St. Lawrence River. In September of that year, a French army was defeated on the Plains of Abraham near Quebec. British forces also seized nearly all the islands in the French Caribbean and established control of India.

William Pitt

A World Transformed

Britain's victory fundamentally reshaped the world balance of power. In the Peace of Paris in 1763, France ceded Canada to Britain, receiving back in return the sugar islands of Guadeloupe and Martinique (far more lucrative colonies from the point of view of French authorities). Spain ceded

The global balance of power

Florida to Britain in exchange for the return of the Philippines and Cuba (seized by the British during the war). Spain also acquired from France the vast Louisiana colony. France's 200-year-old North American empire had come to an end. The entire continent east of the Mississippi River was now in British hands.

The costs of war

Eighteenth-century warfare, conducted on land and sea across the globe, was enormously expensive. The Seven Years' War put strains on all the participants. The war's cost produced a financial crisis in France that almost three decades later would help to spark the French Revolution. The British would try to recoup part of the cost of war by increasing taxes on their American colonies.

Pontiac's Rebellion

Throughout eastern North America, the abrupt departure of the French in the aftermath of the Seven Years' War eliminated the balance-of-power diplomacy that had enabled groups like the Iroquois to maintain a significant degree of autonomy. Domination by any outside power, Indians feared, meant the loss of freedom. Without consulting them, the French had ceded land Indians claimed as their own to British control. The Treaty

Effect on Indians

of Paris left Indians more dependent than ever on the British and ushered in a period of confusion over land claims, control of the fur trade, and tribal relations in general.

In 1763, in the wake of the French defeat, Indians of the Ohio Valley and Great Lakes launched a revolt against British rule. Although known as **Pontiac's Rebellion** after an Ottawa war leader, the rebellion owed at least as much to the teachings of Neolin, a Delaware religious prophet.

Neolin's message

During a religious vision, the Master of Life instructed Neolin that his people must reject European technology, free themselves from commercial ties with whites and dependence on alcohol, clothe themselves in the garb of their ancestors, and drive the British from their territory (although friendly French inhabitants could remain). Neolin combined this message with the relatively new idea of pan-Indian identity. All Indians, he preached, were a single people, and only through cooperation could they regain their lost independence.

The Proclamation Line

In the spring and summer of 1763, Ottawas, Hurons, and other Indians besieged Detroit, then a major British military outpost, seized nine other forts, and killed hundreds of white settlers who had intruded onto Indian

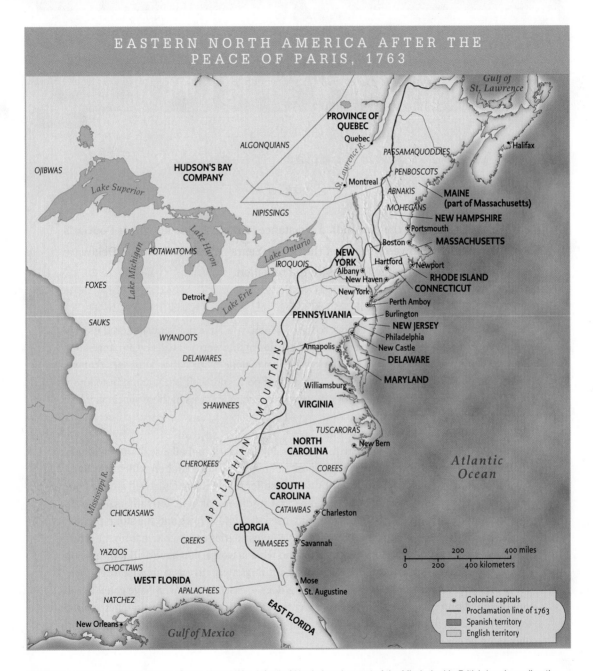

EASTERN NORTH AMERICA AFTER THE PEACE OF PARIS, 1763

OJIBWAS

HUDSON'S BAY COMPANY

Lake Superior

ALGONQUIANS

PROVINCE OF QUEBEC

Quebec

PASSAMAQUODDIES

Halifax

Gulf of St. Lawrence

Montreal

PENBOSCOTS

ABNAKIS

MAINE (part of Massachusetts)

MOHEGANS

NEW HAMPSHIRE

Portsmouth

NIPISSINGS

St. Lawrence R.

Boston

MASSACHUSETTS

POTAWATOMIS

Lake Michigan

Lake Huron

Lake Ontario

IROQUOIS

NEW YORK

Albany

Hartford

New Haven

Newport

RHODE ISLAND

CONNECTICUT

FOXES

Detroit

Lake Erie

New York

Perth Amboy

Burlington

NEW JERSEY

Philadelphia

New Castle

SAUKS

WYANDOTS

DELAWARES

PENNSYLVANIA

Annapolis

DELAWARE

MARYLAND

Williamsburg

SHAWNEES

VIRGINIA

TUSCARORAS

NORTH CAROLINA

New Bern

CHEROKEES

COREES

Atlantic Ocean

APPALACHIAN MOUNTAINS

SOUTH CAROLINA

CATAWBAS

Charleston

CHICKASAWS

GEORGIA

CREEKS

YAMASEES

Savannah

Mississippi R.

YAZOOS

CHOCTAWS

WEST FLORIDA

APALACHEES

NATCHEZ

Mose

St. Augustine

EAST FLORIDA

New Orleans

Gulf of Mexico

| 0 | 200 | 400 miles |
| 0 | 200 | 400 kilometers |

Colonial capitals
Proclamation line of 1763
Spanish territory
English territory

The Peace of Paris, which ended the Seven Years' War, left all of North America east of the Mississippi in British hands, ending the French presence on the continent.

VOICES OF FREEDOM

From Pontiac, Speeches
(1762 and 1763)

Pontiac was a leader of the pan-Indian resistance to English rule known as Pontiac's Rebellion, which followed the end of the Seven Years' War. Neolin was a Delaware religious prophet who helped to inspire the rebellion.

Englishmen, although you have conquered the French, you have not yet conquered us! We are not your slaves. These lakes, these woods, and mountains were left to us by our ancestors. They are our inheritance; and we will part with them to none. Your nation supposes that we, like the white people, cannot live without bread and pork and beef! But you ought to know that He, the Great Spirit and Master of Life, has provided food for us in these spacious lakes, and on these woody mountains.

[The Master of Life has said to Neolin:]

I am the Maker of heaven and earth, the trees, lakes, rivers, and all else. I am the Maker of all mankind; and because I love you, you must do my will. The land on which you live I have made for you and not for others. Why do you suffer the white man to dwell among you? My children, you have forgotten the customs and traditions of your forefathers. Why do you not clothe yourselves in skins, as they did, use bows and arrows and the stone-pointed lances, which they used? You have bought guns, knives, kettles and blankets from the white man until you can no longer do without them; and what is worse, you have drunk the poison firewater, which turns you into fools. Fling all these things away; live as your wise forefathers did before you. And as for these English—these dogs dressed in red, who have come to rob you of your hunting-grounds, and drive away the game—you must lift the hatchet against them. Wipe them from the face of the earth, and then you will win my favor back again, and once more be happy and prosperous.

From The Interesting Narrative of the Life of Olaudah Equiano, or Gustavus Vassa, the African (1789)

Olaudah Equiano's autobiography, published in London, was the most prominent account of the slave experience written in the eighteenth century. In this passage, which comes after Equiano's description of a slave auction in the Caribbean, he calls on white persons to live up to their professed belief in liberty.

We were not many days in the merchant's custody before we were sold after their usual manner, which is this: On a signal given (as the beat of a drum), the buyers rush in at once into the yard where the slaves are confined, and make choice of that parcel they like best. . . . In this manner, without scruple, are relations and friends separated, most of them never to see each other again. I remember in the vessel in which I was brought over, . . . there were several brothers, who, in the sale, were sold in different lots; and it was very moving on this occasion to see and hear their cries at parting.

O, ye nominal Christians! Might not an African ask you, learned you this from your God? Who says unto you, Do unto all men as you would men should do unto you? Is it not enough that we are torn from our country and friends to toil for your luxury and lust of gain? Must every tender feeling be sacrificed to your avarice? Are the dearest friends and relations, now rendered more dear by their separation from their kindred, still to be parted from each other, and thus prevented from cheering the gloom of slavery with the small comfort of being together and mingling their sufferings and sorrows? Why are parents to lose their children, brothers their sisters, or husbands their wives? Surely this is a new refinement in cruelty.

QUESTIONS

1. *What elements of Indian life does Neolin criticize most strongly?*

2. *What aspect of slavery does Equiano emphasize in his account, and why do you think he does so?*

3. *How do Pontiac and Equiano differ in the ways they address white audiences?*

Proclamation of 1763

lands. British forces soon launched a counterattack, and over the next few years the tribes one by one made peace. But the uprising inspired the government in London to issue the Proclamation of 1763, prohibiting further colonial settlement west of the Appalachian Mountains. These lands were reserved exclusively for Indians. Moreover, the Proclamation banned the sale of Indian lands to private individuals.

The British aim was less to protect the Indians than to stabilize the situation on the colonial frontier and to avoid being dragged into an endless series of border conflicts. But the Proclamation enraged both settlers and speculators hoping to take advantage of the expulsion of the French to consolidate their claims to western lands. They ignored the new policy. George Washington himself ordered his agents to buy up as much Indian land as possible, while keeping the transactions "a profound secret" because of their illegality. Failing to offer a viable solution to the question of westward expansion, the Proclamation of 1763 ended up further exacerbating settler-Indian relations.

Pennsylvania and the Indians

Frontier tensions

The Seven Years' War not only redrew the map of the world but produced dramatic changes within the American colonies as well. In Pennsylvania, the conflict shattered the decades-old rule of the Quaker elite and dealt the final blow to the colony's policy of accommodation with the Indians. During the war, with the frontier ablaze with battles between settlers and French and Indian warriors, western Pennsylvanians demanded that colonial authorities adopt a more aggressive stance. When the governor declared war on hostile Delawares, raised a militia, and offered a bounty for Indian scalps, many of the assembly's pacifist Quakers resigned their seats, effectively ending their control of Pennsylvania politics.

The Paxton Boys

In December 1763, while Pontiac's Rebellion still raged, a party of fifty armed men, mostly Scotch-Irish farmers from the vicinity of the Pennsylvania town of Paxton, destroyed the Indian village of Conestoga, massacring half a dozen men, women, and children who lived there under the protection of Pennsylvania's governor. When the Paxton Boys marched on Philadelphia in February 1764, intending to attack Moravian Indians who resided near the city, the governor ordered the expulsion of much of the Indian population. By the 1760s, Pennsylvania's Holy Experiment was at an end and with it William Penn's promise of "true friendship and amity" between colonists and the native population.

Colonial Identities

Before the war, the colonies had been largely isolated from one another. Outside of New England, more Americans probably traveled to England than from one colony to another. The **Albany Plan of Union** of 1754, drafted by Benjamin Franklin at the outbreak of the Seven Years' War, envisioned the creation of a Grand Council composed of delegates from each colony, with the power to levy taxes and deal with Indian relations and the common defense. Rejected by the colonial assemblies, whose powers Franklin's proposal would curtail, the plan was never sent to London for approval.

Participation in the Seven Years' War created greater bonds among the colonies. But the war also strengthened colonists' pride in being members of the British empire. It has been said that Americans were never more British than in 1763. British victory in the Seven Years' War seemed a triumph of liberty over tyranny. The defeat of the Catholic French reinforced the equation of British nationality, Protestantism, and freedom.

The war and American identity

But soon, the American colonists would come to believe that membership in the empire jeopardized their liberty. When they did, they set out on a road that led to independence.

CHAPTER REVIEW AND ONLINE RESOURCES

REVIEW QUESTIONS

1. How did Great Britain's position in North America change relative to the other European powers during the first three-quarters of the eighteenth century?

2. How did the ideas of republicanism and liberalism differ in eighteenth-century British North America?

3. Three distinct slave systems were well entrenched in Britain's mainland colonies. Describe the main characteristics of each system.

4. How and why did the colonists' sense of a collective British identity change during the years before 1764?

5. What ideas generated by the American Enlightenment and the Great Awakening prompted challenges to religious, social, and political authorities in the British colonies?

6. How were colonial merchants in British America involved in the Atlantic economy, and what was the role of the slave trade in that economy?

7. We often consider the impact of the slave trade only on the United States, but its impact extended much further. How did it affect West African nations and society, other regions of the New World, and the nations of Europe?

8. How was an African-American collective identity created in these years and what role did slave rebellions play in that process?

KEY TERMS

Atlantic slave trade (p. 106)
Middle Passage (p. 109)
Stono Rebellion (p. 116)
republicanism (p. 117)
virtue (p. 117)
liberalism (p. 118)
freedom of the press (p. 123)
American Enlightenment (p. 124)
Great Awakening (p. 125)
Father Junípero Serra (p. 128)
"middle ground" (p. 130)
Acadians (p. 131)
Pontiac's Rebellion (p. 132)
Albany Plan of Union (p. 137)

wwnorton.com
/studyspace

VISIT STUDYSPACE FOR THESE
RESOURCES AND MORE

- A chapter outline
- A diagnostic chapter quiz
- Interactive maps
- Map worksheets
- Multimedia documents

CHAPTER 5

THE AMERICAN REVOLUTION

★

1763-1783

A rare print from 1776 depicts George Washington as commander of the American armies, "the supporter of liberty," and "benefactor of mankind." It illustrates the linkage of liberty and American independence, and Americans' conviction that their struggle was of worldwide significance.

On the night of August 26, 1765, a violent crowd of Bostonians assaulted the elegant home of Thomas Hutchinson, chief justice and lieutenant governor of Massachusetts. Hutchinson and his family barely had time to escape before the crowd broke down the front door and proceeded to destroy or carry off most of their possessions, including paintings, furniture, silverware, and notes for a history of Massachusetts Hutchinson was writing. By the time the crowd departed, only the outer walls of the home remained standing.

The immediate cause of the riot was the Stamp Act, a recently enacted British tax that many colonists felt violated their liberty. Only a few days earlier, Hutchinson had helped to disperse a crowd attacking a building owned by his relative Andrew Oliver, a merchant who had been appointed to help administer the new law. Both crowds were led by Ebenezer Mackintosh, a shoemaker who enjoyed a wide following among Boston's working people.

The riot of August 26 was one small episode in a series of events that launched a half-century of popular protest and political upheaval throughout the Western world. The momentous era that came to be called the Age of Revolution began in British North America, spread to Europe and the Caribbean, and culminated in the Latin American wars for independence. In all these struggles, liberty emerged as the foremost rallying cry for popular discontent. Rarely has the idea played so central a role in political debate and social upheaval.

If the attack on Hutchinson's home demonstrated the depths of feeling aroused by Britain's efforts to impose greater control over its empire, it also revealed that revolution is a dynamic process whose consequences no one can anticipate. The crowd's fury expressed resentments against the rich and powerful quite different from colonial leaders' objections to Parliament's attempt to tax the colonies. The Stamp Act crisis inaugurated not only a struggle for colonial liberty in relation to Great Britain but also a multisided battle to define and extend liberty within America.

THE CRISIS BEGINS

Consolidating the Empire

When George III assumed the throne of Great Britain in 1760, no one on either side of the Atlantic imagined that within two decades Britain's American colonies would separate from the empire. Having treated the colonists as allies during the war, Britain reverted in the mid-1760s to seeing them as subordinates whose main role was to enrich the mother country. During this period, the government in London concerned itself with the colonies in unprecedented ways, hoping to make British rule more efficient and systematic and to raise funds to help pay for the war and to finance the empire. Nearly all British political leaders supported the new laws that so enraged the colonists. Americans, Britons felt, should be grateful to the empire. To fight the Seven Years' War, Britain had borrowed from banks and individual investors more than £150 million (the equivalent of tens of trillions of dollars in today's money). It seemed only reasonable that the colonies should help pay this national debt, foot part of the bill for continued British protection, and stop cheating the treasury by violating the Navigation Acts.

According to the doctrine of "virtual representation," the House of Commons represented all residents of the British empire, whether or not they could vote for members. In this 1775 cartoon criticizing the idea, a blinded Britannia, on the far right, stumbles into a pit. Next to her, two colonists complain of being robbed by British taxation. In the background, according to an accompanying explanation of the cartoon, stand the "Catholic" city of Quebec and the "Protestant town of Boston," the latter in flames.

Nearly all Britons, moreover, believed that Parliament represented the entire empire and had a right to legislate for it. Millions of Britons, including the residents of major cities like Manchester and Birmingham, had no representatives in Parliament. But according to the widely accepted theory of **"virtual representation"**—which held that each member represented the entire empire, not just his own district—the interests of all who lived under the British crown were supposedly taken into account. When Americans began to insist that because they were unrepresented in Parliament, the British government could not tax the colonies, they won little support in the mother country.

The British government had already alarmed many colonists by issuing **writs of assistance** to combat smuggling. These were general search warrants that allowed customs officials to search anywhere they chose for smuggled goods. In a celebrated court case in Boston in 1761, the lawyer James Otis insisted that the writs were "an instrument of arbitrary power, destructive to English liberty, and the fundamental principles of the Constitution," and that Parliament therefore had no right to authorize them. ("American independence was then and there born," the Boston lawyer John Adams later remarked—a considerable exaggeration.) Many colonists were also outraged by the Proclamation of 1763 (mentioned in the previous chapter), which barred further settlement on lands west of the Appalachian Mountains.

Outrage in the colonies

Taxing the Colonies

The Sugar Act of 1764

In 1764, the **Sugar Act**, introduced by Prime Minister George Grenville, reduced the existing tax on molasses imported into North America from the French West Indies from six pence to three pence per gallon. But the act also established a new machinery to end widespread smuggling by colonial merchants. And to counteract the tendency of colonial juries to acquit merchants charged with violating trade regulations, it strengthened the admiralty courts, where accused smugglers could be judged without benefit of a jury trial. Thus, colonists saw the measure not as a welcome reduction in taxation but as an attempt to get them to pay a levy they would otherwise have evaded. At the same time, the Currency Act reaffirmed the earlier ban on colonial assemblies' issuing paper as "legal tender"—that is, money that individuals are required to accept in payment of debts.

The Stamp Act of 1765

The Sugar Act was an effort to strengthen the long-established (and long-evaded) Navigation Acts. The Stamp Act of 1765 was a new departure in imperial policy. For the first time, Parliament attempted to raise money from direct taxes in the colonies rather than through the regulation of trade. The act required that all sorts of printed material produced in the colonies—such as newspapers, books, court documents, commercial papers, land deeds, almanacs—carry a stamp purchased from authorities. Its purpose was to help finance the operations of the empire, including the cost of stationing British troops in North America, without seeking revenue from colonial assemblies.

Whereas the Sugar Act had mainly affected residents of colonial ports, the Stamp Act managed to offend virtually every free colonist—rich and poor, farmers, artisans, and merchants. It was especially resented by members of the public sphere who wrote, published, and read books and newspapers and followed political affairs. The prospect of a British army permanently stationed on American soil also alarmed many colonists. And by imposing the stamp tax without colonial consent, Parliament directly challenged the authority of local elites who, through the assemblies they controlled, had established their power over the raising and spending of money. They were ready to defend this authority in the name of liberty.

Opposition to the Stamp Act

Opposition to the Stamp Act was the first great drama of the revolutionary era and the first major split between colonists and Great Britain over the meaning of freedom. Nearly all colonial political leaders opposed the act. In voicing their grievances, they invoked the rights of the freeborn Englishman, which, they insisted, colonists should also enjoy. Opponents of the act occasionally referred to the natural rights of all mankind. More frequently, however, they drew on time-honored British principles such as a community's right not to be taxed except by its elected representatives. Liberty, they insisted, could not be secure where property was "taken away without consent."

Taxation and Representation

At stake were clashing ideas of the British empire itself. American leaders viewed the empire as an association of equals in which free settlers overseas enjoyed the same rights as Britons at home. Colonists in other outposts of the empire, such as India, the West Indies, and Canada, echoed this outlook. All, in the name of liberty, claimed the right to govern their own affairs. The British government and its appointed representatives in America, by contrast, saw the empire as a system of unequal parts in which different principles governed different areas, and all were subject to the authority of Parliament. To surrender the right to tax the colonies would set a dangerous precedent for the empire as a whole.

Views of the British empire

Some opponents of the Stamp Act distinguished between "internal" taxes like the stamp duty, which they claimed Parliament had no right to impose, and revenue legitimately raised through the regulation of trade. But more and more colonists insisted that Britain had no right to tax them at all, since Americans were unrepresented in the House of Commons. "No taxation without representation" became their rallying cry. Virginia's House of Burgesses approved four resolutions offered by the fiery orator Patrick Henry. They insisted that the colonists enjoyed the same "liberties, privileges, franchises, and immunities" as residents of the mother country and that the right to consent to taxation was a cornerstone of "British freedom." (The House of Burgesses rejected as too radical three other resolutions, including Henry's call for outright resistance to unlawful taxation, but these were also reprinted in colonial newspapers.)

"No taxation without representation"

In October 1765, the Stamp Act Congress, with twenty-seven delegates from nine colonies, including some of the most prominent men in America, met in New York and endorsed Virginia's position. Its resolutions began by affirming the "allegiance" of all colonists to the "Crown of Great Britain" and their "due subordination" to Parliament. But they went on to insist that the right to consent to taxation was "essential to the freedom of a people." Soon, merchants throughout the colonies agreed to boycott British goods until Parliament repealed the Stamp Act. This was the first major cooperative action among Britain's mainland colonies. In a sense, by seeking to impose uniformity on the colonies rather than dealing with them individually as in the past, Parliament had inadvertently united America.

This teapot protesting the Stamp Act was produced in England and marketed in colonial America, illustrating the close political and economic connections between the two.

Liberty and Resistance

No word was more frequently invoked by critics of the Stamp Act than "liberty." Throughout the colonies, opponents of the new tax staged mock funerals in which liberty's coffin was carried to a burial ground, only to have the occupant miraculously revived at the last moment, whereupon the assembled crowd repaired to a tavern to celebrate. As the crisis continued, symbols of liberty proliferated. The large elm tree in Boston on which protesters had hanged an effigy of the stamp distributor Andrew Oliver to persuade him to resign his post came to be known as the Liberty Tree. Its image soon appeared in prints and pamphlets throughout the colonies.

The Liberty Tree

Colonial leaders resolved to prevent the new law's implementation, and by and large they succeeded. Even before the passage of the Stamp Act, a **Committee of Correspondence** in Boston communicated with other colonies to encourage opposition to the Sugar and Currency Acts. Now, such committees sprang up in other colonies, exchanging ideas and information about resistance. Initiated by colonial elites, the movement against the Stamp Act quickly drew in a far broader range of Americans. The act, wrote John Adams, who drafted a set of widely reprinted resolutions against the measure, had inspired "the people, even to the lowest ranks," to become "more attentive to their liberties, more inquisitive about them, and more determined to defend them, than they were ever before known."

Organized resistance

Opponents of the Stamp Act, however, did not rely solely on debate. Even before the law went into effect, crowds forced those chosen to administer it to resign and destroyed shipments of stamps. In 1765, New York City residents were organized by the newly created **Sons of Liberty**, who led them in protest processions, posted notices reading "Liberty, Property, and No Stamps," and took the lead in enforcing the boycott of British imports.

A warning by the Sons of Liberty against using the stamps required by the Stamp Act, which are shown on the left.

Stunned by the ferocity of American resistance and pressured by London merchants and manufacturers who did not wish to lose their American markets, the British government retreated. In 1766, Parliament repealed the Stamp Act. But this concession was accompanied by the Declaratory Act, which rejected Americans' claims that only their elected representatives could levy taxes. Parliament, proclaimed this measure, possessed the power to pass laws for "the colonies and people of America . . . in all cases whatsoever." Since the debt-ridden British government continued to need money raised in the colonies, passage of the Declaratory Act promised further conflict.

The Regulators

The Stamp Act crisis was not the only example of violent social turmoil during the 1760s. Many colonies experienced contentious internal divisions as well. As population moved westward, the conflicting land claims of settlers, speculators, colonial governments, and Indians sparked fierce disputes. As in the Stamp Act crisis, "liberty" was the rallying cry, but in this case liberty had less to do with imperial policy than secure possession of land.

Beginning in the mid-1760s, a group of wealthy residents of the South Carolina backcountry calling themselves **Regulators** protested the underrepresentation of western settlements in the colony's assembly and the legislators' failure to establish local governments that could regularize land titles and suppress bands of outlaws.

A parallel movement in North Carolina mobilized small farmers, who refused to pay taxes, kidnapped local officials, assaulted the homes of land speculators, merchants, and lawyers, and disrupted court proceedings. Here, the complaint was not a lack of government, but corrupt county authorities. Demanding the democratization of local government, the Regulators condemned the "rich and powerful" (the colony's elite) who used their political authority to prosper at the expense of "poor industrious" farmers. At their peak, the Regulators numbered around 8,000 armed farmers. The region remained in turmoil until 1771, when, in the "battle of Alamance," the farmers were suppressed by the colony's militia.

Backcountry tensions

The emerging rift between Britain and America eventually superimposed itself on conflicts within the colonies. But the social divisions revealed in the Stamp Act riots and backcountry uprisings made some members of the colonial elite fear that opposition to British measures might unleash turmoil at home. As a result, they were more reluctant to challenge British authority when the next imperial crisis arose.

Social divisions and politics

THE ROAD TO REVOLUTION

The Townshend Crisis

In 1767, the government in London decided to impose a new set of taxes on Americans. They were devised by the chancellor of the Exchequer (the cabinet's chief financial minister), Charles Townshend. In opposing the Stamp Act, some colonists had seemed to suggest that they would not object if Britain raised revenue by regulating trade. Taking them at their word, Townshend persuaded Parliament to impose new taxes on goods imported into the colonies and to create a new board of customs commissioners to collect them and suppress smuggling. Although many merchants objected to the new enforcement procedures, opposition to the Townshend duties developed more slowly than in the case of the Stamp Act. Leaders in several colonies nonetheless decided in 1768 to reimpose the ban on importing British goods.

Homespun clothing, a symbol of American resistance

The boycott began in Boston and soon spread to the southern colonies. Reliance on American rather than British goods, on homespun clothing rather than imported finery, became a symbol of American resistance. It also reflected, as the colonists saw it, a virtuous spirit of self-sacrifice as compared with the self-indulgence and luxury many Americans were coming to associate with Britain. Women who spun and wove at home so as not to purchase British goods were hailed as **Daughters of Liberty**.

Nonimportation

The idea of using homemade rather than imported goods especially appealed to Chesapeake planters, who found themselves owing increasing amounts of money to British merchants. Nonimportation, wrote George Washington, gave "the extravagant man" an opportunity to "retrench his expenses" by reducing the purchase of British luxuries, without having to advertise to his neighbors that he might be in financial distress.

Urban artisans, who welcomed an end to competition from imported British manufactured goods, strongly supported the boycott. Philadelphia and New York merchants at first were reluctant to take part, although they eventually agreed to go along. Nonimportation threatened their livelihoods and raised the prospect of unleashing further lower-class turmoil. As had happened during the Stamp Act crisis, the streets of American cities filled with popular protests against the duties imposed by Parliament. Extralegal local committees attempted to enforce the boycott of British goods.

The Boston Massacre

Royal troops in Boston

Boston once again became the focal point of conflict. Royal troops had been stationed in the city in 1768 after rioting that followed the British seizure of the ship *Liberty* for violating trade regulations. The soldiers, who competed for jobs on Boston's waterfront with the city's laborers, became more and more unpopular. On March 5, 1770, a fight between a snowball-throwing crowd of Bostonians and British troops escalated into an armed confrontation that left five Bostonians dead. One of those who fell in what came to be called the **Boston Massacre** was Crispus Attucks, a sailor of mixed Indian-African-white ancestry. The commanding officer and eight soldiers were put on trial in Massachusetts. Ably defended by John Adams, who viewed lower-class crowd actions as a dangerous method of opposing British policies, seven were found not guilty, while two were convicted of manslaughter. But Paul Revere, a member of the Boston Sons of Liberty and a silversmith and engraver, helped to stir up indignation against the British army by producing a widely circulated (and quite inaccurate) print of the Boston Massacre depicting a line of British soldiers firing into an unarmed crowd.

By 1770, as merchants' profits shriveled and many members of the colonial elite found they could not do without British goods, the non-importation movement was collapsing. British merchants, who wished to remove a possible source of future interruption of trade, pressed for repeal of the Townshend duties. When the British ministry agreed, leaving in place only a tax on tea, and agreed to remove troops from Boston, American merchants quickly abandoned the boycott.

The Boston Massacre. Less than a month after the Boston Massacre of 1770, in which five colonists died, Paul Revere produced this engraving of the event. Although it inaccurately depicts what was actually a disorganized brawl between residents of Boston and British soldiers, this image became one of the most influential pieces of political propaganda of the revolutionary era.

Wilkes and Liberty

Once again, an immediate crisis had been resolved. Nonetheless, many Americans concluded that Britain was succumbing to the same pattern of political corruption and decline of liberty that afflicted other countries. The overlap of the Townshend crisis with a controversy in Britain over the treatment of John Wilkes reinforced this sentiment. A radical journalist known for scandalous writings about the king and ministry, Wilkes had been elected to Parliament from London but was expelled from his seat. "Wilkes and Liberty" became a popular rallying cry on both sides of the Atlantic. In addition, rumors circulated in the colonies that the Anglican Church in England planned to send bishops

William Hogarth's depiction of John Wilkes holding a liberty cap. Wilkes's publication, *North Briton*, bitterly attacked the king and prime minister, for which Wilkes was arrested, tried, and acquitted by a London jury. He became a popular symbol of freedom on both sides of the Atlantic.

to America. Among members of other Protestant denominations, the rumors—strongly denied in London—sparked fears that bishops would establish religious courts like those that had once persecuted Dissenters.

The Tea Act

The next crisis underscored how powerfully events in other parts of Britain's global empire affected the American colonies. The East India Company, a giant trading monopoly, effectively governed recently acquired British possessions in India. Numerous British merchants, bankers, and other individuals had invested heavily in its stock. A classic speculative bubble ensued, with the price of stock in the company rising sharply and then collapsing. To rescue the company and its investors, the British government decided to help it market its enormous holdings of Chinese tea in North America.

To further stimulate its sales and bail out the East India Company, the British government, now headed by Frederick Lord North, offered the company a series of rebates and tax exemptions. These enabled it to dump low-priced tea on the American market, undercutting both established merchants and smugglers.

The tax on tea was not new. But many colonists insisted that to pay it on this large new body of imports would acknowledge Britain's right to tax the colonies. As tea shipments arrived, resistance developed in the major ports. On December 16, 1773, a group of colonists disguised as Indians boarded three ships at anchor in Boston Harbor and threw more than 300 chests of tea into the water. The event became known as the **Boston Tea Party**. The loss to the East India Company was around £10,000 (the equivalent of more than $4 million today).

The Intolerable Acts

British response to the Tea Party

The British government, declared Lord North, must now demonstrate "whether we have, or have not, any authority in that country." Its response to the Boston Tea Party was swift and decisive. Parliament closed the port of Boston to all trade until the tea was paid for. It radically altered the Massachusetts Charter of 1691 by curtailing town meetings and authorizing the governor to appoint members to the council—positions previously filled by election. Parliament also empowered military commanders to lodge soldiers in private homes. These measures, called the Coercive or Intolerable Acts by Americans, united the colonies in opposition to what was widely seen as a direct threat to their political freedom.

At almost the same time, Parliament passed the Quebec Act. This extended the southern boundary of that Canadian province to the Ohio River and granted legal toleration to the Roman Catholic Church in Canada. The act not only threw into question land claims in the Ohio country but persuaded many colonists that the government in London was conspiring to strengthen Catholicism—dreaded by most Protestants—in its American empire.

The Mitred Minuet, a British cartoon from 1774, shows four Roman Catholic bishops dancing around a copy of the Quebec Act. On the left, British officials Lord Bute, Lord North, and Lord Mansfield look on, while the devil oversees the proceedings.

THE COMING OF INDEPENDENCE

The Continental Congress

Opposition to the Intolerable Acts now spread to small towns and rural areas that had not participated actively in previous resistance. In September 1774, in the town of Worcester, Massachusetts, 4,600 militiamen from thirty-seven towns (half the adult male population of the entire county) lined both sides of Main Street as the British-appointed officials walked the gauntlet between them. In the same month, a convention of delegates from Massachusetts towns approved a series of resolutions (called the Suffolk Resolves for the county in which Boston is located) that urged Americans to refuse obedience to the new laws, withhold taxes, and prepare for war.

Suffolk Resolves

To coordinate resistance to the Intolerable Acts, a Continental Congress convened in Philadelphia that month, bringing together the most prominent political leaders of twelve mainland colonies (Georgia did not take part). From Massachusetts came the "brace of Adamses"—John and his more radical cousin Samuel. Virginia's seven delegates included George Washington, Richard Henry Lee, and the renowned orator Patrick Henry. "The distinctions between Virginians, Pennsylvanians, New Yorkers, and New Englanders," Henry declared, "are no more. I am not a Virginian, but an American." In March 1775, Henry concluded a speech urging a Virginia convention to begin military preparations with a legendary credo: "Give me liberty, or give me death!"

Leaders of the Congress

The Continental Association

Before it adjourned at the end of October 1774, the Congress endorsed the Suffolk Resolves and adopted the Continental Association, which called for an almost complete halt to trade with Great Britain and the West Indies (at South Carolina's insistence, exports of rice to Europe were exempted). Congress authorized local Committees of Safety to oversee its mandates and to take action against "enemies of American liberty," including businessmen who tried to profit from the sudden scarcity of goods.

The Committees of Safety

The Committees of Safety began the process of transferring effective political power from established governments whose authority derived from Great Britain to extralegal grassroots bodies reflecting the will of the people. By early 1775, some 7,000 men were serving on local committees throughout the colonies, a vast expansion of the "political nation." The committees became training grounds where small farmers, city artisans, propertyless laborers, and others who had heretofore had little role in government discussed political issues and exercised political power. When the New York assembly refused to endorse the association, local committees continued to enforce it anyway.

The Sweets of Liberty

By 1775, talk of liberty pervaded the colonies. The past few years had witnessed an endless parade of pamphlets with titles like *A Chariot of Liberty* and *Oration on the Beauties of Liberty*. (The latter, a sermon delivered in Boston by Joseph Allen in 1772, became the most popular public address of the years before independence.) Sober men spoke longingly of the "sweets of liberty." One anonymous essayist reported a "night vision" of the word written in the sun's rays. Commented a British emigrant who arrived in Maryland early in 1775: "They are all liberty mad."

Natural rights

As the crisis deepened, Americans increasingly based their claims not simply on the historical rights of Englishmen but on the more abstract language of natural rights and universal freedom. The First Continental Congress defended its actions by appealing to the "principles of the English constitution," the "liberties of free and natural-born subjects within the realm of England," and the "immutable law of nature." John Locke's theory of natural rights offered a powerful justification for colonial resistance, as did Thomas Jefferson in *A Summary View of the Rights of British America*, written in 1774. Americans, Jefferson declared, were "a free people claiming their rights, as derived from the laws of nature, and not as the gift of their chief magistrate."

The Outbreak of War

By the time the Second Continental Congress convened in May 1775, war had broken out between British soldiers and armed citizens of Massachusetts. On April 19, a force of British soldiers marched from Boston toward the nearby town of Concord seeking to seize arms being stockpiled there. Riders from Boston, among them Paul Revere, warned local leaders of the troops' approach. Militiamen took up arms and tried to resist the British advance. Skirmishes between Americans and British soldiers took place at Lexington and again at Concord. By the time the British retreated to the safety of Boston, some forty-nine Americans and seventy-three members of the Royal Army lay dead.

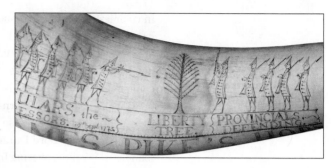

In March 1776, James Pike, a soldier in the Massachusetts militia, carved this scene on his powder horn to commemorate the battles of Lexington and Concord. At the center stands the Liberty Tree.

What the philosopher Ralph Waldo Emerson would later call "the shot heard 'round the world" began the American War of Independence. In May 1775, Ethan Allen and the Green Mountain Boys from Vermont, together with militiamen from Connecticut led by Benedict Arnold, surrounded Fort Ticonderoga in New York and forced it to surrender. The following winter, Henry Knox, George Washington's commander of artillery, arranged for some of the Ticonderoga cannon to be dragged hundreds of miles to the east to reinforce the siege of Boston, where British forces were ensconced. On June 17, 1775, two months after Lexington and Concord, the British had dislodged colonial militiamen from Breed's Hill, although only at a heavy cost in casualties. (The battle came to be named after the nearby Bunker Hill.) But the arrival of American cannon in March 1776 and their entrenchment above the city made the British position in Boston untenable. The British army under the command of Sir William Howe was forced to abandon the city. Before leaving, Howe's forces cut down the original Liberty Tree.

Conflict in Boston

Meanwhile, the Second Continental Congress authorized the raising of an army, printed money to pay for it, and appointed George Washington its commander. In response, Britain declared the colonies in a state of rebellion, dispatched thousands of troops, and ordered the closing of all colonial ports.

The Second Continental Congress

Independence?

By the end of 1775, the breach with Britain seemed irreparable. But many colonists shied away from the idea of independence. Pride in membership in the British empire was still strong, and many political leaders, especially in colonies that had experienced internal turmoil, feared that a complete break with the mother country might unleash further conflict.

Such fears affected how colonial leaders responded to the idea of independence. The elites of Massachusetts and Virginia, who felt supremely confident of their ability to retain authority at home, tended to support a break with Britain. Southern leaders not only were highly protective of their political liberty but also were outraged by a proclamation issued in November 1775 by **Lord Dunmore**, the British governor and military commander in Virginia, offering freedom to any slave who escaped to his lines and bore arms for the king.

The Dunmore proclamation

In New York and Pennsylvania, however, the diversity of the population made it difficult to work out a consensus on how far to go in resisting British measures. Many established leaders drew back from further resistance. Joseph Galloway, a Pennsylvania leader and delegate to the Second Continental Congress who worked to devise a compromise between British and colonial positions, warned that independence would be accompanied by constant disputes within America. He even predicted a war between the northern and southern colonies.

Fear of domestic turmoil

Paine's *Common Sense*

As 1776 dawned, America presented the unusual spectacle of colonists at war against the British empire but still pleading for their rights within it. Ironically, it was a recent emigrant from England, not a colonist from a family long-established on American soil, who grasped the inner logic of the situation and offered a vision of the broad significance of American independence. Thomas Paine had emigrated to Philadelphia late in 1774. He quickly became associated with a group of advocates of the American cause, including John Adams and Dr. Benjamin Rush, a leading Philadelphia physician. It was Rush who suggested to Paine that he write a pamphlet supporting American independence.

Common Sense appeared in January 1776. The pamphlet began not with a recital of colonial grievances but with an attack on the "so much boasted Constitution of England" and the principles of hereditary rule and monarchical government. Rather than being the most perfect system of government in the world, Paine wrote, the English monarchy was headed by "the royal brute of England," and the English constitution was composed in large part of "the base remains of two ancient tyrannies . . . monarchical tyranny in the person of the king [and] aristocratical tyranny in the persons of the peers."

Paine on monarchy and aristocracy

Turning to independence, Paine drew on the colonists' experiences to make his case. "There is something absurd," he wrote, "in supposing a

Continent to be perpetually governed by an island." With independence, moreover, the colonies could for the first time trade freely with the entire world and insulate themselves from involvement in the endless imperial wars of Europe. Membership in the British empire, Paine insisted, was a burden to the colonies, not a benefit.

Toward the close of the pamphlet, Paine moved beyond practical considerations to outline a breathtaking vision of the historical importance of the American Revolution. "The cause of America," he proclaimed in stirring language, "is in great measure, the cause of all mankind." The new nation would become the home of freedom, "an asylum for mankind."

Most of Paine's ideas were not original. What made *Common Sense* unique was his mode of expressing them and the audience he addressed. Previous political writings had generally been directed toward the educated elite. Paine, however, pioneered a new style of political writing, one designed to expand dramatically the public sphere where political discussion took place. He wrote clearly and directly, and he avoided the complex language and Latin phrases common in pamphlets aimed at educated readers. *Common Sense* quickly became one of the most successful and influential pamphlets in the history of political writing, selling, by Paine's estimate, some 150,000 copies. Paine directed that his share of the profits be used to buy supplies for the Continental army.

In the spring of 1776, scores of American communities adopted resolutions calling for a separation from Britain. Only six months elapsed between the appearance of *Common Sense* and the decision by the Second Continental Congress to sever the colonies' ties with Great Britain.

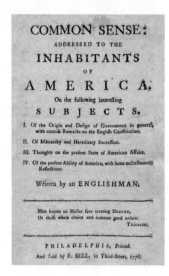

The cover of *Common Sense*, Thomas Paine's influential pamphlet denouncing the idea of hereditary rule and calling for American independence.

The Declaration of Independence

On July 2, 1776, the Congress formally declared the United States an independent nation. Two days later, it approved the **Declaration of Independence**, written by Thomas Jefferson and revised by the Congress before approval. (See the Appendix for the full text.) Most of the Declaration consists of a lengthy list of grievances directed against King George III, ranging from quartering troops in colonial homes to imposing taxes without the colonists' consent. One clause in Jefferson's draft, which condemned the inhumanity of the slave trade and criticized the king for overturning colonial laws that sought to restrict the importation of slaves, was deleted by the Congress at the insistence of Georgia and South Carolina.

Colonial grievances

The Declaration's enduring impact came not from the complaints against George III but from Jefferson's preamble, especially the second paragraph, which begins, "We hold these truths to be self-evident, that all

Jefferson's preamble

men are created equal, that they are endowed by their Creator with certain unalienable Rights, that among these are Life, Liberty, and the pursuit of Happiness." By "unalienable rights," Jefferson meant rights so basic, so rooted in human nature itself, that no government could take them away.

Jefferson then went on to justify the breach with Britain. Government, he wrote, derives its powers from "the consent of the governed." When a government threatens its subjects' natural rights, the people have the authority "to alter or to abolish it." The Declaration of Independence is ultimately an assertion of the right of revolution.

The Declaration and American freedom

The Declaration also changed forever the meaning of American freedom. It completed the shift from the rights of Englishmen to the rights of mankind as the object of American independence. No longer a set of specific rights, no longer a privilege to be enjoyed by a corporate body or people in certain social circumstances, liberty had become a universal entitlement.

When Jefferson substituted the "pursuit of happiness" for property in the familiar triad that opens the Declaration, he tied the new nation's star to an open-ended, democratic process whereby individuals develop their own potential and seek to realize their own life goals. Individual self-fulfillment, unimpeded by government, would become a central element of American freedom. Tradition would no longer rule the present, and Americans could shape their society as they saw fit.

An Asylum for Mankind

A distinctive definition of nationality resting on American freedom was born in the Revolution. From the beginning, the idea of "American exceptionalism"—the belief that the United States has a special mission to be a refuge from tyranny, a symbol of freedom, and a model for the rest of the world—has occupied a central place in American nationalism. The new nation declared itself, in the words of Virginia leader James Madison, the "workshop of liberty to the Civilized World." Countless sermons, political tracts, and newspaper articles of the time repeated this idea. Unburdened by the institutions—monarchy, aristocracy, hereditary privilege—that oppressed the peoples of the Old World, America and America alone was the place where the

America as a Symbol of Liberty, a 1775 engraving from the cover of the *Pennsylvania Magazine*, edited by Thomas Paine soon after his arrival in America. The shield displays the colony's coat of arms. The female figure holding a liberty cap is surrounded by weaponry of the patriotic struggle, including a cartridge box marked "liberty," hanging from a tree (*right*).

principle of universal freedom could take root. This was why Jefferson addressed the Declaration to "the opinions of mankind," not just the colonists themselves or Great Britain.

First to add his name to the Declaration of Independence was the Massachusetts merchant John Hancock, president of the Second Continental Congress, with a signature so large, he declared, according to legend, that King George III could read it without his spectacles.

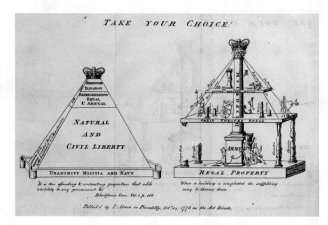

The Global Declaration of Independence

The American colonists were less concerned with securing human rights for all mankind than with winning international recognition in their struggle for independence from Britain. But Jefferson hoped that this rebellion would become "the signal of arousing men to burst the chains . . . and to assume the blessings and security of self-government." And for more than two centuries, the Declaration has remained an inspiration not only to generations of Americans denied the enjoyment of their natural rights but to colonial peoples around the world seeking independence. The Declaration quickly appeared in French and German translations, although not, at first, in Spanish, since the government feared it would inspire dangerous ideas among the peoples of Spain's American empire.

Inspired by the American Revolution, the British reformer John Cartwright published an appeal for the annual election of Parliament as essential to liberty in Britain. He included an engraving contrasting the principles of reform, on the left, with despotism, on the right.

In the years since 1776, numerous anti-colonial movements have modeled their own declarations of independence on America's, often echoing Jefferson's own words. Today more than half the countries in the world, in places as far-flung as China (issued after the revolution of 1911) and Vietnam (1945), have such declarations, though few of them include a list, like Jefferson's, of the rights of citizens that their governments cannot abridge.

Legacy of the Declaration

But even more than the specific language of the Declaration, the principle that legitimate political authority rests on the will of "the people" has been adopted around the world. The idea that "the people" possess rights was quickly internationalized. Slaves in the Caribbean, colonial subjects in India, and indigenous inhabitants of Latin America could all speak this language, to the dismay of those who exercised power over them.

The will of "the people"

VOICES OF FREEDOM

From Thomas Paine, *Common Sense* (1776)

A recent emigrant from England, Thomas Paine in January 1776 published *Common Sense*, a highly influential pamphlet that in stirring language made the case for American independence.

In the following pages I offer nothing more than simple facts, plain arguments, and common sense. . . .

Male and female are the distinctions of nature, good and bad the distinctions of heaven; but how a race of men came into the world so exalted above the rest, and distinguished like some new species, is worth enquiring into, and whether they are the means of happiness or of misery to mankind. . . . One of the strongest *natural* proofs of the folly of hereditary right in kings, is, that nature disapproves it, otherwise she would not so frequently turn it into ridicule, by giving mankind an *ass for a lion.* . . .

The sun never shined on a cause of greater worth. 'Tis not the affair of a city, a country, a province, or a kingdom, but of a continent—of at least one eighth part of the habitable globe. 'Tis not the concern of a day, a year, or an age; posterity are virtually involved in the context, and will be more or less affected, even to the end of time, by the proceedings now. Now is the seed time of continental union, faith and honor. . . .

I challenge the warmest advocate for reconciliation to show a single advantage that this continent can reap by being connected with Great Britain. . . . But the injuries and disadvantages which we sustain by that connection, are without number. . . . Any submission to, or dependence on, Great Britain, tends directly to involve this Continent in European wars and quarrels, and set us at variance with nations who would otherwise seek our friendship, and against whom we have neither anger nor complaint.

O ye that love mankind! Ye that dare oppose, not only the tyranny, but the tyrant, stand forth! Every spot of the old world is overrun with oppression. Freedom hath been hunted round the globe. Asia, and Africa, have long expelled her. Europe regards her like a stranger, and England hath given her warning to depart. O! Receive the fugitive, and prepare in time an asylum for mankind.

From Jonathan Boucher, *A View of the Causes and Consequences of the American Revolution* (1775)

An English-born Episcopal minister, Jonathan Boucher preached in Virginia from 1759 to 1775, when he returned to England after receiving threats on his life because of his loyalty to the crown. In 1797 he published in London a series of sermons he had delivered in 1775 explaining his opposition to the revolutionary movement.

Obedience to government is every man's duty, because it is every man's interest; but it is particularly incumbent on Christians, because . . . it is enjoined by the positive commands of God; and, therefore, when Christians are disobedient to human ordinances, they are also disobedient to God. If the form of government . . . be mild and free, it is our duty to enjoy it with gratitude and with thankfulness and, in particular, to be careful not to abuse it by licentiousness. If it be less indulgent and less liberal than in reason it ought to be, still it is our duty not to disturb and destroy the peace of the community by becoming refractory and rebellious subjects. . . . However humiliating such acquiescence may seem to men of warm and eager minds, the wisdom of God in having made it our duty is manifest. For, as it is the natural temper and bias of the human mind to be impatient under restraint, it was wise and merciful in the blessed Author of our religion . . . with the whole weight of his authority, altogether to discountenance every tendency to disobedience. . . .

Liberty is not the setting at nought and despising established laws—much less the making our own wills the rule of our own actions, or the actions of others . . . but it is the being governed by law and by law only. The Greeks described Eleutheria, or Liberty, as the daughter of Jupiter, the supreme fountain of power and law. . . . Their idea, no doubt, was that liberty was the fair fruit of just authority and that it consisted in men's being subjected to law. The more carefully well-devised restraints of law are enacted, and the more rigorously they are executed in any country, the greater degree of civil liberty does that country enjoy. To pursue liberty, then, in a manner not warranted by law, whatever the pretense may be, is clearly to be hostile to liberty; and those persons who thus *promise you liberty* are themselves *the servants of corruption.*

QUESTIONS

1. *What does Paine see as the global significance of the American struggle for independence?*

2. *Why does Boucher believe that obedience to government is particularly important for Christians?*

3. *How do the two writers differ in their understanding of freedom?*

SECURING INDEPENDENCE

The Balance of Power

Britain's advantages

Declaring Americans independent was one thing; winning independence another. The newly created American army confronted the greatest military power on earth. Viewing the Americans as traitors, Britain resolved to crush the rebellion. On the surface, the balance of power seemed heavily weighted in Britain's favor. It had a well-trained army (supplemented by hired soldiers from German states like Hesse), the world's most powerful navy, and experienced military commanders. The Americans had to rely on local militias and an inadequately equipped Continental army.

American advantages

On the other hand, American soldiers were fighting on their own soil for a cause that inspired devotion and sacrifice. During the eight years of war from 1775 to 1783, some 200,000 men bore arms in the American army (whose soldiers were volunteers) and militias (where service was required of every able-bodied man unless he provided a substitute). The patriots suffered dearly for the cause. Of the colonies' free white male population aged sixteen to forty-five, one in twenty died in the War of Independence, the equivalent of nearly 3 million deaths in today's population. But so long as the Americans maintained an army in the field, the idea of independence remained alive no matter how much territory the British occupied.

The role of France

Despite British power, to conquer the thirteen colonies would be an enormous and expensive task, and it was not at all certain that the public at home wished to pay the additional taxes that a lengthy war would require. Moreover, European rivals, notably France, welcomed the prospect of a British defeat. If the Americans could forge an alliance with France, a world power second only to Britain, it would go a long way toward equalizing the balance of forces.

Blacks in the Revolution

Trading military service for freedom

At the war's outset, George Washington refused to accept black recruits. But he changed his mind after Lord Dunmore's 1775 proclamation, which offered freedom to slaves who joined the British cause. Some 5,000 blacks enlisted in state militias and the Continental army and navy. Since individuals drafted into the militia were allowed to provide a substitute, slaves suddenly gained considerable bargaining power. Not a few acquired their freedom by agreeing to serve in place of an owner or his son. In 1778, Rhode Island, with a higher proportion of slaves in its population than any other New England state, formed a black regiment and promised freedom to slaves who enlisted, while compensating the owners for their loss of property. Blacks who fought under George Washington and in other state militias did so in racially integrated companies (although invariably under white officers). They were the last black American soldiers to do so officially until the Korean War.

Except for South Carolina and Georgia, the southern colonies also enrolled free blacks and slaves to fight. They were not explicitly promised freedom, but many received it individually after the war ended.

American Foot Soldiers, Yorktown Campaign, a 1781 watercolor by a French officer, includes a black soldier from the First Rhode Island Regiment, an all-black unit of 250 men.

Fighting on the side of the British also offered opportunities for freedom. Before his forces were expelled from Virginia, 800 or more slaves had escaped from their owners to join Lord Dunmore's Ethiopian Regiment, wearing uniforms that bore the motto "Liberty to Slaves." Other escaped slaves served the Royal Army as spies, guided their troops through swamps, and worked as military cooks, laundresses, and construction workers. George Washington himself saw seventeen of his slaves flee to the British, some of whom signed up to fight the colonists. "There is not a man of them, but would leave us, if they believed they could make their escape," his cousin Lund Washington reported. "Liberty is sweet."

The First Years of the War

Had the British commander, Sir William Howe, prosecuted the war more vigorously at the outset, he might have nipped the rebellion in the bud by destroying Washington's army. But although Washington suffered numerous defeats in the first years of the war, he generally avoided direct confrontations with the British and managed to keep his army intact. Having abandoned Boston, Howe attacked New York City in the summer of 1776. Washington's army had likewise moved from Massachusetts to Brooklyn to defend the city. Howe pushed American forces back and almost cut off Washington's retreat across the East River.

Early setbacks

Howe pursued the American army but never managed to inflict a decisive defeat. Demoralized by successive failures, however, many American soldiers simply went home. Once 28,000 men, Washington's army dwindled to fewer than 3,000. To restore morale and regain the initiative, he launched successful surprise attacks on Hessian soldiers

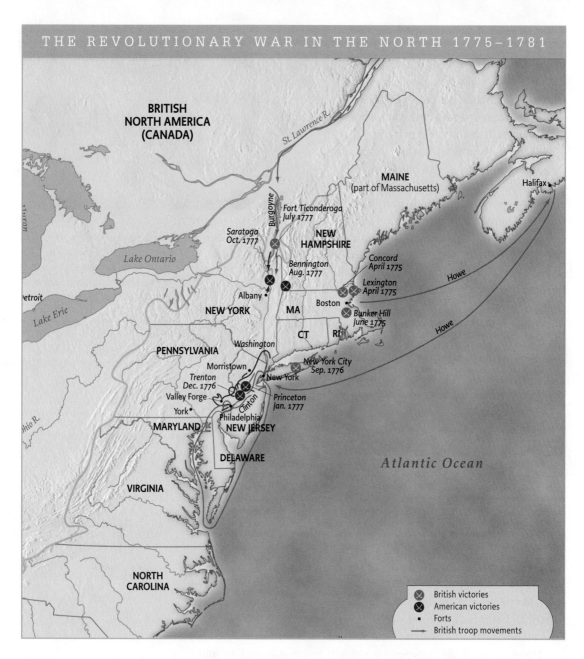

BRITISH
NORTH AMERICA
(CANADA)

St. Lawrence R.

MAINE
(part of Massachusetts)

Halifax

Burgoyne

Fort Ticonderoga
July 1777

Saratoga
Oct. 1777

NEW
HAMPSHIRE

Concord
April 1775

Lake Ontario

Bennington
Aug. 1777

Lexington
April 1775

Howe

Detroit

Lake Erie

Albany

NEW YORK

MA

Boston

Bunker Hill
June 1775

CT

RI

Howe

PENNSYLVANIA

Washington

New York City
Sep. 1776

Morristown

Trenton
Dec. 1776

New York

Valley Forge

Princeton
Jan. 1777

Ohio R.

York

Clinton

Philadelphia

MARYLAND

NEW JERSEY

DELAWARE

Atlantic Ocean

VIRGINIA

NORTH
CAROLINA

⊗ British victories
⊗ American victories
▪ Forts
→ British troop movements

Key battles in the North during the War of Independence included Lexington and Concord, which began the armed conflict; the campaign in New York and New Jersey; and Saratoga, sometimes called the turning point of the war.

at Trenton, New Jersey, on December 26, 1776, and on a British force at Princeton on January 3, 1777. Shortly before crossing the Delaware River to attack the Hessians, Washington had Thomas Paine's inspiring essay *The American Crisis* read to his troops. "These are the times that try men's souls," Paine wrote. "The summer soldier and the sunshine patriot will, in this crisis, shrink from the service of their country; but he that stands it *now*, deserves the love and thanks of man and woman."

The Battle of Saratoga

In the summer of 1777, a second British army, led by General John Burgoyne, advanced south from Canada, hoping to link up with Howe and isolate New England. But in July, Howe instead moved his forces from New York City to attack Philadelphia. In September, the Continental Congress fled to Lancaster in central Pennsylvania, and Howe occupied the City of Brotherly Love. Not having been informed of Burgoyne's plans, Howe had unintentionally abandoned him. American forces blocked Burgoyne's way, surrounded his army, and on October 17, 1777, forced him to surrender at Saratoga. The victory provided a significant boost to American morale.

Howe and Burgoyne

During the winter of 1777–1778, the British army, now commanded by Sir Henry Clinton, was quartered in Philadelphia. (In the Revolution, as in most eighteenth-century wars, fighting came to a halt during the winter.) Meanwhile, Washington's army remained encamped at Valley Forge, where they suffered terribly from the frigid weather. Men who had other options simply went home. By the end of that difficult winter, recent immigrants and African-Americans made up half the soldiers at Valley Forge, and most of the rest were landless or unskilled laborers.

Valley Forge

But Saratoga helped to persuade the French that American victory was possible. In 1778, American diplomats led by Benjamin Franklin concluded a Treaty of Amity and Commerce in which France recognized the United States and agreed to supply military assistance. Soon afterward, Spain also joined the war on the American side. French assistance would play a decisive part in the war's end. At the outset, however, the French fleet showed more interest in attacking British outposts in the West Indies than directly aiding the Americans. Nonetheless, French and Spanish entry transformed the War of Independence into a global conflict. By putting the British on the defensive in places ranging from Gibraltar to the West Indies, it greatly complicated their military prospects.

Alliance with France

The War in the South

In 1778, the focus of the war shifted to the South. Here the British hoped to exploit the social tensions between backcountry farmers and wealthy planters that had surfaced in the Regulator movements, to enlist the support of the numerous colonists in the region who remained loyal to the crown, and to disrupt the economy by encouraging slaves to escape. In December 1778, British forces occupied Savannah, Georgia. In May 1780, Clinton captured Charleston, South Carolina, and with it an American army of 5,000 men.

Setbacks in 1780

The year 1780 was arguably the low point of the struggle for independence. Congress was essentially bankrupt, and the army went months without being paid. The British seemed successful in playing on social conflicts within the colonies, as thousands of southern Loyalists joined up with British forces (fourteen regiments from Savannah alone) and tens of thousands of slaves sought freedom by fleeing to British lines. In August, Lord Charles Cornwallis routed an American army at Camden, South Carolina. The following month one of Washington's ablest commanders, Benedict Arnold, defected and almost succeeded in turning over to the British the important fort at West Point on the Hudson River.

Militia attacks

But the British failed to turn these advantages into victory. British commanders were unable to consolidate their hold on the South. Wherever their forces went, American militias harassed them. Hit-and-run attacks by militiamen under Francis Marion, called the "swamp fox" because his men emerged from hiding places in swamps to strike swiftly and then disappear, eroded the British position in South Carolina. A bloody civil war engulfed North and South Carolina and Georgia, with patriot and Loyalist militias inflicting retribution on each other and plundering the farms of their opponents' supporters. The brutal treatment of civilians by British forces under Colonel Banastre Tarleton persuaded many Americans to join the patriot cause.

Victory at Last

In January 1781, American forces under Daniel Morgan dealt a crushing defeat to Tarleton at Cowpens, South Carolina. Two months later, at Guilford Courthouse, North Carolina, General Nathanael Greene, while conducting a campaign of strategic retreats, inflicted heavy losses on Lord Charles Cornwallis, the British commander in the South. Cornwallis

Yorktown

moved into Virginia and encamped at Yorktown, located on a peninsula

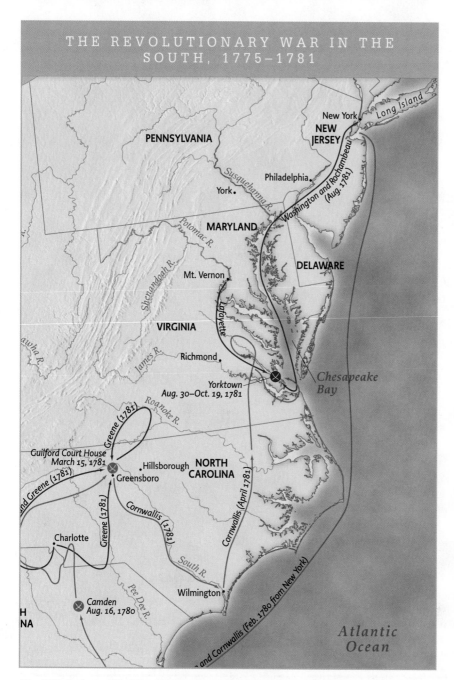

THE REVOLUTIONARY WAR IN THE SOUTH, 1775–1781

PENNSYLVANIA

New York
NEW JERSEY
Long Island

Susquehanna R.

Philadelphia

Washington and Rochambeau (Aug. 1781)

York

Potomac R.

MARYLAND

DELAWARE

Shenandoah R.

Mt. Vernon

Lafayette

VIRGINIA

awha R.

James R.

Richmond

Yorktown
Aug. 30–Oct. 19, 1781

Chesapeake Bay

Roanoke R.

Greene (1781)

Guilford Court House
March 15, 1781

Hillsborough

NORTH CAROLINA

nd Greene (1781)

Greensboro

Greene (1781)

Cornwallis (April 1781)

Cornwallis (1781)

Charlotte

South R.

Pee Dee R.

Wilmington

and Cornwallis (Feb. 1780 from New York)

H
NA

Camden
Aug. 16, 1780

Atlantic Ocean

After 1777, the focus of the War of Independence shifted to the South, where it culminated in 1781 with the British defeat at Yorktown.

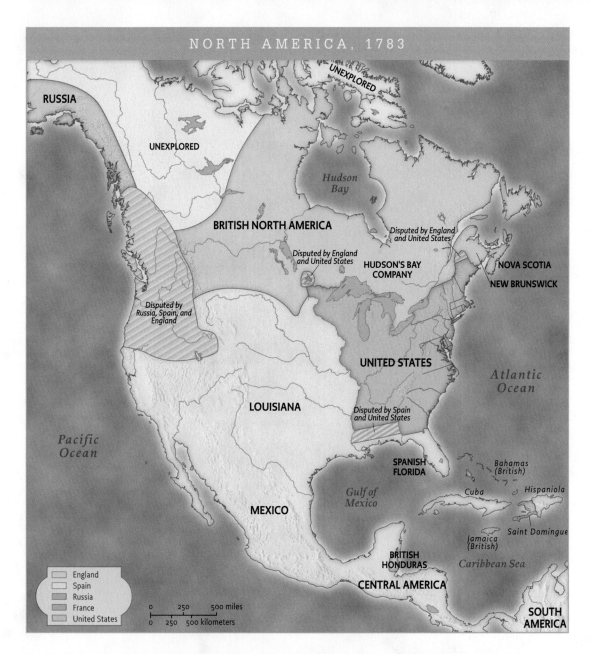

RUSSIA

UNEXPLORED

UNEXPLORED

Hudson
Bay

BRITISH NORTH AMERICA

Disputed by England
and United States

Disputed by England
and United States

HUDSON'S BAY
COMPANY

NOVA SCOTIA

NEW BRUNSWICK

Disputed by
Russia, Spain, and
England

UNITED STATES

Atlantic
Ocean

Pacific
Ocean

LOUISIANA

Disputed by Spain
and United States

SPANISH
FLORIDA

Bahamas
(British)

Cuba

Hispaniola

MEXICO

Gulf of
Mexico

Saint Domingue

Jamaica
(British)

BRITISH
HONDURAS

Caribbean Sea

CENTRAL AMERICA

SOUTH
AMERICA

England
Spain
Russia
France
United States

0   250   500 miles
0   250   500 kilometers

The newly independent United States occupied only a small part of the North American continent in 1783.

that juts into Chesapeake Bay. Brilliantly recognizing the opportunity to surround Cornwallis, Washington rushed his forces, augmented by French troops under the Marquis de Lafayette, to block a British escape by land. Meanwhile, a French fleet controlled the mouth of the Chesapeake, preventing supplies and reinforcements from reaching Cornwallis's army.

Imperial rivalries had helped to create the American colonies. Now, the rivalry of European empires helped to secure American independence. Taking land and sea forces together, more Frenchmen than Americans participated in the decisive Yorktown campaign. On October 19, 1781, Cornwallis surrendered his army of 8,000 men. When the news reached London, public support for the war evaporated and peace negotiations soon began.

A French engraving depicts New Yorkers tearing down the statue of King George III in July 1776, after the approval of the Declaration of Independence. Slaves are doing the work, while whites look on. The statue was later melted down to make bullets for the Continental army.

Two years later, in September 1783, American and British negotiators concluded the **Treaty of Paris**. The American delegation—John Adams, Benjamin Franklin, and John Jay—achieved one of the greatest diplomatic triumphs in the country's history. They not only won recognition of American independence but also gained control of the entire region between Canada and Florida east of the Mississippi River and the right of Americans to fish in Atlantic waters off of Canada (a matter of considerable importance to New Englanders). At British insistence, the Americans agreed that colonists who had remained loyal to the mother country would not suffer persecution and that Loyalists' property that had been seized by local and state governments would be restored.

Territorial gains

Until independence, the thirteen colonies had formed part of Britain's American empire, along with Canada and the West Indies. But Canada rebuffed repeated calls to join the War of Independence, and leaders of the West Indies, fearful of slave uprisings, also remained loyal to the crown. With the Treaty of Paris, the United States of America became the Western Hemisphere's first independent nation. Its boundaries reflected not so much the long-standing unity of a geographical region, but the circumstances of its birth.

CHAPTER REVIEW AND ONLINE RESOURCES

REVIEW QUESTIONS

1. *Patrick Henry proclaimed that he was not a Virginian, but rather an American. What unified the colonists and what divided them at the time of the Revolution?*

2. *Discuss the ramifications of using slaves in the British and Continental armies. Why did the British authorize the use of slaves? Why did the Americans? How did the slaves benefit?*

3. *Why did the colonists reach the conclusion that membership in the empire threatened their freedoms, rather than guaranteed them?*

4. *How did new ideas of liberty contribute to tensions between the social classes in the American colonies?*

5. *Why did people in other countries believe that the American Revolution (or the Declaration of Independence) was important to them or their own countries?*

6. *Summarize the difference of opinion between British officials and colonial leaders over the issues of taxation and representation.*

7. *How did the actions of the British authorities help to unite the American colonists during the 1760s and 1770s?*

KEY TERMS

virtual representation (p. 141)

writs of assistance (p. 141)

Sugar Act (p. 142)

Committee of Correspondence (p. 144)

Sons of Liberty (p. 144)

Regulators (p. 145)

Daughters of Liberty (p. 146)

Boston Massacre (p. 147)

Boston Tea Party (p. 148)

Lord Dunmore (p. 152)

Common Sense (p. 152)

Declaration of Independence (p. 153)

Treaty of Paris (p. 165)

wwnorton.com /studyspace

VISIT STUDYSPACE FOR THESE RESOURCES AND MORE

- A chapter outline
- A diagnostic chapter quiz
- Interactive maps
- Map worksheets
- Multimedia documents

CHAPTER 6

THE REVOLUTION

WITHIN

★

Liberty Displaying the Arts and Sciences. This 1792 painting by Samuel Jennings is one of the few visual images of the early republic explicitly linking slavery with tyranny and liberty with abolition. The female figure offers books to newly freed slaves. Other forms of knowledge depicted include a globe and an artist's palette. Beneath her left foot lies a broken chain. In the background, free slaves enjoy some leisure time.

- *How did equality become a stronger component of American freedom after the Revolution?*

- *How did the expansion of religious liberty after the Revolution reflect the new American ideal of freedom?*

- *How did the definition of economic freedom change after the Revolution, and who benefited from the changes?*

- *How did the Revolution diminish the freedoms of both Loyalists and Native Americans?*

- *What was the impact of the Revolution on slavery?*

- *How did the Revolution affect the status of women?*

Born in Massachusetts in 1744, Abigail Adams became one of the revolutionary era's most articulate and influential women. At a time when educational opportunities for girls were extremely limited, she taught herself by reading books in the library of her father, a Congregational minister. In 1764, she married John Adams. During the War of Independence, with her husband away in Philadelphia and Europe serving the American cause, she stayed behind at their Massachusetts home, raising their four children and managing the family's farm. The letters they exchanged form one of the most remarkable correspondences in American history. A keen observer of public affairs, she kept her husband informed of events in Massachusetts and offered opinions on political matters. Later, when Adams served as president, he relied on her for advice more than on members of his cabinet.

In March 1776, a few months before the Second Continental Congress declared American independence, Abigail Adams wrote her best-known letter to her husband. She began by commenting indirectly on the evils of slavery. How strong, she wondered, could the "passion for Liberty" be among those "accustomed to deprive their fellow citizens of theirs." She went on to urge Congress, when it drew up a "Code of Laws" for the new republic, to "remember the ladies." All men, she warned, "would be tyrants if they could."

It was the leaders of colonial society who initiated resistance to British taxation. But as Abigail Adams's letter illustrates, the struggle for American liberty emboldened other colonists to demand more liberty for themselves. At a time when so many Americans—slaves, indentured servants, women, Indians, apprentices, propertyless men—were denied full freedom, the struggle against Britain threw into question many forms of authority and inequality.

Abigail Adams accepted the prevailing belief that a woman's primary responsibility was to her family. But she resented the "absolute power" husbands exercised over their wives. Her letter is widely remembered today. Less familiar is John Adams's response, which illuminated how the Revolution had unleashed challenges to all sorts of inherited ideas of deference and authority: "We have been told that our struggle has loosened the bands of government everywhere; that children and apprentices were disobedient; that schools and colleges were grown turbulent; that Indians slighted their guardians, and negroes grew insolent to their masters." To John Adams, this upheaval, including his wife's claim to greater freedom, was an affront to the natural order of things. To others, it formed the essence of the American Revolution.

DEMOCRATIZING FREEDOM

The Dream of Equality

The American Revolution took place at three levels simultaneously. It was a struggle for national independence, a phase in a century-long global battle among European empires, and a conflict over what kind of nation an independent America should be.

The Revolution unleashed public debates and political and social struggles that enlarged the scope of freedom and challenged inherited structures of power within America. In rejecting the crown and the principle of hereditary aristocracy, many Americans also rejected the society of privilege, patronage, and fixed status that these institutions embodied. The idea of liberty became a revolutionary rallying cry, a standard by which to judge and challenge homegrown institutions as well as imperial ones.

Abigail Adams, a portrait by Gilbert Stuart, painted over several years beginning in 1800. Stuart told a friend that, as a young woman, Adams must have been a "perfect Venus."

Jefferson's seemingly straightforward assertion in the Declaration of Independence that "all men are created equal" announced a radical principle whose full implications no one could anticipate. In both Britain and its colonies, a well-ordered society was widely thought to depend on obedience to authority—the power of rulers over their subjects, husbands over wives, parents over children, employers over servants and apprentices, slaveholders over slaves. Inequality had been fundamental to the colonial social order; the Revolution challenged it in many ways. Henceforth, American freedom would be forever linked with the idea of equality—equality before the law, equality in political rights, equality of economic opportunity, and, for some, equality of condition. "Whenever I use the words *freedom* or *rights*," wrote Thomas Paine, "I desire to be understood to mean a perfect equality of them. . . . The floor of Freedom is as level as water."

> *The Revolution and equality*

Expanding the Political Nation

In political, social, and religious life, previously marginalized groups challenged the domination by a privileged few. In the end, the Revolution did not undo the obedience to which male heads of household were entitled from their wives and children, and, at least in the southern states, their slaves. For free men, however, the democratization of freedom was dramatic. Nowhere was this more evident than in challenges to the traditional limitation of political participation to those who owned property.

> *Political participation*

In the political thought of the eighteenth century, "democracy" had several meanings. One, derived from the writings of Aristotle, defined democracy as a system in which the entire people governed directly. However, this was thought to mean mob rule. British thinkers sometimes used the word when referring to the House of Commons, the "democratic" branch of a mixed government. In the wake of the American Revolution, the term came into wider use to express the popular aspirations for greater equality inspired by the struggle for independence.

Throughout the colonies, election campaigns became freewheeling debates on the fundamentals of government. Universal male suffrage, religious toleration, and even the abolition of slavery were discussed not only by the educated elite but also by artisans, small farmers, and laborers, now emerging as a self-conscious element in politics. In many colonies-turned-states, members of the militia demanded the right to elect all their officers and to vote for public officials whether or not they met age and property qualifications. They thereby established the tradition that service in the army enabled excluded groups to stake a claim to full citizenship.

The Revolution in Pennsylvania

The Revolution's radical potential was more evident in Pennsylvania than in any other state. Nearly the entire prewar elite opposed independence, fearing that severing the tie with Britain would lead to rule by the "rabble" and to attacks on property. The vacuum of political leadership opened the door for the rise of a new pro-independence grouping, based on the artisan and lower-class communities of Philadelphia, and organized in extralegal committees and the local militia.

Staunch advocates of equality, Pennsylvania's radical leaders particularly attacked property qualifications for voting. "God gave mankind freedom by nature," declared the anonymous author of the pamphlet *The People the Best Governors*, "and made every man equal to his neighbors." The people, therefore, were "the best guardians of their own liberties," and every free man should be eligible to vote and hold office. Three months after independence, Pennsylvania adopted a new state constitution that sought to institutionalize democracy by concentrating power in a one-house legislature elected annually by all men over age twenty-one who paid taxes. It abolished the office of governor, dispensed with property qualifications for officeholding, and provided that schools with low fees be established in every county. It also included clauses guaranteeing "freedom of speech, and of writing," and religious liberty.

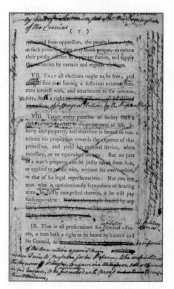

John Dickinson's copy of the Pennsylvania constitution of 1776, with handwritten proposals for changes. Dickinson, one of the more conservative advocates of independence, felt the new state constitution was far too democratic. He crossed out a provision that all "free men" should be eligible to hold office, and another declaring the people not bound by laws that did not promote "the common good."

The New Constitutions

Like Pennsylvania, every state adopted a new constitution in the aftermath of independence. Nearly all Americans now agreed that their governments must be **republics**, meaning that their authority rested on the consent of the governed, and that there would be no king or hereditary aristocracy.

New state constitutions

In part to counteract what he saw as Pennsylvania's excessive radicalism, John Adams in 1776 published ***Thoughts on Government***, which insisted that the new constitutions should create "**balanced governments**" whose structure would reflect the division of society between the wealthy (represented in the upper house) and ordinary men (who would control the lower). A powerful governor and judiciary would ensure that neither class infringed on the liberty of the other. Adams's call for two-house legislatures was followed by every state except Pennsylvania, Georgia, and Vermont. But only his own state, Massachusetts, gave the governor an effective veto over laws passed by the legislature. Americans had come to believe that excessive royal authority had undermined British liberty. They had long resented efforts by appointed governors to challenge the power of colonial assemblies. They preferred power to rest with the legislature.

Power in legislature

The Right to Vote

The issue of requirements for voting and officeholding proved far more contentious. To John Adams, as conservative on the internal affairs of America as he had been radical on independence, freedom and equality were opposites. Men without property, he believed, had no "judgment of their own," and the removal of property qualifications, therefore, would "confound and destroy all distinctions, and prostrate all ranks to one common level." Eliminating traditional social ranks, however, was precisely the aim of the era's radical democrats.

The property qualification for suffrage

Democracy gained the least ground in the southern states, whose highly deferential political traditions enabled the landed gentry to retain their control of political affairs. In Virginia and South Carolina, the new constitutions retained property qualifications for voting and authorized the gentry-dominated legislature to choose the governor.

The most democratic new constitutions moved much of the way toward the idea of voting as an entitlement rather than a privilege, but they generally stopped short of universal **suffrage**, even for free men. Pennsylvania's constitution no longer required ownership of property, but it retained the taxpaying qualification. As a result, it enfranchised nearly all of the state's free male population but still barred a small number, mainly paupers and domestic servants, from voting. Nonetheless, even with the taxpaying requirement, it was a dramatic departure from the colonial practice of restricting the suffrage to those who could claim to be economically independent. It elevated "personal liberty," in the words of one essayist, to a position more important than property ownership in defining the boundaries of the political nation.

Freedom and the right to vote

By the 1780s, except in Virginia, Maryland, and New York, a large majority of the adult white male population could meet voting requirements. New Jersey's new state constitution of 1776 granted the suffrage to all "inhabitants" who met a property qualification. Until the state added the word "male" (along with "white") in 1807, property-owning women, mostly widows, did cast ballots. In the popular language of politics if not in law, freedom and an individual's right to vote had become interchangeable.

TOWARD RELIGIOUS TOLERATION

As remarkable as the expansion of political freedom was the Revolution's impact on American religion. Religious toleration, declared one Virginia patriot, was part of "the common cause of Freedom." We have already seen that some colonies, like Rhode Island and Pennsylvania, had long made a practice of toleration. But freedom of worship before the Revolution arose *Religious pluralism* more from the reality of religious pluralism than from a well-developed theory of religious liberty. Most colonies supported religious institutions with public funds and discriminated in voting and officeholding against

A 1771 image of New York City lists some of the numerous churches visible from the New Jersey shore, illustrating the diversity of religions practiced in the city.

Prospect of the City of NEW-YORK

1 Fort George	6 The Prison.	11 Old Dutch Church	16 Quaker's Meeting
2 Trinity Church	7 New Brick Meeting	12 Jew's Synagogue	17 Calvinist Church
3 Presbyter. Meeting	8 King's College	13 Lutherian Church	18 Anabaptist Meeting
4 North D. Church	9 St. Paul's Church	14 The French Church	19 Moravian Meeting
5 St. George's Chapel	10 N.Dutch Cal.Church	15 New Scot's Meeting	20 N. Lutheran Church
			21 Methodist Meeting

Catholics, Jews, and even dissenting Protestants. On the very eve of independence, Baptists who refused to pay taxes to support local Congregational ministers were still being jailed in Massachusetts. "While our country are pleading so high for liberty," the victims complained, "yet they are denying of it to their neighbors."

Catholic Americans

The War of Independence weakened the deep tradition of American anti-Catholicism. When the Second Continental Congress decided on an ill-fated invasion of Canada, it invited the inhabitants of predominantly Catholic Quebec to join in the struggle against Britain, assuring them that Protestants and Catholics could readily cooperate. In 1778, the United States formed an alliance with France, a Catholic nation. The indispensable assistance provided by France to American victory strengthened the idea that Catholics had a role to play in the newly independent nation. In fact, this was a marked departure from the traditional notion that the full rights of Englishmen applied only to Protestants. When America's first Roman Catholic bishop, John Carroll of Maryland, visited Boston in 1791, he received a cordial welcome.

Anti-Catholicism weakened

In Side of the Old Lutheran Church in 1800, York, Pa. A watercolor by a local artist depicts the interior of one of the numerous churches that flourished after independence. While the choir sings, a man chases a dog out of the building and another man stokes the stove. The institutionalization of religious liberty was one of the most important results of the American Revolution.

Separating Church and State

Many of the leaders of the Revolution considered it essential for the new nation to shield itself from the unruly passions and violent conflicts that religious differences had inspired during the past three centuries. Men like Thomas Jefferson, John Adams, James Madison, and Alexander Hamilton viewed religious doctrines through the Enlightenment lens of rationalism and skepticism. They believed in a benevolent Creator but not in supernatural interventions into the affairs of men.

The drive to separate church and state brought together Deists like Jefferson, who hoped to erect a **"wall of separation"** that would free politics and the exercise of the intellect from religious control, with

members of evangelical sects, who sought to protect religion from the corrupting embrace of government.

Disestablishing churches

The movement toward religious freedom received a major impetus during the revolutionary era. Throughout the new nation, states disestablished their established churches—that is, deprived them of public funding and special legal privileges—although in some cases they appropriated money for the general support of Protestant denominations. The seven state constitutions that began with declarations of rights all declared a commitment to "the free exercise of religion."

To be sure, every state but New York—whose constitution of 1777 established complete religious liberty—kept intact colonial provisions barring Jews from voting and holding public office. Massachusetts retained its Congregationalist establishment well into the nineteenth century. It would not end public financial support for religious institutions until 1833. Throughout the country, however, Catholics gained the right to worship without persecution.

Limits of religious freedom

Jefferson and Religious Liberty

In Virginia, Thomas Jefferson drew up a **Bill for Establishing Religious Freedom**, which was introduced in the House of Burgesses in 1779 and adopted, after considerable controversy, in 1786. Jefferson's bill, whose preamble declared that God "hath created the mind free," eliminated religious requirements for voting and officeholding and government financial support for churches, and barred the state from "forcing" individuals to adopt one or another religious outlook. Late in life, Jefferson would list this measure, along with the Declaration of Independence and the founding of the University of Virginia, as the three accomplishments (leaving out his two terms as president) for which he wished to be remembered.

Definition of "rights"

Religious liberty became the model for the revolutionary generation's definition of "rights" as private matters that must be protected from governmental interference. In an overwhelmingly Christian (though not necessarily churchgoing) nation, the separation of church and state drew a sharp line between public authority and a realm defined as "private," reinforcing the idea that rights exist as restraints on the power of government. It also offered a new justification for the idea of the United States as a beacon of liberty. In successfully opposing a Virginia tax for the general support of Christian churches, James Madison insisted that one reason for the complete separation of church and state was to reinforce the principle that the new nation offered "asylum to the persecuted and oppressed of every nation and religion."

The Revolution did not end the influence of religion on American society—quite the reverse. Thanks to religious freedom, the early republic witnessed an amazing proliferation of religious denominations. The most well-established churches—Anglican, Presbyterian, and Congregationalist—found themselves constantly challenged by upstarts like Free-Will Baptists and Universalists. Today, even as debate continues over the proper relationship between spiritual and political authority, more than 1,300 religions are practiced in the United States.

Circle of the Social and Benevolent Affections, an engraving in *The Columbian Magazine,* 1789, illustrates various admirable qualities radiating outward from the virtuous citizen, including love for one's family, community, nation, and all humanity. Affection only for those of the same religion or "colour" is labeled "imperfect."

Christian Republicanism

Despite the separation of church and state, colonial leaders were not hostile to religion. Indeed, religious and secular language merged in the struggle for independence, producing an outlook scholars have called **Christian Republicanism**. Proponents of evangelical religion and of republican government both believed that in the absence of some kind of moral restraint (provided by religion and government), human nature was likely to succumb to corruption and vice. Samuel Adams, for example, believed the new nation would become a "Christian Sparta," in which Christianity and personal self-discipline underpinned both personal and national progress. American religious leaders interpreted the American Revolution as a divinely sanctioned event, part of God's plan to promote the development of a good society. Rather than being so sinful that it would have to be destroyed before Christ returned, as many ministers had previously preached, the world, the Revolution demonstrated, could be perfected.

A Virtuous Citizenry

Patriot leaders worried about the character of future citizens, especially how to encourage the quality of "virtue," the ability to sacrifice self-interest for the public good. Some, like Jefferson, John Adams, and Benjamin Rush, put forward plans for the establishment of free, state-supported public schools. These would instruct future citizens in what Adams called "the principles of freedom," equipping them for participation in the now-expanded public sphere and for the wise election of representatives. A broad diffusion of

Plans for public schools

knowledge was essential for a government based on the will of the people to survive and for America to avoid the fixed class structure of Europe. No nation, Jefferson wrote, could "expect to be ignorant and free."

DEFINING ECONOMIC FREEDOM

Toward Free Labor

In economic as well as political and religious affairs, the Revolution rewrote the definition of freedom. In colonial America, slavery was one part of a broad spectrum of kinds of unfree labor. In the generation after independence, with the rapid decline of indentured servitude and apprenticeship and the transformation of paid domestic service into an occupation for blacks and white females, the halfway houses between slavery and freedom disappeared, at least for white men.

Unfree labor

The democratization of freedom contributed to these changes. The lack of freedom inherent in apprenticeship and servitude increasingly came to be seen as incompatible with republican citizenship. In 1784, a group of "respectable" New Yorkers released a newly arrived shipload of indentured servants on the grounds that their status was "contrary to . . . the idea of liberty this country has so happily established." By 1800, indentured servitude had all but disappeared from the United States. This development sharpened the distinction between freedom and slavery and between a northern economy relying on what would come to be called "**free labor**" (that is, working for wages or owning a farm or shop) and a southern economy ever more heavily dependent on the labor of slaves.

Decline in indentured servitude

The Soul of a Republic

Americans of the revolutionary generation were preoccupied with the social conditions of freedom. Could a republic survive with a sizable dependent class of citizens? "A general and tolerably equal distribution of landed property," proclaimed the educator and newspaper editor Noah Webster, "is the whole basis of national freedom." "Equality," he added, was "the very soul of a republic." At the Revolution's radical edge, some patriots believed that government had a responsibility to limit accumulations of property in the name of equality. To most free Americans, however, "equality" meant equal opportunity, rather than equality of

Equal opportunity rather than equality of condition

View from Bushongo Tavern, an engraving from *The Columbian Magazine*, 1788, depicts the landscape of York County, Pennsylvania, exemplifying the kind of rural independence many Americans thought essential to freedom.

condition. Many leaders of the Revolution nevertheless assumed that in the exceptional circumstances of the New World, with its vast areas of available land and large population of independent farmers and artisans, the natural workings of society would produce justice, liberty, and equality.

Like many other Americans of his generation, Thomas Jefferson believed that to lack economic resources was to lack freedom. Among his achievements included laws passed by Virginia abolishing entail (the limitation of inheritance to a specified line of heirs to keep an estate within a family) and primogeniture (the practice of passing a family's land entirely to the eldest son). These measures, he believed, would help to prevent the rise of a "future aristocracy."

Abolishing entail and primogeniture

The Politics of Inflation

The Revolution thrust to the forefront of politics debates over whether local or national authorities should take steps to bolster household independence and protect Americans' livelihoods by limiting price increases. To finance the war, Congress issued hundreds of millions of dollars in paper money. Coupled with wartime disruption of agriculture and trade and the hoarding of goods by some Americans hoping to profit from shortages, this produced an enormous increase in prices.

Between 1776 and 1779, more than thirty incidents took place in which crowds confronted merchants accused of holding scarce goods off the market. Often, they seized stocks of food and sold them at the traditional "just price," a form of protest common in eighteenth-century England. In one such incident, a crowd of 100 Massachusetts women accused an "eminent, wealthy, stingy merchant" of hoarding coffee, opened his warehouse, and

Responses to wartime inflation

A cartoon from 1777 illustrates discontent with rising prices. One soldier identifies "extortioners" as "the worst enemies of the country." Another complains about serving "my country for sixteen pence per day."

carted off the goods. "A large concourse of men," wrote Abigail Adams, "stood amazed, silent spectators of the whole transaction."

The Debate over Free Trade

In 1779, with inflation totally out of control (in one month, prices in Philadelphia jumped 45 percent), Congress urged states to adopt measures to fix wages and prices. This request reflected the belief that the task of republican government was to promote the public good, not individuals' self-interest. But when a Committee of Safety tried to enforce price controls, it met spirited opposition from merchants and other advocates of a free market.

In opposition to the traditional view that men should sacrifice for the public good, believers in **free trade** argued that economic development arose from economic self-interest. Adam Smith's great treatise on economics, *The Wealth of Nations*, published in England in 1776, was beginning to become known in the United States. Smith's argument that the "invisible hand" of the free market directed economic life more effectively and fairly than governmental intervention offered intellectual justification for those who believed that the economy should be left to regulate itself.

Advocates of independence had envisioned America, released from the British Navigation Acts, trading freely with all the world. Opponents of price controls advocated free trade at home as well. "Natural liberty" would regulate prices. Here were two competing conceptions of economic freedom—one based on the traditional view that the interests of the community took precedence over the property rights of individuals, the other that unregulated economic freedom would produce social harmony and public gain. After 1779, state and federal efforts to regulate prices ceased. But the clash between these two visions of economic freedom would continue long after independence had been achieved.

Two visions of economic freedom

THE LIMITS OF LIBERTY

Colonial Loyalists

Not all Americans shared in the democratization of freedom brought on by the American Revolution. **Loyalists**—those who retained their allegiance to the crown—experienced the conflict and its aftermath as a loss of liberty. Many leading Loyalists had supported American resistance in the 1760s but drew back at the prospect of independence and war. Altogether, an estimated 20 to 25 percent of free Americans remained loyal to the British, and nearly 20,000 fought on their side.

A sizable Loyalist population

There were Loyalists in every colony, but they were most numerous in New York, Pennsylvania, and the backcountry of the Carolinas and Georgia. Some were wealthy men whose livelihoods depended on close working relationships with Britain—lawyers, merchants, Anglican ministers, and imperial officials. Many feared anarchy in the event of an American victory.

The struggle for independence heightened existing tensions between ethnic groups and social classes within the colonies. Some Loyalist ethnic minorities, like Highland Scots in North Carolina, feared that local majorities would infringe on their cultural autonomy. In the South, many backcountry farmers who had long resented the domination of public affairs by wealthy planters sided with the British, as did numerous slaves, who hoped an American defeat would bring them freedom.

Social bases of loyalism

The Loyalists' Plight

The War of Independence was in some respects a civil war among Americans. The new state governments, or in other instances crowds of patriots, suppressed newspapers thought to be loyal to Britain. Pennsylvania arrested and seized the property of Quakers, Mennonites, and Moravians—pacifist denominations who refused to bear arms because of their religious beliefs. With the approval of Congress, many states required residents to take oaths of allegiance to the new nation. Those who refused were denied the right to vote and in many cases forced into exile. Some wealthy Loyalists saw their land confiscated and sold at auction.

When the war ended, as many as 60,000 Loyalists (including 10,000 slaves) were banished from the United States or emigrated voluntarily—mostly to Britain, Canada, or the West Indies—rather than live in an independent United States. But for those who remained, hostility proved to be short-lived. In the Treaty of Paris of 1783, as noted in Chapter 5, Americans pledged to end the persecution of Loyalists by state and local governments and to restore property seized during the war. Loyalists who did not leave the country were quickly reintegrated

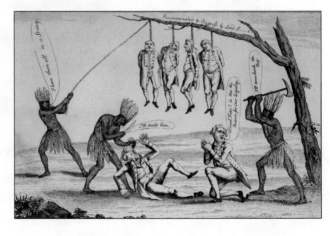

A 1780 British cartoon commenting on the "cruel fate" of American Loyalists. Pro-independence colonists are likened to savage Indians.

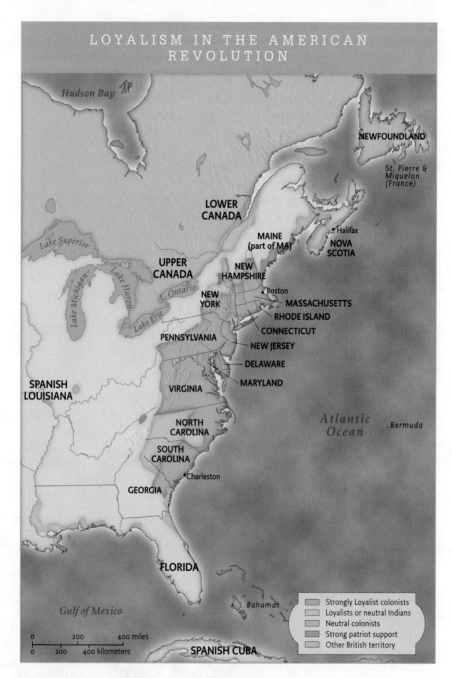

LOYALISM IN THE AMERICAN REVOLUTION

Legend:
- Strongly Loyalist colonists
- Loyalists or neutral Indians
- Neutral colonists
- Strong patriot support
- Other British territory

The Revolutionary War was, in some ways, a civil war within the colonies. There were Loyalists in every colony; they were most numerous in New York and North and South Carolina.

into American society, although confiscated Loyalist property was not returned.

The Indians' Revolution

Another group for whom American independence spelled a loss of freedom—the Indians—was less fortunate. About 200,000 Native Americans lived east of the Mississippi River in 1790. Like white Americans, Indians divided in allegiance during the War of Independence. Some, like the Stockbridge tribe in Massachusetts, suffered heavy losses fighting the British. Many tribes tried to maintain neutrality, only to see themselves break into pro-American and pro-British factions. Most of the Iroquois nations sided with the British, but the Oneida joined the Americans. Despite strenuous efforts to avoid conflict, members of the Iroquois Confederacy for the first time faced each other in battle. (After the war, the Oneida submitted to Congress claims for losses suffered during the war, including sheep, hogs, kettles, frying pans, plows, and pewter plates—evidence of how fully they had been integrated into the market economy.) In the South, younger Cherokee leaders joined the British while older chiefs tended to favor the Americans. Other southern tribes like the Choctaw and Creek remained loyal to the crown.

Indians' allegiances during the War of Independence

Among the grievances Jefferson listed in the Declaration of Independence was Britain's enlisting "savages" to fight on its side. But in the war that raged throughout the western frontier, savagery was not confined to either combatant. In the Ohio country, the British encouraged Indian allies to burn frontier farms and settlements. For their part, otherwise humane patriot leaders ignored the traditional rules of warfare when it came to Indians. Washington dispatched an expedition, led by **General John Sullivan**, against hostile Iroquois, with the aim of "the total destruction and devastation of their settlements and the capture of as many prisoners of every age and sex as possible." After his campaign ended, Sullivan reported that he had burned forty Indian towns, destroyed thousands of bushels of corn, and uprooted a vast number of fruit trees and vegetable gardens.

Savage warfare

Independence created governments democratically accountable to voters who coveted Indian land. But liberty for whites meant loss of liberty for Indians. Independence offered the opportunity to complete the process of dispossessing Indians of their rich lands in upstate New York, the Ohio Valley, and the southern backcountry. The only hope for the Indians, Jefferson wrote, lay in their "removal beyond the Mississippi."

Dispossession of Indian lands

American independence, a group of visiting Indians told the Spanish governor of St. Louis, was "the greatest blow that could have been dealt

The Treaty of Paris and Indian peoples

us." The Treaty of Paris marked the culmination of a century in which the balance of power in eastern North America shifted away from the Indians and toward white Americans. In the treaty, the British abandoned their Indian allies, agreeing to recognize American sovereignty over the entire region east of the Mississippi River, completely ignoring the Indian presence. In the end there seemed to be no permanent place for the descendants of the continent's native population in a new nation bent on creating an empire in the West.

SLAVERY AND THE REVOLUTION

Although Indians experienced American independence as a real threat to their own liberty, African-Americans saw in the ideals of the Revolution and the reality of war an opportunity to claim freedom. When the United States declared its independence in 1776, the slave population had grown to 500,000, about one-fifth of the new nation's inhabitants.

The Language of Slavery and Freedom

Slavery played a central part in the language of revolution. Apart from "liberty," it was the word most frequently invoked in the era's legal and political literature. In the era's debates over British rule, slavery was primarily a political category, shorthand for the denial of one's personal and political rights by arbitrary government. Those who lacked a voice in public affairs, declared a 1769 petition demanding an expansion of the right to vote in Britain, were "enslaved."

Advertisement for newly arrived slaves, in a Savannah newspaper, 1774. Even as colonists defended their own liberty against the British, the buying and selling of slaves continued.

The presence of hundreds of thousands of slaves powerfully affected the meaning of freedom for the leaders of the American Revolution. In a famous speech to Parliament warning against attempts to intimidate the colonies, the British statesman Edmund Burke suggested that familiarity with slavery made colonial leaders unusually sensitive to threats to their own liberties. Where freedom was a privilege, not a common right, he observed, "those who are free are by far the most proud and jealous of their freedom." On the other hand, many British observers

could not resist pointing out the colonists' apparent hypocrisy. "How is it," asked Dr. Samuel Johnson, "that we hear the loudest yelps for liberty from the drivers of negroes?"

Obstacles to Abolition

The contradiction between freedom and slavery seems so self-evident that it is difficult today to appreciate the power of the obstacles to **abolition**. At the time of the Revolution, slavery was already an old institution in America. It existed in every colony and formed the basis of the economy and social structure from Maryland southward. Virtually every founding father owned slaves at one point in his life, including not only southern planters but northern merchants, lawyers, and farmers. (John Adams and Tom Paine were notable exceptions.) Thomas Jefferson owned more than 100 slaves when he wrote of mankind's unalienable right to liberty, and everything he cherished in his own manner of life, from lavish entertainments to the leisure that made possible the pursuit of arts and sciences, ultimately rested on slave labor.

Slavery entrenched

Some patriots, in fact, argued that slavery for blacks made freedom possible for whites. Eliminating the great bulk of the dependent poor from the political nation left the public arena to men of propertied independence. Owning slaves offered a route to the economic autonomy widely deemed necessary for genuine freedom, a point driven home by a 1780 Virginia law that rewarded veterans of the War of Independence with 300 acres of land—and a slave.

Slavery amidst freedom

The Cause of General Liberty

Nonetheless, by imparting so absolute a value to liberty and defining freedom as a universal entitlement rather than a set of rights specific to a particular place or people, the Revolution inevitably raised questions about the status of slavery in the new nation. Before independence, there had been little public discussion of the institution, even though enlightened opinion in the Atlantic world had come to view slavery as morally wrong and economically inefficient, a relic of a barbarous past.

Freedom as universal

Samuel Sewall, a Boston merchant, published *The Selling of Joseph* in 1700, the first antislavery tract printed in America. All "the sons of Adam," Sewall insisted, were entitled to "have equal right unto liberty." During the course of the eighteenth century, antislavery sentiments had spread among Pennsylvania's Quakers, whose belief that all persons possessed the divine "inner light" made them particularly receptive.

But it was during the revolutionary era that slavery for the first time became a focus of public debate. The Pennsylvania patriot Benjamin Rush in 1773 called on "advocates for American liberty" to "espouse the cause of . . . general liberty" and warned that slavery was one of those "national crimes" that one day would bring "national punishment."

Petitions for Freedom

The Revolution inspired widespread hopes that slavery could be removed from American life. Most dramatically, slaves themselves appreciated that by defining freedom as a universal right, the leaders of the Revolution had devised a weapon that could be used against their own bondage. The language of liberty echoed in slave communities, North and South. The most insistent advocates of freedom as a universal entitlement were African-Americans, who demanded that the leaders of the struggle for independence live up to their self-proclaimed creed.

African-Americans advocates for freedom

  The first concrete steps toward emancipation in revolutionary America were "**freedom petitions**"—arguments for liberty presented to New England's courts and legislatures in the early 1770s by enslaved African-Americans. How, one such petition asked, could America "seek release from English tyranny and not seek the same for disadvantaged Africans in her midst?" The turmoil of war offered other avenues to freedom. Many slaves ran away from their masters and tried to pass as free-born. The number of fugitive-slave advertisements in colonial newspapers rose dramatically in the 1770s and 1780s. As one owner put it in accounting for his slave Jim's escape, "I believe he has nothing in view but freedom."

A tray painted by an unknown artist in the early nineteenth century portrays Lemuel Haynes, a celebrated black preacher and critic of slavery.

  In 1776, the year of American independence, **Lemuel Haynes**, a black member of the Massachusetts militia and later a celebrated minister, urged Americans to "extend" their conception of freedom. If liberty were truly "an innate principle" for all mankind, Haynes insisted, "even an African [had] as equally good a right to his liberty in common with Englishmen." Like Haynes, many black writers and leaders sought to make white Americans understand slavery as a concrete reality—the denial of all the essential elements of freedom—not a metaphor for lack of political representation, as many whites used the word.

Most slaves of the revolutionary era were only one or two generations removed from Africa. They did not need the ideology of the Revolution to persuade them that freedom was a birthright—the experience of their parents and grandparents suggested as much. "My love of freedom," wrote the black poet Phillis Wheatley in 1783, arose from the "cruel fate" of being "snatch'd from Afric's" shore. Yet when blacks invoked the Revolution's ideology of liberty to demand their own rights and defined freedom as a universal entitlement, they demonstrated how American they had become.

A portrait of the poet Phillis Wheatley (1753–1784).

British Emancipators

As noted in the previous chapter, some 5,000 slaves fought for American independence, and many thereby gained their freedom. Yet far more slaves obtained liberty from the British. Lord Dunmore's proclamation of 1775, and the Phillipsburgh Proclamation of General Henry Clinton issued four years later, offered sanctuary to slaves who escaped to British lines. All told, nearly 100,000 slaves, including one-quarter of all the slaves in South Carolina and one-third of those in Georgia, deserted their owners and fled to British lines. This was by far the largest exodus from the plantations until the outbreak of the Civil War.

Some of these escaped slaves were recaptured as the tide of battle turned in the patriots' favor. But at the war's end, more than 15,000 black men, women, and children accompanied the British out of the country. They ended up in Nova Scotia, England, and Sierra Leone, a settlement for former slaves from the United States established by the British on the coast of West Africa. Some were re-enslaved in the West Indies.

Freedom through the British

The issue of compensation for the slaves who departed with the British poisoned relations between Britain and the new United States for decades to come. Finally, in 1827, Britain agreed to make payments to 1,100 Americans who claimed they had been improperly deprived of their slave property.

Voluntary Emancipations

For a brief moment, the revolutionary upheaval appeared to threaten the continued existence of slavery. During the War of Independence, nearly every state prohibited or discouraged the further importation of slaves from Africa. The war left much of the plantation South in ruins. During the 1780s and 1790s, a considerable number of slaveholders, especially in Virginia and Maryland, voluntarily emancipated their slaves. In 1796, for example, Richard Randolph, a member of a prominent Virginia family, drafted a will

Voluntary emancipations in the South

VOICES OF FREEDOM

From Abigail Adams to John Adams, Braintree, Mass. (March 31, 1776)

From their home in Massachusetts, Abigail Adams maintained a lively correspondence with her husband while he was in Philadelphia serving in the Continental Congress. In this letter, she suggests some of the limits of the patriots' commitment to liberty.

I wish you would write me a letter half as long as I write you, and tell me if you may where your fleet have gone? What sort of defense Virginia can make against our common enemy? Whether it is so situated as to make an able defense? . . . I have sometimes been ready to think that the passion for Liberty cannot be equally strong in the breasts of those who have been accustomed to deprive their fellow creatures of theirs. Of this I am certain, that it is not founded upon that generous and Christian principle of doing to others as we would that others should do unto us. . . .

I long to hear that you have declared an independency, and by the way in the new Code of Laws which I suppose it will be necessary for you to make I desire you would Remember the Ladies, and be more generous and favorable to them than your ancestors. Do not put such unlimited power into the hands of the husbands. Remember all men would be tyrants if they could. If particular care and attention is not paid to the Ladies we are determined to foment a Rebellion, and will not hold ourselves bound by any such laws in which we have no voice, or representation.

That your sex are naturally tyrannical is a truth so thoroughly established as to admit of no dispute, but such of you as wish to be happy willingly give up the harsh title of Master for the more tender and endearing one of Friend. Why then, not put it out of the power of the vicious and the lawless to use us with cruelty and indignity with impunity? Men of sense in all ages abhor those customs which treat us only as the vassals of your sex. Regard us then as beings placed by providence under your protection and in imitation of the Supreme Being make use of that power only for our happiness.

From Petitions of Slaves to the Massachusetts Legislature (1773 and 1777)

Many slaves saw the struggle for independence as an opportunity to assert their own claims to freedom. Among the first efforts toward abolition were petitions by Massachusetts slaves to their legislature.

The efforts made by the legislative of this province in their last sessions to free themselves from slavery, gave us, who are in that deplorable state, a high degree of satisfaction. We expect great things from men who have made such a noble stand against the designs of their *fellow-men* to enslave them. We cannot but wish and hope Sir, that you will have the same grand object, we mean civil and religious liberty, in view in your next session. The divine spirit of *freedom*, seems to fire every breast on this continent. . . .

* * *

Your petitioners apprehend that they have in common with all other men a natural and unalienable right to that freedom which the great parent of the universe hath bestowed equally on all mankind and which they have never forfeited by any compact or agreement whatever but [they] were unjustly dragged by the hand of cruel power from their dearest friends and . . . from a populous, pleasant, and plentiful country and in violation of laws of nature and of nations and in defiance of all the tender feelings of humanity brought here . . . to be sold like beast[s] of burden . . . among a people professing the mild religion of Jesus. . . .

In imitation of the laudable example of the good people of these states your petitioners have long and patiently waited the event of petition after petition by them presented to the legislative body. . . . They cannot but express their astonishment that it has never been considered that every principle from which America has acted in the course of their unhappy difficulties with Great Britain pleads stronger than a thousand arguments in favor of your petitioners [and their desire] to be restored to the enjoyment of that which is the natural right of all men.

QUESTIONS

1. *What does Abigail Adams have in mind when she refers to the "unlimited power" husbands exercise over their wives?*

2. *How do the slaves employ the principles of the Revolution for their own aims?*

3. *What do these documents suggest about the boundaries of freedom in the era of the American Revolution?*

that condemned slavery as an "infamous practice," provided for the freedom of about 90 slaves, and set aside part of his land for them to own. Farther south, however, voluntary emancipation never got under way. Even during the war, when South Carolina needed more troops, the colony's leaders rejected the idea of emancipating some blacks to aid in the fight against the British. They would rather lose the war than lose their slaves.

Abolition in the North

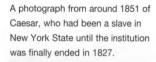

Legislation against slavery

Between 1777 (when Vermont drew up a constitution that banned slavery) and 1804 (when New Jersey acted), every state north of Maryland took steps toward emancipation, the first time in recorded history that legislative power had been invoked to eradicate slavery. But even here, where slavery was peripheral to the economy, the method of abolition reflected how property rights impeded emancipation. Generally, abolition laws did not free living slaves. Instead, they provided for the liberty of any child born in the future to a slave mother, but only after he or she had served the mother's master until adulthood as compensation for the owner's future economic loss.

Because of these legal provisions, abolition in the North was a slow, drawn-out process. The first national census, in 1790, recorded 21,000 slaves still living in New York and 11,000 in New Jersey. The New Yorker John Jay, chief justice of the United States, owned five slaves in 1800. As late as 1830, the census revealed that there were still 3,500 slaves in the North.

A photograph from around 1851 of Caesar, who had been a slave in New York State until the institution was finally ended in 1827.

Free Black Communities

All in all, the Revolution had a contradictory impact on American slavery and, therefore, on American freedom. Gradual as it was, the abolition of slavery in the North drew a line across the new nation, creating the dangerous division between free and slave states. Abolition in the North, voluntary emancipation in the Upper South, and the escape of thousands from bondage created, for the first time in American history, a sizable population of **free blacks** (many of whose members took new family names like Freeman or Freeland).

On the eve of independence, virtually every black person in America had been a slave. Now, free communities, with their own churches, schools, and leaders, came into existence. They formed a standing challenge to the logic of slavery, a haven for fugitives, and a springboard for further efforts at abolition. From 1776 to 1810, the number of free blacks residing in the United States grew from 10,000 to nearly 200,000, and many free black men, especially in the North, enjoyed the right to vote under new state constitutions.

Nonetheless, the stark fact is that slavery survived the War of Independence and, thanks to the natural increase of the slave population, continued to grow. The national census of 1790 revealed that despite all those who had become free through state laws, voluntary emancipation, and escape, the number of slaves in the United States had grown to 700,000— 200,000 more than in 1776.

Growth in slave population

DAUGHTERS OF LIBERTY

Revolutionary Women

The revolutionary generation included numerous women who contributed to the struggle for independence. Deborah Sampson, the daughter of a poor Massachusetts farmer, disguised herself as a man and in 1782, at age twenty-one, enlisted in the Continental army. Ultimately, her commanding officer discovered her secret but kept it to himself, and she was honorably discharged at the end of the war. Years later, Congress awarded her a soldier's pension. Other patriotic women participated in crowd actions against unscrupulous merchants, raised funds to assist soldiers, contributed homespun goods to the army, and passed along information about British army movements.

Within American households, women participated in the political discussions unleashed by independence. "Was not every fireside," John Adams later recalled, "a theater of politics?" Gender, nonetheless, formed a boundary limiting those entitled to the full blessings of American freedom. The principle of "**coverture**" (described in Chapter 1) remained intact in the new nation. The husband still held legal authority over the person, property, and choices of his wife. Despite the expansion of democracy, politics remained overwhelmingly a male realm.

For men, political freedom meant the right to self-government, the power to consent to the individuals and political arrangements that ruled over them. For

The 1781 cipher book (a notebook for mathematics exercises) of Martha Ryan, a North Carolina girl, contains images of ships and a port town and the patriotic slogan "Liberty or Death," illustrating how women shared in the political culture of the revolutionary era.

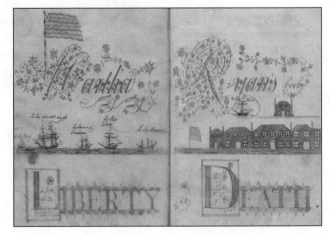

Portrait of John and Elizabeth Lloyd Cadwalader and Their Daughter Anne. This 1772 portrait of a prominent Philadelphia businessman and his family by the American artist Charles Willson Peale illustrates the emerging ideal of the "companionate" marriage, which is based on affection rather than male authority.

women, however, the marriage contract superseded the social contract. A woman's relationship to the larger society was mediated through her relationship with her husband. In both law and social reality, women lacked the essential qualification of political participation—the opportunity for autonomy based on ownership of property or control of one's own person. Overall, the republican citizen was, by definition, male.

Republican Motherhood

The Revolution nonetheless did produce an improvement in status for many women. According to the ideology of "**republican motherhood**" that emerged as a result of independence, women played an indispensable role by training future citizens. Even though republican motherhood ruled out direct female involvement in politics, it encouraged the expansion of educational opportunities for women, so that they could impart political wisdom to their children. Women, wrote Benjamin Rush, needed to have a "suitable education," to enable them to "instruct their sons in the principles of liberty and government."

The idea of republican motherhood reinforced the trend, already evident in the eighteenth century, toward the idea of "companionate" marriage, a voluntary union held together by affection and mutual dependency rather than male authority. In her letter to John Adams quoted above, Abigail Adams recommended that men should willingly give up "the harsh title of Master for the more tender and endearing one of Friend."

A more modern household

The structure of family life itself was altered by the Revolution. In colonial America, those living within the household often included indentured servants, apprentices, and slaves. After independence, southern slaves remained, rhetorically at least, members of the owner's "family." In the North, however, with the rapid decline of various forms of indentured servitude and apprenticeship, a more modern definition of the household as consisting of parents and their children took hold. Hired workers, whether domestic servants or farm laborers, were not considered part of the family.

The Arduous Struggle for Liberty

Significance of the Revolution

The Revolution changed the life of virtually every American. As a result of the long struggle against British rule, the public sphere, and with it the right to vote, expanded markedly. Bound labor among whites declined dramatically, religious groups enjoyed greater liberty, blacks mounted a challenge to slavery in which many won their freedom, and women in

America Triumphant and Britannia in Distress. An elaborate allegory representing American independence as a triumph of liberty, from an almanac published in Boston in 1781. An accompanying key explains the symbolism: (1) America [on the right] holds an olive branch of peace and invites all nations to trade with her. (2) News of America's triumph is broadcast around the world. (3) Britain, seated next to the devil, laments the loss of trade with America. (4) The British flag falls from a fortress. (5) European ships in American waters. (6) Benedict Arnold, the traitor, hangs himself in New York City [in fact, Arnold died of natural causes in London in 1801].

some ways enjoyed a higher status. On the other hand, for Indians, many Loyalists, and the majority of slaves, American independence meant a deprivation of freedom.

The winds of change were sweeping across the Atlantic world. The year 1776 saw not only Paine's *Common Sense* and Jefferson's Declaration but also the publication in England of Adam Smith's *Wealth of Nations*, which attacked the British policy of closely regulating trade, and Jeremy Bentham's *Fragment on Government*, which criticized the nature of British government. Moreover, the ideals of the American Revolution helped to inspire countless subsequent struggles for social equality and national independence, from the French Revolution, which exploded in 1789, to the uprising that overthrew the slave system in Haiti in the 1790s, to the Latin American wars for independence in the early nineteenth century, and numerous struggles of colonial peoples for nationhood in the twentieth. But within the new republic, the debate over who should enjoy the blessings of liberty would continue long after independence had been achieved.

The Revolution's legacy

CHAPTER REVIEW AND ONLINE RESOURCES

REVIEW QUESTIONS

1. *For the lower classes, colonial society had been based on inequality, deference, and obedience. How did the American Revolution challenge that social order?*

2. *Why did the Revolution cause more radical changes in Pennsylvania than elsewhere, and how was this radicalism demonstrated in the new state constitution?*

3. *How did ideas of political freedom affect people's ideas about economic rights and relationships?*

4. *What role did the founders foresee for religion in American government and society?*

5. *What was the impact of the American Revolution on Native Americans?*

6. *What were the most important features of the new state constitutions?*

7. *How did popular views of property rights prevent slaves from enjoying all the freedoms of the social contract?*

8. *How did revolutionary America see both improvements and limitations in women's roles and rights?*

KEY TERMS

republics (p. 171)
Thoughts on Government (p. 171)
balanced government (p. 171)
suffrage (p. 171)
wall of separation (p. 173)
Bill for Establishing Religious Freedom (p. 174)
Christian Republicanism (p. 175)
free labor (p. 176)
inflation (p. 177)
free trade (p. 178)
The Wealth of Nations (p. 178)
Loyalists (p. 178)
General John Sullivan (p. 181)
abolition (p. 183)
freedom petitions (p. 184)
Lemuel Haynes (p. 184)
free blacks (p. 188)
coverture (p. 189)
republican motherhood (p. 190)

wwnorton.com
/studyspace

VISIT STUDYSPACE FOR THESE
RESOURCES AND MORE
- A chapter outline
- A diagnostic chapter quiz
- Interactive maps
- Map worksheets
- Multimedia documents

CHAPTER 7

FOUNDING A NATION

★

1783–1791

Banner of the Society of Pewterers.
A banner carried by one of the many artisan groups that took part in New York City's Grand Federal Procession of 1788 celebrating the ratification of the Constitution. The banner depicts artisans at work in their shop and some of their products. The words "Solid and Pure," and the inscription at the upper right, link the quality of their pewter to their opinion of the new frame of government and hopes for the future. The inscription reads:

The Federal Plan Most Solid and Secure
Americans Their Freedom Will Endure
All Arts Shall Flourish in Columbia's Land
And All Her Sons Join as One Social Band

FOCUS
QUESTIONS

- *What were the achievements and problems of the Confederation government?*

- *What major compromises molded the final content of the Constitution?*

- *How did Anti-Federalist concerns raised during the ratification process lead to the creation of the Bill of Rights?*

- *How did the definition of citizenship in the new republic exclude Native Americans and African-Americans?*

During June and July of 1788, civic leaders in cities up and down the Atlantic coast organized colorful pageants to celebrate the ratification of the U.S. Constitution. For one day, Benjamin Rush commented of Philadelphia's parade, social class "forgot its claims," as thousands of marchers—rich and poor, businessman and apprentice—joined in a common public ceremony. The parades testified to the strong popular support for the Constitution in the nation's cities. Elaborate banners and floats gave voice to the hopes inspired by the new structure of government. "May commerce flourish and industry be rewarded," declared Philadelphia's mariners and shipbuilders.

Throughout the era of the Revolution, Americans spoke of their nation as a "rising empire," destined to populate and control the entire North American continent. Whereas Europe's empires were governed by force, America's would be different. In Jefferson's phrase, it would be "an empire of liberty," bound together by a common devotion to the principles of the Declaration of Independence. Already, the United States exceeded in size Great Britain, Spain, and France combined. As a new nation, it possessed many advantages, including physical isolation from the Old World (a significant asset between 1789 and 1815, when European powers were almost constantly at war), a youthful population certain to grow much larger, and a broad distribution of property ownership and literacy among white citizens.

On the other hand, the nation's prospects at the time of independence were not entirely promising. Control of its vast territory was by no means secure. Nearly all of the 3.9 million Americans recorded in the first national census of 1790 lived near the Atlantic coast. Large areas west of the Appalachian Mountains remained in Indian hands. The British retained military posts on American territory near the Great Lakes, and there were fears that Spain might close the port of New Orleans to American commerce on the Mississippi River.

Away from navigable waterways, communication and transportation were primitive. The country was overwhelmingly rural—fewer than one American in thirty lived in a place with 8,000 inhabitants or more. The population consisted of numerous ethnic and religious groups and some 700,000 slaves, making unity difficult to achieve. No republican government had ever been established over so vast a territory or with so diverse a population. "We have no Americans in America," commented John Adams. It would take time for consciousness of a common nationality to sink deep roots.

Profound questions needed to be answered. What course of development should the United States follow? How could the competing claims of local self-government, sectional interests, and national authority be balanced? Who should be considered full-fledged members of the American people, entitled to the blessings of liberty? These issues became the focus of heated debate as the first generation of Americans sought to consolidate their new republic.

AMERICA UNDER THE CONFEDERATION

The Articles of Confederation

The first written constitution of the United States was the Articles of Confederation, drafted by Congress in 1777 and ratified by the states four years later. The Articles sought to balance the need for national coordination of the War of Independence with widespread fear that centralized political power posed a danger to liberty. It explicitly declared the new national government to be a "perpetual union." But it resembled less a blueprint for a common government than a treaty for mutual defense— in its own words, a "firm league of friendship" among the states. Under the Articles, the thirteen states retained their individual "sovereignty, freedom, and independence." The national government consisted of a one-house Congress, in which each state, no matter how large or populous, cast a single vote. There was no president to enforce the laws and no judiciary to interpret them. Major decisions required the approval of nine states rather than a simple majority.

Limitations of the Articles

The only powers specifically granted to the national government by the Articles of Confederation were those essential to the struggle for independence—declaring war, conducting foreign affairs, and making treaties with other governments. Congress had no real financial resources. It could coin money but lacked the power to levy taxes or regulate commerce. Its revenue came mainly from contributions by the individual states. To amend the Articles required the unanimous consent of the states, a formidable obstacle to change.

But Congress in the 1780s did not lack for accomplishments. The most important was establishing national control over land to the west of the thirteen states and devising rules for its settlement. Citing their original royal charters, which granted territory running all the way to the "South Sea" (the Pacific Ocean), states such as Virginia, the Carolinas, and Connecticut claimed immense tracts of western land. Land speculators, politicians, and prospective settlers from states with clearly

Accomplishments under the Articles

defined boundaries insisted that such land must belong to the nation at large. Only after the land-rich states, in the interest of national unity, ceded their western claims to the central government did the Articles win ratification.

Congress, Settlers, and the West

Establishing rules for the settlement of this national domain—the area controlled by the federal government, stretching from the western boundaries of existing states to the Mississippi River—was critical. Although some Americans spoke of it as if it were empty, some 100,000 Indians inhabited the region. Congress took the position that by aiding the British, Indians had forfeited the right to their lands. But little distinction was made among tribes that had sided with the enemy, aided the patriots, or played no part in the war at all. At peace conferences at Fort Stanwix, New York, in 1784 and Fort McIntosh near Pittsburgh the following year, American representatives demanded and received large surrenders of Indian land north of the Ohio River. Similar treaties soon followed with

Treaties to secure Indian land

the Cherokee, Choctaw, and Chickasaw tribes in the South. The treaties secured national control of a large part of the country's western territory.

When it came to disposing of western land and regulating its settlement, the Confederation government faced conflicting pressures. Many leaders believed that the economic health of the new republic required that farmers have access to land in the West. But they also saw land sales as a potential source of revenue.

The arrival of peace meanwhile triggered a large population move-

Rapid settlement in frontier areas

ment from settled parts of the original states into frontier areas like upstate New York and across the Appalachian Mountains into Kentucky and Tennessee. To settlers, the right to take possession of western lands and use them as they saw fit was an essential element of American freedom. When a group of Ohioans petitioned Congress in 1785, assailing landlords and speculators who monopolized available acreage and asking that preference in land ownership be given to "actual settlements," their motto was "Grant us Liberty."

At the same time, however, like British colonial officials before them,

Frontier fears

many leaders of the new nation feared that an unregulated flow of population across the Appalachian Mountains would provoke constant warfare with Indians. Moreover, they viewed frontier settlers as disorderly and lacking in proper respect for authority.

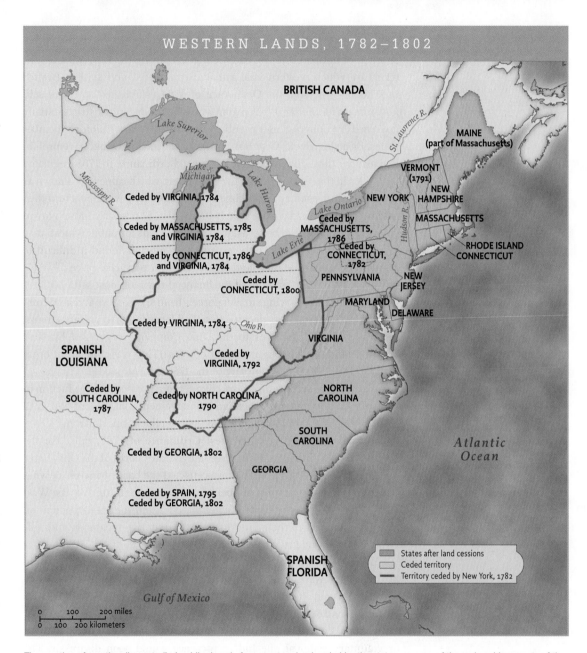

WESTERN LANDS, 1782–1802

BRITISH CANADA

Lake Superior

Lake Michigan

Lake Huron

Mississippi R.

St. Lawrence R.

MAINE
(part of Massachusetts)

VERMONT
(1791)

NEW
HAMPSHIRE

Ceded by VIRGINIA, 1784

Lake Ontario

NEW YORK

Ceded by
MASSACHUSETTS,
1786

MASSACHUSETTS

Ceded by MASSACHUSETTS, 1785
and VIRGINIA, 1784

Hudson R.

RHODE ISLAND
CONNECTICUT

Ceded by CONNECTICUT, 1786
and VIRGINIA, 1784

Lake Erie

Ceded by
CONNECTICUT,
1782

Ceded by
CONNECTICUT, 1800

PENNSYLVANIA

NEW
JERSEY

MARYLAND

DELAWARE

Ceded by VIRGINIA, 1784

Ohio R.

VIRGINIA

SPANISH
LOUISIANA

Ceded by
VIRGINIA, 1792

Ceded by
SOUTH CAROLINA,
1787

Ceded by NORTH CAROLINA,
1790

NORTH
CAROLINA

Ceded by GEORGIA, 1802

SOUTH
CAROLINA

*Atlantic
Ocean*

GEORGIA

Ceded by SPAIN, 1795
Ceded by GEORGIA, 1802

SPANISH
FLORIDA

States after land cessions
Ceded territory
Territory ceded by New York, 1782

Gulf of Mexico

0   100   200 miles
0   100   200 kilometers

The creation of a nationally controlled public domain from western land ceded by the states was one of the main achievements of the federal government under the Articles of Confederation.

The Land Ordinances

Western settlement and self-government

A series of measures approved by Congress during the 1780s defined the terms by which western land would be marketed and settled. Drafted by Thomas Jefferson, the **Ordinance of 1784** established stages of self-government for the West. The region would be divided into districts initially governed by Congress and eventually admitted to the Union as member states. By a single vote, Congress rejected a clause that would have prohibited slavery throughout the West. A second ordinance, in 1785, regulated land sales in the region north of the Ohio River, which came to be known as the Old Northwest. Land would be surveyed by the government and then sold in "sections" of a square mile (640 acres) at $1 per acre. In each township, one section would be set aside to provide funds for public education.

Price of land

Like the British before them, American officials found it difficult to regulate the thirst for new land. The minimum purchase price of $640, however, put public land out of the financial reach of most settlers. They generally ended up buying smaller parcels from speculators and land companies. In 1787, Congress decided to sell off large tracts to private groups, including 1.5 million acres to the Ohio Company, organized by New England land speculators and army officers. (This was a different organization from the Ohio Company of the 1750s, mentioned in Chapter 4.) For many years, actual and prospective settlers pressed for a reduction in the price of government-owned land, a movement that did not end until the Homestead Act of 1862 offered free land on the public domain.

A final measure, the **Northwest Ordinance of 1787**, called for the eventual establishment of from three to five states north of the Ohio River and east of the Mississippi. Thus was enacted the basic principle of what Jefferson called the "**empire of liberty**"—rather than ruling over the West as a colonial power, the United States would admit the area's population as equal members of the political system. Territorial expansion and self-government would grow together.

Territorial expansion and self-government

The Northwest Ordinance pledged that "the utmost good faith" would be observed toward local Indians and that their land would not be taken without consent. "It will cost much less," one congressman noted, "to conciliate the good opinion of the Indians than to pay men for destroying them." But national land policy assumed that whether through purchase, treaties, or voluntary removal, the Indian presence would soon disappear. The ordinance also prohibited slavery in the Old Northwest, a provision that would have far-reaching consequences when the sectional conflict between North and South developed. But for years, owners brought slaves into the area, claiming that they had voluntarily signed long-term labor contracts.

Slavery prohibited

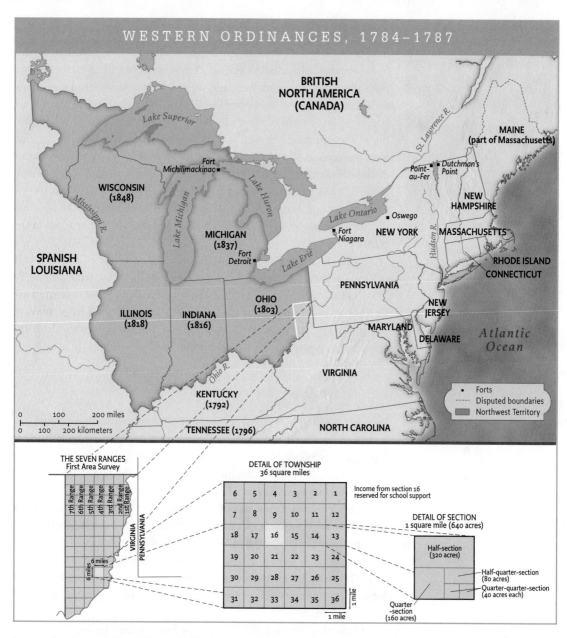

WESTERN ORDINANCES, 1784–1787

A series of ordinances in the 1780s provided for both the surveying and sale of lands in the public domain north of the Ohio River and the eventual admission of states carved from the area as equal members of the Union.

The Confederation's Weaknesses

Whatever the achievements of the Confederation government, in the eyes of many influential Americans they were outweighed by its failings. Both the national government and the country at large faced worsening economic problems. To finance the War of Independence, Congress had borrowed large sums of money by selling interest-bearing bonds and paying soldiers and suppliers in notes to be redeemed in the future. Lacking a secure source of revenue, it found itself unable to pay either interest or the debts themselves. With the United States now outside the British empire, American ships were barred from trading with the West Indies. Imported goods, however, flooded the market, undercutting the business of many craftsmen, driving down wages, and draining money out of the country.

With Congress unable to act, the states adopted their own economic policies. Several imposed tariff duties on goods imported from abroad. In order to increase the amount of currency in circulation and make it easier for individuals to pay their debts, several states printed large sums of paper money. Others enacted laws postponing debt collection. Creditors considered such measures attacks on their property rights.

A Bankruptcy Scene. Creditors repossess the belongings of a family unable to pay its debts, while a woman weeps in the background. Popular fears of bankruptcy led several states during the 1780s to pass laws postponing the collection of debts.

Shays's Rebellion

Uprising in Massachusetts

In late 1786 and early 1787, crowds of debt-ridden farmers closed the courts in western Massachusetts to prevent the seizure of their land for failure to pay taxes. They called themselves "regulators"—a term already used by protesters in the Carolina backcountry in the 1760s. The uprising came to be known as **Shays's Rebellion**, a name affixed to it by its opponents, after Daniel Shays, one of the leaders and a veteran of the War of Independence. The participants in Shays's Rebellion modeled their tactics on the crowd activities of the 1760s and 1770s and employed liberty trees and liberty poles as symbols of their cause. They received no sympathy from Governor James Bowdoin, who dispatched an army headed by the former revolutionary war general Benjamin Lincoln. The rebels were dispersed in January 1787.

Observing Shays's Rebellion from Paris where he was serving as ambassador, Thomas Jefferson refused to be alarmed. "A little rebellion now and then is a good thing," he wrote to a friend. "The tree of liberty must be refreshed from time to time with the blood of patriots and tyrants." But the uprising was the culmination of a series of events in the 1780s that persuaded an influential group of Americans that the national government must be strengthened so that it could develop uniform economic policies and protect property owners from infringements on their rights by local majorities.

Among proponents of stronger national authority, liberty had lost some of its luster. The danger to individual rights, they came to believe, now arose not from a tyrannical central government, but from the people themselves. "Liberty," declared James Madison, "may be endangered by the abuses of liberty as well as the abuses of power." To put it another way, private liberty, especially the secure enjoyment of property rights, could be endangered by public liberty—unchecked power in the hands of the people.

Nationalists of the 1780s

Madison, a diminutive Virginian and the lifelong disciple and ally of Thomas Jefferson, thought deeply and creatively about the nature of political freedom. He was among the group of talented and well-organized men who spearheaded the movement for a stronger national government. Another was Alexander Hamilton, who had come to North America from the West Indies as a youth. Hamilton was perhaps the most vigorous proponent of an "energetic" government that would enable the new nation to become a powerful commercial and diplomatic presence in world affairs. Men like Madison and Hamilton were nation builders. They came to believe during the 1780s that Americans were squandering the fruits of independence and that the country's future greatness depended on enhancing national authority.

The concerns voiced by critics of the Articles found a sympathetic hearing among men who had developed a national consciousness during the Revolution. Nationalists included army officers, members of Congress accustomed to working with individuals from different states, and diplomats who represented the country abroad. Influential economic interests also desired a stronger national government. Among these were bondholders who despaired of being paid so long as Congress lacked a source of revenue, urban artisans seeking tariff protection from foreign imports, merchants desiring access to British markets, and all those who feared that the states were seriously interfering with property rights.

In September 1786, delegates from six states met at Annapolis, Maryland, to consider ways for better regulating interstate and international commerce. The delegates proposed another gathering, in Philadelphia, to amend the Articles of Confederation. Every state except Rhode Island, which had gone the furthest in developing its own debtor relief

James Madison, "father of the Constitution," in a miniature portrait painted by Charles Willson Peale in 1783. Madison was only thirty-six years old when the Constitutional Convention met.

Alexander Hamilton, another youthful leader of the nationalists of the 1780s, was born in the West Indies in 1755. This portrait was painted by Charles Willson Peale in the early 1790s.

The Philadelphia State House (now called Independence Hall), where the Declaration of Independence was signed in 1776 and the Constitutional Convention took place in 1787.

and trade policies, decided to send delegates to the Philadelphia convention. When they assembled in May 1787, they decided to scrap the Articles of Confederation entirely and draft a new constitution for the United States.

A NEW CONSTITUTION

The fifty-five men who gathered for the Constitutional Convention included some of the most prominent Americans. Thomas Jefferson and John Adams, serving as diplomats in Europe, did not take part. But among the delegates were George Washington (whose willingness to lend his prestige to the gathering and to serve as presiding officer was an enormous asset) and Benjamin Franklin (who had returned to Philadelphia after helping to negotiate the Treaty of Paris of 1783, and was now eighty-one years old). John Adams described the convention as a gathering of men of "ability, weight, and experience." He might have added, "and wealth." They earned their livings as lawyers, merchants, planters, and large farmers. Nearly all were quite prosperous by the standards of the day.

Elite convention delegates

At a time when fewer than one-tenth of 1 percent of Americans attended college, more than half the delegates had college educations. Their shared social status and political experiences bolstered their common belief in the need to strengthen national authority and curb what one called "the excesses of democracy." To ensure free and candid debate, the deliberations took place in private. Madison, who believed the outcome would have great consequences for "the cause of liberty throughout the world," took careful notes. They were not published, however, until 1840, four years after he became the last delegate to pass away.

The Structure of Government

Legislature, executive, and national judiciary

It quickly became apparent that the delegates agreed on many points. The new constitution would create a legislature, an executive, and a national judiciary. Congress would have the power to raise money without relying on the states. States would be prohibited from infringing on the rights of property. And the government would represent the people. Most delegates hoped to find a middle ground between the despotism of monarchy and aristocracy and what they considered the excesses of popular self-government. "We had been too democratic," observed George Mason of Virginia, but he warned against the danger of going to "the opposite extreme." The key to stable, effective republican government was finding a way to balance the competing claims of liberty and power.

Differences quickly emerged over the proper balance between the federal and state governments and between the interests of large and small states. Early in the proceedings, Madison presented what came to be called the Virginia Plan. It proposed the creation of a two-house legislature with a state's population determining its representation in each. Smaller states, fearing that populous Virginia, Massachusetts, and Pennsylvania would dominate the new government, rallied behind the New Jersey Plan. This called for a single-house Congress in which each state cast one vote, as under the Articles of Confederation. In the end, a compromise was reached—a two-house Congress consisting of a Senate in which each state had two members, and a House of Representatives apportioned according to population. Senators would be chosen by state legislatures for six-year terms. They were thus insulated from sudden shifts in public opinion. Representatives were to be elected every two years directly by the people.

Large vs. small states

Compromise on a two-house Congress

The Limits of Democracy

Under the Articles of Confederation, no national official had been chosen by popular vote. Thus, the mode of choosing the House of Representatives signaled an expansion of democracy. The Constitution, moreover, imposed neither property nor religious qualifications for voting, leaving it to the states to set voting rules.

Overall, however, the new structure of government was less than democratic. The delegates sought to shield the national government from the popular enthusiasms that had alarmed them during the 1780s and to ensure that the right kind of men held office. The delegates assumed that the Senate would be composed of each state's most distinguished citizens. They made the House of Representatives quite small (initially 65 members, at a time when the Massachusetts assembly had 200), on the assumption that only prominent individuals could win election in large districts.

Less than democratic structure

Nor did the delegates provide for direct election of either federal judges or the president. Members of the Supreme Court would be appointed by the president for life terms. The president would be chosen either by members of an electoral college or by the House of Representatives. A state's electors would be chosen either by its legislature or by popular vote.

The actual system of election seemed a recipe for confusion. Each elector was to cast votes for two candidates for president, with the second-place finisher becoming vice president. If no candidate received a majority of the electoral ballots—as the delegates seem to have assumed would normally be the case—the president would be chosen from among the top three finishers by the House of Representatives, with each state casting one vote. The Senate would then elect the vice president. The delegates devised this extremely cumbersome system of indirect election because they did not trust ordinary voters to choose the president and vice president directly.

Indirect elections

The Division and Separation of Powers

Hammered out in four months of discussion and compromise, the Constitution is a spare document of only 4,000 words that provides only the briefest outline of the new structure of government. (See the Appendix for the full text.) It embodies two basic political principles—**federalism**, sometimes called the "division of powers," and the system of "**checks and balances**" between the different branches of the national government, also known as the "**separation of powers.**"

Federalism

"Federalism" refers to the relationship between the national government and the states. Compared with the Articles of Confederation, the Constitution significantly strengthened national authority. It charged the president with enforcing the law and commanding the military. It empowered Congress to levy taxes, borrow money, regulate commerce, declare war, deal with foreign nations and Indians, and promote the "general welfare." The Constitution also included strong provisions to prevent the states from infringing on property rights. They were barred from issuing paper money, impairing contracts, interfering with interstate commerce, and levying their own import or export duties. On the other hand, most day-to-day affairs of government, from education to law enforcement, remained in the hands of the states. This principle of divided sovereignty was a recipe for debate, which continues to this day, over the balance of power between the national government and the states.

Checks and balances

The "separation of powers," or the system of "checks and balances," refers to the way the Constitution seeks to prevent any branch of the national government from dominating the other two. To prevent an accumulation of power dangerous to liberty, authority within the government is diffused and balanced against itself. Congress enacts laws, but the president can veto them, and a two-thirds majority is required to pass legislation over his objection. Federal judges are nominated by the president and approved by Congress, but to ensure their independence, the judges then serve for life. The president can be impeached by the House and removed from office by the Senate for "high crimes and misdemeanors."

The Debate over Slavery

The structure of government was not the only source of debate at the Constitutional Convention. As Madison recorded, "the institution of slavery and its implications" divided the delegates at many sessions. Those who gathered in Philadelphia included numerous slaveholders, as well as some dedicated advocates of abolition.

The words "slave" and "slavery" did not appear in the Constitution—a concession to the sensibilities of delegates who feared they would "contaminate the glorious fabric of American liberty." Nonetheless, the document contained strong protections for slavery. It prohibited Congress from abolishing the African slave trade for twenty years. It required states to return to their owners fugitives from bondage. And it provided that three-fifths of the slave population would be counted in determining each state's representation in the House of Representatives and its electoral votes for president.

South Carolina's delegates had come to Philadelphia determined to defend slavery, and they had a powerful impact on the final document. They originated the fugitive slave clause and the electoral college. They insisted on strict limits on the power of Congress to levy taxes within the states, fearing future efforts to raise revenue by taxing slave property. Gouverneur Morris, one of Pennsylvania's delegates, declared that he was being forced to decide between offending the southern states or doing injustice to "human nature." For the sake of national unity, he said, he would choose the latter.

South Carolina's influence

Slavery in the Constitution

The Constitution's slavery clauses were compromises, efforts to find a middle ground between the institution's critics and defenders. Taken together, however, they embedded slavery more deeply than ever in American life and politics. The slave trade clause allowed a commerce condemned by civilized society—one that had been suspended during

The slave trade clause

WANTED,
ONE HUNDRED
NEGROES,
From 12 to 30 years old, for which a good
price will be given.
THEY are to be sent out of the state, therefore we shall not be particular respecting the character of any of them—Hearty and well made is all that is necessary.
Moses Austin & Co.
Richmond, Dec. 15, 1787.

This advertisement for the sale of 100 slaves from Virginia to states farther south appeared in a Richmond newspaper only a few months after the signing of the Constitution. Slavery was a major subject of debate at the Constitutional Convention.

the War of Independence—to continue until 1808. On January 1, 1808, the first day that Congress was allowed under the Constitution, it prohibited the further importation of slaves. But in the interim, partly to replace slaves who had escaped to the British and partly to provide labor for the expansion of slavery to fertile land away from the coast, some 170,000 Africans were brought to the new nation as slaves. South Carolina and Georgia imported 100,000. This number accounted for more than one-quarter of all the slaves brought to mainland North America after 1700.

Fugitive slave clause

The fugitive slave clause accorded slave laws "extraterritoriality"— that is, the condition of bondage remained attached to a person even if he or she escaped to a state where slavery had been abolished. The Constitution gave the national government no power to interfere with slavery in the states. And the **three-fifths clause** allowed the white South to exercise far greater power in national affairs than the size of its free population warranted. The clause greatly enhanced the number of southern votes in the House of Representatives and therefore in the electoral college (where the number of electors for each state was determined by adding together its number of senators and representatives). Of the first sixteen presidential elections, between 1788 and 1848, all but four placed a southern slaveholder in the White House.

The Signing of the Constitution, by mid-nineteenth-century American artist Thomas Pritchard Rossiter, depicts the conclusion of the Constitutional Convention of 1787. Among the founding fathers depicted are James Wilson, signing the document at the table in the center, and George Washington, presiding from the dais with an image of the sun behind him.

Nevertheless, some slaveholders detected a potential threat buried in the Constitution. Patrick Henry, who condemned slavery but feared abolition, warned that, in time of war, the new government might take steps to

arm and liberate the slaves. "May Congress not say," he asked, "that every black man must fight?" What Henry could not anticipate was that the war that eventually destroyed slavery would be launched by the South itself to protect the institution.

The Final Document

Gouverneur Morris put the finishing touches on the final draft of the new Constitution, trying to make it, he explained, "as clear as our language would permit." For the original preamble, which began, "We the people of the States of New Hampshire, Massachusetts," etc., he substituted the far more powerful, "We the people of the United States." He added a statement of the Constitution's purposes, including to "establish justice," promote "the general welfare," and "secure the blessings of liberty"—things the Articles of Confederation, in the eyes of most of the delegates, had failed to accomplish.

> *The Preamble*

The last session of the Constitutional Convention took place on September 17, 1787. Benjamin Franklin urged the delegates to put aside individual objections and approve the document, whatever its imperfections. Of the forty-five delegates who remained in Philadelphia, thirty-nine signed the Constitution. It was then sent to the states for ratification.

This satirical engraving by Amos Doolittle depicts some of the issues in the debate over the ratification of the Constitution. The wagon in the center is carrying Connecticut and sinking into the mud under the weight of debts and paper money as "Federals" and "Antifederals" try to pull it out. Federals call for the state to "comply with Congress" (that is, to pay money requisitioned by the national government); the Antifederals reply "tax luxury" and "success to Shays," a reference to Shays's Rebellion. The Connecticut shoreline and the buildings of Manhattan are on the right. Underneath the three merchant ships is a phrase criticizing the tariffs that states were imposing on imports from one another (which the Constitution prohibited). At the bottom is the biblical motto, "A house divided against itself cannot stand," later made famous by Abraham Lincoln.

The Constitution created a new framework for American development. It made possible a national economic market. It created national political institutions, reduced the powers of the states, and sought to place limits on popular democracy. The ratification process, however, unleashed a nationwide debate over the best means of preserving American freedom.

THE RATIFICATION DEBATE AND THE ORIGIN OF THE BILL OF RIGHTS

The Federalist

Even though the Constitution provided that it would go into effect when nine states, not all thirteen as required by the Articles of Confederation, had given their approval, ratification was by no means certain. Each state held an election for delegates to a special ratifying convention. A fierce public battle ensued, producing hundreds of pamphlets and newspaper articles and spirited campaigns to elect delegates. To generate support, Hamilton, Madison, and Jay composed a series of eighty-five essays that appeared in newspapers under the pen name Publius and were gathered as a book, **The Federalist**, in 1788. Today, the essays are regarded as among the most important American contributions to political thought. At the time, however, they were only one part of a much larger national debate over ratification.

For ratification: Alexander Hamilton, James Madison, John Jay

Again and again, Hamilton and Madison repeated that rather than posing a danger to Americans' liberties, the Constitution in fact protected them. Any government, Hamilton insisted, could become oppressive, but with its checks and balances and division of power, the Constitution made political tyranny almost impossible. At the New York ratifying convention, Hamilton assured the delegates that the Constitution had created "the perfect balance between liberty and power."

"Extend the Sphere"

Madison, too, emphasized how the Constitution was structured to prevent abuses of authority. But in several essays, especially *Federalist* nos. 10 and 51, he moved beyond such assurances to develop a strikingly new vision of the relationship between government and society in the United States. Madison identified the essential dilemma, as he saw it, of the new republic—government must be based on the will of the people, yet the people had shown themselves susceptible to dangerous enthusiasms. The problem of balancing democracy and respect for property would only grow in the years ahead because, he warned, economic development would inevitably increase the numbers of poor. What was to prevent them from using their political power to secure "a more equal distribution" of wealth?

The answer, Madison explained, lay not simply in the way power balanced power in the structure of government, but in the nation's size and diversity. Previous republics had existed only in small territories—the Dutch republic or the Italian city-states of the Renaissance. But, argued Madison, the very size of the United States was a source of stability, not, as many feared, weakness. "Extend the sphere," he wrote. The multiplicity of religious denominations, he argued, offered the best security for religious liberty. Likewise, in a nation as large as the United States, so many distinct interests—economic, regional, and political—would arise, that no single one would ever be able to take over the government and oppress the rest.

Madison's writings did much to shape the early nation's understanding of its new political institutions. In arguing that the size of the republic helped to secure Americans' rights, they reinforced the tradition that saw continuous westward expansion as essential to freedom.

In this late-eighteenth-century engraving, Americans celebrate the signing of the Constitution beneath a temple of liberty.

America's size and diversity

The Anti-Federalists

Opponents of ratification, called **Anti-Federalists**, insisted that the Constitution shifted the balance between liberty and power too far in the direction of the latter. Anti-Federalists lacked the coherent leadership of the Constitution's defenders. They included state politicians fearful of seeing their influence diminish, among them such revolutionary heroes as Samuel Adams, John Hancock, and Patrick Henry. Small farmers, many of whom supported the state debtor-relief measures of the 1780s that

Against ratification: Samuel Adams, John Hancock, Patrick Henry

VOICES OF FREEDOM

From David Ramsay, *The History of the American Revolution* (1789)

A member of the Continental Congress from South Carolina, David Ramsay published his history of the Revolution the year after the Constitution was ratified. In this excerpt, he lauds the principles of representative government and the right of future amendment, embodied in the state constitutions and adopted in the national one, as unique American political principles and the best ways of securing liberty.

The world has not hitherto exhibited so fair an opportunity for promoting social happiness. It is hoped for the honor of human nature, that the result will prove the fallacy of those theories that mankind are incapable of self government. The ancients, not knowing the doctrine of representation, were apt in their public meetings to run into confusion, but in America this mode of taking the sense of the people, is so well understood, and so completely reduced to system, that its most populous states are often peaceably convened in an assembly of deputies, not too large for orderly deliberation, and yet representing the whole in equal proportion. These popular branches of legislature are miniature pictures of the community, and from their mode of election are likely to be influenced by the same interests and feelings with the people whom they represent. . . .

In no age before, and in no other country, did man ever possess an election of the kind of government, under which he would choose to live. The constituent parts of the ancient free governments were thrown together by accident. The freedom of modern European governments was, for the most part, obtained by concessions, or liberality of monarchs, or military leaders. In America alone, reason and liberty concurred in the formation of constitutions . . . In one thing they were all perfect. They left the people in the power of altering and amending them, whenever they pleased. In this happy peculiarity they placed the science of politics on a footing with the other sciences, by opening it to improvements from experience, and the discoveries of future ages. By means of this power of amending American constitutions, the friends of mankind have fondly hoped that oppression will one day be no more.

From James Winthrop, Anti-Federalist Essay Signed "Agrippa" (1787)

A local official in Middlesex, Massachusetts, James Winthrop published sixteen public letters between November 1787 and February 1788 opposing ratification of the Constitution.

It is the opinion of the ablest writers on the subject, that no extensive empire can be governed upon republican principles, and that such a government will degenerate into a despotism, unless it be made up of a confederacy of smaller states, each having the full powers of internal regulation. This is precisely the principle which has hitherto preserved our freedom. No instance can be found of any free government of considerable extent which has been supported upon any other plan. Large and consolidated empires may indeed dazzle the eyes of a distant spectator with their splendor, but if examined more nearly are always found to be full of misery. . . . It is under such tyranny that the Spanish provinces languish, and such would be our misfortune and degradation, if we should submit to have the concerns of the whole empire managed by one empire. To promote the happiness of the people it is necessary that there should be local laws; and it is necessary that those laws should be made by the representatives of those who are immediately subject to [them]. . . .

It is impossible for one code of laws to suit Georgia and Massachusetts. They must, therefore, legislate for themselves. Yet there is, I believe, not one point of legislation that is not surrendered in the proposed plan. Questions of every kind respecting property are determinable in a continental court, and so are all kinds of criminal causes. The continental legislature has, therefore, a right to make rules in all cases. . . . No rights are reserved to the citizens. . . . This new system is, therefore, a consolidation of all the states into one large mass, however diverse the parts may be of which it is composed. . . .

A bill of rights . . . serves to secure the minority against the usurpation and tyranny of the majority. . . . The experience of all mankind has proved the prevalence of a disposition to use power wantonly. It is therefore as necessary to defend an individual against the majority in a republic as against the king in a monarchy.

QUESTIONS

1. *Why does Ramsay feel that the power to amend the Constitution is so important a political innovation?*

2. *Why does Winthrop believe that a Bill of Rights is essential in the Constitution?*

3. *How do Ramsay and Winthrop differ concerning how the principle of representation operates in the United States?*

the Constitution's supporters deplored, also saw no need for a stronger central government. Some opponents of the Constitution denounced the document's protections for slavery; others warned that the powers of Congress were so broad that it might enact a law for abolition.

Anti-Federalists repeatedly predicted that the new government would fall under the sway of merchants, creditors, and others hostile to the interests of ordinary Americans. Popular self-government, they claimed, flourished best in small communities, where rulers and ruled interacted daily. The result of the Constitution, warned Melancton Smith of New York, a member of Congress under the Articles of Confederation, would be domination of the "common people" by the "well-born."

Rule by the "well-born"

"Liberty" was the Anti-Federalists' watchword. America's happiness, they insisted, "arises from the freedom of our institutions and the limited nature of our government," both threatened by the new Constitution. To the vision of the United States as an energetic great power, Anti-Federalists counterposed a way of life grounded in local, democratic institutions. Anti-Federalists also pointed to the Constitution's lack of a Bill of Rights, which left unprotected rights such as trial by jury and freedom of speech and the press.

Social bases of support and opposition

In general, pro-Constitution sentiment flourished in the nation's cities and in rural areas closely tied to the commercial marketplace. The Constitution's most energetic supporters were men of substantial property. But what George Bryan of Pennsylvania, a supporter of ratification, called the "golden phantom" of prosperity also swung urban artisans, laborers, and sailors behind the movement for a government that would use its "energy and power" to revive the depressed economy. Anti-Federalism drew its support from small farmers in more isolated rural areas such as the Hudson Valley of New York, western Massachusetts, and the southern backcountry.

Ratification

In the end, the supporters' energy and organization, coupled with their domination of the colonial press, carried the day. Ninety-two newspapers and magazines existed in the United States in 1787. Of these, only twelve published a significant number of Anti-Federalist pieces. Madison also won support for the new Constitution by promising that the first Congress would enact a Bill of Rights. By mid-1788, the required nine states had ratified. Only Rhode Island and North Carolina voted against ratification, and they subsequently had little choice but to join the new government. Anti-Federalism died. But as with other movements in American history that did not immediately achieve their goals—for example, the Populists of the late nineteenth century—some of the Anti-Federalists' ideas eventually entered the political mainstream. To this day, their belief that a too-powerful central government is a threat to liberty continues to influence American political culture.

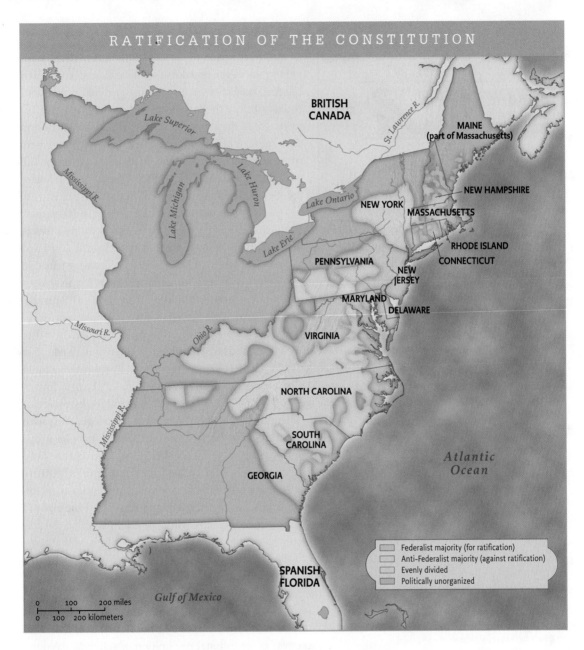

RATIFICATION OF THE CONSTITUTION

Federalists—those who supported the new Constitution—tended to be concentrated in cities and nearby rural areas, whereas backcountry farmers were more likely to oppose the new frame of government.

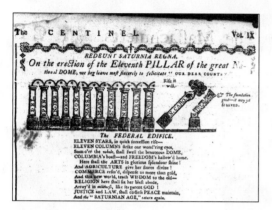

An engraving and poem, published in 1788 in an American newspaper, after New York became the eleventh state to ratify the new Constitution. North Carolina would ratify in 1789 and Rhode Island in 1790.

First Amendment rights

Constitutional recognition of religious freedom

The Bill of Rights

Ironically, the parts of the Constitution Americans most value today—the freedoms of speech, the press, and religion; protection against unjust criminal procedures; equality before the law—were not in the original document. All of these but the last (which was enshrined in the Fourteenth Amendment after the Civil War) were contained in the first ten amendments, known as the **Bill of Rights**. Madison believed a Bill of Rights "redundant or pointless." "Parchment barriers" to the abuse of authority, he observed, would prove least effective when most needed. Madison's prediction would be amply borne out at future times of popular hysteria, such as during the Red Scare following World War I and the McCarthy era of the 1950s, when all branches of government joined in trampling on freedom of expression, and during World War II, when hatred of a foreign enemy led to the internment of more than 100,000 Japanese-Americans, most of them citizens of the United States.

Nevertheless, every new state constitution contained some kind of declaration of citizens' rights, and large numbers of Americans—Federalist and Anti-Federalist alike—believed the new national Constitution should also have one. Madison presented to Congress a series of amendments that became the basis of the Bill of Rights, which was ratified by the states in 1791. The First Amendment prohibited Congress from legislating with regard to religion or infringing on freedom of speech, freedom of the press, or the right of assembly. The Second upheld the people's right to "keep and bear arms" in conjunction with "a well-regulated militia." Others prohibited abuses such as arrests without warrants and forcing a person accused of a crime to testify against himself, and reaffirmed the right to trial by jury. The Tenth Amendment, meant to answer fears that the federal government would ride roughshod over the states, affirmed that powers not delegated to the national government or prohibited to the states continued to reside with the states.

Although the roots and even the specific language of some parts of the Bill of Rights lay far back in English history, other provisions reflected the changes in American life brought about by the Revolution. The most remarkable of these was constitutional recognition of religious freedom. Unlike the Declaration of Independence, which invokes the blessing of divine providence, the Constitution is a purely secular document that contains no reference to God and bars religious tests for federal officeholders. The First Amendment prohibits the federal government from legislating on the subject of religion—a complete departure from British and colonial precedent. Under the Constitution it was and remains possible, as one critic complained, for "a papist, a Mohomatan, a deist, yea an atheist" to become president of the United States. Madison was so adamant about separating church and state that he even opposed the appointment of chaplains to serve Congress and the military.

The Bill of Rights aroused little enthusiasm on ratification and for decades was all but ignored. Not until the twentieth century would it come to be revered as an indispensable expression of American freedom. Nonetheless, the Bill of Rights subtly affected the language of liberty. Applying only to the federal government, not the states, it reinforced the idea that concentrated national power posed the greatest threat to freedom. And it contributed to the long process whereby freedom came to be discussed in the vocabulary of rights.

Legacy of the Bill of Rights

Among the most important rights were freedom of speech and the press, vital building blocks of a democratic public sphere. Once an entitlement of members of Parliament and colonial assemblies, free speech came to be seen as a basic right of citizenship.

"WE THE PEOPLE"

National Identity

The Constitution opens with the words, "We the People." Although one might assume that the "people" of the United States included all those living within the nation's borders, the text made clear that this was not the case. The Constitution identifies three populations inhabiting the United States: Indians, treated as members of independent tribes and not part of the American body politic; "other persons"—that is, slaves; and the "people." Only the third were entitled to American freedom.

Exclusion of Indians and slaves

Indians in the New Nation

The early republic's policies toward Indians and African-Americans illustrate the conflicting principles that shaped American nationality. American leaders agreed that the West should not be left in Indian hands, but they disagreed about the Indians' ultimate fate. The government hoped to encourage the westward expansion of white settlement, which implied one of three things: the removal of the Indian population to lands even farther west, their total disappearance, or their incorporation into white "civilization" with the expectation that they might one day become part of American society.

Political status of Indian tribes

Indian tribes had no representation in the new government, and the Constitution excluded Indians "not taxed" from being counted in determining each state's number of congressmen. The treaty system gave them a unique status within the American political system. But despite this recognition of their sovereignty, treaties were essentially ways of transferring land from Indians to the federal government or the states.

Continuing warfare

Open warfare continued in the Ohio Valley after ratification. In 1791, Little Turtle, leader of the **Miami Confederacy**, inflicted a humiliating defeat on American forces led by Arthur St. Clair, the American governor of the Northwest Territory. With 630 dead, this was the costliest loss ever suffered by the U.S. Army at the hands of Indians. In 1794, 3,000 American troops under Anthony Wayne defeated Little Turtle's forces at the **Battle of Fallen Timbers**. This led directly to the **Treaty of Greenville** of 1795, in which twelve Indian tribes ceded most of Ohio and Indiana to the federal government. The treaty also established the **"annuity" system**—yearly grants of federal money to Indian tribes that institutionalized continuing government influence in tribal affairs and gave outsiders considerable control over Indian life.

Many prominent figures, however, rejected the idea that Indians were innately inferior to white Americans. Thomas Jefferson believed that Indians merely lived at a less advanced stage of civilization. Indians could become full-fledged members of the republic by abandoning communal landholding and hunting in favor of small-scale farming.

To pursue the goal of assimilation, Congress in the 1790s authorized President Washington to distribute agricultural tools and livestock to Indian men and spinning wheels and looms to Indian women. To whites, the adoption of American gender norms, with men working the land and women tending to their homes, would be a crucial sign that the Indians were becoming "civilized." But the American notion of civilization required so great a transformation of Indian life that most tribes rejected it. One missionary was told, "If we want to work, we know how to do it according to our own way and as it pleases us."

The signing of the Treaty of Greenville of 1795, painted by an unknown member of General Anthony Wayne's staff. In the treaty, a group of tribes ceded most of the area of the current state of Ohio, along with the site that became the city of Chicago, to the United States.

To Indians, freedom meant retaining tribal autonomy and identity, including the ability to travel widely in search of game. "Since our acquaintance with our brother white people," declared a Mohawk speaker at a 1796 treaty council, "that which we call freedom and liberty, becomes an entire stranger to us." There was no room for Indians who desired to retain their traditional way of life in the American empire of liberty.

Blacks and the Republic

By 1790, the number of African-Americans far exceeded the Indian population within the United States. The status of free blacks was somewhat indeterminate. Nowhere does the original Constitution define who in fact are citizens of the United States. The individual states were left free to determine the boundaries of liberty. The North's **gradual emancipation** acts assumed that former slaves would remain in the country, not be colonized abroad. During the era of the Revolution, free blacks enjoyed at least some of the legal rights accorded to whites, including, in most states, the right to vote. The large majority of blacks, of course, were slaves, and slavery rendered them all but invisible to those imagining the American community.

One of the era's most widely read books, *Letters from an American Farmer*, published in France in 1782 by Hector St. John de Crèvecoeur, strikingly illustrated this process of exclusion. Born in France, Crèvecoeur eventually married the daughter of a prominent New York landowner and lived with his own family on a farm in Orange County. In this book, Crèvecoeur popularized the idea, which would become so common in the twentieth century, of the United States as a melting pot. "Here," he wrote, "individuals of all nations are melted

TABLE 7.1 Total Population and Black Population of the United States, 1790

STATE	TOTAL POPULATION	SLAVES	FREE BLACKS
New England:			
New Hampshire	141,899	158	630
Vermont*	85,341	0	271
Massachusetts	378,556	0	5,369
Connecticut	237,655	2,764	2,771
Rhode Island	69,112	948	3,484
Maine**	96,643	0	536
Middle States:			
New York	340,241	21,324	4,682
New Jersey	184,139	11,423	2,762
Pennsylvania	433,611	3,737	6,531
South:			
Delaware	59,096	8,887	3,899
Maryland	319,728	103,036	8,043
Virginia	747,610	292,627	12,866
North Carolina	395,005	100,572	5,041
South Carolina	249,073	107,094	1,801
Georgia	82,548	29,264	398
Kentucky*	73,677	12,430	114
Tennessee*	35,691	3,417	361
Total	3,929,625	697,624	59,557

*Vermont, Kentucky, and Tennessee were territories that had not yet been admitted as states.

**Maine was part of Massachusetts in 1790.

into a new one." When he posed the famous question, "What then is the American, this new man?" he answered, "a mixture of English, Scotch, Irish, French, Dutch, Germans, and Swedes. . . . He is either a European, or the descendant of a European." This at a time when fully one-fifth of the population (the highest proportion in U.S. history) consisted of Africans and their descendants.

Like Crèvecoeur, many white Americans excluded blacks from their conception of the American people. The Constitution empowered Congress to create a uniform system by which immigrants became citizens, and the Naturalization Act of 1790 offered the first legislative

definition of American nationality. With no debate, Congress restricted the process of becoming a citizen from abroad to "free white persons." The word "white" in this act excluded a large majority of the world's population from emigrating to the "asylum for mankind" and partaking in the blessings of American freedom. For eighty years, no non-white immigrant could become a naturalized citizen. Africans were allowed to do so in 1870, but not until the 1940s did persons of Asian origin become eligible. (Native Americans were granted American citizenship in 1924.)

Jefferson, Slavery, and Race

The artist John Singleton Copley, best known for his portraits of prominent Americans and Britons, painted this young African-American in the late 1770s. The subject probably worked on a New England fishing boat. This is one of the era's very few portraits of a black person.

Man's liberty, John Locke had written, flowed from "his having reason." To deny liberty to those who were not considered rational beings did not seem to be a contradiction. White Americans increasingly viewed blacks as permanently deficient in the qualities that made freedom possible—the capacity for self-control, reason, and devotion to the larger community. These were the characteristics that Jefferson, in a famous comparison of the races in his book ***Notes on the State of Virginia***, published in 1785, claimed blacks lacked, partly due to natural incapacity and partly because the bitter experience of slavery had (quite understandably, he felt) rendered them disloyal to the nation.

Jefferson was obsessed with the connection between heredity and environment, race and intelligence. His belief that individuals' abilities and achievements are shaped by social conditions inclined him to hope that no group was fixed permanently in a status of inferiority. In the case of blacks, however, he could not avoid the "suspicion" that nature had permanently deprived them of the qualities that made republican citizenship possible. Benjamin Banneker, a free African-American from Maryland who had taught himself the principles of mathematics, sent Jefferson a copy of an astronomical almanac he had published, along with a plea for the abolition of slavery. Jefferson replied, "Nobody wishes more than I do to see such proofs as you exhibit, that nature has given to our black brethren, talents equal to the other colors of men." To his friend Joel Barlow, however, Jefferson suggested that a white person must have helped Banneker with his calculations.

"Nothing is more certainly written in the book of fate," wrote Jefferson, "than that these people are to be free." Yet he felt that America should have a homogeneous citizenry with common experiences, values, and inborn abilities. These contradictions in Jefferson reflected the divided mind of his generation. Some prominent Virginians assumed that blacks could become part of the American nation. Edward Coles, an early governor of Illinois, brought his slaves from Virginia, freed them, and settled them on farms. Washington, who died in 1799, provided in his will that his 277 slaves would become free after the death of his wife, Martha. Believing the slave trade immoral, Jefferson tried to avoid selling slaves to pay off his mounting debts. But his will provided for the freedom of only five, all relatives of his slave Sally Hemings, with whom he appears to have had fathered one or more children.

RUN away from the subscriber in *Albemarle*, a Mulatto slave called *Sandy*, about 35 years of age, his stature is rather low, inclining to corpulence, and his complexion light; he is a shoemaker by trade, in which he uses his left hand principally, can do coarse carpenters work, and is something of a horse jockey; he is greatly addicted to drink, and when drunk is insolent and disorderly, in his conversation he swears much, and in his behaviour is artful and knavish. He took with him a white horse, much scarred with traces, of which it is expected he will endeavour to dispose; he also carried his shoemakers tools, and will probably endeavour to get employment that way. Whoever conveys the said slave to me, in *Albemarle*, shall have 40 s. reward, if taken up within the county, 4 l. if elsewhere within the colony, and 10 l. if in any other colony, from
THOMAS JEFFERSON.

Thomas Jefferson, future author of the Declaration of Independence and in private a sharp critic of slavery, placed this advertisement in a Virginia newspaper in 1769, seeking the return of a runaway slave. Sandy was in fact recaptured, and Jefferson sold him in 1773.

Principles of Freedom

Even as the decline of apprenticeship and indentured servitude narrowed the gradations of freedom among the white population, the Revolution widened the divide between free Americans and those who remained in slavery. Race, one among many kinds of legal and social inequality in colonial America, now emerged as a convenient justification for the existence of slavery in a land that claimed to be committed to freedom. Blacks' "natural faculties," Alexander Hamilton noted in 1779, were "probably as good as ours." But the existence of slavery, he added, "makes us fancy many things that are founded neither in reason or experience."

Emergence of racial distinctions

"We the people" increasingly meant only white Americans. "Principles of freedom, which embrace only half mankind, are only half systems," declared the anonymous author of a Fourth of July speech in Hartford, Connecticut, in 1800. "Declaration of Independence," he wondered, "where art thou now?" The answer came from a Richmond newspaper: "Tell us not of principles. Those principles have been annihilated by the existence of slavery among us."

CHAPTER REVIEW AND ONLINE RESOURCES

REVIEW QUESTIONS

1. *How did the limited central government created by the Articles of Confederation reflect the issues behind the Revolution and fears for individual liberties?*

2. *What were the ideas and motivations that pushed Americans to expand west?*

3. *What events and ideas led to the belief in 1786 and 1787 that the Articles of Confederation were not working well?*

4. *The Constitution has been described as a "bundle of compromises." Which compromises were the most significant in shaping the direction of the new nation and why?*

5. *What were the major arguments in support of the Constitution given by the Federalists?*

6. *What were the major arguments against the Constitution put forth by the Anti-Federalists?*

7. *How accurate was Hector St. John de Crèvecoeur's description of America as a melting pot?*

KEY TERMS

Land Ordinances of 1784 and 1785 (p. 198)

Northwest Ordinance of 1787 (p. 198)

"empire of liberty" (p. 198)

Shays's Rebellion (p. 200)

federalism (p. 204)

checks and balances (p. 204)

separation of powers (p. 204)

three-fifths clause (p. 206)

The Federalist (p. 208)

Anti-Federalists (p. 209)

Bill of Rights (p. 214)

Miami Confederation (p. 216)

Battle of Fallen Timbers (p. 216)

Treaty of Greenville (p. 216)

"annuity" system (p. 216)

gradual emancipation (p. 217)

Letters from an American Farmer (p. 217)

Notes on the State of Virginia (p. 218)

wwnorton.com /studyspace

VISIT STUDYSPACE FOR THESE RESOURCES AND MORE

- A chapter outline
- A diagnostic chapter quiz
- Interactive maps
- Map worksheets
- Multimedia documents

CHAPTER 8

SECURING THE REPUBLIC

★

1791–1815

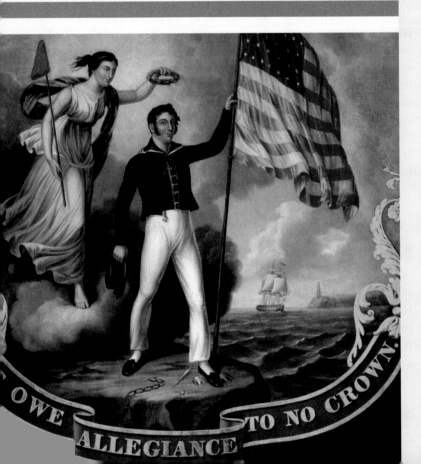

This colorful painting by the artist John Archibald Woodside from around the time of the War of 1812 contains numerous symbols of freedom, among them the goddess of liberty with her liberty cap, a broken chain at the sailor's feet, the fallen crown (under his left foot), a broken royal scepter, and the sailor himself, because English interference with American shipping was one of the war's causes.

FOCUS
QUESTIONS

- *What issues made the politics of the 1790s so divisive?*

- *How did competing views of freedom and global events promote the political divisions of the 1790s?*

- *What were the achievements and failures of Jefferson's presidency?*

- *What were the causes and significant results of the War of 1812?*

O n April 30, 1789, in New York City, the nation's temporary capital, George Washington became the first president under the new Constitution. All sixty-nine electors had awarded him their votes. Dressed in a plain suit of "superfine American broad cloth" rather than European finery, Washington took the oath of office on the balcony of Federal Hall before a large crowd that reacted with "loud and repeated shouts" of approval. He then retreated inside to deliver his inaugural address before members of Congress and other dignitaries.

Washington's speech expressed the revolutionary generation's conviction that it had embarked on an experiment of enormous historical importance, whose outcome was by no means certain. "The preservation of the sacred fire of liberty and the destiny of the republican model of government," Washington proclaimed, depended on the success of the American experiment in self-government.

American leaders believed that maintaining political harmony was crucial to this success. They were especially anxious to avoid the emergence of organized political parties, which had already appeared in several states. Parties were considered divisive and disloyal. "They serve to organize faction," Washington would later declare, and to substitute the aims of "a small but artful" minority for the "will of the nation." The Constitution makes no mention of political parties, and the original method of electing the president assumes that candidates would run as individuals, not on a party ticket (otherwise, the second-place finisher would not have become vice president). Nonetheless, national political parties quickly arose. Originating in Congress, they soon spread to the general populace. Instead of harmony, the 1790s became, in the words of one historian, an "age of passion." Political rhetoric became inflamed because the stakes seemed so high—nothing less than the legacy of the Revolution, the new nation's future, and the survival of American freedom.

POLITICS IN AN AGE OF PASSION

Washington's first administration

President Washington provided a much-needed symbol of national unity. He brought into his cabinet some of the new nation's most prominent political leaders, including Thomas Jefferson as secretary of state and Alexander Hamilton to head the Treasury Department. He also appointed a Supreme Court of six members, headed by John Jay of New York. But harmonious government proved short lived.

Hamilton's Program

Political divisions first surfaced over the financial plan developed by Secretary of the Treasury Hamilton in 1790 and 1791. Hamilton's immediate aims were to establish the nation's financial stability, bring to the government's support the country's most powerful financial interests, and encourage economic development. His long-term purpose was to make the United States a major commercial and military power. The goal of national greatness, he believed, could never be realized if the government suffered from the same weaknesses as under the Articles of Confederation.

Hamilton's program had five parts. The first step was to establish the new nation's credit-worthiness—that is, to create conditions under which persons would loan money to the government by purchasing its bonds, confident that they would be repaid. Hamilton proposed that the federal government assume responsibility for paying off at its full face value the national debt inherited from the War of Independence, as well as outstanding debts of the states. Second, he called for the creation of a new national debt. The old debts would be replaced by new interest-bearing bonds issued to the government's creditors. This would give men of economic substance a stake in promoting the new nation's stability, because the stronger and more economically secure the federal government, the more likely it would be to pay its debts.

The third part of Hamilton's program called for the creation of a **Bank of the United States**, modeled on the Bank of England, to serve as the nation's main financial agent. A private corporation rather than a branch of the government, it would hold public funds, issue bank notes that would serve as currency, and make loans to the government when necessary, all the while returning a tidy profit to its stockholders. Fourth, to raise revenue, Hamilton proposed a tax on producers of whiskey. Finally, in a **Report on Manufactures** delivered to Congress in December 1791, Hamilton called for the imposition of a tariff (a tax on imported foreign goods) and government subsidies to encourage the development of factories that could manufacture products currently purchased from abroad.

Liberty and Washington, painted by an unknown artist around 1800, depicts a female figure of liberty placing a wreath on a bust of the first president. She carries an American flag and stands on a royal crown, which has been thrown to the ground. In the background is a liberty cap. Washington had died in 1799 and was now immortalized as a symbol of freedom, independence, and national pride.

The Emergence of Opposition

Hamilton's vision of a powerful commercial republic won strong support from American financiers, manufacturers, and merchants. But it alarmed those who believed the new nation's destiny lay in charting a different path of development. Hamilton's plans hinged on close ties with Britain, America's main trading partner. To James Madison and Thomas Jefferson,

Support for Hamilton's plan

Venerate the Plough, a medal of the Philadelphia Society for the Promotion of Agriculture, 1786. Americans such as Jefferson and Madison believed that farmers were the most virtuous citizens and therefore agriculture must remain the foundation of American life.

the future lay in westward expansion, not connections with Europe. Their goal was a republic of independent farmers marketing grain, tobacco, and other products freely to the entire world. Jefferson and Madison quickly concluded that the greatest threat to American freedom lay in the alliance of a powerful central government with an emerging class of commercial capitalists, such as Hamilton appeared to envision.

To Jefferson, Hamilton's system "flowed from principles adverse to liberty, and was calculated to undermine and demolish the republic." Hamilton's plans for a standing army seemed to his critics a bold threat to freedom. The national bank and assumption of state debts, they feared, would introduce into American politics the same corruption that had undermined British liberty, and enrich those already wealthy at the expense of ordinary Americans. During the 1780s, speculators had bought up at great discounts (often only a few cents on the dollar) government bonds and paper notes that had been used to pay those who fought in the Revolution or supplied the army. Under Hamilton's plan, speculators would reap a windfall by being paid at face value while the original holders received nothing. Because transportation was so poor, moreover, many backcountry farmers were used to distilling their grain harvest into whiskey, which could then be carried more easily to market. Hamilton's whiskey tax seemed to single them out unfairly in order to enrich bondholders.

The Jefferson-Hamilton Bargain

Opposition to Hamilton's plan

At first, opposition to Hamilton's program arose almost entirely from the South, the region that had the least interest in manufacturing development and the least diversified economy. It also had fewer holders of federal bonds than the Middle States and New England. Because Hamilton insisted that all his plans were authorized by the Constitution's broad "general welfare" clause, many southerners who had supported the new Constitution now became "**strict constructionists**," who insisted that the federal government could exercise only powers specifically listed in the document. Jefferson, for example, believed the new national bank unconstitutional, because the right of Congress to create a bank was not mentioned in the Constitution.

A bargain struck

Opposition in Congress threatened the enactment of Hamilton's plans. Behind-the-scenes negotiations followed. They culminated at a famous dinner in 1790 at which Jefferson brokered an agreement whereby southerners accepted Hamilton's fiscal program (with the exception of subsidies to manufacturers) in exchange for the establishment of the permanent national capital on the Potomac River between Maryland and Virginia. Major Pierre-Charles L'Enfant, a French-born veteran of the War of Independence, designed a grandiose plan for the "federal city" modeled on the great urban centers of Europe, with wide boulevards, parks, and fountains. When it came to constructing public buildings in the nation's new capital, most of the labor was performed by slaves.

The national capital

The Impact of the French Revolution

Political divisions began over Hamilton's fiscal program, but they deepened in response to events in Europe. When it began in 1789, nearly all Americans welcomed the French Revolution, inspired in part by the example of their own rebellion. But in 1793, the revolution took a more radical turn with the execution of King Louis XVI along with numerous aristocrats and other foes of the new government, and war broke out between France and Great Britain.

Events in France became a source of bitter conflict in America. Jefferson and his followers believed that despite its excesses the revolution marked a historic victory for the idea of popular self-government, which must be defended at all costs. Enthusiasm for France inspired a rebirth of symbols of liberty. Liberty poles and caps reappeared on the streets of American towns and cities. To Washington, Hamilton, and their supporters, however, the revolution raised the specter of anarchy.

The rivalry of Britain and France

The rivalry between Britain and France did much to shape early American politics. The "permanent" alliance between France and the United States, which dated to 1778, complicated the situation. No one advocated that the United States should become involved in the European war, and Washington in April 1793 issued a proclamation of American neutrality. Meanwhile, the British seized hundreds of American ships trading with the French West Indies and resumed the hated practice of **impressment**—kidnapping sailors, including American citizens of British origin, to serve in their navy. Sent to London to present objections, while still serving as chief justice, John Jay negotiated an agreement in 1794 that produced the greatest public controversy of Washington's presidency. **Jay's Treaty** contained no British concessions on impressment or the rights of American shipping. Britain did agree to abandon outposts on the western frontier, which it was supposed to have done in 1783. In return, the United States guaranteed favored treatment to British imported goods. Critics of the administration charged that it aligned the United States with

Favored treatment to British imports

monarchical Britain in its conflict with republican France. Ultimately, Jay's Treaty sharpened political divisions in the United States and led directly to the formation of an organized opposition party.

Political Parties

By the mid-1790s, two increasingly coherent parties had appeared in Congress, calling themselves **Federalists and Republicans**. (The latter had no connection with today's Republican Party, which was founded in the 1850s.) Both parties laid claim to the language of liberty, and each accused its opponent of engaging in a conspiracy to destroy it.

Federalists supported Washington and favored Hamilton's economic program

The Federalists, supporters of the Washington administration, favored Hamilton's economic program and close ties with Britain. Prosperous merchants, farmers, lawyers, and established political leaders (especially outside the South) tended to support the Federalists. Their outlook was generally elitist, reflecting the traditional eighteenth-century view of society as a fixed hierarchy and of public office as reserved for men of economic substance—the "rich, the able, and the well-born," as Hamilton put it. Freedom, Federalists insisted, rested on deference to authority. Federalists feared that the "spirit of liberty" unleashed by the American Revolution was degenerating into anarchy and "licentiousness."

The Whiskey Rebellion

The Federalists may have been the only major party in American history forthrightly to proclaim democracy and freedom dangerous in the hands of ordinary citizens. The **Whiskey Rebellion** of 1794, which broke out when backcountry Pennsylvania farmers sought to block collection of the new tax on distilled spirits, reinforced this conviction. The "rebels" invoked the symbols of 1776, displaying liberty poles and banners reading "Liberty or Death." But Washington dispatched 13,000 militiamen to western Pennsylvania (a larger force than he had commanded during the Revolution). He accompanied them part of the way to the scene of the disturbances, the only time in American history that a president has actually commanded an army in the field. The "rebels" offered no resistance.

Opposition to the tax on distilled spirits

The Republican Party

Republicans favored self-government

Republicans, led by Madison and Jefferson, were more sympathetic to France than the Federalists and had more faith in democratic self-government. They drew their support from an unusual alliance of wealthy southern planters and ordinary farmers throughout the country. Enthusiasm for the French Revolution increasingly drew urban artisans into Republican ranks as well. Republicans were far more critical than the Federalists of social and economic inequality, and more accepting of broad democratic participation as essential to freedom.

Political language became more and more heated. Federalists denounced Republicans as French agents, anarchists, and traitors. Republicans called their opponents monarchists intent on transforming the new national government into a corrupt, British-style aristocracy. Each charged the other with betraying the principles of the War of Independence and of American freedom. Washington himself received mounting abuse. When he left office, a Republican newspaper declared that his name had become synonymous with "political iniquity" and "legalized corruption."

GENERAL GEORGE WASHINGTON.
Reviewing the Western army at Fort Cumberland the 18th of Octob. 1794

A 1794 painting by the Baltimore artist and sign painter Frederick Kemmelmayer depicting President George Washington as commander-in-chief of the army dispatched to put down the Whiskey Rebellion.

An Expanding Public Sphere

The debates of the 1790s produced not only one of the most intense periods of partisan warfare in American history but also an enduring expansion of the public sphere and with it the democratic content of American freedom. More and more citizens attended political meetings and became avid readers of pamphlets and newspapers. The establishment of nearly 1,000 post offices made possible the wider circulation of personal letters and printed materials. The era witnessed the rapid growth of the American press—the number of newspapers rose from around 100 to 260 during the 1790s, and reached nearly 400 by 1810.

Growth in American press

Inspired by the Jacobin clubs of Paris, supporters of the French Revolution and critics of the Washington administration in 1793 and 1794 formed nearly fifty Democratic-Republican societies. The Republican press publicized their meetings, replete with toasts to French and American liberty. Federalists saw the societies as another example of how liberty was getting out of hand. The government, not "self-created societies," declared the president, was the authentic voice of the American people. Forced to justify their existence, the societies developed a defense of the right of the people to debate political issues and organize to affect public policy. To the societies, political liberty

Democratic-Republican societies

VOICES OF FREEDOM

From Judith Sargent Murray, "On the Equality of the Sexes" (1790)

A prominent writer of plays, novels, and poetry, Judith Sargent Murray of Massachusetts was one of the first women to demand equal educational opportunities for women.

Is it upon mature consideration we adopt the idea, that nature is thus partial in her distributions? Is it indeed a fact, that she hath yielded to one half of the human species so unquestionable a mental superiority? I know that to both sexes elevated understandings, and the reverse, are common. But, suffer me to ask, in what the minds of females are so notoriously deficient, or unequal. . . .

Are we deficient in reason? We can only reason from what we know, and if an opportunity of acquiring knowledge hath been denied us, the inferiority of our sex cannot fairly be deduced from thence. . . . Will it be said that the judgment of a male of two years old, is more sage than that of a female's of the same age? I believe the reverse is generally observed to be true. But from that period what partiality! How is the one exalted, and the other depressed, by the contrary modes of education which are adopted! The one is taught to aspire, and the other is early confined and limited. As their years increase, the sister must be wholly domesticated, while the brother is led by the hand through all the flowery paths of science. Grant that their minds are by nature equal, yet who shall wonder at the *apparent* superiority. . . . At length arrived at womanhood, the uncultivated fair one feels a void, which the employments allotted her are by no means capable of filling. . . . She herself is most unhappy; she feels the want of a cultivated mind. . . . Should it . . . be vociferated, 'Your domestic employments are sufficient'—I would calmly ask, is it reasonable, that a candidate for immortality, for the joys of heaven, an intelligent being, who is to spend an eternity in contemplating the works of Deity, should at present be so degraded, as to be allowed no other ideas, than those which are suggested by the mechanism of a pudding, or the sewing the seams of a garment? . . .

Yes, ye lordly, ye haughty sex, our souls are by nature *equal* to yours.

From Address of the Democratic-Republican Society of Pennsylvania (December 18, 1794)

The creation of around fifty Democratic-Republican societies in 1793 and 1794 reflected the expansion of the public sphere. The Pennsylvania society issued an address defending itself against critics who questioned its right to criticize the administration of George Washington.

The principles and proceedings of our Association have lately been caluminated [tarred by malicious falsehoods]. We should think ourselves unworthy to be ranked as Freemen, if awed by the name of any man, however he may command the public gratitude for past services, we could suffer in silence so sacred a right, so important a principle, as the freedom of opinion to be infringed, by attack on Societies which stand on that constitutional basis.

Freedom of thought, and a free communication of opinions by speech through the medium of the press, are the safeguards of our Liberties.... By the freedom of opinion, cannot be meant the right of thinking merely; for of this right the greatest Tyrant cannot deprive his meanest slave; but, it is freedom in the communication of sentiments [by] speech or through the press. This liberty is an imprescriptable [unlimitable] right, independent of any Constitution or social compact; it is as complete a right as that which any man has to the enjoyment of his life. These principles are eternal—they are recognized by our Constitution; and that nation is already enslaved that does not acknowledge their truth....

If freedom of opinion, in the sense we understand it, is the right of every Citizen, by what mode of reasoning can that right be denied to an assemblage of Citizens?... The Society are free to declare that they never were more strongly impressed with ... the importance of associations ... than at the present time. The germ of an odious Aristocracy is planted among us—it has taken root.... Let us remain firm in attachment to principles.... Let us be particularly watchful to preserve inviolate the freedom of opinion, assured that it is the most effectual weapon for the protection of our liberty.

QUESTIONS

1. *How does Murray answer the argument that offering education to women will lead them to neglect their "domestic employments"?*

2. *Why does the Democratic-Republican society insist on the centrality of "free communication of opinions" in preserving American liberty?*

3. *How do these documents reflect expanding ideas about who should enjoy the freedom to express one's ideas in the early republic?*

A print shop in the early republic. The increasing number of newspapers played a major role in the expansion of the public sphere.

meant not simply voting in elections but constant involvement in public affairs. It included the right to "exercise watchfulness and inspection, upon the conduct of public officers." Blamed by Federalists for helping to inspire the Whiskey Rebellion, the societies disappeared by the end of 1795. But much of their organization and outlook was absorbed into the emerging Republican Party. They helped to legitimize the right of "any portion of the people," regardless of station in life, to express political opinions and take an active role in public life.

The Rights of Women

Mary Wollstonecraft

The democratic ferment of the 1790s inspired renewed discussion about women's rights. In 1792, Mary Wollstonecraft published in England her extraordinary pamphlet *A Vindication of the Rights of Woman*. Wollstonecraft did not directly challenge traditional gender roles. Her call for greater access to education and to paid employment for women rested on the idea that this would enable single women to support themselves and married women to perform more capably as wives and mothers. But she did "drop a hint," as she put it, that women "ought to have representation" in government. Within two years, American editions of Wollstonecraft's work had appeared, signaling new opportunities for women in the public sphere. Increasing numbers began expressing their thoughts in print. **Judith Sargent Murray**, one of the era's most accomplished American women, wrote essays for the *Massachusetts Magazine* under the pen name "The Gleaner." In her essay "On the Equality of the Sexes," written in 1779 and published in 1790, Murray insisted that women had as much right as men to exercise all their talents and should be allowed equal educational opportunities to enable them to do so.

"On the Equality of the Sexes"

Women were contributing new ideas, but were they part of the new body politic? There was nothing explicitly limiting the rights in the Constitution to men. The Constitution's use of the word "he" to describe officeholders, however, reflected the widespread assumption that politics was a realm for men. The time had not yet come for a broad assault on gender inequality.

The men who wrote the Constitution did not envision the active and continuing involvement of ordinary citizens in affairs of state. But the rise of political parties seeking to mobilize voters in hotly contested elections, the emergence of the "self-created societies," the stirrings of women's political consciousness, and even armed uprisings such as the Whiskey Rebellion broadened and deepened the democratization of public life set in motion by the American Revolution.

THE ADAMS PRESIDENCY

In 1792, Washington won unanimous reelection. Four years later, he decided to retire from public life, in part to establish the precedent that the presidency is not a life office. In his Farewell Address (mostly drafted by Hamilton and published in the newspapers rather than delivered orally; see the Appendix for excerpts from the speech), Washington defended his administration against criticism, warned against the party spirit, and advised his countrymen to steer clear of international power politics by avoiding "permanent alliances with any portion of the foreign world."

The Election of 1796

George Washington's departure unleashed fierce party competition over the choice of his successor. In this, the first contested presidential election, two tickets presented themselves: John Adams, with Thomas Pinckney of South Carolina for vice president, representing the Federalists, and Thomas Jefferson, with Aaron Burr of New York, for the Republicans. Adams received seventy-one electoral votes to Jefferson's sixty-eight. Because of factionalism among the Federalists, Pinckney received only fifty-nine votes, so Jefferson, the leader of the opposition party, became vice president. Voting fell almost entirely along sectional lines: Adams carried New England, New York, and New Jersey, while Jefferson swept the South, along with Pennsylvania.

In 1797, John Adams assumed leadership of a divided nation. His presidency was beset by crises. On the international front, the country was nearly dragged into the ongoing European war. As a neutral nation, the United States claimed the right to trade nonmilitary goods with both Britain and France, but both countries seized American ships with impunity. In 1797, American diplomats were sent to Paris to negotiate a treaty to replace the old alliance of 1778. French officials presented them with a demand for bribes before negotiations could proceed. When Adams made public the envoys' dispatches, the French officials were

An engraving from *The Lady's Magazine and Repository of Entertaining Knowledge*, published in Philadelphia in 1792. A woman identified as the "Genius of the Ladies Magazine" kneels before Liberty, presenting a petition for the "Rights of Women." In the foreground are symbols of the arts, science, and literature—knowledge that should be available to women as well as men.

Adams's presidency beset by crises

designated by the last three letters of the alphabet. This **"XYZ affair"** poisoned America's relations with its former ally. By 1798, the United States and France were engaged in a "quasi-war" at sea. Despite pressure from Hamilton, who desired a declaration of war, Adams in 1800 negotiated peace with France.

Adams was less cautious in domestic affairs. Unrest continued in many rural areas. In 1799, farmers in southeastern Pennsylvania obstructed the assessment of a tax on land and houses that Congress had imposed to help fund an expanded army and navy. A crowd led by John Fries, a local militia leader and auctioneer, released arrested men from prison. The army arrested Fries for treason and proceeded to terrorize his supporters, tear down liberty poles, and whip Republican newspaper editors.

A New Display of the United States, an 1803 engraving by Amos Doolittle, depicts President John Adams surrounded by shields of sixteen states (the original thirteen plus Kentucky, Tennessee, and Vermont), with the population and number of senators and representatives of each. At the top, an eagle holds an arrow, an olive branch, and a banner reading "Millions for our Defence not a Cent for Tribute," a motto that originated during the XYZ affair of 1798 when French officials demanded bribes before entering into negotiations to avoid war with the United States.

Matthew Lyon

The "Reign of Witches"

But the greatest crisis of the Adams administration arose over the **Alien and Sedition Acts of 1798**. Confronted with mounting opposition, some of it voiced by immigrant pamphleteers and editors, Federalists moved to silence their critics. A new Naturalization Act extended from five to fourteen years the residency requirement for immigrants seeking American citizenship. The Alien Act allowed the deportation of persons from abroad deemed "dangerous" by federal authorities. The Sedition Act (which was set to expire in 1801, by which time Adams hoped to have been reelected) authorized the prosecution of virtually any public assembly or publication critical of the government. The new law meant that opposition editors could be prosecuted for almost any political comment they printed. The main target was the Republican press.

The passage of these measures launched what Jefferson—recalling events in Salem, Massachusetts, a century earlier—termed a "reign of witches." Eighteen individuals, including several Republican newspaper editors, were charged under the Sedition Act. Ten were convicted of spreading "false, scandalous, and malicious" information about the government. Matthew Lyon, a member of Congress from Vermont and editor of a Republican newspaper, *The Scourge of Aristocracy*, received a sentence of four months in prison and a fine of $1,000. In Massachusetts, authorities indicted several men for erecting a liberty pole bearing the inscription, "No Stamp Act, no Sedition, no Alien Bill, no Land Tax; Downfall to the Tyrants of America."

The Virginia and Kentucky Resolutions

The Sedition Act thrust freedom of expression to the center of discussions of American liberty. Madison and Jefferson mobilized opposition, drafting resolutions adopted by the Virginia and Kentucky legislatures. Both resolutions attacked the Sedition Act as an unconstitutional violation of the First Amendment. Virginia's, written by Madison, called on the federal courts to protect free speech. The original version of Jefferson's Kentucky resolution went further, asserting that states could nullify laws of Congress that violated the Constitution—that is, states could unilaterally prevent the enforcement of such laws within their borders. The legislature prudently deleted this passage.

> *Opposition to the Sedition Act*

No other state endorsed the **Virginia and Kentucky resolutions**. Many Americans, including many Republicans, were horrified by the idea of state action that might endanger the Union. But the "crisis of freedom" of the late 1790s strongly reinforced the idea that "freedom of discussion" was an indispensable attribute of American liberty and of democratic government. Free speech, as the Massachusetts Federalist Harrison Gray Otis noted, had become the people's "darling privilege."

> *"Freedom of discussion"*

The "Revolution of 1800"

"Jefferson and Liberty" became the watchword of the Republican campaign of 1800. By this time, Republicans had developed effective techniques for mobilizing voters, such as printing pamphlets, handbills, and newspapers and holding mass meetings to promote their cause. The Federalists, who viewed politics as an activity for a small group of elite men, found it difficult to match their opponents' mobilization. Nonetheless, they still dominated New England and enjoyed considerable support in the Middle Atlantic states. Jefferson triumphed, with seventy-three electoral votes to Adams's sixty-five.

Before assuming office, Jefferson was forced to weather an unusual constitutional crisis. Each party arranged to have an elector throw away one of his two votes for president, so that its presidential candidate would come out a vote ahead of the vice presidential. But the designated Republican elector failed to do so. As a result, both Jefferson and his running mate, Aaron Burr, received seventy-three electoral votes. With no candidate having a majority, the election was thrown into the House of Representatives that had been elected in 1798, where the Federalists enjoyed a slight majority. For thirty-five ballots, neither man received a majority of the votes. Finally, Hamilton intervened. He disliked Jefferson

An 1800 campaign banner, with a portrait of Thomas Jefferson and the words, "John Adams is no more."

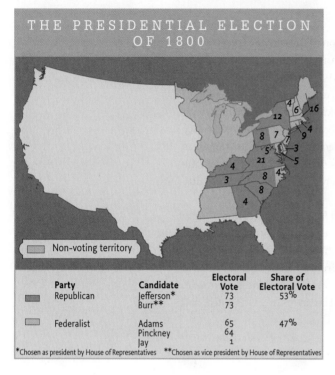

THE PRESIDENTIAL ELECTION
OF 1800

	Party	Candidate	Electoral Vote	Share of Electoral Vote
	Republican	Jefferson*	73	53%
		Burr**	73	
	Federalist	Adams	65	47%
		Pinckney	64	
		Jay	1	

Non-voting territory

*Chosen as president by House of Representatives   **Chosen as vice president by House of Representatives

but believed him enough of a statesman to recognize that the Federalist financial system could not be dismantled.

Hamilton's support for Jefferson tipped the balance. To avoid a repetition of the crisis, Congress and the states soon adopted the Twelfth Amendment to the Constitution, requiring electors to cast separate votes for president and vice president. The election of 1800 also set in motion a chain of events that culminated four years later when Burr killed Hamilton in a duel.

The events of the 1790s demonstrated that a majority of Americans believed ordinary people had a right to play an active role in politics, express their opinions freely, and contest the policies of their government. To their credit, Federalists never considered resistance to the election result. Adams's acceptance of defeat established the vital precedent of a peaceful transfer of power from a defeated party to its successor.

Slavery and Politics

Lurking behind the political battles of the 1790s lay the potentially divisive issue of slavery. Jefferson, after all, received every one of the South's forty-one electoral votes. The triumph of "Jefferson and Liberty" would not have been possible without slavery. Had three-fifths of the slaves not been counted in apportionment, John Adams would have been reelected in 1800.

The issue of slavery would not disappear. The very first Congress under the new Constitution received petitions calling for emancipation. One bore the weighty signature of Benjamin Franklin, who in 1787 had agreed to serve as president of the Pennsylvania Abolition Society. The blessings of liberty, Franklin's petition insisted, should be available "without distinction of color to all descriptions of people." Despite heated debate on both sides of the slavery question, Congress avoided the issue of emancipation. In 1793, to implement the Constitution's fugitive slave clause, Congress enacted a law providing for federal and state judges and local officials to facilitate the return of escaped slaves.

Franklin and abolition

The Haitian Revolution

Events during the 1790s underscored how powerfully slavery defined and distorted American freedom. The same Jeffersonians who hailed the French Revolution as a step in the universal progress of liberty reacted in horror at the slave revolution that began in 1791 in Saint Domingue, the jewel of the French overseas empire situated not far from the southern coast of the United States. Toussaint L'Ouverture, an educated slave on a sugar plantation, forged the rebellious slaves into an army able to defeat British forces seeking to seize the island and then an expedition hoping to reestablish French authority. The slave uprising led to the establishment of Haiti as an independent nation in 1804.

Toussaint L'Ouverture

Although much of the country was left in ruins by years of warfare, the **Haitian Revolution** affirmed the universality of the revolutionary era's creed of liberty. It inspired hopes for freedom among slaves in the United States. Throughout the nineteenth century, black Americans would celebrate the winning of Haitian independence.

Among white Americans, the response to the Haitian Revolution was different. Thousands of refugees from Haiti poured into the United States, fleeing the upheaval. Many spread tales of the massacres of slaveowners and the burning of their plantations, which reinforced white Americans' fears of slave insurrection at home. When Jefferson became president, he sought to quarantine and destroy the hemisphere's second independent republic.

Gabriel's Rebellion

The momentous year of 1800 witnessed not only the "revolution" of Jefferson's election but an attempted real one, a plot by slaves in Virginia itself to gain their freedom. It was organized by a Richmond blacksmith, Gabriel, and his brothers Solomon, also a blacksmith, and Martin, a slave preacher. The conspirators planned to march on the city, which had recently become the state capital, from surrounding plantations. They would kill some white inhabitants and hold the rest, including Governor James Monroe, hostage until their demand for the abolition of slavery was met. The plot was soon discovered and the leaders arrested. Twenty-six slaves, including Gabriel, were hanged and dozens more transported out of the state.

Blacks in 1800 made up half of Richmond's population. One-fifth were free. A black community had emerged in the 1780s and 1790s, and the conspiracy was rooted in its institutions. In cities like Richmond, many skilled slave craftsmen, including Gabriel himself, could read and write

Toussaint L'Overture, leader of the slave revolution in Saint Domingue (modern-day Haiti). Painted in 1800 as part of a series of portraits of French military leaders, it depicts him as a courageous general.

and enjoyed the privilege of hiring themselves out to employers—that is, negotiating their own labor arrangements, with their owner receiving their "wages." Their relative autonomy helps account for slave artisans' prominent role in the conspiracy.

Like other Virginians, the participants in the conspiracy spoke the language of liberty forged in the American Revolution and reinvigorated during the 1790s. "We have as much right," one conspirator declared, "to fight for our liberty as any men." After the rebellion, however, the Virginia legislature tightened controls over the black population—making it illegal for them to congregate on Sundays without white supervision—and severely restricted the possibility that masters could voluntarily free their slaves. Any slave freed after 1806 was required to leave Virginia or be sold back into slavery. The door to emancipation, thrown open during the American Revolution, had been slammed shut.

Tightening control over blacks in Virginia

JEFFERSON IN POWER

The first president to begin his term in Washington, D.C., Jefferson assumed office on March 4, 1801. The city, with its unpaved streets, impoverished residents, and unfinished public buildings, scarcely resembled L'Enfant's grand plan. At one point, part of the roof of the Capitol collapsed, narrowly missing the vice president.

Jefferson's inauguration

Jefferson's inaugural address was conciliatory toward his opponents. "Every difference of opinion," he declared, "is not a difference of principle. . . . We are all Republicans, we are all Federalists." He went on to expound the policies his administration would follow—economy in government, unrestricted trade, freedom of religion and the press, friendship to all nations but "entangling alliances" with none. America, "the world's best hope," would flourish if a limited government allowed its citizens to be "free to regulate their own pursuits."

Dismantling the Federalist system

Jefferson hoped to dismantle as much of the Federalist system as possible. Among his first acts as president was to pardon all those imprisoned under the Sedition Act. During his eight years as president, he reduced the number of government employees and slashed the army and navy. He abolished all taxes except the tariff, including the hated tax on whiskey, and paid off part of the national debt. He aimed to minimize federal power and eliminate government oversight of the economy. His policies ensured that the United States would not become a centralized state on a European model, as Hamilton had envisioned.

Judicial Review

Nonetheless, as Hamilton predicted, it proved impossible to uproot national authority entirely. Jefferson distrusted the unelected judiciary. But during his presidency, and for many years thereafter, the Federalist John Marshall headed the Supreme Court. A strong believer in national supremacy, Marshall established the Court's power to review laws of Congress and the states.

The Marshall court

The first landmark decision of the Marshall Court came in 1803, in the case of **Marbury v. Madison**. On the eve of leaving office, Adams had appointed a number of justices of the peace for the District of Columbia. Madison, Jefferson's secretary of state, refused to issue commissions (the official documents entitling them to assume their posts) to these "midnight judges." Four, including William Marbury, sued for their offices. Marshall's decision declared unconstitutional the section of the Judiciary Act of 1789 that allowed the courts to order executive officials to deliver judges' commissions. It exceeded the power of Congress as outlined in the Constitution and was therefore void. Marbury, in other words, may have been entitled to his commission, but the Court had no power under the Constitution to order Madison to deliver it. The Supreme Court had assumed the right to determine whether an act of Congress violates the Constitution—a power known as "judicial review."

Seven years later, in *Fletcher v. Peck*, the Court extended judicial review to state laws. In 1794, four land companies had paid nearly every member of the state legislature, Georgia's two U.S. senators, and a number of federal judges to secure their right to purchase land in present-day Alabama and Mississippi claimed by Georgia. Two years later, many of the corrupt lawmakers were defeated for reelection, and the new legislature rescinded the land grant and subsequent sales. Whatever the circumstances of the legislature's initial action, Marshall declared, the Constitution prohibited Georgia from taking any action that impaired a contract. Therefore, the individual purchasers could keep their land, and the legislature could not repeal the original grant.

Fletcher v. Peck

The Louisiana Purchase

But the greatest irony of Jefferson's presidency involved his greatest achievement, the **Louisiana Purchase** of 1803. This resulted not from astute American diplomacy but because the rebellious slaves of Saint Domingue defeated forces sent by the ruler of France, Napoleon Bonaparte, to reconquer the island. Moreover, to take advantage of the sudden opportunity to purchase Louisiana, Jefferson had to abandon his conviction that the federal government was limited to powers specifically mentioned in the Constitution, because the document said nothing about buying territory from a foreign power.

This vast Louisiana Territory, which stretched from the Gulf of Mexico to Canada and from the Mississippi River to the Rocky Mountains, had been ceded by France to Spain in 1762 as part of the reshuffling of colonial possessions at the end of the Seven Years' War. France secretly reacquired it in 1800. Soon after taking office, Jefferson learned of the arrangement. He had long been concerned about American access to the port of New Orleans, which lay within Louisiana at the mouth of the Mississippi River. The right to trade through New Orleans, essential to western farmers, had been acknowledged in the Treaty of San Lorenzo (also known as Pinckney's Treaty) of 1795 between the United States and Spain. But Jefferson feared that the far more powerful French might try to interfere with American commerce. Needing money for military campaigns in Europe and with his dreams of American empire in ruins because of his inability to reestablish control over Saint Domingue, Napoleon offered to sell the entire Louisiana Territory. The cost, $15 million (the equivalent of perhaps $250 million in today's money), made the Louisiana Purchase one of history's greatest real estate bargains.

Reasons for the Louisiana Purchase

In a stroke, Jefferson had doubled the size of the United States and ended the French presence in North America. Jefferson admitted that he had "done an act beyond the Constitution." But he believed the benefits justified his transgression. Farmers, Jefferson had written, were "the chosen

Effects of the Purchase

White Hall Plantation, painted around 1800, depicts a Louisiana plantation and the dynamism of the region's economy on the eve of its acquisition by the United States. Black oarsmen man a boat carrying bales of cotton for sale in New Orleans.

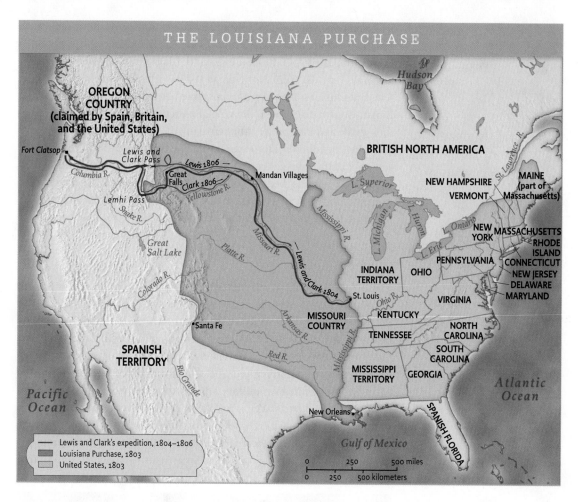

THE LOUISIANA PURCHASE

The Louisiana Purchase of 1803 doubled the land area of the United States.

people of God," and the country would remain "virtuous" as long as it was "chiefly agricultural." Now, Jefferson believed, he had ensured the agrarian character of the United States and its political stability for centuries to come.

Lewis and Clark

Within a year of the purchase, Jefferson dispatched an expedition led by Meriwether Lewis and William Clark, two Virginia-born veterans of Indian wars in the Ohio Valley, to explore the new territory. Their objects were both scientific and commercial—to study the area's plants, animal life, and geography, and to discover how the region could be exploited economically.

Scientific and commercial objectives

A page from William Clark's journal of the Lewis and Clark expedition, depicting a salmon. Among their tasks was to record information about the West's plants, animal life, and geography.

Jefferson hoped the explorers would establish trading relations with western Indians and locate a water route to the Pacific Ocean.

In the spring of 1804, Lewis and Clark's fifty-member "corps of discovery" set out from St. Louis on the most famous exploring party in American history. They were accompanied by a fifteen-year-old Shoshone Indian woman, Sacajawea, the wife of a French fur trader, who served as their guide and interpreter. After crossing the Rocky Mountains, the expedition reached the Pacific Ocean in the area of present-day Oregon. They returned in 1806, bringing with them an immense amount of information about the region as well as numerous plant and animal specimens. The success of their journey helped to strengthen the idea that American territory was destined to reach all the way to the Pacific.

Incorporating Louisiana

The only part of the Louisiana Purchase with a significant non-Indian population in 1803 was the region around New Orleans. When the United States took control, the city had around 8,000 inhabitants, including nearly 3,000 slaves and 1,300 free persons of color. Incorporating this diverse population into the United States was by no means easy. French and Spanish law accorded free blacks, many of whom were the offspring of unions between white military officers and slave women, nearly all the rights of white citizens. Moreover, Spain made it easy for slaves to obtain their freedom through purchase or voluntary emancipation by the owners.

The treaty that transferred Louisiana to the United States promised that all free inhabitants would enjoy "the rights, advantages, and immu-

New Orleans in 1803, at the time of the Louisiana Purchase. The painting shows a view of the city from a nearby plantation. The town houses of merchants and plantation owners line the broad promenade along the waterfront. At the lower center, a slave goes about his work. An eagle holds aloft a banner that suggests the heady optimism of the young republic: Under My Wings Every Thing Prospers.

UNDER MY WINGS EVERY THING PROSPERS

nities of citizens." Spanish and French civil codes, unlike British and American law, recognized women as co-owners of family property. Under American rule, Louisiana retained this principle of "community property" within marriage. But free blacks suffered a steady decline in status. And the local legislature soon adopted one of the most sweeping slave codes in the South. Louisiana's slaves had enjoyed far more freedom under the rule of tyrannical Spain than as part of the liberty-loving United States.

Louisiana slavery

The Barbary Wars

Jefferson hoped to avoid foreign entanglements, but he found it impossible as president to avoid being drawn into the continuing wars of Europe. Even as he sought to limit the power of the national government, foreign relations compelled him to expand it. The first war fought by the United States was to protect American commerce in a dangerous world.

The Barbary states on the northern coast of Africa had long preyed on shipping in the Mediterranean and Atlantic, receiving tribute from several countries, including the United States, to protect their vessels. In 1801, Jefferson refused demands for increased payments, and the pasha of Tripoli declared war on the United States. The naval conflict lasted until 1804, when an American squadron won a victory at Tripoli harbor (a victory commemorated in the official hymn of the Marine Corps, which mentions fighting on "the shores of Tripoli").

Protecting American commerce

The **Barbary Wars** were the new nation's first encounter with the Islamic world. In the 1790s, as part of an attempt to establish peaceful relations, the federal government declared that the United States was "not, in any sense, founded on the Christian religion." But the conflicts helped to establish a long-lasting pattern in which Americans viewed Muslims as an exotic people whose way of life did not adhere to Western standards.

The Embargo

Far more serious in its impact on the United States was warfare between Britain and France, which resumed in 1803 after a brief lull. By 1806, each combatant had declared the other under blockade, seeking to deny trade with America to its rival. The Royal Navy resumed the practice of impressment. By the end of 1807, it had seized more than 6,000 American sailors (claiming they were British citizens and deserters).

Blockades by Britain and France

To Jefferson, the economic health of the United States required freedom of trade with which no foreign government had a right to interfere. American farmers needed access to markets in Europe and the Caribbean.

Deciding to use trade as a weapon, in December 1807 he persuaded Congress to enact the **Embargo**, a ban on all American vessels sailing for foreign ports. For a believer in limited government, this was an amazing exercise of federal power.

In 1808, American exports plummeted by 80 percent. Unfortunately, neither Britain nor France, locked in a death struggle, took much notice. But the Embargo devastated the economies of American port cities. Just before his term ended, in March 1809, Jefferson signed the Non-Intercourse Act, banning trade only with Britain and France but providing that if either side rescinded its edicts against American shipping, commerce with that country would resume.

Effects of the Embargo

Madison and Pressure for War

Jefferson left office at the lowest point of his career. He had won a sweeping reelection in 1804, receiving 162 electoral votes to only 14 for the Federalist candidate, Charles C. Pinckney. With the exception of Connecticut, he even carried the Federalist stronghold of New England. Four years later, his handpicked successor, James Madison, also won an easy victory. The Embargo, however, had failed to achieve its diplomatic aims and was increasingly violated by American shippers. In 1810, Madison adopted a new policy. Congress enacted a measure known as Macon's Bill No. 2, which allowed trade to resume but provided that if either France or Britain ceased interfering with American rights, the president could reimpose an embargo on the other. With little to lose, since Britain controlled the seas, the French emperor Napoleon announced that he had repealed his decrees against neutral shipping. But the British continued to attack American vessels. In the spring of 1812, Madison reimposed the embargo on trade with Britain.

Macon's Bill No. 2

Meanwhile, a group of younger congressmen, mostly from the West, were calling for war with Britain. Known as the War Hawks, this new generation of political leaders had come of age after the winning of independence and were ardent nationalists. Their leaders included Henry Clay of Kentucky, elected Speaker of the House of Representatives in 1810, and John C. Calhoun of South Carolina. The War Hawks spoke passionately of defending the national honor against British insults, but they also had more practical goals in mind, notably the annexation of Canada and the conquest of Florida, a haven for fugitive slaves owned by Britain's ally Spain. Members of Congress also spoke of the necessity of upholding the principle of free trade and liberating the United States once and for all from European infringements on its independence.

War Hawks

THE "SECOND WAR OF INDEPENDENCE"

The growing crisis between the United States and Britain took place against the background of deteriorating Indian relations in the West, which also helped propel the United States down the road to war. Jefferson had long favored the removal beyond the Mississippi River of Indian tribes that refused to cooperate in "civilizing" themselves. He encouraged traders to lend money to Indians, in the hope that accumulating debt would force them to sell some of their holdings west of the Appalachian Mountains, thus freeing up more land for "our increasing numbers." On the other hand, the government continued President Washington's policy of promoting settled farming among the Indians.

Indian relations in the West

The Indian Response

By 1800, nearly 400,000 American settlers lived west of the Appalachian Mountains. They far outnumbered the remaining Indians, whose seemingly irreversible decline in power led some Indians to rethink their opposition to assimilation. Among the Creek and Cherokee, a group led by men of mixed Indian-white ancestry like Major Ridge and John Ross enthusiastically endorsed the federal policy of promoting "civilization." Many had established businesses as traders and slaveowning farmers with the help of their white fathers. Their views, in turn, infuriated "nativists," who strongly opposed assimilation.

Changing attitudes toward assimilation

The period from 1800 to 1812 was an "age of prophecy" among the Indians, as many tribal leaders sought to revitalize Indian life. A militant message was expounded by two Shawnee brothers—**Tecumseh**, a chief who had refused to sign the Treaty of Greenville in 1795, and **Tenskwatawa**, a religious prophet who called for complete separation from whites, the revival of traditional Indian culture, and resistance to federal policies. White people, Tenskwatawa preached, were the source of all evil in the world, and Indians should abandon American alcohol, clothing, food, and manufactured goods. His followers gathered at Prophetstown, located on the Wabash River in Indiana.

Tecumseh meanwhile traversed the Mississippi Valley, pressing the argument that the alternative to Indian resistance was extermination. He repudiated chiefs who had sold land to the federal government: "Sell a country! Why not sell the air, the great sea, as well as the earth? Did not the Great Spirit make them all for the use of his children?" In 1810, Tecumseh called for attacks on American frontier settlements. In November 1811,

Tenskwatawa (the Prophet), in a portrait by the American artist Charles Bird King, who painted numerous Indian leaders.

while he was absent, American forces under William Henry Harrison destroyed Prophetstown in the Battle of Tippecanoe.

The War of 1812

In 1795, James Madison had written that war is the greatest enemy of "true liberty." Nonetheless, Madison became a war president. Reports that the British were encouraging Tecumseh's efforts contributed to the coming of the War of 1812. In June 1812, with assaults on American shipping continuing, Madison asked Congress for a declaration of war. American nationality, the president declared, was at stake—would Americans remain "an independent people" or become "colonists and vassals" of Great Britain? The vote revealed a deeply divided country. Both Federalists and Republicans representing the states from New Jersey northward, where most of the mercantile and financial resources of the country were concentrated, voted against war. The South and West were strongly in favor. The bill passed the House by a vote of 79–49 and the Senate by 19–13. It was the first time the

America's first war declared

United States declared war on another country, and it was approved by the smallest margin of any declaration of war in American history.

In retrospect, it seems remarkably foolhardy for a disunited and militarily unprepared nation to go to war with one of the world's two major powers. Fortunately for the United States, Great Britain at the outset was preoccupied with the struggle in Europe. But it easily repelled two feeble American invasions of Canada and imposed a blockade that all but destroyed American commerce. In 1814, having finally defeated Napoleon, Britain invaded the United States. Its forces seized Washington, D.C., and burned the White House, while the government fled for safety.

Americans did enjoy a few military successes. In August 1812, the American frigate *Constitution* defeated the British warship *Guerriere*. Commodore Oliver H. Perry defeated a British naval force in September 1813 on Lake Erie. In the following year, a British assault on Baltimore was repulsed when Fort McHenry at the entrance to the harbor withstood a British bombardment. This was the occasion when Francis Scott Key composed "The Star-Spangled Banner," an ode to the "land of the free and home of the brave" that became the national anthem during the 1930s.

Fighting the British and the Indians

Like the War of Independence, the War of 1812 was a two-front struggle—against the British and against the Indians. The war produced significant victories over western Indians who sided with the British. In 1813, pan-Indian forces led by Tecumseh (who had been commissioned a general in the British army) were defeated, and he himself was killed, at the Battle of the Thames, near Detroit, by an American force led by William Henry Harrison. In March 1814, an army of Americans and pro-assimilation

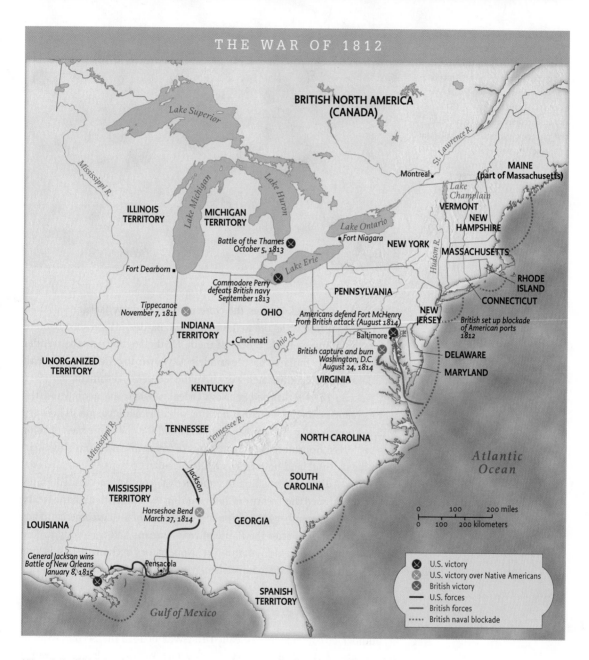

THE WAR OF 1812

BRITISH NORTH AMERICA (CANADA)

Lake Superior

St. Lawrence R.

Montreal

MAINE (part of Massachusetts)

Lake Champlain

ILLINOIS TERRITORY

Lake Michigan

MICHIGAN TERRITORY

Lake Huron

VERMONT

NEW HAMPSHIRE

Mississippi R.

Battle of the Thames
October 5, 1813

Lake Ontario

Fort Niagara

NEW YORK

Hudson R.

MASSACHUSETTS

Fort Dearborn

Commodore Perry
defeats British navy
September 1813

Lake Erie

RHODE ISLAND

CONNECTICUT

Tippecanoe
November 7, 1811

OHIO

PENNSYLVANIA

NEW JERSEY

British set up blockade
of American ports
1812

INDIANA TERRITORY

Cincinnati

Americans defend Fort McHenry
from British attack (August 1814)

Baltimore

DELAWARE

Ohio R.

British capture and burn
Washington, D.C.
August 24, 1814

MARYLAND

UNORGANIZED TERRITORY

KENTUCKY

VIRGINIA

TENNESSEE

Tennessee R.

NORTH CAROLINA

*Atlantic
Ocean*

Mississippi R.

MISSISSIPPI TERRITORY

Jackson

SOUTH CAROLINA

| 0 | 100 | 200 miles |
| 0 | 100 | 200 kilometers |

LOUISIANA

Horseshoe Bend
March 27, 1814

GEORGIA

General Jackson wins
Battle of New Orleans
January 8, 1815

Pensacola

SPANISH TERRITORY

Gulf of Mexico

⊗	U.S. victory
⊗	U.S. victory over Native Americans
⊗	British victory
—	U.S. forces
—	British forces
····	British naval blockade

Although the British burned the nation's capital, the War of 1812 essentially was a military draw.

The Hornet and Peacock, Or, John Bull in Distress, a watercolor by Amos B. Doolittle from 1813, celebrates a victory by the American warship *Hornet* over the British vessel *Peacock* during the War of 1812. Britain is represented as a half-bull, half-peacock creature being stung in the neck by a hornet.

Cherokees and Creeks under the command of Andrew Jackson defeated hostile Creeks known as the Red Sticks at the Battle of Horseshoe Bend in Alabama, killing more than 800 of them. He dictated terms of surrender that required the Indians, hostile and friendly alike, to cede more than half their land, over 23 million acres in all, to the federal government.

Battle of New Orleans

Jackson then proceeded to New Orleans, where he engineered the war's greatest American victory, fighting off a British invasion in January 1815. Although a slaveholder, Jackson recruited the city's free men of color into his forces, appealing to them as "sons of freedom" and promising them the same pay and land bounties as white recruits.

Treaty of Ghent

With neither side wishing to continue the conflict, the United States and Britain signed the Treaty of Ghent, ending the war. Although the treaty was signed in December 1814, ships carrying news of the agreement did not reach America until after the Battle of New Orleans had been fought. The treaty restored the previous status quo. No territory exchanged hands, nor did any provisions relate to impressment or neutral shipping rights.

The War's Aftermath

A number of contemporaries called the War of 1812 the Second War of Independence. Jackson's victory at New Orleans not only made him a national hero but also became a celebrated example of the ability of virtuous citizens of a republic to defeat the forces of despotic Europe.

American control east of the Mississippi

Moreover, the war completed the conquest of the area east of the Mississippi River, which had begun during the Revolution. Never again would the British or Indians pose a threat to American control of this vast region. In its aftermath, white settlers poured into Indiana, Michigan, Alabama, and Mississippi, bringing with them their distinctive forms of social organization.

Britain's defeat of Napoleon inaugurated a long period of peace in Europe. With diplomatic affairs playing less and less of a role in American public life, Americans' sense of separateness from the Old World grew ever stronger.

The End of the Federalist Party

Jefferson and Madison succeeded in one major political aim—the elimination of the Federalist Party. At first, the war led to a revival of Federalist fortunes. With antiwar sentiment at its peak in 1812, Madison had been reelected by the relatively narrow margin of 128 electoral votes to 89 over his Federalist opponent, DeWitt Clinton of New York. But then came a self-inflicted blow. In December 1814, a group of New England Federalists gathered at Hartford, Connecticut, to give voice to their party's long-standing grievances, especially the domination of the federal government by Virginia presidents and their own region's declining influence as new western states entered the Union. Contrary to later myth, the **Hartford Convention** did not call for secession or disunion. But it affirmed the right of a state to "interpose" its authority if the federal government violated the Constitution.

The Hartford Convention had barely adjourned before Jackson electrified the nation with his victory at New Orleans. In speeches and sermons, political and religious leaders alike proclaimed that Jackson's triumph revealed, once again, that a divine hand oversaw America's destiny. The Federalists could not free themselves from the charge of lacking patriotism. Within a few years, their party no longer existed. Yet in their dying moments Federalists had raised an issue—southern domination of the national government—that would long outlive their political party. And the country stood on the verge of a profound economic and social transformation that strengthened the very forces of commercial development that Federalists had welcomed and many Republicans feared.

War Party at Fort Douglas, a watercolor by the Swiss-born Canadian artist Peter Rindisbacher. Painted in 1823, it depicts an incident during the War of 1812 when Indian allies of Great Britain fired rifles into the air to greet their commander, Captain Andrew Bulger, pictured on the far right.

Legacy of Federalist Party

CHAPTER REVIEW AND ONLINE RESOURCES

REVIEW QUESTIONS

1. *Identify the major parts of Hamilton's financial plan, who supported these proposals, and why they aroused such passionate opposition.*

2. *How did the French Revolution and the ensuing global struggle between Great Britain and France shape early American politics?*

3. *How did the United States become involved in foreign affairs in this period?*

4. *How did the expansion of the public sphere and a new language of rights offer opportunities to women?*

5. *What caused the demise of the Federalists?*

6. *What impact did the Haitian Revolution have on the United States?*

7. *How did the Louisiana Purchase affect the situation of Native Americans in that region?*

8. *Whose status was changed the most by the War of 1812— Great Britain, the United States, or Native Americans?*

KEY TERMS

Bank of the United States (p. 223)

Report on Manufactures (p. 223)

strict constructionists (p. 224)

impressment (p. 225)

Jay's Treaty (p. 225)

Federalists and Republicans (p. 226)

Whiskey Rebellion (p. 226)

A Vindication of the Rights of Woman (p. 230)

Judith Sargent Murray (p. 230)

XYZ affair (p. 232)

Alien and Sedition Acts (p. 232)

Virginia and Kentucky resolutions (p. 233)

Haitian Revolution (p. 235)

Gabriel's Rebellion (p. 235)

Marbury v. Madison (p. 237)

Louisiana Purchase (p. 237)

expedition of Lewis and Clark (p. 239)

Barbary Wars (p. 241)

Embargo Act (p. 242)

Tecumseh and Tenskwatawa (p. 243)

Hartford Convention (p. 247)

wwnorton.com /studyspace

VISIT STUDYSPACE FOR THESE RESOURCES AND MORE

- A chapter outline
- A diagnostic chapter quiz
- Interactive maps
- Map worksheets
- Multimedia documents

THE MARKET REVOLUTION

1800–1840

A watercolor from 1829 depicts the Erie Canal five years after it opened. Boats carrying passengers and goods traverse the waterway, along whose banks farms and villages have sprung up.

In 1824, the Marquis de Lafayette visited the United States. Nearly fifty years had passed since, as a youth of twenty, the French nobleman fought at Washington's side in the War of Independence. Since 1784, when he had last journeyed to the United States, the nation's population had tripled to nearly 12 million, its land area had more than doubled, and its political institutions had thrived. The thirteen states of 1784 had grown to twenty-four, and Lafayette visited every one. He traveled up the Mississippi and Ohio rivers by steamboat, a recent invention that was helping to bring economic development to the trans-Appalachian West, and crossed upstate New York via the Erie Canal, the world's longest man-made waterway, which linked the region around the Great Lakes with the Atlantic coast via the Hudson River.

Americans in the first half of the nineteenth century were fond of describing liberty as the defining quality of their new nation, the unique genius of its institutions. Likenesses of the goddess of Liberty, a familiar figure in eighteenth-century British visual imagery, became even more common in the United States, appearing in paintings and sculpture and on folk art from weather vanes to quilts and tavern signs. In *Democracy in America*, the French historian and politician Alexis de Tocqueville wrote of the "holy cult of freedom" he encountered on his own visit to the United States during the early 1830s. "For fifty years," he wrote, "the inhabitants of the United States have been repeatedly and constantly told that they are the only religious, enlightened, and free people. They . . . have an immensely high opinion of themselves and are not far from believing that they form a species apart from the rest of the human race."

Even as Lafayette, Tocqueville, and numerous other visitors from abroad toured the United States, however, Americans' understandings of freedom were changing. Three historical processes unleashed by the Revolution accelerated after the War of 1812: the spread of market relations, the westward movement of the population, and the rise of a vigorous political democracy. (The first two will be discussed in this chapter, the third in Chapter 10.) All helped to reshape the idea of freedom, identifying it ever more closely with economic opportunity, physical mobility, and participation in a vibrantly democratic political system.

But American freedom also continued to be shaped by the presence of slavery. Lafayette, who had purchased a plantation in the West Indies and freed its slaves, once wrote, "I would never have drawn my sword in the cause of America if I could have conceived that thereby I was founding a land of slavery." Yet slavery was moving westward with the young republic. Half a century after the winning of independence, the coexistence of liberty and slavery, and their simultaneous expansion, remained the central contradiction of American life.

A NEW ECONOMY

In the first half of the nineteenth century, an economic transformation known to historians as the market revolution swept over the United States. Its catalyst was a series of innovations in transportation and communication. The market revolution was an acceleration of developments already under way in the colonial era. As noted in previous chapters, southern planters were selling the products of slave labor in the international market as early as the seventeenth century. By the eighteenth, many colonists had been drawn into Britain's commercial empire. Consumer goods like sugar and tea and market-oriented tactics like the boycott of British goods had been central to the political battles leading up to independence.

An economic transformation

Nonetheless, as Americans moved across the Appalachian Mountains and into interior regions of the states along the Atlantic coast, they found themselves more and more isolated from markets. In 1800, American farm families produced at home most of what they needed, from clothing to farm implements. What they could not make themselves, they obtained by bartering with their neighbors or purchasing from local stores and from rural craftsmen like blacksmiths and shoemakers. Those farmers not located near cities or navigable waterways found it almost impossible to market their produce. Many Americans devoted their energies to solving the technological problems that inhibited commerce within the country.

An early version of the great seal of Ohio, which entered the Union in 1803, depicts a canal boat.

Roads and Steamboats

In the first half of the nineteenth century, in rapid succession, the steamboat, canal, railroad, and telegraph wrenched America out of its economic past. These innovations opened new land to settlement, lowered transportation costs, and made it far easier for economic enterprises to sell their products. They linked farmers to national and world markets and made them major consumers of manufactured goods. Americans, wrote Tocqueville, had "annihilated space and time."

In 1806, Congress authorized the construction of the paved National Road from Cumberland, Maryland, to the Old Northwest. It reached Wheeling, on the Ohio River, in 1818 and by 1838 extended to Illinois, where it ended. But it was improved water transportation that most dramatically increased the speed and lowered the expense of commerce.

Robert Fulton, a Pennsylvania-born artist and engineer, had experimented with **steamboat** designs while living in France during the 1790s. But not until 1807, when Fulton's ship, the *Clermont*, navigated the Hudson River from New York City to Albany, was the steamboat's technological and commercial feasibility demonstrated. The invention made possible upstream commerce (that is, travel against the current) on the country's major rivers as well as rapid transport across the Great Lakes and, eventually, the Atlantic Ocean. By 1811, the first steamboat had been introduced on the Mississippi River; twenty years later some 200 plied its waters.

Advantages of the steamboat

The Erie Canal

The completion in 1825 of the 363-mile **Erie Canal** across upstate New York (a remarkable feat of engineering at a time when America's next largest canal was only twenty-eight miles long) allowed goods to flow between the Great Lakes and New York City. Almost instantaneously, the canal attracted an influx of farmers migrating from New England, giving birth to cities like Buffalo, Rochester, and Syracuse along its path.

Connecting New York City and the Old Northwest

New York governor DeWitt Clinton, who oversaw the construction of the state-financed canal, predicted that it would make New York City "the granary of the world, the emporium of commerce, the seat of manufactures, the focus of great moneyed operations." And, indeed, the canal gave

A view of New York City, in 1849, by the noted lithographer Nathaniel Currier. Steamships and sailing vessels of various sizes crowd the harbor of the nation's largest city and busiest port.

THE MARKET REVOLUTION: ROADS AND CANALS, 1840

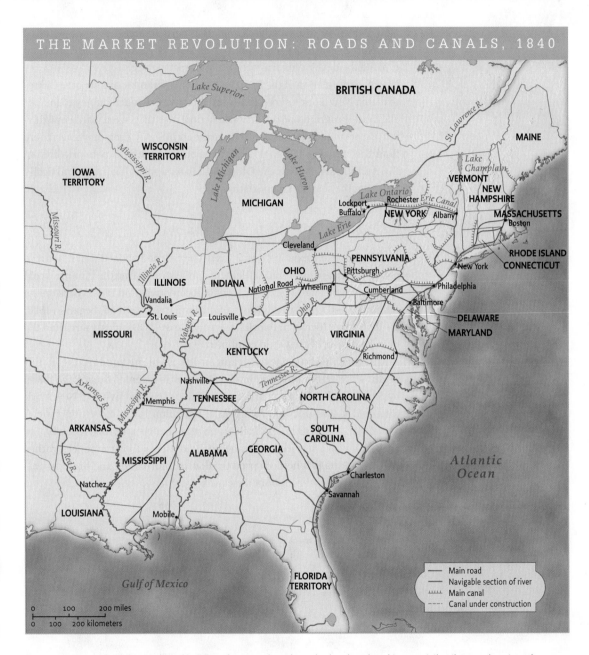

The improvement of existing roads and building of new roads and canals sharply reduced transportation times and costs and stimulated the growth of the market economy.

New York City primacy over competing ports in access to trade with the Old Northwest. In its financing by the state government, the Erie Canal typified the developing transportation infrastructure.

The completion of the Erie Canal set off a scramble among other states to match New York's success. Several borrowed so much money to finance elaborate programs of canal construction that they went bankrupt during the economic depression that began in 1837. By then, however, more than 3,000 miles of canals had been built, creating a network linking the Atlantic states with the Ohio and Mississippi valleys and drastically reducing the cost of transportation.

State spending for internal improvements

Railroads and the Telegraph

Canals connected existing waterways. The **railroad** opened vast new areas of the American interior to settlement, while stimulating the mining of coal for fuel and the manufacture of iron for locomotives and rails. Work on the Baltimore and Ohio, the nation's first commercial railroad, began in 1828. By 1860, the railroad network had grown to 30,000 miles, more than the total in the rest of the world combined.

At the same time, the **telegraph** made possible instantaneous communication throughout the nation. The device was invented during the 1830s by Samuel F. B. Morse, an artist and amateur scientist living in New York City, and it was put into commercial operation in 1844. Within sixteen years, some 50,000 miles of telegraph wire had been strung. Initially, the telegraph was a service for businesses, and especially newspapers, rather than individuals. It helped speed the flow of information and brought uniformity to prices throughout the country.

An 1827 engraving designed to show the feasibility of railroads driven by steam-powered locomotives, and dedicated to the president of the Baltimore and Ohio Railroad, which began construction in the following year. The engraver placed passengers as far from the locomotive as possible to ensure their safety in case of an explosion.

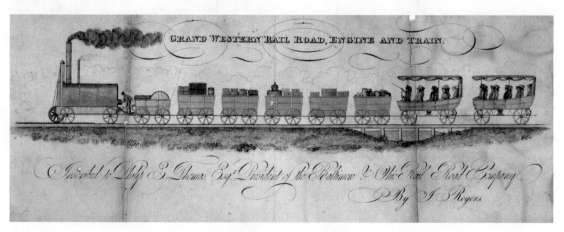

GRAND WESTERN RAIL ROAD, ENGINE AND TRAIN.

The Rise of the West

Improvements in transportation and communication made possible the rise of the West as a powerful, self-conscious region of the new nation. Between 1790 and 1840, some 4.5 million people crossed the Appalachian Mountains—more than the entire U.S. population at the time of Washington's first inauguration. Most of this migration took place after the end of the War of 1812, which unleashed a flood of land-hungry settlers moving from eastern states. In the six years following the end of the war in 1815, six new states entered the Union (Indiana, Illinois, Missouri, Alabama, Mississippi, and Maine—the last an eastern frontier for New England).

Migration west

Few Americans moved west as lone pioneers. More frequently, people traveled in groups and, once they arrived in the West, cooperated with each other to clear land, build houses and barns, and establish communities. One stream of migration, including both small farmers and planters with their slaves, flowed out of the South to create the new Cotton Kingdom of Alabama, Mississippi, Louisiana, and Arkansas. Many farm families from the Upper South crossed into southern Ohio, Indiana, and Illinois. A third population stream moved from New England across New York to the Upper Northwest—northern Ohio, Indiana, and Illinois, and Michigan and Wisconsin.

Some western migrants became "**squatters**," setting up farms on unoccupied land without a clear legal title. Those who purchased land acquired it either from the federal government, at the price, after 1820, of $1.25 per acre payable in cash or from land speculators on long-term credit. The West became the home of regional cultures very much like those the migrants

Regional cultures in the West

A watercolor by the artist Edwin Whitefield depicts a squatter's cabin in the Minnesota woods.

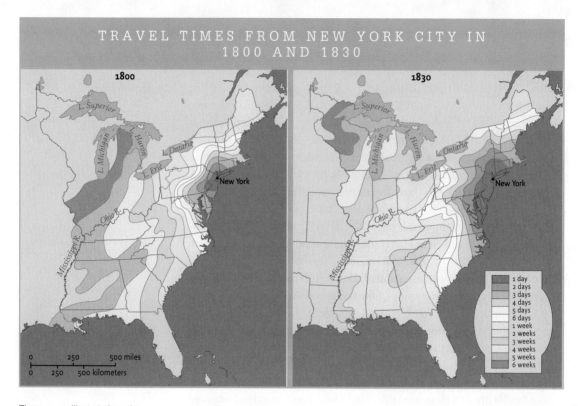

TRAVEL TIMES FROM NEW YORK CITY IN 1800 AND 1830

1800

L. Superior
L. Michigan
L. Huron
L. Ontario
L. Erie
New York
Ohio R.
Mississippi R.

0   250   500 miles
0   250   500 kilometers

1830

L. Superior
L. Michigan
L. Huron
L. Ontario
L. Erie
New York
Ohio R.
Mississippi R.

1 day
2 days
3 days
4 days
5 days
6 days
1 week
2 weeks
3 weeks
4 weeks
5 weeks
6 weeks

These maps illustrate how the transportation revolution of the early nineteenth century made possible much more rapid travel within the United States.

Expansion into Florida

had left behind. Upstate New York and the Upper Northwest resembled New England, with its small towns, churches, and schools, while the Lower South replicated the plantation-based society of the southern Atlantic states.

National boundaries made little difference to territorial expansion—in Florida, and later in Texas and Oregon, American settlers rushed in to claim land under the jurisdiction of foreign countries (Spain, Mexico, and Britain) or Indian tribes, confident that American sovereignty would soon follow in their wake. In 1810, American residents of West Florida rebelled and seized Baton Rouge, and the United States soon annexed the area. The drive for the acquisition of East Florida was spurred by Georgia and Alabama planters who wished to eliminate a refuge for fugitive slaves and hostile Seminole Indians. Andrew Jackson led troops into the area in 1818. While on foreign soil, he created an international crisis by executing two British traders and a number of Indian chiefs. Although Jackson withdrew, Spain, aware that it could not defend the territory, sold it to the United States in the Adams-Onís Treaty of 1819 negotiated by John Quincy Adams.

Successive censuses told the remarkable story of western growth. In 1840, by which time the government had sold to settlers and land companies nearly 43 million acres of land, 7 million Americans—two-fifths of the total population—lived beyond the Appalachian Mountains. Between 1810 and 1830, Ohio's population grew from 231,000 to more than 900,000. It reached nearly 2 million in 1850, when it ranked third among all the states. The careers of the era's leading public figures reflected the westward movement. Andrew Jackson, Henry Clay, and many other statesmen were born in states along the Atlantic coast but made their mark in politics after moving west.

40 percent of Americans west of the Appalachian Mountains

The Cotton Kingdom

Although the market revolution and westward expansion occurred simultaneously in the North and the South, their combined effects heightened the nation's sectional divisions. In some ways, the most dynamic feature of the American economy in the first thirty years of the nineteenth century was the rise of the **Cotton Kingdom**. The early industrial revolution, which began in England and soon spread to parts of the North, centered on factories producing cotton textiles with water-powered spinning and weaving machinery. These factories generated an immense demand for cotton, a crop the Deep South was particularly suited to growing because of its climate and soil fertility. Until 1793, the marketing of cotton had been slowed by the laborious task of removing seeds from the plant itself. But

Cotton and industry

TABLE 9.1 Population Growth of Selected Western States, 1800–1850 (Excluding Indians)

STATE	1810	1830	1850
Alabama	9,000	310,000	772,000
Illinois	12,000	157,000	851,000
Indiana	25,000	343,000	988,000
Louisiana	77,000	216,000	518,000
Mississippi	31,000	137,000	607,000
Missouri	20,000	140,000	682,000
Ohio	231,000	938,000	1,980,000

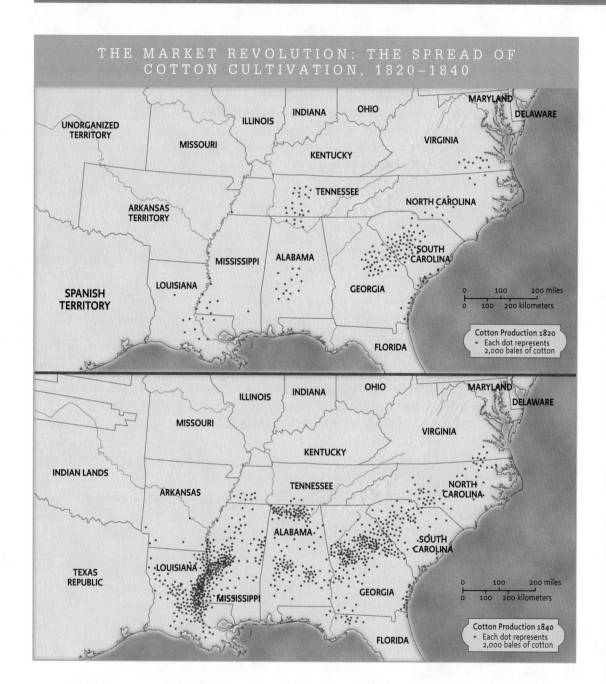

THE MARKET REVOLUTION: THE SPREAD OF COTTON CULTIVATION, 1820–1840

Maps of cotton production graphically illustrate the rise of the Cotton Kingdom stretching from South Carolina to Louisiana.

in that year, Eli Whitney, a Yale graduate working in Georgia as a private tutor, invented the **cotton gin**. A fairly simple device consisting of rollers and brushes, the gin quickly separated the seed from the cotton. Coupled with rising demand for cotton and the opening of new lands in the West, Whitney's invention revolutionized American slavery, an institution that many Americans had expected to die out because its major crop, tobacco, exhausted the soil.

After the War of 1812, the federal government moved to consolidate American control over the Deep South, forcing defeated Indians to cede land, encouraging white settlement, and acquiring Florida. Settlers from the older southern states flooded into the region. Planters monopolized the most fertile land, whereas poorer farmers were generally confined to less productive and less accessible areas in the "hill country" and piney woods. After Congress prohibited the Atlantic slave trade in 1808—the earliest date allowed by the Constitution—a massive trade in slaves developed within the United States, supplying the labor force required by the new Cotton Kingdom.

Slave trading became a well-organized business, with firms gathering slaves in Maryland, Virginia, and South Carolina and shipping them to markets in Mobile, Natchez, and New Orleans. Slave coffles—groups chained to one another on forced marches to the Deep South—became a common sight. Indeed, historians estimate that around 1 million slaves were shifted from the older slave states to the Deep South between 1800 and 1860. A source of greater freedom for many whites, the westward movement meant to African-Americans the destruction of family ties, the breakup of long-standing communities, and receding opportunities for liberty.

In 1793, when Whitney designed his invention, the United States produced 5 million pounds of cotton. By 1820, the crop had grown to nearly 170 million pounds.

Slave Trader, Sold to Tennessee, a watercolor sketch by the artist Lewis Miller from the mid-1850s. Miller depicts a group of slaves being marched from Virginia to Tennessee. Once Congress voted to prohibit the further importation of slaves into the country, slaveowners in newly opened areas of the country had to obtain slaves from other parts of the United States.

Surge in cotton production

MARKET SOCIETY

Since cotton was produced solely for sale in national and international markets, the South was in some ways the most commercially oriented region of the United States. Yet rather than spurring economic change, the South's expansion westward simply reproduced the same agrarian,

A trade card depicts the interior of a chair-manufacturing workshop in New York City. The owner stands at the center, dressed quite differently from his employees. The men are using traditional hand tools; furniture manufacturing had not yet been mechanized.

slave-based social order of the older states. The region remained overwhelmingly rural. In 1860, roughly 80 percent of southerners worked the land—the same proportion as in 1800.

Commercial Farmers

In the North, however, the market revolution and westward expansion set in motion changes that transformed the region into an integrated economy of commercial farms and manufacturing cities. As the Old Northwest became a more settled society, bound by a web of transportation and credit to eastern centers of commerce and banking, farmers found themselves drawn into the new market economy. They increasingly concentrated on growing crops and raising livestock for sale, while purchasing at stores goods previously produced at home.

Western farmers found in the growing cities of the East a market for their produce and a source of credit. Loans originating with eastern banks and insurance companies financed the acquisition of land and supplies and, in the 1840s and 1850s, the purchase of fertilizer and new agricultural machinery to expand production. The **steel plow**, invented by John Deere in 1837 and mass-produced by the 1850s, made possible the rapid subduing of the western prairies. The **reaper**, a horse-drawn machine that greatly increased the amount of wheat a farmer could harvest, was invented by Cyrus McCormick in 1831 and produced in large quantities soon afterward. Eastern farmers, unable to grow wheat and corn as cheaply as their western counterparts, increasingly concentrated on producing dairy products, fruits, and vegetables for nearby urban centers.

The Growth of Cities

From the beginning, cities formed part of the western frontier. Cincinnati was known as "porkopolis," after its slaughterhouses where hundreds of thousands of pigs were butchered each year and processed for shipment to eastern consumers of meat. The greatest of all the western cities was Chicago. In the early 1830s, it was a tiny settlement on the shore of Lake Michigan. By 1860, thanks to the railroad, Chicago had become the nation's fourth largest city, where farm products from throughout the Northwest were gathered to be sent east.

Western cities

Like rural areas, urban centers witnessed dramatic changes due to the market revolution. Urban merchants, bankers, and master craftsmen took advantage of the economic opportunities created by the expanding market among commercial farmers. The drive among these businessmen

A painting of Cincinnati, self-styled Queen City of the West, from 1835. Steamboats line the Ohio River waterfront.

to increase production and reduce labor costs fundamentally altered the nature of work. Traditionally, skilled artisans had manufactured goods at home, where they controlled the pace and intensity of their own labor. Now, entrepreneurs gathered artisans into large workshops in order to oversee their work and subdivide their tasks. Craftsmen who traditionally produced an entire pair of shoes or piece of furniture saw the labor process broken down into numerous steps requiring far less skill and training. They found themselves subjected to constant supervision by their employers and relentless pressure for greater output and lower wages.

A broadside from 1853 illustrates the long hours of work (from 5 AM to 6:30 PM with brief breaks for meals) in the textile mills of Holyoke, Massachusetts. Factory labor was strictly regulated by the clock.

The Factory System

In some industries, most notably textiles, the factory superseded traditional craft production altogether. Factories gathered large groups of workers under central supervision and replaced hand tools with power-driven machinery. Samuel Slater, an immigrant from England, established America's first factory in 1790 at Pawtucket, Rhode Island. Since British law made it illegal to export the plans for industrial machinery, Slater, a skilled mechanic, built from memory a power-driven spinning jenny, one of the key inventions of the early industrial revolution.

Women at work tending machines in the Lowell textile mills.

Spinning factories such as Slater's produced yarn, which was then sent to traditional hand-loom weavers and farm families to be woven into cloth. This "outwork" system, in which rural men and women earned money by taking in jobs from factories, typified early industrialization. Eventually, however, the entire manufacturing process in textiles, shoes, and many other products was brought under a single factory roof.

The cutoff of British imports because of the Embargo of 1807 and the War of 1812 stimulated the establishment of the first large-scale American factory utilizing power looms for weaving cotton cloth. This was constructed in 1814 at Waltham, Massachusetts, by a group of merchants who came to be called the Boston Associates. In the 1820s, they expanded their enterprise by creating an entirely new factory town (incorporated as the city of Lowell in 1836) on the Merrimack River, twenty-seven miles from Boston. Here they built a group of modern textile factories that brought together all phases of production from the spinning of thread to the weaving and finishing of cloth.

Steam power and factories

The earliest factories, including those at Pawtucket, Waltham, and Lowell, were located along the "fall line," where waterfalls and river rapids could be harnessed to provide power for spinning and weaving machinery. By the 1840s, steam power made it possible for factory owners to locate in towns like New Bedford that were nearer to the coast, and in large cities like Philadelphia and Chicago with their immense local markets. In 1850, manufacturers produced in factories not only textiles but also a wide variety of other goods, including tools, firearms, shoes, clocks, ironware, and agricultural machinery. What came to be called the "**American system**

Interchangable parts

of manufactures" relied on the mass production of interchangeable parts that could be rapidly assembled into standardized finished products. More impressive, in a way, than factory production was the wide dispersion of mechanical skills throughout northern society. Every town, it seemed, had its sawmill, paper mill, iron works, shoemaker, hatmaker, tailor, and a host of other such small enterprises.

The "Mill Girls"

Female and child labor

Although some factories employed entire families, the early New England textile mills relied largely on female and child labor. At Lowell, the most famous center of early textile manufacturing, young unmarried women from Yankee farm families dominated the workforce that tended the spinning machines. To persuade parents to allow their daughters to leave home to work in the mills, Lowell owners set up boarding houses with strict rules regulating personal behavior. They also established lecture halls and churches to occupy the women's free time.

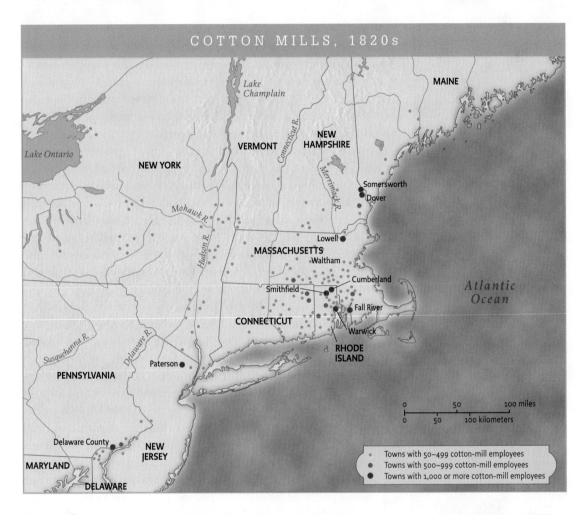

COTTON MILLS, 1820s

The early industrial revolution was concentrated in New England, where factories producing textiles from raw cotton sprang up along the region's many rivers, taking advantage of water power to drive their machinery.

This was the first time in history that large numbers of women left their homes to participate in the public world. Most valued the opportunity to earn money independently at a time when few other jobs were open to women. But these women did not become a permanent class of factory workers. They typically remained in the factories for only a few years, after which they left to return home, marry, or move west.

The Growth of Immigration

Economic expansion fueled a demand for labor, which was met, in part, by increased **immigration** from abroad. Between 1790 and 1830, immigrants contributed only marginally to American population growth. But between

Young women workers from the Amoskeag textile mills in Manchester, New Hampshire, photographed in 1854.

1840 and 1860, over 4 million people (more than the entire population in 1790) entered the United States, the majority from Ireland and Germany. About 90 percent headed for the northern states, where job opportunities were most abundant and the new arrivals would not have to compete with slave labor. In 1860, the 814,000 residents of New York City, the major port of entry, included more than 384,000 immigrants, and one-third of the population of Wisconsin was foreign-born.

Numerous factors inspired this massive flow of population across the Atlantic. In Europe, the modernization of agriculture and the industrial revolution disrupted centuries-old patterns of life, pushing peasants off the land and eliminating the jobs of traditional craft workers. The introduction of the oceangoing steamship and the railroad made long-distance travel more practical. Moreover, America's political and religious freedoms attracted Europeans, including political refugees from the failed revolutions of 1848, who chafed under the continent's repressive governments and rigid social hierarchies.

The largest number of immigrants, however, were refugees from disaster—Irish men and women fleeing the Great Famine of 1845-1851, when a blight destroyed the potato crop on which the island's diet relied. An estimated 1 million persons starved to death and another million emigrated in those years, most of them to the United States. Lacking industrial skills and capital, these impoverished agricultural laborers and small farmers ended up filling the low-wage unskilled jobs native-born Americans sought to avoid. Male Irish immigrants built America's railroads, dug canals, and worked as common laborers, servants, longshoremen, and factory operatives. Irish women frequently went to work as servants in the homes of native-born Americans, although some preferred factory work to domestic service. By the end of the 1850s, the Lowell textile mills had largely replaced Yankee farm women with immigrant Irish families. Four-fifths of Irish immigrants remained in the Northeast.

The second-largest group of immigrants, Germans, included a considerably larger number of skilled craftsmen than the Irish. Germans also settled in tightly knit neighborhoods in eastern cities, but many were able to move to the West, where they established themselves as craftsmen, shopkeepers, and farmers. The "German triangle," as the cities of Cincinnati, St. Louis, and Milwaukee were sometimes called, all attracted large German populations.

Some 40,000 Scandinavians also emigrated to the United States in these years, most of whom settled on farms in the Old Northwest.

TABLE 9.2 Total Number of Immigrants by Five-Year Period

YEARS	NUMBER OF IMMIGRANTS
1841–1845	430,000
1846–1850	1,283,000
1851–1855	1,748,000
1856–1860	850,000

The Rise of Nativism

The idea of the United States as a refuge for those seeking economic opportunity or as an escape from oppression has always coexisted with suspicion of and hostility to foreign newcomers. American history has witnessed periods of intense anxiety over immigration. The Alien Act of 1798 reflected fear of immigrants with radical political views. During the early twentieth century, as will be discussed below, there was widespread hostility to the "new immigration" from southern and eastern Europe. In the early twenty-first century, the question of how many persons should be allowed to enter the United States, and under what circumstances, remains a volatile political issue.

Archbishop John Hughes of New York City made the Catholic Church a more assertive institution. He condemned the use of the Protestant King James Bible in the city's public schools, pressed Catholic parents to send their children to an expanding network of parochial schools, and sought government funding to pay for them. He aggressively sought to win converts from Protestantism.

Many Protestants found such activities alarming. Catholicism, they feared, threatened American institutions and American freedom. In 1834, Lyman Beecher, a prominent Presbyterian minister (and father of the religious leader Henry Ward Beecher and the writers Harriet Beecher Stowe and Catharine Beecher), delivered a sermon in Boston, soon published as "A Plea for the West." Beecher warned that Catholics were seeking to dominate the American West, where the future of Christianity in the

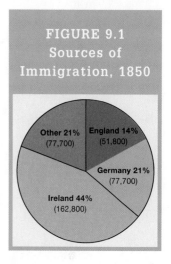

**FIGURE 9.1
Sources of
Immigration, 1850**

Other 21%
(77,700)

England 14%
(51,800)

Germany 21%
(77,700)

Ireland 44%
(162,800)

Lyman Beecher

Riot in Philadelphia, an 1844 lithograph, depicts street battles between nativists and Irish Catholics that left fifteen persons dead. The violence originated in a dispute over the use of the Protestant King James Bible in the city's public schools.

world would be worked out. His sermon inspired a mob to burn a Catholic convent in the city.

The Irish influx of the 1840s and 1850s thoroughly alarmed many native-born Americans and led to violent anti-immigrant riots in New York City and Philadelphia. Those who feared the impact of immigration on American political and social life were called "**nativists**." They blamed immigrants for urban crime, political corruption, and a fondness for intoxicating liquor, and they accused them of undercutting native-born skilled laborers by working for starvation wages. Stereotypes similar to those directed at blacks flourished regarding the Irish as well—childlike, lazy, and slaves of their passions, they were said to be unsuited for republican freedom.

Nativist stereotypes

The Transformation of Law

American law increasingly supported the efforts of entrepreneurs to participate in the market revolution, while shielding them from interference by local governments and liability for some of the less desirable results of economic growth. The corporate form of business organization became central to the new market economy. A corporate firm enjoys special privileges and powers granted in a charter from the government, among them that investors and directors are not personally liable for the company's debts. Unlike companies owned by an individual, family, or limited partnership, in other words, a corporation can fail without ruining its directors and stockholders.

Corporations

Many Americans distrusted corporate charters as a form of government-granted special privilege. But the courts upheld their validity, while opposing efforts by established firms to limit competition from newcomers. In **Dartmouth College v. Woodward** (1819), John Marshall's Supreme Court defined corporate charters issued by state legislatures as contracts, which future lawmakers could not alter or rescind. Five years later, in *Gibbons v. Ogden*, the Court struck down a monopoly the New York legislature had granted for steamboat navigation. And in 1837, with Roger B. Taney now the chief justice, the Court ruled that the Massachusetts legislature did not infringe the charter of an existing company that had constructed a bridge over the Charles River when it empowered a second company to build a competing bridge. The community, Taney declared, had a legitimate interest in promoting transportation and prosperity.

Court decisions on the economy

THE FREE INDIVIDUAL

By the 1830s, the market revolution and westward expansion had produced a society that amazed European visitors: energetic, materialistic,
and seemingly in constant motion. Alexis de Tocqueville was struck by
Americans' restless energy and apparent lack of attachment to place. "No
sooner do you set foot on American soil," he observed, "than you find yourself in a sort of tumult. All around you, everything is on the move."

An energetic society

The West and Freedom

Westward expansion and the market revolution reinforced some older
ideas of freedom and helped to create new ones. American freedom, for
example, had long been linked with the availability of land in the West.
A New York journalist, John L. O'Sullivan, first employed the phrase
"manifest destiny," meaning that the United States had a divinely appointed
mission, so obvious as to be beyond dispute, to occupy all of North America.
Americans, he proclaimed, had a far better title to western lands than could
be provided by any international treaty, right of discovery, or long-term
settlement.

O'Sullivan wrote these words in 1845, but the essential idea was
familiar much earlier. Many Americans believed that the settlement and
economic exploitation of the West would prevent the United States from
following the path of Europe and becoming a society with fixed social
classes and a large group of wage-earning poor. In the West, where land
was more readily available and oppressive factory labor far less common, there continued to be the chance to achieve economic independence,
the social condition of freedom. In national myth and ideology, the West
would long remain, as the writer Wallace Stegner would later put it, "the
last home of the freeborn American."

*The West and economic
independence*

The Transcendentalists

The restless, competitive world of the market revolution strongly encouraged the identification of American freedom with the absence of restraints
on self-directed individuals seeking economic advancement and personal
development. The "one important revolution" of the day, the philosopher
Ralph Waldo Emerson wrote in the 1830s, was "the new value of the private man." In Emerson's definition, rather than a preexisting set of rights

Individual freedom

or privileges, freedom was an open-ended process of self-realization by which individuals could remake themselves and their own lives.

Emerson was perhaps the most prominent member of a group of New England intellectuals known as the **transcendentalists**, who insisted on the primacy of individual judgment over existing social traditions and institutions. Emerson's Concord, Massachusetts, neighbor, the writer Henry David Thoreau, echoed his call for individual self-reliance. "Any man more right than his neighbors," Thoreau wrote, "is a majority of one."

Emerson and Thoreau

In his own life, Thoreau illustrated Emerson's point about the primacy of individual conscience in matters political, social, and personal, and the need to find one's own way rather than following the crowd. Thoreau became persuaded that modern society stifled individual judgment by making men "tools of their tools," trapped in stultifying jobs by their obsession with acquiring wealth. Even in "this comparatively free country," he wrote, most persons were so preoccupied with material things that they had no time to contemplate the beauties of nature.

To escape this fate, Thoreau retreated for two years to a cabin on Walden Pond near Concord, where he could enjoy the freedom of isolation from the "economical and moral tyranny" he believed ruled American society. He subsequently published *Walden* (1854), an account of his experiences and a critique of how the market revolution was, in his opinion, degrading both Americans' values and the natural environment. An area that had been covered with dense forest in his youth, he observed, had been so transformed by woodcutters and farmers that it had become almost completely devoid of trees and wild animals. Thoreau appealed to Americans to "simplify" their lives rather than become obsessed with the accumulation of wealth. Genuine freedom, he insisted, lay within.

The daguerreotype, an early form of photography, required the sitter to remain perfectly still for twenty seconds or longer. The philosopher Ralph Waldo Emerson, depicted here, did not like the result. He complained in his journal that in his "zeal not to blur the image," every muscle had become "rigid" and his face was fixed in a frown as "in madness, or in death."

The Second Great Awakening

The popular religious revivals that swept the country during the **Second Great Awakening** added a religious underpinning to the celebration of personal self-improvement, self-reliance, and self-determination. These revivals, which began at the turn of the century, were originally organized by established religious leaders alarmed by low levels of church attendance in the young republic (perhaps as few as 10 percent of white Americans regularly attended church during the 1790s). But they quickly expanded far beyond existing churches. They reached a crescendo in the 1820s and early 1830s, when the Reverend Charles Grandison Finney held months-long revival meetings in upstate New York and New York City.

Religious Camp Meeting, a watercolor from the late 1830s depicting an evangelical preacher at a revival meeting. Some of the audience members seem inattentive, while others are moved by his fiery sermon.

Like the evangelists (traveling preachers) of the first Great Awakening of the mid-eighteenth century discussed in Chapter 4, Finney warned of hell in vivid language while offering the promise of salvation to converts who abandoned their sinful ways.

The Second Great Awakening democratized American Christianity, making it a truly mass enterprise. At the time of independence, fewer than 2,000 Christian ministers preached in the United States. In 1845, they numbered 40,000. Evangelical denominations such as the Methodists and Baptists enjoyed explosive growth in membership, and smaller sects proliferated. By the 1840s, Methodism, with more than 1 million members, had become the country's largest denomination. At large camp meetings, especially prominent on the frontier, fiery revivalist preachers rejected the idea that man is a sinful creature with a preordained fate, promoting instead the doctrine of human free will. At these gatherings, rich and poor, male and female, and in some instances whites and blacks worshiped alongside one another and pledged to abandon worldly sins in favor of the godly life.

Democratizing American Christianity

Camp meetings

The Awakening's Impact

Even more than its predecessor of several decades earlier, the Second Great Awakening stressed the right of private judgment in spiritual matters and the possibility of universal salvation through faith and good

VOICES OF FREEDOM

From Ralph Waldo Emerson, "The American Scholar" (1837)

Ralph Waldo Emerson was perhaps the most prominent intellectual in mid-nineteenth-century America. In this famous address, delivered at Harvard College, he insisted on the primacy of individual judgment over existing social traditions as the essence of freedom.

Perhaps the time is already come, when . . . the sluggard intellect of this continent will look from under its iron lids and fill the postponed expectation of the world with something better than the exertions of mechanical skill. Our day of dependence, our long apprenticeship to the learning of other lands, draws to a close. . . .

In self-trust, all the virtues are comprehended. Free should the scholar be—free and brave. Free even to the definition of freedom. . . . Not he is great who can alter matter, but he who can alter my state of mind. They are the kings of the world who give the color of their present thought to all nature and all art. . . .

[A] sign of the times . . . is the new importance given to the single individual. Every thing that tends to insulate the individual—to surround him with barriers of natural respect, so that each man shall feel the world is his, and man shall treat with man as a sovereign state with a sovereign state—tends to true union as well as greatness. 'I learned,' said the melancholy Pestalozzi [a Swiss educator], "that no man in God's wide earth is either willing or able to help any other man." Help must come from his bosom alone. . . .

We have listened too long to the courtly muses of Europe. The spirit of the American freeman is already suspected to be timid, imitative, tame. . . . The scholar is decent, indolent, complaisant. See already the tragic consequence. The mind of this country taught to aim at low objects, eats upon itself. Young men . . . do not yet see, that if the single man [should] plant himself indomitably on his instincts, and there abide, the huge world will come round to him. . . . We will walk on our own feet; we will work with our own hands; we will speak our own minds.

From "Factory Life as It Is, by an Operative" (1845)

Beginning in the 1830s, young women who worked in the cotton textile factories in Lowell, Massachusetts, organized to demand shorter hours of work and better labor conditions. In this pamphlet from 1845, a factory worker details her grievances as well as those of female domestic workers, the largest group of women workers.

Philanthropists of the nineteenth century!—shall not the operatives of our country be permitted to speak for themselves? Shall the worthy laborer be awed into silence by wealth and power, and for fear of being deprived of the means of procuring his daily bread? Shall tyranny and cruel oppression be allowed to rivet the chains of physical and mental slavery on the millions of our country who are the real producers of all its improvements and wealth, and they fear to speak out in noble self-defense? Shall they fear to appeal to the sympathies of the people, or the justice of this far-famed republican nation? God forbid!

Much has been written and spoken in woman's behalf, especially in America; and yet a large class of females are, and have been, destined to a state of servitude as degrading as unceasing toil can make it. I refer to the female operatives of New England—the free states of our union—the states where no colored slave can breathe the balmy air, and exist as such—but yet there are those, a host of them, too, who are in fact nothing more nor less than slaves in every sense of the word! Slaves to a system of labor which requires them to toil from five until seven o'clock, with one hour only to attend to the wants of nature, allowed—slaves to ignorance—and how can it be otherwise? What time has the operative to bestow on moral, religious or intellectual culture? Common sense will teach every one the utter impossibility of improving the mind under these circumstances, however great the desire may be for knowledge.

Again, we hear much said on the subject of benevolence among the wealthy and so called, Christian part of community. Have we not cause to question the sincerity of those who, while they talk benevolence in the parlor, compel their help to labor for a mean, paltry pittance in the kitchen? And while they manifest great concern for the souls of the heathen in distant lands, care nothing for the bodies and intellects of those within their own precincts? . . .

In the strength of our united influence we will soon show these drivelling cotton lords, this mushroom aristocracy of New England, who so arrogantly aspire to lord it over God's heritage, that our rights cannot be trampled upon with impunity; that we WILL not longer submit to that arbitrary power which has for the last ten years been so abundantly exercised over us.

QUESTIONS

1. *How does Emerson define the freedom of what he calls "the single individual"?*

2. *Why does the female factory worker compare her conditions with those of slaves?*

3. *What does the contrast between these two documents suggest about the impact of the market revolution on American thought?*

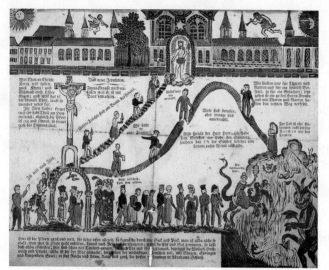

Das neue Jerusalem (The New Jerusalem), an early-nineteenth-century watercolor, in German, illustrates the narrow gateway to heaven and the fate awaiting sinners in hell. These were common themes of preachers in the Second Great Awakening.

works. Every person, Finney insisted, was a "moral free agent"—that is, a person free to choose between a Christian life and sin.

Revivalist ministers seized the opportunities offered by the market revolution to spread their message. They raised funds, embarked on lengthy preaching tours by canal, steamboat, and railroad, and flooded the country with mass-produced, inexpensive religious tracts. The revivals' opening of religion to mass participation and their message that ordinary Americans could shape their own spiritual destinies resonated with the spread of market values.

To be sure, evangelical preachers can hardly be described as cheerleaders for a market society. They regularly railed against greed and indifference to the welfare of others as sins. Yet the revivals thrived in areas caught up in the rapid expansion of the market economy, such as the region of upstate New York along the path of the Erie Canal. Most of Finney's converts here came from the commercial and professional classes. Evangelical ministers promoted what might be called a controlled individualism as the essence of freedom. In stressing the importance of industry, sobriety, and self-discipline as examples of freely chosen moral behavior, evangelical preachers promoted the very qualities necessary for success in a market culture.

The Emergence of Mormonism

The end of governmental support for established churches promoted competition among religious groups that kept religion vibrant and promoted the emergence of new denominations. Among the most successful of the religions that sprang up was the **Church of Latter-Day Saints, or Mormons**, which hoped to create a Kingdom of God on earth. The Mormons were founded in the 1820s by Joseph Smith, a farmer in upstate New York who as a youth began to experience religious visions. He claimed to have been led by an angel to a set of golden plates covered with strange writing. Smith translated and published them as *The Book of Mormon*, after a fourth-century prophet.

The Book of Mormon tells the story of three families who traveled from the ancient Middle East to the Americas, where they eventually evolved into Native American tribes. Jesus Christ plays a prominent role in the

Joseph Smith

book, appearing to one of the family groups in the Western Hemisphere after his death and resurrection. The second coming of Christ would take place in the New World, where Smith was God's prophet.

Mormonism emerged in a center of the Second Great Awakening, upstate New York. The church founded by Smith shared some features with other Christian denominations including a focus on the family and community as the basis of social order and a rejection of alcohol. Gradually, however, Smith began to receive visions that led to more con-

In this 1846 photograph, the massive Mormon temple in Nauvoo, Illinois, towers over the ramshackle wooden buildings of this town along the Mississippi River.

troversial doctrines, notably polygamy, which allows one man to have more than one wife. By the end of his life, Smith had married no fewer than thirty women. Along with the absolute authority Smith exercised over his followers, this doctrine outraged the Mormons' neighbors. Mobs drove Smith and his followers out of New York, Ohio, and Missouri before they settled in 1839 in Nauvoo, Illinois. There, five years later, Smith was arrested on the charge of inciting a riot that destroyed an anti-Mormon newspaper. While in jail awaiting trial, Smith was murdered by a group of intruders. In 1847, his successor as Mormon leader, Brigham Young, led more than 2,000 followers across the Great Plains and Rocky Mountains to the shores of the Great Salt Lake in present-day Utah. By 1852, the number of Mormons in various settlements in Utah reached 16,000. The Mormons' experience revealed the limits of religious toleration in nineteenth-century America but also the opportunities offered by religious pluralism. Today, Mormons constitute the fourth largest church in the United States, and *The Book of Mormon* has been translated into over 100 languages.

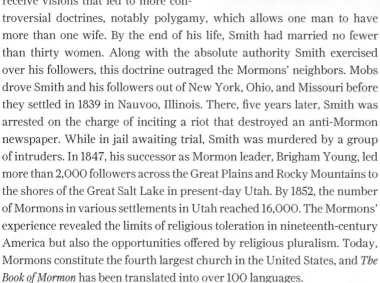

Brigham Young

THE LIMITS OF PROSPERITY

Liberty and Prosperity

As the market revolution progressed, the right to compete for economic advancement became a touchstone of American freedom. Americans celebrated the opportunities open to the "**self-made man**," a term that came

Pat Lyon at the Forge, an 1826–1827 painting of a prosperous blacksmith. Proud of his accomplishments as a self-made man who had achieved success through hard work and skill rather than inheritance, Lyon asked the artist to paint him in his shop wearing his work clothes.

into use at this time. According to this idea, those who achieved success in America did so not as a result of hereditary privilege or government favoritism as in Europe, but through their own intelligence and hard work. The market revolution enriched numerous bankers, merchants, industrialists, and planters. It produced a new middle class—an army of clerks, accountants, and other office employees who staffed businesses in Boston, New York, and elsewhere. It created new opportunities for farmers who profited from the growing demand at home and abroad for American agricultural products, and for skilled craftsmen such as Thomas Rodgers, a machine builder who established a successful locomotive factory in Paterson, New Jersey. New opportunities for talented men opened in professions such as law, medicine, and teaching. By the early 1820s, there were an estimated 10,000 physicians in the United States.

Race and Opportunity

The market revolution affected the lives of all Americans. But not all were positioned to take advantage of its benefits. Most blacks, of course, were slaves, but even free blacks found themselves excluded from the new economic opportunities. The 220,000 blacks living in the free states on the eve of the Civil War (less than 2 percent of the North's population) suffered discrimination in every phase of their lives. The majority of blacks lived in the poorest, unhealthiest sections of cities like New York, Philadelphia, and Cincinnati. And even these neighborhoods were subject to occasional violent assault by white mobs, like the armed bands that attacked blacks and destroyed their homes and businesses in Cincinnati in 1829.

Barred from schools and other public facilities, free blacks laboriously constructed their own institutional life, centered on mutual-aid and educational societies, as well as independent churches, most notably the African Methodist Episcopal Church. Richard Allen of Philadelphia, a Methodist preacher, had been spurred to found the church after being forcibly removed from his former church for praying at the altar rail, a place reserved for whites.

Black institutions

Whereas many white Americans could look forward to a life of economic accumulation and individual advancement, large numbers of free blacks experienced downward mobility. At the time of abolition in the North, because of widespread slave ownership among eighteenth-century artisans, a considerable number of northern blacks possessed craft skills. But it became more and more difficult for blacks to utilize these skills once they became free. Although many white artisans criticized slavery, most

Downward mobility of free blacks

viewed the freed slaves as low-wage competitors and sought to bar them from skilled employment.

Hostility from white craftsmen, however, was only one of many obstacles that kept blacks confined to the lowest ranks of the labor market. White employers refused to hire them in anything but menial positions, and white customers did not wish to be served by them. The result was a rapid decline in economic status until by mid-century, the vast majority of northern blacks labored for wages in unskilled jobs and as domestic servants. The state census of 1855 revealed 122 black barbers and 808 black servants in New York City, but only 1 lawyer and 6 doctors. Nor could free blacks take advantage of the opening of the West to improve their economic status, a central component of American freedom. Federal law barred them from access to public land, and by 1860 four states—Indiana, Illinois, Iowa, and Oregon—prohibited them from entering their territory altogether.

Limited opportunity for free blacks

The Cult of Domesticity

Women, too, found many of the opportunities opened by the market revolution closed to them. As the household declined as a center of economic production, many women saw their traditional roles undermined by the availability of mass-produced goods previously made at home. Some women, as noted above, followed work as it moved from household to factory. Others embraced a new definition of femininity, which glorified not a woman's contribution to the family's economic well-being, but her ability to create a private environment shielded from the competitive tensions of the market economy. Woman's "place" was in the home, a site increasingly emptied of economically productive functions as work moved from the household to workshops and factories. Her role was to sustain nonmarket values like love, friendship, and mutual obligation, providing men with a shelter from the competitive marketplace.

The earlier ideology of "republican motherhood," which allowed women a kind of public role as mothers of future citizens, subtly evolved into the mid-nineteenth-century "**cult of domesticity**." "In whatever situation of life a woman is placed from her cradle to her grave," declared *The Young Lady's Book*, one of numerous popular magazines addressed to female audiences of the 1820s and 1830s, "a spirit of obedience and submission, pliability of temper, and humility of mind, are required from her."

With more and more men leaving the home for work, women did exercise considerable power over personal affairs within the family. The rapid decline in the American birthrate during the nineteenth century

Married, a lithograph from around 1849, depicts a young, middle-class family at home. It exemplifies the cult of domesticity, in which women's social role was to fulfill their family responsibilities.

An image from a female infant's 1830 birth and baptismal certificate depicts a domestic scene, with women at work while men relax.

(from an average of seven children per woman in 1800 to four in 1900) cannot be explained except by the conscious decision of millions of women to limit the number of children they bore. But the idea of domesticity minimized women's even indirect participation in the outside world. Men moved freely between the public and private "spheres"; women were supposed to remain cloistered in the private realm of the family.

Women and Work

Prevailing ideas concerning gender bore little relation to the experience of those women who worked for wages at least some time in their lives. They did so despite severe disadvantages. Women could not compete freely for employment, since only low-paying jobs were available to them. Married women still could not sign independent contracts or sue in their own names, and not until after the Civil War did they, not their husbands, control the wages they earned. Nonetheless, for poor city dwellers and farm families, the labor of all family members was essential to economic survival. Thousands of poor women found jobs as domestic servants, factory workers, and seamstresses.

Expanding middle class

For the expanding middle class, however, it became a badge of respectability for wives to remain at home, outside the disorderly new market economy, while husbands conducted business in their offices, shops, and factories. In larger cities, where families of different social classes had previously lived alongside one another, fashionable middle-class neighborhoods populated by merchants, factory owners, and professionals like lawyers and doctors began to develop. Work in middle-class homes was done by domestic servants, the largest employment category for women in nineteenth-century America. The freedom of the middle-class woman—defined in part as freedom from labor—rested on the employment of other women within her household.

Even though most women were anything but idle, in a market economy where labor increasingly meant work that created monetary value, it became more and more difficult to think of labor as encompassing anyone but men. Discussions of labor rarely mentioned housewives, domestic servants, and female outworkers, except as an indication of how the spread of capitalism was degrading men. The idea that the male head of household

A "family wage"

should command a "family wage" that enabled him to support his wife and children became a popular definition of social justice. It sank deep roots not only among middle-class Americans but among working-class men as well.

The Early Labor Movement

Although many Americans welcomed the market revolution, others felt threatened by its consequences. Surviving members of the revolutionary generation feared that the obsession with personal economic gain was undermining devotion to the public good.

Many Americans experienced the market revolution not as an enhancement of the power to shape their own lives, but as a loss of freedom. The period between the War of 1812 and 1840 witnessed a sharp economic downturn in 1819, a full-fledged depression starting in 1837, and numerous ups and downs in between, during which employment was irregular and numerous businesses failed. The economic transformation significantly widened the gap between wealthy merchants and industrialists on the one hand and impoverished factory workers, unskilled dockworkers, and seamstresses laboring at home on the other. In Massachusetts, the most industrialized state in the country, the richest 5 percent of the population owned more than half the wealth.

Alarmed at the erosion of traditional skills and the threat of being reduced to the status of dependent wage earners, skilled craftsmen in the late 1820s created the world's first Workingmen's Parties, short-lived political organizations that sought to mobilize lower-class support for candidates who would press for free public education, an end to imprisonment for debt, and legislation limiting work to ten hours per day. In the 1830s, a time of rapidly rising prices, union organization spread and strikes became commonplace. Along with demands for higher wages and shorter hours, the early labor movement called for free homesteads for settlers on public land and an end to the imprisonment of union leaders for conspiracy.

The Shoemakers' Strike in Lynn—Procession in the Midst of a Snow-Storm, of Eight Hundred Women Operatives, an engraving from *Frank Leslie's Illustrated Newspaper*, March 17, 1860. The striking women workers carry a banner comparing their condition to that of slaves.

Demands of early labor movement

The "Liberty of Living"

But over and above these specific issues, workers' language of protest drew on older ideas of freedom linked to economic autonomy, public-spirited virtue, and social equality. The conviction of twenty New York tailors in 1835 under the common law of conspiracy for combining to seek higher wages inspired a public procession marking the "burial of liberty." Such actions and language were not confined to male workers. The young mill women of Lowell walked off their jobs in 1834 to protest a reduction in wages and again two years later when employers raised rents at their

Labor actions

boardinghouses. They carried banners affirming their rights as "daughters of free men," and, addressing the factory owners, they charged that "the oppressive hand of avarice [greed] would enslave us."

Rooted in the traditions of the small producer and the identification of freedom with economic independence, labor's critique of the market economy directly challenged the idea that individual improvement—Emerson's "self-trust, self-reliance, self-control, self-culture"—offered an adequate response to social inequality. Orestes Brownson, in his influential essay "The Laboring Classes" (1840), argued that the solution to workers' problems did not require a more complete individualism. What was needed instead, he believed, was a "radical change [in] existing social arrangements" so as to produce "equality between man and man." Here lay the origins of the idea, which would become far more prominent in the late nineteenth and twentieth centuries, that economic security—a standard of life below which no person would fall—formed an essential part of American freedom.

The idea of economic security

Thus, the market revolution transformed and divided American society and its conceptions of freedom. It encouraged a new emphasis on individualism and physical mobility among white men while severely limiting the options available to women and African-Americans. It opened new opportunities for economic freedom for many Americans while leading others to fear that their traditional economic independence was being eroded. In a democratic society, it was inevitable that the debate over the market revolution and its consequences for freedom would be reflected in American politics.

Tensions in the market revolution

CHAPTER REVIEW AND ONLINE RESOURCES

REVIEW QUESTIONS

1. Identify the major transportation improvements in this period, and explain how they influenced the market economy.

2. How did state and local governments promote the national economy in this period?

3. How did the market economy and westward expansion entrench the institution of slavery?

4. How did westward expansion and the market revolution drive each other?

5. What role did immigrants play in the new market society?

6. How did changes in the law promote development in the economic system?

7. As it democratized American Christianity, the Second Great Awakening both took advantage of the market revolution and criticized its excesses. Explain.

8. How did the market revolution change women's work and family roles?

9. Give some examples of the rise of individualism in these years.

KEY TERMS

steamboats (p. 252)

Erie Canal (p. 252)

railroads (p. 254)

telegraph (p. 254)

squatters (p. 255)

Cotton Kingdom (p. 257)

cotton gin (p. 259)

John Deere steel plow (p. 260)

Cyrus McCormick reaper (p. 260)

factory system (p. 261)

"American system of manufactures" (p. 262)

mill girls (p. 262)

immigration (p. 263)

nativists (p. 266)

Dartmouth College v. Woodward (p. 266)

manifest destiny (p. 267)

transcendentalists (p. 268)

Second Great Awakening (p. 268)

Church of Latter-Day Saints, or Mormons (p. 272)

"self-made man" (p. 273)

cult of domesticity (p. 275)

wwnorton.com
/studyspace

VISIT STUDYSPACE FOR THESE
RESOURCES AND MORE
- A chapter outline
- A diagnostic chapter quiz
- Interactive maps
- Map worksheets
- Multimedia documents

CHAPTER 10

DEMOCRACY IN AMERICA

★

1815–1840

Justice's Court in the Back Woods, an 1852 painting by Tompkins Harrison Matteson, depicts the expansion of the public sphere to include ordinary Americans. A court is in session in a local tavern. The justice of the peace, who presides, is a shoemaker who has set aside his tools but still wears his leather work apron. A lawyer appeals to the jury, composed of average (male) citizens. The case has to do with an assault. The plaintiff, his head bandaged, leans on the table at the right, while a woman consoles the defendant on the far left.

T he inauguration of Andrew Jackson on March 4, 1829, made it clear that something had changed in American politics. The swearing-in of the president had previously been a small, dignified event. Jackson's inauguration attracted a crowd of some 20,000 people who poured into the White House after the ceremony, ruining furniture and breaking china and glassware in the crush. It was "the reign of King Mob," lamented Justice Joseph Story of the Supreme Court.

Jackson's career embodied the major developments of his era—the market revolution, the westward movement, the expansion of slavery, and the growth of democracy. He was a symbol of the self-made man. Unlike previous presidents, Jackson rose to prominence from a humble background, reflecting his era's democratic opportunities. Born in 1767 on the South Carolina frontier, he had been orphaned during the American Revolution. While still a youth, he served as a courier for patriotic forces during the War of Independence. His military campaigns against the British and Indians during the War of 1812 helped to consolidate American control over the Deep South, making possible the rise of the Cotton Kingdom. He himself acquired a large plantation in Tennessee. But more than anything else, to this generation of Americans Andrew Jackson symbolized one of the most crucial features of national life—the triumph of political democracy.

Americans pride themselves on being the world's oldest democracy. New Zealand, whose constitution of 1893 gave women and Maoris (the native population) the right to vote, may have a better claim. Europe, however, lagged far behind. Britain did not achieve universal male suffrage until the 1880s. France instituted it in 1793, abandoned it in 1799, reintroduced it in 1848, and abandoned it again a few years later. More to the point, perhaps, democracy became part of the definition of American nationality and the American idea of freedom.

FOCUS QUESTIONS

- *What were the social bases for the flourishing democracy of the early mid-nineteenth century?*

- *What efforts strengthened or hindered the economic integration of the nation?*

- *What were the major areas of conflict between nationalism and sectionalism?*

- *In what ways did Andrew Jackson embody the contradictions of democratic nationalism?*

- *How did the Bank War influence the economy and party competition?*

THE TRIUMPH OF DEMOCRACY

Property and Democracy

The market revolution and territorial expansion were intimately connected with a third central element of American freedom—political democracy. The challenge to property qualifications for voting, begun during

BORN TO COMMAND.

OF VETO MEMORY.

HAD I BEEN CONSULTED.

KING ANDREW THE FIRST.

An anti-Jackson cartoon from 1832 portrays Andrew Jackson as an aspiring monarch, wielding the veto power while trampling on the Constitution.

the American Revolution, reached its culmination in the early nineteenth century. Not a single state that entered the Union after the original thirteen required ownership of property to vote. In the older states, by 1860 all but one had ended property requirements for voting (though several continued to bar persons accepting poor relief, on the grounds that they lacked genuine independence). The personal independence necessary in the citizen now rested not on ownership of property but on ownership of one's self—a reflection of the era's individualism.

The Dorr War

The lone exception to the trend toward democratization was Rhode Island, which required voters to own real estate valued at $134 or rent property for at least $7 per year. A center of factory production, Rhode Island had a steadily growing population of propertyless wage earners unable to vote. In October 1841, proponents of democratic reform organized a People's Convention, which drafted a new state constitution. It enfranchised all adult white men while eliminating entirely blacks (although in a subsequent referendum, blacks' right to vote was restored). When the reformers ratified their constitution in an extralegal referendum and proceeded to inaugurate Thomas Dorr, a prominent Rhode Island lawyer, as governor, President John Tyler dispatched federal troops to the state. The movement collapsed, and Dorr subsequently served nearly two years in prison for treason.

Tocqueville on Democracy

White male suffrage

By 1840, more than 90 percent of adult white men were eligible to vote. A flourishing democratic system had been consolidated. American politics was boisterous, highly partisan, and sometimes violent, and it engaged the energies of massive numbers of citizens. In a country that lacked more traditional bases of nationality—a powerful and menacing neighbor, historic ethnic, religious, or cultural unity—democratic political institutions came to define the nation's sense of its own identity.

Alexis de Tocqueville

Alexis de Tocqueville, the French writer who visited the United States in the early 1830s, returned home to produce ***Democracy in America***, a classic account of a society in the midst of a political transformation. Tocqueville had come to the United States to study prisons. But he soon realized that to understand America, he must understand democracy (which as a person of aristocratic background he rather disliked). His key

Independence Day Celebration in Centre Square, an 1819 painting by John Lewis Krimmel, a German-American artist, depicts a gathering to celebrate the Fourth of July in Philadelphia. On the left, beneath a portrait of George Washington, is a depiction of a naval battle from the War of 1812; on the right, beneath the state flag of Pennsylvania, is an image of the Battle of New Orleans. The celebration, an example of rising American nationalism, includes men and women, soldiers, merchants, and ordinary citizens but is entirely white except for a young black boy in the lower left.

insight was that democracy by this time meant far more than either the right to vote or a particular set of political institutions. It was what scholars call a "habit of the heart," a culture that encouraged individual initiative, belief in equality, and an active public sphere populated by numerous voluntary organizations that sought to improve society. Democracy, Tocqueville saw, had become an essential attribute of American freedom.

Democratic culture

As Tocqueville recognized, the idea that sovereignty belongs to the mass of ordinary citizens was a profound shift in political thought. The founders of the republic, who believed that government must rest on the consent of the governed, also sought to shield political authority from excessive influence by ordinary people (hence the Electoral College, Supreme Court, and other undemocratic features of the Constitution). Nonetheless, thanks to persistent pressure from those originally excluded from political participation, democracy—for white males—had triumphed by the Age of Jackson.

Popular sovereignty

The Information Revolution

The market revolution and political democracy produced a large expansion of the public sphere and an explosion in printing sometimes called the "**information revolution**." The application of steam power to newspaper printing led to a great increase in output and the rise of the mass-circulation "penny press," priced at one cent per issue instead of the traditional six. Newspapers such as the *New York Sun* and *New York Herald* introduced a new style of journalism, appealing to a mass audience by emphasizing sensationalism,

The rise of the mass-circulation press

crime stories, and exposés of official misconduct. By 1840, according to one estimate, the total weekly circulation of newspapers in the United States, whose population was 17 million, exceeded that of Europe, with 233 million people.

Alternative journalism

The reduction in the cost of printing also made possible the appearance of "alternative" newspapers in the late 1820s and early 1830s, including *Freedom's Journal* (the first black newspaper), *Philadelphia Mechanic's Advocate* and other labor publications, the abolitionist weekly *The Liberator*, and *Cherokee Phoenix*, the first Native American newspaper.

The Limits of Democracy

By the 1830s, the time of Andrew Jackson's presidency, the axiom that "the people" ruled had become a universally accepted part of American politics. Those who opposed this principle, wrote Tocqueville, "hide their heads." But the very centrality of democracy to the definition of both freedom and nationality made it all the more necessary to define the boundaries of the political nation. As older economic exclusions fell away, others survived and new ones were added.

"Universal suffrage"

The "principle of universal suffrage," declared the *United States Magazine and Democratic Review* in 1851, meant that "white males of age constituted the political nation." How could the word "universal" be reconciled with barring blacks and women from political participation? As democracy triumphed, the intellectual grounds for exclusion shifted from economic

Democracy, gender, and race

dependency to natural incapacity. Gender and racial differences were widely understood as part of a single, natural hierarchy of innate endowments. White males were considered inherently superior in character and abilities to non-whites and women. The debate over which people are and are not qualified to take part in American democracy lasted well into the twentieth century. Not until 1920 was the Constitution amended to require states to allow women to vote. The Voting Rights Act of 1965 swept away restrictions on black voting imposed by many southern states.

A Racial Democracy

If the exclusion of women from political freedom continued a long-standing practice, the increasing identification of democracy and whiteness marked something of a departure. Blacks were increasingly considered a group apart. Racist imagery became the stock-in-trade of popular theatrical presentations like minstrel shows, in which white actors in blackface entertained the audience by portraying African-Americans as stupid, dishonest, and altogether ridiculous. With the exception of Herman Melville, who portrayed complex, sometimes heroic black characters in works like *Moby Dick* and *Benito Cereno* (the latter a fictionalized account of a shipboard slave rebellion), American authors either ignored blacks entirely or presented them as stereotypes—happy slaves prone to superstition or long-suffering but devout Christians. Meanwhile, the somewhat tentative thinking of the revolutionary era about the status of non-whites flowered into an elaborate ideology of racial superiority and inferiority, complete with "scientific" underpinnings. These developments affected the boundaries of the political nation.

In the revolutionary era, only Virginia, South Carolina, and Georgia explicitly confined the vote to whites, although elsewhere, custom often made it difficult for free blacks to exercise the franchise. As late as 1800, no northern state barred blacks from voting. But every state that entered the Union after that year, with the single exception of Maine, limited the right to vote to white males. And, beginning with Kentucky in 1799 and Maryland two years later, many states that had allowed blacks to vote rescinded the privilege. By 1860, blacks could vote on the same basis as whites in only five New England states, which contained only 4 percent of the nation's free black population.

In effect, race had replaced class as the boundary between those American men who were entitled to enjoy political freedom and those who were not. Even as this focus on race limited America's political community as a whole, it helped to solidify a sense of national identity among the diverse groups of European origin. In a country where the right to vote had become central to the meaning of freedom, it is difficult to overstate the importance of the fact that white male immigrants could vote in some states almost from the moment they landed in America, whereas nearly all free blacks (and, of course, slaves), whose ancestors had lived in the country for centuries, could not vote at all.

"Dandy Jim," a piece of sheet music from 1843. Minstrel shows were a form of nineteenth-century entertainment in which white actors impersonated blacks. Here, the actor makes fun of a black man attempting to adopt the style of middle-class white Americans.

NATIONALISM AND ITS DISCONTENTS

The American System

The War of 1812, which the United States and Great Britain—the world's foremost military power—fought to a draw, inspired an outburst of nationalist pride. But the war also revealed how far the United States still was from being a truly integrated nation. With the Bank of the United

War of 1812 and American nationalism

States having gone out of existence when its charter expired in 1811, the country lacked a uniform currency and found it almost impossible to raise funds for the war effort. Given the primitive state of transportation, it proved very difficult to move men and goods around the country. One shipment of supplies from New England had taken seventy-five days to reach New Orleans. With the coming of peace, the manufacturing enterprises that sprang up while trade with Britain had been suspended faced intense competition from low-cost imported goods. A younger generation of Republicans, led by Henry Clay and John C. Calhoun, believed these **"infant industries"** deserved national protection.

Madison's blueprint for economic development

In his annual message (now known as the State of the Union address) to Congress in December 1815, President James Madison put forward a blueprint for government-promoted economic development that came to be known as the **American System**, a label coined by Henry Clay. The plan rested on three pillars: a new national bank, a tariff on imported manufactured goods to protect American industry, and federal financing of improved roads and canals. The last was particularly important to those worried about the dangers of disunity. "Let us bind the nation together, with a perfect system of roads and canals," John C. Calhoun implored Congress in 1815. "Let us conquer space."

Madison's veto

Congress enacted an **internal-improvements** program drafted by Calhoun, only to be astonished when the president, on the eve of his retirement from office in March 1817, vetoed the bill. Since calling for its enactment, Madison had become convinced that allowing the national government to exercise powers not mentioned in the Constitution would prove dangerous to individual liberty and southern interests. The other

An image from a broadside from the campaign of 1824, promoting the American System of government-sponsored economic development. The illustrations represent industry, commerce, and agriculture. The ship at the center is named the *John Quincy Adams*. Its flag, "No Colonial Subjection," suggests that without a balanced economy, the United States will remain economically dependent on Great Britain.

two parts of his plan, however, became law. The tariff of 1816 offered protection to goods that could be produced in the United States, especially
cheap cotton textiles, while admitting tax-free those that could not be
manufactured at home. Many southerners supported the tariff, believing
that it would enable their region to develop a manufacturing base to rival
New England's. And in 1816, a new Bank of the United States was created,
with a twenty-year charter from Congress.

Tariff of 1816

Banks and Money

The **Second Bank of the United States** soon became the focus of public
resentment. Like its predecessor, it was a private, profit-making corporation that acted as the government's financial agent, issuing paper money,
collecting taxes, and paying the government's debts. It was also charged
with ensuring that paper money issued by local banks had real value. In
the nineteenth century, paper money consisted of notes promising to pay
the bearer on demand a specified amount of "specie" (gold or silver). Since
banks often printed far more money than the specie in their vaults, the value
of paper currency fluctuated wildly. The Bank of the United States was
supposed to correct this problem by preventing the overissuance of money.

Regulating local banks

The Panic of 1819

But instead of effectively regulating the currency and loans issued by local
banks, the Bank of the United States participated in a speculative fever
that swept the country after the end of the War of 1812. The resumption
of trade with Europe created a huge overseas market for American cotton
and grain. Coupled with the rapid expansion of settlement into the West,
this stimulated demand for loans to purchase land, which local banks and
branches of the Bank of the United States were only too happy to meet by
printing more money. The land boom was especially acute in the South,
where the Cotton Kingdom was expanding.

Land boom

Early in 1819, as European demand for American farm products
declined to normal levels, the economic bubble burst. The Bank of the
United States, followed by state banks, began asking for payments from
those to whom it had loaned money. Farmers and businessmen who could
not repay declared bankruptcy, and unemployment rose in eastern cities.

The economic bubble bursts

The **Panic of 1819** lasted little more than a year, but it severely disrupted
the political harmony of the previous years. To the consternation of creditors, many states, especially in the West, suspended the collection of debts.
Kentucky went even further, establishing a state bank that flooded the state
with paper money that creditors were required to accept in repayment of

loans. This eased the burden on indebted farmers but injured those who had loaned them the money. Overall, the panic deepened many Americans' traditional distrust of banks. It undermined the reputation of the Second Bank of the United States, which was widely blamed for causing the panic. Several states retaliated against the national bank by taxing its local branches.

Distrust of banks

These tax laws produced another of John Marshall's landmark Supreme Court decisions, in the case of **McCulloch v. Maryland** (1819). Reasserting his broad interpretation of governmental powers, Marshall declared the Bank a legitimate exercise of congressional authority under the Constitution's clause that allowed Congress to pass "necessary and proper" laws. Marshall's interpretation of the Constitution directly contradicted the "strict construction" view that limited Congress to powers specifically granted in the Constitution.

The Missouri Controversy

In 1816, James Monroe handily defeated the Federalist candidate Rufus King, becoming the last of the Virginia presidents. By 1820, the Federalists fielded electoral tickets in only two states, and Monroe carried the entire country. Monroe's two terms in office were years of one-party government, sometimes called the Era of Good Feelings. Plenty of bad feelings, however, surfaced during his presidency. In the absence of two-party competition, politics was organized along lines of competing sectional interests.

Era of Good Feelings

In 1819, Congress considered a request from Missouri, an area carved out of the Louisiana Purchase, to draft a constitution in preparation for admission to the Union as a state. Missouri's slave population already exceeded 10,000. James Tallmadge, a Republican congressman from New York, moved that the introduction of further slaves be prohibited and that children of those already in Missouri be freed at age twenty-five.

Tallmadge's proposal sparked two years of controversy, during which Republican unity shattered along sectional lines. His restriction passed the House, where most northern congressmen supported it over the objections of southern representatives. It died in the Senate, however. When Congress reconvened in 1820, Senator Jesse Thomas of Illinois proposed a compromise. Missouri would be authorized to draft a constitution without Tallmadge's restriction. Maine, which prohibited slavery, would be admitted to the Union to maintain the sectional balance between free and slave states. And slavery would be prohibited in all remaining territory within the Louisiana Purchase north of latitude 36°30' (Missouri's southern boundary). Congress adopted Thomas's plan as the **Missouri Compromise**.

Sectional division and the spread of slavery

The Missouri controversy raised for the first time what would prove to be a fatal issue—the westward expansion of slavery. The sectional division

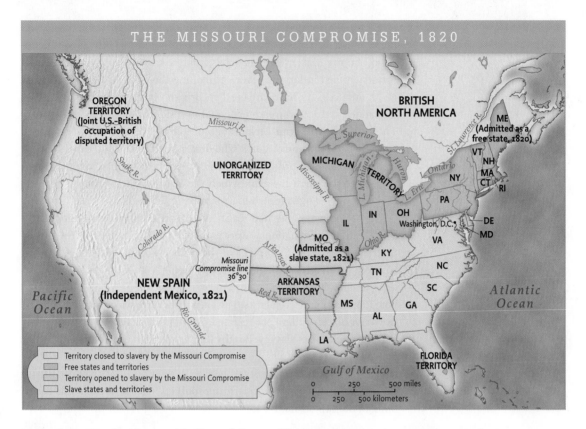

THE MISSOURI COMPROMISE, 1820

OREGON
TERRITORY
(Joint U.S.-British
occupation of
disputed territory)

BRITISH
NORTH AMERICA

ME
(Admitted as a
free state, 1820)

Missouri R.
Snake R.

UNORGANIZED
TERRITORY

MICHIGAN
TERRITORY

L. Superior
Mississippi R.
L. Michigan
L. Huron
L. Ontario
L. Erie
St. Lawrence R.

VT
NH
MA
CT
RI

NY

PA

IN
OH
Washington, D.C.

DE
MD

Colorado R.

Arkansas R.

MO
(Admitted as a
slave state, 1821)

IL

Ohio R.

VA

KY

Missouri
Compromise line
36°30′

NEW SPAIN
(Independent Mexico, 1821)

ARKANSAS
TERRITORY

Red R.

TN

NC

SC

Rio Grande

MS
AL

GA

LA

Pacific
Ocean

Atlantic
Ocean

Gulf of Mexico

FLORIDA
TERRITORY

Territory closed to slavery by the Missouri Compromise
Free states and territories
Territory opened to slavery by the Missouri Compromise
Slave states and territories

0   250   500 miles
0   250   500 kilometers

it revealed aroused widespread feelings of dismay. "This momentous question," wrote Jefferson, "like a fire bell in the night, awakened and filled me with terror. I considered it at once as the knell of the union." For the moment, however, the slavery issue faded once again from national debate.

The Missouri Compromise temporarily settled the question of the expansion of slavery by dividing the Louisiana Purchase into free and slave areas.

NATION, SECTION, AND PARTY

The United States and the Latin American Wars of Independence

Between 1810 and 1822, Spain's Latin American colonies rose in rebellion and established a series of independent nations, including Mexico, Venezuela, Ecuador, and Peru. By 1825, Spain's once vast American empire had been reduced to the islands of Cuba and Puerto Rico. The uprisings inspired a wave of sympathy in the United States. In 1822, the Monroe administration became the first government to extend diplomatic recognition to the new Latin American republics.

The new Latin American republics

Parallels existed between the Spanish-American revolutions and the one that had given birth to the United States. In both cases, the crisis of empire was precipitated by programs launched by the imperial country aimed in large measure at making the colonies contribute more to its finances. As had happened in British North America, local elites demanded status and treatment equal to residents of the imperial power. The Spanish-American declarations of independence borrowed directly from that of the United States. The first, issued in 1811, declared that the "United Provinces" of Venezuela now enjoyed "among the sovereign nations of the earth the rank which the Supreme Being and nature has assigned us"—language strikingly similar to Jefferson's.

Latin American constitutions

In some ways, the new Latin American constitutions—adopted by seventeen different nations—were more democratic than that of the United States. Most sought to implement the trans-Atlantic ideals of rights and freedom by creating a single national "people" out of the diverse populations that made up the Spanish empire. To do so, they extended the right to vote to Indians and free blacks. The Latin American wars of independence, in which black soldiers participated on both sides, also set in motion the gradual abolition of slavery. But the Latin American wars of independence lasted longer—sometimes more than a decade—and were more destructive than the one in the United States had been. As a result, it proved far more difficult for the new Latin American republics to achieve economic development than the United States.

The Monroe Doctrine

John Quincy Adams

John Quincy Adams, who was serving as James Monroe's secretary of state, was devoted to consolidating the power of the national government at home and abroad. Adams feared that Spain would try to regain its Latin American colonies. In 1823, he drafted a section of the president's annual message to Congress that became known as the **Monroe Doctrine**. It expressed three principles. First, the United States would oppose any further efforts at colonization by European powers in the Americas. Second, the United States would abstain from involvement in the wars of Europe. Finally, Monroe warned European powers not to interfere with the newly independent states of Latin America.

America's diplomatic declaration of independence

The Monroe Doctrine is sometimes called America's diplomatic declaration of independence. For many decades, it remained a cornerstone of American foreign policy. Based on the assumption that the Old and New Worlds formed separate political and diplomatic systems, it claimed for the United States the role of dominant power in the Western Hemisphere.

The Election of 1824

The Monroe Doctrine reflected a rising sense of American nationalism. But sectionalism seemed to rule domestic politics. As the election of 1824 approached, only Andrew Jackson could claim truly national support. Jackson's popularity rested not on any specific public policy—few voters knew his views—but on military victories over the British at the Battle of New Orleans, and over the Creek and Seminole Indians. Other candidates included John Quincy Adams, Secretary of the Treasury William H. Crawford of Georgia, and Henry Clay of Kentucky. Adams's support was concentrated in New England and, more generally, in the North, where Republican leaders insisted the time had come for the South to relinquish the presidency. Crawford represented the South's Old Republicans, who wanted the party to reaffirm the principles of states' rights and limited government. Clay was one of the era's most popular politicians, but his support in 1824 lay primarily in the West.

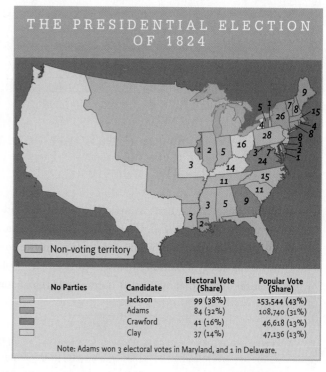

THE PRESIDENTIAL ELECTION OF 1824

Non-voting territory

No Parties	Candidate	Electoral Vote (Share)	Popular Vote (Share)
	Jackson	99 (38%)	153,544 (43%)
	Adams	84 (32%)	108,740 (31%)
	Crawford	41 (16%)	46,618 (13%)
	Clay	37 (14%)	47,136 (13%)

Note: Adams won 3 electoral votes in Maryland, and 1 in Delaware.

Jackson received 153,544 votes and carried states in all the regions outside of New England. But with four candidates in the field, none received a majority of the electoral votes. As required by the Constitution, Clay, who finished fourth, was eliminated, and the choice among the other three fell to the House of Representatives. Sincerely believing Adams to be the most qualified candidate and the one most likely to promote the American System, and probably calculating that the election of Jackson, a westerner, would impede his own presidential ambitions, Clay gave his support to Adams, helping to elect him. He soon became secretary of state in Adams's cabinet. The charge that he had made a "corrupt bargain"—bartering critical votes in the presidential contest for a public office—clung to Clay for the rest of his career, making it all but impossible for him to reach the White House. The election of 1824 laid the groundwork for a new system of political parties. Supporters of Jackson and Crawford would soon unite in the Democratic Party. The alliance of Clay and Adams became the basis for the Whig Party of the 1830s.

The "corrupt bargain"

VOICES OF FREEDOM

From President James Monroe,
Annual Message to Congress (1823)

In the wake of the Latin American struggle for independence, President James Monroe included in his annual message a passage that became known as the Monroe Doctrine. It outlined principles that would help to govern the country's relations with the rest of the world for nearly a century—that the Western Hemisphere was no longer open to European colonization and that the United States would remain uninvolved in the wars of Europe.

[This] occasion has been judged proper for asserting, as a principle, . . . that the American continents, by the free and independent condition which they have assumed and maintain, are henceforth not to be considered as subjects for future colonization by any European powers. . . .

It was stated at the commencement of the last session that a great effort was then making in Spain and Portugal to improve the condition of the people of those countries, and that it appeared to be conducted with extraordinary moderation. It need scarcely be remarked that the results have been so far very different from what was then anticipated. Of events in that quarter of the globe, with which we have so much intercourse and from which we derive our origin, we have always been anxious and interested spectators. The citizens of the United States cherish sentiments the most friendly in favor of the liberty and happiness of their fellow-men on that side of the Atlantic. In the wars of the European powers in matters relating to themselves we have never taken any part, nor does it comport with our policy to do so. It is only when our rights are invaded or seriously menaced that we resent injuries or make preparation for our defense. With the movements in this hemisphere we are of necessity more immediately connected, and by causes which must be obvious to all enlightened and impartial observers. The political system of the allied powers [of Europe] is essentially different in this respect from that of America. . . .

We owe it, therefore, to candor and to the amicable relations existing between the United States and those powers to declare that we should consider any attempt on their part to extend their system to any portion of this hemisphere as dangerous to our peace and safety. With the existing colonies or dependencies of any European power we have not interfered and shall not interfere. But with the Governments who have declared their independence and maintain it, and whose independence we have, on great consideration and on just principles, acknowledged, we could not view any interposition for the purpose of oppressing them, or controlling in any other manner their destiny, by any European power in any other light than as the manifestation of an unfriendly disposition toward the United States.

From John C. Calhoun, "A Disquisition on Government" (ca. 1845)

The most prominent political philosopher in the pre–Civil War South, John C. Calhoun sought to devise ways that the South could retain the power to protect its interests within the Union (especially the institution of slavery) as it fell behind the North in population and political power.

There are two different modes in which the sense of the community may be taken; one, simply by the right of suffrage, unaided; the other, by the right through a proper organism. Each collects the sense of the majority. But one regards numbers only, and considers the whole community as a unit, having but one common interest throughout; and collects the sense of the greater number of the whole, as that of the community. The other, on the contrary, regards interests as well as numbers;—considering the community as made up of different and conflicting interests, as far as the action of the government is concerned; and takes the sense of each, through its majority or appropriate organ, and the united sense of all, as the sense of the entire community. The former of these I shall call the numerical, or absolute majority; and the latter, the concurrent, or constitutional majority. I call it the constitutional majority, because it is an essential element in every constitutional government,—be whatever form it takes. So great is the difference, politically speaking, between the two majorities, that they cannot be confounded, without leading to great and fatal errors; and yet the distinction between them has been so entirely overlooked, that when the term *majority* is used in political discussions, it is applied exclusively to designate the numerical,—as if there were no other. . . .

The first and leading error which naturally arises from overlooking the distinction referred to, is, to confound the numerical majority with the people, and this is so completely as to regard them as identical. This is a consequence that necessarily results from considering the numerical as the only majority. All admit, that a popular government, or democracy, is the government of the people. . . . Those who regard the numerical as the only majority . . . [are] forced to regard the numerical majority as, in effect, the entire people. . . .

The necessary consequence of taking the sense of the community by the concurrent majority is . . . to give to each interest or portion of the community a negative on the others. It is this mutual negative among its various conflicting interests, which invests each with the power of protecting itself; . . . Without this, there can be no constitution.

QUESTIONS

1. *Why does Monroe think that the "systems" of Europe and the Western Hemisphere are fundamentally different?*

2. *Which Americans would be most likely to object to Calhoun's political system?*

3. *How do the two documents differ in their conception of how powerful the national government ought to be?*

The Nationalism of John Quincy Adams

John Quincy Adams in an 1843 daguerreotype.

John Quincy Adams enjoyed one of the most distinguished pre-presidential careers of any American president. The son of John Adams, he had witnessed the Battle of Bunker Hill at age eight and at fourteen had worked as private secretary and French interpreter for an American envoy in Europe. He had gone on to serve as ambassador to Prussia, the Netherlands, Britain, and Russia, and as a senator from Massachusetts.

Adams was not an engaging figure. He described himself as "a man of cold, austere, and foreboding manners." But he had a clear vision of national greatness. At home, he strongly supported the American System of government-sponsored economic development. Abroad, he hoped to encourage American commerce throughout the world and, as illustrated by his authorship of the Monroe Doctrine, enhance American influence in the Western Hemisphere. An ardent expansionist, Adams was certain that the United States would eventually, and peacefully, absorb Canada, Cuba, and at least part of Mexico.

"Liberty Is Power"

Adams held a view of federal power far more expansive than did most of his contemporaries. In his first message to Congress, in December 1825, he set forth a comprehensive program for an activist national state. "The spirit of improvement is abroad in the land," Adams announced, and the federal government should be its patron. He called for legislation promoting agriculture, commerce, manufacturing, and "the mechanical and elegant arts." His plans included the establishment of a national university, an astronomical observatory, and a naval academy. At a time when many Americans felt that governmental authority posed the greatest threat to freedom, Adams astonished many listeners with the bold statement "liberty is power."

Adams's nationalism

Adams's proposals alarmed all believers in strict construction of the Constitution. His administration spent more on internal improvements than those of his five predecessors combined, and it enacted a steep increase in tariff rates in 1828. But the rest of Adams's ambitious ideas received little support in Congress.

Martin Van Buren and the Democratic Party

Adams's program handed his political rivals a powerful weapon. With individual liberty, states' rights, and limited government as their rallying cries, Jackson's supporters began to organize for the election of 1828 almost as soon as Adams assumed office. Martin Van Buren, a senator from New York, supervised the task. The clash between Adams and Van Buren demonstrated how democracy was changing the nature of American politics. Adams typified the old politics—he was the son of a president and, like Jefferson and Madison, a man of sterling intellectual accomplishments. Van Buren represented the new political era. The son of a tavern keeper, he was a talented party manager, not a person of great vision or intellect.

The new politics

But Van Buren did have a compelling idea. Rather than being dangerous and divisive, as the founding generation had believed, political parties, he insisted, were necessary and desirable. Party competition provided a check on those in power and offered voters a real choice in elections. And by bringing together political leaders from different regions in support of common candidates and principles, national parties could counteract the sectionalism that had reared its head during the 1820s. National political parties, Van Buren realized, formed a bond of unity in a divided nation. He set out to reconstruct the Jeffersonian political alliance between "the planters of the South and the plain republicans [the farmers and urban workers] of the North."

Van Buren and political parties

The Election of 1828

By 1828, Van Buren had established the political apparatus of the Democratic Party, complete with local and state party units overseen by a national committee and a network of local newspapers devoted to the party and to the election of Andrew Jackson. Apart from a general commitment to limited government, Jackson's supporters made few campaign promises, relying on their candidate's popularity and the workings of party machinery to get out the vote. The 1828 election campaign was scurrilous. Jackson's supporters praised their candidate's frontier manliness and ridiculed Adams's intellectual attainments. ("Vote for Andrew Jackson who can fight, not John Quincy Adams who can write," declared one campaign slogan.) Jackson's opponents condemned him as a murderer for having executed army deserters and killing men in duels. They questioned the morality of his wife, Rachel, because she had married Jackson before her divorce from her first husband had become final.

Van Buren's Democratic Party machine

Nearly 57 percent of the eligible electorate cast ballots, more than double the percentage four years earlier. Jackson won a resounding victory, carrying the entire South and West, along with Pennsylvania. His election was the first to demonstrate how the advent of universal white

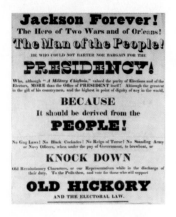

male voting, organized by national political parties, had transformed American politics. For better or worse, the United States had entered the Age of Jackson.

THE AGE OF JACKSON

Andrew Jackson was a man of many contradictions. Although he had little formal education, Jackson was capable of genuine eloquence in his public statements. A self-proclaimed champion of the common man, he held a vision of democracy that excluded any role for Indians, who he believed should be pushed west of the Mississippi River, and African-Americans, who should remain as slaves or be freed and sent abroad. A strong nationalist, Jackson nonetheless believed that the states, not Washington, D.C., should be the focal point of governmental activity.

The Party System

By the time of Jackson's presidency, politics had become more than a series of political contests—it was a spectacle, a form of mass entertainment, a part of Americans' daily lives. Every year witnessed elections to some office—local, state, or national—and millions took part in the parades and rallies organized by the parties. Politicians were popular heroes with mass followings and popular nicknames. Jackson was Old Hickory, Clay was Harry of the West, and Van Buren the Little Magician (or, to his critics, the Sly Fox). Thousands of Americans willingly attended lengthy political orations and debates.

Party machines, headed by professional politicians, reached into every neighborhood, especially in cities. They provided benefits like jobs to constituents and ensured that voters went to the polls on election day. Government posts, Jackson declared, should be open to the people, not reserved for a privileged class of permanent bureaucrats. He introduced

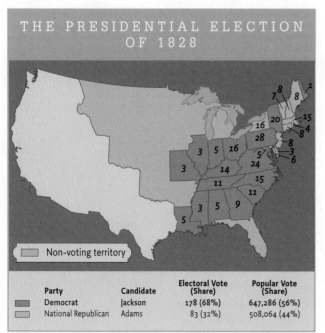

THE PRESIDENTIAL ELECTION OF 1828

Non-voting territory

	Party	Candidate	Electoral Vote (Share)	Popular Vote (Share)
	Democrat	Jackson	178 (68%)	647,286 (56%)
	National Republican	Adams	83 (32%)	508,064 (44%)

the principle of rotation in office (called the "**spoils system**" by opponents) into national government, making loyalty to the party the main qualification for jobs like postmaster and customs official.

Large national conventions where state leaders gathered to hammer out a platform now chose national candidates. Newspapers played a greater and greater role in politics. Every significant town, it seemed, had its Democratic and Whig papers whose job was not so much to report the news as to present the party's position on issues of the day. Jackson's Kitchen Cabinet—an informal group of advisers who helped to write his speeches and supervise communication between the White House and local party officials—mostly consisted of newspaper editors.

Political innovations

Democrats and Whigs

There was more to party politics, however, than spectacle and organization. Jacksonian politics revolved around issues spawned by the market revolution and the continuing tension between national and sectional loyalties. **Democrats** tended to be alarmed by the widening gap between social classes. They warned that "nonproducers"—bankers, merchants, and speculators—were seeking to use connections with government to enhance their wealth to the disadvantage of the "producing classes" of farmers, artisans, and laborers. They believed the government should adopt a hands-off attitude toward the economy and not award special favors to entrenched economic interests. This would enable ordinary Americans to test their abilities in the fair competition of the self-regulating market. The Democratic Party attracted aspiring entrepreneurs who resented government aid to established businessmen, as well as large numbers of farmers and city workingmen suspicious of new corporate enterprises. Poorer farming regions isolated from markets, like the lower Northwest and the southern backcountry, tended to vote Democratic.

Issues for the Democratic Party

Whigs united behind the American System, believing that via a protective tariff, a national bank, and aid to internal improvements, the federal government could guide economic development. They were strongest in the Northeast, the most rapidly modernizing region of the country. Most established businessmen and bankers supported their program of government-promoted economic growth, as did farmers in regions near rivers, canals, and the Great Lakes, who benefited from economic changes or hoped to do so. The counties of upstate New York along the Erie Canal, for example, became a Whig stronghold, whereas more isolated rural communities tended to vote Democratic. Many slaveholders supported

Issues for the Whig Party

the Democrats, believing states' rights to be slavery's first line of defense. But like well-to-do merchants and industrialists in the North, the largest southern planters generally voted Whig.

Public and Private Freedom

The party battles of the Jacksonian era reflected the clash between "public" and "private" definitions of American freedom and their relationship to governmental power, a persistent tension in the nation's history. For Democrats, liberty was a set of private rights best secured by local governments and endangered by powerful national authority. "The limitation of power, in every branch of our government," wrote a Democratic newspaper in 1842, "is the only safeguard of liberty." During Jackson's presidency, Democrats reduced expenditures, lowered the tariff, killed the national bank, and refused pleas for federal aid to internal improvements. By 1835, Jackson had even managed to pay off the national debt. As a result, states replaced the federal government as the country's main economic actors, planning systems of canals and roads and chartering banks and other corporations.

The Democrats: power a threat to liberty

Democrats, moreover, considered individual morality a private matter, not a public concern. They opposed attempts to impose a unified moral vision on society, such as "temperance" legislation, which restricted or outlawed the production and sale of liquor, and laws prohibiting various kinds of entertainment on Sundays. "In this country," declared the New York *Journal of Commerce* in 1848, "liberty is understood to be the *absence* of government from private affairs."

Whigs, for their part, insisted that liberty and power reinforced each other. "A weak government," wrote Francis Lieber, the founding father of American political science, was "a negation of liberty." An activist national government, on the other hand, could enhance the realm of freedom. The government, Whigs believed, should create the conditions for balanced and regulated economic development, thereby promoting a prosperity in which all classes and regions would share.

The Whigs: power allied with liberty

Whigs, moreover, rejected the premise that the government must not interfere in private life. To function as free—that is, self-directed and self-disciplined—moral agents, individuals required certain character traits, which government could help to instill. Many evangelical Protestants supported the Whigs, convinced that via public education, the building of schools and asylums, temperance legislation, and the like, democratic governments could inculcate the "principles of morality." And during the

Government and private life

Jacksonian era, popularly elected local authorities enacted numerous laws, ordinances, and regulations that tried to shape public morals by banning prostitution and the consumption of alcohol, and regulating other kinds of personal behavior. Pennsylvania was as renowned in the nineteenth century for its stringent laws against profanity and desecrating the Sabbath as it had been in the colonial era for its commitment to religious liberty.

Shaping public morals

South Carolina and Nullification

Andrew Jackson, it has been said, left office with many more principles than he came in with. Elected as a military hero backed by an efficient party machinery, he was soon forced to define his stance on public issues. Despite his commitment to states' rights, Jackson's first term was dominated by a battle to uphold the supremacy of federal over state law. The tariff of 1828, which raised taxes on imported manufactured goods made of wool as well as on raw materials such as iron, had aroused considerable opposition in the South, nowhere more than in South Carolina, where it was called the **"tariff of abominations."** The state's leaders no longer believed it possible or desirable to compete with the North in industrial development. Insisting that the tariff on imported manufactured goods raised the prices paid by southern consumers to benefit the North, the legislature threatened to "nullify" it—that is, declare it null and void within their state.

Tariff of 1828

Sectional economic differences

The state with the largest proportion of slaves in its population (55 percent in 1830), South Carolina was controlled by a tightly knit group of large planters. They maintained their grip on power by a state constitution that gave plantation counties far greater representation in the legislature than their population warranted, as well as through high property qualifications for officeholders. Behind their economic complaints against the tariff lay the conviction that the federal government must be weakened lest it one day take action against slavery.

Calhoun's Political Theory

John C. Calhoun soon emerged as the leading theorist of nullification. As the South began to fall behind the rest of the country in population, Calhoun had evolved from the nationalist of 1812 into a powerful defender of southern sectionalism. Having been elected vice president in 1828, Calhoun at first remained behind the scenes, secretly drafting the *Exposition and Protest* in which the South Carolina legislature justified nullification. The national government, Calhoun insisted, had been created by

Calhoun's Exposition and Protest

an agreement, or compact, among sovereign states, each of which retained the right to prevent the enforcement within its borders of acts of Congress that exceeded the powers specifically spelled out in the Constitution.

Almost from the beginning of Jackson's first term, Calhoun's influence in the administration waned, while Secretary of State Martin Van Buren emerged as the president's closest adviser. One incident that helped set Jackson against Calhoun occurred a few weeks after the inauguration. Led by Calhoun's wife, Floride, Washington society women ostracized Peggy Eaton, the wife of Jackson's secretary of war, because she was the daughter of a Washington tavern keeper and, allegedly, a woman of "easy virtue." Jackson identified the criticism of Peggy Eaton with the abuse his own wife had suffered during the campaign of 1828.

Eaton affair

Far weightier matters soon divided Jackson and Calhoun. Debate over nullification raged in Washington. In a memorable exchange in the Senate in January 1830, Daniel Webster, a senator from Massachusetts, responded to South Carolina senator Robert Y. Hayne, a disciple of Calhoun. The people, not the states, declared Webster, created the Constitution, making the federal government sovereign. He called nullification illegal, unconstitutional, and treasonous. Webster's ending was widely hailed throughout the country—"Liberty *and* Union, now and forever, one and inseparable." A few weeks later, at a White House dinner, Jackson delivered a toast while fixing his gaze on Calhoun: "Our Federal Union—it must be preserved." Calhoun's reply came immediately: "The Union—next to our liberty most dear." By 1831, Calhoun had publicly emerged as the leading theorist of states' rights.

Webster-Hayne debate

An 1834 print portrays the United States as a Temple of Liberty. At the center, a figure of liberty rises from the flames, holding the Bill of Rights and a staff with a liberty cap. Justice and Minerva (Roman goddess of war and wisdom) flank the temple, above which flies a banner, "The Union Must and Shall Be Preserved."

The Nullification Crisis

Nullification was not a purely sectional issue. South Carolina stood alone during the crisis, and several southern states passed resolutions condemning its action. Nonetheless, the elaboration of the compact theory of the Constitution gave the South a well-developed political philosophy to which it would turn when sectional conflict became more intense.

To Jackson, nullification amounted to nothing less than disunion. He dismissed Calhoun's constitutional arguments out of hand: "Can anyone of common sense believe the absurdity, that a faction of any state, or a state, has a right to secede and destroy this union, and the liberty of the country with it?" The issue came to a head in 1832, when a new tariff was enacted. Despite a reduction in tariff rates, South Carolina declared the tax on imported goods null and void in the state after the following February. In response, Jackson persuaded Congress to enact a Force Bill authorizing him to use the army and navy to collect customs duties. To avert a confrontation, Henry Clay, with Calhoun's assistance, engineered the passage of a new tariff, in 1833, further reducing duties. South Carolina then rescinded the ordinance of nullification, although it proceeded to "nullify" the **Force Act**. Calhoun abandoned the Democratic Party for the Whigs, where, with Clay and Webster, he became part of a formidable trio of political leaders (even though the three agreed on virtually nothing except hostility toward Jackson).

Jackson's stance

South Carolina and the tariff of 1832

Indian Removal

The nullification crisis underscored Jackson's commitment to the sovereignty of the nation. His exclusion of Indians from the era's assertive democratic nationalism led to the final act in the centuries-long conflict between white Americans and Indians east of the Mississippi River. In the slave states, the onward march of cotton cultivation placed enormous pressure on remaining Indian holdings. One of the early laws of Jackson's administration, the **Indian Removal Act** of 1830, provided funds for uprooting the so-called Five Civilized Tribes—the Cherokee, Chickasaw, Choctaw, Creek, and Seminole—with a population of around 60,000 living in North Carolina, Georgia, Florida, Alabama, and Mississippi.

The law marked a repudiation of the Jeffersonian idea that "civilized" Indians could be assimilated into the American population. These tribes had made great efforts to become everything republican citizens should be. The Cherokee had taken the lead, establishing schools, adopting written laws and a constitution modeled on that of the United States, and becoming

Shift in Indian policy

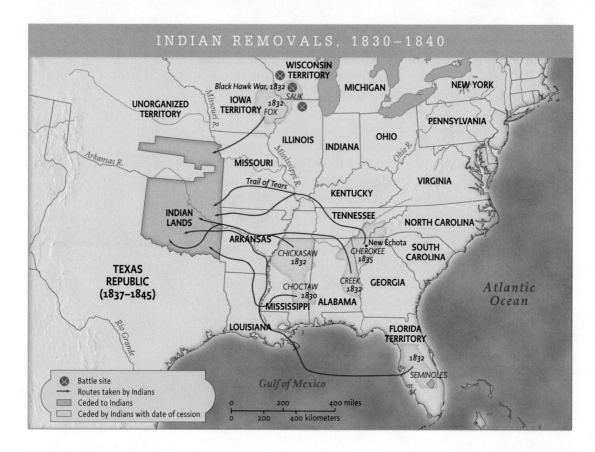

WISCONSIN TERRITORY

Black Hawk War, 1832

SAUK

1832 FOX

UNORGANIZED TERRITORY

IOWA TERRITORY

Missouri R.

Arkansas R.

MICHIGAN

NEW YORK

ILLINOIS

INDIANA

OHIO

PENNSYLVANIA

Ohio R.

MISSOURI

Mississippi R.

Trail of Tears

KENTUCKY

VIRGINIA

INDIAN LANDS

TENNESSEE

NORTH CAROLINA

ARKANSAS

New Echota

CHICKASAW 1832

CHEROKEE 1835

SOUTH CAROLINA

TEXAS REPUBLIC (1837–1845)

CHOCTAW 1830

CREEK 1832

GEORGIA

MISSISSIPPI

ALABAMA

Atlantic Ocean

Rio Grande

LOUISIANA

FLORIDA TERRITORY

1832

SEMINOLES

Gulf of Mexico

⊗ Battle site
→ Routes taken by Indians
▨ Ceded to Indians
▢ Ceded by Indians with date of cession

0   200   400 miles
0   200   400 kilometers

The removal of the so-called Five Civilized Tribes from the Southeast all but ended the Indian presence east of the Mississippi River.

successful farmers, many of whom owned slaves. But in his messages to Congress, Jackson repeatedly referred to them as "savages" and supported Georgia's effort to seize Cherokee land and nullify the tribe's laws. In good American fashion, Cherokee leaders went to court to protect their rights, guaranteed in treaties with the federal government. Their appeals forced the Supreme Court to clarify the unique status of American Indians.

The Supreme Court and the Indians

In a crucial case involving Indians in 1823, *Johnson v. M'Intosh*, the Court had proclaimed that Indians were not in fact owners of their land but merely had a "right of occupancy." Chief Justice John Marshall claimed that from the early colonial era, Indians had lived as nomads and hunters, not farmers. Entirely inaccurate as history, the decision struck a serious blow against Indian efforts to retain their lands. In *Cherokee Nation v. Georgia* (1831), Marshall described Indians as "wards" of the federal government.

"Right of occupancy"

They deserved paternal regard and protection, but they lacked the standing as citizens that would allow the Supreme Court to enforce their rights. The justices could not, therefore, block Georgia's effort to extend its jurisdiction over the tribe.

Marshall, however, believed strongly in the supremacy of the federal government over the states. In 1832, in ***Worcester v. Georgia***, the Court seemed to change its mind, holding that Indian nations were a distinct people with the right to maintain a separate political identity. They must be dealt with by the federal government, not the states, and Georgia's actions violated the Cherokees' treaties with Washington. Jackson, however, refused to recognize the validity of the *Worcester* ruling. "John Marshall has made his decision," he supposedly declared, "now let him enforce it."

With legal appeals exhausted, one faction of the tribe agreed to cede their lands, but the majority, led by John Ross, who had been elected "principal chief" under the Cherokee constitution, adopted a policy of passive resistance. Federal soldiers forcibly removed them during the presidency of Jackson's successor, Martin Van Buren. The army herded 18,000 Cherokee men, women, and children into stockades and then forced them to move west. At least one-quarter perished during the winter of 1838–1839 on the **Trail of Tears**, as the removal route from Georgia to the area of present-day Oklahoma came to be called. (In the Cherokee language, it literally meant "the trail on which we cried.")

A lithograph from 1836 depicts Sequoia, with the alphabet of the Cherokee language that he developed. Because of their written language and constitution, the Cherokee were considered by many white Americans to be a "civilized tribe."

Buffalo Chase over Prairie Bluffs, a painting from the 1830s by George Catlin, who created dozens of works depicting Native Americans in the trans-Mississippi West. Catlin saw himself as recording for posterity a vanishing way of life. At the time, millions of buffalo inhabited the West, providing food and hides for Native Americans.

During the 1830s, most of the other southern tribes bowed to the inevitable and departed peacefully. But with the assistance of escaped slaves, the Seminoles of sparsely settled Florida resisted. In the Second Seminole War, which lasted from 1835 to 1842 (the first had followed American acquisition of Florida in 1819), some 1,500 American soldiers and the same number of Seminoles were killed, and perhaps 3,000 Indians and 500 blacks were forced to move to the West. A small number of Seminoles managed to remain in Florida, a tiny remnant of the once sizable Indian population east of the Mississippi River.

Removal of the Indians powerfully reinforced the racial definition of American nationhood and freedom. At the time of independence, Indians had been a familiar presence in many parts of the United States. But by 1840, in the eyes of most whites east of the Mississippi River, they were simply a curiosity, a relic of an earlier period of American history. Although Indians still dominated the trans-Mississippi West, as American settlement pushed relentlessly westward it was clear that their days of freedom there also were numbered.

THE BANK WAR AND AFTER

Biddle's Bank

The central political struggle of the Age of Jackson was the president's war on the Bank of the United States. The Bank symbolized the hopes and fears inspired by the market revolution. The expansion of banking helped to finance the nation's economic development. But many Americans, including Jackson, distrusted bankers as "nonproducers" who contributed nothing to the nation's wealth but profited from the labor of others. The tendency of banks to overissue paper money, whose deterioration in value reduced the real income of wage earners, reinforced this conviction.

Heading the Bank was Nicholas Biddle of Pennsylvania, who during the 1820s had effectively used the institution's power to curb the overissuing of money by local banks and to create a stable currency throughout the nation. A snobbish, aristocratic Philadelphian, Biddle was as strongwilled as Jackson and as unwilling to back down in a fight. In 1832, he told a congressional committee that his Bank had the ability to "destroy" any state bank. He hastened to add that he had never "injured" any of them. But Democrats wondered whether any institution, public or private, ought to possess such power. Many called it the Monster Bank, an illegitimate union of political authority and entrenched economic privilege. The issue of the Bank's future came to a head in 1832. Although the institution's charter would not expire until 1836, Biddle's allies persuaded Congress to approve a bill extending it for another twenty years. Jackson saw the tactic as a form of blackmail—if he did not sign the bill, the Bank would use its considerable resources to oppose his reelection.

Jackson's veto message is perhaps the central document of his presidency. In a democratic government, Jackson insisted, it was unacceptable for Congress to create a source of concentrated power and economic privilege unaccountable to the people. "It is to be regretted," he declared, "that the rich and powerful too often bend the acts of government to their selfish purposes." Exclusive privileges like the Bank's charter widened the gap between the wealthy and "the humble members of society—the farmers, mechanics, and laborers." Jackson presented himself as the defender of these "humble" Americans.

Jackson's veto of the bank bill

The **Bank War** reflected how Jackson enhanced the power of the presidency during his eight years in office, proclaiming himself the symbolic representative of all the people. He was the first president to use the veto power as a major weapon and to appeal directly to the public for political support, over the head of Congress. Whigs denounced him for usurping the power of the legislature. But Jackson's effective appeal to democratic popular sentiments helped him win a sweeping reelection victory in 1832 over the Whig candidate, Henry Clay. His victory ensured the death of the Bank of the United States.

Enhancing the power of the presidency

The Downfall of Mother Bank, a Democratic cartoon celebrating the destruction of the Second Bank of the United States. President Andrew Jackson topples the building by brandishing his order removing federal funds from the Bank. Led by Nicholas Biddle, with the head of a demon, the Bank's corrupt supporters flee, among them Henry Clay, Daniel Webster, and newspaper editors allegedly paid by the institution.

Pet Banks, the Economy, and the Panic of 1837

What, however, would take the Bank's place? Not content to wait for the charter of the Bank of the United States to expire in 1836, Jackson authorized the removal of federal funds from its vaults and their deposit in select local banks. Not surprisingly, political and personal connections often determined the choice of these "**pet banks**." Two secretaries of the Treasury refused to transfer federal money to the pet banks, since the law creating the Bank had specified that government funds could not be removed except for a good cause as communicated to Congress. Jackson finally appointed Attorney General Roger B. Taney, a loyal Maryland Democrat, to the Treasury post, and he carried out the order. When John Marshall died in 1835, Jackson rewarded Taney by appointing him chief justice.

Consequences of the removal of federal deposits

Without government deposits, the Bank of the United States lost its ability to regulate the activities of state banks. The value of bank notes in circulation rose from $10 million in 1833 to $149 million in 1837. As prices rose dramatically, "real wages"—the actual value of workers' pay—declined. Numerous labor unions emerged, which attempted to protect the earnings of urban workers. Meanwhile, speculators hastened to cash in on rising land prices. Using paper money, they bought up huge blocks of public land, which they resold to farmers or to eastern purchasers of lots in entirely nonexistent western towns.

Inevitably, the speculative boom collapsed. The government sold 20 million acres of federal land in 1836, ten times the amount sold in 1830, nearly all of it paid for in paper money, often of questionable value. In July 1836, the Jackson administration issued the Specie Circular, declaring that henceforth it would only accept gold and silver as payment for public land. At the same time, the Bank of England, increasingly suspicious about the value of American bank notes, demanded that American merchants pay their creditors in London in gold or silver. Then, an economic downturn in Britain dampened demand for American cotton, the country's major export.

The Specie Circular

Taken together, these events triggered an economic collapse in the United States, the **Panic of 1837**, followed by a depression that lasted to 1843. Businesses throughout the country failed, and many farmers, unable to meet mortgage payments because of declining income, lost their land. Tens of thousands of urban workers saw their jobs disappear. The fledgling labor movement collapsed as strikes became impossible, given the surplus of unemployed labor.

Economic collapse

The Times, an 1837 engraving that blames Andrew Jackson's policies for the economic depression. The Custom House is idle, while next door a bank is mobbed by worried depositors. Beneath Jackson's hat, spectacles, and clay pipe (with the ironic word "glory"), images of hardship abound.

Van Buren in Office

The president forced to deal with the depression was Martin Van Buren, who had been elected in 1836 over three regional candidates put forward by the Whigs. Under Van Buren, the hard money, anti-bank wing of the Democratic Party came to power. In 1837, the administration announced its intention to remove federal funds from the pet banks and hold them in the Treasury Department in Washington, under the control of government officials. Not until 1840 did Congress approve the new policy, known as the Independent Treasury, which completely separated the federal government from the nation's banking system. It would be repealed in 1841 when the Whigs returned to power, but it was reinstated under President James K. Polk in 1846.

The Independent Treasury

The Election of 1840

Despite his reputation as a political magician, Van Buren found that without Jackson's personal popularity he could not hold the Democratic coalition together. In 1840, he also discovered that his Whig opponents had mastered the political techniques he had helped to pioneer. Confronting an unprecedented opportunity for victory because of the continuing economic depression, the Whigs abandoned their most prominent leader, Henry Clay, and nominated William Henry Harrison. Harrison's main claim to fame was military success against the British and Indians during the War of 1812.

William Henry Harrison

A political cartoon from the 1840 presidential campaign shows public opinion as the "almighty lever" of politics in a democracy. Under the gaze of the American eagle, "Loco-Foco" Democrats slide into an abyss, while the people are poised to lift William Henry Harrison, the Whig candidate, to victory.

THE ALMIGHTY LEVER

The party nominated Harrison without a platform. In a flood of publications, banners, parades, and mass meetings, they promoted him as the "log cabin" candidate, the champion of the common man. This tactic proved enormously effective, even though it bore little relationship to the actual life of the wealthy Harrison. His running mate was John Tyler, a states'-rights Democrat from Virginia who had joined the Whigs after the nullification crisis and did not follow Calhoun back to the Democrats. On almost every issue of political significance, Tyler held views totally opposed to those of other Whigs. But party leaders hoped he could expand their base in the South.

By 1840, the mass democratic politics of the Age of Jackson had absorbed the logic of the marketplace. Selling candidates and their images was as important as the positions for which they stood. With two highly organized parties competing throughout the country, voter turnout soared to 80 percent of those eligible. Harrison won a sweeping victory. "We have taught them how to conquer us," lamented a Democratic newspaper.

THE PRESIDENTIAL ELECTION OF 1840

Non-voting territory

Party	Candidate	Electoral Vote (Share)	Popular Vote (Share)
Whig	Harrison	234 (80%)	1,275,016 (53%)
Democrat	Van Buren	60 (20%)	1,129,102 (47%)

Whig success proved short-lived. Immediately on assuming office, Harrison contracted pneumonia. He died a month later, and John Tyler succeeded him. When the Whig majority in Congress tried to enact the American System into law, Tyler vetoed nearly every measure, including a new national bank and higher tariff. Most of the cabinet resigned, and his party repudiated him. Tyler's four years in office were nearly devoid of accomplishment. If the campaign that resulted in the election of Harrison and Tyler demonstrated how a flourishing system of democratic politics had come into existence, Tyler's lack of success showed that political parties had become central to American government. Without a party behind him, a president could not govern. But a storm was now gathering that would test the stability of American democracy and the statesmanship of its political leaders.

Importance of political parties

CHAPTER REVIEW AND ONLINE RESOURCES

REVIEW QUESTIONS

1. *What global changes prompted the Monroe Doctrine? What were its key provisions? How does it show America's growing international presence?*

2. *How did Andrew Jackson represent the major developments of the era: westward movement, the market revolution, and the expansion of democracy for some alongside the limits on it for others?*

3. *How did the expansion of white male democracy run counter to the ideals of the founders, who believed government should be sheltered from excessive influence by ordinary people?*

4. *What were the components of the American System, and how were they designed to promote the national economy under the guidance of the federal government?*

5. *How did the Missouri Compromise and the nullification crisis demonstrate increasing sectional competition and disagreements over slavery?*

6. *According to Martin Van Buren, why were political parties a desirable element of public life? What did he do to build the party system?*

7. *What were the major economic, humanitarian, political, and social arguments for and against Indian Removal?*

8. *What were the key issues that divided the Democratic and Whig Parties? Where did each party stand on those issues?*

9. *Explain the causes and effects of the Panic of 1837.*

KEY TERMS

Dorr War (p. 282)

Democracy in America (p. 282)

"information revolution" (p. 283)

"infant industries" (p. 286)

American System (p. 286)

internal improvements (p. 286)

Second Bank of the United States (p. 287)

Panic of 1819 (p. 287)

McCulloch v. Maryland (p. 288)

Missouri Compromise (p. 288)

Monroe Doctrine (p. 290)

"spoils system" (p. 297)

Democratic Party and Whig Party (p. 297)

"tariff of abominations" (p. 299)

nullification crisis (p. 301)

Force Act (p. 301)

Indian Removal Act (p. 301)

Worcester v. Georgia (p. 303)

Trail of Tears (p. 303)

Bank War (p. 305)

"pet banks" (p. 306)

Panic of 1837 (p. 306)

wwnorton.com /studyspace

VISIT STUDYSPACE FOR THESE RESOURCES AND MORE

- A chapter outline
- A diagnostic chapter quiz
- Interactive maps
- Map worksheets
- Multimedia documents

CHAPTER 11

THE PECULIAR INSTITUTION

★

Richmond's Slave Market Auction, by the British artist Eyre Crowe, depicts a scene in an auction house. A slave sale is in progress, while on the right, slaves wait apprehensively for their turn to be sold. A child clings to her mother, perhaps for the last time, while potential buyers examine the seated women. Crowe entered the auction house in March 1853 after seeing an advertisement for a slave sale, and began sketching. When the white crowd realized what he was doing, they "rushed on him savagely and obliged him to quit," Crowe's traveling companion wrote to a friend. The painting is based on his sketches.

I n an age of "self-made" men, no American rose more dramatically from humble origins to national and international distinction than Frederick Douglass. Born into slavery in 1818, he became a major figure in the crusade for abolition, the drama of emancipation, and the effort during Reconstruction to give meaning to black freedom.

Douglass was the son of a slave mother and an unidentified white man, possibly his owner. As a youth in Maryland, he gazed out at the ships in Chesapeake Bay, seeing them as "freedom's swift-winged angels." In violation of Maryland law, Douglass learned to read and write, initially with the assistance of his owner's wife and then, after her husband forbade her to continue, with the help of local white children. "From that moment," he later wrote, he understood that knowledge was "the pathway from slavery to freedom." In 1838, having borrowed the free papers of a black sailor, he escaped to the North.

Frederick Douglass went on to become the most influential African-American of the nineteenth century and the nation's preeminent advocate of racial equality. He also published a widely read autobiography that offered an eloquent condemnation of slavery and racism. Indeed, his own accomplishments testified to the incorrectness of prevailing ideas about blacks' inborn inferiority. Douglass was also active in other reform movements, including the campaign for women's rights. Douglass argued that in their desire for freedom, the slaves were truer to the nation's underlying principles than the white Americans who annually celebrated the Fourth of July while allowing the continued existence of slavery.

THE OLD SOUTH

When Frederick Douglass was born, slavery was already an old institution in America. Two centuries had passed since the first twenty Africans were landed in Virginia from a Dutch ship. After abolition in the North, slavery had become the **"peculiar institution"** of the South—that is, an institution unique to southern society. The Mason-Dixon Line, drawn by two surveyors in the eighteenth century to settle a boundary dispute between Maryland and Pennsylvania, eventually became the dividing line between slavery and freedom.

Mason-Dixon line

Despite the hope of some of the founders that slavery might die out, in fact the institution survived the crisis of the American Revolution and rapidly expanded westward. On the eve of the Civil War, the slave population had risen to nearly 4 million, its high rate of natural increase more than

The expansion of slavery

making up for the prohibition in 1808 of further slave imports from Africa. In the South as a whole, slaves made up one-third of the total population, and in the cotton-producing states of the Deep South, around half. By the 1850s, slavery had crossed the Mississippi River and was expanding rapidly in Arkansas, Louisiana, and eastern Texas.

Cotton Is King

In the nineteenth century, cotton replaced sugar as the world's major crop produced by slave labor. And although slavery survived in Brazil and the Spanish and French Caribbean, its abolition in the British empire in 1833 made the United States indisputably the center of New World slavery.

A photograph of Frederick Douglass, the fugitive slave who became a prominent abolitionist, taken between 1847 and 1852. As a fellow abolitionist noted at the time, "The very look and bearing of Douglass are an irresistible logic against the oppression of his race."

Because the early industrial revolution centered on factories using cotton as the raw material to manufacture cloth, cotton had become by far the most important commodity in international trade. And three-fourths of the world's cotton supply came from the southern United States. Textile manufacturers in places as far flung as Massachusetts, Lancashire in Great Britain, Normandy in France, and the suburbs of Moscow depended on a regular supply of American cotton.

As early as 1803, cotton had become the most important American export. Cotton sales earned the money from abroad that allowed the United States to pay for imported manufactured goods. On the eve of the Civil War, it accounted for well over half of the total value of American exports. In 1860, the economic investment represented by the slave population exceeded the value of the nation's factories, railroads, and banks combined.

Economic value of slavery

COTTON PRESSING IN LOUISIANA

"Cotton Pressing in Louisiana," from *Ballou's Magazine* in 1856, illustrates how slaves were used to supply power for a partially mechanized work process.

The Second Middle Passage

As noted in Chapter 9, to replace the slave trade from Africa, which had been prohibited by Congress in 1808, a massive trade in slaves developed within the United States. More than 2 million slaves were sold between 1820 and 1860. The main business districts of southern cities contained the offices of slave traders, complete with signs reading "Negro Sales" or "Negroes Bought Here." Auctions of slaves took place at public slave markets, as in New Orleans, or at courthouses. Southern newspapers carried advertisements for slave sales, southern banks financed slave trading, southern ships *Slave trade in the South* and railroads carried slaves from buyers to sellers, and southern states and municipalities earned revenue by taxing the sale of slaves.

Slavery and the Nation

Slavery shaped the lives of all Americans, white as well as black. It helped to determine where they lived, how they worked, and under what conditions they could exercise their freedoms of speech, assembly, and the press.

Northern participation   Northern merchants and manufacturers participated in the slave economy and shared in its profits. Money earned in the cotton trade helped to finance industrial development and internal improvements in the North. Northern ships carried cotton to New York and Europe, northern bankers financed cotton plantations, northern companies insured slave property, and northern factories turned cotton into cloth. New York City's rise to commercial prominence depended as much on the establishment of shipping lines that gathered the South's cotton and transported it to Europe as on the Erie Canal.

TABLE 11.1   Growth of the Slave Population

YEAR	SLAVE POPULATION
1790	697,624
1800	893,602
1810	1,191,362
1820	1,538,022
1830	2,009,043
1840	2,487,355
1850	3,204,313
1860	3,953,760

The Southern Economy

There was no single South before the Civil War. In the eight slave states of the Upper South, slaves and slaveowners made up a smaller percentage of the total population than in the seven Deep South states, which stretched from South Carolina west to Texas. The Upper South had major centers of industry in Baltimore, Richmond,

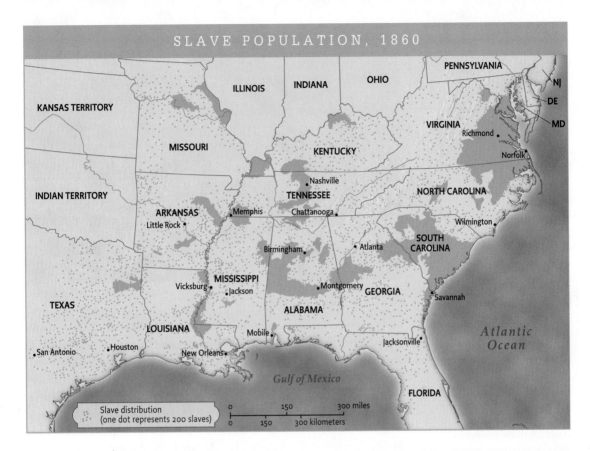

SLAVE POPULATION, 1860

Slave distribution
(one dot represents 200 slaves)

0   150   300 miles
0   150   300 kilometers

and St. Louis, and its economies were more diversified than those in the Deep South, which was heavily dependent on cotton. Not surprisingly, during the secession crisis of 1860–1861, the Deep South states were the first to leave the Union.

Nonetheless, slavery led the South down a very different path of economic development than the North's, limiting the growth of industry, discouraging immigrants from entering the region, and inhibiting technological progress. The South did not share in the urban growth experienced by the rest of the country. In the Cotton Kingdom, the only city of significant size was New Orleans. With a population of 168,000 in 1860, New Orleans ranked as the nation's sixth-largest city. As the gathering point for cotton grown along the Mississippi River and sugar from the plantations of southeastern Louisiana, it was the world's leading exporter of slave-grown crops.

Rather than being evenly distributed throughout the South, the slave population was concentrated in areas with the most fertile soil and easiest access to national and international markets. By 1860, a significant percentage of the slave population had been transported from the Atlantic coast to the Deep South via the internal slave trade.

New Orleans

This 1860 view of New Orleans captures the size and scale of the cotton trade in the South's largest city. More than 3,500 steamboats arrived in New Orleans in 1860.

In 1860, the South produced less than 10 percent of the nation's manufactured goods. Many northerners viewed slavery as an obstacle to American economic progress. But as New Orleans showed, slavery and economic growth could go hand in hand. In general, the southern economy was hardly stagnant, and slavery proved very profitable for most owners. The profits produced by slavery for the South and the nation as a whole formed a powerful obstacle to abolition. Speaking of cotton, Senator James Henry Hammond of South Carolina declared, "No power on earth dares to make war upon it. Cotton is king."

Plain Folk of the Old South

An upcountry family, dressed in homespun, in Cedar Mountain, Virginia. Many white families in the pre–Civil War South were largely isolated from the market economy. This photograph was taken in 1862 but reflects the prewar way of life.

The foundation of the Old South's economy, slavery powerfully shaped race relations, politics, religion, and the law. Its influence was pervasive: "Nothing escaped," writes one historian, "nothing and no one." This was true despite the fact that the majority of white southerners—three out of four white families—owned no slaves. Many southern farmers lived outside the plantation belt in hilly areas unsuitable for cotton production. Using family labor, they raised livestock and grew food for their own use, purchasing relatively few goods at local stores. Unlike northern farmers, therefore, they did not provide a market for manufactured goods. This was one of the main reasons that the South did not develop an industrial base.

Lack of southern market for manufactures

Some poorer whites resented the power and privileges of the great planters. Politicians such as Andrew Johnson of Tennessee and Joseph Brown of Georgia rose to power as self-proclaimed spokesmen of the common man against the "slaveocracy." But most poor whites made their peace with the planters in whose hands economic and social power was concentrated. Racism, kinship ties, common participation in a democratic political culture, and regional loyalty in the face of outside criticism all served to cement bonds between planters and the South's "**plain folk**." Like other white southerners, most small farmers believed their economic and personal freedom rested on slavery. Not until the Civil War would class tensions among the white population threaten the planters' domination.

Planters and "plain folk"

The Planter Class

Even among slaveholders, the planter was far from typical. In 1850, a majority of slaveholding families owned five or fewer slaves. Fewer than 40,000 families possessed the twenty or more slaves that qualified them as planters. Fewer than 2,000 families owned a hundred slaves or more. Nonetheless, even though the planter was not the typical slaveholder or white southerner, his values and aspirations dominated southern life. The plantation, wrote Frederick Douglass, was "a little nation by itself, with its own language, its own rules, regulations, and customs." These rules and customs set the tone for southern society.

Ownership of slaves provided the route to wealth, status, and influence. Planters not only held the majority of slaves but also controlled the most fertile land, enjoyed the highest incomes, and dominated state and local offices and the leadership of both political parties. Slavery, of course, was a profit-making system, and slaveowners kept close watch on world prices for their products, invested in enterprises such as railroads and canals, and carefully supervised their plantations. Their wives—the "plantation mistresses" idealized in southern lore for femininity, beauty, and dependence on men—were hardly idle. They cared for sick slaves, directed the domestic servants, and supervised the entire plantation when their husbands were away. The wealthiest Americans before the Civil War were planters in the South Carolina low country and the cotton region around Natchez, Mississippi.

A slave dealer's place of business in Atlanta. The buying and selling of slaves was a regularized part of the southern economy, and such businesses were a common sight in every southern town.

On the cotton frontier, many planters lived in crude log homes. But in the older slave states, and as settled society developed in the Deep South, they constructed elegant mansions adorned with white columns in the Greek Revival style of architecture. Planters discouraged their sons from entering "lowly" trades such as commerce and manufacturing, one reason that the South remained overwhelmingly agricultural.

The Paternalist Ethos

Plantation hierarchy

The slave plantation was deeply embedded in the world market, and planters sought to accumulate land, slaves, and profits. However, planters' values glorified not the competitive capitalist marketplace but a hierarchical, agrarian society in which slaveholding gentlemen took personal responsibility for the physical and moral well-being of their dependents—women, children, and slaves.

This outlook, known as "**paternalism**" (from the Latin word for "father"), had been a feature of American slavery even in the eighteenth century. But it became more ingrained after the closing of the African slave trade in 1808, which narrowed the cultural gap between master and slave and gave owners an economic interest in the survival of their human property. Unlike the absentee planters of the West Indies, many of whom resided in Great Britain, southern slaveholders lived on their plantations and thus had year-round contact with their slaves.

The paternalist outlook both masked and justified the brutal reality of slavery. It enabled slaveowners to think of themselves as kind, responsible masters even as they bought and sold their human property—a practice at odds with the claim that slaves formed part of the master's "family."

The Proslavery Argument

In the thirty years before the outbreak of the Civil War, even as northern criticism of the "peculiar institution" began to deepen, proslavery thought came to dominate southern public life. Fewer and fewer white southerners shared the view, common among the founding fathers, that slavery was, at best, a "necessary evil."

TABLE 11.2 Slaveholding, 1850 (in Round Numbers)

NUMBER OF SLAVES OWNED	SLAVEHOLDERS
1	68,000
2–4	105,000
5–9	80,000
10–19	55,000
20–49	30,000
50–99	6,000
100–199	1,500
200+	250

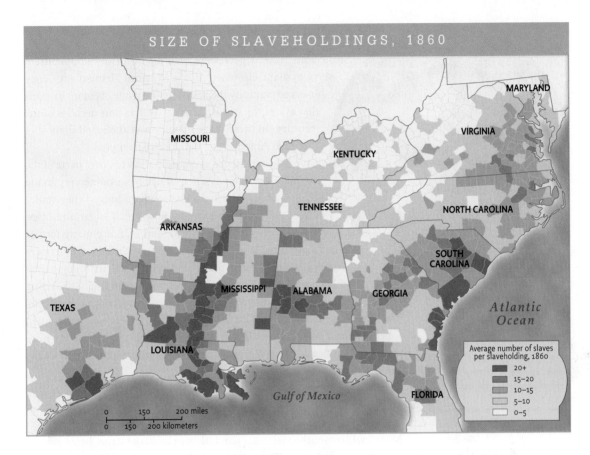

SIZE OF SLAVEHOLDINGS, 1860

Average number of slaves per slaveholding, 1860
- 20+
- 15–20
- 10–15
- 5–10
- 0–5

Even those who had no direct stake in slavery shared with planters a deep commitment to white supremacy. Indeed, racism—the belief that blacks were innately inferior to whites and unsuited for life in any condition other than slavery—formed one pillar of the proslavery ideology. Most slaveholders also found legitimation for slavery in biblical passages such as the injunction that servants should obey their masters. Others argued that slavery was essential to human progress. Without slavery, they believed, planters would be unable to cultivate the arts, sciences, and other civilized pursuits.

Still other defenders of slavery insisted that the institution guaranteed equality for whites by preventing the growth of a class doomed to a life of unskilled labor. Like northerners, they claimed to be committed to the ideal of freedom. Slavery for blacks, they declared, was the surest guarantee of "perfect equality" among whites, liberating them from the "low, menial" jobs such as factory labor and domestic service performed by wage laborers in the North.

Most southern slaveholders owned fewer than five slaves. The largest plantations were concentrated in coastal South Carolina and along the Mississippi River.

Slavery and white supremacy

Equality for whites

Abolition in the Americas

American slaveowners were well aware of developments in slave systems elsewhere in the Western Hemisphere. They observed carefully the results of the wave of emancipations that swept the hemisphere in the first four decades of the century. In these years, slavery was abolished in most of Spanish America and in the British empire.

The experience of emancipation in other parts of the hemisphere strongly affected debates over slavery in the United States. Southern slaveowners judged the vitality of the Caribbean economy by how much sugar and other crops it produced for the world market. Since many former slaves preferred to grow food for their own families, defenders of slavery in the United States charged that British emancipation had been a failure. Abolitionists disagreed, pointing to the rising standard of living of freed slaves, the spread of education among them, and other improvements in their lives. But the stark fact remained that, in a hemispheric perspective, slavery was a declining institution. At midcentury, significant New World slave systems remained only in Cuba, Puerto Rico, Brazil—and the United States.

A plate manufactured in England to celebrate emancipation in the British empire. After a brief period of apprenticeship, the end of slavery came on August 1,1838. At the center, a family of former slaves celebrates outside their cabin.

Slavery and Liberty

Many white southerners declared themselves the true heirs of the American Revolution. They claimed to be inspired by "the same spirit of freedom and independence" that motivated the founding generation. Beginning in the 1830s, however, proslavery writers began to question the ideals of liberty, equality, and democracy so widely shared elsewhere in the nation. South Carolina, the only southern state where a majority of white families owned slaves, became the home of an aggressive defense of slavery that repudiated the idea that freedom and equality were universal entitlements. The language of the Declaration of Independence—that all men were created equal and entitled to liberty—was "the most false and dangerous of all political errors," insisted John C. Calhoun.

Questioning founding ideals

George Fitzhugh

The Virginia writer George Fitzhugh took the argument to its most radical conclusion, repudiating not only Jeffersonian ideals but the notion of America's special mission in the world. Far from being the natural condition of mankind, Fitzhugh wrote, "universal liberty" was the exception, an experiment carried on "for a little while" in "a corner of Europe" and the northern United States. Taking the world and its history as a whole, slavery, "without regard to race and color," was "the general, . . . normal, natural" basis of "civilized society."

After 1830, southern writers, newspaper editors, politicians, and clergymen increasingly devoted themselves to spreading the defense of slavery. The majority of white southerners came to believe that freedom for whites rested on the power to command the labor of blacks. In the words of the Richmond *Enquirer*, "freedom is not possible without slavery."

Spreading defense of slavery

LIFE UNDER SLAVERY

Slaves and the Law

For slaves, the "peculiar institution" meant a life of incessant toil, brutal punishment, and the constant fear that their families would be destroyed by sale. Before the law, slaves were property. Although they had a few legal rights (all states made it illegal to kill a slave except in self-defense, and slaves accused of serious crimes were entitled to their day in court, before all-white judges and juries), these were haphazardly enforced. Slaves could be sold or leased by their owners at will and lacked any voice in the governments that ruled over them. They could not testify in court against a white person, sign contracts or acquire property, own firearms, hold meetings unless a white person was present, or leave the farm or plantation without the permission of their owner. By the 1830s, it was against the law to teach a slave to read or write.

Slaves as property

Legal restrictions on slaves

Not all of these laws were rigorously enforced. Some members of slaveholding families taught slave children to read (although rather few, since well over 90 percent of the slave population was illiterate in 1860). It was quite common throughout the South for slaves to gather without white supervision at crossroads villages and country stores on Sunday, their day of rest.

The slave, declared a Louisiana law, "owes to his master . . . a respect without bounds, and an absolute obedience." No aspect of slaves' lives, from the choice of marriage partners to how they spent their free time, was immune from his interference. The entire system of southern justice, from the state militia and courts down to armed patrols in each locality, was designed to enforce the master's control over the persons and labor of his slaves.

In one famous case, a Missouri court considered the "crime" of Celia, a slave who had killed her master in 1855 while resisting a sexual assault.

A poster advertising the raffle of a horse and a slave, treated as equivalents, at a Missouri store.

State law deemed "any woman" in such circumstances to be acting in self-defense. But Celia, the court ruled, was not a "woman" in the eyes of the law. She was a slave, whose master had complete power over her person. The court sentenced her to death. However, since Celia was pregnant, her execution was postponed until the child was born, so as not to deprive her owner's heirs of their property rights.

Slaves outside their cabin on a South Carolina plantation, probably photographed in the 1850s. They had brought their furniture outdoors to be included in the photo.

Conditions of Slave Life

Compared with their counterparts in the West Indies and Brazil, American slaves enjoyed better diets, lower rates of infant mortality, and longer life expectancies. Many factors contributed to improving material conditions. Most of the South lies outside the geographical area where tropical diseases like malaria, yellow fever, and typhoid fever flourish, so health among all southerners was better than in the Caribbean. And with the price of slaves rising dramatically after the closing of the African slave trade, it made economic sense for owners to become concerned with the health and living conditions of their human property.

Although slaves in the United States enjoyed better material lives than elsewhere in the Western Hemisphere, they had far less access to freedom. In Brazil, it was not uncommon for an owner to free slaves as a form of celebration—on the occasion of a wedding in the owner's family, for example— or to allow slaves to purchase their freedom. In the nineteenth-century South, however, more and more states set limits on voluntary manumission, requiring that such acts be approved by the legislature. Few slave societies in history have so systematically closed off all avenues to freedom as the Old South.

Limiting voluntary manumission

Free Blacks in the Old South

The existence of slavery helped to define the status of those blacks who did enjoy freedom. On the eve of the Civil War, nearly half a million free blacks lived in the United States, a majority in the South. Most were the descendants of slaves freed by southern owners in the aftermath of the Revolution or by the gradual emancipation laws of the northern states. Their numbers were supplemented by slaves who had been voluntarily liberated by their masters, who had been allowed to purchase their freedom, or who succeeded in running away.

When followed by "black" or "Negro," the word "free" took on an entirely new meaning. Free blacks in the South could legally own property and marry and, of course, could not be bought and sold. But many regulations restricting the lives of slaves also applied to them. Free blacks had no voice in selecting public officials. They were not allowed to testify in court or serve on juries, and they had to carry at all times a certificate of freedom. Poor free blacks who required public assistance could be bound out to labor alongside slaves. By the 1850s, most southern states prohibited free blacks from entering their territory. A few states even moved to expel them altogether, offering the choice of enslavement or departure.

In New Orleans and Charleston, on the other hand, relatively prosperous free black communities developed, mostly composed of mixed-race descendants of unions between white men and slave women. Many free blacks in these cities acquired an education and worked as skilled craftsmen such as tailors, carpenters, and mechanics. They established churches for their communities and schools for their children. In the Upper South, where the large majority of southern free blacks lived, they generally worked for wages as farm laborers. Overall, in the words of Willis A. Hodges, a member of a free Virginia family that helped runaways to reach the North, free blacks and slaves were "one man of sorrow."

Slaves were an ever-present part of southern daily life. In this 1826 portrait of the five children of Commodore John Daniel Daniels, a wealthy Baltimore shipowner, a young slave lies on the floor at their side, holding the soap for a game of blowing bubbles, while another hovers in the background, almost depicted as part of the room's design.

Slave Labor

First and foremost, slavery was a system of labor; "from sunup to first dark," with only brief interruptions for meals, work occupied most of the slaves' time. Large plantations were diversified communities, where slaves performed all kinds of work. The 125 slaves on one plantation, for instance, included a butler, two waitresses, a nurse, a dairymaid, a gardener, ten carpenters, and two shoemakers. Other plantations counted among their slaves engineers, blacksmiths, and weavers, as well as domestic workers from cooks to coachmen.

Varieties of slave labor

The large majority of slaves—75 percent of women and nearly 90 percent of men, according to one study—worked in the fields. The precise organization of their labor varied according to the crop and the size of

In this undated photograph, men, women, and children pick cotton under the watchful eye of an overseer. Unlike sugarcane, cotton does not grow to a great height, allowing an overseer to supervise a large number of slaves.

the holding. On small farms, the owner often toiled side by side with his slaves. The largest concentration of slaves, however, lived and worked on plantations in the Cotton Belt, where men, women, and children labored in gangs, often under the direction of an overseer and perhaps a slave "driver" who assisted him. Among slaves, overseers had a reputation for meting out brutal treatment.

The 150,000 slaves who worked in the sugar fields of southern Louisiana also labored in large gangs. Conditions here were among the harshest in the South, for the late fall harvest season required round-the-clock labor to cut and process the sugarcane before it spoiled. On the rice plantations of South Carolina and Georgia, the system of task labor, which had originated in the colonial era, prevailed. With few whites willing to venture into the malaria-infested swamps, slaves were assigned daily tasks and allowed to set their own pace of work. Once a slave's task had been completed, he or she could spend the rest of the day hunting, fishing, or cultivating garden crops.

Slavery in the Cities

Skilled labor

Businessmen, merchants, lawyers, and civil servants owned slaves, and by 1860 some 200,000 worked in industry, especially in the ironworks and tobacco factories of the Upper South. In southern cities, thousands were employed as unskilled laborers and skilled artisans. Most city slaves were servants, cooks, and other domestic laborers. But owners sometimes allowed those with craft skills to "hire their own time." This meant that they could make work arrangements individually with employers, with most of the wages going to the slave's owner. Many urban slaves even lived on their own. But slaveholders increasingly became convinced that, as one wrote, the growing independence of skilled urban slaves "exerts a most injurious influence upon the relation of master and servant." For this reason, many owners in the 1850s sold city slaves to the countryside and sought replacements among skilled white labor.

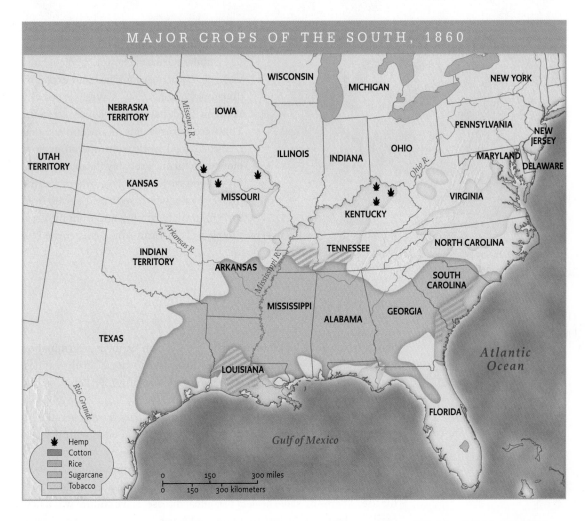

MAJOR CROPS OF THE SOUTH, 1860

Cotton was the major agricultural crop of the South, and, indeed, the nation, but slaves also grew rice, sugarcane, tobacco, and hemp.

Maintaining Order

Slaveowners employed a variety of means in their attempts to maintain order and discipline among their human property and persuade them to labor productively. At base, the system rested on force. Masters had almost complete discretion in inflicting punishment, and rare was the slave who went through his or her life without experiencing a whipping. Any infraction of plantation rules, no matter how minor, could be punished by the lash. One Georgia planter recorded in his journal that he had whipped

A system based on force

A Public Whipping of Slaves in Lexington, Missouri, in 1856, an illustration from the abolitionist publication *The Suppressed Book about Slavery*. Whipping was a common form of punishment for slaves.

a slave "for not bringing over milk for my coffee, being compelled to take it without."

Subtler means of control supplemented violence. Owners encouraged and exploited divisions among the slaves, especially between field hands and house servants. They created systems of incentives that rewarded good work with time off or even money payments. Probably the most powerful weapon wielded by slaveowners was the threat of sale, which separated slaves from their immediate families and from the communities that, despite overwhelming odds, African-Americans created on plantations throughout the South.

SLAVE CULTURE

Slaves never abandoned their desire for freedom or their determination to resist total white control over their lives. In the face of grim realities, they succeeded in forging a semi-independent culture, centered on the family and church. This enabled them to survive the experience of bondage without surrendering their self-esteem and to pass from generation to generation a set of ideas and values fundamentally at odds with those of their masters.

African heritage

Slave culture drew on the African heritage. African influences were evident in the slaves' music and dances, their style of religious worship, and the use of herbs by slave healers to combat disease. Slave culture was a new creation, shaped by African traditions and American values and experiences.

The Slave Family

At the center of the slave community stood the family. On the sugar plantations of the West Indies, the number of males far exceeded that of females, the workers lived in barracks-type buildings, and settled family life was nearly impossible. The United States, where the slave population grew from natural increase rather than continued importation from Africa, had an even male-female ratio, making the creation of families far more possible. To be sure, the law did not recognize the legality of slave marriages. The master had to consent before a man and woman could

Slave marriages

"jump over the broomstick" (the slaves' marriage ceremony), and families stood in constant danger of being broken up by sale.

Nonetheless, most adult slaves married, and their unions, when not disrupted by sale, typically lasted for a lifetime. To solidify a sense of family continuity, slaves frequently named children after cousins, uncles, grandparents, and other relatives. Most slaves lived in two-parent families. But because of constant sales, the slave community had a significantly higher number of female-headed households than among whites, as well as families in which grandparents, other relatives, or even non-kin assumed responsibility for raising children.

The Threat of Sale

As noted above, the threat of sale, which disrupted family ties, was perhaps the most powerful disciplinary weapon slaveholders possessed. As the domestic slave trade expanded with the rise of the Cotton Kingdom, about one slave marriage in three in slave-selling states like Virginia was broken by sale. Many children were separated from their parents by sale.

Slave traders gave little attention to preserving family ties. A public notice, "Sale of Slaves and Stock," announced the 1852 auction of property belonging to a recently deceased Georgia planter. It listed thirty-six individuals ranging from an infant to a sixty-nine-year-old woman and ended with the proviso: "Slaves will be sold separate, or in lots, as best suits the purchaser." Sales like this were a human tragedy.

Sale of Slaves and Stock.

The Negroes and Stock listed below, are a Prime Lot, and belong to the ESTATE OF THE LATE LUTHER McGOWAN, and will be sold on Monday, Sept. 22nd, 1852, at the Fair Grounds, in Savannah, Georgia, at 1:00 P. M. The Negroes will be taken to the grounds two days previous to the Sale, so that they may be inspected by prospective buyers.

On account of the low prices listed below, they will be sold for cash only, and must be taken into custody within two hours after sale.

No.	Name.	Age.	Remarks.	Price.
1	Lunesta	27	Prime Rice Planter,	$1,275.00
2	Violet	16	Housework and Nursemaid,	900.00
3	Lizzie	30	Rice, Unsound,	300.00
4	Minda	27	Cotton, Prime Woman,	1,200.00
5	Adam	28	Cotton, Prime Young Man,	1,100.00
6	Abel	41	Rice Hand, Eyesight Poor,	675.00
7	Tanney	22	Prime Cotton Hand,	950.00
8	Flementina	39	Good Cook. Stiff Knee,	400.00
9	Lanney	34	Prime Cottom Man,	1,000.00
10	Sally	10	Handy in Kitchen,	675.00
11	Maccabey	35	Prime Man, Fair Carpenter,	980.00
12	Dorcas Judy	25	Seamstress, Handy in House,	800.00
13	Happy	60	Blacksmith,	575.00
14	Mowden	15	Prime Cotton Boy,	700.00
15	Bills	21	Handy with Mules,	900.00
16	Theopolis	39	Rice Hand, Gets Fits,	575.00
17	Coolidge	29	Rice Hand and Blacksmith,	1,275.00
18	Bessie	69	Infirm, Sews,	250.00
19	Infant	1	Strong Likely Boy,	400.00
20	Samson	41	Prime Man, Good with Stock,	975.00
21	Callie May	27	Prime Woman, Rice,	1,000.00
22	Honey	14	Prime Girl, Hearing Poor,	850.00
23	Angelina	16	Prime Girl, House or Field,	1,000.00
24	Virgil	21	Prime Field Hand,	1,100.00
25	Tom	40	Rice Hand, Lame Leg,	750.00
26	Noble	11	Handy Boy,	900.00
27	Judge Lesh	55	Prime Blacksmith,	800.00
28	Booster	43	Fair Mason, Unsound,	600.00
29	Big Kate	37	Housekeeper and Nurse,	950.00
30	Melie Ann	19	Housework, Smart Yellow Girl,	1,250.00
31	Deacon	26	Prime Rice Hand,	1,000.00
32	Coming	19	Prime Cotton Hand,	1,000.00
33	Mabel	47	Prime Cotton Hand,	800.00
34	Uncle Tim	60	Fair Hand with Mules,	600.00
35	Abe	27	Prime Cotton Hand,	1,000.00
36	Tennes	29	Prime Rice Hand and Cocahman,	1,250.00

There will also be offered at this sale, twenty head of Horses and Mules with harness, along with thirty head of Prime Cattle. Slaves will be sold separate, or in lots, as best suits the purchaser. Sale will be held rain or shine.

A broadside advertising the public sale of slaves, along with horses, mules, and cattle, after the death of their owner. The advertisement notes that the slaves will be sold individually or in groups "as best suits the purchaser," an indication that families were likely to be broken up. The prices are based on each slave's sex, age, and skill.

Gender Roles among Slaves

In some ways, gender roles under slavery differed markedly from those in the larger society. Slave men and women experienced, in a sense, the equality of powerlessness. The nineteenth century's "cult of domesticity," which defined the home as a woman's proper sphere, did not apply to slave women, who regularly worked in the fields. Slave men could not act as the economic providers for their families. Nor could they protect their

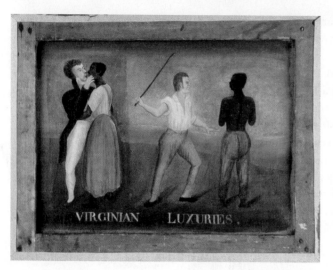

wives from physical or sexual abuse by owners and overseers (a frequent occurrence on many plantations) or determine when and under what conditions their children worked.

When slaves worked "on their own time," however, more conventional gender roles prevailed. Slave men chopped wood, hunted, and fished, while women washed, sewed, and assumed primary responsibility for the care of children. Some planters allowed their slaves small plots of land on which to grow food to supplement the rations provided by the owner; women usually took charge of these "garden plots."

Virginian Luxuries. Originally painted on the back panel of a formal portrait, this image illustrates two "luxuries" of a Virginia slaveowner—the power to sexually abuse slave women and to whip slaves.

Slave Religion

A distinctive version of Christianity also offered solace to slaves in the face of hardship and hope for liberation from bondage. Some blacks, free and slave, had taken part in the Great Awakening of the colonial era, and even more were swept into the South's Baptist and Methodist churches during the religious revivals of the late eighteenth and early nineteenth centuries. As one preacher recalled of the great camp meeting that drew thousands of worshipers to Cane Ridge, Kentucky, in 1801, no distinctions were made "as to age, sex, color, or anything of a temporary nature; old and young, male and female, black and white, had equal privilege to minister the light which they received, in whatever way the Spirit directed."

Black preachers

Even though the law prohibited slaves from gathering without a white person present, every plantation, it seemed, had its own black preacher. Usually the preacher was a "self-called" slave who possessed little or no formal education but whose rhetorical abilities and familiarity with the Bible made him one of the most respected members of the slave community. Especially in southern cities, slaves also worshiped in biracial congregations with white ministers, where they generally were required to sit in the back pews or in the balcony. Urban free blacks established their own churches, sometimes attended by slaves.

Religion and social control

To masters, Christianity offered another means of social control. Many required slaves to attend services conducted by white ministers, who preached that theft was immoral and that the Bible required servants to obey their masters. One slave later recalled being told in a white minister's sermon "how good God was in bringing us over to this country from dark and benighted Africa, and permitting us to listen to the sound of the gospel."

In their own religious gatherings, slaves transformed the Christianity they had embraced, turning it to their own purposes. The biblical story of Exodus, for example, in which God chose Moses to lead the enslaved Jews of Egypt into a promised land of freedom, played a central role in black Christianity. Slaves identified themselves as a chosen people whom God in the fullness of time would deliver from bondage. At the same time, the figure of Jesus Christ represented to slaves a personal redeemer, one who truly cared for the oppressed. And in the slaves' eyes, the Christian message of brotherhood and the equality of all souls before the Creator offered an irrefutable indictment of the institution of slavery.

Kitchen Ball at White Sulphur Springs, Virginia, an 1838 painting by the German-born American artist Christian Mayr. Fashionably dressed domestic slaves celebrate the wedding of a couple, dressed in white at the center.

The Desire for Liberty

Despite their masters' elaborate ideology defending the South's "peculiar institution," slave culture rested on a conviction of the injustices of bondage and the desire for freedom. When slaves sang, "I'm bound for the land of Canaan," they meant not only relief from worldly woes in an afterlife but also escaping to the North or witnessing the breaking of slavery's chains. A fugitive who reached the North later recalled that the "desire for freedom" was the "constant theme" of conversations in the slave quarters.

Most slaves, however, fully understood the impossibility of directly confronting such an entrenched system. Their folk tales had no figures equivalent to Paul Bunyan, the powerful, larger-than-life backwoodsman popular in white folklore. Slaves' folklore, such as the Brer Rabbit stories, glorified the weak hare who outwitted stronger foes like the bear and fox, rather than challenging them outright. Their religious songs, or spirituals, spoke of lives of sorrow ("I've been 'buked and I've been scorned"), while holding out hope for ultimate liberation ("Didn't my Lord deliver Daniel?").

Slave culture

Owners attempted to prevent slaves from learning about the larger world. But slaves created neighborhood networks that transmitted information between plantations. Skilled craftsmen, preachers, pilots

Neighborhood networks

Plantation Burial, a painting from around 1860 by John Antrobus, an English artist who emigrated to New Orleans in 1850 and later married the daughter of a plantation owner. A slave preacher conducts a funeral service while black men, women, and children look on. The well-dressed white man and woman on the far right are, presumably, the plantation owner and his wife. This is a rare eyewitness depiction of black culture under slavery.

on ships, and other privileged slaves spread news of local and national events. James Henry Hammond of South Carolina was "astonished and shocked" to find that his slaves understood the political views of the presidential candidates of 1844, Henry Clay and James K. Polk, and knew "most of what the abolitionists are doing."

The world of most rural slaves was bounded by their local communities and kin. Nor could slaves remain indifferent to the currents of thought unleashed by the American Revolution or to the language of freedom in the society around them. "I am in a land of liberty," wrote Joseph Taper, a Virginia slave who escaped to Canada around 1840. "Here man is as God intended he should be."

RESISTANCE TO SLAVERY

Confronted with federal, state, and local authorities committed to preserving slavery, and outnumbered within the South as a whole by the white population, slaves could only rarely express their desire for freedom by outright rebellion. Compared with revolts in Brazil and the West Indies, which experienced numerous uprisings, involving hundreds or even thousands of slaves, revolts in the United States were smaller and less frequent. Resistance to slavery took many forms in the Old South, from individual acts of defiance to occasional uprisings. These actions posed a constant challenge to the slaveholders' self-image as benign paternalists and their belief that slaves were obedient subjects grateful for their owners' care.

Forms of Resistance

Everyday resistance

The most widespread expression of hostility to slavery was "day-to-day resistance" or "**silent sabotage**"—doing poor work, breaking tools, abusing animals, and in other ways disrupting the plantation routine. Then there was the theft of food, a form of resistance so common that one southern physician diagnosed it as a hereditary disease unique to blacks. Less frequent, but more dangerous, were serious crimes committed by slaves, including arson, poisoning, and armed assaults against individual whites.

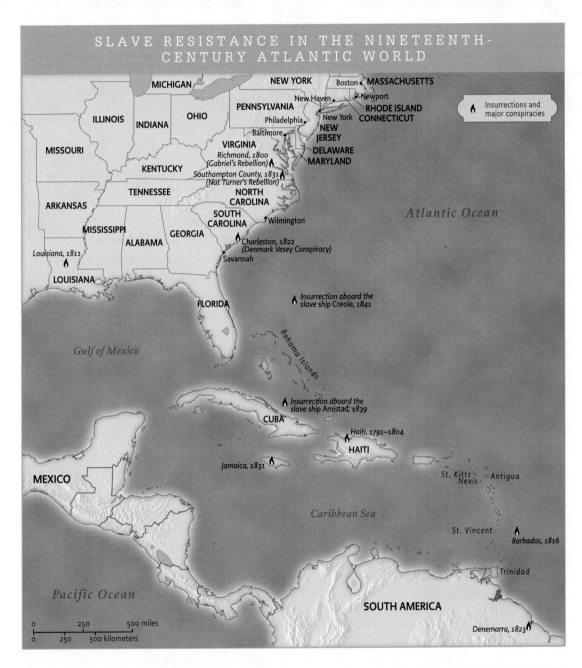

SLAVE RESISTANCE IN THE NINETEENTH-CENTURY ATLANTIC WORLD

MICHIGAN

NEW YORK · Boston · MASSACHUSETTS

New Haven · Newport

PENNSYLVANIA · RHODE ISLAND

ILLINOIS · INDIANA · OHIO · New York · CONNECTICUT

Philadelphia · NEW JERSEY

MISSOURI · Baltimore

KENTUCKY · VIRGINIA · DELAWARE · MARYLAND

Richmond, 1800 (Gabriel's Rebellion)

Southampton County, 1831 (Nat Turner's Rebellion)

TENNESSEE · NORTH CAROLINA

ARKANSAS · SOUTH CAROLINA · Wilmington

MISSISSIPPI · GEORGIA

ALABAMA · Charleston, 1822 (Denmark Vesey Conspiracy)

Louisiana, 1811 · Savannah

LOUISIANA

FLORIDA

Atlantic Ocean

Insurrections and major conspiracies

Insurrection aboard the slave ship Creole, 1841

Gulf of Mexico

Bahama Islands

Insurrection aboard the slave ship Amistad, 1839

CUBA

Haiti, 1791–1804

HAITI

Jamaica, 1831

MEXICO

St. Kitts · Antigua
Nevis

Caribbean Sea

St. Vincent

Barbados, 1816

Trinidad

Pacific Ocean

SOUTH AMERICA

Denemarra, 1823

0   250   500 miles
0   250   500 kilometers

Instances of slave resistance occurred throughout the Western Hemisphere, on land and at sea. This map shows the location of major events in the nineteenth century.

VOICES OF FREEDOM

From Letter by Joseph Taper to Joseph Long (1840)

No one knows how many slaves succeeded in escaping from bondage before the Civil War. Some settled in northern cities like Boston, Cincinnati, and New York. But because the Constitution required that fugitives be returned to slavery, many continued northward until they reached Canada.

One successful fugitive was Joseph Taper, a slave in Frederick County, Virginia, who in 1837 ran away to Pennsylvania with his wife and children. Two years later, learning that a "slave catcher" was in the neighborhood, the Tapers fled to Canada. In 1840, Taper wrote to a white acquaintance in Virginia recounting some of his experiences.

The biblical passage to which Taper refers reads: "And I will come near to you to judgment; and I will be a swift witness against the sorcerers, and against the adulterers, and against false swearers, and against those that oppress the hireling in his wages, the widow, and the fatherless, and that turn aside the stranger from his right, and fear not me, saith the Lord of hosts."

Dear sir,

I now take the opportunity to inform you that I am in a land of liberty, in good health. . . . Since I have been in the Queen's dominions I have been well contented, Yes well contented for Sure, man is as God intended he should be. That is, all are born free and equal. This is a wholesome law, not like the Southern laws which puts man made in the image of God, on level with brutes. O, what will become of the people, and where will they stand in the day of Judgment. Would that the 5th verse of the 3d chapter of Malachi were written as with the bar of iron, and the point of a diamond upon every oppressor's heart that they might repent of this evil, and let the oppressed go free. . . .

We have good schools, and all the colored population supplied with schools. My boy Edward who will be six years next January, is now reading, and I intend keeping him at school until he becomes a good scholar.

I have enjoyed more pleasure within one month here than in all my life in the land of bondage. . . . My wife and self are sitting by a good comfortable fire happy, knowing that there are none to molest [us] or make [us] afraid. God save Queen Victoria. The Lord bless her in this life, and crown her with glory in the world to come is my prayer,

Yours With much respect

most obt, Joseph Taper

From "Slavery and the Bible" (1850)

White southerners developed an elaborate set of arguments defending slavery in the period before the Civil War. One pillar of proslavery thought was the idea that the institution was sanctioned by the Bible, as in this essay from the influential southern magazine *De Bow's Review*.

A very large party in the United States believe that holding slaves is morally wrong; this party founds its belief upon precepts taught in the Bible, and takes that book as the standard of morality and religion.

. . . We think we can show, that the Bible teaches clearly and conclusively that the holding of slaves is right; and if so, no deduction from general principles can make it wrong, if that book is true. . . .

Slavery has existed in some form or under some name, in almost every country of the globe. It existed in every country known, even by name, to any one of the sacred writers, at the time of his writing; yet none of them condemns it in the slightest degree. Would this have been the case had it been wrong in itself? Would not some one of the host of sacred writers have spoken of this alleged crime, in such terms as to show, in a manner not to be misunderstood, that God wished all men to be equal?

Abraham, the chosen servant of God, had his bond servants, whose condition was similar to, or worse than, that of our slaves. He considered them as his property, to be bought and sold as any other property which he owned. . . .

We find . . . that both the Old and New Testaments speak of slavery—that they do not condemn the relation, but, on the contrary, expressly allow it or create it; and they give commands and exhortations, which are based upon its legality and propriety. It can not, then, be wrong.

QUESTIONS

1. *How does Taper's letter reverse the rhetoric, common among white Americans, which saw the United States as a land of freedom and the British empire as lacking in liberty?*

2. *Why does De Bow feel that it is important to show that the Bible sanctions slavery?*

3. *How do Taper and De Bow differ in their understanding of the relationship of slavery and Christianity?*

Even more threatening to the stability of the slave system were slaves who ran away. Formidable obstacles confronted the prospective fugitive. Patrols were constantly on the lookout for runaway slaves. Slaves had little or no knowledge of geography, apart from understanding that following the north star led to freedom. No one knows how many slaves succeeded in reaching the North or Canada—the most common rough estimate is around 1,000 per year. Not surprisingly, most of those who succeeded lived, like Frederick Douglass, in the Upper South, especially Maryland, Virginia, and Kentucky, which bordered on the free states. Douglass, who escaped at age twenty, was also typical in that the large majority of fugitives were young men. Most slave women were not willing to leave children behind, and taking them along on the arduous escape journey was nearly impossible.

In the Deep South, fugitives tended to head for cities like New Orleans or Charleston, where they hoped to lose themselves in the free black community. Other escapees fled to remote areas like the Great Dismal Swamp of Virginia or the Florida Everglades, where the Seminole Indians offered refuge before they were forced to move west. Even in Tennessee, a study of newspaper advertisements for runaways finds that around 40 percent were thought to have remained in the local neighborhood and 30 percent to have headed to other locations in the South, while only 25 percent tried to reach the North.

The **Underground Railroad**, a loose organization of sympathetic abolitionists who hid fugitives in their homes and sent them on to the next "station," assisted some runaway slaves. A few courageous individuals made forays into the South to liberate slaves. The best known was **Harriet Tubman**. Born in Maryland in 1820, Tubman escaped to Philadelphia in 1849 and during the next decade risked her life by making some twenty trips back to her state of birth to lead relatives and other slaves to freedom.

The top part of a typical broadside offering a reward for the capture of four runaway slaves. This was distributed in Mississippi County, Missouri, in 1852. The high reward for George, $1,000, suggests that he is an extremely valued worker.

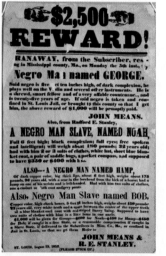

The *Amistad*

In a few instances, large groups of slaves collectively seized their freedom. The most celebrated instance involved fifty-three slaves who in 1839 took control of **the *Amistad***, a ship transporting them from one port in Cuba to another, and tried to force the navigator to steer it to Africa. The *Amistad* wended its way up the Atlantic coast until an American vessel seized it off the coast of Long Island. President Martin Van Buren favored returning the slaves to Cuba. But abolitionists brought their case to the Supreme Court, where the former president John Quincy Adams argued that since

A painting depicting an incident in the Maroon War of 1795 on the island of Jamaica, when British troops were ambushed near a sugar plantation. Maroons were runaway slaves who established independent communities in the mountains, and fought to prevent being returned to slavery.

they had been recently brought from Africa in violation of international treaties banning the slave trade, the captives should be freed. The Court accepted Adams's reasoning, and most of the captives made their way back to Africa.

Success of Amistad *case*

The *Amistad* case had no legal bearing on slaves within the United States. But it may well have inspired a similar uprising in 1841, when 135 slaves being transported by sea from Norfolk, Virginia, to New Orleans seized control of the ship *Creole* and sailed for Nassau in the British Bahamas. Their leader had the evocative name Madison Washington. To the dismay of the Tyler administration, the British gave refuge to the *Creole* slaves.

Slave Revolts

Resistance to slavery occasionally moved beyond such individual and group acts of defiance to outright rebellion. The four largest conspiracies in American history occurred within the space of thirty-one years in the early nineteenth century. The first, organized by the Virginia slave Gabriel in 1800, was discussed in Chapter 8. It was followed eleven years later by an uprising on sugar plantations upriver from New Orleans. Somewhere between 200 and 500 men and women, armed with sugarcane knives, axes, clubs, and a few guns, marched toward the city, destroying property as they proceeded. The white population along the route fled in panic to

Uprising near New Orleans

New Orleans. Within two days, the militia and regular army troops met the rebels and dispersed them in a pitched battle, killing sixty-six.

The next major conspiracy was organized in 1822 by **Denmark Vesey,** a slave carpenter in Charleston, South Carolina, who had purchased his freedom after winning a local lottery. His conspiracy reflected the combination of American and African influences then circulating in the Atlantic world and coming together in black culture. "He studied the Bible a great deal," recalled one of his followers, "and tried to prove from it that slavery and bondage is against the Bible." Vesey also quoted the Declaration of Independence, pored over newspaper reports of the debates in Congress regarding the Missouri Compromise, and made pronouncements like "all men had equal rights, blacks as well as whites." And he read to his conspirators accounts of the successful slave revolution in Haiti. The African heritage was present in the person of Vesey's lieutenant Gullah Jack, a religious "conjurer" from Angola who claimed to be able to protect the rebels against injury or death. The plot was discovered before it could reach fruition.

Vesey's influences

As with many slave conspiracies, evidence about the Vesey plot is contradictory and disputed. Much of it comes from a series of trials in which the court operated in secret and failed to allow the accused to confront those who testified against them.

Nat Turner's Rebellion

The most prominent slave revolt

The best known of all slave rebels was Nat Turner, a slave preacher and religious mystic in Southampton County, Virginia, who came to believe that God had chosen him to lead a black uprising. Turner traveled widely in the county, conducting religious services. He told of seeing black and white angels fighting in the sky and the heavens running red with blood. Perhaps from a sense of irony, Turner initially chose July 4, 1831, for his rebellion, only to fall ill on the appointed day. On August 22, he and a handful of followers marched from farm to farm assaulting the white inhabitants. By the time the militia put down the uprising, about eighty slaves had joined Turner's band, and some sixty whites had been killed. Turner was subsequently captured and, with seventeen other rebels, condemned to die. Asked before his execution whether he regretted what he had done, Turner responded, "Was not Christ crucified?"

Turner's rebellion sent shock waves through the entire South. "A Nat Turner," one white Virginian warned, "might be in any family." In the panic that followed the revolt, hundreds of innocent slaves were whipped, and

Panic among whites

scores executed. For one last time, Virginia's leaders openly debated whether steps ought to be taken to do away with the "peculiar institution." But a proposal to commit the state to gradual emancipation and the removal of the black population from the state failed to win legislative approval. The measure gained overwhelming support in the western part of Virginia, where slaves represented less than 10 percent of the population, but it failed to win sufficient votes in the eastern counties, where slavery was centered.

Instead of moving toward emancipation, the Virginia legislature of 1832 decided to fasten even more tightly the chains of bondage. New laws prohibited blacks, free or slave, from acting as preachers (a measure that proved impossible to enforce), strengthened the militia and patrol systems, banned free blacks from owning firearms, and prohibited teaching slaves to read. Other southern states followed suit.

In some ways, 1831 marked a turning point for the Old South. In that year, Parliament launched a program for abolishing slavery throughout the British empire (a process completed in 1838), underscoring the South's growing isolation in the Western world. Turner's rebellion, following only a few months after the appearance in Boston of William Lloyd Garrison's abolitionist journal, *The Liberator* (discussed in the next chapter), suggested that American slavery faced enemies both within and outside the South. The proslavery argument increasingly permeated southern intellectual and political life, while dissenting opinions were suppressed. Some states made membership in an abolitionist society a criminal offense, while mobs drove critics of slavery from their homes. The South's "great reaction" produced one of the most thoroughgoing suppressions of freedom of speech in American history. Even as reform movements arose in the North that condemned slavery as contrary to Christianity and to basic American values, and national debate over the peculiar institution intensified, southern society closed in defense of slavery.

An engraving depicting Nat Turner's slave rebellion of 1831, from a book published soon after the revolt.

A turning point

An intensifying debate

CHAPTER REVIEW AND ONLINE RESOURCES

REVIEW QUESTIONS

1. Given that most northern states had abolished slavery by the 1830s, how is it useful to think of slavery as a national—rather than regional—economic and political system?

2. Although some poor southern whites resented the dominance of the "slavocracy," most supported the institution and accepted the power of the planter class. Why did the "plain folk" continue to support slavery?

3. How did the planters' paternalism serve to justify the system of slavery? How did it hide the reality of life for slaves?

4. Identify the basic elements of the proslavery defense and those points aimed especially at non-southern audiences.

5. Compare slaves in the Old South with those elsewhere in the world, focusing on health, diet, and opportunities for freedom.

6. Describe the difference between gang labor and task labor for slaves, and explain how slaves' tasks varied by region across the Old South.

7. How did enslaved people create community and a culture that allowed them to survive in an oppressive society?

8. Identify the different types of resistance to slavery. Which ones were the most common, the most effective, and the most demonstrative?

KEY TERMS

wwnorton.com /studyspace

VISIT STUDYSPACE FOR THESE RESOURCES AND MORE

- A chapter outline
- A diagnostic chapter quiz
- Interactive maps
- Map worksheets
- Multimedia documents

CHAPTER 12

AN AGE OF REFORM

★

1820-1840

An abolitionist banner. Antislavery organizations adopted the Liberty Bell as a symbol of their campaign to extend freedom to black Americans. Previously, the bell, forged in Philadelphia in the eighteenth century, had simply been known as the Old State House Bell.

FOCUS QUESTIONS

- *What were the major movements and goals of antebellum reform?*

- *What were the different varieties of abolitionism?*

- *How did abolitionism challenge barriers to racial equality and free speech?*

- *What were the diverse sources of the antebellum women's rights movement and its significance?*

A mong the many Americans who devoted their lives to the crusade against slavery, few were as selfless or courageous as Abby Kelley. As a teacher in Lynn, Massachusetts, she joined the Female Anti-Slavery Society and, like thousands of other northern women, threw herself into the abolitionist movement. In 1838, Kelley began to give public speeches about slavery. Her first lecture outside of Lynn was literally a baptism of fire. Enraged by reports that abolitionists favored "amalgamation" of the races—that is, sexual relations between whites and blacks—residents of Philadelphia stormed the meeting hall and burned it to the ground.

For two decades, Kelley traveled throughout the North, speaking almost daily in churches, public halls, and antislavery homes on "the holy cause of human rights." Her career illustrated the interconnections of the era's reform movements. In addition to abolitionism, she was active in pacifist organizations—which opposed the use of force, including war, to settle disputes—and was a pioneer in the early struggle for women's rights. She forthrightly challenged her era's assumption that woman's "place" was in the home. More than any other individual, remarked Lucy Stone, another women's rights advocate, Kelley "earned for us all the right of free speech."

Abby Kelley's private life was as unconventional as her public career. Happily married to the ardent abolitionist Stephen S. Foster, she gave birth to a daughter in 1847 but soon returned to lecturing. When criticized for not devoting herself to the care of her infant, Kelley replied: "I have done it for the sake of the mothers whose babies are sold away from them. The most precious legacy I can leave my child is a free country."

THE REFORM IMPULSE

Goals of reformers

"In the history of the world," wrote Ralph Waldo Emerson in 1841, "the doctrine of reform has never such hope as at the present hour." Abolitionism was only one of this era's numerous efforts to improve American society. Americans established voluntary organizations that worked to prevent the manufacture and sale of liquor, end public entertainments and the delivery of the mail on Sunday, improve conditions in prisons, expand public education, uplift the condition of wage laborers, and reorganize society on the basis of cooperation rather than competitive individualism.

Nearly all these groups worked to convert public opinion to their cause. They sent out speakers, gathered signatures on petitions, and published

A rare photograph of an abolitionist meeting in New York State around 1850. Frederick Douglass is to the left of the woman at the center.

pamphlets. Some reform movements, like restraining the consumption of liquor and alleviating the plight of the blind and insane, flourished throughout the nation. Others, including women's rights, labor unionism, and educational reform, were weak or nonexistent in the South, where they were widely associated with antislavery sentiment. Reform was an international crusade. Peace, temperance, women's rights, and antislavery advocates regularly crisscrossed the Atlantic to promote their cause.

Reformers adopted a wide variety of tactics to bring about social change. Some relied on "moral suasion" to convert people to their cause. Others, such as opponents of "demon rum," sought to use the power of the government to force sinners to change their ways. Some reformers decided to withdraw altogether from the larger society and establish their own cooperative settlements. They hoped to change American life by creating "heavens on earth," where they could demonstrate by example the superiority of a collective way of life.

Reform tactics

Utopian Communities

About 100 reform communities were established in the decades before the Civil War. Historians call them "utopian" after Thomas More's sixteenth-century novel *Utopia*, an outline of a perfect society. (The word has also

Thomas More

come to imply that such plans are impractical and impossible to realize.) Most communities arose from religious conviction, but others were inspired by the secular desire to counteract the social and economic changes set in motion by the market revolution.

Social harmony

Nearly all the communities set out to reorganize society on a cooperative basis, hoping to restore social harmony to a world of excessive individualism and to narrow the widening gap between rich and poor. Through their efforts, the words "socialism" and "communism," meaning a social organization in which productive property is owned by the community rather than private individuals, entered the language of politics. Most **utopian communities** also tried to find substitutes for conventional gender relations and marriage patterns. Some prohibited sexual relations between men and women altogether; others allowed them to change partners at will. But nearly all insisted that the abolition of private property must be accompanied by an end to men's "property" in women.

In the first half of the nineteenth century, dozens of utopian communities were established in the United States, where small groups of men and women attempted to establish a more perfect social order within the larger society.

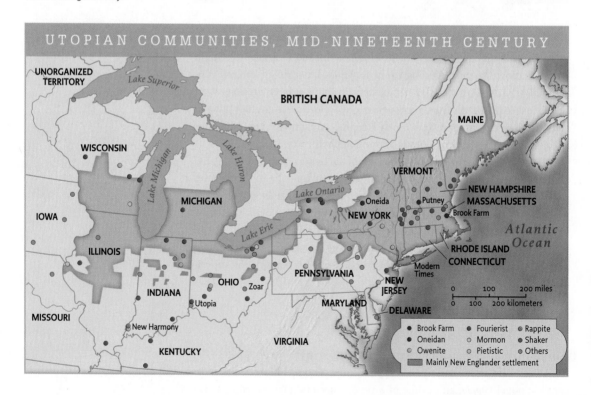

UTOPIAN COMMUNITIES, MID-NINETEENTH CENTURY

An engraving of a Shaker dance, drawn by Benson Lossing, an artist who visited a Shaker community and reported on life there for *Harper's Magazine* in 1857.

The Shakers

Religious communities attracted those who sought to find a retreat from a society permeated by sin. But the Shakers, the most successful of the religious communities, also had a significant impact on the outside world. At their peak during the 1840s, cooperative Shaker settlements, which stretched from Maine to Kentucky, included more than 5,000 members.

God, the Shakers believed, had a "dual" personality, both male and female, and thus the two sexes were spiritually equal. "Virgin purity" formed a pillar of the Shakers' faith. They completely abandoned traditional family life. Men and women lived separately in large dormitory-like structures and ate in communal dining rooms. They increased their numbers by attracting converts and adopting children from orphanages, rather than through natural increase. Although they rejected the individual accumulation of private property, the Shakers proved remarkably successful economically. They were among the first to market vegetable and flower seeds and herbal medicines commercially and to breed cattle for profit. Their beautifully crafted furniture is still widely admired today.

Shaker beliefs

Oneida

Another influential and controversial community was Oneida, founded in 1848 in upstate New York by John Humphrey Noyes, the Vermont-born son of a U.S. congressman. In 1836, Noyes and his followers formed a small

John Humphrey Noyes

community in Putney, Vermont. His community became notorious for what Noyes called "complex marriage," whereby any man could propose sexual relations to any woman, who had the right to reject or accept his invitation, which would then be registered in a public record book. The great danger was "exclusive affections," which, Noyes felt, destroyed the harmony of the community.

After being indicted for adultery by local officials, Noyes in 1848 moved his community to Oneida, where it survived until 1881. Oneida was an extremely dictatorial environment. To become a member of the community, one had to demonstrate command of Noyes's religious teachings and live according to his rules.

Worldly Communities

To outside observers, utopian communities like Oneida seemed cases of "voluntary slavery." But because of their members' selfless devotion to the teachings and rules laid down by their leader, spiritually oriented communities often achieved remarkable longevity. The Shakers survived well into the twentieth century. Communities with a more worldly orientation tended to be beset by internal divisions and therefore lasted for much shorter periods.

The most important secular communitarian (meaning a person who plans or lives in a cooperative community) was Robert Owen, a British factory owner. Appalled by the degradation of workers in the early industrial revolution, Owen created a model factory village at New Lanark, Scotland, which combined strict rules of work discipline with comfortable housing and free public education. Around 1815, its 1,500 employees made New Lanark the largest center of cotton manufacturing in the world. In 1824, he purchased the Harmony community in Indiana—originally founded by the German Protestant religious leader George Rapp, who had emigrated to America with his followers at the beginning of the nineteenth century. Here, Owen established New Harmony, where he hoped to create a "new moral world."

In Owen's scheme, children would be removed at an early age from the care of their parents to be educated in schools where they would be trained to subordinate individual ambition to the common good. Owen also defended women's rights, especially access to education and the right to divorce. At New Harmony, he promised, women would no longer be "enslaved" to their husbands, and "false notions" about innate differences between the sexes would be abandoned.

The Crisis, a publication by the communitarian Robert Owen and his son, Robert Dale Owen. The cover depicts Owen's vision of a planned socialist community.

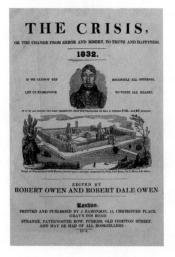

Harmony eluded the residents of New Harmony. They squabbled about everything from the community's constitution to the distribution of property. Owen's settlement survived for only a few years, but it strongly influenced the labor movement, educational reformers, and women's rights advocates. Owen's vision resonated with the widely held American belief that a community of equals could be created in the New World.

Robert Owen's New Harmony

Religion and Reform

Most Americans saw the ownership of property as the key to economic independence—and, therefore, to freedom—and marriage as the foundation of the social order. Few were likely to join communities that required them to surrender both. Far more typical of the reform impulse were movements that aimed at liberating men and women either from restraints external to themselves, such as slavery and war, or from forms of internal "servitude" like drinking, illiteracy, and a tendency toward criminality. Many of these reform movements drew their inspiration from the religious revivalism of the Second Great Awakening, discussed in Chapter 9. If, as the revivalist preachers maintained, God had created man as a "free moral agent," sinners could not only reform themselves but could also remake the world.

Mainstream reform

The revivals popularized the outlook known as **"perfectionism,"** which saw both individuals and society at large as capable of indefinite improvement. Under the impact of the revivals, older reform efforts moved in a new, radical direction. **Temperance** (which literally means moderation in the consumption of liquor) was transformed into a crusade to eliminate drinking entirely. Criticism of war became outright pacifism. And, as will be related below, critics of slavery now demanded not gradual emancipation but immediate and total abolition.

To members of the North's emerging middle-class culture, reform became a badge of respectability, an indication that individuals had taken control of their own lives and had become morally accountable human beings. The American Temperance Society, founded in 1826, directed its efforts to redeeming not only habitual drunkards but also the occasional drinker. It claimed by the 1830s to have persuaded hundreds of thousands of Americans to renounce liquor. By 1840, the consumption of alcohol per person had fallen to less than half the level of a decade earlier. (It had peaked in 1830 at seven gallons per person per year, compared with around two gallons today.)

A temperance banner from around 1850 depicts a young man torn between a woman in white, who illustrates female purity, and a temptress, who offers him a drink of liquor.

LOVE, PURITY & FIDELITY.

GRAND, NATIONAL TEMPERANCE BANNER.

Critics of Reform

Taverns

Many Americans saw the reform impulse as an attack on their own freedom. Taverns were popular meeting places for urban workingmen, sites not only of drinking but also of political discussions, organizational meetings, and recreation. Drinking was a prominent feature of festive celebrations and events like militia gatherings. A "Liberty Loving Citizen" of Worcester, Massachusetts, wondered what gave one group of citizens the right to dictate to others how to conduct their personal lives.

Catholics on reform

American Catholics, their numbers growing because of Irish and German immigration, proved hostile to the reform impulse. Catholics understood freedom in ways quite different from how Protestant reformers did. They viewed sin as an inescapable burden of individuals and society. The perfectionist idea that evil could be banished from the world struck them as an affront to genuine religion, and they bitterly opposed what they saw as reformers' efforts to impose their own version of Protestant morality on their neighbors. Whereas reformers spoke of man as a free moral agent, Catholics tended to place less emphasis on individual independence and more on the importance of communities centered on family and church.

Reformers and Freedom

Tension between liberation and control

Reformers had to reconcile their desire to create moral order and their quest to enhance personal freedom. They did this through a vision of freedom that was liberating and controlling at the same time. On the one hand, reformers insisted that their goal was to enable Americans to enjoy genuine liberty. In a world in which personal freedom increasingly meant the opportunity to compete for economic gain and individual self-improvement, they spoke of liberating Americans from various forms of "slavery" that made it impossible to succeed—slavery to drink, to poverty, to sin.

On the other hand, reformers insisted that self-fulfillment came through **self-discipline**. Their definition of the free individual was the person who internalized the practice of self-control. In some ways, reformers believed, American society suffered from an excess of liberty—the anarchic "natural liberty" John Winthrop had warned against in the early days of Puritan Massachusetts, as opposed to the "Christian liberty" of the morally upright citizen.

Many religious groups in the East worried that settlers in the West and immigrants from abroad lacked self-control and led lives of vice, exhibited by drinking, violations of the Sabbath, and lack of Protestant devotion. They formed the American Tract Society, the American Bible Society, and other groups that flooded eastern cities and the western frontier with copies of the gospel and pamphlets promoting religious virtue. Between 1825 and 1835, the pamphlets distributed by the Tract Society amounted to more than 500 million pages.

American Tract Society

The Invention of the Asylum

The tension between liberation and control in the era's reform movements was vividly evident in the proliferation of new institutions that reformers hoped could remake human beings into free, morally upright citizens. In colonial America, crime had mostly been punished by whipping, fines, or banishment. The poor received relief in their own homes, orphans lived with neighbors, and families took care of mentally ill members.

During the 1830s and 1840s, Americans embarked on a program of institution building—jails for criminals, poorhouses for the destitute, asylums for the insane, and orphanages for children without families. These institutions differed in many respects, but they shared with communitarians and religious believers in "perfectionism" the idea that social ills once considered incurable could in fact be eliminated. Prisons and **asylums** would eventually become overcrowded places where rehabilitating the inmates seemed less important than simply holding them at bay, away from society. At the outset, however, these institutions were inspired by the conviction that those who passed through their doors could eventually be released to become productive, self-disciplined citizens.

Reform institutions

The Common School

The largest effort at institution building before the Civil War came in the movement to establish **common schools**—that is, tax-supported state school systems open to all children. In the early nineteenth century, most children were educated in locally supported schools, private academies, charity schools, or at home. Many had no access to learning at all. School reform reflected the numerous purposes that came together in the era's reform impulse. Horace Mann, a Massachusetts lawyer and Whig politician who served as director of the state's board of education, was the era's leading educational reformer. He hoped that universal **public education** could restore equality to a fractured society by bringing the children of all classes together in a common learning experience and equipping the less fortunate to advance in the social scale.

Horace Mann

With labor organizations, factory owners, and middle-class reformers all supporting the idea, every northern state by 1860 had established tax-supported school systems for its children. The common-school movement created the first real career opportunity for women, who quickly came to dominate the ranks of teachers. The South, where literate blacks were increasingly viewed as a danger to social order and planters had no desire to tax themselves to pay for education for poor white children, lagged far behind in public education. This was one of many ways in which North and South seemed to be growing apart.

The rise of public education

THE CRUSADE AGAINST SLAVERY

Compared with drinking, Sabbath-breaking, and illiteracy, the greatest evil in American society at first appeared to attract the least attention from reformers. For many years, it seemed that the only Americans willing to challenge the existence of slavery were Quakers, slaves, and free blacks.

Colonization

Before the 1830s, those white Americans willing to contemplate an end to bondage almost always coupled calls for abolition with the "colonization" of freed slaves—their deportation to Africa, the Caribbean, or Central America. In 1816, proponents of this idea founded the **American Colonization Society**, which promoted the gradual abolition of slavery and the settlement of black Americans in Africa. It soon established Liberia on the coast of West Africa, an outpost of American influence whose capital, Monrovia, was named for President James Monroe.

Liberia

Colonization struck many observers as totally impractical. Nonetheless, numerous prominent political leaders of the Jacksonian era—including Henry Clay, John Marshall, Daniel Webster, and Jackson himself—supported the Colonization Society. Many colonizationists believed that slavery and racism were so deeply embedded in American life that blacks could never achieve equality if freed and allowed to remain in the country. Like Indian removal, colonization rested on the premise that America is fundamentally a white society.

Beliefs of colonizationists

In the decades before the Civil War, several thousand black Americans did emigrate to Liberia with the aid of the Colonization Society. Some were slaves emancipated by their owners on the condition that they depart, while others left voluntarily, motivated by a desire to spread Christianity in Africa or to enjoy rights denied them in the United States. Having experienced "the legal slavery of the South and the social slavery of the North," wrote one emigrant on leaving for Liberia, he knew he could "never be a free man in this country."

But most African-Americans adamantly opposed the idea of colonization. In fact, the formation of the American Colonization Society galvanized free blacks to claim their rights as Americans. Early in 1817, some 3,000 free blacks assembled in Philadelphia for the first national black convention. Their resolutions insisted that blacks were Americans, entitled to the same freedom and rights enjoyed by whites.

African-American responses to colonization

Militant Abolitionism

The abolitionist movement that arose in the 1830s differed profoundly from its genteel, conservative predecessor. Drawing on the religious conviction that slavery was an unparalleled sin and the secular one that it contradicted the values enshrined in the Declaration of Independence, a new generation of reformers rejected the traditional approach of gradual emancipation and demanded immediate abolition. Also unlike their predecessors, they directed explosive language against slavery and slaveholders and insisted that blacks, once free, should be incorporated as equal citizens of the republic rather than being deported. Perfecting American society, they insisted, meant rooting out not just slavery, but racism in all its forms.

Immediate abolition

The first indication of the new spirit of abolitionism came in 1829 with the appearance of *An Appeal to the Coloured Citizens of the World* by David Walker, a free black who had been born in North Carolina and now operated a used-clothing store in Boston. A passionate indictment of slavery and racial prejudice, the *Appeal* called on black Americans to mobilize for abolition—by force if necessary—and warned whites that the nation faced divine punishment if it did not mend its sinful ways. Walker called on blacks to take pride in the achievements of ancient African civilizations and to claim all their rights as Americans. "Tell us no more about colonization," Walker wrote, addressing white readers, "for America is as much our country as it is yours." Like other reformers, Walker used both secular and religious language. He warned that God would wreak vengeance on the United States for violating the principles of justice and heaped scorn on ministers who defended slavery for violating the golden rule espoused by Jesus Christ ("whatsoever ye would that men should do unto you, do yet even so unto them").

Walker died in mysterious circumstances in 1830. Not until the appearance in 1831 of *The Liberator*, William Lloyd Garrison's weekly

William Lloyd Garrison, editor of *The Liberator* and probably the nation's most prominent abolitionist, in a daguerreotype from around 1850.

journal published in Boston, did the new breed of abolitionism find a permanent voice. "I will be as harsh as truth," Garrison announced, "and as uncompromising as justice. On this subject, I do not wish to think, or speak, or write, with moderation. . . . I will not equivocate—I will not excuse—I will not retreat a single inch—and I will be heard."

And heard he was. Some of Garrison's ideas, such as his suggestion that the North abrogate the Constitution and dissolve the Union to end its complicity in the evil of slavery, were rejected by many abolitionists. But his call for the immediate abolition of slavery echoed throughout antislavery circles. Garrison's pamphlet, *Thoughts on African Colonization*, persuaded many foes of slavery that blacks must be recognized as part of American society, not viewed as aliens to be shipped overseas.

Garrison's Thoughts on African Colonization

Spreading the Abolitionist Message

Beginning with a handful of activists, the abolitionist movement expanded rapidly throughout the North. Antislavery leaders took advantage of the rapid development of print technology and the expansion of literacy due to common-school education to spread their message. Like radical pamphleteers of the American Revolution and evangelical ministers of the Second Great Awakening, they recognized the democratic potential

Pamphlets, broadsides, newspapers

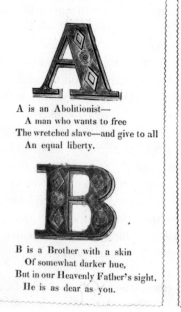

A is an Abolitionist—
A man who wants to free
The wretched slave—and give to all
An equal liberty.

B is a Brother with a skin
Of somewhat darker hue,
But in our Heavenly Father's sight,
He is as dear as you.

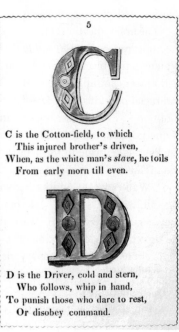

C is the Cotton-field, to which
This injured brother's driven,
When, as the white man's *slave,* he toils
From early morn till even.

D is the Driver, cold and stern,
Who follows, whip in hand,
To punish those who dare to rest,
Or disobey command.

Pages from an abolitionist book for children. Abolitionists sought to convince young and old of the evils of slavery.

in the production of printed material. Abolitionists seized on the recently invented steam printing press to produce millions of copies of pamphlets, newspapers, petitions, novels, and broadsides. Between the formation of the **American Anti-Slavery Society** in 1833 and the end of the decade, some 100,000 northerners joined local groups devoted to abolition. Most were ordinary citizens—farmers, shopkeepers, craftsmen, laborers, along with a few prominent businessmen like the merchants Arthur and Lewis Tappan of New York.

If Garrison was the movement's most notable propagandist, Theodore Weld, a young minister who had been converted by the evangelical preacher Charles G. Finney, helped to create its mass constituency. A brilliant orator, Weld trained a band of speakers who brought the abolitionist message into the heart of the rural and small-town North. Their methods were those of the revivalists—fervent preaching, lengthy meetings, calls for individuals to renounce their immoral ways—and their message was a simple one: slavery was a sin.

Theodore Weld

Slavery and Moral Suasion

Many southerners feared that the abolitionists intended to spark a slave insurrection, a belief strengthened by the outbreak of Nat Turner's Rebellion a few months after *The Liberator* made its appearance. Yet not only was Garrison completely unknown to Turner, but nearly all abolitionists, despite their militant language, rejected violence as a means of ending

Slave Market of America, an engraving produced by the American Anti-Slavery Society in 1836, illustrates how abolitionists sought to identify their cause with American traditions, even as they mocked the nation's claim to be a "land of the free."

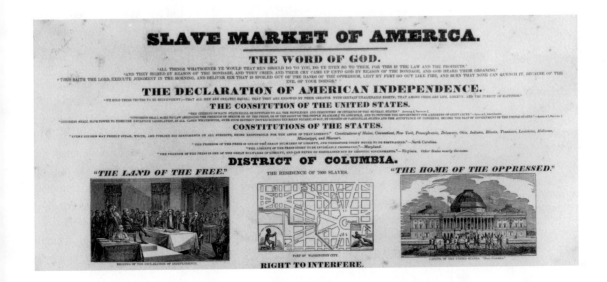

slavery. Many were pacifists or "non-resistants," who believed that coercion should be eliminated from all human relationships and institutions. Their strategy was "**moral suasion**" and their arena the public sphere. Slaveholders must be convinced of the sinfulness of their ways, and the North of its complicity in the peculiar institution.

Awakening the nation

Among the first to appreciate the key role of public opinion in a mass democracy, abolitionists focused their efforts not on infiltrating the existing political parties, but on awakening the nation to the moral evil of slavery. Their language was deliberately provocative, calculated to seize public attention. "Slavery," said Garrison, "will not be overthrown without excitement, without a most tremendous excitement." Abolitionists argued that slavery was so deeply embedded in American life that its destruction would require fundamental changes in the North as well as the South. They insisted that the inherent, natural, and absolute right to personal liberty, regardless of race, took precedence over other forms of freedom, such as the right of citizens to accumulate and hold property or self-government by local political communities.

A New Vision of America

In a society in which the rights of citizenship had become more and more closely associated with whiteness, the antislavery movement sought to reinvigorate the idea of freedom as a truly universal entitlement. The origins of

An American people unbounded by race

the idea of an American people unbounded by race lies not with the founders, who by and large made their peace with slavery, but with the abolitionists. The antislavery crusade viewed slaves and free blacks as members of the national community, a position summarized in the title of Lydia Maria Child's popular treatise of 1833, *An Appeal in Favor of That Class of Americans Called Africans*. The idea that birthplace alone, not race, should determine who was an American, later enshrined in the Fourteenth Amendment, represented a radical departure from the traditions of American life.

Angelina Grimké

The crusade against slavery, wrote Angelina Grimké, who became a leading abolitionist speaker, was the nation's preeminent "school in which human rights are . . . investigated." Abolitionists debated the Constitution's relationship to slavery. William Lloyd Garrison burned the document, calling it a covenant with the devil; Frederick Douglass came to believe that it offered no national protection to slavery. But despite this difference of opinion, abolitionists developed an alternative, rights-oriented view of constitutional law, grounded in their universalistic understanding of liberty. Seeking to define the core rights to which all Americans were entitled—the meaning of freedom in concrete legal terms—abolitionists invented the concept of equality before the law regardless of race, one all but unknown in American life before the Civil War. Abolitionist literature also helped to expand the definition of cruelty. The graphic descriptions of the beatings, brandings, and other physical sufferings of the slaves helped to popularize the idea of bodily integrity as a basic right that slavery violated.

Despite being denounced by their opponents as enemies of American principles, abolitionists consciously identified their movement with the revolutionary heritage. The Declaration of Independence was not as fundamental to public oratory in the early republic as it would later become. Abolitionists seized upon it, interpreting the document's preamble as a condemnation of slavery. The Liberty Bell, later one of the nation's most venerated emblems of freedom, did not achieve that status until abolitionists adopted it as a symbol and gave it its name as part of an effort to identify their principles with those of the founders. Of course, Americans of all regions and political beliefs claimed the Revolution's legacy. Abolitionists never represented more than a small part of the North's population. But as the slavery controversy intensified, the belief spread far beyond abolitionist circles that slavery contradicted the nation's heritage of freedom.

Abolitionism and the Constitution

Abolitionism and the revolutionary heritage

BLACK AND WHITE ABOLITIONISM

Black Abolitionists

Blacks played a leading role in the antislavery movement. Frederick Douglass was only one among many former slaves who published accounts of their lives in bondage; these accounts convinced thousands of northerners of the evils of slavery. Indeed, the most effective piece of antislavery literature of the entire period, Harriet Beecher Stowe's novel *Uncle Tom's Cabin*, was to some extent modeled on the autobiography of the fugitive slave Josiah Henson. Serialized in 1851 in a Washington antislavery newspaper and published as a book the following year, **Uncle Tom's Cabin** sold more than 1 million copies by 1854, and it also inspired numerous stage versions. By portraying slaves as sympathetic men and women, and as Christians at the mercy of slaveholders who split up families and set bloodhounds on innocent mothers and children, Stowe's melodrama gave the abolitionist message a powerful human appeal.

One of many popular lithographs illustrating scenes from Harriet Beecher Stowe's novel *Uncle Tom's Cabin*, the most widely read of all antislavery writings. This depicts the slave Eliza escaping with her child across the ice floes of the Ohio River.

PERILOUS ESCAPE OF ELIZA AND CHILD.

By the 1840s, black abolitionists sought an independent role within the movement, regularly holding their own conventions. The black abolitionist Henry Highland Garnet, who as a child had escaped from slavery in Maryland with his father, proclaimed at one such gathering in 1843 that slaves should rise in rebellion to throw off their shackles. His position was so at odds with the prevailing belief in moral suasion that the published proceedings entirely omitted the speech.

At every opportunity, black abolitionists rejected the nation's pretensions as a land of liberty. Free black communities in the North devised an alternative calendar of "freedom celebrations" centered on January 1, the date in 1808 on which the slave trade became illegal, and August 1, the anniversary of West Indian emancipation, rather than July 4. In doing so, they offered a stinging rebuke to white Americans' claims to live in a land of freedom.

Color-blind citizenship

Even more persistently than their white counterparts, black abolitionists articulated the ideal of color-blind citizenship. "The real battleground between liberty and slavery," wrote Samuel Cornish, "is prejudice against color." (Cornish, a Presbyterian minister, had helped to establish the nation's first black newspaper, *Freedom's Journal*, in New York City in 1827. The first editor, John B. Russwurm, closed the paper after two years and moved to Liberia, explaining, "we consider it a waste of mere words to talk of ever enjoying citizenship in this country.")

Frederick Douglass's Fourth of July speech

The greatest oration on American slavery and American freedom was delivered in Rochester in 1852 by Frederick Douglass. Speaking just after the annual Independence Day celebration, Douglass posed the question, "What, to the Slave, is the Fourth of July?" He answered that Fourth of July festivities revealed the hypocrisy of a nation that proclaimed its belief in liberty yet daily committed "practices more shocking and bloody" than did any other country on earth. Like other abolitionists, however, Douglass also laid claim to the founders' legacy. The Revolution had left a "rich inheritance of justice, liberty, prosperity, and independence" from which subsequent generations had tragically strayed. Only by abolishing slavery and freeing the "great doctrines" of the Declaration of Independence from the "narrow bounds" of race could the United States recapture its original mission.

Gentlemen of Property and Standing

Opposition to abolitionism

At first, abolitionism aroused violent hostility from northerners who feared that the movement threatened to disrupt the Union, interfere with profits wrested from slave labor, and overturn white supremacy. Led by "**gentlemen of property and standing**" (often merchants with close commercial ties to the South), mobs disrupted abolitionist meetings in northern cities.

Destruction by Fire of Pennsylvania Hall, a lithograph depicting the burning of the abolitionist meeting hall by a Philadelphia mob in 1838.

In 1837, antislavery editor Elijah P. Lovejoy became the movement's first martyr when he was killed by a mob in Alton, Illinois, while defending his press. In 1838, a mob in Philadelphia burned to the ground Pennsylvania Hall, which abolitionists had built to hold their meetings. Before starting the fire, however, the mob patriotically carried a portrait of George Washington to safety.

Elijah P. Lovejoy

Elsewhere, crowds of southerners, with the unspoken approval of Andrew Jackson's postmaster general, Amos Kendall, burned abolitionist literature that they had removed from the mails. In 1836, when abolitionists began to flood Washington with petitions calling for emancipation in the nation's capital, the House of Representatives adopted the notorious "**gag rule**," which prohibited their consideration. The rule was repealed in 1844, thanks largely to the tireless opposition of former president John Quincy Adams, who since 1831 had represented Massachusetts in the House.

Far from stemming the movement's growth, however, mob attacks and attempts to limit abolitionists' freedom of speech convinced many northerners that slavery was incompatible with the democratic liberties of white Americans. "We commenced the present struggle," announced abolitionist William Jay, "to obtain the freedom of the slave; we are compelled to continue it to preserve our own. We are now contending . . . for the liberty of speech, of the press, and of conscience."

The abolitionist movement now broadened its appeal so as to win the support of northerners who cared little about the rights of blacks but could be convinced that slavery endangered their own cherished freedoms. The gag rule aroused considerable resentment in the North. "If the government

Am I Not a Man and a Brother? The most common abolitionist depiction of a slave, this image not only presents African-Americans as unthreatening individuals seeking white assistance but also calls upon white Americans to recognize blacks as fellow men unjustly held in bondage.

once begins to discriminate as to what is orthodox and what heterodox in opinion," wrote the *New York Evening Post*, hardly a supporter of abolitionism, "farewell, a long farewell to our freedom."

THE ORIGINS OF FEMINISM

The Rise of the Public Woman

Northern women in abolitionism

"When the true history of the antislavery cause shall be written," Frederick Douglass later recalled, "women will occupy a large space in its pages." Much of the movement's grassroots strength derived from northern women, who joined by the thousands. Most were evangelical Protestants, New England Congregationalists, or Quakers convinced, as Martha Higginson of Vermont wrote, that slavery was "a disgrace in this land of Christian light and liberty."

Women and politics

The public sphere was open to women in ways government and party politics were not. Women's letters and diaries reveal a keen interest in political issues, from slavery to presidential campaigns. Long before they could vote, women circulated petitions, attended mass meetings, marched in political parades, delivered public lectures, and raised money for political causes. They became active in the temperance movement, the building of asylums, and other reform activities. **Dorothea Dix**, a Massachusetts schoolteacher, for example, was the leading advocate of more humane treatment of the insane, who at the time generally were placed in jails alongside debtors and hardened criminals. Thanks to her efforts, twenty-eight states constructed mental hospitals before the Civil War.

Women and Free Speech

Abolitionism and women's rights

All these activities enabled women to carve out a place in the public sphere. But it was participation in abolitionism that inspired the early movement for women's rights. In working for the rights of the slave, not a few women developed a new understanding of their own subordinate social and legal status. The daughters of a prominent South Carolina slaveholder, Angelina and Sarah Grimké had been converted first to Quakerism and then abolitionism while visiting Philadelphia. During the 1830s, they began to deliver popular lectures that offered a scathing condemnation of slavery from the perspective of those who had witnessed its evils firsthand.

Outraged by the sight of females sacrificing all "modesty and delicacy" by appearing on the public lecture platform, a group of Massachusetts clergymen denounced the sisters. In reply, they forthrightly defended not only the right of women to take part in political debate but also their right to share the social and educational privileges enjoyed by men. "Since I engaged in the investigation of the rights of the slave," declared Angelina Grimké, "I have necessarily been led to a better understanding of my own." Her sister Sarah proceeded to publish *Letters on the Equality of the Sexes* (1838), a powerful call for equal rights for women and a critique of the notion of separate spheres. The book raised numerous issues familiar even today, including what later generations would call "equal pay for equal work." Why, Sarah Grimké wondered, did male teachers invariably receive higher wages than women, and a male tailor earn "two or three times as much" as a female counterpart "although the work done by each may be equally good?"

The Grimké sisters

Women's Rights

The Grimké sisters were the first to apply the abolitionist doctrine of universal freedom and equality to the status of women. Although they soon retired from the fray, unwilling to endure the intense criticism to which they were subjected, their writings helped to spark the movement for women's rights, which arose in the 1840s.

Elizabeth Cady Stanton and Lucretia Mott, the key organizers of the Seneca Falls Convention of 1848, were veterans of the antislavery crusade. In 1840, they had traveled to London as delegates to the World Anti-Slavery Convention, only to be barred from participating because of their sex. The Seneca Falls Convention, a gathering on behalf of women's rights held in the upstate New York town where Stanton lived, raised the issue of **woman suffrage** for the first time. Stanton, the principal author, modeled the Seneca Falls Declaration of Sentiments on the Declaration of Independence (see the Appendix for the full text). But the document added "women" to Jefferson's axiom "all men are created equal," and in place of a list of injustices committed by George III, it condemned the "injuries and usurpations on the part of man toward woman." The first to be listed was denying her the right to vote. As Stanton told the convention, only the vote would make woman "free as man is free," since in a democratic society, freedom was impossible without access to the ballot. The argument was simple and irrefutable: in the words of Lydia Maria Child, "either the theory of our government [the democratic principle that government rests on the will of the people] is *false*, or women have a right to vote."

The Seneca Falls Convention

The Declaration of Sentiments

Start of the struggle for suffrage

Seneca Falls marked the beginning of the seventy-year struggle for woman suffrage. The vote, however, was hardly the only issue raised at the convention. The Declaration of Sentiments condemned the entire structure of inequality that denied women access to education and employment, gave husbands control over the property and wages of their wives and custody of children in the event of divorce, deprived women of independent legal status after they married, and restricted them to the home as their "sphere of action." Equal rights became the rallying cry of the early movement for women's rights, and equal rights meant claiming access to all the prevailing definitions of freedom.

Feminism and Freedom

Like abolitionism, temperance, and other reforms, women's rights was an international movement. Lacking broad backing at home, early feminists found allies abroad. "Women alone will say what freedom they want," declared an article in *The Free Woman*, a journal established in Paris in 1832.

Margaret Fuller

Women, wrote Margaret Fuller, had the same right as men to develop their talents, to "grow . . . to live freely and unimpeded." The daughter of a Jeffersonian congressman, Fuller was educated at home, at first under her father's supervision (she learned Latin before the age of six) and later on her own. She became part of New England's transcendentalist circle (discussed in Chapter 9) and from 1840 to 1842 edited *The Dial*, a magazine that reflected the group's views. In 1844, Fuller became literary editor of the *New York Tribune*, the first woman to achieve so important a position in American journalism.

Portrait of feminist Margaret Fuller (1810–1850) from an undated daguerreotype.

In **Woman in the Nineteenth Century**, published in 1845, Fuller sought to apply to women the transcendentalist idea that freedom meant a quest for personal development. "Every path" to self-fulfillment, she insisted, should be "open to woman as freely as to man." Fuller traveled to Europe as a correspondent for the *Tribune*, and there she married an Italian patriot. Along with her husband and baby, she died in a shipwreck in 1850 while returning to the United States.

Women and Work

Women also demanded the right to participate in the market revolution. At an 1851 women's rights convention, the black abolitionist Sojourner Truth insisted that the movement devote attention to the plight of poor and working-class women and repudiate the idea that women were too delicate to engage in work outside the home. Born a slave in New York State around 1799, Truth did not obtain her freedom until the state's emancipation law of 1827. A listener at her 1851 speech (which was not recorded at the time) later recalled that Truth had spoken of her years of hard physical labor, had flexed her arm to show her strength, and exclaimed, "and aren't I a woman?"

Woman's Emancipation, a satirical engraving from *Harper's Monthly*, August 1851, illustrating the much-ridiculed "Bloomer" costume.

Although those who convened at Seneca Falls were predominantly from the middle class—no representatives of the growing number of "factory girls" and domestic servants took part— the participants rejected the identification of the home as the women's "sphere." During the 1850s, some feminists tried to popularize a new style of dress, devised by Amelia Bloomer, consisting of a loose-fitting tunic and trousers. The target of innumerable male jokes, the "bloomer" costume attempted to make a serious point—that the long dresses, tight corsets, and numerous petticoats considered to be appropriate female attire were so confining that they made it almost impossible for women to claim a place in the public sphere or to work outside the home.

The Slavery of Sex

The dichotomy between freedom and slavery powerfully shaped early feminists' political language. Just as the idea of "wage slavery" enabled northern workers to challenge the inequalities inherent in market definitions of freedom, the concept of the "**slavery of sex**" empowered the women's movement to develop an all-encompassing critique of male authority and their own subordination. Feminists of the 1840s and 1850s pointed out that the law of marriage made nonsense of the description of the family as a "private" institution independent of public authority. When the abolitionists and women's rights activists Lucy Stone and Henry Blackwell married, they felt obliged to repudiate New York's laws that clothed the husband "with legal powers which . . . no man should possess." The analogy between free women and slaves gained prominence as it was swept up in the accelerating debate over slavery. For their part, southern defenders of slavery frequently linked slavery and marriage as natural and just forms of inequality. Eliminating the former institution, they charged, would threaten the latter.

Feminists and marriage

VOICES OF FREEDOM

From Angelina Grimké, Letter in *The Liberator* (August 2, 1837)

The daughters of a prominent South Carolina slaveholder, Angelina and Sarah Grimké became abolitionists after being sent to Philadelphia for education. In this article, Angelina Grimké explains how participation in the movement against slavery led her to a greater recognition of women's lack of basic freedoms.

Since I engaged in the investigation of the rights of the slave, I have necessarily been led to a better understanding of my own; for I have found the Anti-Slavery cause to be . . . the school in which human rights are more fully investigated, and better understood and taught, than in any other [reform] enterprise. . . . Here we are led to examine why human beings have any rights. It is because they are moral beings. . . . Now it naturally occurred to me, that if rights were founded in moral being, then the circumstance of sex could not give to man higher rights and responsibilities, than to woman. . . .

When I look at human beings as moral beings, all distinction in sex sinks to insignificance and nothingness; for I believe it regulates rights and responsibilities no more than the color of the skin or the eyes. My doctrine, then is, that whatever it is morally right for man to do, it is morally right for woman to do. . . . This regulation of duty by the mere circumstance of sex . . . has led to all that [numerous] train of evils flowing out of the anti-christian doctrine of masculine and feminine virtues. By this doctrine, man has been converted into the warrior, and clothed in sternness . . . whilst woman has been taught to lean upon an arm of flesh, to . . . be admired for her personal charms, and caressed and humored like a spoiled child, or converted into a mere drudge to suit the convenience of her lord and master. . . . It has robbed woman of . . . the right to think and speak and act on all great moral questions, just as men think and speak and act. . . .

The discussion of the wrongs of slavery has opened the way for the discussion of other rights, and the ultimate result will most certainly be . . . the letting of the oppressed of every grade and description go free.

From Frederick Douglass, Speech on July 5, 1852, Rochester, New York

One of the most prominent reform leaders of his era, Frederick Douglass escaped from slavery in 1838 and soon became an internationally known writer and orator against slavery. His speech of July 1852 condemned the hypocrisy of a nation that proclaimed its devotion to freedom while practicing slavery. It was reprinted in 1855 in his autobiography, *My Bondage and My Freedom*.

Fellow-citizens, pardon me, allow me to ask, why am I called upon to speak here to-day? What have I, or those I represent, to do with your national independence? Are the great principles of political freedom and of natural justice, embodied in that Declaration of Independence, extended to us? . . . Such is not the case. I say it with a sad sense of the disparity between us. I am not included within the pale of this glorious anniversary! Your high independence only reveals the immeasurable distance between us. . . . The rich inheritance of justice, liberty, prosperity and independence, bequeathed by your fathers, is shared by you, not by me. . . .

For the present, it is enough to affirm the equal manhood of the negro race. Is it not astonishing that, while we are ploughing, planting and reaping, using all kinds of mechanical tools, erecting houses, constructing bridges, building ships, . . . acting as clerks, merchants and secretaries . . . confessing and worshiping the Christian's God, and looking hopefully for life and immortality beyond the grave, we are called upon to prove that we are men! . . .

Would you have me argue that man is entitled to liberty? That he is the rightful owner of his body? You have already declared it. Must I argue the wrongfulness of slavery? . . . that men have a natural right to freedom? . . . To do so, would be to make myself ridiculous, and to offer an insult to your understanding. There is not a man beneath the canopy of heaven, that does not know that slavery is wrong *for him*. . . .

What, to the American slave, is your 4th of July? I answer: a day that reveals to him, more than all other days in the year, the gross injustice and cruelty to which he is the constant victim. To him, your celebration is a sham; your boasted liberty, an unholy license; your national greatness, swelling vanity; your sounds of rejoicing are empty and heartless; your denunciations of tyrants, brass fronted impudence; your shouts of liberty and equality, hollow mockery—a thin veil to cover up crimes that would disgrace a nation of savages. There is not a nation on the earth guilty of practices, more shocking and bloody, than are the people of these United States, at this very hour.

QUESTIONS

1. *What consequences does Grimké believe follow from the idea of rights being founded in the individual's "moral being"?*

2. *How does Douglass turn the ideals proclaimed by white Americans into weapons against slavery?*

3. *What do these documents suggest about the language and arguments employed by abolitionists?*

Marriage was not, literally speaking, equivalent to slavery. The married woman, however, did not enjoy the fruits of her own labor—a central element of freedom. Beginning with Mississippi in 1839, numerous states enacted married women's property laws, shielding from a husband's creditors property brought into a marriage by his wife. Such laws initially aimed not to expand women's rights so much as to prevent families from losing their property during the depression that began in 1837. But in 1860, New York enacted a more far-reaching measure, allowing married women to sign contracts, buy and sell property, and keep their own wages. In most states, however, property accumulated after marriage, as well as wages earned by the wife, still belonged to the husband.

Married women's property and the law

"Social Freedom"

Influenced by abolitionism, women's rights advocates turned another popular understanding of freedom—self-ownership, or control over one's own person—in an entirely new direction. The law of domestic relations presupposed the husband's right of sexual access to his wife and to inflict corporal punishment on her. Courts proved reluctant to intervene in cases of physical abuse so long as it was not "extreme" or "intolerable." "Women's Rights," declared a Boston meeting in 1859, included "freedom and equal rights in the family." The demand that women should enjoy the rights to regulate their own sexual activity and procreation and to be protected by the state against violence at the hands of their husbands challenged the notion that claims for justice, freedom, and individual rights should stop at the household's door.

Rights within the family

The issue of women's private freedom revealed underlying differences within the movement for women's rights. Belief in equality between the sexes and in the sexes' natural differences coexisted in antebellum feminist thought. Even as they entered the public sphere and thereby challenged some aspects of the era's "cult of domesticity" (discussed in Chapter 9), many early feminists accepted other elements. Allowing women a greater role in the public sphere, many female reformers argued, would bring their "inborn" maternal instincts to bear on public life, to the benefit of the entire society.

Even feminists critical of the existing institution of marriage generally refrained from raising in public the explosive issue of women's "private" freedom. Not until the twentieth century would the demand that freedom be extended to intimate aspects of life inspire a mass movement. But the dramatic fall in the birthrate over the course of the nineteenth century

Women's private freedom

suggests that many women were quietly exercising "personal freedom" in their most intimate relationships.

The Abolitionist Schism

Even in reform circles, the demand for a greater public role for women remained extremely controversial. Massachusetts physician Samuel Gridley Howe pioneered humane treatment of the blind and educational reform, and he was an ardent abolitionist. But Howe did not support his wife's participation in the movement for female suffrage, which, he complained, caused her to "neglect domestic relations." When organized abolitionism split into two wings in 1840, the immediate cause was a dispute over the proper role of women in antislavery work. Abby Kelley's appointment to the business committee of the American Anti-Slavery Society sparked the formation of a rival abolitionist organization, the American and Foreign Anti-Slavery Society, which believed it wrong for a woman to occupy so prominent a position. The antislavery poet John Greenleaf Whittier compared Kelley to Eve, Delilah, and Helen of Troy, women who had sown the seeds of male destruction.

The role of women in abolitionism

Behind the split lay the fear among some abolitionists that Garrison's radicalism on issues like women's rights, as well as his refusal to support the idea of abolitionists voting or running for public office, impeded

This image appeared on the cover of the sheet music for "Get Off the Track!", a song popularized by the Hutchinson singers, who performed antislavery songs. The trains *Immediate Emancipation* (with *The Liberator* as its front wheel) and *Liberty Party* pull into a railroad station. *The Herald of Freedom* and *American Standard* were antislavery newspapers. The song's lyrics praised William Lloyd Garrison and criticized various politicians, among them Henry Clay. The chorus went: "Roll it along! Through the nation / Freedom's car, Emancipation."

the movement's growth. Determined to make abolitionism a political movement, the seceders formed the **Liberty Party**, which nominated James G. Birney as its candidate for president. He received only 7,000 votes (about one-third of 1 percent of the total). In 1840, antislavery northerners saw little wisdom in "throwing away" their ballots on a third-party candidate.

Achievements of feminism and abolitionism

Although the achievement of most of their demands lay far in the future, the women's rights movement succeeded in making "the woman question" a permanent part of the transatlantic discussion of social reform. As for abolitionism, although it remained a significant presence in northern public life until emancipation was achieved, by 1840 the movement had accomplished its most important work. More than 1,000 local antislavery societies were now scattered throughout the North, representing a broad constituency awakened to the moral issue of slavery. The "great duty of freedom," Ralph Waldo Emerson had declared in 1837, was "to open our halls to discussion of this question." The abolitionists' greatest achievement lay in shattering the conspiracy of silence that had sought to preserve national unity by suppressing public debate over slavery.

CHAPTER REVIEW AND ONLINE RESOURCES

REVIEW QUESTIONS

1. How did the utopian communities challenge existing ideas about property and marriage?

2. How did the supporters and opponents of temperance understand the meaning of freedom differently?

3. What were the similarities and differences between the common school and the institutions like asylums, orphanages, and prisons that were created by reformers?

4. Why did so many prominent white Americans, from both the North and South, support the colonization of freed slaves?

5. How was the abolition movement affected by other social and economic changes such as the rise in literacy, new print technology, and ideas associated with the market revolution?

6. How was racism evident even in the abolitionist movement? What steps did some abolitionists take to fight racism in American society?

7. How could antebellum women participate in the public sphere even though they were excluded from government and politics?

8. How did white women's participation in the abolitionist movement push them to a new understanding of their own rights and oppression?

9. How did advocates for women's rights in these years both accept and challenge existing gender beliefs and social roles?

10. To what degree was antebellum reform international in scope?

KEY TERMS

utopian communities (p. 342)
"perfectionism" (p. 345)
temperance (p. 345)
self-discipline (p. 346)
asylums (p. 347)
common schools (p. 347)
public education (p. 347)
American Colonization Society (p. 348)
American Anti-Slavery Society (p. 351)
"moral suasion" (p. 352)
Uncle Tom's Cabin (p. 353)
"gentlemen of property and standing" (p. 354)
"Am I Not a Man and a Brother?" (p. 355)
gag rule (p. 355)
Dorothea Dix (p. 356)
woman suffrage (p. 357)
Woman in the Nineteenth Century (p. 358)
"slavery of sex" (p. 359)
Liberty Party (p. 364)

wwnorton.com
/studyspace

VISIT STUDYSPACE FOR THESE RESOURCES AND MORE
- A chapter outline
- A diagnostic chapter quiz
- Interactive maps
- Map worksheets
- Multimedia documents

CHAPTER 13

A HOUSE DIVIDE

1840-1861

Abraham Lincoln's nickname, "The Railsplitter," recalled his humble origins. An unknown artist created this larger-than-life portrait. The White House is visible in the distance. The painting is said to have been displayed during campaign rallies in 1860.

I n 1855, Thomas Crawford, one of the era's most prominent American sculptors, was asked to design a statue to adorn the Capitol's dome, still under construction in Washington, D.C. He proposed a statue of Freedom, a female figure wearing a liberty cap. Secretary of War Jefferson Davis of Mississippi, one of the country's largest slaveholders, objected to Crawford's plan. Ancient Romans, he noted, regarded the cap as "the badge of the freed slave." Its use, he feared, might suggest that there was a connection between the slaves' longing for freedom and the liberty of freeborn Americans. Davis ordered the liberty cap replaced with a less controversial military symbol, a feathered helmet.

In 1863, the colossal Statue of Freedom was installed atop the Capitol, where it can still be seen today. By the time it was put in place, the country was immersed in the Civil War and Jefferson Davis had become president of the Confederate States of America. The dispute over the Statue of Freedom offers a small illustration of how, by the mid-1850s, nearly every public question was being swept up into the gathering storm over slavery.

FOCUS QUESTIONS

- *What were the major factors contributing to U.S. territorial expansion in the 1840s?*

- *Why did the expansion of slavery become the most divisive political issue in the 1840s and 1850s?*

- *What combination of issues and events fueled the creation of the Republican Party in the 1850s?*

- *What enabled Lincoln to emerge from the divisive party politics of the 1850s?*

- *What were the final steps on the road to secession?*

The original and final designs for Thomas Crawford's *Statue of Freedom* for the dome of the Capitol building. Secretary of War Jefferson Davis of Mississippi insisted that the liberty cap in the first design, a symbol of the emancipated slave in ancient Rome, be replaced.

FRUITS OF MANIFEST DESTINY

Continental Expansion

In the 1840s, slavery moved to the center stage of American politics. It did so not in the moral language or with the immediatist program of abolitionism, but as a result of the nation's territorial expansion. Between 1840 and 1860, nearly 300,000 men, women, and children had braved disease, starvation, the natural barrier of the Rocky Mountains, and occasional Indian attacks to travel overland to Oregon and California.

During most of the 1840s, the United States and Great Britain jointly administered Oregon, and Utah was part of Mexico. This did not stop Americans from settling in either region. National boundaries meant little to those who moved west. The 1840s witnessed an intensification of the old belief that God intended the American nation to reach all the way to the Pacific Ocean. As noted in Chapter 9, the term that became a shorthand for this expansionist spirit was "manifest destiny."

"Manifest destiny"

The Mexican Frontier: New Mexico and California

Settlement of Oregon did not directly raise the issue of slavery. But the nation's acquisition of part of Mexico did. When Mexico achieved its independence from Spain in 1821, it was nearly as large as the United

A watercolor of a scene on a ranch near Monterey, California, in 1849 depicts *Californios* supervising the work of Native Americans.

States, and its population of 6.5 million was about two-thirds that of its northern neighbor. However, Mexico's northern provinces—California, New Mexico, and Texas—were isolated and sparsely settled outposts surrounded by Indian country. California's non-Indian population in 1821, some 3,200 missionaries, soldiers, and settlers, was vastly outnumbered by about 20,000 Indians living and working on land owned by religious missions and by 150,000 members of unsubdued tribes in the interior. By 1840, California was already linked commercially with the United States, and New England ships were trading with the region. In 1846, Alfred Robinson, who had moved from Boston, published *Life in California*. "In this age of annexation," he wondered, "why not extend the 'area of freedom' by the annexation of California?"

Mexican California

Westward migration in the early and mid-1840s took American settlers across Indian country into the Oregon Territory, ownership of which was disputed with Great Britain. The Mormons migrated west to Salt Lake City, then part of Mexico.

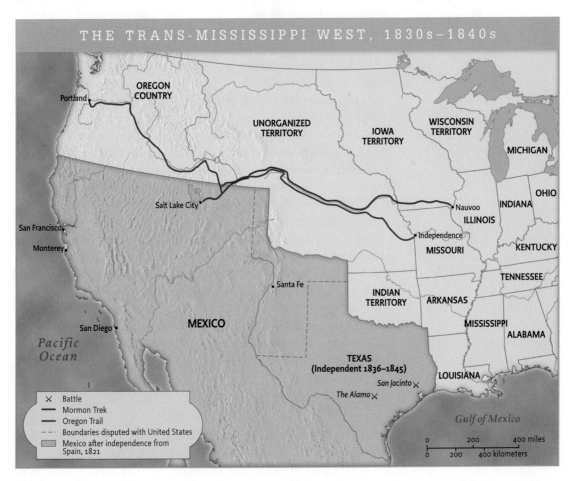

THE TRANS-MISSISSIPPI WEST, 1830s–1840s

Legend:
× Battle
— Mormon Trek
— Oregon Trail
--- Boundaries disputed with United States
⬚ Mexico after independence from Spain, 1821

The Texas Revolt

Moses and Stephen Austin

The first part of Mexico to be settled by significant numbers of Americans was Texas, whose non-Indian population of Spanish origin (called *Tejanos*) numbered only about 2,000 when Mexico became independent. In order to develop the region, the Spanish government had accepted an offer by Moses Austin, a Connecticut-born farmer, to colonize it with Americans. In 1820, Austin received a large land grant. He died soon afterward, and his son Stephen continued the plan, now in independent Mexico, reselling land in smaller plots to American settlers at twelve cents per acre.

Reasons for the Texas revolt

Alarmed that its grip on the area was weakening, the Mexican government in 1830 annulled existing land contracts and barred future emigration from the United States. Led by Stephen Austin, American settlers demanded greater autonomy within Mexico. Part of the area's tiny *Tejano* elite joined them. Mostly ranchers and large farmers, they had welcomed the economic boom that accompanied the settlers and had formed economic alliances with American traders. The issue of slavery further exacerbated matters. Mexico had abolished slavery, but local authorities allowed American settlers to bring slaves with them. Mexico's ruler, General Antonio López de **Santa Anna**, sent an army in 1835 to impose central authority.

Battle of San Jacinto

The appearance of Santa Anna's army sparked a chaotic revolt in Texas. The rebels formed a provisional government that soon called for Texan independence. On March 6, 1836, Santa Anna's army stormed the Alamo, a mission compound in San Antonio, killing its 187 American and *Tejano* defenders. "Remember the Alamo" became the Texans' rallying cry. In April, forces under Sam Houston, a former governor of Tennessee, routed Santa Anna's army at the Battle of San Jacinto and forced him to recognize Texan independence. In 1837, the Texas Congress called for union with the United States. But fearing the political disputes certain to result from an attempt to add another slave state to the Union, Presidents Andrew Jackson and Martin Van Buren shelved the question. Settlers from the United States nonetheless poured into the region, many of them slaveowners taking up fertile cotton land. By 1845, the population of Texas had reached nearly 150,000.

The Election of 1844

The Tyler administration and Texas

Texas annexation remained on the political back burner until President John Tyler revived it in the hope of rescuing his failed administration and securing southern support for renomination in 1844. In April 1844,

The plaza in San Antonio not long after the United States annexed Texas in 1845.

a letter by John C. Calhoun, whom Tyler had appointed secretary of state, was leaked to the press. It linked the idea of absorbing Texas directly to the goal of strengthening slavery in the United States. Some southern leaders, indeed, hoped that Texas could be divided into several states, thus further enhancing the South's power in Congress. Late that month, Henry Clay and former president Van Buren, the prospective Whig and Democratic candidates for president and two of the party system's most venerable leaders, met at Clay's Kentucky plantation. They agreed to issue letters rejecting immediate annexation on the grounds that it might provoke war with Mexico.

Slavery and expansion

Clay went on to receive the Whig nomination, but for Van Buren the letters proved to be a disaster. At the Democratic convention, southerners bent on annexation deserted Van Buren's cause, and he failed to receive the two-thirds majority necessary for nomination. The delegates then turned to the little-known James K. Polk, a former governor of Tennessee whose main assets were his support for annexation and his close association with Andrew Jackson, still the party's most popular figure. To soothe injured feelings among northern Democrats over the rejection of Van Buren, the party platform called not only for the "**reannexation**" of Texas (implying that Texas had been part of the Louisiana Purchase and therefore had once belonged to the United States) but also the "**reoccupation**" of all of Oregon. "Fifty-four forty or fight"—American control of Oregon all the way to its northern boundary at north latitude 54°40'—became a popular campaign slogan.

Emergence of Polk

Polk was the first "dark horse" candidate for president—that is, one whose nomination was completely unexpected. In the fall, he defeated

Clay in an extremely close election. Polk's margin in the popular vote was less than 2 percent. Had not James G. Birney, running again as the Liberty Party candidate, received 16,000 votes in New York, mostly from anti-slavery Whigs, Clay would have been elected. In March 1845, only days before Polk's inauguration, Congress declared Texas part of the United States.

Polk's election

The Road to War

Polk's goals

James K. Polk may have been virtually unknown, but he assumed the presidency with a clearly defined set of goals: to reduce the tariff, reestablish the independent Treasury system, settle the dispute over ownership of Oregon, and bring California into the Union. Congress soon enacted the first two goals, and the third was accomplished in an agreement with Great Britain dividing Oregon at the forty-ninth parallel.

Acquiring California proved more difficult. Polk dispatched an emissary to Mexico offering to purchase the region, but the Mexican government refused to negotiate. By the spring of 1846, Polk was planning for military action. In April, American soldiers under Zachary Taylor moved into the region between the Nueces River and the Rio Grande, land claimed by both countries on the disputed border between Texas and Mexico. This action made conflict with Mexican forces inevitable. When fighting broke out, Polk claimed that the Mexicans had "shed blood upon American soil" and called for a declaration of war.

War News from Mexico, an 1848 painting by Richard C. Woodville, shows how Americans received war news through the popular press.

The War and Its Critics

The Mexican War was the first American conflict to be fought primarily on foreign soil and the first in which American troops occupied a foreign capital. Inspired by the expansionist fervor of manifest destiny, a majority of Americans supported the war. But a significant minority in the North dissented, fearing that far from expanding the "great empire of liberty," the administration's real aim was to acquire new land for the expansion of slavery. Henry David Thoreau was jailed in Massachusetts in 1846 for refusing to pay taxes as a protest against the war. Defending his action, Thoreau wrote an important essay, "On Civil Disobedience," which inspired such later advocates of nonviolent resistance to unjust laws as Martin Luther King Jr.

Among the war's critics was Abraham Lincoln, who had been elected to Congress in 1846 from Illinois. Like many Whigs, Lincoln questioned whether the Mexicans had actually inflicted casualties on American soil, as Polk claimed. But Lincoln was also disturbed by Polk's claiming the right to initiate an invasion of Mexico. Lincoln's stance proved unpopular in Illinois. He had already agreed to serve only one term in Congress, but when Democrats captured his seat in 1848, many blamed the result on Lincoln's criticism of the war. Nonetheless, the concerns he raised regarding the president's power to "make war at pleasure" would continue to echo in the twentieth and twenty-first centuries.

Lincoln as war critic

Combat in Mexico

More than 60,000 volunteers enlisted and did most of the fighting. Combat took place on three fronts. In June 1846, a band of American insurrectionists proclaimed California freed from Mexican control and named Captain John C. Frémont, head of a small scientific expedition in the West, its ruler. Their aim was California's incorporation into the United States, but for the moment they adopted a flag depicting a large bear as the symbol of the area's independence. A month later, the U.S. Navy sailed into Monterey and San Francisco harbors, raised the American flag, and put an end to the "bear flag republic." At almost the same time, 1,600 American troops under General Stephen W. Kearney occupied Sante Fe without resistance and then set out for southern California, where they helped to put down a Mexican uprising against American rule.

The war's three fronts

The bulk of the fighting occurred in central Mexico. In February 1847, Taylor defeated Santa Anna's army at the Battle of Buena Vista. When the Mexican government still refused to negotiate, Polk ordered American forces under Winfield Scott to march inland from the port of Veracruz toward Mexico City. Scott's forces routed Mexican defenders and in September occupied the country's capital. In February 1848, the two governments agreed to the Treaty of Guadalupe Hidalgo, which confirmed the annexation of Texas and ceded California and present-day New Mexico, Arizona, Nevada, and Utah to the United States.

The defeat of Mexico and its consequences

The Mexican War is only a footnote in most Americans' historical memory. Unlike for other wars, few public monuments celebrate the conflict. Mexicans, however, regard the war (or "the dismemberment," as it is called in that country) as a central event of their national history

THE MEXICAN WAR, 1846–1848

Sonoma
San Francisco
Monterey
Santa Barbara
Los Angeles
San Diego
San Pasqual
La Paz
San Lucas · San Jose
San Diego

Fort Leavenworth
UNORGANIZED TERRITORY
Platte R.
Missouri R.
ILLINOIS
MISSOURI
UNITED STATES
ARKANSAS
Bent's Fort
Santa Fe
Las Vegas
Albuquerque
INDIAN TERRITORY
Arkansas R.
Red R.
MISSISSIPPI
LOUISIANA
El Paso
TEXAS
San Antonio
New Orleans
Chihuahua
Corpus Christi
Palo Alto
Buena Vista
Tampico
San Luis Potosí
Mazatlán
Veracruz
Mexico City
Pueblo
Cerro Gordo

CEDED BY MEXICO
Colorado R.
Gila R.
Kearny
MEXICO
Nueces R.
DISPUTED BY TEXAS AND MEXICO
Rio Grande
Pecos R.
Sabine R.

Pacific Ocean
Gulf of Mexico

U.S. Navy
Frémont
Kearny
Santa Anna
Scott
Taylor

0   150   300 miles
0   150   300 kilometers

- ⊗ American victory
- ⊗ Mexican victory
- —— American forces
- ···· American naval blockade
- —— Mexican forces
- —— Treaty of Guadalupe Hidalgo
- ▨ Lands disputed by United States and Mexico
- ☐ Lands ceded by Mexico

The Mexican War was the first in which an American army invaded another country and occupied its capital. As a result of the war, the United States acquired a vast new area in the modern-day Southwest.

and a source of continued resentment over a century and a half after it was fought.

Race and Manifest Destiny

With the end of the Mexican War, the United States absorbed half a million square miles of Mexico's territory, one-third of that nation's total area. A region that for centuries had been united was suddenly split in two, dividing families and severing trade routes. An estimated 75,000 to 100,000 Spanish-speaking Mexicans and more than 150,000 Indians inhabited the land annexed from Mexico, known as the Mexican Cession. The Treaty of Guadalupe Hidalgo guaranteed to "male citizens" of the area "the free enjoyment of their liberty and property" and "all the rights" of Americans—a provision designed to protect the property of large Mexican landowners in California. Thus, in the first half of the nineteenth century, some residents of the area went from being Spaniards to Mexicans to Americans. Although not newcomers, they had to adjust to a new identity as if they were immigrants. As for Indians whose homelands and hunting grounds suddenly became part of the United States, the treaty referred to them only as "savage tribes" whom the United States must prevent from launching incursions into Mexico across the new border.

During the 1840s, territorial expansion came to be seen as proof of the innate superiority of the "Anglo-Saxon race" (a mythical construct defined largely by its opposites: blacks, Indians, Hispanics, and Catholics). "*Race*,"

> *The Mexican Cession*

> *Status of Mexicans and Indians*

By 1853, with the Gadsden Purchase, the present boundaries of the United States in North America, with the exception of Alaska, had been created.

CONTINENTAL EXPANSION THROUGH 1853

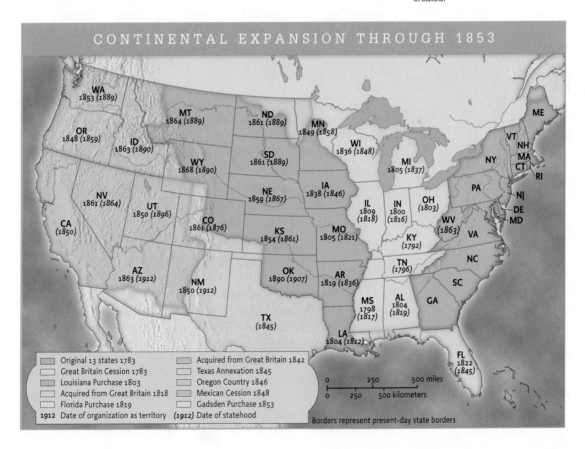

WA 1853 (1889)
MT 1864 (1889)
ND 1861 (1889)
MN 1849 (1858)
ME
OR 1848 (1859)
ID 1863 (1890)
WI 1836 (1848)
VT
NH
NY
MA
CT
RI
WY 1868 (1890)
SD 1861 (1889)
MI 1805 (1837)
NV 1861 (1864)
NE 1859 (1867)
IA 1838 (1846)
IL 1809 (1818)
IN 1800 (1816)
OH (1803)
PA
NJ
UT 1850 (1896)
CO 1861 (1876)
WV (1863)
VA
DE
MD
CA (1850)
KS 1854 (1861)
MO 1805 (1821)
KY (1792)
NC
AZ 1863 (1912)
NM 1850 (1912)
OK 1890 (1907)
AR 1819 (1836)
TN (1796)
SC
TX (1845)
MS 1798 (1817)
AL 1804 (1819)
GA
LA 1804 (1812)
FL 1822 (1845)

Original 13 states 1783
Great Britain Cession 1783
Louisiana Purchase 1803
Acquired from Great Britain 1818
Florida Purchase 1819
Acquired from Great Britain 1842
Texas Annexation 1845
Oregon Country 1846
Mexican Cession 1848
Gadsden Purchase 1853
1912 Date of organization as territory **(1912)** Date of statehood

0   250   500 miles
0   250   500 kilometers

Borders represent present-day state borders

declared John L. O'Sullivan's *Democratic Review*, was the "key" to the "history of nations" and the rise and fall of empires. Newspapers, magazines, and scholarly works popularized the link between American freedom and the supposedly innate liberty-loving qualities of Anglo-Saxon Protestants. Indeed, calls by some expansionists for the United States to annex all of Mexico failed in part because of fear that the nation could not assimilate its large non-white Catholic population, supposedly unfit for citizenship in a republic.

The Texas constitution

Local circumstances affected racial definitions in the former Mexican territories. Although Mexico had abolished slavery and considered all persons equal before the law, the Texas constitution adopted after independence protected slavery and denied civil rights to Indians and persons of African origin. Texas defined "Spanish" Mexicans, however, especially those who occupied important social positions, as white. The residents of New Mexico of both Mexican and Indian origin, on the other hand, were long deemed "too Mexican" for democratic self-government. With white migration lagging, Congress did not allow New Mexico to become a state until 1912.

Gold-Rush California

California had a non-Indian population of less than 15,000 when the Mexican War ended. For most of the 1840s, ten times as many Americans emigrated to Oregon as to California. But this changed dramatically after

Sutter's mill

January 1848, when gold was discovered in the foothills of the Sierra Nevada Mountains at a sawmill owned by the Swiss immigrant Johann A. Sutter. By ship and land, newcomers poured into California. The non-Indian population rose to 200,000 by 1852 and more than 360,000 eight years later.

California's gold-rush population was incredibly diverse. Experienced miners flooded in from Mexico and South America. Tens of thousands of Americans who had never seen a mine arrived from the East, and

Diversity of the gold-rush population

from overseas came Irish, Germans, Italians, and Australians. Nearly 25,000 Chinese landed between 1849 and 1852. Unlike the families who settled farming frontiers, most of the gold-rush migrants were young men. Women played many roles in western mining communities, running restaurants and boardinghouses and working as laundresses, cooks, and prostitutes. But as late as 1860, California's male population outnumbered females by nearly three to one.

As early surface mines quickly became exhausted, they gave way to underground mining that required a large investment of capital. This economic development worsened conflicts among California's many racial and ethnic groups engaged in fierce competition for gold. White miners organized extralegal groups that expelled "foreign miners"—Mexicans, Chileans, Chinese, French, and American Indians—from areas with gold. The state legislature imposed a tax of twenty dollars per month on foreign miners, driving many of them from the state.

Conflicts over gold

For California's Indians, the gold rush and absorption into the United States proved to be disastrous. Gold seekers overran Indian communities. Miners, ranchers, and vigilantes murdered thousands of Indians. Determined to reduce the native population, state officials paid millions in bounties to private militias that launched attacks on the state's Indians. Although California was a free state, thousands of Indian children, declared orphans or vagrants by local courts, were bought and sold as slaves. By 1860, California's Indian population, nearly 150,000 when the Mexican War ended, had been reduced to around 30,000.

The gold rush and California's Indians

In a remarkable coincidence, the California gold rush took place almost simultaneously with another located halfway around the world. In 1851, gold was discovered in Australia, then a collection of British colonies. During the 1850s, California and Australia together produced 80 percent of the world's gold. Like California, Australia attracted gold-seekers from across the globe. As in California, the gold rush was a disaster for the aboriginal peoples (as native Australians are called), whose population, already declining, fell precipitously.

Transportation of Cargo by Westerners at the Port of Yokohama, 1861, by the Japanese artist Utagawa Sadahide, depicts ships in port, including an American one on the left, eight years after Commodore Perry's first voyage to Japan.

Opening Japan

The Mexican War ended with the United States in possession of the magnificent harbors of San Diego and San Francisco, long seen as jumping-off points for trade with the Far East. In the 1850s, the United States took the lead in opening Japan, a country that had closed itself to nearly all foreign contact for more than two centuries. In 1853 and 1854, American warships under the command of **Commodore Matthew Perry** (the younger brother of Oliver Perry, a hero of the War of 1812) sailed into Tokyo Harbor. Perry, who had been sent by President Millard Fillmore to negotiate a trade treaty, demanded that the Japanese deal with him. Alarmed by European intrusions into China and impressed by Perry's armaments as well as a musical pageant he presented that included a blackface minstrel show, Japanese leaders agreed to do so. In 1854, they opened two ports to American shipping. As a result, the United States acquired refueling places on the route to China—seen as Asia's most important trading partner. And Japan soon launched a process of modernization that transformed it into the region's major military power.

A DOSE OF ARSENIC

Slavery in the West

Victory over Mexico added more than 1 million square miles to the United States—an area larger than the Louisiana Purchase. But the acquisition of this vast territory raised the fatal issue that would disrupt the political system and plunge the nation into civil war—whether slavery should be allowed to expand into the West. Events soon confirmed Ralph Waldo Emerson's prediction that if the United States gobbled up part of Mexico, "it will be as the man who swallows arsenic.... Mexico will poison us."

Already, the bonds of Union were fraying. In 1844 and 1845, the Methodists and Baptists, the two largest evangelical churches, divided into northern and southern branches. Once the churches were divided by section, it was easier for the southern branch to move toward a stronger biblical defense of slavery, and the northern toward antislavery, if not necessarily abolitionism. But it was the entrance of the slavery issue into the heart of American politics as the result of the Mexican War that eventually dissolved perhaps the strongest force for national unity—the two-party system.

The Wilmot Proviso

Party vs. section

Before 1846, the status of slavery in all parts of the United States had been settled, either by state law or by the Missouri Compromise, which determined slavery's status in the Louisiana Purchase. The acquisition of new land reopened the question of slavery's expansion. The divisive potential of this issue became clear in 1846, when Congressman David Wilmot of Pennsylvania proposed a resolution prohibiting slavery from all territory acquired from Mexico. Party lines crumbled as every northerner, Democrat and Whig alike, supported what came to be known as the **Wilmot Proviso**, while nearly all southerners opposed it. The measure passed the House, where the more populous North possessed a majority, but failed in the Senate, with its even balance of free and slave states.

In 1848, opponents of slavery's expansion organized the **Free Soil Party** and nominated Martin Van Buren for president and Charles Francis Adams, the son of John Quincy Adams, as his running mate. Democrats nominated Lewis Cass of Michigan, who proposed that the decision on whether to allow slavery should be left to settlers in the new territories (an idea later given the name "popular sovereignty"). Van Buren was motivated in part by revenge against the South for jettisoning him in 1844. But his campaign struck a chord among northerners opposed to the expansion of slavery, and he polled some 300,000 votes, 14 percent of the northern total. Victory in 1848 went to the Whig candidate, Zachary Taylor, a hero of the Mexican War and a Louisiana sugar planter. But the fact that a former president and the son of another abandoned their parties to run on a Free Soil platform showed that antislavery sentiment had spread far beyond abolitionist ranks.

Zachary Taylor

The Free Soil Appeal

The Free Soil position had a popular appeal in the North that far exceeded the abolitionists' demand for immediate emancipation and equal rights for blacks. Many northerners had long resented what they considered southern domination of the federal government. The idea of preventing the creation of new slave states appealed to those who favored policies, such as the protective tariff and government aid to internal improvements, that the majority of southern political leaders opposed.

Economic betterment

For thousands of northerners, moreover, the ability to move to the new western territories held out the promise of economic betterment. "Freedom of the soil," declared George Henry Evans, the editor of a pro-labor newspaper, offered the only alternative to permanent economic dependence for American workers.

Such views merged easily with opposition to the expansion of slavery. If slave plantations were to occupy the fertile lands of the West, northern migration would be effectively blocked. The term "free soil" had a double meaning. The Free Soil platform of 1848 called both for barring slavery from western territories and for the federal government to provide free homesteads to settlers in the new territories. Unlike abolitionism, the "free soil" idea also appealed to the racism so widespread in northern society. Wilmot himself insisted that his controversial proviso was motivated to advance "the cause and rights of the free white man," in part by preventing him from having to compete with "black labor."

The Free Soil platform of 1848

To white southerners, the idea of barring slavery from territory acquired from Mexico seemed a violation of their equal rights as members of the Union. Just as northerners believed westward expansion essential to their economic well-being, southern leaders became convinced that slavery must expand or die. Moreover, the admission of new free states would overturn the delicate political balance between the sections and make the South a permanent minority. Southern interests would not be secure in a Union dominated by non-slaveholding states.

The view of Southern leaders

Crisis and Compromise

Developments in Europe

In world history, the year 1848 is remembered as the "springtime of nations," a time of democratic uprisings against the monarchies of Europe and demands by ethnic minorities for national independence. American principles of liberty and self-government appeared to be triumphing in the Old World. The Chartist movement in Great Britain organized massive demonstrations in support of a proposed Charter that demanded democratic reforms. The French replaced their monarchy with a republic. Hungarians proclaimed their independence from Austrian rule. Patriots in Italy and Germany, both divided into numerous states, demanded national unification. But the revolutionary tide receded. Chartism faded away, Emperor Napoleon III soon restored the French monarchy, and revolts in Budapest, Rome, and other cities were crushed. Would their own experiment in self-government, some Americans wondered, suffer the same fate as the failed revolutions of Europe?

Attempts to resolve sectional differences

With the slavery issue appearing more and more ominous, established party leaders moved to resolve differences between the sections. In 1850, California asked to be admitted to the Union as a free state. Many southerners opposed the measure, fearing that it would upset the sectional balance in Congress. Senator Henry Clay offered a plan with four main provisions that came to be known as the **Compromise of 1850**. California would enter the Union as a free state. The slave trade, but not slavery itself, would be abolished in the nation's capital. A stringent new law would allow southerners to reclaim runaway slaves. And the status of slavery in the remaining territories acquired from Mexico would be left to the decision of the local white inhabitants. The United States would also agree to pay off the massive debt Texas had accumulated while independent.

The Great Debate

In the Senate debate on the Compromise, the divergent sectional positions received eloquent expression. Powerful leaders spoke for and against compromise. Daniel Webster of Massachusetts announced his willingness to abandon the Wilmot Proviso and accept a new fugitive slave law if this were the price of sectional peace. John C. Calhoun, again representing South Carolina, was too ill to speak. A colleague read his remarks rejecting the very idea of compromise. The North must yield, Calhoun insisted, or the Union could not survive. William H. Seward of New York also opposed compromise. To southerners' talk of their constitutional rights, Seward responded that a "higher law" than the Constitution condemned slavery—the law of morality. Here was the voice of abolitionism, now represented in the U.S. Senate.

President Zachary Taylor, like Andrew Jackson a southerner but a strong nationalist, insisted that all Congress needed to do was admit California to the Union. But Taylor died suddenly of an intestinal infection on July 9, 1850. His successor, Millard Fillmore of New York, threw his support to Clay's proposals. Fillmore helped to break the impasse in Congress and secure adoption of the Compromise of 1850.

Senator Daniel Webster of Massachusetts in a daguerreotype from 1850, the year his speech in support of the Compromise of 1850 contributed to its passage.

The Fugitive Slave Issue

For one last time, political leaders had removed the dangerous slavery question from congressional debate. The new **Fugitive Slave Act**, however, made further controversy inevitable. The law allowed special federal commissioners to determine the fate of alleged fugitives without benefit of a jury trial or even testimony by the accused individual. It prohibited local authorities from interfering with the capture of fugitives and required individual citizens to assist in such capture when called upon by federal agents. Thus, southern leaders, usually strong defenders of states' rights and local autonomy, supported a measure that brought federal agents into communities throughout the North, armed with the power to override local law enforcement and judicial procedures to secure the return of runaway slaves. The security of slavery was more important to them than states'-rights consistency.

During the 1850s, federal tribunals heard more than 300 cases throughout the free states and ordered 157 fugitives returned to the South, many at the government's expense. But the law further widened sectional divisions. In a series of dramatic confrontations, fugitives, aided by abolitionist allies, violently resisted recapture. A large crowd in 1851 rescued the escaped slave Jerry from jail in Syracuse, New York, and spirited him off to Canada. In the same year, an owner who attempted to recapture a fugitive was killed in Christiana, Pennsylvania.

In the North, several thousand fugitives and freeborn blacks, worried that they might be swept up in the stringent provisions of the Fugitive Slave Act, fled to safety in Canada. The sight of so many refugees seeking

An 1855 broadside depicting the life of Anthony Burns, a runaway slave captured in Boston and returned to the South in 1854 by federal officials enforcing the Fugitive Slave Act.

liberty in a foreign land challenged the familiar image of the United States as an asylum for freedom.

Douglas and Popular Sovereignty

At least temporarily, the Compromise of 1850 seemed to have restored sectional peace and party unity. In the 1852 presidential election, Democrat Franklin Pierce won a sweeping victory over the Whig Winfield Scott on a platform that recognized the Compromise as a final settlement of the slavery controversy.

Kansas, Nebraska, and slavery

In 1854, however, the old political order finally succumbed to the disruptive pressures of sectionalism. Early in that year, Illinois senator Stephen A. Douglas introduced a bill to provide territorial governments for Kansas and Nebraska, located within the Louisiana Purchase. A strong believer in western development, he hoped that a transcontinental railroad could be constructed through Kansas or Nebraska. Southerners in Congress, however, seemed adamant against allowing the organization of new free territories that might further upset the sectional balance. Douglas hoped to satisfy them by applying the principle of **popular sovereignty**, whereby the status of slavery would be determined by the votes of local settlers, not Congress. To Douglas, popular sovereignty embodied the idea of local self-government and offered a middle ground between the extremes of North and South.

The Kansas-Nebraska Act

Unlike the lands taken from Mexico, Kansas and Nebraska lay in the nation's heartland, directly in the path of westward migration. Slavery, moreover, was prohibited there under the terms of the Missouri Compromise, which Douglas's bill repealed. In response to Douglas's proposal, a group of antislavery congressmen issued the *Appeal of the Independent Democrats*. It arraigned Douglas's bill as a "gross violation of a sacred pledge," part and parcel of "an atrocious plot" to convert free territory into a "dreary region of despotism, inhabited by masters and slaves." It helped to convince millions of northerners that southern leaders aimed at nothing less than extending their peculiar institution throughout the West.

The Appeal of the Independent Democrats

Thanks to Douglas's energetic leadership, the **Kansas-Nebraska Act** became law in 1854. But it shattered the Democratic Party's unity and sparked a profound reorganization of American politics. During the next two years, the Whig Party, unable to develop a unified response to the political crisis, collapsed. From a region divided between the two parties,

Political transformation

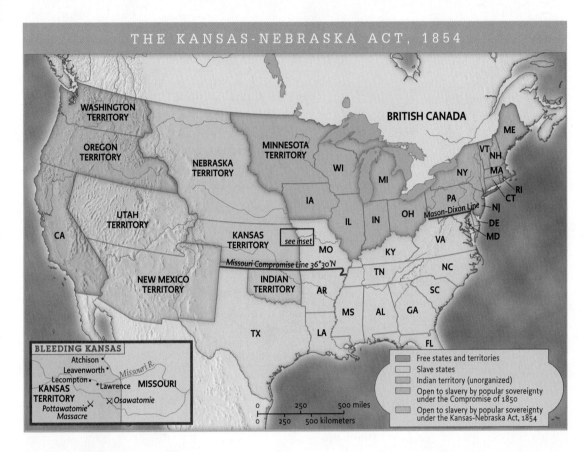

THE KANSAS-NEBRASKA ACT, 1854

Free states and territories
Slave states
Indian territory (unorganized)
Open to slavery by popular sovereignty under the Compromise of 1850
Open to slavery by popular sovereignty under the Kansas-Nebraska Act, 1854

The Kansas-Nebraska Act opened a vast area in the nation's heartland to the possible spread of slavery by repealing the Missouri Compromise and providing that settlers would determine the status of slavery in these territories.

the South became solidly Democratic. Most northern Whigs, augmented by thousands of disgruntled Democrats, joined a new organization, the Republican Party, dedicated to preventing the further expansion of slavery.

THE RISE OF THE REPUBLICAN PARTY

The Northern Economy

The disruptive impact of slavery on the traditional parties was the immediate cause of political transformation in the mid-1850s. But the rise of the Republican Party also reflected underlying economic and social changes, notably the completion of the market revolution and the beginning of mass immigration from Europe.

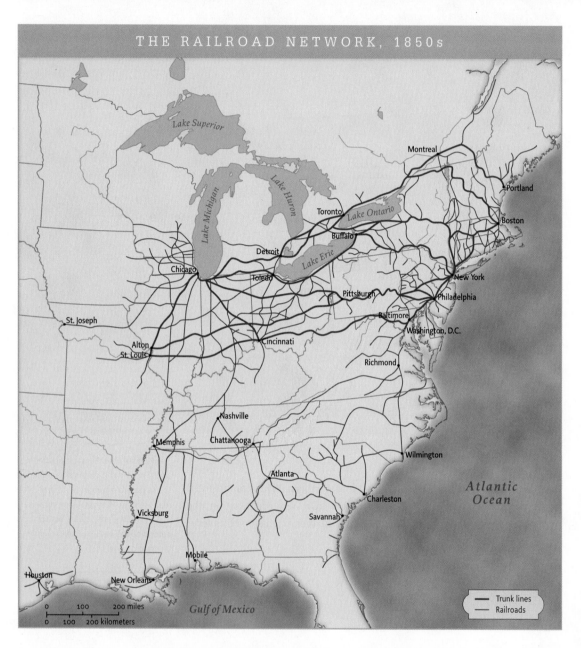

THE RAILROAD NETWORK, 1850s

Trunk lines
Railroads

The rapid expansion of the railroad network in the 1850s linked the Northeast and Old Northwest in a web of commerce. The South's rail network was considerably less developed, accounting for only 30 percent of the nation's track mileage.

The period from 1843 to 1857 witnessed explosive economic growth, especially in the North. The catalyst was the completion of the railroad network. From 5,000 miles in 1848, railroad track mileage grew to 30,000 by 1860, with most of the construction occurring in Ohio, Illinois, and other states of the Old Northwest. Four great trunk railroads now linked eastern cities with western farming and commercial centers. The railroads completed the reorientation of the Northwest's trade from the South to the East. As late as 1850, most western farmers still shipped their produce down the Mississippi River. Ten years later, however, railroads transported nearly all their crops to the East, at a fraction of the previous cost. Eastern industrialists marketed manufactured goods to the commercial farmers of the West, while residents of the region's growing cities consumed the food westerners produced. The economic integration of the Northwest and Northeast created the groundwork for their political unification in the Republican Party.

> *The railroad network in the North*

> *Integration of Northwest and Northeast*

Although most northerners still lived in small towns and rural areas, the majority of the workforce no longer labored in agriculture. Two great areas of industrial production had arisen. One, along the Atlantic coast, stretched from Boston to Philadelphia and Baltimore. A second was centered on or near the Great Lakes, in inland cities like Buffalo, Cleveland, Pittsburgh, and Chicago. Driven by railroad expansion, coal mining and iron manufacturing were growing rapidly. Chicago, the Old Northwest's major rail center and the jumping-off place for settlers heading for the Great Plains, had become a complex manufacturing center. Although the southern economy was also growing and the continuing expansion of cotton production brought wealth to slaveholders, the South did not share in these broad economic changes.

A lithograph from around 1860 depicts the town of Bridgewater, Massachusetts, home of a major iron works. A railroad speeds along in the foreground, while factory smokestacks dot the horizon. The tidy buildings in the center suggest that industrialization has not upset social harmony. Industrial development in the north widened the gap between the sections.

The Rise and Fall of the Know-Nothings

Nativism—hostility to immigrants, especially Catholics—became a national political movement with the sudden appearance in 1854 of the American, or **Know-Nothing, Party** (so called because it began as a secret organization whose members, when asked about its existence, were supposed to respond, "I know nothing"). The party trumpeted its dedication to reserving

The Propagation Society—More Free than Welcome, an anti-Catholic cartoon from the 1850s, illustrates the nativist fear that the Catholic Church poses a threat to American society. Pope Pius IX, cross in hand, steps ashore from a boat that also holds five bishops. Addressing "Young America," who holds a Bible, he says that he has come to "take charge of your spiritual welfare." A bishop adds, "I cannot bear to see that boy, with that horrible book."

political office for native-born Americans and to resisting the "aggressions" of the Catholic Church, such as its supposed efforts to undermine public school systems. The Know-Nothings swept the 1854 state elections in Massachusetts, electing the governor, all of the state's congressmen, and nearly every member of the state legislature. In many states, nativists emerged as a major component of victorious "anti-Nebraska" coalitions of voters opposed to the Kansas-Nebraska Act. In the North, the Know-Nothings' appeal combined anti-Catholic and antislavery sentiment, with opposition to the sale of liquor often added to the equation.

Nativism and antislavery

Despite severe anti-Irish discrimination in jobs, housing, and education, however, it is remarkable how little came of demands that immigrants be barred from the political nation. All European immigrants benefited from being white. The newcomers had the good fortune to arrive after white male suffrage had become the norm and automatically received the right to vote.

Suffrage for European immigrants

The Free Labor Ideology

By 1856, it was clear that the Republican Party—a coalition of antislavery Democrats, northern Whigs, Free Soilers, and Know-Nothings opposed to the further expansion of slavery—would become the major alternative to the Democratic Party in the North. The party's appeal rested on the idea of "free labor." In Republican hands, the antithesis between "free society" and

The Republican Party and free labor

George Catlin's 1827 painting *Five Points* depicts a working-class immigrant neighborhood in New York City that gained a reputation for crime, drinking, and overcrowding.

"slave society" coalesced into a comprehensive worldview that glorified the North as the home of progress, opportunity, and freedom.

The defining quality of northern society, Republicans declared, was the opportunity it offered each laborer to move up to the status of land-owning farmer or independent craftsman, thus achieving the economic independence essential to freedom. Slavery, by contrast, spawned a social order consisting of degraded slaves, poor whites with no hope of advancement, and idle aristocrats. If slavery were to spread into the West, northern free laborers would be barred, and their chances for social advancement severely diminished. Slavery, Republicans insisted, must be kept out of the territories so that free labor could flourish. The Republican platform of 1856 condemned slavery as one of the "twin relics of barbarism" in the United States (the other being Mormon polygamy).

Free labor versus slavery

Republicans were not abolitionists—they focused on preventing the spread of slavery, not attacking it where it existed. Nonetheless, many party leaders viewed the nation's division into free and slave societies as an "irrepressible conflict," as Senator William H. Seward of New York put it in 1858, that eventually would have to be resolved.

Spread of slavery

"Bleeding Kansas" and the Election of 1856

Their free labor outlook, which resonated so effectively with deeply held northern values, helps to explain the Republicans' rapid rise to prominence. But dramatic events in 1855 and 1856 also fueled the party's growth. When

SOUTHERN CHIVALRY — ARGUMENT versus CLUB'S.

A contemporary print denounces South Carolina congressman Preston S. Brooks's assault on Massachusetts senator Charles Sumner in May 1856. The attack on the floor of the Senate was in retaliation for Sumner's speech accusing Senator Andrew P. Butler (Brooks's distant cousin) of having taken "the harlot slavery" as his mistress.

Parties along sectional lines

Kansas held elections in 1854 and 1855, hundreds of proslavery Missourians crossed the border to cast fraudulent ballots. President Franklin Pierce recognized the legitimacy of the resulting proslavery legislature, but settlers from free states soon established a rival government. A sporadic civil war broke out in Kansas in which some 200 persons eventually lost their lives. In one incident, in May 1856, a proslavery mob attacked the free-soil stronghold of Lawrence, burning public buildings and pillaging private homes.

"Bleeding Kansas" seemed to discredit Douglas's policy of leaving the decision on slavery up to the local population, thus aiding the Republicans. The party also drew strength from an unprecedented incident in the halls of Congress. South Carolina representative Preston Brooks, wielding a gold-tipped cane, beat the antislavery senator Charles Sumner of Massachusetts unconscious.

In the election of 1856, the Republican Party chose as its candidate John C. Frémont and drafted a platform that strongly opposed the further expansion of slavery. Stung by the northern reaction to the Kansas-Nebraska Act, the Democrats nominated James Buchanan, who had been minister to Great Britain in 1854 and thus had no direct connection with that divisive measure. The Democratic platform endorsed the principle of popular sovereignty as the only viable solution to the slavery controversy. Meanwhile, the Know-Nothings presented ex-president Millard Fillmore as their candidate. Frémont outpolled Buchanan in the North, carrying eleven of sixteen free states—a remarkable achievement for an organization that had existed for only two years. But Buchanan won the entire South and the key northern states of Illinois, Indiana, and Pennsylvania, enough to ensure his victory. Fillmore carried only Maryland. The 1856 election returns made starkly clear that political parties had reoriented themselves along sectional lines. One major party had been destroyed, another seriously weakened, and a new one had arisen, devoted entirely to the interests of the North.

THE EMERGENCE OF LINCOLN

The final collapse of the party system took place during the administration of a president who epitomized the old political order. Born during George Washington's presidency, James Buchanan had served in Pennsylvania's legislature, in both houses of Congress, and as secretary of state under James K. Polk. A staunch believer in the Union, he committed himself to pacifying inflamed sectional emotions. Few presidents have failed more disastrously in what they set out to accomplish.

The Dred Scott Decision

Even before his inauguration, Buchanan became aware of an impending Supreme Court decision that held out the hope of settling the slavery controversy once and for all. This was the case of Dred Scott. During the 1830s, Scott had accompanied his owner, Dr. John Emerson of Missouri, to Illinois, where slavery had been prohibited by the Northwest Ordinance of 1787 and by state law, and to Wisconsin Territory, where it was barred by the Missouri Compromise. After returning to Missouri, Scott sued for his freedom, claiming that residence on free soil had made him free.

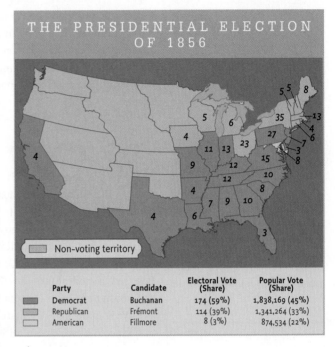

THE PRESIDENTIAL ELECTION OF 1856

Non-voting territory

Party	Candidate	Electoral Vote (Share)	Popular Vote (Share)
Democrat	Buchanan	174 (59%)	1,838,169 (45%)
Republican	Frémont	114 (39%)	1,341,264 (33%)
American	Fillmore	8 (3%)	874,534 (22%)

The **Dred Scott decision**, one of the most famous—or infamous—rulings in the long history of the Supreme Court, was announced in March 1857, two days after Buchanan's inauguration. Speaking for the majority, Chief Justice Roger B. Taney declared that only white persons could be citizens of the United States. The nation's founders, Taney insisted, believed that blacks "had no rights which the white man was bound to respect."

Chief Justice Taney

As for Scott's residence in Wisconsin, the ruling stated that Congress possessed no power under the Constitution to bar slavery from a territory. The Missouri Compromise, recently repealed by the Kansas-Nebraska Act, had been unconstitutional, and so was any measure interfering with southerners' right to bring slaves into the western territories. The decision in effect declared unconstitutional the Republican platform of restricting slavery's expansion. It also seemed to undermine Douglas's doctrine of popular sovereignty. For if Congress lacked the power to prohibit slavery in a territory, how could a territorial legislature created by Congress do so?

Slavery, announced President Buchanan, henceforth existed in all the territories, "by virtue of the Constitution." In 1858, his administration attempted to admit Kansas as a slave state under the Lecompton

The Lecompton battle

Dred Scott as painted in 1857, the year the Supreme Court ruled that he and his family must remain in slavery. (Collection of the New York Historical Society)

Constitution, which had been drafted by a pro-southern convention and never submitted to a popular vote. Outraged by this violation of popular sovereignty, Douglas formed an unlikely alliance with congressional Republicans to block the attempt. The Lecompton battle convinced southern Democrats that they could not trust their party's most popular northern leader.

Lincoln and Slavery

The depth of Americans' divisions over slavery was brought into sharp focus in 1858 in one of the most storied election campaigns in the nation's history. Seeking reelection to the Senate as both a champion of popular sovereignty and the man who had prevented the administration from forcing slavery on the people of Kansas, Douglas faced an unexpectedly strong challenge from Abraham Lincoln, then little known outside of Illinois. Born into a modest farm family in Kentucky in 1809, Lincoln had moved as a youth to frontier Indiana and then Illinois. He had served four terms as a Whig in the state legislature and one in Congress from 1847 to 1849.

Lincoln developed a critique of slavery and its expansion that gave voice to the central values of the emerging Republican Party and the millions of northerners whose loyalty it commanded. His speeches combined the moral fervor of the abolitionists with the respect for order and the Constitution of more conservative northerners. If slavery were allowed to expand, he warned, the "love of liberty" would be extinguished and with it America's special mission to be a symbol of democracy for the entire world.

Lincoln was fascinated and disturbed by the writings of proslavery ideologues like George Fitzhugh (discussed in Chapter 11), and he rose to the defense of northern society. "I want every man to have the chance," said Lincoln, "and I believe a black man is entitled to it, in which he *can* better his condition." Blacks might not be the equal of whites in all respects, but in their "natural right" to the fruits of their labor, they were "my equal and the equal of all others."

The Lincoln-Douglas Campaign

The campaign against Douglas, the North's preeminent political leader, created Lincoln's national reputation. Accepting his party's nomination for the Senate in June 1858, Lincoln announced, "A house divided against itself cannot stand. I believe this government cannot endure, permanently half

"A house divided"

slave and half *free*." Lincoln's point was not that civil war was imminent, but that Americans must choose between favoring and opposing slavery.

The **Lincoln-Douglas debates**, held in seven Illinois towns and attended by tens of thousands of listeners, remain classics of American political oratory. Clashing definitions of freedom lay at their heart. To Lincoln, freedom meant opposition to slavery. Douglas argued, on the other hand, that the essence of freedom lay in local self-government and individual self-determination. A large and diverse nation could only survive by respecting the right of each locality to determine its own institutions. In response to a question posed by Lincoln during the Freeport debate, Douglas insisted that popular sovereignty was not incompatible with the Dred Scott decision. Although territorial legislatures could no longer exclude slavery directly, he argued, if the people wished to keep slaveholders out all they needed to do was refrain from giving the institution legal protection.

Abraham Lincoln in 1858, the year of the Lincoln-Douglas debates.

Lincoln shared many of the racial prejudices of his day. He opposed giving Illinois blacks the right to vote or serve on juries and spoke frequently of colonizing blacks overseas as the best solution to the problems of slavery and race. Yet, unlike Douglas, Lincoln did not use appeals to racism to garner votes. And he refused to exclude blacks from the human family. No less than whites, they were entitled to the inalienable rights of the Declaration of Independence, which applied to "all men, in all lands, everywhere," not merely to Europeans and their descendants.

The 1858 Illinois election returns revealed a state sharply divided, like the nation itself. Southern Illinois, settled from the South, voted strongly Democratic, while the rapidly growing northern part of the state was firmly in the Republican column. Until the adoption of the Seventeenth Amendment in the early twentieth century, each state's legislature chose its U.S. senators. The Democrats emerged with a narrow margin in the legislature, and Douglas was reelected. His victory was remarkable because elsewhere in the North Republicans swept to victory in 1858.

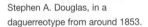

Stephen A. Douglas, in a daguerreotype from around 1853.

John Brown at Harpers Ferry

An armed assault by the abolitionist John Brown on the federal arsenal at **Harpers Ferry**, Virginia, further heightened sectional tensions. During the civil war in Kansas, Brown traveled to the territory. In May 1856, after the attack on Lawrence, he and a few followers murdered five proslavery settlers at Pottawatomie Creek. For the next two years, he traveled through the North and Canada, raising funds and enlisting followers for a war against slavery.

VOICES OF FREEDOM

From the Lincoln-Douglas Debates (1858)

The most famous political campaign in American history, the 1858 race for the U.S. Senate between Senator Stephen A. Douglas (a former Illinois judge) and Abraham Lincoln was highlighted by seven debates in which they discussed the politics of slavery and contrasting understandings of freedom.

DOUGLAS: Mr. Lincoln says that this government cannot endure permanently in the same condition in which it was made by its framers—divided into free and slave states. He says that it has existed for about seventy years thus divided, and yet he tells you that it cannot endure permanently on the same principles and in the same relative conditions in which our fathers made it. . . . One of the reserved rights of the states, was the right to regulate the relations between master and servant, on the slavery question.

Now, my friends, if we will only act conscientiously upon this great principle of popular sovereignty which guarantees to each state and territory the right to do as it pleases on all things local and domestic instead of Congress interfering, we will continue to be at peace one with another.

LINCOLN: Judge Douglas says, "Why can't this Union endure permanently, half slave and half free?" "Why can't we let it stand as our fathers placed it?" That is the exact difficulty between us. . . . I say when this government was first established it was the policy of its founders to prohibit the spread of slavery into the new territories of the United States, where it had not existed. But Judge Douglas and his friends have broken up that policy and placed it upon a new basis by which it is to become national and perpetual. All I have asked or desired anywhere is that it should be placed back again upon the basis that the founders of our government originally placed it—restricting it from the new territories. . . .

Judge Douglas assumes that we have no interest in them—that we have no right to interfere. . . . Do we not wish for an outlet for our surplus population, if I may so express myself? Do we not feel an interest in getting to that outlet with such institutions as we would like to have prevail there? Now irrespective of the moral aspect of this question as to whether there is a right or wrong in enslaving a negro, I am still in favor of our new territories being in such a condition that white men may find a home. I am in favor of this not merely for our own people, but as an outlet for *free white people everywhere*, the world over—in which Hans and Baptiste and Patrick, and all other men from all the world, may find new homes and better their conditions in life.

DOUGLAS: For one, I am opposed to negro citizenship in any and every form. I believe this government was made on the white basis. I believe it was made by white men, for the benefit of white men and their posterity forever . . . I do not believe that the Almighty made the negro capable of self-government. I say to you, my fellow-citizens, that in my opinion the signers of the Declaration of Independence had no reference to the negro whatever when they declared all men to be created equal. They desired to express by that phrase, white men, men of European birth and European descent . . . when they spoke of the equality of men.

LINCOLN: I have no purpose to introduce political and social equality between the white and the black races. There is a physical difference between the two, which in my judgment will probably forever forbid their living together upon the footing of perfect equality, and inasmuch as it becomes a necessity that there must be a difference, I, as well as Judge Douglas, am in favor of the race to which I belong, having the superior position. . . . But I hold that notwithstanding all this, there is no reason in the world why the negro is not entitled to all the natural rights enumerated in the Declaration of Independence, the right to life, liberty, and the pursuit of happiness. I hold that he is as much entitled to these as the white man. I agree with Judge Douglas he is not my equal in many respects—certainly not in color, perhaps not in moral or intellectual endowment. But in the right to eat the bread, without leave of anybody else, which his own hand earns, *he is my equal and the equal of Judge Douglas, and the equal of every living man.*

DOUGLAS: He tells you that I will not argue the question whether slavery is right or wrong. I tell you why I will not do it. . . . I hold that the people of the slaveholding states are civilized men as well as ourselves, that they bear consciences as well as we, and that they are accountable to God and their posterity and not to us. It is for them to decide therefore the moral and religious right of the slavery question for themselves within their own limits. . . . He says that he looks forward to a time when slavery shall be abolished everywhere. I look forward to a time when each state shall be allowed to do as it pleases.

LINCOLN: I suppose that the real difference between Judge Douglas and his friends, and the Republicans, is that the Judge is not in favor of making any difference between slavery and liberty . . . and consequently every sentiment he utters discards the idea that there is any wrong in slavery. . . . That is the real issue. That is the issue that will continue in this country when these poor tongues of Judge Douglas and myself shall be silent. It is the eternal struggle between these two principles—right and wrong—throughout the world.

QUESTIONS

1. *How do Lincoln and Douglas differ on what rights black Americans are entitled to enjoy?*

2. *Why does Lincoln believe the nation cannot exist forever half slave and half free, whereas Douglas believes it can?*

3. *How does each of the speakers balance the right of each state to manage its own affairs against the right of every person to be free?*

John Brown in an 1856 photograph.

On October 16, 1859, with twenty-one men, five of them black, Brown seized Harpers Ferry. The plan made little military sense. Brown's band was soon surrounded and killed or captured by a detachment of federal soldiers headed by Colonel Robert E. Lee. Placed on trial for treason against the state of Virginia, Brown conducted himself with dignity and courage. When Virginia's governor, Henry A. Wise, spurned pleas for clemency and ordered Brown executed, he turned Brown into a martyr to much of the North.

To the South, the failure of Brown's assault seemed less significant than the adulation he seemed to arouse from much of the northern public. His raid and execution further widened the breach between the sections. Brown's last letter was a brief, prophetic statement: "I, John Brown, am quite certain that the crimes of this guilty land will never be purged away but with blood."

The Rise of Southern Nationalism

With the Republicans continuing to gain strength in the North, Democrats might have been expected to put a premium on party unity as the election of 1860 approached. By this time, however, a sizable group of southerners now viewed their region's prospects as more favorable outside the Union than within it. To remain in the Union, secessionists argued, meant to accept "bondage" to the North. But an independent South could become the foundation of a slave empire ringing the Caribbean and embracing Cuba, other West Indian islands, Mexico, and parts of Central America.

Secessionists

More and more southerners were speaking openly of southward expansion. In 1854, Pierre Soulé of Louisiana, the American ambassador to Spain, had persuaded the ministers to Britain and France to join him in signing the Ostend Manifesto, which called on the United States to purchase or seize Cuba, where slavery was still legal, from Spain. Meanwhile, the military adventurer William Walker led a series of **"filibustering" expeditions** (the term derived from the Spanish word for pirate, *filibustero*) in Central America.

Ostend Manifesto

By the late 1850s, southern leaders were bending every effort to strengthen the bonds of slavery. "Slavery is our king," declared a South Carolina politician in 1860. "Slavery is our truth, slavery is our divine right." By early 1860, seven states of the Deep South had gone on record demanding that the Democratic platform pledge to protect slavery in all the territories that had not yet been admitted to the Union as states.

An 1835 painting of the federal arsenal at Harpers Ferry, Virginia (now West Virginia). John Brown's raid on Harpers Ferry in October 1859 helped to bring on the Civil War.

Virtually no northern politician could accept this position. For southern leaders to insist on it would guarantee the destruction of the Democratic Party as a national institution. But southern nationalists, known as **"fire-eaters,"** hoped to split the party and the country and form an independent Southern Confederacy.

The Election of 1860

When the Democratic convention met in April 1860, Douglas's supporters commanded a majority but not the two-thirds required for a presidential nomination. When the convention adopted a platform reaffirming the doctrine of popular sovereignty, delegates from the seven slave states of the Lower South walked out, and the gathering recessed in confusion. Six weeks later, it reconvened, replaced the bolters with Douglas supporters, and nominated him for president. In response, southern Democrats placed their own ticket in the field, headed by John C. Breckinridge of Kentucky. Breckinridge insisted that slavery must be protected in the western territories.

The Democratic Party, the last great bond of national unity, had been shattered. National conventions had traditionally been places where party managers, mindful of the need for unity in the fall campaign, reconciled their differences. But in 1860, neither northern nor southern Democrats were interested in conciliation. Southern Democrats no longer trusted

Democratic Party shattered

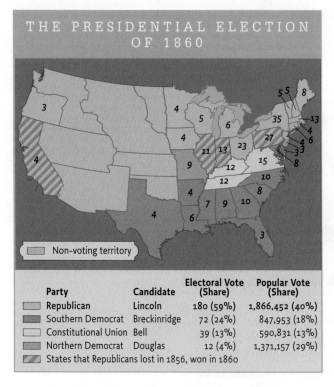

THE PRESIDENTIAL ELECTION OF 1860

Non-voting territory

Party	Candidate	Electoral Vote (Share)	Popular Vote (Share)
Republican	Lincoln	180 (59%)	1,866,452 (40%)
Southern Democrat	Breckinridge	72 (24%)	847,953 (18%)
Constitutional Union	Bell	39 (13%)	590,831 (13%)
Northern Democrat	Douglas	12 (4%)	1,371,157 (29%)
States that Republicans lost in 1856, won in 1860			

their northern counterparts. Douglas's backers, for their part, would not accept a platform that doomed their party to certain defeat in the North.

Meanwhile, Republicans gathered in Chicago and chose Lincoln as their standard-bearer. The party platform denied the validity of the Dred Scott decision, reaffirmed Republicans' opposition to slavery's expansion, and added economic planks designed to appeal to a broad array of northern voters—free homesteads in the West, a protective tariff, and government aid in building a transcontinental railroad.

In effect, two presidential campaigns took place in 1860. In the North, Lincoln and Douglas were the combatants. In the South, the Republicans had no presence, and three candidates contested the election—Douglas, Breckinridge, and John Bell of Tennessee, the candidate of the hastily organized Constitutional Union Party. A haven for Unionist former Whigs, this new party adopted a platform consisting of a single pledge—to preserve "the Constitution as it is [that is, with slavery] and the Union as it was [without sectional discord]."

The election of Lincoln

The most striking thing about the election returns was their sectional character. Lincoln carried all of the North except New Jersey, receiving 1.8 million popular votes (54 percent of the regional total and 40 percent of the national) and 180 electoral votes (a clear majority). Breckinridge captured most of the slave states, although Bell carried three Upper South states and about 40 percent of the southern vote as a whole. Douglas placed first only in Missouri, but he was the only candidate with significant support in all parts of the country. His failure to carry either section, however, suggested that a traditional political career based on devotion to the Union was no longer possible. Without a single vote in ten southern states, Lincoln was elected the nation's sixteenth president. But because of the North's superiority in population, Lincoln would still have carried the electoral college and thus been elected president even if the votes of his three opponents had all been cast for a single candidate.

An 1860 engraving of a mass meeting in Savannah, Georgia, shortly after Lincoln's election as president, which called for the state to secede from the Union. The banner on the obelisk at the center reads, "Our Motto Southern Rights, Equality of the States, Don't Tread on Me"—the last a slogan from the American Revolution.

THE IMPENDING CRISIS

The Secession Movement

In the eyes of many white southerners, Lincoln's victory placed their future at the mercy of a party avowedly hostile to their region's values and interests. Those advocating secession did not believe Lincoln's administration would take immediate steps against slavery in the states. But if, as seemed quite possible, the election of 1860 marked a fundamental shift in power, the beginning of a long period of Republican rule, who could say what the North's antislavery sentiment would demand in five years, or ten? Slaveowners, moreover, feared Republican efforts to extend their party into the South by appealing to non-slaveholders. Rather than accept permanent minority status, Deep South political leaders boldly struck for their region's independence.

Southern response to Lincoln's victory

In the months that followed Lincoln's election, seven states stretching from South Carolina to Texas seceded from the Union. These were the states of the Cotton Kingdom, where slaves represented a larger part of the total population than in the Upper South. First to secede was South Carolina, the state with the highest percentage of slaves in its population and a long history of political radicalism. On December 20, 1860, the legislature unanimously voted to leave the Union. Its *Declaration of the Immediate*

South Carolina

Causes of Secession placed the issue of slavery squarely at the center of the crisis. Experience had proved "that slaveholding states cannot be safe in subjection to nonslaveholding states."

The Secession Crisis

As the Union unraveled, President Buchanan seemed paralyzed. He denied that a state could secede, but he also insisted that the federal government had no right to use force against it. Other political leaders struggled to find a formula to resolve the crisis. Senator John J. Crittenden of Kentucky, a slave state on the border between North and South, offered the most widely supported compromise plan of the secession winter. Embodied in a series of unamendable constitutional amendments, Crittenden's proposal would have guaranteed the future of slavery in the states where it existed and extended the Missouri Compromise line to the Pacific Ocean, dividing between slavery and free soil all territories "now held, or hereafter acquired." The seceding states rejected the compromise as too little, too late. But many in the Upper South and North saw it as a way to settle sectional differences and prevent civil war.

Crittenden compromise

Crittenden's plan, however, foundered on the opposition of Abraham Lincoln. Willing to conciliate the South on issues like the return of fugitive slaves, Lincoln took an unyielding stand against the expansion of slavery. "We have just carried an election," he wrote, "on principles fairly stated to the people. Now we are told in advance that the government shall be broken up unless we surrender to those we have beaten, before we take the offices. . . . If we surrender, it is the end of us and the end of the government."

Lincoln's opposition to the Crittenden plan

Before Lincoln assumed office on March 4, 1861, the seven seceding states formed the Confederate States of America, adopted a constitution, and chose as their president Jefferson Davis of Mississippi. With a few alterations—the president served a single six-year term; cabinet members, as in Britain, could sit in Congress—the Confederate constitution was modeled closely on that of the United States. It departed from the federal Constitution, however, in explicitly guaranteeing slave property both in the states and in any territories the new nation acquired. The "cornerstone" of the Confederacy, announced Davis's vice president, Alexander H. Stephens of Georgia, was "the great truth that the negro is not equal to the white man, that slavery, subordination to the superior race, is his natural and normal condition."

The Confederate States of America

And the War Came

In his inaugural address, delivered on March 4, 1861, Lincoln tried to be conciliatory. He rejected the right of secession but denied any intention of interfering with slavery in the states. He said nothing of retaking the forts, arsenals, and customs houses the Confederacy had seized, although he did promise to "hold" remaining federal property in the seceding states. But Lincoln also issued a veiled warning: "In your hands, my dissatisfied fellow countrymen, and not in mine, is the momentous issue of civil war."

Lincoln's response to secession

In his first month as president, Lincoln walked a tightrope. He avoided any action that might drive more states from the Union, encouraged southern Unionists to assert themselves within the Confederacy, and sought to quiet a growing clamor in the North for forceful action against secession. Knowing that the risk of war existed, Lincoln strove to ensure that if hostilities did break out, the South, not the Union, would fire the first shot. And that is precisely what happened on April 12, 1861, at Fort Sumter, an enclave of Union control in the harbor of Charleston, South Carolina.

A few days earlier, Lincoln had notified South Carolina's governor that he intended to replenish the garrison's dwindling food supplies. Viewing Fort Sumter's presence as an affront to southern nationhood and perhaps hoping to force the wavering Upper South to join the

Fort Sumter

Inauguration of Mr. Lincoln, a photograph taken on March 4, 1861. The unfinished dome of the Capitol building symbolizes the precarious state of the Union at the time Lincoln assumed office.

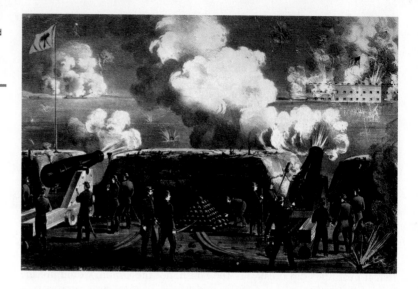

Bombardment of Fort Sumter, a lithograph by Nathaniel Currier and James Ives depicting the beginning of the Civil War.

Confederacy, Jefferson Davis ordered batteries to fire on the fort. On April 14, its commander surrendered. The following day, Lincoln proclaimed that an insurrection existed in the South and called for 75,000 troops to suppress it. Civil war had begun. Within weeks, Virginia, North Carolina, Tennessee, and Arkansas joined the Confederacy. "Both sides deprecated war," Lincoln later said, "but one of them would *make* war rather than let the nation survive; and the other would *accept* war rather than let it perish. And the war came."

The Union created by the founders lay in ruins. The struggle to rebuild it would bring about a new birth of American freedom.

CHAPTER REVIEW AND ONLINE RESOURCES

REVIEW QUESTIONS

1. *Explain the justifications for the doctrine of manifest destiny, including material and idealistic motivations.*

2. *Why did many Americans criticize the Mexican War? How did they see expansion as a threat to American liberties?*

3. *How did the concept of "race" develop by the mid-nineteenth century? How did it enter into the manifest destiny debate?*

4. *How did western expansion affect the sectional tensions between the North and South?*

5. *How did the market revolution contribute to the rise of the Republican Party? How did those economic and political factors serve to unite groups in the Northeast and in the Northwest, and why was that unity significant?*

6. *Based on the Lincoln-Douglas debates, how did the two differ on the expansion of slavery, equal rights, and the role of the national government? Use examples of their words to illustrate your points.*

7. *Why did Stephen Douglas, among others, believe that "popular sovereignty" could resolve sectional divisions of the 1850s? Why did the idea not work out?*

8. *Explain how sectional voting patterns in the 1860 presidential election allowed southern "fire-eaters" to justify secession.*

9. *What do the California gold rush and the opening of Japan reveal about the United States involvement in a global economic system?*

KEY TERMS

Tejanos (p. 370)

Texas revolt (p. 370)

Santa Anna (p. 370)

"reannexation" of Texas and "reoccupation" of Oregon (p. 371)

gold rush (p. 376)

Commodore Matthew Perry (p. 377)

Wilmot Proviso (p. 378)

Free Soil Party (p. 379)

Compromise of 1850 (p. 380)

Fugitive Slave Act (p. 381)

popular sovereignty (p. 382)

Kansas-Nebraska Act (p. 382)

Know-Nothing Party (p. 385)

"Bleeding Kansas" (p. 388)

Dred Scott decision (p. 389)

Lincoln-Douglas debates (p. 391)

Harpers Ferry (p. 391)

"filibustering" expeditions (p. 394)

"fire-eaters" (p. 395)

wwnorton.com
/studyspace

VISIT STUDYSPACE FOR THESE
RESOURCES AND MORE

- A chapter outline
- A diagnostic chapter quiz
- Interactive maps
- Map worksheets
- Multimedia documents

CHAPTER 14

A NEW BIRTH OF FREEDOM

★

THE CIVIL WAR, 1861–1865

Departure of the 7th Regiment, a lithograph from 1861 illustrating the departure of a unit of the New York State militia for service in the Civil War. A contemporary writer captured the exuberant spirit of the early days of the war: "New York was certainly raving mad with excitement. The ladies laughed, smiled, sighed, sobbed, and wept. The men cheered and shouted as never men cheered and shouted before."

ike hundreds of thousands of other Americans, Marcus M. Spiegel volunteered in 1861 to fight in the Civil War. Born into a Jewish family in Germany in 1829, Spiegel emigrated to Ohio, where he married the daughter of a local farmer. When the Civil War broke out, the nation's 150,000 Jews represented less than 1 percent of the total population. But Spiegel shared wholeheartedly in American patriotism. He went to war, he wrote to his brother-in-law, to defend "the flag that was ever ready to protect you and me and every one who sought its protection from oppression." He never wavered in his commitment to the "glorious cause" of preserving the Union and its heritage of freedom.

What one Pennsylvania recruit called "the magic word *Freedom*" shaped how many Union soldiers understood the conflict. But as the war progressed, prewar understandings of liberty gave way to something new. Millions of northerners who had not been abolitionists became convinced that preserving the Union required the destruction of slavery. Marcus Spiegel's changing views mirrored this transformation. Spiegel was an ardent Democrat. He shared the era's racist attitudes and thought Lincoln's Emancipation Proclamation a serious mistake. Yet as the Union army penetrated the heart of the Deep South, Spiegel became increasingly opposed to slavery. "Since I am here," he wrote to his wife from Louisiana in January 1864, "I have learned and seen . . . the horrors of slavery. . . . Never hereafter will I either speak or vote in favor of slavery."

Marcus Spiegel was killed in a minor engagement in Louisiana in May 1864, one of hundreds of thousands of Americans to perish in the Civil War.

FOCUS QUESTIONS

- *Why is the Civil War considered the first modern war?*

- *How did a war to preserve the Union become a war to end slavery?*

- *How did the Civil War transform the national economy and create a stronger nation-state?*

- *How did the war effort affect the society and economy of the Confederacy?*

- *What were the military and political turning points of the war?*

- *What were the most important wartime "rehearsals for Reconstruction"?*

THE FIRST MODERN WAR

The American Civil War is often called the **first modern war**. Never before had mass armies confronted each other on the battlefield with the deadly weapons created by the industrial revolution. The resulting casualties dwarfed anything in the American experience. Beginning as a battle of army versus army, the war became a conflict of society against society, in which the distinction between military and civilian targets often disappeared. In a war of this kind, the effectiveness of political leadership, the ability to mobilize economic resources, and a society's willingness to keep up the fight despite setbacks are as crucial to the outcome as success or failure on individual battlefields.

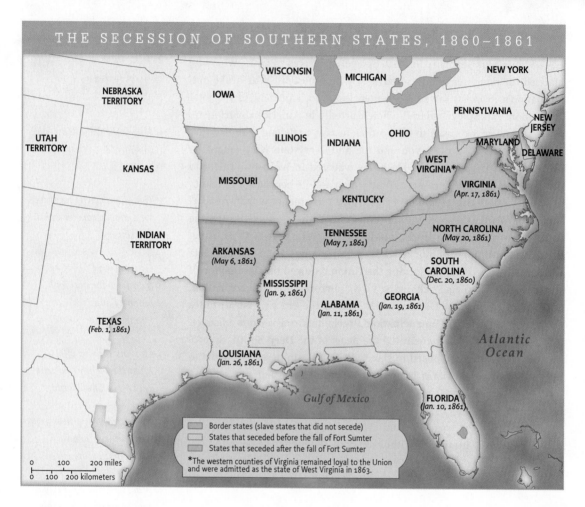

THE SECESSION OF SOUTHERN STATES, 1860–1861

WISCONSIN
MICHIGAN
NEW YORK
NEBRASKA TERRITORY
IOWA
PENNSYLVANIA
NEW JERSEY
UTAH TERRITORY
ILLINOIS
INDIANA
OHIO
MARYLAND
DELAWARE
KANSAS
WEST VIRGINIA*
MISSOURI
VIRGINIA (Apr. 17, 1861)
KENTUCKY
INDIAN TERRITORY
TENNESSEE (May 7, 1861)
NORTH CAROLINA (May 20, 1861)
ARKANSAS (May 6, 1861)
SOUTH CAROLINA (Dec. 20, 1860)
MISSISSIPPI (Jan. 9, 1861)
GEORGIA (Jan. 19, 1861)
ALABAMA (Jan. 11, 1861)
TEXAS (Feb. 1, 1861)
LOUISIANA (Jan. 26, 1861)
Atlantic Ocean
Gulf of Mexico
FLORIDA (Jan. 10, 1861)

Border states (slave states that did not secede)
States that seceded before the fall of Fort Sumter
States that seceded after the fall of Fort Sumter
*The western counties of Virginia remained loyal to the Union and were admitted as the state of West Virginia in 1863.

0   100   200 miles
0   100   200 kilometers

By the time secession ran its course, eleven slave states had left the Union.

Advantages of the North and South

The Two Combatants

Almost any comparison between Union and Confederacy seemed to favor the Union. The population of the North and the loyal border slave states numbered 22 million in 1860, whereas only 9 million persons lived in the Confederacy, 3.5 million of them slaves. In manufacturing, railroad mileage, and financial resources, the Union far outstripped its opponent. On the other hand, the Union confronted by far the greater task. To restore the shattered nation, it had to invade and conquer an area larger than western Europe. Moreover, Confederate soldiers were highly motivated fighters, defending their homes and families.

On both sides, the outbreak of war stirred powerful feelings of patriotism. Recruits rushed to enlist, expecting a short, glorious war. Later, as enthusiasm waned, both sides resorted to a **draft**. By 1865, more

Sergeant James W. Travis, Thirty-eighth Illinois Infantry, Union army, and Private Edwin Francis Jemison, Second Louisiana Regiment, Confederate army, two of the nearly 3 million Americans who fought in the Civil War. Before going off to war, many soldiers sat for photographs like these, reproduced on small cards called *cartes de visite*, which they distributed to friends and loved ones. Jemison was killed in the Battle of Malvern Hill in July 1862.

than 2 million men had served in the Union army and 900,000 in the Confederate army. Each was a cross section of its society: the North's was composed largely of farm boys, shopkeepers, artisans, and urban workers, while the South's consisted mostly of non-slaveholding small farmers, with slaveowners dominating the officer corps.

Soldiers North and South

The Technology of War

Neither the soldiers nor their officers were prepared for the way technology had transformed warfare. The Civil War was the first major conflict in which the railroad transported troops and supplies and the first to see railroad junctions such as Atlanta and Petersburg become major military objectives. The famous sea battle between the Union vessel ***Monitor*** and the Confederate ***Merrimac*** in 1862 was the first demonstration of the superiority of ironclads over wooden ships, revolutionizing naval warfare. The war saw the use of the telegraph for military communication, the introduction of observation balloons to view enemy lines, and even primitive hand grenades and submarines.

Ironclad ships

Perhaps most important, a revolution in arms manufacturing had replaced the traditional musket, accurate at only a short range, with the more modern rifle, deadly at 600 yards or more because of its grooved (or "rifled") barrel. This development changed the nature of combat, emphasizing the importance of heavy fortifications and elaborate trenches and giving those on the defensive—usually southern armies—a significant advantage over attacking forces. The war of rifle and trench produced the appalling casualty statistics of Civil War battles. The most recent estimate

The rifle

An eight-inch cannon, one of the weapons forged in the industrial revolution and deployed in the Civil War.

of those who perished in the war—around 750,000 men—represents the equivalent, in terms of today's population, of more than 7 million men. The death toll in the Civil War nearly equals the total number of Americans who died in all the nation's other wars, from the Revolution to the war in Iraq.

Nor was either side ready for other aspects of modern warfare. Medical care remained primitive. Diseases such as measles, dysentery, malaria, and typhus swept through army camps, killing more men than did combat. The Civil War was the first war in which large numbers of Americans were captured by the enemy and held in dire conditions in military prisons. Some 50,000 men died in these prisons, victims of starvation and disease, including 13,000 Union soldiers at Andersonville, Georgia.

The Public and the War

Propaganda

Another modern feature of the Civil War was that both sides were assisted by a vast propaganda effort to mobilize public opinion. In the Union, an outpouring of lithographs, souvenirs, sheet music, and pamphlets issued

War Spirit at Home, an 1866 painting by the New Jersey artist Lilly M. Spencer, depicts a family reading the news of the Union capture of Vicksburg in 1863. The household is now composed of women and children; the husband may be off in the army. While the children play as soldiers, the cross in the folds of the newspaper suggests a less celebratory reflection on the conflict. Newspapers brought news of the war into American homes.

by patriotic organizations and the War Department reaffirmed northern values, tarred the Democratic Party with the brush of treason, and accused the South of numerous crimes against Union soldiers and loyal civilians. Comparable items appeared in the Confederacy.

At the same time, the war's brutal realities were brought home with unprecedented immediacy to the public at large. War correspondents accompanied the armies, and newspapers reported the results of battles on the following day and quickly published long lists of casualties. The infant art of photography carried images of war into millions of American living rooms.

Mobilizing Resources

The outbreak of the war found both sides unprepared. In 1861, there was no national railroad gauge (the distance separating the two tracks), so trains built for one line could not run on another. There was no national banking system, no tax system capable of raising the enormous funds needed to finance the war, and not even accurate maps of the southern states. Soon after the firing on Fort Sumter, Lincoln proclaimed a naval blockade of the South, part of the so-called Anaconda Plan, which aimed to strangle the South economically. But the navy charged with patrolling the 3,500-mile coastline consisted of only ninety vessels, fewer than half of them steam powered. Not until late in the war did the blockade become effective.

Then there was the problem of purchasing and distributing the food, weapons, and other supplies required by the soldiers. The Union army eventually became the best-fed and best-supplied military force in history. By the war's third year, on the other hand, southern armies were suffering from acute shortages of food, uniforms, and shoes.

Military Strategies

Each side tried to find ways to maximize its advantages. Essentially, the Confederacy adopted a defensive strategy, with occasional thrusts into the North. General Robert E. Lee, the leading southern commander, was a brilliant battlefield tactician who felt confident of his ability to fend off

A defensive strategy

FIGURE 14.1 Resources for War: Union versus Confederacy

Population	22 million
	9 million (including 3.5 million slaves)
Factories	110,000
	18,000
	■ Union
	■ Confederacy
Value of goods produced	1.5 billion
	155 million
Railroad tracks (% of total U.S. mileage)	70%
	30%
Textiles (including cotton cloth and woolen goods)	Ratio 17:1
Firearms	Ratio 32:1
Pig iron	Ratio 20:1

In nearly every resource for warfare, the Union enjoyed a distinct advantage. But this did not make Union victory inevitable; as in the War of Independence, the stronger side sometimes loses.

Union army wagons crossing the Rapidan River in Virginia in May 1864. Supplying Civil War armies required an immense mobilization of economic resources.

attacks by larger Union forces. He hoped that a series of defeats would weaken the North's resolve and lead it eventually to abandon the conflict and recognize southern independence.

Lincoln's early generals initially concentrated on occupying southern territory and attempting to capture Richmond, the Confederate capital. They attacked sporadically and withdrew after a battle, thus sacrificing the North's manpower superiority and allowing the South to concentrate its smaller forces when an engagement impended. Well before his generals did, Lincoln realized that simply capturing and occupying territory would not win the war, and that defeating the South's armies, not capturing its capital, had to be the North's battlefield objective. And when he came to adopt the policy of emancipation, Lincoln acknowledged what Confederate vice president Alexander H. Stephens had already affirmed: slavery was the "cornerstone" of the Confederacy. To win the war, therefore, the Union must make the institution that lay at the economic and social foundation of southern life a military target.

Changing northern strategy

The War Begins

In the East, most of the war's fighting took place in a narrow corridor between Washington and Richmond—a distance of only 100 miles—as a succession of Union generals led the Army of the Potomac (as the main northern force in the East was called) toward the Confederate capital, only to be turned back by southern forces. The first significant engagement, the first Battle of Bull Run, took place in northern Virginia on July 21, 1861. It ended with the chaotic retreat of the Union soldiers, along with the sight-seers and politicians who had come to watch the battle.

First Bull Run

In the wake of Bull Run, George B. McClellan, an army engineer who had recently won a minor engagement with Confederate troops in western Virginia, assumed command of the Union's Army of the Potomac. A brilliant organizer, McClellan succeeded in welding his men into a superb fighting force. He seemed reluctant, however, to commit them to

McClellan

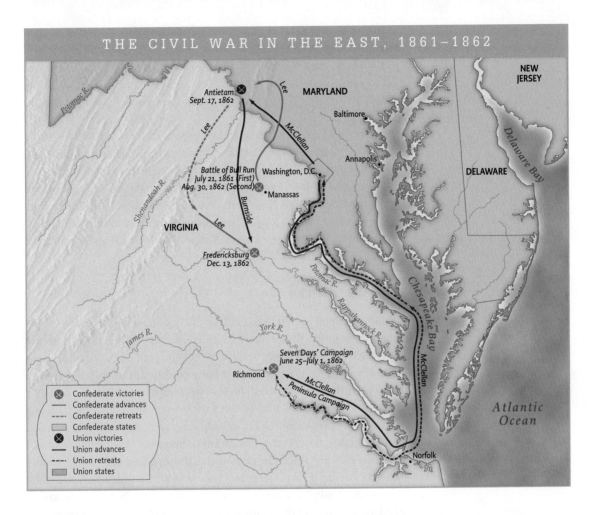

THE CIVIL WAR IN THE EAST, 1861–1862

battle, since he tended to overestimate the size of enemy forces. And as a Democrat, he hoped that compromise might end the war without large-scale loss of life or a weakening of slavery. Months of military inactivity followed.

During the first two years of the war, most of the fighting took place in Virginia and Maryland.

The War in the East, 1862

Not until the spring of 1862, after a growing clamor for action by Republican newspapers, members of Congress, and an increasingly impatient Lincoln, did McClellan lead his army of more than 100,000 men into Virginia. Here they confronted the smaller Army of Northern Virginia under the command of the Confederate general Joseph E. Johnston, and after he was wounded, Robert E. Lee. In the Seven Days' Campaign, a series of engagements in June 1862 on the peninsula south of Richmond, Lee blunted McClellan's attacks and forced him to withdraw back to the vicinity of Washington, D.C. In August 1862, Lee again emerged victorious at the second Battle of Bull Run against Union forces under the command of General John Pope.

Successful on the defensive, Lee now launched an invasion of the North. At the **Battle of Antietam**, in Maryland, McClellan and the Army of the Potomac repelled Lee's advance. In a single day of fighting, nearly 4,000 men were killed and 18,000 wounded (2,000 of whom later died of their injuries). More Americans died on September 17, 1862, when the Battle of Antietam was fought, than on any other day in the nation's history, including Pearl Harbor and D-Day in World War II and the terrorist attacks of September 11, 2001.

The War in the West

While the Union accomplished little in the East in the first two years of the war, events in the West followed a different course. Here, the architect of early success was Ulysses S. Grant. A West Point graduate who had resigned

from the army in 1854, Grant had been notably unsuccessful in civilian life. When the war broke out, he was working as a clerk in his brother's leather store in Galena, Illinois. But after being commissioned as a colonel in an Illinois regiment, Grant quickly displayed the daring, the logical mind, and the grasp of strategy he would demonstrate throughout the war.

In February 1862, Grant won the Union's first significant victory when he captured Forts Henry and Donelson in Tennessee. In April, naval forces under Admiral David G. Farragut steamed into New Orleans, giving the Union control of the South's largest city and the rich sugar plantation parishes to its south and west. At the same time, Grant withstood a surprise Confederate attack at Shiloh, Tennessee. But Union momentum in the West then stalled.

THE COMING OF EMANCIPATION

Slavery and the War

War, it has been said, is the midwife of revolution. And the Civil War produced far-reaching changes in American life. The most dramatic of these was the destruction of slavery, the central institution of southern society.

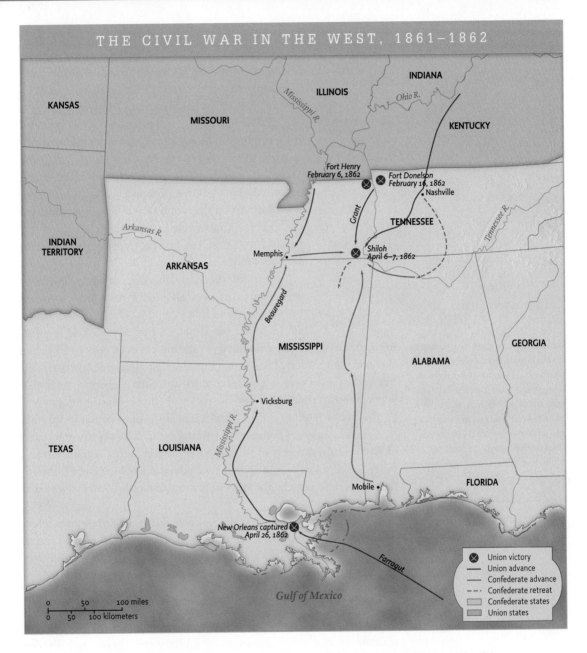

THE CIVIL WAR IN THE WEST, 1861–1862

Most of the Union's victories in the first two years of the war occurred in the West, especially at Shiloh and New Orleans.

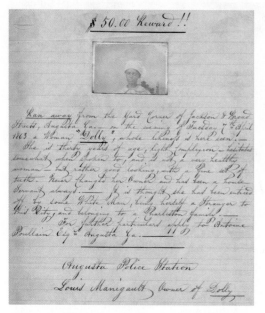

An 1863 advertisement for a runaway domestic slave circulated by Louis Manigault, a member of a prominent Georgia and South Carolina planter family. Manigault blamed an unknown white man for enticing her away, but she most likely escaped with a male slave who had begun to court her. Slaves fled to Union lines from the first days of the Civil War.

The "freedom war"

In numbers, scale, and the economic power of the institution of slavery, American emancipation dwarfed that of any other country (although far more people were liberated in 1861 when Czar Alexander II abolished serfdom in the Russian empire).

Lincoln initially insisted that slavery was irrelevant to the conflict. In the war's first year, his paramount concerns were to keep the border slave states—Delaware, Maryland, Kentucky, and Missouri—in the Union and to build the broadest base of support in the North for the war effort. Action against slavery, he feared, would drive the border, with its white population of 2.6 million and nearly 500,000 slaves, into the Confederacy and alienate conservative northerners.

Thus, in the early days of the war, a nearly unanimous Congress adopted a resolution proposed by Senator John J. Crittenden of Kentucky, which affirmed that the Union had no intention of interfering with slavery. Northern military commanders even returned fugitive slaves to their owners, a policy that raised an outcry in antislavery circles. Yet as the Confederacy set slaves to work as military laborers and blacks began to escape to Union lines, the policy of ignoring slavery unraveled. By the end of 1861, the military had adopted the plan, begun in Virginia by General Benjamin F. Butler, of treating escaped blacks as contraband of war—that is, property of military value subject to confiscation. Butler's order added a word to the war's vocabulary. Escaping slaves ("**contrabands**") were housed by the army in "contraband camps" and educated in new "contraband schools."

Meanwhile, slaves themselves took actions that helped propel a reluctant white America down the road to emancipation. Well before Lincoln made emancipation a war aim, blacks, in the North and the South, were calling the conflict the "freedom war." In 1861 and 1862, as the federal army occupied Confederate territory, slaves by the thousands headed for Union lines. Unlike fugitives before the war, these runaways included large numbers of women and children, as entire families abandoned the plantations. Not a few passed along military intelligence and detailed knowledge of the South's terrain. In southern Louisiana, the arrival of the Union army in 1862 led slaves to sack plantation houses and refuse to work unless wages were paid. Slavery there, wrote a northern reporter, "is forever destroyed and worthless, no matter what Mr. Lincoln or anyone else may say on the subject."

Steps toward Emancipation

The most uncompromising opponents of slavery before the war, abolitionists and **Radical Republicans**, quickly concluded that the institution must become a target of the Union war effort. Outside of Congress, few pressed the case for emancipation more eloquently than Frederick Douglass. From the outset, he insisted that it was futile to "separate the freedom of the slave from the victory of the government."

These appeals won increasing support in a Congress frustrated by lack of military success. In March 1862, Congress prohibited the army from returning fugitive slaves. Then came abolition in the District of Columbia (with monetary compensation for slaveholders) and the territories, followed in July by the Second Confiscation Act, which liberated slaves of disloyal owners in Union-occupied territory, as well as slaves who escaped to Union lines.

Congressional policy against slavery

Throughout these months, Lincoln struggled to retain control of the emancipation issue. In August 1861, John C. Frémont, commanding Union forces in Missouri, a state racked by a bitter guerrilla war between pro-northern and pro-southern bands, decreed the freedom of its slaves. Fearful of the order's impact on the border states, Lincoln swiftly rescinded it. In November, the president proposed that the border states embark on a program of gradual emancipation with the federal government paying owners for their loss of property. He also revived the idea of colonization. In August 1862, Lincoln met at the White House with a delegation of black leaders and urged them to promote emigration from the United States. "You and we are different races," he declared. "It is better for us both to be separated." As late as December, the president signed an agreement with a shady entrepreneur to settle former slaves on an island off the coast of Haiti.

Lincoln's evolving policy

Abe Lincoln's Last Card, an engraving from the British magazine *Punch*, October 18, 1862, portrays the Preliminary Emancipation Proclamation as the last move of a desperate gambler.

Lincoln's Decision

Sometime during the summer of 1862, Lincoln concluded that emancipation had become a political and military necessity. Many factors contributed to his decision—lack of military success, hope that emancipated slaves might help meet the army's growing manpower needs, changing northern public opinion, and the calculation that making slavery a target of the war effort would counteract sentiment in Britain for recognition of the Confederacy. But on the advice of Secretary of State

ABE LINCOLN'S LAST CARD OR, ROUGE-ET-NOIR.

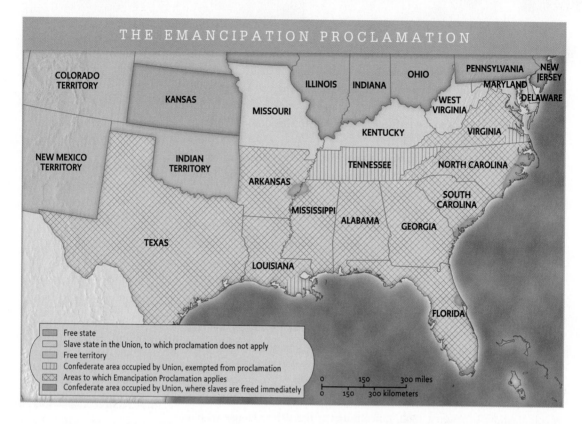

THE EMANCIPATION PROCLAMATION

Legend:
- Free state
- Slave state in the Union, to which proclamation does not apply
- Free territory
- Confederate area occupied by Union, exempted from proclamation
- Areas to which Emancipation Proclamation applies
- Confederate area occupied by Union, where slaves are freed immediately

0   150   300 miles
0   150   300 kilometers

With the exception of a few areas, the Emancipation Proclamation applied only to slaves in parts of the Confederacy not under Union control on January 1, 1863. Lincoln did not "free the slaves" with a stroke of his pen, but the proclamation did change the nature of the Civil War.

William H. Seward, Lincoln delayed his announcement until after a Union victory, lest it seem an act of desperation. On September 22, 1862, five days after McClellan's army forced Lee to retreat at Antietam, Lincoln issued the Preliminary Emancipation Proclamation. It warned that unless the South laid down its arms by the end of 1862, he would decree abolition.

The initial northern reaction was not encouraging. In the fall elections of 1862, Democrats made opposition to emancipation the centerpiece of their campaign. The Republicans suffered sharp reverses. In his annual message to Congress, early in December, Lincoln tried to calm northerners' racial fears: "In giving freedom to the slave, we assure freedom to the free—honorable alike in what we give, and what we preserve."

The Emancipation Proclamation

Effects of the Emancipation Proclamation

On January 1, 1863, after greeting visitors at the annual White House New Year's reception, Lincoln retired to his study to sign the **Emancipation Proclamation**. The document did not liberate all the slaves—indeed, on the day it was issued, it applied to very few. Because its legality derived from the president's authority as military commander-in-chief to combat the South's rebellion, the proclamation exempted areas firmly under Union control (where the war, in effect, had already ended). Thus, it did not apply to the loyal border slave states that had never seceded or to areas of the Confederacy occupied by Union soldiers, such as Tennessee and parts of Virginia and Louisiana. But the vast majority of the South's slaves—more than 3 million men, women, and children—it declared "henceforward shall be free." Since most of these slaves were still behind Confederate lines, however, their liberation would have to await Union victories.

Despite its limitations, the proclamation set off scenes of jubilation among free blacks and abolitionists in the North and "contrabands" and slaves in the South. "Sound the loud timbrel o'er Egypt's dark sea," intoned a black preacher at a celebration in Boston. "Jehovah hath triumphed, his people are free." By making the Union army an agent of emancipation and wedding the goals of Union and abolition, the proclamation sounded the eventual death knell of slavery.

Not only did the Emancipation Proclamation alter the nature of the Civil War and the course of American history, but it also marked a turning point in Lincoln's own thinking. For the first time, it committed the government to enlisting black soldiers in the Union army. He would later refuse suggestions that he rescind or modify the proclamation in the interest of peace. Were he to do so, he told one visitor, "I should be damned in time and eternity."

Like the end of slavery in Haiti and mainland Latin America, abolition in the United States came about as the result of war. But emancipation

Freed Negroes Celebrating President Lincoln's Decree of Emancipation, a fanciful engraving from the French periodical *Le Monde Illustré*, March 21, 1863.

in the United States differed from its counterparts elsewhere in the Western Hemisphere—it was immediate, not gradual, and offered no compensation to slaveholders for their loss of property (with the exception of those in Washington, D.C.). Not until 1888, when Brazil abolished the institution, did slavery come to an end in the entire Western Hemisphere.

The evolution of Lincoln's emancipation policy displayed the hallmarks of his wartime leadership—his capacity for growth and his ability to develop broad public support for his administration.

Enlisting Black Troops

Of the proclamation's provisions, few were more radical in their implications than the enrollment of blacks into military service. Since sailor had been one of the few occupations open to free blacks before the war, Secretary of the Navy Gideon Welles had already allowed African-Americans to serve on Union warships. But at the outset, the Union army refused to accept northern black volunteers. The administration feared that whites would not be willing to fight alongside blacks and that enlisting black soldiers would alienate the border slave states that remained in the Union.

By the end of the war, however, more than 180,000 black men had served in the Union army and 24,000 in the navy. One-third died in battle, or of wounds or disease. Some black units won considerable renown, among them the Fifty-fourth Massachusetts Volunteers, a company of free blacks from throughout the North commanded by Robert Gould Shaw, a young reformer from a prominent Boston family. The bravery of the Fifty-fourth in the July 1863 attack on Fort Wagner, South Carolina, where nearly half the unit, including Shaw, perished, helped to dispel widespread doubts about blacks' ability to withstand the pressures of the Civil War battlefield.

Most black soldiers were emancipated slaves who joined the army in the South. After Union forces in 1863 seized control of the rich plantation lands of the Mississippi Valley, General Lorenzo Thomas raised fifty regiments of black soldiers—some 76,000 men in all. Another large group hailed from the border states exempted from the Emancipation Proclamation, where enlistment was, for most of the war, the only route to freedom. Here black military service undermined slavery, for Congress expanded the Emancipation Proclamation to liberate black soldiers and their families.

The Black Soldier

For black soldiers themselves, military service proved to be a liberating experience. Out of the army came many of the leaders of the Reconstruction era. At least 130 former soldiers served in political office after the Civil

War. In time, the memory of black military service would fade from white America's collective memory. Of the hundreds of Civil War monuments that still dot the northern landscape, fewer than a dozen contain an image of a black soldier. But well into the twentieth century, it remained a point of pride in black families throughout the United States that their fathers and grandfathers had fought for freedom.

Within the army, however, black soldiers received treatment that was anything but equal to that of their white counterparts. Organized into segregated units under sometimes abusive white officers, they initially received lower pay (ten dollars per month, compared to sixteen dollars for white soldiers). They were dispro-portionately assigned to labor rather than combat, and they could not rise to the rank of commissioned officer until the very end of the war. In a notorious incident in 1864, 200 of 262 black soldiers died when southern troops under the command of Nathan B. Forrest overran Fort Pillow in Tennessee. Some of those who perished were killed after surrendering.

This is the only known photograph of a black Union soldier with his family.

Nonetheless, black soldiers played a crucial role not only in winning the Civil War but also in defining the war's consequences. Thanks in part to black military service, many Republicans in the last two years of the war came to believe that emancipation must bring with it equal protection of the laws regardless of race. One of the first acts of the federal government to recognize this principle was the granting of retroactive equal pay to black soldiers early in 1865.

The illustration accompanying *The American Flag*, a piece of patriotic Civil War sheet music, exemplifies how the war united the ideals of liberty and nationhood.

The service of black soldiers affected Lincoln's own outlook. In 1864, Lincoln, who before the war had never supported suffrage for African-Americans, urged the governor of Union-occupied Louisiana to work for the partial enfranchisement of blacks, singling out soldiers as especially deserving. At some future time, he observed, they might again be called upon to "keep the *jewel of Liberty* in the family of freedom."

THE SECOND AMERICAN REVOLUTION

The changing status of black Americans was only one dramatic example of what some historians call the **Second American Revolution**—the transformation of American government and society brought about by the Civil War.

A songbook compiled and illustrated by a Union soldier includes "John Brown's Body," sung to the melody of a Methodist hymn.

Liberty, Union, and Nation

Never was freedom's contested nature more evident than during the Civil War. "We all declare for liberty," Lincoln observed in 1864, "but in using the same *word* we do not all mean the same *thing*." To the North, he continued, freedom meant for "each man" to enjoy "the product of his labor." To southern whites, it conveyed mastership—the power to do "as they please with other men, and the product of other men's labor." The Union's triumph consolidated the northern understanding of freedom as the national norm.

But it was Lincoln himself who linked the conflict with the deepest beliefs of northern society. It is sometimes said that the American Civil War was part of a broader nineteenth-century process of nation building. Throughout the world, powerful, centralized nation-states developed in old countries, and new nations emerged where none had previously existed. The Civil War took place as modern states were consolidating their power and reducing local autonomy. The Meiji Restoration in Japan saw the emperor reclaim power from local lords, or shoguns. Lincoln has been called the American equivalent of Giuseppe Mazzini or Otto von Bismarck, who during this same era created nation-states in Italy and Germany from disunited collections of principalities. But Lincoln's nation was different from those being constructed in Europe. They were based on the idea of unifying a particular people with a common ethnic, cultural, and linguistic heritage. To Lincoln, the American nation embodied a set of universal ideas, centered on political democracy and human liberty.

The Gettysburg Address

Lincoln summarized his conception of the war's meaning in November 1863 in brief remarks at the dedication of a military cemetery at the site of the war's greatest battle. The Gettysburg Address is considered his finest speech (see the Appendix for the full text). In less than three minutes, he identified the nation's mission with the principle that "all men are created equal," spoke of the war as bringing about a "new birth of freedom," and defined the essence of democratic government. The sacrifices of Union soldiers, he declared, would ensure that "government of the people, by the people, for the people, shall not perish from the earth."

Expansion of the American nation-state

The mobilization of the Union's resources for modern war brought into being a new American nation-state with greatly expanded powers and responsibilities. The United States remained a federal republic with sovereignty divided between the state and national governments. But the war forged a new national self-consciousness, reflected in the increasing use of the word "nation"—a unified political entity—in place of the older "Union" of separate states. In his inaugural address in 1861, Lincoln used the word "Union" twenty times, while making no mention of the "nation." By

1863, "Union" does not appear at all in the 269-word Gettysburg Address, while Lincoln referred five times to the "nation."

The War and American Religion

The upsurge of patriotism, and of national power, was reflected in many aspects of American life. Even as the war produced unprecedented casualties, the northern Protestant clergy strove to provide it with a religious justification and to reassure their congregations that the dead had not died in vain. The religious press now devoted more space to military and political developments than to spiritual matters. In numerous wartime sermons, Christianity and patriotism were joined in a **civic religion** that saw the war as God's mechanism for ridding the United States of slavery and enabling it to become what it had never really been—a land of freedom. Of course, the southern clergy was equally convinced that the Confederate cause represented God's will.

Religious beliefs enabled Americans to cope with the unprecedented mass death the war involved. Coping with death, moreover, required unprecedented governmental action, from notifying next of kin to accounting for the dead and missing. Both the Union and Confederacy established elaborate systems for gathering statistics and maintaining records of dead and wounded soldiers, an effort supplemented by private philanthropic organizations. After the war ended, the federal government embarked on

Lincoln and the Female Slave, by the free black artist David B. Bowser. Working in Philadelphia, Bowser painted flags for a number of black Civil War regiments. Lincoln confers freedom on a kneeling slave, an image that downplays blacks' role in their own emancipation.

A priest conducts mass for the Sixty-ninth New York State militia, stationed in Washington, D.C., in June 1861. The famed photographer Mathew Brady took this photo, which illustrates how the war mitigated the anti-Catholic bias so prominent in the 1850s.

VOICES OF FREEDOM

From Letter of Thomas F. Drayton
(April 17, 1861)

A South Carolina plantation owner and ardent supporter of secession, Thomas F. Drayton explained the Confederate cause in this letter to his brother Percival, an officer in the U.S. Navy, written from Charleston shortly after the firing on Fort Sumter. Drayton went on to serve as a brigadier general in the Confederate army.

My dear Percy

And so Sumter is at last ours, and this too without the loss of a *single* life upon either side.... Before this dispute is over however, I look for abundance of death & blood....

You say I don't yet understand the position you have taken. I do fully, but certainly differ from you when you say that to side with us, would be "battling for slavery against freedom." On the contrary, by siding with us, you likewise defend yourselves at the North against a far greater danger than we are threatened with, which is the enslavement of the *whites*; for the tendency with you is towards consolidation & the abrogation of State rights.... All these evils & horrors will be laid to your doors, because you have encouraged . . . in the form of abolition lecturers, fanatical preachers, unscrupulous editors, selfish politicians; . . . and by voting for men . . . with the *avowed object* of abolishing slavery throughout the Southern States . . . who made a merit of John Brown's murderous invasion; set at defiance all fugitive slave laws, . . . and whose clergy denounced us indiscriminately as barbarians....

We are fighting for home & liberty. Can the North say as much? Good night. And don't say again, that in siding for us, you would be defending slavery and fighting for what is abhorrent to your feelings & convictions. On the contrary, in fighting on our side, you will be battling for law & order & against abstract fanatical ideas which will certainly bring about vastly greater evils upon our race, than could possibly result from the perpetuation of slavery among us.

From Abraham Lincoln, Address at Sanitary Fair, Baltimore (April 18, 1864)

Abraham Lincoln's speech at a Sanitary Fair (a grand bazaar that raised money for the care of Union soldiers) offers a dramatic illustration of the contested meaning of freedom during the Civil War.

The world has never had a good definition of the word liberty, and the American people, just now, are much in want of one. We all declare for liberty; but in using the same *word* we do not all mean the same *thing*. With some the word liberty may mean for each man to do as he pleases with himself, and the product of his labor; while with others the same word may mean for some men to do as they please with other men, and the product of other men's labor. Here are two, not only different, but incompatible things, called by the same name—liberty. And it follows that each of the things is, by the respective parties, called by two different and incompatible names—liberty and tyranny.

The shepherd drives the wolf from the sheep's throat, for which the sheep thanks the shepherd as a *liberator*, while the wolf denounces him for the same act as the destroyer of liberty, especially as the sheep was a black one. Plainly the sheep and the wolf are not agreed upon a definition of the word liberty; and precisely the same difference prevails today among us human creatures, even in the North, and all professing to love liberty. Hence we behold the process by which thousands are daily passing from under the yoke of bondage, hailed by some as the advance of liberty, and bewailed by others as the destruction of all liberty. Recently, as it seems, the people of Maryland have been doing something to define liberty [abolishing slavery in the state]; and thanks to them that, in what they have done, the wolf's dictionary, has been repudiated.

QUESTIONS

1. *Why does Drayton deny that the Confederacy is fighting to defend slavery?*

2. *What does Lincoln identify as the essential difference between northern and southern definitions of freedom?*

3. *How do Drayton and Lincoln differ in their definitions of liberty and whether it applies to African-Americans?*

A girl in mourning dress holds a framed photograph of her father, a cavalryman.

a program to locate and re-bury hundreds of thousands of Union soldiers in national military cemeteries. Between 1865 and 1871, the government reinterred more than 300,000 Union (but not Confederate) soldiers—including black soldiers, who were buried, as they had fought, in segregated sections of military cemeteries.

Liberty in Wartime

This intense new nationalism made criticism of the war effort—or of the policies of the Lincoln administration—seem to Republicans equivalent to treason. During the conflict, declared the Republican *New York Times*, "the safety of the nation is the supreme law." Arbitrary arrests numbered in the thousands. They included opposition newspaper editors, Democratic politicians, individuals who discouraged enlistment in the army, and ordinary civilians like the Chicago man briefly imprisoned for calling the president a "damned fool." With the Constitution unclear as to who possessed the power to suspend the writ of habeas corpus (thus allowing prisoners to be held without charge), Lincoln claimed the right under the presidential war powers and twice suspended the writ throughout the entire Union for those accused of "disloyal activities." Not until 1866, after the fighting had ended, did the Supreme Court, in the case ***Ex parte Milligan***, declare it unconstitutional to bring accused persons before military tribunals where civil courts were operating. The Constitution, declared Justice David Davis, is not suspended in wartime—it remains "a law for rulers and people, equally in time of war and peace."

Arbitrary arrests and the suspension of habeas corpus

Lincoln was not a despot. Most of those arrested were quickly released, the Democratic press continued to flourish, and contested elections were held throughout the war. But the policies of the Lincoln administration offered proof—to be repeated during later wars—of the fragility of civil liberties in the face of assertive patriotism and wartime demands for national unity.

The North's Transformation

Even as he invoked traditional values, Lincoln presided over far-reaching changes in northern life. The effort to mobilize the resources of the Union greatly enhanced the power not only of the federal government but also of a rising class of capitalist entrepreneurs. Unlike the South, which suffered economic devastation, the North experienced the war as a time of prosperity.

Northern prosperity in wartime

Nourished by wartime inflation and government contracts, the profits of industry boomed. New England mills worked day and night to supply the army with blankets and uniforms, and Pennsylvania coal mines and ironworks rapidly expanded their production. Mechanization proceeded apace in many industries, especially those, such as boot and shoe production and meatpacking, that supplied the army's ever-increasing needs. Agriculture also flourished, for even as farm boys by the hundreds of thousands joined the army, the frontier of cultivation pushed westward, with machinery and immigrants replacing lost labor.

Government and the Economy

The new American nation-state that emerged during the Civil War was committed to rapid economic development. Congress adopted policies that promoted economic growth and permanently altered the nation's financial system. To spur agricultural development, the **Homestead Act** offered 160 acres of free public land to settlers in the West. It took effect on January 1, 1863, the same day as the Emancipation Proclamation, and like the proclamation, tried to implement a vision of freedom. By the 1930s, more than 400,000 families had acquired farms under its provisions. In addition, the Land Grant College Act assisted the states in establishing "agricultural and mechanic colleges."

Congress also made huge grants of money and land for internal improvements, including up to 100 million acres to the Union Pacific and Central Pacific, two companies chartered in 1862 and charged with building a railroad from the Missouri River to the Pacific coast. (These were the first corporate charters issued by the federal government since the Second Bank of the United States in 1816.) It required some 20,000 men to lay the tracks across prairies and mountains, a substantial number of them immigrant Chinese contract laborers, called "coolies" by many Americans. Hundreds of Chinese workers died blasting tunnels and building bridges through this treacherous terrain. When it was completed in 1869, the **transcontinental railroad**, which ran from Omaha, Nebraska, to San Francisco, expanded the national market, facilitated the spread of settlement and investment in the West, and heralded the doom of the Plains Indians.

The War and Native Americans

One of Lincoln's first orders as president was to withdraw federal troops from the West so that they could protect Washington, D.C. Recognizing that this would make it impossible for the army to keep white interlopers from intruding on Indian land, as treaties required it to do, Indian leaders

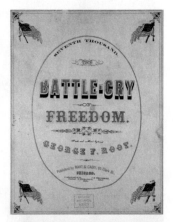

Sheet music for two of the best-known patriotic songs written during the Civil War.

Effects of the transcontinental railroad

A lithograph depicts the hanging of thirty-eight Sioux Indians in December 1862, the largest mass execution in American history.

begged Lincoln to reverse this decision, but to no avail. Inevitably, conflict flared in the West between Native Americans and white settlers, with disastrous results. During the Civil War, the Sioux killed hundreds of white farmers in Minnesota before being subdued by the army. After a military court sentenced more than 300 Indians to death, Lincoln commuted the sentences of all but 38. But their hanging in December 1862 remains the largest official execution in American history.

The Union army also launched a campaign against the Navajo in the Southwest, destroying their orchards and sheep and forcing 8,000 people to move to a reservation set aside by the government. The **Navajo's Long Walk** became as central to their historical experience as the Trail of Tears to the Cherokee (see Chapter 10). Unlike the eastern Indians, however, the Navajo were eventually allowed to return to a portion of their lands.

Some tribes that owned slaves, like the Cherokee, sided with the Confederacy. After 1865, they were forced to cede much of their land to the federal government and to accept former slaves into the Cherokee nation and give them land (the only slaveowners required to do so). Their status remains a point of controversy to this day. The Cherokee constitution was recently amended to exclude descendants of slaves from citizenship, leading to lawsuits that have yet to be resolved.

A Union soldier stands guard over a group of Indians during the Navajo's Long Walk, in which the army removed them from their New Mexico homeland to a reservation hundreds of miles away.

A New Financial System

The need to pay for the war produced dramatic changes in financial policy. To raise money, the government increased the tariff to unprecedented heights (thus promoting the further growth of northern industry), imposed new taxes on the production and consumption of goods, and enacted the nation's first income tax. It also borrowed more than $2 billion by selling interest-bearing bonds, thus creating an immense national debt. And it printed more than $400 million worth of paper money, called "greenbacks," declared to be legal tender—that is, money that must be accepted for nearly all public and private payments and debts. To rationalize the banking system, Congress established a system of nationally chartered banks, which were required to purchase government bonds and were given the right to issue bank notes as currency.

Financing the war

Numerous Americans who would take the lead in reshaping the nation's postwar economy created or consolidated their fortunes during the Civil War, among them the iron and steel entrepreneur Andrew Carnegie, the oil magnate John D. Rockefeller, the financiers Jay Gould and J. P. Morgan, and Philip D. Armour, who earned millions supplying beef to the Union army. These and other "captains of industry" managed to escape military service, sometimes by purchasing exemptions or hiring substitutes, as allowed by the draft law.

"Captains of industry"

Taken together, the Union's economic policies vastly increased the power and size of the federal government. The federal budget for 1865 exceeded $1 billion—nearly twenty times that of 1860. With its new army of clerks, tax collectors, and other officials, the government became the nation's largest employer. And although much of this expansion proved temporary, the government would never return to its weak and fragmented condition of the prewar period.

Filling Cartridges at the U.S. Arsenal of Watertown, Massachusetts, an engraving from *Harper's Weekly,* September 21, 1861. Both men and women were drawn to work in the booming war-related industries of the North.

Women and the War

For many northern women, the conflict opened new doors of opportunity. Women took advantage of the wartime labor shortage to move into jobs in factories and into certain largely male professions, particularly nursing. The expansion of the activities of the national government opened new jobs for women as clerks in government offices. Many of these wartime gains were short lived, but in white-collar government jobs, retail sales, and nursing, women found a permanent place in the workforce.

Hundreds of thousands of northern women took part in organizations that gathered money and medical supplies for soldiers and sent books, clothing, and food to freedmen. The U.S. Sanitary Commission emerged as a centralized national relief agency to coordinate donations on the northern home front. Although control at the national level remained in male hands, patriotic women did most of the grassroots work. Women played the leading role in organizing **Sanitary Fairs**—grand bazaars that displayed military banners, uniforms, and other relics of the war and sold goods to raise money for soldiers' aid.

Northern women volunteers and the public sphere

Many men understood women's war work as an extension of their "natural" capacity for self-sacrifice. But the very act of volunteering for the war effort brought many northern women into the public sphere and offered them a taste of independence. From the ranks of this wartime mobilization came many of the leaders of the postwar movement for women's rights. Clara Barton, for example, organized supply lines and nursed wounded soldiers in northern Virginia. After the war, she became not only an advocate of woman suffrage but also, as president of the American National Red Cross, a strong proponent of the humane treatment of battlefield casualties.

The Divided North

Despite Lincoln's political skills, the war and his administration's policies divided northern society. Republicans labeled those opposed to the war Copperheads, after a poisonous snake that strikes without warning. Mounting casualties and rapid societal changes divided the North.

Copperheads

Whimsical potholders expressing hope for a better life for emancipated slaves were sold at the Chicago Sanitary Fair of 1865 to raise money for soldiers' aid.

Disaffection was strongest among the large southern-born population of states like Ohio, Indiana, and Illinois and working-class Catholic immigrants in eastern cities.

As the war progressed, it heightened existing social tensions and created new ones. The growing power of the federal government challenged traditional notions of local autonomy. The Union's draft law, which allowed individuals to provide a substitute or buy their way out of the army, caused widespread indignation. Workers resented manufacturers and financiers who reaped large profits while their own real incomes dwindled because of inflation. The prospect of a sweeping change in the status of blacks called forth a racist reaction in many parts of the North. Throughout the war, the Democratic Party subjected Lincoln's policies to withering criticism, although it remained divided between "War Democrats," who supported the military effort while criticizing emancipation and the draft, and those who favored immediate peace.

Social tensions in the North

On occasion, dissent degenerated into outright violence. In July 1863, the introduction of the draft provoked four days of rioting in New York City. The mob, composed largely of Irish immigrants, assaulted symbols of the new order being created by the war—draft offices, the mansions of wealthy Republicans, industrial establishments, and the city's black population, many of whom fled to New Jersey or took refuge in Central Park. Only the arrival of Union troops quelled the uprising, but not before more than 100 persons had died.

The New York City draft riots

The Riots in New York: The Mob Lynching a Negro in Clarkson Street, an engraving from the British magazine *Illustrated London News*, August 8, 1863, reveals how the New York City draft riots escalated from an attempt to obstruct the draft into an assault on the city's black population.

THE CONFEDERATE NATION

Leadership and Government

Jefferson Davis

The man charged with the task of rallying public support for the Confederacy proved unequal to the task. Jefferson Davis had moved to Mississippi as a youth, attended West Point, and acquired a large plantation. Aloof and stubborn, Davis lacked Lincoln's political flexibility and ability to communicate the war's meaning effectively to ordinary men and women.

Centralizing the South

Under Davis, the Confederate nation became far more centralized than the Old South had been. The government raised armies from scratch, took control of southern railroads, and built manufacturing plants. But it failed to find an effective way of utilizing the South's major economic resource, cotton. In the early part of the war, the administration tried to suppress cotton production, urging planters to grow food instead and banning cotton exports. This, it was hoped, would promote economic self-sufficiency and force Great Britain, whose textile mills could not operate without southern cotton, to intervene on the side of the Confederacy.

"**King Cotton diplomacy**" turned out to be ineffective. But the Confederate policy had far-reaching global consequences. Recognizing their overdependence on southern cotton, other nations moved to expand production. Britain promoted cultivation of the crop in Egypt and India, and Russia did the same in parts of Central Asia. As a result, the resumption of American cotton production after the war led directly to a worldwide crisis of overproduction that drove down the price of cotton, impoverishing farmers around the world.

The Inner Civil War

As the war progressed, social change and internal turmoil engulfed much of the Confederacy. At the outset, most white southerners rallied to the Confederate cause. No less fervently than northern troops, southern soldiers spoke of their cause in the language of freedom. "We are fighting for our liberty," wrote one volunteer, without any sense of contradiction, "against tyrants of the North . . . who are determined to destroy slavery."

Social change in the South

But even as it waged a desperate struggle for independence, the South found itself increasingly divided. One grievance was the draft. Like the Union, the Confederacy allowed individuals to provide a substitute.

Because of the accelerating disintegration of slavery, it also exempted one white male for every twenty slaves on a plantation (thus releasing many overseers and planters' sons from service). The "twenty-negro" provision convinced many yeomen that the struggle for southern independence had become "a rich man's war and a poor man's fight."

Economic Problems

Economic deprivation also sparked disaffection. As the blockade tightened, areas of the Confederacy came under Union occupation, and production by slaves declined, shortages arose of essential commodities such as salt, corn, and meat. The war left countless farms, plantations, businesses, and railroads in ruins. The economic crisis, which stood in glaring contrast to the North's boom, was an unavoidable result of the war. But Confederate policies exaggerated its effects. War requires sacrifice, and civilian support for war depends, in part, on the belief that sacrifice is being fairly shared. Many non-slaveholders, however, became convinced that they were bearing an unfair share of the war's burdens.

Declining southern production

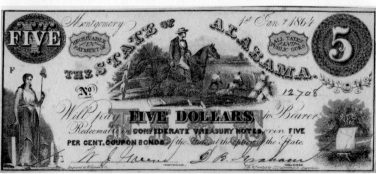

The centrality of slavery to the Confederacy is illustrated by the paper money issued by state governments and private banks, which frequently juxtaposed scenes of slaves at work with other revered images. The ten-dollar note of the Eastern Bank of Alabama depicts slaves working in the field and at a port, along with an idealized image of southern white womanhood. Alabama's five-dollar bill includes an overseer directing slaves in the field and a symbol of liberty.

An engraving in the *New York Illustrated News* depicts the bread riot that took place in Mobile, Alabama, in the fall of 1863.

Like the Union, the Confederacy borrowed heavily to finance the war. Unlike federal lawmakers, however, the planter-dominated Confederate Congress proved unwilling to levy heavy taxes that planters would have to pay. It relied on paper money, of which it issued $1.5 billion, far more than the North's greenbacks. The Confederate Congress also authorized military officers to seize farm goods to supply the army, paying with increasingly worthless Confederate money. Small farmers deeply resented this practice, known as "impressment." Food riots broke out in many places, including Richmond, Virginia, and Mobile, Alabama, where in 1863 large crowds of women plundered army food supplies. As the war progressed, desertion became what one officer called a "crying evil" for the southern armies. By the war's end, more than 100,000 men had deserted, almost entirely from among "the poorest class of nonslaveholders whose labor is indispensable to the daily support of their families."

By 1864, organized peace movements had appeared in several southern states, and secret pro-Union societies such as the Heroes of America were actively promoting disaffection.

Women and the Confederacy

Wartime roles for women in the Confederacy

Even more than in the North, the war placed unprecedented burdens on southern white women. Left alone on farms and plantations, they were often forced to manage business affairs and discipline slaves, previously the responsibility of men. As in the North, women mobilized to support soldiers in the field and stepped out of their traditional "sphere" to run commercial establishments and work in arms factories. In Richmond, "government girls" staffed many of the clerkships in the new Confederate bureaucracy.

All Confederate women struggled to cope as their loved ones were drawn off into the army. The war led to the political mobilization, for the first time, of non-slaveholding white women. Lacking the aid of slave labor, they found that the absence of their husbands from their previously self-sufficient farms made it impossible to feed their families. They flooded

Confederate authorities with petitions seeking assistance, not as charity but as a right. Politicians could not ignore the pleas of soldiers' wives, and state governments began to distribute supplies to needy families.

Southern women's self-sacrificing devotion to the cause became legendary. But as the war went on and the death toll mounted, increasing numbers of women came to believe that the goal of independence was not worth the cost. The growing disaffection of southern white women, conveyed in letters to loved ones at the front, contributed to the decline in civilian morale and encouraged desertion from the army.

Black Soldiers for the Confederacy

The growing shortage of white manpower eventually led Confederate authorities to a decision no one could have foreseen when the war began: they authorized the arming of slaves to fight for the South. Many slaveholders fiercely resisted this idea, and initially, the Confederate Senate rejected it. Not until March 1865, after Robert E. Lee had endorsed the plan, did the Confederate Congress authorize the arming of slaves.

Southern debate over arming the slaves

The war ended before the recruitment of black soldiers actually began. But the Confederate army did employ numerous blacks, nearly all of them slaves, as laborers. This later led to some confusion over whether blacks actually fought for the Confederacy—apart from a handful who "passed" for white, none in fact did. But the South's decision to raise black troops illustrates how the war undermined not only slavery but also the proslavery ideology. Declared Howell Cobb, a Georgia planter and politician, "If slaves make good soldiers, our whole theory of slavery is wrong."

TURNING POINTS

Gettysburg and Vicksburg

Despite the accelerating demise of slavery and the decline of morale in the South, the war's outcome remained very much in doubt for much of its third and fourth years. In April 1863, "Fighting Joe" Hooker, who had succeeded Ambrose E. Burnside as the Union commander in the East, brought the Army of the Potomac into central Virginia to confront Lee. Outnumbered two to one, Lee repelled Hooker's attack at Chancellorsville,

"Fighting Joe" Hooker

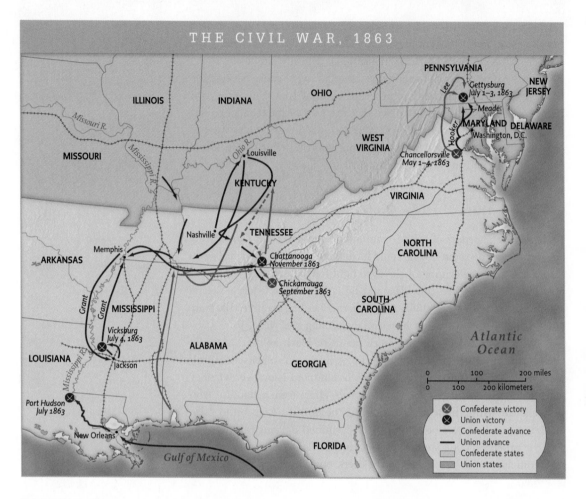

THE CIVIL WAR, 1863

In July 1863, the Union won major victories at Gettysburg and Vicksburg.

Gettysburg

although he lost his ablest lieutenant, "Stonewall" Jackson, mistakenly killed by fire from his own soldiers.

Lee now gambled on another invasion of the North, although his strategic objective remains unclear. Perhaps he believed a defeat on its own territory would destroy the morale of the northern army and public. In any event, the two armies, with Union soldiers now under the command of General George G. Meade, met at Gettysburg, Pennsylvania, on the first three days of July 1863. With 165,000 troops involved, Gettysburg remains the largest battle ever fought on the North American continent. On July 3, Confederate forces, led by Major General George E. Pickett's crack division, marched across an open field toward Union forces. Withering artillery and rifle fire met the charge, and most of Pickett's soldiers never reached Union lines. Pickett's Charge was Lee's greatest blunder. His army retreated to Virginia, never again to set foot on northern soil.

On the same day that Lee began his retreat from Gettysburg, the Union achieved a significant victory in the West. Late in 1862, Grant had moved into Mississippi toward the city of Vicksburg. From its heights, defended by miles of trenches and earthworks, the Confederacy commanded the central Mississippi River. When direct attacks failed, Grant launched a siege. On July 4, 1863, Vicksburg surrendered, and with it John C. Pemberton's army of 30,000 men, a loss the Confederacy could ill afford. The entire Mississippi Valley now lay in Union hands.

The surrender of Vicksburg

Generals Robert E. Lee and Ulysses S. Grant, leaders of the opposing armies in the East, 1864–1865.

1864

Nearly two years, however, would pass before the war ended. Brought east to take command of Union forces, Grant in 1864 began a war of attrition against Lee's army in Virginia. That is, he was willing to accept high numbers of casualties, knowing that the North could replace its manpower losses, whereas the South could not. Grant understood that to bring the North's manpower advantage into play, he must attack continuously "all along the line," thereby preventing the enemy from concentrating its forces or retreating to safety after an engagement.

In May 1864, the 115,000-man Army of the Potomac crossed the Rapidan River to do battle with Lee's forces in Virginia. At the end of six weeks of fighting, Grant's casualties stood at 60,000—almost the size of Lee's entire army—while Lee had lost 30,000 men. The sustained fighting in Virginia was a turning point in modern warfare. With daily combat and a fearsome casualty toll, it had far more in common with the trench warfare of World War I (discussed in Chapter 19) than the almost gentlemanly fighting with which the Civil War began.

Grant had become the only Union general to maintain the initiative against Lee but at a cost that led critics to label him a "butcher of men." Victory still eluded him. Grant attempted to capture Petersburg, which controlled the railway link to Richmond, but Lee got to Petersburg first, and Grant settled in for a prolonged siege. Meanwhile, General William T. Sherman, who had moved his forces into Georgia from Tennessee, encountered dogged resistance from Confederate troops. Not until September 1864 did he finally enter Atlanta, seizing Georgia's main railroad center.

As casualty rolls mounted in the spring and summer of 1864, northern morale sank to its lowest point of the war. Lincoln for a time believed he would be unable to win reelection. In May, hoping to force Lincoln to

A sketch by William Waud, an artist who covered the war for *Harper's Weekly*, depicts Pennsylvania soldiers voting in their army camp in the 1864 election.

step aside, Radical Republicans nominated John C. Frémont on a platform calling for a constitutional amendment to abolish slavery, federal protection of the freedmen's rights, and confiscation of the land of leading Confederates. The Democratic candidate for president, General George B. McClellan, was hampered from the outset of the campaign by a platform calling for an immediate cease-fire and peace conference—a plan that even war-weary northerners viewed as equivalent to surrender. In the end, Frémont withdrew, and buoyed by Sherman's capture of Atlanta, Lincoln won a sweeping victory. He captured every state but Kentucky, Delaware, and New Jersey. The result ensured that the war would continue until the Confederacy's defeat.

REHEARSALS FOR RECONSTRUCTION AND THE END OF THE WAR

As the war drew toward a close and more and more parts of the Confederacy came under Union control, federal authorities found themselves presiding over the transition from slavery to freedom. In South Carolina, Louisiana, and other parts of the South, debates took place over issues—access to land, control of labor, and the new structure of political power—that would reverberate in the postwar world.

The Sea Islands Experiment

The most famous "rehearsal for Reconstruction" took place on the Sea Islands just off the coast of South Carolina. The war was only a few months old when, in November 1861, the Union navy occupied the islands. Nearly the entire white population fled, leaving behind some 10,000 slaves. The navy was soon followed by other northerners—army officers, Treasury agents, prospective investors in cotton land, and a group known as Gideon's Band, which included black and white reformers and teachers committed to uplifting the freed slaves. Northern-born teachers like Charlotte Forten, a member of one of Philadelphia's most prominent black families, and Laura M. Towne, a white native of Pittsburgh, devoted themselves to teaching the freed blacks.

Many northerners believed that the transition from slave to free labor meant enabling blacks to work for wages in more humane conditions than

Gideon's Band

under slavery. When the federal government put land on the islands up for sale, most was acquired not by former slaves but by northern investors bent on demonstrating the superiority of free wage labor and turning a tidy profit at the same time. By 1865, the **Sea Islands experiment** was widely held to be a success. But the experiment also bequeathed to postwar Reconstruction the contentious issue of whether landownership should accompany black freedom.

Wartime Reconstruction in the West

A very different rehearsal for Reconstruction, involving a far larger area and population than the Sea Islands, took place in Louisiana and the Mississippi Valley. After the capture of Vicksburg, the Union army established regulations for plantation labor. Military authorities insisted that the emancipated slaves must sign labor contracts with plantation owners who took an oath of loyalty. But, unlike before the war, they would be paid wages and provided with education, physical punishment was prohibited, and their families were safe from disruption by sale.

Teachers in the Freedmen's Schools in Norfolk, 1863, a photograph of a group of black and white teachers who brought education to former slaves in a Union-occupied part of Virginia.

Neither side was satisfied with the new labor system. Blacks resented having to resume working for whites and being forced to sign labor contracts. Planters complained that their workers were insubordinate. But only occasionally did army officers seek to implement a different vision of freedom. At Davis Bend, Mississippi, site of the cotton plantations of Jefferson Davis and his brother Joseph, the emancipated slaves saw the land divided among themselves. In addition, a system of government was established that allowed the former slaves to elect their own judges and sheriffs.

The Politics of Wartime Reconstruction

As the Civil War progressed, the future political status of African-Americans emerged as a key dividing line in public debates. Events in Union-occupied Louisiana brought the issue to national attention. Hoping to establish a functioning civilian government in the state, Lincoln in 1863 announced his **Ten-Percent Plan of Reconstruction**. He essentially offered an amnesty and full restoration of rights, including property except for slaves, to nearly all white southerners who took an oath affirming loyalty to the Union and support for emancipation. When 10 percent of the voters of 1860 had taken the oath, they could elect a new state government, which would be required to abolish slavery. Lincoln's plan offered no role to blacks in shaping the post-slavery order.

Lincoln's Ten-Percent Plan

Another group now stepped onto the stage of politics—the free blacks of New Orleans, who saw the Union occupation as a golden opportunity to press for equality before the law and a role in government for themselves. Their complaints at being excluded under Lincoln's Reconstruction plan won a sympathetic hearing from Radical Republicans in Congress. By the summer of 1864, dissatisfaction with events in Louisiana helped to inspire the Wade-Davis Bill, named for two leading Republican members of Congress. This bill required a majority (not one-tenth) of white male southerners to pledge support for the Union before Reconstruction could begin in any state, and it guaranteed blacks equality before the law, although not the right to vote. The bill passed Congress only to die when Lincoln refused to sign it and Congress adjourned. As the war drew to a close, it was clear that although slavery was dead, no agreement existed as to what social and political system should take its place.

Wade-Davis Bill

Victory at Last

After Lincoln's reelection, the war hastened to its conclusion. In November 1864, Sherman and his army of 60,000 set out from Atlanta on their March to the Sea. Cutting a sixty-mile-wide swath through the heart of Georgia, they destroyed railroads, buildings, and all the food and supplies they could not use. His aim, Sherman wrote, was "to whip the rebels, to humble their pride, to follow them to their innermost recesses, and make them fear and dread us." Here was modern war in all its destructiveness, even though few civilians were physically harmed. In January 1865, after capturing Savannah, Sherman moved into South Carolina, bringing even greater destruction.

Sherman's March to the Sea

On January 31, 1865, Congress approved the Thirteenth Amendment, which abolished slavery throughout the entire Union—and in so doing, introduced the word "slavery" into the Constitution for the first time. In March, in his second inaugural address, Lincoln called for reconciliation: "with malice toward none, with charity for all, . . . let us . . . bind up the nation's wounds." Yet he also leveled a harsh judgment on the nation's past. Perhaps, Lincoln suggested, God had brought on the war to punish the entire nation, not just the South, for the sin of slavery. And if God willed that the war continue until all the wealth created by 250 years of slave labor had been destroyed, and "every drop of blood drawn with the lash shall be paid by another drawn with the sword," this too would be an act of justice (see the Appendix for the full text).

General William T. Sherman photographed in 1864.

April 1865 brought some of the most momentous events in American history. On April 2, Grant finally broke through Lee's lines at Petersburg,

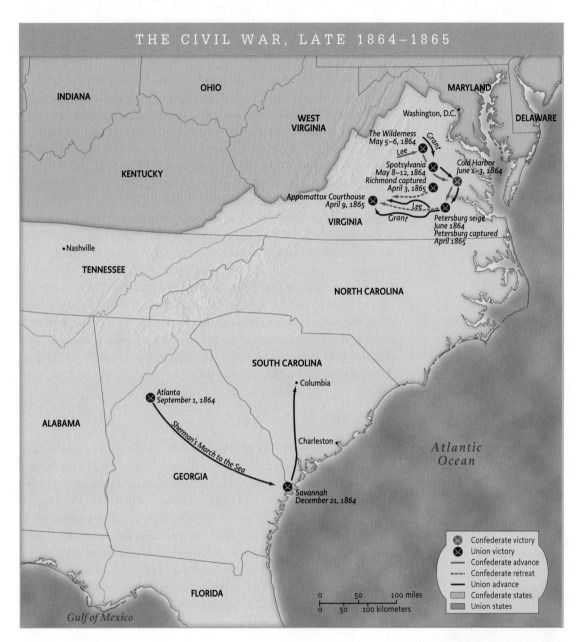

THE CIVIL WAR, LATE 1864–1865

INDIANA

OHIO

MARYLAND

Washington, D.C.

WEST VIRGINIA

DELAWARE

The Wilderness
May 5–6, 1864

Grant

Lee

Cold Harbor
June 1–3, 1864

KENTUCKY

Spotsylvania
May 8–12, 1864

Richmond captured
April 3, 1865

Appomattox Courthouse
April 9, 1865

Lee

Grant

Petersburg seige
June 1864
Petersburg captured
April 1865

VIRGINIA

Nashville

TENNESSEE

NORTH CAROLINA

SOUTH CAROLINA

Columbia

Atlanta
September 1, 1864

ALABAMA

Sherman's March to the Sea

Charleston

Atlantic
Ocean

GEORGIA

Savannah
December 21, 1864

FLORIDA

Gulf of Mexico

⊗	Confederate victory
⊗	Union victory
—	Confederate advance
- - -	Confederate retreat
—	Union advance
	Confederate states
	Union states

0   50   100 miles
0   50   100 kilometers

The military defeat of the Confederacy came in the East, with Sherman's March to the Sea, Grant's occupation of Richmond, and the surrender of Robert E. Lee's army.

forcing the Army of Northern Virginia to abandon the city and leaving Richmond defenseless. The following day, Union soldiers occupied the southern capital. On April 4, heedless of his own safety, Lincoln walked the streets of Richmond accompanied only by a dozen sailors. At every step he was besieged by former slaves, some of whom fell on their knees before the embarrassed president, who urged them to remain standing. On April 9, realizing that further resistance was useless, Lee surrendered at Appomattox Courthouse, Virginia. Although some Confederate units remained in the field, the Civil War was over.

Surrender at Appomattox

Lincoln did not live to savor victory. On April 11, in what proved to be his last speech, he called publicly for the first time for limited black suffrage. Three days later, while attending a performance at Ford's Theatre in Washington, D.C., the president was mortally wounded by John Wilkes Booth, one of the nation's most celebrated actors. Lincoln died the next morning. A train carried the president's body to its final resting place in Illinois on a winding 1,600-mile journey that illustrated how tightly the railroad now bound the northern states. Grieving crowds lined the train route, and solemn processions carried the president's body to lie in state in major cities so that mourners could pay their respects. It was estimated that 300,000 persons passed by the coffin in Philadelphia, 500,000 in New York, and 200,000 in Chicago.

The assassination of Lincoln

The War and the World

In 1877, soon after retiring as president, Ulysses S. Grant embarked with his wife on a two-year tour of the world. At almost every location, he was greeted as a modern-day hero. What did America in the aftermath of the Civil War represent to the world? In England, the son of the duke of Wellington greeted Grant as a military genius. In Newcastle, parading English workers hailed him as the man whose military prowess had saved the world's leading experiment in democratic government and as a "Hero of Freedom." In Berlin, Otto von Bismarck, the chancellor of Germany, welcomed Grant as a nation-builder, who had accomplished on the battlefield something—national unity—that Bismarck was attempting to create for his own people.

A redesign of the American flag proposed in 1863 illustrates the linkage of nationalism and freedom that was solidified by the Civil War. The thirty-five stars forming the word "FREE" include the eleven Confederate states.

The War in American History

The Civil War laid the foundation for modern America, guaranteeing the Union's permanence, destroying slavery, and shifting power in the nation from the South to the North (and, more specifically, from slaveowning

Winslow Homer's painting, *The Veteran in a New Field*, completed in the fall of 1865, offers a reflection on the Civil War and its legacy. The one-armed former Union soldier, whose army jacket lies in the right corner, is at work cutting wheat. The scythe brings to mind the grim reaper, a symbol of death, perhaps a reference not only to war casualties but also Lincoln's assassination. But the bountiful field suggests national regeneration.

planters to northern capitalists). It dramatically increased the power of the federal government and accelerated the modernization of the northern economy. And it placed on the postwar agenda the challenge of defining and protecting African-American freedom. "Verily," as Frederick Douglass declared, "the work does not *end* with the abolition of slavery, but only *begins*."

Paradoxically, both sides lost something they had gone to war to defend. Slavery was the cornerstone of the Confederacy, but the war led inexorably to slavery's destruction. In the North, the war hastened the transformation of Lincoln's America—the world of free labor, of the small shop and independent farmer—into an industrial giant. Americans, in the words of the abolitionist Wendell Phillips, would "never again . . . see the republic in which we were born."

Slavery destroyed

CHAPTER REVIEW AND ONLINE RESOURCES

REVIEW QUESTIONS

1. *What made the American Civil War the first modern war?*

2. *How was the North's victory over the South tied to the different ways the market revolution had developed in the North and South?*

3. *Describe how President Lincoln's war aims evolved between 1861 and 1863, changing from simply preserving the Union to also ending slavery.*

4. *How did the actions of slaves themselves, as well as northern military strategy and the Emancipation Proclamation, combine to end slavery?*

5. *What role did blacks play in both winning the Civil War and in defining the war's consequences?*

6. *How did federal policies undertaken during the Civil War transform the United States into a stronger nation-state—economically, politically, and ideologically?*

7. *What was the impact of the Civil War on civil liberties?*

8. *Compare and contrast women's efforts in the North and South to support the war effort and their families.*

9. *In what ways did the outcome of the Civil War change the United States' status in the world?*

KEY TERMS

first modern war (p. 403)

the draft (p. 404)

Monitor v. *Merrimac* (p. 405)

Battle of Antietam (p. 410)

"contrabands" (p. 412)

Radical Republicans (p. 413)

Emancipation Proclamation (p. 414)

black soldiers and sailors (p. 416)

Second American Revolution (p. 417)

civic religion (p. 419)

Ex parte Milligan (p. 422)

Homestead Act (p. 423)

transcontinental railroad (p. 423)

Navajo's Long Walk (p. 424)

national banking system (p. 425)

women and war work (p. 425)

Sanitary Fairs (p. 426)

"King Cotton diplomacy" (p. 428)

Sea Islands experiment (p. 435)

Ten-Percent Plan of Reconstruction (p. 435)

wwnorton.com /studyspace

VISIT STUDYSPACE FOR THESE RESOURCES AND MORE

- A chapter outline
- A diagnostic chapter quiz
- Interactive maps
- Map worksheets
- Multimedia documents

CHAPTER 15

"WHAT IS FREEDOM?"

★

RECONSTRUCTION, 1865–1877

The Shackle Broken—by the Genius of Freedom. This 1874 lithograph depicts Robert B. Elliott, a black congressman from South Carolina, delivering celebrated speech supporting the bill that became the Civil Rights Act of 1875.

On the evening of January 12, 1865, less than a month after Union forces captured Savannah, Georgia, twenty leaders of the city's black community gathered for a discussion with General William T. Sherman and Secretary of War Edwin M. Stanton. The conversation revealed that the black leaders brought out of slavery a clear definition of freedom. Asked what he understood by slavery, Garrison Frazier, a Baptist minister chosen as the group's spokesman, responded that it meant one person's "receiving by irresistible power the work of another man, and not by his consent." Freedom he defined as "placing us where we could reap the fruit of our own labor, and take care of ourselves." The way to accomplish this was "to have land, and turn it and till it by our own labor."

Sherman's meeting with the black leaders foreshadowed some of the radical changes that would take place during the era known as Reconstruction (meaning, literally, the rebuilding of the shattered nation). In the years following the Civil War, former slaves and their white allies, North and South, would seek to redefine the meaning and boundaries of American freedom. Previously an entitlement of whites, freedom would be expanded to include black Americans. The laws and Constitution would be rewritten to guarantee African-Americans, for the first time in the nation's history, recognition as citizens and equality before the law. Black men would be granted the right to vote, ushering in a period of interracial democracy throughout the South. Black schools, churches, and other institutions would flourish, laying the foundation for the modern African-American community. Many of the advances of Reconstruction would prove temporary, swept away during a campaign of violence in the South and the North's retreat from the ideal of equality. But Reconstruction laid the foundation for future struggles to extend freedom to all Americans.

Four days after the meeting, Sherman responded to the black delegation by issuing Special Field Order 15. This set aside the Sea Islands and a large area along the South Carolina and Georgia coasts for the settlement of black families on forty-acre plots of land. He also offered them broken-down mules that the army could no longer use. In Sherman's order lay the origins of the phrase, "forty acres and a mule," which would reverberate across the South in the next few years. Among the emancipated slaves, Sherman's order raised hopes that the end of slavery would be accompanied by the economic independence that they, like other Americans, believed essential to genuine freedom.

THE MEANING OF FREEDOM

"What is freedom?" asked Congressman James A. Garfield in 1865. "Is it the bare privilege of not being chained? If this is all, then freedom is a bitter mockery, a cruel delusion." Did freedom mean simply the absence of slavery, or did it imply other rights for the former slaves, and if so, which ones? Equal civil rights, the vote, ownership of property? During Reconstruction, freedom became a terrain of conflict, its substance open to different, often contradictory interpretations.

Conflicts over freedom

African-Americans' understanding of freedom was shaped by their experiences as slaves and their observation of the free society around them. To begin with, freedom meant escaping the numerous injustices of slavery—punishment by the lash, the separation of families, denial of access to education, the sexual exploitation of black women by their owners—and sharing in the rights and opportunities of American citizens. "If I cannot do like a white man," Henry Adams, an emancipated slave in Louisiana, told his former master in 1865, "I am not free."

Family Record, a lithograph marketed to former slaves after the Civil War, centers on an idealized portrait of a middle-class black family, with scenes of slavery and freedom.

Families in Freedom

With slavery dead, institutions that had existed before the war, like the black family, free blacks' churches and schools, and the secret slave church, were strengthened, expanded, and freed from white supervision. The family was central to the postemancipation black community. Former slaves made remarkable efforts to locate loved ones from whom they had been separated under slavery. One northern reporter in 1865 encountered a freedman who had walked more than 600 miles from Georgia to North Carolina, searching for the wife and children from whom he had been sold away before the war.

While freedom helped to stabilize family life, it also subtly altered relationships within the family. Immediately after the Civil War, planters complained that freedwomen had "withdrawn" from field labor and work as house servants. Many black women preferred to devote more time to their families than had been possible under slavery, and men considered it a badge of

Five Generations of a Black Family, an 1862 photograph that suggests the power of family ties among emancipated slaves.

honor to see their wives remain at home. Eventually, the dire poverty of the black community would compel a far higher proportion of black women than white women to go to work for wages.

Church and School

At the same time, blacks abandoned white-controlled religious institutions to create churches of their own. On the eve of the Civil War, 42,000 black Methodists worshiped in biracial South Carolina churches; by the end of Reconstruction, only 600 remained. As the major institution independent of white control, the church played a central role in the black community. A place of worship, it also housed schools, social events, and political gatherings. Black ministers came to play a major role in politics. Some 250 held public office during Reconstruction.

Another striking example of the freedpeople's quest for individual and community improvement was their desire for education. The thirst for learning sprang from many sources—a desire to read the Bible, the need to prepare for the economic marketplace, and the opportunity, which arose in 1867, to take part in politics. Blacks of all ages flocked to the schools established by northern missionary societies, the Freedmen's Bureau, and groups of ex-slaves themselves. Reconstruction also witnessed the creation of the nation's first black colleges, including Fisk University in Tennessee, Hampton Institute in Virginia, and Howard University in the nation's capital.

Mother and Daughter Reading, Mt. Meigs, Alabama, an 1890 photograph by Rudolph Eickemeyer. During Reconstruction and for years thereafter, former slaves exhibited a deep desire for education, and learning took place outside of school as well as within.

Political Freedom

In a society that had made political participation a core element of freedom, the right to vote inevitably became central to the former slaves' desire for empowerment and equality. As Frederick Douglass put it soon after the South's surrender in 1865, "Slavery is not abolished until the black man has the ballot." In a "monarchial government," Douglass explained, no "special" disgrace applied to those denied the right to vote. But in a democracy, "where universal suffrage is the rule," excluding any group meant branding them with "the stigma of inferiority."

Anything less than full citizenship, black spokesmen insisted, would betray the nation's democratic promise and the war's meaning. To demonstrate their patriotism, blacks throughout the South organized Fourth of July celebrations. For years after the Civil War, white southerners would

The First African Church, Richmond, as depicted in *Harper's Weekly*, June 27, 1874. The establishment of independent black churches was an enduring accomplishment of Reconstruction.

"shut themselves within doors" on Independence Day, as a white resident of Charleston recorded in her diary, while former slaves commemorated the holiday themselves.

Land, Labor, and Freedom

Like those of rural people throughout the world, former slaves' ideas of freedom were directly related to landownership. On the land they would develop independent communities free of white control. Many former slaves insisted that through their unpaid labor, they had acquired a right to the land. "The property which they hold," declared an Alabama black convention, "was nearly all earned by the sweat of *our* brows." In some parts of the South, blacks in 1865 seized property, insisting that it belonged to them.

Freedom and landownership

In its individual elements and much of its language, former slaves' definition of freedom resembled that of white Americans—self-ownership, family stability, religious liberty, political participation, and economic autonomy. But these elements combined to form a vision very much their own. For whites, freedom, no matter how defined, was a given, a birthright to be defended. For African-Americans, it was an open-ended process, a transformation of every aspect of their lives and of the society and culture that had sustained slavery in the first place. Although the freedpeople failed to achieve full freedom as they understood it, their definition did much to shape national debate during the turbulent era of Reconstruction.

Freedom's meaning for former slaves

Masters without Slaves

Most white southerners reacted to military defeat and emancipation with dismay, not only because of the widespread devastation but also because they must now submit to northern demands. "The demoralization is

The southern white reaction to emancipation

Two maps of the Barrow plantation illustrate the effects of emancipation on rural life in the South. In 1860, slaves lived in communal quarters near the owner's house. Twenty years later, former slaves working as sharecroppers lived scattered across the plantation and had their own church and school.

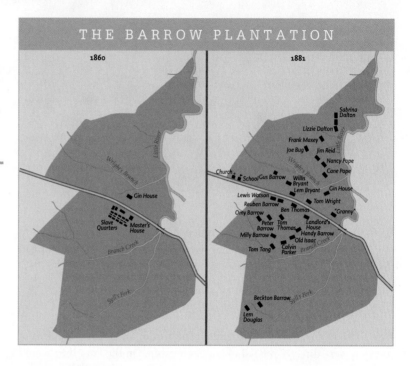

THE BARROW PLANTATION

1860

1881

complete," wrote a Georgia girl. "We are whipped, there is no doubt about it." The appalling loss of life, a disaster without parallel in the American experience, affected all classes of southerners. Nearly 260,000 men died for the Confederacy—more than one-fifth of the South's adult male white population. The widespread destruction of work animals, farm buildings, and machinery ensured that economic revival would be slow and painful. In 1870, the value of property in the South, not counting that represented by slaves, was 30 percent lower than before the war.

Confederate deaths

Planters

Planter families faced profound changes in the war's aftermath. Many lost not only their slaves but their life savings, which they had patriotically invested in now-worthless Confederate bonds. Some, whose slaves departed the plantation, for the first time found themselves compelled to do physical labor.

Southern planters sought to implement an understanding of freedom quite different from that of the former slaves. As they struggled to accept the reality of emancipation, most planters defined black freedom in the narrowest manner. As journalist Sidney Andrews discovered late in 1865, "The whites seem wholly unable to comprehend that freedom for the negro means the same thing as freedom for them."

The Free Labor Vision

Along with former slaves and former masters, the victorious Republican North tried to implement its own vision of freedom. Central to its definition was the antebellum principle of free labor, now further strengthened as a definition of the good society by the Union's triumph. In the free labor vision of a reconstructed South, emancipated blacks, enjoying the same opportunities for advancement as northern workers, would labor more productively than they had as slaves. At the same time, northern capital and migrants would energize the economy. The South would eventually come to resemble the "free society" of the North, complete with public schools, small towns, and independent farmers.

Free labor and the good society

With planters seeking to establish a labor system as close to slavery as possible, and former slaves demanding economic autonomy and access to land, a long period of conflict over the organization and control of labor followed on plantations throughout the South. It fell to the **Freedmen's Bureau**, an agency established by Congress in March 1865, to attempt to establish a working free labor system.

The Freedmen's Bureau

Under the direction of O. O. Howard, a graduate of Bowdoin College in Maine and a veteran of the Civil War, the bureau took on responsibilities that can only be described as daunting. The bureau was an experiment in government social policy that seems to belong more comfortably to the New Deal of the 1930s or the Great Society of the 1960s (see Chapters 21 and 25, respectively) than to nineteenth-century America. Bureau agents were supposed to establish schools, provide aid to the poor and aged, settle disputes between whites and blacks and among the freedpeople, and secure for former slaves and white Unionists equal treatment before the courts. "It is not . . . in your power to fulfill one-tenth of the expectations of those who framed the Bureau," General William T. Sherman wrote to Howard. "I fear you have Hercules' task."

The bureau lasted from 1865 to 1870. Even at its peak, there were fewer than

Winslow Homer's 1876 painting, *A Visit from the Old Mistress*, depicts an imaginary meeting between a southern white woman and her former slaves. Their stance and gaze suggest the tensions arising from the birth of a new social order. Homer places his subjects on an equal footing, yet maintains a space of separation between them. He exhibited the painting to acclaim at the Paris Universal Exposition in 1878.

The Freedmen's Bureau, an engraving from *Harper's Weekly*, July 25, 1868, depicts the bureau agent as a promoter of racial peace in the violent postwar South.

Achievements of the Freedmen's Bureau

1,000 agents in the entire South. Nonetheless, the bureau's achievements in some areas, notably education and health care, were striking. By 1869, nearly 3,000 schools, serving more than 150,000 pupils in the South, reported to the bureau. Bureau agents also ran hospitals established during the war and provided medical care and drugs to both black and white southerners.

The Failure of Land Reform

One provision of the law establishing the bureau gave it the authority to divide abandoned and confiscated land into forty-acre plots for rental and eventual sale to the former slaves. In the summer of 1865, however, President Andrew Johnson, who had succeeded Lincoln, ordered nearly all land in federal hands returned to its former owners. A series of confrontations followed, notably in South Carolina and Georgia, where the army forcibly evicted blacks who had settled on "Sherman land." When O. O. Howard, head of the Freedmen's Bureau, traveled to the Sea Islands to inform blacks of the new policy, he was greeted with disbelief and protest. A committee of former slaves drew up petitions to Howard and President Johnson. Land, the freedmen insisted, was essential to the meaning of freedom. Without it, they declared, "we have not bettered our condition" from the days of slavery—"you will see, this is not the condition of really free men."

Andrew Johnson and land reform

Because no land distribution took place, the vast majority of rural freedpeople remained poor and without property during Reconstruction.

They had no alternative but to work on white-owned plantations, often for their former owners. Far from being able to rise in the social scale through hard work, black men were largely confined to farm work, unskilled labor, and service jobs, and black women to positions in private homes as cooks and maids. The failure of land reform produced a deep sense of betrayal that survived among the former slaves and their descendants long after the end of Reconstruction. "No sir," Mary Gaffney, an elderly ex-slave, recalled in the 1930s, "we were not given a thing but freedom."

Out of the conflict on the plantations, new systems of labor emerged in the different regions of the South. **Sharecropping** came to dominate the Cotton Belt and much of the Tobacco Belt of Virginia and North Carolina. Sharecropping initially arose as a compromise between blacks' desire for land and planters' demand for labor discipline. The system allowed each black family to rent a part of a plantation, with the crop divided between worker and owner at the end of the year. Sharecropping guaranteed the planters a stable resident labor force. Former slaves preferred it to gang labor because it offered them the prospect of working without day-to-day white supervision. But as the years went on, sharecropping became more and more oppressive. Sharecroppers' economic opportunities were severely limited by a world market in which the price of farm products suffered a prolonged decline.

A nursemaid and her charge, from a daguerreotype around 1865.

The White Farmer

The plight of the small farmer was not confined to blacks in the postwar South. Wartime devastation set in motion a train of events that permanently altered the independent way of life of white yeomen, leading to what they considered a loss of freedom. To obtain supplies from merchants, farmers were forced to take up the growing of cotton and pledge a part of the crop as collateral (property the creditor can seize if a debt is not paid). This system became known as the "**crop lien**." Since interest rates were extremely high and the price of cotton fell steadily, many farmers found themselves still in debt after marketing their portion of the crop at year's end. They had no choice but to continue to plant cotton to obtain new loans. By the mid-1870s, white farmers, who cultivated only 10 percent of the South's cotton crop in 1860, were growing 40 percent, and many who had owned their land had fallen into dependency as sharecroppers who now rented land owned by others.

The crop-lien system

Both black and white farmers found themselves caught in the sharecropping and crop-lien systems. The workings of sharecropping and the

The burden of debt

VOICES OF FREEDOM

From Petition of Committee in Behalf of the Freedmen to Andrew Johnson (1865)

In the summer of 1865, President Andrew Johnson ordered land that had been distributed to freed slaves in South Carolina and Georgia returned to its former owners. A committee of freedmen drafted a petition asking for the right to obtain land. Johnson did not, however, change his policy.

We the freedmen of Edisto Island, South Carolina, have learned from you through Major General O. O. Howard . . . with deep sorrow and painful hearts of the possibility of [the] government restoring these lands to the former owners. We are well aware of the many perplexing and trying questions that burden your mind, and therefore pray to god (the preserver of all, and who has through our late and beloved President [Lincoln's] proclamation and the war made us a free people) that he may guide you in making your decisions and give you that wisdom that cometh from above to settle these great and important questions for the best interests of the country and the colored race.

Here is where secession was born and nurtured. Here is where we have toiled nearly all our lives as slaves and treated like dumb driven cattle. This is our home, we have made these lands what they were, we are the only true and loyal people that were found in possession of these lands. We have been always ready to strike for liberty and humanity, yea to fight if need be to preserve this glorious Union. Shall not we who are freedmen and have always been true to this Union have the same rights as are enjoyed by others? . . . Are not our rights as a free people and good citizens of these United States to be considered before those who were found in rebellion against this good and just government? . . .

[Are] we who have been abused and oppressed for many long years not to be allowed the privilege of purchasing land but be subject to the will of these large land owners? God forbid. Land monopoly is injurious to the advancement of the course of freedom, and if government does not make some provision by which we as freedmen can obtain a homestead, we have not bettered our condition. . . .

We look to you . . . for protection and equal rights with the privilege of purchasing a homestead—a homestead right here in the heart of South Carolina.

From a Sharecropping Contract (1866)

Few former slaves were able to acquire land in the post–Civil War South. Most ended up as sharecroppers, working on white-owned land for a share of the crop at the end of the growing season. This contract, typical of thousands of others, originated in Tennessee. The laborers signed with an X, as they were illiterate.

Thomas J. Ross agrees to employ the Freedmen to plant and raise a crop on his Rosstown Plantation. . . . On the following Rules, Regulations and Remunerations.

The said Ross agrees to furnish the land to cultivate, and a sufficient number of mules & horses and feed them to make and house said crop and all necessary farming utensils to carry on the same and to give unto said Freedmen whose names appear below one half of all the cotton, corn and wheat that is raised on said place for the year 1866 after all the necessary expenses are deducted out that accrues on said crop. Outside of the Freedmen's labor in harvesting, carrying to market and selling the same the said Freedmen . . . covenant and agrees to and with said Thomas J. Ross that for and in consideration of one half of the crop before mentioned that they will plant, cultivate, and raise under the management control and Superintendence of said Ross, in good faith, a cotton, corn and oat crop under his management for the year 1866. And we the said Freedmen agrees to furnish ourselves & families in provisions, clothing, medicine and medical bills and all, and every kind of other expenses that we may incur on said plantation for the year 1866 free of charge to said Ross. Should the said Ross furnish us any of the above supplies or any other kind of expenses, during said year, [we] are to settle and pay him out of the net proceeds of our part of the crop the retail price of the county at time of sale or any price we may agree upon—The said Ross shall keep a regular book account, against each and every one or the head of every family to be adjusted and settled at the end of the year.

We furthermore bind ourselves to and with said Ross that we will do good work and labor ten hours a day on an average, winter and summer. . . . We further agree that we will lose all lost time, or pay at the rate of one dollar per day, rainy days excepted. In sickness and women lying in childbed are to lose the time and account for it to the other hands out of his or her part of the crop. . . .

We furthermore bind ourselves that we will obey the orders of said Ross in all things in carrying out and managing said crop for said year and be docked for disobedience . . . and are also responsible to said Ross if we carelessly, maliciously maltreat any of his stock for said year to said Ross for damages to be assessed out of our wages.

Samuel (X) Johnson, Thomas (X) Richard, Tinny (X) Fitch, Jessie (X) Simmons, Sophe (X) Pruden, Henry (X) Pruden, Frances (X) Pruden, Elijah (X) Smith.

QUESTIONS

1. *Why do the black petitioners believe that owning land is essential to the enjoyment of freedom?*

2. *In what ways does the contract limit the freedom of the laborers?*

3. *What do these documents suggest about competing definitions of black freedom in the aftermath of slavery?*

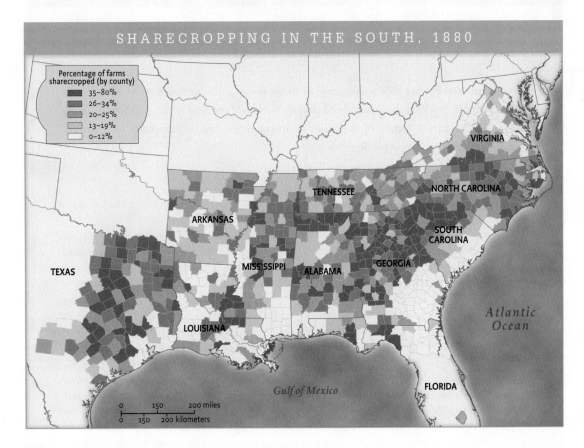

SHARECROPPING IN THE SOUTH, 1880

Percentage of farms
sharecropped (by county)

- 35–80%
- 26–34%
- 20–25%
- 13–19%
- 0–12%

VIRGINIA

TENNESSEE

NORTH CAROLINA

ARKANSAS

SOUTH CAROLINA

TEXAS

MISSISSIPPI ALABAMA

GEORGIA

Atlantic Ocean

LOUISIANA

FLORIDA

Gulf of Mexico

0   150   200 miles

0   150   200 kilometers

By 1880, sharecropping had become the dominant form of agricultural labor in large parts of the South. The system involved both white and black farmers.

crop-lien system are illustrated by the case of Matt Brown, a Mississippi farmer who borrowed money each year from a local merchant. He began 1892 with a debt of $226 held over from the previous year. By 1893, although he produced cotton worth $171, Brown's debt had increased to $402, because he had borrowed $33 for food, $29 for clothing, $173 for supplies, and $112 for other items. Brown never succeeded in getting out of debt. He died in 1905; the last entry under his name in the merchant's account book is a coffin.

Growth of southern cities

Even as the rural South stagnated economically, southern cities experienced remarkable growth after the Civil War. As railroads penetrated the interior, they enabled merchants in market centers like Atlanta to trade directly with the North, bypassing coastal cities that had traditionally monopolized southern commerce. A new urban middle class of merchants, railroad promoters, and bankers reaped the benefits of the spread of cotton production in the postwar South.

The cotton depot at Guthrie, Texas. Bales of cotton have been loaded onto trains for shipment. After the Civil War, more and more white farmers began growing cotton to support their families, permanently altering their formerly self-sufficient way of life.

Aftermath of Slavery

The United States, of course, was not the only society to confront the problem of the transition from slavery to freedom. Indeed, many parallels exist between the debates during Reconstruction and struggles that followed slavery in other parts of the Western Hemisphere over the same issues of land, control of labor, and political power. Planters elsewhere held the same stereotypical views of black laborers as were voiced by their counterparts in the United States—former slaves were supposedly lazy and lacking in ambition, and thought that freedom meant an absence of labor.

Emancipation in the Western Hemisphere

For their part, former slaves throughout the hemisphere tried to carve out as much independence as possible, both in their daily lives and in their labor. On small Caribbean islands like Barbados, where no unoccupied land existed, former slaves had no alternative but to return to plantation labor. Elsewhere, the plantations either fell to pieces, as in Haiti, or continued operating with a new labor force composed of indentured servants from India and China, as in Jamaica, Trinidad, and British Guiana. Southern planters in the United States brought in a few Chinese laborers in an attempt to replace freedmen, but since the federal government opposed such efforts, the Chinese remained only a tiny proportion of the southern workforce.

But if struggles over land and labor united its postemancipation experience with that of other societies, in

Chinese laborers at work on a Louisiana plantation during Reconstruction.

one respect the United States was unique. Only in the United States were former slaves, within two years of the end of slavery, granted the right to vote and, thus, given a major share of political power. Few anticipated this development when the Civil War ended. It came about as the result of one of the greatest political crises of American history—the battle between President Andrew Johnson and Congress over Reconstruction. The struggle resulted in profound changes in the nature of citizenship, the structure of constitutional authority, and the meaning of American freedom.

Emancipation and the right to vote

THE MAKING OF RADICAL RECONSTRUCTION

Andrew Johnson

To Lincoln's successor, Andrew Johnson, fell the task of overseeing the restoration of the Union. Born in poverty in North Carolina, as a youth Johnson worked as a tailor's apprentice. Becoming a successful politician after moving to Tennessee, Johnson identified himself as the champion of his state's "honest yeomen" and a foe of large planters, whom he described as a "bloated, corrupted aristocracy." A strong defender of the Union, he became the only senator from a seceding state to remain at his post in Washington, D.C., when the Civil War began in 1861. When northern forces occupied Tennessee, Abraham Lincoln named him military governor. In 1864, Republicans nominated him to run for vice president as a symbol of the party's hope of extending its organization into the South.

Johnson's background

In personality and outlook, Johnson proved unsuited for the responsibilities he shouldered after Lincoln's death. A lonely, stubborn man, he was intolerant of criticism and unable to compromise. He lacked Lincoln's political skills and keen sense of public opinion. Moreover, while Johnson had supported emancipation once Lincoln made it a goal of the war effort, he held deeply racist views. African-Americans, Johnson believed, had no role to play in Reconstruction.

Outlook

The Failure of Presidential Reconstruction

A little over a month after Lee's surrender at Appomattox, and with Congress out of session until December, Johnson in May 1865 outlined his plan for reuniting the nation. He issued a series of proclamations that began the period of Presidential Reconstruction (1865–1867). Johnson offered a pardon (which restored political and property rights, except for slaves) to nearly all white southerners who took an oath of allegiance. He excluded Confederate leaders and wealthy planters whose prewar property had been valued at more than $20,000. Most of those exempted, however, soon received individual pardons from the president. Johnson also appointed provisional governors and ordered them to call state conventions, elected by whites alone, that would establish loyal governments in the South. Apart from the requirement that they abolish slavery, repudiate secession, and refuse to pay the Confederate debt—all unavoidable consequences of southern defeat—he granted the new governments a free hand in managing local affairs.

Johnson's program

The conduct of the southern governments elected under Johnson's program turned most of the Republican North against the president. By and large, white voters returned prominent Confederates and members of the old elite to power. Reports of violence directed against former slaves and northern visitors in the South further alarmed Republicans.

The Black Codes

But what aroused the most opposition to Johnson's Reconstruction policy were the **Black Codes**, laws passed by the new southern governments that attempted to regulate the lives of the former slaves. These laws granted blacks certain rights, such as legalized marriage, ownership of property, and limited access to the courts. But they denied them the rights to testify

Regulating former slaves

Selling a Freedman to Pay His Fine at Monticello, Florida, an engraving from *Frank Leslie's Illustrated Newspaper*, January 19, 1867. Under the Black Codes enacted by southern legislatures immediately after the Civil War, blacks convicted of "vagrancy"—often because they refused to sign contracts to work on plantations—were fined and, if unable to pay, auctioned off to work for the person who paid the fine.

against whites, to serve on juries or in state militias, or to vote. And in response to planters' demands that the freedpeople be required to work on the plantations, the Black Codes declared that those who failed to sign yearly labor contracts could be arrested and hired out to white landowners.

Clearly, the death of slavery did not automatically mean the birth of freedom. But the Black Codes so completely violated free labor principles that they called forth a vigorous response from the Republican North. In general, few groups of rebels in history have been treated more leniently than the defeated Confederates. A handful of southern leaders were arrested, but most were quickly released. Only one was executed—Henry Wirz, the commander of Andersonville prison, where thousands of Union prisoners of war had died. Most of the Union army was swiftly demobilized. What motivated the North's turn against Johnson's policies was not a desire to "punish" the white South, but the inability of the South's political leaders to accept the reality of emancipation as evidenced by the Black Codes.

Thaddeus Stevens, leader of the Radical Republicans in the House of Representatives during Reconstruction.

Reaction to Black Codes

The Radical Republicans

When Congress assembled in December 1865, Johnson announced that with loyal governments functioning in all the southern states, the nation had been reunited. In response, Radical Republicans, who had grown increasingly disenchanted with Johnson during the summer and fall, called for the dissolution of these governments and the establishment of new ones with "rebels" excluded from power and black men guaranteed the right to vote. Radicals shared the conviction that Union victory created a golden opportunity to institutionalize the principle of equal rights for all, regardless of race.

The most prominent Radicals in Congress were Charles Sumner, a senator from Massachusetts, and Thaddeus Stevens, a lawyer and iron manufacturer who represented Pennsylvania in the House of Representatives. Before the Civil War, both had been outspoken foes of slavery and defenders of black rights. Stevens's most cherished aim was to confiscate the land of disloyal planters and divide it among former slaves and northern migrants to the South. But his plan to make "small independent landholders" of the former slaves proved too radical even for many of his Radical colleagues and failed to pass.

The Origins of Civil Rights

With the South unrepresented, Republicans enjoyed an overwhelming majority in Congress. Most Republicans were moderates, not Radicals. Moderates believed that Johnson's plan was flawed, but they desired to work with the president to modify it. They feared that neither northern nor southern whites would accept black suffrage. Moderates and Radicals joined in refusing to seat the southerners recently elected to Congress, but moderates broke with the Radicals by leaving the Johnson governments in place.

Radical Republicans versus moderates

Early in 1866, Senator Lyman Trumbull of Illinois proposed two bills that reflected the moderates' belief that Johnson's policy required modification. The first extended the life of the Freedmen's Bureau, which had originally been established for only one year. The second, the **Civil Rights Bill**, was described by one congressman as "one of the most important bills ever presented to the House for its action." It defined all persons born in the United States as citizens and spelled out rights they were to enjoy without regard to race. Equality before the law was central to the measure—no longer could states enact laws like the Black Codes discriminating between white and black citizens. So were free labor values. According to the law, no state could deprive any citizen of the right to make contracts, bring lawsuits, or enjoy equal protection of one's person and property. These, said Trumbull, were the "fundamental rights belonging to every man as a free man." The bill made no mention of the right to vote for blacks. In constitutional terms, the Civil Rights Bill represented the first attempt to define in law the essence of freedom.

The Civil Rights Bill of 1866

To the surprise of Congress, Johnson vetoed both bills. Both, he said, would centralize power in the national government and deprive the states of the authority to regulate their own affairs. Moreover, he argued, blacks did not deserve the rights of citizenship. Congress failed by a single vote to muster the two-thirds majority necessary to override the veto of the Freedmen's Bureau Bill (although later in 1866, it did extend the bureau's life to 1870). But in April 1866, the Civil Rights Bill became the first major law in American history to be passed over a presidential veto.

The Fourteenth Amendment

Congress now proceeded to adopt its own plan of Reconstruction. In June, it approved and sent to the states for ratification the **Fourteenth Amendment**, which placed in the Constitution the principle of citizenship for all persons born in the United States, and which empowered the federal government to protect the rights of all Americans. The amendment prohibited the states from abridging the "privileges and immunities" of citizens or denying them the "equal protection of the law." This broad language opened the door for future Congresses and the federal courts to breathe meaning into the guarantee of legal equality.

President Andrew Johnson, in an 1868 lithograph by Currier and Ives. Because of Johnson's stubborn opposition to the congressional Reconstruction policy, one disgruntled citizen drew a crown on his head with the words, "I am King."

In a compromise between the radical and moderate positions on black suffrage, the amendment did not grant blacks the right to vote. But it did provide that if a state denied the vote to any group of men, that state's representation in Congress would be reduced. (This provision did not apply when states barred women from voting.) The abolition of slavery threatened to increase southern political power, since now all blacks, not merely three-fifths as in the case of slaves, would be counted in determining a state's representation in Congress. The Fourteenth Amendment offered the leaders of the white South a choice—allow black men to vote and keep their state's full representation in the House of Representatives, or limit the vote to whites and sacrifice part of their political power.

Black suffrage and political power

By writing into the Constitution the principle that equality before the law regardless of race is a fundamental right of all American citizens, the amendment made the most important change in that document since the adoption of the Bill of Rights.

Significance of the Fourteenth Amendment

The Reconstruction Act

The Fourteenth Amendment became the central issue of the political campaign of 1866. Johnson embarked on a speaking tour of the North. Denouncing his critics, the president made wild accusations that the Radicals were plotting to assassinate him. His behavior further undermined public support for his policies, as did riots that broke out in Memphis and New Orleans, in which white policemen and citizens killed dozens of blacks.

In the northern congressional elections that fall, Republicans opposed to Johnson's policies won a sweeping victory. Nonetheless, at the president's urging, every southern state but Tennessee refused to ratify the Fourteenth Amendment. The intransigence of Johnson and the bulk of the white South pushed moderate Republicans toward the Radicals. In March 1867, over Johnson's veto, Congress adopted the **Reconstruction Act**, which temporarily divided the South into five military districts and called for the creation of new state governments, with black men given the right to vote. Thus began the period of Radical Reconstruction, which lasted until 1877.

Radical Reconstruction

Impeachment and the Election of Grant

In March 1867, Congress adopted the Tenure of Office Act, barring the president from removing certain officeholders, including cabinet members, without the consent of the Senate. Johnson considered this an unconstitutional restriction on his authority. In February 1868, he removed

A Democratic Party broadside from the election of 1866 in Pennsylvania uses racist imagery to argue that government assistance aids lazy former slaves at the expense of hardworking whites.

Secretary of War Edwin M. Stanton, an ally of the Radicals. The House of Representatives responded by approving articles of impeachment—that is, it presented charges against Johnson to the Senate, which had to decide whether to remove him from office.

That spring, for the first time in American history, a president was placed on trial before the Senate for "high crimes and misdemeanors." By this point, virtually all Republicans considered Johnson a failure as president. But some moderates feared that conviction would damage the constitutional separation of powers between Congress and the executive. Johnson's lawyers assured moderate Republicans that, if acquitted, he would stop interfering with Reconstruction policy. The final tally was 35-19 to convict Johnson, one vote short of the two-thirds necessary to remove him. Seven Republicans had joined the Democrats in voting to acquit the president.

The trial of Andrew Johnson

A few days after the vote, Republicans nominated Ulysses S. Grant, the Union's most prominent military hero, as their candidate for president. Grant's Democratic opponent was Horatio Seymour, the former governor of New York. Reconstruction became the central issue of the bitterly fought 1868 campaign. Democrats denounced Reconstruction as unconstitutional and condemned black suffrage as a violation of America's political traditions. They appealed openly to racism. Seymour's running mate, Francis P. Blair Jr., charged Republicans with placing the South under the rule of "a

Ulysses Grant

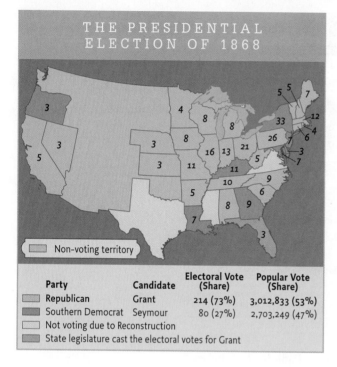

THE PRESIDENTIAL ELECTION OF 1868

Non-voting territory

Party	Candidate	Electoral Vote (Share)	Popular Vote (Share)
Republican	Grant	214 (73%)	3,012,833 (53%)
Southern Democrat	Seymour	80 (27%)	2,703,249 (47%)
Not voting due to Reconstruction			
State legislature cast the electoral votes for Grant			

semi-barbarous race" who longed to "subject the white women to their unbridled lust."

The Fifteenth Amendment

Grant won the election of 1868, although by a margin—300,000 of 6 million votes cast—that many Republicans found uncomfortably slim. The result led Congress to adopt the **Fifteenth Amendment**, which prohibited the federal and state governments from denying any citizen the right to vote because of race. Bitterly opposed by the Democratic Party, it was ratified in 1870.

Although the Fifteenth Amendment opened the door to suffrage restrictions not explicitly based on race—literacy tests, property qualifications, and poll taxes—and did not extend the right to vote to women, it marked the culmination of four decades of abolitionist agitation. "Nothing in all history," exclaimed veteran abolitionist William Lloyd Garrison, equaled "this wonderful, quiet, sudden transformation of four millions of human beings from . . . the auction-block to the ballot-box."

The Fifteenth Amendment, an 1870 lithograph marking the ratification of the constitutional amendment prohibiting states from denying citizens the right to vote because of race. Surrounding an image of a celebration parade are portraits of Abraham Lincoln; President Ulysses S. Grant and his vice president, Schuyler Colfax; the abolitionists John Brown, Martin R. Delany, and Frederick Douglass; and Hiram Revels, the first black to serve in the U.S. Senate. At the bottom are scenes of freedom—education, family, political representation, and church life.

The "Great Constitutional Revolution"

The laws and amendments of Reconstruction reflected the intersection of two products of the Civil War era—a newly empowered national state, and the idea of a national citizenry enjoying equality before the law. What Republican leader Carl Schurz called the "great Constitutional revolution" of Reconstruction transformed the federal system and with it, the language of freedom so central to American political culture.

Effects of Reconstruction amendments

Before the Civil War, American citizenship had been closely linked to race. But the laws and amendments of Reconstruction repudiated the idea that citizenship was an entitlement of whites alone. And, as one congressman noted, the amendments expanded the liberty of whites as well as blacks, including "the millions of people of foreign birth who will flock to our shores."

Race and citizenship

The new amendments also transformed the relationship between the federal government and the states. The Bill of Rights had linked civil liberties to the autonomy of the states. Its language—"Congress shall make no law"—reflected the belief that concentrated national power posed the greatest threat to freedom. The authors of the Reconstruction amendments assumed that rights required national power to enforce them. Rather than a threat to liberty, the federal government, in Charles Sumner's words, had become "the custodian of freedom."

The Reconstruction amendments transformed the Constitution from a document primarily concerned with federal-state relations and the rights of property into a vehicle through which members of vulnerable minorities could stake a claim to freedom and seek protection against misconduct by all levels of government. In the twentieth century, many of the Supreme Court's most important decisions expanding the rights of American citizens were based on the Fourteenth Amendment, perhaps most notably the 1954 *Brown* ruling that outlawed school segregation (see Chapter 24).

Constitutional significance

The Rights of Women

"The contest with the South that destroyed slavery," wrote the Philadelphia lawyer Sidney George Fisher in his diary, "has caused an immense increase in the popular passion for liberty and equality." But advocates of **women's rights** encountered the limits of the Reconstruction commitment to equality. Women activists saw Reconstruction as the moment to claim their own emancipation. The rewriting of the Constitution, declared suffrage leader Olympia Brown, offered the opportunity to sever the blessings of freedom from sex as well as race and to "bury the black man and the woman in the citizen."

Women and the limits of equality

A Delegation of Advocates of Woman Suffrage Addressing the House Judiciary Committee, an engraving from *Frank Leslie's Illustrated Newspaper*, February 4, 1871. The group includes Elizabeth Cady Stanton, seated just to the right of the speaker, and Susan B. Anthony, at the table on the extreme right.

Even Radical Republicans insisted that Reconstruction was the "Negro's hour" (the hour, that is, of the black male). The Fourteenth Amendment for the first time introduced the word "male" into the Constitution, in its clause penalizing a state for denying any group of men the right to vote. The Fifteenth Amendment outlawed discrimination in voting based on race but not gender. These measures produced a bitter split both between feminists and Radical Republicans, and within feminist circles. Some leaders, like Elizabeth Cady Stanton and Susan B. Anthony, denounced their former abolitionist allies and moved to sever the women's rights movement from its earlier moorings in the antislavery tradition.

Thus, even as it rejected the racial definition of freedom that had emerged in the first half of the nineteenth century, Reconstruction left the gender boundary largely intact. When women tried to use the rewritten legal code and Constitution to claim equal rights, they found the courts unreceptive. Myra Bradwell invoked the idea of free labor in challenging an Illinois statute limiting the practice of law to men, but the Supreme Court in 1873 rebuffed her claim. Free labor principles, the justices declared, did not apply to women, since "the law of the Creator" had assigned them to "the domestic sphere."

> *America's great departure*

Despite their limitations, the Fourteenth and Fifteenth Amendments and the Reconstruction Act of 1867 marked a radical departure in American and world history. Alone among the nations that abolished slavery in the nineteenth century, the United States, within a few years of emancipation, clothed its former slaves with citizenship rights equal to those of whites. The Reconstruction Act of 1867 inaugurated America's first real experiment in interracial democracy.

RADICAL RECONSTRUCTION IN THE SOUTH

"The Tocsin of Freedom"

> *Political action by African-Americans*

Among the former slaves, the passage of the Reconstruction Act inspired an outburst of political organization. At mass political meetings—community gatherings attended by men, women, and children—African-Americans

Electioneering at the South, an engraving from *Harper's Weekly*, July 25, 1868, depicts a speaker at a political meeting in the rural South. Women as well as men took part in these grassroots gatherings.

staked their claim to equal citizenship. Blacks, declared an Alabama meeting, deserved "exactly the same rights, privileges and immunities as are enjoyed by white men. We ask for nothing more and will be content with nothing less."

Determined to exercise their new rights as citizens, thousands joined the Union League, an organization closely linked to the Republican Party, and the vast majority of eligible African-Americans registered to vote. James K. Green, a former slave in Hale County, Alabama, and a League organizer, went on to serve eight years in the Alabama legislature. In the 1880s, Green looked back on his political career. Before the war, he declared, "I was entirely ignorant; I knew nothing more than to obey my master; and there were thousands of us in the same attitude. . . . But the tocsin [warning bell] of freedom sounded and knocked at the door and we walked out like free men and shouldered the responsibilities."

The First Vote, an engraving from *Harper's Weekly*, November 16, 1867, depicts the first biracial elections in southern history. The voters represent key sources of the black political leadership that emerged during Reconstruction—the artisan carrying his tools, the well-dressed city person (probably free before the war), and the soldier.

By 1870, all the former Confederate states had been readmitted to the Union, and in a region where the Republican Party had not existed before the war, nearly all were under Republican control. Their new state constitutions, drafted in 1868 and 1869 by the first public bodies in American history with substantial black representation, marked a considerable improvement over those they replaced. The constitutions greatly expanded public responsibilities. They established the region's first state-funded systems of free public education, and they created new penitentiaries, orphan asylums, and homes for the insane. The constitutions guaranteed equality of civil and political rights and abolished practices of the antebellum era such as whipping as a punishment for crime, property qualifications for officeholding, and imprisonment for debt. A few states initially barred former Confederates from voting, but this policy was quickly abandoned by the new state governments.

The Black Officeholder

African-Americans in public office

Throughout Reconstruction, black voters provided the bulk of the Republican Party's support. But African-Americans did not control Reconstruction politics, as their opponents frequently charged. The highest offices remained almost entirely in white hands, and only in South Carolina, where blacks made up 60 percent of the population, did they form a majority of the legislature. Nonetheless, the fact that some 2,000 African-Americans held public office during Reconstruction marked a fundamental shift of power in the South and a radical departure in American government.

African-Americans were represented at every level of government. Fourteen were elected to the national House of Representatives. Two blacks served in the U.S. Senate during Reconstruction, both representing Mississippi. Hiram Revels, who had been born free in North Carolina, in 1870 became the first black senator in American history. The second, Blanche K. Bruce, a former slave, was elected in 1875. At state and local levels, the presence of black officeholders and their white allies made a real difference in southern life, ensuring that blacks accused of crimes would be tried before juries of their peers and enforcing fairness in such aspects of local government as road repair, tax assessment, and poor relief.

In South Carolina and Louisiana, homes of the South's wealthiest and best-educated free black communities, most prominent Reconstruction officeholders had never experienced slavery. In addition, a number of black Reconstruction officials, like Pennsylvania-born Jonathan J. Wright, who served on the South Carolina Supreme Court, had come from the North after the Civil War. The majority, however, were former slaves who had established their leadership in the black community by serving in the Union army; working as ministers, teachers, or skilled craftsmen; or engaging in Union League organizing.

A portrait of Hiram Revels, the first black U. S. senator, by Theodore Kaufmann, a German-born artist who emigrated to the United States in 1855. Lithograph copies sold widely in the North during Reconstruction. Frederick Douglass, commenting on the dignified image, noted that African-Americans "so often see ourselves described and painted as monkeys, that we think it a great piece of fortune to find an exception to this general rule."

Carpetbaggers and Scalawags

The new southern governments also brought to power new groups of whites. Many Reconstruction officials were northerners who for one reason or another had made their homes in the South after the war. Their opponents dubbed them "**carpetbaggers**," implying that they had packed all their belongings in a suitcase and left their homes in order to reap the spoils of office in the South. Some carpetbaggers were undoubtedly corrupt adventurers. The large majority, however, were former Union soldiers who decided to remain in the South when the war ended, before there was any prospect of going into politics.

Most white Republicans, however, had been born in the South. Former Confederates reserved their greatest scorn for these **"scalawags,"** whom they considered traitors to their race and region. Some southern-born Republicans were men of stature and wealth, like James L. Alcorn, the owner of one of Mississippi's largest plantations and the state's first Republican governor. Most "scalawags," however, were non-slaveholding white farmers from the southern upcountry. Many had been wartime Unionists, and they now cooperated with the Republicans in order to prevent "rebels" from returning to power.

Southern Republicans

Southern Republicans in Power

In view of the daunting challenges they faced, the remarkable thing is not that Reconstruction governments in many respects failed, but how much they did accomplish. Perhaps their greatest achievement lay in establishing the South's first state-supported public schools. The new educational systems served both black and white children, although generally in schools segregated by race. Only in New Orleans were the public schools integrated during Reconstruction, and only in South Carolina did the state university admit black students (elsewhere, separate colleges were established). The new governments also pioneered civil rights legislation. Their laws made it illegal for railroads, hotels, and other institutions to discriminate on the basis of race. Enforcement varied considerably from locality to locality, but Reconstruction established for the first time at the state level a standard of equal citizenship and a recognition of blacks' right to a share of public services.

State-supported public schools

Civil rights legislation

Republican governments also took steps to strengthen the position of rural laborers and promote the South's economic recovery. They passed laws to ensure that agricultural laborers and sharecroppers had the first claim on harvested crops, rather than merchants to whom the landowner owed money. South Carolina created a state Land Commission, which by 1876 had settled 14,000 black families and a few poor whites on their own farms.

The Quest for Prosperity

Rather than on land distribution, however, the Reconstruction governments pinned their hopes for southern economic growth and opportunity for African-Americans and poor whites alike on regional economic development.

Economic development during Reconstruction

A group of black students and their teacher in a picture taken by an amateur photographer, probably a Union army veteran, while touring Civil War battlefields.

Railroad construction

Railroad construction, they believed, was the key to transforming the South into a society of booming factories, bustling towns, and diversified agriculture. Every state during Reconstruction helped to finance railroad construction, and through tax reductions and other incentives tried to attract northern manufacturers to invest in the region. The program had mixed results. Economic development in general remained weak.

To their supporters, the governments of Radical Reconstruction presented a complex pattern of disappointment and accomplishment. A revitalized southern economy failed to materialize, and most African-Americans remained locked in poverty. On the other hand, biracial demo-

Biracial democracy

cratic government, a thing unknown in American history, for the first time functioned effectively in many parts of the South. The conservative elite that had dominated southern government from colonial times to 1867 found itself excluded from political power, while poor whites, newcomers from the North, and former slaves cast ballots, sat on juries, and enacted and administered laws. It is a measure of how far change had progressed that the reaction against Reconstruction proved so extreme.

THE OVERTHROW OF RECONSTRUCTION

Reconstruction's Opponents

The South's traditional leaders—planters, merchants, and Democratic politicians—bitterly opposed the new governments. "Intelligence, virtue,

Sources of opposition

and patriotism" in public life, declared a protest by prominent southern

Democrats, had given way to "ignorance, stupidity, and vice." Corruption did exist during Reconstruction, but it was confined to no race, region, or party. The rapid growth of state budgets and the benefits to be gained from public aid led in some states to a scramble for influence that produced bribery, insider dealing, and a get-rich-quick atmosphere. Southern frauds, however, were dwarfed by those practiced in these years by the Whiskey Ring, which involved high officials of the Grant administration, and by New York's Tweed Ring, controlled by the Democrats, whose thefts ran into the tens of millions of dollars. (These are discussed in the next chapter.) The rising taxes needed to pay for schools and other new public facilities and to assist railroad development were another cause of opposition to Reconstruction. Many poor whites who had initially supported the Republican Party turned against it when it became clear that their economic situation was not improving.

The most basic reason for opposition to Reconstruction, however, was that most white southerners could not accept the idea of former slaves voting, holding office, and enjoying equality before the law. Opponents launched a campaign of violence in an effort to end Republican rule. Their actions posed a fundamental challenge both for Reconstruction governments in the South and for policymakers in Washington, D.C.

A cartoon from around 1870 illustrates a key theme of the racist opposition to Reconstruction—that blacks had forced themselves upon whites and gained domination over them. A black school teacher inflicts punishment on a white student in an integrated classroom, and a racially mixed jury judges a white defendant.

"A Reign of Terror"

The Civil War ended in 1865, but violence remained widespread in large parts of the postwar South. In the early years of Reconstruction, violence was mostly local and unorganized. Blacks were assaulted and murdered for refusing to give way to whites on city sidewalks, using "insolent" language, challenging end-of-year contract settlements, and attempting to buy land. The violence that greeted the advent of Republican governments after 1867, however, was far more pervasive and more directly motivated by politics. In wide areas of the South, secret societies sprang up with the aim of preventing blacks from voting and destroying the organization of the Republican Party by assassinating local leaders and public officials.

Campaigns of violence

The most notorious such organization was the **Ku Klux Klan**, which in effect served as a military arm of the Democratic Party in the South. From its founding in 1866 in Tennessee, the Klan was a terrorist organization. It committed some of the most brutal criminal acts in American history. In many counties throughout the South, it launched what one victim called a "reign of terror" against Republican leaders, black and white.

The Klan's victims included white Republicans, among them wartime Unionists and local officeholders, teachers, and party organizers. But African-Americans—local political leaders, those who managed to acquire land, and others who in one way or another defied the norms of white supremacy—bore the brunt of the violence. On occasion, violence escalated from assaults on individuals to mass terrorism and even local insurrections. The bloodiest act of violence during Reconstruction took place in **Colfax**, Louisiana, in 1873, where armed whites assaulted the town with a small cannon. Hundreds of former slaves were murdered, including fifty members of a black militia unit after they had surrendered.

In 1870 and 1871, Congress adopted three **Enforcement Acts**, outlawing terrorist societies and allowing the president to use the army against them. These laws continued the expansion of national authority during Reconstruction. In 1871, President Grant dispatched federal marshals, backed up by troops in some areas, to arrest hundreds of accused Klansmen. Many Klan leaders fled the South. After a series of well-publicized trials, the Klan went out of existence. In 1872, for the first time since the Civil War, peace reigned in most of the former Confederacy.

A Prospective Scene in the City of Oaks, a cartoon in the September 1, 1868, issue of the *Independent Monitor,* a Democratic newspaper published in Tuscaloosa, Alabama. The cartoon sent a warning to the Reverend A. S. Lakin, who had moved from Ohio to become president of the University of Alabama, and Dr. N. B. Cloud, a southern-born Republican serving as Alabama's superintendent of public education. The Ku Klux Klan forced both men from their positions.

The Liberal Republicans

Despite the Grant administration's effective response to Klan terrorism, the North's commitment to Reconstruction waned during the 1870s. Northerners increasingly felt that the South should be able to solve its own problems without constant interference from Washington. The federal government had freed the slaves, made them citizens, and given them the right to vote. Now, blacks should rely on their own resources, not demand further assistance.

Waning commitment to the North

In 1872, an influential group of Republicans, alienated by corruption within the Grant administration and believing that the growth of federal power during and after the war needed to be curtailed, formed their own party. They included Republican founders like Lyman Trumbull and prominent editors and journalists such as E. L. Godkin of *The Nation*. Calling themselves Liberal Republicans, they nominated Horace Greeley, editor of the *New York Tribune*, for president.

Liberal Republicans

Democratic criticisms of Reconstruction found a receptive audience among the Liberals. As in the North, they became convinced, the "best men" of the South had been excluded from power while "ignorant" voters controlled politics, producing corruption and misgovernment. Greeley had spent most of his career, first as a Whig and then as a Republican, denouncing the Democratic Party. But with the

Changes in graphic artist Thomas Nast's depiction of blacks in *Harper's Weekly* mirrored the evolution of Republican sentiment in the North. *And Not This Man?* August 5, 1865, shows the black soldier as an upstanding citizen deserving of the vote. *Colored Rule in a Reconstructed (?) State*, March 14, 1874, suggests that Reconstruction legislatures had become travesties of democratic government.

Republican split presenting an opportunity to repair their political fortunes, Democratic leaders endorsed Greeley as their candidate. But many rank-and-file Democrats, unable to bring themselves to vote for Greeley, stayed at home on election day. As a result, Greeley suffered a devastating defeat by Grant, whose margin of more than 700,000 popular votes was the largest in a nineteenth-century presidential contest. But Greeley's campaign placed on the northern agenda the one issue on which the Liberal reformers and the Democrats could agree—a new policy toward the South.

The North's Retreat

The Liberal attack on Reconstruction, which continued after 1872, contributed to a resurgence of racism in the North. Journalist James S. Pike, a leading Greeley supporter, in 1874 published *The Prostrate State*, an influential account of a visit to South Carolina. The book depicted a state engulfed by political corruption, drained by governmental extravagance, and under the control of "a mass of black barbarism." Resurgent racism offered a convenient explanation for the alleged "failure" of Reconstruction. The solution, for many, was to restore leading whites to political power.

Other factors also weakened northern support for Reconstruction. In 1873, the country plunged into a severe economic depression. Distracted by economic problems, Republicans were in no mood to devote further attention to the South. The depression dealt the South a severe blow and further weakened the prospect that Republicans could revitalize the region's economy. Democrats made substantial gains throughout the nation in the elections of 1874. For the first time since the Civil War, their party took control of the House of Representatives. Before the new Congress met, the old one enacted a final piece of Reconstruction legislation, the **Civil Rights Act of 1875**. This outlawed racial discrimination in places of public accommodation like hotels and theaters. But it was clear that the northern public was retreating from Reconstruction.

The Supreme Court whittled away at the guarantees of black rights Congress had adopted. In the ***Slaughterhouse Cases*** (1873), the justices ruled that the Fourteenth Amendment had not altered traditional federalism. Most of the rights of citizens, it declared, remained under state control. Three years later, in *United States v. Cruikshank*, the Court gutted the Enforcement Acts by throwing out the convictions of some of those responsible for the Colfax Massacre of 1873.

The Triumph of the Redeemers

By the mid-1870s, Reconstruction was clearly on the defensive. Democrats had already regained control of states with substantial white voting majorities such as Tennessee, North Carolina, and Texas. The victorious Democrats called themselves **Redeemers**, since they claimed to have "redeemed" the white South from corruption, misgovernment, and northern and black control.

Democratic victories at the polls

In those states where Reconstruction governments survived, violence again erupted. This time, the Grant administration showed no desire to intervene. In Mississippi, in 1875, armed Democrats destroyed ballot boxes and drove former slaves from the polls. The result was a Democratic landslide and the end of Reconstruction in Mississippi. Similar events

Return of violence

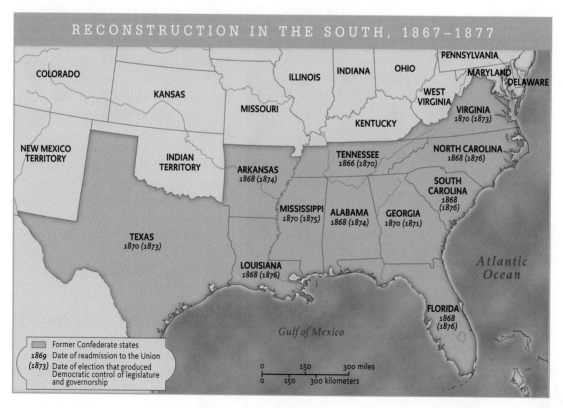

RECONSTRUCTION IN THE SOUTH, 1867–1877

Former Confederate states

1869 Date of readmission to the Union

(1873) Date of election that produced Democratic control of legislature and governorship

0   150   300 miles
0   150   300 kilometers

took place in South Carolina in 1876. Democrats nominated for governor former Confederate general Wade Hampton. Hampton promised to respect the rights of all citizens of the state, but his supporters, inspired by Democratic tactics in Mississippi, launched a wave of intimidation. Democrats intended to carry the election, one planter told a black official, "if we have to wade in blood knee-deep."

The Disputed Election and Bargain of 1877

Events in South Carolina directly affected the outcome of the presidential campaign of 1876. To succeed Grant, the Republicans nominated Governor Rutherford B. Hayes of Ohio. The Democrats chose as his opponent New York's governor, Samuel J. Tilden. By this time, only South Carolina, Florida, and Louisiana remained under Republican control. The election turned out to be so close that whoever captured these states—which both parties claimed to have carried—would become the next president.

Rutherford B. Hayes

Unable to resolve the impasse on its own, Congress in January 1877 appointed a fifteen-member Electoral Commission, composed of senators, representatives, and Supreme Court justices. Republicans enjoyed an 8-7 majority on the commission, and to no one's surprise, the members decided by that margin that Hayes had carried the disputed southern states and had been elected president.

Even as the commission deliberated, however, behind-the-scenes negotiations took place between leaders of the two parties. Hayes's representatives agreed to recognize Democratic control of the entire South and to avoid further intervention in local affairs. For their part, Democrats promised not to dispute Hayes's right to office and to respect the civil and political rights of blacks.

Thus was concluded the **Bargain of 1877**. Hayes became president and quickly ordered federal troops to stop guarding the state houses in Louisiana and South Carolina, allowing Democratic claimants to become governors. (Contrary to legend,

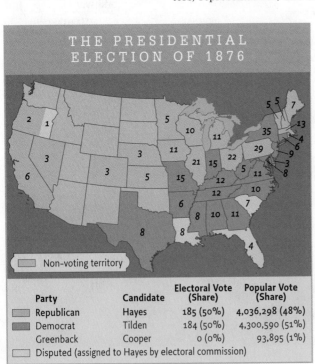

THE PRESIDENTIAL ELECTION OF 1876

Non-voting territory

Party	Candidate	Electoral Vote (Share)	Popular Vote (Share)
Republican	Hayes	185 (50%)	4,036,298 (48%)
Democrat	Tilden	184 (50%)	4,300,590 (51%)
Greenback	Cooper	0 (0%)	93,895 (1%)
Disputed (assigned to Hayes by electoral commission)			

Hayes did not remove the last soldiers from the South—he simply ordered them to return to their barracks.) The triumphant southern Democrats failed to live up to their pledge to recognize blacks as equal citizens.

The End of Reconstruction

As a historical process—the nation's adjustment to the destruction of slavery—Reconstruction continued well after 1877. Blacks continued to vote and, in some states, hold office into the 1890s. But as a distinct era of national history—when Republicans controlled much of the South, blacks exercised significant political power, and the federal government accepted the responsibility for protecting the fundamental rights of all American citizens—Reconstruction had come to an end. Despite its limitations, Reconstruction was a remarkable chapter in the story of American freedom. Nearly a century would pass before the nation again tried to bring equal rights to the descendants of slaves. The civil rights era of the 1950s and 1960s would sometimes be called the Second Reconstruction.

Is This a Republican Form of Government?, a cartoon by Thomas Nast in *Harper's Weekly,* September 2, 1876, illustrates his conviction that the overthrow of Reconstruction meant that the United States was not prepared to live up to its democratic ideals or protect the rights of black citizens threatened by violence.

CHAPTER REVIEW AND ONLINE RESOURCES

REVIEW QUESTIONS

1. In 1865, the former Confederate general Robert Richardson remarked that "the emancipated slaves own nothing, because nothing but freedom has been given to them." Explain whether this would be an accurate assessment of Reconstruction twelve years later.

2. The women's movement split into two separate national organizations in part because the Fifteenth Amendment did not give women the vote. Explain why the two groups split.

3. How did black families, churches, schools, and other institutions contribute to the development of African-American culture and political activism in this period?

4. Why did ownership of land and control of labor become major points of contention between former slaves and whites in the South?

5. By what methods did southern whites seek to limit African-American civil rights and liberties? How did the federal government respond?

6. How did the failure of land reform and continued poverty lead to new forms of servitude for both blacks and whites?

7. What caused the confrontation between President Johnson and Congress over Reconstruction policies?

8. What national issues and attitudes combined to bring an end to Reconstruction by 1877?

9. By 1877, how did the condition of former slaves in the United States compare with that of freedmen around the globe?

KEY TERMS

Freedmen's Bureau (p. 447)

sharecropping (p. 449)

crop-lien system (p. 449)

Black Codes (p. 455)

Civil Rights Bill of 1866 (p. 457)

Fourteenth Amendment (p. 457)

Reconstruction Act (p. 458)

Fifteenth Amendment (p. 460)

women's rights (p. 461)

carpetbaggers and scalawags (p. 464)

Ku Klux Klan (p. 468)

Colfax Massacre (p. 468)

Enforcement Acts (p. 468)

Civil Rights Act of 1875 (p. 470)

Slaughterhouse Cases (p. 470)

Redeemers (p. 471)

Bargain of 1877 (p. 472)

wwnorton.com
/studyspace

VISIT STUDYSPACE FOR THESE RESOURCES AND MORE

- A chapter outline
- A diagnostic chapter quiz
- Interactive maps
- Map worksheets
- Multimedia documents

CHAPTER 16

AMERICA'S GILDED AGE

★

1870-1890

Forging the Shaft, a painting from the 1870s by the American artist John Ferguson Weir, depicts workers in a steel factory making a propeller shaft for an ocean liner. Weir illustrates both the dramatic power of the factory at a time when the United States was overtaking European countries in manufacturing, and the fact that industrial production still required hard physical labor.

FOCUS QUESTIONS

- *What factors combined to make the United States a mature industrial society after the Civil War?*

- *How was the West transformed economically and socially in this period?*

- *Was the Gilded Age political system effective in meeting its goals?*

- *How did the economic development of the Gilded Age affect American freedom?*

- *How did reformers of the period approach the problems of an industrial society?*

An immense crowd gathered in New York Harbor on October 28, 1886, for the dedication of *Liberty Enlightening the World*, a fitting symbol for a nation now wholly free. The idea for the statue originated in 1865 with Édouard de Laboulaye, a French educator and the author of several books on the United States, as a response to the assassination of Abraham Lincoln. Measuring more than 150 feet from torch to toe and standing atop a huge pedestal, the edifice was the tallest man-made structure in the Western Hemisphere.

In time, the Statue of Liberty, as it came to be called, would become Americans' most revered national icon. For over a century it has stood as a symbol of freedom. The statue has welcomed millions of immigrants—the "huddled masses yearning to breathe free" celebrated in a poem by Emma Lazarus inscribed on its base in 1903. In the years since its dedication, the statue's familiar image has been reproduced by folk artists in every conceivable medium and has been used by advertisers to promote everything from cigarettes and lawn mowers to war bonds. It has become a powerful international symbol as well.

The year of the statue's dedication, 1886, also witnessed the "**great upheaval**," a wave of strikes and labor protests that touched every part of the nation. The 600 dignitaries (598 of them men) who gathered on what is now called Liberty Island for the dedication hoped the Statue of Liberty would inspire renewed devotion to the nation's political and economic system. But for all its grandeur, the statue could not conceal the deep social divisions and fears about the future of American freedom that accompanied the country's emergence as the world's leading industrial power. Crucial questions moved to the center stage of American public life during the 1870s and 1880s and remained there for decades to come: What are the social conditions that make freedom possible, and what role should the national government play in defining and protecting the liberty of its citizens?

THE SECOND INDUSTRIAL REVOLUTION

Between the end of the Civil War and the early twentieth century, the United States underwent one of the most rapid and profound economic revolutions any country has ever experienced. There were numerous causes for this explosive economic growth. The country enjoyed abundant natural resources, a growing supply of labor, an expanding market for manufactured goods, and the availability of capital for investment. In

Roots of economic change

addition, the federal government actively promoted industrial and agricultural development. It enacted high tariffs that protected American industry from foreign competition, granted land to railroad companies to encourage construction, and used the army to remove Indians from western lands desired by farmers and mining companies.

The Industrial Economy

The rapid expansion of factory production, mining, and railroad construction in all parts of the country except the South signaled the transition from Lincoln's America—a world centered on the small farm and artisan

A changing America

TABLE 16.1 Indicators of Economic Change, 1870–1920

	1870	1900	1920
Farms (millions)	2.7	5.7	6.4
Land in farms (million acres)	408	841	956
Wheat grown (million bushels)	254	599	843
Employment (millions)	14	28.5	44.5
In manufacturing (millions)	2.5	5.9	11.2
Percentage in workforce[a]			
Agricultural	52		27
Industry[b]	29		44
Trade, service, administration[c]	20		27
Railroad track (thousands of miles)	53	258	407
Steel produced (thousands of tons)	0.8	11.2	46
GNP (billions of dollars)	7.4	18.7	91.5
Per capita (in 1920 dollars)	371	707	920
Life expectancy at birth (years)	42	47	54

[a] Percentages are rounded and do not total 100

[b] Includes manufacturing, transportation, mining, construction

[c] Includes trade, finance, public administration

workshop—to a mature industrial society. By 1913, the United States produced one-third of the world's industrial output—more than Great Britain, France, and Germany combined. By 1880, for the first time, the U.S. Census Bureau found a majority of the workforce engaged in non-farming jobs.

Industrial growth

The traditional dream of economic independence seemed obsolete. By 1890, two-thirds of Americans worked for wages, rather than owning a farm, business, or craft shop. Drawn to factories by the promise of employment, a new working class emerged in these years. Between 1870 and 1920, almost 11 million Americans moved from farm to city, and another 25 million immigrants arrived from overseas.

Most manufacturing now took place in industrial cities. The heartland of what is sometimes called the "second industrial revolution" was the region around the Great Lakes, with its factories producing iron and steel, machinery, chemicals, and packaged foods. Pittsburgh had become the world's center of iron and steel manufacturing. Chicago, by 1900 the nation's second-largest city with 1.7 million inhabitants, was home to factories producing steel and farm machinery and giant stockyards where cattle were processed into meat products for shipment east in refrigerated rail cars.

The industrial Great Lakes region

Railroads and the National Market

The railroad made possible the second industrial revolution. Spurred by private investment and massive grants of land and money by federal, state, and local governments, the number of miles of railroad track in the United States tripled between 1860 and 1880 and tripled again by 1920, opening vast new areas to commercial farming and creating a truly national market for manufactured goods. The railroads even reorganized time itself. In 1883, the major companies divided the nation into the four time zones still in use today.

Key role of railroads

The growing population formed an ever-expanding market for the mass production, mass distribution, and mass marketing of goods, essential elements of a modern industrial economy. The spread of national brands like Ivory Soap and Quaker Oats symbolized the continuing integration of the economy. So did the growth of national chains, most prominently the Atlantic and Pacific Tea Company, better known as A & P grocery stores. Based in Chicago, the national mail-order firms Montgomery Ward and Sears, Roebuck & Co. sold clothing, jewelry, farm equipment, and numerous other goods to rural families throughout the country.

The rise of national brands

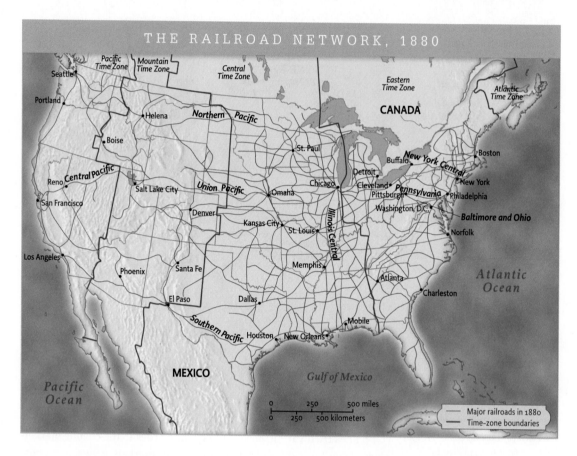

THE RAILROAD NETWORK, 1880

The Spirit of Innovation

A remarkable series of technological innovations spurred rapid communication and economic growth. The opening of the Atlantic cable in 1866 made it possible to send electronic telegraph messages instantaneously between the United States and Europe. During the 1870s and 1880s, the telephone, typewriter, and handheld camera came into use.

Scientific breakthroughs poured forth from research laboratories in Menlo Park and Orange, New Jersey, created by the era's greatest inventor, Thomas A. Edison. During the course of his life, Edison helped to establish entirely new industries that transformed private life, public entertainment, and economic activity. Among Edison's innovations were the phonograph, lightbulb, motion picture, and a system for generating and distributing electric power. The spread of electricity was essential to industrial and urban growth, providing a more reliable and flexible source of power than water or steam.

By 1880, the transnational rail network made possible the creation of a truly national market for goods.

Edison's innovations

Electricity

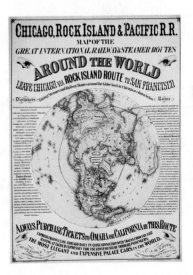

(*Left*) Travel became globalized in the second half of the nineteenth century. This advertisement promotes an around-the-world route by railroad and steamboat, beginning in Chicago. (*Right*) The cover of the 1897 Sears, Roebuck & Co. catalog. One of the country's largest mail-order companies, Sears, Roebuck processed 100,000 orders per day at the end of the nineteenth century. The cornucopia at the center suggests the variety of items one could order by mail: furniture, a piano, a bicycle, and farm tools.

Competition and Consolidation

Economic growth was dramatic but highly volatile. The combination of a market flooded with goods and the federal monetary policies (discussed later) that removed money from the national economy led to a relentless fall in prices. The world economy suffered prolonged downturns in the 1870s and 1890s.

Businesses engaged in ruthless competition. Railroads and other companies tried various means of bringing order to the chaotic marketplace. They formed "pools" that divided up markets between supposedly competing firms and fixed prices. They established "**trusts**"—legal devices whereby the affairs of several rival companies were managed by a single director. Such efforts to coordinate the economic activities of independent companies generally proved short lived.

To avoid cutthroat competition, more and more corporations battled to control entire industries. Between 1897 and 1904, some 4,000 firms fell by the wayside or were gobbled up by others. By the time the wave of mergers had been completed, giant corporations like U.S. Steel (created by financier J. P. Morgan in 1901 by combining eight large steel companies into the first billion-dollar economic enterprise), Standard Oil,

The Electricity Building at the Chicago World's Fair of 1893, painted by Childe Hassam. The electric lighting at the fair astonished visitors and illustrated how electricity was changing the visual landscape.

and International Harvester (a manufacturer of agricultural machinery) dominated major parts of the economy.

The Rise of Andrew Carnegie

In an era without personal or corporate income taxes, some business leaders accumulated enormous fortunes and economic power. During the depression that began in 1873, Andrew Carnegie set out to establish a **"vertically integrated"** steel company—that is, one that controlled every phase of the business from raw materials to transportation, manufacturing, and distribution. By the 1890s, he dominated the steel industry and had accumulated a fortune worth hundreds of millions of dollars. Carnegie's complex of steel factories at Homestead, Pennsylvania, were the most technologically advanced in the world.

Vertical integration

Believing that the rich had a moral obligation to promote the advancement of society, Carnegie denounced the "worship of money" and distributed much of his wealth to various philanthropies, especially the creation of public libraries in towns throughout the country. But he ran his companies with a dictatorial hand. His factories operated nonstop, with two twelve-hour shifts every day of the year except the Fourth of July.

Philanthropy

The Triumph of John D. Rockefeller

If any single name became a byword for enormous wealth, it was John D. Rockefeller, who began his working career as a clerk for a Cleveland merchant and rose to dominate the oil industry. He drove out rival firms through cutthroat competition, arranging secret deals with railroad companies, and fixing prices and production quotas. Like Carnegie, he soon established a vertically integrated monopoly, which controlled the drilling, refining, storage, and distribution of oil. By the 1880s, his Standard Oil Company controlled 90 percent of the nation's oil industry. Like Carnegie, Rockefeller gave much of his fortune away, establishing foundations to promote education and medical research. And like Carnegie, he bitterly fought his employees' efforts to organize unions.

These and other industrial leaders inspired among ordinary Americans a combination of awe, admiration, and hostility.

Next!, a cartoon from the magazine *Puck,* September 7, 1904, depicts the Standard Oil Company as an octopus with tentacles wrapped around the copper, steel, and shipping industries, as well as a state house and Congress. One tentacle reaches for the White House.

Depending on one's point of view, they were "**captains of industry**," whose energy and vision pushed the economy forward, or "**robber barons**," who wielded power without any accountability in an unregulated marketplace. Their dictatorial attitudes, unscrupulous methods, repressive labor policies, and exercise of power without any democratic control led to fears that they were undermining political and economic freedom. Concentrated wealth degraded the political process, declared Henry Demarest Lloyd in *Wealth against Commonwealth* (1894), an exposé of how Rockefeller's Standard Oil Company made a mockery of economic competition and political democracy by manipulating the market and bribing legislators. "Liberty and monopoly," Lloyd concluded, "cannot live together."

Henry Demarest Lloyd's Wealth against Commonwealth

Workers' Freedom in an Industrial Age

Striking as it was, the country's economic growth distributed its benefits very unevenly. For a minority of workers, the rapidly expanding industrial system created new forms of freedom. In some industries, skilled workers commanded high wages and exercised considerable control over the production process. A worker's economic independence now rested on technical skill rather than ownership of one's own shop and tools as in earlier times. Through their union, skilled iron- and steelworkers fixed output quotas and controlled the training of apprentices in the technique of iron rolling. These workers often knew more about the details of production than their employers did.

Economic insecurity

For most workers, however, economic insecurity remained a basic fact of life. During the depressions of the 1870s and 1890s, millions of workers lost their jobs or were forced to accept reductions of pay. The "tramp" became a familiar figure on the social landscape as thousands of men took to the roads in search of work. Between 1880 and 1900, an average of 35,000 workers perished each year in factory and mine accidents, the highest rate in the industrial world. Much of the working class remained desperately poor and to survive needed income from all family members.

By 1890, the richest 1 percent of Americans received the same total income as the bottom half of the population and owned more property than the remaining 99 percent. Many of the wealthiest Americans consciously pursued an aristocratic lifestyle, building palatial homes, attending exclusive social clubs, schools, and colleges, holding fancy-dress balls, and marrying into each other's families. In 1899, the economist and social historian Thorstein Veblen published *The Theory*

Thorstein Veblen's The Theory of the Leisure Class

A turn-of-the-century photograph of the Casino Grounds, Newport, Rhode Island, an exclusive country club for rich socialites of the Gilded Age.

of the Leisure Class, a devastating critique of an upper-class culture focused on "conspicuous consumption"—that is, spending money not on needed or even desired goods, but simply to demonstrate the possession of wealth.

At the same time much of the working class lived in desperate conditions. Jacob Riis, in *How the Other Half Lives* (1890), offered a shocking account of living conditions among the urban poor, complete with photographs of apartments in dark, airless, overcrowded tenement houses.

Jacob Riis and tenements

THE TRANSFORMATION OF THE WEST

Nowhere did capitalism penetrate more rapidly or dramatically than in the trans-Mississippi West, whose "vast, trackless spaces," as the poet Walt Whitman called them, were now absorbed into the expanding economy. At the close of the Civil War, the frontier of continuous white settlement did not extend far beyond the Mississippi River. To the west lay millions of acres of fertile and mineral-rich land roamed by giant herds of buffalo whose meat and hides provided food, clothing, and shelter for a population of more than 250,000 Indians.

Ever since the beginning of colonial settlement in British North America, the West—a region whose definition shifted as the population expanded—had been seen as a place of opportunity for those seeking to improve their condition in life. From farmers moving into Ohio, Indiana, and Illinois in the decades after the American Revolution to prospectors

The West as place of opportunity

Baxter Street Court, 1890, one of numerous photographs by Jacob Riis depicting living conditions in New York City's slums.

who struck it rich in the California gold rush of the mid-nineteenth century, millions of Americans and immigrants from abroad found in the westward movement a path to economic opportunity. But the West was hardly a uniform paradise of small, independent farmers. Beginning in the eighteenth century, for example, California was the site of forced Indian labor on missions run by members of religious orders, a system that helped establish the pattern of large agricultural landholdings in that region. Landlords, railroads, and mining companies in the West also utilized Mexican migrant and indentured labor, Chinese working on long-term contracts, and, until the end of the Civil War, African-American slaves.

A Diverse Region

The West, of course, was hardly a single area. West of the Mississippi River lay a variety of regions, all marked by remarkable physical beauty—the "vast, trackless" Great Plains, the Rocky Mountains, the desert of the Southwest, the Sierra Nevada, and the valleys and coastline of California and the Pacific Northwest. It would take many decades before individual settlers and corporate business enterprises penetrated all these areas. But the process was far advanced by the end of the nineteenth century.

The worldwide fate of indigenous peoples

The political and economic incorporation of the American West was part of a global process. In many parts of the world, indigenous inhabitants—the Zulu in South Africa, aboriginal peoples in Australia, American Indians—were pushed aside (often after fierce resistance) as centralizing governments brought large interior regions under their control. In the United States, the incorporation of the West required the active intervention of the federal government, which acquired Indian land by war and treaty, administered land sales, regulated territorial politics, and distributed land and money to farmers, railroads, and mining companies.

Role of government in the West

In the twentieth century, the construction of federally financed irrigation systems and dams would open large areas to commercial farming. Ironically, the West would become known (not least to its own inhabitants) as a place of rugged individualism and sturdy independence. But without active governmental assistance, the region could never have been settled and developed.

Across the Continent, a lithograph from 1868 by the British-born female artist Frances F. Palmer, celebrates post–Civil War westward expansion as the spread of civilization—represented by the railroad, telegraph, school, church, and wagon trains—into a wilderness that appears totally uninhabited except for two Indians in the far distance and a herd of buffalo.

Farming in the Trans-Mississippi West

Even as sporadic Indian wars raged, settlers poured into the West. Territorial and state governments eager for population and railroad companies anxious to sell the immense tracts of land they had acquired from the government flooded European countries and eastern cities with promotional literature promising easy access to land. More land came into cultivation in the thirty years after the Civil War than in the previous two and a half centuries of American history. Hundreds of thousands of families acquired farms under the Homestead Act, and even more purchased land from speculators and from railroad companies. A new agricultural empire producing wheat and corn arose on the Middle Border (Minnesota, the Dakotas, Nebraska, and Kansas), whose population rose from 300,000 in 1860 to 5 million in 1900. The farmers were a diverse group, including native-born easterners, blacks escaping the post-Reconstruction South, and immigrants from Canada, Germany, Scandinavia, and Great Britain. In the late nineteenth century the most multicultural state in the Union was North Dakota.

The new agricultural empire of the West

Despite the promises of promotional pamphlets, farming on the Great Plains was not an easy task. Much of the burden fell on women. Farm families generally invested in the kinds of labor-saving machinery that would bring in cash, not machines that would ease women's burdens in the household (like the back-breaking task of doing laundry). A farm woman in Arizona described her morning chores in her diary: "Get up, turn out my chickens, draw a pail of water . . . make a fire, put potatoes to cook, brush and sweep half inch of dust off floor, feed three litters of chickens, then mix

Farm women

biscuits, get breakfast, milk, besides work in the house, and this morning had to go half mile after calves."

Despite the emergence of a few **"bonanza farms"** that covered thousands of acres and employed large numbers of agricultural wage workers, family farms still dominated the trans-Mississippi West. Even small farmers, however, became increasingly oriented to national and international markets, specializing in the production of single crops for sale in faraway places. At the same time, railroads brought factory-made goods to rural people, replacing items previously produced in farmers' homes. Farm families became more and more dependent on loans to purchase land, machinery, and industrial products, and increasingly vulnerable to the ups and downs of prices for agricultural goods in the world market. Agriculture reflected how the international economy was becoming more integrated. The combination of economic depressions and expanding agricultural production in places like Argentina, Australia, and the American West pushed prices of farm products steadily downward. Small farmers throughout the world suffered severe difficulties in the last quarter of the nineteenth century. Many joined the migration to cities within their countries or the increasing international migration of labor.

The future of western farming ultimately lay with giant agricultural enterprises relying heavily on irrigation, chemicals, and machinery—investments far beyond the means of family farmers. A preview of the agricultural future was already evident in California, where, as far back as Spanish and Mexican days, landownership had been concentrated in large units. In the late nineteenth century, California's giant fruit and vegetable farms, owned by corporations like the Southern Pacific Railroad, were tilled not by agricultural laborers who could expect to acquire land of their own, but by migrant laborers from China, the Philippines, Japan, and Mexico, who tramped from place to place following the ripening crops.

Family farms

Vulnerability to global market prices

The family of David Hilton on their Nebraska homestead in 1887. The Hiltons insisted on being photographed with their organ, away from the modest sod house in which they lived, to better represent their aspiration for prosperity.

The Cowboy and the Corporate West

The two decades following the Civil War also witnessed the golden age of the cattle kingdom. The Kansas Pacific Railroad's stations at Abilene, Dodge City, and Wichita, Kansas, became destinations for the fabled drives of millions of cattle from Texas. A collection of white, Mexican, and black men who conducted the cattle drives, the cowboys became symbols of a life of freedom on the open range. Their exploits would later serve as the theme of many a Hollywood movie, and their clothing inspired fashions that remain popular today. But there was nothing romantic about the life of the cowboys, most of whom were low-paid wage workers. (Texas cowboys even went on strike for higher pay in 1883.) The days of the long-distance cattle drive ended in the mid-1880s, as farmers enclosed more and more of the open range with barbed-wire fences, making it difficult to graze cattle on the grasslands of the Great Plains, and two terrible winters destroyed millions of cattle. When the industry recuperated, it was reorganized in large, enclosed ranches close to rail connections.

The West was more than a farming empire. By 1890, a higher percentage of its population lived in cities than was the case in other regions. Large corporate enterprises appeared throughout the West. Western mining, from Michigan iron ore and copper to gold and silver in California, Nevada, and Colorado, fell under the sway of companies that mobilized eastern and European investment to introduce advanced technology. Gold and silver rushes took place in the Dakotas in 1876, Idaho in 1883, and Alaska at the end of the century.

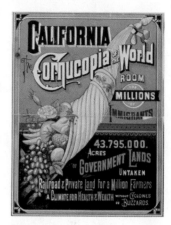

In the late 1800s, California tried to attract immigrants by advertising its pleasant climate and the availability of land, although large-scale corporate farms were coming to dominate the state's agriculture.

Conflict on the Mormon Frontier

The Mormons had moved to the Great Salt Lake Valley in the 1840s, hoping to practice their religion free of the persecution they had encountered in the East. They envisioned their community in Utah as the foundation of a great empire they called Deseret. Given the widespread unpopularity of Mormon polygamy and the close connection of church and state in Mormon theology, conflict with the growing numbers of non-Mormon settlers moving west became inevitable. When President James Buchanan removed the Mormon leader Brigham Young as Utah's territorial governor and Young refused to comply, federal troops entered the Salt Lake Valley, where they remained until the beginning of the Civil War. In 1857, during this time of tension, a group of Mormons attacked a wagon train of non-Mormon settlers traveling through Utah toward California. What came to be called the Mountain Meadows Massacre resulted in the death of all the adults and older children in the wagon train—over 100 persons. Nearly twenty years later, one leader of the assault was convicted of murder and executed.

After the Civil War, Mormon leaders sought to avoid further antagonizing the federal government. In the 1880s, Utah banned the practice of polygamy (although the practice persists to this day among

Deseret community

Mountain Meadows Massacre

some fundamentalist Mormons living in isolated areas). But sporadic conflict continued between Mormon families, who spread out across the Southwest, and Native Americans as well as other settlers.

The Subjugation of the Plains Indians

The incorporation of the West into the national economy spelled the doom of the Plains Indians and their world. Their lives had already undergone profound transformations. In the eighteenth century, the spread of horses, originally introduced by the Spanish, led to a wholesale shift from farming and hunting on foot to mounted hunting of buffalo.

Most migrants on the Oregon and California Trails before the Civil War encountered little hostility from Indians, often trading with them for food and supplies. But as settlers encroached on Indian lands, bloody conflict between the army and Plains tribes began in the 1850s and continued for decades.

In 1869, President Ulysses S. Grant announced a new "peace policy" in the West, but warfare soon resumed. Drawing on methods used to defeat the Confederacy, Civil War generals like Philip H. Sheridan set out to destroy the foundations of the Indian economy—villages, horses, and

especially the buffalo. Hunting by mounted Indians had already reduced the buffalo population—estimated at 30 million in 1800—but it was army campaigns and the depredations of hunters seeking buffalo hides that rendered the vast herds all but extinct.

Albert Bierstadt's 1863 painting, *The Rocky Mountains, Lander's Peak*, depicts Indians as an integral part of the majestic landscape of the West.

"Let Me Be a Free Man"

The army's relentless attacks broke the power of one tribe after another. In 1877, troops commanded by former Freedmen's Bureau commissioner O. O. Howard pursued the Nez Percé Indians on a 1,700-mile chase across the Far West. The Nez Percé (whose name was given them by Lewis and Clark in 1805 and means "pierced noses" in French) were seeking to escape to Canada after fights with settlers who had encroached on tribal lands in Oregon and Idaho. After four months, Howard forced the Indians to surrender, and they were removed to Oklahoma.

The Nez Percé

Two years later, the Nez Percé leader, Chief Joseph, delivered a speech in Washington to a distinguished audience that included President Rutherford B. Hayes. Condemning the policy of confining Indians to reservations, Joseph adopted the language of freedom and equal rights before the law so powerfully reinforced by the Civil War and Reconstruction. "Treat all men alike," he pleaded. "Give them the same law. . . . Let me be a free man—free to travel, free to stop, free to work, free to trade where I choose, free to . . . think and talk and act for myself." Until his death in 1904, Joseph would unsuccessfully petition successive presidents for his people's right to return to their beloved Oregon homeland.

Chief Joseph

Indians occasionally managed to inflict costly delay and even defeat on army units. The most famous Indian victory took place in June 1876 at Little Bighorn, when General George A. Custer and his entire command of 250 men perished. The Sioux and Cheyenne warriors, led by Sitting Bull and Crazy Horse, were defending tribal land in the Black Hills of the Dakota Territory.

Events like these delayed only temporarily the onward march of white soldiers, settlers, and prospectors. Between the end of the Civil War and 1890, eight new western states entered the Union (Nebraska, Colorado, North and South Dakota, Montana, Washington, Idaho, and Wyoming). Railroads now crisscrossed the Great Plains, farmers and cattlemen exploited land formerly owned by Indians, and the Plains tribes had been concentrated on reservations, where they lived in poverty, preyed on by unscrupulous traders and government agents.

Remaking Indian Life

"The life my people want is a life of freedom," Sitting Bull declared. The Indian idea of freedom, however, which centered on preserving their cultural and political autonomy and control of ancestral lands, conflicted with the interests and values of most white Americans.

Sitting Bull, probably the best-known Native American of the late nineteenth century, in a photograph from 1885.

In 1871, Congress eliminated the treaty system that dated back to the revolutionary era, by which the federal government negotiated agreements with Indians as if they were independent nations. The federal government also pressed forward with its assault on Indian culture. The Bureau of Indian Affairs established boarding schools where Indian children, removed from the "negative" influences of their parents and tribes, were dressed in non-Indian clothes, given new names, and educated in white ways.

The Dawes Act and Wounded Knee

The crucial step in attacking "tribalism" came in 1887 with the passage of the **Dawes Act**, named for Senator Henry L. Dawes of Massachusetts, chair of the Senate's Indian Affairs Committee. The act broke up the land of nearly all tribes into small parcels to be distributed to Indian families, with the remainder auctioned off to white purchasers. Indians who accepted the farms and "adopted the habits of civilized life" would become full-fledged American citizens. The policy proved to be a disaster, leading to the loss of much tribal land and the erosion of Indian cultural traditions. When the government made 2 million acres of Indian land available in Oklahoma, 50,000 white settlers poured into the territory to claim farms on the single day of April 22, 1889. Further land rushes followed in the 1890s. In the half century after the passage of the Dawes Act, Indians lost 86 million of the 138 million acres of land in their possession in 1887.

A quilt created by a Sioux woman who lived on a reservation in South Dakota around 1900, possibly as a gift for a nearby white family. It depicts scenes of traditional daily life among the Indians, including hunting buffalo and cooking game. The bird's eggs at the top left corner have hatched at the bottom right.

Some Indians sought solace in the **Ghost Dance**, a religious revitalization campaign. Its leaders foretold a day when whites disappear, the buffalo would return, and Indians could once again practice their ancestral customs "free from misery, death, and disease." Large numbers of Indians gathered for days of singing, dancing, and religious observances. Fearing a general uprising, the government sent troops to the reservations. On December 29, 1890, soldiers opened fire on Ghost Dancers encamped near Wounded Knee Creek in South Dakota, killing between 150 and 200 Indians, mostly women and children. The Wounded Knee massacre was widely applauded in the press. An army court of inquiry essentially exonerated the troops and their commander, and twenty soldiers were later awarded the Medal of Honor, a recognition of exceptional heroism in battle, for their actions at Wounded Knee.

The Wounded Knee massacre marked the end of four centuries of armed conflict between the continent's native population and European

Despite white efforts to remake Indian life, traditional crafts survived. This photograph, taken in 1903, depicts a pottery maker in the Isleta Pueblo near Albuquerque, New Mexico.

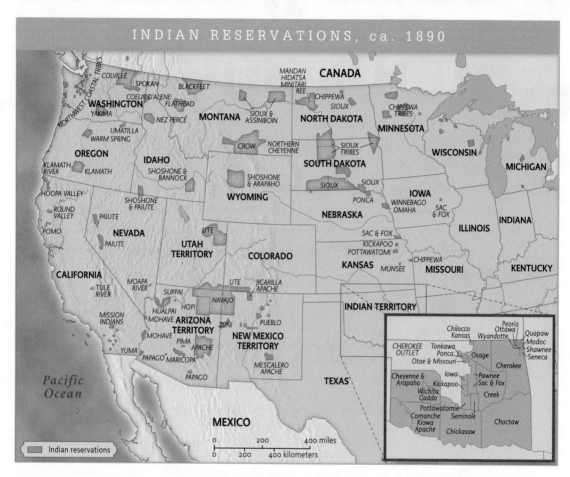

INDIAN RESERVATIONS, ca. 1890

☐ Indian reservations

settlers and their descendants. By 1900, the Indian population had fallen to 250,000, the lowest point in American history. Of that number, 53,000 had become American citizens by accepting land allotments under the Dawes Act. The following year, Congress granted citizenship to 100,000 residents of Indian Territory (in present-day Oklahoma). The remainder would have to wait until 1919 (for those who fought in World War I) and 1924, when Congress made all Indians American citizens.

By 1890, the vast majority of the remaining Indian population had been removed to reservations scattered across the western states.

Settler Societies and Global Wests

The conquest of the American West was part of a global process whereby settlers moved boldly into the interior of regions in temperate climates around the world, bringing their familiar crops and livestock and establishing

A global process

VOICES OF FREEDOM

From Andrew Carnegie, "Wealth" (1889)

One of the richest men in Gilded Age America, Andrew Carnegie promoted what he called the gospel of wealth, the idea that those who accumulated money had an obligation to use it to promote the advancement of society. He explained his outlook in this article in the *North American Review*, one of the era's most prominent magazines.

The problem of our age is the proper administration of wealth, so that the ties of brotherhood may still bind together the rich and poor in harmonious relationship. The conditions of human life have not only been changed, but revolutionized, within the past few hundred years. . . . The contrast between the palace of the millionaire and the cottage of the laborer with us to-day measures the change which has come with civilization.

This change, however, is not to be deplored, but welcomed as highly beneficial. It is well, nay, essential for the progress of the race, that the houses of some should be homes for all that is highest and best in literature and the arts, and for all the refinements of civilization, rather than that none should be so. . . .

In bestowing charity, the main consideration should be to help those who will help themselves. . . . He is the only true reformer who is as careful and as anxious not to aid the unworthy as he is to aid the worthy, and, perhaps, even more so, for in alms-giving more injury is probably done by rewarding vice than by relieving virtue. . . .

The best means of benefitting the community is to place within its reach the ladders upon which the aspiring can rise—parks, and means of recreation, by which men are helped in body and mind; works of art, certain to give pleasure and improve the public taste, and public institutions of various kinds, which will improve the general condition of the people—in this manner returning their surplus wealth to the mass of their fellows in the forms best calculated to do them lasting good.

Thus is the problem of Rich and Poor to be solved. The laws of accumulation will be left free; the laws of distribution free. Individualism will continue, but the millionaire will be but a trustee for the poor.

From Ira Steward, "A Second Declaration of Independence" (1879)

At a Fourth of July celebration in Chicago in 1879, Ira Steward, the most prominent labor leader associated with the movement for the eight-hour day, invoked the legacy of the Declaration of Independence and the abolition of slavery during the Civil War to discuss labor's grievances.

Resolved, That the practical question for an American Fourth of July is not between freedom and slavery, but between wealth and poverty. For if it is true that laborers ought to have as little as possible of the wealth they produce, South Carolina slaveholders were right and the Massachusetts abolitionists were wrong. Because, when the working classes are denied everything but the barest necessities of life, they have no decent use for liberty. . . .

Slavery is . . . the child of poverty, instead of poverty the child of slavery: and freedom is the child of wealth, instead of wealth the child of freedom. The only road, therefore, to universal freedom is the road that leads to universal wealth.

Resolved, That while the Fourth of July was heralded a hundred years ago in the name of Liberty, we now herald this day in behalf of the great economic measure of Eight Hours, or shorter day's work for wageworkers everywhere . . . because more leisure, rest and thought will cultivate habits, customs, and expenditures that mean higher wages: and the world's highest paid laborers now furnish each other with vastly more occupations or days' work than the lowest paid workers can give to one another. . . . [And] if the worker's power to buy increases with his power to do, granaries and warehouses will empty their pockets, and farms and factories fill up with producers. . . .

And we call to the workers of the whole civilized world, especially those of France, Germany, and Great Britain, to join hands with the laborers of the United States in this mighty movement. . . .

On the . . . issue of eight hours, therefore, or less hours, we join hands with all, regardless of politics, nationality, color, religion, or sex; knowing no friends or foes except as they aid or oppose this long-postponed and world-wide movement.

And for the soundness of our political economy, as well as the rectitude of our intentions, we confidently and gladly appeal to the wiser statesmanship of the civilized world.

QUESTIONS

1. *Why does Carnegie think it is better to build public institutions than to give charity to the poor?*

2. *Why does Ira Steward appeal to other countries for assistance and understanding?*

3. *Compare the views of Carnegie and Stewart about how the economy should operate.*

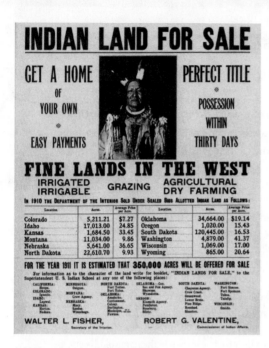

INDIAN LAND FOR SALE

GET A HOME
OF
YOUR OWN
❖
EASY PAYMENTS

PERFECT TITLE

POSSESSION
WITHIN
THIRTY DAYS

FINE LANDS IN THE WEST

| IRRIGATED IRRIGABLE | GRAZING | AGRICULTURAL DRY FARMING |

IN 1910 THE DEPARTMENT OF THE INTERIOR SOLD UNDER SEALED BIDS ALLOTTED INDIAN LANDS AS FOLLOWS:

Location	Acres	Average Price per Acre	Location	Acres	Average Price per Acre
Colorado	5,211.21	$7.27	Oklahoma	34,664.00	$19.14
Idaho	17,013.00	24.85	Oregon	1,020.00	15.43
Kansas	1,684.50	33.45	South Dakota	120,445.00	16.53
Montana	11,034.00	9.86	Washington	4,879.00	41.37
Nebraska	5,641.00	36.65	Wisconsin	1,069.00	17.00
North Dakota	22,610.70	9.93	Wyoming	865.00	20.64

FOR THE YEAR 1911 IT IS ESTIMATED THAT 350,000 ACRES WILL BE OFFERED FOR SALE

For information as to the character of the land write for booklet, "INDIAN LANDS FOR SALE," to the Superintendent U. S. Indian School at any one of the following places:

| CALIFORNIA: | MINNESOTA: | NORTH DAKOTA: | OKLAHOMA—Con. | SOUTH DAKOTA: | WASHINGTON: |
Hoopa. | Onigum. | Fort Totten. | Sac and Fox Agency. | Cheyenne Agency. | Fort Simcoe. |
COLORADO: | MONTANA: | Fort Yates. | Shawnee. | Crow Creek. | Fort Spokane. |
Ignacio. | Crow Agency. | OKLAHOMA: | Wyandotte. | Greenwood. | Tulalip. |
IDAHO: | NEBRASKA: | Anadarko. | OREGON: | Lower Brule. | Tulalip. |
Lapwai. | Macy. | Cantonment. | Klamath Agency. | Pine Ridge. | WISCONSIN: |
KANSAS: | Santee. | Colony. | Pendleton. | Rosebud. | Oneida. |
Horton. | Winnebago. | Darlington. | Roseburg. | Sisseton. |
Nadeau. | | Muskogee, etc. | Siletz. |
| | Pawnee. |

WALTER L. FISHER, Secretary of the Interior.   **ROBERT G. VALENTINE,** Commissioner of Indian Affairs.

A 1911 poster advertising the federal government's sale of land formerly possessed by Indians. Under the Dawes Act of 1887, Indian families were allotted individual farms and the remaining land on reservations, so-called surplus land, was made available to whites.

mining and other industries. Countries such as Argentina, Australia, Canada, and New Zealand, as well as the United States, are often called "settler societies," because immigrants from overseas quickly outnumbered and displaced the original inhabitants—unlike in India and most parts of colonial Africa, where fewer Europeans ventured and those who did relied on the labor of the indigenous inhabitants.

In many settler societies, native peoples were subjected to cultural reconstruction similar to policies in the United States. In Australia, the government gathered the Aboriginal populations—their numbers devastated by disease—in "reserves" reminiscent of American Indian reservations. Australia went further than the United States in the forced assimilation of surviving Aboriginal peoples. The government removed large numbers of children from their families to be adopted by whites—a policy abandoned only in the 1970s.

POLITICS IN A GILDED AGE

The era from 1870 to 1890 is the only period of American history commonly known by a derogatory name—the Gilded Age, after the title of an 1873 novel by Mark Twain and Charles Dudley Warner. "Gilded" means covered with a layer of gold, but it also suggests that the glittering surface covers a core of little real value and is therefore deceptive.

The Corruption of Politics

As they had earlier in the nineteenth century, Americans during the Gilded Age saw their nation as an island of political democracy in a world still dominated by undemocratic governments. In Europe, only France and Switzerland enjoyed universal male suffrage. Even in Britain, most of the working class could not vote until the passage of the Reform Act of 1884.

The new corporation and political power

Nonetheless, the power of the new corporations, seemingly immune to democratic control, raised disturbing questions for the American understanding of political freedom as popular self-government. Political corruption was rife. In Pennsylvania's legislature, the "third house" of railroad

The Bosses of the Senate, a cartoon from *Puck*, January 23, 1889, shows well-fed monopolists towering over the obedient senators. Above them, a sign rewrites the closing words of Lincoln's Gettysburg Address: "This is the Senate of the Monopolists, by the Monopolists, and for the Monopolists."

lobbyists supposedly exerted as much influence as the elected chambers. In the West, many lawmakers held stock or directorships in lumber companies and railroads that received public aid.

Urban politics fell under the sway of corrupt political machines like New York's Tweed Ring, which plundered the city of tens of millions of dollars. "Boss" William M. Tweed's organization reached into every neighborhood. He won support from the city's immigrant poor by fashioning a kind of private welfare system that provided food, fuel, and jobs in hard times. A combination of political reformers and businessmen tired of paying tribute to the ring ousted Tweed in the early 1870s, although he remained popular among the city's poor, who considered him an urban Robin Hood.

"Boss" Tweed of New York

At the national level, the most notorious example of corruption came to light during Grant's presidency. This was Crédit Mobilier, a corporation formed by an inner ring of Union Pacific Railroad stockholders to oversee the line's government-assisted construction. Essentially, it enabled the participants to sign contracts with themselves, at an exorbitant profit, to build the new line. The arrangement was protected by the distribution of stock to influential politicians.

The Crédit Mobilier scandal

The Politics of Dead Center

In national elections, party politics bore the powerful imprint of the Civil War. Republicans controlled the industrial North and Midwest and the agrarian West and were particularly strong among members of revivalist churches, Protestant immigrants, and blacks. Organizations of Union

Republican strength

Non-voting territory

Elections of 1876–1892
Voted Democrat 4–5 times
Voted Republican 4–5 times
Voted more irregularly

veterans formed a bulwark of Republican support. Every Republican candidate for president from 1868 to 1900 had fought in the Union army. By 1893, a lavish system of pensions for Union soldiers and their widows and children consumed more than 40 percent of the federal budget. Democrats, after 1877, dominated the South and did well among Catholic voters, especially Irish-Americans, in the nation's cities.

The parties were closely divided. In three of the five presidential elections between 1876 and 1892, the margin separating the major candidates was less than 1 percent of the popular vote. Twice, in 1876 and 1888, the candidate with an electoral-college majority trailed in the popular vote. Only for brief periods did the same party control the White House and both houses of Congress. More than once, Congress found itself paralyzed as important bills shuttled back and forth between House and Senate, and special sessions to complete legislation became necessary. Gilded Age presidents made little effort to mobilize public opinion or extend executive leadership.

Party activism

In some ways, though, American democracy in the Gilded Age seemed remarkably healthy. Elections were closely contested, party loyalty was intense, and 80 percent or more of eligible voters turned out to cast ballots.

Government and the Economy

The nation's political structure, however, proved ill equipped to deal with the problems created by the economy's rapid growth. Despite its expanded scope and powers arising from the Civil War, the federal government remained remarkably small by modern standards. The federal workforce in 1880 numbered 100,000 (today, it exceeds 2.5 million).

The parties and business interest

Nationally, both parties came under the control of powerful political managers with close ties to business interests. Republicans strongly supported a high tariff to protect American industry, and throughout the 1870s they pursued a fiscal policy based on reducing federal spending, repaying much of the national debt, and withdrawing **greenbacks**—the paper money issued by the Union during the Civil War—from circulation. Democrats opposed the high tariff, but the party's national leadership remained closely linked to New York bankers and financiers and resisted demands from debt-ridden agricultural areas for an increase in the money supply. In 1879, for the first time since the war, the United States returned to the gold standard—that is, paper currency became exchangeable for gold at a fixed rate.

Republican economic policies strongly favored the interests of eastern industrialists and bankers. These policies worked to the disadvantage of southern and western farmers, who had to pay a premium for manufactured goods while the prices they received for their produce steadily declined.

Reform Legislation

Gilded Age national politics did not entirely lack accomplishments. Inspired in part by President Garfield's assassination by a disappointed office seeker, the Civil Service Act of 1883 created a merit system for federal employees, with appointment via competitive examinations rather than political influence. Although it applied at first to only 10 percent of the more than 100,000 government workers, the act marked the first step in establishing a professional civil service and removing officeholding from the hands of political machines. (However, since funds raised from political appointees had helped to finance the political parties, civil service reform had the unintended result of increasing politicians' dependence on donations from business interests.)

This political cartoon from the 1884 presidential campaign depicts Republican nominee James G. Blaine as a champion of a high tariff that would protect American workers from cheap foreign labor. Blaine's attire is a reference to the nominating speech at the Republican convention by Robert G. Ingersoll, who referred to the candidate as a "plumed knight."

In 1887, in response to public outcries against railroad practices, Congress established the **Interstate Commerce Commission** (ICC) to ensure that the rates railroads charged farmers and merchants to transport their goods were "reasonable" and did not offer more favorable treatment to some shippers over others. The ICC was the first federal agency intended to regulate economic activity, but since it lacked the power to establish rates on its own—it could only sue companies in court—it had little impact on railroad practices. Three years later, Congress passed the **Sherman Antitrust Act**, which banned all combinations and practices that restrained free trade. But the language was so vague that the act proved almost impossible to enforce. Weak as they were, these laws helped to establish the precedent that the national government could regulate the economy to promote the public good.

Legacy of economic reform legislation

Political Conflict in the States

At the state and local level the Gilded Age was an era of political ferment and conflict over the proper uses of governmental authority. In the immediate aftermath of the Civil War, state governments in the North, like

Laying Tracks at Union Square for a Railroad, an 1890 painting, depicts one of the era's many public works assisted by state and local governments.

those in the Reconstruction South, greatly expanded their responsibility for public health, welfare, and education, and cities invested heavily in public works such as park construction and improved water and gas services.

The policies of railroad companies produced a growing chorus of protest, especially in the West. Farmers and local merchants complained of excessively high freight rates, discrimination in favor of large producers and shippers, and high fees charged by railroad-controlled grain warehouses. Critics of the railroads came together in the **Patrons of Husbandry**, or Grange (1867), which moved to establish cooperatives for storing and marketing farm output in the hope of forcing the carriers "to take our produce at a fair price."

At the same time, the labor movement, revitalized during the Civil War, demanded laws establishing eight hours as a legal day's work. Seven northern legislatures passed such laws, but since most lacked strong means of enforcement they remained dead letters. Nevertheless, the efforts of workers, like those of farmers, inspired a far-reaching national debate.

FREEDOM IN THE GILDED AGE

The Social Problem

As the United States matured into an industrial economy, Americans struggled to make sense of the new social order. Debates over political economy engaged the attention of millions of Americans, reaching far beyond the tiny academic world into the public sphere inhabited by self-educated workingmen and farmers, reformers of all kinds, newspaper editors, and politicians. This broad public discussion produced thousands of books, pamphlets, and articles on such technical issues as land taxation and currency reform, as well as widespread debate over the social and ethical implications of economic change.

Social unrest

Many Americans sensed that something had gone wrong in the nation's social development. Talk of "better classes," "respectable classes," and "dangerous classes," dominated public discussion, and bitter labor strikes seemed to have become the rule. In 1881, the Massachusetts Bureau of Labor Statistics reported that virtually every worker it interviewed in Fall River, the nation's largest center of textile production, complained of overwork, poor housing, and tyrannical employers.

With factory workers living on the edge of poverty alongside a growing class of millionaires, it became increasingly difficult to view wage labor as a temporary resting place on the road to economic independence. Yet given the vast expansion of the nation's productive capacity, many Americans viewed the concentration of wealth as inevitable, natural, and justified by progress. By the turn of the century, advanced economics taught that wages were determined by the iron law of supply and demand and that wealth rightly flowed not to those who worked the hardest but to men with business skills and access to money. The close link between freedom and equality, forged in the Revolution and reinforced during the Civil War, appeared increasingly out of date.

Freedom and equality disconnected

Social Darwinism in America

The idea of the natural superiority of some groups to others, which before the Civil War had been invoked to justify slavery in an otherwise free society, now reemerged in the vocabulary of modern science to explain the success and failure of individuals and social classes. In 1859, the British scientist Charles Darwin published *On the Origin of Species*. One of the most influential works of science ever to appear, it expounded the theory of evolution whereby plant and animal species best suited to their environment took the place of those less able to adapt.

Charles Darwin

In a highly oversimplified form, language borrowed from Darwin, such as "natural selection," "the struggle for existence," and "the survival of the fittest," entered public discussion of social problems in the Gilded Age. According to what came to be called **Social Darwinism**, evolution was as natural a process in human society as in nature, and government must not interfere. Especially misguided, in this view, were efforts to uplift those at the bottom of the social order, such as laws regulating conditions of work or public assistance to the poor. The giant industrial corporation, Social Darwinists believed, had emerged because it was better adapted to its environment than earlier forms of enterprise. To restrict its operations by legislation would reduce society to a more primitive level.

The misapplication of Darwin's theory of evolution

Even the depressions of the 1870s and 1890s did not shake the widespread view that the poor were essentially responsible for their own fate. Failure to advance in society was widely thought to indicate a lack of character, an absence of self-reliance and determination in the face of adversity.

The era's most influential Social Darwinist was Yale professor William Graham Sumner. For Sumner, freedom required frank acceptance of inequality. Society faced two and only two alternatives: "liberty, inequality, survival of the fittest; not-liberty, equality, survival of the unfittest." Government, Sumner believed, existed only to protect "the property of men and the honor of women," not to upset social arrangements decreed by nature.

Liberty of Contract and the Courts

The growing influence of Social Darwinism helped to popularize an idea that would be embraced by the business and professional classes in the last quarter of the nineteenth century—a "negative" definition of freedom as limited government and an unrestrained free market. Central to this social vision was the idea of contract. So long as labor relations were governed by contracts freely arrived at by independent individuals, neither the government nor unions had a right to interfere with working conditions, and Americans had no grounds to complain of a loss of freedom. Thus the principle of free labor, which originated as a celebration of the independent small producer in a society of broad equality and social harmony, was transformed into a defense of the unrestrained operations of the capitalist marketplace.

State and federal courts regularly struck down state laws regulating economic enterprise as an interference with the right of the free laborer to choose his employment and working conditions, and of the entrepreneur to utilize his property as he saw fit. For decades, the courts viewed state regulation of business—especially laws establishing maximum hours of work and safe working conditions—as an insult to free labor.

The courts generally sided with business enterprises that complained of a loss of economic freedom. In 1885, the New York Court of Appeals invalidated a state law that prohibited the manufacture of cigars in tenement dwellings on the grounds that such legislation deprived the worker of the "liberty" to work "where he will." Although women still lacked political rights, they were increasingly understood to possess the same economic "liberty," defined in this way, as men. The Illinois Supreme Court in 1895 declared unconstitutional a state law that outlawed the production of garments in sweatshops and established a forty-eight-hour work week for women and children.

In 1895 in *United States v. E. C. Knight Co.*, the U.S. Supreme Court ruled that the Sherman Antitrust Act of 1890, which barred combinations in restraint of trade, could not be used to break up a sugar refining monopoly, because the Constitution empowered Congress to regulate commerce but not manufacturing. Their unwillingness to allow regulation of the economy, however, did not prevent the courts from acting to impede labor organization. The Sherman Act, intended to prevent business mergers that stifled competition, was used by judges primarily to issue injunctions prohibiting strikes on the grounds that they illegally interfered with the freedom of trade.

In a 1905 case that became almost as notorious as *Dred Scott*, the Supreme Court in *Lochner v. New York* voided a state law establishing ten hours per day or sixty per week as the maximum hours of work for bakers. By this time, the Court was invoking "liberty" in ways that could easily seem absurd. In one case, it overturned as a violation of "personal liberty" a Kansas law prohibiting "yellow-dog" contracts, which made nonmembership in a union a condition of employment. In another, it struck down state laws requiring payment of coal miners in money rather than paper usable only at company-owned stores. Workers, observed mine union leader John P. Mitchell, could not but feel that "they are being guaranteed the liberties they do not want and denied the liberty that is of real value to them."

> Lochner v. New York

LABOR AND THE REPUBLIC

"The Overwhelming Labor Question"

As Mitchell's remark suggests, public debate in the late nineteenth century, more than at almost any other moment in American history, divided along class lines. The shift from the slavery controversy to what one politician called "the overwhelming labor question" was dramatically illustrated in 1877, the year of both the end of Reconstruction and also the first national labor walkout— the Great Railroad Strike. When workers protesting a pay cut paralyzed rail traffic in much of the country, militia units tried to force them back to work. After troops fired on strikers in Pittsburgh, killing twenty people, workers responded by burning the city's railroad yards, destroying millions of dollars in property. General strikes paralyzed Chicago and St. Louis. The strike revealed both a strong sense of solidarity among workers and the close ties between the Republican Party and the new class of industrialists. President Rutherford B. Hayes, who a few months earlier had ordered federal troops in the South to end their involvement in local politics, ordered the army into the North. The workers, the president wrote in his diary, were "put down by force."

Ruins of the Pittsburgh Round House, a photograph published in the July 1895 issue of *Scribner's Magazine*, shows the widespread destruction of property during the Great Railroad Strike of July 1877.

The Great Labor Parade of September 1, from *Frank Leslie's Illustrated Newspaper*, *September 13, 1884*. A placard illustrates how the labor movement identified Gilded Age employers with the Slave Power of the pre–Civil War era.

In the aftermath of 1877, the federal government constructed armories in major cities to ensure that troops would be on hand in the event of further labor difficulties. Henceforth, national power would be used not to protect beleaguered former slaves but to guarantee the rights of property.

The Knights of Labor and the "Conditions Essential to Liberty"

The 1880s witnessed a new wave of labor organizing. At its center stood the **Knights of Labor**, led by Terence V. Powderly. The Knights were the first group to try to organize unskilled workers as well as skilled, women alongside men, and blacks as well as whites (although even the Knights excluded the despised Asian immigrants on the West Coast). The group reached a peak membership of nearly 800,000 in 1886 and involved millions of workers in strikes, boycotts, political action, and educational and social activities.

Labor reformers of the Gilded Age put forward a wide array of programs, from the eight-hour day to public employment in hard times, currency reform, anarchism, socialism, and the creation of a vaguely defined "cooperative commonwealth." Labor raised the question whether meaningful freedom could exist in a situation of extreme economic inequality.

Middle-Class Reformers

Social thought in the Gilded Age

Dissatisfaction with social conditions in the Gilded Age extended well beyond aggrieved workers. Alarmed by fear of class warfare and the growing power of concentrated capital, social thinkers offered numerous plans for change. In the last quarter of the century, more than 150 utopian or cataclysmic novels appeared, predicting that social conflict would end either in a new, harmonious social order or in total catastrophe.

Of the many books proposing more optimistic remedies for the unequal distribution of wealth, the most popular were *Progress and Poverty* (1879) by Henry George, *The Cooperative Commonwealth* (1884) by Laurence Gronlund, and Edward Bellamy's *Looking Backward* (1888). All three were among the century's greatest best-sellers, their extraordinary success testifying to what George called "a wide-spread consciousness . . . that there is something *radically* wrong in the present social organization." All three writers, though in very different ways, sought to reclaim an imagined golden age of social harmony and American freedom.

Progress and Poverty probably commanded more public attention than any book on economics in American history. Henry George began with a famous statement of "the problem" suggested by its title—the growth of "squalor and misery" alongside material progress. His solution was the "single tax," which would replace other taxes with a levy on increases in the value of real estate. No one knows how many of Henry George's readers actually believed in this way of solving the nation's ills. But millions responded to his clear explanation of economic relationships and his stirring account of how the "social distress" long thought to be confined to the Old World had made its appearance in the New.

> *Henry George's* Progress and Poverty

Quite different in outlook was *The Cooperative Commonwealth*, the first book to popularize socialist ideas for an American audience. Its author, Laurence Gronlund, was a lawyer who had emigrated from Denmark in 1867. Socialism—the belief that private control of economic enterprises should be replaced by government ownership in order to ensure a fairer distribution of the benefits of the wealth produced—became a major political force in western Europe in the late nineteenth century. In the United States, however, where access to private property was widely considered essential to individual freedom, socialist beliefs were largely confined to immigrants, whose writings, frequently in foreign languages, attracted little attention.

> *Socialism*

Gronlund began the process of socialism's Americanization. Whereas Karl Marx, the nineteenth century's most influential socialist theorist, had predicted that socialism would come into being via a working-class revolution, Gronlund portrayed it as the end result of a process of peaceful evolution, not violent upheaval. He thus made socialism seem more acceptable to middle-class Americans who desired an end to class conflict and the restoration of social harmony.

Not until the early twentieth century would socialism become a significant presence in American public life. As Gronlund himself noted, the most important result of *The Cooperative Commonwealth* was to prepare an audience for Edward Bellamy's *Looking Backward*, which promoted socialist ideas while "ignoring that name" (Bellamy wrote of nationalism, not socialism). In *Looking Backward*, his main character falls asleep in the late nineteenth century only to awaken in the year 2000, in a world where cooperation has replaced class strife, "excessive individualism," and cutthroat competition. Freedom, Bellamy insisted, was a social condition resting on interdependence, not autonomy.

Edward Bellamy, author of the utopian novel *Looking Backward*.

The book inspired the creation of hundreds of nationalist clubs devoted to bringing into existence the world of 2000 and left a profound mark on a generation of reformers and intellectuals. Bellamy held out the hope of retaining the material abundance made possible by industrial capitalism while eliminating inequality.

Protestants and Moral Reform

Mainstream Protestants played a major role in seeking to stamp out sin during the Gilded Age. What one historian calls a "Christian lobby" promoted political solutions to what they saw as the moral problems raised by labor conflict and the growth of cities, and threats to religious faith by Darwinism and other scientific advances.

Legislation on morals

Unlike the pre–Civil War period, when "moral suasion" was the preferred approach of many reformers, powerful national organizations like the Women's Christian Temperance Union, National Reform Association, and Reform Bureau now campaigned for federal legislation that would "christianize the government" by outlawing sinful behavior. Among the proposed targets were the consumption of alcohol, gambling, prostitution, polygamy, and birth control. In a striking departure from the prewar situation, southerners joined in the campaign for federal regulation of individual behavior, something whites in the region had strongly opposed before the Civil War, fearing it could lead to action against slavery. The key role played by the white South in the campaign for moral legislation

The Bible Belt

helped earn the region a reputation as the Bible Belt—a place where political action revolved around religious principles. Although efforts to enact a national law requiring businesses to close on Sunday failed, the Christian lobby's efforts set the stage for later legislation such as the Mann Act of 1910, banning the transportation of women across state lines for immoral purposes (an effort to suppress prostitution), and Prohibition.

A Social Gospel

Most of the era's Protestant preachers concentrated on attacking individual sins like drinking and Sabbath-breaking and saw nothing immoral about the pursuit of riches. But the outlines of what came to be called the **Social**

Rauschenbusch and Gladden

Gospel were taking shape in the writings of Walter Rauschenbusch, a Baptist minister in New York City; Washington Gladden, a Congregational clergyman in Columbus, Ohio; and others. They insisted that freedom and spiritual self-development required an equalization of wealth and power and that unbridled competition mocked the Christian ideal of brotherhood.

The Social Gospel movement originated as an effort to reform Protestant churches by expanding their appeal in poor urban neighborhoods and making them more attentive to the era's social ills. The movement's adherents established missions and relief programs in urban areas that attempted to alleviate poverty, combat child labor, and encourage the construction of better working-class housing. Within American Catholicism as well, a group of priests and bishops emerged who attempted to alter the church's traditional hostility to movements for social reform and its isolation from contemporary currents of social thought. With most of its parishioners working men and women, they argued, the church should lend its support to the labor movement.

The Haymarket Affair

The year of the dedication of the Statue of Liberty, 1886, also witnessed an unprecedented upsurge in labor activity. On May 1, 1886, some 350,000 workers in cities across the country demonstrated for an eight-hour day. Having originated in the United States, May 1, or May Day as it came to be called, soon became an annual date of parades, picnics, and protests, celebrated around the world by organized labor.

The first May Day

The most dramatic events of 1886 took place in Chicago, a city with a large and vibrant labor movement that brought together native-born and immigrant workers, whose outlooks ranged from immigrant socialism and anarchism to American traditions of equality and anti-monopoly. On May 3, 1886, four strikers were killed by police. The next day, a rally was held in Haymarket Square to protest the killings. Near the end of the speeches, someone—whose identity has never been determined—threw a bomb into the crowd, killing a policeman. The panicked police opened fire, shooting several bystanders and a number of their own force. Soon after, police raided the offices of labor and radical groups and arrested their leaders. Employers took the opportunity to paint the labor movement as a dangerous and un-American force, prone to violence and controlled by foreign-born radicals. Eight anarchists were charged with plotting and carrying out the bombing. Even though the evidence against them was extremely weak, a jury convicted the "Haymarket martyrs." Four were hanged, one committed suicide in prison, and the remaining three were imprisoned until John Peter Altgeld, a pro-labor governor of Illinois, commuted their sentences in 1893.

Haymarket protests

Seven of the eight men accused of plotting the Haymarket bombing were foreign-born—six Germans and an English immigrant. The last was Albert Parsons, a native of Alabama who had served in the Confederate

In this pro-labor cartoon from 1888, a workingman rescues liberty from the stranglehold of monopolies and the pro-business major parties.

army in the Civil War, married a black woman, and edited a Republican newspaper in Texas during Reconstruction. Having survived the Ku Klux Klan in Reconstruction Texas, Parsons perished on the Illinois gallows for a crime that he, like the other "Haymarket martyrs," did not commit.

Labor and Politics

The Haymarket affair took place amid an outburst of independent labor political activity. In Kansas City, for example, a coalition of black and Irish-American workers and middle-class voters elected Tom Hanna as mayor. He proceeded to side with unions rather than employers in industrial disputes.

The most celebrated labor campaign took place in New York City, where in 1886, somewhat to his own surprise, Henry George found himself thrust into the role of labor's candidate for mayor. George's aim in running was to bring attention to the single tax on land. The labor leaders who organized the United Labor Party had more immediate goals in mind, especially stopping the courts from barring strikes and jailing unionists for conspiracy. A few days after the dedication of the Statue of Liberty, New Yorkers flocked to the polls to elect their mayor. Nearly 70,000 voted for George, who finished second, eclipsing the total of the Republican candidate, Theodore Roosevelt, and coming close to defeating Democrat Abram Hewitt.

The events of 1886 suggested that labor might be on the verge of establishing itself as a permanent political force. In fact, that year marked the high point of the Knights of Labor. Facing increasing employer hostility and linked by employers and the press to the violence and radicalism associated with the Haymarket events, the Knights soon declined. The major parties, moreover, proved remarkably resourceful in appealing to labor voters.

Decline of Knights of Labor

In the early twentieth century, reformers would turn to new ways of addressing the social conditions of freedom and new means of increasing ordinary Americans' political and economic liberty. But before this, in the 1890s, the nation would face its gravest crisis since the Civil War, and the boundaries of freedom would once again be redrawn.

CHAPTER REVIEW AND ONLINE RESOURCES

REVIEW QUESTIONS

1. *The American economy thrived because of federal involvement, not the lack of it. How did the federal government actively promote industrial and agricultural development in this period?*

2. *Why were railroads so important to America's second industrial revolution? What events demonstrate their influence on society and politics as well as the economy?*

3. *Why did organized efforts of farmers, workers, and local reformers largely fail to achieve substantive change in the Gilded Age?*

4. *Describe the involvement of American family farmers in the global economy after 1870 and its effects on their independence.*

5. *How successfully did third parties lead movements for reform at the state level?*

6. *How did American political leaders seek to remake Indians and change the ways they lived?*

7. *How do the ideas of Henry George, Edward Bellamy, and other authors conflict with Social Darwinism?*

8. *How did social reformers such as Edward Bellamy, Henry George, and advocates of the Social Gospel movement conceive of liberty and freedom differently than the proponents of the liberty of contract ideal and laissez-faire?*

9. *In what ways did the West provide a "safety valve" for the problems in the industrial East? In what ways did it reveal some of the same problems?*

KEY TERMS

"great upheaval" of 1886 (p. 476)

"trusts" (p. 480)

vertical integration (p. 481)

"captains of industry" vs. "robber barons" (p. 482)

"bonanza farms" (p. 486)

Dawes Act (p. 490)

Ghost Dance (p. 490)

gospel of wealth (p. 492)

greenbacks (p. 496)

Interstate Commerce Commission (p. 497)

Sherman Antitrust Act (p. 497)

Patrons of Husbandry (p. 498)

Social Darwinism (p. 499)

liberty of contract (p. 500)

Knights of Labor (p. 502)

Social Gospel (p. 504)

Haymarket Affair (p. 505)

wwnorton.com
/studyspace

VISIT STUDYSPACE FOR THESE
RESOURCES AND MORE

- A chapter outline
- A diagnostic chapter quiz
- Interactive maps
- Map worksheets
- Multimedia documents

CHAPTER 17

FREEDOM'S BOUNDARIES, AT HOME AND ABROAD

★

1890–1900

A Trifle Embarrassed, a cartoon from the magazine *Puck* in 1898, depicts Uncle Sam and a female figure of liberty standing at the gate of a Foundling [Orphan] Asylum and being presented with orphans representing Puerto Rico, Hawaii, Cuba, and the Philippines. These were the territories acquired by the United States during the Spanish-American War. (All but Cuba remained American possessions.) The artist seems to question whether the United States is prepared to assume the role of imperial power.

One of the most popular songs of 1892 bore the title "Father Was Killed by a Pinkerton Man." It was inspired by an incident during a bitter strike at Andrew Carnegie's steelworks at Homestead, Pennsylvania, the nineteenth century's most widely publicized confrontation between labor and capital.

Homestead's twelve steel mills were the most profitable and technologically advanced in the world. The union contract gave the Amalgamated Association a considerable say in their operation, including the right to approve the hiring of new workers and to regulate the pace of work. In 1892, Carnegie and Henry Clay Frick, his local supervisor, decided to operate the plant on a nonunion basis. Henceforth, only workers who agreed not to join the union could work at Homestead. In response, the workers blockaded the steelworks and mobilized support from the local community. The battle memorialized in song took place on July 6, 1892, when armed strikers confronted 300 private policemen from the Pinkerton Detective Agency. Seven workers and three Pinkerton agents were killed, and the Pinkertons were forced to retreat. Four days later, the governor of Pennsylvania dispatched 8,000 militiamen to open the complex on management's terms. In the end, the Amalgamated Association was destroyed.

Homestead demonstrated that neither a powerful union nor public opinion could influence the conduct of the largest corporations. Moreover, two American ideas of freedom collided at Homestead—the employers' definition, based on the idea that property rights, unrestrained by union rules or public regulation, sustained the public good; and the workers' conception, which stressed economic security and independence from what they considered the "tyranny" of employers. During the 1890s, many Americans came to believe that they were being denied economic independence and democratic self-government, long central to the popular understanding of freedom.

Millions of farmers joined the Populist movement in an attempt to reverse their declining economic prospects and to rescue the government from what they saw as control by powerful corporate interests. The 1890s witnessed the imposition of a new racial system in the South that locked African-Americans into the status of second-class citizenship, denying them many of the freedoms white Americans took for granted. Increasing immigration produced heated debates over whether the country should reconsider its traditional self-definition as a refuge for foreigners seeking greater

FOCUS QUESTIONS

- *What were the origins and the significance of Populism?*

- *How did the liberties of blacks after 1877 give way to legal segregation across the South?*

- *In what ways did the boundaries of American freedom grow narrower in this period?*

- *How did the United States emerge as an imperial power in the 1890s?*

Andrew Carnegie's ironworks at Homestead, Pennsylvania.

freedom on American shores. At the end of the 1890s, in the Spanish-American War, the United States for the first time acquired overseas possessions and found itself ruling over subject peoples from Puerto Rico to the Philippines. Was the democratic republic, many Americans wondered, becoming an empire like those of Europe? Rarely has the country experienced at one time so many debates over both the meaning of freedom and freedom's boundaries.

THE POPULIST CHALLENGE

The Farmers' Revolt

Even as labor unrest crested, a different kind of uprising was ripening in the South and the trans-Mississippi West, a response to falling agricultural prices and growing economic dependency in rural areas. In the South, the sharecropping system, discussed in Chapter 15, locked millions of tenant farmers, white and black, into perpetual poverty. The interruption of cotton exports during the Civil War had led to the rapid *Causes of unrest* expansion of production in India, Egypt, and Brazil. The glut of cotton on the world market led to declining prices, throwing millions of small farmers deep into debt and threatening them with the loss of their land. In the West, farmers who had mortgaged their property to purchase seed, fertilizer, and equipment faced the prospect of losing their farms when unable to repay their bank loans. Farmers increasingly believed that their plight derived from the high freight rates charged by railroad companies, excessive interest rates for loans from merchants and bankers, and the fiscal policies of the federal government (discussed in the previous chapter) that reduced the supply of money and helped to push down farm prices.

The Farmers' Alliance   Through the Farmers' Alliance, the largest citizens' movement of the nineteenth century, farmers sought to remedy their condition. Founded in Texas in the late 1870s, the Alliance spread to forty-three states by 1890. The Alliance proposed that the federal government establish warehouses where farmers could store their crops until they were sold. Using the crops as collateral, the government would then issue loans to farmers at low interest rates, thereby ending their dependence on bankers and merchants. Since it would have to be enacted by Congress, the "subtreasury plan," as this proposal was called, led the Alliance into politics.

The People's Party

In the early 1890s, the Alliance evolved into the **People's Party (or Populists)**, the era's greatest political insurgency. Attempting to speak for all "producing classes," the party did not just appeal to farmers. It achieved some of its greatest successes in states like Colorado and Idaho, where it won the support of miners and industrial workers. But its major base lay in the cotton and wheat belts of the South and West.

The Populists embarked on a remarkable effort of community organization and education. To spread their message they published numerous pamphlets on political and economic questions, established more than 1,000 local newspapers, and sent traveling speakers throughout rural America. At great gatherings on the western plains, similar in some ways to religious revival meetings, and in small-town southern country stores, one observer wrote, "people commenced to think who had never thought before, and people talked who had seldom spoken." Here was the last great political expression of the nineteenth-century vision of America as a commonwealth of small producers whose freedom rested on the ownership of productive property and respect for the dignity of labor.

Populist organizing

But although the Populists used the familiar language of nineteenth-century radicalism, they were hardly a backward-looking movement. They embraced the modern technologies that made large-scale cooperative enterprise possible—the railroad, the telegraph, and the national market—while looking to the federal government to regulate those technologies in the public interest. They promoted agricultural education and believed farmers should adopt modern scientific methods of cultivation.

The Populist message

A group of Kansas Populists, perhaps on their way to a political gathering, in a photograph from the 1890s.

The Populist Platform

Proposals of reform

The Populist platform of 1892, adopted at the party's Omaha convention, remains a classic document of American reform. Written by Ignatius Donnelly, a Minnesota editor, it spoke of a nation "brought to the verge of moral, political, and material ruin" by political corruption and economic inequality. The platform put forth a long list of proposals to restore democracy and economic opportunity, many of which would be adopted during the next half-century: the direct election of U.S. senators, government control of the currency, a graduated income tax, a system of low-cost public financing to enable farmers to market their crops, and recognition of the right of workers to form labor unions. In addition, Populists called for public ownership of the railroads to guarantee farmers inexpensive access to markets for their crops. A generation would pass before a major party offered so sweeping a plan for political action to create the social conditions of freedom.

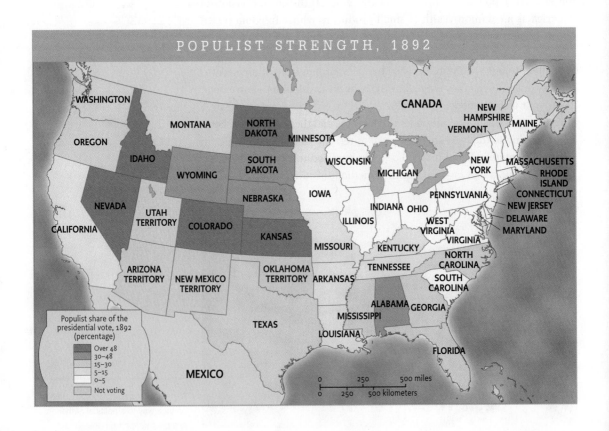

POPULIST STRENGTH, 1892

Populist share of the presidential vote, 1892 (percentage)

- Over 48
- 30–48
- 15–30
- 5–15
- 0–5
- Not voting

The Populist Coalition

In some southern states, the Populists made remarkable efforts to unite black and white small farmers on a common political and economic program. In general, southern white Populists' racial attitudes did not differ significantly from those of their non-Populist neighbors. Nonetheless, recognizing the need for allies to break the Democratic Party's stranglehold on power in the South, some white Populists insisted that black and white farmers shared common grievances and could unite for common goals. Tom Watson, Georgia's leading Populist, worked the hardest to forge a black-white alliance. "You are kept apart," he told interracial audiences, "that you may be separately fleeced of your earnings." While many blacks refused to abandon the party of Lincoln, others were attracted by the Populist appeal. In most of the South, however, Democrats fended off the Populist challenge by resorting to the tactics they had used to retain power since the 1870s—mobilizing whites with warnings about "Negro supremacy," intimidating black voters, and stuffing ballot boxes on election day.

Populism and race

The Populist movement also engaged the energies of thousands of reform-minded women from farm and labor backgrounds. Some, like Mary Elizabeth Lease, a former homesteader and one of the first female lawyers in Kansas, became prominent organizers, campaigners, and strategists. During the 1890s, referendums in Colorado and Idaho approved extending the vote to women, whereas in Kansas and California the proposal went down in defeat. Populists in all these states endorsed woman suffrage.

Women reformers

Populist presidential candidate James Weaver received more than 1 million votes in 1892. The party carried five western states. In his inaugural address in 1893, Lorenzo Lewelling, the new Populist governor of Kansas, anticipated a phrase made famous seventy years later by Martin Luther King Jr.: "I have a dream. . . . A time is foreshadowed when . . . liberty, equality, and justice shall have permanent abiding places in the republic."

Presidential election of 1892

The Government and Labor

Were the Populists on the verge of replacing one of the two major parties? The severe depression that began in 1893 led to increased conflict between capital and labor and seemed to create an opportunity for expanding the Populist vote. Time and again, employers brought state or federal authority to bear to protect their own economic power or put down threats to public order. In May 1894, the federal government deployed soldiers to disperse **Coxey's Army**—a band of several hundred unemployed men led by Ohio businessman Jacob Coxey, who marched to Washington demanding economic relief.

Also in 1894, workers in the company-owned town of Pullman, Illinois, where railroad sleeping cars were manufactured, called a strike to protest a reduction in wages. The American Railway Union announced that its members would refuse to handle trains with Pullman cars. When the boycott crippled national rail service, President Grover Cleveland's attorney general, Richard Olney (himself on the board of several railroad companies), obtained a federal court injunction ordering the strikers back to work. Federal troops and U.S. marshals soon occupied railroad centers like Chicago and Sacramento.

The Pullman Strike

The strike collapsed when the union's leaders, including its charismatic president, Eugene V. Debs, were jailed for contempt of court for violating the judicial order. In the case of *In re Debs*, the Supreme Court unanimously confirmed the sentences and approved the use of injunctions against striking labor unions. On his release from prison in November 1895, more than 100,000 persons greeted Debs at a Chicago railroad depot.

Eugene Debs

Populism and Labor

Federal troops pose atop a railroad engine after being sent to Chicago to help suppress the Pullman strike of 1894.

In 1894, Populists made determined efforts to appeal to industrial workers. Governor Davis Waite of Colorado, who had edited a labor newspaper before his election, sent the militia to protect striking miners against

company police. In the state and congressional elections of that year, as the economic depression deepened, voters by the millions abandoned the Democratic Party of President Cleveland.

In rural areas, the Populist vote increased in 1894. But urban workers did not rally to the Populists, whose core issues—the subtreasury plan and lower mortgage interest rates—had little meaning for them. Urban working-class voters instead shifted en masse to the Republicans, who claimed that raising tariff rates (which Democrats had recently reduced) would restore prosperity by protecting manufacturers and industrial workers from the competition of imported goods and cheap foreign labor. In one of the most decisive shifts in congressional power in American history, the Republicans gained 117 seats in the House of Representatives.

Labor votes

Bryan and Free Silver

In 1896, Democrats and Populists joined to support William Jennings Bryan for the presidency. A thirty-six-year-old congressman from Nebraska, Bryan won the Democratic nomination after delivering to the national convention an electrifying speech that crystallized the farmers' pride and grievances. "Burn down your cities and leave our farms," Bryan proclaimed, "and your cities will spring up again as if by magic; but destroy our farms and grass will grow in the streets of every city in the country." Bryan called for the "free coinage" of silver—the unrestricted minting of silver money. In language ringing with biblical imagery, Bryan condemned the gold standard: "You shall not crucify mankind upon a cross of gold."

Bryan's demand for **"free silver"** was the latest expression of the view that increasing the amount of currency in circulation would raise the prices farmers received for their crops and make it easier to pay off their debts. His nomination wrested control of the Democratic Party from long-dominant leaders like President Grover Cleveland, who were closely tied to eastern businessmen.

There was more to Bryan's appeal, however, than simply free silver. A devoutly religious man, he was strongly influenced by the Social Gospel movement (discussed in the previous chapter). He championed a vision of the government helping ordinary Americans that anticipated provisions of the New Deal of the 1930s, including a progressive income tax, banking regulation, and the right of workers to form unions. Bryan also broke with tradition and embarked on a nationwide speaking tour, seeking to rally farmers and workers to his cause.

A cartoon from the magazine *Judge*, September 14, 1896, condemns William Jennings Bryan and his "cross of gold" speech for defiling the symbols of Christianity. Bryan tramples on the Bible while holding his golden cross; a vandalized church is visible in the background.

The Campaign of 1896

Republicans met the silverite challenge head on, insisting that gold was the only "honest" currency. Abandoning the gold standard, they insisted, would destroy business confidence and prevent recovery from the depression by making creditors unwilling to extend loans, because they could not be certain of the value of the money in which they would be repaid. The party nominated for president Ohio governor William McKinley, who as a congressman in 1890 had shepherded to passage the strongly protectionist McKinley Tariff.

The election of 1896 is sometimes called the first modern presidential campaign because of the amount of money spent by the Republicans and the efficiency of their national organization. Eastern bankers and industrialists, thoroughly alarmed by Bryan's call for monetary inflation and his fiery speeches denouncing corporate arrogance, poured millions of dollars into Republican coffers. (McKinley's campaign raised some $10 million; Bryan's around $300,000.) While McKinley remained at his Ohio home, his political manager Mark Hanna created a powerful national political machine that flooded the country with pamphlets, posters, and campaign buttons.

The results revealed a nation as divided along regional lines as in 1860. Bryan carried the South and West and received 6.5 million votes. McKinley swept the more populous industrial states of the Northeast and Midwest, attracting 7.1 million. Industrial America, from financiers and managers to workers, now voted solidly Republican, a loyalty reinforced when prosperity returned after 1897.

McKinley's victory shattered the political stalemate that had persisted since 1876 and created one of the most enduring political majorities in American history. During McKinley's presidency, Republicans placed their stamp on economic policy by passing the Dingley Tariff of 1897, raising rates to the highest level in history, and the Gold Standard Act of 1900. Not until 1932, in the midst of another economic depression, would the Democrats become the nation's majority party.

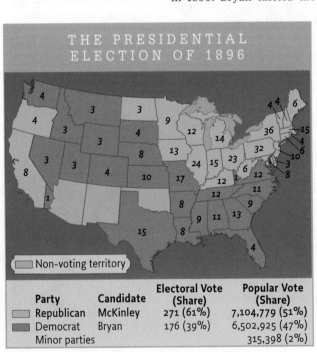

THE PRESIDENTIAL ELECTION OF 1896

Non-voting territory

Party	Candidate	Electoral Vote (Share)	Popular Vote (Share)
Republican	McKinley	271 (61%)	7,104,779 (51%)
Democrat	Bryan	176 (39%)	6,502,925 (47%)
Minor parties			315,398 (2%)

THE SEGREGATED SOUTH

The Redeemers in Power

The failure of Populism in the South opened the door for the full imposition of a new racial order. The coalition of merchants, planters, and business entrepreneurs who dominated the region's politics after 1877 called themselves Redeemers, since they claimed to have redeemed the region from the alleged horrors of misgovernment and "black rule." On achieving power, they had moved to undo as much as possible of Reconstruction. Hardest hit were the new public school systems. Louisiana spent so little on education that it became the only state in the Union in which the percentage of whites unable to read and write actually increased between 1880 and 1900. Black schools, however, suffered the most, as the gap between expenditures for black and white pupils widened steadily.

Undoing Reconstruction

New laws authorized the arrest of virtually any person without employment and greatly increased the penalties for petty crimes. As the South's prison population rose, the renting out of convicts became a profitable business. Every southern state placed at least a portion of its convicted criminals, the majority of them blacks imprisoned for minor offenses, in the hands of private businessmen. Railroads, mines, and lumber companies competed for this new form of cheap, involuntary labor. Conditions in labor camps were often barbaric, with disease rife and the death rates high. "One dies, get another" was the motto of the system's architects.

Convict labor

The Failure of the New South Dream

During the 1880s, Atlanta editor Henry Grady tirelessly promoted the promise of a New South, an era of prosperity based on industrial expansion and agricultural diversification. In fact, while planters, merchants, and industrialists prospered, the region as a whole sank deeper and deeper into poverty. Some industry did develop, such as new upcountry cotton factories that offered jobs to entire families of poor whites from the surrounding countryside. But since the main attractions for investors were the South's low wages and taxes and the availability of convict labor, these enterprises made little contribution to regional economic development. With the exception of Birmingham, Alabama, which by 1900 had developed into an important center for the manufacture of iron and steel, southern cities were mainly export centers for cotton, tobacco, and rice,

A group of Florida convict laborers. Southern states notoriously used convicts for public labor or leased them out to work in dire conditions for private employers.

with little industry or skilled labor. Overall, the region remained dependent on the North for capital and manufactured goods. As late as the 1930s, President Franklin D. Roosevelt would declare the South the nation's "number one" economic problem.

Black Life in the South

Black farmers

As the most disadvantaged rural southerners, black farmers suffered the most from the region's condition. In the Upper South, economic development offered some opportunities—mines, iron furnaces, and tobacco factories employed black laborers, and a good number of black farmers managed to acquire land. In the rice kingdom of coastal South Carolina and Georgia, most of the great plantations had fallen to pieces by the turn of the century, and many blacks acquired land and took up self-sufficient farming. In most

Declining landownership

of the Deep South, however, African-Americans owned a smaller percentage of land in 1900 than they had at the end of Reconstruction.

In southern cities, the network of institutions created after the Civil War—schools and colleges, churches, businesses, women's clubs, and the like—served as the foundation for increasingly diverse black urban communities. They supported the growth of a black middle class, mostly professionals like teachers and physicians, or businessmen like undertakers and shopkeepers serving the needs of black customers. But the labor market was rigidly divided along racial lines. Black men were excluded from supervisory positions in factories and workshops and white-collar jobs such as clerks in offices. A higher percentage of black women than white worked for wages, but mainly as domestic servants. In most occupations, the few unions that existed in the South excluded blacks, forming yet another barrier to their economic advancement.

Coal miners, in a photograph by Lewis Hine. Mining was one occupation in which blacks and whites often worked side by side.

The Kansas Exodus

Trapped at the bottom of a stagnant economy, some blacks sought a way out through emigration from the South. In 1879 and 1880, an estimated 40,000 to 60,000 African-Americans migrated to Kansas, seeking political equality, freedom from violence, access to education, and economic opportunity. Those promoting the **Exodus**, including former fugitive slave Benjamin "Pap" Singleton, the organizer of a real estate company, distributed flyers and lithographs picturing Kansas as an idyllic land of rural plenty. Lacking the capital to take up farming, however, most black migrants ended up as unskilled laborers in towns and cities. But few chose to return to the South. In the words of one minister active in the movement, "We had rather suffer and be free."

Despite deteriorating prospects in the South, most African-Americans had little alternative but to stay in the region. The real expansion of job opportunities was taking place in northern cities. But most northern employers refused to offer jobs to blacks in the expanding industrial economy, preferring to hire white migrants from rural areas and immigrants from Europe.

Northern jobs

The Decline of Black Politics

Neither black voting nor black officeholding came to an abrupt end in 1877. A few blacks even served in Congress in the 1880s and 1890s. Nonetheless, political opportunities became more and more restricted. Not until the 1990s would the number of black legislators in the South approach the level seen during Reconstruction.

Benjamin "Pap" Singleton (on the left), who helped to organize the "Exodus" of 1879, superimposed on a photograph of a boat carrying African-Americans emigrating from the South to Kansas.

With black men of talent and ambition turning away from politics, the banner of political leadership passed to black women activists. The National Association of Colored Women, founded in 1896, brought together local and regional women's clubs to press for both women's rights and racial uplift. They aided poor families, offered lessons in home life and childrearing, and battled gambling and drinking in black communities. By insisting on the right of black women to be considered as "respectable" as their white counterparts, the women reformers challenged the racial ideology that consigned all blacks to the status of degraded second-class citizens.

Black women reformers

For nearly a generation after the end of Reconstruction, despite fraud and violence, black southerners continued to cast ballots in large numbers. In some states, such as Virginia, Tennessee, Arkansas, and North Carolina, the Republican Party remained competitive and formed biracial political coalitions that challenged Democratic Party rule. Despite the limits of these alliances, especially those involving the Populists, the threat of a biracial political insurgency frightened the ruling Democrats and contributed greatly to the disenfranchisement movement.

Biracial politics

The Elimination of Black Voting

Between 1890 and 1906, every southern state enacted laws or constitutional provisions meant to eliminate the black vote. Since the Fifteenth Amendment prohibited the use of race as a qualification for the suffrage, how were such measures even possible? Southern legislatures drafted laws that on paper appeared color-blind but that were actually designed to end black voting. The most popular devices were the poll tax (a fee that each citizen had to pay in order to retain the right to vote), literacy tests, and the requirement that a prospective voter demonstrate to election officials an "understanding" of the state constitution. Six southern states also adopted a "grandfather clause," exempting from the new requirements descendants of persons eligible to vote before the Civil War (when only whites, of course, could cast ballots in the South). The racial intent of the grandfather clause was so clear that the Supreme Court in 1915 invalidated such laws for violating the Fifteenth Amendment. The other methods of limiting black voting, however, remained on the books.

Poll tax

Grandfather clause

Although election officials often allowed whites who did not meet the new qualifications to register, numerous poor and illiterate whites also lost the right to vote, a result welcomed by many planters and urban reformers. Louisiana, for example, reduced the number of blacks registered to vote from 130,000 in 1894 to 1,342 a decade later. But 80,000 white voters also lost the right. **Disenfranchisement** led directly to the rise of a generation of southern demagogues, who mobilized white voters by extreme appeals to racism.

Scope of disenfranchisement

As late as 1940, only 3 percent of adult black southerners were registered to vote. The elimination of black and many white voters, which reversed the nineteenth-century trend toward more inclusive suffrage, could not have been accomplished without the approval of the North and the Supreme Court, both of which gave their approval to disenfranchisement laws, in clear violation of the Fourteenth Amendment. As a result, southern congressmen wielded far greater power on the national scene than their tiny electorates warranted.

The Law of Segregation

Along with disenfranchisement, the 1890s saw the widespread imposition of segregation in the South. Laws and local customs requiring the separation of the races had numerous precedents. They had existed in many parts of the pre–Civil War North. Southern schools and many other institutions had been segregated during Reconstruction. In the 1880s, however, southern race relations remained unsettled. Some railroads, theaters, and hotels admitted blacks and whites on an equal basis while others separated them by race or excluded blacks altogether.

In 1883, in the *Civil Rights Cases*, the Supreme Court invalidated the Civil Rights Act of 1875, which had outlawed racial discrimination by hotels, theaters, railroads, and other public facilities. In 1896, in the landmark decision in ***Plessy v. Ferguson***, the Court gave its approval to state laws requiring separate facilities for blacks and whites. The case arose in Louisiana, where the legislature had required railroad companies to maintain a separate car or section for black passengers. In an 8-1 decision, the Court upheld the Louisiana law, arguing that segregated facilities did not discriminate so long as they were "**separate but equal.**" The lone dissenter, John Marshall Harlan, reprimanded the majority with an oft-quoted comment: "Our constitution is color-blind." Segregation, he insisted, violated the principle of equal liberty. To Harlan, freedom for the former slaves meant the right to participate fully and equally in American society.

Civil Rights Cases

As Harlan predicted, states reacted to the *Plessy* decision by passing laws mandating racial segregation in every aspect of southern life, from schools to hospitals, waiting rooms, toilets, and cemeteries. Some states

Spread of segregation

In *Plessy v. Ferguson* (1896), the U.S. Supreme Court ruled that laws establishing racial segregation did not violate the equal protection clause of the Fourteenth Amendment so long as facilities were "separate but equal." In fact, this was almost never the case, as illustrated by these photographs of the elementary schools for black and white children in South Boston, Virginia, in the early twentieth century.

Segregation and other minority groups

forbade taxi drivers to carry members of different races at the same time. Despite the "thin disguise" (Harlan's phrase) of equality required by the Court's "separate but equal" doctrine, facilities for blacks were either non-existent or markedly inferior.

More than a form of racial separation, segregation was one part of an all-encompassing system of white domination, in which each component—disenfranchisement, unequal economic status, inferior education—reinforced the others.

Segregation affected other groups as well as blacks. In some parts of Mississippi where Chinese laborers had been brought in to work the fields after the Civil War, three separate school systems—white, black, and Chinese—were established. In California, black, Hispanic, and American Indian children were frequently educated alongside whites, but state law required separate schools for those of "mongolian or Chinese descent." In Texas and California, although Mexicans were legally considered "white," they found themselves barred from many restaurants, places of entertainment, and other public facilities.

The Rise of Lynching

Mob violence

Those blacks who sought to challenge the system faced not only overwhelming political and legal power but also the threat of violent reprisal. In every year between 1883 and 1905, more than fifty persons, the vast majority of them black men, were lynched in the South—that is, murdered by a mob. **Lynching** continued well into the twentieth century. By mid-century, the total number of victims since 1880 had reached nearly 5,000. Some lynchings occurred secretly at night; others were advertised in advance and attracted large crowds of onlookers. Mobs engaged in activities that shocked the civilized world. In 1899, Sam Hose, a plantation laborer who killed his employer in self-defense, was brutally murdered near Newman, Georgia, before 2,000 onlookers, some of whom arrived on a special excursion train from Atlanta. A crowd including young children watched as his executioners cut off Hose's ears, fingers, and genitals, burned him alive, and then fought over pieces of his bones as souvenirs.

Like many victims of lynchings, Hose was accused after his death of having raped a white woman. Yet in nearly all cases, as activist Ida B. Wells argued in a newspaper editorial after a Memphis lynching in 1892, the charge of rape was a "bare lie." Born a slave in Mississippi in 1862, Wells had become a schoolteacher and editor. Her essay condemning the lynching of three black men in Memphis led a mob to destroy her newspaper, the *Memphis Free Press*, while she was out of the city. Wells moved to the North, where she became the nation's leading antilynching crusader. She bluntly insisted that given the conditions of southern blacks, the United States had no right to call itself the "land of the free."

TABLE 17.1 States with Over 200 Lynchings, 1889–1918	
STATE	NUMBER OF LYNCHINGS
Georgia	386
Mississippi	373
Texas	335
Louisiana	313
Alabama	276
Arkansas	214

Politics, Religion, and Memory

As the white North and South moved toward reconciliation in the 1880s and 1890s, one cost was the abandonment of the dream of racial equality spawned by the Civil War and written into the laws and Constitution during Reconstruction. In popular literature and memoirs by participants, at veterans' reunions and in public memorials, the Civil War came to be remembered as a tragic family quarrel among white Americans in which blacks had played no significant part. It was a war of "brother against brother" in which both sides fought gallantly for noble causes—local rights on the part of the South, preservation of the Union for the North. Slavery increasingly came to be viewed as a minor issue, not the war's fundamental cause, and Reconstruction as a regrettable period of "Negro rule."

Part of the crowd of 10,000 that watched the 1893 lynching of Henry Smith in Paris, Texas. Smith was accused of raping and murdering a four-year-old girl. The word "justice" was painted on the platform.

This carving by an unknown southerner from around 1875 juxtaposes Robert E. Lee and the crucified Christ, illustrating the strong religious overtones in the ideology of the Lost Cause.

Southern governments erected monuments to the **Lost Cause**, a romanticized version of slavery, the Old South, and the Confederate experience. Religion was central to the development of Lost Cause mythology— it offered a way for white southerners to come to terms with defeat in the Civil War without abandoning white supremacy. According to the Lost Cause, Confederate leaders like Robert E. Lee and Thomas "Stonewall" Jackson were sterling representatives of Christian virtue, while the Yankees had represented the forces of evil. The death of the Confederacy, in many sermons, was equated with the death of Christ, who gave his life for the sins of mankind. Southern churches played a key role in keeping the values of the Old South alive by refusing to reunite with northern branches. In the 1840s, the Methodist and Baptist churches had divided into northern and southern branches. Methodists would not reunite until well into the twentieth century; Baptists have yet to do so.

REDRAWING THE BOUNDARIES

As the nineteenth century drew to a close, American society seemed to be fracturing along lines of both class and race. The result, commented economist Simon Patten, was a widespread obsession with redrawing the boundary of freedom by identifying and excluding those unworthy of the blessings of liberty. "The South," he wrote, "has its negro, the city has its slums. . . . The friends of American institutions fear the ignorant immigrant, and the workingman dislikes the Chinese."

The New Immigration and the New Nativism

The 1890s witnessed a major shift in the sources of immigration to the United States. Despite the prolonged depression, 3.5 million newcomers entered the United States during the decade, seeking jobs in the industrial centers of the North and Midwest. Over half arrived not from Ireland, England, Germany, and Scandinavia, the traditional sources of immigration, but from southern and eastern Europe, especially Italy and the Russian and Austro-Hungarian empires. The "new immigrants" were widely described by native-born Americans as members of distinct "races," whose lower level of civilization explained everything from their willingness to work for substandard wages to their supposed inborn tendency toward criminal behavior.

Southern and eastern Europe

A cartoon from the magazine *Judge* illustrates anti-immigrant sentiment. A tide of newcomers representing the criminal element of other countries washes up on American shores, to the consternation of Uncle Sam.

Founded in 1894 by a group of Boston professionals, the **Immigration Restriction League** called for reducing immigration by barring the illiterate from entering the United States. Such a measure was adopted by Congress early in 1897 but was vetoed by President Cleveland. Like the South, northern and western states experimented with ways to eliminate undesirable voters. Nearly all the states during the 1890s adopted the secret or "Australian" ballot, meant both to protect voters' privacy and to limit the participation of illiterates (who could no longer receive help from party officials at polling places). Suffrage throughout the country was increasingly becoming a privilege, not a right.

Restricting the vote

Chinese Exclusion and Chinese Rights

The boundaries of nationhood, expanded so dramatically in the aftermath of the Civil War, slowly contracted. Leaders of both parties expressed vicious opinions regarding immigrants from China—they were "odious, abominable, dangerous, revolting," declared Republican leader James G. Blaine. Between 1850 and 1870, nearly all Chinese immigrants had been unattached men, brought in by labor contractors to work in western gold fields, railroad construction, and factories. In the early 1870s, entire Chinese families began to immigrate, leading Congress in 1875 to exclude Chinese women from entering the country.

Anti-Chinese opinion

Beginning in 1882, Congress temporarily excluded immigrants from China from entering the country altogether. Although non-whites had long been barred from becoming naturalized citizens, this was the first

A Chinese vegetable peddler in Idaho City, Idaho.

time that race had been used to exclude an entire group of people from entering the United States. Congress renewed the restriction ten years later and made it permanent in 1902.

At the time of exclusion, 105,000 persons of Chinese descent lived in the United States. Nearly all of them resided on the West Coast, where they suffered intense discrimination and periodic mob violence. In the late-nineteenth-century West, thousands of Chinese immigrants were expelled from towns and mining camps, and mobs assaulted Chinese residences and businesses. Between 1871 and 1885, San Francisco provided no public education for Chinese children. In 1885, the California Supreme Court, in *Tape v. Hurley*, ordered the city to admit Chinese students to public schools. The state legislature responded by passing a law authorizing segregated education. But Joseph and Mary Tape, who had lived in the United States since the 1860s, insisted that their daughter be allowed to attend her neighborhood school like other children. "Is it a disgrace to be born a Chinese?" Mary Tape wrote. "Didn't God make us all!" But her protest failed. Not until 1947 did California repeal the law authorizing separate schools for the Chinese.

Expulsion without due process

The U.S. Supreme Court also considered the status of Chinese-Americans. In *United States v. Wong Kim Ark* (1898), the Court ruled that the Fourteenth Amendment awarded citizenship to children of Chinese immigrants born on American soil. Yet the justices also affirmed the right of Congress to set racial restrictions on immigration. And in its decision in *Fong Yue Ting* (1893), the Court authorized the federal government to expel Chinese aliens without due process of law. In his dissent, Justice David J. Brewer acknowledged that the power was now directed against a people many Americans found "obnoxious." But "who shall say," he continued, "it will not be exercised tomorrow against other classes and other people?" Brewer proved to be an accurate prophet. In 1904, the Court cited *Fong Yue Ting* in upholding a law barring anarchists from entering the

Result of an anti-Chinese riot in Seattle, Washington.

United States, demonstrating how restrictions on the rights of one group can become a precedent for infringing on the rights of others.

The Emergence of Booker T. Washington

The social movements that had helped to expand the nineteenth-century boundaries of freedom now redefined their objectives so that they might be realized within the new economic and intellectual framework. Prominent black leaders, for example, took to emphasizing economic self-help and individual advancement into the middle class as an alternative to political agitation.

Symbolizing the change was the juxtaposition, in 1895, of the death of Frederick Douglass with Booker T. Washington's widely praised speech at the Atlanta Cotton Exposition that urged blacks to adjust to segregation and abandon agitation for civil and political rights. Born a slave in 1856, Washington had studied as a young man at Hampton Institute, Virginia. He adopted the outlook of Hampton's founder, General Samuel Armstrong, who emphasized that obtaining farms or skilled jobs was far more important to African-Americans emerging from slavery than the rights of citizenship. Washington put this view into practice when he became head of Tuskegee Institute in Alabama, a center for vocational education (education focused on training for a job rather than broad learning).

Booker T. Washington, advocate of industrial education and economic self-help.

In his Atlanta speech, Washington repudiated the abolitionist tradition, which stressed ceaseless agitation for full equality. He urged blacks not to try to combat segregation. Washington's ascendancy rested in large part on his success in channeling aid from wealthy northern whites to Tuskegee and to black politicians and newspapers who backed his program. But his support in the black community also arose from a widespread sense that in the world of the late nineteenth century, frontal assaults on white power were impossible and that blacks should concentrate on building up their segregated communities.

Washington's appeal

The Rise of the AFL

Within the labor movement, the demise of the Knights of Labor and the ascendancy of the **American Federation of Labor** (AFL) during the 1890s reflected a similar shift away from a broadly reformist past to more limited goals. As the Homestead and Pullman strikes demonstrated, direct confrontations with the large corporations were likely to prove suicidal. Unions, declared Samuel Gompers, the AFL's founder and longtime president, should not pursue the Knights' utopian dream of creating a "cooperative commonwealth." Rather, the labor movement should devote itself to negotiating with employers for higher wages and better working conditions for its members. Like Washington, Gompers spoke the language of the era's business culture. Indeed, the AFL policies he pioneered were known as "business unionism."

Samuel Gompers

During the 1890s, union membership rebounded from its decline in the late 1880s. But at the same time, the labor movement became less and less inclusive. Abandoning the Knights' ideal of labor solidarity, the AFL restricted membership to skilled workers—a small minority of the labor force—effectively excluding the vast majority of unskilled workers and, therefore, nearly all blacks, women, and new European immigrants. AFL membership centered on sectors of the economy like printing and building construction that were dominated by small competitive businesses with workers who frequently were united by craft skill and ethnic background. AFL unions had little presence in basic industries like steel and rubber, or in the large-scale factories that now dominated the economy.

The Women's Era

Changes in the women's movement reflected the same combination of expanding activities and narrowing boundaries. The 1890s launched what would later be called the "**women's era**"—three decades during which women, although still denied the vote, enjoyed larger opportunities than in the past for economic independence and played a greater and greater role in public life. Nearly 5 million women worked for wages in 1900.

Although most were young, unmarried, and concentrated in traditional jobs such as domestic service and the garment industry, a generation of college-educated women was beginning to take its place in better-paying clerical and professional positions.

Through a network of women's clubs, temperance associations, and social reform organizations, women exerted a growing influence on public affairs. Founded in 1874, the Women's Christian Temperance Union

(WCTU) grew to become the era's largest female organization, with a membership by 1890 of 150,000. Under the banner of Home Protection, it moved from demanding the prohibition of alcoholic beverages (blamed for leading men to squander their wages on drink and treat their wives abusively) to a comprehensive program of economic and political reform, including the right to vote. Women, insisted Frances Willard, the group's president, must abandon the idea that "weakness" and dependence were their nature and join assertively in movements to change society.

At the same time, the center of gravity of feminism shifted toward an outlook more in keeping with prevailing racial and ethnic norms. The movement continued to argue for women's equality in employment, education, and politics. But with increasing frequency, the native-born, middle-class women who dominated the suffrage movement claimed the vote as educated members of a "superior race."

Immigrants and former slaves had been enfranchised with "ill-advised haste," declared Carrie Chapman Catt, president of the National American Woman Suffrage Association (created in 1890 to reunite the rival suffrage organizations formed after the Civil War). Indeed, Catt suggested, extending the vote to native-born white women would help to counteract the growing power of the "ignorant foreign vote" in the North and the dangerous potential for a second Reconstruction in the South. In 1895, the same year that Booker T. Washington delivered his Atlanta address, the National American Woman Suffrage Association held its annual convention in that segregated city. Like other American institutions, the organized movement for woman suffrage had made its peace with nativism and racism.

"A woman's liquor raid," an illustration in the *National Police Gazette* in 1879, depicts a group of temperance crusaders destroying liquor containers in a Frederickstown, Ohio, saloon.

BECOMING A WORLD POWER

The New Imperialism

In world history, the last quarter of the nineteenth century is known as the age of imperialism, when rival European empires carved up large parts of the world among themselves. For most of this period, the United States remained a second-rate power.

The "new imperialism" that arose after 1870 was dominated by European powers and Japan. Belgium, Great Britain, and France consolidated their hold on colonies in Africa, and newly unified Germany acquired colonies there as well. By the early twentieth century, most of Asia, Africa, the Middle East, and the Pacific had been divided among these empires.

The global context

American Expansionism

Territorial expansion, of course, had been a feature of American life from well before independence. But the 1890s marked a major turning point in America's relationship with the rest of the world. Americans were increasingly aware of themselves as an emerging world power. "We are a great imperial Republic destined to exercise a controlling influence upon the actions of mankind and to affect the future of the world," proclaimed Henry Watterson, an influential newspaper editor.

"A great imperial Republic"

Until the 1890s, American expansion had taken place on the North American continent. Ever since the Monroe Doctrine (see Chapter 10), to be sure, many Americans had considered the Western Hemisphere an American sphere of influence. The last territorial acquisition before the 1890s had been Alaska, purchased from Russia by Secretary of State William H. Seward in 1867.

Expanding trade

Most Americans who looked overseas were interested in expanded trade, not territorial possessions. The country's agricultural and industrial production could no longer be absorbed entirely at home. By 1890, companies like Singer Sewing Machines and John D. Rockefeller's Standard Oil Company aggressively marketed their products abroad. Especially during economic downturns, business leaders insisted on the necessity of greater access to foreign customers. Middle-class American women, moreover, were becoming more and more desirous of clothing and food from abroad, and their demand for consumer goods such as "Oriental" fashions and exotic spices for cooking spurred the economic penetration of the Far East.

The Lure of Empire

Missionaries

One group of Americans who spread the nation's influence overseas were religious missionaries, thousands of whom ventured abroad in the late nineteenth century to spread Christianity, prepare the world for the second coming of Christ, and uplift the poor. Inspired by Dwight Moody, a Methodist evangelist, the Student Volunteer Movement for Foreign Missions sent more than 8,000 missionaries to "bring light to heathen worlds" across the globe.

A small group of late-nineteenth-century thinkers actively promoted American expansionism, warning that the country must not allow itself to be shut out of the scramble for empire. Naval officer **Alfred T. Mahan**, in *The Influence of Sea Power upon History* (1890), argued that no nation could prosper without a large fleet of ships engaged in international trade, protected by a powerful navy operating from overseas bases. His arguments influenced the outlook of James G. Blaine, who served as secretary of state during Benjamin Harrison's presidency (1889–1893). Blaine urged the president to try to acquire Hawaii, Puerto Rico, and Cuba as strategic naval bases.

Hawaii

Although independent, Hawaii was already closely tied to the United States through treaties that exempted imports of its sugar from tariff duties and provided for the establishment of an American naval base at Pearl Harbor. Hawaii's economy was dominated by American-owned sugar plantations that employed a workforce of native islanders and Chinese,

Japanese, and Filipino laborers under long-term contracts. Early in 1893, a group of American planters organized a rebellion that overthrew the Hawaii government of Queen Liliuokalani. On the eve of leaving office, Harrison submitted a treaty of annexation to the Senate. After determining that a majority of Hawaiians did not favor the treaty, Harrison's successor, Grover Cleveland, withdrew it. In July 1898, in the midst of the Spanish-American War, the United States finally annexed the Hawaiian Islands.

The depression that began in 1893 heightened the belief that a more aggressive foreign policy was necessary to stimulate American exports. Fears of economic and ethnic disunity fueled an assertive nationalism. These were the years when rituals like the Pledge of Allegiance and the practice of standing for the playing of "The Star-Spangled Banner" came into existence. New, mass-circulation newspapers also promoted nationalistic sentiments. By the late 1890s, papers like William Randolph Hearst's *New York Journal* and Joseph Pulitzer's *New York World*—dubbed the "**yellow press**" by their critics after the color in which Hearst printed a popular comic strip—were selling a million copies each day by mixing sensational accounts of crime and political corruption with aggressive appeals to patriotic sentiments.

A cartoon in *Puck*, December 1, 1897, imagines the annexation of Hawaii by the United States as a shotgun wedding. The minister, President McKinley, reads from a book entitled *Annexation Policy*. The Hawaiian bride appears to be looking for a way to escape. Most Hawaiians did not support annexation.

The "Splendid Little War"

All these factors contributed to America's emergence as a world power in the Spanish-American War of 1898. But the immediate origins of the war lay not at home but in the long Cuban struggle for independence from Spain. Ten years of guerrilla war had followed a Cuban revolt in 1868. The movement for independence resumed in 1895. As reports circulated of widespread suffering caused by the Spanish policy of rounding up civilians and moving them into detention camps, the Cuban struggle won growing support in the United States.

Demands for intervention escalated after February 15, 1898, when an explosion—probably accidental, a later investigation concluded—destroyed the American battleship **Maine** in Havana Harbor, with the loss of nearly 270 lives. After Spain rejected an American demand for a cease-fire on the island and eventual Cuban independence, President McKinley in April asked Congress for a declaration of war. The purpose, declared Senator Henry Teller of Colorado, was to aid Cuban patriots in their struggle for "liberty and freedom." To underscore the government's humanitarian intentions, Congress adopted the Teller Amendment, stating that the United States had no intention of annexing or dominating the island.

The U.S.S. Maine

The Teller Amendment

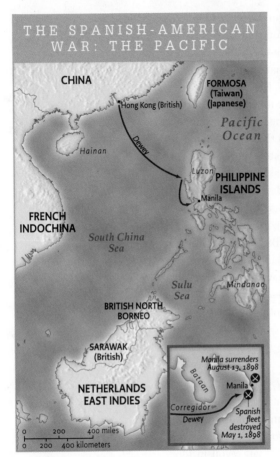

In both the Caribbean and the Pacific, the United States achieved swift victories over Spain in the Spanish-American War.

The Spanish-American War

Rough Riders

Secretary of State John Hay called the Spanish-American conflict a "splendid little war." It lasted only four months and resulted in fewer than 400 American combat deaths. The war's most decisive engagement took place not in Cuba but at Manila Bay, a strategic harbor in the Philippine Islands in the distant Pacific Ocean. Here, on May 1, the American navy under Admiral George Dewey defeated a Spanish fleet. Soon afterward, soldiers went ashore, becoming the first American army units to engage in combat outside the Western Hemisphere. July witnessed another naval victory off Santiago, Cuba, and the landing of American troops on Cuba and Puerto Rico.

Roosevelt at San Juan Hill

The most highly publicized land battle of the war took place in Cuba. This was the charge up San Juan Hill, outside Santiago, by Theodore Roosevelt's Rough Riders. An ardent expansionist, Roosevelt had long believed that a war would reinvigorate the nation's unity and sense of manhood, which had suffered, he felt, during the 1890s. A few months shy of his fortieth birthday when war broke out, Roosevelt resigned his post as assistant secretary of the navy to raise a volunteer cavalry unit, which rushed to Cuba to participate in the fighting. His exploits made Roosevelt a national hero. He was elected governor of New York that fall and in 1900 became McKinley's vice president.

Theodore Roosevelt

An American Empire

With the backing of the yellow press, the war quickly escalated from a crusade to aid the suffering Cubans to an imperial venture that ended with the United States in possession of a small overseas empire. McKinley became convinced that the United States could neither return the Philippines to Spain nor grant them independence, for which he believed the inhabitants unprepared. In an interview with a group of Methodist ministers, the president spoke of receiving a divine revelation that Americans had a duty to "uplift and civilize" the Filipino people and to train them for self-government. In the treaty with Spain that ended the war, the United States acquired the Philippines, Puerto Rico, and the Pacific island of Guam. As for Cuba, before recognizing its independence, McKinley forced the island's new government to approve the **Platt Amendment** to the new Cuban constitution (drafted by Senator Orville H. Platt of Connecticut), which authorized the United States to intervene militarily whenever it saw fit. The United States also acquired a permanent lease on naval stations in Cuba, including what is now the facility at Guantánamo Bay.

Acquiring possessions

Charge of the Rough Riders at San Juan Hill, a painting by Frederic Remington, depicts the celebrated unit, commanded by Theodore Roosevelt, in action in Cuba during the Spanish-American War of 1898. Roosevelt, on horseback, leads the troops. Remington had been sent to the island the previous year by publisher William Randolph Hearst to provide pictures of Spanish atrocities during the Cuban war for independence in the hope of boosting the *New York Journal*'s circulation.

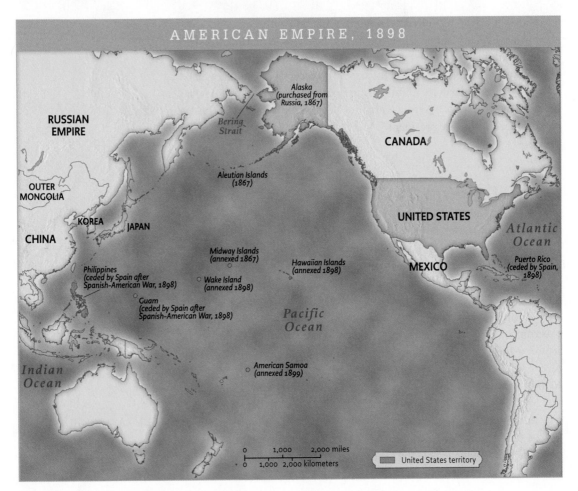

AMERICAN EMPIRE, 1898

RUSSIAN EMPIRE

Alaska (purchased from Russia, 1867)

Bering Strait

CANADA

OUTER MONGOLIA

Aleutian Islands (1867)

KOREA JAPAN

CHINA

UNITED STATES

Atlantic Ocean

Midway Islands (annexed 1867)

Hawaiian Islands (annexed 1898)

MEXICO

Puerto Rico (ceded by Spain, 1898)

Philippines (ceded by Spain after Spanish-American War, 1898)

Wake Island (annexed 1898)

Guam (ceded by Spain after Spanish-American War, 1898)

Pacific Ocean

American Samoa (annexed 1899)

Indian Ocean

0   1,000   2,000 miles
0 1,000 2,000 kilometers

United States territory

As a result of the Spanish-American War, the United States became the ruler of a far-flung overseas empire.

Spheres of influence

America's interest in its new possessions had more to do with trade than with gaining wealth from natural resources or large-scale American settlement. Puerto Rico and Cuba were gateways to Latin America, strategic outposts from which American naval and commercial power could be projected throughout the hemisphere. The Philippines, Guam, and Hawaii lay astride shipping routes to the markets of Japan and China. In 1899, soon after the end of the Spanish-American War, Secretary of State John Hay announced the **Open Door policy**, demanding that European powers that had recently divided China into commercial spheres of influence grant equal access to American exports. The Open Door referred to the free movement of goods and money, not people. Even as the United States banned the immigration of Chinese into this country, it insisted on access to the markets and investment opportunities of Asia.

The Philippine War

Many Cubans, Filipinos, and Puerto Ricans had welcomed American intervention as a way of breaking Spain's long hold on these colonies. Large planters looked forward to greater access to American markets. Nationalists and labor leaders admired America's democratic ideals and believed that American participation in the destruction of Spanish rule would lead to social reform and political self-government.

In this cartoon comment on the American effort to suppress the movement for Philippine independence, Uncle Sam tries to subdue a knife-wielding insurgent.

But the American determination to exercise continued control, direct or indirect, led to a rapid change in local opinion, nowhere more so than in the Philippines. Filipinos had been fighting a war against Spain since 1896. After Dewey's victory at Manila Bay, their leader, Emilio Aguinaldo, established a provisional government with a constitution modeled on that of the United States. But once McKinley decided to retain possession of the islands, the Filipino movement turned against the United States. The result was a second war, far longer (it lasted from 1899 to 1903) and bloodier (it cost the lives of more than 100,000 Filipinos and 4,200 Americans) than the Spanish-American conflict. Today, this is perhaps the least remembered of all American wars.

Once in control of the Philippines, the colonial administration took seriously the idea of modernizing the islands. It expanded railroads and harbors, brought in American schoolteachers and public health officials, and sought to modernize agriculture (although efforts to persuade local farmers to substitute corn for rice ran afoul of Filipino climate and cultural traditions).

The United States, said President McKinley, had an obligation to its "little brown brothers." Yet in all the new possessions, American policies tended to serve the interests of land-based local elites—and bequeathed enduring poverty to the majority of the rural population. Under American rule, Puerto Rico, previously an island of diversified small farmers, became a low-wage plantation economy controlled by absentee American corporations. By the 1920s, its residents were among the poorest in the entire Caribbean.

Emilio Aguinaldo, leader of the Philippine War against American occupation, in a more dignified portrayal than in the cartoon above.

VOICES OF FREEDOM

From Josiah Strong,

Our Country (1885)

The Congregational minister Josiah Strong promoted both the Social Gospel—a desire, grounded in religious belief, to solve the nation's social problems—and an updated version of manifest destiny and American expansionism strongly connected to ideas of racial superiority and a Christian missionary impulse.

It seems to me that God, with infinite wisdom and skill, is training the Anglo-Saxon race for an hour sure to come in the world's future. Heretofore there has always been in the history of the world a comparatively unoccupied land westward, into which the crowded countries of the East have poured their surplus populations. But the widening waves of migration, which millenniums ago rolled east and west from the valley of the Euphrates meet to-day on our Pacific coast. There are no more new worlds. The unoccupied arable lands of the earth are limited, and will soon be taken. The time is coming when the pressure of population on the means of subsistence will be felt here as it is now felt in Europe and Asia.

Then will the world enter upon a new stage of its history—the *final competition of races, for which the Anglo-Saxon is being schooled*. Long before the thousand millions are here, the mighty *centrifugal* tendency, inherent in this stock and strengthened in the United States, will assert itself. Then this race of unequaled energy, with all the majesty of numbers and the might of wealth behind it—the representative, let us hope, of the largest liberty, the purest Christianity, the highest civilization—having developed peculiarly aggressive traits calculated to impress its institutions upon mankind, will spread itself over the earth. If I read not amiss, this powerful race will move down upon Mexico, down upon Central and South America, out upon the islands of the sea, over upon Africa and beyond. And can any one doubt that the results of this competition of races will be the "survival of the fittest?". . .

Some of the stronger races, doubtless, may be able to preserve their integrity; but, in order to compete with the Anglo-Saxon, they will probably be forced to adopt his methods and instruments, his civilization and his religion.

From "Aguinaldo's Case against the United States" (1899)

Emilio Aguinaldo, who led the Filipino armed struggle for independence against Spain and then another war against the United States when President McKinley decided to annex the Philippines, explained his reasons for opposing American imperialism in an article in the widely read magazine the *North American Review*. He contrasted American traditions of self-government with the refusal to grant this right to the Philippines.

We Filipinos have all along believed that if the American nation at large knew exactly, as we do, what is daily happening in the Philippine Islands, they would rise en masse, and demand that this barbaric war should stop [and] . . . she would cease to be the laughing stock of other civilized nations, as she became when she abandoned her traditions and set up a double standard of government—government by consent in America, government by force in the Philippine Islands. . . .

You have been greatly deceived in the personality of my countrymen. You went to the Philippines under the impression that their inhabitants were ignorant savages. . . . We have been represented by your popular press as if we were Africans or Mohawk Indians. . . .

You repeat constantly the dictum that we cannot govern ourselves. . . . With equal reason, you might have said the same thing some fifty or sixty years ago of Japan; and, little over a hundred years ago, it was extremely questionable, when you, also, were rebels against the English Government, if you could govern yourselves. . . . Now, the moral of all this obviously is: Give us the chance; treat us exactly as you demanded to be treated at the hands of England when you rebelled against her autocratic methods.

Now, here is a unique spectacle—the Filipinos fighting for liberty, the American people fighting them to give them liberty. . . . You promised us your aid and protection in our attempt to form a government on the principles and after the model of the government of the United States. . . . In combination with our forces, you compelled Spain to surrender. . . . Joy abounded in every heart, and all went well . . . until . . . the Government at Washington . . . commenc[ed] by ignoring all promises that had been made and end[ed] by ignoring the Philippine people, their personality and rights, and treating them as a common enemy. . . . In the face of the world you emblazon humanity and Liberty upon your standard, while you cast your political constitution to the winds and attempt to trample down and exterminate a brave people whose only crime is that they are fighting for their liberty.

QUESTIONS

1. *How does Strong justify the idea of world domination by Anglo-Saxons?*

2. *Why does Aguinaldo think that the United States is betraying its own values?*

3. *How do these documents reflect different definitions of liberty?*

Citizens or Subjects?

American rule also brought with it American racial attitudes. In an 1899 poem, the British writer Rudyard Kipling urged the United States to take up the "white man's burden" of imperialism. American proponents of empire agreed that the domination of non-white peoples by whites formed part of the progress of civilization.

America's triumphant entry into the ranks of imperial powers sparked an intense debate over the relationship among political democracy, race, and American citizenship. The American system of government had no provision for permanent colonies. The right of every people to self-government was one of the main principles of the Declaration of Independence. The idea of an "empire of liberty" assumed that new territories would eventually be admitted as equal states and their residents would be American citizens. In the aftermath of the Spanish-American War, however, nationalism, democracy, and American freedom emerged more closely identified than ever with notions of Anglo-Saxon superiority.

The Foraker Act of 1900 declared Puerto Rico an "insular territory," different from previous territories in the West. Its 1 million inhabitants were defined as citizens of Puerto Rico, not the United States, and denied a future path to statehood. Filipinos occupied a similar status. In a series of cases decided between 1901 and 1904 and known collectively as the **Insular Cases**, the Supreme Court held that the Constitution did not fully apply to the territories recently acquired by the United States—a significant limitation of the scope of American freedom. Thus, two principles central to American freedom since the War of Independence—no taxation without representation and government based on the consent of the governed—were abandoned when it came to the nation's new possessions.

In the twentieth century, the territories acquired in 1898 would follow different paths. Hawaii, which had a sizable population of American missionaries and planters, became a traditional territory. Its population, except for Asian immigrant laborers, became American citizens, and it was admitted as a state in 1959. After nearly a half-century of American rule, the Philippines achieved independence in 1946. Until 1950, the U.S. Navy administered Guam, which remains today an "unincorporated" territory. As for Puerto Rico,

Colonies in the American framework

This propaganda photograph from 1898 depicts the Spanish-American War as a source of national reconciliation in the United States (with Confederate and Union soldiers shaking hands) and of freedom for Cuba (personified by a girl whose arm holds a broken chain).

it is sometimes called "the world's oldest colony," because ever since the Spanish conquered the island in 1493 it has lacked full self-government. It elects its own government but lacks a voice in Congress (and in the election of the U.S. president).

Puerto Rico

Drawing the Global Color Line

Just as American ideas about liberty and self-government had circulated around the world in the Age of Revolution, American racial attitudes had a global impact in the age of empire. The turn of the twentieth century was a time of worldwide concern about immigration, race relations, and the **"white man's burden,"** all of which inspired a global sense of fraternity among "Anglo-Saxon" nations. Chinese exclusion in the United States strongly influenced anti-Chinese laws adopted in Canada, and American segregation and disenfranchisement became models for Australia and South Africa as they formed new governments; they read in particular the proceedings of the Mississippi constitutional convention of 1890, which pioneered ways to eliminate black voting rights.

The Union of South Africa, inaugurated in 1911, saw its own policy of racial separation—later known as apartheid—as following in the footsteps of segregation in the United States. South Africa, however, went much further, enacting laws that limited skilled jobs to whites and dividing the country into areas where black Africans could and could not live.

An advertisement employs the idea of a "white man's burden" (borrowed from a poem by Rudyard Kipling) as a way of promoting the virtues of Pears' Soap. Accompanying text claims that Pears' is "the ideal toilet soap" for "the cultured of all nations," and an agent of civilization in "the dark corners of the earth."

The first step towards lightening

The White Man's Burden

is through teaching the virtues of cleanliness.

Pears' Soap

"Republic or Empire?"

The emergence of the United States as an imperial power sparked intense debate. Opponents formed the **Anti-Imperialist League**. It united writers and social reformers who believed American energies should be directed at home, businessmen fearful of the cost of maintaining overseas outposts, and racists who did not wish to bring non-white populations into the United States. America's historic mission, the League declared, was to "help the world by an example of successful self-government," not to conquer other peoples.

In 1900, Democrats again nominated William Jennings Bryan to run against McKinley. The Democratic platform opposed the Philippine War for placing the United States in the "un-American" position of "crushing with military force" another people's desire for "liberty and self-government." George S. Boutwell, president of the Anti-Imperialist League, declared that the most pressing question in the election was the nation's future character—"republic or empire?"

But without any sense of contradiction, proponents of an imperial foreign policy also adopted the language of freedom. America's was a "benevolent" imperialism, they claimed, rooted in a national mission to uplift backward cultures and spread liberty across the globe. Riding the wave of patriotic sentiment inspired by the war, and with the economy having recovered from the depression of 1893–1897, McKinley in 1900 repeated his 1896 triumph.

At the dawn of the twentieth century, the United States seemed poised to take its place among the world's great powers. In 1900, many features that would mark American life for much of the twentieth century were already apparent. The United States had surpassed Britain, France, and Germany in industrial production. The political system had stabilized. The white North and South had achieved reconciliation, while rigid lines of racial exclusion—the segregation of blacks, Chinese exclusion, Indian reservations—limited the boundaries of freedom and citizenship.

A Republican campaign poster from the election of 1900 links prosperity at home and benevolent imperialism abroad as achievements of William McKinley's first term in office.

Yet the questions central to nineteenth-century debates over freedom—the relationship between political and economic liberty, the role of government in creating the conditions of freedom, and the definition of those entitled to enjoy the rights of citizens—had not been permanently answered. Nor had the dilemma of how to reconcile America's role as an empire with traditional ideas of freedom. These were the challenges bequeathed by the nineteenth century to the first generation of the twentieth.

CHAPTER REVIEW AND ONLINE RESOURCES

REVIEW QUESTIONS

1. What economic and political issues gave rise to the Populist Party, and what changes did the party advocate?

2. How did employers use state and federal forces to protect their own economic interests, and what were the results?

3. Compare and contrast the goals, strategies, and membership of the American Federation of Labor and the Knights of Labor (you may want to refer back to Chapter 16).

4. Who were the Redeemers, and how did they change society and politics in the New South?

5. Explain how changes in politics, economics, social factors, and violence interacted to affect the situation of African-Americans in the New South.

6. How did religion and the idea of the Lost Cause give support to a new understanding of the Civil War?

7. What ideas and interests motivated the United States to create an empire in the late nineteenth century?

8. Compare the arguments for and against U.S. imperialism. Be sure to consider the views of Josiah Strong and Emilio Aguinaldo.

9. What rights did Chinese immigrants and Chinese Americans gain in these years, and what limitations did they experience? How did their experiences set the stage for other restrictions on immigration?

KEY TERMS

People's Party (or Populists) (p. 511)

Coxey's Army (p. 514)

"free silver" (p. 515)

Kansas Exodus (p. 518)

disenfranchisement (p. 521)

Plessy v. Ferguson (p. 521)

"separate but equal" (p. 521)

lynching (p. 522)

the Lost Cause (p. 524)

Immigration Restriction League (p. 525)

Washington's Atlanta Speech (p. 526)

American Federation of Labor (p. 527)

"women's era" (p. 528)

Alfred T. Mahan (p. 530)

"yellow press" (p. 531)

U.S.S. *Maine* (p. 531)

Platt Amendment (p. 533)

Open Door policy (p. 534)

Insular Cases (p. 538)

"white man's burden" (p. 539)

Anti-Imperialist League (p. 539)

wwnorton.com
/studyspace

VISIT STUDYSPACE FOR THESE
RESOURCES AND MORE

- A chapter outline
- A diagnostic chapter quiz
- Interactive maps
- Map worksheets
- Multimedia documents

CHAPTER 18

THE PROGRESSIVE ERA

★

1900-1916

Sixth Avenue and Thirtieth Street, a 1907 painting by John Sloan, depicts a busy street in New York City in an area known as the Tenderloin, with an elevated railroad overhead. Sloan was one of a group of painters called the Ashcan School because of their focus on everyday city life. Here, he emphasizes the vitality of the city and the mingling of people of different social classes on its streets.

It was late afternoon on March 25, 1911, when fire broke out at the Triangle Shirtwaist Company. The factory occupied the top three floors of a ten-story building in the Greenwich Village neighborhood of New York City. Here some 500 workers, mostly young Jewish and Italian immigrant women, toiled at sewing machines producing ladies' blouses, some earning as little as three dollars per week. Those who tried to escape the blaze discovered that the doors to the stairwell had been locked—the owner's way, it was later charged, of discouraging theft and unauthorized bathroom breaks. The fire department rushed to the scene with high-pressure hoses. But their ladders reached only to the sixth floor. Onlookers watched in horror as girls leaped from the upper stories. By the time the blaze had been put out, 46 bodies lay on the street and 100 more were found inside the building.

The Triangle fire was not the worst fire disaster in American history (seven years earlier, over 1,000 people had died in a blaze on the *General Slocum* excursion boat in New York Harbor). But it had an unrivaled impact on public consciousness. In its wake, efforts to organize the city's workers accelerated, and the state legislature passed new factory inspection laws and fire safety codes.

Triangle focused attention on the social divisions that plagued American society during the first two decades of the twentieth century, a period known as the Progressive era. These were years when economic expansion produced millions of new jobs and brought an unprecedented array of goods within reach of American consumers. Cities expanded rapidly—by 1920, for the first time, more Americans lived in towns and cities than in rural areas. Yet severe inequality remained the most visible feature of the urban landscape, and persistent labor strife raised anew the question of government's role in combating social inequality.

The word "Progressive" came into common use around 1910 as a way of describing a broad, loosely defined political movement of individuals and groups who hoped to bring about significant change in American social and political life. Progressives included forward-looking businessmen who realized that workers must be accorded a voice in economic decision making, and labor activists bent on empowering industrial workers. Other major contributors to Progressivism were members of female reform organizations who hoped to protect women and children from exploitation, social scientists who believed that academic research would help to solve social problems, and members of an anxious middle class who feared that their status was threatened by the rise of big business.

As this and the following chapter will discuss, Progressive reformers addressed issues of American freedom in varied, contradictory ways. The era saw the expansion of political and economic freedom through the reinvigoration of the movement for woman suffrage, the use of political power to expand workers' rights, and efforts to improve democratic government by weakening the power of city bosses and giving ordinary citizens more influence on legislation. It witnessed the flowering of understandings of freedom based on individual fulfillment and personal self-determination. At the same time, many Progressives supported efforts to limit the full enjoyment of freedom to those deemed fit to exercise it properly. The new system of white supremacy born in the 1890s became fully consolidated in the South. Growing numbers of native-born Americans demanded that immigrants abandon their traditional cultures and become fully "Americanized." And efforts were made at the local and national levels to place political decision making in the hands of experts who did not have to answer to the electorate. Even as the idea of freedom expanded, freedom's boundaries contracted in Progressive America.

AN URBAN AGE AND A CONSUMER SOCIETY

Farms and Cities

The Progressive era was a period of explosive economic growth, fueled by increasing industrial production, a rapid rise in population, and the continued expansion of the consumer marketplace. In the first decade of the twentieth century, the economy's total output rose by about 85 percent. For the last time in American history, farms and cities grew together. Farm families poured into the western Great Plains. More than 1 million claims for free government land were filed under the Homestead Act of 1862—more than in the previous forty years combined. Irrigation transformed the Imperial Valley of California and parts of Arizona into major areas of commercial farming.

Economic growth

But it was the city that became the focus of Progressive politics and of a new mass-consumer society. The United States counted twenty-one cities whose population exceeded 100,000 in 1910, the largest of them

Growth of the cities

TABLE 18.1 Rise of the City, 1880–1920		
YEAR	URBAN POPULATION (PERCENTAGE)	NUMBER OF CITIES WITH 100,000+ POPULATION
1880	20%	12
1890	28	15
1900	38	18
1910	50	21
1920	68	26

New York, with 4.7 million residents. The twenty-three square miles of Manhattan Island were home to over 2 million people, more than lived in thirty-three of the states.

The stark urban inequalities of the 1890s continued into the Progressive era. Immigrant families in New York's downtown tenements often had no electricity or indoor toilets. Three miles to the north stood the mansions of Fifth Avenue's Millionaire's Row. According to one estimate, J. P. Morgan's financial firm directly or indirectly controlled 40 percent of all financial and industrial capital in the United States.

The Muckrakers

Lewis Hine used his camera to chronicle the plight of child laborers such as this young spinner in a southern cotton factory.

Some observers saw the city as a place where corporate greed undermined traditional American values. At a time when more than 2 million children under the age of fifteen worked for wages, Lewis Hine photographed child laborers to draw attention to persistent social inequality. A new generation of journalists writing for mass-circulation national magazines exposed the ills of industrial and urban life. *The Shame of the Cities* (1904) by Lincoln Steffens showed how party bosses and business leaders profited from political corruption. Theodore Roosevelt disparaged such writing as "**muckraking**," the use of journalistic skills to expose the underside of American life.

Major novelists took a similar unsparing approach to social ills. Perhaps the era's most influential novel was Upton Sinclair's *The Jungle* (1906), whose description of unsanitary slaughterhouses and the sale of rotten meat stirred public outrage and led directly to the passage of the Pure Food and Drug Act and the Meat Inspection Act of 1906.

Immigration as a Global Process

If one thing characterized early-twentieth-century cities, it was their immigrant character. The "new immigration" from southern and eastern Europe (discussed in Chapter 17) had begun around 1890 but reached its peak during the Progressive era. Between 1901 and the outbreak of World

War I in Europe in 1914, some 13 million immigrants came to the United States, the majority from Italy, Russia, and the Austro-Hungarian empire. In fact, Progressive-era immigration formed part of a larger process of worldwide migration set in motion by industrial expansion and the decline of traditional agriculture.

Worldwide migration

During the years from 1840 to 1914 (when immigration to the United States would be virtually cut off, first by the outbreak of World War I and then by legislation), perhaps 40 million persons emigrated to the United States and another 20 million to other parts of the Western Hemisphere, including Canada, Argentina, Brazil, and the Caribbean. Millions of persons migrated to Southeast Asia and the South Pacific, mainly from India and China.

Numerous causes inspired this massive uprooting of population. Rural southern and eastern Europe and large parts of Asia were regions marked by widespread poverty and illiteracy, burdensome taxation, and declining economies. Political turmoil at home, like the revolution that engulfed Mexico after 1911, also inspired emigration.

Causes of emigration

Most European immigrants to the United States entered through **Ellis Island**. Located in New York Harbor, this became in 1892 the nation's main facility for processing immigrants. Millions of Americans today trace their ancestry to immigrants who passed through Ellis Island.

At the same time, an influx of Asian and Mexican newcomers was taking place in the West. After the exclusion of immigrants from China in the late nineteenth century, approximately 72,000 Japanese arrived, primarily to work as agricultural laborers in California's fruit and vegetable fields and on Hawaii's sugar plantations. Between 1910 and 1940, **Angel Island** in San Francisco Bay—the "Ellis Island of the West"—served as the main entry point for immigrants from Asia. Far larger was Mexican immigration. Between 1900 and 1930, some 1 million Mexicans (more than 10 percent of that country's population) entered the United States—a number exceeded by only a few European countries.

By 1910, one-seventh of the American population was foreign-born, the highest percentage in the country's history.

TABLE 18.2 Immigrants and Their Children as Percentage of Population, Ten Major Cities, 1920

CITY	PERCENTAGE
New York City	76%
Cleveland	72
Boston	72
Chicago	71
Detroit	65
San Francisco	64
Minneapolis	63
Pittsburgh	59
Seattle	55
Los Angeles	45

The Immigrant Quest for Freedom

Like their nineteenth-century predecessors, the new immigrants arrived imagining the United States as a land of freedom, where all persons enjoyed equality before the law, could worship as they pleased, enjoyed economic opportunity, and had been emancipated from the oppressive social hierarchies of their homelands. "America is a free country," one Polish immigrant wrote home. "You don't have to be a serf to anyone." Agents sent abroad by the American government to investigate the reasons for large-scale immigration reported that the main impetus was a desire to share in the "freedom and prosperity enjoyed by the people of the United States." Although some of the new immigrants, especially Jews fleeing religious persecution in the Russian empire, thought of themselves as permanent emigrants, the majority initially planned to earn enough money to return home and purchase land. Groups like Mexicans and Italians included many "birds of passage," who remained only temporarily in the United States.

A greeting card for Rosh Hashanah, the Jewish New Year, marketed to early-twentieth-century immigrants, depicts Americanized Jews welcoming traditionally dressed new arrivals from Russia. The American eagle holds a banner reading, "Shelter us in the shadow of your wings." Above the immigrants is the Imperial Russian coat of arms.

The new immigrants clustered in close-knit "ethnic" neighborhoods with their own shops, theaters, and community organizations, and often continued to speak their native tongues. Although most immigrants earned more than was possible in the impoverished regions from which they came, they endured low wages, long hours, and dangerous working conditions. In the mines and factories of Pennsylvania and the Midwest, eastern European immigrants performed low-wage unskilled labor, whereas native-born workers dominated skilled and supervisory jobs. The vast majority of Mexican immigrants became poorly paid agricultural, mine, and railroad laborers, with little prospect of upward economic mobility. "My people are not in America," remarked one Slavic priest, "they are under it."

Consumer Freedom

The rise of mass consumption

Cities, however, were also the birthplace of a mass-consumption society that added new meaning to American freedom. During the Progressive era, large downtown department stores, neighborhood chain stores, and retail mail-order houses made available to consumers throughout the country the vast array of goods now pouring from the nation's factories. By 1910, Americans could purchase, among many other items, electric sewing machines, washing machines, vacuum cleaners, and record players.

Leisure activities also took on the characteristics of mass consumption. Amusement parks, dance halls, and theaters attracted large crowds of city dwellers. By 1910, 25 million Americans per week, mostly working-class urban residents, were attending "nickelodeons"—motion-picture theaters whose five-cent admission charge was far lower than that of vaudeville shows.

The Working Woman

The new visibility of women in urban public places—at work, as shoppers, and in places of entertainment like cinemas and dance halls—indicated that traditional gender roles were changing dramatically in Progressive America. As the Triangle fire revealed, more and more women were working for wages. Immigrant women were largely confined to low-paying factory employment. But for native-born white women, the kinds of jobs available expanded enormously. By 1920, around 25 percent of employed women were office workers or telephone operators. Female work was no longer confined to young, unmarried white women and adult black women. In 1920, of 8 million women working for wages, one-quarter were married and living with their husbands. The working woman—immigrant and native, working-class and professional—became a symbol of female emancipation. "We enjoy our independence and freedom" was the assertive statement of the Bachelor Girls Social Club, a group of female mail-order clerks in New York.

The desire to participate in the consumer society produced remarkably similar battles within immigrant families of all nationalities between parents and their self-consciously "free" children, especially daughters.

Women at work in a shoe factory, 1908.

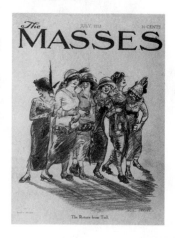

The Return from Toil, a drawing by John Sloan for the radical magazine *The Masses*, pictures working women not as downtrodden but as independent-minded, stylish, and self-confident.

TABLE 18.3 Percentage of Women 14 Years and Older in the Labor Force

YEAR	ALL WOMEN	MARRIED WOMEN	WOMEN AS % OF LABOR FORCE
1900	20.4%	5.6%	18%
1910	25.2	10.7	24
1920	23.3	9.0	24
1930	24.3	11.7	25

TABLE 18.4 Percentage of Women Workers in Various Occupations

OCCUPATION	1900	1920
Professional, technical	8.2%	11.7%
Clerical	4.0	18.7
Sales workers	4.3	6.2
Unskilled and semiskilled manufacturing	23.7	20.2
Household workers	28.7	15.7

One of the numerous advertisements of the early twentieth century that invoked the Statue of Liberty to market consumer goods, in this case a brand of crackers.

Contemporaries, native and immigrant, noted how "the novelties and frivolities of fashion" appealed to young working women, who spent part of their meager wages on clothing and makeup and at places of entertainment. Daughters considered parents who tried to impose curfews or to prevent them from going out alone to dances or movies as old-fashioned and not sufficiently "American."

The Rise of Fordism

If any individual exemplified the new consumer society, it was Henry Ford. Ford did not invent the automobile, but he developed the techniques of production and marketing that brought it within the reach of ordinary Americans. In 1905, he established the Ford Motor Company, one of dozens of small automobile manufacturing firms that emerged in these years. Three years later, he introduced the Model T, a simple, light vehicle sturdy enough to navigate the country's poorly maintained roads.

In 1913, Ford's factory in Highland Park, Michigan, adopted the method of production known as the moving assembly line, in which car frames were brought to workers on a continuously moving conveyor belt. The process enabled Ford to expand output by greatly reducing the time it took to produce each car. In 1914, he raised wages at his factory to the unheard-of level of five dollars per day (more than double the pay of most industrial workers), enabling him to attract a steady stream of skilled laborers. When other businessmen criticized him for endangering profits by paying high wages, Ford replied that workers must be able to afford the goods being turned out by American factories. Ford's output rose from 34,000 cars, priced at $700 each, in 1910, to 730,000 Model T's that sold at a price of $316 (well within the reach of many workers) in 1916. The economic system based on mass production and mass consumption came to be called **Fordism**.

The Promise of Abundance

As economic production shifted from capital goods (steel, railroad equipment, etc.) to consumer products, the new advertising industry perfected ways of increasing sales, often by linking goods with the idea of freedom.

Numerous products took "liberty" as a brand name or used an image of the Statue of Liberty as a sales device. Economic abundance would eventually come to define the "American way of life," in which personal fulfillment was to be found through acquiring material goods.

The maturation of the consumer economy gave rise to concepts—a "living wage" and an "American standard of living"—that offered a new language for criticizing the inequalities of wealth and power in Progressive America. Father John A. Ryan's influential book *A Living Wage* (1906) described a decent standard of living (one that enabled a person to participate in the consumer economy) as a "natural and absolute" right of citizenship. His book sought to translate into American terms Pope Leo XIII's powerful statement of 1894, **Rerum Novarum**, which criticized the divorce of economic life from ethical considerations, endorsed the right of workers to organize unions, and repudiated competitive individualism in favor of a more cooperative vision of the good society. For the first time in the nation's history, mass consumption came to occupy a central place in descriptions of American society and its future.

TABLE 18.5 Sales of Passenger Cars	
YEAR	NUMBER OF CARS (IN THOUSANDS)
1900	4.1
1905	24.2
1910	181.0
1915	895.9
1920	1,905.5
1925	3,735.1

An advertisement for Palmolive soap illustrates how companies marketed goods to consumers by creating anxiety and invoking exotic images. The accompanying text promises "a perfect skin" and includes an imagined image of Cleopatra, claiming that the soap embodies "ancient beauty arts." By 1915, Palmolive was the best-selling soap in the world.

VARIETIES OF PROGRESSIVISM

The immediate task, in the Progressives' view, was to humanize industrial capitalism and find common ground in a society still racked by labor conflict and experiencing massive immigration from abroad. Some Progressives proposed to return to a competitive marketplace populated by small producers. Others accepted the permanence of the large corporation and looked to the government to reverse the growing concentration of wealth and to ensure social justice. Still others would relocate freedom from the economic and political worlds to a private realm of personal fulfillment and unimpeded self-expression. But nearly all Progressives agreed that freedom must be infused with new meaning to deal with the economic and social conditions of the early twentieth century.

Industrial Freedom

In Progressive America, complaints of a loss of freedom came not only from the most poorly paid factory workers but from better-off employees as well. Large firms in the automobile, electrical, steel, and other industries sought to implement greater control over the work process. Efficiency expert Frederick W. Taylor pioneered what he called "**scientific management**." Through scientific study, Taylor believed, the "one best way" of producing goods could be determined and implemented. The role of workers was to obey the detailed instructions of supervisors. Not surprisingly, many skilled workers saw the erosion of their traditional influence over the work process as a loss of freedom.

Roller skaters with socialist leaflets during a New York City strike in 1916. A "scab" is a worker who crosses the picket line during a strike.

These developments helped to place the ideas of "industrial freedom" and "industrial democracy," which had entered the political vocabulary in the Gilded Age, at the center of political discussion during the Progressive era. Lack of "industrial freedom" was widely believed to lie at the root of the much-discussed "labor problem." Many Progressives believed that the key to increasing industrial freedom lay in empowering workers to participate in economic decision making via strong unions. Louis D. Brandeis, an active ally of the labor movement whom President Woodrow Wilson appointed to the Supreme Court in 1916, maintained that unions embodied an essential principle of freedom—the right of people to govern themselves. The contradiction between "political liberty" and "industrial slavery," Brandeis insisted, was America's foremost social problem.

The Socialist Presence and Eugene Debs

Peak of American socialism

Economic freedom was also a rallying cry of American socialism, which reached its greatest influence during the Progressive era. Founded in 1901, the Socialist Party called for immediate reforms such as free college education, legislation to improve the condition of laborers, and, as an ultimate goal, democratic control over the economy through public ownership of railroads and factories.

Centers of socialist strength

By 1912, the Socialist Party claimed 150,000 dues-paying members, published hundreds of newspapers, enjoyed substantial support in the American Federation of Labor, and had elected scores of local officials. Socialism flourished in diverse communities throughout the country. On the Lower East Side of New York City, it arose from the economic exploitation of immigrant workers and Judaism's tradition of social reform. Here, a vibrant socialist culture developed, complete with Yiddish-language newspapers and theaters, as well as large public meetings and street demonstrations. In 1914, the district elected socialist Meyer London to

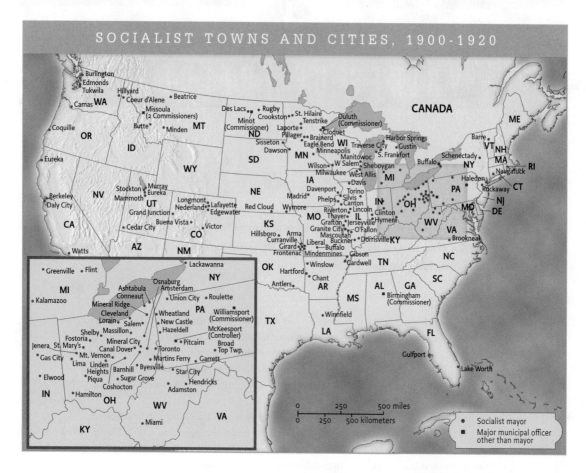

SOCIALIST TOWNS AND CITIES, 1900-1920

Socialist mayor

■ Major municipal officer other than mayor

Congress. Another center of socialist strength was Milwaukee, where Victor Berger, a German-born teacher and newspaper editor, mobilized local AFL unions into a potent political force. Socialism also made inroads among tenant farmers in old Populist areas like Oklahoma, and in the mining regions of Idaho and Montana.

No one was more important in spreading the socialist gospel or linking it to ideals of equality, self-government, and freedom than Eugene V. Debs, the railroad union leader who, as noted in the previous chapter, had been jailed during the Pullman Strike of 1894. For two decades, Debs crisscrossed the country preaching that control of the economy by a democratic government held out the hope of uniting "political equality and economic freedom." "While there is a lower class," proclaimed Debs, "I am in it, . . . while there is a soul in prison, I am not free."

Throughout the Atlantic world of the early twentieth century, socialism was a rising presence. Debs would receive more than 900,000 votes

Although the Socialist Party never won more than 6 percent of the vote nationally, it gained control of numerous small and medium-sized cities between 1900 and 1920.

Debs and socialism

VOICES OF FREEDOM

From Charlotte Perkins Gilman, *Women and Economics* (1898)

Women and Economics, by the prolific feminist social critic and novelist Charlotte Perkins Gilman, influenced the new generation of women aspiring to greater independence. It insisted that how people earned a living shaped their entire lives and that therefore women must free themselves from the home to achieve genuine freedom.

It is not motherhood that keeps the housewife on her feet from dawn till dark; it is house service, not child service. Women work longer and harder than most men. . . . A truer spirit is the increasing desire of young girls to be independent, to have a career of their own, at least for a while, and the growing objection of countless wives to the pitiful asking for money, to the beggary of their position. More and more do fathers give their daughters, and husbands their wives, a definite allowance,—a separate bank account,—something . . . all their own.

The spirit of personal independence in the women of today is sure proof that a change has come. . . . The radical change in the economic position of women is advancing upon us. . . . The growing individualization of democratic life brings inevitable change to our daughters as well as to our sons. . . . One of its most noticeable features is the demand in women not only for their own money, but for their own work for the sake of personal expression. Few girls today fail to manifest some signs of this desire for individual expression. . . .

Economic independence for women necessarily involves a change in the home and family relation. But, if that change is for the advantage of individual and race, we need not fear it. It does not involve a change in the marriage relation except in withdrawing the element of economic dependence, nor in the relation of mother to child save to improve it. But it does involve the exercise of human faculty in women, in social service and exchange rather than in domestic service solely. . . . [Today], when our still developing social needs call for an ever-increasing . . . freedom, the woman in marrying becomes the house-servant, or at least the housekeeper, of the man. . . . When women stand free as economic agents, they will [achieve a] much better fulfilment of their duties as wives and mothers and [contribute] to the vast improvement in health and happiness of the human race.

From John Mitchell, "The Workingman's Conception of Industrial Liberty" (1910)

During the Progressive era, the idea of "industrial liberty" moved to the center of political discussion. Progressive reformers and labor leaders like John Mitchell, head of the United Mine Workers, condemned the prevailing idea of liberty of contract in favor of a broader definition of economic freedom.

While the Declaration of Independence established civil and political liberty, it did not, as you all know, establish industrial liberty. . . . Liberty means more than the right to choose the field of one's employment. He is not a free man whose family must buy food today with the money that is earned tomorrow. He is not really free who is forced to work unduly long hours and for wages so low that he can not provide the necessities of life for himself and his family; who must live in a crowded tenement and see his children go to work in the mills, the mines, and the factories before their bodies are developed and their minds trained. To have freedom a man must be free from the harrowing fear of hunger and want; he must be in such a position that by the exercise of reasonable frugality he can provide his family with all of the necessities and the reasonable comforts of life. He must be able to educate his children and to provide against sickness, accident, and old age. . . .

A number of years ago the legislatures of several coal producing States enacted laws requiring employers to pay the wages of their workmen in lawful money of the United States and to cease the practice of paying wages in merchandise. From time immemorial it had been the custom of coal companies to conduct general supply stores, and the workingmen were required, as a condition of employment, to accept products in lieu of money in return for services rendered. This system was a great hardship to the workmen. . . . The question of the constitutionality of this legislation was carried into the courts and by the highest tribunal it was declared to be an invasion of the workman's liberty to deny him the right to accept merchandise in lieu of money as payment of his wages. . . . [This is] typical of hundreds of instances in which laws that have been enacted for the protection of the workingmen have been declared by the courts to be unconstitutional, on the grounds that they invaded the liberty of the working people. . . . Is it not natural that the workingmen should feel that they are being guaranteed the liberties they do not want and denied the liberty that is of real value to them? May they not exclaim, with Madame Roland [of the French Revolution], "O Liberty! Liberty! How many crimes are committed in thy name!"

QUESTIONS

1. *What does Gilman see as the main obstacles to freedom for women?*

2. *What does Mitchell believe will be necessary to establish "industrial liberty"?*

3. *How do the authors differ in their view of the relationship of the family to individual freedom?*

for president (6 percent of the total) in 1912. In that year, the socialist *Appeal to Reason*, published in Girard, Kansas, with a circulation of 700,000, was the largest weekly newspaper in the country.

AFL and IWW

American Federation of Labor (AFL)

Socialism was only one example of widespread discontent in Progressive America. Having survived the depression of the 1890s, the American Federation of Labor saw its membership triple to 1.6 million between 1900 and 1904. At the same time, its president, Samuel Gompers, sought to forge closer ties with forward-looking corporate leaders willing to deal with unions as a way to stabilize employee relations. Most employers nonetheless continued to view unions as an intolerable interference with their authority and resisted them stubbornly.

Industrial Workers of the World (IWW)

The AFL mainly represented the most privileged American workers—skilled industrial and craft laborers, nearly all of them white, male, and native-born. In 1905, a group of unionists who rejected the AFL's exclusionary policies formed the **Industrial Workers of the World** (IWW). Part trade union, part advocate of a workers' revolution that would seize the means of production and abolish the state, the IWW made solidarity its guiding principle. The organization sought to mobilize those excluded from the AFL—the immigrant factory-labor force, migrant timber and agricultural workers, women, blacks, and even the despised Chinese on the West Coast.

The New Immigrants on Strike

The right to collective bargaining

A series of mass strikes among immigrant workers placed labor's demand for the right to bargain collectively at the forefront of the reform agenda. These strikes demonstrated that although ethnic divisions among workers impeded labor solidarity, ethnic cohesiveness could also be a basis of unity, so long as strikes were organized on a democratic basis. The IWW did not originate these confrontations but was sometimes called in by local unionists to solidify the strikers. IWW organizers printed leaflets, posters, and banners in multiple languages and insisted that each nationality enjoy representation on the committee coordinating a walkout. It drew on the sense of solidarity within immigrant communities to persuade local religious leaders, shopkeepers, and officeholders to support the strikes.

The labor conflict that had the greatest impact on public consciousness took place in Lawrence, Massachusetts. The city's huge woolen mills employed 32,000 men, women, and children representing twenty-five nationalities. When the state legislature in January 1912 enacted a fifty-four-hour limit to the workweek, employers reduced the weekly take-home pay of those who had been laboring longer hours. Workers spontaneously went on strike.

In February, strikers devised the idea of sending strikers' children out of the city for the duration of the walkout. Socialist families in New York City agreed to take them in. The sight of the children, many of whom appeared pale and half-starved, marching up Fifth Avenue from the train station led to a wave of sympathy for the strikers. The governor of Massachusetts soon intervened, and the strike was settled on the workers' terms. A banner carried by the Lawrence strikers gave a new slogan to the labor movement:

"We want bread and roses, too"—a declaration that workers sought not only higher wages but the opportunity to enjoy the finer things of life.

Striking New York City garment workers carrying signs in multiple languages, 1913.

Labor and Civil Liberties

The fiery organizer Mary "Mother" Jones, who at the age of eighty-three had been jailed after addressing striking Colorado miners, later told a New York audience that the union "had only the Constitution; the other side had the bayonets." Yet the struggle of workers for the right to strike and of labor radicals against restraints on open-air speaking made free speech a significant public issue in the early twentieth century. By and large, the courts rejected their claims. But these battles laid the foundation for the rise of civil liberties as a central component of freedom in twentieth-century America.

The right to strike and the right to free speech

The IWW's battle for freedom of expression is a case in point. Lacking union halls, its organizers relied on songs, street theater, impromptu organizing meetings, and street corner gatherings to spread their message and attract support. In response to IWW activities, officials in Los Angeles, Spokane, Denver, and more than a dozen other cities limited or prohibited outdoor meetings. To arouse popular support, the IWW filled the jails with members who defied local law by speaking in public. In nearly all the free-speech fights, however, the IWW eventually forced local officials to give way. "Whether they agree or disagree with its methods or aims," wrote one journalist, "all lovers of liberty everywhere owe a debt to this organization for . . . [keeping] alight the fires of freedom."

Forms of political activity

The New Feminism

Isadora Duncan brought a new freedom to an old art form.

During the Progressive era, the word "feminism" first entered the political vocabulary. In 1914, a mass meeting at New York's Cooper Union debated the question "What is Feminism?" Feminism, said one speaker, meant women's emancipation "both as a human being and a sex-being." Feminists' forthright attack on traditional rules of sexual behavior added a new dimension to the discussion of personal freedom.

One symbol of the new era was Isadora Duncan, who brought from California a new, expressive dance based on the free movement of a body liberated from the constraints of traditional technique and costume. "I beheld the dance I had always dreamed of," wrote the novelist Edith Wharton on seeing a Duncan performance, "satisfying every sense as a flower does, or a phrase of Mozart's."

During this era, as journalist William M. Reedy jested, it struck "sex o'clock" in America. Issues of intimate personal relations previously confined to private discussion blazed forth in popular magazines and public debates. For the generation of women who adopted the word "feminism" to express their demand for greater liberty, free sexual expression and reproductive choice emerged as critical definitions of women's emancipation.

The Birth-Control Movement

The much-beloved and much-feared Emma Goldman, speaking in favor of birth control to an almost entirely male crowd in New York City in 1916.

The growing presence of women in the labor market reinforced demands for access to **birth control**, an issue that gave political expression to changing sexual behavior. Emma Goldman, who had emigrated to the United States from Lithuania at the age of sixteen, toured the country lecturing on subjects from anarchism to the need for more enlightened attitudes toward homosexuality. She regularly included the right to birth control in her speeches and distributed pamphlets with detailed information about various contraceptive devices.

By forthrightly challenging the laws banning contraceptive information and devices, Margaret Sanger, one of eleven children of an Irish-American working-class family, placed the issue of birth control at the heart of the new feminism. In 1911, she began a column on sex education, "What Every Girl Should Know," for *The Call*, a New York socialist newspaper. Postal officials barred one issue, containing a column on venereal disease, from the mails. The next issue of *The Call* included a blank page with the headline: "What Every Girl Should Know—Nothing; by order of the U. S. Post Office."

By 1914, the intrepid Sanger was openly advertising birth-control devices in her own journal, *The Woman Rebel*. "No woman can call herself free," she proclaimed, "who does not own and control her own body [and] can choose consciously whether she will or will not be a mother." In 1916, Sanger opened a clinic in a working-class neighborhood of Brooklyn and began distributing contraceptive devices to poor Jewish and Italian women, an action for which she was sentenced to a month in prison.

Native American Progressivism

Many groups participated in the Progressive impulse. Founded in 1911, the **Society of American Indians** was a reform organization typical of the era. It brought together Indian intellectuals to promote discussion of the plight of Native Americans in the hope that public exposure would be the first step toward remedying injustice. It created a pan-Indian public space independent of white control.

Many of these Indian intellectuals were not unsympathetic to the basic goals of federal Indian policy, including the transformation of communal landholdings on reservations into family farms. But Carlos Montezuma, a founder of the Society of American Indians, became an outspoken critic. Born in Arizona, he had been captured as a child by members of a neighboring tribe and sold to a traveling photographer, who brought him to Chicago. There Montezuma attended school and eventually obtained a medical degree.

Goals of federal Indian policy

In 1916, Montezuma established a newsletter, *Wassaja* (meaning "signaling"), that called for the abolition of the Bureau of Indian Affairs. Convinced that outsiders exerted too much power over life on the reservations, he insisted that self-determination was the only way for Indians to escape poverty and marginalization. But he also demanded that Indians be granted full citizenship and all the constitutional rights of other Americans. Indian activists would later rediscover him as a forerunner of Indian radicalism.

THE POLITICS OF PROGRESSIVISM

Effective Freedom

Progressivism was an international movement. In the early twentieth century, cities throughout the world experienced similar social strains arising from rapid industrialization and urban growth. Reformers across the globe exchanged ideas and envisioned new social policies. The Chinese

Worldwide progressivism

leader Sun Yat-Sen, for example, was influenced by the writings of Henry George and Edward Bellamy.

As governments in Britain, France, and Germany instituted old-age pensions, minimum-wage laws, unemployment insurance, and the regulation of workplace safety, American reformers came to believe they had much to learn from the Old World. The term "**social legislation**," meaning governmental action to address urban problems and the insecurities of working-class life, originated in Germany but soon entered the political vocabulary of the United States.

European social legislation

Drawing on the reform programs of the Gilded Age and the example of European legislation, Progressives sought to reinvigorate the idea of an activist, socially conscious government. Progressives could reject the traditional assumption that powerful government posed a threat to freedom, because their understanding of freedom was itself in flux. "Effective freedom," wrote the philosopher John Dewey, was far different from the "highly formal and limited concept of liberty" as protection from outside restraint. Freedom was a positive, not a negative, concept—the "power to do specific things." It sometimes required the government to act on behalf of those with little wealth or power. Thus, freedom in the Progressive era inevitably became a political question.

Dewey and freedom

Children at play at the Hudson-Bank Gymnasium, built in 1898 in a New York immigrant neighborhood by the Outdoor Recreation League, one of many Progressive-era groups that sought to improve life in urban centers.

State and Local Reforms

In the United States, with a political structure more decentralized than in European countries, state and local governments enacted most of the era's reform measures. In cities, Progressives worked to reform the structure of government to reduce the power of political bosses, establish public control of "natural monopolies" like gas and water works, and improve public transportation. They raised property taxes in order to spend more money on schools, parks, and other public facilities.

Gilded Age mayors and governors pioneered urban Progressivism. A former factory worker who became a successful shoe manufacturer, Hazen Pingree served as mayor of Detroit from 1889 to 1897. He battled the business interests that had dominated city government, forcing gas and telephone companies to lower their rates, and established a municipal power plant. Hiram Johnson, who as public prosecutor had secured the conviction for bribery of a San Francisco political boss, was elected governor of California in 1910. Having promised to "kick the Southern Pacific [Railroad] out of politics," he secured passage of the Public Utilities Act, one of the country's strongest railroad-regulation measures, as well as laws banning child labor and limiting the working hours of women.

Public Utilities Act

The most influential Progressive administration at the state level was that of Robert M. La Follette, who made Wisconsin a "laboratory for democracy." After serving as a Republican member of Congress, La Follette became convinced that an alliance of railroad and lumber companies controlled state politics. Elected governor in 1900, he instituted a series of measures known as the Wisconsin Idea, including nominations of candidates for office through primary elections rather than by political bosses, the taxation of corporate wealth, and state regulation of railroads and public utilities. To staff his administration, he drew on nonpartisan faculty members from the University of Wisconsin.

Robert La Follette and the Wisconsin Idea

Progressive Democracy

Progressives hoped to reinvigorate democracy by restoring political power to the citizenry and civic harmony to a divided society. Alarmed by the upsurge in violent class conflict and the unrestricted power of corporations, they believed that political reforms could help to create a unified "people" devoted to greater democracy and social reconciliation. Yet increasing the responsibilities of government made it all the more important to identify who was entitled to political participation and who was not.

Civic harmony

The Progressive era saw a host of changes implemented in the political process, many seemingly contradictory in purpose. The electorate was simultaneously expanded and contracted, empowered and removed from direct influence on many functions of government. Democracy was enhanced by the **Seventeenth Amendment** (1917)—which provided that U.S. senators be chosen by popular vote rather than by state legislatures—by widespread adoption of the popular election of judges, and by the use of primary elections among party members to select candidates for office. Several states, including California under Hiram Johnson, adopted the initiative and referendum (the former allowed voters to propose legislation, the latter to vote directly on it) and the recall, by which officials could be removed from office by popular vote. The era culminated with a constitutional amendment enfranchising women—the largest expansion of democracy in American history.

Initiative and referendum

But the Progressive era also witnessed numerous restrictions on democratic participation, most strikingly the disenfranchisement of blacks in the South, as noted in Chapter 17. To make city government more honest and efficient, many localities replaced elected mayors with appointed nonpartisan commissions or city managers—a change that insulated officials from machine domination but also from popular control. New literacy tests and residency and registration requirements, common in northern as well as southern states, limited the right to vote among the poor. In the eyes of many Progressives, the "fitness" of voters, not their absolute numbers, defined a functioning democracy.

Restricting democratic participation

Most Progressive thinkers were highly uncomfortable with the real world of politics, which seemed to revolve around the pursuit of narrow class, ethnic, and regional interests. Robert M. La Follette's reliance on college professors to staff important posts in his administration reflected a larger Progressive faith in expertise. The government could best exercise intelligent control over society through a democracy run by impartial experts who were in many respects unaccountable to the citizenry. Political freedom was less a matter of direct participation in government than of qualified persons devising the best public policies.

Government by experts

Jane Addams and Hull House

But alongside this elitist politics, Progressivism also included a more democratic vision of the activist state. As much as any other group, organized women reformers spoke for the more democratic side of Progressivism. Still barred from voting and holding office in most states, women nonetheless became central to the political history of the Progressive era. The immediate catalyst was a growing awareness among women reformers of the plight of poor immigrant communities and the emergence of the condition of women and child laborers as a major focus of public concern.

A staff member greets an immigrant family at Hull House, the settlement house established in Chicago by Jane Addams.

The era's most prominent female reformer was Jane Addams, who had been born in 1860, the daughter of an Illinois businessman. In 1889, she founded Hull House in Chicago, a "settlement house" devoted to improving the lives of the immigrant poor. Unlike previous reformers who had aided the poor from afar, settlement-house workers moved into poor neighborhoods. They built kindergartens and playgrounds for children, established employment bureaus and health clinics, and showed female victims of domestic abuse how to gain legal protection. By 1910, more than 400 settlement houses had been established in cities throughout the country.

Addams was typical of the Progressive era's "new woman." By 1900, there were more than 80,000 college-educated women in the United

States. Many found a calling in providing social services, nursing, and education to poor families in the growing cities. The efforts of middle-class women to uplift the poor, and of laboring women to uplift themselves, helped to shift the center of gravity of politics toward activist government. Women like Addams discovered that even well-organized social work was not enough to alleviate the problems of inadequate housing, income, and health. Government action was essential. Hull House instigated an array of reforms in Chicago, soon adopted elsewhere, including stronger building and sanitation codes, shorter working hours and safer labor conditions, and the right of labor to organize.

Hull House

The settlement houses have been called "spearheads for reform." Florence Kelley, a veteran of Hull House, went on to mobilize women's power as consumers as a force for social change. Under Kelley's leadership, the National Consumers' League became the nation's leading advocate of laws governing the working conditions of women and children.

Florence Kelley

The Campaign for Woman Suffrage

After 1900, the campaign for woman suffrage moved beyond the elitism of the 1890s to engage a broad coalition ranging from middle-class members of women's clubs to unionists, socialists, and settlement house workers. For the first time, it became a mass movement. Membership in the National American Woman Suffrage Association grew from 13,000 in 1893 to more than 2 million by 1917. By 1900, more than half the states allowed women to vote in local elections dealing with school issues, and

A mass movement

A "suffrage float" promotes equal rights for women in Nebraska. Although most of its neighboring states had extended the right to vote to women, Nebraska's male voters rejected woman suffrage in a 1914 referendum.

THE POLITICS OF PROGRESSIVISM | 563

Wyoming, Colorado, Idaho, and Utah had adopted full woman suffrage. Between 1910 and 1914, seven more western states enfranchised women. In 1913, Illinois became the first state east of the Mississippi River to allow women to vote in presidential elections.

State campaigns for suffrage

These campaigns, which brought women aggressively into the public sphere, were conducted with a new spirit of militancy. They also made effective use of the techniques of advertising, publicity, and mass entertainment characteristic of modern consumer society. California's successful 1911 campaign utilized automobile parades, numerous billboards and electric signs, and countless suffrage buttons and badges. Nonetheless, state campaigns were difficult, expensive, and usually unsuccessful. The movement increasingly focused its attention on securing a national constitutional amendment giving women the right to vote.

Maternalist Reform

Ironically, the desire to exalt women's role within the home did much to inspire the reinvigoration of the suffrage movement. Female reformers helped to launch a mass movement for direct government action to improve the living standards of poor mothers and children. Laws providing for mothers' pensions (state aid to mothers of young children who lacked male support) spread rapidly after 1910. These "**maternalist**" **reforms** rested on the assumption that the government should encourage women's capacity for bearing and raising children and enable them to be economically independent at the same time. Both feminists and believers

Government aid to women and children

Louisine Havemeyer, one of New York City's wealthiest women, was a strong advocate of woman suffrage. Here, in a 1915 photograph, she passes the Torch of Liberty to a group of New Jersey women.

in conventional domestic roles supported such measures. The former hoped that these laws would subvert women's dependence on men, the latter that they would strengthen traditional families and the mother-child bond.

Other Progressive legislation recognized that large numbers of women did in fact work outside the home but defined them as a dependent group (like children) in need of state protection in ways male workers were not. In 1908, in the landmark case of **Muller v. Oregon**, Louis D. Brandeis filed a famous brief citing scientific and sociological studies to demonstrate that because they had less strength and endurance than men, long hours of labor were dangerous for women, while their unique ability to bear children gave the government a legitimate interest in their working conditions. Persuaded by Brandeis's argument, the Supreme Court unanimously upheld the constitutionality of an Oregon law setting maximum working hours for women.

Louis D. Brandeis and Muller v. Oregon

Thus, three years after the notorious *Lochner* decision invalidating a New York law limiting the working hours of male bakers (discussed in Chapter 16), the Court created the first large breach in "liberty of contract" doctrine. But the cost was high: at the very time that women in unprecedented numbers were entering the labor market and earning college degrees, Brandeis's brief and the Court's opinion solidified the view of women workers as weak, dependent, and incapable of enjoying the same economic rights as men. By 1917, thirty states had enacted laws limiting the hours of labor of female workers.

The unintended effects of Muller

The maternalist agenda that built gender inequality into the early foundations of the welfare state by extension raised the idea that government should better the living and working conditions of men as well. Indeed, Brandeis envisioned the welfare state as one rooted in the notion of universal economic entitlements, including the right to a decent income and protection against unemployment and work-related accidents.

This vision, too, enjoyed considerable support in the Progressive era. By 1913, twenty-two states had enacted **workmen's compensation laws** to benefit workers, male or female, injured on the job. This legislation was the first wedge that opened the way for broader programs of social insurance. But state minimum-wage laws and most laws regulating working hours applied only to women. Women and children may have needed protection, but interference with the freedom of contract of adult male workers was still widely seen as degrading. The establishment of a standard of living and working conditions beneath which no American should be allowed to fall would await the coming of the New Deal.

A form of social insurance

THE PROGRESSIVE PRESIDENTS

Despite creative experiments in social policy at the city and state levels, the tradition of localism seemed to most Progressives an impediment to a renewed sense of national purpose. Poverty, economic insecurity, and lack of industrial democracy were national problems that demanded national solutions. The democratic national state, wrote *New Republic* editor Herbert Croly, offered an alternative to control of Americans' lives by narrow interests that manipulated politics or by the all-powerful corporations. Croly proposed a new synthesis of American political traditions. To achieve the "Jeffersonian ends" of democratic self-determination and individual freedom, he insisted, the country needed to employ the "Hamiltonian means" of government intervention in the economy. Each in his own way, the Progressive presidents—Theodore Roosevelt, William Howard Taft, and Woodrow Wilson—tried to address this challenge.

Herbert Croly

Theodore Roosevelt

McKinley's assassination

In September 1901, the anarchist Leon Czolgosz assassinated William McKinley while the president visited the Pan-American Exposition in Buffalo, New York. At the age of forty-two, Vice President Theodore Roosevelt became the youngest man ever to hold the office of president. In many ways, he became the model for the twentieth-century president, an official actively and continuously engaged in domestic and foreign affairs. (The foreign policies of the Progressive presidents will be discussed in the next chapter.) He moved aggressively to set the political agenda.

Roosevelt's domestic program, which he called the Square Deal, attempted to confront the problems caused by economic consolidation by distinguishing between "good" and "bad" corporations. The former, among which he included U.S. Steel and Standard Oil, served the public interest. The latter were run by greedy financiers interested only in profit and had no right to exist.

Soon after assuming office, Roosevelt shocked the corporate world by announcing his intention to prosecute under the Sherman Antitrust Act the Northern Securities Company. Created by financier J. P. Morgan, this "holding company" owned the stock and directed the affairs of three major western railroads. It monopolized transportation between the Great Lakes and the Pacific. In 1904, the Supreme Court ordered Northern Securities dissolved, a major victory for the antitrust movement.

President Theodore Roosevelt addressing a crowd in Evanston, Illinois, in 1902.

Reelected that same year, Roosevelt pushed for more direct federal regulation of the economy. He proposed to strengthen the Interstate Commerce Commission, which the Supreme Court had essentially limited to collecting economic statistics. By this time, journalistic exposés, labor unrest, and the agitation of Progressive reformers had created significant public support for Roosevelt's regulatory program. In 1906, Congress passed the Hepburn Act, giving the ICC the power to examine railroads' business records and to set reasonable rates, a significant step in the development of federal intervention in the corporate economy. That year, as has been noted, also saw the Pure Food and Drug Act. Many businessmen supported these measures, recognizing that they would benefit from greater public confidence in the quality and safety of their products. But they were alarmed by Roosevelt's calls for federal inheritance and income taxes and the regulation of all interstate businesses.

Putting the Screws on Him, a 1904 cartoon, depicts President Theodore Roosevelt squeezing ill-gotten gains out of the trusts.

John Muir and the Spirituality of Nature

If the United States lagged behind Europe in many areas of social policy, it led the way in the **conservation** of natural resources. The first national park, Yellowstone in Wyoming, was created in 1872, partly to preserve an area of remarkable natural beauty and partly at the urging of the Northern Pacific Railroad, which was anxious to promote western tourism. In the 1890s, the Scottish-born naturalist John Muir organized the Sierra Club to help preserve forests from uncontrolled logging by timber companies.

Muir's love of nature stemmed from deep religious feelings. Nearly blinded in an accident in an Indianapolis machine shop where he worked in his twenties, he found in the restoration of his sight an inspiration to appreciate God's creation. He called forests "God's first temples." In nature, he believed, men could experience directly the presence of God. Muir was inspired by the Transcendentalists of the pre–Civil War era—like Henry David Thoreau, he lamented the intrusions of civilization on the natural environment. But unlike them, Muir developed a broad following. As more and more Americans lived in cities, they came to see nature less as something to conquer and more as a place for recreation and personal growth. Muir's spiritual understanding of nature resonated with these urbanites.

The Old Faithful geyser, the most famous site in Yellowstone, the nation's first national park, in a photograph from the 1880s.

The Conservation Movement

In the 1890s, Congress authorized the president to withdraw "forest reserves" from economic development, a restriction on economic freedom in the name of a greater social good. But it was under Theodore Roosevelt

Theodore Roosevelt and the conservationist John Muir at Glacier Point, Yosemite Valley, California, in 1906. Yosemite was set aside as a national park in 1890.

that conservation became a concerted federal policy. A dedicated outdoorsman who built a ranch in North Dakota in the 1880s, Roosevelt moved to preserve parts of the natural environment from economic exploitation.

Relying for advice on Gifford Pinchot, the head of the U.S. Forest Service, he ordered that millions of acres be set aside as wildlife preserves and encouraged Congress to create new national parks. In some ways, conservation was a typical Progressive reform. Manned by experts, the government could stand above political and economic battles, serving the public good while preventing "special interests" from causing irreparable damage to the environment. The aim was less to end the economic utilization of natural resources than to develop responsible, scientific plans for their use. Pinchot halted timber companies' reckless assault on the nation's forests. But unlike Muir, he believed that development and conservation could go hand in hand and that logging, mining, and grazing on public lands should be controlled, not eliminated.

Taft in Office

Having served nearly eight years as president, Roosevelt did not run again in 1908. His chosen successor, William Howard Taft, defeated William Jennings Bryan, making his third unsuccessful race for the White House.

Taft's antitrust policy

Although temperamentally more conservative than Roosevelt, Taft pursued antitrust policy even more aggressively. He persuaded the Supreme Court in 1911 to declare John D. Rockefeller's Standard Oil Company (one of Roosevelt's "good" trusts) in violation of the Sherman Antitrust Act and to order its breakup into separate marketing, producing, and refining companies. The government also won a case against American Tobacco, which the Court ordered to end pricing policies that were driving smaller firms out of business.

The income tax

Taft supported the **Sixteenth Amendment** to the Constitution, which authorized Congress to enact a graduated income tax (one whose rate of taxation is higher for wealthier citizens). It was ratified shortly before he left office. A 2 percent tax on incomes over $4,000 had been included in a tariff enacted in 1894 but had been quickly declared unconstitutional by the Supreme Court as a "communistic threat to property." A key step in the modernization of the federal government, the income tax provided a reliable and flexible source of revenue for a national state whose powers, responsibilities, and expenditures were growing rapidly.

Despite these accomplishments, Taft seemed to gravitate toward the more conservative wing of the Republican Party. Taft's rift with Progressives grew deeper when Richard A. Ballinger, the new secretary of the interior, concluded that Roosevelt had exceeded his authority in placing land in forest reserves. Ballinger decided to return some of this land to the public domain, where mining and lumber companies would have access to it. Gifford Pinchot accused Ballinger of colluding with business interests and repudiating the environmental goals of the Roosevelt administration. When Taft fired Pinchot in 1910, the breach with party Progressives became irreparable. In 1912, Roosevelt challenged Taft for the Republican nomination. Defeated, Roosevelt launched an independent campaign as the head of the new Progressive Party.

Ballinger and Pinchot

The Election of 1912

All the crosscurrents of Progressive-era thinking came together in the presidential campaign of 1912. The four-way contest between Taft, Roosevelt, Democrat Woodrow Wilson, and Socialist Eugene V. Debs became a national debate on the relationship between political and economic freedom in the age of big business. At one end of the political spectrum stood Taft, who stressed that economic individualism could remain the foundation of the social order so long as government and private entrepreneurs cooperated in addressing social ills. At the other end was Debs. Relatively few Americans supported the Socialist Party's goal of abolishing the "capitalistic system" altogether, but its immediate demands—including public ownership of the railroads and banking system, government aid to the unemployed, and laws establishing shorter working hours and a minimum wage—summarized forward-looking Progressive thought.

A key election

Eugene V. Debs, the Socialist Party candidate, speaking in Chicago during the 1912 presidential campaign.

But it was the battle between Wilson and Roosevelt over the role of the federal government in securing economic freedom that galvanized public attention in 1912. The two represented competing strands of Progressivism. Both believed government action necessary to preserve individual freedom, but they differed over the dangers of increasing the government's power and the inevitability of economic concentration.

New Freedom and New Nationalism

Strongly influenced by Louis D. Brandeis, with whom he consulted frequently during the campaign, Wilson insisted that democracy must be reinvigorated by restoring market competition and freeing government from domination by big business. Wilson feared big government as much as he feared the power of the corporations. The **New Freedom**, as he called his program, envisioned the federal government strengthening antitrust laws, protecting the right of workers to unionize, and actively encouraging small businesses—creating, in other words, the conditions for the renewal of economic competition without increasing government regulation of the economy. Wilson warned that corporations were as likely to corrupt government as to be managed by it, a forecast that proved remarkably accurate.

Woodrow Wilson's New Freedom

To Roosevelt's supporters, Wilson seemed a relic of a bygone era; his program, they argued, served the needs of small businessmen but ignored the inevitability of economic concentration and the interests of professionals, consumers, and labor. Espousing the **New Nationalism**, his program of 1912, Roosevelt insisted that only the "controlling and directing power of the government" could restore "the liberty of the oppressed." He called for heavy taxes on personal and corporate fortunes and federal regulation of industries, including railroads, mining, and oil.

Roosevelt's New Nationalism

The Progressive Party platform offered numerous proposals to promote social justice. Drafted by a group of settlement-house activists, labor reformers, and social scientists, the platform laid out a blueprint for a modern, democratic welfare state, complete with woman suffrage, federal supervision of corporate enterprise, national labor and health legislation for women and children, an eight-hour day and "living wage" for all workers, and a national system of social insurance covering unemployment, medical care, and old age. Roosevelt's campaign helped to give freedom a modern social and economic content and established an agenda that would define political liberalism for much of the twentieth century.

The Progressive Party Platform of 1912

Wilson's First Term

The Republican split ensured a sweeping victory for Wilson, who won about 42 percent of the popular vote, although Roosevelt humiliated Taft by winning about 27 percent to the president's 23 percent. In office, Wilson proved himself a strong executive leader. He was the first president to hold regular press conferences, and he delivered messages personally to Congress rather than sending them in written form, as did all his predecessors since John Adams.

With Democrats in control of Congress, Wilson moved aggressively to implement his version of Progressivism. The first significant measure of his presidency was the Underwood Tariff, which substantially reduced duties on imports and, to make up for lost revenue, imposed a graduated income tax on the richest 5 percent of Americans. There followed the Clayton Act of 1914, which exempted labor unions from antitrust laws and barred courts from issuing injunctions curtailing the right to strike. In 1916 came the Keating-Owen Act, outlawing child labor in the manufacture of goods sold in interstate commerce; the Adamson Act, establishing an eight-hour workday on the nation's railroads; and the Warehouse Act, reminiscent of the Populist subtreasury plan, which extended credit to farmers when they stored their crops in federally licensed warehouses.

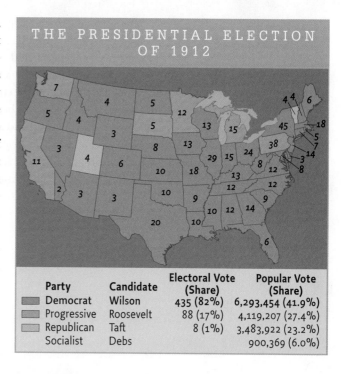

THE PRESIDENTIAL ELECTION OF 1912

Party	Candidate	Electoral Vote (Share)	Popular Vote (Share)
Democrat	Wilson	435 (82%)	6,293,454 (41.9%)
Progressive	Roosevelt	88 (17%)	4,119,207 (27.4%)
Republican	Taft	8 (1%)	3,483,922 (23.2%)
Socialist	Debs		900,369 (6.0%)

The Expanding Role of Government

Some of Wilson's policies seemed more in tune with Roosevelt's New Nationalism than the New Freedom of 1912. Wilson presided over the creation of two powerful new public agencies. In 1913, Congress created the Federal Reserve System, consisting of twelve regional banks. They were overseen by a central board appointed by the president and empowered to handle the issuance of currency, aid banks in danger of failing, and influence interest rates so as to promote economic growth.

The Federal Reserve System

A second expansion of national power occurred in 1914, when Congress established the **Federal Trade Commission** (FTC) to investigate and prohibit "unfair" business activities such as price-fixing and monopolistic practices. Both the Federal Reserve and the FTC were welcomed by many business leaders as a means of restoring order to the economic marketplace and warding off more radical measures for curbing corporate power. But they reflected the remarkable expansion of the federal role in the economy during the Progressive era.

By 1916, the social ferment and political mobilizations of the Progressive era had given birth to a new American state. With new laws, administrative agencies, and independent commissions, government at the local, state, and national levels had assumed the authority to protect and advance "industrial freedom." Government had established rules for labor relations, business behavior, and financial policy, protected citizens from market abuses, and acted as a broker among the groups whose conflicts threatened to destroy social harmony. But a storm was already engulfing Europe that would test the Progressive faith in empowered government as the protector of American freedom.

CHAPTER REVIEW AND ONLINE RESOURCES

REVIEW QUESTIONS

1. Identify the main groups and ideas that drove the Progressive movement.

2. Explain how immigration to the United States in this period was part of a global movement of peoples.

3. Describe how Fordism transformed American industrial and consumer society.

4. Socialism was a rising force across the globe in the early twentieth century. How successful was the movement in the United States?

5. Explain why the Industrial Workers of the World (IWW) grew so rapidly and aroused so much opposition.

6. How did immigrants adjust to life in America? What institutions or activities became important to their adjustment, and why?

7. What did Progressive era feminists want to change in society, and how did their actions help to spearhead broader reforms?

8. How did ideas of women's roles, shared by maternalist reformers, lead to an expansion of activism by and rights for women?

9. How did each Progressive era president view the role of the federal government?

10. Pick a Progressive era reform (a movement, a specific legislation, or an organization) and describe how it shows how Progressives could work for both the expansion of democracy and restrictions on it.

KEY TERMS

muckrakers (p. 546)

Ellis Island and Angel Island (p. 547)

Fordism (p. 550)

Rerum Novarum (p. 551)

"scientific management" (p. 552)

Industrial Workers of the World (p. 556)

collective bargaining (p. 556)

new feminism (p. 558)

birth-control movement (p. 558)

Society of American Indians (p. 559)

"social legislation" (p. 560)

Seventeenth Amendment (p. 561)

"maternalist" reforms (p. 564)

Muller v. Oregon (p. 565)

workmen's compensation laws (p. 565)

Conservation Movement (p. 567)

Sixteenth Amendment (p. 568)

New Freedom and New Nationalism (p. 569)

Federal Trade Commission (p. 571)

wwnorton.com /studyspace

VISIT STUDYSPACE FOR THESE RESOURCES AND MORE

- A chapter outline
- A diagnostic chapter quiz
- Interactive maps
- Map worksheets
- Multimedia documents

The Greatest Department Store on Earth, a cartoon from *Puck*, November 29, 1899, depicts Uncle Sam selling goods, mostly manufactured products, to the nations of the world. The search for markets overseas would be a recurring theme of twentieth-century American foreign policy.

CHAPTER 19

SAFE FOR DEMOCRACY

THE UNITED STATES

AND WORLD WAR I

★

1916-1920

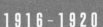

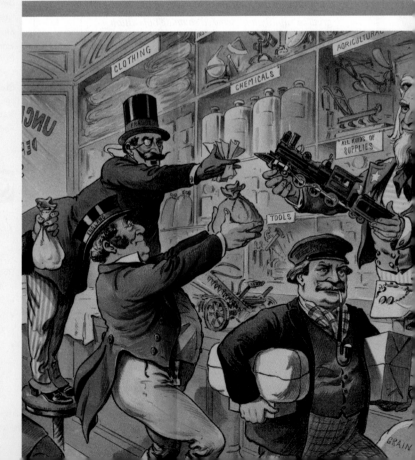

In 1902, W. T. Stead published a short volume with the arresting title *The Americanization of the World; or, the Trend of the Twentieth Century*, in which he predicted that the United States would soon emerge as "the greatest of world-powers." But what was most striking about his work was that Stead located the source of American power less in the realm of military might or territorial acquisition than in the country's single-minded commitment to the "pursuit of wealth" and the relentless international spread of American culture—art, music, journalism, even ideas about religion and gender relations. He foresaw a future in which the United States promoted its interests and values through an unending involvement in the affairs of other nations. Stead proved to be an accurate prophet.

The Spanish-American War had established the United States as an international empire. Despite the conquest of the Philippines and Puerto Rico, however, the country's overseas holdings remained tiny compared to those of Britain, France, and Germany. And no more were added, except for a strip of land surrounding the Panama Canal, acquired in 1903, and the Virgin Islands, purchased from Denmark in 1917. In 1900, Great Britain ruled over more than 300 million people in possessions scattered across the globe, and France had nearly 50 million subjects in Asia and Africa. Compared with these, the American presence in the world seemed very small. As Stead suggested, America's empire differed significantly from those of European countries—it was economic, cultural, and intellectual, rather than territorial.

The world economy at the dawn of the twentieth century was already highly globalized. An ever-increasing stream of goods, investments, and people flowed from country to country. Although Britain still dominated world banking and the British pound remained the major currency of international trade, the United States had become the leading industrial power. By 1914, it produced more than one-third of the world's manufactured goods. Spearheads of American culture like movies and popular music were not far behind.

Europeans were fascinated by American ingenuity and mass-production techniques. Many feared American products and culture would overwhelm their own. "What are the chief new features of London life?" one British writer asked in 1901. "They are the telephone, the portable camera, the phonograph, the electric street car, the automobile, the typewriter. . . . In every one of these the American maker is supreme."

America's growing connections with the outside world led to increasing military and political involvement. In the two decades after 1900, many of the basic principles that would guide American foreign

• In what ways did the Progressive presidents promote the expansion of American power overseas?

• How did the United States get involved in World War I?

• How did the United States mobilize resources and public opinion for the war effort?

• How did the war affect race relations in the United States?

• Why was 1919 such a watershed year for the United States and the world?

policy for the rest of the century were formulated. The "open door"—the free flow of trade, investment, information, and culture—emerged as a key principle of American foreign relations.

Americans in the twentieth century often discussed foreign policy in the language of freedom. A supreme faith in America's historic destiny and in the righteousness of its ideals enabled the country's leaders to think of the United States simultaneously as an emerging great power and as the worldwide embodiment of freedom.

More than any other individual, Woodrow Wilson articulated this vision of America's relationship to the rest of the world. His foreign policy, called by historians **"liberal internationalism,"** rested on the conviction that economic and political progress went hand in hand. Thus, greater worldwide freedom would follow inevitably from increased American investment and trade abroad. Frequently during the twentieth century, this conviction would serve as a mask for American power and self-interest. It would also inspire sincere efforts to bring freedom to other peoples. In either case, liberal internationalism represented a shift from the nineteenth-century tradition of promoting freedom primarily by example to active intervention to remake the world in the American image.

AN ERA OF INTERVENTION

Just as they expanded the powers of the federal government in domestic affairs, the Progressive presidents were not reluctant to project American power outside the country's borders. At first, their interventions were confined to the Western Hemisphere, whose affairs the United States had claimed a special right to oversee ever since the Monroe Doctrine of 1823.

The Caribbean

Between 1901 and 1920, U.S. marines landed in Caribbean countries more than twenty times. Usually, they were dispatched to create a welcoming economic environment for American companies that wanted stable access to raw materials like bananas and sugar, and for bankers nervous that their loans to local governments might not be repaid.

"I Took the Canal Zone"

Theodore Roosevelt became far more active in international diplomacy than most of his predecessors, helping, for example, to negotiate a settlement of the Russo-Japanese War of 1905, a feat for which he was awarded

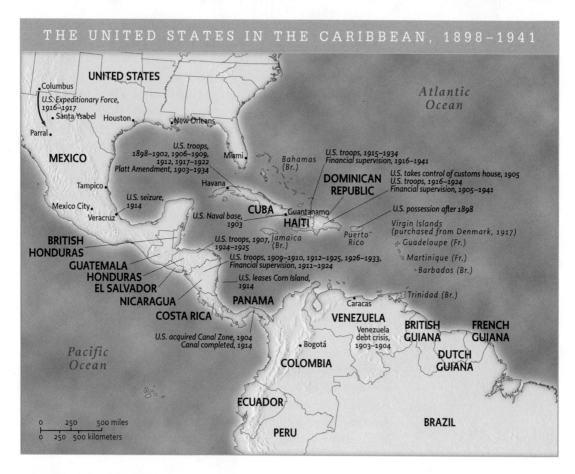

THE UNITED STATES IN THE CARIBBEAN, 1898–1941

the Nobel Peace Prize. Closer to home, his policies were more aggressive. "I have always been fond of the West African proverb," he wrote, "'Speak softly and carry a big stick.'"

The idea of a canal across the fifty-one-mile-wide Isthmus of Panama had a long history. A long-time proponent of American naval development, Roosevelt was convinced that a canal would facilitate the movement of naval and commercial vessels between the two oceans. In 1903, when Colombia, of which Panama was a part, refused to cede land for the project, Roosevelt helped set in motion an uprising by Panamanian conspirators. An American gunboat prevented the Colombian army from suppressing the rebellion.

On establishing its independence, Panama signed a treaty giving the United States both the right to construct and operate a canal and sovereignty over the **Canal Zone**, a ten-mile-wide strip of land through

Between 1898 and 1941, the United States intervened militarily numerous times in Caribbean countries, generally to protect the economic interests of American banks and investors.

The Panama Canal

which the route would run. A remarkable feat of engineering, the canal was the largest construction project in history to that date. Like the building of the transcontinental railroad in the 1860s and much construction work today, it involved the widespread use of immigrant labor. Most of the 60,000 workers came from the Caribbean islands of Barbados and Jamaica, but others hailed from Europe, Asia, and the United States. When completed in 1914, the canal reduced the sea voyage between the East and West Coasts of the United States by 8,000 miles. "I took the Canal Zone," Roosevelt exulted. But the manner in which the canal had been initiated, and the continued American rule over the Canal Zone, would long remain a source of tension. In 1977, President Jimmy Carter negotiated treaties that led to turning over the canal's operation and control of the Canal Zone to Panama in the year 2000 (see Chapter 26).

Immigrant labor

The Roosevelt Corollary

Roosevelt's actions in Panama reflected a principle that came to be called the **Roosevelt Corollary** to the Monroe Doctrine. This held that the United States had the right to exercise "an international police power" in the Western Hemisphere—a significant expansion of James Monroe's pledge to defend the hemisphere against European intervention. In 1904, Roosevelt ordered American forces to seize the customs houses of the Dominican Republic to ensure payment of its debts to European and American investors. In 1906, he dispatched troops to Cuba to oversee a disputed election; they remained in the country until 1909.

An international police power

The World's Constable, a cartoon commenting on Theodore Roosevelt's "new diplomacy," *in Judge*, January 14, 1905, portrays Roosevelt as an impartial policeman, holding in one hand the threat of force and in the other the promise of the peaceful settlement of disputes. Roosevelt stands between the undisciplined non-white peoples of the world and the imperialist powers of Europe and Japan.

Roosevelt's successor, William Howard Taft, landed marines in Nicaragua to protect a government friendly to American economic interests. In general, however, Taft emphasized economic investment and loans from American banks, rather than direct military intervention, as the best way to spread American influence. As a result, his foreign policy became known as **Dollar Diplomacy**.

Moral Imperialism

The son of a Presbyterian minister, Woodrow Wilson brought to the presidency a missionary zeal and a sense of his own and the nation's moral righteousness. He appointed as secretary of state William Jennings Bryan, a strong anti-imperialist. Wilson promised a new foreign policy that would respect Latin America's independence and free it from foreign economic domination. But Wilson could not abandon the conviction that the United States had a responsibility to teach other peoples the lessons of democracy.

Woodrow Wilson

Wilson's "**moral imperialism**" produced more military interventions in Latin America than any president before or since. In 1915, he sent marines to occupy Haiti after the government refused to allow American banks to oversee its financial dealings. In 1916, he established a military government in the Dominican Republic, with the United States controlling the country's customs collections and paying its debts. American soldiers remained in the Dominican Republic until 1924 and in Haiti until 1934. Wilson's foreign policy underscored a paradox of modern American history: the presidents who spoke the most about freedom were likely to intervene most frequently in the affairs of other countries.

Wilson's military interventions in Latin America

Wilson and Mexico

Wilson's major preoccupation in Latin America was Mexico, where in 1911 a revolution led by Francisco Madero overthrew the government of dictator Porfirio Díaz. Two years later, without Wilson's knowledge but with the backing of the U.S. ambassador and of American companies that controlled Mexico's oil and mining industries, military commander Victoriano Huerta assassinated Madero and seized power.

Political turmoil

Wilson was appalled. He would "teach" Latin Americans, he added, "to elect good men." When civil war broke out in Mexico, Wilson ordered American troops to land at Vera Cruz to prevent the arrival of weapons meant for Huerta's forces. But to Wilson's surprise, Mexicans greeted the marines as invaders rather than liberators.

Pancho Villa

In 1916, the war spilled over into the United States when "Pancho" Villa, the leader of one faction, attacked Columbus, New Mexico, where he killed seventeen Americans. Wilson ordered 10,000 troops into northern Mexico on an expedition that unsuccessfully sought to arrest Villa. Mexico was a warning that it might be difficult to use American might to reorder the internal affairs of other nations.

AMERICA AND THE GREAT WAR

In June 1914, a Serbian nationalist assassinated Archduke Franz Ferdinand, heir to the throne of the Austro-Hungarian empire, in Sarajevo, Bosnia. This deed set in motion a chain of events that plunged Europe into the most devastating war the world had ever seen. In the years before 1914, European nations had engaged in a scramble to obtain colonial possessions overseas and had constructed a shifting series of alliances seeking military domination within Europe. Within a little more than a month, because of the European powers' interlocking military alliances, Britain, France, Russia, and Japan (the Allies) found themselves at war with the Central Powers—Germany, Austria-Hungary, and the Ottoman empire, whose holdings included modern-day Turkey and much of the Middle East.

Outbreak of war

German forces quickly overran Belgium and part of northern France. The war then settled into a prolonged stalemate, with bloody, indecisive battles succeeding one another. New military technologies—submarines, airplanes, machine guns, tanks, and poison gas—produced unprecedented slaughter. In one five-month battle at Verdun, in 1916, 600,000 French

New technologies

In this painting from 1917, the Austrian painter Albin Egger-Leinz portrays World War I soldiers as faceless automatons marching in unison to the slaughter. By this time, the massive loss of life had produced widespread revulsion against the war.

and German soldiers perished—nearly as many combatants as in the entire American Civil War. By the time the war ended, an estimated 10 million soldiers, and uncounted millions of civilians, had perished. And the war was followed by widespread famine and a worldwide epidemic of influenza that killed an estimated 21 million people more.

Casualties of the Great War

The Great War, or World War I as it came to be called, dealt a severe blow to the optimism and self-confidence of Western civilization. For decades, philosophers, reformers, and politicians had hailed the triumph of reason and human progress, an outlook hard to reconcile with the mass slaughter of World War I. The conflict was also a shock to European socialist and labor movements. Karl Marx had called on the "workers of the world" to unite against their oppressors. Instead, they marched off to kill each other.

Neutrality and Preparedness

As war engulfed Europe, Americans found themselves sharply divided. British-Americans sided with their nation of origin, as did many other Americans who associated Great Britain with liberty and democracy and Germany with repressive government. On the other hand, German-Americans identified with Germany, and Irish-Americans bitterly opposed any aid to the British. Immigrants from the Russian empire, especially Jews, had no desire to see the United States aid the czar's regime.

Americans divided

When war broke out in 1914, President Wilson proclaimed American neutrality. But naval warfare in Europe reverberated in the United States. Britain declared a naval blockade of Germany and began to stop American merchant vessels. Germany launched submarine warfare against ships entering and leaving British ports. In May 1915, a German submarine sank the British liner **Lusitania** (which was carrying a large cache of arms) off the coast of Ireland, causing the death of 1,198 passengers, including 124 Americans. Wilson composed a note of protest so strong that Bryan resigned as secretary of state, fearing that the president was laying the foundation for military intervention.

The liner *Lusitania*, pictured on a "peace" postcard. Its sinking by a German submarine in 1915 strengthened the resolve of those who wished to see the United States enter the European war.

The sinking of the *Lusitania* outraged American public opinion and strengthened the hand of those who believed that the United States must prepare for possible entry into the war. Wilson himself had strong pro-British sympathies and viewed Germany as "the natural foe of liberty." By the end of 1915, he had embarked on a policy of "preparedness"—a crash program to expand the American army and navy.

The Road to War

In May 1916, Germany announced the suspension of submarine warfare against noncombatants. Wilson's preparedness program seemed to have succeeded in securing the right of Americans to travel freely on the high seas. "He kept us out of war" became the slogan of his campaign for reelection. With the Republican Party reunited after its split in 1912, the election proved to be one of the closest in American history. Wilson defeated Republican candidate Charles Evans Hughes by only twenty-three electoral votes and about 600,000 popular votes out of more than 18 million cast. Partly because he seemed to promise not to send American soldiers to Europe, Wilson carried ten of the twelve states that had adopted woman suffrage. Without the votes of women, Wilson would not have been reelected.

Wilson's reelection

Almost immediately, however, Germany announced its intention to resume submarine warfare against ships sailing to or from the British Isles, and several American merchant vessels were sunk. In March 1917, British spies intercepted and made public the **Zimmerman Telegram**, a message by German foreign secretary Arthur Zimmerman calling on Mexico to join in a coming war against the United States and promising to help it recover territory lost in the Mexican War of 1846–1848. On April 2, Wilson went before Congress to ask for a declaration of war against Germany. "The world," he proclaimed, "must be made safe for democracy." The war resolution passed the Senate 82–6 and the House 373–50.

A 1916 Wilson campaign truck (a new development in political campaigning), promising peace, prosperity, and preparedness.

The Fourteen Points

Not until the spring of 1918 did American forces arrive in Europe in large numbers. By then, the world situation had taken a dramatic turn. In November 1917, a communist revolution headed by Vladimir Lenin overthrew the Russian government. Shortly thereafter, Lenin withdrew Russia from the war and published the secret treaties by which the Allies had agreed to divide up

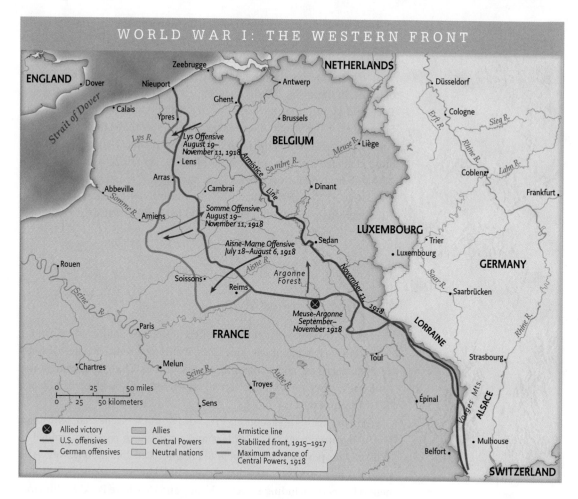

WORLD WAR I: THE WESTERN FRONT

After years of stalemate on the western front in World War I, the arrival of American troops in 1917 and 1918 shifted the balance of power and made possible the Allied victory.

conquered territory after the war—an embarrassment for Wilson, who had promised a just peace.

Partly to assure the country that the war was being fought for a moral cause, Wilson in January 1918 issued the **Fourteen Points**, the clearest statement of American war aims and of his vision of a new international order. Among the key principles were self-determination for all nations, freedom of the seas, free trade, open diplomacy (an end to secret treaties), the readjustment of colonial claims with colonized people given "equal weight" in deciding their futures, and the creation of a "general association of nations" to preserve the peace. Wilson envisioned this last provision, which led to the establishment after the war of the League of Nations, as a kind of global counterpart to the regulatory commissions Progressives had created

League of Nations

at home to maintain social harmony. The Fourteen Points established the agenda for the peace conference that followed the war.

Turning the tide of battle

The United States threw its economic resources and manpower into the war. When American troops finally arrived in Europe, they turned the tide of battle. In the spring of 1918, they helped repulse a German advance near Paris and by July were participating in a major Allied counteroffensive. In September, in the Meuse-Argonne campaign, more than 1 million American soldiers under General John J. Pershing helped push back the outnumbered and exhausted German army. With his forces in full retreat, the German kaiser abdicated on November 9. Two days later, Germany sued for peace. Over 100,000 Americans had died, a substantial number, but they were only 1 percent of the 10 million soldiers killed in the Great War.

THE WAR AT HOME

The Progressives' War

For most Progressives, the war offered the possibility of reforming American society along scientific lines, instilling a sense of national unity and self-sacrifice, and expanding social justice. That American power could now disseminate Progressive values around the globe heightened the war's appeal.

Almost without exception, Progressive intellectuals and reformers, joined by prominent labor leaders and native-born socialists, rallied to Wilson's support. The roster included intellectuals like John Dewey, AFL head Samuel Gompers, socialist writers like Upton Sinclair, and prominent reformers including Florence Kelley and Charlotte Perkins Gilman.

The Wartime State

An expanded state

Like the Civil War, World War I created, albeit temporarily, a national state with unprecedented powers and a sharply increased presence in Americans' everyday lives. Under the **Selective Service Act** of May 1917, 24 million men were required to register with the draft. New federal agencies moved to regulate industry, transportation, labor relations, and agriculture. Headed by Wall Street financier Bernard Baruch, the **War Industries Board** presided over all elements of war production from the distribution of raw materials to the prices of manufactured goods. To spur efficiency, it established standardized specifications for everything from automobile tires to shoe colors (three were permitted—black, brown, and white). The Railroad Administration took control of the nation's transportation system, and the Fuel Agency rationed coal and oil. The Food Administration instructed farmers on modern methods of cultivation and promoted the more efficient preparation of meals.

The War Labor Board, which included representatives of government, industry, and the American Federation of Labor, pressed for the establishment of a minimum wage, an eight-hour workday, and the right to form unions. During the war, wages rose substantially, working conditions in many industries improved, and union membership doubled. To finance the war, corporate and individual income taxes rose enormously. By 1918, the wealthiest Americans were paying 60 percent of their income in taxes. Tens of millions of Americans answered the call to demonstrate their patriotism by purchasing Liberty bonds.

The Propaganda War

During the Civil War, it had been left to private agencies—Union Leagues, the Loyal Publication Society, and others—to mobilize prowar public opinion. But the Wilson administration decided that patriotism was too important to leave to the private sector. Many Americans opposed American participation, notably the Industrial Workers of the World (IWW) and the bulk of the Socialist Party, which in 1917 condemned the declaration of war as "a crime against the people of the United States" and called on "the workers of all countries" to refuse to fight.

In April 1917, the Wilson administration created the Committee on Public Information (CPI) to explain to Americans and the world, as its director, George Creel, put it, "the cause that compelled America to take arms in defense of its liberties and free institutions." The CPI flooded the country with prowar propaganda, using every available medium from pamphlets (of which it issued 75 million) to posters, newspaper advertisements, and motion pictures.

The CPI couched its appeal in the Progressive language of social cooperation and expanded democracy. Abroad, this meant a peace based on the principle of national self-determination. At home, it meant improving "industrial democracy." The CPI distributed pamphlets foreseeing a postwar society complete with a "universal eight-hour day" and a living wage for all.

Although "democracy" served as the key term of wartime mobilization, "freedom" also took on new significance. The war, a CPI advertisement proclaimed, was being fought in "the great cause of freedom." The most common visual image in wartime propaganda was the Statue of Liberty, employed especially to rally support among immigrants. Buying

All combatants raised money by selling war bonds. In the German poster, the text reads: "The war loan is the way to peace. The enemies want it this way [referring to the mailed fist]. So subscribe." The fist conveys sheer power—it offers an image rather different from the representation of liberty on the American war poster.

Liberty bonds became a demonstration of patriotism. Wilson's speeches cast the United States as a land of liberty fighting alongside a "concert of free people" to secure self-determination for the oppressed peoples of the world. Government propaganda whipped up hatred of the wartime foe by portraying Germany as a nation of barbaric Huns.

The Coming of Woman Suffrage

The enlistment of "democracy" and "freedom" as ideological war weapons inevitably inspired demands for their expansion at home. In 1916, Wilson had cautiously endorsed votes for women. America's entry into the war threatened to tear the suffrage movement apart, because many advocates had been associated with opposition to American involvement. Indeed, among those who voted against the declaration of war was the first woman member of Congress, the staunch pacifist Jeannette Rankin of Montana. Although defeated in her reelection bid in 1918, Rankin would return to Congress in 1940. She became the only member to oppose the declaration of war against Japan in 1941, which ended her political career. In 1968, at the age of eighty-five, Rankin took part in a giant march on Washington to protest the war in Vietnam.

Jeannette Rankin

As during the Civil War, however, most leaders of woman suffrage organizations enthusiastically enlisted in the effort. Women sold war bonds, organized patriotic rallies, and went to work in war production jobs. Some 22,000 served as clerical workers and nurses with American forces in Europe.

Women and the war

At the same time, a new generation of college-educated activists, organized in the National Women's Party, pressed for the right to vote with militant tactics many older suffrage advocates found scandalous. The party's

The National Women's Party

THE AWAKENING

A 1915 cartoon showing the western states where women had won the right to vote. Women in the East reach out to a western woman carrying a torch of liberty.

leader, Alice Paul, had studied in England between 1907 and 1910, when the British suffrage movement adopted a strategy that included arrests, imprisonments, and vigorous denunciations of a male-dominated political system. Paul compared Wilson to the kaiser, and a group of her followers chained themselves to the White House fence, resulting in a seven-month prison sentence. When they began a hunger strike, the prisoners were force-fed.

The combination of women's patriotic service and widespread outrage over the treatment of Paul and her fellow prisoners pushed the administration toward full-fledged support of woman suffrage. In 1920, the long struggle ended with the ratification of the Nineteenth Amendment, which barred states from using sex as a qualification for the suffrage. The United States became the twenty-seventh country to allow women to vote.

The Nineteenth Amendment

Prohibition

The war gave a powerful impulse to other campaigns that had engaged the energies of many women in the Progressive era. Prohibition, a movement inherited from the nineteenth century that had gained new strength and militancy in Progressive America, finally achieved national success during the war. Employers hoped it would create a more disciplined labor force. Urban reformers believed that it would promote a more orderly city environment and undermine urban political machines, which used saloons as places to organize. Women reformers hoped Prohibition would protect wives and children from husbands who engaged in domestic violence when drunk or who squandered their wages at saloons. Many native-born Protestants saw Prohibition as a way of imposing "American" values on immigrants.

After some success at the state level, Prohibitionists came to see national legislation as their best strategy. The war gave them added ammunition. Many prominent breweries were owned by German-Americans, making beer seem unpatriotic. The Food Administration insisted that grain must be used to produce food, not brewed into beer or distilled into liquor. In December 1917, Congress passed the Eighteenth Amendment, prohibiting the manufacture and sale of intoxicating liquor. It was ratified by the states in 1919 and went into effect at the beginning of 1920.

A 1916 cartoon from the publication of the Women's Christian Temperance Union shows petitions for Prohibition flooding into Congress.

ON TO WASHINGTON!
STORM THE CAPITOL WITH PETITIONS FOR NATIONAL CONSTITUTIONAL PROHIBITION—NOW IS THE TIME FOR ACTION

Liberty in Wartime

World War I raised questions already glimpsed during the Civil War that would trouble the nation again during the

VOICES OF FREEDOM

From Eugene V. Debs, Speech to the Jury before Sentencing under the Espionage Act (1918)

The most prominent spokesman for American socialism and a fervent opponent of American participation in World War I, Eugene V. Debs was arrested for delivering an antiwar speech and convicted of violating the Espionage Act. In his speech to the jury, he defended the right of dissent in wartime.

I wish to admit the truth of all that has been testified to in this proceeding. . . . Gentlemen, you have heard the report of my speech at Canton on June 16, and I submit that there is not a word in that speech to warrant the charges set out in the indictment. . . . In what I had to say there my purpose was to have the people understand something about the social system in which we live and to prepare them to change this system by perfectly peaceable and orderly means into what I, as a Socialist, conceive to be a real democracy. . . . I have never advocated violence in any form. I have always believed in education, in intelligence, in enlightenment; and I have always made my appeal to the reason and to the conscience of the people.

In every age there have been a few heroic souls who have been in advance of their time, who have been misunderstood, maligned, persecuted, sometimes put to death. . . . Washington, Jefferson, Franklin, Paine, and their compeers were the rebels of their day. . . . But they had the moral courage to be true to their convictions. . . .

William Lloyd Garrison, Wendell Phillips, Elizabeth Cady Stanton . . . and other leaders of the abolition movement who were regarded as public enemies and treated accordingly, were true to their faith and stood their ground. . . . You are now teaching your children to revere their memories, while all of their detractors are in oblivion.

This country has been engaged in a number of wars and every one of them has been condemned by some of the people. The war of 1812 was opposed and condemned by some of the most influential citizens; the Mexican War was vehemently opposed and bitterly denounced, even after the war had been declared and was in progress, by Abraham Lincoln, Charles Sumner, Daniel Webster. . . . They were not indicted; they were not charged with treason. . . .

I believe in the Constitution. Isn't it strange that we Socialists stand almost alone today in upholding and defending the Constitution of the United States? The revolutionary fathers . . . understood that free speech, a free press and the right of free assemblage by the people were fundamental principles in democratic government. . . . I believe in the right of free speech, in war as well as in peace.

From W. E. B. Du Bois, "Returning Soldiers," *The Crisis* (1919)

Scholar, poet, activist, and founder of the National Association for the Advancement of Colored People and editor of its magazine, *The Crisis*, W. E. B. Du Bois was the most prominent black leader of the first half of the twentieth century. He supported black participation in World War I, but he insisted that black soldiers must now join in the struggle for freedom at home.

We are returning from war! *The Crisis* and tens of thousands of black men were drafted into a great struggle. For bleeding France and what she means and has meant and will mean to us and humanity and against the threat of German race arrogance, we fought gladly and to the last drop of blood; for America and her highest ideals, we fought in far-off hope; for the dominant southern oligarchy entrenched in Washington, we fought in bitter resignation. For the America that represents and gloats in lynching, disfranchisement, caste, brutality and devilish insult—for this, in the hateful upturning and mixing of things, we were forced by vindictive fate to fight, also.

But today we return! . . . We sing: This country of ours, despite all its better souls have done and dreamed, is yet a shameful land.

It *lynches*.

And lynching is barbarism of a degree of contemptible nastiness unparalleled in human history. Yet for fifty years we have lynched two Negroes a week, and we have kept this up right through the war.

It *disfranchises* its own citizens.

Disfranchisement is the deliberate theft and robbery of the only protection of poor against rich and black against white. The land that disfranchises its citizens and calls itself a democracy lies and knows it lies.

It encourages *ignorance*.

It has never really tried to educate the Negro. A dominate minority does not want Negroes educated. It wants servants. . . .

It *insults* us.

It has organized a nationwide and latterly a worldwide propaganda of deliberate and continuous insult and defamation of black blood wherever found. . . .

This is the country to which we Soldiers of Democracy return. This is the fatherland for which we fought! But it is *our* fatherland. It was right for us to fight. . . .

We *return fighting*.

Make way for Democracy!

QUESTIONS

1. *Why does Debs relate the history of wartime dissent in America?*

2. *What connections does Du Bois draw between blacks fighting abroad in the war and returning to fight at home?*

3. *In what ways does each author point up the contradiction between America's professed values and its actual conduct?*

McCarthy era and in the aftermath of the terrorist attacks of 2001: What is the balance between security and freedom? Does the Constitution protect citizens' rights during wartime? Should dissent be equated with lack of patriotism?

Despite the administration's idealistic language of democracy and freedom, the war inaugurated the most intense repression of civil liberties the nation has ever known. "It is a fearful thing to lead this great peaceful people into war," Wilson remarked in his speech asking Congress to bring America into the conflict. Even he could not have predicted how significant an impact the war would have on American freedom.

The Espionage Act

Restrictions on freedom of speech

For the first time since the Alien and Sedition Acts of 1798, the federal government enacted laws to restrict freedom of speech. **The Espionage Act** of 1917 prohibited not only spying and interfering with the draft but also "false statements" that might impede military success. The postmaster general barred from the mails numerous newspapers and magazines critical of the administration. In 1918, the **Sedition Act** made it a crime to make spoken or printed statements that intended to cast "contempt, scorn, or disrepute" on the "form of government," or that advocated interference with the war effort. The government charged more than 2,000 persons with violating these laws. Over half were convicted. A court sentenced Ohio farmer John White to twenty-one months in prison for saying that the murder of innocent women and children by German soldiers was no worse than what the United States had done in the Philippines in the war of 1899–1903.

The most prominent victim was Eugene V. Debs, convicted in 1918 under the Espionage Act for delivering an antiwar speech. Germany sent a socialist leader to prison for four years for opposing the war; in the United States, Debs's sentence was ten years. After the war's end, Wilson rejected the advice of his attorney general that he commute Debs's sentence. Debs ran for president while still in prison in 1920 and received 900,000 votes. It was left to Wilson's successor, Warren G. Harding, to release Debs from prison in 1921.

Coercive Patriotism

Even more extreme repression took place at the hands of state governments and private groups. During the war, thirty-three states outlawed the possession or display of red or black flags (symbols, respectively, of communism and anarchism), and

Douglas Fairbanks, one of the era's most celebrated movie stars, addressing a 1918 rally urging people to buy Liberty Bonds.

twenty-three outlawed a newly created offense, "criminal syndicalism," the advocacy of unlawful acts to accomplish political change or "a change in industrial ownership."

"Who is the real patriot?" Emma Goldman asked when the United States entered the war. She answered, those who "love America with open eyes," who were not blind to "the wrongs committed in the name of patriotism." But from the federal government to local authorities and private groups, patriotism came to be equated with support for the government, the war, and the American economic system. Throughout the country, schools revised their course offerings to ensure their patriotism and required teachers to sign loyalty oaths.

The 250,000 members of the newly formed American Protective League (APL) helped the Justice Department identify radicals and critics of the war by spying on their neighbors and carrying out "slacker raids" in which thousands of men were stopped on the streets of major cities and required to produce draft registration cards. Employers cooperated with the government in crushing the Industrial Workers of the World (IWW), a move long demanded by business interests. In September 1917, operating under one of the broadest warrants in American history, federal agents swooped down on IWW offices throughout the country, arresting hundreds of leaders and seizing files and publications.

The American Protective League

Although some Progressives protested individual excesses, most failed to speak out against the broad suppression of freedom of expression. Civil liberties, by and large, had never been a major concern of Progressives, who had always viewed the national state as the embodiment of democratic purpose and insisted that freedom flowed from participating in the life of society, not standing in opposition. Strong believers in the use of national power to improve social conditions, Progressives found themselves ill prepared to develop a defense of minority rights against majority or governmental tyranny.

Progressives and civil liberties

WHO IS AN AMERICAN?

The "Race Problem"

Even before American participation in World War I, what contemporaries called the "race problem"—the tensions that arose from the country's increasing ethnic diversity—had become a major subject of public concern. "Race" referred to far more than black-white relations. The *Dictionary of Races of Peoples*, published in 1911 by the U.S. Immigration Commission, listed no fewer than forty-five immigrant "races," each supposedly with its own inborn characteristics. They ranged from Anglo-Saxons at the top down to Hebrews, Northern Italians, and, lowest of all, Southern Italians—supposedly violent, undisciplined, and incapable of assimilation. The new science of eugenics, which studied the alleged mental characteristics of different races, gave anti-immigrant sentiment an air of professional expertise.

Demands for Americanization

Somehow, the very nationalization of politics and economic life served to heighten awareness of ethnic and racial difference and spurred demands for "Americanization"—the creation of a more homogeneous national culture. A 1908 play by the Jewish immigrant writer Israel Zangwill, *The Melting Pot*, gave a popular name to the process by which newcomers were supposed to merge their identity into existing American nationality. Public and private groups of all kinds—including educators, employers, labor leaders, social reformers, and public officials—took up the task of Americanizing new immigrants. Fearful that adult newcomers remained too stuck in their Old World ways, public schools paid great attention to Americanizing immigrants' children. Moreover, the federal and state governments demanded that immigrants demonstrate their unwavering devotion to the United States.

Randolph Bourne's "Trans-National America"

A minority of Progressives questioned Americanization efforts and insisted on respect for immigrant subcultures. Probably the most penetrating critique issued from the pen of Randolph Bourne, whose 1916 essay, "Trans-National America," exposed the fundamental flaw in the Americanization model. "There is no distinctive American culture," Bourne pointed out. Interaction between individuals and groups had produced the nation's music, poetry, and other cultural expressions. Bourne envisioned a democratic, cosmopolitan society in which immigrants and natives alike submerged their group identities in a new "trans-national" culture.

The Anti-German Crusade

German-Americans bore the brunt of forced Americanization. The first wave of German immigrants had arrived before the Civil War. By 1914, German-Americans numbered nearly 9 million, including immigrants and persons of German parentage. They had created thriving ethnic institutions including clubs, sports associations, schools, and theaters. On the eve of the war, many Americans admired German traditions in literature, music, and philosophy, and one-quarter of all the high school students in the country studied the German language. But after American entry into the war, the use of German and expressions of German culture became a target of prowar organizations.

German culture in America

By 1919, the vast majority of the states had enacted laws restricting the teaching of foreign languages. Popular words of German origin were changed: "hamburger" became "liberty sandwich," and "sauerkraut" was renamed "liberty cabbage." The government jailed Karl Müch, the director of the Boston Symphony and a Swiss citizen, as an enemy alien after he insisted on including the works of German composers like Beethoven in his concerts.

A 1919 cartoon, *Close the Gate*, warns that unrestricted immigration allows dangerous radicals to enter the United States.

Toward Immigration Restriction

Even as Americanization programs sought to assimilate immigrants into American society, the war strengthened the conviction that certain kinds of undesirable persons ought to be excluded altogether. The new immigrants, one advocate of restriction declared, appreciated the values of democracy and freedom far less than "the Anglo-Saxon." Stanford University psychologist Lewis Terman introduced the term "IQ" (intelligence quotient) in 1916, claiming that this single number could measure an individual's mental capacity. Intelligence tests administered to recruits by the army seemed to confirm scientifically that blacks and the new immigrants stood far below native white Protestants on the IQ scale, further spurring demands for immigration restriction.

The war accelerated other efforts to upgrade the American population. Some were inspired by the idea of improving the human race by discouraging reproduction among less "desirable" persons. Indiana in 1907 had passed a law authorizing doctors to sterilize insane and "feeble-minded" inmates in mental institutions so that they would not pass their "defective" genes on to children. Numerous other states now followed suit. In *Buck v. Bell* (1927), the Supreme Court upheld the constitutionality of these laws. Justice Oliver Wendell Holmes's opinion included the famous statement, "three generations of imbeciles are enough." By the time the practice ended in the 1960s, some 63,000 persons had been involuntarily sterilized.

> Buck v. Bell

Groups Apart: Mexicans and Asian-Americans

No matter how coercive, Americanization programs assumed that European immigrants and especially their children could eventually adjust to the conditions of American life, embrace American ideals, and become productive citizens enjoying the full blessings of American freedom. This assumption did not apply to non-white immigrants or to blacks.

The war led to further growth of the Southwest's Mexican population. Wartime demand for labor from the area's mine owners and large farmers led the government to exempt Mexicans temporarily from the

> *Mexicans in the Southwest*

literacy test enacted in 1917. Segregation, by law and custom, was common in schools, hospitals, theaters, and other institutions in states with significant Mexican populations. By 1920, nearly all Mexican children in California and the Southwest were educated in their own schools or classrooms. Phoenix, Arizona, established separate public schools for Indians, Mexicans, blacks, and whites.

Even more restrictive were policies toward Asian-Americans. In 1906, the San Francisco school board ordered all Asian students confined to a single public school. When the Japanese government protested, President Theodore Roosevelt persuaded the city to rescind the order.

The Gentlemen's Agreement

He then negotiated the Gentlemen's Agreement of 1907, whereby Japan agreed to end migration to the United States except for the wives and children of men already in the country. In 1913, California barred all aliens incapable of becoming naturalized citizens (that is, Asians) from owning or leasing land.

The Color Line

By far the largest non-white group, African-Americans, were excluded from nearly every Progressive definition of freedom described in Chapter 18. After their disenfranchisement in the South, few could participate in

Exclusion of blacks

American democracy. Barred from joining most unions and from skilled employment, black workers had little access to "industrial freedom." Nor could blacks, the majority desperately poor, participate fully in the emerging consumer economy, either as employees in the new department stores (except as janitors and cleaning women) or as purchasers of the consumer goods now flooding the marketplace.

Progressives and race

Progressive intellectuals, social scientists, labor reformers, and suffrage advocates displayed a remarkable indifference to the black condition. Most settlement house reformers accepted segregation as natural and equitable. White leaders of the woman suffrage movement said little about black disenfranchisement. The amendment that achieved woman suffrage left the states free to limit voting by poll taxes and literacy tests. Living in the South, the vast majority of the country's black women did not enjoy its benefits.

Roosevelt, Wilson, and Race

The Progressive presidents shared prevailing attitudes concerning blacks. Theodore Roosevelt shocked white opinion by inviting Booker T. Washington to dine with him in the White House and by appointing a

Brownsville affair

number of blacks to federal offices. But in 1906, when a small group of black soldiers shot off their guns in Brownsville, Texas, killing one resident, and none of their fellows would name them, Roosevelt ordered the dishonorable discharge of three black companies—156 men in all, including six winners of the Congressional Medal of Honor.

Woodrow Wilson, a native of Virginia, could speak without irony of the South's "genuine representative government" and its exalted "standards of liberty." His administration imposed racial segregation in federal departments in Washington, D.C., and dismissed numerous black federal employees. Wilson allowed D. W. Griffith's film *Birth of a Nation*, which glorified the Ku Klux Klan as the defender of white civilization during Reconstruction, to have its premiere at the White House in 1915.

Blacks subject to disenfranchisement and segregation were understandably skeptical of the nation's claim to embody freedom. In one of hundreds of lynchings during the Progressive era, a white mob in Springfield, Missouri, in 1906 falsely accused three black men of rape, hanged them from an electric light pole, and burned their bodies in a public orgy of violence. Atop the pole stood a replica of the Statue of Liberty.

A cartoon from the *St. Louis Post-Dispatch*, April 17, 1906, commenting on the lynching of three black men in Springfield, Missouri. The shadow cast by the Statue of Liberty forms a gallows on the ground.

W. E. B. Du Bois and the Revival of Black Protest

Black leaders struggled to find a strategy to rekindle the national commitment to equality that had flickered brightly, if briefly, during Reconstruction. No one thought more deeply, or over so long a period, about the black condition and the challenge it posed to American democracy than the scholar and activist W. E. B. Du Bois. Born in 1868, and educated at Fisk and Harvard universities, Du Bois lived to his ninety-fifth year. The unifying theme of Du Bois's career was his effort to reconcile the contradiction between what he called "American freedom for whites and the continuing subjection of Negroes." His book *The Souls of Black Folk* (1903) issued a clarion call for blacks dissatisfied with the accommodationist policies of Booker T. Washington to press for equal rights. Du Bois believed that educated African-Americans like himself—the "talented tenth" of the black community—must use their education and training to challenge inequality.

The Souls of Black Folk

In some ways, Du Bois was a typical Progressive who believed that investigation, exposure, and education would lead to solutions for social problems. But he also understood the necessity of political action. In 1905, Du Bois gathered a group of black leaders at Niagara Falls (meeting on the Canadian side because no American hotel would provide accommodations) and organized the Niagara movement, which sought to reinvigorate the abolitionist tradition. "We claim for ourselves," Du Bois

The *Niagara movement*

wrote in the group's manifesto, "every single right that belongs to a free-born American." Four years later, Du Bois joined with a group of mostly white reformers shocked by a lynching in Springfield, Illinois (Lincoln's adult home), to create the **National Association for the Advancement of Colored People**. The NAACP, as it was known, launched a long struggle for the enforcement of the Fourteenth and Fifteenth Amendments.

The NAACP

The NAACP's legal strategy won a few victories. In *Bailey v. Alabama* (1911), the Supreme Court overturned southern "peonage" laws that made it a crime for sharecroppers to break their labor contracts. Six years later, it ruled unconstitutional a Louisville zoning regulation excluding blacks from living in certain parts of the city (primarily because it interfered with whites' right to sell their property as they saw fit). Overall, however, the Progressive era witnessed virtually no progress toward racial justice.

Closing Ranks

Among black Americans, the wartime language of freedom inspired hopes for a radical change in the country's racial system. The black press rallied to the war. Du Bois himself, in a widely reprinted editorial in the NAACP's monthly magazine, *The Crisis*, called on African-Americans to "close ranks" and enlist in the army, to help "make our own America a real land of the free."

A 1918 poster celebrates black soldiers in World War I as "True Sons of Freedom." At the upper right, Abraham Lincoln looks on, with a somewhat modified quotation from the Gettysburg Address.

Black participation in the Civil War had helped to secure the destruction of slavery and the achievement of citizenship. But during World War I, closing ranks did not bring significant gains. The navy barred blacks entirely, and the segregated army confined most of the 400,000 blacks who served in the war to supply units rather than combat. Contact with African colonial soldiers fighting alongside the British and French did widen the horizons of black American soldiers. But although colonial troops marched in the victory parade in Paris, the Wilson administration did not allow black Americans to participate.

The Great Migration

Nonetheless, the war unleashed social changes that altered the contours of American race relations. The combination of increased wartime production and a drastic falloff in immigration from Europe once war broke out opened thousands of industrial jobs to black

TABLE 19.1 The Great Migration

CITY	BLACK POPULATION, 1910	BLACK POPULATION, 1920	PERCENT INCREASE
New York	91,709	152,467	66.3%
Philadelphia	84,459	134,229	58.9
Chicago	44,103	109,458	148.2
St. Louis	43,960	69,854	58.9
Detroit	5,741	40,838	611.3
Pittsburgh	25,623	37,725	47.2
Cleveland	8,448	34,451	307.8

laborers for the first time, inspiring a large-scale migration from South to North. On the eve of World War I, 90 percent of the African-American population still lived in the South. But between 1910 and 1920, half a million blacks left the South. The black population of Chicago more than doubled, New York City's rose 66 percent, and smaller industrial cities like Akron, Buffalo, and Trenton showed similar gains. Many motives sustained the **Great Migration**—higher wages in northern factories than were available in the South (even if blacks remained confined to menial and unskilled positions), opportunities for educating their children, escape from the threat of lynching, and the prospect of exercising the right to vote.

Higher wages in northern factories

The black migrants, mostly young men and women, carried with them "a new vision of opportunity, of social and economic freedom," as Alain Locke explained in the preface to his influential book, *The New Negro* (1925). Yet the migrants encountered vast disappointments—severely restricted employment opportunities, exclusion from unions, rigid housing segregation, and outbreaks of violence that made it clear that no region of the country was free from racial hostility. The new black presence, coupled with demands for change inspired by the war, created a racial tinderbox that needed only an incident to trigger an explosion.

Racial restrictions in the North

Racial Violence, North and South

Dozens of blacks were killed during a 1917 riot in East St. Louis, Illinois, where employers had recruited black workers in an attempt to weaken unions (most of which excluded blacks from membership). In 1919, more

Buildings in Tulsa, Oklahoma, burn during the city's riot of June 1921. An estimated 300 people died when white mobs destroyed the city's black neighborhood in the worst outbreak of racial violence in American history.

than 250 persons died in riots in the urban North. Most notable was the violence in Chicago, touched off by the drowning by white bathers of a black teenager who accidentally crossed the unofficial dividing line between black and white beaches on Lake Michigan. By the time the National Guard restored order, 38 persons had been killed and more than 500 injured.

Violence was not confined to the North. In the year after the war ended, seventy-six persons were lynched in the South, including several returning black veterans wearing their uniforms. The worst race riot in American history occurred in Tulsa, Oklahoma, in 1921, when more than 300 blacks were killed and over 10,000 left homeless after a white mob, including police and National Guardsmen, burned an all-black section of the city to the ground.

The Rise of Garveyism

World War I kindled a new spirit of militancy. The East St. Louis riot of 1917 inspired a widely publicized Silent Protest Parade on New York's Fifth Avenue in which 10,000 blacks silently carried placards reading, "Mr. President, Why Not Make America Safe for Democracy?" In the new densely populated black ghettos of the North, widespread support emerged for the Universal Negro Improvement Association, a movement for African independence and black self-reliance launched by Marcus Garvey, a recent immigrant from Jamaica. To **Garveyites**, freedom meant national self-determination. Blacks, they insisted, should enjoy the same internationally recognized identity enjoyed by other peoples in the aftermath of the war. Du Bois and other established black leaders viewed Garvey as little more than a demagogue. They applauded when the government deported him after a conviction for mail fraud. But the massive following his movement achieved testified to the sense of betrayal that had been kindled in black communities during and after the war.

The "silent parade" down Fifth Avenue, July 28, 1917, in which 10,000 black marchers protested the East St. Louis race riot.

1919

A Worldwide Upsurge

The combination of militant hopes for social change and disappointment with the war's outcome was evident far beyond the black community. In the Union of Soviet Socialist Republics (or Soviet Union), as Russia had been renamed after the revolution, Lenin's government had nationalized landholdings, banks, and factories and proclaimed the socialist dream of a workers' government. The Russian Revolution and the democratic aspirations unleashed by World War I sent tremors of hope and fear throughout the world. General strikes demanding the fulfillment of wartime promises of "industrial democracy" took place in Belfast, Glasgow, and Winnipeg. In Spain, anarchist peasants began seizing land. Crowds in India challenged British rule, and nationalist movements in other colonies demanded independence.

Global uprisings

The worldwide revolutionary upsurge produced a countervailing mobilization by opponents of radical change. Despite Allied attempts to overturn its government, the Soviet regime survived, but in the rest of the world the tide of change receded. By the fall, the mass strikes had been suppressed and conservative governments had been installed in central Europe.

Upheaval in America

In the United States, 1919 also brought unprecedented turmoil. It seemed all the more disorienting for occurring in the midst of a worldwide **flu epidemic** that killed between 20 and 40 million persons, including nearly 700,000 Americans. Racial violence, as noted above, was widespread. In June, bombs exploded at the homes of prominent Americans, including the attorney general, A. Mitchell Palmer, who escaped uninjured. Among aggrieved American workers, wartime language linking patriotism with democracy and freedom inspired hopes that an era of social justice and economic empowerment was at hand. In 1917, Wilson had told the AFL, "While we are fighting for freedom, we must see to it among other things that labor is free." Labor took him seriously—more seriously, it seems, than Wilson intended.

In 1919, more than 4 million workers engaged in strikes—the greatest wave of labor unrest in American history. There were walkouts, among many others, by textile workers, telephone operators, and Broadway actors. They were met by an unprecedented mobilization of employers, government, and private patriotic organizations.

Wave of strikes

Local police with literature seized from a Communist Party office in Cambridge, Massachusetts, November 1919.

The wartime rhetoric of economic democracy and freedom helped to inspire the era's greatest labor uprising, the 1919 steel strike. Centered in Chicago, it united some 365,000 mostly immigrant workers in demands for union recognition, higher wages, and an eight-hour workday. Before 1917, the steel mills were little autocracies where managers arbitrarily established wages and working conditions and suppressed all efforts at union organizing. During the war, workers won an eight-hour day. "For why this war?" asked one Polish immigrant steelworker at a union meeting. "For why we buy Liberty bonds? For the mills? No, for freedom and America—for everybody."

In response to the strike, steel magnates launched a concerted counterattack. Employers appealed to anti-immigrant sentiment among native-born workers, many of whom returned to work, and conducted a propaganda campaign that associated the strikers with the IWW, communism, and disloyalty. With middle-class opinion having turned against the labor movement and the police in Pittsburgh assaulting workers on the streets, the strike collapsed in early 1920.

The Red Scare

Wartime repression of dissent reached its peak with the **Red Scare of 1919–1920**, a short-lived but intense period of political intolerance inspired by the postwar strike wave and the social tensions and fears generated by the Russian Revolution. Convinced that episodes like the steel strike were part of a worldwide communist conspiracy, Attorney General A. Mitchell Palmer in November 1919 and January 1920 dispatched federal agents to raid the offices of radical and labor organizations throughout the country. More than 5,000 persons were arrested, most of them without warrants, and held for months without charge. The government deported hundreds of immigrant radicals, including Emma Goldman, the prominent radical speaker mentioned in the previous chapter.

A. Mitchell Palmer

The abuse of civil liberties in early 1920 was so severe that Palmer came under heavy criticism from Congress and much of the press. Even the explosion of a bomb outside the New York Stock Exchange in September 1920, which killed forty persons, failed to rekindle the repression of the Red Scare years. (The perpetrators of this terrorist explosion, the worst on American soil until the Oklahoma City bombing of 1995, were never identified.)

Effects of Red Scare

The reaction to the Palmer Raids planted the seeds for a new appreciation of the importance of civil liberties that would begin to flourish during the 1920s. But in their immediate impact, the events of 1919 and

1920 dealt a devastating setback to radical and labor organizations of all kinds and kindled an intense identification of patriotic Americanism with support for the political and economic status quo. The IWW had been effectively destroyed, and many moderate unions lay in disarray. The Socialist Party crumbled under the weight of governmental repression (the New York legislature expelled five Socialist members, and Congress denied Victor Berger the seat to which he had been elected from Wisconsin) and internal differences over the Russian Revolution.

Part of the crowd that greeted President Woodrow Wilson in November 1918 when he traveled to Paris to take part in the peace conference. An electric sign proclaims "Long Live Wilson."

Wilson at Versailles

The beating back of demands for fundamental social change was a severe rebuke to the hopes with which so many Progressives had enlisted in the war effort. Wilson's inability to achieve a just peace based on the Fourteen Points compounded the sense of failure. Late in 1918, the president traveled to France to attend the Versailles peace conference. But he proved a less adept negotiator than his British and French counterparts, David Lloyd George and Georges Clemenceau.

Although the Fourteen Points had called for "open covenants openly arrived at," the negotiations were conducted in secret. The **Versailles Treaty** did accomplish some of Wilson's goals. It established the League of Nations, the body central to his vision of a new international order. It applied the principle of self-determination to eastern Europe and redrew the map of that region. From the ruins of the Austro-Hungarian empire and parts of Germany and czarist Russia, new European nations emerged from the war—Finland, Poland, Czechoslovakia, Austria, Hungary, Latvia, Lithuania, Estonia, and Yugoslavia. Some enjoyed ethno-linguistic unity, whereas others comprised unstable combinations of diverse nationalities.

New boundaries in Eastern Europe

Despite Wilson's pledge of a peace without territorial acquisitions or vengeance, the Versailles Treaty was a harsh document that all but guaranteed future conflict in Europe. Lloyd George persuaded Wilson to agree to a clause declaring Germany morally responsible for the war and setting astronomical reparations payments (they were variously estimated at between $33 billion and $56 billion), which crippled the German economy.

German reparations

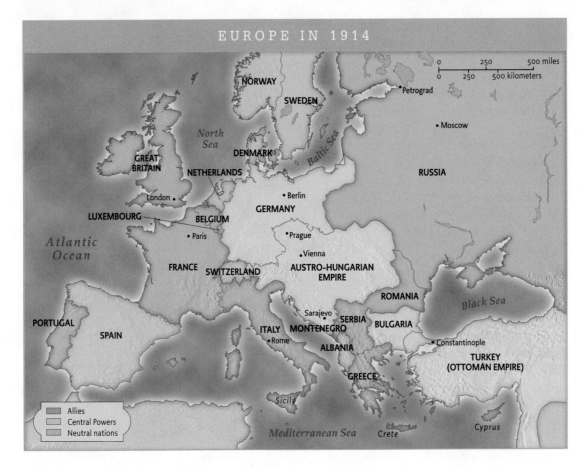

EUROPE IN 1914

World War I and the Versailles Treaty redrew the map of Europe and the Middle East. The Austro-Hungarian and Ottoman empires ceased to exist, and Germany and Russia were reduced in size. A group of new states emerged in eastern Europe, embodying the principle of self-determination, one of Woodrow Wilson's Fourteen Points.

Wilsonian ideals around the world

The Wilsonian Moment

Like the ideals of the American Revolution, the Wilsonian rhetoric of self-determination reverberated across the globe, especially among oppressed minorities (including blacks in the United States) and colonial peoples seeking independence. In fact, these groups took Wilson's rhetoric more seriously than he did. Despite his belief in self-determination, he had supported the American annexation of the Philippines, believing that colonial peoples required a long period of tutelage before they were ready for independence.

Nonetheless, Wilsonian ideals quickly spread around the globe. In eastern Europe, whose people sought to carve new, independent nations from the ruins of the Austro-Hungarian and Ottoman empires, many considered Wilson a "popular saint." The leading Arabic newspaper *Al-Ahram*, published in Egypt, then under British rule, gave extensive coverage to Wilson's

EUROPE IN 1919

New nations
Demilitarized or Allied occupied zone

speech asking Congress to declare war in the name of democracy, and to the Fourteen Points. In Beijing, students demanding that China free itself of foreign domination gathered at the American embassy shouting, "Long live Wilson." Japan proposed to include in the charter of the new League of Nations a clause recognizing the equality of all people, regardless of race.

Outside of Europe, however, the idea of "self-determination" was stillborn. When the Paris peace conference opened, Secretary of State Robert Lansing warned that the phrase was "loaded with dynamite" and would "raise hopes which can never be realized." As Lansing anticipated, advocates of colonial independence descended on Paris to lobby the peace negotiators. Arabs demanded that a unified independent state be carved from the old Ottoman empire in the Middle East. Nguyen That Thanh, a young Vietnamese patriot working in Paris, pressed his people's claim for

Self-determination

greater rights within the French empire. W. E. B. Du Bois organized a Pan-African Congress in Paris that put forward the idea of a self-governing nation to be carved out of Germany's African colonies. Koreans, Indians, Irish, and others also pressed claims for self-determination.

Imperial interests

The British and French, however, had no intention of applying this principle to their own empires. During the war, the British had encouraged Arab nationalism as a weapon against the Ottoman empire and had also pledged to create a homeland in Palestine for the persecuted Jews of Europe. In fact, the victors of World War I divided Ottoman territory into a series of new territories, including Syria, Lebanon, Iraq, and Palestine, controlled by the victorious Allies under League of Nations "mandates." South Africa, Australia, and Japan acquired former German colonies in Africa and Asia. Nor did Ireland achieve its independence at Versailles. Only at the end of 1921 did Britain finally agree to the creation of the Irish Free State while continuing to rule the northeastern corner of the island. As for the Japanese proposal to establish the principle of racial equality, Wilson, with the support of Great Britain and Australia, engineered its defeat.

The Seeds of Wars to Come

Disappointment at the failure to apply the Fourteen Points to the non-European world created a pervasive cynicism about Western use of the language of freedom and democracy. Wilson's apparent willingness to accede to the demands of the imperial powers helped to spark a series of popular protest movements across the Middle East and Asia, and

The rise of anti-Western nationalism

the rise of a new anti-Western nationalism. Some leaders, like Nguyen That Thanh, who took the name Ho Chi Minh, turned to communism, in whose name he would lead Vietnam's long and bloody struggle for independence. The Soviet leader Lenin, in fact, had spoken of "the right of nations to self-determination" before Wilson, and with the collapse of the Wilsonian moment, Lenin's reputation in the colonial world began to eclipse that of the American president. But whether communist or not, these movements announced the emergence of anticolonial nationalism as a major force in world affairs, which it would remain for the rest of the twentieth century.

"Your liberalness," one Egyptian leader remarked, speaking of Britain and America, "is only for yourselves." Yet ironically, when colonial peoples demanded to be recognized as independent members of the international community, they would invoke the heritage of the American Revolution—the first colonial struggle that produced an independent nation.

World War I sowed the seeds not of a lasting peace but of wars to come. German resentment over the peace terms would help to fuel the rise of Adolf Hitler and the coming of World War II. In the breakup of Czechoslovakia and Yugoslavia, violence over the status of Northern Ireland, and the seemingly unending conflict in the Middle East between Arabs and Israelis, the world was still haunted by the ghost of Versailles.

The Treaty Debate

One final disappointment awaited Wilson on his return from Europe. He viewed the new League of Nations as the war's finest legacy. But many Americans feared that membership in the League would commit the United States to an open-ended involvement in the affairs of other countries.

A considerable majority of senators would have accepted the treaty with "reservations" ensuring that the obligation to assist League members against attack did not supersede the power of Congress to declare war. Convinced, however, that the treaty reflected "the hand of God," Wilson refused to negotiate with congressional leaders. In October 1919, in the midst of the League debate, Wilson suffered a serious stroke. Although the extent of his illness was kept secret, he remained incapacitated for the rest of his term. In effect, his wife, Edith, headed the government for the next seventeen months. In November 1919 and again in March 1920, the Senate rejected the Versailles Treaty.

American involvement in World War I lasted barely nineteen months, but it cast a long shadow over the following decade—and, indeed, the rest of the century. In its immediate aftermath, the country retreated from international involvements. But in the long run, Wilson's combination of idealism and power politics had an enduring impact. His appeals to democracy, open markets, and a special American mission to instruct the world in freedom, coupled with a willingness to intervene abroad militarily to promote American interests and values, would create the model for twentieth-century American international relations.

On its own terms, the war to make the world safe for democracy failed. It also led to the eclipse of Progressivism. Republican candidate Warren

Interrupting the Ceremony, a 1918 cartoon from the *Chicago Tribune*, depicts Senate opponents of the Versailles Treaty arriving just in time to prevent the United States from becoming permanently ensnared in "foreign entanglements" through the League of Nations.

The enduring impact of Wilsonian policy

"Return to normalcy"

G. Harding, who had no connection with the party's Progressive wing, swept to victory in the presidential election of 1920. Harding's campaign centered on a "return to normalcy" and a repudiation of what he called "Wilsonism." He received 60 percent of the popular vote. Begun with idealistic goals and grand hopes for social change, American involvement in the Great War laid the foundation for one of the most conservative decades in the nation's history.

CHAPTER REVIEW AND ONLINE RESOURCES

REVIEW QUESTIONS

1. Explain the role of the United States in the global economy by 1920.

2. What were the assumptions underlying the Roosevelt Corollary? How did the doctrine affect our relations with European nations and those in the Western Hemisphere?

3. What did President Wilson mean by "moral imperialism," and what measures were taken to apply this to Latin America?

4. How did the ratification of the Eighteenth and Nineteenth Amendments show the restrictive and democratizing nature of Progressivism?

5. Why did Progressives see in the expansion of governmental powers in wartime an opportunity to reform American society?

6. What were the goals and methods of the Committee on Public Information during World War I?

7. What are governmental and private examples of coercive patriotism during the war? What were the effects of those efforts?

8. What were the major causes—both real and imaginary—of the Red Scare?

9. How did World War I and its aftermath provide African-Americans with opportunities?

10. Describe how World War I and the U.S. failure to join the League of Nations sowed the seeds of future twentieth-century wars.

11. Identify the goals of those pressing for global change in 1919, and of those who opposed them.

KEY TERMS

"liberal internationalism" (p. 576)

Panama Canal Zone (p. 577)

Roosevelt Corollary (p. 578)

Dollar Diplomacy (p. 579)

"moral imperialism" (p. 579)

sinking of the *Lusitania* (p. 581)

Zimmerman Telegram (p. 582)

Fourteen Points (p. 582)

Selective Service Act (p. 584)

War Industries Board (p. 584)

Espionage Act (p. 590)

Sedition Act (p. 590)

National Association for the Advancement of Colored People (p. 596)

Great Migration (p. 596)

Tulsa riot of 1921 (p. 598)

Garveyites (p. 598)

flu epidemic (p. 599)

Red Scare of 1919–1920 (p. 600)

Versailles Treaty (p. 601)

wwnorton.com /studyspace

VISIT STUDYSPACE FOR THESE RESOURCES AND MORE

- A chapter outline
- A diagnostic chapter quiz
- Interactive maps
- Map worksheets
- Multimedia documents

CHAPTER 20

FROM BUSINESS CULTURE TO GREAT DEPRESSION

★

THE TWENTIES, 1920-1932

City Activities with Dance Hall. This mural, painted in 1930 by Thomas Hart Benton for the New School for Social Research in New York City, portrays aspects of 1920s urban life. On the left, hands reach for a bottle of liquor, a businessman reads a stock ticker, and patrons enjoy themselves at a dance hall and movie theater. Images on the right include a circus, a woman at a soda fountain, and scenes of family life.

I n May 1920, at the height of the postwar Red Scare, police arrested two Italian immigrants accused of participating in a robbery at a South Braintree, Massachusetts, factory in which a security guard was killed. Nicola Sacco, a shoemaker, and Bartolomeo Vanzetti, an itinerant unskilled laborer, were anarchists who dreamed of a society in which government, churches, and private property would be abolished. They saw violence as an appropriate weapon of class warfare. But very little evidence linked them to this particular crime. In the atmosphere of anti-radical and anti-immigrant fervor, however, their conviction was a certainty.

Although their 1921 trial had aroused little public interest outside the Italian-American community, the case of Sacco and Vanzetti attracted considerable attention during the lengthy appeals that followed. There were mass protests in Europe against their impending execution. On August 23, 1927, Sacco and Vanzetti died in the electric chair.

The **Sacco-Vanzetti case** laid bare some of the fault lines beneath the surface of American society during the 1920s. To many native-born Americans, the two men symbolized an alien threat to their way of life. To Italian-Americans, including respectable middle-class organizations like the Sons of Italy that raised money for the defense, the outcome symbolized the nativist prejudices and stereotypes that haunted immigrant communities.

FOCUS QUESTIONS

- *Who benefited and who suffered in the new consumer society of the 1920s?*

- *In what ways did the government promote business interests in the 1920s?*

- *Why did the protection of civil liberties gain importance in the 1920s?*

- *What were the major flash points between fundamentalism and pluralism in the 1920s?*

- *What were the causes of the Great Depression, and how effective were the government's responses by 1932?*

A 1927 photograph shows Nicola Sacco and Bartolomeo Vanzetti outside the courthouse in Dedham, Massachusetts, surrounded by security agents and onlookers. They are about to enter the courthouse, where the judge will pronounce their death sentence.

The way to his heart

Advertisements, like this one for a refrigerator, promised that consumer goods would enable Americans to fulfill their hearts' desires.

In popular memory, the decade that followed World War I is recalled as the Jazz Age or the Roaring Twenties. With its flappers (young, sexually liberated women), speakeasies (nightclubs that sold liquor in violation of Prohibition), and a soaring stock market fueled by easy credit and a get-rich-quick outlook, it was a time of revolt against moral rules inherited from the nineteenth century. Observers from Europe, where class divisions were starkly visible in work, politics, and social relations, marveled at the uniformity of American life. Factories poured out standardized consumer goods, their sale promoted by national advertising campaigns. Conservatism dominated a political system from which radical alternatives seemed to have been purged. Radio and the movies spread mass culture throughout the nation.

Many Americans, however, did not welcome the new secular, commercial culture. They resented and feared the ethnic and racial diversity of America's cities and what they considered the lax moral standards of urban life. The 1920s was a decade of profound social tensions—between rural and urban Americans, traditional and "modern" Christianity, participants in the burgeoning consumer culture and those who did not fully share in the new prosperity.

THE BUSINESS OF AMERICA

A Decade of Prosperity

"The chief business of the American people," said Calvin Coolidge, who became president after Warren G. Harding's sudden death from a heart attack in 1923, "is business." Rarely in American history had economic growth seemed more dramatic, cooperation between business and government so close, and business values so widely shared. Productivity and economic output rose dramatically as new industries—chemicals, aviation, electronics—flourished and older ones like food processing and the manufacture of household appliances adopted Henry Ford's moving assembly line. Annual automobile production tripled during the 1920s, from 1.5 to 4.8 million, stimulating steel, rubber, and oil production, and other sectors of the economy. By 1929, half of all Americans owned a car.

Industrial growth

Multinational corporations

During the 1920s, American multinational corporations extended their sway throughout the world. With Europe still recovering from the Great War, American investment overseas far exceeded that of other countries. The dollar replaced the British pound as the most important currency of international trade. American companies produced 85 percent of the world's cars and 40 percent of its manufactured goods. General Electric and International Telephone and Telegraph bought up companies in other countries. International Business Machines (IBM) was the world's leader in office supplies. American companies took control of raw materials abroad, from rubber in Liberia to oil in Venezuela.

A New Society

During the 1920s, consumer goods of all kinds proliferated, marketed by salesmen and advertisers who promoted them as ways of satisfying Americans' psychological desires and everyday needs. Frequently purchased on credit through new installment buying plans, they rapidly altered daily life. Telephones made communication easier. Vacuum cleaners, washing machines, and refrigerators transformed work in the home and reduced the demand for domestic servants. Boosted by Prohibition and an aggressive advertising campaign that, according to the company's sales director, made it "impossible for the consumer to *escape*" the product, Coca-Cola became a symbol of American life.

Consumer goods

Americans spent more and more of their income on leisure activities like vacations, movies, and sporting events. By 1929, weekly movie attendance had reached 80 million, double the figure of 1922. Hollywood films now dominated the world movie market.

Leisure activities

Radios and phonographs brought mass entertainment into American living rooms. The number of radios in American homes rose from 190,000 in 1923 to just under 5 million in 1929. These developments helped create and spread a new celebrity culture, in which recording, film, and sports stars moved to the top of the list of American heroes. During the 1920s, more than 100 million records were sold each year. RCA Victor sold so many recordings of the great opera tenor Enrico Caruso that he is sometimes called the first modern celebrity. He was soon joined by the film actor Charlie Chaplin, baseball player Babe Ruth, and boxer Jack Dempsey. Perhaps the decade's greatest celebrity, in terms of intensive press coverage, was the aviator Charles Lindbergh, who in 1927 made the first solo nonstop flight across the Atlantic.

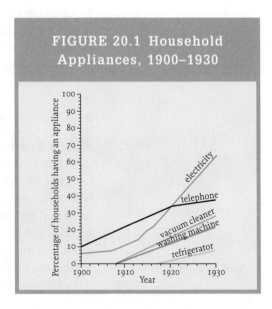

FIGURE 20.1 Household Appliances, 1900–1930

Widespread acceptance of going into debt to purchase consumer goods replaced the values of thrift and self-denial, central to nineteenth-century notions of upstanding character. Work, once seen as a source of pride in craft skill or collective empowerment via trade unions, now came to be valued as a path to individual fulfillment through consumption and entertainment.

The Limits of Prosperity

But signs of future trouble could be seen beneath the prosperity of the 1920s. The fruits of increased production were very unequally distributed. Real wages for industrial workers (wages adjusted to take account of inflation) rose by one-quarter between 1922 and 1929, but corporate profits rose at more than twice that rate. The process of economic concentration continued unabated. A handful of firms dominated numerous sectors of the economy. In 1929, 1 percent of the nation's banks controlled half of its financial resources. Most of the small auto companies that had existed earlier in the century had fallen by the wayside. General Motors, Ford, and Chrysler now controlled four-fifths of the industry.

Economic concentration and its consequences

At the beginning of 1929, a majority of families had no savings, and an estimated 40 percent of the population remained in poverty, unable to participate in the flourishing consumer economy. Improved productivity meant that goods could be produced with fewer workers. During the 1920s, more Americans worked in the professions, retailing, finance, and education, but the number of manufacturing workers declined by 5 percent, the first such drop in the nation's history. Parts of New England were already experiencing the chronic unemployment caused by deindustrialization. Many of the region's textile companies failed in the face of low-wage competition from southern factories or shifted production to take advantage of the South's cheap labor.

Economic weakness

The Farmers' Plight

Nor did farmers share in the decade's prosperity. The "golden age" of American farming had reached its peak during World War I, when the need to feed war-torn Europe and government efforts to maintain high farm prices had raised farmers' incomes and promoted the purchase of more land on credit. Thanks to mechanization and the increased use of fertilizer and insecticides, agricultural production continued to rise even when government subsidies ended and world demand stagnated. As a result, farm incomes in the 1920s declined steadily, and banks foreclosed tens of thousands of farms.

Rural depression

Facing dire conditions, some 3 million persons migrated out of rural areas. Many headed for southern California, whose rapidly growing economy needed new labor. The population of Los Angeles, the West's leading industrial center, a producer of oil, automobiles, aircraft, and, of course, Hollywood movies, rose from 575,000 to 2.2 million during the decade, largely because of an influx of displaced farmers from the Midwest. Well before the 1930s, rural America was in an economic depression.

Farmers, such as this family of potato growers in rural Minnesota, did not share in the prosperity of the 1920s.

The Image of Business

Despite America's underlying economic problems, businessmen like Henry Ford and engineers like Herbert Hoover were cultural heroes. Photographers like Lewis Hine and Margaret Bourke-White and painters like Charles Sheeler celebrated the beauty of machines and factories.

Numerous firms established public relations departments. They aimed to justify corporate practices to the public and counteract its longstanding distrust of big business. They even succeeded in changing popular attitudes toward Wall Street.

In the 1920s, as the steadily rising price of stocks made front-page news, the market attracted more investors. Many assumed that stock values would keep rising forever. By 1928, an estimated 1.5 million Americans owned stock—still a small minority of the country's 28 million families, but far more than in the past.

Rise of the stock market

The Decline of Labor

With the defeat of the labor upsurge of 1919 and the dismantling of the wartime regulatory state, business appropriated the rhetoric of Americanism and "industrial freedom" as weapons against labor unions. Some corporations during the 1920s implemented a new style of management. They provided their employees with private pensions and medical insurance plans, job security, and greater workplace safety. They spoke of "**welfare capitalism**," a more socially conscious kind of business leadership, and

River Rouge Plant, by the artist Charles Sheeler, exemplifies the "machine-age aesthetic" of the 1920s. Sheeler found artistic beauty in Henry Ford's giant automobile assembly factory.

trumpeted the fact that they now paid more attention to the "human factor" in employment.

The American Plan

At the same time, however, employers in the 1920s embraced the American Plan, at whose core stood the open shop—a workplace free of both government regulation and unions, except, in some cases, "company unions" created and controlled by management. Even the most forward-looking companies continued to employ strikebreakers, private detectives, and the blacklisting of union organizers to prevent or defeat strikes.

The decline of unions

During the 1920s, organized labor lost more than 2 million members, and unions agreed to demand after demand by employers in an effort to stave off complete elimination. Uprisings by the most downtrodden workers did occur sporadically throughout the decade. Southern textile mills witnessed desperate strikes by workers who charged employers with "making slaves out of the men and women" who labored there. Facing the combined opposition of business, local politicians, and the courts, as well as the threat of violence, such strikes were doomed to defeat.

The Equal Rights Amendment

Like the labor movement, feminists struggled to adapt to the new political situation. The achievement of suffrage in 1920 eliminated the bond of unity among various activists, each "struggling for her own conception of freedom," in the words of labor reformer Juliet Stuart Poyntz. Black feminists insisted that the movement must now demand enforcement of the Fifteenth Amendment in the South, but they won little support from their white counterparts.

The long-standing division between two competing conceptions of woman's freedom—one based on motherhood, the other on individual autonomy and the right to work—now crystallized in the debate over an **Equal Rights Amendment** (ERA) to the Constitution promoted by Alice Paul and the National Women's Party. This amendment proposed to eliminate all legal distinctions "on account of sex." In Paul's opinion, the ERA followed logically from winning the right to vote. Having gained political equality, she insisted, women no longer required special legal protection—they needed equal access to employment, education, and all the other opportunities of citizens. To supporters of mothers' pensions and laws limiting women's hours of labor, which the ERA would sweep away, the proposal represented a giant step backward. Apart from the National Women's Party, every major female organization opposed the ERA.

The ERA campaign failed, and only six states ratified a proposed constitutional amendment giving Congress the power to prohibit child labor, which farm groups and business organizations opposed. In 1929, Congress repealed the Sheppard-Towner Act of 1921, a major achievement of the maternalist reformers that had provided federal assistance to programs for infant and child health.

Women's Freedom

If political feminism faded, the prewar feminist demand for personal freedom survived in the vast consumer marketplace and in the actual behavior of the decade's much-publicized liberated young women. No longer one element in a broader program of social reform, sexual freedom now meant individual autonomy or personal rebellion. With her bobbed hair, short skirts, public smoking and drinking, and unapologetic use of birth-control methods such as the diaphragm, the young, single **"flapper"** epitomized the change in standards of sexual behavior, at least in large cities. She frequented dance halls and attended sexually charged Hollywood films

> *Debate over the ERA*

Tipsy, a 1930 painting by the Japanese artist Kobayakawa Kiyoshi, illustrates the global appeal of the "new woman" of the 1920s. The subject, a *moga* ("modern girl" in Japanese), sits alone in a nightclub wearing Western clothing, makeup, and hairstyle and enjoying a cigarette and a martini. The title of the work suggests that Kiyoshi does not entirely approve of her behavior, but he presents her as self-confident and alluring. Japanese police took a dim view of "modern" women, arresting those who applied makeup in public.

(*Left*) Advertisers marketed cigarettes to women as symbols of female independence. This 1929 ad for Lucky Strike reads: "Legally, politically and socially, woman has been emancipated from those chains which bound her. . . . Gone is that ancient prejudice against cigarettes." (*Right*) An ad for Procter & Gamble laundry detergent urges modern women to modernize the methods of their employees. The text relates how a white woman in the Southwest persuaded Felipa, her Mexican-American domestic worker, to abandon her "primitive washing methods." Felipa, according to the ad, agrees that the laundry is now "whiter, cleaner, and fresher."

featuring stars like Clara Bow, the provocative "'It' Girl," and Rudolph Valentino, the original on-screen "Latin Lover."

Women's self-conscious pursuit of personal pleasure became a device to market goods from automobiles to cigarettes. In 1904, a woman had been arrested for smoking in public in New York City. Two decades later, Edward Bernays, the "father" of modern public relations, masterminded a campaign to persuade women to smoke, dubbing cigarettes women's "torches of freedom." The new freedom, however, was available only during one phase of a woman's life. Marriage, according to one advertisement, remained "the one pursuit that stands foremost in the mind of every girl and woman." Having found husbands, women were expected to seek freedom within the confines of the home.

Marriage and the new freedom

BUSINESS AND GOVERNMENT

Robert and Helen Lynd,
Middletown

In 1929, the sociologists Robert and Helen Lynd published *Middletown*, a classic study of life in Muncie, Indiana, a typical community in the American heartland. The Lynds found that new leisure activities and a new emphasis on consumption had replaced politics as the focus of public concern. Elections were no longer "lively centers" of public attention as in the nineteenth century, and voter participation had fallen dramatically. National statistics bore out their point; the turnout of eligible voters, over 80 percent in 1896, had dropped to less than 50 percent in 1924. Many factors helped to explain this decline, including the consolidation of one-party politics in the South, the long period of Republican dominance in national elections, and the enfranchisement of women, who for many years voted in lower numbers than men. But the shift from public to private concerns also played a part. "The American citizen's first importance to his country," declared a Muncie newspaper, "is no longer that of a citizen but that of a consumer."

Decline in voter participation

The Republican Era

Government policies reflected the pro-business ethos of the 1920s. Business lobbyists dominated national conventions of the Republican Party. They called on the federal government to lower taxes on personal incomes and business profits, maintain high tariffs, and support employers' continuing campaign against unions. The administrations of Warren G. Harding and Calvin Coolidge obliged. Under William Howard Taft, appointed chief justice in 1921, the Supreme Court remained strongly conservative. A resurgence of laissez-faire jurisprudence eclipsed the Progressive ideal of a socially active national state. The Court struck down a federal law that barred goods produced by child labor from interstate commerce. It even repudiated *Muller v. Oregon* (see Chapter 18) in a 1923 decision overturning a minimum wage law for women in Washington, D.C. Now that women enjoyed the vote, the justices declared, they were entitled to the same workplace freedom as men.

Pro-business government policies

Corruption in Government

Warren G. Harding took office as president in 1921 promising a return to "normalcy" after an era of Progressive reform and world war. Reflecting the prevailing get-rich-quick ethos, his administration quickly became one of the most corrupt in American history. Although his cabinet included men of integrity and talent, like Secretary of State Charles Evans Hughes and Secretary of Commerce Herbert Hoover, Harding also surrounded himself with cronies who used their offices for private gain. Attorney General Harry Daugherty accepted payments not to prosecute accused criminals. The most notorious scandal involved Secretary of the Interior Albert Fall, who accepted nearly $500,000 from private businessmen to whom he leased government oil reserves at Teapot Dome, Wyoming. Fall became the first cabinet member in history to be convicted of a felony.

The policies of President Calvin Coolidge were music to the ears of big business, according to one 1920s cartoonist.

A 1924 cartoon commenting on the scandals of the Harding administration. The White House, Capitol, and Washington Monument have been sold to the highest bidder.

The Election of 1924

Harding's successor, Calvin Coolidge, who as governor of Massachusetts had won national fame for using state troops against striking Boston policemen in 1919, was a dour man of few words. But in contrast to his predecessor he seemed to exemplify Yankee honesty. In 1924, Coolidge was elected in a landslide, defeating John W. Davis, a Wall Street lawyer nominated on the 103rd ballot by a badly divided Democratic convention. (This was when the comedian Will Rogers made the quip, often repeated in future years, "I am a member of no organized political party; I am a Democrat.")

One-sixth of the electorate in 1924 voted for Robert La Follette, running as the candidate of a new Progressive Party, which called for greater taxation of wealth, the conservation of natural resources, public ownership of the railroads, farm relief, and the end of child labor. La Follette carried only his native Wisconsin. But his candidacy demonstrated the survival of some currents of dissent in a highly conservative decade.

Economic Diplomacy

Foreign affairs also reflected the close working relationship between business and government. The 1920s marked a retreat from Wilson's goal of internationalism in favor of unilateral American actions mainly designed to increase exports and investment opportunities overseas. Indeed, what is sometimes called the "isolationism" of the 1920s represented a reaction against the disappointing results of Wilson's military and diplomatic pursuit of freedom and democracy abroad. The United States did play host to the Washington Naval Arms Conference of 1922, which negotiated reductions in the navies of Britain, France, Japan, Italy, and the United States. But the country remained outside the League of Nations. Even as American diplomats continued to press for access to markets overseas, the Fordney-McCumber Tariff of 1922 raised taxes on imported goods to their highest levels in history, a repudiation of Wilson's principle of promoting free trade.

As before World War I, the government dispatched soldiers when a change in government in the Caribbean threatened American economic interests. Having been stationed in Nicaragua since 1912, American marines withdrew in 1925. But the troops soon returned in an effort to suppress a nationalist revolt headed by General Augusto César Sandino. Having created a National Guard headed by General Anastasio Somoza, the marines finally departed in 1933. A year later, Somoza assassinated Sandino and seized power. For the next forty-five years, he and his family ruled and plundered Nicaragua. Somoza was overthrown in 1978 by a popular movement calling itself the Sandinistas (see Chapter 26).

Intervention in Nicaragua

THE BIRTH OF CIVIL LIBERTIES

Among the casualties of World War I and the 1920s was Progressivism's faith that an active federal government embodied the national purpose and enhanced the enjoyment of freedom. Wartime and postwar repression, Prohibition, and the pro-business policies of the 1920s all illustrated, in the eyes of many Progressives, how public power could go grievously wrong.

This lesson opened the door to a new appreciation of civil liberties— rights an individual may assert even against democratic majorities—as essential elements of American freedom. In the name of a "new freedom for the individual," the 1920s saw the birth of a coherent concept of civil liberties and the beginnings of significant legal protection for freedom of speech against the government.

Rights of the individual

Wartime repression continued into the 1920s. Artistic works with sexual themes were subjected to rigorous censorship. The Postal Service removed from the mails books it deemed obscene. The Customs

Service barred works by the sixteenth-century French satirist Rabelais, the modern novelist James Joyce, and many others from entering the country. A local crusade against indecency made the phrase "Banned in Boston" a term of ridicule among upholders of artistic freedom. Boston's Watch and Ward Committee excluded sixty-five books from the city's bookstores, including works by the novelists Upton Sinclair, Theodore Dreiser, and Ernest Hemingway. In 1922, the film industry adopted the **Hays code**, a sporadically enforced set of guidelines that prohibited movies from depicting nudity, long kisses, and adultery, and barred scripts that portrayed clergymen in a negative light or criminals sympathetically.

Disillusionment with the conservatism of American politics and the materialism of the culture inspired some American artists and writers to emigrate to Paris. The Lost Generation of cultural exiles included novelists and poets like Ernest Hemingway, Gertrude Stein, and F. Scott Fitzgerald. Europe, they felt, valued art and culture, and appreciated unrestrained freedom of expression (and, of course, allowed individuals to drink legally).

The Lost Generation

A "Clear and Present Danger"

The arrest of antiwar dissenters under the Espionage and Sedition Acts inspired the formation in 1917 of the Civil Liberties Bureau, which in 1920 became the **American Civil Liberties Union** (ACLU). For the rest of the century, the ACLU would take part in most of the landmark cases that helped to bring about a "rights revolution." Its efforts helped to give meaning to traditional civil liberties like freedom of speech and invented new ones, like the right to privacy. When it began, however, the ACLU was a small, beleaguered organization.

Prior to World War I, the Supreme Court had done almost nothing to protect the rights of unpopular minorities. Now, it was forced to address the question of the permissible limits on political and economic dissent. In 1919, the Court upheld the constitutionality of the Espionage Act and the conviction of Charles T. Schenck, a socialist who had distributed antidraft leaflets through the mails. Speaking for the Court, Justice Oliver Wendell Holmes declared that the First Amendment did not prevent Congress from prohibiting speech that presented a **"clear and present danger"** of inspiring illegal actions. A week after *Schenck v. United States*, the Court unanimously upheld the conviction of Eugene V. Debs for a speech condemning the war.

Schenck v. United States

The Court and Civil Liberties

Also in 1919, the Court upheld the conviction of Jacob Abrams and five other men for distributing pamphlets critical of American intervention in Russia after the Bolshevik revolution. This time, however, Holmes and Louis Brandeis dissented, marking the emergence of a court minority committed to a broader defense of free speech.

The tide of civil-liberties decision making slowly began to turn. By the end of the 1920s, the Supreme Court had voided a Kansas law that made it a crime to advocate unlawful acts to change the political or economic system and one from Minnesota authorizing censorship of the press. The new regard for free speech went beyond political expression. In 1933, a federal court overturned the Customs Service's ban on James Joyce's novel *Ulysses*, a turning point in the battle against the censorship of works of literature.

A broader defense of free speech

A judicial defense of civil liberties was slowly being born. As Brandeis insisted, "Those who won our independence believed . . . that freedom to think as you will and to speak as you think are indispensable to the discovery and spread of political truth. . . . The greatest menace to freedom is an inert people."

THE CULTURE WARS

The Fundamentalist Revolt

Although many Americans embraced modern urban culture with its religious and ethnic pluralism, mass entertainment, and liberated sexual rules, others found it alarming. Many evangelical Protestants felt threatened by the decline of traditional values and the increased visibility of Catholicism and Judaism because of immigration. They also resented the growing presence within mainstream Protestant denominations of "modernists" who sought to integrate science and religion and adapt Christianity to the new secular culture.

Convinced that the literal truth of the Bible formed the basis of Christian belief, fundamentalists launched a campaign to rid Protestant denominations of modernism and to combat the new individual freedoms that seemed to contradict traditional morality. Their most flamboyant apostle was Billy Sunday, a talented professional baseball player who became a revivalist preacher. Between 1900 and 1930, Sunday drew huge crowds with a highly theatrical preaching style and a message denouncing

Billy Sunday

A 1923 lithograph by George Bellows captures the dynamic style of the most prominent evangelical preacher of the 1920s, Billy Sunday.

sins ranging from Darwinism to alcohol. **Fundamentalism** remained an important strain of 1920s culture and politics. Prohibition, which fundamentalists strongly supported, succeeded in reducing the consumption of alcohol as well as public drunkenness and drink-related diseases.

Prohibition, however, remained a deeply divisive issue. The greatest expansion of national authority since Reconstruction, it raised major questions of local rights, individual freedom, and the wisdom of attempting to impose religious and moral values on the entire society through legislation. It divided the Democratic Party into "wet" and "dry" wings, leading to bitter internal battles at the party's 1924 and 1928 national conventions.

Too many Americans deemed Prohibition a violation of individual freedom for the flow of illegal liquor to stop. In urban areas, Prohibition led to large profits for the owners of illegal speakeasies and the "bootleggers" who supplied them. It produced widespread corruption as police and public officials accepted bribes to turn a blind eye to violations of the law.

The Scopes Trial

In 1925, a trial in Tennessee threw into sharp relief the division between traditional values and modern, secular culture.

Federal agents with confiscated liquor in Colorado in 1920, shortly after the advent of Prohibition.

John Scopes, a teacher in a Tennessee public school, was arrested for violating a state law that prohibited the teaching of Charles Darwin's theory of evolution. His trial became a national sensation.

The **Scopes trial** reflected the enduring tension between two American definitions of freedom. Fundamentalist Christians, strongest in rural areas of the South and West, clung to the traditional idea of "moral" liberty—voluntary adherence to time-honored religious beliefs. The theory that man had evolved over millions of years from ancestors like apes contradicted the biblical account of creation. To Scopes's defenders, including the American Civil Liberties Union, freedom meant above all the right to independent thought and individual self-expression. To them, the Tennessee law offered a lesson in the dangers of religious intolerance and the merger of church and state.

Because of extreme heat, some sessions of the Scopes trial were held outdoors, in front of the courthouse in Dayton, Tennessee. A photographer snapped this picture of the trial's climactic moment, when Clarence Darrow (standing at the center) questioned William Jennings Bryan (seated) about his interpretation of the Bible.

The renowned labor lawyer Clarence Darrow defended Scopes. The trial's highlight came when Darrow called William Jennings Bryan to the stand as an "expert witness" on the Bible. Bryan revealed an almost complete ignorance of modern science and proved unable to respond effectively to Darrow's sarcastic questioning. Asked whether God had actually created the world in six days, Bryan replied that these should be understood as ages, "not six days of twenty-four hours"—thus opening the door to the very nonliteral interpretation of the Bible that the fundamentalists rejected.

Clarence Darrow and William Jennings Bryan

The jury found Scopes guilty, although the Tennessee supreme court later overturned the decision on a technicality. Fundamentalists retreated for many years from battles over public education, preferring to build their own schools and colleges where teaching could be done as they saw fit. The battle would be rejoined, however, toward the end of the twentieth century. To this day, the teaching of the theory of evolution in public schools arouses intense debate in parts of the United States.

The Second Klan

Few features of urban life seemed more alien to rural and small-town native-born Protestants than their immigrant populations and cultures. The wartime obsession with "100 percent Americanism" continued into the 1920s. In 1922, Oregon became the only state ever to require

"100 percent Americanism"

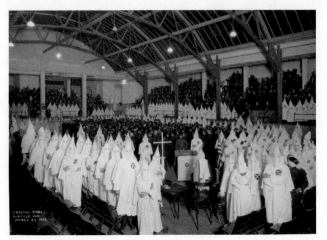

A Ku Klux Klan gathering in Seattle, Washington, in 1923. The unrobed members of the audience are covering their faces to avoid identification. Unlike the Klan of the Reconstruction era, the second Ku Klux Klan was more powerful in the North and West than the South.

all students to attend public schools—a measure aimed, said the state's attorney general, at abolishing parochial education and preventing "bolshevists, syndicalists and communists" from organizing their own schools.

Perhaps the most menacing expression of the idea that enjoyment of American freedom should be limited on religious and ethnic grounds was the resurgence of the Ku Klux Klan in the early 1920s. The Klan had been reborn in Atlanta in 1915 after the lynching of Leo Frank, a Jewish factory manager accused of killing a teenage girl. By the mid-1920s, it claimed more than 3 million members, nearly all white, native-born Protestants, many of whom held respected positions in their communities. Unlike the Klan of Reconstruction, the organization now sank deep roots in parts of the North and West. It became the largest private organization in Indiana and for a time controlled the state Republican Party. American civilization, the new Klan insisted, was endangered not only by blacks but by immigrants (especially Jews and Catholics) and all the forces (feminism, unions, immorality, even, on occasion, the giant corporations) that endangered "individual liberty."

Closing the Golden Door

The Klan's influence faded after 1925, when its leader in Indiana was convicted of assaulting a young woman. But the Klan's attacks on modern secular culture and political radicalism and its demand that control of the nation be returned to "citizens of the old stock" reflected sentiments widely shared in the 1920s.

The 1920s produced a fundamental change in immigration policy. Prior to World War I virtually all the white persons who wished to pass through the "golden door" into the United States and become citizens were able to do so. During the 1920s, however, the pressure for wholesale **immigration restriction** became irresistible.

Restrictions on European immigration

In 1921, a temporary measure restricted immigration from Europe to 357,000 per year (one-third of the annual average before the war). Three years later, Congress permanently limited European immigration to 150,000 per year, distributed according to a series of national quotas that severely restricted the numbers from southern and eastern Europe. However, to satisfy the demands of large farmers in California who relied heavily on seasonal Mexican labor, the 1924 law established no limits on immigration from the Western Hemisphere.

The immigration law did bar the entry of all those ineligible for naturalized citizenship—that is, the entire population of Asia, even though Japan had fought on the American side in World War I.

Although a few Chinese had tried to enter the country in the past in spite of exclusion legislation, the law of 1924 established, in effect, for the first time a new category—the "**illegal alien**." With it came a new enforcement mechanism, the Border Patrol, charged with policing the land boundaries of the United States and empowered to arrest and deport persons who entered the country in violation of the new nationality quotas or other restrictions. A term later associated almost exclusively with Latinos, "illegal aliens" at first referred mainly to southern and eastern Europeans who tried to sneak across the border from Mexico or Canada.

The immigration law of 1924 established the Border Patrol to stop those barred from entry from sneaking into the United States from Mexico. At first, the patrol was a modest operation. Here, two officers police the California-Mexico border.

Race and the Law

The new immigration law reflected the heightened emphasis on "race" as a determinant of public policy. By the early 1920s, political leaders of both North and South agreed on the relegation of blacks to second-class citizenship. But "race policy" meant far more than black-white relations. When President Coolidge signed the new law, his secretary of labor, James J. Davis, commented that immigration policy must now rest on a biological definition of the ideal population. Although enacted by a highly conservative Congress strongly influenced by nativism, the 1924 immigration law also reflected the Progressive desire to improve the "quality" of democratic citizenship and to employ scientific methods to set public policy. It revealed how these aims were overlaid with pseudo-scientific assumptions about the superiority and inferiority of particular "races."

A "biologically ideal" population

But the entire concept of race as a basis for public policy lacked any rational foundation. The Supreme Court admitted as much in 1923 when it rejected the claim of Bhagat Singh Thind, an Indian-born World War I

TABLE 20.1 Selected Annual Immigration Quotas under the 1924 Immigration Act

COUNTRY	QUOTA	IMMIGRANTS IN 1914
Northern and Western Europe:		
Great Britain and Northern Ireland	65,721	48,729 (Great Britain only)
Germany	25,957	35,734
Ireland	17,853	24,688 (includes Northern Ireland)
Scandinavia (Sweden, Norway, Denmark, Finland)	7,241	29,391
Southern and Eastern Europe:		
Poland	6,524	(Not an independent state; included in Germany, Russia, and Austria-Hungary)
Italy	5,802	283,738
Russia	2,784	255,660
Other:		
Africa (total of various colonies and countries)	1,000	1,539
Western Hemisphere	No quota limit	122,695
Asia (China, India, Japan, Korea)	0	11,652

veteran, who asserted that as a "pure Aryan," he was actually white and could therefore become an American citizen. "White," the Court declared, was not a scientific concept at all, but part of "common speech, to be interpreted with the understanding of the common man" (a forthright statement of what later scholars would call the "social construction" of race).

Promoting Tolerance

In the face of immigration restriction, Prohibition, a revived Ku Klux Klan, and widespread anti-Semitism and anti-Catholicism, immigrant groups asserted the validity of cultural diversity and identified toleration of difference—religious, cultural, and individual—as the essence of American freedom. In effect, they reinvented themselves as "ethnic" Americans, claiming an equal share in the nation's life but, in addition, the right to remain in

Ethnic Americans

many respects culturally distinct. The Roman Catholic Church urged immigrants to learn English and embrace "American principles," but it continued to maintain separate schools and other institutions. Throughout the country, organizations like the Anti-Defamation League of B'nai B'rith (founded in 1916 to combat anti-Semitism) and the National Catholic Welfare Council lobbied, in the name of "personal liberty," for laws prohibiting discrimination against immigrants by employers, colleges, and government agencies.

The efforts of immigrant communities to resist coerced Americanization and of the Catholic Church to defend its school system broadened the definition of liberty for all Americans. In landmark decisions, the Supreme Court struck down Oregon's law, mentioned earlier, requiring all students to attend public schools and Nebraska's law prohibiting teaching in a language other than English—one of the anti-German measures of World War I. The *Meyer v. Nebraska* (1923) decision expanded the freedom of all immigrant groups. In its aftermath, federal courts overturned various Hawaii laws imposing special taxes and regulations on private Japanese-language schools. In these cases, the Court also interpreted the Fourteenth Amendment's guarantee of equal liberty to include the right to "marry, establish a home and bring up children" and to practice religion as one chose, "without interference from the state." The decisions gave pluralism a constitutional foundation.

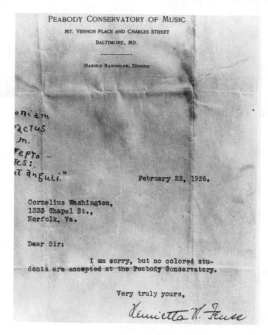

PEABODY CONSERVATORY OF MUSIC
MT. VERNON PLACE AND CHARLES STREET
BALTIMORE, MD.

HAROLD RANDOLPH, Director

February 22, 1926.

Cornelius Washington,
1333 Chapel St.,
Norfolk, Va.

Dear Sir:

I am sorry, but no colored students are accepted at the Peabody Conservatory.

Very truly yours,

Henrietta N. Fuss

Racism severely limited the opportunities open to black Americans. Here, the internationally renowned Peabody Conservatory of Music informs a black applicant that he cannot pursue his musical education there.

The Emergence of Harlem

The 1920s also witnessed an upsurge of self-consciousness among black Americans, especially in the North's urban ghettos. With European immigration all but halted, the Great Migration of World War I continued apace as nearly 1 million blacks left the South during the decade. New York's Harlem gained an international reputation as the "capital" of black America, a mecca for migrants from the South and immigrants from the West Indies, 150,000 of whom entered the United States between 1900 and 1930. Unlike the southern newcomers, most of whom had been agricultural workers, the West Indians included a large number of well-educated professional and white-collar workers. Their encounter with American racism appalled them. "I had heard of prejudice in America," wrote the poet and novelist Claude McKay, who emigrated from Jamaica in 1912, "but never dreamed of it being so intensely bitter."

Caribbean immigrants

VOICES OF FREEDOM

From André Siegfried, "The Gulf Between,"
Atlantic Monthly (March 1928)

The French writer André Siegfried in 1928 commented on the rise of an industrial economy and consumer culture and the changes they produced in American society.

Never has Europe more eagerly observed, studied, discussed America; and never . . . have the two continents been wider apart in their aspirations and ideals. . . . Europe, after all, is not very different from what it was a generation ago; but there has been born since then a new America. . . .

The conquest of the continent has been completed, and—all recent American historians have noted the significance of the event—the western frontier has disappeared; the pioneer is no longer needed, and, with him, the mystic dream of the West . . . has faded away. Thus came the beginning of the era of organization: the new problem was not to conquer adventurously but to produce methodically. The great man of the new generation was no longer a pioneer like Lincoln . . . but . . . Henry Ford. From this time on, America has been no more an unlimited prairie with pure and infinite horizons, in which free men may sport like wild horses, but a huge factory of prodigious efficiency. . . .

In the last twenty-five or thirty years America has produced a new civilization. . . . From a *moral point of view*, it is obvious that Americans have come to consider their standard of living as a somewhat sacred acquisition, which they will defend at any price. This means that they would be ready to make many an intellectual or even moral concession in order to maintain that standard.

From a *political point of view*, it seems that the notion of efficiency of production is on the way to taking [precedence over] the very notion of liberty. In the name of efficiency, one can obtain, from the American, all sorts of sacrifices in relation to his personal and even to certain of his political liberties. . . .

Mass production and mass civilization, its natural consequence, are the true characteristics of the new American society. . . . Lincoln, with his Bible and classical tradition, was easier for Europe to understand than Ford, with his total absence of tradition and his proud creation of new methods and new standards, especially conceived for a world entirely different from our own.

From Majority Opinion, Justice James C. McReynolds, in *Meyer v. Nebraska* (1923)

A landmark in the development of civil liberties, the Supreme Court's decision in *Meyer v. Nebraska* rebuked the coercive Americanization impulse of World War I, overturning a Nebraska law that required all school instruction to take place in English.

The problem for our determination is whether the statute [prohibiting instruction in a language other than English] as construed and applied unreasonably infringes the liberty guaranteed . . . by the Fourteenth Amendment. . . .

The American people have always regarded education and acquisition of knowledge as matters of supreme importance which should be diligently promoted. . . . The calling always has been regarded as useful and honorable, essential, indeed, to the public welfare. Mere knowledge of the German language cannot reasonably be regarded as harmful. Heretofore it has been commonly looked upon as helpful and desirable. [Meyer] taught this language in school as part of his occupation. His right to teach and the right of parents to engage him so to instruct their children, we think, are within the liberty of the Amendment.

It is said the purpose of the legislation was to promote civil development by inhibiting training and education of the immature in foreign tongues and ideals before they could learn English and acquire American ideals. . . . It is also affirmed that the foreign born population is very large, that certain communities commonly use foreign words, follow foreign leaders, move in a foreign atmosphere, and that the children are therefore hindered from becoming citizens of the most useful type and the public safety is impaired.

That the State may do much, go very far, indeed, in order to improve the quality of its citizens, physically, mentally, and morally, is clear; but the individual has certain fundamental rights which must be respected. The protection of the Constitution extends to all, to those who speak other languages as well as to those born with English on the tongue. Perhaps it would be highly advantageous if all had ready understanding of our ordinary speech, but this cannot be coerced by methods which conflict with the Constitution. . . . No emergency has arisen which rendered knowledge by a child of some language other than English so clearly harmful as to justify its inhibition with the consequent infringement of rights long freely enjoyed.

QUESTIONS

1. *Why does Siegfried feel that Europeans no longer find America understandable?*

2. *How does the decision in* Meyer v. Nebraska *expand the definition of liberty protected by the Fourteenth Amendment?*

3. *How do the two excerpts reflect the changes American society experienced in the 1910s and 1920s?*

A black family arriving in Chicago in 1922, as part of the Great Migration from the rural South.

The 1920s became famous for "slumming," as groups of whites visited Harlem's dance halls, jazz clubs, and speakeasies in search of exotic adventure. The Harlem of the white imagination was a place of primitive passions, free from the puritanical restraints of mainstream American culture. The real Harlem was a community of widespread poverty, its residents confined to low-wage jobs and, because housing discrimination barred them from other neighborhoods, forced to pay exorbitant rents.

The Harlem Renaissance

Vibrant culture

But Harlem also was home to a vibrant black cultural community that established links with New York's artistic mainstream. Poets and novelists such as Countee Cullen, Langston Hughes, and Claude McKay were befriended and sponsored by white intellectuals and published by white presses. Broadway for the first time presented black actors in serious dramatic roles, as well as shows such as *Dixie to Broadway* and *Blackbirds* that featured great entertainers such as the singers Florence Mills and Ethel Waters and the tap dancer Bill Robinson.

The term "**New Negro**," associated in politics with pan-Africanism and the militancy of the Garvey movement, in art meant the rejection of established stereotypes and a search for black values to put in their place. This quest led the writers of what came to be called the Harlem Renaissance to the roots of the black experience—Africa, the rural South's folk traditions, and the life of the urban ghetto. Harlem Renaissance writings also contained a strong element of protest. This mood was exemplified by McKay's poem "If We Must Die," a response to the race riots of 1919. The poem affirmed that blacks would no longer allow themselves to be murdered defenselessly by whites:

> If we must die, let it not be like hogs
> Hunted and penned in an inglorious spot,
> While round us bark the mad and hungry dogs,
> Making their mock at our accursed lot. . . .
> Like men we'll face the murderous, cowardly pack,
> Pressed to the wall, dying, but fighting back!

Winston Churchill would invoke McKay's words to inspire the British public during World War II.

THE GREAT DEPRESSION

The Election of 1928

Few men elected to the presidency have seemed destined for a more successful term in office than Herbert Hoover. Born in Iowa in 1874, Hoover accumulated a fortune as a mining engineer working for firms in Asia, Africa, and Europe. During and immediately after World War I, he gained international fame by coordinating overseas food relief. In 1922, while serving as secretary of commerce, he published *American Individualism*, which condemned government regulation as an interference with the economic opportunities of ordinary Americans but also insisted that self-interest should be subordinated to public service. Hoover considered himself a Progressive, although he preferred what he called "associational action," in which private agencies directed regulatory and welfare policies, to government intervention in the economy.

After "silent Cal" Coolidge in 1927 handed a piece of paper to a group of reporters that stated, "I do not choose to run for president in 1928," Hoover quickly emerged as his successor. Accepting the Republican nomination, Hoover celebrated the decade's prosperity and promised that poverty would "soon be banished from this earth." His Democratic opponent was Alfred E. Smith, the first Catholic to be nominated by a major

A 1928 campaign poster for the Republican ticket of Herbert Hoover and Charles Curtis.

VOTE FOR HERBERT HOOVER
& CHARLES   CURTIS
for the Prosperity   *and the Happiness*
of your Country   *and your home....*

President Herbert Hoover (at center, next to the woman), at the opening day baseball game in Washington, D.C., April 17, 1929.

party. Although he had no family connection with the new immigrants from southern and eastern Europe (his grandparents had emigrated from Ireland), Smith emerged as their symbolic spokesman. He served three terms as governor of New York, securing passage of laws limiting the hours of working women and children and establishing widows' pensions. Smith denounced the Red Scare and called for the repeal of Prohibition.

Smith's Catholicism became the focus of the race. Many Protestant ministers and religious publications denounced him for his faith. For the first time since Reconstruction, Republicans carried several southern states, reflecting the strength of anti-Catholicism and nativism among religious fundamentalists. On the other hand, Smith carried the nation's twelve largest cities and won significant support in economically struggling farm areas. With more than 58 percent of the vote, Hoover was elected by a landslide. But Smith's campaign helped to lay the foundation for the triumphant Democratic coalition of the 1930s, based on urban ethnic voters, farmers, and the South.

The Coming of the Depression

On October 21, 1929, President Hoover traveled to Michigan to take part in the Golden Anniversary of the Festival of Light, organized by Henry Ford to commemorate the invention of the lightbulb by Thomas Edison fifty years earlier. Eight days later, on Black Tuesday, the stock market crashed. As panic selling set in, more than $10 billion in market value (equivalent to more than ten times that amount in today's money) vanished in five hours. Soon, the United States and, indeed, the entire world found itself in the grip of the Great Depression, the greatest economic disaster in modern history.

Even before 1929, signs of economic trouble had become evident. Southern California and Florida experienced frenzied real-estate speculation and then spectacular busts, with banks failing, land remaining undeveloped, and mortgages foreclosed. The highly unequal distribution of income and the prolonged depression in farm regions reduced American purchasing

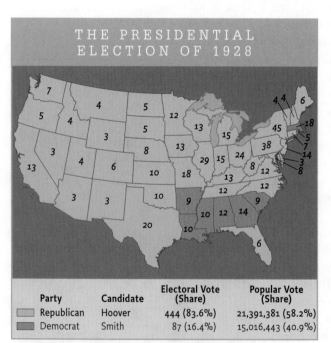

THE PRESIDENTIAL ELECTION OF 1928

Party	Candidate	Electoral Vote (Share)	Popular Vote (Share)
Republican	Hoover	444 (83.6%)	21,391,381 (58.2%)
Democrat	Smith	87 (16.4%)	15,016,443 (40.9%)

power. Sales of new autos and household consumer goods stagnated after 1926. European demand for American goods also declined, partly because industry there had recovered from wartime destruction.

A fall in the bloated stock market, driven ever higher during the 1920s by speculators, was inevitable. But it came with such severity that it destroyed many of the investment companies that had been created to buy and sell stock, wiping out thousands of investors, and it greatly reduced business and consumer confidence.

The global financial system was ill-equipped to deal with the down- *Global crisis* turn. Germany defaulted on reparations payments to France and Britain, leading these governments to stop repaying debts to American banks. Throughout the industrial world, banks failed as depositors withdrew money, fearful that they could no longer count on the promise to redeem paper money in gold. Millions of families lost their life savings.

Although stocks recovered somewhat in 1930, they soon resumed *A deepening recession* their relentless downward slide. Between 1929 and 1932, the price of a share of U.S. Steel fell from $262 to $22, and General Motors from $73 to $8. Four-fifths of the Rockefeller family fortune disappeared. In 1932, the economy hit rock bottom. Since 1929, the gross national product (the value of all the goods and services in the country) had fallen by one-third, prices by nearly 40 percent, and more than 11 million Americans— 25 percent of the labor force—could not find work. U.S. Steel, which had employed 225,000 full-time workers in 1929, had none at the end of 1932. Those who retained their jobs confronted reduced hours and dramatically reduced wages. Every industrial economy suffered, but the United States, which had led the way in prosperity in the 1920s, was hit hardest of all.

Americans and the Depression

The Depression transformed American life. Hundreds of thousands of people took to the road in search of work. Hungry men and women lined the streets of major cities. In Detroit, 4,000 children stood in bread lines each day seeking food. Thousands of families, evicted from their homes, moved into ramshackle shanty-towns, dubbed Hoovervilles, that sprang

Three months before the stock market crash, *The Magazine of Wall Street* was avidly encouraging readers to purchase stocks.

BUY! REPEATED
BUY! PERSISTENT
BUY! ADVICES

The American Institute of Finance *repeatedly* and *persistently* recommends the purchase of *the same* stock. This persistent repetition on the same stock makes it practically impossible for the advice to escape the attention of clients.

The following nine stocks have been definitely recommended for purchase no less than 113 times in a twenty-month period—an average of over five recommendations a month.

Have *YOU* made *REAL PROFITS* in These Stocks? Did *YOU* BUY

(14 advices in 18 mos.)	Allied Chemical	@	140 up—now 290
(12 advices in 19 mos.)	Air Reduction	@	138 up—now 330
(11 advices in 18 mos.)	American Smelting	@	155 up—now 360
(10 advices in 20 mos.)	Chicago, R. I. & Pacific	@	70 up—now 135
(10 advices in 18 mos.)	Gold Dust Corp.	@	45 up—now 150
(11 advices in 19 mos.)	Inter. Harvester	@	135 up—now 400
(10 advices in 18 mos.)	Jewel Tea	@	58 up—now 170*
(18 advices in 20 mos.)	Mathieson Alkali	@	86 up—now 190
(17 advices in 19 mos.)	Peoples Gas	@	128 up—now 250

* Price includes recent "rights."

Unemployed men lined up outside a Chicago soup kitchen in 1931. Charitable institutions like this one were overwhelmed by the advent of the Great Depression.

up in parks and on abandoned land. In Chicago, where half the working population was unemployed at the beginning of 1932, Mayor Anton Cermak telephoned people individually, begging them to pay their taxes. When the Soviet Union advertised its need for skilled workers, it received more than 100,000 applications from the United States.

The Depression actually reversed the long-standing movement of population from farms to cities. Many Americans left cities to try to grow

A Hooverville—a shantytown created by homeless squatters—outside Seattle, Washington, in 1933.

food for their families. In 1935, 33 million people lived on farms—more than at any previous point in American history. But rural areas, already poor, saw families reduce the number of meals per day and children go barefoot. With the future shrouded in uncertainty, the American suicide rate rose to the highest level in the nation's history, and the birthrate fell to the lowest.

The image of big business, carefully cultivated during the 1920s, collapsed as congressional investigations revealed massive irregularities committed by bankers and stockbrokers. Banks had knowingly sold worthless bonds. Prominent Wall Streeters had unloaded their own portfolios while advising small investors to maintain their holdings. Richard Whitney, the president of the New York Stock Exchange, was convicted of stealing funds from customers, including from a fund to aid widows and orphans. He ended up in jail.

Resignation and Protest

Many Americans reacted to the Depression with resignation or blamed themselves for economic misfortune. Others responded with protests that were at first spontaneous and uncoordinated, since unions, socialist organizations, and other groups that might have provided disciplined leadership had been decimated during the 1920s. In the spring of 1932, 20,000 unemployed World War I veterans descended on Washington to demand early payment of a bonus due in 1945, only to be driven away by federal soldiers. That summer, led by the charismatic Milo Reno, a former Iowa Populist, the National Farmers' Holiday Association protested low prices by temporarily blocking roads in the Midwest to prevent farm goods from getting to market.

Only the minuscule Communist Party seemed able to give a political focus to the anger and despair. One labor leader later recalled that the Communists "brought misery out of hiding," forming unemployed councils, sponsoring marches and demonstrations for public assistance, and protesting the eviction of unemployed families from their homes.

Communist Party headquarters in New York City, 1932. The banners illustrate the variety of activities the party organized in the early 1930s.

Hoover's Response

Andrew Mellon

In the eyes of many Americans, President Hoover's response to the Depression seemed inadequate and uncaring. Leading advisers, including Andrew Mellon, the wealthy secretary of the treasury, told Hoover that economic downturns were a normal part of capitalism, which weeded out unproductive firms and encouraged moral virtue among the less fortunate. Businessmen strongly opposed federal aid to the unemployed, and many publications called for individual "belt-tightening" as the road to recovery.

The federal government had never faced an economic crisis as severe as the Great Depression. Few political leaders understood how important consumer spending had become in the American economy. In 1931, Hoover quoted former president Grover Cleveland from four decades earlier: "The Government should not support the people. . . . Federal aid . . . weakens the sturdiness of our national character."

Hoover and associational action

Strongly opposed on principle to direct federal intervention in the economy, Hoover remained committed to "associational action." He put his faith in voluntary steps by business to maintain investment and employment—something few found it possible to do—and efforts by local charity organizations to assist needy neighbors. He attempted to restore public confidence, making frequent public statements that "the tide had turned." But these made him increasingly seem out of touch with reality. About the unemployed men who appeared on city streets offering apples at five cents apiece, Hoover would later write, "Many persons left their jobs for the more profitable one of selling apples."

An unemployed man and woman selling apples on a city street during the Great Depression.

The Worsening Economic Outlook

Some administration remedies, like the Hawley-Smoot Tariff, which Hoover signed with some reluctance in 1930, made the economic situation worse. Raising the already high taxes on imported goods, it inspired similar increases abroad, further reducing international trade.

By 1932, Hoover had to admit that voluntary action had failed to stem the Depression. He signed laws creating the

Reconstruction Finance Corporation, which loaned money to failing banks, railroads, and other businesses, and the Federal Home Loan Bank System, which offered aid to home owners threatened with foreclosure. Having vetoed previous bills to create employment through public-works projects like road and bridge construction, he now approved a measure appropriating nearly $2 billion for such initiatives and helping to fund local relief efforts. These were dramatic departures from previous federal economic policy. But he adamantly opposed offering direct relief to the unemployed.

Government action

Freedom in the Modern World

In 1927, the New School for Social Research in New York City organized a series of lectures on the theme of freedom in the modern world. The lectures painted a depressing portrait of American freedom on the eve of the Great Depression. The "sacred dogmas of patriotism and Big Business," said the educator Horace Kallen, dominated teaching, the press, and public debate. A definition of freedom reigned supreme that celebrated the unimpeded reign of economic enterprise yet tolerated the surveillance of private life and individual conscience.

The prosperity of the 1920s had reinforced this definition of freedom. With the economic crash, compounded by the ineffectiveness of the Hoover administration's response, it would be discredited. By 1932, the seeds had already been planted for a new conception of freedom that combined two different elements in a sometimes uneasy synthesis. One was the Progressive belief in a socially conscious state making constructive changes in economic arrangements. The other, which arose in the 1920s, centered on respect for civil liberties and cultural pluralism and declared that realms of life like group identity, personal behavior, and the free expression of ideas lay outside legitimate state concern. These two principles would become the hallmarks of modern liberalism, which during the 1930s would redefine American freedom.

A new conception of freedom

CHAPTER REVIEW AND ONLINE RESOURCES

REVIEW QUESTIONS

1. How did consumerism and the idea of the "American way of life" affect people's understanding of American values, including the meaning of freedom, in the 1920s?

2. Which groups did not share in the prosperity of the 1920s and why?

3. How did business practices and policies lead to a decline in union membership in the 1920s?

4. President Calvin Coolidge said, "The chief business of the American people is business." How did the federal government's policies and practices in the 1920s reflect this understanding of the importance of business interests?

5. Who supported restricting immigration in the 1920s and why? Why were they more successful in gaining federal legislation to limit immigration in these years?

6. Did U.S. society in the 1920s reflect the concept of cultural pluralism as explained by Horace Kallen? Why or why not?

7. Identify the causes of the Great Depression.

8. What principles guided President Hoover's response to the Great Depression, and how did this restrict his ability to help the American people?

9. What issues were of particular concern to fundamentalists in these years and why?

10. In what ways did the ideas about (and the reality of) proper roles for women change in these years?

KEY TERMS

Sacco-Vanzetti case (p. 609)

rise of the stock market (p. 613)

"welfare capitalism" (p. 613)

Equal Rights Amendment (p. 615)

"flapper" (p. 615)

Teapot Dome scandal (p. 617)

Hays code (p. 620)

American Civil Liberties Union (p. 620)

"clear and present danger" (p. 620)

fundamentalism (p. 622)

Scopes trial (p. 623)

second Ku Klux Klan (p. 624)

immigration restriction (p. 624)

"illegal alien" (p. 625)

"New Negro" (p. 631)

stock market crash (p. 632)

bonus marchers (p. 635)

Reconstruction Finance Corporation (p. 637)

wwnorton.com
/studyspace

VISIT STUDYSPACE FOR THESE RESOURCES AND MORE

- A chapter outline
- A diagnostic chapter quiz
- Interactive maps
- Map worksheets
- Multimedia documents

CHAPTER 21

THE NEW DEAL

★

1932-1940

This panel depicting the construction of a dam was painted in 1939 by William Gropper as part of a mural for the new Department of Interior building in Washington, D.C. Like other artists who found it difficult to obtain work during the Depression, Gropper was hired by the Works Projects Administration to paint murals for government buildings. This one was inspired by the construction of the Grand Coulee Dam on the Columbia River, one of the many New Deal projects that expanded the nation's infrastructure and provided employment to victims of the Depression.

- *What were the major policy initiatives of the New Deal in the Hundred Days?*

- *Who were the main proponents of economic justice in the 1930s, and what measures did they advocate?*

- *What were the major initiatives of the Second New Deal?*

- *How did the New Deal recast the meaning of American freedom?*

- *How did New Deal benefits apply to women and minorities?*

- *How did the Popular Front influence American culture in the 1930s?*

The Columbia River winds its way on a 1,200-mile course from Canada through Washington and Oregon to the Pacific Ocean. Because of its steep descent from uplands to sea level, it produces an immense amount of energy. Residents of the economically underdeveloped Pacific Northwest had long dreamed of tapping this unused energy for electricity and irrigation. But not until the 1930s did the federal government launch the program of dam construction that transformed the region. The project created thousands of jobs for the unemployed, and the network of dams produced abundant cheap power.

When the Grand Coulee Dam went into operation in 1941, it was the largest man-made structure in world history. It eventually produced more than 40 percent of the nation's hydroelectric power. The project also had less appealing consequences. From time immemorial, the Columbia River had been filled with salmon. But the Grand Coulee Dam made no provision for the passage of fish, and the salmon all but vanished. This caused little concern during the Depression but became a source of controversy later in the century as Americans became more concerned about preserving the natural environment.

The Columbia River project reflected broader changes in American life and thought during the New Deal of the 1930s. Franklin D. Roosevelt believed regional economic development like that in the Northwest would promote economic growth, ease the domestic and working lives of ordinary Americans, and keep control of key natural resources in public rather than private hands. The Roosevelt administration spent far more money on building roads, dams, airports, bridges, and housing than on any other activity.

Roosevelt also oversaw the transformation of the Democratic Party into a coalition of farmers, industrial workers, the reform-minded urban middle class, liberal intellectuals, northern African-Americans, and, somewhat incongruously, the white supremacist South, united by the belief that the federal government must provide Americans with protection against the dislocations caused by modern capitalism. "Liberalism," traditionally understood as limited government and free market economics, took on its modern meaning. Thanks to the New Deal, it now referred to active efforts by the national government to uplift less fortunate members of society.

Freedom, too, underwent a transformation during the 1930s. The New Deal elevated a public guarantee of economic security to the forefront of American discussions of freedom. Regional economic planning reflected this understanding of freedom. So did other New Deal measures, including the Social Security Act, which offered aid to the unemployed and aged, and the Fair Labor Standards Act, which established a national minimum wage.

Yet although the New Deal significantly expanded the meaning of freedom, it did not erase freedom's boundaries. Its benefits flowed to industrial workers but not tenant farmers, to men far more fully than women, and to white Americans more than blacks, who, in the South, still were deprived of the basic rights of citizenship.

THE FIRST NEW DEAL

FDR and the Election of 1932

FDR, as he liked to be called, was born in 1882, a fifth cousin of Theodore Roosevelt. After serving as undersecretary of the navy during World War I, he ran for vice president on the ill-fated Democratic ticket of 1920 headed by James M. Cox. In 1921, he contracted polio and lost the use of his legs, a fact carefully concealed from the public in that pre-television era. Very few Americans realized that the president who projected an image of vigorous leadership during the 1930s and World War II was confined to a wheelchair.

Franklin Delano Roosevelt

In his speech accepting the Democratic nomination for president in 1932, Roosevelt promised a "new deal" for the American people. But his campaign offered only vague hints of what this might entail. He advocated a balanced federal budget and criticized his opponent, President Hoover, for excessive government spending. The biggest difference between the parties during the campaign was the Democrats' call for the repeal of Prohibition, although Roosevelt certainly suggested a greater awareness of the plight of ordinary Americans. Battered by the economic crisis, Americans in 1932 were desperate for new leadership, and Roosevelt won a resounding victory.

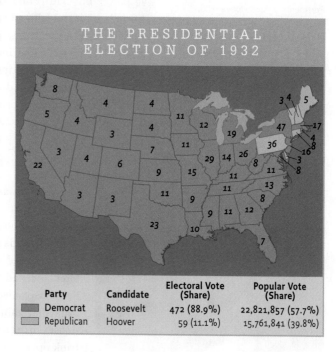

THE PRESIDENTIAL ELECTION OF 1932

Party	Candidate	Electoral Vote (Share)	Popular Vote (Share)
Democrat	Roosevelt	472 (88.9%)	22,821,857 (57.7%)
Republican	Hoover	59 (11.1%)	15,761,841 (39.8%)

He received 57 percent of the popular vote, and Democrats swept to a commanding majority in Congress.

The Coming of the New Deal

Roosevelt conceived of the New Deal as an alternative to socialism on the left, Nazism on the right, and the inaction of upholders of unregulated capitalism. He hoped to reconcile democracy, individual liberty, and economic recovery and development. He did not, however, enter office with a blueprint for dealing with the Depression. At first, he relied heavily for advice on a group of intellectuals and social workers who took up key positions in his administration. They included Secretary of Labor Frances Perkins, a veteran of Hull House and the New York Consumers' League; Harry Hopkins, who had headed emergency relief efforts during Roosevelt's term as governor of New York; Secretary of the Interior Harold Ickes, a veteran of Theodore Roosevelt's Progressive campaign of 1912; and Louis Brandeis, who had advised Woodrow Wilson during the 1912 campaign and now offered political advice to FDR while serving on the Supreme Court.

FDR's advisers

Brandeis believed that large corporations not only wielded excessive power but had contributed to the Depression by keeping prices artificially high and failing to increase workers' purchasing power. They should be broken up, he insisted, not regulated. But the "brains trust"—a group of academics that included a number of Columbia University professors—saw bigness as inevitable in a modern economy. Large firms needed to be managed and directed by the government, not dismantled. Their view prevailed during what came to be called the First New Deal.

The Banking Crisis

"This nation asks for action and action now," Roosevelt announced on taking office on March 4, 1933. The new president confronted a banking system on the verge of collapse. As bank funds invested in the stock market lost their value and panicked depositors withdrew their savings, bank after bank had closed its doors. By March 1933, banking had been suspended in a majority of the states—that is, people could not gain access to money in their bank accounts. Roosevelt declared a "**bank holiday**," temporarily halting all bank operations, and called Congress into special session.

Presidents Herbert Hoover and Franklin D. Roosevelt on their way to the latter's inauguration on March 4, 1933. The two men strongly disliked one another. They barely spoke during the ride and never saw each other again after that day.

A "run" on a bank: crowds of people wait outside a New York City bank, hoping to withdraw their money.

On March 9, it rushed to pass the **Emergency Banking Act**, which provided funds to shore up threatened institutions.

Further measures soon followed that transformed the American financial system. The Glass-Steagall Act barred commercial banks from becoming involved in the buying and selling of stocks. Until its repeal in the 1990s, the law prevented many of the irresponsible practices that had contributed to the stock market crash. The same law established the Federal Deposit Insurance Corporation (FDIC), a government system that insured the accounts of individual depositors. Together, these measures rescued the financial system and greatly increased the government's power over it.

The Glass-Steagall Act

The NRA

The Emergency Banking Act was the first of an unprecedented flurry of legislation during the first three months of Roosevelt's administration, a period known as the **Hundred Days**. Seizing on the sense of crisis and the momentum of his electoral victory, Roosevelt won rapid passage of laws he hoped would promote economic recovery. He persuaded Congress to create a host of new agencies, whose initials soon became part of the language of politics—NRA, AAA, CCC.

A flurry of legislation

The centerpiece of Roosevelt's plan for combating the Depression, the National Industrial Recovery Act, was to a large extent modeled on the government–business partnership established by the War Industries Board of World War I. The act established the **National Recovery Administration**

(NRA), which would work with groups of business leaders to establish industry codes that set standards for output, prices, and working conditions.

In effect, FDR had repudiated the older idea of liberty based on the idea that the best way to encourage economic activity and ensure a fair distribution of wealth was to allow market competition to operate, unrestrained by the government. And to win support from labor, section 7a of the new law recognized the workers' right to organize unions—a departure from the "open shop" policies of the 1920s and a step toward government support for what workers called "industrial freedom."

Industrial freedom

Headed by Hugh S. Johnson, a retired general and businessman, the NRA quickly established codes that set standards for production, prices, and wages in the textile, steel, mining, and auto industries. But the NRA became mired in controversy. Large companies dominated the code-writing process. They used the NRA to drive up prices, limit production, lay off workers, and divide markets among themselves at the expense of smaller competitors. The NRA produced neither economic recovery nor peace between employers and workers. It did, however, combat the pervasive sense that the government was doing nothing to deal with the economic crisis.

NRA codes

Government Jobs

The Hundred Days also brought the government into providing relief to those in need. Roosevelt and most of his advisers shared the widespread fear that direct government payments to the unemployed would undermine individual self-reliance. But with nearly a quarter of the workforce unemployed, spending on relief was unavoidable. In May 1933, Congress created the Federal Emergency Relief Administration, to make grants to local agencies that aided those impoverished by the Depression. FDR, however, much preferred to create temporary jobs, thereby combating unemployment while improving the nation's infrastructure of roads, bridges, public buildings, and parks.

In March 1933, Congress established the **Civilian Conservation Corps** (CCC), which set unemployed young men to work on projects like forest preservation, flood control, and the improvement of national parks and wildlife preserves. By the time

A Civilian Conservation Corps workforce in Yosemite National Park, 1935.

the program ended in 1942, more than 3 million persons had passed through CCC camps, where they received government wages of $30 per month.

Public-Works Projects

One section of the National Industrial Recovery Act created the **Public Works Administration** (PWA), with an appropriation of $3.3 billion. Directed by Secretary of the Interior Harold Ickes, it built roads, schools, hospitals, and other public facilities, including New York City's Triborough Bridge and the Overseas Highway between Miami and Key West, Florida. In November, yet another agency, the Civil Works Administration (CWA), was launched. By January 1934, it employed more than 4 million persons in the construction of highways, tunnels, courthouses, and airports. But as the cost spiraled upward and complaints multiplied that the New Deal was creating a class of Americans permanently dependent on government jobs, Roosevelt ordered the CWA dissolved.

The Tennessee Valley Authority (TVA), another product of the Hundred Days, built a series of dams to prevent floods and deforestation along the Tennessee River and to provide cheap electric power for homes and factories in a seven-state region where many families still lived in

A map published by the Public Works Administration in 1935 depicts some of the numerous infrastructure projects funded by the New Deal. Among the most famous public-works projects are the Triborough Bridge in New York City, the Key West Highway in Florida, and the Grand Coulee Dam in Washington. Overall, the New Deal spent $250 billion (in today's money) to construct, among other things, 40,000 public buildings, 72,000 schools, 80,000 bridges, and 8,000 parks.

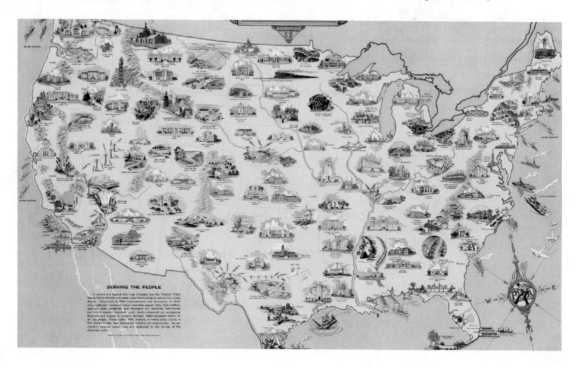

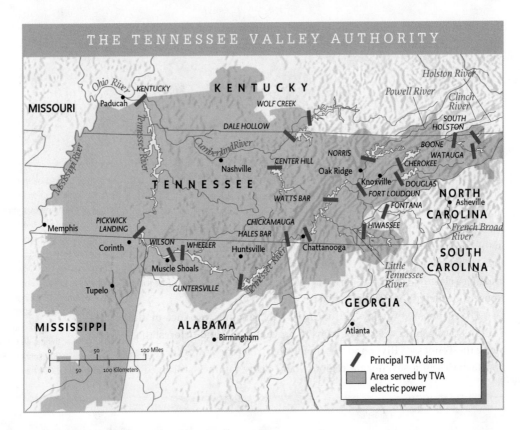

THE TENNESSEE VALLEY AUTHORITY

A map showing the reach of the Tennessee Valley Authority, covering all or parts of seven southeastern states. Numerous reservoirs and power plants dot the landscape.

isolated log cabins. The TVA put the federal government, for the first time, in the business of selling electricity in competition with private companies.

The New Deal and Agriculture

Another policy initiative of the Hundred Days addressed the disastrous plight of American farmers. The Agricultural Adjustment Act (AAA) authorized the federal government to try to raise farm prices by setting production quotas for major crops and paying farmers to plant less. Many crops already in the field were destroyed. In 1933, the government ordered more than 6 million pigs slaughtered as part of the policy, a step critics found strange at a time of widespread hunger.

Efforts to raise farm prices

The AAA succeeded in significantly raising farm prices and incomes. But not all farmers benefited. Benefits flowed to property-owning farmers, ignoring the large number who worked on land owned by others. The AAA policy of paying landowning farmers not to grow crops encouraged the eviction of thousands of poor tenants and sharecroppers. Many joined the rural exodus to cities or to the farms of the West Coast.

The onset in 1930 of a period of unusually dry weather in the nation's heartland worsened the Depression's impact on rural America. By mid-decade, the region suffered from the century's most severe drought. Mechanized agriculture in this semi-arid region had pulverized the topsoil and killed native grasses that prevented erosion. Winds now blew much of the soil away, creating the **Dust Bowl**, as the affected areas of Oklahoma, Texas, Kansas, and Colorado were called. The drought and dust storms displaced more than 1 million farmers.

A giant dust storm engulfs a town in western Kansas on April 14, 1935, known as Black Sunday in the American West.

The New Deal and Housing

The Depression devastated the American housing industry. The construction of new residences all but ceased, and banks and savings and loan associations that had financed home ownership collapsed or, to remain afloat, foreclosed on many homes (a quarter of a million in 1932 alone). Millions of Americans lived in overcrowded, unhealthy urban slums or in ramshackle rural dwellings. Private enterprise alone, it seemed clear, was unlikely to solve the nation's housing crisis.

Roosevelt spoke of "the security of the home" as a fundamental right. In 1933 and 1934, his administration moved energetically to protect home owners from foreclosure and to stimulate new construction. The Home Owners Loan Corporation and **Federal Housing Administration** (FHA) insured millions of long-term mortgages issued by private banks. At the same time, the federal government itself built thousands of units of low-rent housing. Thanks to the FHA and, later, the Veterans' Administration, home ownership came within the reach of tens of millions of families. It became cheaper for most Americans to buy single-family homes than to rent apartments.

Other important measures of Roosevelt's first two years in office included the ratification of the Twenty-first Amendment to the Constitution, which repealed Prohibition; the establishment

As it did in other sectors of the economy, the Great Depression led to a collapse in the construction industry.

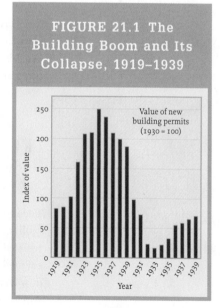

FIGURE 21.1 The Building Boom and Its Collapse, 1919–1939

The Illegal Act, a cartoon critical of the Supreme Court's decision declaring the NRA unconstitutional. FDR tells a drowning Uncle Sam, "I'm sorry, but the Supreme Court says I must chuck you back in."

of the Federal Communications Commission to oversee the nation's broadcast airwaves and telephone communications; and the creation of the Securities and Exchange Commission to regulate the stock and bond markets. Taken together, the First New Deal was a series of experiments, some of which succeeded and some of which did not. They transformed the role of the federal government, constructed numerous public facilities, and provided relief to millions of needy persons. But they did not end the Depression. Some 10 million Americans—more than 20 percent of the workforce—remained unemployed when 1934 came to an end.

The Court and the New Deal

In 1935, the Supreme Court, still controlled by conservative Republican judges who held to the nineteenth-century understanding of freedom as liberty of contract, began to invalidate key New Deal laws. First came the NRA, declared unconstitutional in May in a case brought by the Schechter Poultry Company of Brooklyn, which had been charged with violating the code adopted by the chicken industry. In a unanimous decision, the Court declared the NRA unlawful because in its codes and other regulations it delegated legislative powers to the president and attempted to regulate local businesses that did not engage in interstate commerce. In January 1936, the AAA fell in *United States v. Butler*, which declared it an unconstitutional exercise of congressional power over local economic activities.

Having failed to end the Depression or win judicial approval, the First New Deal ground to a halt. Meanwhile, pressures were mounting outside Washington that propelled the administration toward more radical departures in policy.

End of the First New Deal

THE GRASSROOTS REVOLT

Labor's Great Upheaval

The most striking development of the mid-1930s was the mobilization of millions of workers in mass-production industries that had successfully resisted unionization. "Labor's great upheaval," as this era of unprecedented militancy was called, came as a great surprise. Unlike in the past, however, the federal government now seemed to be on the side of labor. American-born children of the new immigrants now dominated the indus-

Industrial labor

trial labor force, and organizers no longer had to distribute materials in numerous languages as the IWW had done. And a cadre of militant labor leaders, many of them socialists and communists, had survived the repression of the 1920s. They provided leadership to the labor upsurge.

American factories at the outset of the New Deal were miniature dictatorships in which unions were rare, workers could be beaten by supervisors and fired at will, and management determined the length of the workday and speed of the assembly line. Workers' demands during the 1930s went beyond better wages. They included an end to employers' arbitrary power in the workplace, and basic civil liberties for workers, including the right to picket, distribute literature, and meet to discuss their grievances. All these goals required union recognition.

Conditions in American factories

Roosevelt's inauguration unleashed a flood of poignant letters to the federal government describing what a Louisiana sugar laborer called the "terrible and inhuman condition" of many workers. Labor organizers spread the message that the "political liberty for which our forefathers fought" had been "made meaningless by economic inequality" and "industrial despotism."

Labor's great upheaval exploded in 1934, a year that witnessed no fewer than 2,000 strikes. Many produced violent confrontations between workers and the local police. San Francisco experienced the country's first general strike since 1919. It began with a walkout of dockworkers led by the fiery communist Harry Bridges. Workers demanded recognition of the International Longshoremen's Association and an end to the hated "shape up" system in which they had to gather en masse each day to wait for work assignments. The year 1934 also witnessed a strike of 400,000 textile workers in states from New England to the Deep South, demanding recognition of the United Textile Workers. Many of these walkouts won at least some of the workers' demands. But the textile strike failed.

A year of strikes

The Rise of the CIO

The labor upheaval posed a challenge to the American Federation of Labor's traditional policy of organizing workers by craft rather than seeking to mobilize all the workers in a given industry, such as steel manufacturing. In 1934, thirty AFL leaders called for the creation of unions of industrial workers. When the AFL convention of 1935 refused, the head of the United Mine Workers, John L. Lewis, led a walkout that produced a new labor organization, the **Congress of Industrial Organizations** (CIO). It aimed, said Lewis, at nothing less than to secure "economic freedom and industrial democracy" for American workers—a fair share in the wealth

John L. Lewis

produced by their labor, and a voice in determining the conditions under which they worked.

The UAW's sit-down strike

In December 1936, unions, most notably the United Auto Workers (UAW), a fledgling CIO union, unveiled the **sit-down**, a strikingly effective tactic that the IWW had pioneered three decades earlier. Rather than walking out of the Fisher Body Plant in Cleveland, thus enabling management to bring in strikebreakers, workers halted production but remained inside. Sit-downs soon spread to General Motors plants in Flint, Michigan, the nerve center of automobile production. Demonstrating a remarkable spirit of unity, the strikers cleaned the plant, oiled the idle machinery, and settled disputes among themselves. Workers' wives shuttled food into the plant. On February 11, General Motors agreed to negotiate with the UAW. By the end of 1937, the UAW claimed 400,000 members.

The victory in the auto industry reverberated throughout industrial America. Steelworkers had suffered memorable defeats in the struggle for unionization, notably at Homestead in 1892 and in the Great Steel Strike of 1919. But in March 1937, fearing a sit-down campaign and aware that it could no longer count on the aid of state and federal authorities, U.S. Steel, the country's single most important business firm, agreed to recognize the Steel Workers Organizing Committee (forerunner of the United Steelworkers of America). Smaller steel firms, however, refused to follow suit.

Growth in union membership

Union membership nonetheless reached 9 million by 1940, more than double the number in 1930. Workers gained new grievance procedures and seniority systems governing hiring, firing, and promotions. The CIO unions helped to stabilize a chaotic employment situation and offered members a sense of dignity and freedom.

Sit-down strike at a General Motors factory in Flint, Michigan, 1937.

Labor and Politics

Throughout the industrial heartland, the labor upsurge altered the balance of economic power and propelled to the forefront of politics labor's goal of a fairer, freer, more equal America. The CIO put forward an ambitious program for federal action to shield Americans from economic and social insecurity, including public housing, universal health care, and unemployment and old age insurance.

Building on the idea, so prominent in the 1920s, that the key to prosperity lay in an American standard of living based on mass consumption, CIO leaders explained the Depression as the result of an imbalance of wealth and income. The pathbreaking 1937 agreement between the UAW and General Motors spoke of a "rate of pay commensurate with an American standard of living." By mid-decade, many New Dealers accepted the "underconsumptionist" explanation of the Depression, which saw lack of sufficient consumer demand as its underlying cause.

Voices of Protest

Other popular movements of the mid-1930s also placed the question of economic justice on the political agenda. In California, the novelist Upton Sinclair won the Democratic nomination for governor in 1934 as the head of the End Poverty in California movement. Sinclair called for the state to use idle factories and land in cooperative ventures that would provide jobs for the unemployed. He lost the election after being subjected to one of the first modern "negative" media campaigns. Sinclair's opponents circulated false newsreels showing armies of unemployed men marching to California to support his candidacy and a fake endorsement from the Communist Party.

The rise to national prominence of Huey Long offered another sign of popular dissatisfaction with the slow pace of economic recovery. Driven by intense ambition and the desire to help uplift Louisiana's "common people," Long won election as governor in 1928 and in 1930 took a seat in the U.S. Senate. From Washington, he dominated every branch of state government. He used his dictatorial power to build roads, schools, and hospitals and to increase the tax burden on Louisiana's oil companies.

In 1934, Long launched the **Share Our Wealth movement**, with the slogan "Every Man a King." He called for the confiscation of most of the wealth of the richest Americans in order to finance an immediate grant of $5,000 and a guaranteed job and annual income for all citizens. He was on the verge of announcing a run for president when the son of a defeated political rival assassinated him in 1935.

Dr. Francis Townsend, a California physician, meanwhile won wide support for a plan by which the government would make a monthly payment of $200 to older Americans, with the requirement that they spend it immediately. This, he argued, would boost the economy. Along with the rise of the CIO, these signs of popular discontent helped spark the Second New Deal.

Religion on the Radio

Religious leaders of various denominations took advantage of the mass media to spread their beliefs. Ironically, many fundamentalists used the most modern techniques of communication, including the radio and

Pennsylvania Steelworkers outside the Local Headquarters of the Steel Workers Organizing Committee, a 1938 photograph by Arnold Rothstein.

Huey Long, the "Kingfish" of Louisiana politics, in full rhetorical flight. This photo was probably taken in 1934, when Long was in the Senate but still running the state government.

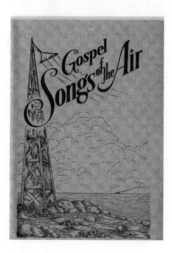

The cover of a songbook to accompany a radio broadcast from the Chicago Gospel Tabernacle. A radio tower dominates the image.

popular entertainment, to promote their anti-modernist message. They found in the radio a way to bypass established churches and their leaders. Aimee Semple McPherson, a Los Angeles revivalist, had her own radio station, which broadcast sermons from the International Church of the Foursquare Gospel she had founded. By the 1940s, national religious broadcast networks emerged, with a reliable and dedicated listening audience.

Also in the mid-1930s, the "radio priest," Father Charles E. Coughlin, attracted millions of listeners with weekly broadcasts attacking Wall Street bankers and greedy capitalists, and calling for government ownership of key industries as a way of combating the Depression. Initially a strong supporter of FDR, Coughlin became increasingly critical of the president for what he considered the failure of the New Deal to promote social justice. His crusade would later shift to anti-Semitism and support for European fascism.

THE SECOND NEW DEAL

Buoyed by Democratic gains in the midterm elections of 1934, Roosevelt in 1935 launched the Second New Deal. The First had focused on economic recovery. The emphasis of the Second was economic security—a guarantee that Americans would be protected against unemployment and poverty.

Economic security

The idea that lack of consumer demand caused the Depression had been popularized by Huey Long, Francis Townsend, and the CIO. By 1935, more and more New Dealers had concluded that the government should no longer try to plan business recovery but should try to redistribute the national income so as to sustain mass purchasing power in the consumer economy. A series of measures in 1935 attacked head-on the problem of weak demand and economic inequality. Congress levied a highly publicized tax on large fortunes and corporate profits—a direct response to the popularity of Huey Long's Share Our Wealth campaign. It created the Rural Electrification Agency (REA) to bring electric power to homes that lacked it—80 percent of farms were still without electricity in 1934—in part to enable more Americans to purchase household appliances.

The Rural Electrification Agency

By 1950, 90 percent of the nation's farms had been wired for electricity, and almost all now possessed radios, electric stoves, refrigerators, and mechanical equipment to milk cows. In addition, the federal government under the Second New Deal tried to promote soil conservation and family farming. This effort resulted from the belief that the country would never achieve prosperity so long as farmers' standard of living lagged well behind that of city dwellers, and that rural poverty resulted mainly from the poor use of natural resources. Thus, farmers received federal assistance in reducing soil loss in their fields. These measures (like those of the AAA) mainly benefited landowners, not sharecroppers, tenants, or migrant workers. In the long run, the Second New Deal failed to arrest the trend toward larger farms and fewer farmers.

The WPA and the Wagner Act

In 1934, Roosevelt had severely curtailed federal employment for those in need. Now, he approved the establishment of the **Works Progress Administration** (WPA), which hired some 3 million Americans, in virtually every walk of life, each year until it ended in 1943. It constructed thousands of public buildings and bridges, more than 500,000 miles of roads, and 600 airports. It built stadiums, swimming pools, and sewage treatment plants. Unlike previous work relief programs, the WPA employed many out-of-work white-collar workers and professionals, even doctors and dentists.

Perhaps the most famous WPA projects were in the arts. The WPA set hundreds of artists to work decorating public buildings with murals. It hired writers to produce local histories and guidebooks to the forty-eight states and to record the recollections of ordinary Americans, including hundreds of former slaves. Thanks to the WPA, audiences across the

A poster by the artist Vera Bock for the Federal Art Project of the Works Progress Administration depicts farmers and laborers joining hands to produce prosperity.

An art exhibit in a New York City alley in 1938. The Works Progress Administration tried to broaden the audience for art by displaying it in unusual venues.

country enjoyed their first glimpse of live musical and theatrical performances and their first opportunity to view exhibitions of American art.

The Wagner Act

Another major initiative of the Second New Deal, the Wagner Act, brought democracy into the American workplace by empowering the National Labor Relations Board to supervise elections in which employees voted on union representation. It also outlawed "unfair labor practices," including the firing and blacklisting of union organizers.

The American Welfare State: Social Security

The centerpiece of the Second New Deal was the **Social Security Act** of 1935. It embodied Roosevelt's conviction that the national government had a responsibility to ensure the material well-being of ordinary Americans. It created a system of unemployment insurance, old age pensions, and aid to the disabled, the elderly poor, and families with dependent children.

Progressive legacy

None of these were original ideas. The Progressive platform of 1912 had called for old age pensions. Assistance to poor families with dependent children descended from the mothers' pensions promoted by maternalist reformers. Many European countries had already adopted national unemployment insurance plans. What was new, however, was that in the name of economic security, the American government would now supervise not simply temporary relief but a permanent system of social insurance.

The Social Security Act launched the American version of the **welfare state**—a term that originated in Britain during World War II to refer to a system of income assistance, health coverage, and social services for all citizens. Compared with similar programs in Europe, the American welfare state has always been far more decentralized, involved lower levels of public spending, and covered fewer citizens. The original Social Security bill, for example, envisioned a national system of health insurance. But Congress dropped this after ferocious opposition from the American Medical Association, which feared government regulation of doctors' activities and incomes. And the fact that domestic and agricultural workers were not covered by unemployment and old age benefits meant that Social Security at first excluded large numbers of Americans, especially unmarried women and non-whites.

Nonetheless, Social Security represented a dramatic departure from the traditional functions of government. The Second New Deal transformed the relationship between the federal government and American citizens. Before the 1930s, national political debate often revolved around the question of *whether* the federal government should intervene in the economy. After the New Deal, debate rested on *how* it should intervene. In addition, the government assumed a responsibility, which it has never

A 1935 poster promoting the new Social Security system.

wholly relinquished, for guaranteeing Americans a living wage and protecting them against economic and personal misfortune.

A RECKONING WITH LIBERTY

The Depression made inevitable, in the words of one writer, a "reckoning with liberty." For too many Americans, Roosevelt proclaimed, "life was no longer free, liberty no longer real, men could no longer follow the pursuit of happiness."

Along with being a superb politician, Roosevelt was a master of political communication. At a time when his political opponents controlled most newspapers, he harnessed radio's power to bring his message directly into American homes. By the mid-1930s, more than two-thirds of American families owned radios. They listened avidly to Roosevelt's radio addresses, known as "fireside chats."

FDR's "fireside chats"

Roosevelt adeptly appealed to traditional values in support of new policies. He gave the term "liberalism" its modern meaning. As we have seen, in the nineteenth century, liberalism had been a shorthand for limited government and free-market economics. Roosevelt consciously chose to employ it to describe a large, active, socially conscious state. He reclaimed the word "freedom" from conservatives and made it a rallying cry for the New Deal. In his second fireside chat, Roosevelt juxtaposed his own definition of liberty as "greater security for the average man" to the older notion of liberty of contract, which served the interests of "the privileged few." Henceforth, he would consistently link freedom with economic security and identify entrenched economic inequality as its greatest enemy. "The liberty of a democracy," he declared in 1938, was not safe if citizens could not "sustain an acceptable standard of living."

FDR delivering one of his "fireside chats" in 1938. Roosevelt was the first president to make effective use of the radio to promote his policies.

Even as Roosevelt invoked the word to uphold the New Deal, "liberty"—in the sense of freedom from powerful government—became the fighting slogan of his opponents. When conservative businessmen and politicians in 1934 formed an organization to mobilize opposition to Roosevelt's policies, they called it the American Liberty League.

The Election of 1936

By 1936, with working-class voters providing massive majorities for the Democratic Party and businesses large and small bitterly estranged from the New Deal, politics reflected class divisions more completely than at any

VOICES OF FREEDOM

From Franklin D. Roosevelt, "Fireside Chat" (1934)

President Roosevelt pioneered the use of the new mass medium of radio to speak directly to Americans in their homes. He used his "fireside chats" to mobilize support for New Deal programs, link them with American traditions, and outline his definition of freedom.

To those who say that our expenditures for public works and other means for recovery are a waste that we cannot afford, I answer that no country, however rich, can afford the waste of its human resources. Demoralization caused by vast unemployment is our greatest extravagance. Morally, it is the greatest menace to our social order. Some people try to tell me that we must make up our minds that in the future we shall permanently have millions of unemployed just as other countries have had them for over a decade. What may be necessary for those countries is not my responsibility to determine. But as for this country, I stand or fall by my refusal to accept as a necessary condition of our future a permanent army of unemployed. . . .

In our efforts for recovery we have avoided, on the one hand, the theory that business should and must be taken over into an all-embracing Government. We have avoided, on the other hand, the equally untenable theory that it is an interference with liberty to offer reasonable help when private enterprise is in need of help. The course we have followed fits the American practice of Government, a practice of taking action step by step, of regulating only to meet concrete needs, a practice of courageous recognition of change. I believe with Abraham Lincoln, that "the legitimate object of Government is to do for a community of people whatever they need to have done but cannot do at all or cannot do so well for themselves in their separate and individual capacities."

I am not for a return to that definition of liberty under which for many years a free people were being gradually regimented into the service of the privileged few. I prefer and I am sure you prefer that broader definition of liberty under which we are moving forward to greater freedom, to greater security for the average man than he has ever known before in the history of America.

From John Steinbeck, *The Harvest Gypsies: On the Road to the Grapes of Wrath* (1938)

John Steinbeck's popular novel *The Grapes of Wrath* (1939), and the film version that followed shortly thereafter, focused national attention on the plight of homeless migrants displaced from their farms as a result of the Great Depression. Before that book appeared, Steinbeck had published a series of newspaper articles based on eyewitness accounts of the migrants, which became the basis for his novel.

In California, we find a curious attitude toward a group that makes our agriculture successful. The migrants are needed, and they are hated. . . . The migrants are hated for the following reasons, that they are ignorant and dirty people, that they are carriers of disease, that they increase the necessity for police and the tax bill for schooling in a community, and that if they are allowed to organize they can, simply by refusing to work, wipe out the season's crops. . . .

Let us see what kind of people they are, where they come from, and the routes of their wanderings. In the past they have been of several races, encouraged to come and often imported as cheap labor. Chinese in the early period, then Filipinos, Japanese and Mexicans. These were foreigners, and as such they were ostracized and segregated and herded about. . . . But in recent years the foreign migrants have begun to organize, and at this danger they have been deported in great numbers, for there was a new reservoir from which a great quantity of cheap labor could be obtained.

The drought in the middle west has driven the agricultural populations of Oklahoma, Nebraska and parts of Kansas and Texas westward. . . . Thousands of them are crossing the borders in ancient rattling automobiles, destitute and hungry and homeless, ready to accept any pay so that they may eat and feed their children. . . .

The earlier foreign migrants have invariably been drawn from a peon class. This is not the case with the new migrants. They are small farmers who have lost their farms, or farm hands who have lived with the family in the old American way. . . . They have come from the little farm districts where democracy was not only possible but inevitable, where popular government, whether practiced in the Grange, in church organization or in local government, was the responsibility of every man. And they have come into the country where, because of the movement necessary to make a living, they are not allowed any vote whatever, but are rather considered a properly unprivileged class. . . .

As one little boy in a squatter's camp said, "When they need us they call us migrants, and when we've picked their crop, we're bums and we got to get out."

other time in American history. Conceptions of freedom divided sharply as well.

A fight for the possession of "the ideal of freedom," reported the *New York Times*, emerged as the central issue of the presidential campaign of 1936. In his speech accepting renomination, Roosevelt launched a blistering attack against "economic royalists" who, he charged, sought to establish a new tyranny over the "average man." Economic rights, he went on, were the precondition of liberty—poor men "are not free men." Throughout the campaign, FDR would insist that the threat posed to economic freedom by the "new despotism" of large corporations was the main issue of the election.

Economic freedom

As Roosevelt's opponent, Republicans chose Kansas governor Alfred Landon, a former Theodore Roosevelt Progressive. Landon denounced Social Security and other measures as threats to individual liberty. Opposition to the New Deal planted the seeds for the later flowering of an antigovernment conservatism bent on upholding the free market and dismantling the welfare state. But in 1936 Roosevelt won a landslide reelection, with more than 60 percent of the popular vote. His success stemmed from strong backing from organized labor and his ability to unite southern white and northern black voters, Protestant farmers and urban Catholic and Jewish ethnics, industrial workers and middle-class home owners. These groups made up the so-called New Deal coalition, which would dominate American politics for nearly half a century.

The New Deal coalition

The Court Fight

Fall In!, a cartoon commenting on Roosevelt's proposal to "pack" the Supreme Court, from the *Richmond Times-Dispatch*, January 8, 1937.

Roosevelt's second inaugural address was the first to be delivered on January 20. In order to shorten a newly elected president's wait before taking office, the recently ratified Twentieth Amendment had moved inauguration day from March 4. The Depression, he admitted, had not been conquered: "I see one-third of a nation ill-housed, ill-clad, and ill-nourished." Emboldened by his electoral triumph, Roosevelt now made what many considered a serious political miscalculation. On the pretext that several members of the Supreme Court were too old to perform their functions, he proposed that the president be allowed to appoint a new justice for each one who remained on the Court past age seventy (an age that six of the nine had already passed). FDR's aim, of course, was to change the balance of power on a Court that, he feared, might well invalidate Social Security, the Wagner Act, and other measures of the Second New Deal.

Congress rejected the plan. But Roosevelt accomplished his underlying purpose. Coming soon after Roosevelt's landslide victory of 1936, the threat of "**court packing**" inspired an astonishing about-face by key justices. Beginning in March 1937, the Court suddenly revealed a new willingness to support economic regulation by both the federal government and the states. It turned aside challenges to Social Security and the Wagner Act. In subsequent cases, the Court affirmed federal power to regulate wages, hours, child labor, agricultural production, and numerous other aspects of economic life.

The about-face for the Court

The Court's new attitude marked a permanent change in judicial policy. Having declared dozens of economic laws unconstitutional in the decades leading up to 1937, the justices have rarely done so since.

The End of the Second New Deal

Even as the Court made its peace with Roosevelt's policies, the momentum of the Second New Deal slowed. The landmark United States Housing Act did pass in 1937, initiating the first major national effort to build homes for the poorest Americans. But the Fair Labor Standards bill failed to reach the floor for over a year. When it finally passed in 1938, it banned goods produced by child labor from interstate commerce, set forty cents as the hourly **minimum wage**, and required overtime pay for hours of work exceeding forty per week. This last major piece of New Deal legislation established the practice of federal regulation of wages and working conditions, another radical departure from pre-Depression policies.

The year 1937 also witnessed a sharp downturn of the economy. With economic conditions improving in 1936, Roosevelt had reduced federal funding for farm subsidies and WPA work relief. The result was disastrous. Unemployment, still 14 percent at the beginning of 1937, rose to nearly 20 percent by year's end.

In 1936, in *The General Theory of Employment, Interest, and Money*, John Maynard Keynes had challenged economists' traditional belief in the sanctity of balanced budgets. Large-scale government spending, he insisted, was necessary to sustain purchasing power and stimulate economic activity during downturns. Such spending should be enacted even at the cost of a budget deficit (a situation in which the government spends more money than it takes in). By 1938, Roosevelt was ready to follow this prescription, which would later be known as Keynesian economics. In April, he asked Congress for billions more for work relief and farm aid. The events of 1937–1938 marked a major shift in New Deal philosophy. Public spending would now be the government's major tool for combating unemployment and stimulating economic growth. The Second New Deal had come to an end.

The New Deal did not really solve the problem of unemployment, which fell below 10 percent only in 1941, as the United States prepared to enter World War II.

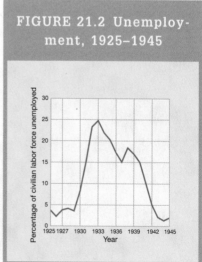

FIGURE 21.2 Unemployment, 1925–1945

THE LIMITS OF CHANGE

Roosevelt conceived of the Second New Deal, and especially Social Security, as expanding the meaning of freedom by extending assistance to broad groups of needy Americans—the unemployed, elderly, and dependent—as a right of citizenship, not charity or special privilege. But political realities, especially the power of inherited ideas about gender and black disenfranchisement in the South, powerfully affected the drafting of legislation. Different groups of Americans experienced the New Deal in radically different ways.

The New Deal and American Women

The New Deal brought more women into government than ever before in American history. A number of talented women, including Secretary of Labor Frances Perkins, advised the president and shaped public policy. Most prominent of all was Eleanor Roosevelt, FDR's distant cousin, whom *Eleanor Roosevelt* he had married in 1905. She transformed the role of First Lady, turning a position with no formal responsibilities into a base for political action. She traveled widely, spoke out on public issues, wrote a regular newspaper column, and worked to enlarge the scope of the New Deal in areas like civil rights, labor legislation, and work relief.

But even as the New Deal increased women's visibility in national politics, organized feminism, already in disarray during the 1920s, disappeared as a political force. Indeed, the Depression inspired widespread demands for women to remove themselves from the labor market to make room for unemployed men. Because the Depression hit industrial employment harder than low-wage clerical and service jobs where women predominated, the proportion of the workforce made up of women rose. The government tried to reverse this trend. The Economy Act of 1933 prohibited both members of a married couple from holding federal jobs. Until its repeal in 1937, it led to the dismissal of numerous female civil service employees whose husbands worked for the government. Employers from banks to public school systems barred married women from jobs.

Most New Deal programs did not exclude women from benefits (although the CCC restricted its camps to men). But the ideal of the male-headed household powerfully shaped social policy. Since paying taxes on one's

Eleanor Roosevelt transformed the role of First Lady by taking an active and visible part in public life. Here she visits a West Virginia coal mine in 1933.

wages made one eligible for the most generous Social Security programs—old age pensions and unemployment insurance—they left most women uncovered, because they did not work outside the home. The program excluded the 3 million mostly female domestic workers altogether.

The Southern Veto

Roosevelt made the federal government the symbolic representative of all the people, including racial and ethnic groups generally ignored by previous administrations. Yet the power of the Solid South helped to mold the New Deal welfare state into an entitlement of white Americans. After the South's blacks lost the right to vote around the turn of the century, Democrats enjoyed a political monopoly in the region. Democratic members of Congress were elected again and again. Committee chairmanships in Congress rest on seniority—how many years a member has served in office. Thus, beginning in 1933, when Democrats took control of Congress, southerners took the key leadership positions. At their insistence, the Social Security law excluded agricultural and domestic workers, the largest categories of black employment.

Black organizations like the Urban League and the NAACP lobbied strenuously for a system that enabled agricultural and domestic workers to receive unemployment and old age benefits and that established national relief standards. The Social Security Act, however, complained the *Pittsburgh Courier*, a black newspaper, reflected the power of "reactionary elements in the South who cannot bear the thought of Negroes getting pensions and compensations" and who feared that the inclusion of black workers would disrupt the region's low-wage, racially divided labor system.

The Stigma of Welfare

Because of the "southern veto," the majority of black workers found themselves confined to the least generous and most vulnerable wing of the new welfare state. The public assistance programs established by Social Security, notably aid to dependent children and to the poor elderly, were open to all Americans who could demonstrate financial need. But they set benefits at extremely low levels and authorized the states to determine eligibility standards, including "moral" behavior as defined by local authorities. As a result, public assistance programs allowed for widespread discrimination in the distribution of benefits. Recipients came to bear the humiliating stigma of dependency on government handouts, which would soon come to be known as "welfare."

The situation seemed certain to stigmatize blacks as recipients of unearned government assistance, and welfare as a program for minorities, thus dooming it forever to inadequate "standards of aid." Over time, this is precisely what happened, until the federal government abolished its responsibility for welfare in 1996, during the presidency of Bill Clinton.

The Indian New Deal

Overall, the Depression and New Deal had a contradictory impact on America's racial minorities. Under Commissioner of Indian Affairs John Collier, the administration launched an **Indian New Deal**. Collier ended the policy of forced assimilation and allowed Indians unprecedented cultural autonomy. He replaced boarding schools meant to eradicate the tribal heritage of Indian children with schools on reservations, and dramatically increased spending on Indian health. He secured passage of the Indian Reorganization Act of 1934, ending the policy, dating back to the Dawes Act of 1887, of dividing Indian lands into small plots for individual families and selling off the rest. Federal authorities once again recognized Indians' right to govern their own affairs.

The New Deal marked the most radical shift in Indian policy in the nation's history. But living conditions on the desperately poor reservations did not significantly improve.

Changes in Indian policy

The New Deal and Mexican-Americans

For Mexican-Americans, the Depression was a wrenching experience. With demand for their labor plummeting, more than 400,000 (one-fifth of the population of Mexican origin) returned to Mexico, some voluntarily, others at the strong urging of local authorities in the Southwest. A majority of those "encouraged" to leave the country were recent immigrants, but they included perhaps 200,000 Mexican-American children who had been born in the United States and were therefore citizens. Those who remained mostly worked in grim conditions in California's vegetable and fruit fields, whose corporate farms benefited enormously from New Deal dam construction that provided them with cheap electricity and water for irrigation. The Wagner and Social Security acts did not apply to agricultural laborers.

Mexican-American leaders struggled to develop a consistent strategy for their people. They sought greater rights by claiming to be white Americans—in order not to suffer the same discrimination as African-Americans—but also sought the backing of the Mexican government and

Repatriation of Mexican-Americans

promoted a mystical sense of pride and identification with Mexican heritage later given the name *la raza*.

Last Hired, First Fired

As the "last hired and first fired," African-Americans were hit hardest by the Depression. Even those who retained their jobs now faced competition from unemployed whites who had previously considered positions like waiter and porter beneath them. With an unemployment rate double that of whites, blacks benefited disproportionately from direct government relief and, especially in northern cities, jobs on New Deal public-works projects. Half of the families in Harlem received public assistance during the 1930s. Demonstrations in Harlem demanded jobs in the neighborhood's white-owned stores, with the slogan "Don't Buy Where You Can't Work."

Unemployment for blacks

Although Roosevelt seems to have had little personal interest in race relations or civil rights, he appointed Mary McLeod Bethune, a prominent black educator, as a special adviser on minority affairs and a number of other blacks to important federal positions. Key members of his administration, including his wife, Eleanor, and Secretary of the Interior Harold Ickes, a former president of the Chicago chapter of the NAACP, directed national attention to the injustices of segregation, disenfranchisement, and lynching. In 1939, Eleanor Roosevelt resigned from the Daughters

Future congressman Adam Clayton Powell, Jr. (at center with billboard) taking part in a "Don't Buy Where You Can't Work" demonstration in Harlem during the Depression. The campaign targeted stores that served black customers but refused to hire black employees.

A map of Philadelphia prepared by the Home Owners' Loan Corporation illustrates how federal agencies engaged in "redlining" of neighborhoods containing blue-collar and black residents. The colors correspond to the agency's perception of an area's real-estate prospects. Wealthy neighborhoods, colored green and given the best credit ratings, were expected to be racially and ethnically homogenous. White-collar districts, in blue, were second best. Red districts, the worst, had an "undesirable population." The Corporation prepared maps like this for many cities and shared them with private lenders and the Federal Housing Administration, resulting in massive disinvestment in "red" neighborhoods, whose residents found it almost impossible to obtain housing loans.

of the American Revolution when the organization refused to allow the black singer Marian Anderson to present a concert at Constitution Hall in Washington. The president's wife arranged for Anderson to sing on the steps of the Lincoln Memorial and for the concert to be broadcast nationally on the radio.

The decade witnessed a historic shift in black voting patterns. In the North and West, where they enjoyed the right to vote, blacks in 1934 and 1936 abandoned their allegiance to the party of Lincoln and emancipation in favor of Democrats and the New Deal. But despite a massive lobbying campaign, southern congressmen prevented passage of a federal antilynching law. FDR offered little support. Because of the exclusion of agricultural and domestic workers, Social Security's old age pensions and unemployment benefits and the minimum wages established by the Fair Labor Standards Act left uncovered 60 percent of all employed blacks and 85 percent of black women.

Federal Discrimination

Federal housing policy, which powerfully reinforced residential segregation, revealed the limits of New Deal freedom. As in the case of Social Security, local officials put national housing policy into practice in a way that reinforced existing racial boundaries. Nearly all municipalities, North as well as South, insisted that housing built or financially aided by the federal government be racially segregated. The Federal Housing Administration, moreover, had no hesitation about insuring mortgages that contained clauses barring future sales to non-white buyers, and it refused to channel money into integrated neighborhoods. Along with discriminatory practices by private banks and real estate companies, federal policy became a major factor in further entrenching housing segregation in the United States.

Federal employment practices also discriminated on the basis of race. As late as 1940, of the 150,000 blacks holding federal jobs, only 2 percent occupied positions other than clerk or custodian. In the South, many New Deal construction projects refused to hire blacks at all. The New Deal began the process of modernizing southern agriculture, but tenants, black and white, footed much of the bill. Tens of thousands of sharecroppers, as noted earlier, were driven off the land as a result of the AAA policy of raising crop prices by paying landowners to reduce cotton acreage.

Not until the Great Society of the 1960s would those left out of Social Security and other New Deal programs—racial minorities, many women, migrants and other less privileged workers—win inclusion in the American welfare state.

A NEW CONCEPTION OF AMERICA

But if the New Deal failed to dismantle the barriers that barred non-whites from full participation in American life, the 1930s witnessed the absorption of other groups into the social mainstream. With Catholics and Jews occupying prominent posts in the Roosevelt administration and new immigrant voters forming an important part of its electoral support, the New Deal made ethnic pluralism a living reality in American politics.

Ethnic pluralism

Thanks to the virtual cutoff of southern and eastern European immigration in 1924; the increasing penetration of movies, chain stores, and mass advertising into ethnic communities; and the common experience of economic crisis, the 1930s witnessed an acceleration of cultural assimilation. For the children of the new immigrants, labor and political activism became agents of a new kind of Americanization. "Unionism is Americanism" became a CIO rallying cry.

The Heyday of American Communism

In the mid-1930s, for the first time in American history, the left—an umbrella term for socialists, communists, labor radicals, and many New Deal liberals—enjoyed a shaping influence on the nation's politics and culture. The CIO and Communist Party became focal points for a broad social and intellectual impulse that helped to redraw the boundaries of American freedom. An obscure, faction-ridden organization when the Depression began, the Communist Party experienced remarkable growth during the 1930s. The party's membership never exceeded 100,000, but several times that number passed through its ranks.

The left

It was not so much the party's ideology as its vitality—its involvement in a mind-boggling array of activities, including demonstrations by the unemployed, struggles for industrial unionism, and a renewed movement for black civil rights—that for a time made it the center of gravity for a broad democratic upsurge. At the height of the **Popular Front**—a period during the mid-1930s when the Communist Party sought to ally itself with socialists and New Dealers in movements for social change, urging reform of the capitalist system rather than revolution—Communists gained an unprecedented respectability.

Respectability for Communists

Redefining the People

In theater, film, and dance, the Popular Front vision of American society sank deep roots and survived much longer than the political moment from which it sprang. In this broad left-wing culture, social and economic radicalism, not support for the status quo, defined true Americanism. Ethnic and racial diversity was the glory of American society, and the "American way of life" meant unionism and social citizenship, not the unbridled pursuit of wealth.

During the 1930s, artists and writers who strove to create socially meaningful works eagerly took up the task of depicting the daily lives of ordinary farmers and city dwellers. Art about the people—such as Dorothea Lange's photographs of migrant workers and sharecroppers—and art created by the people—such as black spirituals—came to be seen as expressions of genuine Americanism. Films celebrated populist figures who challenged and defeated corrupt businessmen and politicians, as in *Mr. Deeds Goes to Town* (1936) and *Mr. Smith Goes to Washington* (1939). Earl Robinson's song "Ballad for Americans," a typical expression of Popular Front culture that celebrated the religious, racial, and ethnic diversity of American society, became a national hit and was performed in 1940 at the Republican national convention.

History of Southern Illinois, a mural sponsored by the Illinois Federal Art Project, illustrates the widespread fascination during the 1930s with American traditions and the lives of ordinary Americans. On the left, a man strums a guitar, while workers labor on the waterfront.

Challenging the Color Line

It was fitting that "Ballad for Americans" reached the top of the charts in a version performed by the magnificent black singer Paul Robeson. Popular Front culture moved well beyond New Deal liberalism in condemning racism as incompatible with true Americanism. In the 1930s, groups like the American Jewish Committee and the National Conference of Christians and Jews actively promoted ethnic and religious tolerance, defining pluralism as "the American way." But whether in Harlem or East Los Angeles, the Communist Party was the era's only predominantly white organization to make fighting racism a top priority. Communist influence spread even to the South. The Communist-dominated International Labor Defense mobilized popular support for black defendants victimized by a racist criminal justice system. It helped to make the Scottsboro case an international cause célèbre. The case revolved around nine young black men arrested for the rape of two white women in Alabama in 1931. Despite the weakness of the evidence against the **Scottsboro boys** and the fact that one of the two accusers recanted, Alabama authorities three times put them on trial and three times won convictions. Landmark Supreme Court decisions overturned the first two verdicts and established legal principles that greatly expanded the definition of civil liberties—that defendants have a constitutional right to effective legal representation and that states cannot systematically exclude blacks from juries. But the Court allowed the third set of convictions to stand, which led to prison sentences for five of the defendants.

The CIO brought large numbers of black industrial workers into the labor movement for the first time and ran extensive educational campaigns to persuade white workers to recognize the interests they shared with their black counterparts. Black workers, many of them traditionally hostile to unions because of their long experience of exclusion, responded with enthusiasm to CIO organizing efforts.

A Dorothea Lange photograph of a sharecropper and his family outside their modest home.

The "Scottsboro boys," flanked by two prison guards, with their lawyer, Samuel Liebowitz.

Labor and Civil Liberties

Another central element of Popular Front public culture was its mobilization for civil liberties, especially the right of labor to organize. The struggle to launch industrial unions encountered sweeping local restrictions on freedom of speech as well as repression by private and public police forces.

Labor militancy

Labor militancy helped to produce an important shift in the understanding of civil liberties. Previously conceived of as individual rights that must be protected against infringement by the government, the concept now expanded to include violations of free speech and assembly by powerful private groups. As a result, just as the federal government emerged as a guarantor of economic security, it also became a protector of freedom of expression.

By the eve of World War II, civil liberties had assumed a central place in the New Deal understanding of freedom. In 1939, Attorney General Frank Murphy established a Civil Liberties Unit in the Department of Justice. Meanwhile, the same Supreme Court that in 1937 relinquished its role as a judge of economic legislation moved to expand its authority over

Free expression

civil liberties. The justices insisted that constitutional guarantees of free thought and expression were essential to "nearly every other form of freedom" and therefore deserved special protection by the courts. Since 1937, the large majority of state and national laws overturned by the courts have been those that infringe on civil liberties, not the property rights of business.

The new appreciation of free expression was hardly universal. In 1938, the House of Representatives established an **Un-American Activities Committee** to investigate disloyalty. Its expansive definition of "un-American" included communists, labor radicals, and the left of the Democratic Party, and its hearings led to the dismissal of dozens of federal employees on charges of subversion. Two years later, Congress enacted the **Smith Act**, which made it a federal crime to "teach, advocate, or encourage" the overthrow of the government.

The End of the New Deal

By then the New Deal, as an era of far-reaching social reform, had already begun to recede. One reason was that more and more southern Democrats were finding themselves at odds with Roosevelt's policies. In 1938, the administration released a "Report on Economic Conditions in the South," along with a letter by the president referring to the region as "the nation's No. 1 economic problem." The document revealed that the South lagged far behind other parts of the country in industrialization and investment in education and public health. Also in 1938, a new generation of home-grown radicals—southern New Dealers, black activists, labor leaders, communists, even a few elected officials—founded the Southern

Southern leaders and the New Deal

Conference for Human Welfare to work for unionization, unemployment relief, and racial justice.

Southern business and political leaders feared that continuing federal intervention in their region would encourage unionization and upset race relations. Roosevelt concluded that the enactment of future New Deal measures required a liberalization of the southern Democratic Party. In 1938, he tried to persuade the region's voters to replace conservative congressmen with ones who would support his policies. The South's small electorate dealt him a stinging rebuke.

A period of political stalemate followed the congressional election of 1938. For many years, a conservative coalition of southern Democrats and northern Republicans dominated Congress. Further reform initiatives became almost impossible, and Congress moved to abolish existing ones. It repealed an earlier tax on corporate profits and rejected a proposed program of national medical insurance. The administration, moreover, increasingly focused its attention on the storm gathering in Europe. Even before December 1941, when the United States entered World War II, "Dr. Win the War," as Roosevelt put it, had replaced "Dr. New Deal."

"Dr. Win the War"

The New Deal in American History

Given the scope of the economic calamity it tried to counter, the New Deal seems in many ways limited. Compared with later European welfare states, Social Security remained restricted in scope and modest in cost. The New Deal failed to address the problem of racial inequality, which in some ways it actually worsened.

Yet even as the New Deal receded, its substantial accomplishments remained. It greatly expanded the federal government's role in the American economy and made it an independent force in relations between industry and labor. The government influenced what farmers could and could not plant, required employers to deal with unions, insured bank deposits, regulated the stock market, loaned money to home owners, and provided payments to a majority of the elderly and unemployed. It transformed the physical environment through hydroelectric dams, reforestation projects, rural electrification, and the construction of innumerable public facilities. It restored faith in democracy and made the government an institution directly experienced in Americans' daily lives and directly concerned with their welfare. It redrew the map of American politics. It helped to inspire, and was powerfully influenced by, a popular upsurge that recast the idea of freedom to include a public guarantee of economic

Failures and accomplishments of the New Deal

security for ordinary citizens and that identified economic inequality as the greatest threat to American freedom.

Legacy of the New Deal

The New Deal certainly improved economic conditions in the United States. But it did not generate sustained prosperity. More than 15 percent of the workforce remained unemployed in 1940. Only the mobilization of the nation's resources to fight World War II would finally end the Great Depression.

CHAPTER REVIEW AND ONLINE RESOURCES

REVIEW QUESTIONS

1. Discuss how regional development such as the Tennessee Valley Authority and the Columbia River project reflected broader changes in American life during the New Deal.

2. What actions did President Roosevelt and Congress take to help the banking system recover as well as to reform how it operated in the long run?

3. How did the actions of the AAA benefit many farmers, injure others, and provoke attacks by conservatives?

4. Explain what labor did in the 1930s to secure "economic freedom and industrial democracy" for American workers.

5. How did the emphasis of the Second New Deal differ from that of the First New Deal?

6. How did the entrenched power of southern white conservatives limit African-Americans' ability to enjoy the full benefits of the New Deal and eliminate racial violence and discrimination? Why did African-Americans still support the Democratic Party?

7. Analyze the effects of the Indian Reorganization Act of 1934 on Native Americans.

8. Explain how New Deal programs contributed to the stigma of blacks as welfare dependent.

9. How did the New Deal build on traditional ideas about the importance of homeownership to Americans, and how did it change Americans' ability to own their own homes?

10. What were the major characteristics of liberalism by 1939?

KEY TERMS

"bank holiday" (p. 642)
Emergency Banking Act (p. 643)
Hundred Days (p. 643)
National Recovery Administration (p. 643)
Civilian Conservation Corp. (p. 644)
Public Works Administration (p. 645)
Dust Bowl (p. 647)
Federal Housing Administration (p. 647)
Congress of Industrial Organizations (p. 649)
sit-down strike (p. 650)
Share Our Wealth movement (p. 651)
Works Progress Administration (p. 653)
Social Security Act (p. 654)
welfare state (p. 654)
court-packing plan (p. 658)
minimum wage (p. 659)
Indian New Deal (p. 662)
Popular Front (p. 666)
"Scottsboro boys" (p. 667)
House Un-American Activities Committee (p. 668)
Smith Act (p. 668)

wwnorton.com /studyspace

VISIT STUDYSPACE FOR THESE RESOURCES AND MORE
- A chapter outline
- A diagnostic chapter quiz
- Interactive maps
- Map worksheets
- Multimedia documents

CHAPTER 22

FIGHTING FOR THE FOUR FREEDOMS: WORLD WAR II

★

1941–1945

Freedom of Speech

Freedom of Worship

Freedom from Want

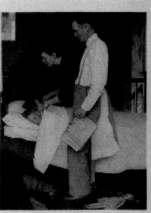
Freedom from Fear

The immensely popular Office of War Information poster reproducing Norman Rockwell's paintings of the Four Freedoms, President Franklin D. Roosevelt's shorthand for American purposes in World War II.

By far the most popular works of art produced during World War II were paintings of the **Four Freedoms** by the magazine illustrator Norman Rockwell. In his State of the Union Address, delivered before Congress on January 6, 1941, President Roosevelt spoke eloquently of a future world order founded on the "essential human freedoms": freedom of speech, freedom of worship, freedom from want, and freedom from fear. The Four Freedoms became Roosevelt's favorite statement of Allied aims. They embodied, Roosevelt declared in a 1942 radio address, the "rights of men of every creed and every race, wherever they live," and made clear "the crucial difference between ourselves and the enemies we face today."

Rockwell's paintings succeeded in linking the Four Freedoms with the defense of traditional American values. Drawing on the lives of his Vermont neighbors, Rockwell translated the Four Freedoms into images of real people situated in small-town America. Each of the paintings focuses on an instantly recognizable situation. An ordinary citizen rises to speak at a town meeting; members of different religious groups are seen at prayer; a family enjoys a Thanksgiving dinner; a mother and father stand over their sleeping children.

Even as Rockwell invoked images of small-town life to rally Americans to the war effort, however, the country experienced changes as deep as at any time in its history. As during World War I, but on a far larger scale, wartime mobilization expanded the size and scope of government and energized the economy. The gross national product more than doubled and unemployment disappeared as war production finally conquered the Depression. The demand for labor drew millions of women into the workforce and sent a tide of migrants from rural America to the industrial cities of the North and West, permanently altering the nation's social geography.

World War II gave the country a new and lasting international role and greatly strengthened the idea that American security was global in scope and could be protected only by the worldwide triumph of core American values. Government military spending sparked the economic development of the South and West, laying the foundation for the rise of the modern Sunbelt. The war created a close link between big business and a militarized federal government—a "military-industrial complex," as President Dwight D. Eisenhower would later call it—that long survived the end of fighting.

FOCUS QUESTIONS

- *What steps led to American participation in World War II?*

- *How did the United States mobilize economic resources and promote popular support for the war effort?*

- *What visions of America's postwar role began to emerge during the war?*

- *How did American minorities face threats to their freedom at home and abroad during World War II?*

- *How did the end of the war begin to shape the postwar world?*

1778 1943

AMERICANS
will **always** fight for liberty

One of the patriotic war posters issued by the Office of War Information during World War II, linking modern-day soldiers with patriots of the American Revolution as fighters for freedom, a major theme of government efforts to mobilize support for the war.

World War II also redrew the boundaries of American nationality. In contrast to World War I, the government recognized the "new immigrants" of the early twentieth century and their children as loyal Americans. Black Americans' second-class status assumed, for the first time since Reconstruction, a prominent place on the nation's political agenda. But toleration had its limits. With the United States at war with Japan, the federal government removed more than 100,000 Japanese-Americans, the majority of them American citizens, from their homes and confined them to internment camps.

As a means of generating support for the struggle, the Four Freedoms provided a crucial language of national unity. But this unity obscured underlying divisions concerning freedom. Although some Americans looked forward to a worldwide New Deal, others envisioned "free enterprise" replacing government intervention in the economy. The movement of women into the labor force challenged traditional gender relations, but most men and not a few women longed for the restoration of family life with a male breadwinner and a wife responsible for the home.

FIGHTING WORLD WAR II

Good Neighbors

During the 1930s, with Americans preoccupied by the economic crisis, international relations played only a minor role in public affairs. From the outset of his administration, nonetheless, FDR embarked on a number of departures in foreign policy. In 1933, hoping to stimulate American trade, he exchanged ambassadors with the Soviet Union, whose government his Republican predecessors had stubbornly refused to recognize.

Roosevelt also formalized a policy initiated by Herbert Hoover by which the United States repudiated the right to intervene militarily in the internal affairs of Latin American countries. This **Good Neighbor Policy**, as it was called, offered a belated recognition of the sovereignty of America's neighbors. But the United States lent its support to dictators like Anastasio Somoza in Nicaragua, Rafael Trujillo Molina in the Dominican Republic, and Fulgencio Batista in Cuba. "He may be a son of a bitch, but he's *our* son of a bitch," FDR said of Somoza.

Latin America

The Road to War

Ominous developments in Asia and Europe quickly overshadowed events in Latin America. By the mid-1930s, it seemed clear that the rule of law was disintegrating in international relations and that war was on the horizon. In 1931, seeking to expand its military and economic power in Asia, Japan invaded Manchuria, a province of northern China. Six years later, its troops moved farther into China. When the Japanese overran the city of Nanjing, they massacred an estimated 300,000 Chinese prisoners of war and civilians.

Aggression in Europe and Asia

An aggressive power threatened Europe as well. After brutally consolidating his rule in Germany, Adolf Hitler embarked on a campaign to control the entire continent. In 1936, he sent troops to occupy the Rhineland, a demilitarized zone between France and Germany established after World War I. The failure of Britain, France, and the United States to oppose this action convinced Hitler that the democracies could not muster the will to halt his aggressive plans. The Italian leader Benito Mussolini, the founder of fascism, a movement similar to Hitler's Nazism, invaded and conquered Ethiopia. As part of a campaign to unite all Europeans of German origin in a single empire, Hitler in 1938 annexed Austria and the Sudetenland, an ethnically German part of Czechoslovakia. Shortly thereafter, he gobbled up all of that country.

Adolf Hitler

As the 1930s progressed, Roosevelt became more and more alarmed at Hitler's aggression as well as his accelerating campaign against Germany's Jews, whom the Nazis stripped of citizenship and property and began to deport to concentration camps. But Roosevelt had little choice but to follow the policy of "appeasement" adopted by Britain and France, which hoped that agreeing to Hitler's demands would prevent war.

Isolationism

To most Americans, the threat arising from Japanese and German aggression seemed very distant. Moreover, Hitler had more than a few admirers in the United States.

In a 1940 cartoon, war clouds engulf Europe, while Uncle Sam observes that the Atlantic Ocean no longer seems to shield the United States from involvement.

Obsessed with the threat of communism, some Americans approved his expansion of German power as a counterweight to the Soviet Union. Businessmen did not wish to give up profitable overseas markets. Henry Ford did business with Nazi Germany throughout the 1930s. Trade with Japan also continued, including shipments of American trucks and aircraft and considerable amounts of oil.

Many Americans remained convinced that involvement in World War I had been a mistake. Ethnic allegiances reinforced Americans' traditional reluctance to enter foreign conflicts. Many Americans of German and Italian descent celebrated the expansion of national power in their countries of origin, even as they disdained their dictatorial governments. Irish-Americans remained strongly anti-British.

Isolationism—the 1930s version of Americans' long-standing desire to avoid foreign entanglements—dominated Congress. Beginning in 1935, lawmakers passed a series of neutrality acts that banned travel on belligerents' ships and the sale of arms to countries at war. These policies, Congress hoped, would allow the United States to avoid the conflicts over freedom of the seas that had contributed to involvement in World War I.

The Neutrality Acts

War in Europe

In the Munich agreement of 1938, Britain and France had caved in to Hitler's aggression. In 1939, the Soviet Union proposed an international agreement to oppose further German demands for territory. Britain and France, who distrusted Stalin and saw Germany as a bulwark against the spread of communist influence in Europe, refused. Stalin then astonished the world by signing a nonaggression pact with Hitler, his former sworn enemy. On September 1, immediately after the signing of the Nazi–Soviet pact, Germany invaded Poland. This time, Britain and France, which had pledged to protect Poland against aggression, declared war. But Germany appeared unstoppable. Within a year, the Nazi *blitzkrieg* (lightning war) had overrun Poland and much of Scandinavia, Belgium, and the Netherlands. On June 14, 1940, German troops occupied Paris. Hitler now dominated nearly all of Europe, as well as North Africa. In September 1940, Germany, Italy, and Japan created a military alliance known as the Axis.

For one critical year, Britain stood virtually alone in fighting Germany. In the Battle of Britain of 1940–1941, the German air force launched devastating attacks on London and other cities. The Royal Air Force eventually turned back the air assault.

A newsreel theater in New York's Times Square announces Hitler's *blitzkrieg* in Europe in the spring of 1940.

Toward Intervention

Roosevelt viewed Hitler as a mad gangster whose victories posed a direct threat to the United States. But most Americans remained desperate to stay out of the conflict. After a tumultuous debate, Congress in 1940 agreed to allow the sale of arms to Britain on a "cash and carry" basis—that is, they had to be paid for in cash and transported in British ships. It also approved plans for military rearmament. But with a presidential election looming, Roosevelt was reluctant to go further. Opponents of involvement in Europe organized the America First Committee, with hundreds of thousands of members and a leadership that included well-known figures like Henry Ford, Father Coughlin, and Charles A. Lindbergh.

"Cash and carry"

In 1940, breaking with a tradition that dated back to George Washington, Roosevelt announced his candidacy for a third term as president. The international situation was too dangerous and domestic recovery too fragile, he insisted, for him to leave office. Republicans chose as his opponent a political amateur, Wall Street businessman and lawyer Wendell Willkie. Willkie, who endorsed New Deal social legislation, captured more votes than Roosevelt's previous opponents. But FDR still emerged with a decisive victory. Soon after his victory, in a fireside chat in December 1940, Roosevelt announced that the United States would become the "arsenal of democracy," providing Britain and China with military supplies in their fight against Germany and Japan.

A third term

During 1941, the United States became more and more closely allied with those fighting Germany and Japan. At Roosevelt's urging, Congress passed the **Lend-Lease Act**, which authorized military aid so long as countries promised somehow to return it all after the war. Under the law's provisions, the United States funneled billions of dollars worth of arms to Britain and China, as well as the Soviet Union, after Hitler renounced his nonaggression pact and invaded that country in June 1941. FDR also froze Japanese assets in the United States, halting virtually all trade between the countries, including the sale of oil vital to Japan.

Financial support

Pearl Harbor

Until November 1941, the administration's attention focused on Europe. But at the end of that month, intercepted Japanese messages revealed that an assault in the Pacific was imminent. No one, however, knew where it would come. On December 7, 1941, Japanese planes, launched from aircraft carriers, bombed the naval base at Pearl Harbor in Hawaii, the first attack by a foreign power on American soil since the War of 1812. Pearl Harbor

Pearl Harbor attack

was a complete and devastating surprise. In a few hours, more than 2,000 American servicemen were killed, and 187 aircraft and 18 naval vessels, including 8 battleships, had been destroyed or damaged.

Secretary of Labor Frances Perkins, who saw the president after the attack, remarked that he seemed calm—"his terrible moral problem had been resolved." Terming December 7 "a date which will live in infamy," Roosevelt asked Congress for a declaration of war against Japan. The combined vote in Congress was 477 in favor and 1 against—pacifist Jeanette Rankin of Montana, who had also voted against American entry into World War I. The next day, Germany declared war on the United States. America had finally joined the largest war in human history.

Members of the U.S. Marine Corps, Navy, and Coast Guard taking part in an amphibious assault during the "island hopping" campaign in the Pacific theater of World War II.

The War in the Pacific

World War II has been called a "gross national product war," meaning that its outcome turned on which coalition of combatants could outproduce the other. In retrospect, it appears inevitable that the entry of the United States, with its superior industrial might, would ensure the defeat of the Axis powers. But the first few months of American involvement witnessed an unbroken string of military disasters. Japan in early 1942 conquered Burma (Myanmar) and Siam (Thailand). Japan also took control of the Dutch East Indies (Indonesia), whose extensive oil fields could replace supplies from the United States. And it occupied Guam, the Philippines, and other Pacific islands. At Bataan, in the Philippines, the Japanese forced 78,000 American and Filipino troops to lay down their arms—the largest surrender in American military history. Thousands perished on the ensuing "death march" to a prisoner-of-war camp. At the same time, German submarines sank hundreds of Allied merchant and naval vessels during the Battle of the Atlantic.

Soon, however, the tide of battle began to turn. In May 1942, in the Battle of the Coral Sea, the American navy turned back a Japanese fleet intent on attacking Australia. The following month, it inflicted devastating losses on the Japanese navy in the Battle of Midway Island. These victories allowed American forces to launch the bloody campaigns that

Battle of Midway Island

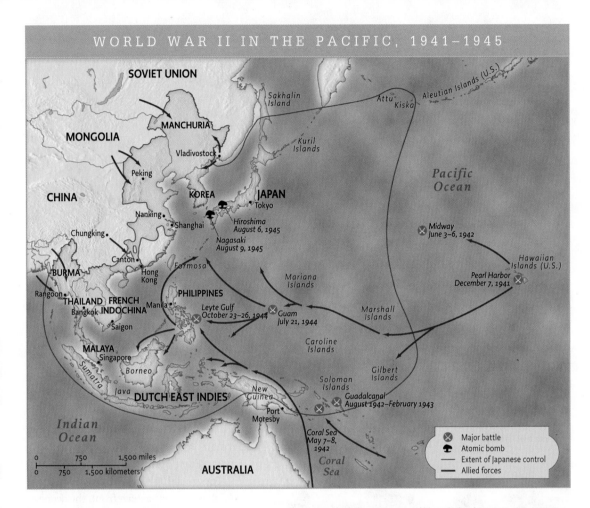

WORLD WAR II IN THE PACIFIC, 1941–1945

one by one drove the Japanese from fortified islands like Guadalcanal and the Solomons in the western Pacific and brought American troops ever closer to Japan.

Although the Japanese navy never fully recovered from its defeats at the Coral Sea and Midway in 1942, it took three more years for American forces to near the Japanese homeland.

The War in Europe

By the spring of 1943, the Allies also gained the upper hand in the Atlantic, as British and American destroyers and planes devastated the German submarine fleet. In July 1943, American and British forces invaded Sicily, beginning the liberation of Italy. A popular uprising in Rome overthrew the Mussolini government, whereupon Germany occupied most of the country. Fighting there raged throughout 1944.

Ben Hurwitz, a soldier from New York City who fought in North Africa and Italy during World War II, made numerous sketches of his experiences. Here American troops pass a wrecked German tank in southern Italy in June 1944.

German prisoners of war guarded by an American soldier shortly after D-Day in June 1944. By this time, the Germans were drafting very young men into their armies.

The major involvement of American troops in Europe did not begin until June 6, 1944. On that date, known as **D-Day**, nearly 200,000 American, British, and Canadian soldiers under the command of General Dwight D. Eisenhower landed in Normandy in northwestern France. More than a million troops followed them ashore in the next few weeks, in the most massive sea–land operation in history. After fierce fighting, German armies retreated eastward. By August, Paris had been liberated.

The crucial fighting in Europe, however, took place on the eastern front, the scene of an epic struggle between Germany and the Soviet Union. More than 3 million German soldiers took part in the 1941 invasion. After sweeping through western Russia, German armies in August 1942 launched a siege of Stalingrad, a city located deep inside Russia on the Volga River. This proved to be a catastrophic mistake. Bolstered by an influx of military supplies from the United States, the Russians surrounded the German troops and forced them to surrender in January 1943. Stalingrad marked the turning point of the European war.

WORLD WAR II IN EUROPE, 1942–1945

Most of the land fighting in Europe during World War II took place on the eastern front between the German and Soviet armies.

Of 13.6 million German casualties in World War II, 10 million came on the Russian front. They were only part of the war's vast toll in human lives. Millions of Poles and at least 20 million Russians, probably many more, perished—not only soldiers but civilian victims of starvation, disease, and massacres by German soldiers. After his armies had penetrated eastern Europe in 1941, moreover, Hitler embarked on the "final solution"—the mass extermination of "undesirable" peoples—Slavs, gypsies, homosexuals, and, above all, Jews. By 1945, 6 million Jewish men, women, and children had died in Nazi death camps. What came to be called the **Holocaust** was the horrifying culmination of the Nazi belief that Germans constituted a "master race" destined to rule the world.

Hitler's "final solution"

THE HOME FRONT

Mobilizing for War

At home, World War II transformed the role of the national government. FDR created federal agencies like the War Production Board, the War Manpower Commission, and the Office of Price Administration to regulate the allocation of labor, control the shipping industry, establish manufacturing quotas, and fix wages, prices, and rents. The number of federal workers rose from 1 million to 4 million, helping to push the unemployment rate down from 14 percent in 1940 to 2 percent three years later.

A list of jobs available in Detroit in July 1941 illustrates how war-related production ended the Great Depression even before the United States entered the conflict.

The government built housing for war workers and forced civilian industries to retool for war production. Michigan's auto factories now turned out trucks, tanks, and jeeps for the army. The gross national product rose from $91 billion to $214 billion during the war, and the federal government's expenditures amounted to twice the combined total of the previous 150 years. The government marketed billions of dollars worth of war bonds, increased taxes, and began the practice of withholding income tax directly from weekly paychecks.

Business and the War

Americans marveled at the achievements of wartime manufacturing. Thousands of aircraft, 100,000 armored vehicles, and 2.5 million trucks rolled off American assembly lines, and entirely new products like synthetic rubber replaced natural resources now controlled by Japan. Government-sponsored scientific research perfected inventions like radar, jet engines, and early computers that helped to win the war and would have a large impact on postwar life. These accomplishments not only made it possible to win a two-front war but also helped to restore the reputation of business and businessmen, which had reached a low point during the Depression.

Wartime technology

Federal funds reinvigorated established manufacturing areas and created entirely new industrial centers. World War II saw the West Coast emerge as a focus of military-industrial production. The government invested billions of dollars in the shipyards of Seattle, Portland, and San Francisco and in the steel plants and aircraft factories of southern California. By the war's end, California had received one-tenth of all federal spending. Nearly 2 million Americans moved to California for jobs in defense-related industries, and millions more passed through for military training and embarkation to the Pacific war.

War production in the West

M-5 tanks on the assembly line at a Detroit Cadillac plant, in a 1942 photograph. During the war, General Motors and other automakers produced vehicles for the armed forces rather than cars for consumers.

TABLE 22.1 Labor Union Membership	
YEAR	NUMBER OF MEMBERS
1933	2,857,000
1934	3,728,000
1935	3,753,000
1936	4,107,000
1937	5,780,000
1938	8,265,000
1939	8,980,000
1940	8,944,000
1941	10,489,000
1942	10,762,000
1943	13,642,000
1944	14,621,000
1945	14,796,000

In the South, the combination of rural out-migration and government investment in military-related factories and shipyards hastened a shift from agricultural to industrial employment. The South remained very poor when the war ended. Much of its rural population still lived in small wooden shacks with no indoor plumbing.

Labor in Wartime

During the war, labor entered a three-sided arrangement with government and business that allowed union membership to soar to unprecedented levels. In order to secure industrial peace and stabilize war production, the federal government forced reluctant employers to recognize unions. In 1944, when Montgomery Ward, the large mail-order company, defied a pro-union order, the army seized its headquarters and physically evicted its president. For their part, union leaders agreed not to strike.

By 1945, union membership stood at nearly 15 million, one-third of the non-farm labor force and the highest proportion in American history. But if labor became a partner in government, it was very much a junior partner. Congress continued to be dominated by a conservative alliance of Republicans and southern Democrats. Despite the "no-strike" pledge, 1943 and 1944 witnessed numerous brief walkouts in which workers protested the increasing speed of assembly-line production and the disparity between wages frozen by government order and expanding corporate profits.

Fighting for the Four Freedoms

The Good War

Previous conflicts, including the Mexican War and World War I, had deeply divided American society. In contrast, World War II came to be remembered as the Good War, a time of national unity in pursuit of indisputably noble goals. But all wars require the mobilization of patriotic public opinion. By 1940, "To sell *goods*, we must sell *words*" had become a motto of advertisers. Foremost among the words that helped to "sell" World War II was "freedom."

Talk of freedom pervaded wartime America. In 1941, the administration celebrated with considerable fanfare the 150th anniversary of the Bill of Rights (the first ten amendments to the Constitution). FDR described their protections against tyrannical government as defining characteristics of American life, central to the rights of "free men and free women."

The "most ambiguous" of the Four Freedoms, *Fortune* magazine remarked, was freedom from want. Yet this "great inspiring phrase," as a Pennsylvania steelworker put it in a letter to the president, seemed to strike the deepest chord in a nation just emerging from the Depression. Roosevelt initially meant it to refer to the elimination of barriers to international trade. But he quickly came to link freedom from want to an economic goal more relevant to the average citizen—protecting the future "standard of living of the American worker and farmer" by guaranteeing that the Depression would not resume after the war. This, he declared, would bring "real freedom for the common man."

The Fifth Freedom

Under the watchful eye of the War Advertising Council, private companies joined in the campaign to promote wartime patriotism, while positioning themselves and their brand names for the postwar world. Alongside advertisements urging Americans to purchase war bonds, guard against revealing military secrets, and grow "victory gardens" to allow food to be sent to the army, the war witnessed a burst of messages marketing

In this recruitment poster for the Boy Scouts, a svelte Miss Liberty prominently displays the Bill of Rights, widely celebrated during World War II as the centerpiece of American freedom.

In this advertisement by the Liberty Motors and Engineering Corporation, published in the February 1944 issue of *Fortune*, Uncle Sam offers the Fifth Freedom—"free enterprise"—to war-devastated Europe. To spread its message, the company offered free enlargements of its ad.

advertisers' definition of freedom. Without directly criticizing Roosevelt, they repeatedly suggested that he had overlooked a fifth freedom. The National Association of Manufacturers and individual companies bombarded Americans with press releases, radio programs, and advertisements attributing the amazing feats of wartime production to "free enterprise."

With the memory of the Depression still very much alive, businessmen predicted a postwar world filled with consumer goods, with "freedom of choice" among abundant possibilities assured if only private enterprise were liberated from government controls.

A female lathe operator in a Texas plant that produced transport planes.

Women at War

Unlike the lathe operator in the above illustration, the woman operating industrial machinery on the cover of the September 1942 issue of McCall's magazine remains glamorous, with makeup in place and hair unruffled.

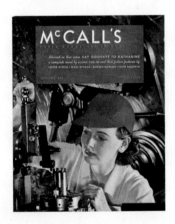

During the war, the nation engaged in an unprecedented mobilization of "womanpower" to fill industrial jobs vacated by men. Hollywood films glorified the independent woman, and private advertising celebrated the achievements of **Rosie the Riveter**, the female industrial laborer depicted as muscular and self-reliant in Norman Rockwell's famous magazine cover. With 15 million men in the armed forces, women in 1944 made up more than one-third of the civilian labor force, and 350,000 served in auxiliary military units.

Even though most women workers still labored in clerical and service jobs, new opportunities suddenly opened in industrial, professional, and government positions previously restricted to men. On the West Coast, one-third of the workers in aircraft manufacturing and shipbuilding were women. For the first time in history, married women in their thirties outnumbered the young and single among female workers. Women forced unions like the United Auto Workers to confront issues like equal pay for equal work, maternity leave, and child-care facilities for working mothers. Having enjoyed what one wartime worker called "a taste of freedom"—doing "men's" jobs for men's wages and, sometimes, engaging in sexual activity while unmarried—many women hoped to remain in the labor force once peace returned.

"We as a nation," proclaimed one magazine article, "must change our basic attitude toward the work of women." But change proved difficult.

The government, employers, and unions depicted work as a temporary necessity, not an expansion of women's freedom. When the war ended, most female war workers, especially those in better-paying industrial employment, did indeed lose their jobs.

Despite the upsurge in the number of working women, the advertisers' "world of tomorrow" rested on a vision of family-centered prosperity. Advertisements portrayed working women dreaming of their boyfriends in the army and emphasized that with the proper makeup, women could labor in a factory and remain attractive to men. Men in the army seem to have assumed that they would return home to resume traditional family life.

This is America... ...where the family is a sacred institution. Where children love, honor and respect their parents ...where a man's home is his castle * This is your America ... *Keep it Free!*

VISIONS OF POSTWAR FREEDOM

Toward an American Century

The prospect of an affluent future provided a point of unity between New Dealers and conservatives, business and labor. And the promise of prosperity to some extent united two of the most celebrated blueprints for the postwar world. One was *The American Century*, the publisher Henry Luce's 1941 effort to mobilize the American people both for the coming war and for an era of postwar world leadership. Americans, Luce's book insisted, must embrace the role history had thrust on them as the "dominant power in the world." After the war, American power and American values would underpin a previously unimaginable prosperity—"the abundant life," Luce called it—produced by "free economic enterprise."

Luce's essay anticipated important aspects of the postwar world. But its bombastic rhetoric and a title easily interpreted as a call for an American imperialism aroused immediate opposition among liberals and the left. Henry Wallace offered their response in "The Price of Free World Victory," an address delivered in May 1942 to the Free World Association. Wallace, secretary of agriculture during the 1930s, had replaced Vice President John Nance Garner as Roosevelt's running mate in 1940. In contrast to Luce's American Century, a world of business dominance no less than of American power, Wallace predicted that the war would usher in a "century of the common man." Governments acting to "humanize" capitalism and redistribute economic resources would eliminate hunger, illiteracy, and poverty.

Despite the new independence enjoyed by millions of women, propaganda posters during World War II emphasized the male-dominated family as an essential element of American freedom.

Luce's The American Century

Henry Wallace

Luce and Wallace had one thing in common—a new conception of America's role in the world, tied to continued international involvement, the promise of economic abundance, and the idea that the American experience should serve as a model for all other nations.

"The Way of Life of Free Men"

Even as Congress moved to dismantle parts of the New Deal, liberal Democrats and their left-wing allies unveiled plans for a postwar economic policy that would allow all Americans to enjoy freedom from want. In 1942 and 1943, the reports of the National Resources Planning

NRPB

Board (NRPB) offered a blueprint for a peacetime economy based on full employment, an expanded welfare state, and a widely shared American standard of living. The board called for a "new bill of rights" that would include all Americans in an expanded Social Security system and guarantee access to education, health care, adequate housing, and jobs for able-bodied adults. The NRPB's plan for a "full-employment economy" with a "fair distribution of income," said *The Nation*, embodied "the way of life of free men."

Mindful that public-opinion polls showed a large majority of Americans favoring a guarantee of employment for those who could not

An Economic Bill of Rights

find work, the president in 1944 called for an "Economic Bill of Rights." The original Bill of Rights restricted the power of government in the name of liberty. FDR proposed to expand its power in order to secure full employment, an adequate income, medical care, education, and a decent home for all Americans.

Already ill and preoccupied with the war, Roosevelt spoke only occasionally of the Economic Bill of Rights during the 1944 presidential campaign. The replacement of Vice President Henry Wallace by Harry S. Truman, then a little-known senator from Missouri, suggested that the president did not intend to do battle with Congress over social policy. Congress did not enact the Economic Bill of Rights. But in 1944, it extended to the millions of returning veterans an array of benefits, including unemployment pay, scholarships for further education, low-cost mortgage loans, pensions, and job training. The Servicemen's

GI Bill

Readjustment Act, or **GI Bill of Rights**, was one of the farthest-reaching pieces of social legislation in American history. Aimed at rewarding members of the armed forces for their service and preventing the widespread unemployment and economic disruption that had followed World War I, it profoundly shaped postwar society. By 1946, more than 1 million veterans were attending college under its provisions, making up half of total college enrollment. Almost 4 million would receive home mortgages, spurring the postwar suburban housing boom.

The Road to Serfdom

The Road to Serfdom (1944), a surprise best-seller by Friedrich A. Hayek, a previously obscure Austrian-born economist, claimed that even the best-intentioned government efforts to direct the economy posed a threat to individual liberty. Coming at a time when the miracles of war production had reinvigorated belief in the virtues of capitalism, and with the confrontation with Nazism highlighting the danger of merging economic and political power, Hayek offered a new intellectual justification for opponents of active government. In a complex economy, he insisted, no single person or group of experts could possibly possess enough knowledge to direct economic activity intelligently. A free market, he wrote, mobilizes the fragmented and partial knowledge scattered throughout society far more effectively than a planned economy.

Friedrich A. Hayek and laissez-faire economics

By equating fascism, socialism, and the New Deal and by identifying economic planning with a loss of freedom, he helped lay the foundation for the rise of modern conservatism and a revival of laissez-faire economic thought. As the war drew to a close, the stage was set for a renewed battle over the government's proper role in society and the economy, and the social conditions of American freedom.

THE AMERICAN DILEMMA

In this patriotic war poster the words of Abraham Lincoln are linked to the struggle against Nazi tyranny.

The unprecedented attention to freedom as the defining characteristic of American life had implications that went far beyond wartime mobilization. The struggle against Nazi tyranny and its theory of a master race discredited ethnic and racial inequality. A pluralist vision of American society now became part of official rhetoric. What set the United States apart from its wartime foes, the government insisted, was not only dedication to the ideals of the Four Freedoms but also the principle that Americans of all races, religions, and national origins could enjoy those freedoms equally. Racism was the enemy's philosophy; Americanism rested on toleration of diversity and equality for all. By the end of the war, the new immigrant groups had been fully accepted as loyal ethnic Americans, rather than members of distinct and inferior "races." And the contradiction between the principle of equal freedom and the actual status of blacks had come to the forefront of national life.

Arthur Poinier's cartoon for the *Detroit Free Press*, June 19, 1941, illustrates how, during World War II, white ethnics (of British, German, Irish, French, Polish, Italian and Scandinavian descent) were incorporated within the boundaries of American freedom.

The persistence of prejudice

Patriotic Assimilation

Among other things, World War II created a vast melting pot, especially for European immigrants and their children. Millions of Americans moved out of urban ethnic neighborhoods and isolated rural enclaves into the army and industrial plants, where they came into contact with people of very different backgrounds. What one historian has called their **"patriotic assimilation"** differed sharply from the forced Americanization of World War I.

Horrified by the uses to which the Nazis put the idea of inborn racial difference, biological and social scientists abandoned belief in a link among race, culture, and intelligence, an idea only recently central to their disciplines. Ruth Benedict's *Races and Racism* (1942) described racism as "a travesty of scientific knowledge." By the war's end, racism and nativism had been stripped of intellectual respectability, at least outside the South, and were viewed as psychological disorders.

Intolerance, of course, hardly disappeared from American life. Many business and government circles still excluded Jews. Along with the fact that early reports of the Holocaust were too terrible to be believed, anti-Semitism contributed to the government's unwillingness to allow more than a handful of European Jews (21,000 during the course of the war) to find refuge in the United States. Roosevelt himself learned during the war of the extent of Hitler's "final solution" to the Jewish presence in Europe. But he failed to authorize air strikes that might have destroyed German death camps.

The *Bracero* Program

The war had a far more ambiguous meaning for non-white groups than for whites. On the eve of Pearl Harbor, racial barriers remained deeply entrenched in American life. Southern blacks were still trapped in a rigid system of segregation. Asians could not emigrate to the United States or become naturalized citizens. Most American Indians still lived on reservations in dismal poverty.

Mexican contract workers

The war set in motion changes that would reverberate in the postwar years. Under the ***bracero* program** agreed to by the Mexican and American governments in 1942 (the name derives from *brazo*, the Spanish word for arm), tens of thousands of contract laborers crossed into the United States to take up jobs as domestic and agricultural workers. Initially designed as a temporary response to the wartime labor shortage, the program lasted until 1964. During that period, more than 4.5 million Mexicans entered the

United States under labor contracts (while a slightly larger number were arrested for illegal entry by the Border Patrol).

Although the *bracero* program reinforced the status of immigrants from Mexico as an unskilled labor force, wartime employment opened new opportunities for second-generation Mexican-Americans. Hundreds of thousands of men and women emerged from ethnic neighborhoods, or *barrios*, to work in defense industries and serve in the army (where, unlike blacks, they fought alongside whites). Contact with other groups led many to learn English and sparked a rise in interethnic marriages.

New opportunities for Mexican-Americans

The **"zoot suit" riots** of 1943, in which club-wielding sailors and policemen attacked Mexican-American youths wearing flamboyant clothing on the streets of Los Angeles, illustrated the limits of wartime tolerance. But the contrast between the war's rhetoric of freedom and pluralism and the reality of continued discrimination inspired a heightened consciousness of civil rights. For example, Mexican-Americans brought complaints of discrimination before the Fair Employment Practices Commission (FEPC) to fight the practice in the Southwest of confining them to the lowest-paid work or paying them lower wages than white workers doing the same jobs. "Our Latin American boys," complained one activist, "are not segregated at the front line. . . . They are dying that democracy may live." Perhaps half a million Mexican-American men and women served in the armed forces.

Indians during the War

The war also brought many American Indians closer to the mainstream of American life. Some 25,000 served in the army (including the famous Navajo "code-talkers," who transmitted messages in their complex native language, which the Japanese could not decipher). Insisting that the United States lacked the authority to draft Indian men into the army, the Iroquois issued their own declaration of war against the Axis powers. Tens of thousands of Indians left reservations for jobs in war industries. Exposed for the first time to urban life and industrial society, many chose not to return to the reservations after the war ended. (Indeed, the reservations did not share in wartime prosperity.) Some Indian veterans took advantage of the GI Bill to attend college after the war, an opportunity that had been available to very few Indians previously.

The Navajo "code-talkers"

Asian-Americans in Wartime

Asian-Americans' war experience was paradoxical. More than 50,000—the children of immigrants from China, Japan, Korea, and the

What are YOU going to do about it?

5200 Yank Prisoners Killed by Jap Torture In Philippines; Cruel 'March of Death' Described

STAY ON THE JOB UNTIL EVERY MURDERING JAP IS WIPED OUT!

Wartime propaganda in the United States sought to inspire hatred against the Pacific foe. This poster, issued by the U.S. Army, recalls the Bataan death march in the Philippines.

Philippines—fought in the army, mostly in all-Asian units. With China an ally in the Pacific war, Congress in 1943 ended decades of complete exclusion by establishing a nationality quota for Chinese immigrants. The annual limit of 105 hardly suggested a desire for a large-scale influx. But the image of the Chinese as gallant fighters defending their country against Japanese aggression called into question long-standing racial stereotypes.

The experience of Japanese-Americans was far different. Both sides saw the Pacific war as a race war. Japanese propaganda depicted Americans as a self-indulgent people contaminated by ethnic and racial diversity as opposed to the racially "pure" Japanese. In the United States, long-standing prejudices and the shocking attack on Pearl Harbor combined to produce an unprecedented hatred of Japan. Government propaganda and war films portrayed the Japanese foe as rats, dogs, gorillas, and snakes—bestial and subhuman. They blamed Japanese aggression on a violent racial or national character, not, as in the case of Germany and Italy, on tyrannical rulers.

About 70 percent of Japanese-Americans in the continental United States lived in California, where they dominated vegetable farming in the Los Angeles area. One-third were first-generation immigrants, or *issei*, but a substantial majority were *nisei*—American-born, and therefore citizens. Many of the latter spoke only English, had never been to Japan, and had tried to assimilate despite prevailing prejudice. The government bent over backward to include German-Americans and Italian-Americans in the war effort. It ordered the arrest of only a handful of the more than 800,000 German and Italian nationals in the United States when the war began. But it viewed every person of Japanese ethnicity as a potential spy.

Japanese-American Internment

Inspired by exaggerated fears of a Japanese invasion of the West Coast and pressured by whites who saw an opportunity to gain possession of Japanese-American property, the military persuaded FDR to issue **Executive Order 9066**. Promulgated in February 1942, this ordered the relocation of all persons of Japanese descent from the West Coast. That spring and summer, authorities removed more than 110,000 men, women, and children—nearly two-thirds of them American citizens—to camps far from their homes. The order did not apply to persons of Japanese descent living in Hawaii, where they made up nearly 40 percent of the population. Despite Hawaii's vulnerability, its economy could not function without Japanese-American labor.

Internment camps

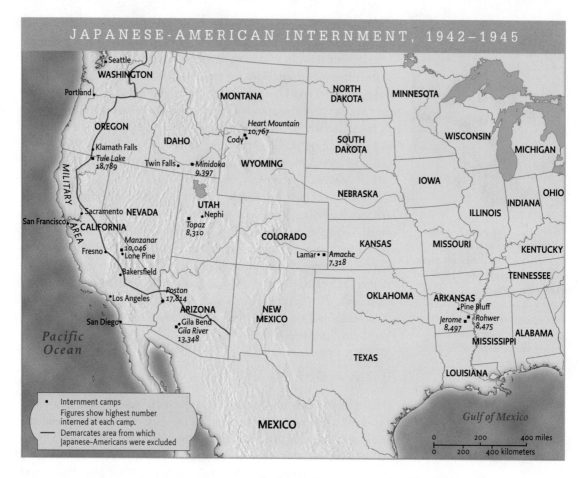

JAPANESE-AMERICAN INTERNMENT, 1942–1945

Seattle
WASHINGTON
Portland
MONTANA
NORTH DAKOTA
MINNESOTA
OREGON
Heart Mountain
10,767
Cody
IDAHO
SOUTH DAKOTA
WISCONSIN
MICHIGAN
Klamath Falls
Tule Lake
18,789
Twin Falls
Minidoka
9,397
WYOMING
IOWA
OHIO
MILITARY
Sacramento NEVADA
UTAH
Nephi
NEBRASKA
INDIANA
San Francisco
CALIFORNIA
AREA
Topaz
8,310
ILLINOIS
Manzanar
10,046
Lone Pine
COLORADO
KANSAS
MISSOURI
KENTUCKY
Fresno
Lamar
Amache
7,318
Bakersfield
TENNESSEE
Poston
17,814
Los Angeles
OKLAHOMA
ARKANSAS
Pine Bluff
ARIZONA
NEW MEXICO
San Diego
Gila Bend
Gila River
13,348
Jerome
8,497
Rohwer
8,475
ALABAMA
MISSISSIPPI
Pacific Ocean
TEXAS
LOUISIANA
MEXICO
Gulf of Mexico

- Internment camps
  Figures show highest number interned at each camp.
— Demarcates area from which Japanese-Americans were excluded

0   200   400 miles
0   200   400 kilometers

The internees were subjected to a quasi-military discipline in the camps. Living in former horse stables, makeshift shacks, or barracks behind barbed-wire fences, they were awakened for roll call at 6:45 each morning and ate their meals (which rarely involved the Japanese cooking to which they were accustomed) in giant mess halls. Nonetheless, the internees did their best to create an atmosphere of home, decorating their accommodations with pictures, flowers, and curtains, planting vegetable gardens, and setting up activities like sports clubs and art classes for themselves.

Internment revealed how easily war can undermine basic freedoms. There were no court hearings, no due process, and no writs of habeas corpus. One searches the wartime record in vain for public protests among non-Japanese against the gravest violation of civil liberties since the end of slavery.

More than 100,000 Japanese-Americans—the majority American citizens—were forcibly moved from their homes to internment camps during World War II.

The courts refused to intervene. In 1944, in *Korematsu v. United States*, the Supreme Court denied the appeal of Fred Korematsu, a Japanese-American citizen who had been arrested for refusing to present himself for internment. Speaking for a 6-3 majority, Justice Hugo Black, usually an avid defender of civil liberties, upheld the legality of the internment policy, insisting that an order applying only to persons of Japanese descent was not based on race. The Court has never overturned the *Korematsu* decision. As Justice Robert H. Jackson warned in his dissent, it "lies about like a loaded weapon ready for the hand of any authority that can bring forward a plausible claim" of national security.

Fumiko Hayashida holds her thirteen-month-old daughter, while waiting for relocation to an internment camp. Both wear baggage tags, as if they were pieces of luggage. This photo, taken by a journalist for the *Seattle Post-Intelligencer*, came to symbolize the entire internment experience. Ms. Hayashida celebrated her 100th birthday in 2011.

The government established a loyalty oath program, expecting Japanese-Americans to swear allegiance to the government that had imprisoned them and to enlist in the army. Some young men refused, and about 200 were sent to prison for resisting the draft. But 20,000 Japanese-Americans joined the armed forces from the camps, along with another 13,000 from Hawaii. A long campaign for acknowledgment of the injustice done to Japanese-Americans followed the end of the war. In 1988, Congress apologized for internment and provided $20,000 in compensation to each surviving victim.

Blacks and the War

Although the treatment of Japanese-Americans revealed the stubborn hold of racism in American life, the wartime message of freedom portended a major transformation in the status of blacks. Nazi Germany cited American practices as proof of its own race policies. Washington remained a rigidly segregated city, and the Red Cross refused to mix blood from blacks and whites in its blood banks (thereby, critics charged, in effect accepting Nazi race theories). Charles Drew, the black scientist who pioneered the techniques of storing and shipping blood plasma—a development of immense importance to the treatment of wounded soldiers—protested bitterly against this policy, pointing out that it had no scientific basis.

Segregation during wartime

Second Great Migration

The war spurred a movement of black population from the rural South to the cities of the North and West that dwarfed the Great Migration of World War I and the 1920s. About 700,000 black migrants poured out of the South on what they called "liberty trains," seeking jobs in the industrial heartland. They encountered sometimes violent hostility, nowhere more so than in Detroit, where angry white residents forced authorities to evict black tenants from a new housing project. In 1943, a fight at a Detroit city park spiraled into a race riot that left thirty-four persons dead, and a "hate strike" of 20,000 workers protested the upgrading of black employees in a plant manufacturing aircraft engines.

Blacks and Military Service

When World War II began, the air force and marines had no black members. The army restricted the number of black enlistees and contained only five black officers, three of them chaplains. The navy accepted blacks only as waiters and cooks.

During the war, more than 1 million blacks served in the armed forces. They did so in segregated units, largely confined to construction, transport, and other noncombat tasks. Black soldiers sometimes had to give up their seats on railroad cars to accommodate Nazi prisoners of war.

When southern black veterans returned home and sought benefits through the GI Bill, they encountered even more evidence of racial discrimination. On the surface, the GI Bill contained no racial differentiation in offering benefits like health care, college tuition assistance, job training, and loans to start a business or purchase a farm. But local authorities who administered its provisions allowed southern black veterans to use its education benefits only at segregated colleges, limited their job training to unskilled work and low-wage service jobs, and limited loans for farm purchase to white veterans.

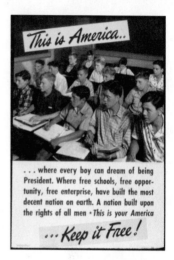

... where every boy can dream of being President. Where free schools, free opportunity, free enterprise, have built the most decent nation on earth. A nation built upon the rights of all men • *This is your America*

... *Keep it Free!*

Another *This Is America* propaganda poster emphasizes the American dream of equal opportunity for all. All the children in the classroom, however, are white.

Birth of the Civil Rights Movement

The war years witnessed the birth of the modern civil rights movement. Angered by the almost complete exclusion of African-Americans from jobs in the rapidly expanding war industries (of 100,000 aircraft workers in 1940, fewer than 300 were blacks), the black labor leader A. Philip Randolph in July 1941 called for a March on Washington. His demands included access to defense employment, an end to segregation, and a national antilynching law.

Randolph's March on Washington

The prospect of thousands of angry blacks descending on Washington, remarked one official, "scared the government half to death." To persuade Randolph to call off the march, Roosevelt issued **Executive Order 8802**, which banned discrimination in defense jobs and established a Fair Employment Practices Commission (FEPC) to monitor compliance. The first federal agency since Reconstruction to campaign for equal opportunity for black Americans, the FEPC played an important role in obtaining jobs for black workers in industrial plants and shipyards. By 1944, more

FEPC

than 1 million blacks, 300,000 of them women, held manufacturing jobs. ("My sister always said that Hitler was the one that got us out of the white folks' kitchen," recalled one black woman.)

The Double-V

CORE

During the war, NAACP membership grew from 50,000 to nearly 500,000. The Congress of Racial Equality (CORE), founded by an interracial group of pacifists in 1942, held sit-ins in northern cities to integrate restaurants and theaters. In February of that year, the *Pittsburgh Courier* coined the phrase that came to symbolize black attitudes during the war—the "**double-V**." Victory over Germany and Japan, it insisted, must be accompanied by victory over segregation at home. Whereas the Roosevelt administration and the white press saw the war as an expression of American ideals, black newspapers pointed to the gap between those ideals and reality.

Surveying wartime public opinion, a political scientist concluded that "symbols of national solidarity" had very different meanings to white and black Americans. To blacks, freedom from fear meant, among other things, an end to lynching, and freedom from want included doing away with "discrimination in getting jobs." If, in whites' eyes, freedom was a "possession to be defended," he observed, to blacks and other racial minorities it remained a "goal to be achieved."

This is the Enemy, a 1942 poster by Victor Ancona and Karl Koehler, suggests a connection between Nazism abroad and lynching at home.

The War and Race

During the war, a broad political coalition centered on the left but reaching well beyond it called for an end to racial inequality in America. The NAACP and American Jewish Congress cooperated closely in advocating laws to ban discrimination in employment and housing. Despite considerable resistance from rank-and-file white workers, CIO unions, especially those with strong left-liberal and communist influence, made significant efforts to organize black workers and win them access to skilled positions.

The new black militancy alarmed southern politicians. The "war emergency," insisted Governor Frank Dixon of Alabama, "should not be used as a pretext to bring about the abolition of the color line." Even as the war gave birth to the modern civil rights movement, it also planted the seeds for the South's "massive resistance" to desegregation during the 1950s.

Although progress was slow, it was measurable. The National War Labor Board banned racial wage differentials. In *Smith v. Allwright* (1944),

Paul Robeson, the black actor, singer, and battler for civil rights, leading Oakland dockworkers in singing the national anthem in 1942. World War II gave a significant boost to the vision, shared by Robeson and others on the left, of an America based on genuine equality.

the Supreme Court outlawed all-white primaries, one of the mechanisms by which southern states deprived blacks of political rights. In the same year, the navy began assigning small numbers of black sailors to previously all-white ships. In the final months of the war, it ended segregation altogether, and the army established a few combat units that included black and white soldiers.

Progress on race

An American Dilemma

No event reflected the new concern with the status of black Americans more than the publication in 1944 of *An American Dilemma*, a sprawling account of the country's racial past, present, and future written by the Swedish social scientist Gunnar Myrdal. The book offered an uncompromising portrait of how deeply racism was entrenched in law, politics, economics, and social behavior. But Myrdal combined this sobering analysis with admiration for what he called the American Creed—belief in equality, justice, equal opportunity, and freedom. He concluded that "there is bound to be a redefinition of the Negro's status as a result of this War."

The American Creed

Myrdal's notion of a conflict between American values and American racial policies was hardly new—Frederick Douglass and W. E. B. Du Bois had said much the same thing. But in the context of a worldwide struggle against Nazism and rising black demands for equality at home, his book struck a chord. It identified a serious national problem and seemed to offer

VOICES OF FREEDOM

From Henry R. Luce, *The American Century* (1941)

Even before the United States entered World War II, some Americans were thinking of a postwar world in which the United States would exert its influence throughout the globe. One influential call for Americans to accept the burden of world leadership was a short book by Henry R. Luce, the publisher of *Life* and *Time* magazines.

In the field of national policy, the fundamental trouble with America has been, and is, that whereas their nation became in the 20th Century the most powerful and the most vital nation in the world, nevertheless Americans were unable to accommodate themselves spiritually and practically to that fact. Hence they have failed to play their part as a world power—a failure which has had disastrous consequences for themselves and for all mankind. And the cure is this: to accept wholeheartedly our duty and our opportunity as the most powerful and vital nation in the world and in consequence to exert upon the world the full impact of our influence, for such purposes as we see fit and by such means as we see fit. . . .

Our world of 2,000,000,000 human beings is for the first time in history one world, fundamentally indivisible. . . . Our world, again for the first time in human history, is capable of producing all the material needs of the entire human family. . . . The world of the 20th Century, if it is to come to life in any nobility of health and vigor, must be to a significant degree an American Century. . . .

In postulating the indivisibility of the contemporary world, one does not necessarily imagine that anything like a world state—a parliament of men—must be brought about in this century. Nor need we assume that war can be abolished. . . . Large sections of the human family may be effectively organized into opposition to one another. Tyrannies may require a large amount of living space. But Freedom requires and will require far greater living space than Tyranny. . . . Justice will come near to losing all meaning in the minds of men unless Justice can have approximately the same fundamental meanings in many lands and among many peoples. . . .

As to the . . . promise of adequate production for all mankind, the "more abundant life," be it noted that this is characteristically an American promise. . . . What we must insist on is that the abundant life is predicated on Freedom. . . . Without Freedom, there will be no abundant life. With Freedom, there can be.

And finally there is the belief—shared let us remember by most men living—that the 20th Century must be to a significant degree an American Century. . . . As America enters dynamically upon the world scene, we need most of all to seek and to bring forth a vision of America as a world power and to bring forth a vision . . . which will guide us to the authentic creation of the 20th Century—our Century.

From Charles H. Wesley, "The Negro Has Always Wanted the Four Freedoms," in *What the Negro Wants* (1944)

In 1944, the University of North Carolina Press published *What the Negro Wants*, a book of essays by fourteen prominent black leaders. Virtually every contributor called for the right to vote in the South, the dismantling of segregation, and access to the "American standard of living." Several essays also linked the black struggle for racial justice with movements against European imperialism in Africa and Asia. When he read the manuscript, W. T. Couch, the director of the press, was stunned. "If this is what the Negro wants," he told the book's editor, "nothing could be clearer than what he needs, and needs most urgently, is to revise his wants." In this excerpt, the historian Charles H. Wesley explains that blacks are denied each of the Four Freedoms and also illustrates how the war strengthened black internationalism.

[Negroes] have wanted what other citizens of the United States have wanted. They have wanted freedom and opportunity. They have wanted the pursuit of the life vouchsafed to all citizens of the United States by our own liberty documents. They have wanted freedom of speech, [but] they were supposed to be silently acquiescent in all aspects of their life. . . . They have wanted freedom of religion, for they had been compelled to "steal away to Jesus" . . . in order to worship God as they desired. . . . They have wanted freedom from want. . . . However, the Negro has remained a marginal worker and the competition with white workers has left him in want in many localities of an economically sufficient nation. They have wanted freedom from fear. They have been cowed, browbeaten or beaten, as they have marched through the years of American life. . . .

The Negro wants democracy to begin at home. . . . The future of our democratic life is insecure so long as the hatred, disdain and disparagement of Americans of African ancestry exist. . . .

The Negro wants not only to win the war but also to win the peace. . . . He wants the peace to be free of race and color restrictions, of imperialism and exploitation, and inclusive of the participation of minorities all over the world in their own governments. When it is said that we are fighting for freedom, the Negro asks, "Whose freedom?" Is it the freedom of a peace to exploit, suppress, exclude, debase and restrict colored peoples in India, China, Africa, Malaya in the usual ways? . . . Will Great Britain and the United States specifically omit from the Four Freedoms their minorities and subject peoples? The Negro does not want such a peace.

QUESTIONS

1. *What values does Luce wish America to spread to the rest of the world?*

2. *Why does Wesley believe that black Americans are denied the Four Freedoms?*

3. *Do Luce and Wesley envision different roles for the United States in the post-war world?*

an almost painless path to peaceful change, in which the federal government would take the lead in outlawing discrimination.

Black Internationalism

Black international consciousness

In the nineteenth century, black radicals like David Walker and Martin Delany had sought to link the fate of African-Americans with that of peoples of African descent in other parts of the world, especially the Caribbean and Africa. In the first decades of the twentieth century, this kind of international consciousness was reinvigorated. In a sense, the global imposition of white supremacy brought forth a feeling of racial solidarity across national and geographic lines. At the home of George Padmore, a West Indian labor organizer and editor living in London, black American leaders like W. E. B. Du Bois and Paul Robeson came into contact with future leaders of African independence movements such as Jomo Kenyatta (Kenya), Kwame Nkrumah (Ghana), and Nnamdi Azikiwe (Nigeria).

A global cause

Through these gatherings, Du Bois, Robeson, and others developed an outlook that linked the plight of black Americans with that of people of color worldwide. Freeing Africa from colonial rule, they came to believe, would encourage greater equality at home. World War II stimulated among African-Americans an even greater awareness of the links between racism in the United States and colonialism abroad.

THE END OF THE WAR

As 1945 opened, Allied victory was assured. In December 1944, in a desperate gamble, Hitler launched a surprise counterattack in France that pushed Allied forces back fifty miles, creating a large bulge in their lines. The largest single battle ever fought by the U.S. Army, the Battle of the Bulge produced more than 70,000 American casualties. But by early 1945 the assault had failed.

V-E Day

In March, American troops crossed the Rhine River and entered the industrial heartland of Germany. Hitler took his own life, and shortly afterward Soviet forces occupied Berlin. On May 8, known as V-E Day (for victory in Europe), came the formal end to the war against Germany. In the Pacific, American forces moved ever closer to Japan.

"The Most Terrible Weapon"

Franklin D. Roosevelt defeated Republican nominee Thomas E. Dewey, the governor of New York, to win an unprecedented fourth term in 1944. But FDR did not live to see the Allied victory. He succumbed to a stroke on April 12, 1945. To his successor, Harry S. Truman, fell one of the most momentous decisions ever confronted by an American president— whether to use the atomic bomb against Japan. Truman did not know about the bomb until after he became president. Then, Secretary of War Henry L. Stimson informed him that the United States had secretly developed "the most terrible weapon ever known in human history."

Truman and the atomic bomb

The bomb was a practical realization of the theory of relativity, a rethinking of the laws of physics developed early in the twentieth century by the German scientist Albert Einstein. Energy and matter, Einstein showed, were two forms of the same phenomenon. By using certain forms of uranium, or the man-made element plutonium, scientists could create an atomic reaction that transformed part of the mass into energy. This energy could be harnessed to provide a form of controlled power—or it could be unleashed in a tremendous explosion.

Albert Einstein

In 1940, FDR authorized what came to be known as the **Manhattan Project**, a top-secret program in which American scientists developed an atomic bomb during World War II. The weapon was tested successfully in New Mexico in July 1945.

The Dawn of the Atomic Age

On August 6, 1945, an American plane dropped an atomic bomb that detonated over Hiroshima, Japan—a target chosen because almost alone among major Japanese cities, it had not yet suffered damage. In an instant, nearly every building in the city was destroyed. Of the city's population of 280,000 civilians and 40,000 soldiers, approximately 70,000 died immediately. Because atomic bombs release deadly radiation, the death toll kept rising in the months that followed. By the end of the year, it reached at least 140,000. On August 9, the United States exploded a second bomb over Nagasaki, killing 70,000 persons. On the same day, the Soviet Union declared war on Japan and invaded Manchuria. Within a week, Japan surrendered.

Hiroshima and Nagasaki

Because of the enormous cost in civilian lives—more than twice America's military fatalities in the entire Pacific war—the use of the bomb remains controversial. An American invasion of Japan, some advisers warned Truman, might cost as many as 250,000 American lives. No such invasion was planned to begin, however, until 1946, and considerable evidence had accumulated that Japan was nearing surrender. Japan's economy had been crippled and its fleet destroyed, and it would now have to fight the Soviet Union as well as the United States. Some of the scientists who had worked on the bomb urged Truman to demonstrate its power to international observers. But Truman did not hesitate. The bomb was a weapon, and weapons are created to be used.

The Nature of the War

The dropping of the atomic bombs was the logical culmination of the way World War II had been fought. All wars inflict suffering on non-combatants. But never before had civilian populations been so ruthlessly targeted. Of the estimated 50 million persons who perished during World War II (including 400,000 American soldiers), perhaps 20 million were civilians. Germany had killed millions of members of "inferior races." The Allies carried out deadly air assaults on civilian populations. Early in 1945, the firebombing of Dresden killed some 100,000 people, mostly women, children, and elderly men. On March 9, nearly the same number died in an inferno caused by the bombing of Tokyo.

The war and civilian populations

After the dropping of the atomic bomb on Hiroshima, Japan, the federal government restricted the circulation of images of destruction. But soon after the end of the war, it dispatched photographers to compile a Strategic Bombing Survey to assess the bomb's impact. This photograph, which long remained classified, shows the remains of an elementary school.

Four years of war propaganda had dehumanized the Japanese in American eyes, and few persons criticized Truman's decision in 1945. But public doubts began to surface, especially after John Hersey published *Hiroshima* (1946), a graphic account of the horrors suffered by the civilian population. General Dwight D. Eisenhower, who thought the use of the bomb unnecessary, later wrote, "I hated to see our country be the first to use such a weapon."

Hersey's Hiroshima

Planning the Postwar World

Even as the war raged, a series of meetings between Allied leaders formulated plans for the postwar world. Churchill, Roosevelt, and Soviet chief Josef Stalin met at Tehran, Iran, in 1943, and at Yalta, in the southern Soviet Union, early in 1945, to hammer out agreements. The final "Big Three" conference took place at Potsdam, near Berlin, in July 1945. It involved Stalin, Truman, and Churchill (replaced midway in the talks by Clement Attlee, who became prime minister when his Labour Party swept the British elections). At Potsdam, the Allied leaders established a military administration for Germany and agreed to place top Nazi leaders on trial for war crimes.

The "Big Three" conferences

Relations among the three Allies were often uneasy, as each maneuvered to maximize its postwar power. Neither Britain nor the United States trusted Stalin. But since Stalin's troops had won the war on the eastern front, it was difficult to resist his demand that eastern Europe become a Soviet sphere of influence (a region whose governments can be counted on to do a great power's bidding).

Yalta and Bretton Woods

At Yalta, Roosevelt and Churchill entered only a mild protest against Soviet plans to retain control of the Baltic states (Estonia, Latvia, and Lithuania) and a large part of eastern Poland, in effect restoring Russia's pre–World War I western borders. Stalin agreed to enter the war against Japan later in 1945 and to allow "free and unfettered elections" in Poland, but he was intent on establishing communism in eastern Europe. Yalta saw the high-water mark of wartime American–Soviet cooperation. But it planted seeds of conflict, since the participants soon disagreed over the fate of eastern Europe.

The Big Three—Stalin, Roosevelt, and Churchill—at their first meeting, in Tehran, Iran, in 1943, where they discussed the opening of a second front against Germany in western Europe.

Tension also existed between Britain and the United States. Churchill rejected American pressure to place India and other British colonies on the road to independence. He concluded private deals with Stalin to divide southern and eastern Europe into British and Soviet spheres of influence.

Shaping the postwar economic order

Britain also resisted, unsuccessfully, American efforts to reshape and dominate the postwar economic order. A meeting of representatives of forty-five nations at **Bretton Woods**, New Hampshire, in July 1944 replaced the British pound with the dollar as the main currency for international transactions. The conference also created two American-dominated financial institutions. The World Bank would provide money to developing countries and to help rebuild Europe. The International Monetary Fund would work to prevent governments from devaluing their currencies to gain an advantage in international trade, as many had done during the Depression. Both of these institutions, American leaders believed, would encourage free trade and the growth of the world economy, an emphasis that remains central to American foreign policy to this day.

The United Nations

Early in the war, the Allies also agreed to establish a successor to the League of Nations. In a 1944 conference at Dumbarton Oaks, near Washington, D.C., they developed the structure of the **United Nations** (UN). There would be a General Assembly—essentially a forum for discussion where each member enjoyed an equal voice—and a Security Council responsible for maintaining world peace. Along with six rotating members, the Council would have five permanent ones—Britain, China, France, the Soviet Union, and the United States—each with the power to veto resolutions. In June 1945, representatives of fifty-one countries met in San Francisco to adopt the UN Charter, which outlawed force or the threat of force as a means of settling international disputes. In July, the U.S. Senate endorsed the charter. In contrast to the bitter dispute over membership in the League of Nations after World War I, only two members of the U.S. Senate voted against joining the UN.

Structure of the UN

Peace, but Not Harmony

World power redistributed

World War II produced a radical redistribution of world power. Japan and Germany, the two dominant military powers in their regions before the war, were utterly defeated. Britain and France, though victorious, were substantially weakened. Only the United States and the Soviet Union were able to project significant influence beyond their national borders.

Atlantic Charter For Whom?

This 1943 cartoon from the *Chicago Defender*, a black newspaper, questions whether non-white peoples will be accorded the right to choose their own government, as promised in the Atlantic Charter agreed to two years earlier by Franklin D. Roosevelt and Winston Churchill. Churchill insisted the principle only applied to Europeans.

Overall, however, the United States was clearly the dominant world power. But peace did not usher in an era of international harmony. The Soviet occupation of eastern Europe created a division soon to be solidified in the Cold War. The dropping of the atomic bombs left a worldwide legacy of fear.

The dominant world power

The Four Freedoms speech had been intended primarily to highlight the differences between Anglo-American ideals and Nazism. Nonetheless, it had unanticipated consequences. As one of Roosevelt's speechwriters remarked, "when you state a moral principle, you are stuck with it, no matter how many fingers you have kept crossed at the moment." The language with which World War II was fought helped to lay the foundation for postwar ideals of human rights that extend to all mankind.

Human rights

During the war, Mahatma Gandhi, the Indian nationalist leader, wrote to Roosevelt that the idea "that the Allies are fighting to make the world safe for freedom of the individual and for democracy seems hollow, so long as India, and for that matter, Africa, are exploited by Great Britain, and America has the Negro problem in her own home." Allied victory saved mankind from a living nightmare—a worldwide system of dictatorial rule and slave labor in which peoples deemed inferior suffered the fate of European Jews and of the victims of Japanese outrages in Asia. But disputes over the freedom of colonial peoples overseas and non-whites in the United States foretold more wars and social upheavals to come.

Unresolved disputes

CHAPTER REVIEW AND ONLINE RESOURCES

REVIEW QUESTIONS

1. *Why did most Americans support isolationism in the 1930s?*

2. *What factors after 1939 led to U.S. involvement in World War II?*

3. *How did government, business, and labor work together to promote wartime production? How did the war affect each group?*

4. *How did different groups understand or experience the Four Freedoms differently?*

5. *Explain how conservatives in Congress and business used the war effort to attack the goals and legacy of the New Deal.*

6. *How did the war alter the lives of women on the home front, and what did different groups think would happen after the war?*

7. *How did a war fought to bring "essential human freedoms" to the world fail to protect the home front liberties of blacks, Indians, Japanese-Americans, and Mexican-Americans?*

8. *Explain how World War II promoted an awareness of the links between racism in the United States and colonialism around the world.*

9. *What was the impact of the GI Bill of Rights on American society, including minorities?*

10. *Describe how the decisions made at the Bretton Woods conference in 1944 created the framework for postwar U.S. economic and foreign policy.*

KEY TERMS

Four Freedoms (p. 673)
Good Neighbor Policy (p. 674)
isolationism (p. 676)
Lend-Lease Act (p. 677)
D-Day (p. 680)
Holocaust (p. 682)
Rosie the Riveter (p. 686)
GI Bill of Rights (p. 688)
"patriotic assimilation" (p. 690)
bracero program (p. 690)
"zoot suit" riots (p. 691)
Executive Order 9066 (p. 692)
Second Great Migration (p. 694)
Executive Order 8802 (p. 695)
"double-V" (p. 696)
Manhattan Project (p. 701)
Bretton Woods Conference (p. 704)
United Nations (p. 704)

wwnorton.com
/studyspace

VISIT STUDYSPACE FOR THESE RESOURCES AND MORE

- A chapter outline
- A diagnostic chapter quiz
- Interactive maps
- Map worksheets
- Multimedia documents

CHAPTER 23

THE UNITED STATES AND THE COLD WAR

★

1945-1953

ERICA UNDER COMMUNISM!

The Cold War led to widespread fears of a communist takeover in the United States (a task far beyond the capacity of the minuscule American Communist Party). This image is the cover of a comic book warning of the danger that communists might overthrow the government and detailing the horrors of life in a communist America. It was published in 1947 by the Catechetical Guild Educational Society of St. Paul, Minnesota, a religious organization. Church groups distributed some 4 million copies.

On September 16, 1947, the 160th anniversary of the signing of the Constitution, the Freedom Train opened to the public in Philadelphia. A traveling exhibition of 133 historical documents, the train, bedecked in red, white, and blue, soon embarked on a sixteen-month tour that took it to more than 300 American cities. Never before or since have so many cherished pieces of Americana—among them the Mayflower Compact, the Declaration of Independence, and the Gettysburg Address—been assembled in one place.

The idea for the Freedom Train originated in 1946 with the Department of Justice. President Harry S. Truman endorsed it as a way of contrasting American freedom with "the destruction of liberty by the Hitler tyranny." Since direct government funding raised fears of propaganda, however, the administration turned the project over to a nonprofit group, the American Heritage Foundation.

By any measure, the Freedom Train was an enormous success. Behind the scenes, however, the Freedom Train demonstrated that the meaning of freedom remained as controversial as ever.

The liberal staff members at the National Archives who proposed the initial list of documents had included the Wagner Act of 1935, which guaranteed workers the right to form unions, as well as President Roosevelt's Four Freedoms speech of 1941, with its promise to fight "freedom from want." The more conservative American Heritage Foundation removed these documents. They also deleted from the original list the Fourteenth and Fifteenth Amendments, which had established the principle of equal civil and political rights regardless of race after the Civil War. In the end, nothing on the train referred to organized labor or any twentieth-century social legislation. The only documents relating to African-Americans were the Emancipation Proclamation, the Thirteenth Amendment, and a 1776 letter by South Carolina patriot Henry Laurens criticizing slavery.

On the eve of the train's unveiling, the poet Langston Hughes wondered whether there would be "Jim Crow on the Freedom Train." "When it stops in Mississippi," Hughes asked, "will it be made plain/Everybody's got a right to board the Freedom Train?" In fact, with the Truman administration about to make civil rights a major priority, the train's organizers announced that they would not permit segregated viewing. In an unprecedented move, the American Heritage Foundation canceled visits to Memphis, Tennessee, and Birmingham, Alabama, when local authorities insisted on separating visitors by race. The Freedom Train visited forty-seven other southern cities without incident.

Even as the Freedom Train reflected a new sense of national unease about expressions of racial inequality, its journey also revealed the growing impact of the Cold War. In the spring of 1947, a few months before the train was dedicated, President Truman committed the United States to the worldwide containment of Soviet power and inaugurated a program to root out "disloyal" persons from government employment. The Federal Bureau of Investigation began compiling reports on those who found the train objectionable. The Freedom Train revealed how the Cold War helped to reshape freedom's meaning, identifying it ever more closely with anticommunism, "free enterprise," and the defense of the social and economic status quo.

The cover of a comic book promoting the Freedom Train in 1948. The image links the train to Paul Revere's ride and, more broadly, the Revolutionary era.

ORIGINS OF THE COLD WAR

The Two Powers

The United States emerged from World War II as by far the world's greatest power. The United States accounted for half the world's manufacturing capacity. It alone possessed the atomic bomb. American leaders believed that the nation's security depended on the security of Europe and Asia, and that American prosperity required global economic reconstruction.

The only power that in any way could rival the United States was the Soviet Union, whose armies now occupied most of eastern Europe, including the eastern part of Germany. Its crucial role in defeating Hitler and its claim that communism had wrested a vast backward nation into modernity gave the Soviet Union considerable prestige in Europe and among colonial peoples struggling for independence. Having lost more than 20 million dead and suffered immense devastation during the war, however, Stalin's government was in no position to embark on new military adventures. But the Soviet government remained determined to establish a sphere of influence in eastern Europe, through which Germany had twice invaded Russia in the past thirty years.

Soviet power

The Roots of Containment

In retrospect, it seems all but inevitable that the two major powers to emerge from the war would come into conflict. Born of a common foe rather than common long-term interests, values, or history, the wartime alliance between the United States and the Soviet Union began to unravel almost from the day that peace was declared.

The Cold War in the Middle East

The first confrontation of the Cold War took place in the Middle East. At the end of World War II, Soviet troops had occupied parts of northern Iran, hoping to pressure that country to grant it access to its rich oil fields. Under British and American pressure, however, Stalin quickly withdrew Soviet forces. At the same time, however, the Soviets installed procommunist governments in Poland, Romania, and Bulgaria, a step they claimed was no different from American domination of Latin America or Britain's determination to maintain its own empire.

George Kennan

Early in 1946, in his famous **Long Telegram** from Moscow, American diplomat George Kennan advised the Truman administration that the Soviets could not be dealt with as a normal government. Communist ideology drove them to try to expand their power throughout the world, he claimed, and only the United States had the ability to stop them. His telegram laid the foundation for what became known as the policy of "**containment**," according to which the United States committed itself to preventing any further expansion of Soviet power.

Shortly afterward, in a speech at Fulton, Missouri, Britain's former wartime prime minister Winston Churchill declared that an "**iron curtain**" had descended across Europe, partitioning the free West from the communist East. But not until March 1947, in a speech announcing what came to be known as the **Truman Doctrine**, did the president officially embrace the Cold War as the foundation of American foreign policy and describe it as a worldwide struggle over the future of freedom.

President Harry S Truman delivering his Truman Doctrine speech before Congress on March 12, 1947.

The Truman Doctrine

Harry S Truman never expected to become president. When he assumed the presidency after Roosevelt's death in April 1945, Truman found himself forced to decide foreign policy debates in which he had previously played virtually no role.

Convinced that Stalin could not be trusted and that the United States had a responsibility to provide leadership to a world that he tended to view in stark, black-and-white terms, Truman soon determined to put the policy of containment into effect. The immediate occasion for this epochal decision came early in 1947 when Britain informed the United States that because its economy had been shattered by the war, it had no choice but to end military and financial aid to two crucial governments—Greece, a monarchy threatened by a communist-led rebellion, and Turkey, from which the Soviets were demanding joint control of the straits linking the Black Sea and the Mediterranean. Britain asked the United States to fill the vacuum.

Aid to Greece and Turkey

The Soviet Union had little to do with the internal problems of Greece and Turkey, where opposition to corrupt, undemocratic regimes was largely homegrown. But the two countries occupied strategically important sites at the gateway to southeastern Europe and the oil-rich Middle East. Truman had been told by Senate leader Arthur Vandenberg that the only way a reluctant public and Congress would support aid to these governments was for the president to "scare hell" out of the American people. Truman rolled out the heaviest weapon in his rhetorical arsenal—the defense of freedom. As the leader of the "free world," the United States must now shoulder the responsibility of supporting "freedom-loving peoples" wherever communism threatened them. Twenty-four times in the eighteen-minute speech, Truman used the words "free" or "freedom."

Freedom and containment

Truman succeeded in persuading both Republicans and Democrats in Congress to support his policy, beginning a long period of bipartisan support for the containment of communism. As Truman's speech to Congress suggested, the Cold War was, in part, an ideological conflict. Both sides claimed to be promoting freedom and social justice while defending their own security, and each offered its social system as a model the rest of the world should follow.

Truman's rhetoric suggested that the United States had assumed a permanent global responsibility. The speech set a precedent for American assistance to anticommunist regimes throughout the world, no matter how undemocratic, and for the creation of a set of global military alliances directed against the Soviet Union. There soon followed the creation of new national security bodies immune from democratic oversight, such as the Atomic Energy Commission, **National Security Council**, and Central Intelligence Agency (CIA), the last established in 1947 to gather intelligence and conduct secret military operations abroad.

Consequences of the Truman Doctrine

The Marshall Plan

The threat of American military action overseas formed only one pillar of containment. Secretary of State George C. Marshall spelled out the other in a speech at Harvard University in June 1947. Marshall pledged the United States to contribute billions of dollars to finance the economic recovery of Europe. Two years after the end of the war, much of the continent still lay

Postwar foreign aid to Europe

Bales of American cotton in a warehouse at the French port of Le Havre, 1949. Part of the Marshall Plan aid program, the shipment helped to revive the French cotton industry.

in ruins with widespread food shortages and rampant inflation. The economic chaos had strengthened the communist parties of France and Italy. American policymakers feared that these countries might fall into the Soviet orbit.

The **Marshall Plan** offered a positive vision to go along with containment. Avoiding Truman's language of a world divided between free and unfree blocs, Marshall insisted, "Our policy is directed not against any country or doctrine, but against hunger, poverty, desperation, and chaos."

The Marshall Plan proved to be one of the most successful foreign aid programs in history. By 1950, western European production exceeded prewar levels and the region was poised to follow the United States down the road to a mass-consumption society. Because the Soviet Union refused to participate, fearing American control over the economies of eastern Europe, the Marshall Plan further solidified the division of the continent. At the same time, the United States worked out with twenty-three other Western nations the **General Agreement on Tariffs and Trade** (GATT), which proposed to stimulate freer trade among the participants, creating an enormous market for American goods and investment.

The Reconstruction of Japan

A democratic constitution

Under the guidance of General Douglas MacArthur, the "supreme commander" in Japan until 1948, that country adopted a new, democratic constitution. Thanks to American insistence, and against the wishes of most Japanese leaders, the new constitution gave women the right to vote for the first time in Japan's history. Furthermore, Article 9 of the new constitution stated that Japan would renounce forever the policy of war and armed aggression, and would maintain only a modest self-defense force.

Japan's recovery

The United States also oversaw the economic reconstruction of Japan. Initially, the United States proposed to dissolve Japan's giant industrial corporations, which had contributed so much to the nation's war effort. But this plan was abandoned in 1948 in favor of an effort to rebuild Japan's industrial base as a bastion of anticommunist strength in Asia. By the 1950s, thanks to American economic assistance, the adoption of new technologies, and low spending on the military, Japan's economic recovery was in full swing.

The Berlin Blockade and NATO

Meanwhile, the Cold War intensified and, despite the Marshall Plan, increasingly took a militaristic turn. At the end of World War II, each of the four victorious powers assumed control of a section of occupied Germany, and of Berlin, located deep in the Soviet zone. In June 1948, the United States, Britain, and France introduced a separate currency in their zones, a prelude to the creation of a new West German government that would be aligned with them in the Cold War. In response, the Soviets cut off road and rail traffic from the American, British, and French zones of occupied Germany to Berlin.

Occupation of Germany

An eleven-month airlift followed, with Western planes supplying fuel and food to their zones of the city. When Stalin lifted the blockade in May 1949, the Truman administration had won a major victory. Soon, two new nations emerged, East and West Germany, each allied with a side in the Cold War. Berlin itself remained divided. Not until 1991 would Germany be reunified.

The Berlin airlift

Also in 1949, the Soviet Union tested its first atomic bomb, ending the American monopoly of that weapon. In the same year, the United States, Canada, and ten western European nations established the **North Atlantic Treaty Organization** (NATO), pledging mutual defense against any future Soviet attack. Soon, West Germany became a crucial part of NATO. The North Atlantic Treaty was the first long-term military alliance between the United States and Europe since the Treaty of Amity and Commerce with France during the American Revolution. The Soviets formalized their own eastern European alliance, the Warsaw Pact, in 1955.

The Growing Communist Challenge

In 1949, communists led by Mao Zedong emerged victorious in the long Chinese civil war—a serious setback for the policy of containment. Assailed by Republicans for having "lost" China (which, of course, the United States never "had" in the first place), the Truman administration refused to recognize the new government—the People's Republic of China—and blocked it from occupying China's seat at the United Nations. Until the 1970s, the United States insisted that the ousted regime, which

"Losing" China

COLD WAR EUROPE, 1956

Occupation Zones
- American
- British
- French
- Soviet

West Berlin · Berlin Wall, 1961 · East Berlin

ICELAND

SWEDEN · FINLAND

NORWAY

North Sea

Baltic Sea

IRELAND

DENMARK

SOVIET UNION

GREAT BRITAIN
London

NETHERLANDS

Berlin

EAST GERMANY · POLAND
Warsaw

Atlantic Ocean

BELGIUM · Bonn

WEST GERMANY · Prague

Paris

LUXEMBOURG

CZECHOSLOVAKIA

FRANCE

SWITZERLAND · AUSTRIA · Budapest

HUNGARY · ROMANIA

Bucharest

PORTUGAL · SPAIN

Lisbon

Corsica

ITALY

YUGOSLAVIA

Sofia

Black Sea

BULGARIA

Tirane

ALBANIA

Sardinia

GREECE

Ankara

TURKEY

MOROCCO

Sicily

Athens

SYRIA

IRAQ

TUNISIA

Mediterranean Sea

Crete

CYPRUS LEBANON
(Great Britain)

ISRAEL · JORDAN

ALGERIA
(France)

SAUDI ARABIA

NATO countries
Warsaw Pact countries

LIBYA

EGYPT

Red Sea

0   250   500 miles
0   250   500 kilometers

The division of Europe between communist and noncommunist nations, solidified by the early 1950s, would last for nearly forty years.

had been forced into exile on the island of Taiwan, remained the legitimate government of China.

In the wake of Soviet-American confrontations in Europe, the communist victory in China, and Soviet success in developing an atomic bomb, the National Security Council approved a call for a permanent military build-up to enable the United States to pursue a global crusade against communism. Known as **NSC-68**, this 1950 manifesto described the Cold War as an epic struggle between "the idea of freedom" and the "idea of slavery under the grim oligarchy of the Kremlin."

A global crusade against communism

The Korean War

Initially, American postwar policy focused on Europe. But it was in Asia that the Cold War suddenly turned hot. Occupied by Japan during World War II, Korea had been divided in 1945 into Soviet and American zones. These zones soon evolved into two governments: communist North Korea and anticommunist South Korea, undemocratic but aligned with the United States. In June 1950, the North Korean army invaded the south, hoping to reunify the country under communist control. North Korean soldiers soon occupied most of the peninsula. The Truman administration persuaded the United Nations Security Council to authorize the use of force to repel the invasion. (The Soviets, who could have vetoed the resolution, were boycotting Security Council meetings to protest the refusal to seat communist China.)

A divided Korea

American troops did the bulk of the fighting on this first battlefield of the Cold War. In September 1950, General Douglas MacArthur launched a daring counterattack at Inchon, behind North Korean lines. MacArthur's army soon occupied most of North Korea. Truman now hoped to unite Korea under a pro-American government. But in October 1950, when UN forces neared the Chinese border, hundreds of thousands of Chinese troops intervened, driving them back in bloody fighting. MacArthur demanded the right to push north again and possibly even invade China and use nuclear weapons against it. But Truman, fearing an all-out war on the Asian mainland, refused. MacArthur did not fully accept the principle of civilian control of the military. When he went public with criticism of the president, Truman removed him from command. The war then settled into a stalemate around the thirty-eighth parallel, the original boundary between the two Koreas. Not until 1953 was an armistice agreed to, essentially restoring the prewar status quo. There has never been a formal peace treaty ending the Korean War.

McArthur in Korea

The Chinese in Korea

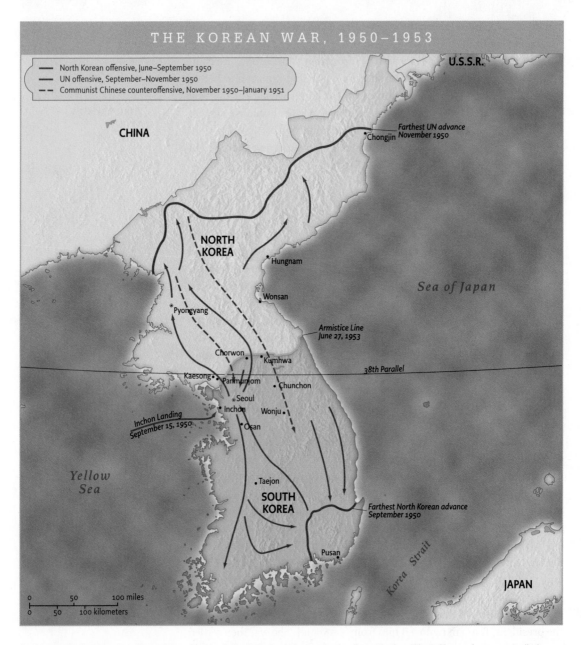

THE KOREAN WAR, 1950–1953

— North Korean offensive, June–September 1950
— UN offensive, September–November 1950
-- Communist Chinese counteroffensive, November 1950–January 1951

U.S.S.R.

CHINA

*Farthest UN advance
November 1950*
Chongjin

NORTH
KOREA

Hungnam

Sea of Japan

Wonsan

Pyongyang

*Armistice Line
June 27, 1953*

Chorwon
Kumhwa

Kaesong
Panmunjom
38th Parallel

Chunchon

Seoul
Inchon
Wonju

*Inchon Landing
September 15, 1950*

Osan

*Yellow
Sea*

Taejon

SOUTH
KOREA

*Farthest North Korean advance
September 1950*

Pusan

Korea Strait

JAPAN

0   50   100 miles
0   50   100 kilometers

As this map indicates, when General Douglas MacArthur launched his surprise landing at Inchon, North Korean forces controlled nearly the entire Korean peninsula.

More than 33,000 Americans died in Korea. The Asian death toll reached an estimated 1 million Korean soldiers and 2 million civilians, along with hundreds of thousands of Chinese troops. Korea made it clear that the Cold War, which began in Europe, had become a global conflict.

Cold War Critics

In the Soviet Union, Stalin had consolidated a brutal dictatorship that jailed or murdered millions of Soviet citizens. With its one-party rule, stringent state control of the arts and intellectual life, and government-controlled economy, the Soviet Union presented a stark opposite of democracy and "free enterprise." As a number of contemporary critics, few of them sympathetic to Soviet communism, pointed out, however, casting the Cold War in terms of a worldwide battle between freedom and slavery had unfortunate consequences.

A photograph of a street battle in Seoul, South Korea, during the Korean War illustrates the ferocity of the fighting.

Walter Lippmann

In a penetrating critique of Truman's policies, Walter Lippmann, one of the nation's most prominent journalists, objected to turning foreign policy into an "ideological crusade." To view every challenge to the status quo as part of a contest with the Soviet Union, Lippmann correctly predicted, would require the United States to recruit and subsidize an "array of satellites, clients, dependents and puppets." It would have to intervene continuously in the affairs of nations whose political problems did not arise from Moscow and could not be easily understood in terms of the battle between freedom and slavery. World War II, he went on, had shaken the foundations of European empires. In the tide of revolutionary nationalism now sweeping the world, communists were certain to play an important role.

Imperialism and Decolonization

World War II had increased American awareness of the problem of imperialism. Many movements for colonial independence borrowed the language of the American Declaration of Independence in demanding the right to self-government. Liberal Democrats and black leaders urged the Truman administration to take the lead in promoting worldwide **decolonization**, insisting that a Free World worthy of the name should not include colonies

The Free World

VOICES OF FREEDOM

From Will Herberg, *Protestant,*
Catholic, Jew (1955)

The Jewish philosopher Will Herberg was one of the more influential writers of the 1950s. In this excerpt, he analyzes the concept of the American way of life, a key slogan of the Cold War.

What is this American Way of Life that we have said constitutes the "common religion" of American society? . . . The American Way of Life is the symbol by which Americans define themselves and establish their unity. . . . On its political side it means the Constitution; on its economic side, "free enterprise"; on its social side, an equalitarianism which is not only compatible with but indeed actually implies vigorous economic competition and high mobility. . . .

The American Way of Life is humanitarian, "forward looking," optimistic. Americans are easily the most generous and philanthropic people in the world, in terms of their ready and unstinting response to suffering anywhere on the globe. The American believes in progress, in self-improvement, and quite fanatically in education. But above all, the American is idealistic. . . . And because they are so idealistic, Americans tend to be moralistic: they are inclined to see all issues as plain and simple, black and white, issues of morality. Every struggle in which they are seriously engaged becomes a "crusade." To Mr. Eisenhower, who in many ways exemplifies American religion in a particularly representative way, the second world war was a "crusade" (as was the first to Woodrow Wilson); . . . and so is his administration—a "battle for the republic" against "godless Communism" abroad and against "corruption and materialism" at home. . . . It is the secret of what outsiders must take to be the incredible self-righteousness of the American people, who tend to see the world divided into an innocent, virtuous America confronted with a corrupt, devious, and guileful Europe and Asia.

From Henry Steele Commager, "Who Is Loyal to America?" *Harper's* (September 1947)

In a sharply worded essay written in 1947, the prominent historian Henry Steele Commager commented on how the anticommunist crusade was stifling the expression of dissent and promoting an idea of patriotism that equated loyalty to the nation with the uncritical acceptance of American society and institutions.

Increasingly, Congress is concerned with the eradication of disloyalty and the defense of Americanism, and scarcely a day passes . . . that the outlines of the new loyalty and the new Americanism are not etched more sharply in public policy. . . . In the making is a revival of the red hysteria of the early 1920s, one of the shabbiest chapters in the history of American democracy, and more than a revival, for the new crusade is designed not merely to frustrate Communism but to formulate a positive definition of Americanism, and a positive concept of loyalty.

What is this new loyalty? It is, above all, conformity. It is the uncritical and unquestioning acceptance of America as it is—the political institutions, the social relationships, the economic practices. It rejects inquiry into the race question or socialized medicine, or public housing, or into the wisdom or validity of our foreign policy. It regards as particularly heinous any challenge to what is called "the system of private enterprise," identifying that system with Americanism. It abandons . . . the once popular concept of progress, and regards America as a finished product, perfect and complete.

It is, it must be added, easily satisfied. For it wants not intellectual conviction nor spiritual conquest, but mere outward conformity. In matters of loyalty, it takes the word for the deed, the gesture for the principle. It is content with the flag salute. . . . It is satisfied with membership in respectable organizations and, as it assumes that every member of a liberal organization is a Communist, concludes that every member of a conservative one is a true American. It has not yet learned that not everyone who saith Lord, Lord, shall enter into the kingdom of Heaven. It is designed neither to discover real disloyalty nor to foster true loyalty.

The concept of loyalty as conformity is a false one. It is narrow and restrictive, denies freedom of thought and of conscience. . . . What do men know of loyalty who make a mockery of the Declaration of Independence and the Bill of Rights?

QUESTIONS

1. *What does Herberg think are the strengths and weaknesses of the American outlook?*

2. *Why does Commager feel that the new patriotism makes "a mockery" of the Bill of Rights?*

3. *How does Herberg's analysis help to explain the violations of civil liberties deplored by Commager?*

and empires. But as the Cold War developed, the United States backed away from pressuring its European allies to grant self-government to colonies like French Indochina, the Dutch East Indies, and British possessions like the Gold Coast and Nigeria in Africa and Malaya in Asia.

No matter how repressive to its own people, if a nation joined the worldwide anticommunist alliance led by the United States, it was counted as a member of the Free World. The Republic of South Africa, for example, was considered a part of the Free World even though its white minority had deprived the black population of nearly all their rights.

THE COLD WAR AND THE IDEA OF FREEDOM

Among other things, the Cold War was an ideological struggle, a battle, in a popular phrase of the 1950s, for the "hearts and minds" of people throughout the world. During the 1950s, freedom became an inescapable theme of academic research, popular journalism, mass culture, and official pronouncements.

The Cold War in the movies

One of the more unusual Cold War battlefields involved American history and culture. National security agencies encouraged Hollywood to produce anticommunist movies, such as *The Red Menace* (1949) and *I Married a Communist* (1950), and urged that film scripts be changed to remove references to less-than-praiseworthy aspects of American history, such as Indian removal and racial discrimination.

To counteract the widespread European view of the United States as a cultural backwater, the CIA secretly funded an array of overseas publications, conferences, publishing houses, concerts, and art exhibits. And to try to improve the international image of American race relations, the government sent jazz musicians and other black performers abroad, especially to Africa and Asia.

Freedom and Totalitarianism

Along with freedom, the Cold War's other great mobilizing concept was **"totalitarianism."** The term originated in Europe between the world wars to describe fascist Italy and Nazi Germany—aggressive, ideologically driven states that sought to subdue all of civil society, including churches, unions, and other voluntary associations, to their control. By the 1950s, the term had become shorthand for describing those on the Soviet side in the Cold War. As the eventual collapse of communist governments in eastern Europe and the Soviet Union would demonstrate, the idea of totalitarianism greatly exaggerated the totality of government control of private life and thought in these countries.

Just as the conflict over slavery redefined American freedom in the nineteenth century and the confrontation with the Nazis shaped understandings of freedom during World War II, the Cold War reshaped them once again. Whatever Moscow stood for was by definition the opposite of freedom, including anything to which the word "socialized" could be attached. In the largest public relations campaign in American history, the American Medical Association raised the specter of "socialized medicine" to defeat Truman's proposal for national health insurance.

The Rise of Human Rights

The Cold War also affected the emerging concept of human rights. The idea that there are rights that are applicable to all of humanity originated during the eighteenth century in the Enlightenment and the American and French Revolutions. The atrocities committed during World War II, as well as the global language of the Four Freedoms, forcefully raised the issue of human rights in the postwar world. After the war, the victorious Allies put numerous German officials on trial before special courts at Nuremberg for crimes against humanity. For the first time, individuals were held directly accountable to the international community for violations of human rights. The trials resulted in prison terms for many Nazi officials and the execution of ten leaders.

In 1948, the UN General Assembly approved the Universal Declaration of Human Rights, drafted by a committee chaired by Eleanor Roosevelt. It identified a broad range of rights to be enjoyed by people everywhere, including freedom of speech, religious toleration, and protection against arbitrary government, as well as social and economic entitlements like the right to an adequate standard of living and access to housing, education, and medical care. The document had no enforcement mechanism. Some considered it an exercise in empty rhetoric. But the core principle—that a nation's treatment of its own citizens should be subject to outside evaluation—slowly became part of the language in which freedom was discussed.

A poster for *The Red Menace,* one of numerous anticommunist films produced by Hollywood during the 1950s.

The Universal Declaration of Human Rights

Ambiguities of Human Rights

One reason for the lack of an enforcement mechanism in the Universal Declaration of Human Rights was that both the United States and the Soviet Union refused to accept outside interference in their internal affairs or restraints on their ability to conduct foreign policy as they desired. In 1947, the NAACP did file a petition with the United Nations asking it to investigate racism in the United States as a violation of human rights. But the UN decided that it lacked jurisdiction. Nonetheless, since the end of World War II, the enjoyment of human rights has increasingly taken its place in definitions of freedom across the globe, especially, perhaps, where such rights are flagrantly violated.

Human rights in world affairs

After the Cold War ended, the idea of human rights would play an increasingly prominent role in world affairs. But during the 1950s, Cold War imperatives shaped the concept. Neither the United States nor the Soviet Union could resist emphasizing certain provisions of the Universal Declaration while ignoring others. The Soviets claimed to provide all citizens with social and economic rights, but violated democratic rights and civil liberties. Many Americans condemned these nonpolitical rights as a path to socialism.

THE TRUMAN PRESIDENCY

The Fair Deal

Economic transition

With the end of World War II, President Truman's first domestic task was to preside over the transition from a wartime to a peacetime economy. More than 12 million men remained in uniform in August 1945. They wanted nothing more than to return home to their families. Some returning soldiers found the adjustment to civilian life difficult. The divorce rate in 1945 rose to double its prewar level. Others took advantage of the GI Bill of Rights (discussed in the previous chapter) to obtain home mortgages, set up small businesses, and embark on college educations. The majority of returning soldiers entered the labor force—one reason why more than 2 million women workers lost their jobs. The government abolished wartime agencies that regulated industrial production and labor relations, and it dismantled wartime price controls, leading to a sharp rise in prices.

In the immediate aftermath of World War II, President Truman, backed by party liberals and organized labor, moved to revive the stalled momentum of the New Deal. Truman's program, which he announced in September 1945 and would later call the **Fair Deal**, focused on improving the social safety net and raising the standard of living of ordinary Americans. He called on Congress to increase the minimum wage, enact a program of national health insurance, and expand public housing, Social Security, and aid to education.

A few of the numerous World War II veterans who attended college after the war, thanks to the GI Bill.

The Postwar Strike Wave

In 1946, a new wave of labor militancy swept the country. The AFL and CIO launched Operation Dixie, a campaign to bring unionization to the South and, by so doing, shatter the hold of anti-labor conservatives on the region's politics. More than 200 labor organizers entered the region, seeking support especially in the southern textile industry, the steel industry in the Birmingham region, and agriculture. As inflation soared following the removal of price controls, the resulting drop in workers' real income sparked the largest strike wave in American history. Nearly 5 million workers—including those in the steel, auto, coal, and other key industries—walked off their jobs, demanding wage increases. The strike of 750,000 steelworkers represented the largest single walkout in American history to that date.

The Republican Resurgence

In the congressional elections of 1946, large numbers of middle-class voters, alarmed by the labor turmoil, voted Republican. For the first time since the 1920s, Republicans swept to control of both houses of Congress. Meanwhile, in the face of vigorous opposition from southern employers and public officials and the reluctance of many white workers to join interracial labor unions, Operation Dixie had failed to unionize the South or dent the political control of conservative Democrats in the region. The election of 1946 ensured that a conservative coalition of Republicans and southern Democrats would continue to dominate Congress.

A conservative coalition

Congress turned aside Truman's Fair Deal program. It enacted tax cuts for wealthy Americans and, over the president's veto, in 1947 passed the **Taft-Hartley Act**, which sought to reverse some of the gains made by organized labor in the past decade. The measure authorized the president to suspend strikes by ordering an eighty-day "cooling-off period," and it banned sympathy strikes and secondary boycotts (labor actions directed not at an employer but at those who did business with him). It outlawed the closed shop, which required a worker to be a union member when taking up a job, and authorized states to pass "right-to-work" laws, prohibiting other forms of compulsory union membership. It also forced union officials to swear that they were not communists. Over time, as population and capital investment shifted to states with "right-to-work" laws like Texas, Florida, and North Carolina, Taft-Hartley contributed to the decline of organized labor's share of the nation's workforce.

Decline of organized labor

Postwar Civil Rights

During his first term, Truman reached out in unprecedented ways to the nation's black community. In the years immediately following World War II, the status of black Americans enjoyed a prominence in national affairs unmatched since Reconstruction.

The status of black Americans

Between 1945 and 1951, eleven states from New York to New Mexico established fair employment practices commissions, and numerous cities passed laws against discrimination in access to jobs and public accommodations. A broad civil rights coalition involving labor, religious groups, and black organizations supported these measures. By 1952, 20 percent of black southerners were registered to vote, nearly a seven-fold increase since 1940. (Most of the gains took place in the Upper South—in Alabama and Mississippi, the heartland of white supremacy, the numbers barely budged.) Also in 1952, for the first time since record keeping began seventy years earlier, no lynchings took place in the United States.

An NAACP youth march against racial segregation in Houston, Texas, in 1947 illustrates the civil rights upsurge of the years immediately following the end of World War II.

In another indication that race relations were in flux, the Brooklyn Dodgers in 1947 challenged the long-standing exclusion of black players from major league baseball by adding Jackie Robinson to their team. Robinson, who possessed both remarkable athletic ability and a passion for equality, had been tried and acquitted for insubordination in 1944 when he refused to move to the back of a bus at Fort Hood, Texas, while serving in the army. But he promised Dodger owner Branch Rickey that he would not retaliate when subjected to racist taunts by opposing fans and players. His dignity in the face of constant verbal abuse won Robinson nationwide respect, and his baseball prowess earned him the Rookie of the Year award. His success opened the door to the integration of baseball and led to the demise of the Negro Leagues, to which black players had previously been confined.

To Secure These Rights

In October 1947, a Commission on Civil Rights appointed by the president issued *To Secure These Rights*, one of the most devastating indictments ever published of racial inequality in America. It called on the federal government to assume the responsibility for abolishing segregation and ensuring equal treatment in housing, employment, education, and the criminal justice system.

Jackie Robinson sliding into third base, 1949.

In February 1948, Truman presented an ambitious civil rights program to Congress, calling for a permanent federal civil rights commission, national laws against lynching and the poll tax, and action to ensure equal access to jobs and education. Congress, as Truman anticipated, approved none of his proposals. But in July 1948, just as the presidential campaign was getting under way, Truman issued an executive order desegregating the armed forces. The armed services became the first large institution in American life to promote racial integration actively and to attempt to root out long-standing racist practices. The Korean War would be the first American conflict fought by an integrated army since the War of Independence.

Desegregating the armed forces

The Democratic platform of 1948 was the most progressive in the party's history. Led by Hubert Humphrey, the young mayor of Minneapolis, party liberals overcame southern resistance and added a strong civil rights plank to the platform.

The Dixiecrat and Wallace Revolts

"I say the time has come," Humphrey told the Democratic national convention, "to walk out of the shadow of states' rights and into the sunlight of human rights." Whereupon numerous southern delegates—dubbed **Dixiecrats** by the press—walked out of the gathering. They soon formed the States' Rights Democratic Party and nominated for president Governor

Blacks, led by A. Philip Randolph *(left)*, picketing at the 1948 Democratic national convention. The delegates' adoption of a strong civil rights plank led representatives of several southern states to withdraw and nominate their own candidate for president, Strom Thurmond.

Strom Thurmond of South Carolina. His platform called for the "complete segregation of the races" and his campaign drew most of its support from those alarmed by Truman's civil rights initiatives.

Also in 1948, a group of left-wing critics of Truman's foreign policy formed the Progressive Party and nominated former vice president Henry A. Wallace for president. Wallace advocated an expansion of social welfare programs at home and denounced racial segregation even more vigorously than Truman. When he campaigned in the South, angry white crowds attacked him. But his real difference with the president concerned the Cold War. Wallace called for international control of nuclear weapons and a renewed effort to develop a relationship with the Soviet Union based on economic co-operation rather than military confrontation. The influence of the now much-reduced Communist Party in Wallace's campaign led to an exodus of New Deal liberals and severe attacks on his candidacy. A vote for Wallace, Truman declared, was in effect a vote for Stalin.

Wallace threatened to draw votes from Truman on the left, and Thurmond to undermine the president's support in the South, where whites had voted solidly for the Democrats throughout the twentieth century. But Truman's main opponent, fortunately for the president, was the colorless Republican Thomas A. Dewey. Certain of victory and an ineffective speaker and campaigner, Dewey seemed unwilling to commit himself on controversial issues. Truman, by contrast, ran an aggressive campaign. He crisscrossed the country by train, delivering fiery attacks on the Republican-controlled "do-nothing Congress."

Truman's victory

Virtually every public-opinion poll and newspaper report predicted a Dewey victory. Truman's success—by 303 to 189 electoral votes—represented one of the greatest upsets in American political history. For the first time since 1868, blacks (in the North, where they enjoyed the right to vote) played a decisive role in the outcome. Thurmond carried four Deep South states, demonstrating that the race issue, couched in terms of individual freedom, had the potential to lead traditionally Democratic white voters to desert their party. In retrospect, the States' Rights campaign offered a preview of the political transformation that by the end of the twentieth century would leave every southern state in the Republican column. As for Wallace, he suffered the humiliation of polling fewer popular votes than Thurmond.

THE ANTICOMMUNIST CRUSADE

For nearly half a century, the Cold War profoundly affected American life. There would be no return to "normalcy" as after World War I. The military-industrial establishment created during World War II would become permanent, not temporary. National security became the stated reason for a host of government projects, including aid to higher education and the building of a new national highway system (justified by the need to speed the evacuation of major cities in the event of nuclear war). The Cold War encouraged a culture of secrecy and dishonesty. American nuclear tests, conducted on Pacific islands and in Nevada, exposed thousands of civilians to radiation that caused cancer and birth defects.

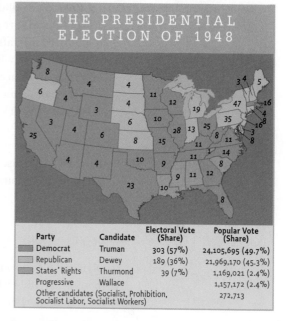

THE PRESIDENTIAL ELECTION OF 1948

Party	Candidate	Electoral Vote (Share)	Popular Vote (Share)
Democrat	Truman	303 (57%)	24,105,695 (49.7%)
Republican	Dewey	189 (36%)	21,969,170 (45.3%)
States' Rights	Thurmond	39 (7%)	1,169,021 (2.4%)
Progressive	Wallace		1,157,172 (2.4%)
Other candidates (Socialist, Prohibition, Socialist Labor, Socialist Workers)			272,713

A postcard promoting tourism to Las Vegas highlights as one attraction the city's proximity to a nuclear test site. Witnessing nearby atomic explosions became a popular pastime in the city. The government failed to issue warnings of the dangers of nuclear fallout and only years later did it admit that many onlookers had contracted diseases from radiation.

Cold War military spending helped to fuel economic growth and support scientific research that not only perfected weaponry but also led to improved aircraft, computers, medicines, and other products with a large impact on civilian life. The Cold War reshaped immigration policy, with refugees from communism being allowed to enter the United States regardless of national-origin quotas. The international embarrassment caused by American racial policies contributed to the dismantling of segregation. And like other wars, the Cold War encouraged the drawing of a sharp line between patriotic Americans and those accused of being disloyal. At precisely the moment when the United States celebrated freedom as the foundation of American life, the right to dissent came under attack.

Loyalty and Disloyalty

Dividing the world between liberty and slavery automatically made those who could be linked to communism enemies of freedom. Although the assault on civil liberties came to be known as McCarthyism, it began before Senator Joseph R. McCarthy of Wisconsin burst onto the national scene in 1950. In 1947, less than two weeks after announcing the Truman Doctrine, the president established a **loyalty review system** in which government employees were required to demonstrate their patriotism without being allowed to confront accusers or, in some cases, knowing the charges against them. Along with persons suspected of disloyalty, the new

Gays and the loyalty review system

national security system also targeted homosexuals who worked for the government. They were deemed particularly susceptible to blackmail by Soviet agents as well as supposedly lacking the manly qualities needed to maintain the country's resolve in the fight against communism. Ironically, the government conducted an anti-gay campaign at the very time that gay men enjoyed a powerful presence in realms of culture and commercial life being promoted as expressions of American freedom—modern art and ballet, fashion, and advertising. The loyalty program failed to uncover any cases of espionage. But the federal government dismissed several hundred persons from their jobs.

The HUAC hearings on Hollywood

Also in 1947, the House Un-American Activities Committee (HUAC) launched a series of hearings about communist influence in Hollywood. Calling well-known screenwriters, directors, and actors to appear before the committee ensured it a wave of national publicity, which its members relished. Celebrities like producer Walt Disney and actors Gary Cooper and Ronald Reagan testified that the movie industry harbored numerous communists. But ten "unfriendly witnesses" refused to answer the committee's questions about their political beliefs or to "name names" (identify individual communists) on the grounds that the hearings violated the First Amendment's guarantees of freedom of speech and political association. The committee charged the **Hollywood Ten**, who included the prominent screenwriters Ring Lardner Jr. and Dalton Trumbo, with contempt of Congress, and they served jail terms of six months to a year. Hollywood studios blacklisted them (denied them employment), along with more than 200 others who were accused of communist sympathies or who refused to name names.

Movie stars, led by actors Humphrey Bogart and Lauren Bacall, on their way to attend the 1947 hearings of the House Un-American Activities Committee, in a demonstration of support for those called to testify about alleged communist influence in Hollywood.

The Spy Trials

A series of highly publicized legal cases followed, which fueled the growing anticommunist hysteria. Whittaker Chambers, an editor at *Time* magazine, testified before HUAC that during the 1930s, Alger Hiss, a high-ranking State Department official, had given him secret government documents to pass to agents of the Soviet Union. Hiss vehemently denied the charge, but a jury convicted him of perjury and he served five years in prison. A young congressman from California and a member of HUAC, Richard Nixon achieved national prominence because of his dogged pursuit of Hiss.

The most sensational trial involved Julius and Ethel Rosenberg, a working-class Jewish communist couple from New York City (quite different from Hiss, a member of the eastern Protestant "establishment"). In 1951, a jury convicted the Rosenbergs of conspiracy to pass secrets concerning the atomic bomb to Soviet agents during World War II (when the Soviets were American allies). Their chief accuser was David Greenglass, Ethel Rosenberg's brother, who had worked at the Los Alamos nuclear research center.

The trial of Julius and Ethel Rosenberg

The case against Julius Rosenberg rested on highly secret documents that could not be revealed in court. (When they were released many years later, the scientific information they contained seemed too crude to justify the government's charge that Julius had passed along the "secret of the atomic bomb," although he may have helped the Soviets speed up their atomic program.) The government had almost no evidence against Ethel

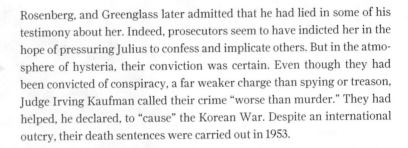

Rosenberg, and Greenglass later admitted that he had lied in some of his testimony about her. Indeed, prosecutors seem to have indicted her in the hope of pressuring Julius to confess and implicate others. But in the atmosphere of hysteria, their conviction was certain. Even though they had been convicted of conspiracy, a far weaker charge than spying or treason, Judge Irving Kaufman called their crime "worse than murder." They had helped, he declared, to "cause" the Korean War. Despite an international outcry, their death sentences were carried out in 1953.

Anticommunist hysteria

McCarthy and McCarthyism

In this atmosphere, a little-known senator from Wisconsin suddenly emerged as the chief national pursuer of subversives and gave a new name to the anticommunist crusade. Joseph R. McCarthy had won election to the Senate in 1946, partly on the basis of a fictional war record (he falsely claimed to have flown combat missions in the Pacific). In a speech at Wheeling, West Virginia, in February 1950, McCarthy announced that he had a list of 205 communists working for the State Department. The charge was preposterous, the numbers constantly changed, and McCarthy never identified a single person guilty of genuine disloyalty. But with a genius for self-promotion, McCarthy used the Senate subcommittee he chaired to hold hearings and level wild charges against numerous individuals as well as the Defense Department, the Voice of America, and other government agencies.

Joseph McCarthy

McCarthy's downfall came in 1954, when a Senate committee investigated his charges that the army had harbored and "coddled" communists. The nationally televised **Army-McCarthy hearings** revealed McCarthy as a bully who browbeat witnesses and made sweeping accusations with no basis in fact. The dramatic high point came when McCarthy attacked the loyalty of a young lawyer in the firm of Joseph Welch, the army's chief lawyer. "Let us not assassinate this lad further," Welch pleaded. "You have done enough. Have you no sense of decency, sir?" After the hearings ended, the Republican-controlled

Senator Joseph R. McCarthy at the Army-McCarthy hearings of 1954. McCarthy points to a map detailing charges about the alleged extent of the communist menace, while the army's lawyer, Joseph Welch, listens in disgust.

Senate voted to "condemn" McCarthy for his behavior. But the word "McCarthyism" had entered the political vocabulary, a shorthand for character assassination, guilt by association, and abuse of power in the name of anticommunism.

An Atmosphere of Fear

States created their own committees, modeled on HUAC, that investigated suspected communists and other dissenters. States and localities required loyalty oaths of teachers, pharmacists, and members of other professions, and they banned communists from fishing, holding a driver's license, and, in Indiana, working as professional wrestlers. Throughout the country in the late 1940s and 1950s, those who failed to testify about their past and present political beliefs and to inform on possible communists frequently lost their jobs.

Local anticommunist groups forced public libraries to remove from their shelves "un-American" books like the tales of Robin Hood, who took from the rich to give to the poor. Universities refused to allow left-wing speakers to appear on campus and fired teachers who refused to sign loyalty oaths or to testify against others.

"Fire!" The cartoonist Herbert Block, known as "Herblock," offered this comment in 1949 on the danger to American freedom posed by the anticommunist crusade.

The Uses of Anticommunism

There undoubtedly were Soviet spies in the United States. Yet the tiny U.S. Communist Party hardly posed a threat to American security. And the vast majority of those jailed or deprived of their livelihoods during the McCarthy era were guilty of nothing more than holding unpopular beliefs and engaging in lawful political activities.

Anticommunism had many faces and purposes. A popular mass movement, it grew especially strong among ethnic groups like Polish-Americans, with roots in eastern European countries now dominated by the Soviet Union, and among American Catholics in general, who resented and feared communists' hostility to religion. Government agencies like the Federal Bureau of Investigation (FBI) used anticommunism to expand their power. Under director J. Edgar Hoover, the FBI developed files on thousands of American citizens, including political dissenters, homosexuals, and others, most of whom had no connection to communism. For business, anticommunism became part of a campaign to identify labor unions and government intervention in the economy with socialism. White supremacists employed anticommunism as a weapon against black civil rights. Upholders of sexual

Anticommunist groups and goals

morality and traditional gender roles raised the cry of subversion against feminism and homosexuality, both supposedly responsible for eroding the country's fighting spirit. (Those barred from government service now included homosexuals and members of nudist colonies.)

Anticommunist Politics

At its height, from the late 1940s to around 1960, the anticommunist crusade powerfully structured American politics and culture. After launching the government's loyalty program in 1947, Truman had become increasingly alarmed at the excesses of the anticommunist crusade. He vetoed the McCarran Internal Security Bill of 1950, which required "subversive" groups to register with the government, allowed the denial of passports to their members, and authorized their deportation or detention on presidential order. But Congress quickly gave the measure the two-thirds majority necessary for it to become law.

Immigration quotas retained

The **McCarran-Walter Act** of 1952, the first major piece of immigration legislation since 1924, also passed over the president's veto. Truman had called for replacing the quotas based on national origins with a more flexible system taking into account family reunion, labor needs, and political asylum. But the McCarran-Walter Act kept the quotas in place. It also authorized the deportation of immigrants identified as communists, even if they had become citizens. But the renewed fear of aliens sparked by the anticommunist crusade went far beyond communists. In 1954, the federal government launched Operation Wetback, which employed the military to invade Mexican-American neighborhoods and round up and deport illegal aliens. Within a year, some 1 million Mexicans had been deported.

The privatization of social benefits

Truman did secure passage of a 1950 law that added previously excluded self-employed and domestic workers to Social Security. Otherwise, however, the idea of expanding the New Deal welfare state faded. In its place, private welfare arrangements proliferated. The labor contracts of unionized workers established health insurance plans, automatic cost-of-living wage increases, paid vacations, and pension plans that supplemented Social Security. Western European governments provided these benefits to all citizens. In the United States, union members in major industries enjoyed them, but not the nonunionized majority of the population, a situation that created increasing inequality among laboring Americans.

Organized labor emerged as a major supporter of the foreign policy of the Cold War. Internal battles over the role of communists and their allies led to the purging of some of the most militant union leaders, often the ones most committed to advancing equal rights to women and racial minorities in the workplace. This left organized labor less able to respond to the economy's shift to an emphasis on service rather than manufacturing, and to the rise of the civil rights movement.

Cold War Civil Rights

The civil rights movement also underwent a transformation. Although a few prominent black leaders, notably the singer and actor Paul Robeson and the veteran crusader for equality W. E. B. Du Bois, became outspoken critics of the Cold War, most felt they had no choice but to go along. The NAACP purged communists from local branches. When the government deprived Robeson of his passport and indicted Du Bois for failing to register as an agent of the Soviet Union, few prominent Americans, white or black, protested. (The charge against Du Bois was so absurd that even at the height of McCarthyism, the judge dismissed it.)

Black organizations and the Cold War

Black organizations embraced the language of the Cold War and used it for their own purposes. They insisted that by damaging the American image abroad, racial inequality played into the Russians' hands. Thus, they helped to cement Cold War ideology as the foundation of the political culture, while complicating the idea of American freedom.

President Truman, as noted above, had called for greater attention to civil rights in part to improve the American image abroad. All in all, however, the height of the Cold War was an unfavorable time to raise questions about the imperfections of American society. In 1947, two months after the Truman Doctrine speech, Undersecretary of State Dean Acheson delivered a major address defending the president's pledge to aid "free peoples" seeking to preserve their "democratic institutions." Acheson chose as his audience the Delta Council, an organization of Mississippi planters, bankers, and merchants. He seemed unaware that to make the case for the Cold War, he had ventured into what one historian has called the "American Siberia," a place of grinding poverty whose black population (70 percent of the total) enjoyed neither genuine freedom nor democracy. Most of the Delta's citizens were denied the very liberties supposedly endangered by communism.

By 1948, the Truman administration's civil rights flurry had subsided. State and local laws banning discrimination in employment and housing remained largely unenforced. In 1952, the Democrats showed how quickly the issue had faded by nominating for president Adlai

The waning civil rights impulse

Stevenson of Illinois, a candidate with little interest in civil rights, with southern segregationist John Sparkman as his running mate.

Time would reveal that the waning of the civil rights impulse was only temporary. Yet it came at a crucial moment—the late 1940s and early 1950s, when the United States experienced the greatest economic boom in its history. The rise of an "affluent society" transformed American life, opening new opportunities for tens of millions of white Americans in rapidly expanding suburbs. But it left blacks trapped in the declining rural areas of the South and urban ghettos of the North. The contrast between new opportunities and widespread prosperity for whites and continued discrimination for blacks would soon inspire a civil rights revolution and, with it, yet another redefinition of American freedom.

Rising affluence

CHAPTER REVIEW AND ONLINE RESOURCES

REVIEW QUESTIONS

1. *What major ideological conflicts, security interests, and events brought about the Cold War?*

2. *President Truman referred to the Truman Doctrine and the Marshall Plan as "two halves of the same walnut." Explain the similarities and differences between these two aspects of containment.*

3. *How did the tendency of both the United States and the Soviet Union to see all international events through the lens of the Cold War lessen each country's ability to understand what was happening in various countries around the world?*

4. *Why did the United States not support movements for colonial independence around the world?*

5. *How did the government attempt to shape public opinion during the Cold War?*

6. *Explain the differences between the United States' and the Soviet Union's application of the UN Universal Declaration of Human Rights.*

7. *How did the anticommunist crusade affect organized labor in the postwar period?*

8. *What accounts for the Republican resurgence in these years?*

9. *What were the major components of Truman's Fair Deal? Which ones were implemented, and which ones were not?*

10. *How did the Cold War affect civil liberties in the United States?*

KEY TERMS

Long Telegram (p. 710)

"containment" (p. 710)

"iron curtain" speech (p. 710)

Truman Doctrine (p. 710)

National Security Council (p. 711)

Marshall Plan (p. 712)

General Agreement on Tariffs and Trade (p. 712)

North Atlantic Treaty Organization (p. 713)

NSC-68 (p. 715)

decolonization (p. 717)

"totalitarianism" (p. 720)

Fair Deal (p. 723)

Taft-Hartley Act (p. 723)

Dixiecrats (p. 725)

loyalty review system (p. 728)

Hollywood Ten (p. 729)

Army-McCarthy hearings (p. 730)

McCarran-Walter Act (p. 732)

wwnorton.com
/studyspace

VISIT STUDYSPACE FOR THESE RESOURCES AND MORE

- A chapter outline
- A diagnostic chapter quiz
- Interactive maps
- Map worksheets
- Multimedia documents

CHAPTER 24

AN AFFLUENT SOCIETY

1953–1960

A portrait of affluence: In this photograph by Alex Henderson, Steve Czekalinski, an employee of the DuPont Corporation, poses with his family and the food they consumed in a single year, 1951. The family spent $1,300 (around $11,000 in today's money) on food, including 699 bottles of milk, 578 pounds of meat, and 131 dozen eggs. Nowhere else in the world in 1951 was food so available and inexpensive.

In 1958, during a "thaw" in the Cold War, the United States and the Soviet Union agreed to exchange national exhibitions in order to allow citizens of each "superpower" to become acquainted with life in the other. The Soviet Exhibition, unveiled in New York City in June 1959, featured factory machinery, scientific advances, and other illustrations of how communism had modernized a backward country. The following month, the American National Exhibition opened in Moscow. A showcase of consumer goods and leisure equipment, complete with stereo sets, a movie theater, home appliances, and twenty-two different cars, the exhibit, *Newsweek* observed, hoped to demonstrate the superiority of "modern capitalism with its ideology of political and economic freedom." Yet the exhibit's real message was not freedom but consumption—or, to be more precise, the equating of the two. Vice President Richard Nixon opened the exhibit with an address entitled "What Freedom Means to Us." He spoke of the "extraordinarily high standard of living" in the United States, with its 56 million cars and 50 million television sets.

The Moscow exhibition became the site of a classic Cold War confrontation over the meaning of freedom—the "kitchen debate" between Nixon and Soviet premier Nikita Khrushchev. Nixon and Khrushchev engaged in unscripted debate, first in the kitchen of a model suburban ranch house, then in a futuristic "miracle kitchen" complete with a mobile robot that swept the floors. Supposedly the home of an average steelworker, the ranch house represented, Nixon declared, the mass enjoyment of American freedom within a suburban setting—freedom

FOCUS QUESTIONS

- *What were the main characteristics of the affluent society of the 1950s?*

- *How were the 1950s a period of consensus in both domestic policies and foreign affairs?*

- *What were the major thrusts of the civil rights movement in this period?*

- *What was the significance of the presidential election of 1960?*

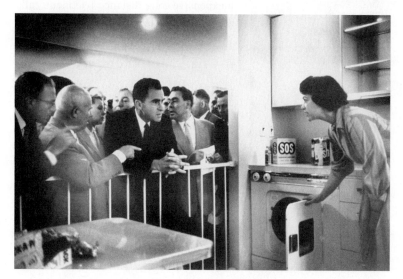

Vice President Richard Nixon and Soviet premier Nikita Khrushchev during the "kitchen debate," a discussion, among other things, of the meaning of freedom, which took place in 1959 at the American National Exposition in Moscow. Khrushchev makes a point while a woman demonstrates a washing machine.

of choice among products, colors, styles, and prices. It also implied a particular role for women. Throughout his exchanges with Khrushchev, Nixon used the words "women" and "housewives" interchangeably. His stance reflected the triumph during the 1950s of a conception of freedom centered on economic abundance and consumer choice within the context of traditional family life—a vision that seemed to offer far more opportunities for the "pursuit of happiness" to men than women.

THE GOLDEN AGE

The end of World War II was followed by what one scholar has called the "golden age" of capitalism, a period of economic expansion, stable prices, low unemployment, and rising standards of living that continued

Economic growth

until 1973. Between 1946 and 1960, the American gross national product more than doubled. Much of the benefit flowed to ordinary citizens in rising wages. In every measurable way—diet, housing, income, education, recreation—most Americans lived better than their parents and grandparents had. The official poverty rate, 30 percent of all families in 1950, had declined to 22 percent a decade later (still, to be sure, representing more than one in five Americans).

Numerous innovations came into widespread use in these years, transforming Americans' daily lives. They included television, home air-conditioning, automatic dishwashers, inexpensive long-distance telephone calls, and jet air travel.

A Changing Economy

Like other wars, the Cold War fueled U.S. industrial production and promoted a redistribution of the nation's population and economic resources. The West, especially the Seattle area, southern California, and the Rocky Mountain states, benefited enormously from government contracts for aircraft, guided missiles, and radar systems. The South became the home of numerous military bases and government-funded shipyards.

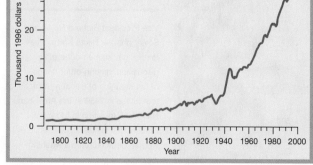

FIGURE 24.1   Real Gross Domestic Product per Capita, 1790–2000

In retrospect, the 1950s appear as the last decade of the industrial age in the United States. Since then, the American economy has shifted rapidly toward services, education, information, finance, and entertainment, while employment in manufacturing has declined. Unions' very success in raising wages inspired employers to mechanize more and more elements of manufacturing in order to reduce labor costs. In 1956, for the first time in American history, white-collar workers outnumbered blue-collar factory and manual laborers.

Industrial strength

The decade witnessed an acceleration of the transformation of southern life that had begun during World War II. New tractors and harvesting machinery and a continuing shift from cotton production to less labor-intensive soybean and poultry raising reduced the need for farm workers. More than 3 million black and white hired hands and sharecroppers migrated out of the region. The large corporate farms of California, worked by Latino and Filipino migrant laborers, poured forth an endless supply of fruits and vegetables for the domestic and world markets. Items like oranges and orange juice, once luxuries, became an essential part of the American diet.

Regional changes

A Suburban Nation

The main engines of economic growth during the 1950s, however, were residential construction and spending on consumer goods. The postwar baby boom (discussed later) and the shift of population from cities to suburbs created an enormous demand for housing, television sets, home appliances, and cars.

Consumer demand

During the 1950s, the number of houses in the United States doubled, nearly all of them built in the suburbs that sprang up across the landscape. William and Alfred Levitt, who shortly after the war built the first **Levittown** on 1,200 acres of potato fields on Long Island near New York City, became the most famous suburban developers. Levittown's more than 10,000 houses were assembled quickly from prefabricated parts and priced well within the reach of most Americans. Levittown was soon home to 40,000 people. At the same time, suburbs required a new form of shopping center—the mall—to which people drove in their cars.

The automobile, the pivot on which suburban life turned, transformed the nation's daily life, just as the interstate highway system (discussed later) transformed Americans' travel habits, making possible long-distance vacationing by car and commuting to work from ever-increasing distances. The result was an altered American landscape, leading to the construction

Suburbs and the automobile

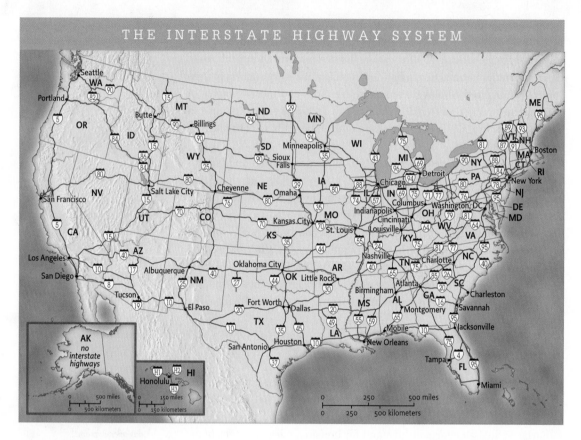

THE INTERSTATE HIGHWAY SYSTEM

Begun in 1956 and completed in 1993, the interstate highway system dramatically altered the American landscape and Americans' daily lives. It made possible more rapid travel by car and stimulated the growth of suburbs along its many routes.

of motels, drive-in movie theaters, and roadside eating establishments. The first McDonald's fast food restaurant opened in Illinois in 1954. Within ten years, having been franchised by the California business-man Ray Kroc, approximately 700 McDonald's stands had been built, which had sold over 400 million hamburgers. The car symbolized the identification of freedom with individual mobility and private choice. Americans could imagine themselves as modern versions of western pioneers, able to leave behind urban crowds and workplace pressures for the "open road."

The Growth of the West

Indeed, it was California that became the most prominent symbol of the postwar suburban boom. Between World War II and 1975, more than 30 million Americans moved west of the Mississippi River. In 1963, California surpassed New York to become the nation's most populous state.

"Centerless" western cities like Houston, Phoenix, and Los Angeles differed greatly from traditional urban centers in the East. Rather than consisting of downtown business districts linked to residential neighborhoods by public transportation, western cities were decentralized clusters of single-family homes and businesses united by a web of highway. Life centered around the car; people drove to and from work and did their shopping at malls reachable only by driving. In other sections of the country as well, shopping shifted to suburban centers, and old downtown business districts stagnated. The spread of suburban homes created millions of new lawns. Today, more land is cultivated in grass than any agricultural crop in the United States.

Ernst Haas's 1969 photograph of Albuquerque, New Mexico, could have been taken in any one of scores of American communities. As cities spread out, "strips," consisting of motels, gas stations, and nationally franchised businesses, became common. Meanwhile, older downtown business sections stagnated.

The TV World

Thanks to television, images of middle-class life and advertisements for consumer goods blanketed the country. By the end of the 1950s, nearly nine of ten American families owned a TV set. Television replaced newspapers as the most common source of information about public events, and TV watching became the nation's leading leisure activity. Television changed Americans' eating habits (the frozen TV dinner, heated and eaten while diners watched a program, went on sale in 1954), and it provided Americans of all regions and backgrounds with a common cultural experience.

With a few exceptions, like the Army-McCarthy hearings mentioned in the previous chapter, TV avoided controversy and projected a bland image of middle-class life. The dominant programs were quiz shows, westerns, and comedies set in suburban homes, like *Leave It to Beaver* and *The Adventures of Ozzie and Harriet*. Television also became the most effective advertising medium ever invented.

Women at Work and at Home

The emergence of suburbia placed pressure on the family—and especially on women—to live up to freedom's promise. After a sharp postwar drop in female employment, the number of women at work soon began to rise. By

FIGURE 24.2
Average Daily
Television Viewing

| 1950 | 1960 | 1970 |
| 4 hrs. 36 mins. | 5 hrs. 6 mins. | 5 hrs. 54 mins. |

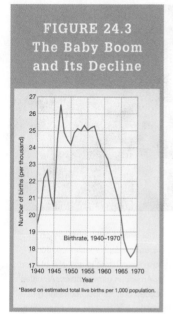

FIGURE 24.3
The Baby Boom
and Its Decline

Number of births (per thousand)

27
26
25
24
23
22
21
20
19
18
17
1940 1945 1950 1955 1960 1965 1970

Year

Birthrate, 1940–1970*

*Based on estimated total live births per 1,000 population.

1955, it exceeded the level during World War II. But the nature and aims of women's work had changed. The modern woman worked part-time to help support the family's middle-class lifestyle, not to help pull it out of poverty or to pursue personal fulfillment or an independent career. Working women in 1960 earned, on average, only 60 percent of the income of men.

Despite the increasing numbers of wage-earning women, the suburban family's breadwinner was assumed to be male, while the wife remained at home. Films, TV shows, and advertisements portrayed marriage as the most important goal of American women. And during the 1950s, men and women married younger (at an average age of twenty-two for men and twenty for women), divorced less frequently than in the past, and had more children (3.2 per family). A **"baby boom"** that lasted into the mid-1960s followed the end of the war. At a time of low immigration, the American population rose by nearly 30 million (almost 20 percent) during the 1950s.

Like other forms of dissent, feminism seemed to have disappeared from American life or was widely dismissed as evidence of mental disorder. Prominent psychologists insisted that the unhappiness of individual women or even the desire to work for wages stemmed from a failure to accept the "maternal instinct."

A Segregated Landscape

For millions of city dwellers, the suburban utopia fulfilled the dream, postponed by depression and war, of home ownership and middle-class incomes. The move to the suburbs also promoted Americanization, cutting residents off from urban ethnic communities and bringing them fully into the world of mass consumption. But if the suburbs offered a new site for the enjoyment of American freedom, they retained at least one familiar characteristic—rigid racial boundaries.

Suburbia has never been as uniform as either its celebrants or its critics claimed. There are upper-class suburbs, working-class suburbs, industrial suburbs, and "suburban" neighborhoods within city limits. But suburbia's racial uniformity was all too real. As late as the 1990s, nearly 90 percent of suburban whites lived in communities with non-white populations of less than 1 percent—the legacy of decisions by government, real-estate developers, banks, and residents.

Racial uniformity

During the postwar suburban boom, federal agencies continued to insure mortgages that barred resale of houses to non-whites, thereby financing **housing segregation**. Even after the Supreme Court in 1948 declared such provisions legally unenforceable, banks and private developers barred non-whites from the suburbs. The government refused to subsidize their mortgages, except in segregated enclaves. The vast new communities built by William Levitt refused to allow blacks, including army veterans, to rent or purchase homes. A lawsuit forced Levitt to begin selling to non-whites in the 1960s, but by 1990, his Long Island community, with a population of 53,000, included only 127 black residents.

At the same time, under programs of "**urban renewal**," cities demolished poor neighborhoods in city centers that occupied potentially valuable real estate. In their place, developers constructed retail centers and all-white middle-income housing complexes, and states built urban public universities like Wayne State in Detroit and the University of Illinois at Chicago. White residents displaced by urban renewal often moved to the suburbs. Non-whites, unable to do so, found housing in rundown city neighborhoods.

The Divided Society

Suburbanization hardened the racial lines of division in American life. Between 1950 and 1970, about 7 million white Americans left cities for the suburbs. Meanwhile, nearly 3 million blacks moved from the South to the North, greatly increasing the size of existing urban ghettos and creating entirely new ones. And half a million Puerto Ricans, mostly small coffee and tobacco farmers and agricultural laborers forced off the land when American sugar companies expanded their landholdings on the island, moved to the mainland.

The process of racial exclusion became self-reinforcing. Non-whites remained concentrated in manual and unskilled jobs, the result of employment discrimination and their virtual exclusion from educational opportunities at public and private universities, including those outside the South. As the white population and industrial jobs fled the old city centers for the suburbs, poorer blacks and Latinos remained trapped in urban ghettos, seen by many whites as places of crime, poverty, and welfare.

Religion and Anticommunism

Both Protestant and Roman Catholic religious leaders played crucial roles in the spread of anticommunism and Cold War culture. Official American values celebrated the nation's religiosity as opposed to "godless" communism. During the 1950s, a majority of

Students at an East Harlem elementary school in 1947. Most have recently migrated from Puerto Rico to the mainland with their families, although some are probably children of the area's older Italian-American community.

Advertisers during the 1950s sought to convey the idea that women would enjoy their roles as suburban homemakers, as in this ad for a vacuum cleaner, which equates housework with a game of golf.

Americans—the highest percentage in the nation's history—were affiliated with a church or synagogue. In 1954, to "strengthen our national resistance to communism," Congress added the words "under God" to the Pledge of Allegiance. In 1957, "**In God We Trust**" was included on paper money. Big-budget Hollywood films like *The Ten Commandments* and *Ben Hur* celebrated early Judaism and Christianity. Leading clerics like Bishop Fulton J. Sheen of the Catholic church and Protestant evangelist Billy Graham used radio and television to spread to millions a religious message heavily imbued with anticommunism. Communism, Graham declared, was not only an economic and political outlook but a religion—one "inspired, directed and motivated by the Devil himself."

An image from a booklet issued by the American Economic Foundation illustrates the linkage of anticommunism and religious faith during the Cold War. The hairy hand in the bottom half of the drawing represents the communist threat, which endangers religious freedom in the United States. Most of the booklet, however, dealt with the superiority of free enterprise to communism.

Selling Free Enterprise

The economic content of Cold War freedom increasingly came to focus on consumer capitalism, or, as it was now universally known, "free enterprise." More than political democracy or freedom of speech, which many allies of the United States outside western Europe lacked, an economic system resting on private ownership united the nations of the Free World.

Free enterprise seemed an odd way of describing an economy in which a few large corporations dominated key sectors. Until well into the twentieth century, most ordinary Americans had been deeply suspicious of big business, associating it with images of robber barons who manipulated politics, suppressed economic competition, and treated their workers unfairly.

In 1953, 4.5 million Americans—only slightly more than in 1928—owned shares of stock. By the mid-1960s, the number had grown to 25 million. In the face of widespread abundance, who could deny that the capitalist marketplace embodied individual freedom or that poverty would soon be a thing of the past? "It was American Freedom," proclaimed *Life* magazine, "by which and through which this amazing achievement of wealth and power was fashioned."

The Libertarian Conservatives and the New Conservatives

During the 1950s, a group of thinkers began the task of reviving conservatism and reclaiming the idea of freedom from liberals. Although largely ignored outside their own immediate circle, they developed ideas that would define conservative thought for the next half-century. One was opposition to a strong national government, an outlook that had been given new political life in conservatives' bitter reaction against the New

Opposition to strong national government

Deal. To these "libertarian" conservatives, freedom meant individual autonomy, limited government, and unregulated capitalism. These ideas had great appeal to conservative entrepreneurs, especially in the rapidly growing South and West, who desired to pursue their economic fortunes free of government regulation, high taxes, and labor unions.

A second strand of thought became increasingly prominent in the 1950s. Convinced that the Free World needed to arm itself morally and intellectually, not just militarily, for the battle against communism, "new conservatives" insisted that toleration of difference—a central belief of modern liberalism—offered no substitute for the search for absolute truth. The West, they warned, was suffering from moral decay, and they called for a return to a civilization based on values grounded in the Christian tradition and in timeless notions of good and evil. The "new conservatives" understood freedom as first and foremost a moral condition. It required a decision by independent men and women to lead virtuous lives or governmental action to force them to do so.

Freedom and morality

Here lay the origins of a division in conservative ranks that would persist into the twenty-first century. Unrestrained individual choice and moral virtue are radically different starting points from which to discuss freedom. Was the purpose of conservatism, one writer wondered, to create the "free man" or the "good man"? Libertarian conservatives spoke the language of progress and personal autonomy; the "new conservatives" emphasized tradition, community, and moral commitment. The former believed that too many barriers existed to the pursuit of individual liberty. The latter condemned an excess of individualism and a breakdown of common values.

Fortunately for conservatives, political unity often depends less on intellectual coherence than on the existence of a common foe. And two powerful enemies became focal points for the conservative revival—the Soviet Union abroad and the federal government at home. Republican control of the presidency did not lessen conservatives' hostility to the federal government, partly because they did not consider President Eisenhower one of their own.

THE EISENHOWER ERA

Ike and Nixon

Dwight D. Eisenhower, or "Ike," as he was affectionately called, emerged from World War II as the military leader with the greatest political appeal, partly because his public image of fatherly warmth set him apart

Dwight D. Eisenhower

from other successful generals like the arrogant Douglas MacArthur. Eisenhower became convinced that Senator Robert A. Taft of Ohio, a leading contender for the Republican nomination, would lead the United States back toward isolationism. Eisenhower entered the contest and won the Republican nomination.

Richard Nixon

For his running mate, Eisenhower chose Richard Nixon of California, a World War II veteran who had made a name for himself with his vigorous anticommunism. Nixon won election to the U.S. Senate in 1950 in a campaign in which he suggested that the Democratic candidate, Congresswoman Helen Gahagan Douglas, had communist sympathies.

These tactics gave Nixon a lifelong reputation for opportunism and dishonesty. But Nixon was also a shrewd politician who pioneered efforts to transform the Republican Party's image from defender of business to

The Republican message

champion of the "forgotten man"—the hardworking citizen burdened by heavy taxation and unresponsive government bureaucracies. In using populist language to promote free market economics, Nixon helped to lay the foundation for the triumph of conservatism a generation later.

The 1952 Campaign

Television was beginning to transform politics by allowing candidates to bring carefully crafted images directly into Americans' living rooms. The 1952 campaign became the first to make extensive use of TV ads. Parties, one observer complained, were "selling the president like toothpaste."

Dwight D. Eisenhower's popularity was evident at this appearance in Baltimore during the 1952 presidential campaign.

More important to the election's outcome, however, was Eisenhower's popularity (invoked in the Republican campaign slogan "I Like Ike") and the public's weariness with the Korean War. Ike's pledge to "go to Korea" in search of peace signaled his intention to bring the conflict to an end. He won a resounding victory over the Democratic candidate, Adlai Stevenson. Four years later, Eisenhower again defeated Stevenson by an even wider margin. His popularity, however, did not extend to his party. Republicans won a razor-thin majority in Congress in 1952, but Democrats regained control in 1954 and retained it for the rest of the decade. In 1956, Eisenhower became the first president to be elected without his party controlling either house of Congress.

During the 1950s, voters at home and abroad seemed to find reassurance in selecting familiar, elderly leaders to govern them. At age sixty-two, Eisenhower was one of the oldest men ever elected president. But he seemed positively youthful compared with Winston Churchill, who returned to office as prime minister of Great Britain at age seventy-seven; Charles De Gaulle, who assumed the presidency of France at sixty-eight; and Konrad Adenauer, who served as chancellor of West Germany from age seventy-three until well into his eighties. In retrospect, Eisenhower's presidency seems almost uneventful, at least in domestic affairs—an interlude between the bitter party battles of the Truman administration and the social upheavals of the 1960s.

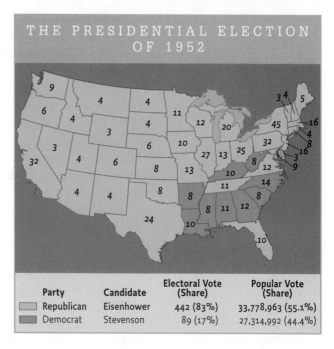

THE PRESIDENTIAL ELECTION OF 1952

Party	Candidate	Electoral Vote (Share)	Popular Vote (Share)
Republican	Eisenhower	442 (83%)	33,778,963 (55.1%)
Democrat	Stevenson	89 (17%)	27,314,992 (44.4%)

Modern Republicanism

With a Republican serving as president for the first time in twenty years, the tone in Washington changed. Wealthy businessmen dominated Eisenhower's cabinet. Defense Secretary Charles Wilson, the former president of General Motors, made the widely publicized statement: "What is good for the country is good for General Motors, and vice versa." A champion of the business community and a fiscal conservative, Ike worked to scale back government spending, including the military budget. But although right-wing Republicans saw his victory as an invitation to roll back the New Deal, Eisenhower realized that such a course would be disastrous. "Should any political party attempt to abolish Social Security, unemployment insurance, and eliminate labor laws and farm programs," he declared, "you would not hear of that party again in our political history."

Eisenhower called his domestic agenda Modern Republicanism. It aimed to sever his party's identification in the minds of many Americans with the Great Depression. The core New Deal programs not only remained in place but expanded.

Accepting the New Deal

Eisenhower presided over the largest public-works enterprise in American history, the building of the 41,000-mile **interstate highway system**. As noted in the previous chapter, Cold War arguments—especially the need to provide rapid exit routes from cities in the event of nuclear war—justified this multibillion-dollar project. But automobile manufacturers, oil companies, suburban builders, and construction unions had very practical reasons for supporting highway construction regardless of any Soviet threat. When the Soviets launched *Sputnik*, the first artificial earth satellite, in 1957, the administration responded with the **National Defense Education Act**, which for the first time offered direct federal funding to higher education.

All in all, rather than dismantling the New Deal, Eisenhower's modern Republicanism consolidated and legitimized it. By accepting its basic premises, he ensured that its continuation no longer depended on Democratic control of the presidency.

The Social Contract

The 1950s also witnessed an easing of the labor conflict of the two previous decades. The passage of the Taft-Hartley Act in 1947 (discussed in the previous chapter) had reduced labor militancy. In 1955, the AFL and CIO merged to form a single organization representing 35 percent of all

Labor and management cooperation

nonagricultural workers. In leading industries, labor and management hammered out what has been called a new "social contract." Unions signed long-term agreements that left decisions regarding capital investment, plant location, and output in management's hands. Employers stopped trying to eliminate existing unions and granted wage increases and fringe benefits such as private pension plans, health insurance, and automatic cost-of-living adjustments to pay.

Unionized workers shared fully in 1950s prosperity. Although the social contract did not apply to the majority of workers, who did not belong to unions, it did bring benefits to those who labored in nonunion

Nonunion workers

jobs. For example, trade unions in the 1950s and 1960s were able to use their political power to win a steady increase in the minimum wage, which was earned mostly by nonunion workers at the bottom of the employment pyramid. But the majority of workers did not enjoy anything close to the wages, benefits, and job security of unionized workers in such industries as automobiles and steel.

By the end of the 1950s, the social contract was weakening. In 1959, the steel industry sought to tighten work rules and limit wage increases in an attempt to boost profits battered by a recession that hit two years earlier. The plan sparked a strike of 500,000 steelworkers, which successfully beat back the proposed changes.

Massive Retaliation

Soon after he entered office, Eisenhower approved an armistice that ended fighting in Korea. But this failed to ease international tensions. Ike took office at a time when the Cold War had entered an extremely dangerous phase. In 1952, the United States exploded the first hydrogen bomb—a weapon far more powerful than those that had devastated Hiroshima and Nagasaki. The following year, the Soviets matched this achievement. Both sides feverishly developed long-range bombers capable of delivering weapons of mass destruction around the world.

The hydrogen bomb

A professional soldier, Ike hated war, which he viewed as a tragic waste. "Every gun that is made," he said in 1953, "every warship launched . . . signifies a theft from those who hunger and are not fed." But his secretary of state, John Foster Dulles, was a grim Cold Warrior. In 1954, Dulles announced an updated version of the doctrine of containment. "**Massive retaliation**," as it was called, declared that any Soviet attack on an American ally would be countered by a nuclear assault on the Soviet Union itself.

John Foster Dulles

Massive retaliation ran the risk that any small conflict, or even a miscalculation, could escalate into a war that would destroy both the United States and the Soviet Union. The reality that all-out war would result in "mutual assured destruction" (or MAD, in military shorthand) did succeed in making both great powers cautious in their direct dealings with one another. But it also inspired widespread fear of impending nuclear war. Government programs encouraging Americans to build bomb shelters in their backyards and school drills that trained children to hide under their desks in the event of an atomic attack aimed to convince Americans that nuclear war was survivable.

Ike and the Russians

The end of the Korean War and the death of Stalin, both of which occurred in 1953, convinced Eisenhower that rather than being blind zealots, the Soviets were reasonable and could be dealt with in conventional diplomatic terms. In 1955, Ike met in Geneva, Switzerland, with Nikita Khrushchev, the new Soviet leader, at the first "summit" conference since Potsdam a decade earlier. The following year, Khrushchev delivered a speech to the Communist Party Congress in Moscow that detailed Stalin's crimes, including purges of political opponents numbering in the millions.

Khrushchev's call in the same 1956 speech for "peaceful coexistence" with the United States raised the possibility of an easing of the Cold War. The "thaw" was abruptly shaken that fall, however, when Soviet troops

A man helps his daughter into a backyard bomb shelter in Garden City, Long Island, New York, in a photograph from 1955. Manufacturers of such shelters assured purchasers that occupants could survive for five days after a nuclear attack.

put down an anticommunist uprising in Hungary. Eisenhower refused to extend aid to the Hungarian rebels, an indication that he believed it impossible to "roll back" Soviet domination of eastern Europe.

In 1958, the two superpowers agreed to a voluntary halt to the testing of nuclear weapons. The pause lasted until 1961. It had been demanded by the National Committee for a Sane Nuclear Policy, which publicized the danger to public health posed by radioactive fallout from nuclear tests. But the spirit of cooperation ended abruptly in 1960, when the Soviets shot down an American U-2 spy plane over their territory. Eisenhower first denied that the plane had been involved in espionage and refused to apologize even after the Russians produced the captured pilot. The incident torpedoed another planned summit meeting.

The Emergence of the Third World

Even as Europe, where the Cold War began, settled into what appeared to be a permanent division between a communist East and a capitalist West, an intense rivalry, which sometimes took a military form, persisted in what came to be called the Third World. The term was invented to describe

developing countries aligned with neither of the two Cold War powers and desirous of finding their own model of development between Soviet centralized economic planning and free market capitalism. But none of these countries could avoid being strongly affected by the political, military, and economic contest of the Cold War.

The post–World War II era witnessed the crumbling of European

empires. Decolonization began when India and Pakistan (the latter carved out of India to give Muslims their own nation) achieved independence in 1947. Ten years later, Britain's Gold Coast colony in West Africa emerged as the independent nation of Ghana. Other new nations— including Indonesia, Malaysia, Nigeria, Kenya, and Tanzania—soon followed.

The Soviet Union strongly supported the dissolution of Europe's overseas empires, and communists participated in movements for colonial independence. Most of the new Third World nations resisted alignment with either major power bloc, hoping to remain neutral in the Cold War.

By the end of the 1950s, much of the focus of the Cold War shifted to the

Third World. The policy of containment easily slid over into opposition to any government, whether communist or not, that seemed to threaten American strategic or economic interests. Jacobo Arbenz Guzmán in Guatemala and Mohammed Mossadegh in Iran were elected, homegrown nationalists, not agents of Moscow. But they were determined to reduce foreign corporations' control over their countries' economies. Arbenz embarked on a sweeping land-reform policy that threatened the domination of Guatemala's economy by the American-owned United Fruit Company. Mossadegh nationalized the Anglo-Iranian Oil Company, whose refinery in Iran was Britain's largest remaining overseas asset. In 1953 and 1954, the Central Intelligence Agency organized the ouster of both governments—a clear violation of the UN Charter, which barred a member state from taking military action against another except in self-defense.

The military junta installed in Guatemala by the CIA in 1954 enters Guatemala City in a Jeep driven by CIA agent Carlos Castillo Armas. Although hailed by the Eisenhower administration as a triumph for freedom, the new government suppressed democracy in Guatemala and embarked on a murderous campaign to stamp out opposition.

In 1956, Israel, France, and Britain—without prior consultation with the United States—invaded Egypt after the country's nationalist leader, Gamal Abdel Nasser, nationalized the Suez Canal, jointly owned by Britain and France. A furious Eisenhower forced them to abandon the invasion. After the Suez fiasco, the United States moved to replace Britain as the dominant Western power in the Middle East.

Origins of the Vietnam War

In Vietnam, the expulsion of the Japanese in 1945 led not to independence but to a French military effort to preserve France's Asian empire against Ho Chi Minh's nationalist forces. Anticommunism led the United States into deeper and deeper involvement. Following a policy initiated by Truman, the Eisenhower administration funneled billions of dollars in aid to bolster French efforts. By the early 1950s, the United States was paying four-fifths of the cost of the war. Wary of becoming bogged down in another land war in Asia immediately after Korea, however, Ike declined to send in American troops when France requested them to avert defeat in 1954, leaving France no alternative but to agree to Vietnamese independence.

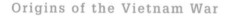

The U.S. and French forces

A peace conference in Geneva divided Vietnam temporarily into northern and southern districts, with elections scheduled for 1956 to unify the country. But the staunchly anticommunist southern leader Ngo Dinh Diem, urged on by the United States, refused to hold elections, which would almost certainly have resulted in a victory for Ho Chi Minh's communists. American aid poured into South Vietnam in order to bolster the

Geneva agreements

Diem regime. By the time Eisenhower left office, Diem nevertheless faced a full-scale guerrilla revolt by the communist-led National Liberation Front.

U.S. interventions

Little by little, the United States was becoming accustomed to intervention, both open and secret, in far-flung corners of the world. Despite the Cold War rhetoric of freedom, American leaders seemed more comfortable dealing with reliable military regimes than democratic governments. A series of military governments succeeded Arbenz in Guatemala. The shah of Iran replaced Mossadegh and remained in office until 1979 as one of the world's most tyrannical rulers, until his overthrow in a revolution led by the fiercely anti-American radical Islamist Ayatollah Khomeini. In Vietnam, the American decision to prop up Diem's regime laid the groundwork for what would soon become the most disastrous military involvement in American history.

Mass Society and Its Critics

The fatherly Eisenhower seemed the perfect leader for the placid society of the 1950s. Consensus was the dominant ideal in an era in which McCarthyism had defined criticism of the social and economic order as disloyalty and most Americans located the enjoyment of freedom in private pleasures rather than the public sphere. Even *Life* magazine commented that American freedom might be in greater danger from "disuse" than from communist subversion.

Commuters returning from work in downtown Chicago, leaving the railroad station at suburban Park Forest, Illinois, in 1953. Social critics of the 1950s claimed that Americans had become "organization men," too conformist to lead independent lives.

Dissenting voices could be heard. The sociologist C. Wright Mills challenged the self-satisfied vision of democratic pluralism that dominated mainstream social science in the 1950s. Mills wrote of a "power elite"—an interlocking directorate of corporate leaders, politicians, and military men whose domination of government and society had made political democracy obsolete. Freedom, Mills insisted, rested on the ability "to formulate the available choices," and this most Americans were effectively denied.

Other writers worried that modern mass society inevitably produced loneliness and anxiety, causing mankind to yearn for stability and authority, not freedom. In *The Lonely Crowd* (1950), the decade's most influential work of social analysis, the sociologist David Riesman described Americans as "other-directed" conformists who lacked the inner resources to lead truly independent lives. Other social critics charged that corporate bureaucracies had transformed employees into "organization men" incapable of independent thought.

Rebels without a cause. Teenage members of a youth gang, photographed at Coney Island, Brooklyn, in the late 1950s.

William Whyte's *The Organization Man* (1956) and Vance Packard's *The Hidden Persuaders* (1957), which criticized the monotony of modern work, the emptiness of suburban life, and the pervasive influence of advertising, created the vocabulary for an assault on the nation's social values that lay just over the horizon.

Rebels without a Cause

The social critics did not offer a political alternative or have any real impact on the parties or government. Nor did other stirrings of dissent. With teenagers a growing part of the population thanks to the baby boom, the rise of a popular culture geared to the emerging youth market suggested that significant generational tensions lay beneath the bland surface of 1950s life. The 1955 films *Blackboard Jungle* and *Rebel without a Cause* (the latter starring James Dean as an aimlessly rebellious youth) highlighted the alienation of at least some young people from the world of adult respectability. These works helped to spur a mid-1950s panic about **juvenile delinquency**.

Cultural life during the 1950s seemed far more daring than politics. Teenagers wore leather jackets and danced to **rock-and-roll music** that brought the hard-driving rhythms and sexually provocative movements of black musicians and dancers to enthusiastic young white audiences. They made Elvis Presley, a rock-and-roll singer with an openly sexual performance style, an immensely popular entertainment celebrity.

Elvis Presley's gyrating hips appealed to teenagers but alarmed many adults during the 1950s.

A Beat coffeehouse in San Francisco, photographed in 1958, where poets, artists, and others who rejected 1950s mainstream culture gathered.

Allen Ginsberg

In New York City and San Francisco, as well as college towns like Madison, Wisconsin, and Ann Arbor, Michigan, **the Beats**, a small group of poets and writers, railed against mainstream culture. "I saw the best minds of my generation destroyed by madness, starving hysterical naked," wrote the Beat poet Allen Ginsberg in *Howl* (1955), a brilliant protest against materialism and conformism written while the author was under the influence of hallucinogenic drugs. Ginsberg became nationally known when San Francisco police in 1956 confiscated his book and arrested bookstore owners for selling an obscene work. (A judge later overturned the ban on the grounds that *Howl* possessed redeeming social value.) Rejecting the work ethic, the "desperate materialism" of the suburban middle class, and the militarization of American life by the Cold War, the Beats celebrated impulsive action, immediate pleasure (often enhanced by drugs), and sexual experimentation. Despite Cold War slogans, they insisted, personal and political repression, not freedom, were the hallmarks of American society.

THE FREEDOM MOVEMENT

Not until the 1960s would young white rebels find their cause, as the seeds of dissent planted by the social critics and Beats flowered in an outpouring of political activism, new attitudes toward sexuality, and a full-fledged generational rebellion. A more immediate challenge to the complacency of the 1950s arose from the twentieth century's greatest citizens' movement—the black struggle for equality.

Origins of the Movement

Today, with the birthday of Martin Luther King Jr. a national holiday and the struggles of Montgomery, Little Rock, Birmingham, and Selma celebrated as heroic episodes in the history of freedom, it is easy to forget that at the time, the civil rights revolution came as a great surprise. Few predicted the emergence of the southern mass movement for civil rights.

With blacks' traditional allies on the left decimated by McCarthyism, most union leaders unwilling to challenge racial inequalities within their own ranks, and the NAACP concentrating on court battles, new constituencies and new tactics were sorely needed. The movement found in the southern black church the organizing power for a militant, nonviolent assault on segregation.

The southern black church

The United States in the 1950s was still a segregated, unequal society. Half of the nation's black families lived in poverty. In the South, evidence of Jim Crow abounded—in separate public institutions and the signs "white" and "colored" at entrances to buildings, train carriages, drinking fountains, restrooms, and the like. In the North and West, the law did not require segregation, but custom barred blacks from many colleges, hotels, and restaurants, and from most suburban housing. Las Vegas, Nevada, for example, was as strictly segregated as any southern city. Hotels and casinos did not admit blacks except in the most menial jobs. Lena Horne, Sammy Davis Jr., Louis Armstrong, and other black entertainers played the hotel-casinos on the "strip" but could not stay as guests where they performed.

The persistence of Jim Crow

In 1950, seventeen southern and border states and Washington, D.C., had laws requiring the racial segregation of public schools, and several others permitted local districts to impose it. In northern communities housing patterns and school district lines created de facto segregation—separation in fact if not in law. Few white Americans felt any urgency about confronting racial inequality.

The Legal Assault on Segregation

With the Eisenhower administration reluctant to address the issue, it fell to the courts to confront the problem of racial segregation. In the Southwest, the **League of United Latin American Citizens** (LULAC), the

A segregated school in West Memphis, Arkansas, photographed for *Life* magazine in 1949. Education in the South was separate but hardly equal.

equivalent of the NAACP, challenged restrictive housing, employment discrimination, and the segregation of Latino students. They won an important victory in 1946 in the case of *Mendez v. Westminster,* when the California Supreme Court ordered the schools of Orange County desegregated. In response, the state legislature repealed all school laws requiring racial segregation. The governor who signed the measure, Earl Warren, had presided over the internment of Japanese-Americans during World War II as the state's attorney general. After the war, he became convinced that racial inequality had no place in American life. When Chief Justice Fred Vinson died in 1953, Eisenhower appointed Earl Warren to replace him on the U.S. Supreme Court.

Desegregation in California

For years, the NAACP, under the leadership of attorneys Charles Hamilton Houston and Thurgood Marshall, had pressed legal challenges to the "separate but equal" doctrine laid down by the Court in 1896 in *Plessy v. Ferguson* (see Chapter 17). At first, the NAACP sought to gain admission to white institutions of higher learning for which no black equivalent existed. In 1938, the Supreme Court ordered the University of Missouri Law School to admit Lloyd Gaines, a black student, because the state had no such school for blacks. Missouri responded by setting up a segregated law school, satisfying the courts. But in 1950, the Supreme Court unanimously ordered Heman Sweatt admitted to the University of Texas Law School even though the state had established a "school" for him in a basement containing three classrooms and no library.

Thurgood Marshall and the NAACP

The *Brown* Case

Marshall now launched a frontal assault on segregation itself. He brought the NAACP's support to local cases that had arisen when black parents challenged unfair school policies. To do so required remarkable courage. In Clarendon County, South Carolina, Levi Pearson, a black farmer who brought a lawsuit on behalf of his children, saw his house burned to the ground. The Clarendon case attacked not segregation itself but the unequal funding of schools. Black children attended class in buildings with no running water or indoor toilets and were not provided with buses to transport them to classes. Five such cases from four states and the District of Columbia were combined in a single appeal that reached the Supreme Court late in 1952.

When cases are united, they are listed alphabetically and the first case gives the entire decision its name. In this instance, the first case arose from a state outside the old Confederacy. Oliver Brown went to court because his daughter, a third grader, was forced to walk across dangerous railroad tracks each morning rather than being allowed to attend a nearby school restricted to whites. His lawsuit became *Brown v. Board of Education of Topeka, Kansas.*

Linda Brown's parents sued the school board of Topeka, Kansas, demanding that it admit their daughter to a school near her home restricted to whites, rather than requiring her to walk across dangerous railroad tracks each day, as in this photograph, to attend a black school. The result was the Supreme Court's landmark *Brown* decision outlawing school segregation.

Thurgood Marshall decided that the time had come to attack the "separate but equal" doctrine itself. Even with the same funding and facilities, he insisted, segregation was inherently unequal because it stigmatized one group of citizens as unfit to associate with others. In its legal brief, the Eisenhower administration did not directly support Marshall's position, but it urged the justices to consider "the problem of racial discrimination . . . in the context of the present world struggle between freedom and tyranny." Other peoples, it noted, "cannot understand how such a practice can exist in a country which professes to be a staunch supporter of freedom, justice, and democracy."

The Warren Court

The new chief justice, Earl Warren, managed to create unanimity on a divided Court, some of whose members disliked segregation but feared that a decision to outlaw it would spark widespread violence. On May 17, 1954, Warren himself read aloud the decision, only eleven pages long. Segregation in public education, he concluded, violated the equal protection of the laws guaranteed by the Fourteenth Amendment. "In the field of education, the doctrine of 'separate but equal' has no place. Separate educational facilities are inherently unequal."

The decision did not order immediate implementation but instead called for hearings as to how segregated schooling should be dismantled. But *Brown* marked the emergence of the Warren Court as an active agent of social change. And it inspired a wave of optimism that discrimination would soon disappear.

The Montgomery Bus Boycott

Brown did not cause the modern civil rights movement, which, as noted in the previous two chapters, began during World War II and continued in cities like New York after the war. But the decision did ensure that when the movement resumed after waning in the early 1950s, it would have the backing of the federal courts. Mass action against Jim Crow soon reappeared. On December 1, 1955, Rosa Parks, a black tailor's assistant who had just completed her day's work in a Montgomery, Alabama, department store, refused to surrender her seat on a city bus to a white rider, as required by local law. Parks's arrest sparked a yearlong bus boycott, the beginning of the mass phase of the civil rights movement in the South. In 2000, *Time* magazine named Rosa Parks one of the 100 most significant persons of the twentieth century.

The mug shot of Rosa Parks, taken in December 1955 at a Montgomery, Alabama, police station after she was arrested for refusing to give up her seat on a city bus to a white passenger.

Rosa Parks

Parks is widely remembered today as a "seamstress with tired feet," a symbol of ordinary blacks' determination to resist the daily injustices and indignities of the Jim Crow South. In fact, her life makes clear that the civil rights revolution built on earlier struggles. Parks was a veteran of black politics. During the 1930s, she took part in meetings protesting the conviction of the Scottsboro Boys. She served for many years as secretary to E. D. Nixon, the local leader of the NAACP. In 1943, she tried to register to vote, only to be turned away because she supposedly failed a literacy test. After two more attempts, Parks succeeded in becoming one of the few blacks in Montgomery able to cast a ballot.

When news of Parks's arrest spread, hundreds of blacks gathered in a local church and vowed to refuse to ride the buses until accorded equal treatment. For 381 days, despite legal harassment and occasional violence, black maids, janitors, teachers, and students walked to their destinations or rode an informal network of taxis. Finally, in November 1956, the Supreme Court ruled segregation in public transportation unconstitutional. The boycott ended in triumph.

Successful boycott

The Daybreak of Freedom

The Montgomery bus boycott marked a turning point in postwar American history. It launched the movement for racial justice as a nonviolent crusade based in the black churches of the South. It gained the support of northern liberals and focused unprecedented and unwelcome international attention on the country's racial policies. And it marked the emergence of the twenty-six-year-old Martin Luther King Jr., who had recently arrived in Montgomery to become pastor of a Baptist church, as the movement's national symbol. On the night of the first protest meeting, King's call to action electrified the audience: "We, the disinherited of this land, we who have been oppressed so long, are tired of going through the long night of captivity. And now we are reaching out for the daybreak of freedom and justice and equality."

The rise of Martin Luther King Jr.

From the beginning, the language of freedom pervaded the black movement. It resonated in the speeches of civil rights leaders and in the hand-lettered placards of the struggle's foot soldiers. During the summer of 1964, when civil rights activists established "freedom schools" for black children across Mississippi, lessons began with students being asked to define the word. Some gave specific answers ("going to public libraries"), some more abstract ("standing up for your rights"). Some insisted that freedom meant legal equality, others saw it as liberation from years of deference to and fear of whites. "Freedom of the mind," wrote one, was the greatest freedom of all.

For adults as well, freedom had many meanings. It meant enjoying the political rights and economic opportunities taken for granted by whites. It required eradicating historic wrongs such as segregation, disenfranchisement, confinement to low-wage jobs, and the ever-present threat of violence. It meant the right to be served at lunch counters and downtown department stores, central locations in the consumer culture, and to be addressed as "Mr.," "Miss," and "Mrs.," rather than "boy" and "auntie."

The movement and freedom

The Leadership of King

In King's soaring oratory, the protesters' understandings of freedom fused into a coherent whole. His most celebrated oration, the "I Have a Dream" speech of 1963, began by invoking the unfulfilled promise of emancipation ("one hundred years later, the Negro still is not free") and closed with a cry borrowed from a black spiritual: "Free at last! Free at last! Thank God Almighty, we are free at last!"

King presented the case for black rights in a vocabulary that merged the black experience with that of the nation. Having studied the writings of Henry David Thoreau and Mahatma Gandhi on peaceful civil disobedience, King outlined a philosophy of struggle in which evil must be met with good, hate with Christian love, and violence with peaceful demands for change.

Peaceful civil disobedience

Echoing Christian themes derived from his training in the black church, King's speeches resonated deeply in both black communities and the broader culture. He repeatedly invoked the Bible to preach justice and forgiveness, even toward those "who desire to deprive you of freedom." Like Frederick Douglass before him, King appealed to white America by stressing the protesters' love of country and devotion to national values. If Africa was gaining its freedom, he asked, why must black America lag behind?

Massive Resistance

Southern Christian Leadership Conference

Buoyed by success in Montgomery, King in 1956 took the lead in forming the Southern Christian Leadership Conference, a coalition of black ministers and civil rights activists, to press for desegregation. But despite the movement's success in popular mobilization, the fact that Montgomery's city fathers agreed to the boycott's demands only after a Supreme Court ruling indicated that without national backing, local action might not be enough to overturn Jim Crow. The white South's refusal to accept the *Brown* decision reinforced the conviction that black citizens could not gain their constitutional rights without Washington's intervention. This was not immediately forthcoming. When the Supreme Court finally issued its implementation ruling in 1955, the justices declared that desegregation should proceed "with all deliberate speed." This vague formulation unintentionally encouraged a campaign of "massive resistance" that paralyzed civil rights progress in much of the South.

In 1956, 82 of 106 southern congressmen—and every southern senator except Lyndon B. Johnson of Texas and Albert Gore and Estes Kefauver of Tennessee—signed a **Southern Manifesto**, denouncing the *Brown* decision as a "clear abuse of judicial power," and calling for resistance to "forced integration" by "any lawful means." State after state passed laws to block desegregation. Virginia pioneered the strategy of closing any public schools ordered to desegregate and offering funds to enable white pupils, but not black, to attend private institutions. Prince Edward County, Virginia, shut its schools entirely in 1959; not until 1964 did the Supreme Court order them reopened.

Eisenhower and Civil Rights

The federal government tried to remain aloof from the black struggle. Thanks to the efforts of Senate majority leader Lyndon B. Johnson, who hoped to win liberal support for a run for president in 1960, Congress

Opponents of racial integration raised all sorts of lurid fears about the consequences if blacks and whites attended school together.

in 1957 passed the first national civil rights law since Reconstruction. It targeted the denial of black voting rights in the South, but with weak enforcement provisions it added few voters to the rolls. President Eisenhower failed to provide moral leadership. He called for Americans to abide by the law, but he made it clear that he found the whole civil rights issue distasteful.

In 1957, however, after Governor Orval Faubus of Arkansas used the National Guard to prevent the court-ordered integration of Little Rock's Central High School, Eisenhower dispatched federal troops to the city. In the face of a howling mob, soldiers of the 101st Airborne Division escorted nine black children into the school. Events in Little Rock showed that in the last instance, the federal government would not allow the flagrant violation of court orders. But because of massive resistance, the pace of the movement slowed in the final years of the 1950s. When Eisenhower left office, fewer than 2 percent of black students attended desegregated schools in the states of the old Confederacy.

Little Rock

Ever since the beginning of the Cold War, American leaders had worried about the impact of segregation on the country's international reputation. Foreign nations and colonies paid close attention to the unfolding of the American civil rights movement. The global reaction to the *Brown* decision was overwhelmingly positive. But the slow pace of change led to criticism that embarrassed American diplomats seeking to win the loyalty

Segregation and America's reputation abroad

Federal troops escort black children to Little Rock Central High School, enforcing a court order for integration in 1957.

VOICES OF FREEDOM

From Martin Luther King Jr., Speech at Montgomery, Alabama (December 5, 1955)

On the evening of Rosa Parks's arrest for refusing to give up her seat on a Montgomery bus to a white passenger, a mass rally of local African-Americans decided to boycott city buses in protest. In his speech to the gathering, the young Baptist minister Martin Luther King Jr. invoked Christian and American ideals of justice and democracy—themes he would strike again and again during his career as the leading national symbol of the civil rights struggle.

We are here this evening . . . because first and foremost we are American citizens, and we are determined to apply our citizenship to the fullness of its means. We are here also because of our love for democracy. . . . Just the other day . . . one of the finest citizens in Montgomery—not one of the finest Negro citizens but one of the finest citizens in Montgomery—was taken from a bus and carried to jail and arrested because she refused to give her seat to a white person. . . .

Mrs. Rosa Parks is a fine person. And since it had to happen I'm happy that it happened to a person like Mrs. Parks, for nobody can doubt the boundless outreach of her integrity! Nobody can doubt the height of her character, nobody can doubt that depth of her Christian commitment and devotion to the teachings of Jesus. And I'm happy since it had to happen, it happened to a person that nobody can call a disturbing factor in the community. Mrs. Parks is a fine Christian person, unassuming, and yet there is integrity and character there. And just because she refused to get up, she was arrested.

I want to say, that we are not here advocating violence. We have never done that. . . . We believe in the teachings of Jesus. The only weapon that we have in our hands this evening is the weapon of protest. . . . There will be no white persons pulled out of their homes and taken out to some distant road and lynched. . . .

We are not wrong in what we are doing. If we are wrong, then the Supreme Court of this nation is wrong. If we are wrong, the Constitution of the United States is wrong. If we are wrong, God Almighty is wrong. . . . If we are wrong, justice is a lie. . . .

We, the disinherited of this land, we who have been oppressed so long, are tired of going through the long night of captivity. And now we are reaching out for the daybreak of freedom and justice and equality. . . . Right here in Montgomery when the history books are written in the future, somebody will have to say, "There lived a race of people, a black people, . . . a people who had the moral courage to stand up for their rights. And thereby they injected a new meaning into the veins of history and of civilization."

From The Southern Manifesto (1956)

Drawn up early in 1956 and signed by 101 southern members of the Senate and House of Representatives, the Southern Manifesto repudiated the Supreme Court decision in *Brown v. Board of Education* and offered support to the campaign of resistance in the South.

The unwarranted decision of the Supreme Court in the public school cases is now bearing the fruit always produced when men substitute naked power for established law. . . .

We regard the decisions of the Supreme Court in the school cases as a clear abuse of judicial power. It climaxes a trend in the Federal Judiciary undertaking to legislate, in derogation [violation] of the authority of Congress, and to encroach upon the reserved rights of the States and the people.

The original Constitution does not mention education. Neither does the 14th Amendment nor any other amendment. The debates preceding the submission of the 14th Amendment clearly show that there was no intent that it should affect the system of education maintained by the States.

In the case of *Plessy v. Ferguson* in 1896 the Supreme Court expressly declared that under the 14th Amendment no person was denied any of his rights if the States provided separate but equal facilities. This decision . . . restated time and again, became a part of the life of the people of many of the States and confirmed their habits, traditions, and way of life. It is founded on elemental humanity and commonsense, for parents should not be deprived by Government of the right to direct the lives and education of their own children.

Though there has been no constitutional amendment or act of Congress changing this established legal principle almost a century old, the Supreme Court of the United States, with no legal basis for such action, undertook to exercise their naked judicial power and substituted their personal political and social ideas for the established law of the land.

This unwarranted exercise of power by the Court, contrary to the Constitution, is creating chaos and confusion in the States principally affected. It is destroying the amicable relations between the white and Negro races that have been created through 90 years of patient effort by the good people of both races. It has planted hatred and suspicion where there has been heretofore friendship and understanding.

With the gravest concern for the explosive and dangerous condition created by this decision and inflamed by outside meddlers: . . . we commend the motives of those States which have declared the intention to resist forced integration by any lawful means. . . .

QUESTIONS

1. *How do religious convictions shape King's definition of freedom?*

2. *Why does the Southern Manifesto claim that the Supreme Court decision is a threat to constitutional government?*

3. *How do these documents illustrate contrasting understandings of freedom at the dawn of the civil rights movement?*

of people in the non-white world. Of course, the Soviet Union played up American race relations as part of the global "battle for hearts and minds of men" that was a key part of the Cold War.

THE ELECTION OF 1960

Kennedy and Nixon

JFK

The presidential campaign of 1960 turned out to be one of the closest in American history. Republicans chose Vice President Richard Nixon as their candidate to succeed Eisenhower. Democrats nominated John F. Kennedy, a senator from Massachusetts and a Roman Catholic, whose father, a millionaire Irish-American businessman, had served as ambassador to Great Britain during the 1930s. Kennedy's chief rivals for the nomination were Hubert Humphrey, leader of the party's liberal wing, and Lyndon B. Johnson of Texas, the Senate majority leader, who accepted Kennedy's offer to run for vice president.

Kennedy's Catholicism

The atmosphere of tolerance promoted by World War II had weakened traditional anti-Catholicism. But many Protestants remained reluctant to vote for a Catholic, fearing that Kennedy would be required to support church doctrine on controversial public issues or, in a more extreme version, take orders from the pope. Kennedy addressed the question directly. "I do not speak for my church on public matters," he insisted,

The 1960 presidential campaign produced a flood of anti-Catholic propaganda. Kennedy's victory, the first for an American Catholic, was a major step in the decline of this long-standing prejudice.

and "the church does not speak for me." At age forty-three, Kennedy became the youngest major-party nominee for president in the nation's history.

Both Kennedy and Nixon were ardent Cold Warriors. But Kennedy pointed to Soviet success in putting *Sputnik*, the first earth satellite, into orbit and subsequently testing the first intercontinental ballistic missile (ICBM) as evidence that the United States had lost the sense of national purpose necessary to fight the Cold War. He warned that Republicans had allowed a "**missile gap**" to develop in which the Soviets had achieved technological and military superiority over the United States. In fact, as both Kennedy and Nixon well knew, American economic and military capacity far exceeded that of the Soviets. But the charge persuaded many Americans that the time had come for new leadership. The stylishness of Kennedy's wife, Jacqueline, reinforced the impression that Kennedy would conduct a more youthful, vigorous presidency.

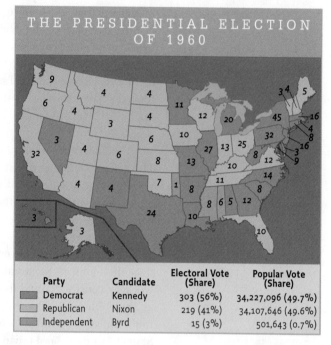

THE PRESIDENTIAL ELECTION OF 1960

Party	Candidate	Electoral Vote (Share)	Popular Vote (Share)
Democrat	Kennedy	303 (56%)	34,227,096 (49.7%)
Republican	Nixon	219 (41%)	34,107,646 (49.6%)
Independent	Byrd	15 (3%)	501,643 (0.7%)

In the first televised debate between presidential candidates, judging by viewer response, the handsome Kennedy bested Nixon, who was suffering from a cold and appeared tired and nervous. Those who heard the encounter on the radio thought Nixon had won, but, on TV, image counted for more than substance. In November, Kennedy eked out a narrow victory, winning the popular vote by only 120,000 out of 69 million votes cast (and, Republicans charged, benefiting from a fraudulent vote count by the notoriously corrupt Chicago Democratic machine).

The End of the 1950s

In January 1961, shortly before leaving office, Eisenhower delivered a televised Farewell Address, modeled to some extent on George Washington's address of 1796. Knowing that the missile gap was a myth, Ike warned against the drumbeat of calls for a new military buildup. He urged Americans to think about the dangerous power of what he called the "**military-industrial complex**"—the conjunction of "an immense military establishment" with a "permanent arms industry"—with an

A photograph of John F. Kennedy and his wife, Jacqueline, strolling along the pier at Hyannisport, Massachusetts, illustrates their youthful appeal.

influence felt in "every office" in the land. "We must never let the weight of this combination," he advised his countrymen, "endanger our liberties or democratic processes." Few Americans shared Ike's concern—far more saw the alliance of the Defense Department and private industry as a source of jobs and national security rather than a threat to democracy. A few years later, however, with the United States locked in an increasingly unpopular war in Vietnam, Eisenhower's warning would come to seem prophetic.

By then, other underpinnings of 1950s life were also in disarray. The tens of millions of cars that made suburban life possible were spewing toxic lead, an additive to make gasoline more efficient, into the atmosphere. Penned in to the east by mountains that kept automobile emissions from being dispersed by the wind, Los Angeles had become synonymous with smog, a type of air pollution produced by cars. The chemical insecticides that enabled agricultural conglomerates to produce the country's remarkable abundance of food were poisoning farm workers, consumers, and the water supply. Housewives were rebelling against a life centered in suburban dream houses. Blacks were increasingly impatient with the slow progress of racial change. The United States, in other words, had entered that most turbulent of decades, the 1960s.

CHAPTER REVIEW AND ONLINE RESOURCES

REVIEW QUESTIONS

1. Explain the meaning of the "American standard of living" during the 1950s.

2. Describe how the automobile transformed American communities and culture in the 1950s.

3. Identify the prescribed roles and aspirations for women during the social conformity of the 1950s.

4. How did governmental policies, business practices, and individual choices contribute to racially segregated suburbs?

5. Explain the ideological rifts among conservatives in the 1950s. Why did many view President Eisenhower as "not one of them"?

6. What was the new "social contract" between labor and management, and how did it benefit both sides as well as the nation as a whole?

7. How did the United States and Soviet Union shift the focus of the Cold War to the Third World?

8. What were the most significant factors that contributed to the growing momentum of the civil rights movement in the 1950s?

9. How did many southern whites, led by their elected officials, resist desegregation and civil rights in the name of "freedom"?

10. How and why did the federal government's concern with U.S. relations overseas shape its involvement with the Brown v. Board of Education case?

KEY TERMS

Levittown (p. 739)

"baby boom" (p. 742)

housing segregation (p. 742)

"urban renewal" (p. 743)

"In God We Trust" (p. 744)

Interstate highway system (p. 747)

Sputnik (p. 748)

National Defense Education Act (p. 748)

massive retaliation (p. 749)

Iranian coup (p. 751)

Geneva Accords (p. 752)

juvenile delinquency (p. 753)

rock-and-roll music (p. 753)

the Beats (p. 754)

League of United Latin American Citizens (p. 755)

Brown v. Board of Education (p. 757)

Montgomery bus boycott (p. 758)

"Southern Manifesto" (p. 760)

"missile gap" (p. 765)

"military-industrial complex" (p. 765)

wwnorton.com /studyspace

VISIT STUDYSPACE FOR THESE RESOURCES AND MORE

- A chapter outline
- A diagnostic chapter quiz
- Interactive maps
- Map worksheets
- Multimedia documents

CHAPTER 25

THE SIXTIES

★

1960-1968

An antiwar demonstrator offers a flower to Military Police stationed outside the Pentagon at a 1967 rally against the Vietnam War. Some 100,000 protesters took part in this demonstration.

On the afternoon of February 1, 1960, four students from North Carolina Agricultural and Technical State University, a black college in Greensboro, North Carolina, entered the local Woolworth's department store. After making a few purchases, they sat down at the lunch counter, an area reserved for whites. Told that they could not be served, they remained in their seats until the store closed. They returned the next morning and the next. After resisting for five months, Woolworth's in July agreed to serve black customers at its lunch counters.

More than any other event, the Greensboro sit-in launched the 1960s: a decade of political activism and social change. Similar demonstrations soon took place throughout the South as activists demanded the integration not only of lunch counters but of parks, pools, restaurants, bowling alleys, libraries, and other facilities as well. By the end of 1960, some 70,000 demonstrators had taken part in sit-ins. Angry whites often assaulted them. But having been trained in nonviolent resistance, the protesters did not strike back.

Even more than elevating blacks to full citizenship, declared the writer James Baldwin, the civil rights movement challenged the United States to rethink "what it really means by freedom"—including whether freedom applied to all Americans or only to part of the population. With

FOCUS QUESTIONS

- *What were the major events in the civil rights movement of the early 1960s?*

- *What were the major crises and policy initiatives of the Kennedy presidency?*

- *What were the purposes and strategies of Johnson's Great Society programs?*

- *How did the civil rights movement change in the mid-1960s?*

- *How did the Vietnam War transform American politics and culture?*

- *What were the sources and significance of the rights revolution of the late 1960s?*

- *In what ways was 1968 a climactic year for the Sixties?*

Participants in a sit-in in Raleigh, North Carolina, in 1960. The protesters, probably students from a local college, brought books and newspapers to emphasize the seriousness of their intentions and their commitment to nonviolence.

Civil rights demonstrators in Orangeburg, South Carolina, in 1960.

their freedom rides, freedom schools, freedom marches, and the insistent cry "freedom now," black Americans and their white allies risked physical and economic retribution to lay claim to freedom. Their courage inspired a host of other challenges to the status quo, including a student movement known as the New Left, the "second wave" of feminism, and activism among other minorities.

By the time the decade ended, these movements had challenged the 1950s' understanding of freedom linked to the Cold War abroad and consumer choice at home. They made American society confront the fact that certain groups, including students, women, members of racial minorities, and homosexuals, felt themselves excluded from full enjoyment of American freedom.

Reflecting back years later on the struggles of the 1960s, one black organizer in Memphis remarked, "All I wanted to do was to live in a free country." Of the movement's accomplishments, he added, "You had to fight for every inch of it. Nobody gave you anything. Nothing."

THE CIVIL RIGHTS REVOLUTION

The Rising Tide of Protest

Ella Baker and SNCC

With the sit-ins, college students for the first time stepped onto the stage of American history as the leading force for social change. In April 1960, Ella Baker, a longtime civil rights organizer, called a meeting of young activists in Raleigh, North Carolina. Out of the gathering came the **Student Non-Violent Coordinating Committee** (SNCC), dedicated to replacing the culture of segregation with a "beloved community" of racial justice and to empowering ordinary blacks to take control of the decisions that affected their lives.

In 1961, the Congress of Racial Equality (CORE) launched the **Freedom Rides**. Integrated groups traveled by bus into the Deep South to test compliance with court orders banning segregation on interstate buses and trains and in terminal facilities. Violent mobs assaulted them. Near Anniston, Alabama, a firebomb was thrown into the vehicle and the passengers beaten as they escaped. In Birmingham, Klansmen attacked riders with bats and chains while police refused to intervene. But the Interstate Commerce Commission ordered buses and terminals desegregated.

James Meredith

As protests escalated, so did the resistance of local authorities. In September 1962, a court ordered the University of Mississippi to admit James Meredith, a black student. The state police stood aside as a mob,

A police officer takes picket signs from young demonstrators in downtown Birmingham, Alabama, during the civil rights campaign of 1963. One sign illustrates how religious beliefs helped to inspire the protesters.

encouraged by Governor Ross Barnett, rampaged through the streets of Oxford, where the university is located. Two bystanders lost their lives in the riot. President Kennedy was forced to dispatch the army to restore order.

Birmingham

The high point of protest came in the spring of 1963, when demonstrations took place in towns and cities across the South. In one week in June, there were more than 15,000 arrests in 186 cities. The dramatic culmination came in Birmingham, Alabama, a citadel of segregation. Even for the Deep South, Birmingham was a violent city—there had been over fifty bombings of black homes and institutions since World War II.

With the movement flagging, some of its leaders invited Martin Luther King Jr. to come to Birmingham. While serving a nine-day prison term in April 1963 for violating a ban on demonstrations, King composed one of his most eloquent pleas for racial justice, the "Letter from Birmingham Jail." Responding to local clergymen who counseled patience, King related the litany of abuses faced by black southerners, from

A fireman assaulting young African-American demonstrators with a high-pressure hose during the climactic demonstrations in Birmingham. Broadcast on television, such pictures proved a serious problem for the United States in its battle for the "hearts and minds" of people around the world and forced the Kennedy administration to confront the contradiction between the rhetoric of freedom and the reality of racism.

police brutality to the daily humiliation of having to explain to their children why they could not enter amusement parks or public swimming pools. The "white moderate," King declared, must put aside fear of disorder and commit himself to racial justice.

Confrontations in Birmingham

In May, King made the bold decision to send black schoolchildren into the streets of Birmingham. Police chief Eugene "Bull" Connor unleashed his forces against the thousands of young marchers. The images, broadcast on television, of children being assaulted with nightsticks, high-pressure fire hoses, and attack dogs produced a wave of revulsion throughout the world. It led President Kennedy, as will be related later, to endorse the movement's goals. Leading businessmen, fearing that the city was becoming an international symbol of brutality, brokered an end to the demonstrations that desegregated downtown stores and restaurants and promised that black salespeople would be hired.

In June 1963, a sniper killed Medgar Evers, field secretary of the NAACP in Mississippi. In September, a bomb exploded at a black Baptist church in Birmingham, killing four young girls. (Not until the year 2002 was the last of those who committed this act of domestic terrorism tried and convicted.)

The March on Washington

On August 28, 1963, two weeks before the Birmingham church bombing, 250,000 black and white Americans converged on the nation's capital for the **March on Washington**, often considered the high point of the nonviolent civil rights movement. Calls for the passage of a civil rights bill pending before Congress took center stage. But the march's goals also included a public-works program to reduce unemployment, an increase in the minimum wage, and a law barring discrimination in employment. These demands, and the marchers' slogan, "Jobs and Freedom," revealed how the black movement had, for the moment, forged an alliance with white liberal groups. On the steps of the Lincoln Memorial, King delivered his most famous speech, including the words, "I have a dream that one day this nation will rise up and live out the true meaning of its creed: 'We hold these truths to be self-evident, that all men are created equal.' "

The movement was not without internal tensions. March organizers ordered SNCC leader John Lewis (later a congressman from Georgia) to tone down his speech, the original text of which called on blacks to "free ourselves of the chains of political and economic slavery" and march "through the heart of Dixie the way Sherman did . . . and burn Jim Crow to the ground." Lewis's rhetoric forecast the more militant turn many in the movement would soon be taking.

Three participants in the 1963 March on Washington stand in front of the White House with signs invoking freedom and the memory of slavery.

Civil rights activists also resurrected the Civil War–era vision of national authority as the custodian of American freedom. Despite the fact that the federal government had for many decades promoted segregation, blacks' historical experience suggested that they had more hope for justice from national power than from local governments or civic institutions—home owners' associations, businesses, private clubs—still riddled with racism. It remained unclear whether the federal government would take up this responsibility.

THE KENNEDY YEARS

John F. Kennedy served as president for less than three years and, in domestic affairs, had few tangible accomplishments. But his administration is widely viewed today as a moment of youthful glamour, soaring hopes, and dynamic leadership at home and abroad.

Kennedy's inaugural address of January 1961 announced a watershed in American politics: "The torch has been passed," he declared, "to a new generation of Americans" who would "pay any price, bear any burden," to "assure the survival and success of liberty." But although the sit-ins were by now a year old, the speech said nothing about segregation or race. At the outset of his presidency, Kennedy regarded civil rights as a distraction from his main concern—vigorous conduct of the Cold War.

"The torch has been passed"

Kennedy and the World

Kennedy's agenda envisioned new initiatives aimed at countering communist influence in the world. One of his first acts was to establish the Peace Corps, which sent young Americans abroad to aid in the economic and educational progress of developing countries and to improve the image of the United States there. When the Soviets in April 1961 launched a satellite carrying the first man into orbit around the earth, Kennedy announced that the United States would mobilize its resources to land a man on the moon by the end of the decade. The goal seemed almost impossible when announced, but it was stunningly accomplished in 1969.

The Peace Corps

Like his predecessors, Kennedy viewed the entire world through the lens of the Cold War. This outlook shaped his dealings with Fidel Castro, who had led a revolution that in 1959 ousted Cuban dictator Fulgencio Batista. Until Castro took power, Cuba was an economic dependency of

Kennedy as Cold Warrior

the United States. When his government began nationalizing American landholdings and other investments and signed an agreement to sell sugar to the Soviet Union, the Eisenhower administration suspended trade with the island. The CIA began training anti-Castro exiles for an invasion of Cuba.

In April 1961, Kennedy allowed the CIA to launch its invasion at a site known as the **Bay of Pigs**. But the assault proved to be a total failure and only strengthened Cuba's ties to the Soviet Union. The Kennedy administration tried other methods, including assassination attempts, to get rid of Castro's government.

The Missile Crisis

Meanwhile, relations between the two "superpowers" deteriorated. In August 1961, in order to stem a growing tide of emigrants fleeing from East to West Berlin, the Soviets constructed a wall separating the two parts of the city. Until its demolition in 1989, the **Berlin Wall** would stand as a tangible symbol of the Cold War and the division of Europe.

A Cold War symbol

The most dangerous crisis of the Kennedy administration, and in many ways of the entire Cold War, came in October 1962, when American spy planes discovered that the Soviet Union was installing missiles in Cuba capable of reaching the United States with nuclear weapons. Rejecting advice from military leaders that he authorize an attack on Cuba, which would almost certainly have triggered a Soviet response in Berlin and perhaps a nuclear war, Kennedy imposed a blockade, or "quarantine," of the island and demanded the missiles' removal. After tense behind-the-scenes negotiations, Soviet premier Nikita Khrushchev agreed to withdraw the missiles; Kennedy pledged that the United States would not invade Cuba and secretly agreed to remove American Jupiter missiles from Turkey, from which they could reach the Soviet Union.

The Cuba blockade

The crisis seems to have lessened Kennedy's passion for the Cold War. Indeed, he appears to have been shocked by the casual way military leaders spoke of "winning" a nuclear exchange in which tens of millions of Americans and Russians were certain to die. In 1963, he called for greater cooperation with the Soviets. That summer, the two countries agreed to a treaty banning the testing of nuclear weapons in the atmosphere and in space. In announcing the agreement, Kennedy paid tribute to the small movement against nuclear weapons that had been urging such a ban for several years.

The 1963 nuclear test-ban treaty

James Meredith, the first black student to attend the University of Mississippi, in a classroom where white classmates refused to sit near him.

Kennedy and Civil Rights

In his first two years in office, Kennedy was preoccupied with foreign policy. But in 1963, the crisis over civil rights eclipsed other concerns. Until then, Kennedy had been reluctant to take a forceful stand on black demands. He used federal force when obstruction of civil rights law became acute, as at the University of Mississippi. But he failed to protect activists from violence, insisting that law enforcement was a local matter.

Events in Birmingham in May 1963 forced Kennedy's hand. In June, he went on national television to call for the passage of a law banning discrimination in all places of public accommodation, a major goal of the civil rights movement. The nation, he asserted, faced a moral crisis: "We preach freedom around the world, . . . but are we to say to the world, and much more importantly, to each other, that this is a land of the free except for Negroes?"

Kennedy did not live to see his civil rights bill enacted. On November 22, 1963, while riding in a motorcade through Dallas, Texas, he was shot and killed. Most likely, the assassin was Lee Harvey Oswald, a troubled former marine. Partly because Oswald was murdered two days later by a local

New York City train passengers reading the news of President Kennedy's assassination, November 22, 1963.

nightclub owner while in police custody, speculation about a possible conspiracy continues to this day. In any event, Kennedy's death brought an abrupt and utterly unexpected end to his presidency. It fell to his successor, Lyndon B. Johnson, to secure passage of the civil rights bill and to launch a program of domestic liberalism far more ambitious than anything Kennedy had envisioned.

LYNDON JOHNSON'S PRESIDENCY

Unlike John F. Kennedy, raised in a wealthy and powerful family, Lyndon Johnson grew up in one of the poorest parts of the United States, the central Texas hill country. Johnson never forgot the poor Mexican and white children he had taught in a Texas school in the early 1930s. Far more interested than Kennedy in domestic reform, he continued to hold the New Deal view that government had an obligation to assist less-fortunate members of society.

Texas background

The Civil Rights Act of 1964

Just five days after Kennedy's assassination, Johnson called on Congress to enact the civil rights bill as the most fitting memorial to his slain predecessor.

Landmark legislation

In 1964, Congress passed the **Civil Rights Act**, which prohibited racial discrimination in employment, institutions like hospitals and schools, and privately owned public accommodations such as restaurants, hotels, and theaters. It also banned discrimination on the grounds of sex—a provision added by opponents of civil rights in an effort to derail the entire bill and embraced by liberal and female members of Congress as a way to broaden its scope. Johnson knew that many whites opposed the new law. After signing it, he turned to an aide and remarked, "I think we delivered the South to the Republican Party."

Freedom Summer

The 1964 voter registration drive

The 1964 law did not address a major concern of the civil rights movement—the right to vote in the South. That summer, a coalition of civil rights groups launched a voter registration drive in Mississippi. Hundreds of white college students from the North traveled to the state to take part in Freedom Summer. An outpouring of violence greeted the campaign, including thirty-five bombings and numerous beatings of civil rights workers. In June, three young activists—Michael Schwerner and

Andrew Goodman, white students from the North, and James Chaney, a local black youth, were kidnapped by a group headed by a deputy sheriff and murdered near Philadelphia, Mississippi. Although many black lives had been lost in the movement, the deaths of the two white students now focused unprecedented attention on Mississippi and on the apparent inability of the federal government to protect citizens seeking to exercise their constitutional rights.

Mississippi

Freedom Summer led directly to one of the most dramatic confrontations of the civil rights era—the campaign by the Mississippi Freedom Democratic Party (MFDP) to take the seats of the state's all-white official party at the 1964 Democratic national convention in Atlantic City, New Jersey. The civil rights movement in Mississippi had created the MFDP, open to all residents of the state. At televised hearings before the credentials committee, Fannie Lou Hamer of the MFDP held a national audience spellbound with her account of growing up in poverty in the Yazoo-Mississippi Delta and of the savage beatings she had endured at the hands of police. Party liberals, including Johnson's running mate, Hubert Humphrey, pressed for a compromise in which two black delegates would be granted seats. But the MFDP rejected the proposal.

The MFDP

Fannie Lou Hamer

The 1964 Election

The events at Atlantic City severely weakened black activists' faith in the responsiveness of the political system and forecast the impending

Fannie Lou Hamer testifying at the Democratic national convention of 1964 on behalf of the Mississippi Freedom Democratic Party.

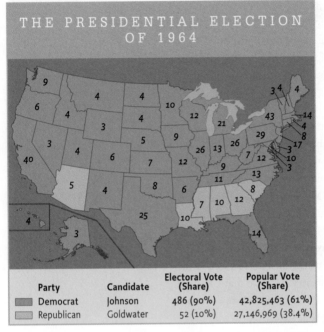

THE PRESIDENTIAL ELECTION OF 1964

Party	Candidate	Electoral Vote (Share)	Popular Vote (Share)
Democrat	Johnson	486 (90%)	42,825,463 (61%)
Republican	Goldwater	52 (10%)	27,146,969 (38.4%)

breakup of the coalition between the civil rights movement and the liberal wing of the Democratic Party. For the moment, however, the movement rallied behind Johnson's campaign for reelection. Johnson's opponent, Senator Barry Goldwater of Arizona, demanded a more aggressive conduct of the Cold War. But Goldwater directed most of his critique against "internal" dangers to freedom, especially the New Deal welfare state, which he believed stifled individual initiative and independence. He voted against the Civil Rights Act of 1964. His acceptance speech at the Republican national convention contained the explosive statement, "Extremism in the defense of liberty is no vice."

Stigmatized by the Democrats as an extremist who would repeal Social Security and risk nuclear war, Goldwater went down to a disastrous defeat. Johnson received almost 43 million votes to Goldwater's 27 million. Democrats swept to two-to-one majorities in both houses of Congress. But Goldwater's message enabled him to carry five Deep South states, and segregationist governor George Wallace of Alabama showed in several Democratic primaries that politicians could strike electoral gold by appealing to white opposition to the civil rights movement. Although few realized it, the 1964 campaign marked a milestone in the resurgence of American conservatism.

The Conservative Sixties

The 1960s, today recalled as a decade of radicalism, clearly had a conservative side as well. With the founding in 1960 of Young Americans for Freedom (YAF), conservative students emerged as a force in politics. There were striking parallels between the Sharon Statement, issued by ninety young people who gathered at the estate of conservative intellectual William F. Buckley in Sharon, Connecticut, to establish YAF, and the Port Huron Statement of SDS of 1962 (discussed later in this chapter). Both manifestos portrayed youth as the cutting edge of a new radicalism, and both claimed to offer a route to greater freedom. The Sharon

Young Americans for Freedom

A 1967 rally by members of Young Americans for Freedom, a conservative group that flourished in the 1960s.

Statement summarized beliefs that had circulated among conservatives during the past decade—the free market underpinned "personal freedom," government must be strictly limited, and "international communism," the gravest threat to liberty, must be destroyed.

Goldwater also brought new constituencies to the conservative cause. His campaign aroused enthusiasm in the rapidly expanding suburbs of southern California and the Southwest. Orange County, California, many of whose residents had recently arrived from the East and Midwest and worked in defense-related industries, became a nationally known center of grassroots conservative activism. And by carrying five states of the Deep South, Goldwater showed that the civil rights revolution had redrawn the nation's political map, opening the door to a "southern strategy" that would eventually lead the entire region into the Republican Party.

Conservative strength

Well before the rise of Black Power, a reaction against civil rights gains offered conservatives new opportunities and threatened the stability of the Democratic coalition. In 1962, YAF bestowed its Freedom Award on Senator Strom Thurmond of South Carolina, one of the country's most prominent segregationists. During the 1960s, most conservatives abandoned talk of racial superiority and inferiority. But conservative appeals to law and order, "freedom of association," and the evils of welfare often had strong racial overtones. Racial divisions would prove to be a political gold mine for conservatives.

Strom Thurmond

The Voting Rights Act

Selma, Alabama

One last legislative triumph, however, lay ahead for the civil rights movement. In January 1965, King launched a voting rights campaign in Selma, Alabama, a city where only 355 of 15,000 black residents had been allowed to register to vote. In March, defying a ban by Governor Wallace, King attempted to lead a march from Selma to the state capital, Montgomery. When the marchers reached the bridge leading out of the city, state police assaulted them with cattle prods, whips, and tear gas.

LBJ's support

Once again, violence against nonviolent demonstrators flashed across television screens throughout the world. Calling Selma a milestone in "man's unending search for freedom," Johnson asked Congress to enact a law securing the right to vote. He closed his speech by quoting the demonstrators' song, "We Shall Overcome." Never before had the movement received so powerful an endorsement from the federal government. Congress quickly passed the **Voting Rights Act of 1965**, which allowed federal officials to register voters. In addition, the Twenty-fourth Amendment to the Constitution outlawed the poll tax, which had long prevented poor blacks (and some whites) from voting in the South.

Immigration Reform

The Hart-Celler Act and its consequences

By 1965, the civil rights movement had succeeded in eradicating the legal bases of second-class citizenship. The belief that racism should no longer serve as a basis of public policy spilled over into other realms. In 1965, the **Hart-Celler Act** abandoned the national-origins quota system of immigration, which had excluded Asians and severely restricted southern and eastern Europeans. The law established new, racially neutral criteria for immigration, notably family reunification and possession of skills in demand in the United States. On the other hand, because of growing hostility in the Southwest to Mexican immigration, the law established the first limit, 120,000, on newcomers from the Western Hemisphere.

New wave of immigration

The new law had many unexpected results. At the time, immigrants represented only 5 percent of the American population—the lowest proportion since the 1830s. No one anticipated that the new quotas not only would lead to an explosive rise in immigration but also would spark a dramatic shift in which newcomers from Latin America, the Caribbean, and Asia came to outnumber those from Europe. Taken together, the civil rights revolution and immigration reform marked the triumph of a pluralist conception of Americanism. By 1976, 85 percent of respondents to a public-opinion survey agreed with the statement, "The United States was meant to be...a country made up of many races, religions, and nationalities."

American pluralism

The Great Society

After his landslide victory of 1964, Johnson outlined the most sweeping proposal for governmental action to promote the general welfare since the New Deal. Johnson's initiatives of 1965–1967, known collectively as the **Great Society**, provided health services to the poor and elderly in the new Medicaid and Medicare programs and poured federal funds into education and urban development. New agencies, such as the Equal Employment Opportunity Commission, the National Endowments for the Humanities and for the Arts, and a national public broadcasting network, were created. These measures greatly expanded the powers of the federal government, and they completed and extended the social agenda (with the exception of national health insurance) that had been stalled in Congress since 1938.

Expanding social programs

Unlike the New Deal, the Great Society was a response to prosperity, not depression. The mid-1960s were a time of rapid economic expansion, fueled by increased government spending and a tax cut on individuals and businesses initially proposed by Kennedy and enacted in 1964. Johnson and Democratic liberals believed that economic growth made it possible to fund ambitious new government programs and to improve the quality of life.

The War on Poverty

The centerpiece of the Great Society, however, was the crusade to eradicate poverty, launched by Johnson early in 1964. Michael Harrington's 1962 book *The Other America* revealed that 40 to 50 million Americans lived in poverty.

During the 1930s, Democrats had attributed poverty to an imbalance of economic power and flawed economic institutions. In the 1960s, the administration attributed it to an absence of skills and a lack of proper attitudes and work habits. Thus, the **War on Poverty** did not address the economic changes that were reducing the number of well-paid manufacturing jobs and leaving poor families in rural areas like Appalachia and decaying urban ghettos with little hope of economic advancement.

One of the Great Society's most popular and successful components, food stamps, offered direct aid to the poor. But, in general, the War on

As part of his War on Poverty, President Lyndon Johnson visited Appalachia, one of the poorest places in the United States.

Poverty concentrated not on direct economic aid but on equipping the poor with skills and rebuilding their spirit and motivation. It provided Head Start (an early childhood education program), job training, legal services, and scholarships for poor college students. It also created VISTA, a domestic version of the Peace Corps for the inner cities. The War on Poverty required that poor people play a leading part in the design and implementation of local policies, a recipe for continuing conflict with local political leaders accustomed to controlling the flow of federal dollars.

Freedom and Equality

Recognizing that black poverty was fundamentally different from white, because its roots lay in "past injustice and present prejudice," Johnson sought to redefine the relationship between freedom and equality. Economic liberty, he insisted, meant more than equal opportunity: "You do not wipe away the scars of centuries by saying: Now you are free to go where you want, do as you desire, and choose the leaders you please. . . . We seek . . . not just equality as a right and a theory, but equality as a fact and as a result."

Johnson's Great Society may not have achieved equality "as a fact," but it represented the most expansive effort in the nation's history to mobilize the powers of the national government to address the needs of the least-advantaged Americans.

Coupled with the decade's high rate of economic growth, the War on Poverty succeeded in reducing the incidence of poverty from 22 percent to 13 percent of American families during the 1960s. It has fluctuated around the latter figure ever since. By the 1990s, thanks to the civil rights movement and the Great Society, the historic gap between whites and blacks in education, income, and access to skilled employment narrowed considerably. But nearly a quarter of all black children still lived in poverty.

FIGURE 25.1 Percentage of Population below Poverty Level, by Race, 1959–1969*

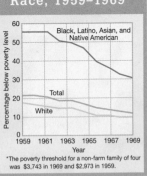

*The poverty threshold for a non-farm family of four was $3,743 in 1969 and $2,973 in 1959.

During the 1960s, an expanding economy and government programs assisting the poor produced a steady decrease in the percentage of Americans living in poverty.

THE CHANGING BLACK MOVEMENT

In the mid-1960s, economic issues rose to the forefront of the civil rights agenda. Violent outbreaks in black ghettos outside the South drew attention to the national scope of racial injustice and to inequalities in jobs, education, and housing that the dismantling of legal segregation left intact.

A semblance of normal life resumes amid the rubble of the Watts uprising of August 1965.

The Ghetto Uprisings

The first riots—really, battles between angry blacks and the predominantly white police (widely seen by many ghetto residents as an occupying army)—erupted in Harlem in 1964. Far larger was the Watts uprising of 1965, which took place in the black ghetto of Los Angeles only days after Johnson signed the Voting Rights Act. An estimated 50,000 persons took part in this "rebellion," attacking police and firemen, looting white-owned businesses, and burning buildings. It required 15,000 police and National Guardsmen to restore order, by which time thirty-five people lay dead, 900 were injured, and $30 million worth of property had been destroyed.

Watts riots

By the summer of 1967, urban uprisings left twenty-three dead in Newark and forty-three in Detroit, where entire blocks went up in flames and property damage ran into the hundreds of millions of dollars. The violence led Johnson to appoint a commission headed by Illinois governor Otto Kerner to study the causes of urban rioting. Released in 1968, the Kerner Report blamed the violence on "segregation and poverty" and offered a powerful indictment of "white racism." But the report failed to offer any clear proposals for change.

Detroit and Newark

With black unemployment twice that of whites and the average black family income little more than half the white norm, the movement looked for ways to "make freedom real" for black Americans. In 1964, King called for a "Bill of Rights for the Disadvantaged" to mobilize the nation's resources to abolish economic deprivation. His proposal was directed against poverty in general, but King also insisted that after "doing something special *against* the Negro for hundreds of years," the United States had an obligation to "do something special *for* him now"—an early call for what would come to be known as "affirmative action."

Affirmative action

In 1966, King launched the Chicago Freedom Movement, with demands quite different from its predecessors in the South—an end to discrimination by employers and unions, equal access to mortgages, the integration of public housing, and the construction of low-income housing scattered throughout the region. Confronting the entrenched power of Mayor Richard J. Daley's political machine and the ferocious opposition of white home owners, the movement failed.

Malcolm X

The civil rights movement's first phase had produced a clear set of objectives, far-reaching accomplishments, and a series of coherent if sometimes competitive organizations. The second witnessed political fragmentation and few significant victories. Even during the heyday of the integration struggle, the fiery orator Malcolm X had insisted that blacks must control the political and economic resources of their communities and rely on their own efforts rather than working with whites. Malcolm Little dropped his "slave surname" in favor of "X," symbolizing blacks' separation from their African ancestry. He became a spokesman for the Nation of Islam, or Black Muslims, and a sharp critic of the ideas of integration and nonviolence.

Black control

On a 1964 trip to Mecca, Saudi Arabia, Islam's spiritual home, Malcolm X witnessed harmony among Muslims of all races. He now began to speak of the possibility of interracial cooperation for radical change in the United States. But when members of the Nation of Islam assassinated him in February 1965 after he had formed his own Organization of Afro-American Unity, Malcolm X left neither a consistent ideology nor a coherent movement. However, his call for blacks to rely on their own resources struck a chord among the urban poor and younger civil rights activists.

Legacy of Malcolm X

The Rise of Black Power

Malcolm X was the intellectual father of "**Black Power**," a slogan that came to national attention in 1966 when SNCC leader Stokely Carmichael used it during a civil rights march in Mississippi.

A highly imprecise idea, Black Power suggested everything from the election of more black officials (hardly a radical notion) to the belief that black Americans were a colonized people whose freedom could be won only through a revolutionary struggle for self-determination. But however employed, the idea reflected the radicalization of young civil rights activists and sparked an explosion of racial self-assertion, reflected in the slogan "black is beautiful." The abandonment of the word "Negro" in favor of "Afro-American," as well as the popularity of African styles of dress and the "natural," or "Afro," hairdo among both men and women reflected a new sense of racial pride and a rejection of white norms.

Female students on the campus of Howard University in Washington, D.C., sport the Afro, a hairstyle representative of the "black is beautiful" campaign of the 1960s.

Inspired by the idea of black self-determination, SNCC and CORE repudiated their previous interracialism, and new militant groups sprang into existence. Most prominent of the new groups, in terms of publicity, if not numbers, was the Black Panther Party. Founded in Oakland, California, in 1966, it became notorious for advocating armed self-defense in response to police brutality. The party's youthful members alarmed whites by wearing military garb, although they also ran health clinics, schools, and children's breakfast programs. But internal disputes and a campaign against the Black Panthers by police and the FBI, which left several leaders dead in shootouts, destroyed the organization.

By 1967, with the escalation of U.S. military involvement in Vietnam, the War on Poverty had ground to a halt. By then, with ghetto uprisings punctuating the urban landscape, the antiwar movement assuming massive proportions, and millions of young people ostentatiously rejecting mainstream values, American society faced its greatest crisis since the Depression.

Social crisis

VIETNAM AND THE NEW LEFT

Old and New Lefts

To most Americans, the rise of a protest movement among white youth came as a complete surprise. If blacks' grievances appeared self-evident, those of white college students were difficult to understand. What persuaded large numbers of children of affluence to reject the values and institutions of their society? In part, the answer lay in a redefinition of the meaning of freedom by what came to be called the New Left.

The New Left

The New Left challenged not only mainstream America but also what it dismissively called the Old Left. Unlike the Communist Party, it did not take the Soviet Union as a model or see the working class as the main agent of social change. Instead of economic equality, the language of New Deal liberals, the New Left spoke of loneliness, isolation, and alienation, of powerlessness in the face of bureaucratic institutions and a hunger for authenticity that affluence could not provide. By 1968, thanks to the coming of age of the baby-boom generation and the growing number of jobs that required post–high school skills, more than 7 million students attended college, more than the number of farmers or steelworkers.

Rising college attendance

The New Left's greatest inspiration was the black freedom movement. More than any other event, the sit-ins catalyzed white student activism. Here was the unlikely combination that created the upheaval known as The Sixties—the convergence of society's most excluded members demanding full access to all its benefits, with the children of the middle class rejecting the social mainstream.

The Fading Consensus

The years 1962 and 1963 witnessed the appearance of several pathbreaking books that challenged one or another aspect of the 1950s consensus. James Baldwin's *The Fire Next Time* gave angry voice to the black revolution. Rachel Carson's *Silent Spring* exposed the environmental costs of economic growth. Michael Harrington's *The Other America* revealed the persistence of poverty amid plenty. *The Death and Life of Great American Cities*, by Jane Jacobs, criticized urban renewal, the removal of the poor from city centers, and the destruction of neighborhoods to build highways.

Members of Students for a Democratic Society (SDS) at a 1963 National Council meeting in Indiana. Despite their raised fists, they appear eminently respectable compared to radicals who emerged later in the decade. The group is entirely white.

Yet in some ways the most influential critique of all arose in 1962 from Students for a Democratic Society (SDS), an offshoot of the socialist League for Industrial Democracy. Meeting at Port Huron, Michigan, some sixty college students adopted a document that captured the mood and summarized the beliefs of this generation of student protesters.

The **Port Huron Statement** offered a new vision of social change. "We seek the establishment," it proclaimed, of "a democracy of individual participation, [in which] the individual shares in those social decisions determining the quality and direction of his life." Freedom, for the New Left, meant "participatory democracy." Although rarely defined with precision, this became a standard by which students judged existing social arrangements—workplaces, schools, government—and found them wanting.

Mario Savio, a leader of the 1964 Free Speech Movement at the University of California, Berkeley, addressing a crowd on campus from the roof of a police car.

In 1964, events at the University of California, Berkeley, revealed the possibility for a mobilization of students in the name of participatory democracy. Berkeley was an immense, impersonal institution where enrollments in many classes approached 1,000 students. The spark that set student protests alight was a new rule prohibiting political groups from using a central area of the campus to spread their ideas. Students responded by creating the Free Speech movement.

Thousands of Berkeley students became involved in the protests in the months that followed. Their program moved from demanding a repeal of the new rule to a critique of the entire structure of the university and of an education geared toward preparing graduates for corporate jobs. The university gave in on the speech ban early in 1965.

America and Vietnam

By 1965 the black movement and the emergence of the New Left had shattered the climate of consensus of the 1950s. But what transformed protest into a full-fledged generational rebellion was the war in Vietnam. The war tragically revealed the danger that Walter Lippmann had warned of at the outset of the Cold War—viewing the entire world and every local situation within it through the either-or lens of an anticommunist crusade. A Vietnam specialist in the State Department who attended a policy meeting in August 1963 later recalled "the abysmal ignorance around the table of the particular facts of Vietnam. . . . They [believed] that we could manipulate other states and build nations; that we knew all the answers."

Vietnam and anticommunism

As noted in the previous chapter, the Truman and Eisenhower administrations had cast their lot with French colonialism in the region. After the French defeat, they financed the creation of a pro-American South

VOICES OF FREEDOM

Although the 1960s is usually thought of as a decade of youthful radicalism, it also witnessed the growth of conservative movements. The Sharon Statement marked the emergence of Young Americans for Freedom as a force for conservatism in American politics.

In this time of moral and political crisis, it is the responsibility of the youth of America to affirm certain eternal truths. We, as young conservatives, believe:

That foremost among the transcendent values is the individual's use of his God-given free will, whence derives his right to be free from the restrictions of arbitrary force;

That liberty is indivisible, and that political freedom cannot long exist without economic freedom;

That the purposes of government are to protect those freedoms through the preservation of internal order, the provision of national defense, and the administration of justice;

That when government ventures beyond these lawful functions, it accumulates power which tends to diminish order and liberty; . . .

That the market economy, allocating resources by the free play of supply and demand, is the single economic system compatible with the requirements of personal freedom and constitutional government, and that it is at the same time the most productive supplier of human needs; . . .

That the forces of international Communism are, at present, the greatest single threat to these liberties;

That the United States should stress victory over, rather than coexistence with, this menace.

From Tom Hayden and Others, The Port Huron Statement (June 1962)

One of the most influential documents of the 1960s emerged in 1962 from a meeting sponsored by the Students for a Democratic Society in Port Huron, Michigan. Its call for a "democracy of individual participation" inspired many of the social movements of the decade and offered a critique of institutions ranging from the government to universities that failed to live up to this standard.

We are the people of this generation, bred in at least modest comfort, housed now in universities, looking uncomfortably to the world we inherit.... Freedom and equality for each individual, government of, by, and for the people—these American values we found good principles by which we could live as men.

As we grew, however, our comfort was penetrated by events too troubling to dismiss. First, the ... Southern struggle against racial bigotry compelled most of us from silence to activism. Second, ... the proclaimed peaceful intentions of the United States contradicted its economic and military investments in the Cold War.... The conventional moral terms of the age, the politician moralities—"free world," "people's democracies"—reflect realities poorly if at all, and seem to function more as ruling myths than as descriptive principles. But neither has our experience in the universities brought us moral enlightenment. Our professors and administrators sacrifice controversy to public relations; ... their skills and silence are purchased by investors in the arms race....

We regard *men* as infinitely precious and possessed of unfulfilled capacities for reason, freedom, and love. In affirming these principles we are aware of countering perhaps the dominant conceptions of man in the twentieth century: that he is a thing to be manipulated, and that he is inherently incapable of directing his own affairs. We oppose the depersonalization that reduces human beings to the status of things—if anything, the brutalities of the twentieth century teach that means and ends are intimately related, that vague appeals to "posterity" cannot justify the mutilations of the present.... We see little reason why men cannot meet with increasing skill the complexities and responsibilities of their situation, if society is organized not for minority, but for majority, participation in decision-making.

We would replace power rooted in possession, privilege, or circumstance by power and uniqueness rooted in love, reflectiveness, reason, and creativity. As a social system we seek the establishment of a democracy of individual participation [so] that the individual [can] share in those social decisions determining the quality and direction of his life.... A new left must consist of younger people.... [It] must start controversy throughout the land, if national policies and national apathy are to be reversed.

QUESTIONS

1. *How do the young conservatives who wrote the Sharon Statement understand freedom?*

2. *What do the authors of the Port Huron Statement appear to mean by participatory democracy?*

3. *What are the main differences, and are there any similarities, between the outlooks of the young conservatives and the young radicals?*

Commitment to South Vietnam

Vietnamese government. By the 1960s, the United States was committed to the survival of this corrupt regime.

Fear that the public would not forgive them for "losing" Vietnam made it impossible for presidents Kennedy and Johnson to remove the United States from an increasingly untenable situation. Kennedy's foreign policy advisers saw Vietnam as a test of whether the United States could, through "counterinsurgency"—intervention to counter internal uprisings in non-communist countries—halt the spread of Third World revolutions. South Vietnamese leader Ngo Dinh Diem resisted American advice to broaden his government's base of support. In October 1963, after large Buddhist demonstrations against his regime, the United States approved a military coup that led to Diem's death. When Kennedy was assassinated the following month, there were 17,000 American military advisers in South Vietnam.

Lyndon Johnson's War

Lyndon B. Johnson came to the presidency with little experience in foreign relations. But he knew that Republicans had used the "loss" of China as a weapon against Truman.

In August 1964, North Vietnamese vessels encountered an American ship on a spy mission off its coast. When North Vietnamese patrol boats fired on the American vessel, Johnson proclaimed that the United States was a victim of "aggression." In response, Congress passed the **Gulf of Tonkin resolution**, authorizing the president to take "all necessary measures to repel armed attack" in Vietnam. Only two members—senators Ernest Gruening of Alaska and Wayne Morse of Oregon—voted against giving Johnson this blank check. (Over forty years later, in December 2005, the National Security Agency finally released hundreds of pages of secret documents that made it clear that no North Vietnamese attack had actually taken place.)

Immediately after Johnson's 1964 election, the National Security Council recommended that the United States begin air strikes against North Vietnam and introduce American ground troops in the south. Johnson put the plan into effect. At almost the same time, he intervened in the Dominican Republic. Here, military leaders in 1963 had overthrown the left-wing but noncommunist Juan Bosch, the country's first elected president since 1924.

Secretary of Defense Robert McNamara, on the left, and his deputy, Cyrus Vance, at a May 1965 meeting at the White House where the war in Vietnam was discussed. A bust of President Kennedy stands in the background. McNamara later wrote in his memoirs that his misgivings only grew as the war progressed.

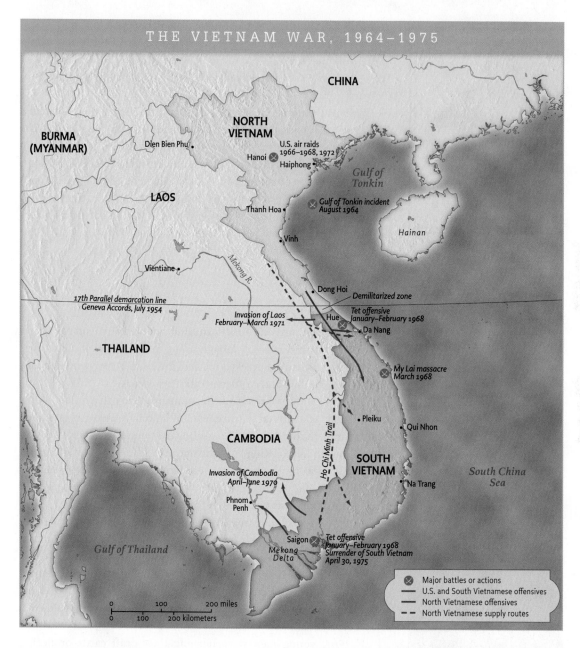

THE VIETNAM WAR, 1964–1975

CHINA

BURMA
(MYANMAR)

NORTH
VIETNAM

Dien Bien Phu

Hanoi — U.S. air raids
1966–1968, 1972

Haiphong

*Gulf of
Tonkin*

LAOS

Thanh Hoa — Gulf of Tonkin incident
August 1964

Vinh

Hainan

Vientiane

Mekong R.

Dong Hoi — Demilitarized zone

17th Parallel demarcation line
Geneva Accords, July 1954

Invasion of Laos
February–March 1971

Hue — Tet offensive
January–February 1968

Da Nang

THAILAND

My Lai massacre
March 1968

Pleiku

Qui Nhon

CAMBODIA

Ho Chi Minh Trail

SOUTH
VIETNAM

*South China
Sea*

Invasion of Cambodia
April–June 1970

Na Trang

Phnom
Penh

Gulf of Thailand

Saigon — Tet offensive
January–February 1968
Surrender of South Vietnam
April 30, 1975

*Mekong
Delta*

	Major battles or actions
---	U.S. and South Vietnamese offensives
	North Vietnamese offensives
	North Vietnamese supply routes

0   100   200 miles
0 100   200 kilometers

A war of aerial bombing and small guerrilla skirmishes rather than fixed land battles, Vietnam was the longest war in American history and the only one the United States has lost.

An antiwar placard parodies a famous army recruiting poster from World War I. The original read, "I Want You."

In April 1965, another group of military men attempted to restore Bosch to power but were defeated by the ruling junta. Fearing the unrest would lead to "another Cuba," Johnson dispatched 22,000 American troops. The operation's success seemed to bolster Johnson's determination in Vietnam.

By 1968, the number of American troops in Vietnam exceeded half a million, and the conduct of the war had become more and more brutal. The North Vietnamese mistreated American prisoners of war held in a camp known sardonically by the inmates as the Hanoi Hilton. American planes dropped more tons of bombs on the small countries of North and South Vietnam than both sides had used in all of World War II. They spread chemicals that destroyed forests to deprive the Viet Cong of hiding places and dropped bombs filled with napalm, a gelatinous form of gasoline that burns the skin of anyone exposed to it.

The Antiwar Movement

Opposition to the Vietnam War

As casualties mounted and American bombs poured down on North and South Vietnam, the Cold War foreign policy consensus began to unravel. By 1968, the war had sidetracked much of the Great Society and had torn families, universities, and the Democratic Party apart.

Opposition to the war became the organizing theme that united people with all kinds of doubts and discontents. With college students exempted from the draft, the burden of fighting fell on the working class and the poor. In 1967, Martin Luther King Jr. condemned the administration's Vietnam policy as an unconscionable use of violence and for draining resources from needs at home. At this point, King was the most prominent American to speak out against the war.

Two young members of the counterculture at their wedding in New Mexico.

As for SDS, the war seemed the opposite of participatory democracy, since American involvement had come through secret commitments and decisions made by political elites, with no real public debate. In April 1965, SDS invited opponents of American policy in Vietnam to assemble in Washington, D.C. The turnout of 25,000 amazed the organizers, offering the first hint that the antiwar movement would soon enjoy a mass constituency.

By 1967, young men were burning their draft cards or fleeing to Canada to avoid fighting in what they considered an unjust war. In October of that year, 100,000 antiwar protesters assembled at the Lincoln Memorial in Washington, D.C. Many marched across the Potomac River to the Pentagon, where photographers captured them

THE NEW MOVEMENTS AND THE RIGHTS REVOLUTION

The civil rights revolution, soon followed by the rise of the New Left, inspired other Americans to voice their grievances and claim their rights. By the late 1960s, new social movements dotted the political landscape.

The counterculture's notion of liberation centered on the free individual. Starting in 1960, the mass marketing of birth-control pills made possible what "free lovers" had long demanded—the separation of sex from procreation. By the late 1960s, sexual freedom had become as much an element of the youth rebellion as long hair and drugs. The sexual revolution was central to another mass movement that emerged in the 1960s— the "second wave" of feminism.

"Second wave" feminism

The Feminine Mystique

During the 1950s, some commentators had worried that the country was wasting its "woman power," a potential weapon in the Cold War. But the public reawakening of feminist consciousness did not get its start until the publication in 1963 of Betty Friedan's ***The Feminine Mystique***. Friedan had written pioneering articles during the 1940s on pay discrimination against women workers and racism in the workplace for the newspaper of the United Electrical Workers' union. But, like other social critics of the 1950s, she now took as her themes the emptiness of consumer culture and the discontents of the middle class. Her opening chapter, "The Problem That Has No Name," painted a devastating picture of talented, educated women trapped in a world that viewed marriage and motherhood as their primary goals.

Betty Friedan

Few books have had the impact of *The Feminine Mystique*. Friedan was deluged by desperate letters from female readers relating how the suburban dream had become a nightmare.

The law slowly began to address feminist concerns. In 1963, Congress passed the Equal Pay Act, barring sex discrimination among holders of the same jobs. The Civil Rights Act of 1964, as noted earlier, prohibited inequalities based on sex as well as race. Deluged with complaints of discrimination by working women, the Equal Employment Opportunity Commission established by the law became a major force in breaking down barriers to female employment. In 1966 the **National Organization for Women** (NOW) was formed, with Friedan as president. Modeled on

Sex discrimination and the law

civil rights organizations, it demanded equal opportunity in jobs, education, and political participation and attacked the "false image of women" spread by the mass media.

Women's Liberation

A different female revolt was brewing within the civil rights and student movements. Young women who had embraced an ideology of social equality and personal freedom and learned methods of political organizing encountered inequality and sexual exploitation in organizations like SNCC and SDS. Many women in the movement found themselves relegated to typing, cooking, and cleaning for male coworkers.

Raising consciousness

By 1967, women throughout the country were establishing "consciousness-raising" groups to discuss the sources of their discontent. The new feminism burst onto the national scene at the Miss America beauty pageant of 1968, when protesters filled a "freedom trash can" with objects of "oppression"—girdles, brassieres, high-heeled shoes, and copies of *Playboy* and *Cosmopolitan*. (Contrary to legend, they did not set the contents on fire, but the media invented a new label for radical women—"bra burners.") Inside the hall, demonstrators unfurled banners carrying the slogans "Freedom for Women" and "Women's Liberation."

In 1967, in a celebrated incident arising from the new feminism, a race official tried to eject Kathrine Switzer from the Boston Marathon, only to be pushed aside by other runners. Considered too fragile for the marathon (whose course covers more than twenty-six miles), women were prohibited from running. Switzer completed the race, and today hundreds of thousands of women around the world compete in marathons each year.

Personal Freedom

The women's liberation movement inspired a major expansion of the idea of freedom by insisting that it should be applied to the most intimate realms of life. They contended that sexual relations, conditions of marriage, and standards of beauty were as much "political" questions as the war, civil rights, and the class tensions that had traditionally inspired the Left to action. The idea that family life is not off limits to considerations of power and justice repudiated the family-oriented public culture of the 1950s, and it permanently changed Americans' definition of freedom.

Radical feminists' first public campaign demanded the repeal of state laws that underscored women's lack of self-determination by banning abortions or leaving it up to physicians to decide whether a pregnancy could be terminated. In 1969, a group of feminists disrupted legislative hearings on New York's law banning abortions, where the experts scheduled to testify consisted of fourteen men and a Roman Catholic nun.

By this time, feminist ideas had entered the mainstream. In 1962, a poll showed that two-thirds of American women did not feel themselves to be victims of discrimination. By 1974, two-thirds did.

Gay Liberation

In a decade full of surprises, perhaps the greatest of all was the emergence of the movement for gay liberation. Gay men and lesbians had long been stigmatized as sinful or mentally disordered. Most states made homosexual acts illegal, and police regularly harassed the gay subcultures that existed in major cities like San Francisco and New York. Although homosexuals had achieved considerable success in the arts and fashion, most kept their sexual orientation secret, or "in the closet."

Part of the Gay Liberation Day demonstration in New York City in June 1970.

Stonewall

If one moment marked the advent of "gay liberation," it was a 1969 police raid on the Stonewall Bar in New York's Greenwich Village, a gathering place for homosexuals. Rather than bowing to police harassment, as in the past, gays fought back. Five days of rioting followed, and a militant movement was born. Gay men and lesbians stepped out of the "closet" to insist that sexual orientation is a matter of rights, power, and identity. Prejudice against homosexuals persisted. But within a few years, "gay pride" marches were being held in numerous cities.

Latino Activism

As in the case of blacks, a movement for legal rights had long flourished among Mexican-Americans. But the mid-1960s saw the flowering of a new militancy challenging the group's second-class economic status. Like Black Power advocates, the movement emphasized pride in both the Mexican past and the new Chicano culture that had arisen in the United States. Unlike the Black Power movement and SDS, it was closely linked to labor struggles. Beginning in 1965, César Chavez, the son of migrant farm workers and a disciple of King, led a series of nonviolent protests, including marches, fasts, and a national boycott of California grapes, to pressure growers to agree to labor contracts with the United Farm Workers union (UFW). The UFW was as much a mass movement for civil rights as a campaign for economic betterment. The boycott mobilized Latino communities

Chicano culture

UFW

throughout the Southwest and drew national attention to the pitifully low wages and oppressive working conditions of migrant laborers. In 1970, the major growers agreed to contracts with the UFW.

Red Power

The 1960s also witnessed an upsurge of Native American militancy. The Truman and Eisenhower administrations had sought to dismantle the reservation system and integrate Indians into the American mainstream—a policy known as "termination," since it meant ending recognition of the remaining elements of Indian sovereignty. Many Indian leaders protested vigorously against this policy, and it was abandoned by President Kennedy. Johnson's War on Poverty channeled increased federal funds to reservations. But like other minority groups, Indian activists demanded not simply economic aid but self-determination.

Founded in 1968, the **American Indian movement** staged protests demanding greater tribal self-government and the restoration of economic resources guaranteed in treaties. In 1969, a group calling itself "Indians of All Nations" occupied (or from their point of view, re-occupied) Alcatraz Island in San Francisco Bay, claiming that it had been illegally seized from its original inhabitants. In the years that followed, many Indian tribes would win greater control over education and economic development on the reservations. Indian activists would bring land claims suits, demanding and receiving monetary settlements for past dispossession. In an atmosphere of rising Native American pride, the number of Americans identifying themselves as Indians doubled between 1970 and 1990.

The occupation of Alcatraz Island in San Francisco Bay in 1969 by "Indians of All Tribes" symbolized the emergence of a new militancy among Native Americans.

Silent Spring

Another movement, environmentalism, called into question different pillars of American life—the equation of progress with endless increases in consumption and the faith that science, technology, and economic growth would advance social welfare. In keeping with the spirit of the Sixties, the new environmentalism reflected the very affluence celebrated by proponents of the American Way. As the "quality of life"—including physical fitness, health, and opportunities to enjoy leisure activities—occupied a greater role in the lives of middle-class Americans, the environmental consequences of economic growth received increased attention.

The publication in 1962 of *Silent Spring* by the marine biologist Rachel Carson brought home to millions of readers the effects of DDT, an insecti-

cide widely used by home owners and farmers against mosquitoes, gypsy moths, and other insects. In chilling detail, Carson related how DDT killed birds and animals and caused sickness among humans.

Carson's work launched the modern environmental movement. The Sierra Club, founded in the 1890s to preserve forests, saw its membership more than triple, and other groups sprang into existence to alert the country to the dangers of water contamination, air pollution, lead in paint, and the extinction of animal species. Nearly every state quickly banned the use of DDT.

Despite vigorous opposition from business groups that considered its proposals a violation of property rights, environmentalism attracted the broadest bipartisan support of any of the new social movements. Under Republican president Richard Nixon, Congress during the late 1960s and early 1970s passed a series of measures to protect the environment, including the Clean Air and Clean Water Acts and the Endangered Species Act. On April 22, 1970, the first Earth Day, some 20 million people, most of them under the age of thirty, participated in rallies, concerts, and teach-ins.

> *Environmental legislation*

Closely related to environmentalism was the consumer movement, spearheaded by the lawyer Ralph Nader. His book *Unsafe at Any Speed* (1965) exposed how auto manufacturers produced highly dangerous vehicles. General Motors, whose Chevrolet Corvair Nader singled out for its tendency to roll over in certain driving situations, hired private investigators to discredit him.

Nader's campaigns laid the groundwork for the numerous new consumer protection laws and regulations of the 1970s. Unlike 1960s movements that emphasized personal liberation, environmentalism and the consumer movement called for limiting some kinds of freedom—especially the right to use private property in any way the owner desired—in the name of a greater common good.

Karl Hubenthal's December 8, 1976, cartoon for the *Los Angeles Herald-Examiner* celebrates the rights revolution as an expansion of American liberty.

The Rights Revolution

It is one of the more striking ironies of the 1960s that although the "rights revolution" began in the streets, it achieved constitutional legitimacy through the Supreme Court, historically the most conservative branch of government. Under the guidance of Chief Justice Earl Warren, the Court vastly expanded the rights enjoyed by all Americans and placed them beyond the reach of legislative and local majorities.

The Court moved to rein in the anticommunist crusade. The justices overturned convictions of individuals for advocating the overthrow of the government, failing to answer questions before the House Un-American Activities Committee, and refusing to disclose their political beliefs to state officials. By the time Warren retired in 1969, the Court had reaffirmed the right of even the most unpopular viewpoints to First Amendment protection.

New York Times v. Sullivan

The landmark ruling in *New York Times v. Sullivan* (1964) overturned a libel judgment by an Alabama jury against the nation's leading newspaper for carrying an advertisement critical of how local officials treated civil rights demonstrators. Before the 1960s, few Supreme Court cases had dealt with newspaper publishing. *Sullivan* created the modern constitutional law of freedom of the press.

Loving v. Virginia

The Court in the 1960s continued the push toward racial equality, overturning numerous local Jim Crow laws. In *Loving v. Virginia* (1967), it declared unconstitutional the laws still on the books in sixteen states that prohibited interracial marriage. This aptly named case arose from the interracial marriage of Richard and Mildred Loving. Barred by Virginia law from marrying, they did so in Washington, D.C., and later returned to their home state. Two weeks after their arrival, the local sheriff entered their home in the middle of the night, roused the couple from bed, and arrested them.

Miranda v. Arizona

The Court simultaneously pushed forward the process of imposing on the states the obligation to respect the liberties outlined in the Bill of Rights. Among the most important of these decisions was the 5-4 ruling in *Miranda v. Arizona* (1966). This held that an individual in police custody must be informed of the rights to remain silent and to confer with a lawyer before answering questions and must be told that any statements might be used in court. The decision made "Miranda warnings" standard police practice.

"One man, one vote"

The Court also assumed the power to oversee the fairness of democratic procedures at the state and local levels. *Baker v. Carr* (1962) established the principle that districts electing members of state legislatures must be equal in population. This "one-man, one-vote" principle overturned apportionment systems in numerous states that had allowed individuals in sparsely inhabited rural areas to enjoy the same representation as residents of populous city districts.

The justices also moved to reinforce the "wall of separation" between church and state. In *Engle v. Vitole*, they decreed that prayers and Bible readings in public schools violated the First Amendment.

Richard and Mildred Loving with their children in a 1965 photograph by Grey Villet. Their desire to live in Virginia as husband and wife led to a Supreme Court decision declaring unconstitutional state laws that barred interracial marriages.

These rulings proved to be the most unpopular of all the Warren Court's decisions.

The Right to Privacy

The Warren Court not only expanded existing liberties but also outlined entirely new rights in response to the rapidly changing contours of American society. Most dramatic was its assertion of a constitutional right to privacy in *Griswold v. Connecticut* (1965), which overturned a state law prohibiting the use of contraceptives. Justice William O. Douglas, who wrote the decision, had once declared, "The right to be let alone is the beginning of all freedom."

Griswold linked privacy to the sanctity of marriage. But the Court soon transformed it into a right of individuals. It extended access to birth control to unmarried adults and ultimately to minors—an admission by the Court that law could not reverse the sexual revolution. These decisions led directly to the most controversial decision that built on the rulings of the Warren Court (even though it occurred in 1973, four years after Warren's retirement). This was *Roe v. Wade*, which created a constitutional right to terminate a pregnancy. *Roe* provoked vigorous opposition that has continued to this day.

The rights revolution completed the transformation of American freedom from a set of entitlements enjoyed mainly by white men into an open-ended claim to equality, recognition, and self-determination.

The cartoonist Herblock's comment on critics of the Supreme Court's decision barring prayer in public schools.

"WHAT DO THEY EXPECT US TO DO — LISTEN TO THE KIDS PRAY AT HOME?"

1968

A Year of Turmoil

The Sixties reached their climax in 1968, a year when momentous events succeeded each other so rapidly that the foundations of society seemed to be dissolving. Late January 1968 saw the **Tet offensive**, in which Viet Cong and North Vietnamese troops launched well-organized uprisings in cities throughout South Vietnam, completely surprising American military leaders. The intensity of the fighting, brought into America's homes on television, shattered public confidence in the Johnson administration, which had repeatedly proclaimed victory to be "just around the corner." Eugene McCarthy, an antiwar senator from Minnesota, announced that he would seek the Democratic nomination. In March, aided by a small army of student volunteers, McCarthy received more than 40 percent of the vote in the New Hampshire primary. In March, Johnson stunned the nation by announcing that he had decided not to seek reelection.

Eugene McCarthy's challenge

Meanwhile, Martin Luther King Jr. was organizing a Poor People's March, hoping to bring thousands of demonstrators to Washington to demand increased anti-poverty efforts. On April 4, having traveled to Memphis to support a strike of the city's grossly underpaid black garbage collectors, King was killed by a white assassin. The greatest outbreak of urban violence in the nation's history followed in black neighborhoods

Martin Luther King Jr.'s assassination

Striking sanitation workers in Memphis, Tennessee. As their signs suggest, they demanded respect as well as higher wages. Having traveled to Memphis to support the strikers, Martin Luther King Jr. was assassinated on April 4, 1968.

across the country. Washington, D.C., had to be occupied by soldiers before order was restored.

In June, a young Palestinian nationalist assassinated Robert F. Kennedy, who was seeking the Democratic nomination as an opponent of the war. In August, tens of thousands of antiwar activists descended on Chicago for protests at the Democratic national convention, where the delegates nominated Vice President Hubert Humphrey as their presidential candidate. The city's police, never known for restraint, assaulted the marchers with nightsticks, producing hundreds of injuries outside the convention hall and pandemonium inside it.

> *Robert F. Kennedy's assassination*

> *The 1968 Democratic national convention*

The Global 1968

Like 1848 and 1919, 1968 was a year of worldwide upheaval. In many countries, young radicals challenged existing power structures, often borrowing language and strategies from the decade's social movements in the United States and adapting them to their own circumstances.

Massive antiwar demonstrations took place in London, Rome, Paris, Munich, and Tokyo, leading to clashes with police and scores of injuries. In Paris, a nationwide student uprising began in May 1968 that echoed American demands for educational reform and personal liberation. Unlike in the United States, millions of French workers soon joined the protest, adding their own demands for higher wages and greater democracy in the workplace. The result was a general strike that paralyzed the country. In communist Czechoslovakia, leaders bent on reform came to power by promising to institute "socialism with a human face," only to be ousted by a Soviet invasion. Soldiers fired on students demonstrating for greater democracy on the eve of the opening of the Olympic Games in Mexico City, leading to more than 500 deaths. In Northern Ireland, which remained part of Great Britain after the rest of Ireland achieved independence, the police attacked a peaceful march of Catholics demanding an end to religious discrimination who were inspired by the American civil rights movement. This event marked the beginning of the Troubles, a period of both peaceful protest and violent conflict in the region that did not end until the turn of the twenty-first century.

A mural in Belfast, Northern Ireland, depicts the black American abolitionist Frederick Douglass, illustrating how the movement for Catholic civil rights associated itself with the struggle for racial justice in the United States. The text points out that Douglass lectured in Ireland in the 1840s on abolitionism, women's rights, and Irish independence.

Nixon's Comeback

The 1968 presidential election

In the United States, instead of radical change, the year's events opened the door for a conservative reaction. Turmoil in the streets produced a demand for public order. Black militancy produced white "backlash."

In August, Richard Nixon capped a remarkable political comeback by winning the Republican nomination. He called for a renewed commitment to "law and order." With 43 percent of the vote, Nixon had only a razor-thin margin over his Democratic rival. But George Wallace, running as an independent and appealing to resentments against blacks' gains, Great Society programs, and the Warren Court, received an additional 13 percent. Taken together, the Nixon and Wallace totals indicated that four years after Johnson's landslide election ushered in the Great Society, liberalism was on the defensive.

The Legacy of the Sixties

The 1960s transformed American life in ways unimaginable when the decade began. It produced new rights and new understandings of freedom. It made possible the entrance of numerous members of racial minorities into the mainstream of American life, while leaving unsolved the problem of urban poverty. It set in motion a transformation of the status of women.

As the country became more conservative, the Sixties would be blamed for every imaginable social ill, from crime and drug abuse to a decline of respect for authority. Yet during the 1960s, the United States had become a more open, more tolerant—in a word, a freer—country.

CHAPTER REVIEW AND ONLINE RESOURCES

REVIEW QUESTIONS

1. *How did the idea of a "zone of privacy" build on or change earlier notions of rights and freedom?*

2. *In what ways were President Kennedy's foreign policy decisions shaped by Cold War ideology?*

3. *How did immigration policies change in these years, and what were the consequences for the makeup of the population in the United States?*

4. *Explain why many blacks, especially in the North, did not believe that civil rights legislation went far enough in promoting black freedom.*

5. *What were the effects of President Johnson's Great Society and War on Poverty programs?*

6. *In what ways was the New Left not as new as it claimed?*

7. *How did the goals and actions of the United States in Vietnam cause controversy at home and abroad?*

8. *Discuss the impact of the civil rights movement on at least two other movements for social change in the 1960s.*

9. *Identify the origins, goals, and composition of the feminist, or women's liberation, movement.*

10. *Describe how the social movements of the 1960s in the United States became part of global movements for change by 1968. How did those connections affect the United States' position in the world?*

11. *How did the counterculture expand the meaning of freedom in these years?*

KEY TERMS

Student Non-Violent Coordinating Committee (p. 770)

Freedom Rides (p. 770)

March on Washington (p. 772)

Bay of Pigs (p. 774)

Berlin Wall (p. 774)

Cuban missile crisis (p. 774)

Civil Rights Act of 1964 (p. 776)

Voting Rights Act of 1965 (p. 780)

Hart-Celler Act (p. 780)

Great Society (p. 781)

War on Poverty (p. 781)

"Black Power" (p. 784)

Port Huron Statement (p. 786)

Gulf of Tonkin resolution (p. 790)

counterculture (p. 793)

The Feminine Mystique (p. 795)

National Organization for Women (p. 795)

American Indian movement (p. 798)

Silent Spring (p. 798)

wwnorton.com
/studyspace

VISIT STUDYSPACE FOR THESE
RESOURCES AND MORE

- A chapter outline
- A diagnostic chapter quiz
- Interactive maps
- Map worksheets
- Multimedia documents

CHAPTER 26

THE TRIUMPH OF CONSERVATISM

1969–1988

Ronald Reagan addressing the Republican national convention of 1980, which nominated him for president. His election that fall brought modern conservatism to the White House and launched the Reagan Revolution.

Beginning with the dramatic 1960 contest between John F. Kennedy and Richard M. Nixon, the journalist Theodore White published best-selling accounts of four successive races for the presidency. Covering the 1964 election, White attended civil rights demonstrations and rallies for Barry Goldwater, the Republican nominee. White noticed something that struck him as odd: "The dominant word of these two groups, which loathe each other, is 'freedom.'"

White had observed firsthand the struggle over the meaning of freedom set in motion by the 1960s, as well as the revival of conservatism in the midst of an era known for radicalism.

The second half of the 1960s and the 1970s would witness pivotal developments that reshaped American politics—the breakup of the political coalition forged by Franklin D. Roosevelt; an economic crisis that traditional liberal remedies seemed unable to solve; a shift of population and economic resources to conservative strongholds in the Sunbelt of the South and West; the growth of an activist, conservative Christianity increasingly aligned with the Republican Party; and a series of setbacks for the United States overseas. Together, they led to growing popularity for conservatives' ideas, including their understanding of freedom.

PRESIDENT NIXON

From the vantage point of the early twenty-first century, it is difficult to recall how marginal conservatism seemed at the end of World War II. Associated in many minds with conspiracy theories, anti-Semitism, and preference for social hierarchy over democracy and equality, conservatism seemed a relic of a discredited past.

Nonetheless, as noted in the previous two chapters, the 1950s and 1960s witnessed a conservative rebirth. And in 1968, a "backlash" among formerly Democratic voters against both black assertiveness and antiwar demonstrations helped to propel Richard Nixon into the White House. But conservatives found Nixon no more to their liking than his predecessors. In office, he expanded the welfare state and moved to improve American relations with the Soviet Union and China. During his presidency, the social changes set in motion by the 1960s—seen by conservatives as forces of moral decay—continued apace.

FOCUS QUESTIONS

- *What were the major policies of the Nixon administration on social and economic issues?*

- *How did Vietnam and the Watergate scandal affect popular trust in the government?*

- *In what ways did the opportunities of most Americans diminish in the 1970s?*

- *What were the roots of the rise of conservatism in the 1970s?*

- *How did the Reagan presidency affect Americans both at home and abroad?*

Nixon's Domestic Policies

Having won the presidency by a very narrow margin, Nixon moved toward the political center on many issues. A shrewd politician, he worked to solidify his support among Republicans while reaching out to disaffected elements of the Democratic coalition. Mostly interested in foreign policy, he had no desire to battle Congress, still under Democratic control, on domestic issues. Just as Eisenhower had helped to institutionalize the New Deal, Nixon accepted and even expanded many elements of the Great Society.

Nixon's New Federalism

Conservatives applauded Nixon's New Federalism, which offered federal "block grants" to the states to spend as they saw fit, rather than for specific purposes dictated by Washington. On the other hand, the Nixon administration created a host of new federal agencies. The Environmental Protection Agency oversaw programs to combat water and air pollution, cleaned up hazardous wastes, and required "environmental impact" statements from any project that received federal funding. The Occupational Safety and Health Administration sent inspectors into the nation's workplaces. The National Transportation Safety Board instructed automobile makers on how to make their cars safer.

Environmental Protection Agency

Nixon also signed measures that expanded the food stamp program and made Social Security benefits adjust automatically to the rising cost of living. His environmental initiatives included the Endangered Species Act and the Clean Air Act, which set air quality standards for carbon monoxide and other chemicals released by cars and factories.

Richard Nixon (on the right) and former Alabama governor George Wallace at an "Honor America" celebration in February 1974. Nixon's "southern strategy" sought to woo Wallace's supporters into the Republican Party.

Nixon and Welfare

Perhaps Nixon's most startling initiative was his proposal for a Family Assistance Plan, or "negative income tax," that would replace Aid to Families with Dependent Children (AFDC) by having the federal government guarantee a minimum income for all Americans. Originally a New Deal program that mainly served the white poor, welfare had come to be associated with blacks, who by 1970 accounted for nearly half the recipients. The AFDC rolls expanded rapidly during the 1960s. This arose from an increase in births to unmarried women, which produced a sharp rise in the number of poor female-headed households, and from an aggressive campaign by welfare rights groups to encourage people to apply for benefits. Conservative politicians now attacked recipients of welfare as people who preferred to live at the expense of honest taxpayers rather than by working. A striking example of Nixon's willingness to break the political mold, his plan to replace welfare with a guaranteed annual income failed to win approval by Congress.

Nixon and Race

Nixon's racial policies offer a similarly mixed picture. To consolidate support in the white South, he nominated to the Supreme Court Clement Haynsworth and G. Harold Carswell, conservative southern jurists with records of support for segregation. Both were rejected by the Senate. On the other hand, in Nixon's first three years in office, the proportion of southern black students attending integrated schools rose from 32 percent to 77 percent.

Rise in southern school integration

For a time, the Nixon administration also pursued "**affirmative action**" programs to upgrade minority employment. The Philadelphia Plan required that construction contractors on federal projects hire specific numbers of minority workers. Secretary of Labor George Shultz, who initiated the idea, sincerely hoped to open more jobs for black workers. Nixon seems to have viewed the plan mainly as a way of fighting inflation by weakening the power of the building trades unions. Their control over the labor market, he believed, pushed wages to unreasonably high levels, raising the cost of construction.

Trade unions of skilled workers like plumbers and electrical workers, which had virtually no black members, strongly opposed the Philadelphia Plan. After a widely publicized incident in May 1970, when a group of construction workers assaulted antiwar demonstrators in New York City, Nixon suddenly decided that he might be able to woo blue-collar workers in preparation for his 1972 reelection campaign. He soon abandoned the Philadelphia Plan in favor of an ineffective one that stressed voluntary local efforts toward minority hiring instead of federal requirements.

The Burger Court

When Earl Warren retired as chief justice in 1969, Nixon appointed Warren Burger, a federal court-of-appeals judge, to succeed him.

Warren Burger

In 1971, in *Swann v. Charlotte-Mecklenburg Board of Education*, which arose from North Carolina, the justices unanimously approved a lower court's plan that required the extensive transportation of students to achieve school integration. The decision led to hundreds of cases in

The busing issue

which judges throughout the country ordered the use of **busing** as a tool to achieve integration. With many white parents determined to keep their children in neighborhood schools and others willing to move to the suburbs or enroll them in private academies to avoid integration, busing became a lightning rod for protests. One of the most bitter fights took place in Boston in the mid-1970s. Residents of the tightly knit Irish-American community of South Boston demonstrated vociferously and sometimes violently against a busing plan decreed by a local judge.

The Supreme Court soon abandoned the idea of overturning local control of schools or moving students great distances to achieve integration. In *Milliken v. Bradley* (1974), the justices overturned a lower court order that required Detroit's predominantly white suburbs to enter into a regional desegregation plan with the city's heavily minority school system. By absolving suburban districts of responsibility for assisting in integrating urban schools, the decision guaranteed that housing segregation would be mirrored in public education. Indeed, by the 1990s, public schools in the North were considerably more segregated than those in the South.

Many whites came to view affirmative action programs as a form of **"reverse discrimination."** Even as affirmative action programs quickly spread from blacks to encompass women, Latinos, Asian-Americans, and Native Americans, conservatives demanded that the Supreme Court invalidate all such policies.

The justices proved increasingly hostile to governmental affirmative action policies. In *Regents of the University of California v. Bakke* (1978), the Court overturned an admissions program of the University of California at Davis, a public university, which set aside 16 of 100 places in the entering medical school class for minority students. Justice Lewis F. Powell, a Nixon appointee who cast the deciding vote in the 5-4 decision, rejected the idea of fixed affirmative action quotas. He added, however, that race could be used as one factor among many in admissions decisions, so affirmative action continued at most colleges and universities.

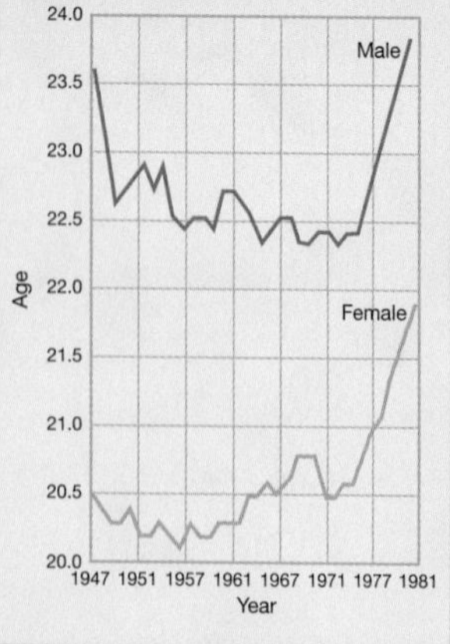

The Continuing Sexual Revolution

To the alarm of conservatives, during the 1970s the sexual revolution passed from the counterculture into the social mainstream. The number of divorces soared, reaching more than 1 million in 1975, double the number ten years earlier. The age at which both men and women married rose dramatically. As a result of women's changing aspirations

Milliken v. Bradley

FIGURE 26.1
Median Age at First Marriage, 1947–1981

and the availability of birth control and legal abortions, the American birthrate declined dramatically. By 1976, the average woman was bearing 1.7 children during her lifetime, less than half the figure of 1957 and below the level at which a population reproduces itself. A 1971 survey of the last five graduating classes at Bryn Mawr, an elite women's college, reported the birth of more than seventy children. A similar survey covering the classes of 1971 through 1975 found that only three had been born.

During the Nixon years, women made inroads into areas from which they had long been excluded. In 1972, Congress approved **Title IX**, which banned gender discrimination in higher education. The giant corporation American Telephone and Telegraph (AT&T) entered into a landmark agreement in which it paid millions of dollars to workers who had suffered gender discrimination and to upgrade employment opportunities for women. The number of women at work continued its upward climb. Working women were motivated by varied aims. Some sought careers in professions and skilled jobs previously open only to men. Others, spurred by the need to bolster family income as the economy faltered, flooded into the traditional, low-wage, "pink-collar" sector, working as cashiers, secretaries, and telephone operators.

In addition, the gay and lesbian movement, born at the end of the 1960s, expanded greatly during the 1970s and became a major concern of the right. In 1969, there had been about fifty local gay rights groups in the United States; ten years later, their numbers reached into the thousands. They began to elect local officials, persuaded many states to decriminalize homosexual relations, and succeeded in convincing cities with large gay populations to pass antidiscrimination laws. They actively encouraged gay men and lesbians to "come out of the closet"—that is, to reveal their sexual orientation.

Daryl Koehn of Kansas celebrates in 1977 on learning that she has been chosen as one of the first group of women allowed to study at Oxford University as a Rhodes Scholar. Since their establishment in 1903, the scholarships had been limited to men.

Nixon and Détente

Just as domestic policies and social trends under Nixon disappointed conservatives, they viewed his foreign policy as dangerously "soft" on communism. To be sure, Nixon and Henry Kissinger, his national security adviser and secretary of state, continued their predecessors' policy of attempting to undermine Third World governments deemed dangerous to American strategic or economic interests. Nixon funneled arms to dictatorial pro-American regimes in Iran, the Philippines, and South Africa. After Chile in 1970 elected socialist Salvador Allende as

The Allende affair

president, the CIA worked with his domestic opponents to destabilize the regime. On September 11, 1973, Allende was overthrown and killed in a military coup, which installed a bloody dictatorship under General Augusto Pinochet. Thousands of Allende backers, including a few Americans then in Chile, were tortured and murdered, and many others fled the country. The Nixon administration continued to back Pinochet despite his brutal policies. Democracy did not return to Chile until the end of the 1980s.

Nixon and Kissinger's "realist" foreign policy

In his relations with the major communist powers, however, Nixon fundamentally altered Cold War policies. In the language of foreign relations, he and Kissinger were "realists." They had more interest in power than ideology and preferred international stability to relentless conflict. Nixon also hoped that if relations with the Soviet Union improved, the Russians would influence North Vietnam to agree to an end to the Vietnam War on terms acceptable to the United States.

Nixon in China

Nixon realized that far from being part of a unified communist bloc, China had its own interests, different from those of the Soviet Union, and was destined to play a major role on the world stage. The policy of refusing to recognize China's communist government had reached a dead end. In 1971, Kissinger flew secretly to China, paving the way for Nixon's own astonishing public visit of February 1972. The trip led to the Beijing government's taking up China's seat at the United Nations, previously occupied by the exiled regime on Taiwan.

Three months after his trip to Beijing, Nixon became the first American president to visit the Soviet Union, where he engaged in intense negotiations with his Soviet counterpart, Leonid Brezhnev. Out of this summit meeting came agreements for increased trade and two landmark arms-control treaties. SALT (named for the **Strategic Arms Limitation Talks** under way since 1969) froze each country's arsenal of intercontinental missiles capable of carrying nuclear warheads. The Anti–Ballistic Missile Treaty banned the development of systems designed to intercept incoming missiles, so that neither side would be tempted to attack the other without fearing devastating retaliation. Nixon and Brezhnev proclaimed a new era of "peaceful coexistence," in which "**détente**" (cooperation) would replace the hostility of the Cold War.

Richard Nixon at a banquet celebrating his visit to China in February 1972. To his right is Premier Chou En-lai.

VIETNAM AND WATERGATE

Nixon and Vietnam

Despite Nixon's foreign policy triumphs, one issue would not go away—Vietnam. On taking office, he announced a new policy, Vietnamization. Under this plan, American troops would gradually be withdrawn while South Vietnamese soldiers, backed by continued American bombing, did more and more of the fighting. But Vietnamization neither limited the war nor ended the antiwar movement. Hoping to cut North Vietnamese supply lines, Nixon in 1970 ordered American troops into neutral Cambodia. The invasion did not achieve its military goals, but it destabilized the Cambodian government and set in motion a chain of events that eventually brought to power the Khmer Rouge. Before being ousted by a Vietnamese invasion in 1979, this local communist movement attempted to force virtually all Cambodians into rural communes and committed widespread massacres in that unfortunate country.

The invasion of Cambodia and its consequences

As the war escalated, protests again spread on college campuses. In the wake of the killing of four antiwar protesters at Kent State University by the Ohio National Guard and two by police at Jackson State University in Mississippi, the student movement reached its high-water mark. In the spring of 1970, more than 350 colleges and universities experienced strikes, and troops occupied 21 campuses. The protests at Kent State, a public university with a largely working-class student body, and Jackson State, a black institution, demonstrated how antiwar sentiment had spread far beyond elite campuses.

Violence on campus

The same social changes sweeping the home front were evident among troops in Vietnam. Soldiers experimented with drugs, openly wore peace and Black-Power symbols, refused orders, and even assaulted unpopular officers. In 1971, thousands deserted the army, while at home Vietnam veterans held antiwar demonstrations. The decline of discipline within the army convinced increasing numbers of high-ranking officers that the United States must extricate itself from Vietnam.

Public support for the war was rapidly waning. In 1969, the *New York Times* published details of the **My Lai massacre**

Tear gas envelops the campus as members of the Ohio National Guard prepare to fire on student demonstrators at Kent State University. Shortly after this photo was taken, four students lay dead.

of 1968, in which a company of American troops had killed some 350 South Vietnamese civilians. After a military investigation, one soldier, Lieutenant William Calley, was found guilty of directing the atrocity. (The courts released him from prison in 1974.) In 1971, the *Times* began publishing the

The Pentagon Papers

Pentagon Papers, a classified report prepared by the Defense Department that traced American involvement in Vietnam back to World War II and revealed how successive presidents had misled the American people about it. In a landmark freedom-of-the-press decision, the Supreme Court rejected Nixon's request for an injunction to halt publication. In 1973, Congress passed the **War Powers Act**. The most vigorous assertion of congressional control over foreign policy in the nation's history, it required the president to seek congressional approval for the commitment of American troops overseas.

The End of the Vietnam War

The Paris peace agreement

Early in 1973, Nixon achieved what had eluded his predecessors—a negotiated settlement in Vietnam. The Paris peace agreement, the result of five years of talks, made possible the final withdrawal of American troops. The compromise left in place the government of South Vietnam, but it also left North Vietnamese and Viet Cong soldiers in control of parts of the South. The U.S. military draft came to an end. Henceforth, volunteers would make up the armed forces. But in the spring of 1975, the North Vietnamese launched a final military offensive. The government of South Vietnam collapsed. The United States did not intervene except to evacuate the American embassy, and Vietnam was reunified under communist rule.

Buttons and flags for sale at a rally in the early 1970s illustrate the linkage of support for the Vietnam War and strong feelings of patriotism, building blocks of the new conservatism.

The only war the United States has ever lost, Vietnam was a military, political, and social disaster. By the time it ended, 58,000 Americans had been killed, along with 3 million to 4 million Vietnamese. Vietnam undermined Americans' confidence in their own institutions and challenged long-standing beliefs about the country and its purposes.

Two decades after the war ended, former secretary of defense Robert McNamara published a memoir in which he admitted that the policy he had helped to shape had been "terribly wrong." Ignorance of the history and culture of Vietnam and a misguided belief that every communist movement in the world was a puppet of Moscow, he wrote, had led the country into a war that he now profoundly regretted. The political establishment had supported the war for most of its duration. For far too long, they had accepted its basic premise—that the United States had the right to decide the fate of a far-away people about whom it knew almost nothing.

Watergate

By the time the war ended, Richard Nixon was no longer president. His domestic policies and foreign policy successes had contributed greatly to his reelection in 1972. He won a landslide victory over liberal Democrat George McGovern, receiving 60 percent of the popular vote. Nixon made deep inroads into former Democratic strongholds in the South and among working-class white northerners. He carried every state but Massachusetts. But his triumph soon turned into disaster.

Nixon's reelection

Nixon was obsessed with secrecy. He viewed every critic as a threat to national security and developed an "enemies list" that included reporters, politicians, and celebrities unfriendly to the administration. In June 1972, five former employees of Nixon's reelection committee took part in a break-in at Democratic Party headquarters in the **Watergate** apartment complex in Washington, D.C. A security guard called police, who arrested the intruders.

The break-in

No one knows precisely what the Watergate burglars were looking for (perhaps they intended to install listening devices), and the botched robbery played little role in the 1972 presidential campaign. But in 1973, Judge John J. Sirica, before whom the burglars were tried, determined to find out who had sponsored the break-in. A pair of *Washington Post* journalists began publishing investigative stories that made it clear that persons close to the president had ordered the burglary and then tried to "cover up" White House involvement. Congressional hearings followed that revealed a wider pattern of wiretapping, break-ins, and attempts to sabotage political opposition. When it became known that Nixon had made tape recordings of conversations in his office, Archibald Cox, a special prosecutor the president had reluctantly appointed to investigate the Watergate affair, demanded the tapes. In October 1973, Nixon proposed to allow Senator John C. Stennis of Mississippi to review the tapes, rather than releasing them. When Cox refused to agree, Nixon fired him, whereupon Attorney General Elliot Richardson and his deputy resigned in protest. These events, known as the Saturday Night Massacre, further undermined Nixon's standing. The Supreme Court unanimously ordered Nixon to provide the tapes—a decision that reaffirmed the principle that the president is not above the law.

The Watergate hearings

Nixon's Fall

Week after week, revelations about the scandal unfolded. By mid-1974, it had become clear that whether or not Nixon knew in advance of the

Watergate break-in, he had become involved immediately afterward in authorizing payments to the burglars to remain silent or commit perjury, and he had ordered the FBI to halt its investigation of the crime. In August 1974, the House Judiciary Committee voted to recommend that Nixon be impeached for conspiracy to obstruct justice. His political support having evaporated, Nixon became the only president in history to resign.

Nixon's resignation

Nixon's presidency remains a classic example of the abuse of political power. In 1973, his vice president, Spiro T. Agnew, resigned after revelations that he had accepted bribes from construction firms while serving as governor of Maryland. Nixon's attorney general, John Mitchell, and White House aides H. R. Haldeman and John Ehrlichman were convicted of obstruction of justice in the Watergate affair and went to jail. As for the president, he insisted that he had done nothing wrong.

The aftermath of Watergate

His departure from office was followed by Senate hearings headed by Frank Church of Idaho that laid bare a history of abusive actions involving every administration since the beginning of the Cold War. In violation of the law, the FBI had spied on millions of Americans and had tried to disrupt the civil rights movement. The CIA had conducted secret operations to overthrow foreign governments and had tried to assassinate foreign leaders. Abuses of power, in other words, went far beyond the misdeeds of a single president.

The Church Committee revelations led Congress to enact new restrictions on the power of the FBI and CIA to spy on American citizens or conduct operations abroad without the knowledge of lawmakers. Congress also strengthened the Freedom of Information Act (FOIA), initially enacted in 1966. Since 1974, the FOIA has allowed scholars, journalists, and ordinary citizens to gain access to millions of pages of records of federal agencies.

Freedom of Information Act

Liberals, who had despised Nixon throughout his career, celebrated his downfall. Nixon's fall and the revelations of years of governmental misconduct helped to convince many Americans that conservatives were correct when they argued that to protect liberty it was necessary to limit Washington's power over Americans' lives.

THE END OF THE GOLDEN AGE

The Decline of Manufacturing

During the 1970s, the long period of postwar economic expansion and consumer prosperity came to an end, succeeded by slow growth and high inflation. For the only time in the twentieth century, other than the 1930s,

TABLE 26.1 The Misery Index, 1970–1980

YEAR	RATE OF INFLATION (%)	RATE OF UNEMPLOYMENT (%)	MISERY INDEX (%)
1970	5.9	4.9	10.8
1971	4.3	5.9	10.2
1972	3.3	5.6	8.9
1973	6.2	4.9	11.1
1974	11.0	5.6	16.6
1975	9.1	8.5	17.6
1976	5.8	7.7	13.5
1977	6.5	7.1	13.6
1978	7.7	6.1	13.8
1979	11.3	5.8	17.1
1980	13.5	7.1	20.6

the average American ended the 1970s poorer than when the decade began. There were many reasons for the end of capitalism's "golden age." With American prosperity seemingly unassailable and the military-industrial complex thriving, successive administrations had devoted little attention to the less positive economic consequences of the Cold War. To strengthen its anticommunist allies, the United States promoted the industrial reconstruction of Japan and Germany and the emergence of new centers of manufacturing in places like South Korea and Taiwan. It encouraged American companies to invest in overseas plants. The strong dollar, linked to gold by the Bretton Woods agreement of 1944, made it harder to sell American goods overseas (discussed in Chapter 22).

Economic weakness

In 1971, for the first time in the twentieth century, the United States experienced a merchandise trade deficit—that is, it imported more goods than it exported. By 1980, nearly three-quarters of goods produced in the United States were competing with foreign-made products, and the number of manufacturing workers, 38 percent of the American workforce in 1960, had fallen to 28 percent.

Trade deficit

In 1971, Nixon announced the most radical change in economic policy since the Great Depression. He took the United States off the gold standard, ending the Bretton Woods agreement that fixed the value of the dollar and other currencies in terms of gold. Henceforth, the world's currencies would "float" in relation to one another, their worth determined not by treaty but by

Currency values and trade

Drivers lining up to purchase gas during the oil crisis of 1973–1974.

The World Trade Center under construction in New York City in the 1970s.

international currency markets. Nixon hoped that lowering the dollar's value in terms of the German mark and Japanese yen would promote exports by making American goods cheaper overseas and reduce imports, because foreign products would be more expensive in the United States. But the end of fixed currency rates injected a new element of instability into the world economy. Nixon also ordered wages and prices frozen for ninety days.

Stagflation

Nixon's policies temporarily curtailed inflation and reduced imports. But in 1973, a brief war broke out between Israel and its neighbors Egypt and Syria. Middle Eastern Arab states retaliated against Western support of Israel by quadrupling the price of oil and suspending the export of oil to the United States for several months. Long lines of cars appeared at American gas stations, which either ran out of fuel or limited how much a customer could buy. A second "oil shock" occurred in 1979 as a result of the revolution that overthrew the shah of Iran, discussed later.

Rising oil prices rippled through the world economy, contributing to the combination of stagnant economic growth and high inflation known as "**stagflation**." Between 1973 and 1981, the rate of inflation in developed countries was 10 percent per year and the rate of economic growth only 2.4 percent, a sharp deterioration from the economic conditions of the 1960s. The so-called **misery index**—the sum of the unemployment and inflation rates—stood at 10.8 when the decade began. By 1980, it had almost doubled. As oil prices rose, many Americans shifted from large, domestically produced cars, known for high gasoline consumption, to smaller, more fuel-efficient imports. By the end of the decade, Japan had become the world's leading automobile producer, and imports accounted for nearly 25 percent of car sales in the United States.

The Beleaguered Social Compact

The economic crisis contributed to a breakdown of the postwar social compact. Faced with declining profits and rising overseas competition, corporations stepped up the trend, already under way before 1970, toward eliminating well-paid manufacturing jobs through automation and shifting production to low-wage areas of the United States and overseas. By 1980, Detroit and Chicago had lost more than half the manufacturing jobs in existence three decades earlier.

The accelerating flow of jobs, investment, and population to the nonunion, low-wage states of the **Sunbelt** increased the political influence of this conservative region.

In some manufacturing centers, political and economic leaders welcomed the opportunity to remake their cities as finance, information, and entertainment hubs. In New York, the construction of the World Trade Center, completed in 1977, symbolized this shift in the economy. Until destroyed by terrorists twenty-four years later, the 110-story "twin towers" stood as a symbol of New York's grandeur. But to make way for the World Trade Center, the city displaced hundreds of small electronics, printing, and other firms, causing the loss of thousands of manufacturing jobs.

Always a junior partner in the Democratic coalition, the labor movement found itself forced onto the defensive. It has remained there ever since.

The weakening of unions and the continuation of the economy's long-term shift from manufacturing to service employment had an adverse impact on ordinary Americans. Between 1953 and 1973, median family income had doubled. But beginning in 1973, real wages essentially did not rise for twenty years.

Ford as President

Economic problems dogged the presidencies of Nixon's successors. Gerald Ford, who had been appointed to replace Vice President Agnew, succeeded to the White House when Nixon resigned. Ford named Nelson Rockefeller of New York as his own vice president. Thus, for the only time in American history, both offices were occupied by persons for whom no one had actually voted. Among his first acts as president, Ford pardoned Nixon, shielding him from prosecution for obstruction of justice. Ford claimed that he wanted the country to put the Watergate scandal behind it. But the pardon proved to be widely unpopular.

In domestic policy, Ford's presidency lacked significant accomplishment. To combat inflation, Ford urged Americans to shop wisely, reduce expenditures, and wear WIN buttons (for "Whip Inflation Now"). Although inflation fell, joblessness continued to rise. During the steep recession of 1974–1975 unemployment exceeded 9 percent, the highest level since the Depression.

In the international arena, 1975 witnessed the major achievement of Ford's presidency. In a continuation of Nixon's policy of détente, the United States and Soviet Union signed an agreement at Helsinki, Finland,

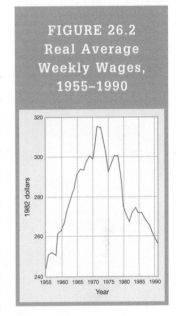

**FIGURE 26.2
Real Average
Weekly Wages,
1955–1990**

Because of economic dislocations and deindustrialization, Americans' real wages (wages adjusted to take account of inflation) peaked in the early 1970s and then began a sharp, prolonged decline.

President Gerald Ford tried to enlist Americans in his "Whip Inflation Now" program. It did not succeed.

Dear President Ford:

I enlist as an Inflation Fighter and Energy Saver for the duration. I will do the very best I can for America.

(Please Print.)

Name_____Date_____

Address_____

City_____State_____Zip Code_____

that recognized the permanence of Europe's post–World War II boundaries (including the division of Germany). In addition, both superpowers agreed to respect the basic liberties of their citizens. Secretary of State Henry Kissinger and his Soviet counterpart, Andrey Gromyko, assumed that this latter pledge would have little practical effect. But over time, the Helsinki Accords inspired movements for greater freedom within the communist countries of eastern Europe.

The Carter Administration

In the presidential election of 1976, Jimmy Carter, a former governor of Georgia, narrowly defeated Ford. A graduate of the U.S. Naval Academy

who later became a peanut farmer, Carter was virtually unknown outside his state when he launched his campaign for the Democratic nomination. But realizing that Watergate and Vietnam had produced a crisis in confidence in the federal government, he turned his obscurity into an advantage. Carter ran for president as an "outsider," making a virtue of the fact that he had never held federal office. A devout "born-again" Baptist, he spoke openly of his religious convictions. His promise, "I'll never lie to you," resonated with an electorate tired of official dishonesty.

Carter had much in common with Progressives of the early twentieth century. His passions were making government more efficient, protecting the environment, and raising the moral tone of politics. Unlike the Progressives, however, he embraced the aspirations of black Americans. As president, Carter appointed an unprecedented number of blacks to important positions, including Andrew Young, a former lieutenant of Martin Luther King Jr., as ambassador to the United Nations.

Carter and the Economic Crisis

The Democratic party found itself ill-equipped to deal with the economic crisis. The social upheavals of the 1960s had led to the emergence of politicians known collectively as the New Democrats. Representing affluent

urban and suburban districts, they viewed issues like race relations, gender equality, the environment, and improving the political process as more central than traditional economic matters. Although his party controlled both houses, Carter often found himself at odds with Congress. He viewed inflation, not unemployment, as the country's main economic problem, and to combat it he promoted cuts in spending on domestic programs. In the hope that increased competition would reduce prices, his administration **deregulated** the trucking and airline industries. In 1980, with Carter's approval, Congress repealed usury laws—laws that limit how much interest lenders can charge—allowing credit card companies to push their interest rates up to twenty percent or even higher.

Carter also believed that expanded use of nuclear energy could help reduce dependence on imported oil. For years, proponents of nuclear power had hailed it as an inexpensive way of meeting the country's energy needs. By the time Carter took office, more than 200 nuclear plants were operating or on order. But in 1979 the industry suffered a near-fatal blow when an accident at the Three Mile Island plant in Pennsylvania released a large amount of radioactive steam into the atmosphere. The Three Mile Island mishap reinforced fears about the environmental hazards associated with nuclear energy and put a halt to the industry's expansion.

Since the New Deal, Democrats had presented themselves as the party of affluence and economic growth. But Carter seemed to be presiding over a period of national decline. It did not help his popularity when, in a speech in 1979, he spoke of a national "crisis of confidence" and seemed to blame it on the American people themselves and their "mistaken idea of freedom" as "self-indulgence and consumption."

The deregulation of the airline industry brought lower fares but also a drastic decline in service. Before deregulation, with prices fixed, airlines sought to attract customers by providing good service. Today, fares may be lower, but passengers are jammed in like sardines and have to pay for checked baggage, onboard meals, and other amenities.

The Emergence of Human Rights Politics

Under Carter, a commitment to promoting human rights became a centerpiece of American foreign policy for the first time. He was influenced by the proliferation of information about global denials of human rights spread by nongovernmental agencies like Amnesty International and the International League for Human Rights. Their reports marked a significant break with dominant ideas about international affairs since World War II, which had viewed the basic division in the world as between communist and noncommunist countries. Such reports, along with congressional hearings, exposed misdeeds not only by communist countries but also by American allies, especially the death squads of Latin American dictatorships.

Carter's human rights foreign policy

In 1978, Carter cut off aid to the brutal military dictatorship governing Argentina, which in the name of anticommunism had launched a "dirty war" against its own citizens, kidnapping off the streets and secretly murdering an estimated 10,000 to 30,000 persons. Carter's action was a dramatic gesture, as Argentina was one of the most important powers in Latin America, and previous American administrations had turned a blind eye to human rights abuses by Cold War allies. By the end of his presidency, the phrase "human rights" had acquired political potency.

Argentina

President Jimmy Carter (*center*), Egyptian president Anwar Sadat (*left*), and Israeli prime minister Menachem Begin (*right*) celebrating the signing of the 1979 peace treaty between Israel and Egypt.

Carter believed that in the post-Vietnam era, American foreign policy should de-emphasize Cold War thinking. Combating poverty in the Third World, preventing the spread of nuclear weapons, and promoting human rights should take priority over what he called "the inordinate fear of communism that once led us to embrace any dictator who joined us in that fear." In one of his first acts as president, he offered an unconditional pardon to Vietnam-era draft resisters.

Carter's emphasis on pursuing peaceful solutions to international problems and his willingness to think outside the Cold War framework yielded important results. In 1979, he brought the leaders of Egypt and Israel to the presidential retreat at Camp David and brokered a historic peace agreement between the two countries. He improved American relations with Latin America by agreeing to a treaty, ratified by the Senate in 1978, that provided for the transfer of the Panama Canal to local control by the year 2000. Carter attempted to curb the murderous violence of death squads allied to the right-wing government of El Salvador, and in 1980 he suspended military aid after the murder of four American nuns by members of the country's army.

Carter's effectiveness

Both conservative Cold Warriors and foreign policy "realists" severely criticized Carter's emphasis on human rights. He himself found it impossible to translate rhetoric into action. He criticized American arms sales to the rest of the world. But with thousands of jobs and billions of dollars in corporate profits at stake, he did nothing to curtail them. The United States continued its support of allies with records of serious human rights violations such as the governments of Guatemala, the Philippines, South Korea, and Iran. Indeed, the American connection with the shah of Iran, whose secret police regularly jailed and tortured political opponents, proved to be Carter's undoing.

The Iran Crisis and Afghanistan

Occupying a strategic location on the southern border of the Soviet Union, Iran was a major supplier of oil and an importer of American military equipment. At the end of 1977, Carter traveled there to help celebrate the shah's rule, causing the internal opposition to become more and more anti-American. Early in 1979, a popular revolution inspired by the exiled

Muslim cleric Ayatollah Khomeini overthrew the shah and declared Iran an Islamic republic.

When Carter in November 1979 allowed the deposed shah to seek medical treatment in the United States, Khomeini's followers invaded the American embassy in Tehran and seized sixty-six hostages. They did not regain their freedom until January 1981, on the day Carter's term as president ended. Events in Iran made Carter seem helpless and inept and led to a rapid fall in his popularity.

Another crisis that began in 1979 undermined American relations with Moscow. At the end of that year, the Soviet Union sent thousands of troops into Afghanistan to support a friendly government threatened by an Islamic rebellion. In the long run, Afghanistan became the Soviet Vietnam, an unwinnable conflict whose mounting casualties seriously weakened the government at home. Initially, however, it seemed another example of declining American power.

Declaring the invasion the greatest crisis since World War II (a considerable exaggeration), the president announced the Carter Doctrine, declaring that the United States would use military force, if necessary, to protect its interests in the Persian Gulf. He organized a Western boycott of the 1980 Olympics, which took place in Moscow, and dramatically increased American military spending. In a reversion to the Cold War principle that any opponent of the Soviet Union deserved American support, the United States funneled aid to fundamentalist Muslims in Afghanistan who fought a decade-long guerrilla war against the Soviets. The alliance had unforeseen consequences. A faction of Islamic fundamentalists known as the Taliban eventually came to power in Afghanistan. Tragically, they would prove as hostile to the United States as to Moscow.

American hostages being paraded by their Iranian captors on the first day of the occupation of the American embassy in Tehran in 1979. Television gave extensive coverage to the plight of the hostages, leading many Americans to view the Carter administration as weak and inept.

Actions in Afghanistan

THE RISING TIDE OF CONSERVATISM

The combination of domestic and international dislocations during the 1970s created a widespread sense of anxiety among Americans and offered conservatives new political opportunities. Economic problems heightened the appeal of lower taxes, reduced government regulation, and

VOICES OF FREEDOM

From Redstockings Manifesto (1969)

Redstockings was one of the radical feminist movements that arose in the late 1960s. Based in New York, it issued this manifesto. In language typical of the era, it illustrates how at its most radical edge feminism had evolved from demands for equal treatment for women to a total critique of male power and a call for women's "liberation."

After centuries of individual and preliminary political struggle, women are uniting to achieve their final liberation from male supremacy. Redstockings is dedicated to building this unity and winning our freedom.

Women are an oppressed class. Our oppression is total, affecting every facet of our lives. We are exploited as sex objects, breeders, domestic servants, and cheap labor. We are considered inferior beings, whose only purpose is to enhance men's lives. Our humanity is denied. Our prescribed behavior is enforced by the threat of physical violence.

Because we have lived so intimately with our oppressors, in isolation from each other, we have been kept from seeing our personal suffering as a political condition. . . .

We identify the agents of our oppression as men. Male supremacy is the oldest, most basic form of domination. . . . Men have controlled all political, economic, and cultural institutions and backed up this control with physical force. . . .

Our chief task at present is to develop female class consciousness through sharing experience and publicly exposing the sexist foundation of all our institutions. Consciousness-raising is not "therapy," which implies the existence of individual solutions and falsely assumes that the male-female relationship is purely personal, but the only method by which we can ensure that our program for liberation is based on the concrete realities of our lives. . . . The first requirement for raising class consciousness is honesty, in private and in public, with ourselves and other women.

We identify with all women. We define our best interest as that of the poorest, most brutally exploited women. . . .

We call on all our sisters to unite with us in struggle.

We call on all men to give up their male privileges and support women's liberation in the interest of our humanity and their own.

July 7, 1969, New York City

From Jerry Falwell, *Listen, America!* (1980)

The Reverend Jerry Falwell, a Virginia minister who in 1979 founded the self-proclaimed Moral Majority, was one of the leading conservative activists of the 1970s and 1980s. In language reminiscent of Puritan jeremiads about the decline of moral values, Falwell helped mobilize evangelical Christians to ally with the Republican Party.

We must reverse the trend America finds herself in today. Young people between the ages of twenty-five and forty have been born and reared in a different world than Americans of years past. The television set has been their primary baby-sitter. From the television set they have learned situation ethics and immorality—they have learned a loss of respect for human life. They have learned to disrespect the family as God has established it. They have been educated in a public-school system that is permeated with secular humanism. They have been taught that the Bible is just another book of literature. They have been taught that there are no absolutes in our world today. They have been introduced to the drug culture. They have been reared by the family and the public school in a society that is greatly void of discipline and character-building. . . .

Every American who looks at the facts must share a deep concern and burden for our country. . . . If Americans will face the truth, our nation can be turned around and can be saved from the evils and the destruction that have fallen upon every other nation that has turned its back on God. . . .

I personally feel that the home and the family are still held in reverence by the vast majority of the American public. I believe there is still a vast number of Americans who love their country, are patriotic, and are willing to sacrifice for her. . . . I believe that Americans want to see this country come back to basics, back to values, back to biblical morality, back to sensibility, and back to patriotism. . . .

It is now time to take a stand on certain moral issues, and we can only stand if we have leaders. We must stand against the Equal Rights Amendment, the feminist revolution, and the homosexual revolution. . . . The hope of reversing the trends of decay in our republic now lies with the Christian public in America. We cannot expect help from the liberals. They certainly are not going to call our nation back to righteousness and neither are the pornographers, the smut peddlers, and those who are corrupting our youth. Moral Americans must be willing to put their reputations, their fortunes, and their very lives on the line for this great nation of ours. Would that we had the courage of our forefathers who knew the great responsibility that freedom carries with it.

QUESTIONS

1. *How do the authors of the Redstockings Manifesto seem to define women's freedom?*

2. *What does Falwell see as the main threats to moral values?*

3. *How do the two documents differ in their views about the role of women in American society?*

cuts in social spending to spur business investment. Fears about a decline of American power in the world led to calls for a renewal of the Cold War. The civil rights and sexual revolutions produced resentments that undermined the Democratic coalition. Rising urban crime rates reinforced demands for law and order and attacks on courts considered too lenient toward criminals. These issues brought new converts to the conservative cause.

Conservatives and freedom

As the 1970s went on, conservatives abandoned overt opposition to the black struggle for racial justice. The fiery rhetoric and direct confrontation tactics of Bull Connor, George Wallace, and other proponents of massive resistance were succeeded by appeals to freedom of association, local control, and resistance to the power of the federal government. This language of individual freedom resonated throughout the country, appealing especially to the growing, predominantly white, suburban population that was fleeing the cities and their urban problems. The suburbs would become one of the bastions of modern conservatism.

One set of recruits was the "**neoconservatives**," a group of intellectuals who charged that the 1960s had produced a decline in moral standards and respect for authority. Once supporters of liberalism, they had come to believe that even well-intentioned government social programs did more harm than good. Neoconservatives repudiated the attempts by Nixon, Ford, and Carter to reorient foreign policy away from the Cold War. Conservative "think tanks" created during the 1970s, like the Heritage Foundation and the American Enterprise Institute, refined and spread these ideas.

The Religious Right

The rise of religious fundamentalism during the 1970s expanded conservatism's popular base. Even as membership in mainstream denominations like Episcopalianism and Presbyterianism declined, evangelical Protestantism flourished. Some observers spoke of a Third Great Awakening (like those of the 1740s and early nineteenth century). The election of Carter, the first "born-again" Christian to become president, highlighted the growing influence of evangelical religion. But unlike Carter, most fundamentalists who entered politics did so as conservatives.

Evangelical religion

Evangelical Christians had become more and more alienated from a culture that seemed to them to trivialize religion and promote immorality. Although it spoke of restoring traditional values, the Religious Right proved remarkably adept at using modern technology, including mass mailings and televised religious programming, to raise funds for its crusade and spread its message. In 1979, Jerry Falwell, a Virginia minister,

Conservatism and the evangelicals

founded the self-styled Moral Majority, devoted to waging a "war against sin" and electing "pro-life, pro-family, pro-America" candidates to office.

Christian conservatives seemed most agitated by the ongoing sexual revolution, which they saw as undermining the traditional family and promoting immorality. As a result of the 1960s, they believed, American freedom was out of control.

The Battle over the Equal Rights Amendment

During the 1970s, "family values" moved to the center of conserva-tive politics, nowhere more so than in the battle over the Equal Rights Amendment (ERA). Originally proposed during the 1920s by Alice Paul and the Women's Party, the ERA had been revived by second-wave femi-nists. In the wake of the rights revolution, the amendment's affirmation that "equality of rights under the law" could not be abridged "on account of sex" hardly seemed controversial. In 1972, with little opposition, Congress approved the ERA and sent it to the states for ratification. Designed to eliminate obstacles to the full participation of women in public life, it aroused unexpected protest from those who claimed it would discredit the role of wife and homemaker.

The ERA

The ERA debate reflected a division among women as much as a battle of the sexes. To its supporters, the amendment offered a guarantee of women's freedom in the public sphere. To its foes, freedom for women still resided in the divinely appointed roles of wife and mother. They claimed that the ERA would let men "off the hook" by denying their responsibility

Women divided

Doug Marlette's cartoon comments on the continuing gap in pay between men and women, the kind of inequality that inspired support for the proposed Equal Rights Amendment.

Women demonstrating in support for abortion rights.

to provide for their wives and children. Polls consistently showed that a majority of Americans, male and female, favored the ERA. But thanks to the mobilization of conservative women, the amendment failed to achieve ratification by the required thirty-eight states.

The Abortion Controversy

An even more bitter battle emerged in the 1970s over abortion rights, another example, to conservatives, of how liberals in office promoted sexual immorality at the expense of moral values. The movement to reverse the 1973 *Roe v. Wade* decision began among Roman Catholics, whose church condemned abortion under any circumstances. But it soon enlisted evangelical Protestants and social conservatives more generally. Life, the movement insisted, begins at conception, and abortion is nothing less than murder. Between this position and the feminist insistence that a woman's right to control her body includes the right to a safe, legal abortion, compromise was impossible.

The abortion issue drew a bitter, sometimes violent line through American politics. It affected battles over nominees to judicial positions and led to demonstrations at family-planning and abortion clinics. The anti-abortion movement won its first victory in 1976 when Congress, over President Ford's veto, ended federal funding for abortions for poor women through the Medicaid program. By the 1990s, a few fringe anti-abortion activists were placing bombs at medical clinics and murdering doctors who terminated pregnancies.

A 1979 anti-abortion rally in Washington, D.C., on the sixth anniversary of the Supreme Court's decision in *Roe v. Wade*, which barred states from limiting a woman's right to terminate a pregnancy.

The Tax Revolt

With liberals unable to devise an effective policy to counteract deindustrialization and declining real wages, economic anxieties also created a growing constituency for conservative economics. Unlike during the Great Depression, economic distress inspired a critique of government rather than of business. New environmental regulations led to calls for less government intervention in the economy. These were most strident in the West, where measures to protect the environment threatened irrigation projects and private access to public lands. But everywhere, the economy's descent from affluence to "stagflation" increased the appeal of the conservative argument that government regulation raised business costs and eliminated jobs.

Conservative economics

Economic decline also broadened the constituency receptive to demands for lower taxes. To conservatives, tax reductions served the dual purposes of enhancing business profits and reducing the resources available to government, thus making new social programs financially impossible.

In 1978, conservatives sponsored and California voters approved Proposition 13, a ban on further increases in property taxes. The vote demonstrated that the level of taxation could be a powerful political issue. Proposition 13 proved to be a windfall for businesses and home owners while reducing funds available for schools, libraries, and other public services. Many voters, however, proved willing to accept this result of lower taxes. As anti-tax sentiment flourished throughout the country, many states followed California's lead.

California's Proposition 13

The Election of 1980

By 1980, Carter's approval rating had fallen to 21 percent—lower than Nixon's at the time of his resignation. Ronald Reagan's 1980 campaign for the presidency brought together the many strands of 1970s conservatism. He pledged to end stagflation and restore the country's dominant role in the world and its confidence in itself. "Let's make America great again," he proclaimed. "The era of self-doubt is over."

Reagan's appeal

Reagan also appealed skillfully to "white backlash." He kicked off his campaign in Philadelphia, Mississippi, where three civil rights workers had been murdered in 1964, with a speech emphasizing his belief in states' rights. Many white southerners understood this doctrine as including opposition to federal intervention on behalf of civil rights. During the campaign, Reagan repeatedly condemned welfare "cheats," school busing, and affirmative action. The Republican platform reversed the party's long-standing support for the Equal Rights Amendment and condemned

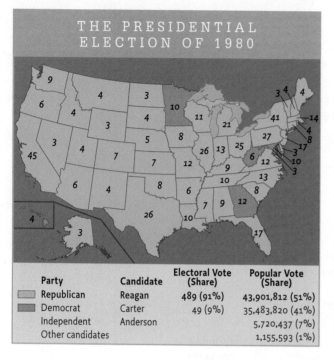

THE PRESIDENTIAL ELECTION OF 1980

Party	Candidate	Electoral Vote (Share)	Popular Vote (Share)
Republican	Reagan	489 (91%)	43,901,812 (51%)
Democrat	Carter	49 (9%)	35,483,820 (41%)
Independent	Anderson		5,720,437 (7%)
Other candidates			1,155,593 (1%)

moral permissiveness. Although not personally religious and the first divorced man to run for president, Reagan won the support of the Religious Right and conservative upholders of "family values."

Riding a wave of dissatisfaction with the country's condition, Reagan swept into the White House. Because moderate Republican John Anderson, running for president as an independent, received about 7 percent of the popular vote, Reagan won only a bare majority, although he commanded a substantial margin in the electoral college. Carter received 41 percent, a humiliating defeat for a sitting president.

The election of 1980 launched the **Reagan Revolution**, which completed the transformation of freedom from the rallying cry of the left to a possession of the right.

THE REAGAN REVOLUTION

Before entering politics, Ronald Reagan was a prominent actor and a spokesperson for General Electric. In this 1958 photograph, he demonstrates the use of a GE oven.

Ronald Reagan followed a most unusual path to the presidency. Originally a New Deal Democrat and head of the Screen Actors Guild (he was the only union leader ever to reach the White House), he emerged in the 1950s as a spokesman for the General Electric Corporation, preaching the virtues of unregulated capitalism. His nominating speech for Barry Goldwater at the 1964 Republican convention brought Reagan to national attention. Two years later, California voters elected Reagan as governor, establishing him as the conservatives' best hope of capturing the presidency. His victory in 1980 brought to power a diverse coalition of old and new conservatives: Sunbelt suburbanites and urban working-class ethnics, antigovernment crusaders and advocates of a more aggressive foreign policy, libertarians who believed in freeing the individual from restraint, and the Christian Right, which sought to restore what they considered traditional moral values to American life.

Reagan and American Freedom

Reagan's opponents often underestimated him. By the time he left office at the age of seventy-seven, he had become the oldest man ever to serve as president. Unlike most modern presidents, he was content to outline broad policy themes and leave their implementation to others.

Reagan, however, was hardly a political novice. An excellent public speaker, his optimism and affability appealed to large numbers of Americans. Reagan made conservatism seem progressive, rather than an attempt to turn back the tide of progress. Reagan repeatedly invoked the idea that America has a divinely appointed mission as a "beacon of liberty and freedom." Freedom, indeed, became the watchword of the Reagan Revolution. In his public appearances and state papers, Reagan used the word more often than any president before him.

Reagan reshaped the nation's agenda and political language more effectively than any president since Franklin D. Roosevelt. On issues ranging from taxes to government spending, national security, crime, welfare, and "traditional values," he put Democrats on the defensive. But he also proved to be a pragmatist, recognizing when to compromise so as not to fragment his diverse coalition of supporters.

A delegate to the Republican national convention of 1980 wears a hat festooned with the flags of the United States and Texas and a button with a picture of her hero, Ronald Reagan.

Reaganomics

In 1981, Reagan persuaded Congress to reduce the top tax rate from 70 percent to 50 percent and to index tax brackets to take inflation into account. Five years later, the Tax Reform Act reduced the rate on the wealthiest Americans to 28 percent. These measures marked a sharp retreat from the principle of progressivity (the idea that the wealthy should pay a higher percentage of their income in taxes than other citizens), one of the ways twentieth-century societies tried to address the unequal distribution of wealth. Reagan also appointed conservative heads of regulatory agencies, who cut back on environmental protection and workplace safety rules, about which business had complained for years.

Tax reform

Since the New Deal, liberals had tried to promote economic growth by using the power of the government to bolster ordinary Americans' purchasing power. Reagan's economic program, known as "supply-side economics" by proponents and "trickle-down economics" by critics, relied on high interest rates to curb inflation and lower tax rates, especially for businesses and high-income Americans, to stimulate private investment. The policy assumed that cutting taxes would inspire Americans at all income levels to work harder, because they would keep more of the money they earned.

Supply-side economics

Reagan and Labor

Reagan inaugurated an era of hostility between the federal government and organized labor. In August 1981, when 13,000 members of PATCO,

The air traffic controllers' strike

the union of air traffic controllers, began a strike in violation of federal law, Reagan fired them all. He used the military to oversee the nation's air traffic system until new controllers could be trained. Reagan's action inspired many private employers to launch anti-union offensives. The hiring of workers to replace permanently those who had gone on strike, a rare occurrence before 1980, became widespread. Manufacturing employment, where union membership was concentrated, meanwhile continued its long-term decline. By the mid-1990s, the steel industry employed only 170,000 persons—down from 600,000 in 1973.

"**Reaganomics**," as critics dubbed the administration's policies, initially produced the most severe recession since the 1930s. A long period of economic expansion, however, followed the downturn of 1981–1982. As companies "downsized" their workforces, shifted production overseas, and took advantage of new technologies such as satellite communications, they became more profitable. At the same time, the rate of inflation, 13.5 percent at the beginning of 1981, declined to 3.5 percent in 1988, partly because a period of expanded oil production that drove down prices succeeded the shortages of the 1970s.

The wealthiest American families benefited the most from economic expansion during the 1980s, whereas the poorest 40 percent of the population saw their real incomes decline. (Real income indicates income adjusted to take account of inflation.)

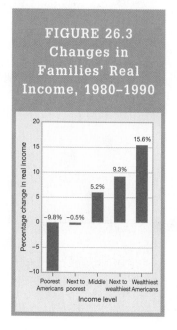

FIGURE 26.3 Changes in Families' Real Income, 1980–1990

Percentage change in real income

- Poorest Americans: –9.8%
- Next to poorest: –0.5%
- Middle: 5.2%
- Next to wealthiest: 9.3%
- Wealthiest Americans: 15.6%

Income level

The Problem of Inequality

Together, Reagan's policies, rising stock prices, and deindustrialization resulted in a considerable rise in economic inequality. By the mid-1990s, the richest 1 percent of Americans owned 40 percent of the nation's wealth, twice their share twenty years earlier. Most spent their income not on productive investments and charity as supply-side economists had promised, but on luxury goods, real-estate speculation, and corporate buyouts that often led to plant closings as operations were consolidated. The income of middle-class families, especially those with a wife who did not work outside the home, stagnated while that of the poorest one-fifth of the population declined.

During the 1970s, Jim Crow had finally ended in many workplaces and unions. But just as decades of painful efforts to obtain better jobs bore fruit, hundreds of thousands of black workers lost their jobs when factories closed their doors. In South Gate, a working-class suburb of Los Angeles, for example, the giant Firestone tire factory shut down in 1980, only a few years after black and Latino workers had made their first breakthroughs in employment. When the national unemployment rate reached 8.9 percent at the end of 1981, the figure for blacks exceeded 20 percent.

This photograph of the remains of the Bethlehem Steel plant in Lackawana, New York, which closed in 1982, depicts the aftermath of deindustrialization. Today, the site is a wind farm, with eight windmills helping to provide electricity for the city.

The Second Gilded Age

In retrospect, the 1980s, like the 1890s, would be widely remembered as a decade of misplaced values. Buying out companies generated more profits than running them; making deals, not making products, became the way to get rich. The merger of Nabisco and R. J. Reynolds Tobacco Company in 1988 produced close to $1 billion in fees for lawyers, economic advisers, and stockbrokers. "Greed is healthy," declared Wall Street financier Ivan Boesky (who ended up in prison for insider stock trading). "Yuppie"—the young urban professional who earned a high income working in a bank or stock-brokerage firm and spent lavishly on designer clothing and other trappings of the good life—became a household word.

Taxpayers footed the bill for some of the consequences. The deregulation of savings and loan associations—banks that had generally confined themselves to financing home mortgages—allowed those institutions to invest in unsound real-estate ventures and corporate mergers. Losses piled up, and the Federal Savings and Loan Insurance Corporation, which insured depositors' accounts, faced bankruptcy. After Reagan left office, the federal government bailed out the savings and loan institutions at a cost to taxpayers estimated at $250 billion.

Supply-side advocates insisted that lowering taxes would enlarge government revenue by stimulating economic activity. But spurred by large increases in funds for the military, federal spending far outstripped income,

A homeless Los Angeles family, forced to live in their car, photographed in 1983.

First lady Nancy Reagan promoting her "Just Say No" campaign against the use of drugs, in a photo from 1986.

producing large budget deficits, despite assurances by supply-siders that this would not happen. During Reagan's presidency, the national debt tripled to $2.7 trillion.

Nonetheless, Reagan remained immensely popular. He won a triumphant reelection in 1984. His opponent, Walter Mondale (best remembered for choosing Congresswoman Geraldine Ferraro of New York as his running mate, the first woman candidate on a major-party presidential ticket), carried only his home state of Minnesota and the District of Columbia.

Conservatives and Reagan

Reagan's social policies

Although he implemented their economic policies, Reagan in some ways disappointed ardent conservatives. The administration left intact core elements of the welfare state, such as Social Security, Medicare, and Medicaid, which many conservatives wished to curtail significantly or repeal. The Reagan era did little to advance the social agenda of the Christian Right. Abortion remained legal, women continued to enter the labor force in unprecedented numbers, and Reagan even appointed the first female member of the Supreme Court, Sandra Day O'Connor. In 1986, in *Bowers v. Hardwick*, in a rare victory for cultural conservatives, the Supreme Court did uphold the constitutionality of state laws outlawing homosexual acts. (In 2003, the justices would reverse the *Bowers* decision, declaring unconstitutional laws that criminalized homosexuality.)

Hollywood joined enthusiastically in the revived Cold War. The 1984 film *Red Dawn* depicted a Soviet invasion of the United States.

Reagan and the Cold War

In foreign policy, Reagan resumed vigorous denunciation of the Soviet Union—calling it an "evil empire"—and sponsored the largest military buildup in American history, including new long-range bombers and missiles. In 1983, he proposed an entirely new strategy, the Strategic Defense Initiative, which would develop a space-based system to intercept and destroy enemy missiles. The idea was not remotely feasible technologically, and, if

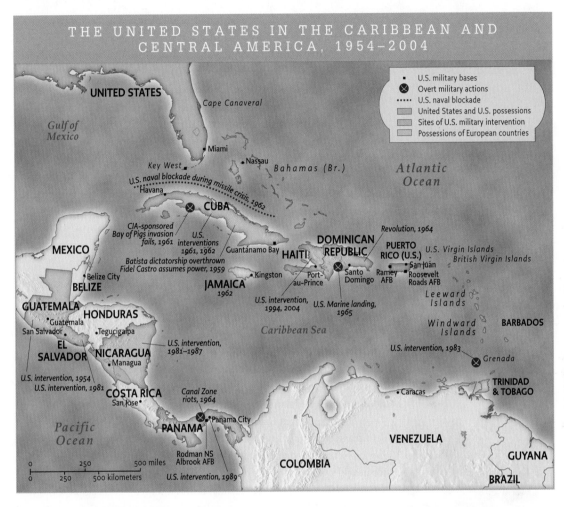

THE UNITED STATES IN THE CARIBBEAN AND CENTRAL AMERICA, 1954–2004

- ∎ U.S. military bases
- ⊗ Overt military actions
- ⋯⋯ U.S. naval blockade
- ▢ United States and U.S. possessions
- ▢ Sites of U.S. military intervention
- ▢ Possessions of European countries

UNITED STATES

Cape Canaveral

Gulf of Mexico

Miami

Key West · · Nassau · Bahamas (Br.)

U.S. naval blockade during missile crisis, 1962

Havana

CUBA

CIA-sponsored Bay of Pigs invasion fails, 1961

U.S. interventions 1961, 1962

MEXICO

Guantánamo Bay

Batista dictatorship overthrown Fidel Castro assumes power, 1959

Belize City

BELIZE

Kingston

JAMAICA 1962

HAITI

Port-au-Prince

DOMINICAN REPUBLIC

Santo Domingo

Revolution, 1964

PUERTO RICO (U.S.)

San Juan

Ramey AFB

U.S. Virgin Islands

British Virgin Islands

Roosevelt Roads AFB

Atlantic Ocean

GUATEMALA

Guatemala

San Salvador

HONDURAS

Tegucigalpa

U.S. intervention, 1994, 2004

U.S. Marine landing, 1965

Leeward Islands

EL SALVADOR

NICARAGUA

U.S. intervention, 1981–1987

Managua

Caribbean Sea

Windward Islands

BARBADOS

U.S. intervention, 1954

U.S. intervention, 1981

COSTA RICA

San José

Canal Zone riots, 1964

U.S. intervention, 1983

Grenada

TRINIDAD & TOBAGO

Pacific Ocean

PANAMA

Panama City

Caracas

VENEZUELA

GUYANA

Rodman NS Albrook AFB

U.S. intervention, 1989

COLOMBIA

BRAZIL

0 · 250 · 500 miles

0 · 250 · 500 kilometers

deployed, it would violate the Anti-Ballistic Missile Treaty of 1972. But it appealed to Reagan's desire to reassert America's worldwide power.

Reagan came into office determined to overturn the **"Vietnam syndrome"**—as widespread public reluctance to commit American forces overseas was called. He sent American troops to the Caribbean island of Grenada to oust a pro-Cuban government. In 1982, Reagan dispatched marines as a peacekeeping force to Lebanon, where a civil war raged between the Christian government, supported by Israeli forces, and Muslim insurgents. But he quickly withdrew them after a bomb exploded at their barracks, killing 241 Americans. The public, Reagan realized, would support minor operations like Grenada but remained unwilling to sustain heavy casualties abroad.

As in the first part of the twentieth century, the United States intervened frequently in Caribbean and Central American countries during and immediately after the Cold War.

Troops overseas

THE REAGAN REVOLUTION | 835

Abandoning the Carter administration's emphasis on human rights, Reagan embraced the idea, advanced in 1979 by neoconservative writer Jeane Kirkpatrick, that the United States should oppose "totalitarian" communists but assist "authoritarian" noncommunist regimes. The United Nations and the United States stepped up its alliances with Third World anticommunist dictatorships like the governments of Chile and South Africa. The administration poured in funds to combat insurgencies against the governments of El Salvador and Guatemala, whose armies and associated death squads committed flagrant abuses against their own citizens. When El Salvador's army massacred hundreds of civilians in the town of El Mozote in 1981, the State Department denied that the event, widely reported in the press, had taken place.

Latin America

The Iran-Contra Affair

American involvement in Central America produced the greatest scandal of Reagan's presidency, the **Iran-Contra affair**. In 1984, Congress banned military aid to the Contras (derived from the Spanish word for "against") fighting the Sandinista government of Nicaragua, which had ousted the American-backed dictator Anastasio Somoza in 1979. In 1985, Reagan secretly authorized the sale of arms to Iran—now involved in a war with its neighbor, Iraq—in order to secure the release of a number of American hostages held by Islamic groups in the Middle East. CIA director William Casey and Lieutenant Colonel Oliver North of the National Security Council set up a system that diverted some of the proceeds to buy military supplies for the Contras in defiance of the congressional ban. The scheme continued for nearly two years.

In 1987, after a Middle Eastern newspaper leaked the story, Congress held televised hearings that revealed a pattern of official duplicity and violation of the law reminiscent of the Nixon era. Eleven members of the administration eventually were convicted of perjury or destroying documents, or pleaded guilty before being tried. Reagan denied knowledge of the illegal proceedings, but the Iran-Contra affair undermined confidence that he controlled his own administration.

President Reagan visited Moscow in 1988, cementing his close relationship with Soviet leader Mikhail Gorbachev. They were photographed in Red Square.

Reagan and Gorbachev

In his second term, to the surprise of both his foes and his supporters, Reagan softened his anticommunist rhetoric and established good relations with Soviet premier Mikhail Gorbachev. Gorbachev had come to power in 1985, bent on reforming the Soviet Union's repressive political system and reinvigorating its economy. Gorbachev inaugurated policies known as *glasnost* (political openness) and *perestroika* (economic reform).

Gorbachev realized that significant change would be impossible without reducing his country's military budget. Reagan was ready to negotiate. A series of talks between 1985 and 1987 yielded more progress on arms control than in the entire postwar period to that point, including an agreement to eliminate intermediate- and short-range nuclear missiles in Europe. In 1988, Gorbachev began pulling Soviet troops out of Afghanistan. Having entered office as an ardent Cold Warrior, Reagan left with hostilities between the superpowers much diminished. He even repudiated his earlier comment that the Soviet Union was an "evil empire," saying that it referred to "another era."

Diminished hostilities

Reagan's Legacy

Reagan's presidency revealed the contradictions at the heart of modern conservatism. In some ways, the Reagan Revolution undermined the very values and institutions conservatives held dear. Intended to discourage reliance on government handouts by rewarding honest work and business initiative, Reagan's policies inspired a speculative frenzy that enriched architects of corporate takeovers and investors in the stock market while leaving in their wake plant closings, job losses, and devastated communities. Nothing proved more threatening to local traditions or family stability than deindustrialization, insecurity about employment, and the relentless downward pressure on wages.

Nonetheless, few figures have so successfully changed the landscape and language of politics. Reagan's vice president, George H. W. Bush, defeated Michael Dukakis, the governor of Massachusetts, in the 1988 election partly because Dukakis could not respond effectively to the charge that he was a "liberal"—now a term of political abuse. Conservative assumptions about the virtues of the free market and the evils of "big government" dominated the mass media and political debates. During the 1990s, these and other conservative ideas would be embraced almost as fully by President Bill Clinton, a Democrat, as by Reagan and the Republicans.

Reagan's impact

The Election of 1988

The 1988 election seemed to show politics sinking to new lows. Television advertisements and media exposés now dominated political campaigns. The race for the Democratic nomination had hardly begun before the front-runner, Senator Gary Hart of Colorado, withdrew after a newspaper reported that he had spent the night at his Washington town house with a woman other than his wife. Democrats ridiculed the Republican vice presidential nominee, Senator Dan Quayle of Indiana, for factual and linguistic mistakes. Republicans spread unfounded rumors that Michael Dukakis's wife had burned an American flag during the 1960s. The low point of the campaign came in a Republican television ad depicting the threatening image of Willie Horton, a black murderer and rapist who had been furloughed from prison during Dukakis's term as governor of Massachusetts. Rarely in the modern era had a major party appealed so blatantly to racial fears.

A dismal campaign

Bush achieved a substantial majority, winning 54 percent of the popular vote. Democratic success in retaining control of Congress suggested that an electoral base existed for a comeback. But this would only occur if the party fashioned a new appeal to replace traditional liberalism, which had been eclipsed by the triumph of conservatism.

CHAPTER REVIEW AND ONLINE RESOURCES

REVIEW QUESTIONS

1. *Why were social issues associated with the sexual revolution so contested by all sides?*

2. *What were continuing challenges to the cohesiveness of the Democratic (New Deal) coalition? What were the consequences of those divisions?*

3. *What were the main features of Nixon's policy of "realism" in dealing with China and the Soviet Union?*

4. *Describe the basic events and the larger significance of the Watergate scandal.*

5. *What were the major causes for the decline of the U.S. economy during the 1970s?*

6. *What were the causes and consequences of the public's disillusionment with the federal government in the 1970s and 1980s?*

7. *Identify the groups and their agendas that combined to create the new conservative base in the 1970s and 1980s.*

8. *What impact did Ronald Reagan have on the American political scene?*

9. *Why was there growth in economic inequality in the 1980s?*

10. *How did various groups see the relationship between women's rights and freedom differently?*

KEY TERMS

affirmative action (p. 809)
busing (p. 810)
"reverse discrimination" (p. 810)
Title IX (p. 811)
Strategic Arms Limitation Talks (p. 812)
détente (p. 812)
My Lai massacre (p. 813)
War Powers Act (p. 814)
Watergate (p. 815)
stagflation (p. 818)
misery index (p. 818)
Sunbelt (p. 819)
Nixon pardon (p. 819)
Helsinki Accords (p. 820)
deregulation (p. 820)
Camp David Accords (p. 822)
"neoconservatives" (p. 826)
Reagan Revolution (p. 830)
Reaganomics (p. 832)
"Vietnam syndrome" (p. 834)
Iran-Contra affair (p. 836)

wwnorton.com /studyspace

VISIT STUDYSPACE FOR THESE RESOURCES AND MORE

- A chapter outline
- A diagnostic chapter quiz
- Interactive maps
- Map worksheets
- Multimedia documents

CHAPTER 27

GLOBALIZATION AND ITS DISCONTENTS

★

1989 - 2000

The Goddess of Democracy and Freedom, a statue reminiscent of the Statue of Liberty, was displayed by pro-democracy advocates during the 1989 demonstrations in Beijing's Tiananmen Square. After allowing it to continue for two months, the Chinese government sent troops to crush the peaceful occupation of the square.

I n December 1999, delegates from around the world gathered in
    Seattle for a meeting of the World Trade Organization (WTO), a
    135-nation group created five years earlier to reduce barriers to
international commerce and settle trade disputes. To the astonishment
of residents of the city, more than 30,000 persons gathered to protest
the meeting. Their marches and rallies brought together factory workers,
who claimed that global free trade encouraged corporations to shift
production to low-wage centers overseas, and "tree-huggers," as some
reporters called environmentalists, who complained about the impact on
the earth's ecology of unregulated economic development.

Once a center of labor radicalism, the Seattle area in 1999 was
best known as the home of Microsoft, developer of the Windows
operating system used in most of the world's computers. The company's
worldwide reach symbolized "**globalization**," the process by which
people, investment, goods, information, and culture increasingly flowed
across national boundaries. Globalization has been called "*the* concept of
the 1990s."

Globalization, of course, was hardly a new phenomenon. The
internationalization of commerce and culture and the reshuffling of the
world's peoples had been going on since the explorations of the fifteenth
century. But the scale and scope of late-twentieth-century globalization
was unprecedented. Thanks to satellites and the Internet, information
and popular culture flowed instantaneously to every corner of the world.

FOCUS QUESTIONS

- *How did Bush and Clinton transform America's world role?*

- *What forces drove the economic resurgence of the 1990s?*

- *What cultural conflicts emerged in the 1990s?*

- *How did a divisive political partisanship affect the election of 2000?*

- *What were the prevailing ideas of American freedom at the end of the twentieth century?*

Protesters dressed as sea turtles, an endangered species, at the demonstrations against the World Trade Organization in Seattle, December 1999.

Manufacturers and financial institutions scoured the world for profitable investment opportunities.

Perhaps most important, the collapse of communism between 1989 and 1991 opened almost the entire world to the spread of market capitalism and to the idea that government should interfere as little as possible with economic activity. American politicians and social commentators increasingly criticized the regulation of wages and working conditions, assistance to the less fortunate, and environmental protections as burdens on international competitiveness. During the 1990s, presidents George H. W. Bush, a Republican, and Bill Clinton, a Democrat, both spoke of an American mission to create a single global free market as the path to rising living standards, the spread of democracy, and greater worldwide freedom.

Global markets and freedom

The media called the loose coalition of groups who organized the Seattle protests and others like it the "antiglobalization" movement. In fact, they challenged not globalization itself but its social consequences. Globalization, the demonstrators claimed, accelerated the worldwide creation of wealth but widened gaps between rich and poor countries and between haves and have-nots within societies. Decisions affecting the day-to-day lives of millions of people were made by institutions—the World Trade Organization, International Monetary Fund, World Bank, and multinational corporations—that operated without any democratic input. Demonstrators demanded not an end to global trade and capital flows but the establishment of international standards for wages, labor conditions, and the environment, and greater investment in health and education in poor countries.

The Battle of Seattle placed on the national and international agendas a question that promises to be among the most pressing concerns of the twenty-first century—the relationship between globalization, economic justice, and freedom.

THE POST-COLD WAR WORLD

The Crisis of Communism

Tiananmen Square

The year 1989 was one of the most momentous of the twentieth century. In April, tens of thousands of student demonstrators occupied Tiananmen Square in the heart of Beijing, demanding greater democracy in China. The students erected a figure reminiscent of the Statue of Liberty, calling it "The Goddess of Democracy and Freedom." In June, Chinese troops crushed the protest, killing an unknown number of people, possibly thousands.

In the fall of 1989, pro-democracy demonstrations spread across eastern Europe. Gorbachev made it clear that unlike in the past, the Soviet Union would not intervene. The climactic event took place on November 9 when crowds breached the Berlin Wall, which since 1961 had stood as the Cold War's most prominent symbol. One by one, the region's communist governments agreed to give up power. In 1990, a reunified German nation absorbed East Germany. The remarkably swift and almost entirely peaceful collapse of communism in eastern Europe became known as the "velvet revolution."

The fall of the Berlin Wall

Meanwhile, the Soviet Union itself slipped deeper and deeper into crisis. One after another, the republics of the Soviet Union declared themselves sovereign states. By the end of 1991, the Soviet Union ceased to exist; in its place were fifteen new independent nations.

The breakup of the Soviet Union

The sudden and unexpected collapse of communism marked the end of the Cold War and a stunning victory for the United States and its allies. For the first time since 1917, there existed a truly worldwide capitalist system. Even China, though remaining under Communist Party rule, had already embarked on market reforms and rushed to attract foreign investment. Other events suggested that the 1990s would also be a "decade of democracy." In 1990, South Africa released Nelson Mandela, head of the African National Congress, from prison. Four years later, as a result of the

Decade of democracy

Demonstrators dancing atop the Berlin Wall on November 10, 1989. The next day, crowds began dismantling it, in the most dramatic moment of the collapse of communist rule in eastern Europe.

THE POST–COLD WAR WORLD | 843

The end of the Cold War and breakup of the Soviet Union, Czechoslovakia, and Yugoslavia redrew the map of eastern Europe (compare this map with the map of Cold War Europe in Chapter 23). Two additional nations that emerged from the Soviet Union lie to the east and are not indicated here: Kyrgyzstan and Tajikistan.

first democratic elections in the country's history, Mandela became president, ending the system of state-sponsored racial inequality, known as "apartheid," and white minority government. Throughout Latin America and Africa, civilian governments replaced military rule.

A New World Order?

The sudden shift from a bipolar world to one of unquestioned American predominance promised to redefine the country's global role. President George H. W. Bush spoke of the coming of a "new world order." But no one knew what its characteristics would be.

Intervention in Panama

Bush's first major foreign policy action was a throwback to the days of American interventionism in the Western Hemisphere. At the end of 1989, he dispatched troops to Panama to overthrow the government of General Manuel Antonio Noriega, a former ally of the United States who had become involved in the international drug trade.

The Gulf War

A far more serious crisis arose in 1990 when Iraq invaded and annexed Kuwait, an oil-rich sheikdom on the Persian Gulf. Fearing that Iraqi dictator Saddam Hussein might next attack Saudi Arabia, a longtime ally that supplied more oil to the United States than any other country, Bush rushed troops to defend the kingdom and warned Iraq to withdraw from Kuwait or face war.

Iraq crisis

In February 1991, the United States launched Operation Desert Storm, which quickly drove the Iraqi army from Kuwait. The United Nations ordered Iraq to disarm and imposed economic sanctions that produced widespread civilian suffering for the rest of the decade. But Hussein remained in place. So did a large American military establishment in Saudi Arabia, to the outrage of Islamic fundamentalists who deemed its presence an affront to their faith. In the war's immediate aftermath, Bush's public approval rating rose to an unprecedented 89 percent.

Operation Desert Storm

Visions of America's Role

In a speech to Congress, President Bush identified the Gulf War as the first step in the struggle to create a world rooted in democracy and global free trade. But it remained unclear how this broad vision would be translated into policy. Soon after the end of the war, General Colin Powell, chairman of the Joint Chiefs of Staff, and Dick Cheney, the secretary of defense, outlined different visions of the future. Powell predicted that the post–Cold War world would be a dangerous environment with conflicts popping up in unexpected places. To avoid being drawn into an unending role as global policeman, he insisted, the United States should not commit its troops abroad without clear objectives and a timetable for withdrawal. Cheney argued that with the demise of the Soviet Union, the United States possessed the power to reshape the world and prevent hostile states from achieving regional power. For the rest of the 1990s, it was not certain which definition of the American role in the post–Cold War world would predominate.

President Bush, with Defense Secretary Dick Cheney *(left)* and General Colin Powell *(right)*, chair of the Joint Chiefs of Staff, at a meeting in January 1991, shortly before the beginning of the Gulf War. Cheney and Powell would play major roles in the administration of Bush's son, President George W. Bush.

The Election of Clinton

Had a presidential election been held early in 1991, Bush would undoubtedly have been victorious. But later that year, the economy slipped into recession. Despite victory in the Cold War and the Gulf, public-opinion polls showed that more and more Americans believed the country was on the wrong track. No one seized more effectively on this widespread sense of unease than Bill Clinton, a former governor of Arkansas. In 1992, Clinton won the Democratic nomination by combining social liberalism (he supported abortion rights, gay rights, and affirmative action for racial minorities) with elements of conservatism (he pledged to reduce government bureaucracy and, borrowing a page from Republicans, promised to "end welfare as we know it").

Bill Clinton's appeal

A charismatic campaigner, Clinton conveyed sincere concern for voters' economic anxieties. Bush, by contrast, seemed out of touch with the day-to-day lives of ordinary Americans. On the wall of Democratic headquarters, Clinton's campaign director posted the slogan, "It's the Economy, Stupid"—a reminder that the economic downturn was the Democrats' strongest card. Bush was further weakened when conservative leader Pat Buchanan delivered a fiery televised speech at the Republican national convention that declared cultural war against gays, feminists, and supporters of abortion rights. This rhetoric seemed to confirm the Democratic portrait of Republicans as intolerant and divisive.

Bush's weaknesses

A third candidate, the eccentric Texas billionaire Ross Perot, also entered the fray. He attacked Bush and Clinton as lacking the economic know-how to deal with the recession and the ever-increasing national debt. That millions of Americans considered Perot a credible candidate—at one point, polls showed him leading both Clinton and Bush—testified to widespread dissatisfaction with the major parties. Perot's support faded, but he still received 19 percent of the popular vote, the best result for a third-party candidate since Theodore Roosevelt in 1912. Clinton won by a substantial margin, a humiliating outcome for Bush, given his earlier popularity.

Clinton in Office

Clinton's domestic policy

In his first two years in office, Clinton turned away from some of the social and economic policies of the Reagan and Bush years. He appointed several blacks and women to his cabinet, including Janet Reno, the first female attorney general, and named two supporters of abortion rights, Ruth Bader Ginsburg and Stephen Breyer, to the Supreme Court. He modified the military's strict ban on gay soldiers, instituting a **"don't ask, don't tell"** policy by which officers would not seek out gays for dismissal from the armed forces. His first budget raised taxes on the wealthy and significantly expanded the Earned Income Tax Credit (EITC)—a cash payment for low-income workers begun during the Ford administration. The most effective antipoverty policy since the Great Society, the EITC raised more than 4 million Americans, half of them children, above the poverty line during Clinton's presidency.

Earned Income Tax Credit

Clinton shared his predecessor's passion for free trade. Despite strong opposition from unions and environmentalists, he obtained congressional approval in 1993 of the **North American Free Trade Agreement** (NAFTA), a treaty negotiated by Bush that created a free-trade zone consisting of Canada, Mexico, and the United States.

The major policy initiative of Clinton's first term was a plan devised by a panel headed by his wife, Hillary, to address the rising cost of health care and the increasing number of Americans who lacked health insurance. In Canada and western Europe, governments provided universal medical coverage. The United States had the world's most advanced medical technology but a woefully incomplete system of health insurance. Tens of millions of Americans lacked any coverage at all. Beginning in the 1980s, moreover, businesses shifted their employees from individual doctors to health maintenance organizations (HMOs), which reduced costs by limiting physicians' fees and, critics charged, denying patients needed medical procedures.

Announced with great fanfare by Hillary Rodham Clinton at congressional hearings in 1993, Clinton's plan would have provided universal coverage through large groupings of organizations like the HMOs. Doctors and health insurance and drug companies attacked it vehemently, fearing government regulations that would limit reimbursement for medical procedures, insurance rates, and the cost of drugs. Too complex to be easily understood by most voters, and vulnerable to criticism for further expanding the unpopular federal bureaucracy, the plan died in 1994.

Edward Sorel's illustration for the cover of the *New Yorker* depicts Bill Clinton at his 1993 inauguration, flanked by some of his presidential predecessors.

The "Freedom Revolution"

With the economy recovering slowly from the recession and Clinton's first two years in office seemingly lacking in significant accomplishments, voters in 1994 turned against the administration. For the first time since the 1950s, Republicans won control of both houses of Congress. They proclaimed their triumph the "Freedom Revolution." Newt Gingrich, a conservative congressman from Georgia who became the new Speaker of the House, masterminded their campaign. Gingrich had devised a platform called the "**Contract with America**," which promised to curtail the scope

VOICES OF FREEDOM

From Bill Clinton, Speech on Signing of NAFTA (1993)

The North American Free Trade Agreement was signed by President Bill Clinton early in his first term. It created a free-trade zone (an area where goods can travel freely without import duties) composed of Canada, the United States, and Mexico. Clinton asked Americans to accept economic globalization as an inevitable form of progress and the path to future prosperity. "There will be no job loss," he promised. Things did not entirely work out that way.

As President, it is my duty to speak frankly to the American people about the world in which we now live. Fifty years ago, at the end of World War II, an unchallenged America was protected by the oceans and by our technological superiority and, very frankly, by the economic devastation of the people who could otherwise have been our competitors. We chose then to try to help rebuild our former enemies and to create a world of free trade supported by institutions which would facilitate it. . . . As a result, jobs were created, and opportunity thrived all across the world. . . .

For the last 20 years, in all the wealthy countries of the world—because of changes in the global environment, because of the growth of technology, because of increasing competition—the middle class that was created and enlarged by the wise policies of expanding trade at the end of World War II has been under severe stress. Most Americans are working harder for less. They are vulnerable to the fear tactics and the averseness to change that are behind much of the opposition to NAFTA. But I want to say to my fellow Americans: When you live in a time of change, the only way to recover your security and to broaden your horizons is to adapt to the change—to embrace, to move forward. . . . The only way we can recover the fortunes of the middle class in this country so that people who work harder and smarter can, at least, prosper more, the only way we can pass on the American dream of the last 40 years to our children and their children for the next 40, is to adapt to the changes which are occurring.

In a fundamental sense, this debate about NAFTA is a debate about whether we will embrace these changes and create the jobs of tomorrow or try to resist these changes, hoping we can preserve the economic structures of yesterday. . . . I believe that NAFTA will create 1 million jobs in the first 5 years of its impact. . . . NAFTA will generate these jobs by fostering an export boom to Mexico by tearing down tariff walls. . . . There will be no job loss.

From Global Exchange, Seattle, Declaration for Global Democracy (December 1999)

The demonstrations that disrupted the December 1999 meeting of the World Trade Organization in Seattle brought to public attention a widespread dissatisfaction with the effects of economic globalization. In this declaration, organizers of the protest offered their critique.

As citizens of global society, recognizing that the World Trade Organization is unjustly dominated by corporate interests and run for the enrichment of the few at the expense of all others, we demand:

Representatives from all sectors of society must be included in all levels of trade policy formulations. All global citizens must be democratically represented in the formulation, implementation, and evaluation of all global social and economic policies.

Global trade and investment must not be ends in themselves, but rather the instruments for achieving equitable and sustainable development including protection for workers and the environment.

Global trade agreements must not undermine the ability of each nation-state or local community to meet its citizens' social, environmental, cultural or economic needs.

The World Trade Organization must be replaced by a democratic and transparent body accountable to citizens—not to corporations.

No globalization without representation!

QUESTIONS

1. *Why does Clinton feel that free trade is necessary to American prosperity?*

2. *Why do the Seattle protesters feel that the World Trade Organization is a threat to democracy?*

3. *How do these documents reflect contradictory arguments about the impact of globalization in the United States?*

Congressman Newt Gingrich of Georgia announcing the "Contract with America" on the steps of the Capitol in Washington. The Republican program for the congressional elections of 1994, the contract helped to produce a Republican sweep that resulted in Gingrich's selection as Speaker of the House.

of government, cut back on taxes and economic and environmental regulations, overhaul the welfare system, and end affirmative action.

Republicans moved swiftly to implement its provisions. The House approved deep cuts in social, educational, and environmental programs, including the popular Medicare system. With the president and Congress unable to reach agreement on a budget, the government in December 1995 shut down all nonessential operations, including Washington, D.C., museums and national parks.

Government shutdown

Most Americans blamed Congress for the impasse, however, and Gingrich's popularity plummeted.

Clinton's Political Strategy

Like Truman after the Republican sweep of 1946, Clinton rebuilt his popularity by campaigning against a radical Congress. He opposed the most extreme parts of his opponents' program, while adopting others. In his state of the union address of January 1996, he announced that "the era of big government is over," in effect turning his back on the tradition of Democratic Party liberalism and embracing the antigovernment outlook associated with Republicans.

Ending AFDC

Also in 1996, ignoring the protests of most Democrats, Clinton signed into law a Republican bill that abolished the program of Aid to Families with Dependent Children (AFDC), commonly known as "welfare." Grants of money to the states, with strict limits on how long recipients could receive payments, replaced it. At the time of its abolition, AFDC assisted 14 million individuals, 9 million of them children. Thanks to stringent new eligibility requirements imposed by the states and the economic boom of the late 1990s, welfare rolls plummeted. But the number of children living in poverty remained essentially unchanged.

Clinton's strategy enabled him to neutralize Republican claims that Democrats were the party of high taxes and lavish spending on persons who preferred dependency to honest labor. Clinton's passion for free trade alienated many working-class Democrats but convinced middle-class voters that the party was not beholden to the unions.

The presidential election of 1996

Clinton easily defeated Republican Bob Dole in the presidential contest of 1996, becoming the first Democrat elected to two terms since FDR. Clinton had accomplished for Reaganism what Eisenhower had done for the New Deal and Nixon for the Great Society—consolidating a basic shift in American politics by accepting many of the premises of his opponents.

Clinton and World Affairs

Like Jimmy Carter before him, Clinton took steps to encourage the settlement of long-standing international conflicts and tried to elevate support for human rights to a central place in international relations. He met only mixed success.

Like Carter, Clinton found it difficult to balance concern for human rights with strategic and economic interests and to formulate clear guidelines for humanitarian interventions overseas. For example, the United States did nothing in 1994 when tribal massacres racked Rwanda, in central Africa. More than 800,000 people were slaughtered, and 2 million refugees fled the country.

Massacres in Rwanda

The most complex foreign policy crisis of the Clinton years arose from the disintegration of Yugoslavia, a multi-ethnic state in southeastern Europe that had been carved from the old Austro-Hungarian empire after World War I. As in the rest of eastern Europe, the communist government that had ruled Yugoslavia since the 1940s collapsed in 1989. Within a few years, the country's six provinces dissolved into five new states. Ethnic conflict plagued several of these new nations. "**Ethnic cleansing**"—a terrible new term meaning the forcible expulsion from an area of a particular ethnic group—now entered the international vocabulary.

The Balkan crisis

With the Cold War over, protection of human rights in the Balkans gave NATO a new purpose. In 1998, Yugoslavian troops and local Serbs conducted ethnic cleansing against the Albanian population of Kosovo, a province of Serbia. More than 800,000 Albanians fled the region. To halt the bloodshed, NATO launched a two-month war in 1999 against Yugoslavia that led to the deployment of American and UN forces in Kosovo.

Human Rights

During Clinton's presidency, human rights played an increasingly important role in international affairs. Hundreds of nongovernmental agencies throughout the world defined themselves as protectors of human rights. During the 1990s, the agenda of international human rights organizations expanded to include access to health care, women's rights, and the rights of indigenous peoples like the Aborigines of Australia and the descendants of the original inhabitants of the Americas. The United States dispatched the military to distant parts of the world to assist in international missions to protect civilians.

New institutions

New institutions emerged that sought to punish violations of human rights. The **Rwandan genocide** produced a UN-sponsored war crimes court that sentenced the country's former prime minister to life in prison. An international tribunal put Yugoslav president Slobodan Miloševič on trial for sponsoring the massacre of civilians. It remained to be seen whether these initiatives would grow into an effective international system of protecting human rights across national boundaries.

Serbian refugees fleeing a Croat offensive during the 1990s. By the fall of 1995, the wars that followed the breakup of Yugoslavia and accompanying "ethnic cleansing" had displaced over 3 million people.

A NEW ECONOMY?

Clinton's popularity rested in part on the American economy's remarkable performance in the mid- and late 1990s. After recovery from the recession of 1990–1991, economic expansion continued for the rest of the decade. By 2000, unemployment stood below 4 percent, a figure not seen since the 1960s. Because Reagan and Bush had left behind massive budget deficits, Clinton worked hard to balance the federal budget—a goal traditionally associated with fiscal conservatives. Because economic growth produced rising tax revenues, Clinton during his second term not only balanced the budget but actually produced budget surpluses.

Economic growth

The Computer Revolution

Many commentators spoke of the 1990s as the dawn of a "new economy," in which computers and the Internet would produce vast new efficiencies and the production and sale of information would occupy the central place once held by the manufacture of goods. Computers had first been developed during and after World War II to solve scientific problems and do calculations involving enormous amounts of data. The early ones were extremely large, expensive, and, by modern standards, slow. Research for the space program of the 1960s spurred the development of the microchip, on which circuits could be imprinted.

Origins of computers

Microchips made possible the development of entirely new consumer products. Video cassette recorders, handheld video games, cellular phones, and digital cameras were mass produced at affordable prices during the 1990s, mostly in Asia and Latin America rather than the United States. But it was the computer that transformed American life. As computers became smaller, faster, and less expensive, they found a place in businesses of every kind. They also changed private life. By the year 2000, nearly half of all American households owned a personal computer, used for entertainment, shopping, and sending and receiving electronic mail. Centers of computer technology, such as Silicon Valley south of San Francisco, the Seattle and Austin metropolitan areas, and lower Manhattan, boomed during the 1990s.

Two architects of the computer revolution, Steve Jobs (on the left), the head of Apple Computer, and Bill Gates, founder of Microsoft, which makes the operating system used in most of the world's computers.

The Internet, first developed as a high-speed military communications network, was simplified and opened to commercial and individual use through personal computers. The Internet expanded the flow of information and communications more radically than any invention since the printing press. The fact that anyone with a computer could post his or her ideas for worldwide circulation led "netizens" ("citizens" of the Internet) to hail the advent of a new, democratic public sphere in cyberspace.

The Stock Market Boom and Bust

Economic growth and talk of a new economy sparked a frenzied boom in the stock market that was reminiscent of the 1920s. Investors, large and small, poured funds into stocks, spurred by the rise of discount and online firms that advertised aggressively and charged lower fees than traditional brokers. By 2000, a majority of American households owned stocks outright or through investment in mutual funds and pension and retirement accounts.

Investors were especially attracted to the new "dot coms"—companies that conducted business via the Internet and seemed to symbolize the promise of the new economy. The NASDAQ, a stock exchange dominated by new technology companies, rose more than 500 percent from 1998 to 1999. Many of these "high-tech" companies never turned a profit. But economic journalists and stockbrokers explained that the new economy had so revolutionized business that traditional methods of assessing a company's value no longer applied.

Inevitably, the bubble burst. On April 14, 2000, stocks suffered their largest one-day point drop in history. For the first time since the Depression, stock prices declined for three successive years (2000–2002), wiping out billions of dollars in Americans' net worth and pension funds. The value of NASDAQ stocks fell by nearly 80 percent between 2000 and 2002. Not until 2006 would the general stock index again reach the level of early 2000. The NASDAQ still remains far below its record high. By 2001, the American economy had fallen into a recession. Talk of a new economy, it appeared, had been premature.

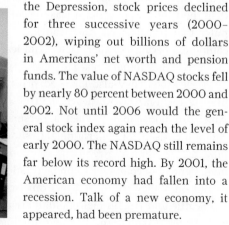

Technicians at the offices of FHP Wireless in Belmont, California, one of numerous technology companies launched with great fanfare in the late 1990s. Unlike many, FHP survived. In 2002, *Fortune* magazine listed it as one of the country's "cool companies." It is now called Tropos Networks.

The Enron Syndrome

Only after the market dropped did it become apparent that the stock boom of the 1990s had been fueled in part by fraud. During the late 1990s, accounting firms like Arthur Andersen, giant banks like JPMorgan, Chase, and Citigroup, and corporate lawyers pocketed extravagant fees for devising complex schemes to help push up companies' stock prices by hiding their true financial condition. Enron, a Houston-based energy company that epitomized the new economy—it bought and sold electricity rather than actually producing it—reported as profits billions of dollars in operating losses.

Corporate fraud

In the early twenty-first century, the bill came due for many corporate criminals. Kenneth Lay and Jeffrey Skilling, chief officers of Enron, were convicted by a Texas jury of multiple counts of fraud. Even reputable firms like JPMorgan, Chase, and Citigroup agreed to pay billions of dollars to compensate investors on whom they had pushed worthless stocks.

Fruits of Deregulation

At the height of the 1990s boom, with globalization in full swing, stocks rising, and the economy expanding, the economic model of free trade and deregulation appeared unassailable. But the retreat from government economic regulation, a policy embraced by both the Republican Congress and President Clinton, left no one to represent the public interest. The sectors of the economy most affected by the scandals—energy, telecommunications, and stock trading—had all been subjects of deregulation.

Cartoonist David Jacobson's comment on the Enron scandal.

Many stock frauds stemmed from the repeal in 1999 of the Glass-Steagall Act, a New Deal measure that had separated commercial banks, which accept deposits and make loans, from investment banks, which invest in stocks and real estate and take larger risks.

Banks took their new freedom as an invitation to engage in all sorts of misdeeds, knowing that they had become so big that if disaster struck, the federal government would have no choice but to rescue them. They poured money into risky mortgages. When the housing bubble collapsed in

"Let's say I was Enron, how would you do my taxes?"

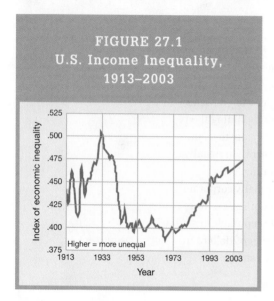
Outsourcing jobs

2007–2008, the banks suffered losses that threatened to bring down the entire financial system. The George W. Bush and Obama administrations felt they had no choice but to expend hundreds of billions of dollars of taxpayer money to save the banks from their own misconduct.

Rising Inequality

The boom that began in 1995 benefited nearly all Americans. For the first time since the early 1970s, average real wages and family incomes began to grow significantly. Economic expansion at a time of low unemployment brought rapid increases in wages for families at all income levels. Yet, despite these gains, average wages for nonsupervisory workers, adjusted for inflation, remained below the level of the 1970s.

Overall, in the last two decades of the twentieth century, the poor and the middle class became worse off while the rich became significantly richer.

The wealth of the richest Americans exploded during the 1990s. Sales of luxury goods like yachts and mansions boomed. Bill Gates, head of Microsoft and the country's richest person, owned as much wealth as the bottom 40 percent of the American population put together.

Companies continued to shift manufacturing jobs overseas. Thanks to NAFTA, which eliminated barriers to imports from Mexico, a thriving industrial zone emerged just across the southern border of the United States, where American manufacturers built plants to take advantage of cheap labor and weak environmental and safety regulations. Despite low unemployment, companies' threats to shut down and move exerted downward pressure on American wages. Business, moreover, increasingly relied on financial operations for profits rather than making things. The financial sector of the economy accounted for around 10 percent of total profits in 1950; by 2000 the figure was up to 40 percent. Companies like Ford and General Electric made more money from interest on loans to customers and other financial operations than selling their products.

The outsourcing of jobs soon moved from manufacturing to other areas, including accounting, legal services, banking, and other skilled positions where companies could employ workers overseas for a fraction of their cost in the United States. All this lowered prices for consumers but also threw millions of American workers into competition with those around the globe, producing a relentless downward pressure on American wages. In 2000, the United States no longer led the world in the hourly wages of manufacturing workers, lagging behind several countries in Europe.

In 1970, General Motors had been the country's largest corporate employer. In the early twenty-first century, it had been replaced by Wal-Mart, a giant discount retail chain that paid most of its 1.6 million workers slightly more than the minimum wage. Wal-Mart aggressively opposed efforts at collective bargaining. Not a single one of its employees belonged to a union. Thanks to NAFTA, which enabled American companies to expand their business in Mexico, by 2010 Walmart was also the largest employer in Mexico.

Overall, between 1990 and 2008, companies that did business in global markets contributed almost nothing to job growth in the United States. Those that did hire new workers tended to be those not facing global competition, such as health care, government agencies, retailers, and hotels and restaurants.

At the end of the twentieth century, the United States, more than ever before, was a suburban nation. Two-thirds of new jobs were created in the suburbs. Suburbs were no longer places from which people commuted to jobs in central cities—their office parks, industrial plants, and huge shopping malls employed many local residents. Nor were suburbs as racially segregated as in the past. In 2000, one-quarter of the suburban population was black, and Hispanics represented a majority of the population in the suburbs of Los Angeles and Miami.

Barbie's Liberty, a satirical work by the artist Hans Haacke, recasts the Barbie doll, one of America's most successful toys, in the image of the Statue of Liberty to comment on the loss of manufacturing jobs to low-wage areas overseas.

CULTURE WARS

The end of the Cold War ushered in hopes for a new era of global harmony. Instead, what one observer called a "rebellion of particularisms"—renewed emphasis on group identity and insistent demands for group recognition and power—racked the international arena during the 1990s. The declining power of nation-states arising from globalization seemed to unleash long-simmering ethnic and religious antagonisms. Partly in reaction to the global spread of a secular culture based on consumption and mass entertainment, intense religious movements attracted increasing numbers of followers—Hindu nationalism in India, orthodox Judaism in Israel, Islamic fundamentalism in much of the Muslim world, and evangelical Christianity in the United States. Like other nations, although in a far less

A "rebellion of particularisms"

Recent immigrants reciting the Pledge of Allegiance during a naturalization ceremony.

Shifts in immigration

extreme way and with little accompanying violence, the United States experienced divisions arising from the intensification of ethnic and racial identities and religious fundamentalism.

The Newest Immigrants

Because of shifts in immigration, cultural and racial diversity became increasingly visible in the United States. Until the immigration law of 1965, the vast majority of twentieth-century newcomers had hailed from Europe. Between 1965 and 2010, nearly 38 million immigrants entered the United States, substantially more than the 27 million during the peak period of immigration between 1880 and 1924. About 50 percent came from Latin America and the Caribbean, 35 percent from Asia, and smaller numbers from the Middle East and Africa. Only 10 percent arrived from Europe, mostly from the war-torn Balkans and the former Soviet Union.

The immigrant influx changed the country's religious and racial map. By 2010, more than 4 million Muslims resided in the United States, and the combined population of Buddhists and Hindus exceeded 1 million.

Unlike in the past, rather than being concentrated in one or two parts of city centers, immigrants quickly moved into outlying neighborhoods and older suburbs. By the turn of the century, more than half of all Latinos lived in suburbs. Orange County, California, which had been a stronghold of suburban conservatism between 1960 and 1990, elected a Latina Democrat to Congress in the late 1990s. Immigrants brought cultural and racial diversity to once-homogeneous communities in the American heartland.

Post-1965 immigration formed part of the worldwide uprooting of labor arising from globalization. In 2000, the global immigrant population was estimated at 100 million. Those who migrated to the United States

TABLE 27.1 Immigration to the United States, 1960–2010

DECADE	TOTAL	EUROPE	ASIA	WESTERN HEMISPHERE	OTHER AREAS
1961–1970	3,321,584	1,123,492	427,642	1,716,374	54,076
1971–1980	4,493,302	800,368	1,588,178	1,982,735	122,021
1981–1990	7,336,940	761,550	2,738,157	3,615,225	222,008
1991–2000	9,042,999	1,359,737	2,795,672	4,486,806	400,784
2001–2010	14,974,975	1,165,176	4,088,455	8,582,601	1,138,743

included poor, illiterate refugees from places of economic and political crisis—Central Americans escaping the region's civil wars and poverty, Haitians and Cambodians fleeing repressive governments. But many immigrants were well-educated professionals from countries like India and South Korea, where the availability of skilled jobs had not kept pace with the spread of higher education. In the year 2000, more than 40 percent of all immigrants to the United States had a college education.

For the first time in American history, women made up the majority of newcomers, reflecting the decline of manufacturing jobs that had previously absorbed immigrant men, as well as the spread of employment opportunities in traditionally female fields like care of children and the elderly and retail sales. Thanks to cheap global communications and jet travel, modern-day immigrants retained strong ties with their countries of origin, frequently phoning and visiting home.

The New Diversity

Latinos formed the largest single immigrant group. This term was invented in the United States and included people of quite different origins— Mexicans, Central and South Americans, and migrants from Spanish-speaking Caribbean island nations such as Cuba, the Dominican Republic, and Puerto Rico (although the last group, of course, were American citizens, not immigrants). With 95 million people, Mexico in 2000 had become the world's largest Spanish-speaking nation. Its poverty, high birthrate, and proximity to the United States made it a source of massive legal and illegal immigration. In 2000, Mexican-Americans made up a majority of the Hispanic population of the United States and nearly half the residents of Los Angeles.

Latina nannies pushing baby carriages in Beverly Hills, California, in the 1990s. For the first time in American history, female immigrants outnumbered male immigrants.

Numbering around 50 million in 2010, Latinos had become the largest minority group in the United States. Between 1990 and 2010, 30 million Hispanics were added to the American population, representing half the nation's total growth. Latinos were highly visible in entertainment, sports, and politics. Indeed, the Hispanic presence transformed American life. José was now the most common name for baby boys in

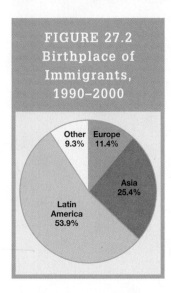

FIGURE 27.2
Birthplace of Immigrants, 1990–2000

Other 9.3%
Europe 11.4%
Asia 25.4%
Latin America 53.9%

During the 1990s, immigration from Latin America and Asia eclipsed immigration from Europe, traditionally the main source of newcomers to the United States.

Texas and the third most popular in California. Smith remained the most common American surname, but Garcia, Rodriguez, Gonzales, and other Hispanic names were all in the top fifty.

Latino communities remained far poorer than the rest of the country. The influx of legal and illegal immigrants swelled the ranks of low-wage urban workers and agricultural laborers. Latinos lagged far behind other Americans in education. In 2010, their poverty rate stood at nearly double the national figure of 15 percent. Living and working conditions among predominantly Latino farm workers in the West fell back to levels as dire as when César Chavez established the United Farm Workers union in the 1960s.

Asian-Americans also became increasingly visible in the 1990s. There had long been a small population of Asian ancestry in California and New York City, but only after 1965 did immigration from Asia assume large proportions. Asian-Americans were a highly diverse population, including well-educated Koreans, Indians, and Japanese, as well as poor refugees from Cambodia, Vietnam, and China. Growing up in tight-knit communities that placed great emphasis on education, young Asian-Americans poured into American colleges and universities. Once subjected to harsh discrimination, Asian-Americans now achieved remarkable success. White Americans hailed them as a "model minority." By 2007, the median family income of Asian-Americans, $66,000, surpassed that of whites. But more than any other group, Asian-Americans clustered at opposite ends of the income spectrum.

The United States, of course, had long been a multiracial society. But for centuries race relations had been shaped by the black-white divide

Young Korean girls rehearsing a dance at the Veterans' Administration Medical Center in Columbia, South Carolina, an illustration of the growing diversity of American society.

and the experience of slavery and segregation. The growing visibility of Latinos and Asians suggested that a two-race system no longer adequately described American life. Interracial marriage, at one time banned in forty-two states, became more common and acceptable. Among Asian-Americans at the turn of the century, half of all marriages involved a non-Asian partner. The figure for Latinos was 30 percent.

One thing seemed clear at the dawn of the twenty-first century: diversity was here to stay. In 2000, whites made up around 70 percent of the population, blacks and Hispanics around 13 percent each, and Asians 6 percent. Because the birthrate of racial minorities is higher than that of whites, the Census Bureau projected that by 2050, only 50 percent of the American population would be white, a little less than 25 percent would be Hispanic, and blacks and Asians would account for around 13 percent each.

African-Americans in the 1990s

Compared with the situation in 1900 or 1950, the most dramatic change in American life at the turn of the century was the absence of legal segregation and the presence of blacks in areas of American life from which they had once been almost entirely excluded. Thanks to the decline in overt discrimination and the effectiveness of many affirmative action programs, blacks now worked in unprecedented numbers alongside whites in corporate board rooms, offices, and factories.

One major change in black life was the growing visibility of Africans among the nation's immigrants. Between 1970 and 2000, twice as many Africans immigrated to the United States as had entered during the entire period of the Atlantic slave trade. For the first time, all the elements of the African diaspora—natives of Africa, Caribbean, Central and South Americans of African descent, Europeans with African roots—could be found in the United States alongside the descendants of American slaves.

More than half the African newcomers had college educations, the highest percentage for any immigrant group. Indeed, some African countries complained of a "brain drain" as physicians, teachers, and other highly skilled persons sought opportunities in the United States that did not exist in their own underdeveloped countries.

Most African-Americans, nonetheless, remained in a more precarious situation than whites or many recent immigrants. In 2007 their median family income of $34,000 and poverty rate of 25 percent put them behind whites, Asians, and Latinos. Half of all black children lived in poverty,

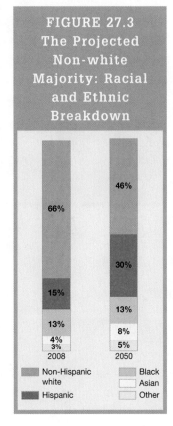

FIGURE 27.3
The Projected Non-white Majority: Racial and Ethnic Breakdown

2008: Non-Hispanic white 66%, Hispanic 15%, Black 13%, Asian 4%, Other 3%
2050: Non-Hispanic white 46%, Hispanic 30%, Black 13%, Asian 8%, Other 5%

Non-Hispanic white | Black
Hispanic | Asian | Other

African immigration

TABLE 27.2 Home Ownership Rates by Group, 1970–2000

	1970	1980	1990	2000
Whites	65.0%	67.8%	68.2%	73.8%
Blacks	41.6	44.4	43.4	47.2
Latinos	43.7	43.4	42.4	46.3
All families	62.9	64.4	64.2	67.4

two-thirds were born out of wedlock, and in every index of social well-being from health to quality of housing, blacks continued to lag. Housing segregation remained pervasive.

Despite the nation's growing racial diversity, school segregation—now resulting from housing patterns and the divide between urban and suburban school districts rather than laws requiring racial separation—was on the rise. Most city public school systems consisted overwhelmingly of minority students, large numbers of whom failed to receive an adequate education. By 2000, the nation's black and Latino students were more isolated from white pupils than in 1970. Since school funding rested on property taxes, poor communities continued to have less to spend on education than wealthy ones.

The Spread of Imprisonment

During the 1960s, the nation's prison population had declined. But in the 1970s, with urban crime rates rising, politicians of both parties sought to convey the image of being "**tough on crime**." They insisted that the judicial system should focus on locking up criminals for long periods rather than rehabilitating them. They treated drug addiction as a violation of the law

The prison population

rather than as a disease. As a result, the number of Americans in prison rose dramatically, most of them incarcerated for nonviolent drug offenses.

During the 1990s, thanks to the waning of the crack epidemic and more effective urban police tactics, crime rates dropped dramatically across the country. But this did nothing to stem the increase of the prison population. In 2008, it reached 2.3 million. Ten times the figure of 1970, this number represented one-quarter of the entire world's inmates and far exceeded the number in any other country. Several million more Americans were on parole, probation, or under some other kind of criminal supervision.

Racial minorities and incarceration

Members of racial minorities experienced most strongly the paradox of growing islands of unfreedom in a nation that prided itself on liberty. In 1950, whites accounted for 70 percent of the nation's prison population and non-whites 30 percent. By 2010, these figures had been reversed. One reason was that severe penalties faced those convicted of using or selling

A private, for-profit, maximum-security prison under construction in 1999 in California City, in the Mohave Desert, illustrates the expansion of the "prison-industrial complex."

crack, a particularly potent form of cocaine concentrated among the urban poor, whereas the use of powder cocaine, the drug of choice in suburban America, led to far lighter sentences.

The percentage of the black population in prison stood five times higher than the proportion of white Americans. More than one-quarter of all black men could expect to serve time in prison at some time during their lives. Partly because so many young men were in prison, blacks had a significantly lower rate of marriage than other Americans.

The continuing frustration of urban blacks exploded in 1992 when an all-white suburban jury found four Los Angeles police officers not guilty in the beating of black motorist Rodney King, even though an onlooker had captured their assault on videotape. The deadliest urban uprising since the New York draft riots of 1863 followed. Some fifty-two people died, and property damage approached $1 billion. Many Latino youths, who shared blacks' resentment over mistreatment by the police, joined in the violence. The uprising suggested that despite the civil rights revolution, the nation had failed to address the plight of the urban poor.

The AIDS quilt, each square of which represents a person who died of AIDS, on display in Washington, D.C. The quilt was exhibited throughout the country, heightening public awareness of the AIDS epidemic.

The Continuing Rights Revolution

Reflecting the continued power of the rights revolution, the 1990s also witnessed the emergence of new movements for public recognition. In 1990, newly organized disabled Americans won passage of the **Americans with Disabilities Act**. This far-reaching measure prohibited discrimination in hiring and promotion against persons with disabilities and required that entrances to public buildings be redesigned so as to ensure access for the disabled.

Some movements that were descended from the late 1960s achieved their greatest visibility in the 1990s. Prominent among these was the campaign for gay rights, which turned its attention to combating acquired immunodeficiency syndrome (AIDS), a fatal disease spread by sexual contact, drug use, and transfusions of contaminated blood. AIDS first emerged in the early 1980s. It quickly became epidemic among homosexual men. The gay movement mobilized to promote "safe sex" and press the federal government to devote greater resources to fighting the disease. By 2000, even though more than 400,000 Americans had died of AIDS, its spread among gays had been sharply curtailed.

Gay groups also played an increasing role in politics. In cities with large gay populations, such as New York and San Francisco, politicians vied to attract their votes. Overall, the growth of public tolerance of homosexuality was among the most striking changes in American social attitudes in the last two decades of the century.

AIDS

This "public sculpture" by the Native American artist Lewis DeSoto links his own surname with more than four centuries of American history. The wall label invokes the depredations of the sixteenth-century Spanish conquistador Hernando de Soto. The car reminds the viewer that the Chrysler Corporation chose the name DeSoto for a now-defunct automobile. On the rear of the car is an insignia based on traditional Indian basket designs, encircled by the Latin word for smallpox, which the conquistadores transmitted to the Indian population.

Native Americans

Another social movement spawned by the 1960s that continued to flourish was the American Indian Movement. The Indian population reached over 5 million (including people choosing more than one race) in the 2010 Census—a sign not only of population growth but also of a renewed sense of pride that led many Indians for the first time to identify themselves as such to census enumerators.

The legal position of Indians as American citizens who enjoy a kind of quasi-sovereignty still survives in some cases. Notable examples are the lucrative Indian casinos now operating in states that otherwise prohibit gambling. Indian casinos take in around $15 billion each year, making some tribes very rich. One such group is the Pequot tribe of Connecticut. In 1637, as the result of a brief, bloody war, Puritan New Englanders exterminated or sold into slavery most of the tribe's members. The treaty that restored peace decreed that the tribe's name should be wiped from the historical record. Today, the few hundred members of the Pequot tribe operate Foxwoods, reputedly the world's largest casino.

Although some tribes have reinvested casino profits in improved housing and health care and college scholarships for Native American students, most Indian casinos are marginal operations whose low-wage jobs as cashiers, waitresses, and the like have done little to relieve Indian poverty. Native Americans continue to occupy the lowest rung on the economic ladder.

Multiculturalism

Public opinion polls revealed a remarkable growth of tolerance. The number of respondents who accepted interracial dating without objection rose from 45 percent in 1987 to 78 percent in 2003. Those who believed gays should automatically be fired from teaching jobs fell from 50 to 35 percent over the same period. In addition, popular television shows portrayed gay characters in a sympathetic light.

Increasing tolerance

Among some Americans, the heightened visibility of immigrants, racial minorities, and inheritors of the sexual revolution inspired not celebration of pluralism but alarm over perceived cultural fragmentation.

Increased cultural diversity and changes in educational policy inspired harsh debates over whether immigrant children should be required to learn English and whether further immigration should be discouraged. These issues entered politics most dramatically in California, whose voters in 1994 approved Proposition 187, which denied illegal immigrants and their children access to welfare, education, and most health services. A federal judge soon barred implementation of the measure on the grounds that control over immigration policy rests with the federal government. By 2000, twenty-three states had passed laws establishing English as their official language.

But efforts to appeal to prejudice for political gain often backfired. In California, Republicans' anti-immigrant campaigns inspired minorities to mobilize politically and offended many white Americans. In 2000, Republican presidential candidate George W. Bush emphasized that his brand of conservatism was multicultural, not exclusionary.

Immigration occupied only one front in what came to be called the **Culture Wars**—battles over moral values that raged throughout the 1990s. The Christian Coalition, founded by evangelical minister Pat Robertson, launched crusades against gay rights, abortion, secularism in public schools, and government aid to the arts.

It sometimes appeared during the 1990s that the country was refighting old battles between traditional religion and modern secular culture. In an echo of the 1920s, a number of localities required the teaching of creationism, a religious alternative to Darwin's theory of evolution. Many

At the beginning of the twenty-first century, less than one-quarter of American households consisted of a "traditional" family—a married couple living with their children.

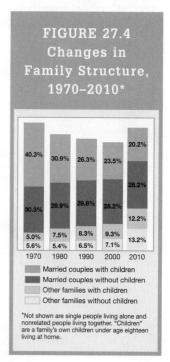

FIGURE 27.4 Changes in Family Structure, 1970–2010*

40.3%	30.9%	26.3%	23.5%	20.2%
				28.2%
30.3%	29.9%	29.8%	28.2%	12.2%
5.0%	7.5%	8.3%	9.3%	13.2%
5.6%	5.4%	6.5%	7.1%	
1970	1980	1990	2000	2010

■ Married couples with children
■ Married couples without children
□ Other families with children
□ Other families without children

*Not shown are single people living alone and nonrelated people living together. "Children" are a family's own children under age eighteen living at home.

conservatives railed against the erosion of the nuclear family, the changing racial landscape produced by immigration, and what they considered a general decline of traditional values.

"Family Values" in Retreat

Rise in divorce

The censuses of 2000 and 2010 showed "**family values**" increasingly in disarray. Half of all marriages ended in divorce (70 percent on the West Coast). In 2010, over 40 percent of births were to unmarried women, not only sexually active teenagers but growing numbers of professional women in the thirties and forties as well. For the first time, less than half of all households consisted of married couples, and only one-fifth were "traditional" families—a wife, husband, and their children. Two-thirds of married women worked outside the home. The pay gap between men and women, although narrowing, persisted. In 2010, the weekly earnings of women with full-time jobs stood at 82 percent of those of men—up from 63 percent in 1980. In only two occupational categories did women earn more than men: postal service clerks and special education teachers.

By 2000, women made up nearly half of the American workforce. Unlike in the nineteenth century, a majority of women working outside the home were married.

Although dominated by conservatives, the Supreme Court, in *Casey v. Planned Parenthood of Pennsylvania* (1992), reaffirmed a woman's right to obtain an abortion. The decision allowed states to enact mandatory waiting periods and anti-abortion counseling, but it overturned a requirement that the husband be given notification before the procedure was undertaken. "At the heart of liberty," said the Court, "is the right to . . . make the most intimate and personal choices" without outside interference.

In the early twenty-first century, women received more than 60 percent of all college degrees (as opposed to 35 percent in 1960) and over 40 percent of advanced law, medical, and business degrees (up from around 5 percent forty years earlier).

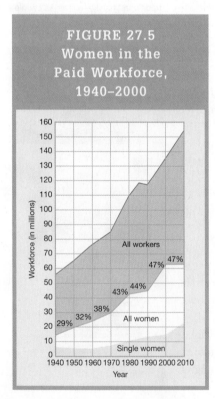

FIGURE 27.5
Women in the
Paid Workforce,
1940–2000

The Antigovernment Extreme

At the radical fringe of conservatism, the belief that the federal government posed a threat to American freedom led to the creation of private militias who armed themselves to fend off oppressive authority. Groups like Aryan Nation, Posse Comitatus, and other self-proclaimed "Christian patriots" spread a mixture of racist, anti-Semitic, and antigovernment ideas.

Rescue workers sifting the wreckage of a federal office building in Oklahoma City after it was heavily damaged by a bomb in 1995, the worst act of terrorism in the United States during the twentieth century.

Although such organizations had been growing for years, they burst into the national spotlight in 1995 when Timothy McVeigh, a member of the militant antigovernment movement, exploded a bomb at a federal office building in Oklahoma City. The blast killed 168 persons, including numerous children at a day-care center. McVeigh was captured, convicted, and executed. The bombing alerted the nation to the danger of violent antigovernment right-wing groups.

The Oklahoma City bombing

IMPEACHMENT AND THE
ELECTION OF 2000

The unusually intense partisanship of the 1990s seemed ironic, given Clinton's move toward the political center. Republicans' intense dislike of Clinton could be explained only by the fact that he seemed to symbolize everything conservatives hated about the 1960s. As a college student, the president had smoked marijuana and participated in antiwar demonstrations. He had married a feminist, made a point of leading a multicultural administration, and supported gay rights. Clinton's popularity puzzled and frustrated conservatives, reinforcing their conviction that something was deeply amiss in American life. From the very outset of

Clinton and the Right

BALANCE

BUDGET

Herbert Block's 1998 cartoon comments humorously on Clinton's talent for political survival.

his administration, Clinton's political opponents and a scandal-hungry media stood ready to pounce. Clinton himself provided the ammunition.

The Impeachment of Clinton

From the day Clinton took office, charges of misconduct bedeviled him. In 1993, an investigation began of an Arkansas real-estate deal known as Whitewater, from which he and his wife had profited. The following year, an Arkansas woman, Paula Jones, filed a civil suit charging that Clinton had sexually harassed her while he served as governor of that state. In 1998, it became known that Clinton had carried on an affair with Monica Lewinsky, a White House intern. Kenneth Starr, the special counsel who had been appointed to investigate Whitewater, shifted his focus to Lewinsky. He issued a lengthy report containing details of Clinton's sexual acts with the young woman. In December 1998, the Republican-controlled House of Representatives voted to **impeach** Clinton for perjury and obstruction of justice. He became the second president to be tried before the Senate. Early in 1999, the vote took place. Neither charge mustered a simple majority, much less than the two-thirds required to remove Clinton from office.

Polls suggested that the obsession of Kenneth Starr and members of Congress with Clinton's sexual acts appalled Americans far more than the president's irresponsible behavior. Clinton's continuing popularity throughout the impeachment controversy demonstrated how profoundly traditional attitudes toward sexual morality had changed.

The Disputed Election

Had Clinton been eligible to run for reelection in 2000, he would probably have won. But after the death of FDR, the Constitution had been amended to limit presidents to two terms in office. Democrats nominated Vice President Al Gore to succeed Clinton (pairing him with Senator Joseph Lieberman of Connecticut, the first Jewish

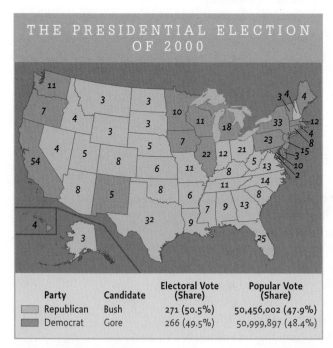

THE PRESIDENTIAL ELECTION OF 2000

Party	Candidate	Electoral Vote (Share)	Popular Vote (Share)
Republican	Bush	271 (50.5%)	50,456,002 (47.9%)
Democrat	Gore	266 (49.5%)	50,999,897 (48.4%)

vice presidential nominee). Republicans chose George W. Bush, the governor of Texas and son of Clinton's predecessor, as their candidate, with former secretary of defense Dick Cheney as his running mate.

The election proved to be one of the closest in the nation's history. The outcome remained uncertain until a month after the ballots had been cast. Gore won the popular vote by a tiny margin—540,000 votes of 100 million cast, or one-half of 1 percent. Victory in the electoral college hinged on which candidate had carried Florida. There, amid widespread confusion at the polls and claims of irregularities in counting the ballots, Bush claimed a margin of a few hundred votes. In the days after the election, Democrats demanded a hand recount of the Florida ballots for which machines could not determine a voter's intent.

It fell to Supreme Court justices to decide the outcome. On December 12, 2000, by a 5-4 vote, the Court ordered a halt to the recounting of Florida ballots, allowing the state's governor Jeb Bush (George W. Bush's brother) to certify that the Republican candidate had carried the state and had therefore won the presidency.

The decision in *Bush v. Gore* was one of the oddest in Supreme Court history. Many observers did not expect the justices to consider the matter at all, since it did not seem to raise a federal constitutional question. They justified their decision by insisting that the "equal protection" clause of the Fourteenth Amendment required that all ballots within a state be counted in accordance with a single standard, something impossible given the wide variety of machines and paper ballots used in Florida. Perhaps recognizing that this new constitutional principle threatened to throw into question results throughout the country—since many states had voting systems as complex as Florida's—the Court added that it applied only in this single case.

The most remarkable thing about the election of 2000 was not so much its controversial ending as the even division of the country it revealed. Bush and Gore each received essentially half of the popular vote. The final count in the electoral college stood at 271–266, the narrowest margin since 1876. The Senate ended up divided 50-50 between the two parties.

A Challenged Democracy

Coming at the end of the "decade of democracy," the 2000 election revealed troubling features of the American political system. The electoral college, devised by the founders to enable the country's prominent men rather than ordinary voters to choose the president, gave the White House to a candidate

> *The election of 2000*

> Bush v. Gore

A member of a Florida election board trying to determine a voter's intent during the recount of presidential ballots in November 2000. The U.S. Supreme Court eventually ordered the recount halted.

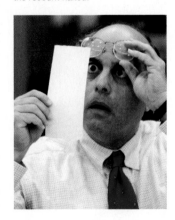

At the beginning of the twenty-first century, more than 7 million American families lived in gated communities, where the wealthy, and some members of the middle class as well, walled themselves off from the rest of society. This one is in the Brentwood section of Los Angeles.

who did not receive the most votes, an odd result in a political democracy. A country that prided itself on modern technology had a voting system in which citizens' choices could not be reliably determined. Counting both congressional and presidential races, the campaign cost more than $1.5 billion, mostly raised from wealthy individuals and corporate donors. This amount reinforced the widespread belief that money dominated the political system.

Evidence abounded of a broad disengagement from public life. As governments at all levels competed to turn their activities over to private contractors, and millions of Americans walled themselves off from their fellow citizens by taking up residence in socially homogeneous gated communities, the very idea of a shared public sphere seemed to dissolve. Nearly half the eligible voters did not bother to go to the polls. In state and local elections, turnouts typically ranged between only 20 and 30 percent. More people watched the televised Nixon-Kennedy debates of 1960 than the Bush-Gore debates of 2000, even though the population had risen by 100 million. Major issues like health care, race relations, and economic inequality went virtually unmentioned during the campaign.

A shrinking public sphere

FREEDOM AND THE NEW CENTURY

The century that ended with the 2000 election witnessed vast human progress and unimaginable human tragedy. It saw the decolonization of Asia and Africa, the emergence of women into full citizenship in most parts of the world, and amazing advances in science, medicine, and technology. Thanks to the spread of new products, available at ever-cheaper prices, it brought more improvement in the daily conditions of life to more human beings than any other century in history. But the twentieth century also witnessed the death of uncounted millions in wars and genocides and the widespread degradation of the natural environment, the underside of progress.

Exceptional America

In the United States, people lived longer and healthier lives in 2000 compared with previous generations, and they enjoyed a level of material comfort unimagined a century before. In 1900, the typical American had no indoor plumbing, no telephone or car, and had not graduated from high school. As late as 1940, one-third of American households did not have running water. In 2000, health conditions had improved so much that the average life expectancy for men had risen to seventy-four and for women to seventy-nine (from forty-six and forty-eight in 1900). On the other hand, poverty, income inequality, and infant mortality in the United States considerably exceeded that of other economically advanced countries, and fewer than 10 percent of workers in private firms belonged to unions, a figure not seen since the nineteenth century.

America from 1900 to 2000

Many of the changes affecting American life have taken place in all economically advanced societies. In other ways, however, the United States at the dawn of the twenty-first century differed sharply from other developed countries. Prevailing ideas of freedom in the United States seemed more attuned to individual advancement than to broad social welfare. The United States was a far more religious country. Sixty percent of Americans agreed with the statement, "religion plays a very important part in my life," whereas the comparable figure was 32 percent in Britain, 26 percent in Italy, and only 11 percent in France.

Individual freedom

Other forms of **American exceptionalism** had a darker side. Among advanced countries, the United States has by far the highest rate of murder using guns. In 1998, there were 11,789 murders with guns in the United States as opposed to 373 in Germany, 151 in Canada, 54 in Great Britain, and 19 in Japan. The United States continued to lag behind other countries in providing social rights to its citizens. In Europe, workers are guaranteed by law a paid vacation each year and a number of paid sick days. American employers are not required to offer either to their workers. Only four countries in the world have no national provision for paid maternity leave after a woman gives birth to a child: Liberia, Papua New Guinea, Swaziland, and the United States.

Global comparisons

It was an irony of late-twentieth-century life that Americans enjoyed more personal freedom than ever before but less of what earlier generations called "industrial freedom." The sustained recovery from the recession of the early 1990s did not entirely relieve a widespread sense of economic insecurity. Globalization—which treated workers at home and abroad as interchangeable factors of production, capable of being uprooted or dismissed without warning—seemed to render individual and even national sovereignty all but meaningless. Because economic liberty has long been associated with economic security, and rights have historically been linked to democratic participation and membership in a nation-state, these processes had ominous implications for traditional understandings of freedom. It remained to be seen whether a conception of freedom grounded in access to the consumer marketplace and the glorification of individual self-fulfillment unrestrained by government, social citizenship, or a common public culture could provide an adequate way to comprehend the world of the twenty-first century.

The approach of a new millennium inspired writers, artists, and politicians to reflect on the history and symbolism of freedom. In a work entitled *Chillin' With Liberty*, the artist Renée Cox poses herself atop the Statue of Liberty, audaciously staking her own claim to American freedom.

CHAPTER REVIEW AND ONLINE RESOURCES

REVIEW QUESTIONS

1. *Why was the year 1989 one of the most momentous in the twentieth century?*

2. *Describe the different visions of the U.S. role in the post–Cold War world as identified by President George H. W. Bush and President Clinton.*

3. *Explain Clinton's political strategy of combining social liberalism with conservative economic ideas.*

4. *Identify the factors that, in the midst of 1990s prosperity, increased the levels of inequality in the United States.*

5. *What are the similarities and differences between immigration patterns of the 1990s and earlier?*

6. *What main issues gave rise to the Culture Wars of the 1990s?*

7. *Assess the role of the Supreme Court in the presidential election of 2000.*

8. *What is globalization, and how did it affect the United States in the 1990s?*

9. *What is meant by American exceptionalism? In what ways is the United States different from the rest of the world, and how is it similar?*

KEY TERMS

globalization (p. 841)

Gulf War (p. 845)

the Perot candidacy (p. 846)

"don't ask, don't tell" (p. 846)

North American Free Trade Agreement (p. 847)

Contract with America (p. 847)

welfare reform (p. 850)

Balkan crisis (p. 851)

"ethnic cleansing" (p. 851)

Rwandan genocide (p. 852)

"tough on crime" (p. 862)

Americans with Disabilities Act (p. 863)

multiculturalism (p. 865)

Culture Wars (p. 865)

"family values" (p. 866)

Clinton impeachment (p. 868)

American exceptionalism (p. 871)

wwnorton.com /studyspace

VISIT STUDYSPACE FOR THESE RESOURCES AND MORE

- A chapter outline
- A diagnostic chapter quiz
- Interactive maps
- Map worksheets
- Multimedia documents

CHAPTER 28

A NEW CENTURY AN
NEW CRISES

★

Barack Obama and his family greet enthusiastic supporters at an outdoor celebration in Chicago on the night of his election as president on November 4, 2008.

No member of the present generation will ever forget when he or she first learned of the events of September 11, 2001. That beautiful late-summer morning began with the sun rising over the East Coast of the United States in a crystal-clear sky. But September 11 soon became one of the most tragic dates in American history.

Around 8 A.M., hijackers seized control of four jet airliners filled with passengers. They crashed two into the World Trade Center in New York City, igniting infernos that soon caused these buildings, which dominated the lower Manhattan skyline, to collapse. A third plane hit a wing of the Pentagon, the country's military headquarters, in Washington, D.C. On the fourth aircraft, passengers who had learned of these events via their cell phones overpowered the hijackers. The plane crashed in a field near Pittsburgh, killing all aboard. Counting the nineteen hijackers, the more than 200 passengers, pilots, and flight attendants, and the victims on the ground, around 3,000 people died on September 11. The victims included nearly 400 police and firefighters who had rushed to the World Trade Center in a rescue effort.

The administration of George W. Bush quickly blamed Al Qaeda, a shadowy terrorist organization headed by Osama bin Laden, for the attacks. A wealthy Islamic fundamentalist from Saudi Arabia, bin Laden had joined the fight against the Soviet occupation of Afghanistan in the 1980s. He had developed a relationship with the Central Intelligence Agency and received American funds to help build his mountain bases. But after the Gulf War of 1991, his anger increasingly turned against the United States. Bin Laden was especially outraged by the presence of American military bases in Saudi Arabia and by American support for Israel in its ongoing conflict with the Palestinians.

Terrorists associated with Al Qaeda exploded a truck bomb at the World Trade Center in 1993, killing six persons, and set off blasts in 1998 at two American embassies in Africa, killing over 200 persons. Nonetheless, the attack of September 11 came as a complete surprise. With the end of the Cold War in 1991, most Americans felt more secure, especially within their own borders, than they had for decades.

September 11 enveloped the country in a cloud of fear. In the months that followed, as the government periodically issued "alerts" concerning possible new attacks, national security remained at the forefront of Americans' consciousness, and fear of terrorism powerfully affected their daily lives.

FOCUS QUESTIONS

- *What were the major policy elements of the war on terror in the wake of September 11, 2001?*

- *How did the war in Iraq unfold in the wake of 9/11?*

- *How did the war on terror affect the economy and American liberties?*

- *What events eroded support for President Bush's policies during his second term?*

- *What kinds of change did voters hope for when they elected Barack Obama?*

In the immediate aftermath the Bush administration announced a "war on terrorism." Over the next two years, the United States embarked on wars in Afghanistan and Iraq, the second with very limited international support. It created a new Department of Homeland Security to coordinate efforts to improve security at home, and it imposed severe limits on the civil liberties of those suspected of a connection with terrorism and, more generally, on immigrants from the Middle East.

The attacks and events that followed also lent new urgency to questions that had recurred many times in American history: Should the United States act in the world as a republic or an empire? What is the proper balance between liberty and security? Who deserves the full enjoyment of American freedom? None had an easy answer.

THE WAR ON TERRORISM

The twin towers of the World Trade Center after being struck by hijacked airplanes on September 11, 2001. Shortly after this photograph was taken, the towers collapsed.

Bush before September 11

From the outset, Bush pursued a strongly conservative agenda. In 2001, he persuaded Congress to enact the largest tax cut in American history. With the economy slowing, he promoted the plan as a way of stimulating renewed growth. In keeping with the "supply-side" economic outlook embraced twenty years earlier by Ronald Reagan, most of the tax cuts were directed toward the wealthiest Americans, on the assumption that they would invest the money they saved in taxes in economically productive activities.

In foreign policy, Bush emphasized American freedom of action, unrestrained by international treaties and institutions. To great controversy, the Bush administration announced that it would not abide by the **Kyoto Protocol** of 1997, which sought to combat global warming—a slow rise in the earth's temperature that scientists warned could have disastrous effects on the world's climate. Global warming is caused when gases released by burning fossil fuels such as coal and oil remain in the upper atmosphere, trapping heat reflected from the earth. Most scientists consider global warming a serious situation. Climate change threatens to disrupt long-established patterns of agriculture, and the melting of glaciers and the polar ice caps because of rising temperatures may raise ocean levels and flood coastal cities.

Global warming

By the time Bush took office, some 180 nations, including the United States, had agreed to accept the goals set in the Kyoto Protocol for reducing the output of greenhouse gases from fossil fuels. Because the United States burns far more fossil fuel than any other nation, Bush's repudiation of the treaty, on the grounds that it would weaken the American economy, infuriated much of the world, as well as environmentalists at home.

A bystander gazes at some of the missing-persons posters with photographs of those who died on September 11.

"They Hate Freedom"

September 11 transformed the international situation, the domestic political environment, and the Bush presidency. An outpouring of popular patriotism followed the attacks, all the more impressive because it was spontaneous, not orchestrated by the government or private organizations. Throughout the country, people demonstrated their sense of resolve and their sympathy for the victims by displaying the American flag.

The Bush administration benefited from this patriotism and identification with government. The president's popularity soared. Bush seized the opportunity to give his administration a new direction and purpose. Like presidents before him, he made freedom the rallying cry for a nation at war.

On September 20, 2001, Bush addressed a joint session of Congress and a national television audience. His speech echoed the words of FDR, Truman, and Reagan: "Freedom and fear are at war. The advance of human freedom . . . now depends on us." The country's antagonists, Bush went on, "hate our freedoms, our freedom of religion, our freedom of speech, our freedom to assemble and disagree with each other." In later speeches, he repeated this theme. Why did terrorists attack the United States, the president repeatedly asked. His answer: "Because we love freedom, that's why. And they hate freedom."

The Bush Doctrine

Bush's speech announced a new foreign policy principle, which quickly became known as the **Bush Doctrine**. The United States would launch a war on terrorism. Unlike previous wars, this one had a vaguely defined enemy—terrorist groups around the world that might threaten the United States or its allies—and no predictable timetable for victory. The new war would recognize no middle ground: "Either you are with us, or you are with the terrorists." Bush demanded that Afghanistan, ruled by a group of Islamic fundamentalists called the Taliban, surrender Osama bin Laden, who had established a base in the country. When the Taliban refused, the

A war on terrorism

United States on October 7, 2001, launched air strikes against its strongholds.

By the end of the year, the Taliban had been driven from power. A new government, friendly to and dependent on the United States, took its place. It repealed Taliban laws denying women the right to attend school and banning movies, music, and other expressions of Western culture but found it difficult to establish full control over the country. By early 2007, the Taliban had reasserted their power in some parts of Afghanistan. No end was in sight to the deployment of American troops there.

Supporters of the Bush administration who turned out in Washington, D.C., late in 2001 to confront demonstrators opposed to the war in Afghanistan.

The "Axis of Evil"

In his State of the Union address of January 2002, the president accused Iraq, Iran, and North Korea of harboring terrorists and developing "weapons of mass destruction"—nuclear, chemical, and biological—that posed a potential threat to the United States. He called the three countries an **"axis of evil,"** even though no evidence connected them with the attacks of September 11 and they had never cooperated with one another.

Steve Benson's 2003 cartoon, which alters a renowned World War II photograph of soldiers raising an American flag, illustrates widespread skepticism about American motivations in the Iraq War.

AN AMERICAN EMPIRE?

The "axis of evil" speech sent shock waves around the world. In the immediate aftermath of September 11, a wave of sympathy for the United States had swept across the globe. Most of the world supported the war in Afghanistan as a legitimate response to the terrorist attacks. By late 2002, however, many persons overseas feared that the United States was claiming the right to act as a world policeman in violation of international law.

Critics, including leaders of close American allies, wondered whether dividing the world into friends and enemies of freedom ran the danger of repeating some of the mistakes of the Cold War. Charges quickly arose that the United States was bent on establishing itself as a new global empire. Indeed, September 11 and its aftermath highlighted not only the vulnerability of the United States but also its overwhelming strength. In every index of power—military, economic, cultural—the United States far outpaced the rest of the world. It was not surprising that in such circumstances many American policymakers felt that the country had a responsibility to impose order in a dangerous world, even if this meant establishing its own rules of international conduct. The need to "shoulder the burdens of empire" emerged as a common theme in discussions among foreign policy analysts and political commentators.

Confronting Iraq

These tensions became starkly evident in the Bush administration's next initiative. The Iraqi dictatorship of Saddam Hussein had survived its defeat in the Gulf War of 1991. Hussein's opponents charged that he had flouted United Nations resolutions barring his regime from developing new weapons.

Saddam Hussein

From the outset of the Bush administration, a group of conservative policymakers including Vice President Dick Cheney, Secretary of Defense Donald Rumsfeld, and Deputy Defense Secretary Paul D. Wolfowitz were determined to oust Hussein from power. They insisted that the oppressed Iraqi people would welcome an American army as liberators and quickly establish a democratic government, allowing for the early departure of American soldiers. Secretary of State Colin Powell, who believed the conquest and stabilization of Iraq would require hundreds of thousands of American soldiers and should not be undertaken without the support of America's allies, found himself marginalized in the administration.

Even though Hussein was not an Islamic fundamentalist and no known evidence linked him to the terrorist attacks of September 11, the Bush administration in 2002 announced a goal of "regime change" in Iraq. Hussein, administration spokesmen insisted, must be ousted from power because he had developed an arsenal of chemical and bacterial "weapons of mass destruction" and was seeking to acquire nuclear arms. American newspaper and television journalists repeated these claims with almost no independent investigation. Early in 2003, despite his original misgivings, Secretary of State Powell delivered a speech before the UN outlining the administration's case. He claimed that Hussein possessed a mobile chemical weapons laboratory, had hidden weapons of mass destruction in his many palaces, and was seeking to acquire uranium in Africa to build nuclear weapons. (Every one of these assertions later turned out to be false.) Shortly after Powell's address, the president announced his intention to go to war with or without the approval of the United Nations. Congress passed a resolution authorizing the president to use force if he deemed it necessary.

Regime change in Iraq

The Iraq War

Part of the massive crowd that gathered in New York City on February 15, 2003, a day of worldwide demonstrations against the impending war against Iraq.

The decision to go to war split the Western alliance and inspired a massive antiwar movement throughout the world. In February 2003, between 10 million and 15 million people across the globe demonstrated against the impending war.

Foreign policy "realists," including members of previous Republican administrations like Brent Scowcroft, the national security adviser under the first President Bush, warned that the administration's preoccupation with Iraq deflected attention from its real foe, Al Qaeda, which remained capable of launching terrorist attacks. They insisted that the United States could not unilaterally transform the Middle East into a bastion of democracy, as the administration claimed was its long-term aim.

Both traditional foes of the United States like Russia and China and traditional allies like Germany and France refused to support a "preemptive" strike against Iraq. Unable to obtain approval from the United Nations for attacking Iraq, the United States went to war anyway in March 2003, with Great Britain as its sole significant ally. President Bush called the war "Operation Iraqi Freedom." Within a month, American troops occupied Baghdad. After hiding out for several months, Hussein was captured by American forces and subsequently put on trial before an Iraqi court. Late in 2006, he was found guilty of ordering the killing of many Iraqis during his reign, and was sentenced to death and executed.

Soon after the fall of Baghdad, a triumphant President Bush appeared on the deck of an aircraft carrier beneath a banner reading "Mission Accomplished." But after the fall of Hussein, everything seemed to go wrong. Rather than parades welcoming American liberators, looting and chaos followed the fall of the Iraqi regime. An insurgency quickly developed that targeted American soldiers and Iraqis cooperating with them. Sectarian violence soon swept throughout Iraq, with militias of Shiite and Sunni Muslims fighting each other. (Under Hussein, Sunnis, a minority of Iraq's population, had dominated the government and army; now, the Shiite majority sought to exercise power and exact revenge.)

With no end in sight to the conflict, comparisons with the American experience in Vietnam became commonplace. In both wars, American policy was made by officials who had little or no knowledge of the countries to which they were sending troops and distrusted State Department experts on these regions, who tended to be skeptical about the possibility of achieving quick military and long-term political success.

President Bush standing on the deck of the aircraft carrier *Abraham Lincoln* on May 10, 2003, announcing the end of combat operations in Iraq. A banner proclaims, "Mission Accomplished." Unfortunately, the war was not in fact over.

The World and the War

The war marked a departure in American foreign policy. The United States had frequently intervened unilaterally in the affairs of Latin American countries. But outside the Western Hemisphere it had previously been reluctant to use force except as part of an international coalition. Never before had it occupied a nation in the center of the world's most volatile region.

Rarely in its history had the United States found itself so isolated from world public opinion. Initially, the war in Iraq proved to be popular in the United States. Unlike earlier wars, this one brought no calls for public sacrifice from the administration. There were no tax increases and no reintroduction of the draft to augment the hard-pressed all-volunteer army. Many Americans believed the administration's claims that Saddam Hussein had something to do with September 11 and had stockpiled weapons of mass destruction. The realization that in fact Hussein had no such weapons discredited the administration's rationale for the war. By early 2007, polls showed that a large majority of Americans considered the invasion of Iraq a mistake and the war a lost cause.

Much of the outside world now viewed the United States as a superpower unwilling to abide by the rules of international law. The fact that Iraq possessed the world's second-largest reserves of oil reinforced suspicions that American motives had less to do with freedom than self-interest.

In 2008, a church in Miami displayed nearly 4,500 small American flags in honor of each of the American soldiers who to that date had died in Afghanistan and Iraq.

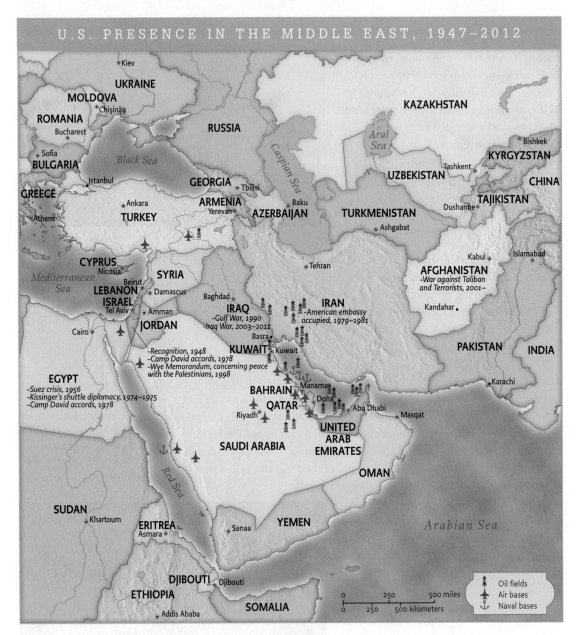

U.S. PRESENCE IN THE MIDDLE EAST, 1947–2012

*Kiev

UKRAINE

MOLDOVA
*Chișinău

ROMANIA
Bucharest

RUSSIA

KAZAKHSTAN

*Sofia

BULGARIA

*Bishkek

Black Sea

KYRGYZSTAN

Istanbul

GREECE

*Athens

GEORGIA
*Tbilisi

*Ankara

TURKEY

ARMENIA
Yerevan*

AZERBAIJAN

*Baku

Tashkent
*

UZBEKISTAN

CHINA

Aral Sea

Dushanbe*

TAJIKISTAN

TURKMENISTAN
*Ashgabat

Caspian Sea

CYPRUS
*Nicosia

Mediterranean Sea

SYRIA
Beirut *Damascus

LEBANON
ISRAEL
Tel Aviv*

JORDAN
*Amman

Cairo *

Baghdad *

IRAQ
-Gulf War, 1990
-Iraq War, 2003–2012
Basra *

*Tehran

IRAN
-American embassy
occupied, 1979–1981

Kabul *

*Islamabad

AFGHANISTAN
-War against Taliban
and Terrorists, 2001–

Kandahar .

KUWAIT *Kuwait

-Recognition, 1948
-Camp David accords, 1978
-Wye Memorandum, concerning peace
with the Palestinians, 1998

PAKISTAN

INDIA

*Karachi

EGYPT
-Suez crisis, 1956
-Kissinger's shuttle diplomacy, 1974–1975
-Camp David accords, 1978

BAHRAIN *Manama

QATAR
Riyadh* *Doha
*Abu Dhabi

*Masqat

UNITED ARAB EMIRATES

SAUDI ARABIA

OMAN

Red Sea

SUDAN
*Khartoum

ERITREA
Asmara *

*Sanaa

YEMEN

Arabian Sea

DJIBOUTI *Djibouti

ETHIOPIA

SOMALIA

*Addis Ababa

| 0 | | 250 | 500 miles |
| 0 | 250 | 500 kilometers | |

⛏ Oil fields
✈ Air bases
⚓ Naval bases

Since World War II, the United States has become more and more deeply involved in the affairs of the Middle East, whose countries are together the world's largest exporters of oil.

THE AFTERMATH OF SEPTEMBER 11 AT HOME

Security and Liberty

Like earlier wars, the war on terrorism raised anew the problem of balancing security and liberty. In the immediate aftermath of the attacks, Congress rushed to pass the **USA PATRIOT Act**, a mammoth bill (it ran to more than 300 pages) that few members of the House or Senate had actually read. It conferred unprecedented powers on law enforcement agencies charged with preventing the new, vaguely defined crime of "domestic terrorism," including the authority to wiretap, spy on citizens, open letters, read e-mail, and obtain personal records from third parties like universities and libraries without the knowledge of a suspect. At least 5,000 foreigners with Middle Eastern connections were rounded up and more than 1,200 arrested. Many with no link to terrorism were held for months, without either a formal charge or a public notice of their fate. The administration also set up a detention camp at the U.S. naval base at **Guantánamo Bay**, Cuba, for persons captured in Afghanistan or otherwise accused of terrorism. More than 700 persons, nationals of many foreign countries, were detained there.

> *"Domestic terrorism"*

In November 2001, the Bush administration issued an executive order authorizing the holding of secret military tribunals for noncitizens deemed to have assisted terrorism. In such trials, traditional constitutional protections, such as the right of the accused to choose a lawyer and see all the evidence, would not apply.

Before the Cuban Revolution of 1959, Guantánamo Bay was mostly known as an American naval base where the families of servicemen enjoyed a slice of suburban life, as in this photograph from the 1950s. Today, Guantánamo is famous as the site of the world's most notorious prison.

The Power of the President

In the new atmosphere of heightened security, numerous court orders and regulations of the 1970s, inspired by abuses of the CIA, FBI, and local police forces, were rescinded, allowing these agencies to resume surveillance of Americans without evidence that a crime had been committed. Some of these measures were authorized by Congress, but the president implemented many of them unilaterally, claiming the authority to ignore laws that restricted his power as commander-in-chief in wartime.

Two centuries earlier, in the 1790s, James Madison had predicted that no nation could preserve its freedom "in the midst of continual warfare." Madison's remarkable warning about how presidents might seize the power afforded them in war to limit freedom has been borne out at many points in American history—from Lincoln's suspension of the writ of habeas corpus to Wilson's suppression of free speech and Franklin D. Roosevelt's internment of Japanese-Americans. The administration of George W. Bush was no exception. The debate over liberty and security seemed certain to last as long as the war on terrorism itself.

The Torture Controversy

The U.S. and international law

Officials of the Bush administration also insisted in the aftermath of September 11 that the United States need not be bound by international law in pursuing the war on terrorism. They were especially eager to sidestep the Geneva Conventions and the International Convention Against Torture, which regulate the treatment of prisoners of war and prohibit torture and other forms of physical and mental coercion. In January 2002, the Justice Department produced a memorandum stating that these rules did not apply to captured members of Al Qaeda as they were "unlawful combatants," not members of regularly constituted armies. The Defense Department approved methods of interrogation that most observers considered torture.

In this atmosphere and lacking clear rules of behavior, some military personnel—in Afghanistan, at Abu Ghraib prison in Iraq, and at Guantánamo—beat prisoners who were being held for interrogation, subjected them to electric shocks and simulated drowning (so-called waterboarding), let them be attacked by dogs, and forced them to strip naked and lie atop other prisoners. Some prisoners in U.S. custody died from their maltreatment. Photographs of the abuse of prisoners eventually became public. Their publication around the world in newspapers, on television, and on the Internet undermined the reputation of the United States as a country that adheres to standards of civilized behavior and the rule of law.

Late in 2008 and early the following year, previously secret government documents were released demonstrating that torture was the result not of missteps by a few "bad apples," as the administration had

Based on an infamous photograph circulated around the world of an Iraqi prisoner abused while in American custody, this 2004 cartoon suggests how such mistreatment damaged the image of the United States.

claimed, but decisions at the highest levels of government. Secretary of Defense Donald Rumsfeld, Attorney General Alberto Gonzales, and other officials had authorized the torture of persons captured in the war on terrorism, over the objections of many in the military.

The Economy under Bush

Continuing chaos in Iraq began to undermine support for Bush's foreign policy. But the main threat to the president's reelection appeared to be the condition of the American economy. During 2001, the economy slipped into a recession—that is, it contracted rather than grew. Growth resumed at the end of the year, but, with businesses reluctant to make new investments after the overexpansion of the 1990s, it failed to generate new jobs. Talk of "economic pain" reappeared in public discussions.

Recession

Ninety percent of the jobs lost during the recession of 2001–2002 were in manufacturing. Despite the renewed spirit of patriotism, deindustrialization continued. Textile firms closed southern plants and shifted production to cheap-labor factories in China and India. Maytag, a manufacturer of washing machines, refrigerators, and other home appliances, announced plans to close its factory in Galesburg, Illinois, where wages averaged fifteen dollars per hour, to open a new one in Mexico, where workers earned less than one-seventh that amount.

The Bush administration responded to economic difficulties by supporting the Federal Reserve Board's policy of reducing interest rates and by proposing another round of tax cuts. In 2003, the president signed into law a $320 billion tax reduction, one of the largest in American history. In accordance with supply-side theory, the cuts were again geared to reducing the tax burden on wealthy individuals and corporations. Left to future generations were the questions of how to deal with a rapidly mounting federal deficit (which exceeded $400 billion, a record, in 2004) and how to pay for the obligations of the federal government and the needs of American society.

Tax cuts

THE WINDS OF CHANGE

The 2004 Election

With Bush's popularity sliding because of the war in Iraq and a widespread sense that many Americans were not benefiting from economic growth, Democrats in 2004 sensed a golden opportunity to retake the

White House. They nominated as their candidate John Kerry, a senator from Massachusetts and the first Catholic to run for president since John F. Kennedy in 1960. A decorated combat veteran in Vietnam, Kerry had joined the antiwar movement after leaving the army.

Kerry proved a surprisingly ineffective candidate. An aloof man who lacked the common touch, he failed to generate the same degree of enthusiasm among his supporters as Bush did among his. The Bush campaign consistently and successfully appealed to fear, with continuous reminders of September 11 and warnings of future attacks.

Bush won a narrow victory, with a margin of 2 percent of the popular vote and thirty-four electoral votes. The results revealed a remarkable electoral stability. Both sides had spent tens of millions of dollars in advertising and had mobilized new voters—nearly 20 million since 2000. But in the end, only three states voted differently from four years earlier—New Hampshire, which Kerry carried, and Iowa and New Mexico, which swung to Bush.

Bush's Second Term

A more conciliatory foreign policy

In his second inaugural address, in January 2005, Bush outlined a new American goal—"ending tyranny in the world." Striking a more conciliatory tone than during his first administration, he promised that the United States would not try to impose "our style of government" on others and that it would in the future seek the advice of allies. He said nothing specific about Iraq but tried to shore up falling support for the war by invoking the ideal of freedom: "The survival of liberty in our land increasingly depends on the success of liberty in other lands." In his first inaugural, in January 2001, Bush had used the words "freedom," "free," or "liberty" seven times. In his second, they appeared forty-nine times. But the ongoing chaos in Iraq, coupled with a spate of corruption scandals surrounding Republicans in Congress and the White House, eroded Bush's standing.

Domestic scandals

Hurricane Katrina

Disasters, natural and man-made

A further blow to the Bush administration's came in August 2005, when **Hurricane Katrina** slammed ashore near New Orleans. Situated below sea level between the Mississippi River and Lake Pontchartrain and protected by levees, New Orleans has always been vulnerable to flooding. For years, scientists had predicted a catastrophe if a hurricane hit the city. When the storm hit on August 29 the levees broke. Nearly the entire city, with a population of half a million, was inundated. Nearby areas of the Louisiana and Mississippi Gulf Coast were also hard hit.

The natural disaster quickly became a man-made one, with ineptitude evident from local government to the White House. The mayor of New Orleans had been slow to order an evacuation, fearing it would damage the city's tourist trade. In November 2002, the new Department of Homeland Security had been created, absorbing many existing intelligence agencies, including the Federal Emergency Management Agency (FEMA), which is responsible for disaster planning and relief within the United States. FEMA was headed by Michael Brown, who lacked experience in disaster management and had apparently been appointed because he was a college friend of his predecessor in the office. Although warned of impending disaster by the National Weather Service, FEMA had made almost no preparations. If the Bush administration had prided itself on anything, it was competence in dealing with disaster. Katrina shattered that image.

FEMA's ineptitude

For days, vast numbers of people, most of them poor African-Americans, remained abandoned amid the floodwaters. Bodies floated in the streets, and people died in city hospitals and nursing homes. By the time aid began to arrive, damage stood at $80 billion, the death toll was around 1,500, and two-thirds of the city's population had been displaced. The televised images of misery in the streets of New Orleans shocked the world and shamed the country.

Hurricane Katrina also shone a bright light on the heroic side of American life. Where government failed, individual citizens stepped into the breach. People with boats rescued countless survivors from rooftops and attics, private donations flowed in to aid the victims, and neighboring states like Texas opened their doors to thousands of refugees.

Residents of New Orleans, stranded on a rooftop days after flood waters engulfed the city, frantically attempt to attract the attention of rescue helicopters.

The Immigration Debate

In the spring of 2006, an issue as old as the American nation suddenly burst again onto the center stage of politics—immigration. Alongside legal immigrants, millions of undocumented newcomers had made their way to the United States, mostly from Mexico. Economists disagree about their impact. It seems clear that the presence of large numbers of uneducated, low-skilled workers pushes down wages at the bottom of the economic ladder, especially affecting African-Americans. On the other hand, immigrants both legal and illegal receive regular paychecks, spend money, and pay taxes. They fill jobs for which American workers seem to be unavailable because the wages are so low. It is estimated that more than one-fifth

of construction workers, domestic workers, and agricultural workers are in the United States illegally.

In 2006, with many Americans convinced that the United States had lost control of its borders and that immigration was in part responsible for the stagnation of real wages, the House of Representatives approved a bill making it a felony to be in the country illegally and a crime to offer aid to illegal immigrants. The response was utterly unexpected: a series of massive demonstrations in the spring of 2006 by immigrants—legal and illegal—and their supporters, demanding the right to remain in the country as citizens. In cities from New York to Chicago, Los Angeles, Phoenix, and Dallas, hundreds of thousands of protesters took to the streets. An Iraq War veteran who marched with his parents, who had come to the country illegally, said, "I've fought for freedom overseas. Now I'm fighting for freedom here."

Demonstrations for immigrant rights

At the same time, church groups used to sheltering and feeding the destitute denounced the proposed bill as akin to the Fugitive Slave Law of 1850 for making it a crime to help a suffering human being and vowed to resist it. On the other hand, many conservatives condemned the marches as "ominous" and their display of the flags of the marchers' homelands as "repellent." All Congress could agree on was a measure to build a 700-mile wall along part of the U.S.-Mexico border. The immigration issue was at a stalemate.

Policy stalemate

Islam, America, and the "Clash of Civilizations"

The events of September 11, 2001, placed new pressures on religious liberty. Even before the terrorist attacks, the political scientist Samuel P. Huntington had published a widely noted book, *The Clash of Civilizations*

In April 2006, millions of people demonstrated for immigrant rights. This photograph shows part of the immense crowd in Chicago, bearing the flags of many nations.

and the Remaking of the World Order (1996), which argued that with the Cold War over, a new global conflict impended between Western and Islamic "civilizations."

The idea of such a clash reduces politics and culture to a single characteristic—in this case, religion—that remains forever static, divorced from historical development. "Islam," for example, consists of well over a billion people, in very different countries ranging from South Asia to the Middle East, Africa, Europe, and the Americas. Nonetheless, in the aftermath of 9/11, Huntington's formula that pitted a freedom-loving United States against militant, authoritarian Muslims became popular as a way of making sense of the terrorist attacks.

What did this mean for the nearly 5 million Americans who practiced the Muslim religion? President Bush insisted that the war on terror was not a war against Islam. But many Americans found it difficult to separate the two, even though most American Muslims were as appalled by the terrorist attacks as their fellow countrymen. Some critics claimed that Islam was fundamentally incompatible with American life—a position reminiscent of prejudice in the nineteenth century against Catholics and Mormons. In a number of states, politicians appealed for votes by opposing the construction of new mosques and raising the nonexistent threat that courts would impose "sharia law"—the religious rules laid down in the Koran—on all Americans.

Islam and terrorism

The Constitution and Liberty

Two significant Supreme Court decisions in June 2003 revealed how the largely conservative justices had come to accept that the social revolution that began during the 1960s could not be undone.

In two cases arising from challenges to the admissions policies of the University of Michigan, the Supreme Court issued its most important rulings on affirmative action since the *Bakke* case twenty-five years earlier. A 5-4 majority upheld the right of colleges and universities to take race into account in admissions decisions. Writing for the majority, Justice Sandra Day O'Connor argued that such institutions have a legitimate interest in creating a "diverse" student body to enhance education.

Revisiting the Bakke *case*

In the second decision, in ***Lawrence v. Texas***, a 6-3 majority declared unconstitutional a Texas law making homosexual acts a crime. Written by Justice Anthony Kennedy, the majority opinion overturned the Court's 1986 ruling in *Bowers v. Hardwick*, which had upheld a similar Georgia law. Today, Kennedy insisted, the idea of liberty includes not only "freedom of thought, belief, [and] expression" but "intimate

Freedom and "intimate conduct"

conduct" as well. The decision was a triumph for the feminist and gay movements, which had long campaigned to extend the idea of freedom into the most personal realms of life. Kennedy reaffirmed the liberal view of the Constitution as a living document whose protections expand as society changes. "Times can blind us to certain truths," he wrote, "and later generations can see that laws once thought necessary and proper in fact serve only to oppress. As the Constitution endures, persons in every generation can invoke its principles in their own search for greater freedom."

The Court and the President

Nor did the Supreme Court prove receptive to President Bush's claim of authority to disregard laws and treaties and to suspend constitutional protections of individual liberties. In a series of decisions, the Court reaffirmed the rule of law both for American citizens and for foreigners held prisoner by the United States. It ruled that an American citizen who had moved to Saudi Arabia and been captured in Afghanistan had a right to a judicial hearing. The justices offered a stinging rebuke to the key presumptions of the Bush administration—that the Geneva Conventions do not apply to prisoners captured in the war on terrorism, that the president can unilaterally set up secret military tribunals in which defendants have very few if any rights, and that the Constitution does not apply at Guantánamo.

The right to a hearing

In June 2008, the Supreme Court rebuffed the Bush administration's strategy of denying detainees at Guantánamo Bay the normal protections guaranteed by the Constitution. Written by Justice Anthony Kennedy, the 5-4 decision in *Boumediene v. Bush* affirmed the detainees' right to challenge their detention in U.S. courts. "The laws and Constitution are designed," Kennedy wrote, "to survive, and remain in force, in extraordinary times." Security, he added, consists not simply in military might, but "in fidelity to freedom's first principles," including freedom from arbitrary arrest and the right of a person to go to court to challenge his or her imprisonment.

Rights of detainees

The Midterm Elections of 2006

With President Bush's popularity having plummeted because of the war in Iraq and the Hurricane Katrina disaster, Congress beset by scandal after scandal, and public-opinion polls revealing that a majority of Americans believed the country to be "on the wrong track," Democrats expected to reap major gains in the congressional elections of 2006. They were not disappointed. In a sweeping repudiation of the administration, voters

Democratic majorities in Congress

gave Democrats control of both houses of Congress for the first time since the Republican sweep of 1994. In January 2007, Democrat Nancy Pelosi of California became the first female Speaker of the House in American history.

As the end of his second term approached, Bush's popularity sank to historic lows. In January 2009, as Bush's presidency came to an end, only 22 percent of Americans approved of his performance in office—the lowest figure since such polls began in the mid-twentieth century. Indeed, it was difficult to think of many substantive achievements during Bush's eight years in office. His foreign policy alienated most of the world, leaving the United States militarily weakened and diplomatically isolated. Because of the tax cuts for the wealthy that he pushed through Congress during his first term, as well as the cost of the wars in Iraq and Afghanistan, the large budget surplus he had inherited was transformed into an immense deficit.

George W. Bush's legacy

The Housing Bubble

At one point in his administration, Bush might have pointed to the economic recovery that began in 2001 as a major success. But late in 2007, the economy entered a recession. And in 2008, the American banking system suddenly found itself on the brink of collapse, threatening to drag the national and world economies into a repeat of the Great Depression.

The economy in crisis

The roots of the crisis of 2008 lay in a combination of public and private policies that favored economic speculation, free-wheeling spending, and get-rich-quick schemes over more traditional avenues to economic growth and personal advancement. For years, the Federal Reserve Bank kept interest rates at unprecedented low levels, first to help the economy recover from the bursting of the technology bubble in 2000 and then to enable more Americans to borrow money to purchase homes. Housing prices rose rapidly. Consumer indebtedness also rose dramatically as people who owned houses took out second mortgages or simply spent to the limits on their credit cards. In mid-2008, when the median family income was around $50,000, the average American family owed an $84,000 home mortgage, $14,000 in auto and student loans, $8,500 to credit card companies, and $10,000 in home equity loans.

All this borrowing fueled increased spending. An immense influx of cheap goods from China accelerated the loss of manufacturing jobs in the United States but also enabled Americans to keep buying, even though for most, household income stagnated during the Bush years. Indeed, China helped to finance the American spending spree by buying up hundreds of billions of dollars worth of federal bonds—in effect loaning

The rise in consumer debt

An Arizona house left unfinished when the housing bubble collapsed. When prices were at their peak, housing developers rushed to build new residences; many were abandoned when prices plunged.

money to the United States so that it could purchase Chinese-made goods. Banks and other lending institutions issued more and more "subprime" mortgages—risky loans to people who lacked the income to meet their monthly payments.

Wall Street bankers developed complex new ways of repackaging and selling these mortgages to investors. Insurance companies, including the world's largest, American International Group (AIG), insured these new financial products against future default. Credit-rating agencies gave these securities their highest ratings, even though they were based on loans that clearly would never be repaid. Believing that the market must be left to regulate itself, the Federal Reserve Bank and other regulatory agencies did nothing to slow the speculative frenzy. Banks and investment firms reported billions of dollars in profits and rewarded their executives with unheard-of bonuses.

Selling debt

The Great Recession

In 2006 and 2007, overbuilding had reached the point where home prices began to fall. More and more home owners found themselves owing more money than their homes were worth. As mortgage rates reset, increasing numbers of borrowers defaulted—that is, they could no longer meet their monthly mortgage payments. Banks suddenly found themselves with billions of dollars of worthless investments on their books. In 2008, the situation became a full-fledged crisis, as banks stopped making loans, business dried up, and the stock market collapsed. Once above 14,000, the Dow Jones Industrial Average plunged to around 8,000—the worst percentage decline since 1931. Some $7 trillion in shareholder wealth was wiped

Causes of the depression

out. Lehman Brothers, a venerable investment house, recorded a $2.3 billion loss and went out of existence in history's biggest bankruptcy. Leading banks seemed to be on the verge of failure.

With the value of their homes and stock market accounts in free fall, Americans cut back on spending, leading to business failures and a rapid rise in unemployment. By the end of 2008, 2.5 million jobs had been lost—the most in any year since the end of World War II. Unemployment was concentrated in manufacturing and construction, sectors dominated by men. As a result, by mid-2009, for the first time in American history, more women than men in the United States held paying jobs.

Even worse than the economic meltdown was the meltdown of confidence as millions of Americans lost their jobs and/or their homes and saw their retirement savings and pensions, if invested in the stock market, disappear. In April 2009, the recession that began in December 2007 became the longest since the Great Depression.

FIGURE 28.1
Portrait of a Recession

These graphs offer a vivid visual illustration of the steep decline in the American economy in 2008 and the first part of 2009, and the slow recovery to 2012.

"A Conspiracy against the Public"

In *The Wealth of Nations* (1776), Adam Smith wrote: "People of the same trade seldom meet together, even for merriment and diversion, but the conversation ends in a conspiracy against the public." This certainly seemed an apt description of the behavior of leading bankers and investment houses whose greed helped bring down the American economy.

Fueled by revelations of corporate misdeeds, the reputation of stockbrokers and bankers fell to lows last seen during the Great Depression. One poll showed that of various social groups, bankers ranked third from the bottom in public esteem—just above prostitutes and convicted felons. Resentment was fueled by the fact that Wall Street had long since abandoned the idea that pay should be linked to results. By the end of 2008, the worst year for the stock market since the Depression, Wall Street firms had fired 240,000 employees. But they also paid out $20 billion in bonuses to top executives.

Resentment towards Wall Street

In 2010, Goldman Sachs, the Wall Street banking and investment firm, paid a fine of half a billion dollars to settle charges that it had knowingly marketed to clients mortgage-based securities it knew were bound to fail and then in effect bet on their failure. (This was like a real-estate

ALL THOSE IN
FAVOR OF A
LITTLE MORE
REGULATION
SAY 'AYE'.

This cartoon suggests that the near-collapse of the financial system in 2008 indicates the need for "a little more regulation."

agency selling an unsuspecting customer a house with faulty wiring and then taking out insurance so that the agency would be paid when the house burned down.) But no changes followed in management, and the fine represented only two weeks' profit for the mighty firm.

It was also revealed that Bernard Madoff, a Wall Street investor who claimed to have made enormous profits for his clients, had in fact run a Ponzi scheme in which investors who wanted to retrieve their money were paid with funds from new participants. Madoff sent fictitious monthly financial statements to his clients, but he never actually made stock purchases for them. When the scheme collapsed, Madoff's investors suffered losses amounting to around $50 billion. The crisis exposed the dark side of market fundamentalism—the ethos of deregulation that had dominated world affairs for the preceding thirty years.

Every president from Ronald Reagan onward had lectured the rest of the world on the need to adopt the American model of unregulated economic competition and berated countries like Japan and Germany for assisting failing businesses. Now, the American model lay in ruins and a new role for government in regulating economic activity seemed inevitable.

Bush and the Crisis

In the fall of 2008, with the presidential election campaign in full swing, the Bush administration seemed unable to come up with a response to the crisis. In keeping with the free market ethos, it allowed Lehman Brothers to fail. But this immediately created a domino effect, with the stock prices of other banks and investment houses collapsing, and the administration

The bailout

quickly reversed course. It persuaded a reluctant Congress to appropriate $700 billion dollars to bail out other floundering firms. Insurance companies like AIG, banks like Citigroup and Bank of America, and giant financial companies like the Federal Home Loan Mortgage Corporation (popularly known as Freddie Mac) and the Federal National Mortgage Association (Fannie Mae), which insured most mortgages in the country,

"Too big to fail"

were deemed "too big to fail"—that is, they were so interconnected with other institutions that their collapse would drive the economy into a full-fledged depression. Through the **federal bailout**, taxpayers in effect took temporary ownership of these companies, absorbing the massive losses created by the companies' previous malfeasance.

Few of the rescued firms used the public funds to assist home owners threatened with foreclosure; indeed, because they pocketed lucrative fees from those who could not pay their mortgages, they had no incentive to help them keep their homes or sell them. Giant banks and investment houses that received public money redirected some of it to enormous bonuses to top employees. But despite the bailout, the health of the banking system remained fragile. Firms still had balance sheets weighed down with "toxic assets"—billions and billions of dollars in worthless loans.

The crisis also revealed the limits of the American social "safety net" compared with those of other industrialized countries. In western Europe, workers who lose their jobs typically receive many months of unemployment insurance amounting to a significant percentage of their lost wages. In the United States, only one-third of out-of-work persons even qualify for unemployment insurance, and it runs out after a few months. The abolition of "welfare" (the national obligation to assist the neediest Americans) during the Clinton administration left the American safety net a patchwork of a few national programs such as food stamps, supplemented by locally administered aid. The poor were dependent on aid from the states, which found their budgets collapsing as revenues from property and sales taxes dried up.

The limits of the American social safety net

THE RISE OF OBAMA

With the economy in crisis and President Bush's popularity at low ebb, the time was ripe for a Democratic victory in the election of 2008. To the surprise of nearly all political pundits, the long series of winter and spring caucuses and primary elections resulted in the nomination not of **Hillary Rodham Clinton**, the initial favorite, but of Barack Obama, a relatively little-known forty-seven-year-old senator from Illinois when the campaign began. Obama was the first black candidate to win the nomination of a major party. His triumph was a tribute both to his own exceptional skills as a speaker and campaigner and to how American politics had changed.

Obama's life story exemplified the enormous changes American society had undergone since 1960. Without the civil rights movement, his election would have been inconceivable. He was the product of an interracial marriage, which ended in divorce when he was two years old, between a Kenyan immigrant and a white American woman. When Obama was born in 1961, his parents' marriage was still illegal in many states. He attended

Obama's background

A cartoon in the *Boston Globe* suggests the progress that has been made since Rosa Parks refused to give her seat on a bus to a white passenger.

Columbia College and Harvard Law School, and worked in Chicago as a community organizer before going into politics. Obama was elected to the U.S. Senate in 2004 and first gained national attention with an eloquent speech at the Democratic national convention that year.

Clinton sought the Democratic nomination by emphasizing her political experience, both as First Lady and as a senator from New York. Obama realized that in 2008 people were hungry for change, not experience. Indeed, although Clinton's nomination would also have been pathbreaking—no woman has ever been the presidential candidate of a major party—Obama succeeded in making her seem a representative of the status quo. His early opposition to the Iraq War, for which Clinton had voted in the Senate, won the support of the party's large antiwar element; his race galvanized the support of black voters; and his youth and promise of change appealed to the young.

Obama recognized how the Internet had changed politics. He established an e-mail list containing the names of millions of voters with whom he could communicate instantaneously, and his campaign used Web-based networks to raise enormous sums of money in small donations. With its widespread use of modern technology and massive mobilization of new voters, Obama's was the first political campaign of the twenty-first century.

The 2008 Campaign

John McCain

Having won the nomination, Obama faced Senator John McCain, the Republican nominee, in the general election. At age seventy-two, McCain was the oldest man ever to run for president, and he seemed even more a representative of the old politics than Clinton. He surprised virtually everyone by choosing as his running mate Sarah Palin, the little-known governor of Alaska, in part as an attempt to woo Democratic women disappointed at their party's rejection of Hillary Clinton. Palin proved extremely popular with the Republican Party's conservative base. But her performances in speeches and interviews soon made it clear that she lacked familiarity with many of the domestic and foreign issues a new administration would confront.

But the main obstacles for the McCain campaign were President Bush's low popularity and the financial crisis that reached bottom in September and October. Obama's promise of change seemed more appealing than ever. On election day, he swept to victory with 53 percent of the popular vote and a large majority in the electoral college. His election redrew the nation's political map. Obama carried not only Democratic strongholds in New England, the mid-Atlantic states, the industrial Midwest, and the West Coast, but also states that had been reliably Republican for years. He cracked the solid South, winning Virginia, North Carolina, and Florida. He did extremely well in suburbs throughout the country. He even carried Indiana, where Bush had garnered 60 percent of the vote in 2004 but which now was hard hit by unemployment. He did exceptionally well among young voters. Obama carried every age group except persons over 65. Thus, he was elected even though he received only 43 percent of the nation's white vote.

Obama's victory

The Age of Obama?

Obama's victory seemed to mark the end of a political era that began with Richard Nixon and his "southern strategy." Instead of using control of the South as the base to build a national majority, Republicans now ran the danger of becoming a regional and marginalized southern party. In the wake of the Iraq War, the economic meltdown, and the enthusiasm aroused by Obama's candidacy, Republican appeals to patriotism, low taxes, and resentment against the social changes sparked by the 1960s seemed oddly out of date. Democrats not only regained the presidency but ended up with 60 of the 100 seats in the Senate and a large majority in the House. The groups carried by Obama—young voters, Hispanics, suburbanites—represented the growing parts of the population, auguring well for future Democratic success.

The election of the nation's first African-American president represented a historic watershed. Only time would tell whether Obama's election announced the end of the Age of Reagan—the era of economic deregulation, the demonization of the federal government, and an aggressive foreign policy abroad—and the beginning of something fundamentally different.

On inauguration day, January 20, 2009, a photograph of the outgoing president, George W. Bush, is replaced by one of Barack Obama at the headquarters of the U.S. naval station at Guantánamo, Cuba.

Obama's First Inauguration

Few presidents have come into office facing as serious a set of problems as did Barack Obama. The economy was in crisis and the country involved in two wars. But

VOICES OF FREEDOM

From The National Security Strategy of the United States (September 2002)

The National Security Strategy, issued in 2002 by the Bush administration, outlined a new foreign and military policy for the United States in response to the terrorist attacks of September 11, 2001. It announced the doctrine of preemptive war—that the United States retained the right to use its military power against countries that might pose a threat in the future. The document began with a statement of the administration's definition of freedom and its commitment to spreading freedom to the entire world.

The great struggles of the twentieth century between liberty and totalitarianism ended with a decisive victory for the forces of freedom—and a single sustainable model for national success: freedom, democracy, and free enterprise. . . . These values of freedom are right and true for every person, in every society. . . .

Today, the international community has the best chance since the rise of the nation-state in the seventeenth century to build a world where great powers compete in peace instead of continually prepare for war. . . . The United States will use this moment of opportunity to extend the benefits of freedom across the globe. We will actively work to bring the hope of democracy, development, free markets, and free trade to every corner of the world. . . .

In building a balance of power that favors freedom, the United States is guided by the conviction that all nations have important responsibilities. Nations that enjoy freedom must actively fight terror. Nations that depend on international stability must help prevent the spread of weapons of mass destruction. . . . Throughout history, freedom has been threatened by war and terror; it has been challenged by the clashing wills of powerful states and the evil designs of tyrants; and it has been tested by widespread poverty and disease. Today, humanity holds in its hands the opportunity to further freedom's triumph over all these foes. The United States welcomes our opportunity to lead in this great mission.

From President Barack Obama, Speech on the Middle East (2011)

In the wake of the Arab Spring of 2011, the United States found itself caught between its traditional alliances with dictatorial regimes throughout the Middle East and the principles of democracy and human rights. In May 2011, President Obama announced what he called "a new chapter in American diplomacy" and sought to link the spring uprisings with the tradition of protest in the United States.

For six months, we have witnessed an extraordinary change taking place in the Middle East and North Africa. Square by square, town by town, country by country, the people have risen up to demand their basic human rights. . . . The story of this revolution . . . should not have come as a surprise. The nations of the Middle East and North Africa won their independence long ago, but . . . in too many countries, power has been concentrated in the hands of a few. . . . But the events of the past six months show us that strategies of repression and strategies of diversion will not work anymore. Satellite television and the Internet provide a window into the wider world. . . . Cell phones and social networks allow young people to connect and organize like never before. And so a new generation has emerged. And their voices tell us that change cannot be denied. . . .

The United States supports a set of universal rights. And these rights include free speech, the freedom of peaceful assembly, the freedom of religion, equality for men and women under the rule of law, and the right to choose your own leaders. . . . History shows that countries are more prosperous and more peaceful when women are empowered. And that's why we will continue to insist that universal rights apply to women as well as men. . . .

For the American people, the scenes of upheaval in the region may be unsettling, but the forces driving it are not unfamiliar. Our own nation was founded through a rebellion against an empire. Our people fought a painful Civil War that extended freedom and dignity to those who were enslaved. And I would not be standing here today unless past generations turned to the moral force of nonviolence as a way to perfect our union—organizing, marching, protesting peacefully together to make real those words that declared our nation: "We hold these truths to be self-evident, that all men are created equal."

QUESTIONS

1. *How does the National Security Strategy define the global mission of the United States?*

2. *How does President Obama hope to change American diplomacy in the Middle East?*

3. *What are the areas of agreement and disagreement between these two statements about the role of the United States in the world?*

Americans, including many who had not voted for him, viewed Obama's election as a cause for optimism. On January 20, 2009, a day after the Martin Luther King Jr. holiday and more than forty-five years after King's "I Have a Dream" speech, Obama was inaugurated as president. More than 1 million people traveled to Washington to view the historic event. In his inaugural address Obama offered a stark rebuke to eight years of Bush policies and, more broadly, to the premises that had shaped government policy since the election of Reagan. He promised a foreign policy based on diplomacy rather than unilateral force, pledged to protect the environment, spoke of the need to combat income inequality and lack of access to health care, and blamed a culture of "greed and irresponsibility" for helping to bring on the economic crisis. He promised to renew respect for the Constitution. Instead of freedom, he spoke of community and responsibility. His address harked back to the revolutionary-era ideal of putting the common good before individual self-interest.

Obama's first inaugural address

Obama in Office

In many ways, Obama's first policy initiatives lived up to the promise of change. In his first three months, he barred the use of torture, launched a diplomatic initiative to repair relations with the Muslim world, reversed the previous administration's executive orders limiting women's reproductive rights, and abandoned Bush's rhetoric about a God-given American mission to spread freedom throughout the world. When Supreme Court justice David Souter announced his retirement, Obama named **Sonia Sotomayor**, the first Hispanic and third woman in the Court's history, to replace him. In 2010, Obama appointed a second woman, Elena Kagan, to the Court.

Obama's first budget recalled the New Deal and Great Society. Breaking with the Reagan-era motto, "Government is the problem, not the solution," it anticipated active government support for health-care reform, clean energy, and public education, paid for in part by allowing Bush's tax cuts for the wealthy to expire in 2010. He pushed through Congress a **"stimulus" package** amounting to nearly $800 billion in new government spending—for construction projects, the extension of unemployment benefits, and aid to the states to enable them to balance their budgets. The largest single spending appropriation in American history, the bill was meant to pump

In the spring of 2009, Republicans and independents opposed to President Obama's "stimulus" plan held "tea parties" around the country, seeking to invoke the tradition of the Boston Tea Party and its opposition to taxation. In this demonstration in Austin, Texas, some participants wore hats reminiscent of the revolutionary era. One participant carries a sign urging the state to secede from the Union.

money into the economy in order to save and create jobs and to ignite a resumption of economic activity.

For most of Obama's first year in office, congressional debate revolved around a plan to restructure the nation's health care system so as to provide insurance coverage to the millions of Americans who lacked it, and to end abusive practices by insurance companies, such as their refusal to cover patients with existing illnesses. After months of increasingly bitter debate, in March 2010, Congress passed a sweeping health-care bill that required all Americans to purchase health insurance and most businesses to provide it to their employees. It also offered subsidies to persons of modest incomes so they could afford insurance and required insurance companies to accept all applicants. The legislation aroused strong partisan opposition. Claiming that it amounted to a "government takeover" of the health-care industry, every Republican in Congress voted against the bill.

Another far-reaching piece of legislation followed in July 2010. This was a law to overhaul regulation of the financial industry so as to prevent a repetition of the abuses that had led to the economic crash. It subjected to public oversight the huge market in derivatives—exotic financial instruments that were basically bets that some element of the economy would fail; limited banks' speculative investments; and established a consumer protection agency to stop predatory lending and fees by banks, credit cards, and mortgage companies. The law marked an end to several decades when banks had been given a free hand to engage in any practice, honest or dishonest, they deemed profitable.

Obama had come into office promising an era of cooperation between the parties. But with Republicans overwhelmingly opposing every one of his policy initiatives, the atmosphere in Washington became more and more partisan. One of his key proposals, a plan to combat global warming by limiting factory emissions, had to be abandoned because it could not muster the 60 votes needed to end debate in the Senate. Immigration reform remained stalled, as the recession inflamed hostility to illegal immigrants and to any proposal that offered them a path to legalized status.

Taken together, the measures of Obama's first year and a half in office saw the most dramatic domestic reform legislation since the Great Society of the 1960s. "Change"—the slogan of his election campaign—was significant but did not go far enough for many of his supporters. The health care bill failed to include a "public option," in which the government itself would offer medical insurance to those who desired it (much like Medicare for elderly Americans). Obama chose his economic advisers from Wall Street and continued the Bush administration policy of pouring taxpayer money into the banks. Little was done to help home owners facing foreclosure.

The design for the Freedom Tower at the World Trade Center One. The building illustrates the juxtaposition of optimism and fear a decade after the terrorist attacks of 2001. The soaring tower underscores Americans' capacity for recovery and regeneration. But at the insistence of the New York City police, the base consists of reinforced concrete, giving the building, at ground level, the appearance of a fortress. The two rectangles, planned as reflecting pools, mark the "footprints" of the original twin towers.

OBAMA'S FIRST TERM

The Continuing Economic Crisis

During 2008 and 2009 the economy lost 8 million jobs. Although the recession officially ended in mid-2009, economic growth was so anemic that unemployment remained stubbornly high throughout Obama's first term in office. The poverty rate in 2011 exceeded 15 percent, its highest level in twenty years. With housing prices still falling, Americans found their net worth reduced by trillions of dollars from the height of the housing bubble. Thus, they cut back on borrowing and spending, adding to the economy's malaise.

A weak recovery

The deep recession and feeble recovery exacerbated structural trends long under way. Manufacturing employment, which once offered a route into the middle class for those (mostly men) with limited education, remained several million jobs lower than in 2000. Job growth was concentrated at either the high or low ends of the pay scale. Indeed, the Bureau of Labor Statistics in 2012 projected that over the next decade, the largest areas of job growth would be in office work, sales, food preparation and service, child care, home health aides, and janitors—every one of which paid less than the median annual wage. All this exacerbated the tendency toward economic inequality.

African-Americans and the recession

Ironically, under the nation's first black president, African-Americans suffered most severely from the recession. A far higher proportion of blacks' family wealth was in their homes compared with whites, so the collapse of the housing bubble devastated their economic status. In 2011, the median family wealth of white families was $92,000, that of blacks only $4,900.

Obama and the World

The most dramatic achievement of Obama's presidency in foreign affairs was fulfilment of his campaign promise to end American involvement in the Iraq War. At the end of 2011, the last American soldiers came home. Nearly 5,000 Americans and, according to the estimates of U.S. and Iraqi analysts, hundreds of thousands of Iraqis, most of them civilians, had died during this eight-year conflict. The war had cost the United States nearly $2 trillion, an almost unimaginable sum. Whether it would produce a stable, democratic Iraq remained to be seen.

End of Iraq War

At the same time, Obama continued many of the policies of his predecessor. He dramatically increased the American troop presence in Afghanistan, while pledging to withdraw American forces by the end of

2014. By 2012, polls showed that a large majority of Americans felt the war was a mistake and wanted it to end.

Like many of his predecessors, Obama found that criticizing presidential power from outside is one thing, dismantling it another. As noted above, in his first weeks in office he banned the use of torture. But he reversed his previous promise to abolish the military tribunals Bush had established and to close the military prison at Guantánamo, Cuba. And in 2011 he signed a four-year extension of key provisions of the USA PATRIOT Act originally passed under Bush. In May 2011, to wide acclaim in the United States, Obama authorized an armed raid into Pakistan that resulted in the death of Osama bin Laden, who had been hiding there for years. More controversially, Obama claimed the right to order the assassination of American citizens in foreign countries if evidence indicated their connection with terrorism. And in 2011, when he sent the air force to participate in a NATO campaign that assisted rebels who overthrew Libyan dictator Muammar Gaddafi, Obama did not seek congressional approval of the action. All told, Obama's conduct of foreign affairs proved to be considerably more bellicose than either his supporters or opponents had expected.

Fighting terrorism

Events overseas presented new challenges and opportunities for the Obama administration. To the surprise of almost everyone, beginning in 2011 popular revolts swept the Middle East. Uprisings brought millions of people into the streets, toppling long-serving dictators in Tunisia, Egypt, and Libya. Freedom emerged as the rallying cry of those challenging autocratic governments. "I'm in Tahrir Square," one demonstrator yelled into his cell phone while standing at the epicenter of the Egyptian revolution. "In freedom, in freedom, in freedom." Once again, the tension between the ideals of freedom and democracy and American strategic interests posed a difficult challenge for policymakers. After some hesitation, the United States sided with those seeking the ouster of Egyptian dictator Hosni Moubarak, a staunch American ally. It then stood on the sidelines throughout 2011 and 2012 as Egypt lurched from popular uprising to military rule to electoral victory by the Muslim Brotherhood, a previously illegal Islamic group, to a military coup in 2013, with the final outcome of the revolution always in doubt. In Bahrain, however, an oil-rich principality

Millions of Egyptians took part in the popular uprising of 2011 that overthrew the long-serving dictator Hosni Mubarak.

in the Persian Gulf and home base of the American Fifth Fleet, the Obama administration looked the other way when the autocratic government suppressed popular discontent with force.

The Republican Revival

In nearly all midterm elections in American history the party in power has lost seats in Congress. But Democrats faced more serious difficulties than usual in the midterm elections of 2010. Grassroots Republicans were energized by hostility to Obama's sweeping legislative enactments. The **Tea Party**, named for the Boston tea party of the 1770s and inspired by its opposition to taxation by a far-away government, mobilized grassroots opposition to the administration. For a time, some activists denied that Obama was legally president at all, claiming that he had been born in Africa, not in the United States. (In fact, he was born in Hawaii.)

Grassroots support

With their opponents energized and their own supporters demoralized by the slow pace of economic recovery, Democrats suffered a severe reversal. Republicans swept to control of the House of Representatives and substantially reduced the Democratic majority in the Senate. The result produced two years of political gridlock.

But if Tea Party–inspired conservative Republicans could not get their way in Washington, their gains at the state level in 2010 unleashed a rash of new legislation. Several states moved to curtail abortion rights. In the name of combating a supposed epidemic of voting fraud, several required voters to present a state-issued photo identification card such as a driver's license, an obstacle for poor Americans who did not own such a document, and restricted the ability of groups like the League of Women Voters to register new members of the electorate. Taken together, these measures represented the strongest effort to limit the right to vote since the early twentieth century.

The immigration issue

New conservative legislatures also took aim at undocumented immigrants. Alabama, which has no land border with a foreign country and a small population of immigrants, enacted the harshest measure, making it a crime for illegal immigrants to apply for a job and for anyone to transport them, even to a church or hospital. During the contest for the Republican presidential nomination in early 2012, candidates vied with each other to demonstrate their determination to drive illegal immigrants from the country. Oddly, all this took place at a time when illegal immigration from Mexico, the largest source of undocumented workers, had ceased almost completely because of stricter controls at the border and the drying up of available jobs because of the recession. These measures associated the Republican Party with intense nativism in the minds of many Hispanic voters. In 2008, Obama had received around 70 percent of the Hispanic vote, and in 2012 he seemed likely to come close to that figure again.

The Occupy Movement

While most grassroots activism in 2011 and 2012 came from the right, these years also witnessed the emergence of a movement that targeted the depredations of Wall Street banks. On September 17, 2011, a few dozen young protesters unrolled sleeping bags in Zuccotti Park, in the heart of New York City's financial district. They vowed to remain—to **Occupy Wall Street** as they put it—as a protest against growing economic inequality, declining opportunity, and the banks' malfeasance.

Over the next few weeks, hundreds of people camped out in the park, and thousands took part in rallies organized by the Occupy movement. Similar encampments sprang up in cities across the country. Using social media and the Internet, the Occupy movement spread its message far and wide. In the spring of 2012, public authorities began to evict the protesters. But its language, especially the charge that "the one percent" (the very richest Americans) dominated political and economic life, had entered the political vocabulary.

An Occupy Wall Street demonstrator expresses her concern about rising economic inequality.

"The one percent"

The 2012 Campaign

Despite the continuing economic crisis, sociocultural issues played a major role in the campaign for the Republican presidential nomination, as candidates vied to win the support of the evangelical Christians who formed a major part of the party's base. The front-runner was Mitt Romney, the former governor of Massachusetts. Romney had made a fortune directing Bain Capital, a firm that specialized in buying up other companies and then reselling them at a profit after restructuring them, which often involved firing large numbers of employees. But the party's powerful conservative wing disliked Romney because of his moderate record (as governor he had instituted a state health care plan remarkably similar to Obama's 2010 legislation) and a distrust of his Mormon faith among many evangelical Christians.

Mitt Romney

Eventually, using his personal fortune to outspend his rivals by an enormous amount, Romney emerged as the Republican candidate, the first Mormon to win a major party's nomination—a significant moment in the history of religious toleration in the United States. He chose as his running mate Congressman Paul D. Ryan of Wisconsin, a favorite of the Tea Party and a Roman Catholic. For the first time in its history, the Republican Party's ticket did not contain a traditional Protestant.

President Obama began the 2012 campaign with numerous liabilities. The enthusiasm that greeted his election had long since faded as the worst economic slump since the Great Depression dragged on, and voters became fed up with both president and Congress because of the intensity of partisanship and legislative gridlock. The war in Afghanistan was increasingly unpopular and his signature health care law under ferocious assault by Republicans (although to the surprise of many observers, the Supreme Court in June 2012 held most of the law's provisions constitutional, with the conservative chief justice, John G. Roberts Jr., writing the opinion).

Obama's reelection

Nonetheless, after a heated campaign, Obama emerged victorious, winning 332 electoral votes to Romney's 206, and 51 percent of the popular vote to his opponent's 47 percent. At the same time, while Democrats gained a few seats in the House and Senate, the balance of power in Washington remained unchanged with a Democratic president and Senate and a Republican House. This set the stage for continued partisan infighting and political gridlock during Obama's second term.

Obama's victory stemmed from many causes, including an extremely efficient get-out-the-vote organization on election day and Romney's weaknesses as a campaigner. Romney never managed to shed the image of a millionaire who used loopholes to avoid paying taxes (his federal tax rate of 14 percent was lower than that of most working-class Americans). Many people believed he held ordinary people in contempt, particularly after he was videotaped making an off-the-cuff remark that 47 percent of the people would not vote for him because they were "victims" dependent on government payments like Medicare and Social Security. But more important, as in 2008, the result reflected the new diversity of the American population in the twenty-first century. Romney won 60 percent of the white vote, which in previous elections would have guaranteed victory. But Obama carried over 90 percent of the black vote and over 70 percent of Asians

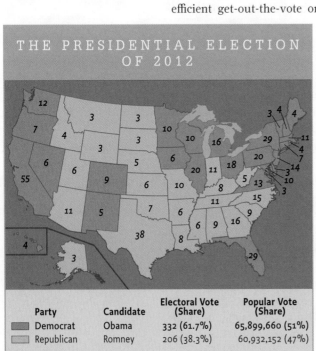

THE PRESIDENTIAL ELECTION OF 2012

Party	Candidate	Electoral Vote (Share)	Popular Vote (Share)
Democrat	Obama	332 (61.7%)	65,899,660 (51%)
Republican	Romney	206 (38.3%)	60,932,152 (47%)

and Hispanics. In 1990, only 2 percent of the electorate was Hispanic. In 2012 that figure had risen to 10 percent, which gave Obama a margin of over 5 million votes. With the minority population on the increase, these figures heralded future difficulties for the Republican Party unless it modified its strong anti-immigration rhetoric.

A rising Hispanic population

The 2012 election reflected the new diversity in other ways as well. Hawaii elected Tulsi Gabbard, the first Hindu to serve in Congress, and the first Buddhist, Mazie K. Hirono, to the Senate. And for the first time, popular referendums in Maine and Maryland registered approval of gay marriage, bringing to nine the number of states where such marriages were now lawful. But perhaps the most striking feature of the 2012 election was the unprecedented amount of money spent on the campaign. In 2010, in *Citizens United v. Federal Elections Commission*, the conservative majority on the Supreme Court had overturned federal restrictions on political con- tributions by corporations. At the same time, **political action committees** were allowed to spend as much money as they wished supporting or denigrating candidates for office so long as they did not coordinate their activities with the candidates' campaigns. Meanwhile, the Romney and Obama campaigns themselves raised and spent hundreds of millions of dol- lars from individual donors. All this resulted in an election that cost, tak- ing presidential and congressional races combined, some 6 billion dollars.

Campaign funding

LEARNING FROM HISTORY

"The owl of Minerva takes flight at dusk." Minerva was the Roman god- dess of wisdom, and this saying suggests that the meaning of events only becomes clear once they are over. It is still far too soon to assess the full impact of September 11 on American life and the long-term consequences of the changes at home and abroad it inspired.

Seeking the lessons of history: a young visitor at the Civil Rights Memorial in Montgomery, Alabama.

As of early 2013 the world seemed far more unstable than anyone could have pre- dicted when the Cold War ended nearly twenty years earlier. An end to the war on terror seemed as remote as ever. The future of Iraq and Afghanistan remained uncer- tain. No settlement of the long-standing conflict between Israel and its Arab neigh- bors seemed in sight. Iran, its power in the region enhanced by the American removal

...UNTIL JUSTICE ROLLS DOWN LIKE WATERS AND RIGHTEOUSNESS LIKE A MIGHTY STREAM
MARTIN LUTHER KING JR

of its chief rival, Saddam Hussein's regime in Iraq, appeared to be bent on acquiring nuclear weapons, which the United States vowed to prevent, raising the prospect of future conflict.

Other regions of the world also presented daunting problems for American policymakers, most notably China's rapidly growing economic power, which challenged American predominance.

No one could predict how any of these crises, or others yet unimagined, would be resolved.

An evolving concept of freedom

What *is* clear is that September 11 and its aftermath drew new attention to essential elements of the history of American freedom. As in the past, freedom is central to Americans' sense of themselves as individuals and as a nation. Americans continue to debate contemporary issues in a political landscape shaped by ideas of freedom. Indeed, freedom remains, as it has always been, an evolving concept, its definition open to disagreement, its boundaries never fixed or final. Freedom is neither self-enforcing nor self-correcting. It cannot be taken for granted, and its preservation requires eternal vigilance, especially in times of crisis.

More than half a century ago, the African-American poet Langston Hughes urged Americans both to celebrate the freedoms they enjoy and to remember that freedom has always been incomplete:

> There are words like *Freedom*
> Sweet and wonderful to say.
> On my heartstrings freedom sings
> All day everyday.
>
> There are words like *Liberty*
> That almost make me cry.
> If you had known what I know
> You would know why.

CHAPTER REVIEW AND ONLINE RESOURCES

REVIEW QUESTIONS

1. How did the foreign policy initiatives of the George W. Bush administration depart from the policies of other presidents since World War II?

2. How did the September 11 attacks transform Americans' understanding of their security? How did the response compare to that after Pearl Harbor?

3. What are the similarities of and differences between America's involvement in Afghanistan and Iraq since 2001?

4. In what ways did Americans—leaders and citizens—draw lessons from Vietnam when considering U.S. involvement in Iraq?

5. What does the war on terrorism suggest about the tension between freedom and security as priorities of the United States?

6. What were the goals and impact of the Bush administration's economic policies?

7. How did Supreme Court decisions since 2001 indicate that the rights revolution was here to stay?

8. What were the political and social effects of Hurricane Katrina? Which were lasting?

9. In what ways did the Obama administration diverge from the policies of other recent administrations? In what ways was it similar?

10. How did the 2012 election reveal changes in American political and social practices? How did it represent continuities?

KEY TERMS

Kyoto Protocol (p. 876)
Bush Doctrine (p. 877)
war in Afghanistan (p. 878)
"war on terror" (p. 878)
"axis of evil" (p. 878)
Iraq War (p. 880)
USA PATRIOT Act (p. 883)
Guantánamo Bay detention camp (p. 883)
Hurricane Katrina (p. 886)
Lawrence v. Texas (p. 889)
housing bubble (p. 891)
Great Recession (p. 892)
federal bailout (p. 894)
Hillary Rodham Clinton (p. 895)
Sonia Sotomayor (p. 900)
"stimulus" package (p. 900)
Tea Party (p. 904)
Occupy Wall Street (p. 905)
political action committees (p. 907)

wwnorton.com /studyspace

VISIT STUDYSPACE FOR THESE RESOURCES AND MORE

- A chapter outline
- A diagnostic chapter quiz
- Interactive maps
- Map worksheets
- Multimedia documents

APPENDIX

THE DECLARATION OF INDEPENDENCE (1776)

When in the course of human events, it becomes necessary for one people to dissolve the political bands which have connected them with another, and to assume among the Powers of the earth, the separate and equal station to which the Laws of Nature and of Nature's God entitle them, a decent respect to the opinions of mankind requires that they should declare the causes which impel them to the separation.

We hold these truths to be self-evident, that all men are created equal, that they are endowed by their Creator with certain unalienable rights, that among these are Life, Liberty, and the pursuit of Happiness. That to secure these rights, Governments are instituted among Men, deriving their just powers from the consent of the governed. That whenever any Form of Government becomes destructive of these ends, it is the Right of the People to alter or to abolish it, and to institute new Government, laying its foundation on such principles and organizing its powers in such form, as to them shall seem most likely to effect their Safety and Happiness. Prudence, indeed, will dictate that Governments long established should not be changed for light and transient causes; and accordingly all experience hath shown, that mankind are more disposed to suffer, while evils are sufferable, than to right themselves by abolishing the forms to which they are accustomed. But when a long train of abuses and usurpations, pursuing invariably the same Object evinces a design to reduce them under absolute Despotism, it is their right, it is their duty, to throw off such Government, and to provide new Guards for their future security.—Such has been the patient sufferance of these Colonies; and such is now the necessity which constrains them to alter their former Systems of Government. The history of the present King of Great Britain is a history of repeated injuries and usurpations, all having in direct object the establishment of an absolute Tyranny over these States. To prove this, let Facts be submitted to a candid world.

He has refused his Assent to Laws, the most wholesome and necessary for the public good.

He has forbidden his Governors to pass Laws of immediate and pressing importance, unless suspended in their operation till his Assent should be obtained; and when so suspended, he has utterly neglected to attend to them.

He has refused to pass other Laws for the accommodation of large districts of people, unless those people would relinquish the right of Representation in the Legislature, a right inestimable to them and formidable to tyrants only.

He has called together legislative bodies at places unusual, uncomfortable, and distant from the depository of their public Records, for the sole purpose of fatiguing them into compliance with his measures.

He has dissolved Representative Houses repeatedly, for opposing with manly firmness his invasions on the rights of the people.

He has refused for a long time, after such dissolutions, to cause others to be elected; whereby the Legislative powers, incapable of Annihilation, have returned to the People at large for their exercise; the State remaining in the mean time exposed to all dangers of invasion from without, and convulsions within.

He has endeavoured to prevent the population of these States; for that purpose obstructing the Laws of Naturalization of Foreigners; refusing to pass others to encourage their migrations hither, and raising the conditions of new Appropriations of Lands.

He has obstructed the Administration of Justice, by refusing his Assent to Laws for establishing Judiciary powers.

He has made Judges dependent on his Will alone, for the tenure of their offices, and the amount and payment of their salaries.

He has erected a multitude of New Offices, and sent hither swarms of Officers to harass our People, and eat out their substance.

He has kept among us, in times of peace, Standing Armies without the Consent of our legislatures.

He has affected to render the Military independent of and superior to the Civil Power.

He has combined with others to subject us to a jurisdiction foreign to our constitution, and unacknowledged by our laws; giving his Assent to their Acts of pretended Legislation:

For quartering large bodies of armed troops among us:

For protecting them, by a mock Trial, from Punishment for any Murders which they should commit on the Inhabitants of these States:

For cutting off our Trade with all parts of the world:

For imposing taxes on us without our Consent:

For depriving us of many cases, of the benefits of Trial by jury:

For transporting us beyond Seas to be tried for pretended offences:

For abolishing the free System of English Laws in a neighbouring Province, establishing therein an Arbitrary government, and enlarging its Boundaries so as to render it at once an example and fit instrument for introducing the same absolute rule into these Colonies:

For taking away our Charters, abolishing our most valuable Laws, and altering fundamentally the Forms of our Governments:

For suspending our own Legislatures, and declaring themselves invested with Power to legislate for us in all cases whatsoever.

He has abdicated Government here, by declaring us out of his Protection and waging War against us.

He has plundered our seas, ravaged our Coasts, burnt our towns, and destroyed the lives of our people.

He is at this time transporting large armies of foreign mercenaries to compleat the works of death, desolation, and tyranny, already begun with circumstances of Cruelty & perfidy scarcely paralleled in the most barbarous ages, and totally unworthy the Head of a civilized nation.

He has constrained our fellow Citizens taken Captive on the high Seas to bear Arms against their Country, to become the executioners of their friends and Brethren, or to fall themselves by their Hands.

He has excited domestic insurrections amongst us, and has endeavoured to bring on the inhabitants of our frontiers, the merciless Indian Savages, whose known rule of warfare, is an undistinguished destruction of all ages, sexes, and conditions.

In every stage of these Oppressions We have Petitioned for Redress in the most humble terms: Our repeated Petitions have been answered only by repeated injury. A Prince, whose character is thus marked by every act which may define a Tyrant, is unfit to be the ruler of a free people.

Nor have We been wanting in attention to our British brethren. We have warned them from time to time of attempts by their legislature to extend an unwarrantable jurisdiction over us. We have reminded them of the circumstances of our emigration and settlement here. We have appealed to their native justice and magnanimity, and we have conjured them by the ties of our common kindred to disavow these usurpations, which, would inevitably interrupt our connections and correspondence. They too must have been deaf to the voice of justice and of consanguinity. We must, therefore, acquiesce in the necessity, which denounces our Separation, and hold them, as we hold the rest of mankind, Enemies in War, in Peace Friends.

WE, THEREFORE, the Representatives of the UNITED STATES OF AMERICA, in General Congress, Assembled, appealing to the Supreme Judge of the world for the rectitude of our intentions, do, in the Name, and by Authority of the good People of these Colonies, solemnly publish and declare, That these United Colonies are, and of Right ought to be FREE AND INDEPENDENT STATES; that they are Absolved from all Allegiance to the British Crown, and that all political connection between them and the State of Great Britain, is and ought to be totally dissolved; and that as Free and Independent States, they have full Power to levy War, conclude Peace, contract Alliances, establish Commerce, and to do all other Acts and Things which Independent States may of right do. And for the support of this Declaration, with a firm reliance on the Protection of Divine Providence, we mutually pledge to each other our Lives, our Fortunes, and our sacred Honor.

The foregoing Declaration was, by order of Congress, engrossed, and signed by the following members:

John Hancock

NEW HAMPSHIRE	NEW YORK	DELAWARE	NORTH CAROLINA
Josiah Bartlett	William Floyd	Caesar Rodney	William Hooper
William Whipple	Philip Livingston	George Read	Joseph Hewes
Matthew Thornton	Francis Lewis	Thomas M'Kean	John Penn
	Lewis Morris		
MASSACHUSETTS BAY		MARYLAND	SOUTH CAROLINA
Samuel Adams	NEW JERSEY	Samuel Chase	Edward Rutledge
John Adams	Richard Stockton	William Paca	Thomas Heyward, Jr.
Robert Treat Paine	John Witherspoon	Thomas Stone	Thomas Lynch, Jr.
Elbridge Gerry	Francis Hopkinson	Charles Carroll, of	Arthur Middleton
	John Hart	Carrollton	
RHODE ISLAND	Abraham Clark		GEORGIA
Stephen Hopkins		VIRGINIA	Button Gwinnett
William Ellery	PENNSYLVANIA	George Wythe	Lyman Hall
	Robert Morris	Richard Henry Lee	George Walton
CONNECTICUT	Benjamin Rush	Thomas Jefferson	
Roger Sherman	Benjamin Franklin	Benjamin Harrison	
Samuel Huntington	John Morton	Thomas Nelson, Jr.	
William Williams	George Clymer	Francis Lightfoot Lee	
Oliver Wolcott	James Smith	Carter Braxton	
	George Taylor		
	James Wilson		
	George Ross		

Resolved, That copies of the Declaration be sent to the several assemblies, conventions, and committees, or councils of safety, and to the several commanding officers of the continental troops; that it be proclaimed in each of the United States, at the head of the army.

THE CONSTITUTION OF THE UNITED STATES (1787)

We the People of the United States, in order to form a more perfect Union, establish Justice, insure domestic Tranquility, provide for the common defence, promote the general Welfare, and secure the Blessings of Liberty to ourselves and our Posterity, do ordain and establish this Constitution for the United States of America.

ARTICLE. I.

Section. 1. All legislative Powers herein granted shall be vested in a Congress of the United States, which shall consist of a Senate and House of Representatives.

Section. 2. The House of Representatives shall be composed of Members chosen every second Year by the People of the several States, and the Electors in each State shall have the Qualifications requisite for Electors of the most numerous Branch of the State Legislature.

No Person shall be a Representative who shall not have attained to the Age of twenty five Years, and been seven Years a Citizen of the United States, and who shall not, when elected, be an Inhabitant of that State in which he shall be chosen.

Representatives and direct Taxes shall be apportioned among the several States which may be included within this Union, according to their respective Numbers, which shall be determined by adding to the whole Number of free Persons, including those bound to Service for a Term of Years, and excluding Indians not taxed, three fifths of all other Persons. The actual Enumeration shall be made within three Years after the first Meeting of the Congress of the United States, and within every subsequent Term of ten Years, in such Manner as they shall by Law direct. The Number of Representatives shall not exceed one for every thirty Thousand, but each State shall have at Least one Representative; and until such enumeration shall be made, the State of New Hampshire shall be entitled to chuse three, Massachusetts eight, Rhode-Island and Providence Plantations one, Connecticut five, New York six, New Jersey four, Pennsylvania eight, Delaware one, Maryland six, Virginia ten, North Carolina five, South Carolina five, and Georgia three.

When vacancies happen in the Representation from any state, the Executive Authority thereof shall issue Writs of Election to fill such Vacancies.

The House of Representatives shall chuse their Speaker and other Officers; and shall have the sole Power of Impeachment.

Section. 3. The Senate of the United States shall be composed of two Senators from each State, chosen by the legislature thereof, for six Years; and each Senator shall have one Vote.

Immediately after they shall be assembled in Consequence of the first Election, they shall be divided as equally as may be into three Classes. The Seats of the Senators of the first Class shall be vacated at the Expiration of the second Year, of the second Class at the Expiration of the fourth Year, and of the third Class at the Expiration of the sixth Year, so that one third may be chosen every second Year; and if Vacancies happen by Resignation, or otherwise, during the Recess of the Legislature of any State, the Executive thereof may make temporary Appointments until the next Meeting of the Legislature, which shall then fill such Vacancies.

No Person shall be a Senator who shall not have attained to the Age of thirty Years, and been nine Years a Citizen of the United States, and who shall not, when elected, be an Inhabitant of that State for which he shall be chosen.

The Vice President of the United States shall be President of the Senate, but shall have no Vote, unless they be equally divided.

The Senate shall chuse their other Officers, and also a President pro tempore, in the Absence of the

Vice President, or when he shall exercise the Office of President of the United States.

The Senate shall have the sole Power to try all Impeachments. When sitting for that Purpose, they shall be on Oath or Affirmation. When the President of the United States is tried, the Chief Justice shall preside: And no Person shall be convicted without the Concurrence of two thirds of the Members present.

Judgment in Cases of Impeachment shall not extend further than to removal from Office, and disqualification to hold and enjoy any Office of honor, Trust or Profit under the United States: but the Party convicted shall nevertheless be liable and subject to Indictment, Trial, Judgment and Punishment, according to Law.

Section. 4. The Times, Places and Manner of holding Elections for Senators and Representatives, shall be prescribed in each State by the Legislature thereof; but the Congress may at any time by Law make or alter such Regulations, except as to the Places of chusing Senators.

The Congress shall assemble at least once in every Year, and such Meeting shall be on the first Monday in December, unless they shall by Law appoint a different Day.

Section. 5. Each House shall be the Judge of the Elections, Returns and Qualifications of its own Members, and a Majority of each shall constitute a Quorum to do Business; but a smaller Number may adjourn from day to day, and may be authorized to compel the Attendance of absent Members, in such Manner, and under such Penalties as each House may provide.

Each House may determine the Rules of its Proceedings, punish its Members for disorderly Behaviour, and, with the Concurrence of two thirds, expel a Member.

Each House shall keep a Journal of its Proceedings, and from time to time publish the same, excepting such Parts as may in their Judgment require Secrecy; and the Yeas and Nays of the Members of either House on any question shall, at the Desire of one fifth of those Present, be entered on the Journal.

Neither House, during the Session of Congress, shall, without the Consent of the other, adjourn for more than three days, not to any other Place than that in which the two Houses shall be sitting.

Section. 6. The Senators and Representatives shall receive a Compensation for their Services, to be ascertained by Law, and paid out of the Treasury of the United States. They shall in all Cases, except Treason, Felony and Breach of the Peace, be privileged from Arrest during their Attendance at the Session of their respective Houses, and in going to and returning from the same; and for any Speech or Debate in either House, they shall not be questioned in any other Place.

No Senator or Representative shall, during the Time for which he was elected, be appointed to any civil Office under the Authority of the United States, which shall have been created, or the Emoluments whereof shall have been encreased during such time; and no Person holding any Office under the United States, shall be a Member of either House during his Continuance in Office.

Section. 7. All Bills for raising Revenue shall originate in the House of Representatives; but the Senate may propose or concur with Amendments as on other Bills.

Every Bill which shall have passed the House of Representatives and the Senate shall, before it become a Law, be presented to the President of the United States; If he approve he shall sign it, but if not he shall return it, with his Objections to that House in which it shall have originated, who shall enter the Objections at large on their Journal, and proceed to reconsider it. If after such Reconsideration two thirds of that House shall agree to pass the Bill, it shall be sent, together with the Objections, to the other House, by which it shall likewise be reconsidered, and if approved by two thirds of that House, it shall become a Law. But in all such Cases the Votes of both Houses shall be determined by Yeas and Nays, and the Names of the Persons voting for and against the Bill shall be entered on the Journal of each House respectively. If any Bill shall not be returned by the President within ten Days (Sundays excepted) after it shall have been presented to him, the Same shall be a Law, in like Manner as if he had signed it, unless the Congress by their Adjournment prevent its Return, in which Case it shall not be a Law.

Every Order, Resolution, or Vote to which the Concurrence of the Senate and House of Representatives may be necessary (except on a question of Adjournment) shall be presented to the President of the United States; and before the Same shall take Effect, shall be approved by him, or being disapproved by him, shall be repassed by two thirds of the Senate and House of Representatives, according to the Rules and Limitations prescribed in the Case of a Bill.

Section. 8. The Congress shall have Power To lay and collect Taxes, Duties, Imposts and Excises, to pay the Debts and provide for the common Defence and general Welfare of the United States; but all Duties, Imposts and Excises shall be uniform throughout the United States;

To borrow Money on the credit of the United States;

To regulate Commerce with foreign Nations, and among the several States, and with the Indian Tribes;

To establish an uniform Rule of Naturalization, and uniform Laws on the subject of Bankruptcies throughout the United States;

To coin Money, regulate the Value thereof, and of foreign Coin, and fix the Standard of Weights and Measures;

To provide for the Punishment of counterfeiting the Securities and current Coin of the United States;

To establish Post Offices and Post Roads;

To promote the Progress of Science and useful Arts, by securing for limited Times to Authors and Inventors the exclusive Right to their respective Writings and Discoveries;

To constitute Tribunals inferior to the supreme Court;

To define and punish Piracies and Felonies committed on the high Seas, and Offences against the Law of Nations;

To declare War, grant Letters of Marque and Reprisal, and make Rules concerning Captures on Land and Water;

To raise and support Armies, but no Appropriation of Money to that Use shall be for a longer Term than two Years;

To provide and maintain a Navy;

To make Rules for the Government and Regulation of the land and naval Forces;

To provide for calling forth the Militia to execute the Laws of the Union, suppress Insurrections and repel Invasions;

To provide for organizing, arming, and disciplining, the Militia, and for governing such Part of them as may be employed in the Service of the United States, reserving to the States respectively, the Appointment of the Officers, and the Authority of training the Militia according to the discipline prescribed by Congress;

To exercise exclusive Legislation in all Cases whatsoever, over such District (not exceeding ten Miles square) as may, by Cession of Particular States, and the Acceptance of Congress, become the Seat of the Government of the United States, and to exercise like Authority over all Places purchased by the Consent of the Legislature of the State in which the Same shall be, for the Erection of Forts, Magazines, Arsenals, dock-Yards, and other needful Buildings;—And

To make all Laws which shall be necessary and proper for carrying into Execution the foregoing Powers, and all other Powers vested by this Constitution in the Government of the United States, or in any Department or Officer thereof.

Section. 9. The Migration or Importation of such Persons as any of the States now existing shall think proper to admit, shall not be prohibited by the Congress prior to the Year one thousand eight hundred and eight, but a Tax or duty may be imposed on such Importation, not exceeding ten dollars for each Person.

The Privilege of the Writ of Habeas Corpus shall not be suspended, unless when in Cases of Rebellion or Invasion the public Safety may require it.

No Bill of Attainder or ex post facto Law shall be passed.

No Capitation, or other direct, Tax shall be laid, unless in Proportion to the Census or Enumeration herein before directed to be taken.

No Tax or Duty shall be laid on Articles exported from any State.

No Preference shall be given by any Regulation of Commerce or Revenue to the Ports of one State over those of another: nor shall Vessels bound to, or from, one State, be obliged to enter, clear, or pay Duties in another.

No Money shall be drawn from the Treasury, but in Consequence of Appropriations made by Law; and a regular Statement and Account of the Receipts and Expenditures of all public Money shall be published from time to time.

No Title of Nobility shall be granted by the United States: And no Person holding any Office of Profit or Trust under them, shall, without the Consent of the Congress, accept of any present, Emolument, Office, or Title, of any kind whatever, from any King, Prince, or foreign State.

Section. 10. No State shall enter into any Treaty, Alliance, or Confederation; grant Letters of Marque and Reprisal; coin Money; emit Bills of Credit; make any Thing but gold and silver Coin a Tender in Payment of Debts; pass any Bill of Attainder, ex post facto Law, or Law impairing the Obligation of Contracts, or grant any Title of Nobility.

No State shall, without the Consent of the Congress, lay any Imposts or Duties on Imports or Exports, except what may be absolutely necessary for executing its inspection Laws: and the net Produce of all Duties and Imposts, laid by any State on Imports or Exports, shall be for the Use of the Treasury of the United States; and all such Laws shall be subject to the Revision and Controul of the Congress.

No State shall, without the Consent of Congress, lay any Duty of Tonnage, keep Troops, or Ships of War in time of Peace, enter into any Agreement or Compact with another State, or with a foreign Power, or engage in War, unless actually invaded, or in such imminent Danger as will not admit of delay.

ARTICLE. II.

Section. 1. The executive Power shall be vested in a President of the United States of America. He shall hold his Office during the term of four Years, and,

together with the Vice President, chosen for the same Term, be elected, as follows:

Each State shall appoint, in such Manner as the Legislature thereof may direct, a Number of Electors, equal to the whole Number of Senators and Representatives to which the State may be entitled in the Congress: but no Senator or Representative, or Person holding an Office of Trust or Profit under the United States, shall be appointed an Elector.

The Electors shall meet in their respective States, and vote by Ballot for two Persons, of whom one at least shall not be an Inhabitant of the same State with themselves. And they shall make a List of all the Persons voted for, and of the Number of Votes for each; which List they shall sign and certify, and transmit sealed to the Seat of the Government of the United States, directed to the President of the Senate. The President of the Senate shall, in the Presence of the Senate and House of Representatives, open all the Certificates, and the Votes shall then be counted. The Person having the greatest Number of Votes shall be the President, if such Number be a Majority of the whole Number of Electors appointed; and if there be more than one who have such Majority, and have an equal Number of Votes, then the House of Representatives shall immediately chuse by Ballot one of them for President; and if no Person have a Majority, then from the five highest on the List the said House shall in like Manner chuse the President. But in chusing the President, the Votes shall be taken by States, the Representation from each State having one Vote; A quorum for this Purpose shall consist of a Member or Members from two thirds of the States, and a Majority of all the States shall be necessary to a Choice. In every Case, after the Choice of the President, the Person having the greatest Number of Votes of the Electors shall be the Vice President. But if there should remain two or more who have equal Votes, the Senate shall chuse from them by Ballot the Vice President.

The Congress may determine the Time of chusing the Electors, and the Day on which they shall give their Votes; which Day shall be the same throughout the United States.

No Person except a natural born Citizen, or a Citizen of the United States, at the time of the Adoption of this Constitution, shall be eligible to the Office of

President; neither shall any Person be eligible to that Office who shall not have attained to the Age of thirty five Years, and been fourteen Years a Resident within the United States.

In Case of the Removal of the President from Office, or of his Death, Resignation, or Inability to discharge the Powers and Duties of the said Office, the Same shall devolve on the Vice President, and the Congress may by Law provide for the Case of Removal, Death, Resignation or Inability, both of the President and Vice President, declaring what Officer shall then act as President, and such Officer shall act accordingly, until the Disability be removed, or a President shall be elected.

The President shall, at stated Times, receive for his Services, a Compensation, which shall neither be encreased or diminished during the Period for which he shall have been elected, and he shall not receive within that Period any other Emolument from the United States, or any of them.

Before he enters on the Execution of his Office, he shall take the following Oath or Affirmation:—"I do solemnly swear (or affirm) that I will faithfully execute the Office of President of the United States, and will to the best of my Ability, preserve, protect and defend the Constitution of the United States."

Section. 2. The President shall be Commander in Chief of the Army and Navy of the United States, and of the Militia of the several States, when called into the actual Service of the United States; he may require the Opinion, in writing, of the principal Officer in each of the executive Departments, upon any Subject relating to the Duties of their respective Offices, and he shall have Power to grant Reprieves and Pardons for Offences against the United States, except in Cases of Impeachment.

He shall have Power, by and with the Advice and Consent of the Senate, to make Treaties, provided two thirds of the Senators present concur; and he shall nominate, and by and with the Advice and Consent of the Senate, shall appoint Ambassadors, other public Ministers and Consuls, Judges of the supreme Court, and all other Officers of the United States, whose Appointments are not herein otherwise

provided for, and which shall be established by Law; but the Congress may by Law vest the Appointment of such inferior Officers, as they think proper, in the President alone, in the Courts of Law, or in the Heads of Departments.

The President shall have Power to fill up all Vacancies that may happen during the Recess of the Senate, by granting Commissions which shall expire at the End of their next Session.

Section. 3. He shall from time to time give to the Congress Information of the State of the Union, and recommend to their Consideration such Measures as he shall judge necessary and expedient; he may, on extraordinary Occasions, convene both Houses, or either of them, and in Case of Disagreement between them, with Respect to the Time of Adjournment, he may adjourn them to such Time as he shall think proper; he shall receive Ambassadors and other public Ministers; he shall take Care that the Laws be faithfully executed, and shall Commission all the Officers of the United States.

Section. 4. The President, Vice President and all civil Officers of the United States, shall be removed from Office on Impeachment for, and Conviction of, Treason, Bribery, or other high Crimes and Misdemeanors.

ARTICLE. III.

Section. 1. The judicial Power of the United States, shall be vested in one supreme Court, and in such inferior Courts as the Congress may from time to time ordain and establish. The Judges, both of the supreme and inferior Courts, shall hold their Offices during good Behavior, and shall, at stated Times, receive for their Services, a Compensation, which shall not be diminished during their Continuance in Office.

Section. 2. The judicial Power shall extend to all Cases, in Law and Equity, arising under this Constitution, the Laws of the United States, and Treaties made, or which shall be made, under their Authority;—to all Cases affecting Ambassadors, other public Ministers and Consuls;—to all Cases of admiralty and maritime Jurisdiction;—the Controversies to which the United States shall be a Party;—to Controversies between two or more States;—between a State and Citizens of another State;—between Citizens of different States;—between Citizens of the same State claiming Lands under Grants of different States, and between a State, or the Citizens thereof, and foreign States, Citizens or Subjects.

In all cases affecting Ambassadors, other public Ministers and Consuls, and those in which a State shall be Party, the supreme Court shall have original Jurisdiction. In all the other Cases before mentioned, the supreme Court shall have appellate Jurisdiction, both as to Law and Fact, with such Exceptions, and under such Regulations as the Congress shall make.

The Trial of all Crimes, except in Cases of Impeachment, shall be by Jury; and such Trial shall be held in the State where the said Crimes shall have been committed; but when not committed within any State, the Trial shall be at such Place or Places as the Congress may by Law have directed.

Section. 3. Treason against the United States, shall consist only in levying War against them, or in adhering to their Enemies, giving them Aid and Comfort. No Person shall be convicted of Treason unless on the Testimony of two Witnesses to the same overt Act, or on Confession in open Court.

The Congress shall have Power to declare the Punishment of Treason, but no Attainder of Treason shall work Corruption of Blood, or Forfeiture except during the Life of the Person attainted.

ARTICLE. IV.

Section. 1. Full Faith and Credit shall be given in each State to the public Acts, Records, and judicial Proceedings of every other State. And the Congress may by general Laws prescribe the Manner in which such Acts, Records and Proceedings shall be proved, and the Effect thereof.

Section. 2. The Citizens of each State shall be entitled to all Privileges and Immunities of Citizens in the several States.

A Person charged in any State with Treason, Felony, or other Crime, who shall flee from Justice, and be found in another State, shall on Demand of the executive Authority of the State from which he fled, be delivered up, to be removed to the State having Jurisdiction of the Crime.

No Person held to Service or Labour in one State, under the Laws thereof, escaping into another, shall, in Consequence of any Law or Regulation therein, be discharged from such Service or Labour, but shall be delivered up on Claim of the Party to whom such Service or Labour may be due.

Section. 3. New States may be admitted by the Congress into this Union; but no new State shall be formed or erected within the Jurisdiction of any other State; nor any State be formed by the Junction of two or more States, or Parts of States, without the consent of the Legislatures of the States concerned as well as of the Congress.

The Congress shall have Power to dispose of and make all needful Rules and Regulations respecting the Territory or other Property belonging to the United States; and nothing in this Constitution shall be so construed as to Prejudice any Claims of the United States, or of any particular States.

Section. 4. The United States shall guarantee to every State in this Union a Republican Form of Government, and shall protect each of them against Invasion; and on Application of the Legislature, or of the Executive (when the Legislature cannot be convened) against domestic Violence.

ARTICLE. V.

The Congress, whenever two thirds of both Houses shall deem it necessary, shall propose Amendments to this Constitution, or, on the Application of the Legislatures of two thirds of the several States, shall call a Convention for proposing Amendments, which, in either Case, shall be valid to all Intents and Purposes, as Part of this Constitution, when ratified by the Legislatures of three fourths of the several States, or by Conventions in three fourths thereof, as the one or the other Mode of Ratification may be proposed by the Congress; Provided that no Amendment which may be made prior to the Year One thousand eight hundred and eight shall in any Manner affect the first and fourth Clauses in the Ninth Section of the first Article; and that no State, without its Consent, shall be deprived of its equal Suffrage in the Senate.

ARTICLE. VI.

All Debts contracted and Engagements entered into, before the Adoption of this Constitution, shall be as valid against the United States under this Constitution, as under the Confederation.

This Constitution, and the Laws of the United States which shall be made in Pursuance thereof; and all Treaties made, or which shall be made, under the Authority of the United States, shall be the supreme Law of the Land; and the Judges in every State shall be bound thereby, any Thing in the Constitution or Laws of any State to the Contrary notwithstanding.

The Senators and Representatives before mentioned, and the Members of the several State Legislatures, and all executive and judicial Officers, both of the United States and of the several States, shall be bound by Oath or Affirmation, to support this Constitution; but no religious Test shall ever be required as a Qualification to any Office or public Trust under the United States.

ARTICLE. VII.

The Ratification of the Conventions of nine States, shall be sufficient for the Establishment of this Constitution between the States so ratifying the Same.

Done in Convention by the Unanimous Consent of the States present the Seventeenth Day of September in the Year of our Lord one thousand seven hundred and Eighty seven and of the Independence of the United States of America the Twelfth. In witness thereof We have hereunto subscribed our Names,

G^o. WASHINGTON—Presd^t.
and deputy from Virginia

NEW HAMPSHIRE
John Langdon
Nicholas Gilman

MASSACHUSETTS
Nathaniel Gorham
Rufus King

CONNECTICUT
Wm Saml Johnson
Roger Sherman

NEW YORK
Alexander Hamilton

NEW JERSEY
Wil: Livingston
David A. Brearley
Wm Paterson
Jona: Dayton

PENNSYLVANIA
B Franklin
Thomas Mifflin
Robt Morris
Geo. Clymer
Thos FitzSimons
Jared Ingersoll
James Wilson
Gouv Morris

DELAWARE
Geo: Read
Gunning Bedford jun
John Dickinson
Richard Bassett
Jaco: Broom

MARYLAND
James McHenry
Dan of St Thos Jenifer
Danl Carroll

VIRGINIA
John Blair—
James Madison Jr.

NORTH CAROLINA
Wm Blount
Richd Dobbs Spaight
Hu Williamson

SOUTH CAROLINA
J. Rutledge
Charles Cotesworth
      Pinckney
Charles Pinckney
Pierce Butler

GEORGIA
William Few
Abr Baldwin

AMENDMENTS TO THE CONSTITUTION

Articles in addition to, and Amendment of the Constitution of the United States of America, proposed by Congress, and ratified by the Legislatures of the several States, pursuant to the fifth Article of the original Constitution.

AMENDMENT I.

Congress shall make no law respecting an establishment of religion, or prohibiting the free exercise thereof; or abridging the freedom of speech, or of the press; or the right of the people peaceably to assemble, and to petition the Government for a redress of grievances.

AMENDMENT II.

A well regulated Militia, being necessary to the security of a free State, the right of the people to keep and bear Arms, shall not be infringed.

AMENDMENT III.

No Soldier shall, in time of peace be quartered in any house, without the consent of the Owner, nor in time of war, but in a manner to be prescribed by law.

AMENDMENT IV.

The right of the people to be secure in their persons, houses, papers, and effects, against unreasonable searches and seizures, shall not be violated, and no Warrants shall issue, but upon probable cause, supported by Oath or affirmation, and particularly describing the place to be searched, and the persons or things to be seized.

AMENDMENT V.

No person shall be held to answer for a capital, or otherwise infamous crime, unless on a presentment or indictment of a Grand Jury, except in cases arising in the land or naval forces, or in the Militia, when in actual service in time of War or public danger; nor shall any person be subject for the same offence to be twice put in jeopardy of life or limb; nor shall be compelled in any criminal case to be a witness against himself, nor be deprived of life, liberty, or property, without due process of law; nor shall private property be taken for public use, without just compensation.

AMENDMENT VI.

In all criminal prosecutions, the accused shall enjoy the right to a speedy and public trial, by an impartial jury of the State and district wherein the crime shall have been committed, which district shall have been previously ascertained by law, and to be informed of the nature and cause of the accusation; to be confronted with the witnesses against him; to have compulsory process for obtaining witnesses in his favor, and to have the Assistance of Counsel for his defence.

AMENDMENT VII.

In Suits at common law, where the value in controversy shall exceed twenty dollars, the right of trial by jury shall be preserved, and no fact tried by a jury, shall be otherwise re-examined in any Court of the United States, than according to the rules of the common law.

AMENDMENT VIII.

Excessive bail shall not be required, nor excessive fines imposed, nor cruel and unusual punishments inflicted.

AMENDMENT IX.

The enumeration in the Constitution, of certain rights, shall not be construed to deny or disparage others retained by the people.

AMENDMENT X.

The powers not delegated to the United States by the Constitution, nor prohibited by it to the States, are reserved to the States respectively, or to the people.

AMENDMENT XI.

The Judicial power of the United States shall not be construed to extend to any suit in law or equity, commenced or prosecuted against one of the United States by Citizens of another State, or by Citizens or Subjects of any Foreign State. [January 8, 1798]

AMENDMENT XII.

The Electors shall meet in their respective states, and vote by ballot for President and Vice-President, one of whom, at least, shall not be an inhabitant of the same state with themselves; they shall name in their ballots the person voted for as President, and in distinct ballots the person voted for as Vice-President, and they shall make distinct lists of all persons voted for as President, and of all persons voted for as Vice President, and of the number of votes for each, which lists they shall sign and certify, and transmit sealed to the seat of the government of the United States, directed to the President of the Senate;—The President of the Senate shall, in the presence of the Senate and House of Representatives, open all the certificates and the votes shall then be counted;—The person having the greatest number of votes for President, shall be the President, if such number be a majority of the whole number of Electors appointed; and if no person have such majority, then from the persons having the highest numbers not exceeding three on the list of those voted for as President, the House of Representatives shall choose immediately, by ballot, the President. But in choosing the President, the votes shall be taken by states, the representation from each state having one vote; a quorum for this purpose shall consist of a member or members from two-thirds of the states, and a majority of all the states shall be necessary to a choice. And if the House of Representatives shall not choose a President whenever the right of choice shall devolve upon them, before the fourth day of March next following, then the Vice-President shall act as President, as in the case of the death or other constitutional disability of the President.—The person having the greatest number of votes as Vice-President, shall be the Vice-President, if such number be a majority of the whole number of Electors appointed, and if no person have a majority, then from the two highest numbers on the list, the Senate shall choose the Vice-President; a quorum for the purpose shall consist of two-thirds of the whole number of Senators, and a majority of the whole number shall be necessary to a choice. But no person constitutionally ineligible to the office of President shall be eligible to that of Vice-President of the United States. [September 25, 1804]

AMENDMENT XIII.

Section 1. Neither slavery nor involuntary servitude, except as a punishment for crime whereof the party shall have been duly convicted, shall exist within the United States, or any place subject to their jurisdiction.

Section 2. Congress shall have power to enforce this article by appropriate legislation. [December 18, 1865]

AMENDMENT XIV.

Section 1. All persons born or naturalized in the United States, and subject to the jurisdiction thereof, are citizens of the United States and of the State wherein they reside. No State shall make or enforce any law which shall abridge the privileges or immunities of citizens of the United States; nor shall any State deprive any person of life, liberty, or property, without due process of law; nor deny to any person within its jurisdiction the equal protection of the laws.

Section 2. Representatives shall be apportioned among the several States according to their respective numbers, counting the whole number of persons in each State, excluding Indians not taxed. But when the right to vote at any election for the choice of electors for President and Vice President of the United States, Representatives in Congress, the Executive and Judicial officers of a State, or the members of the Legislature thereof, is denied to any of the male inhabitants of such State, being twenty-one years of age, and citizens of the United States, or in any way abridged, except for participation in rebellion, or other crime, the basis of representation therein shall be reduced in the proportion which the number of such male citizens shall bear to the whole number of male citizens twenty-one years of age in such State.

Section 3. No person shall be a Senator or Representative in Congress, or elector of President and Vice President, or hold any office, civil or military, under the United States, or under any State, who, having previously taken an oath, as a member of Congress, or as an officer of the United States, or as a member of any State legislature, or as an executive or judicial officer of any State, to support the Constitution of the United States, shall have engaged in insurrection or rebellion against the same, or given aid or comfort to the enemies thereof. But Congress may by a vote of two-thirds of each House, remove such disability.

Section 4. The validity of the public debt of the United States, authorized by law, including debts incurred for payment of pensions and bounties for services in suppressing insurrection or rebellion, shall not be questioned. But neither the United States nor any State shall assume or pay any debt or obligation incurred in aid of insurrection or rebellion against the United States, or any claim for the loss or emancipation of any slave; but all such debts, obligations and claims shall be held illegal and void.

Section 5. The Congress shall have power to enforce, by appropriate legislation, the provisions of this article. [July 28, 1868]

AMENDMENT XV.

Section 1. The right of citizens of the United States to vote shall not be denied or abridged by the United States or by any State on account of race, color, or previous condition of servitude—

Section 2. The Congress shall have power to enforce this article by appropriate legislation. [March 30, 1870]

AMENDMENT XVI.

The Congress shall have power to lay and collect taxes on incomes, from whatever source derived, without apportionment among the several States, and without regard to any census or enumeration. [February 25, 1913]

AMENDMENT XVII.

The Senate of the United States shall be composed of two senators from each State, elected by the people thereof, for six years; and each Senator shall have one vote. The electors in each State shall have the qualifications requisite for electors of the most numerous branch of the State legislatures.

When vacancies happen in the representation of any State in the Senate, the executive authority of such State shall issue writs of election to fill such vacancies: *Provided*, That the legislature of any State may empower the executive thereof to make temporary appointments until the people fill the vacancies by election as the legislature may direct.

This amendment shall not be so construed as to affect the election or term of any senator chosen before it becomes valid as part of the Constitution. [May 31, 1913]

AMENDMENT XVIII.

After one year from the ratification of this article, the manufacture, sale, or transportation of intoxicating liquors within, the importation thereof into, or the exportation thereof from the United States and all territory subject to the jurisdiction thereof for beverage purposes is hereby prohibited.

The Congress and the several States shall have concurrent power to enforce this article by appropriate legislation.

This article shall be inoperative unless it shall have been ratified as an amendment to the Constitution by the legislatures of the several States, as provided in the Constitution, within seven years from the date of the submission thereof to the States by Congress. [January 29, 1919]

AMENDMENT XIX.

The right of citizens of the United States to vote shall not be denied or abridged by the United States or by any State on account of sex.

The Congress shall have power by appropriate legislation to enforce the provisions of this article. [August 26, 1920]

AMENDMENT XX.

Section 1. The terms of the President and Vice-President shall end at noon on the twentieth day of January, and the terms of Senators and Representatives at noon on the third day of January, of the years in which such terms would have ended if this article had not been ratified; and the terms of their successors shall then begin.

Section 2. The Congress shall assemble at least once in every year, and such meeting shall begin at noon on the third day of January, unless they shall by law appoint a different day.

Section 3. If, at the time fixed for the beginning of the term of the President, the President-elect shall have died, the Vice-President-elect shall become President. If a President shall not have been chosen before the time fixed for the beginning of his term, or if the President-elect shall have failed to qualify, then the Vice-President-elect shall act as President until a President shall have qualified; and the Congress may by law provide for the case wherein neither a President-elect nor a Vice-President-elect shall have qualified, declaring who shall then act as President, or the manner in which one who is to act shall be selected, and such person shall act accordingly until a President or Vice-President shall have qualified.

Section 4. The Congress may by law provide for the case of the death of any of the persons from whom the House of Representatives may choose a President whenever the right of choice shall have devolved upon them, and for the case of the death of any of the persons from whom the Senate may choose a Vice-President whenever the right of choice shall have devolved upon them.

Section 5. Sections 1 and 2 shall take effect on the 15th day of October following the ratification of this article.

Section 6. This article shall be inoperative unless it shall have been ratified as an amendment to the Constitution by the legislatures of three-fourths of the several States within seven years from the date of its submission. [February 6, 1933]

AMENDMENT XXI.
Section 1. The eighteenth article of amendment to the Constitution of the United States is hereby repealed.

Section 2. The transportation or importation into any State, Territory or possession of the United States for delivery or use therein of intoxicating liquors, in violation of the laws thereof, is hereby prohibited.

Section 3. This article shall be inoperative unless it shall have been ratified as an amendment to the Constitution by convention in the several States, as provided in the Constitution, within seven years from the date of the submission thereof to the States by the Congress. [December 5, 1933]

AMENDMENT XXII.
Section 1. No person shall be elected to the office of the President more than twice, and no person who has held the office of President, or acted as President, for more than two years of a term to which some other person was elected President shall be elected to the office of the President more than once. But this Article shall not apply to any person holding the office of President when this Article was proposed by the Congress, and shall not prevent any person who may be holding the office of President, or acting as President, during the term within which this Article becomes operative from holding the office of President or acting as President during the remainder of such term.

Section 2. This article shall be inoperative unless it shall have been ratified as an amendment to the Constitution by the legislatures of three-fourths of the several States within seven years from the date of its submission to the States by the Congress. [February 27, 1951]

AMENDMENT XXIII.
Section 1. The District constituting the seat of government of the United States shall appoint in such manner as the Congress may direct:

A number of electors of President and Vice-President equal to the whole number of Senators and Representatives in Congress to which the District would be entitled if it were a State, but in no event more than the least populous State; they shall be in addition to those appointed by the States, but they shall be considered, for the purposes of the election of President and Vice-President, to be electors appointed by a State; and they shall meet in the District and perform such duties as provided by the twelfth article of amendment.

Section 2. The Congress shall have the power to enforce this article by appropriate legislation. [March 29, 1961]

AMENDMENT XXIV.

Section 1. The right of citizens of the United States to vote in any primary or other election for President or Vice President, for electors for President or Vice President, or for Senator or Representative in Congress, shall not be denied or abridged by the United States or any State by reason of failure to pay any poll tax or other tax.

Section 2. The Congress shall have power to enforce this article by appropriate legislation. [January 23, 1964]

AMENDMENT XXV.

Section 1. In case of the removal of the President from office or of his death or resignation, the Vice President shall become President.

Section 2. Whenever there is a vacancy in the office of Vice President, the President shall nominate a Vice President who shall take office upon confirmation by a majority vote of both Houses of Congress.

Section 3. Whenever the President transmits to the President pro tempore of the Senate and the Speaker of the House of Representatives his written declaration that he is unable to discharge the powers and duties of his office, and until he transmits to them a written declaration to the contrary, such powers and duties shall be discharged by the Vice President as Acting President.

Section 4. Whenever the Vice President and a majority of either the principal officers of the executive departments or of such other body as Congress may by law provide, transmit to the President pro tempore of the Senate and the Speaker of the House of Rep-

resentatives their written declaration that the President is unable to discharge the powers and duties of his office, the Vice President shall immediately assume the powers and duties of the office as Acting President.

Thereafter, when the President transmits to the President pro tempore of the Senate and the Speaker of the House of Representatives his written declaration that no inability exists, he shall resume the powers and duties of his office unless the Vice President and a majority of either the principal officers of the executive departments or of such other body as Congress may by law provide, transmit within four days to the President pro tempore of the Senate and the Speaker of the House of Representatives their written declaration that the President is unable to discharge the powers and duties of his office. Thereupon Congress shall decide the issue, assembling within forty-eight hours for that purpose if not in session. If the Congress, within twenty-one days after receipt of the latter written declaration, or, if Congress is not in session, within twenty-one days after Congress is required to assemble, determines by two-thirds vote of both Houses that the President is unable to discharge the powers and duties of his office, the Vice President shall continue to discharge the same as Acting President; otherwise, the President shall resume the powers and duties of his office. [February 10, 1967]

AMENDMENT XXVI.

Section 1. The right of citizens of the United States, who are eighteen years of age or older, to vote shall not be denied or abridged by the United States or by any State on account of age.

Section 2. The Congress shall have power to enforce this article by appropriate legislation. [June 30, 1971]

AMENDMENT XXVII.

No law, varying the compensation for the services of the Senators and Representatives shall take effect, until an election of Representatives shall have intervened. [May 8, 1992]

FROM GEORGE WASHINGTON'S FAREWELL ADDRESS (1796)

Friends and Citizens:

The period for a new election of a citizen to administer the executive government of the United States being not far distant, and the time actually arrived when your thoughts must be employed in designating the person who is to be clothed with that important trust, it appears to me proper, especially as it may conduce to a more distinct expression of the public voice, that I should now apprise you of the resolution I have formed, to decline being considered among the number of those out of whom a choice is to be made.

★ ★ ★

In looking forward to the moment which is intended to terminate the career of my public life, my feelings do not permit me to suspend the deep acknowledgment of that debt of gratitude which I owe to my beloved country for the many honors it has conferred upon me; still more for the steadfast confidence with which it has supported me; and for the opportunities I have thence enjoyed of manifesting my inviolable attachment, by services faithful and persevering, though in usefulness unequal to my zeal. If benefits have resulted to our country from these services, let it always be remembered to your praise, and as an instructive example in our annals, that under circumstances in which the passions, agitated in every direction, were liable to mislead, amidst appearances sometimes dubious, vicissitudes of fortune often discouraging, in situations in which not unfrequently want of success has countenanced the spirit of criticism, the constancy of your support was the essential prop of the efforts, and a guarantee of the plans by which they were effected. Profoundly penetrated with this idea, I shall carry it with me to my grave, as a strong incitement to unceasing vows that heaven may continue to you the choicest tokens of its beneficence; that your union and brotherly affection may be perpetual; that the free Constitution, which is the work of your hands, may be sacredly maintained; that its administration in every department may be stamped with wisdom and virtue; that, in fine, the happiness of the people of these States, under the auspices of liberty, may be made complete by so careful a preservation and so prudent a use of this blessing as will acquire to them the glory of recommending it to the applause, the affection, and adoption of every nation which is yet a stranger to it.

Here, perhaps, I ought to stop. But a solicitude for your welfare, which cannot end but with my life, and the apprehension of danger, natural to that solicitude, urge me, on an occasion like the present, to offer to your solemn contemplation, and to recommend to your frequent review, some sentiments which are the result of much reflection, of no inconsiderable observation, and which appear to me all-important to the permanency of your felicity as a people. These will be offered to you with the more freedom, as you can only see in them the disinterested warnings of a parting friend, who can possibly have no personal motive to bias his counsel. Nor can I forget, as an encouragement to it, your indulgent reception of my sentiments on a former and not dissimilar occasion.

Interwoven as is the love of liberty with every ligament of your hearts, no recommendation of mine is necessary to fortify or confirm the attachment.

The unity of government which constitutes you one people is also now dear to you. It is justly so, for it is a main pillar in the edifice of your real independence, the support of your tranquility at home, your peace abroad; of your safety; of your prosperity; of that very liberty which you so highly prize. But as it is easy to foresee that, from different causes and from different quarters, much pains will be taken, many artifices employed to weaken in your minds the conviction of this truth; as this is the point in your political fortress against which the batteries of internal and external enemies will be most constantly and actively (though often covertly and insidiously) directed, it is of infinite moment that you should properly estimate the immense value of your national union to your collective and individual happiness; that you should cherish a cordial, habitual, and immovable attachment to it; accustoming yourselves to think and speak of it as of the palladium of your political safety and prosperity; watching for its preservation with jealous anxiety; discountenancing whatever may suggest even a suspicion that it can in any event be abandoned; and indignantly frowning upon the first dawning of every attempt to alienate any portion of our country from the rest, or to enfeeble the sacred ties which now link together the various parts.

For this you have every inducement of sympathy and interest. Citizens, by birth or choice, of a common country, that country has a right to concentrate your affections. The name of American, which belongs to you in your national capacity, must always exalt the just pride of patriotism more than any appellation derived from local discriminations. With slight shades of difference, you have the same religion, manners, habits, and political principles. You have in a common cause fought and triumphed together; the independence and liberty you possess are the work of joint counsels, and joint efforts of common dangers, sufferings, and successes.

But these considerations, however powerfully they address themselves to your sensibility, are greatly outweighed by those which apply more immediately to your interest. Here every portion of our country finds the most commanding motives for carefully guarding and preserving the union of the whole.

The North, in an unrestrained intercourse with the South, protected by the equal laws of a common government, finds in the productions of the latter great additional resources of maritime and commercial enterprise and precious materials of manufacturing industry. The South, in the same intercourse, benefiting by the agency of the North, sees its agriculture grow and its commerce expand. Turning partly into its own channels the seamen of the North, it finds its particular navigation invigorated; and, while it contributes, in different ways, to nourish and increase the general mass of the national navigation, it looks forward to the protection of a maritime strength, to which itself is unequally adapted. The East, in a like intercourse with the West, already finds, and in the progressive improvement of interior communications by land and water, will more and more find a valuable vent for the commodities which it brings from abroad, or manufactures at home. The West derives from the East supplies requisite to its growth and comfort, and, what is perhaps of still greater consequence, it must of necessity owe the secure enjoyment of indispensable outlets for its own productions to the weight, influence, and the future maritime strength of the Atlantic side of the Union, directed by an indissoluble community of interest as one nation. Any other tenure by which the West can hold this essential advantage, whether derived from its own separate strength, or from an apostate and unnatural connection with any foreign power, must be intrinsically precarious.

While, then, every part of our country thus feels an immediate and particular interest in union, all the parts combined cannot fail to find in the united mass of means and efforts greater strength, greater resource, proportionably greater security from external danger, a less frequent interruption of their peace by foreign nations; and, what is of inestimable value, they must derive from union an exemption from those broils and wars between themselves, which so frequently afflict neighboring countries not tied together by the same governments, which their own rival ships alone would be sufficient to produce, but which opposite foreign alliances, attachments, and intrigues would stimulate and embitter. Hence, likewise, they will avoid the necessity of those overgrown military establishments which, under any form of government, are inauspicious to liberty, and which are to be regarded as particularly hostile to republican liberty. In this sense it is that your union ought to be considered as a main prop of your liberty, and that the love of the one ought to endear to you the preservation of the other.

These considerations speak a persuasive language to every reflecting and virtuous mind, and exhibit the continuance of the Union as a primary object of patriotic desire. Is there a doubt whether a common government can embrace so large a sphere? Let experience solve it. To listen to mere speculation in such a case were criminal. We are authorized to hope that a proper organization of the whole with the auxiliary agency of governments for the respective subdivisions, will afford a happy issue to the experiment. It is well worth a fair and full experiment. With such powerful and obvious motives to union, affecting all parts of our country, while experience shall not have demonstrated its impracticability, there will always be reason to distrust the patriotism of those who in any quarter may endeavor to weaken its bands.

★ ★ ★

To the efficacy and permanency of your Union, a government for the whole is indispensable. No alliance, however strict, between the parts can be an adequate substitute; they must inevitably experience the infractions and interruptions which all alliances in all times have experienced. Sensible of this momentous truth, you have improved upon your first essay, by the adoption of a constitution of government better calculated than your former for an intimate union, and for the efficacious management of your common concerns. This government, the offspring of our own choice, uninfluenced and unawed, adopted upon full investigation and mature deliberation, completely free in its principles, in the distribution of its powers, uniting security with energy, and containing within itself a provision for its own amendment, has a just claim to your confidence and your support. Respect for its authority, compliance with its laws, acquiescence in its measures, are duties enjoined by the fundamental maxims of true liberty. The basis of our political systems is the right of the people to make and to alter their constitutions of government. But the Constitution which at any time exists, till changed by an explicit and authentic act of the whole people, is sacredly obligatory upon all. The very idea of the power and the right of the people to establish government presupposes the duty of every individual to obey the established government.

★ ★ ★

I have already intimated to you the danger of parties in the State, with particular reference to the founding of them on geographical discriminations. Let me now take a more comprehensive view, and warn you in the most solemn manner against the baneful effects of the spirit of party generally.

This spirit, unfortunately, is inseparable from our nature, having its root in the strongest passions of the human mind. It exists under different shapes in all governments, more or less stifled, controlled, or repressed; but, in those of the popular form, it is seen in its greatest rankness, and is truly their worst enemy.

The alternate domination of one faction over another, sharpened by the spirit of revenge, natural to party dissension, which in different ages and countries has perpetrated the most horrid enormities, is itself a frightful despotism. But this leads at length to a more formal and permanent despotism. The disorders and miseries which result gradually incline the minds of men to seek security and repose in the absolute power of an individual; and sooner or later the chief of some prevailing faction, more able or more fortunate than his competitors, turns this disposition to the purposes of his own elevation, on the ruins of public liberty.

Without looking forward to an extremity of this kind (which nevertheless ought not to be entirely out of sight), the common and continual mischiefs of the spirit of party are sufficient to make it the interest and duty of a wise people to discourage and restrain it.

It serves always to distract the public councils and enfeeble the public administration. It agitates the community with ill-founded jealousies and false alarms, kindles the animosity of one part against another, foments occasionally riot and insurrection. It opens the door to foreign influence and corruption, which finds a facilitated access to the government itself through the channels of party passions. Thus the policy and the will of one country are subjected to the policy and will of another.

There is an opinion that parties in free countries are useful checks upon the administration of the government and serve to keep alive the spirit of liberty. This within certain limits is probably true; and in governments of a monarchical cast, patriotism may look with indulgence, if not with favor, upon the spirit of party. But in those of the popular character, in governments purely elective, it is a spirit not to be encouraged. From their natural tendency, it is certain there will always be enough of that spirit for every salutary purpose. And there being constant danger of excess, the effort ought to be by force of public opinion, to mitigate and assuage it. A fire not to be quenched, it demands a uniform vigilance to prevent its bursting into a flame, lest, instead of warming, it should consume.

It is important, likewise, that the habits of thinking in a free country should inspire caution in those entrusted with its administration, to confine themselves within their respective constitutional spheres, avoiding in the exercise of the powers of one department to encroach upon another. The spirit of encroachment tends to consolidate the powers of all the departments in one, and thus to create, whatever the form of government, a real despotism. A just estimate of that love of power, and proneness to abuse it, which predominates in the human heart, is sufficient to satisfy us of the truth of this position. The necessity of reciprocal checks in the exercise of political power, by dividing and distributing it into different depositaries, and constituting each the guardian of the public weal against invasions by the others, has been evinced by experiments ancient and modern; some of them in our country and under our own eyes. To preserve them must be as necessary as to institute them. If, in the opinion of the people, the distribution or modification of the constitutional powers be in any particular wrong, let it be corrected by an amendment in the way which the Constitution designates. But let there be no change by usurpation; for though this, in one instance, may be the instrument of good, it is the customary weapon by which free governments are destroyed. The precedent must always greatly overbalance in permanent evil any partial or transient benefit, which the use can at any time yield.

★ ★ ★

Observe good faith and justice towards all nations; cultivate peace and harmony with all. Religion and morality enjoin this conduct; and can it be, that good policy does not equally enjoin it? It will be worthy of

a free, enlightened, and at no distant period, a great nation, to give to mankind the magnanimous and too novel example of a people always guided by an exalted justice and benevolence. Who can doubt that, in the course of time and things, the fruits of such a plan would richly repay any temporary advantages which might be lost by a steady adherence to it? Can it be that Providence has not connected the permanent felicity of a nation with its virtue? The experiment, at least, is recommended by every sentiment which ennobles human nature. Alas! is it rendered impossible by its vices?

In the execution of such a plan, nothing is more essential than that permanent, inveterate antipathies against particular nations, and passionate attachments for others, should be excluded; and that, in place of them, just and amicable feelings towards all should be cultivated. The nation which indulges towards another a habitual hatred or a habitual fondness is in some degree a slave. It is a slave to its animosity or to its affection, either of which is sufficient to lead it astray from its duty and its interest. Antipathy in one nation against another disposes each more readily to offer insult and injury, to lay hold of slight causes of umbrage, and to be haughty and intractable, when accidental or trifling occasions of dispute occur. Hence, frequent collisions, obstinate, envenomed, and bloody contests. The nation, prompted by ill-will and resentment, sometimes impels to war the government, contrary to the best calculations of policy. The government sometimes participates in the national propensity, and adopts through passion what reason would reject; at other times it makes the animosity of the nation subservient to projects of hostility instigated by pride, ambition, and other sinister and pernicious motives. The peace often, sometimes perhaps the liberty, of nations, has been the victim.

★ ★ ★

The great rule of conduct for us in regard to foreign nations is in extending our commercial relations, to have with them as little political connection as possible. So far as we have already formed engagements, let them be fulfilled with perfect good faith. Here let us stop. Europe has a set of primary interests which to us have none; or a very remote relation. Hence she must be engaged in frequent controversies, the causes of which are essentially foreign to our concerns. Hence, therefore, it must be unwise in us to implicate ourselves by artificial ties in the ordinary vicissitudes of her politics, or the ordinary combinations and collisions of her friendships or enmities.

Our detached and distant situation invites and enables us to pursue a different course. If we remain one people under an efficient government, the period is not far off when we may defy material injury from external annoyance; when we may take such an attitude as will cause the neutrality we may at any time resolve upon to be scrupulously respected; when belligerent nations, under the impossibility of making acquisitions upon us, will not lightly hazard the giving us provocation; when we may choose peace or war, as our interest, guided by justice, shall counsel.

Why forego the advantages of so peculiar a situation? Why quit our own to stand upon foreign ground? Why, by interweaving our destiny with that of any part of Europe, entangle our peace and prosperity in the toils of European ambition, rivalship, interest, humor or caprice?

It is our true policy to steer clear of permanent alliances with any portion of the foreign world; so far, I mean, as we are now at liberty to do it; for let me not be understood as capable of patronizing infidelity to existing engagements. I hold the maxim no less applicable to public than to private affairs, that honesty is always the best policy. I repeat it, therefore, let those engagements be observed in their genuine sense. But, in my opinion, it is unnecessary and would be unwise to extend them.

Taking care always to keep ourselves by suitable establishments on a respectable defensive posture, we may safely trust to temporary alliances for extraordinary emergencies.

Harmony, liberal intercourse with all nations, are recommended by policy, humanity, and interest. But even our commercial policy should hold an equal and impartial hand; neither seeking nor granting exclusive favors or preferences; consulting the natural course of things; diffusing and diversifying by gentle means the streams of commerce, but forcing nothing; establishing (with powers so disposed, in order to give trade a stable course, to define the rights of our merchants, and to enable the government to support them) conventional rules of intercourse, the best that present circumstances and mutual opinion will permit, but temporary, and liable to be from time to time abandoned or varied, as experience and circumstances shall dictate; constantly keeping in view that it is folly in one nation to look for disinterested favors from another; that it must pay with a portion of its independence for whatever it may accept under that character; that, by such acceptance, it may place itself in the condition of having given equivalents for nominal favors, and yet of being reproached with ingratitude for not giving more.

★ ★ ★

Relying on its kindness in this as in other things, and actuated by that fervent love towards it, which is so natural to a man who views in it the native soil of himself and his progenitors for several generations, I anticipate with pleasing expectation that retreat in which I promise myself to realize, without alloy, the sweet enjoyment of partaking, in the midst of my fellow-citizens, the benign influence of good laws under a free government, the ever-favorite object of my heart, and the happy reward, as I trust, of our mutual cares, labors, and dangers.

Geo. Washington

THE SENECA FALLS DECLARATION OF SENTIMENTS AND RESOLUTIONS (1848)

1. DECLARATION OF SENTIMENTS

When, in the course of human events, it becomes necessary for one portion of the family of man to assume among the people of the earth a position different from that which they have hitherto occupied, but one to which the laws of nature and of nature's God entitle them, a decent respect to the opinions of mankind requires that they should declare the causes that impel them to such a course.

We hold these truths to be self-evident: that all men and women are created equal; that they are endowed by their Creator with certain inalienable rights; that among these are life, liberty, and the pursuit of happiness; that to secure these rights governments are instituted, deriving their just powers from the consent of the governed. Whenever any form of government becomes destructive of these ends, it is the right of those who suffer from it to refuse allegiance to it, and to insist upon the institution of a new government, laying its foundation on such principles, and organizing its powers in such form, as to them shall seem most likely to effect their safety and happiness. Prudence, indeed, will dictate that governments long established should not be changed for light and transient causes; and accordingly all experience hath shown that mankind are more disposed to suffer, while evils are sufferable, than to right themselves by abolishing the forms to which they are accustomed. But when a long train of abuses and usurpations, pursuing invariably the same object, evinces a design to reduce them under absolute despotism, it is their duty to throw off such government, and to provide new guards for their future security. Such has been the patient sufferance of the women under this government, and such is now the necessity which constrains them to demand the equal station to which they are entitled. The history of mankind is a history of repeated injuries and usurpations on the part of man toward woman, having in direct object the establishment of an absolute tyranny over her. To prove this, let facts be submitted to a candid world.

He has never permitted her to exercise her inalienable right to the elective franchise.

He has compelled her to submit to laws, in the formation of which she had no voice.

He has withheld from her rights which are given to the most ignorant and degraded men—both natives and foreigners.

Having deprived her of this first right of a citizen, the elective franchise, thereby leaving her without representation in the halls of legislation, he has oppressed her on all sides.

He has made her, if married, in the eye of the law, civilly dead. He has taken from her all right in property, even to the wages she earns.

He has made her, morally, an irresponsible being, as she can commit many crimes with impunity, provided they be done in the presence of her husband.

In the covenant of marriage, she is compelled to promise obedience to her husband, he becoming, to all intents and purposes, her master—the law giving him power to deprive her of her liberty, and to administer chastisement.

He has so framed the laws of divorce, as to what shall be the proper causes, and in case of separation, to whom the guardianship of the children shall be given, as to be wholly regardless of the happiness of women—the law, in all cases, going upon a false supposition of the supremacy of man, and giving all power into his hands.

After depriving her of all rights as a married woman, if single, and the owner of property, he has taxed her to support a government which recognizes her only when her property can be made profitable to it.

He has monopolized nearly all the profitable employments, and from those she is permitted to follow, she receives but a scanty remuneration. He closes against her all the avenues to wealth and distinction which he considers most honorable to himself. As a teacher of theology, medicine, or law, she is not known.

He has denied her the facilities for obtaining a thorough education, all colleges being closed against her.

He allows her in Church, as well as State, but a subordinate position, claiming Apostolic authority for her exclusion from the ministry, and, with some exceptions, from any public participation in the affairs of the Church.

He has created a false public sentiment by giving to the world a different code of morals for men and women, by which moral delinquencies which exclude women from society, are not only tolerated, but deemed of little account in man.

He has usurped the prerogative of Jehovah himself, claiming it as his right to assign for her a sphere of action, when that belongs to her conscience and to her God.

He has endeavored, in every way that he could, to destroy her confidence in her own powers, to lessen her self-respect and to make her willing to lead a dependent and abject life.

Now, in view of this entire disfranchisement of one-half the people of this country, their social and religious degradation—in view of the unjust laws above mentioned, and because women do feel themselves aggrieved, oppressed, and fraudulently deprived of their most sacred rights, we insist that they have immediate admission to all the rights and privileges which belong to them as citizens of the United States.

In entering upon the great work before us, we anticipate no small amount of misconception, misrepresentation, and ridicule; but we shall use every instrumentality within our power to effect our object. We shall employ agents, circulate tracts, petition the State and National legislatures, and endeavor to enlist the pulpit and the press in our behalf. We hope this Convention will be followed by a series of Conventions embracing every part of the country.

2. RESOLUTIONS

WHEREAS, The great precept of nature is conceded to be, that "man shall pursue his own true and substantial happiness." Blackstone in his Commentaries remarks, that this law of Nature being coeval with mankind, and dictated by God himself, is of course superior in obligation to any other. It is binding over all the globe, in all countries and at all times; no human laws are of any validity if contrary to this, and such of them as are valid, derive all their force, and all their validity, and all their authority, mediately and immediately, from this original; therefore,

Resolved, That such laws as conflict, in any way, with the true and substantial happiness of woman, are contrary to the great precept of nature and of no validity, for this is "superior in obligation to any other."

Resolved, That all laws which prevent woman from occupying such a station in society as her conscience shall dictate, or which place her in a position inferior to that of man, are contrary to the great precept of nature, and therefore of no force or authority.

Resolved, That woman is man's equal—was intended to be so by the Creator, and the highest good of the race demands that she should be recognized as such.

Resolved, That the women of this country ought to be enlightened in regard to the laws under which they live, that they may no longer publish their degradation by declaring themselves satisfied with their present position, nor their ignorance, by asserting that they have all the rights they want.

Resolved, That inasmuch as man, while claiming for himself intellectual superiority, does accord to woman moral superiority, it is pre-eminently his duty to encourage her to speak and teach, as she has an opportunity, in all religious assemblies.

Resolved, That the same amount of virtue, delicacy, and refinement of behavior that is required of woman in the social state, should also be required of man, and the same transgressions should be visited with equal severity on both man and woman.

Resolved, That the objection of indelicacy and impropriety, which is so often brought against woman when she addresses a public audience, comes with a very ill-grace from those who encourage, by their attendance, her appearance on the stage, in the concert. Or in feats of the circus.

Resolved, That woman has too long rested satisfied in the circumscribed limits which corrupt customs and a perverted application of the Scriptures have marked out for her, and that it is time she should move in the enlarged sphere which her great Creator has assigned her.

Resolved, That it is the duty of the women of this country to secure to themselves their sacred right to the elective franchise.

Resolved, That the equality of human rights results necessarily from the fact of the identity of the race in capabilities and responsibilities.

Resolved, therefore, That, being invested by the Creator with the same capabilities, and the same consciousness of responsibility for their exercise, it is demonstrably the right and duty of woman, equally with man, to promote every righteous cause by every righteous means; and especially in regard to the great subjects of morals and religion, it is self-evidently her right to participate with her brother in teaching them, both in private and in public, by writing and by speaking, by any instrumentalities proper to be used, and in any assemblies proper to be held; and this being a self-evident truth growing out of the divinely implanted principles of human nature, any custom or authority adverse to it, whether modern or wearing the hoary sanction of antiquity, is to be regarded as a self-evident falsehood, and at war with mankind.

Resolved, That the speedy success of our cause depends upon the zealous and untiring efforts of both men and women, for the overthrow of the monopoly of the pulpit, and for the securing to women an equal participation with men in the various trades, professions, and commerce.

FROM FREDERICK DOUGLASS'S "WHAT, TO THE SLAVE, IS THE FOURTH OF JULY?" SPEECH (1852)

★ ★ ★

This, for the purpose of this celebration, is the Fourth of July. It is the birthday of your National Independence, and of your political freedom. This, to you, is what the Passover was to the emancipated people of God. It carries your minds back to the day, and to the act of your great deliverance; and to the signs and to the wonders associated with that act and that day. This celebration also marks the beginning of another year of your national life; and reminds you that the Republic of America is now seventy-six years old. I am glad, fellow citizens, that your nation is so young. Seventy-six years, though a good old age for a man, is but a mere speck in the life of a nation. Three score years and ten is the allotted time for individual men; but nations number their years by thousands. According to this fact, you are, even now, only in the beginning of your national career, still lingering in the period of childhood. I repeat, I am glad this is so. There is hope in the thought, and hope is much needed, under the dark clouds which lower above the horizon. The eye of the reformer is met with angry flashes, portending disastrous times; but his heart may well beat lighter at the thought that America is young, and that she is still in the impressible stage of her existence. May he not hope that high lessons of wisdom, of justice and of truth, will yet give direction to her destiny? Were the nation older, the patriot's heart might be sadder and the reformer's brow heavier. Its future might be shrouded in gloom and the hope of its prophets go out in sorrow. There is consolation in the thought that America is young. Great streams are not easily turned from channels worn deep in the course of ages. They may sometimes rise in quiet and stately majesty, and inundate the land, refreshing and fertilizing the earth with their mysterious properties. They may also rise in wrath and fury, and bear away on their angry waves the accumulated wealth of years of toil and hardship. They, however, gradually flow back to the same old channel and flow on as serenely as ever. But, while the river may not be turned aside, it may dry up and leave nothing behind but the withered branch and the unsightly rock, to howl in the abyss-sweeping wind, the sad tale of departed glory. As with rivers, so with nations.

Fellow citizens, I shall not presume to dwell at length on the associations that cluster about this day. The simple story of it is, that seventy-six years ago the people of this country were British subjects. The style and title of your "sovereign people" (in which you now glory) was not then born. You were under the British Crown. Your fathers esteemed the English government as the home government, and England as the fatherland. This home government, you know, although a considerable distance from your home, did, in the exercise of its parental prerogatives, impose upon its colonial children such restraints, burdens and limitations as, in its mature judgment, it deemed wise, right and proper.

★ ★ ★

Feeling themselves harshly and unjustly treated by the home government, your fathers, like men of honesty and men of spirit, earnestly sought redress. They petitioned and remonstrated, they did so in a decorous, respectful and loyal manner. Their conduct was wholly unexceptionable. This, however, did not answer the purpose. They saw themselves treated with sovereign indifference, coldness and scorn. Yet they persevered. They were not the men to look back.

★ ★ ★

Citizens, your fathers . . . succeeded; and today you reap the fruits of their success. The freedom gained is yours; and you, therefore, may properly celebrate this anniversary. The Fourth of July is the first great fact in your nation's history—the very ringbolt in the chain of your yet undeveloped destiny.

Pride and patriotism, not less than gratitude, prompt you to celebrate and to hold it in perpetual remembrance. I have said that the Declaration of Independence is the ringbolt to the chain of your nation's destiny; so, indeed, I regard it. The principles contained in that instrument are saving principles. Stand by those principles, be true to them on all occasions, in all places, against all foes, and at whatever cost.

★ ★ ★

[The fathers of this republic] were peace men, but they preferred revolution to peaceful submission to bondage. They were quiet men; but they did not shrink from agitating against oppression. They showed forbearance, but that they knew its limits. They believed in order, but not in the order of tyranny. With them, nothing was "settled" that was not right. With them, justice, liberty and humanity were "final," not slavery and oppression. You may well cherish the memory of such men. They were great in their day and generation. Their solid manhood stands out the more as we contrast it with these degenerate times.

★ ★ ★

Fellow citizens, pardon me, allow me to ask, why am I called upon to speak here today? What have I, or those I represent, to do with your national independence? Are the great principles of political freedom and of natural justice, embodied in that Declaration of Independence, extended to us? and am I, therefore, called upon to bring our humble offering to the national altar and to confess the benefits and express devout gratitude for the blessings resulting from your independence to us?

★ ★ ★

But such is not the state of the case. I say it with a sad sense of the disparity between us. I am not included within the pale of this glorious anniversary! Your high independence only reveals the immeasurable distance between us. The blessings in which you, this day, rejoice, are not enjoyed in common. The rich inheritance of justice, liberty, prosperity and independence, bequeathed by your fathers, is shared by you, not by me. The sunlight that brought light and healing to you, has brought stripes and death to me. This Fourth of July is *yours*, not *mine*. *You* may rejoice, *I* must mourn.

★ ★ ★

Fellow citizens, above your national, tumultuous joy I hear the mournful wail of millions! whose chains, heavy and grievous yesterday, are today rendered more intolerable by the jubilee shouts that reach them. If I do forget, if I do not faithfully remember those bleeding children of sorrow this day, "may my right hand forget her cunning, and may my tongue cleave to the roof of my mouth!" To forget them, to pass lightly over their wrongs and to chime in with the popular theme would be treason most scandalous and shocking and would make me a reproach before God and the world. My subject, then, fellow citizens, is American slavery. I shall see this day and its popular characteristics from the slave's point of view. Standing there identified with the American bondman, making his wrongs mine, I do not hesitate to declare, with all my soul, that the character and conduct of this nation never looked blacker to me than on this Fourth of July. Whether we turn to the declarations of the past or to the professions of the present, the conduct of the nation seems equally hideous and revolting. America is false to the past, false to the present, and solemnly binds herself to be false to the future.

★ ★ ★

For the present, it is enough to affirm the equal manhood of the Negro race. It is not astonishing that, while we are plowing, planting and reaping, using all kinds of mechanical tools, erecting houses, constructing bridges, building ships, working in metals of brass, iron, copper, silver and gold; that, while we are reading, writing and ciphering, acting as clerks, merchants and secretaries, having among us lawyers, doctors, ministers, poets, authors, editors, orators and teachers; that, while we are engaged in all manner of enterprises common to other men, digging gold in California, capturing the whale in the Pacific, feeding sheep and cattle on the hillside, living, moving, acting, thinking, planning, living in families as husbands, wives and children, and, above all, confessing and worshiping the Christian's God and looking hopefully for life and immortality beyond the grave, we are called upon to prove that we are men!

Would you have me argue that man is entitled to liberty? that he is the rightful owner of his own body? You have already declared it. Must I argue the wrongfulness of slavery? Is that a question for republicans? Is it to be settled by the rules of logic and argumentation, as a matter beset with great difficulty, involving a doubtful application of the principle of justice, hard to be understood? How should I look today, in the presence of Americans, dividing and subdividing a discourse, to show that men have a natural right to freedom, speaking of it relatively and positively, negatively and affirmatively? To do so would be to make myself ridiculous and to offer an insult to your understanding. There is not a man beneath the canopy of heaven that does not know that slavery is wrong *for him*.

★ ★ ★

What, to the American slave, is your Fourth of July? I answer: a day that reveals to him, more than all other days in the year, the gross injustice and cruelty to which he is the constant victim. To him, your celebration is a sham; your boasted liberty an unholy license; your national greatness swelling vanity; your sounds of rejoicing are empty and heartless; your denunciation of tyrants brass-fronted impudence; your shouts of liberty and equality hollow mockery; your prayers and hymns, your sermons and thanksgivings, with all your religious parade and solemnity, are to Him mere bombast, fraud, deception, impiety and hypocrisy—a thin veil to cover up crimes which would disgrace a nation of savages. There is not a nation on the earth guilty of practices more shocking and bloody than are the people of the United States at this very hour.

Go where you may, search where you will, roam through all the monarchies and despotisms of the Old World, travel through South America, search out every abuse, and when you have found the last, lay your facts by the side of the everyday practices of this nation, and you will say with me, that, for revolting barbarity and shameless hypocrisy, America reigns without a rival.

★ ★ ★

Americans! your republican politics, not less than your republican religion, are flagrantly inconsistent. You boast of your love of liberty, your superior civilization and your pure Christianity, while the whole political power of the nation (as embodied in the two great political parties) is solemnly pledged to support and perpetuate the enslavement of three millions of your countrymen. You hurl your anathemas at the crowned-headed tyrants of Russia and Austria and pride yourselves on your democratic institutions, while you yourselves consent to be the mere *tools* and *bodyguards* of the tyrants of Virginia and Carolina. You invite to your shores fugitives of oppression from abroad, honor them with banquets, greet them with ovations, cheer them, toast them, salute them, protect them, and pour out your money to them like water; but the fugitives from your own land you advertise, hunt, arrest, shoot and kill. You glory in your refinement and your universal education; yet you maintain a system as barbarous and dreadful as ever stained the character of a nation—a system begun in avarice, supported in pride, and perpetuated in cruelty. You shed tears over fallen Hungary, and make the sad story of her wrongs the theme of your poets, statesmen and orators, till your gallant sons are ready to fly to arms to vindicate her cause against the oppressor; but, in regard to the ten thousand wrongs of the American slave, you would enforce the strictest silence and would hail him as an enemy of the nation who dares to make those wrongs the subject of public discourse! You are all on fire at the mention of liberty for France or for Ireland, but are as cold as an iceberg at the thought of liberty for the enslaved of America. You discourse eloquently on the dignity of labor; yet, you sustain a system which, in its very essence, casts a stigma upon labor. You can bare your bosom to the storm of British artillery to throw off a three-penny tax on tea, and yet wring the last hard-earned farthing from the grasp of the black laborers of your country. You profess to believe "that of one blood God made all nations of men to dwell on the face of all the earth"[†] and hath commanded all men, everywhere, to love one another; yet you notoriously hate (and glory in your hatred) all men whose skins are not colored like your own. You declare before the world, and are understood by the world to declare, that you "*hold these truths to be self-evident, that all men are created equal; and are endowed by their Creator with certain unalienable rights; and that among these are, life, liberty and the pursuit of happiness*"; *and yet, you hold securely, in a bondage which, according to your own Thomas Jefferson, "is worse than ages of that which your fathers rose in rebellion to oppose," a seventh part* of the inhabitants of your country.

Fellow citizens, I will not enlarge further on your national inconsistencies. The existence of slavery in this country brands your republicanism as a sham, your humanity as a base pretense, and your Christianity as a lie. It destroys your moral power abroad; it corrupts your politicians at home. It saps the foundation of religion; it makes your name a hissing and a byword to a mocking earth. It is the antagonistic force in your government, the only thing that seriously disturbs and endangers your union. It fetters your progress; it is the enemy of improvement; the deadly foe of education; it fosters pride; it breeds insolence; it promotes vice; it shelters crime; it is a curse to the earth that supports it; and yet you cling to it as if it were the sheet anchor of all your hopes.

★ ★ ★

Allow me to say, in conclusion, notwithstanding the dark picture I have this day presented, of the state of the nation, I do not despair of this country. There are forces in operation which must inevitably work the downfall of slavery.

---

*The fledgling Hungarian republic was invaded by Austria and Russia in 1849.

†Acts 17:26.

THE GETTYSBURG ADDRESS (1863)

Four score and seven years ago our fathers brought forth on this continent, a new nation, conceived in Liberty, and dedicated to the proposition that all men are created equal.

Now we are engaged in a great civil war, testing whether that nation, or any nation so conceived and so dedicated, can long endure. We are met on a great battle field of that war. We have come to dedicate a portion of that field, as a final resting place for those who here gave their lives that that nation might live. It is altogether fitting and proper that we should do this.

But, in a larger sense, we can not dedicate—we can not consecrate—we can not hallow—this ground. The brave men, living and dead, who struggled here, have consecrated it, far above our poor power to add or detract. The world will little note, nor long remember what we say here, but it can never forget what they did here. It is for us the living, rather, to be dedicated here to the unfinished work which they who fought here have thus far so nobly advanced. It is rather for us to be here dedicated to the great task remaining before us—that from these honored dead we take increased devotion to that cause for which they gave the last full measure of devotion—that we here highly resolve that these dead shall not have died in vain—that this nation, under God, shall have a new birth of freedom—and that government of the people, by the people, for the people, shall not perish from the earth.

Abraham Lincoln
November 19, 1863

ABRAHAM LINCOLN'S SECOND INAUGURAL ADDRESS (1865)

Fellow Countrymen:

At this second appearing to take the oath of the presidential office, there is less occasion for an extended address than there was at the first. Then a statement, somewhat in detail, of a course to be pursued, seemed fitting and proper. Now, at the expiration of four years, during which public declarations have been constantly called forth on every point and phase of the great contest which still absorbs the attention, and engrosses the energies of the nation, little that is new could be presented. The progress of our arms, upon which all else chiefly depends, is as well known to the public as to myself; and it is, I trust, reasonably satisfactory and encouraging to all. With high hope for the future, no prediction in regard to it is ventured.

On the occasion corresponding to this four years ago, all thoughts were anxiously directed to an impending civil war. All dreaded it—all sought to avert it. While the inaugural address was being delivered from this place, devoted altogether to *saving* the Union without war, insurgent agents were in the city seeking to *destroy* it without war—seeking to dissolve the Union, and divide effects, by negotiation. Both parties deprecated war; but one of them would *make* war rather than let the nation survive; and the other would *accept* war rather than let it perish. And the war came.

One eighth of the whole population were colored slaves, not distributed generally over the Union, but localized in the southern part of it. These slaves constituted a peculiar and powerful interest. All knew that this interest was, somehow, the cause of the war. To strengthen, perpetuate, and extend this interest was the object for which the insurgents would rend the Union, even by war; while the government claimed no right to do more than to restrict the territorial enlargement of it. Neither party expected for the war, the magnitude, or the duration, which it has already attained. Neither anticipated that the *cause* of the conflict might cease with, or even before, the conflict itself should cease. Each looked for an easier triumph, and a result less fundamental and astounding. Both read the same Bible, and pray to the same God; and each invokes His aid against the other. It may seem strange that any men should dare to ask a just God's assistance in wringing their bread from the sweat of other men's faces; but let us judge not that we be not judged. The prayers of both could not be answered; that of neither has been answered fully. The Almighty has His own purposes. "Woe unto the world because of offences! for it must needs be that offences come; but woe to that man by whom the offence cometh." If we shall suppose that American slavery is one of those offences which, in the providence of God, must needs come, but which, having continued through His appointed time, He now wills to remove, and that He gives to both North and South, this terrible war, as the woe due to those by whom the offence came, shall we discern therein any departure from those divine attributes which the believers in a living God always ascribe to Him? Fondly do we hope, fervently do we pray—that this mighty scourge of war may speedily pass away. Yet, if God wills that it continue until all the wealth piled by the bondsman's two hundred and fifty years of unrequited toil shall be sunk, and until every drop of blood drawn with the lash shall be paid by another drawn with the sword, as was said three thousand years ago, so still it must be said "the judgments of the Lord are true and righteous altogether."

With malice toward none; with charity for all; with firmness in the right as God gives us to see the right, let us strive on to finish the work we are in; to bind up the nation's wounds; to care for him who shall have borne the battle and for his widow and his orphan, to do all which may achieve and cherish a just and a lasting peace, among ourselves and with all nations.

THE POPULIST PLATFORM OF 1892

Assembled upon the 116th anniversary of the Declaration of Independence, the People's Party of America, in their first national convention, invoking upon their action the blessing of Almighty God, puts forth in the name and on behalf of the people of this country, the following preamble and declaration of principles:

PREAMBLE

The conditions which surround us best justify our co-operation; we meet in the midst of a nation brought to the verge of moral, political, and material ruin. Corruption dominates the ballot-box, the Legislatures, the Congress, and touches even the ermine of the bench. The people are demoralized; most of the States have been compelled to isolate the voters at the polling places to prevent universal intimidation and bribery. The newspapers are largely subsidized or muzzled, public opinion silenced, business prostrated, homes covered with mortgages, labor impoverished, and the land concentrating in the hands of the capitalists. The urban workmen are denied the right to organize for self-protection, imported pauperized labor beats down their wages, a hireling standing army, unrecognized by our laws, is established to shoot them down, and they are rapidly degenerating into European conditions. The fruits of the toil of millions are boldly stolen to build up the fortunes for a few, unprecedented in the history of mankind; and the possessors of these, in turn, despise the Republic and endanger liberty. From the same prolific womb of governmental injustice we breed the two great classes—tramps and millionaires.

The national power to create money is appropriated to enrich bondholders; a vast public debt, payable in legal tender currency, has been funded into gold-bearing bonds, thereby adding millions to the burdens of the people. Silver, which has been accepted as coin since the dawn of history, has been demonetized to add to the purchasing power of gold by decreasing the value of all forms of property as well as human labor, and the supply of currency is purposely abridged to fatten usurers, bankrupt enterprise, and enslave industry. A vast conspiracy against mankind has been organized on two continents, and it is rapidly taking possession of the world. If not met and overthrown at once it forebodes terrible social convulsions, the destruction of civilization, or the establishment of an absolute despotism.

We have witnessed for more than a quarter of a century the struggles of the two great political parties for power and plunder, while grievous wrongs have been inflicted upon the suffering people. We charge that the controlling influences dominating both these parties have permitted the existing dreadful conditions to develop without serious effort to prevent or restrain them. Neither do they now promise us any substantial reform. They have agreed together to ignore in the coming campaign every issue but one. They propose to drown the outcries of a plundered people with the uproar of a sham battle over the tariff, so that capitalists, corporations, national banks, rings, trusts, watered stock, the demonetization of silver, and the oppressions of the usurers may all be lost sight of. They propose to sacrifice our homes, lives, and children on the altar of mammon; to destroy the multitude in order to secure corruption funds from the millionaires.

Assembled on the anniversary of the birthday of the nation, and filled with the spirit of the grand general and chief who established our independence, we seek to restore the government of the Republic to the hands of "the plain people," with which class it originated. We assert our purpose to be identical with the purposes of the National Constitution, "to form a more perfect union and establish justice, insure domestic tranquility, provide for the common defense, promote the general welfare, and secure the blessings of liberty for ourselves and our posterity." We declare that this Republic can only endure as a free government while built upon the love of the whole people for each other and for the nation; that it cannot be pinned together by bayonets; that the civil war is over, and that every passion and resentment which grew out of it must die with it; and that we must be in fact, as we are in name, one united brotherhood of free men.

Our country finds itself confronted by conditions for which there is no precedent in the history of the world; our annual agricultural productions amount to billions of dollars in value, which must, within a few weeks or months, be exchanged for billions of dollars of commodities consumed in their production; the existing currency supply is wholly inadequate to make this exchange; the results are falling prices, the formation of combines and rings, the impoverishment of the producing class. We pledge ourselves, if given power, we will labor to correct these evils by wise and reasonable legislation, in accordance with the terms of our platform. We believe that the power of government—in other words, of the people—should be expanded (as in the case of the postal service) as rapidly and as far as the good sense of an intelligent people and the teaching of experience shall justify, to the end that oppression, injustice, and poverty shall eventually cease in the land.

While our sympathies as a party of reform are naturally upon the side of every proposition which will tend to make men intelligent, virtuous, and temperate, we nevertheless regard these questions—important as they are—as secondary to the great issues now pressing for solution, and upon which not only our individual prosperity but the very existence of free institutions depend; and we ask all men to first help us to determine whether we are to have a republic to administer before we differ as to the conditions upon which it is to be administered, believing that the forces of reform this day organized will never cease to move forward until every wrong is remedied, and equal rights and equal privileges securely established for all the men and women of this country.

PLATFORM

We declare, therefore—

First.—That the union of the labor forces of the United States this day consummated shall be permanent and perpetual; may its spirit enter into all hearts for the salvation of the Republic and the uplifting of mankind!

Second.—Wealth belongs to him who creates it, and every dollar taken from industry without an equivalent is robbery. "If any will not work, neither shall he eat." The interests of rural and civic labor are the same; their enemies are identical.

Third.—We believe that the time has come when the railroad corporations will either own the people or the people must own the railroads; and, should the government enter upon the work of owning and managing all railroads, we should favor an amendment to the Constitution by which all persons engaged in the government service shall be placed under a civil-service regulation of the most rigid character, so as to prevent the increase of the power of the national administration by the use of such additional government employees.

FINANCE.—We demand a national currency, safe, sound, and flexible, issued by the general government only, a full legal tender for all debts, public and private, and that without the use of banking corporations, a just, equitable, and efficient means of distribution direct to the people, at a tax not to exceed two per cent per annum, to be provided as set forth in the sub-treasury plan of the Farmers' Alliance, or a better system; also by payments in discharge of its obligations for public improvements.

1. We demand free and unlimited coinage of silver and gold at the present legal ratio of 16 to 1.

2. We demand that the amount of circulating medium be speedily increased to not less than $50 per capita.

3. We demand a graduated income tax.

4. We believe that the money of the country should be kept as much as possible in the hands of the people, and hence we demand that all State and national revenues shall be limited to the necessary expenses of the government, economically and honestly administered.

5. We demand that postal savings banks be established by the government for the safe deposit of the earnings of the people and to facilitate exchange.

TRANSPORTATION.—Transportation being a means of exchange and a public necessity, the government should own and operate the railroads in the interest of the people. The telegraph and telephone, like the post-office system, being a necessity for the transmission of news, should be owned and operated by the government in the interest of the people.

LAND.—The land, including all the natural sources of wealth, is the heritage of the people, and should not be monopolized for speculative purposes, and alien ownership of land should be prohibited. All land now held by railroads and other corporations in excess of their actual needs, and all lands now owned by aliens should be reclaimed by the government and held for actual settlers only.

EXPRESSION OF SENTIMENTS

Your committee on Platform and Resolutions beg leave unanimously to report the following:

Whereas, Other questions have been presented for our consideration, we hereby submit the following, not as a part of the Platform of the People's Party, but as resolutions expressive of the sentiment of this Convention:

1. *Resolved*, That we demand a free ballot and a fair count in all elections, and pledge ourselves to secure it to every legal voter without federal intervention, through the adoption by the States of the unperverted Australian or secret ballot system.

2. *Resolved*, That the revenue derived from a graduated income tax should be applied to the reduction of the burden of taxation now levied upon the domestic industries of this country.

3. *Resolved*, That we pledge our support to fair and liberal pensions to ex-Union soldiers and sailors.

4. *Resolved*, That we condemn the fallacy of protecting American labor under the present system, which opens our ports to the pauper and criminal classes of the world, and crowds out our wage-earners; and we denounce the present ineffective laws against contract labor, and demand the further restriction of undesirable emigration.

5. *Resolved*, that we cordially sympathize with the efforts of organized workingmen to shorten the hours of labor, and demand a rigid enforcement of the existing eight-hour law on Government work, and ask that a penalty clause be added to the said law.

6. *Resolved*, That we regard the maintenance of a large standing army of mercenaries, known as the Pinkerton system, as a menace to our liberties, and we demand its abolition; and we condemn the recent invasion of the Territory of Wyoming by the hired assassins of plutocracy, assisted by federal officers.

7. *Resolved*, That we commend to the favorable consideration of the people and the reform press the legislative system known as the initiative and referendum.

8. *Resolved*, That we favor a constitutional provision limiting the office of President and Vice-President to one term, and providing for the election of Senators of the United States by a direct vote of the people.

9. *Resolved*, That we oppose any subsidy or national aid to any private corporation for any purpose.

10. *Resolved*, That this convention sympathizes with the Knights of Labor and their righteous contest with the tyrannical combine of clothing manufacturers of Rochester, and declare it to be the duty of all who hate tyranny and oppression to refuse to purchase the goods made by the said manufacturers, or to patronize any merchants who sell such goods.

FRANKLIN D. ROOSEVELT'S FIRST INAUGURAL ADDRESS (1933)

I am certain that my fellow Americans expect that on my induction into the Presidency I will address them with a candor and a decision which the present situation of our Nation impels. This is preeminently the time to speak the truth, the whole truth, frankly and boldly. Nor need we shrink from honestly facing conditions in our country today. This great Nation will endure as it has endured, will revive and will prosper. So, first of all, let me assert my firm belief that the only thing we have to fear is fear itself—nameless, unreasoning, unjustified terror which paralyzes needed efforts to convert retreat into advance. In every dark hour of our national life a leadership of frankness and vigor has met with that understanding and support of the people themselves which is essential to victory. I am convinced that you will again give that support to leadership in these critical days.

In such a spirit on my part and on yours we face our common difficulties. They concern, thank God, only material things. Values have shrunken to fantastic levels; taxes have risen; our ability to pay has fallen; government of all kinds is faced by serious curtailment of income; the means of exchange are frozen in the currents of trade; the withered leaves of industrial enterprise lie on every side; farmers find no markets for their produce; the savings of many years in thousands of families are gone.

More important, a host of unemployed citizens face the grim problem of existence, and an equally great number toil with little return. Only a foolish optimist can deny the dark realities of the moment.

Yet our distress comes from no failure of substance. We are stricken by no plague of locusts. Compared with the perils which our forefathers conquered because they believed and were not afraid, we have still much to be thankful for. Nature still offers her bounty and human efforts have multiplied it. Plenty is at our doorstep, but a generous use of it languishes in the very sight of the supply. Primarily this is because the rulers of the exchange of mankind's goods have failed, through their own stubbornness and their own incompetence, have admitted their failure, and abdicated. Practices of the unscrupulous money changers stand indicted in the court of public opinion, rejected by the hearts and minds of men.

True they have tried, but their efforts have been cast in the pattern of an outworn tradition. Faced by failure of credit they have proposed only the lending of more money. Stripped of the lure of profit by which to induce our people to follow their false leadership, they have resorted to exhortations, pleading tearfully for restored confidence. They know only the rules of a generation of self-seekers. They have no vision, and when there is no vision the people perish.

The money changers have fled from their high seats in the temple of our civilization. We may now restore that temple to the ancient truths. The measure of the restoration lies in the extent to which we apply social values more noble than mere monetary profit.

Happiness lies not in the mere possession of money; it lies in the joy of achievement, in the thrill of creative effort. The joy and moral stimulation of work no longer must be forgotten in the mad chase of evanescent profits. These dark days will be worth all they cost us if they teach us that our true destiny is not to be ministered unto but to minister to ourselves and to our fellow men.

Recognition of the falsity of material wealth as the standard of success goes hand in hand with the abandonment of the false belief that public office and high political position are to be valued only by the standards of pride of place and personal profit; and there must be an end to a conduct in banking and in business which too often has given to a sacred trust the likeness of callous and selfish wrongdoing. Small wonder that confidence languishes, for it thrives only on honesty, on honor, on the sacredness of obligations, on faithful protection, on unselfish performance; without them it cannot live.

Restoration calls, however, not for changes in ethics alone. This Nation asks for action, and action now.

Our greatest primary task is to put people to work. This is no unsolvable problem if we face it wisely and courageously. It can be accomplished in part by direct recruiting by the Government itself, treating the task as we would treat the emergency of a war, but at the same time, through this employment, accomplishing greatly needed projects to stimulate and reorganize the use of our natural resources.

Hand in hand with this we must frankly recognize the overbalance of population in our industrial centers and, by engaging on a national scale in a redistribution, endeavor to provide a better use of the land for those best fitted for the land. The task can be helped by definite efforts to raise the values of agricultural products and with this the power to purchase the output of our cities. It can be helped by preventing realistically the tragedy of the growing loss through foreclosure of our small homes and our farms. It can be helped by insistence that the Federal, State, and local governments act forthwith on the demand that their cost be drastically reduced. It can be helped by the unifying of relief activities which today are often scattered, uneconomical, and unequal. It can be helped by national planning for and supervision of all forms of transportation and of communications and other utilities which have a definitely public character. There are many ways in which it can be helped, but it can never be helped merely by talking about it. We must act and act quickly.

Finally, in our progress toward a resumption of work we require two safeguards against a return of the evils of the old order; there must be a strict supervision of all banking and credits and investments; there must be an end to speculation with other people's money, and there must be provision for an adequate but sound currency.

There are the lines of attack. I shall presently urge upon a new Congress, in special session, detailed measures for their fulfillment, and I shall seek the immediate assistance of the several States.

Through this program of action we address ourselves to putting our own national house in order and making income balance outgo. Our international trade relations, though vastly important, are in point of time and necessity secondary to the establishment of a sound national economy. I favor as a practical policy the putting of first things first. I shall spare no effort to restore world trade by international economic readjustment, but the emergency at home cannot wait on that accomplishment.

The basic thought that guides these specific means of national recovery is not narrowly nationalistic. It is the insistence, as a first consideration, upon the interdependence of the various elements in all parts of the United States—a recognition of the old and permanently important manifestation of the American spirit of the pioneer. It is the way to recovery. It is the immediate way. It is the strongest assurance that the recovery will endure.

In the field of world policy I would dedicate this Nation to the policy of the good neighbor—the neighbor who resolutely respects himself and, because he does so, respects the rights of others—the neighbor who respects his obligations and respects the sanctity of his agreements in and with a world of neighbors.

If I read the temper of our people correctly, we now realize as we have never realized before our interdependence on each other; that we cannot merely take but we must give as well; that if we are to go forward, we must move as a trained and loyal army willing to sacrifice for the good of a common discipline, because without such discipline no progress is made, no leadership becomes effective. We are, I know, ready and willing to submit our lives and property to such discipline, because it makes possible a leadership which aims at a larger good. This I propose to offer, pledging that the larger purposes will bind upon us all as a sacred obligation with a unity of duty hitherto evoked only in time of armed strife.

With this pledge taken, I assume unhesitatingly the leadership of this great army of our people dedicated to a disciplined attack upon our common problems.

Action in this image and to this end is feasible under the form of government which we have inherited from our ancestors. Our Constitution is so simple and practical that it is possible always to meet extraordinary needs by changes in emphasis and arrangement without loss of essential form. That is why our constitutional system has proved itself the most superbly enduring political mechanism the modern world has produced. It has met every stress of vast expansion of territory, of foreign wars, of bitter internal strife, of world relations.

It is to be hoped that the normal balance of executive and legislative authority may be wholly adequate to meet the unprecedented task before us. But it may be that an unprecedented demand and need for undelayed action may call for temporary departure from that normal balance of public procedure.

I am prepared under my constitutional duty to recommend the measures that a stricken nation in the midst of a stricken world may require. These measures, or such other measures as the Congress may build out of its experience and wisdom, I shall seek, within my constitutional authority, to bring to speedy adoption.

But in the event that the Congress shall fail to take one of these two courses, and in the event that the national emergency is still critical, I shall not evade the clear course of duty that will then confront me. I shall ask the Congress for the one remaining instrument to meet the crisis—broad Executive power to wage a war against the emergency, as great as the power that would be given to me if we were in fact invaded by a foreign foe.

For the trust reposed in me I will return the courage and the devotion that befit the time. I can do no less.

We face the arduous days that lie before us in the warm courage of national unity; with the clear consciousness of seeking old and precious moral values; with the clean satisfaction that comes from the stern performance of duty by old and young alike. We aim at the assurance of a rounded and permanent national life.

We do not distrust the future of essential democracy. The people of the United States have not failed. In their need they have registered a mandate that they want direct, vigorous action. They have asked for discipline and direction under leadership. They have made me the present instrument of their wishes. In the spirit of the gift I take it.

In this dedication of a Nation we humbly ask the blessing of God. May He protect each and every one of us. May He guide me in the days to come.

FROM THE PROGRAM FOR THE MARCH ON WASHINGTON FOR JOBS AND FREEDOM (1963)

WHAT WE DEMAND*

1. Comprehensive and effective *civil rights legislation* from the present Congress—without compromise or filibuster—to guarantee all Americans

> access to all public accommodations
> decent housing
> adequate and integrated education
> the right to vote

2. Withholding of Federal funds from all programs in which discrimination exists.

3. *Desegregation of all school districts in 1963.*

4. Enforcement of the *Fourteenth Amendment*—reducing Congressional representation of states where citizens are disfranchised.

5. A new *Executive Order* banning discrimination in all housing supported by federal funds.

6. Authority for the Attorney General to institute *injunctive suits* when any constitutional right is violated.

7. A massive federal program to train and place all unemployed workers—Negro and white—on meaningful and dignified jobs at decent wages.

8. A national *minimum wage* act that will give all Americans a decent standard of living. (Government surveys show that anything less than $2.00 an hour fails to do this.)

9. A broadened *Fair Labor Standards Act* to include all areas of employment which are presently excluded.

10. A federal *Fair Employment Practices Act* barring discrimination by federal, state, and municipal governments, and by employers, contractors, employment agencies, and trade unions.

*Support of the March does not necessarily indicate endorsement of every demand listed. Some organizations have not had an opportunity to take an official position on all of the demands advocated here.

RONALD REAGAN'S FIRST INAUGURAL ADDRESS (1981)

WEST FRONT OF THE U.S. CAPITOL JANUARY 20, 1981

Senator Hatfield, Mr. Chief Justice, Mr. President, Vice President Bush, Vice President Mondale, Senator Baker, Speaker O'Neill, Reverend Moomaw, and my fellow citizens.

To a few of us here today this is a solemn and most momentous occasion, and yet in the history of our nation it is a commonplace occurrence. The orderly transfer of authority as called for in the Constitution routinely takes place, as it has for almost two centuries, and few of us stop to think how unique we really are. In the eyes of many in the world, this every-four-year ceremony we accept as normal is nothing less than a miracle.

Mr. President, I want our fellow citizens to know how much you did to carry on this tradition. By your gracious cooperation in the transition process, you have shown a watching world that we are a united people pledged to maintaining a political system which guarantees individual liberty to a greater degree than any other, and I thank you and your people for all your help in maintaining the continuity which is the bulwark of our republic. The business of our nation goes forward. These United States are confronted with an economic affliction of great proportions. We suffer from the longest and one of the worst sustained inflations in our national history. It distorts our economic decisions, penalizes thrift, and crushes the struggling young and the fixed-income elderly alike. It threatens to shatter the lives of millions of our people.

Idle industries have cast workers into unemployment, human misery, and personal indignity. Those who do work are denied a fair return for their labor by a tax system which penalizes successful achievement and keeps us from maintaining full productivity. But great as our tax burden is, it has not kept pace with public spending. For decades we have piled deficit upon deficit, mortgaging our future and our children's future for the temporary convenience of the present. To continue this long trend is to guarantee tremendous social, cultural, political, and economic upheavals.

You and I, as individuals, can, by borrowing, live beyond our means, but for only a limited period of time. Why, then, should we think that collectively, as a nation, we're not bound by that same limitation? We must act today in order to preserve tomorrow. And let there be no misunderstanding: We are going to begin to act, beginning today. The economic ills we suffer have come upon us over several decades. They will not go away in days, weeks, or months, but they will go away. They will go away because we as Americans have the capacity now, as we've had in the past, to do whatever needs to be done to preserve this last and greatest bastion of freedom.

In this present crisis, government is not the solution to our problem; government is the problem. From time to time we've been tempted to believe that society has become too complex to be managed by self-rule, that government by an elite group is superior to government for, by, and of the people. Well, if no one among us is capable of governing himself, then who among us has the capacity to govern someone else? All of us together, in and out of government, must bear the burden. The solutions we seek must be equitable, with no one group singled out to pay a higher price.

We hear much of special interest groups. Well, our concern must be for a special interest group that has been too long neglected. It knows no sectional boundaries or ethnic and racial divisions, and it crosses political party lines. It is made up of men and women who raise our food, patrol our streets, man our mines and factories, teach our children, keep our homes, and heal us when we're sick—professionals, industrialists, shopkeepers, clerks, cabbies, and truck drivers. They are, in short, "we the people," this breed called Americans.

Well, this administration's objective will be a healthy, vigorous, growing economy that provides equal opportunities for all Americans, with no barriers born of bigotry or discrimination. Putting America back to work means putting all Americans back to work. Ending inflation means freeing all Americans from the terror of runaway living costs. All must share in the productive work of this "new beginning," and all must share in the bounty of a revived economy. With the idealism and fair play which are the core of our system and our strength, we can have a strong and prosperous America, at peace with itself and the world.

So, as we begin, let us take inventory. We are a nation that has a government—not the other way around. And this makes us special among the nations of the Earth. Our government has no power except that granted it by the people. It is time to check and reverse the growth of government, which shows signs of having grown beyond the consent of the governed.

It is my intention to curb the size and influence of the federal establishment and to demand recognition of the distinction between the powers granted to the federal government and those reserved to the states or to the people. All of us need to be reminded that the federal government did not create the states; the states created the federal government.

Now, so there will be no misunderstanding, it's not my intention to do away with government. It is rather to make it work—work with us, not over us; to stand by our side, not ride on our back. Government can and must provide opportunity, not smother it; foster productivity, not stifle it.

If we look to the answer as to why for so many years we achieved so much, prospered as no other people on earth, it was because here in this land we unleashed the energy and individual genius of man to a greater extent than has ever been done before. Freedom and the dignity of the individual have been more available and assured here than in any other place on earth. The price for this freedom at times has been high, but we have never been unwilling to pay the price.

It is no coincidence that our present troubles parallel and are proportionate to the intervention and intrusion in our lives that result from unnecessary and excessive growth of government. It is time for us to realize that we're too great a nation to limit ourselves to small dreams. We're not, as some would have us believe, doomed to an inevitable decline. I do not believe in a fate that will fall on us no matter what we do. I do believe in a fate that will fall on us if we do nothing. So, with all the creative energy at our command, let us begin an era of national renewal. Let us renew our determination, our courage, and our strength. And let us renew our faith and our hope.

We have every right to dream heroic dreams. Those who say that we're in a time when there are no heroes, they just don't know where to look. You can see heroes every day going in and out of factory gates. Others, a handful in number, produce enough food to feed all of us and then the world beyond. You meet heroes across a counter, and they're on both sides of that counter. There are entrepreneurs with faith in themselves and faith in an idea who create new jobs, new wealth and opportunity. They're individuals and families whose taxes support the government and whose voluntary gifts support church, charity, culture, art, and education. Their patriotism is quiet, but deep. Their values sustain our national life.

Now, I have used the words "they" and "their" in speaking of these heroes. I could say "you" and "your," because I'm addressing the heroes of whom I speak—you, the citizens of this blessed land. Your dreams, your hopes, your goals are going to be the dreams, the hopes, and the goals of this administration, so help me God.

We shall reflect the compassion that is so much a part of your makeup. How can we love our country and not love our countrymen; and loving them, reach out a hand when they fall, heal them when they're sick, and provide opportunity to make them self-sufficient so they will be equal in fact and not just in theory?

Can we solve the problems confronting us? Well, the answer is an unequivocal and emphatic "yes." To paraphrase Winston Churchill, I did not take the oath I've just taken with the intention of presiding over the dissolution of the world's strongest economy.

In the days ahead I will propose removing the roadblocks that have slowed our economy and reduced productivity. Steps will be taken aimed at restoring the balance between the various levels of government. Progress may be slow, measured in inches and feet, not miles, but we will progress. It is time to reawaken this industrial giant, to get government back within its means, and to lighten our punitive tax burden. And these will be our first priorities, and on these principles there will be no compromise.

On the eve of our struggle for independence a man who might have been one of the greatest among the Founding Fathers, Dr. Joseph Warren, president of the Massachusetts Congress, said to his fellow Americans, "Our country is in danger, but not to be despaired of . . . On you depend the fortunes of America. You are to decide the important questions upon which rests the happiness and the liberty of millions yet unborn. Act worthy of yourselves." Well, I believe we, the Americans of today, are ready to act worthy of ourselves, ready to do what must be done to ensure happiness and liberty for ourselves, our children, and our children's children. And as we renew ourselves here in our own land, we will be seen as having greater strength throughout the world. We will again be the exemplar of freedom and a beacon of hope for those who do not now have freedom.

To those neighbors and allies who share our freedom, we will strengthen our historic ties and assure them of our support and firm commitment. We will match loyalty with loyalty. We will strive for mutually beneficial relations. We will not use our friendship to impose on their sovereignty, for our own sovereignty is not for sale. As for the enemies of freedom, those who are potential adversaries, they will be reminded that peace is the highest aspiration of the American people. We will negotiate for it, sacrifice for it; we will not surrender for it, now or ever.

Our forbearance should never be misunderstood. Our reluctance for conflict should not be misjudged as a failure of will. When action is required to preserve our national security, we will act. We will maintain sufficient strength to prevail if need be, knowing that if we do so we have the best chance of never having to use that strength. Above all, we must realize that no arsenal or no weapon in the arsenals of the world is so formidable as the will and moral courage of free men

and women. It is a weapon our adversaries in today's world do not have. It is a weapon that we as Americans do have. Let that be understood by those who practice terrorism and prey upon their neighbors. I'm told that tens of thousands of prayer meetings are being held on this day, and for that I'm deeply grateful. We are a nation under God, and I believe God intended for us to be free. It would be fitting and good, I think, if on each Inaugural Day in future years it should be declared a day of prayer.

This is the first time in our history that this ceremony has been held, as you've been told, on the West Front of the Capitol. Standing here, one faces a magnificent vista, opening up on the city's special beauty and history. At the end of this open mall are those shrines to the giants on whose shoulders we stand.

Directly in front of me, the monument to a monumental man, George Washington, father of our country. A man of humility who came to greatness reluctantly. He led Americans out of revolutionary victory into infant nationhood. Off to one side, the stately memorial to Thomas Jefferson. The Declaration of Independence flames with his eloquence. And then, beyond the Reflecting Pool, the dignified columns of the Lincoln Memorial. Whoever would understand in his heart the meaning of America will find it in the life of Abraham Lincoln.

Beyond those monuments to heroism is the Potomac River, and on the far shore the sloping hills of Arlington National Cemetery, with its row upon row of simple white markers bearing crosses and Stars of David. They add up to only a tiny fraction of the price that has been paid for our freedom. Each one of those markers is a monument to the kind of hero I spoke of earlier. Their lives ended in places called Belleau Wood, the Argonne, Omaha Beach, Salerno, and halfway around the world on Guadalcanal, Tarawa, Pork Chop Hill, the Chosin Reservoir, and in a hundred rice paddies and jungles of a place called Vietnam.

Under one such marker lies a young man, Martin Treptow, who left his job in a small town barbershop in 1917 to go to France with the famed Rainbow Division. There, on the western front, he was killed trying to carry a message between battalions under heavy artillery fire.

We're told that on his body was found a diary. On the flyleaf under the heading "My Pledge," he had written these words: "America must win this war. Therefore I will work, I will save, I will sacrifice, I will endure, I will fight cheerfully and do my utmost, as if the issue of the whole struggle depended on me alone."

The crisis we are facing today does not require of us the kind of sacrifice that Martin Treptow and so many thousands of others were called upon to make. It does require, however, our best effort and our willingness to believe in ourselves and to believe in our capacity to perform great deeds, to believe that together with God's help we can and will resolve the problems which now confront us.

And after all, why shouldn't we believe that? We are Americans.

God bless you, and thank you.

BARACK OBAMA'S FIRST INAUGURAL ADDRESS (2009)

My fellow citizens: I stand here today humbled by the task before us, grateful for the trust you've bestowed, mindful of the sacrifices borne by our ancestors.

I thank President Bush for his service to our nation—(*applause*)—as well as the generosity and cooperation he has shown throughout this transition.

Forty-four Americans have now taken the presidential oath. The words have been spoken during rising tides of prosperity and the still waters of peace. Yet, every so often, the oath is taken amidst gathering clouds and raging storms. At these moments, America has carried on not simply because of the skill or vision of those in high office, but because we, the people, have remained faithful to the ideals of our forebears and true to our founding documents.

So it has been: so it must be with this generation of Americans.

That we are in the midst of crisis is now well understood. Our nation is at war against a far-reaching network of violence and hatred. Our economy is badly weakened, a consequence of greed and irresponsibility on the part of some, but also our collective failure to make hard choices and prepare the nation for a new age. Homes have been lost, jobs shed, businesses shuttered. Our health care is too costly, our schools fail too many—and each day brings further evidence that the ways we use energy strengthen our adversaries and threaten our planet.

These are the indicators of crisis, subject to data and statistics. Less measurable, but no less profound, is a sapping of confidence across our land; a nagging fear that America's decline is inevitable, that the next generation must lower its sights.

Today I say to you that the challenges we face are real. They are serious and they are many. They will not be met easily or in a short span of time. But know this America: They will be met. (*Applause*)

On this day, we gather because we have chosen hope over fear, unity of purpose over conflict and discord. On this day, we come to proclaim an end to the petty grievances and false promises, the recriminations and worn-out dogmas that for far too long have strangled our politics. We remain a young nation. But in the words of Scripture, the time has come to set aside childish things. The time has come to reaffirm our enduring spirit; to choose our better history; to carry forward that precious gift, that noble idea passed on from generation to generation; the God-given promise that all are equal, all are free, and all deserve a chance to pursue their full measure of happiness. (*Applause*)

In reaffirming the greatness of our nation we understand that greatness is never a given. It must be earned. Our journey has never been one of short-cuts or settling for less. It has not been the path for the faint-hearted, for those that prefer leisure over work, or seek only the pleasures of riches and fame. Rather, it has been the risk-takers, the doers, the makers of things—some celebrated, but more often men and women obscure in their labor—who have carried us up the long rugged path towards prosperity and freedom.

For us, they packed up their few worldly possessions and traveled across oceans in search of a new life. For us, they toiled in sweatshops, and settled the West, endured the lash of the whip, and plowed the hard earth. For us, they fought and died in places like Concord and Gettysburg, Normandy and Khe Sahn.

Time and again these men and women struggled and sacrificed and worked till their hands were raw so that we might live a better life. They saw America as bigger than the sum of our individual ambitions, greater than all the differences of birth or wealth or faction.

This is the journey we continue today. We remain the most prosperous, powerful nation on Earth. Our workers are no less productive than when this crisis began. Our minds are no less inventive, our goods and services no less needed than they were last week, or last month, or last year. Our capacity remains undiminished. But our time of standing pat, of protecting narrow interests and putting off unpleasant decisions—that time has surely passed. Starting today, we must pick ourselves up, dust ourselves off, and begin again the work of remaking America. (*Applause*)

For everywhere we look, there is work to be done. The state of our economy calls for action, bold and swift. And we will act, not only to create new jobs, but to lay a new foundation for growth. We will build the roads and bridges, the electric grids and digital lines that feed our commerce and bind us together. We'll restore science to its rightful place, and wield technology's wonders to raise health care's quality and lower its cost. We will harness the sun and the winds and the soil to fuel our cars and run our factories. And we will transform our schools and colleges and universities to meet the demands of a new age. All this we can do. All this we will do.

Now, there are some who question the scale of our ambitions, who suggest that our system cannot tolerate too many big plans. Their memories are short, for they have forgotten what this country has already done, what free men and women can achieve when imagination is joined to common purpose, and necessity to courage. What the cynics fail to understand is that the ground has shifted beneath them, that the stale political arguments that have consumed us for so long no longer apply.

The question we ask today is not whether our government is too big or too small, but whether it works—whether it helps families find jobs at a decent wage, care they can afford, a retirement that is dignified. Where the answer is yes, we intend to move forward. Where the answer is no, programs will end. And those of us who manage the public's dollars will be held to account, to spend wisely, reform bad habits, and do our business in the light of day, because only then can we restore the vital trust between a people and their government.

Nor is the question before us whether the market is a force for good or ill. Its power to generate wealth and expand freedom is unmatched. But this crisis has reminded us that without a watchful eye, the market can spin out of control. The nation cannot prosper long when it favors only the prosperous. The success of our economy has always depended not just on the size of our gross domestic product, but on the reach of our prosperity, on the ability to extend opportunity to every willing heart—not out of charity, but because it is the surest route to our common good. (*Applause*)

As for our common defense, we reject as false the choice between our safety and our ideals. Our Founding Fathers—(*Applause*)—our Founding Fathers, faced with perils that we can scarcely imagine, drafted a charter to assure the rule of law and the rights of man—a charter expanded by the blood of generations. Those ideals still light the world, and we will not give them up for expedience sake. (*Applause*)

And so, to all the other peoples and governments who are watching today, from the grandest capitals to the small village where my father was born, know that America is a friend of each nation, and every man, woman and child who seeks a future of peace and dignity. And we are ready to lead once more. (*Applause*)

Recall that earlier generations faced down fascism and communism not just with missiles and tanks, but with the sturdy alliances and enduring convictions. They understood that our power alone cannot protect us, nor does it entitle us to do as we please. Instead they knew that our power grows through its prudent use; our security emanates from the justness of our cause, the force of our example, the tempering qualities of humility and restraint.

We are the keepers of this legacy. Guided by these principles once more we can meet those new threats that demand even greater effort, even greater cooperation and understanding between nations. We will begin to responsibly leave Iraq to its people and forge a hard-earned peace in Afghanistan. With old friends and former foes, we'll work tirelessly to lessen the nuclear threat, and roll back the specter of a warming planet.

We will not apologize for our way of life, nor will we waver in its defense. And for those who seek to advance their aims by inducing terror and slaughtering innocents, we say to you now that our spirit is stronger and cannot be broken—you cannot outlast us, and we will defeat you. (*Applause*)

For we know that our patchwork heritage is a strength, not a weakness. We are a nation of Christians and Muslims, Jews and Hindus, and non-believers. We are shaped by every language and culture, drawn from every end of this Earth: and because we have tasted the bitter swill of civil war and segregation, and emerged from that dark chapter stronger and more united, we cannot help but believe that the old hatreds shall someday pass; that the lines of tribe shall soon dissolve; that as the world grows smaller, our common humanity shall reveal itself; and that America must play its role in ushering in a new era of peace.

To the Muslim world, we seek a new way forward, based on mutual interest and mutual respect. To those leaders around the globe who seek to sow conflict, or blame their society's ills on the West, know that your people will judge you on what you can build, not what you destroy. (*Applause*)

To those who cling to power through corruption and deceit and the silencing of dissent, know that you are on the wrong side of history, but that we will extend a hand if you are willing to unclench your fist. (*Applause*)

To the people of poor nations, we pledge to work alongside you to make your farms flourish and let clean waters flow; to nourish starved bodies and feed hungry minds. And to those nations like ours that enjoy relative plenty, we say we can no longer afford indifference to the suffering outside our borders, nor can we consume the world's resources without regard to effect. For the world has changed, and we must change with it.

As we consider the role that unfolds before us, we remember with humble gratitude those brave Americans who at this very hour patrol far-off deserts and distant mountains. They have something to tell us, just as the fallen heroes who lie in Arlington whisper through the ages.

We honor them not only because they are the guardians of our liberty, but because they embody the spirit of service—a willingness to find meaning in something greater than themselves.

And yet at this moment, a moment that will define a generation, it is precisely this spirit that must inhabit us all. For as much as government can do, and must do, it is ultimately the faith and determination of the American people upon which this nation relies. It is the kindness to take in a stranger when the levees break, the selflessness of workers who would rather cut their hours than see a friend lose their job which sees us through our darkest hours. It is the firefighter's courage to storm a stairway filled with smoke, but also a parent's willingness to nurture a child that finally decides our fate.

Our challenges may be new. The instruments with which we meet them may be new. But those values upon which our success depends—honesty and hard work, courage and fair play, tolerance and curiosity, loyalty and patriotism—these things are old. These things are true. They have been the quiet force of progress throughout our history.

What is demanded, then, is a return to these truths. What is required of us now is a new era of responsibility—a recognition on the part of every American that we have duties to ourselves, our nation and the world; duties that we do not grudgingly accept, but rather seize gladly, firm in the knowledge that there is nothing so satisfying to the spirit, so defining of our character than giving our all to a difficult task.

This is the price and the promise of citizenship. This is the source of our confidence—the knowledge that God calls on us to shape an uncertain destiny. This is the meaning of our liberty and our creed, why men and women and children of every race and every faith can join in celebration across this magnificent mall; and why a man whose father less than 60 years ago might not have been served in a local restaurant can now stand before you to take a most sacred oath. (*Applause*)

So let us mark this day with remembrance of who we are and how far we have traveled. In the year of America's birth, in the coldest of months, a small band of patriots huddled by dying campfires on the shores of an icy river. The capital was abandoned. The enemy was advancing. The snow was stained with blood. At the moment when the outcome of our revolution was most in doubt, the father of our nation ordered these words to be read to the people:

"Let it be told to the future world . . . that in the depth of winter, when nothing but hope and virtue could survive . . . that the city and the country, alarmed at one common danger, came forth to meet [it]."

America: In the face of our common dangers, in this winter of our hardship, let us remember these timeless words. With hope and virtue, let us brave once more the icy currents, and endure what storms may come. Let it be said by our children's children that when we were tested we refused to let this journey end, that we did not turn back nor did we falter; and with eyes fixed on the horizon and God's grace upon us, we carried forth that great gift of freedom and delivered it safely to future generations.

Thank you. God bless you. And God bless the United States of America. (*Applause*)

PRESIDENTIAL ELECTIONS

Year	Number of States	Candidates	Parties	Popular Vote	% of Popular Vote	Electoral Vote	% Voter Participation
1789	11	**GEORGE WASHINGTON**	NO PARTY			69	
		John Adams	DESIGNATIONS			34	
		Other candidates				35	
1792	15	**GEORGE WASHINGTON**	NO PARTY			132	
		John Adams	DESIGNATIONS			77	
		George Clinton				50	
		Other candidates				5	
1796	16	**JOHN ADAMS**	FEDERALIST			71	
		Thomas Jefferson	Republican			68	
		Thomas Pinckney	Federalist			59	
		Aaron Burr	Republican			30	
		Other candidates				48	
1800	16	**THOMAS JEFFERSON**	REPUBLICAN			73	
		Aaron Burr	Republican			73	
		John Adams	Federalist			65	
		Charles C. Pinckney	Federalist			64	
		John Jay	Federalist			1	
1804	17	**THOMAS JEFFERSON**	REPUBLICAN			162	
		Charles C. Pinckney	Federalist			14	
1808	17	**JAMES MADISON**	REPUBLICAN			122	
		Charles C. Pinckney	Federalist			47	
		George Clinton	Republican			6	
1812	18	**JAMES MADISON**	REPUBLICAN			128	
		DeWitt Clinton	Federalist			89	

Year	Number of States	Candidates	Parties	Popular Vote	% of Popular Vote	Electoral Vote	% Voter Participation
1816	19	**JAMES MONROE** Rufus King	REPUBLICAN Federalist			183 34	
1820	24	**JAMES MONROE** John Quincy Adams	REPUBLICAN Independent			231 1	
1824	24	**JOHN QUINCY ADAMS** Andrew Jackson William H. Crawford Henry Clay	NO PARTY DESIGNATIONS	108,740 153,544 46,618 47,136	31.0 43.0 13.0 13.0	84 99 41 37	26.9
1828	24	**ANDREW JACKSON** John Quincy Adams	DEMOCRAT National Republican	647,286 508,064	56.0 44.0	178 83	57.6
1832	24	**ANDREW JACKSON** Henry Clay William Wirt John Floyd	DEMOCRAT National Republican Anti-Masonic Democrat	687,502 530,189 101,051	54.5 37.5 8.0	219 49 7 11	55.4
1836	26	**MARTIN VAN BUREN** William H. Harrison Hugh L. White Daniel Webster William P. Mangum	DEMOCRAT Whig Whig Whig Whig	765,483 739,795	51.0 49.0	170 73 26 14 11	57.8
1840	26	**WILLIAM H. HARRISON** Martin Van Buren	WHIG Democrat	1,274,624 1,127,781	53.0 47.0	234 60	80.2

Year	Number of States	Candidates	Parties	Popular Vote	% of Popular Vote	Electoral Vote	% Voter Participation
1844	26	**JAMES K. POLK**	DEMOCRAT	1,338,464	50.0	170	78.9
		Henry Clay	Whig	1,300,097	48.0	105	
		James G. Birney	Liberty	62,300	2.0		
1848	30	**ZACHARY TAYLOR**	WHIG	1,360,967	47.5	163	72.7
		Lewis Cass	Democrat	1,222,342	42.5	127	
		Martin Van Buren	Free Soil	291,263	10.0		
1852	31	**FRANKLIN PIERCE**	DEMOCRAT	1,601,117	51.0	254	69.6
		Winfield Scott	Whig	1,385,453	44.0	42	
		John P. Hale	Free Soil	155,825	5.0		
1856	31	**JAMES BUCHANAN**	DEMOCRAT	1,832,955	45.0	174	78.9
		John C. Frémont	Republican	1,339,932	33.0	114	
		Millard Fillmore	American	871,731	22.0	8	
1860	33	**ABRAHAM LINCOLN**	REPUBLICAN	1,865,593	40.0	180	81.2
		Stephen A. Douglas	Northern Democrat	1,382,713	29.0	12	
		John C. Breckinridge	Southern Democrat	848,356	18.0	72	
		John Bell	Constitutional Union	592,906	13.0	39	
1864	36	**ABRAHAM LINCOLN**	REPUBLICAN	2,206,938	55.0	212	73.8
		George B. McClellan	Democrat	1,803,787	45.0	21	
1868	37	**ULYSSES S. GRANT**	REPUBLICAN	3,013,421	53.0	214	78.1
		Horatio Seymour	Democrat	2,706,829	47.0	80	

Year	Number of States	Candidates	Parties	Popular Vote	% of Popular Vote	Electoral Vote	% Voter Participation
1872	37	**ULYSSES S. GRANT**	REPUBLICAN	3,596,745	55.6	286	71.3
		Horace Greeley	Democrat	2,843,446	43.9	66	
1876	38	**RUTHERFORD B. HAYES**	REPUBLICAN	4,036,572	48.0	185	81.8
		Samuel J. Tilden	Democrat	4,284,020	51.0	184	
1880	38	**JAMES A. GARFIELD**	REPUBLICAN	4,453,295	48.4	214	79.4
		Winfield S. Hancock	Democrat	4,414,082	48.3	155	
		James B. Weaver	Greenback-Labor	308,578	3.5		
1884	38	**GROVER CLEVELAND**	DEMOCRAT	4,879,507	48.5	219	77.5
		James G. Blaine	Republican	4,850,293	48.2	182	
		Benjamin F. Butler	Greenback-Labor	175,370	1.8		
		John P. St. John	Prohibition	150,369	1.5		
1888	38	**BENJAMIN HARRISON**	REPUBLICAN	5,447,129	47.9	233	79.3
		Grover Cleveland	Democrat	5,537,857	48.6	168	
		Clinton B. Fisk	Prohibition	249,506	2.2		
		Anson J. Streeter	Union Labor	146,935	1.3		
1892	44	**GROVER CLEVELAND**	DEMOCRAT	5,555,426	46.1	277	74.7
		Benjamin Harrison	Republican	5,182,690	43.0	145	
		James B. Weaver	People's	1,029,846	8.5	22	
		John Bidwell	Prohibition	264,133	2.2		
1896	45	**WILLIAM McKINLEY**	REPUBLICAN	7,102,246	51.0	271	79.3
		William J. Bryan	Democrat	6,492,559	47.0	176	

Year	Number of States	Candidates	Parties	Popular Vote	% of Popular Vote	Electoral Vote	% Voter Participation
1900	45	**WILLIAM McKINLEY**	REPUBLICAN	7,218,491	52.0	292	73.2
		William J. Bryan	Democrat; Populist	6,356,734	46.0	155	
		John C. Wooley	Prohibition	208,914	1.5		
1904	45	**THEODORE ROOSEVELT**	REPUBLICAN	7,628,461	56.4	336	65.2
		Alton B. Parker	Democrat	5,084,223	37.6	140	
		Eugene V. Debs	Socialist	402,283	3.0		
		Silas C. Swallow	Prohibition	258,536	1.9		
1908	46	**WILLIAM H. TAFT**	REPUBLICAN	7,675,320	52.0	321	65.4
		William J. Bryan	Democrat	6,412,294	43.4	162	
		Eugene V. Debs	Socialist	420,793	2.8		
		Eugene W. Chafin	Prohibition	253,840	1.7		
1912	48	**WOODROW WILSON**	DEMOCRAT	6,296,547	41.9	435	58.8
		Theodore Roosevelt	Progressive	4,118,571	27.4	88	
		William H. Taft	Republican	3,486,720	23.2	8	
		Eugene V. Debs	Socialist	900,672	6.0		
		Eugene W. Chafin	Prohibition	206,275	1.4		
1916	48	**WOODROW WILSON**	DEMOCRAT	9,127,695	49.4	277	61.6
		Charles E. Hughes	Republican	8,533,507	46.2	254	
		A. L. Benson	Socialist	585,113	3.2		
		J. Frank Hanly	Prohibition	220,506	1.2		
1920	48	**WARREN G. HARDING**	REPUBLICAN	16,153,115	60.6	404	49.2
		James M. Cox	Democrat	9,133,092	34.3	127	
		Eugene V. Debs	Socialist	915,490	3.4		
		P. P. Christensen	Farmer-Labor	265,229	1.0		
1924	48	**CALVIN COOLIDGE**	REPUBLICAN	15,719,921	54.0	382	48.9
		John W. Davis	Democrat	8,386,704	29.0	136	
		Robert M. La Follette	Progressive	4,832,532	16.5	13	

Year	Number of States	Candidates	Parties	Popular Vote	% of Popular Vote	Electoral Vote	% Voter Participation
1928	48	**HERBERT C. HOOVER**	REPUBLICAN	21,437,277	58.2	444	56.9
		Alfred E. Smith	Democrat	15,007,698	40.9	87	
1932	48	**FRANKLIN D. ROOSEVELT**	DEMOCRAT	22,829,501	57.7	472	56.9
		Herbert C. Hoover	Republican	15,760,684	39.8	59	
		Norman Thomas	Socialist	884,649	2.2		
1936	48	**FRANKLIN D. ROOSEVELT**	DEMOCRAT	27,757,333	60.8	523	61.0
		Alfred M. Landon	Republican	16,684,231	36.6	8	
		William Lemke	Union	892,267	2.0		
1940	48	**FRANKLIN D. ROOSEVELT**	DEMOCRAT	27,313,041	54.9	449	62.5
		Wendell L. Willkie	Republican	22,348,480	44.9	82	
1944	48	**FRANKLIN D. ROOSEVELT**	DEMOCRAT	25,612,610	53.5	432	55.9
		Thomas E. Dewey	Republican	22,017,617	46.0	99	
1948	48	**HARRY S. TRUMAN**	DEMOCRAT	24,179,345	49.7	303	53.0
		Thomas E. Dewey	Republican	21,991,291	45.3	189	
		J. Strom Thurmond	States' Rights	1,176,125	2.4	39	
		Henry A. Wallace	Progressive	1,157,326	2.4		
1952	48	**DWIGHT D. EISENHOWER**	REPUBLICAN	33,936,234	55.1	442	63.3
		Adlai E. Stevenson	Democrat	27,314,992	44.4	89	

Year	Number of States	Candidates	Parties	Popular Vote	% of Popular Vote	Electoral Vote	% Voter Participation
1956	48	**DWIGHT D. EISENHOWER**	REPUBLICAN	35,590,472	57.6	457	60.6
		Adlai E. Stevenson	Democrat	26,022,752	42.1	73	
1960	50	**JOHN F. KENNEDY**	DEMOCRAT	34,226,731	49.7	303	62.8
		Richard M. Nixon	Republican	34,108,157	49.6	219	
1964	50	**LYNDON B. JOHNSON**	DEMOCRAT	43,129,566	61.0	486	61.9
		Barry M. Goldwater	Republican	27,178,188	38.4	52	
1968	50	**RICHARD M. NIXON**	REPUBLICAN	31,785,480	43.2	301	60.9
		Hubert H. Humphrey	Democrat	31,275,166	42.6	191	
		George C. Wallace	American Independent	9,906,473	12.9	46	
1972	50	**RICHARD M. NIXON**	REPUBLICAN	47,169,911	60.7	520	55.2
		George S. McGovern	Democrat	29,170,383	37.5	17	
		John G. Schmitz	American	1,099,482	1.4		
1976	50	**JIMMY CARTER**	DEMOCRAT	40,830,763	50.0	297	53.5
		Gerald R. Ford	Republican	39,147,793	48.0	240	
1980	50	**RONALD REAGAN**	REPUBLICAN	43,904,153	50.9	489	52.6
		Jimmy Carter	Democrat	35,483,883	41.1	49	
		John B. Anderson	Independent	5,720,060	6.6		
		Ed Clark	Libertarian	921,299	1.1		

Year	Number of States	Candidates	Parties	Popular Vote	% of Popular Vote	Electoral Vote	% Voter Participation
1984	50	**RONALD REAGAN**	REPUBLICAN	54,455,075	58.8	525	53.1
		Walter F. Mondale	Democrat	37,577,185	40.5	13	
1988	50	**GEORGE H. BUSH**	REPUBLICAN	48,886,097	53.4	426	50.1
		Michael Dukakis	Democrat	41,809,074	45.6	111	
1992	50	**BILL CLINTON**	DEMOCRAT	44,909,326	42.9	370	55.0
		George H. Bush	Republican	39,103,882	37.4	168	
		H. Ross Perot	Independent	19,741,657	18.9		
1996	50	**BILL CLINTON**	DEMOCRAT	47,402,357	49.2	379	49.0
		Bob Dole	Republican	39,198,755	40.7	159	
		H. Ross Perot	Reform Party	8,085,402	8.4		
2000	50	**GEORGE W. BUSH**	REPUBLICAN	50,455,156	47.9	271	50.4
		Albert Gore	Democrat	50,992,335	48.4	266	
		Ralph Nader	Green Party	2,882,738	2.7		
2004	50	**GEORGE W. BUSH**	REPUBLICAN	62,040,610	50.7	286	56.2
		John F. Kerry	Democrat	59,028,111	48.3	251	
2008	50	**BARACK H. OBAMA**	DEMOCRAT	66,882,230	53	365	56.8
		John S. McCain	Republican	58,343,671	46	173	
2012	50	**BARACK H. OBAMA**	DEMOCRAT	62,611,250	51	332	53.6
		W. Mitt Romney	Republican	59,134,475	48	206	

ADMISSION OF STATES

Order of Admission	State	Date of Admission	Order of Admission	State	Date of Admission
1	Delaware	December 7, 1787	26	Michigan	January 26, 1837
2	Pennsylvania	December 12, 1787	27	Florida	March 3, 1845
3	New Jersey	December 18, 1787	28	Texas	December 29, 1845
4	Georgia	January 2, 1788	29	Iowa	December 28, 1846
5	Connecticut	January 9, 1788	30	Wisconsin	May 29, 1848
6	Massachusetts	February 7, 1788	31	California	September 9, 1850
7	Maryland	April 28, 1788	32	Minnesota	May 11, 1858
8	South Carolina	May 23, 1788	33	Oregon	February 14, 1859
9	New Hampshire	June 21, 1788	34	Kansas	January 29, 1861
10	Virginia	June 25, 1788	35	West Virginia	June 30, 1863
11	New York	July 26, 1788	36	Nevada	October 31, 1864
12	North Carolina	November 21, 1789	37	Nebraska	March 1, 1867
13	Rhode Island	May 29, 1790	38	Colorado	August 1, 1876
14	Vermont	March 4, 1791	39	North Dakota	November 2, 1889
15	Kentucky	June 1, 1792	40	South Dakota	November 2, 1889
16	Tennessee	June 1, 1796	41	Montana	November 8, 1889
17	Ohio	March 1, 1803	42	Washington	November 11, 1889
18	Louisiana	April 30, 1812	43	Idaho	July 3, 1890
19	Indiana	December 11, 1816	44	Wyoming	July 10, 1890
20	Mississippi	December 10, 1817	45	Utah	January 4, 1896
21	Illinois	December 3, 1818	46	Oklahoma	November 16, 1907
22	Alabama	December 14, 1819	47	New Mexico	January 6, 1912
23	Maine	March 15, 1820	48	Arizona	February 14, 1912
24	Missouri	August 10, 1821	49	Alaska	January 3, 1959
25	Arkansas	June 15, 1836	50	Hawaii	August 21, 1959

POPULATION OF THE UNITED STATES

Year	Number of States	Population	% Increase	Population per Square Mile
1790	13	3,929,214		4.5
1800	16	5,308,483	35.1	6.1
1810	17	7,239,881	36.4	4.3
1820	23	9,638,453	33.1	5.5
1830	24	12,866,020	33.5	7.4
1840	26	17,069,453	32.7	9.8
1850	31	23,191,876	35.9	7.9
1860	33	31,443,321	35.6	10.6
1870	37	39,818,449	26.6	13.4
1880	38	50,155,783	26.0	16.9
1890	44	62,947,714	25.5	21.1
1900	45	75,994,575	20.7	25.6
1910	46	91,972,266	21.0	31.0
1920	48	105,710,620	14.9	35.6
1930	48	122,775,046	16.1	41.2
1940	48	131,669,275	7.2	44.2
1950	48	150,697,361	14.5	50.7
1960	50	179,323,175	19.0	50.6
1970	50	203,235,298	13.3	57.5
1980	50	226,504,825	11.4	64.0
1985	50	237,839,000	5.0	67.2
1990	50	250,122,000	5.2	70.6
1995	50	263,411,707	5.3	74.4
2000	50	281,421,906	6.8	77.0
2005	50	296,410,404	5.3	81.7
2010	50	308,745,538	4.2	87.4

LABOR FORCE—SELECTED CHARACTERISTICS EXPRESSED AS A PERCENTAGE OF THE LABOR FORCE: 1800–2000

Year	Agriculture	Manufacturing	Domestic service	Clerical, sales, and service	Professions	Slave	Nonwhite	Foreign-born	Female
1800	74.4	—	2.4	—	—	30.2	32.6	—	21.4
1860	55.8	13.8	5.4	4.8[1]	3.0[1]	21.7	23.6	24.5[1]	19.6
1910	30.7	20.8	5.5	14.1	4.7	—	13.4	22.0	20.8
1950	12.0	26.4	2.5	27.3	8.9	—	10.0	8.7	27.9
2000	2.4	14.7	0.6	38.0[2]	15.6	—	16.5	10.3[2]	46.6
2010	1.6	10.1	1.6	40.2	22.2	—	18.7	15.8	46.7

[1]Values for 1870 are presented here because the available data for 1860 exclude slaves.
[2]1990.
Note: "Clerical, sales, and service" excludes domestic service.

IMMIGRATION, BY ORIGIN (in thousands)

Period	Europe	Americas	Asia
1820–30	106	12	—
1831–40	496	33	—
1841–50	1,597	62	—
1851–60	2,453	75	42
1861–70	2,065	167	65
1871–80	2,272	404	70
1881–90	4,735	427	70
1891–1900	3,555	39	75
1901–10	8,065	362	324
1911–20	4,322	1,144	247
1921–30	2,463	1,517	112
1931–40	348	160	16
1941–50	621	355	32
1951–60	1,326	997	150
1961–70	1,123	1,716	590
1971–80	800	1,983	1,588
1981–90	762	3,616	2,738
1991–2000	1,100	3,800	2,200

UNEMPLOYMENT RATE, 1890–2013

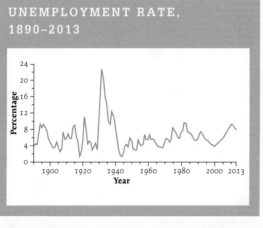

UNION MEMBERSHIP AS A PERCENTAGE OF NONAGRICULTURAL EMPLOYMENT, 1880–2012

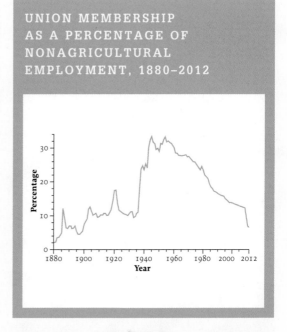

VOTER PARTICIPATION IN PRESIDENTIAL ELECTIONS, 1824–2012

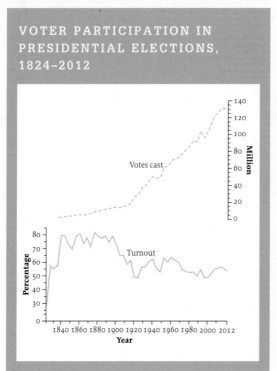

BIRTHRATE, 1820–2011

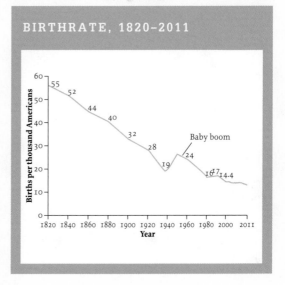

SUGGESTED READING

CHAPTER 1: A NEW WORLD

Books

Bender, Thomas. *A Nation among Nations: America's Place in World History* (2006). Attempts to place American history in an international context; the opening chapters offer a global portrait of the age of exploration and conquest.

Crosby, Alfred J. *The Columbian Exchange: Biological and Cultural Consequences of 1492* (1972). Examines the flow of goods and diseases across the Atlantic and their consequences.

Elliott, J. H. *Empires of the Atlantic World: Britain and Spain in America 1492–1830* (2006). A fascinating comparison of the development of two New World empires.

Fernández-Armesto, Felipe. *Pathfinders: A Global History of Exploration* (2006). A history of explorations throughout the centuries, including those of the fifteenth and sixteenth centuries.

Gutiérrez, Ramón A. *When Jesus Came, the Corn Mothers Went Away: Marriage, Sexuality, and Power in New Mexico, 1500–1846* (1991). Discusses the changes in Indian life in New Mexico as a result of Spanish colonization.

Mann, Charles C. *1491: New Revelations of the Americas before Columbus* (2005). A comprehensive portrait of life in the Western Hemisphere before the arrival of Europeans.

Richter, Daniel K. *Facing East from Indian Country* (2001). Examines the era of exploration and settlement as viewed through the experience of Native Americans.

Websites

Archive of Early American Images: www.brown.edu/Facilities/John_Carter_ Brown_ Library/pages/ea_hmpg.html

Exploring the Early Americas: www.loc.gov/exhibits/earlyamericas/

France in America: http://international.loc.gov/intldl/fiahtml/fiahome.html

Jamestown, Québec, Santa Fe: Three North American Beginnings: http://american history.si.edu/exhibitions/small _exhibition.cfm?key=1267&exkey=244

CHAPTER 2: BEGINNINGS OF ENGLISH AMERICA, 1607–1660

Books

Anderson, Victoria D. *New England's Generation: The Great Migration and the Formation of Society and Culture in the Seventeenth Century* (1991). A careful study of emigration from England to New England.

Brown, Kathleen. *Good Wives, Nasty Wenches, and Anxious Patriarchs: Gender, Race, and Power in Colonial Virginia* (1996). A pioneering study of gender relations and their impact on Virginia society.

Cronon, William. *Changes in the Land: Colonists and the Ecology of New England* (1983). A path-breaking examination of how English colonization affected the natural environment in New England.

Gleach, Frederic W. *Powhatan's World and Colonial Virginia: A Conflict of Cultures* (1997). A study of Indian culture and the impact of European colonization on it.

Pestana, Carla G. *The English Atlantic in an Age of Revolution, 1640–1661* (2001). Analyzes how the English Civil War reverberated in the American colonies.

Philbrick, Nathaniel. *Mayflower* (2006). An account of one of the most celebrated voyages of the colonial era, and the early history of the Plymouth colony.

Taylor, Alan. *American Colonies* (2001). A comprehensive survey of the history of North American colonies from their beginnings to 1763.

Websites

Plymouth Colony Archive Project: www.histarch.uiuc.edu/plymouth/index.html

Virtual Jamestown: www.virtualjamestown.org

CHAPTER 3: CREATING ANGLO-AMERICA, 1660–1750

Books

Bailyn, Bernard. *The Peopling of British North America* **(1986).** A brief survey of the movement of peoples across the Atlantic.

Berlin, Ira. *Many Thousands Gone: The First Two Centuries of Slavery in North America* (1998). The most extensive study of the origins and development of colonial slavery.

Lemon, James T. *The Best Poor Man's Country: A Geographical Study of Early Southeastern Pennsylvania* (1972). A study of agriculture and the environment in one of the most successful farming areas of colonial America.

Lepore, Jill. *The Name of War: King Philip's War and the Origin of American Identity* (1998). An examination not only of the war itself but also of its long-term consequences for Indian-white relations.

Mintz, Sidney. *Sweetness and Power: The Place of Sugar in Modern History* (1985). A global history of the significance of sugar in the making of the modern world.

Morgan, Edmund S. *American Slavery, American Freedom: The Ordeal of Colonial Virginia* (1975). An influential study of the slow development of slavery in seventeenth-century Virginia.

Norton, Mary Beth. *In the Devil's Snare: The Salem Witchcraft Crisis of 1692* (2002). A study of the witch trials that places them in the context of anxieties over Indian warfare on the Massachusetts frontier.

Saxton, Martha. *Being Good: Women's Moral Values in Early America* (2003). Examines social standards for women's behavior and how women tried to live up to them.

Websites

The Atlantic Slave Trade and Slave Life in the Americas: http://hitchcock.itc.virginia.edu/Slavery/index.php

Afro-Louisiana History and Genealogy: www.ibiblio.org/laslave/

CHAPTER 4: SLAVERY, FREEDOM, AND THE STRUGGLE FOR EMPIRE TO 1763

Books

Anderson, Fred. *Crucible of War: The Seven Years' War and the Fate of Empire in British North America, 1754–1766* (2000). A general history of the Seven Years' War and its consequences.

Clark, Charles E. *The Public Prints: The Newspaper in Anglo-American Culture, 1665–1740* (1994). Presents the early history of newspapers in colonial America.

Gomez, Michael A. *Exchanging Our Country Marks: The Transformation of African Identities in the Colonial and Antebellum South* (1998). The most detailed study of the process by which Africans became African-Americans.

Greene, Jack P. *The Quest for Power: The Lower Houses of Assembly in the Southern Royal Colonies, 1689–1776* (1963). A careful examination of how elected assemblies expanded their authority in the eighteenth-century South.

Noll, Mark. *The Rise of Evangelicalism: The Age of Edwards, Whitefield, and the Wesleys* (2004). Explores the Great Awakening on both sides of the Atlantic and its impact on religious life.

Rediker, Marcus. *The Slave Ship: A Human History* (2007). A fascinating and disturbing account of the Atlantic slave trade that focuses on the captains, sailors, and slaves aboard the slave ships.

White, Richard. *The Middle Ground: Indians, Empires, and Republics in the Great Lakes Region, 1650–1815* (1991). The book that developed the idea of a middle ground where Europeans and Indians both exercised authority.

Websites

Africans in America: www.pbs.org/wgbh/aia/

Web de Anza: http://anza.uoregon.edu

CHAPTER 5: THE AMERICAN REVOLUTION, 1763–1783

Books

Armitage, David. *The Declaration of Independence: A Global History* (2007). Traces the international impact of the Declaration of Independence in the years since it was written.

Bailyn, Bernard. *The Ideological Origins of the American Revolution* (1967). A classic study of the ideas that shaped the movement for independence.

Breen, T. H. *Marketplace of Revolution: How Consumer Politics Shaped American Independence* (2004). An examination of how the colonists' very dependence on British consumer goods led them to resent interference with trade.

Countryman, Edward. *The American Revolution* (rev. ed., 2002). A brief summary of the Revolution's causes, conduct, and consequences.

Foner, Eric. *Tom Paine and Revolutionary America* (1976). Examines the ideas of the era's greatest pamphleteer of revolution and how they contributed to the struggle for independence.

Nash, Gary. *The Urban Crucible: Social Change, Political Consciousness, and the Origins of the American Revolution* (1979). Explores how the social history of American cities contributed to the coming of the Revolution.

Royster, Charles. *A Revolutionary People at War: The Continental Army and American Character* (1979). A social history of the army and the impact of military service on American soldiers.

Websites

Declaring Independence: www.loc.gov/exhibits/declara/declara1.html

The American Revolution and Its Era: Maps and Charts of North America and the West Indies: http://memory.loc.gov /ammem/gmdhtml/armhtml/armhome.html

The Coming of the American Revolution: www.masshist.org/revolution/

CHAPTER 6: THE REVOLUTION WITHIN

Books

Berkin, Carol. *Revolutionary Mothers: Women in the Struggle for American Independence* (2005). Presents profiles of women who took part in the movement for independence.

Calloway, Colin. *The American Revolution in Indian Country* (1995). Examines how the Revolution affected Indians in each region of the United States.

Frey, Sylvia R. *Water from the Rock: Black Resistance in a Revolutionary Age* (1991). A study of the many ways blacks sought to gain freedom for themselves during the Revolution.

Hatch, Nathan O. *The Democratization of American Christianity* (1989). A comprehensive account of the Revolution's impact on religion, and its aftermath.

Kruman, Marc. *Between Authority and Liberty: State Constitution Making in Revolutionary America* (1997). The most detailed account of how state constitutions were changed during the era.

Schama, Simon. *Rough Crossing: Britain, the Slaves and the American Revolution* (2006). A detailed look at the experience of the thousands of slaves who escaped to British lines and their fate after the end of the War of Independence.

Taylor, Alan. *The Divided Ground: Indians, Settlers, and the Northern Borderland of the American Revolution* (2006). Examines the Revolution and its consequence in the Iroquois region of upstate New York.

Wood, Gordon. *The Radicalism of the American Revolution* (1992). An influential work that sees the Revolution as transforming a hierarchical society into a democratic one.

Websites

Creating the United States: http://myloc.gov/exhibitions/creatingtheus/Pages/ default.aspx

Religion and the Founding of the American Republic: www.loc.gov/exhibits/ religion/religion.html

The Geography of Slavery in Virginia: www2.vcdh.virginia.edu/gos/

CHAPTER 7: FOUNDING A NATION, 1783–1789

Books

Amar, Akhil Reed. *Bill of Rights: Creation and Reconstruction* (1998). Presents the history of the Bill of Rights from its ratification through the Reconstruction era.

Berkin, Carol. *A Brilliant Solution: Inventing the American Constitution* (2002). A lively account of the proceedings of the Constitutional Convention.

Cornell, Saul. *The Other Founders: Anti-Federalism and the Dissenting Tradition in America, 1788–1828* (1999). A careful examination of the ideas of those who opposed ratification of the Constitution.

MacLeod, Duncan J. *Slavery, Race, and the American Revolution* (1974). A British scholar's interpretation of the role of race and slavery in the revolutionary era.

Nedelsky, Jennifer. *Private Property and the Limits of American Constitutionalism* (1990). Analyzes how the protection of private property shaped the writing of the Constitution.

Rakove, Jack. *Original Meanings: Politics and Ideas in the Making of the Constitution* (1996). An influential interpretation of the ideas that went into the drafting of the Constitution.

Wood, Gordon S. *The Creation of the American Republic, 1776–1789* (1969). Presents the evolution of American political ideas and institutions from the Declaration of Independence to the ratification of the Constitution.

Websites

Creating the United States: http://myloc.gov/exhibitions/creatingtheus/Pages/ default.aspx

National Constitution Center www.constitutioncenter.org

CHAPTER 8: SECURING THE REPUBLIC, 1790–1815

Books

Appleby, Joyce. *Capitalism and a New Social Order: The Republican Vision of the 1790s* (1984). Explores how the Jeffersonians sought simultaneously to expand economic enterprise and equality of opportunity.

Hofstadter, Richard. *The Idea of a Party System: The Rise of Legitimate Opposition in the United States, 1780–1840* (1969). Considers how Americans began by rejecting the idea of organized political parties and ended up accepting their legitimacy.

Kerber, Linda K. *Women of the Republic: Intellect and Ideology in Revolutionary America* (1980). A study of prevailing ideas about women's place in the new republic.

McCoy, Drew. *The Elusive Republic: Political Economy in Jeffersonian America* (1980). An influential study of the economic and political outlooks and policies of Federalists and Jeffersonians.

Miller, John C. *Crisis in Freedom: The Alien and Sedition Acts* (1952). Examines how the Adams administration sought to use the power of the federal government to stifle dissent and the free press.

Rothman, Adam. *Slave Country: American Expansion and the Origins of the Deep South* (2005). A pioneering study of how the United States secured control of what are now the Gulf states, opening the door for the expansion of slavery.

Waldstreicher, David. *In the Midst of Perpetual Fetes: The Making of American Nationalism, 1776–1820* (1997). Explores how Americans celebrated and thought about their nation's independence in the years of the early republic.

Websites

Rivers, Edens, Empires: Lewis and Clark and the Revealing of America: www.loc.gov/exhibits/lewisandclark /lewisandclark.html

CHAPTER 9: THE MARKET REVOLUTION, 1800–1840

Books

Butler, Jon. *Awash in a Sea of Faith: Christianizing the American People* (1990). A history of American religion with emphasis on evangelical movements, including the Second Great Awakening.

Clark, Christopher. *The Roots of Rural Capitalism: Western Massachusetts, 1780–1860* (1990). Considers how the market revolution transformed economic and social life in one region of the North.

Dublin, Thomas. *Women at Work: The Transformation of Work in Lowell, Massachusetts, 1826–1860* (1975). A pioneering study of the working and nonworking lives of Lowell "factory girls."

Faragher, John M. *Sugar Creek: Life on the Illinois Prairie* (1986). Traces the growth of a frontier community from early settlement to market society.

Harris, Leslie. *In the Shadow of Slavery: African-Americans in New York City, 1626–1863* (2003). A study that emphasizes the exclusion of African-Americans from the economic opportunities offered by the market revolution.

Ryan, Mary P. *Cradle of the Middle Class: The Family in Oneida County, New York, 1790–1865* (1981). Examines how economic change helped to produce a new kind of middle-class family structure centered on women's dominance of the household.

Wilentz, Sean. *Chants Democratic: New York City and the Rise of the American Working Class, 1788–1850* (1984). A study of the early labor movement in one of its key centers in antebellum America.

Websites

American Transcendentalism Web: www.vcu.edu/engweb/transcendentalism/index.html

Erie Canal Time Machine: www.archives.nysed.gov/projects/eriecanal/

Women in America, 1820–1842: http://xroads.virginia.edu/~HYPER/ DETOC/fem/home.htm

CHAPTER 10: DEMOCRACY IN AMERICA, 1815–1840

Books

Ashworth, John. *"Agrarians" and "Aristocrats": Party Ideology in the United States, 1837–1846* (1983). A careful study of political ideas in the last years of Jacksonian politics, stressing increasing class divisions between the parties.

Freehling, William G. *Prelude to Civil War: The Nullification Controversy in South Carolina, 1816–1836* (1966). Still the standard account of the nullification crisis during Jackson's presidency.

Howe, Daniel W. *The Political Culture of the American Whigs* (1979). Illuminates the key ideas that held the Whig Party together.

Keyssar, Alexander. *The Right to Vote: The Contested History of Democracy in the United States* (2000). The most up-to-date history of the right to vote in America from the colonial era to the present.

Wallace, Anthony. *The Long, Bitter Trail: Andrew Jackson and the Indians* (1993). A brief history of Jackson's Indian policies, especially Indian Removal in the southern states.

Watson, Harry. *Liberty and Power: The Politics of Jacksonian America* (1990). A valuable brief account of the politics of the 1820s and 1830s.

Wilentz, Sean. *The Rise of American Democracy: Jefferson to Lincoln* (2005). A comprehensive history of democratic ideas and politics from the American Revolution to the Civil War.

Websites

Democracy in America, Alexis de Tocqueville: http://xroads.virginia.edu/~HYPER/DETOC/home.html

George Catlin and His Indian Gallery: http://americanart.si.edu/exhibitions/online/catlin/index.html

Legacy: Spain and the United States in the Age of Independence, 1763–1848: http://latino.si.edu/SpainLegacy/Archive/index.html

CHAPTER 11: THE PECULIAR INSTITUTION

Books

Berlin, Ira. *Slaves without Masters: The Free Negro in the Antebellum South* (1974). A careful study of the status of free blacks, stressing differences between the Upper and Lower South.

Davis, David Brion. *Inhuman Bondage: The Rise and Fall of Slavery in the New World* (2006). Places the history of slavery in the United States firmly in a hemispheric context.

Genovese, Eugene D. *Roll, Jordan, Roll: The World the Slaves Made* (1974). A classic study of the paternalist ethos and the culture that developed under slavery.

Gutman, Herbert G. *The Black Family in Slavery and Freedom* (1976). A pioneering examination of how slaves created and sustained families under the harsh conditions of slavery.

Johnson, Walter. *Soul by Soul: Life inside the Antebellum Slave Market* (1999). Considers the operations of the New Orleans slave market as a window into slavery as a whole.

Joyner, Charles D. *Down by the Riverside: A South Carolina Slave Community* (1984). Studies slave communities in coastal South Carolina, emphasizing the blend of African and American influences.

McCurry, Stephanie. *Masters of Small Worlds: Yeoman Households, Gender Relations, and the Political Culture of Antebellum South Carolina* (1995). Studies the lives of men and women in non-slaveholding families, to explore their links with the planter class.

Websites

Born in Slavery: Slave Narratives from the Federal Writers' Project: http://lcweb2.loc. gov/ammem/snhtml/snhome.html

Documenting the American South: http://docsouth.unc.edu

Gilder Lehrman Center for the Study of Slavery, Resistance, and Abolition: www.yale.edu/glc/index.htm

Slaves and the Courts, 1740–1860: http://memory.loc.gov/ammem/sthtml/sthome.html

CHAPTER 12: AN AGE OF REFORM, 1820–1840

Books

Boylan, Anne M. *The Origins of Women's Activism: New York and Boston, 1797–1840* (2002). Considers how middle-class urban women organized numerous associations for social improvement and thereby gained a place in the public sphere.

Bushman, Claudia L. and Richard L. Bushman. *Building the Kingdom: A History of Mormons in America* (2001). A survey of the history of American Mormons.

Goodman, Paul. *Of One Blood: Abolitionists and the Origins of Racial Equality* (1998). Explores the origins of racial egalitarianism in the movement against slavery.

Harding, Vincent. *There Is a River: The Black Struggle for Freedom in America* (1981). A study that links slave resistance and black abolitionism as phases of a common struggle for freedom.

Nye, Russell B. *Fettered Freedom: Civil Liberties and the Slavery Controversy, 1830–1860* (1949). Examines the impact of mob activities and other violations of civil liberties on the growth of abolitionism.

Rothman, David J. *The Discovery of the Asylum: Social Order and Disorder in the New Republic* (1971). Relates the rise of prisons, orphanages, and asylums and their common characteristics.

Tyrrell, Ian. *Sobering Up: From Temperance to Prohibition in Antebellum America, 1800–1860* (1979). Traces the movement against the sale and use of liquor and how it changed in the first part of the nineteenth century.

Websites

Samuel J. May Anti-Slavery Collection: http://ebooks.library.cornell.edu/m/mayantislavery//

Women and Social Movements in the United States, 1600–2000: http://asp6new.alexanderstreet.com/wam2/wam2 .index.map.aspx

CHAPTER 13: A HOUSE DIVIDED, 1840–1861

Books

Anbinder, Tyler. *Nativism and Slavery: The Northern Know-Nothings and the Politics of the 1850s* (1992). A detailed study of the relationship between nativism and antislavery politics in the North.

Cronon, William. *Nature's Metropolis: Chicago and the Great West* (1992). An influential account of the rise of Chicago and the city's relationship to its agricultural hinterland.

Foner, Eric. *Free Soil, Free Labor, Free Men: The Ideology of the Republican Party before the Civil War* (1970). A discussion of the basic ideas that united Republicans in the 1850s, especially their "free labor ideology."

Potter, David M. *The Impending Crisis, 1848–1861* (1976). Still the standard account of the nation's history in the years before the Civil War.

Sinha, Manisha. *The Counterrevolution of Slavery: Politics and Ideology in Antebellum South Carolina* (2002). A detailed study of how a vigorous defense of slavery developed in South Carolina, which justified the decision for secession.

Stampp, Kenneth. *And the War Came: The North and the Secession Crisis, 1860–61* (1950). An examination of Northern actions and attitudes during the secession crisis.

Stephanson, Anders. *Manifest Destiny: American Expansionism and the Empire of Right* (1995). Considers how the idea of an American mission to spread freedom and democracy has affected American foreign policy throughout the country's history.

Websites

Getting the Message Out: National Campaign Materials, 1840–1860: http://dig.lib.niu.edu/message/

Gold Rush!: http://museumca.org/goldrush/

The Mexican-American War and the Media: www.history.vt.edu/MxAmWar/INDEX.HTM#

The Oregon Trail: www.isu.edu/~trinmich/Oregontrail.html

Uncle Tom's Cabin and American Culture: http://jefferson.village.virginia.edu/utc/

CHAPTER 14: A NEW BIRTH OF FREEDOM: THE CIVIL WAR, 1861–1865

Books

Berlin, Ira, ed. *Slaves No More: Three Essays on Emancipation and the Civil War* (1992). A careful account of the causes and consequences of emancipation during the war.

Faust, Drew G. *This Republic of Suffering* (2008). A powerful account of how the experience of mass death affected American culture, religion, and politics.

Lawson, Melinda. *Patriot Fires: Forging a New Nationalism in the Civil War North* (2002). Considers how both public and private groups, in order to mobilize support for the war effort, promoted a new idea of American nationalism.

McPherson, James M. *Battle Cry of Freedom: The Civil War Era* (1988). The standard account of the coming of the war, its conduct, and its consequences.

Neely, Mark E. *The Fate of Liberty: Abraham Lincoln and Civil Liberties* (1991). Explores how the Lincoln administration did and did not meet the challenge of preserving civil liberties while fighting the war.

Quarles, Benjamin. *Lincoln and the Negro* (1962). A judicious account of the evolution of Lincoln's policies regarding slavery, emancipation, and the rights of African-Americans.

Richardson, Heather C. *Greatest Nation of the Earth: Republican Economic Policies during the Civil War* (1997). Considers the far-reaching impact of the economic measures adopted by the Union during the war.

Rubin, Anne S. *Shattered Nation: The Rise and Fall of the Confederacy, 1861–1868* (2005). An up-to-date account of the Confederate experience.

Websites

A House Divided: America in the Age of Lincoln: www.digitalhistory.uh.edu/ahd/index.html

Civil War Women: http://library.duke.edu/specialcollections/collections/digitized/civil-war-women/

The American Civil War Homepage: http://sunsite.utk.edu/civil-war/

The Valley of the Shadow: Two Communities in the American Civil War: http://valley.vcdh.virginia.edu

CHAPTER 15: "WHAT IS FREEDOM?": RECONSTRUCTION,1865–1877

Books

Butchart, Ronald E. *Schooling the Freed People: Teaching, Learning, and the Struggle for Black Freedom* (2010). Relates the efforts of black and white teachers to educate the former slaves and some of the conflicts that arose over the purposes of such education.

DuBois, Ellen C. *Feminism and Suffrage: The Emergence of an Independent Women's Movement in America, 1848–1869* (1978). Explores how the split over the exclusion of women from the Fourteenth and Fifteenth Amendments gave rise to a movement for woman suffrage no longer tied to the abolitionist tradition.

Foner, Eric. *Nothing but Freedom: Emancipation and Its Legacy* (1983). Includes a comparison of the emancipation experience in different parts of the Western Hemisphere.

Foner, Eric. *Reconstruction: America's Unfinished Revolution, 1863–1877* (1988). A comprehensive account of the Reconstruction era.

Hahn, Steven. *A Nation under Our Feet: Black Political Struggles in the Rural South from Slavery to the Great Migration* (2003). A detailed study of black political activism, stressing nationalist consciousness and emigration movements.

Hyman, Harold M. *A More Perfect Union: The Impact of the Civil War and Reconstruction on the Constitution* (1973). Analyzes how the laws and constitutional amendments of Reconstruction changed the Constitution and the rights of all Americans.

Litwack, Leon F. *Been in the Storm So Long: The Aftermath of Slavery* (1979). A detailed look at the immediate aftermath of the end of slavery and the variety of black and white responses to emancipation.

Rable, George C. *But There Was No Peace: The Role of Violence in the Politics of Reconstruction* (1984). The only full-scale study of violence in the Reconstruction South.

Websites

After Slavery: Race, Labor, and Politics in the Post-Emancipation Carolinas: www.afterslavery.com

America's Reconstruction: People and Politics after the Civil War: www.digitalhistory.uh.edu/reconstruction/index.html

Freedmen and Southern Society Project: www.history.umd.edu/Freedmen/

The Andrew Johnson Impeachment Trial: www.law.umkc.edu/faculty/projects/ftrials/impeach/impeachmt.htm

CHAPTER 16: AMERICA'S GILDED AGE, 1870–1890

Books

Blackhawk, Ned. *Violence Over the Land: Indians and Empires in the Early American West* (2006). A history of the long conflict between Native Americans and the federal government for control of the trans-Mississippi West.

Fink, Leon. *Workingmen's Democracy: The Knights of Labor and American Politics* (1983). Examines the rise of the Knights of Labor and their forays into local politics in the mid-1880s.

Hamalainen, Pekka. *The Comanche Empire* (2008). The rise and fall of Comanche domination over much of the southwestern United States.

Hofstadter, Richard. *Social Darwinism in American Thought* (1944). A classic study of a major tendency in American thought during the Gilded Age.

Jeffrey, Julie R. *Frontier Women: "Civilizing" the West? 1840–1880* (rev. ed., 1998). A study, based on letters and diaries, of the experience of women on the western frontier.

Morgan, H. Wayne. *From Hayes to McKinley: National Party Politics, 1877–1896* (1969). The standard narrative of national politics during these years.

Thomas, John L. *Alternative Americas: Henry George, Edward Bellamy, Henry Demarest Lloyd and the Adversary Tradition* (1983). A thorough exposition of the thought of three critics of Gilded Age society.

Trachtenberg, Alan. *The Incorporation of America: Culture and Society in the Gilded Age* (1982). An influential survey of how economic change affected American life during the Gilded Age.

White, Richard. *Railroaded: The Transcontinentals and the Making of Modern America* (2011). A careful study of the building of the transcontinental railroad and how it epitomized the political corruption and financial mismanagement so widespread in the Gilded Age.

Websites

Indian Peoples of the Northern Great Plains: www.lib.montana.edu/digital/nadb/

The Dramas of Haymarket: www.chicagohistory.org/dramas/overview/over.htm

Western History Genealogy Digital Collections: http://digital.dewerlibrary.org

CHAPTER 17: FREEDOM'S BOUNDARIES, AT HOME AND ABROAD, 1890–1900

Books

Blight, David. *Race and Reunion: The Civil War in American Memory* (2001). Examines how a memory of the Civil War that downplayed the issue of slavery played a part in sectional reconciliation and the rise of segregation.

Hoganson, Kristin L. *Consumers' Imperium: The Global Production of American Domesticity, 1865–1920* (2007). Shows how the consumer desires of middle-class women helped to spur the consolidation of an American empire.

LaFeber, Walter. *The New Empire: An Interpretation of American Expansion, 1860–1898* (1963). A classic examination of the forces that led the United States to acquire an overseas empire.

Lake, Marilyn, and Henry Reynolds. *Drawing the Global Color Line* (2008). Traces the global transmission of ideas about white supremacy in the late nineteenth century.

McClain, Charles J. *In Search of Equality: The Chinese Struggle against Discrimination in Nineteenth-Century America* (1994). Explores how Chinese-Americans worked to combat the discrimination to which they were subjected and to assert their rights.

Perez, Louis A. *The War of 1898: The United States and Cuba in History and Historiography* (1998). Presents the Cuban side of the Spanish-American War, including a detailed discussion of the Cuban movement for independence and how American intervention affected it.

Postel, Charles. *The Populist Vision* (2007). A history of the Populist movement that stresses how it anticipated many public policies of the twentieth century.

Woodward, C. Vann. *Origins of the New South, 1877–1913* (1951). A classic treatment of the New South, emphasizing how its rulers failed to meet the needs of most southerners, white as well as black.

Websites

1896: The Presidential Campaign: http://projects.vassar.edu/1896/1896home.html

The Chinese in California, 1850–1925: http://memory.loc.gov/ammem/award99/cubhtml/cichome.html

The History of Jim Crow: www.jimcrowhistory.org

The World of 1898: The Spanish-American War: www.loc.gov/rr/hispanic/1898

CHAPTER 18: THE PROGRESSIVE ERA, 1900–1916

Books

Bodnar, John. *The Transplanted: A History of Immigrants in Urban America* (1985). A comprehensive account of American immigration.

Cott, Nancy F. *The Grounding of Modern Feminism* (1987). A careful study of feminist ideas in the Progressive era.

Dawley, Alan. *Struggles for Justice: Social Responsibility and the Liberal State* (1991). Examines the varieties of Progressive reform and various efforts to use the power of government for social betterment.

Hofstadter, Richard. *The Age of Reform: From Bryan to F. D. R.* (1955). A classic account of the ideas of reformers from Populism to the New Deal.

Johnston, Robert D. *The Radical Middle Class: Populist Democracy and the Question of Capitalism in Progressive Era Portland* (2003). Analyzes how Progressivism operated in one important city.

Lears, Jackson. *Rebirth of a Nation: The Making of Modern America, 1877–1920* (2009). A comprehensive history of the Gilded Age and Progressive eras, stressing the extent of social and cultural change.

Recchiuti, John L. *Civic Engagement: Social Science and Progressive-Era Reform in New York City* (2006). Examines the influence of a group of reform-minded scholars on the politics of the Progressive era.

Rodgers, Daniel T. *Atlantic Crossings: Social Politics in a Progressive Age* (1998). A comprehensive study of the flow of Progressive ideas and policies back and forth across the Atlantic.

Websites

Evolution of the Conservation Movement, 1860–1920: http://memory.loc.gov/ ammem/amrvhtml/conshome.html

Immigration to the United States, 1789–1930: http://ocp.hul.harvard.edu/ immigration/

Triangle Shirtwaist Factory Fire: www.ilr.cornell.edu/trianglefire/

Urban Experience in Chicago: Hull House and Its Neighborhoods: www.uic.edu/ jaddams/hull/urbanexp/index.htm

Votes for Women: http://memory.loc.gov/ammem/naw/nawshome.html

CHAPTER 19: SAFE FOR DEMOCRACY: THE UNITED STATES AND WORLD WAR I, 1916–1920

Books

Bederman, Gail. *Manliness and Civilization: A Cultural History of Race and Gender in the United States, 1880–1917* (1995). Explores how ideas concerning civilization and gender affected American foreign policy.

Capozzola, Christopher. *Uncle Sam Wants You: World War I and the Making of the Modern American Citizen* (2008). A careful study of public and private efforts to enforce patriotic ideas and actions during World War I.

Dawley, Alan. *Changing the World: American Progressives in War and Revolution* (2003). Presents the war as a fulfillment and betrayal of the Progressive impulse.

Greene, Julie. *The Canal Builders: Making American Empire at the Panama Canal* (2009). Tells the story of the construction of the Panama Canal and the tens of thousands of workers who did the work.

Grossman, James R. *Land of Hope: Chicago, Black Southerners, and the Great Migration* (1989). An in-depth study of the migration of blacks to one American city.

Kennedy, David M. *Over Here: The First World War and American Society* (1980). A comprehensive account of how the war affected domestic life in the United States.

Manela, Erez. *The Wilsonian Moment* (2007). Details how the Wilsonian ideal of self-determination was received around the world, with results Wilson did not anticipate.

Preston, William, Jr. *Aliens and Dissenters: Federal Suppression of Radicals, 1903–1933* (1963). An influential study of the federal government's efforts to suppress dissenting ideas, especially during and immediately after World War I.

Websites

Alcohol, Temperance, and Prohibition: http://dl.lib.brown.edu/temperance/

First World War.com: www.firstworldwar.com/index.htm

Red Scare: http://newman.baruch.cuny.edu/digital/redscare/default.htm

The Bisbee Deportation of 1917: www.library.arizona.edu/exhibits/bisbee/

CHAPTER 20: FROM BUSINESS CULTURE TO GREAT DEPRESSION: THE TWENTIES, 1920–1932

Books

Dumenil, Lynn. *The Modern Temper: America in the Twenties* (1995). A brief survey of the main political and cultural trends of the decade.

Garraty, John A. *The Great Depression* (1986). Places the Depression in a global context and compares various governments' responses to it.

Gerstle, Gary. *American Crucible: Race and Nation in the Twentieth Century* (2002). A sweeping survey of how changing ideas of race have affected the concept of American nationality, with a strong account of the debates of the 1920s.

Lerner, Michael A. *Dry Manhattan: Prohibition in New York City* (2007). An account of the success and failure of Prohibition in the nation's largest city.

Lewis, David L. *When Harlem Was in Vogue* (1981). A lively account of the Harlem Renaissance of the 1920s.

Marsden, George M. *Fundamentalism and American Culture: The Shaping of Twentieth-Century Evangelicism, 1870–1925* (1980). Traces the ups and downs of American fundamentalism, culminating in the Scopes trial.

Murphy, Paul L. *World War I and the Origin of Civil Liberties in the United States* (1979). An analysis of how the repression of free speech during World War I paved the way for a heightened awareness of the importance of civil liberties.

Ngai, Mae. *Impossible Subjects: Illegal Aliens and the Making of Modern America* (2004). An influential examination of immigration policy toward Mexicans and Asians, and the development of the legal category of "illegal alien."

Websites

Emergence of Advertising in America: http://library.duke.edu/digitalcollections/eaa/

Harlem History: www.columbia.edu/cu/iraas/harlem/index.html

Pluralism and Unity: www.expo98.msu.edu/

Prosperity and Thrift: Coolidge Era and the Consumer Economy: http://memory.loc.gov/ammem/coolhtml/coolhome.html

CHAPTER 21: THE NEW DEAL, 1932–1940

Books

Brinkley, Alan. *Voices of Protest: Huey Long, Father Coughlin, and the Great Depression* (1982). An account of the political careers of two key figures of the New Deal era and their influence on national events.

Denning, Michael. *The Cultural Front: The Laboring of American Culture in the Twentieth Century* (1996). A comprehensive account of the rise of cultural activity associated with the political left and the New Deal.

Kessler-Harris, Alice. *In Pursuit of Equity: Men, Women, and the Quest for Economic Citizenship in 20th-Century America* (2001). Explores how assumptions regarding the proper roles of men and women helped to shape New Deal measures such as Social Security.

Leuchtenberg, William E. *Franklin D. Roosevelt and the New Deal, 1932–1940* (1963). Still the standard one-volume account of Roosevelt's first two terms as president.

Maher, Neil. *Nature's New Deal: The Civilian Conservation Corps and the Roots of the American Environmental Movement* (2007). A history of one of the most significant New Deal agencies and how it affected attitudes toward the natural environment.

Naison, Mark. *Communists in Harlem during the Depression* (1983). Examines the rise and decline of the Communist Party in a center of black life, and its impact on the movement for racial justice.

Phillips, Sarah T. *The Land, This Nation: Conservation, Rural America, and the New Deal* (2007). Examines New Deal policies regarding agricultural development, rural conservation, and land use, and its attempt to modernize and uplift rural life.

Sanchez, George. *Becoming Mexican American: Ethnicity, Culture, and Identity in Chicano Los Angeles, 1900–1945* (1995). A careful study of Mexican-Americans in Los Angeles, including their participation in the social unrest of the 1930s and the movement for deporting them during that decade.

Sitkoff, Harvard. *A New Deal for Blacks: The Emergence of Civil Rights as a National Issue* (1978). Discusses the changing approach of the Roosevelt administration toward black Americans.

Websites

America from the Great Depression to World War II: http://memory.loc.gov/ammem/fsowhome.html

FDR Cartoon Archive: www.nisk.k12.ny.us/fdr/FDRcartoons.html

Flint Sit-Down Strike: www.historicalvoices.org/flint/

New Deal Network: http://newdeal.feri.org

CHAPTER 22: FIGHTING FOR THE FOUR FREEDOMS: WORLD WAR II, 1941–1945

Books

Anderson, Karen. *Wartime Women: Sex Roles, Family Relations, and the Status of Women during World War II* (1981). Explores how the experience of World War II opened new opportunities for women and challenged existing gender conventions.

Borgwardt, Elizabeth. *A New Deal for the World: America's Vision for Human Rights* (2005). The emergence during the war of the idea of human rights as an international entitlement.

Brinkley, Alan. *The End of Reform: New Deal Liberalism in Recession and War* (1995). Describes how liberals' ideas and policies moved away, during the late New Deal and the war, from combating inequalities of economic power.

Daniels, Rogers. *Prisoners without Trial: Japanese Americans in World War II* (1993). A brief history of the internment of Japanese-Americans during the war.

Dower, John W. *War without Mercy: Race and Power in the Pacific War* (1986). Explores how racial fears and antagonisms motivated both sides in the Pacific theater.

Kennedy, David M. *Freedom from Fear: The American People in Depression and War, 1929–1945* (1999). A detailed and lively account of American history from the Great Depression through the end of World War II.

Von Eschen, Penny. *Race against Empire: Black Americans and Anticolonialism, 1937–1957* (1997). Examines how black Americans responded to the rise of movements for colonial independence overseas during and after World War II.

Zelizer, Julian E. *Arsenal of Democracy: The Politics of National Security—From World War II to the War on Terrorism* (2009). Traces the origins of the national security state from Roosevelt's "arsenal of democracy" speech of 1940 to the present, stressing the tension between the two elements, arsenal and democracy.

Websites

A More Perfect Union: Japanese Americans and the U.S. Constitution: http://americanhistory.si.edu/perfectunion/experience/index.html

A People at War: www.archives.gov/exhibits/a_people_at_war/a_people_at_war. html

"A Summons to Comradeship": World War I and World War II Posters and Postcards: http://digital.lib.umn.edu/warposters/warpost.html

Remembering Nagasaki: www.exploratorium.edu/nagasaki/

CHAPTER 23: THE UNITED STATES AND THE COLD WAR, 1945–1953

Books

Biondi, Martha. *To Stand and Fight: The Struggle for Civil Rights in Postwar New York City* (2003). A comprehensive account of the broad coalition that battled for racial justice in New York City, in areas such as jobs, education, and housing.

Canaday, Margot. *The Straight State: Sexuality and Citizenship in Twentieth-Century America* (2009). Details the federal government's efforts to stigmatize and punish homosexuality.

Gaddis, John. *Strategies of Containment: A Critical Analysis of Postwar American National Security* (1982). An influential analysis of the development of the containment policy central to American foreign policy during the Cold War.

Glendon, Mary Ann. *A World Made New: Eleanor Roosevelt and the Universal Declaration of Human Rights* (2001). Relates the drafting of the Universal Declaration of Human Rights and the response of governments around the world, including that of the United States.

Leffler, Melvyn P. *A Preponderance of Power: National Security, the Truman Administration, and the Cold War* (1992). An influential account of the origins of the Cold War.

Saunders, Frances S. *The Cultural Cold War: The CIA and the World of Arts and Letters* (2000). Describes how the CIA and other government agencies secretly funded artists and writers as part of the larger Cold War.

Schrecker, Ellen. *Many Are the Crimes: McCarthyism in America* (1998). A full account of the anticommunist crusade at home and its impact on American intellectual and social life.

Stueck, William. *The Korean War: An International History* (1995). Studies the Korean War in its full global context.

Websites

Cold War International History Project: www.wilsoncenter.org/index.cfm? fuseaction=topics.home&topic_id=1409

The Korean War and Its Origins, 1945–1953: http://www.trumanlibrary.org/whistlestop/study_collections/koreanwar/index.php

CHAPTER 24: AN AFFLUENT SOCIETY, 1953–1960

Books

Branch, Taylor. *Parting the Waters: America in the King Years, 1954–1963* (1988). A comprehensive account of the civil rights movement from the *Brown* decision to the early 1960s.

Cohen, Lizabeth. *A Consumer's Republic: The Politics of Mass Consumption in Postwar America* (2003). Considers how the glorification of consumer freedom shaped American public policy and the physical landscape.

Freeman, Joshua B. *Working-Class New York: Life and Labor since World War II* (2000). An account of the lives of laborers in the nation's largest city, tracing the rise and decline of the labor movement.

Inboden, William. *Religion and American Foreign Policy, 1945–1960: The Soul of Containment* (2008). How religious groups influenced American diplomacy at the height of the Cold War.

Jackson, Kenneth T. *Crabgrass Frontier: The Suburbanization of America* (1985). The standard account of the development of American suburbia.

May, Elaine T. *Homeward Bound: American Families in the Cold War Era* (1988). Studies the nuclear family as a bastion of American freedom during the Cold War, at least according to official propaganda.

Nicolaides, Becky M. *My Blue Heaven: Life and Politics in the Working-Class Suburbs of Los Angeles, 1920–1965* (2002). Traces the transformation of Southgate, an industrial neighborhood of Los Angeles, into an all-white suburb, and the political results.

Phillips-Fein, Kim. *Invisible Hands: The Making of the Conservative Movement from the New Deal to Reagan* (2009). Relates how a group of economic thinkers and businessmen worked to fashion a conservative movement in an attempt to reverse many of the policies of the New Deal.

Westad, Odd Arne. *The Global Cold War* (2005). A wide-ranging analysis of how the Cold War played out in the Third World.

Websites

Brown v. Board of Education: www.lib.umich.edu/brown-versus-board-education/

Herblock's History: Political Cartoons from the Crash to the Millennium: www.loc.gov/rr/print/swann/herblock/

Levittown: Documents of an Ideal American Suburb: http://uic.edu/~pbhales/Levittown.html

CHAPTER 25: THE SIXTIES, 1960–1968

Books

Anderson, John A., III. *The Other Side of the Sixties: Young Americans for Freedom and the Rise of Conservative Politics* (1997). Considers conservative students of the 1960s and how they laid the groundwork for the later growth of their movement.

Anderson, Terry H. *The Movement and the Sixties: Protest in America from Greensboro to Wounded Knee* (1995). Offers an account of the numerous social protests that took place during the 1960s.

Dierenfield, Bruce. *The Battle Over School Prayer: How* Engle v. Vitale *Changed America* (2007). One controversial Supreme Court decision of the 1960s and its long-term consequences.

Dittmer, John. *Local People: The Struggle for Civil Rights in Mississippi* (1994). Traces the civil rights movement in one state, looked at from the experience of grassroots activists.

Herring, George C. *America's Longest War: The United States and Vietnam, 1950–1975* (2002 ed.). The fullest study of how the United States became involved in the war in Vietnam, and the course of the conflict.

Isserman, Maurice, and Michael Kazin. *America Divided: The Civil War of the 1960s* (2000). A comprehensive account of the social movements and political debates of the 1960s.

Rosen, Ruth. *The World Split Open: How the Modern Women's Movement Changed America* (2000). Considers how the "second wave" of feminism transformed the lives of American women and men.

Sale, Kirkpatrick. *The Green Revolution: The American Environmental Movement, 1962–1992* (1993). A brief history of one of the most significant movements to emerge from the 1960s.

Websites

A Visual Journey: Photographs by Lisa Law, 1965–1971: http://americanhistory.si.edu/lisalaw/

Free Speech Movement Digital Archive: http://bancroft.berkeley.edu/FSM/

Freedom Now!: www.stg.brown.edu/projects/FreedomNow/

The Wars for Vietnam, 1945–1975: http://vietnam.vassar.edu/index.html

CHAPTER 26: THE TRIUMPH OF CONSERVATISM, 1969–1988

Books

Dallek, Matthew. *The Right Moment: Ronald Reagan's First Victory and the Decisive Turning Point in American Politics* (2000). An examination of the causes of Reagan's election in 1980 and its impact on American politics.

Greenberg, David. *Nixon's Shadow: The History of an Image* (2003). Explores how Nixon's supporters and enemies thought about him during his long political career.

Kruse, Kevin. *White Flight: Atlanta and the Making of Modern Conservatism* (2005). Explores how conservative politics took root in the predominantly white suburbs of Atlanta, with implications for similar communities across the country.

Martin, William. *With God on Our Side: The Rise of the Religious Right in America* (1996). Traces the development of religious conservatism and its impact on American society.

McGirr, Lisa. *Suburban Warriors: The Origins of the New American Right* (2001). An influential study of the rise of conservatism in Orange County, California, once one of its more powerful centers.

Schulman, Bruce J. *The Seventies: The Great Shift in American Culture, Society, and Politics* (2001). A survey of the numerous political, social, and economic changes that took place during the 1970s.

Stein, Judith. *Pivotal Decade: How the United States Traded Factories for Finance in the Seventies* (2010). A careful analysis of the economic transformations of the 1970s.

————. *Running Steel, Running America: Race, Economic Policy, and the Decline of Liberalism* (1998). Examines the decline of the American steel industry and how the Cold War and presidential policies from Eisenhower to Carter contributed to it.

Wilentz, Sean. *The Age of Reagan: A History, 1974–2008* (2008). Explores how Ronald Reagan set the terms of public debate during and after his presidency.

Websites

China and the United States: From Hostility to Engagement, 1960–1998: www.gwu.edu/~nsarchiv/nsa/publications/china-us/

National Security Archive: www.gwu.edu/~nsarchiv/

CHAPTER 27: GLOBALIZATION AND ITS DISCONTENTS, 1989–2000

Books

Foner, Nancy. *From Ellis Island to JFK: New York's Two Great Waves of Immigration* (2000). Studies the new immigration of the 1980s and 1990s and considers how it does and does not differ from earlier waves of newcomers.

Hodgson, Godfrey. *More Equal Than Others: America from Nixon to the New Century* (2004). A survey of recent American history that identifies growing inequality as a major trend of these years.

Judis, John B. *The Paradox of American Democracy* (2000). Discusses how the democratic tradition has been weakened by the growing influence of money and declining voter participation.

Levitas, Daniel. *The Terrorist Next Door: The Militia Movement and the Radical Right* (2003). A careful study of right-wing extremism of the 1990s.

Lichtenstein, Nelson. *The Retail Revolution: How Wal-Mart Created a Brave New World of Business* (2009). How Walmart became the largest employer in the United States and one of the most profitable.

Phillips, Kevin. *Wealth and Democracy* (2002). A critique of the influence of money on American politics.

Roberts, Sam. *Who We Are Now: The Changing Face of America in the Twenty-First Century* (2004). A social portrait of the American people, based on the 2000 Census.

Stiglitz, Joseph. *Globalization and Its Discontents* (2002). A leading economist's criticism of some of the consequences of economic globalization.

Websites

Global Exchange: www.globalexchange.org

Making the Macintosh: Technology and Culture in Silicon Valley: http://library.stanford.edu/mac/

CHAPTER 28: SEPTEMBER 11 AND THE NEXT AMERICAN CENTURY

Books

Bacevich, Andrew. *American Empire: The Realities and Consequences of U.S. Diplomacy* (2003). Examines how the idea of an American empire reemerged after September 11, and some of the results.

Brinkley, Douglas. *The Great Deluge: Hurricane Katrina, New Orleans, and the Mississippi Gulf Coast* (2006). A scathing account of how government at all levels failed the people of New Orleans.

Cole, David. *Terrorism and the Constitution* (rev. ed., 2006). Explores the constitutional issues raised by the war on terrorism.

Krugman, Paul, *The Return of Depression Economics and the Crisis of 2008* (2009). A leading economist explains the origins of the Great Recession.

Lansley, Stewart. *Divided We Stand: Why Inequality Keeps Rising* (2011). A prominent economist explains the reasons for rising economic inequality.

Little, Douglas. *American Orientalism: The United States and the Middle East since 1945* (2003). A careful study of American relations with a volatile region since World War II.

Packer, George. *The Assassin's Gate: America in Iraq* (2005). An early supporter of the war in Iraq explains what went wrong.

Zakaria, Fareed. *The Future of Freedom: Illiberal Democracy at Home and Abroad* (2003). A foreign policy analyst discusses how the United States should respond to threats to freedom in the world.

Websites

September 11 Digital Archive: http://911digitalarchive.org

The White House: www.whitehouse.gov

GLOSSARY

Abolitionism Social movement of the pre–Civil War era that advocated the immediate emancipation of the slaves and their incorporation into American society as equal citizens.

Affirmative action Policy efforts to promote greater employment opportunities for minorities.

Agricultural Adjustment Act (1933) New Deal legislation that established the Agricultural Adjustment Administration (AAA) to improve agricultural prices by limiting market supplies; declared unconstitutional in United States v. Butler (1936).

Aid to Families with Dependent Children Federal program, also known as "welfare," of financial assistance to needy American families; created in 1935 as part of the Social Security Act; abolished in 1996.

Alamo, Battle of the Siege in the Texas War for Independence, 1836, in which the San Antonio mission fell to the Mexicans.

Alien and Sedition Acts (1798) Four measures passed during the undeclared war with France that limited the freedoms of speech and press and restricted the liberty of noncitizens.

America First Committee Largely midwestern isolationist organization supported by many prominent citizens, 1940–1941.

American Civil Liberties Union Organization founded during World War I to protest the suppression of freedom of expression in wartime; played a major role in court cases that achieved judicial recognition of Americans' civil liberties.

American Colonization Society Organized in 1816 to encourage colonization of free blacks to Africa; West African nation of Liberia founded in 1822 to serve as a homeland for them.

"American exceptionalism" The belief that the United States has a special mission to serve as a refuge from tyranny, a symbol of freedom, and a model for the rest of the world.

American Federation of Labor Founded in 1881 as a federation of trade unions composed mostly of skilled, white, native-born workers; its long-term president was Samuel Gompers.

American System Program of internal improvements and protective tariffs promoted by Speaker of the House Henry Clay in his presidential campaign of 1824; his proposals formed the core of Whig ideology in the 1830s and 1840s.

Amistad Ship that transported slaves from one port in Cuba to another, seized by the slaves in 1839. They made their way northward to the United States, where the status of the slaves became the subject of a celebrated court case; eventually most were able to return to Africa.

Anarchism Belief that all institutions that exercise power over individuals, especially government, are illegitimate; it flourished among certain native-born individualists in the nineteenth century and radical immigrants in the early twentieth century.

Antietam, Battle of One of the bloodiest battles of the Civil War, fought to a standoff on September 17, 1862, in western Maryland.

Antifederalists Opponents of the Constitution who saw it as a limitation on individual and states' rights; their demands led to the addition of a Bill of Rights to the document.

Appomattox Courthouse, Virginia Site of the surrender of Confederate general Robert E. Lee to Union general Ulysses S. Grant on April 9, 1865, marking the end of the Civil War.

Arab Spring Revolutionary demonstrations and protests that swept the Middle East in 2011.

Army-McCarthy hearings Televised U.S. Senate hearings in 1954 on Senator Joseph McCarthy's charges of disloyalty in the army; his tactics contributed to his censure by the Senate.

Articles of Confederation First frame of government for the United States; in effect from 1781 to 1788, it provided for a weak central authority and was soon replaced by the Constitution.

Atlanta Compromise Speech to the Cotton States and International Exposition in 1895 by educator Booker T. Washington, the leading black spokesman of the day; black scholar W. E. B. Du Bois gave the speech its derisive name and criticized Washington for encouraging blacks to accommodate segregation and disenfranchisement.

Atlantic Charter Issued August 12, 1941, following meetings in Newfoundland between President Franklin D. Roosevelt and British prime minister Winston Churchill, the charter signaled the Allies' cooperation and stated their war aims.

Atlantic slave trade The systematic importation of African slaves from their native continent across the Atlantic Ocean to the New World, largely fuelled by rising demand for sugar, rice, coffee, and tobacco.

Atomic Energy Commission Created in 1946 to supervise peacetime uses of atomic energy.

Axis powers In World War II, the nations of Germany, Italy, and Japan.

Aztec Mesoamerican people who were conquered by the Spanish under Hernán Cortés, 1519–1528.

Baby boom Markedly higher birthrate in the years following World War II; led to the biggest demographic "bubble" in American history.

Bacon's Rebellion Unsuccessful 1676 revolt led by planter Nathaniel Bacon against Virginia governor William Berkeley's administration because of governmental corruption and because Berkeley had failed to protect settlers from Indian raids and did not allow them to occupy Indian lands.

***Baker v. Carr* (1962)** U.S. Supreme Court decision that established the principle of "one man, one vote," that is, that legislative districts must be equal in population.

***Bakke v. Regents of the University of California* (1978)** Case in which the U.S. Supreme Court ruled against the California university system's use of racial quotas in admissions but allowed the use of race as one factor in admissions decisions.

Balance of trade Ratio of imports to exports.

Bank of the United States Proposed by the first secretary of the treasury, Alexander Hamilton, the bank opened in 1791 and operated until 1811 to issue a uniform currency, make business loans, and collect tax monies. The Second Bank of the United States was chartered in 1816 but President Andrew Jackson vetoed the recharter bill in 1832.

Barbary pirates Plundering pirates off the Mediterranean coast of Africa; President Thomas Jefferson's refusal to pay them tribute to protect American ships sparked an undeclared naval war with North African nations, 1801–1805.

Barbed wire First practical fencing material for the Great Plains was invented in 1873 and rapidly spelled the end of the open range.

Bay of Pigs invasion Hoping to inspire a revolt against Fidel Castro, the CIA sent 1,500 Cuban exiles to invade their homeland on April 17, 1961, but the mission was a spectacular failure.

The Beats A term coined by Jack Kerouac for a small group of poets and writers who railed against 1950s mainstream culture.

Bill of Rights First ten amendments to the U.S. Constitution, adopted in 1791 to guarantee individual rights against infringement by the federal government.

Black Codes (1865–1866) Laws passed in southern states to restrict the rights of former slaves; to nullify the codes, Congress passed the Civil Rights Act of 1866 and the Fourteenth Amendment.

Black Legend Idea that the Spanish New World empire was more oppressive toward the Indians than other European empires; was used as a justification for English imperial expansion.

Black Power Post-1966 rallying cry of a more militant civil rights movement.

Bland-Allison Act (1878) Passed over President Rutherford B. Hayes's veto, the inflationary measure authorized the purchase each month of 2 to 4 million dollars' worth of silver for coinage.

"Bleeding Kansas" Violence between pro- and antislavery settlers in the Kansas Territory, 1856.

Boston Massacre Clash between British soldiers and a Boston mob, March 5, 1770, in which five colonists were killed.

Boston Tea Party On December 16, 1773, the Sons of Liberty, dressed as Indians, dumped hundreds of chests of tea into Boston Harbor to protest the Tea Act of 1773, under which the British exported to the colonies millions of pounds of cheap—but still taxed—tea, thereby undercutting the price of smuggled tea and forcing payment of the tea duty.

Boxer Rebellion Chinese nationalist protest against Western commercial domination and cultural influence, 1900; a coalition of American, European, and Japanese forces put down the rebellion and reclaimed captured embassies in Peking (Beijing) within the year.

Bracero program System agreed to by Mexican and American governments in 1942 under which tens of thousands of Mexicans entered the United States to work temporarily in agricultural jobs in the Southwest; lasted until 1964 and inhibited labor organization among farm workers since braceros could be deported at any time.

Brains trust Group of advisers—many of them academics—assembled by Franklin D. Roosevelt to recommend New Deal policies during the early months of his presidency.

Bretton Woods Town in New Hampshire and site of international agreement in 1944 by which the American dollar replaced the British pound as the most important international currency, and the World Bank and International Monetary Fund were created to promote rebuilding after World War II and to ensure that countries did not devalue their currencies.

Brook Farm Transcendentalist commune in West Roxbury, Massachusetts, populated from 1841 to 1847 principally by writers (Nathaniel Hawthorne, for one) and other intellectuals.

Brown v. Board of Education of Topeka (1954) U.S. Supreme Court decision that struck down racial segregation in public education and declared "separate but equal" unconstitutional.

Bull Run, Battles of (First and Second Manassas) First land engagement of the Civil War took place on July 21, 1861, at Manassas Junction, Virginia, at which Union troops quickly retreated; one year later, on August 29–30, Confederates captured the federal supply depot and forced Union troops back to Washington.

Bunker Hill, Battle of First major battle of the Revolutionary War; it actually took place at nearby Breed's Hill, Massachusetts, on June 17, 1775.

"Burned-over district" Area of western New York strongly influenced by the revivalist fervor of the Second Great Awakening; Disciples of Christ and Mormons are among the many sects that trace their roots to the phenomenon.

Bush Doctrine President George W. Bush's foreign policy principle wherein the United States would launch a war on terrorism.

***Bush v. Gore* (2000)** U.S. Supreme Court case that determined the winner of the disputed 2000 presidential election.

Busing The means of transporting students via buses to achieve school integration in the 1970s.

Calvinism Doctrine of predestination expounded by Swiss theologian John Calvin in 1536; influenced the Puritan, Presbyterian, German and Dutch Reformed, and Huguenot churches in the colonies.

Camp David accords Peace agreement between the leaders of Israel and Egypt, brokered by President Jimmy Carter in 1978.

Caravel A fifteenth-century European ship capable of long-distance travel.

Carpetbaggers Derisive term for northern emigrants who participated in the Republican governments of the Reconstruction South.

Chancellorsville, Battle of Confederate general Robert E. Lee won his last major victory and General "Stonewall" Jackson died in this Civil War battle in northern Virginia on May 1–4, 1863.

Checks and balances A systematic balance to prevent any one branch of the national government from dominating the other two.

Chinese Exclusion Act (1882) Halted Chinese immigration to the United States.

Civil Rights Act of 1866 Along with the Fourteenth Amendment, guaranteed the rights of citizenship to former slaves.

Civil Rights Act of 1957 First federal civil rights law since Reconstruction; established the Civil Rights Commission and the Civil Rights Division of the Department of Justice.

Civil Rights Act of 1964 Outlawed discrimination in public accommodations and employment.

Civil Service Act of 1883 Established the Civil Service Commission and marked the end of the spoils system.

Closed shop Hiring requirement that all workers in a business must be union members.

Coercive Acts/Intolerable Acts (1774) Four parliamentary measures in reaction to the Boston Tea Party that forced payment for the tea, disallowed colonial trials of British soldiers, forced their quartering in private homes, and reduced the number of elected officials in Massachusetts.

Cold War Term for tensions, 1945–1989, between the Soviet Union and the United States, the two major world powers after World War II.

Collective bargaining The process of negotiations between an employer and a group of employees to regulate working conditions.

Columbian exchange The transatlantic flow of goods and people that began with Columbus's voyages in 1492.

Common school Tax-supported state schools of the early nineteenth century open to all children.

Common Sense A pamphlet anonymously written by Thomas Paine in January 1776 that attacked the English principles of hereditary rule and monarchical government.

Commonwealth v. Hunt (1842) Landmark ruling of the Massachusetts Supreme Court establishing the legality of labor unions.

Communitarianism Social reform movement of the nineteenth century driven by the belief that by establishing small communities based on common ownership of property, a less competitive and individualistic society could be developed.

Compromise of 1850 Complex compromise devised by Senator Henry Clay that admitted California as a free state, included a stronger fugitive slave law, and delayed determination of the slave status of the New Mexico and Utah territories.

Compromise of 1877 Deal made by a Republican and Democratic special congressional commission to resolve the disputed presidential election of 1876; Republican Rutherford B. Hayes, who had lost the popular vote, was declared the winner in exchange for the withdrawal of federal troops from involvement in politics in the South, marking the end of Reconstruction.

Congress of Industrial Organizations (CIO) Umbrella organization of semiskilled industrial unions, formed in 1935 as the Committee for Industrial Organization and renamed in 1938.

Congress of Racial Equality (CORE) Civil rights organization started in 1942 and best known for its Freedom Rides, bus journeys challenging racial segregation in the South in 1961.

Conspicuous consumption Phrase referring to extravagant spending to raise social standing, coined by Thorstein Veblen in The Theory of the Leisure Class (1899).

Constitutional Convention Meeting in Philadelphia, May 25–September 17, 1787, of representatives from twelve colonies—excepting Rhode Island—to revise the existing Articles of Confederation; convention soon resolved to produce an entirely new constitution.

Containment General U.S. strategy in the Cold War that called for containing Soviet expansion; originally devised by U.S. diplomat George F. Kennan.

Continental army Army authorized by the Continental Congress in 1775 to fight the British; commanded by General George Washington.

Continental Congress Representatives of the colonies met first in Philadelphia in 1774 to formulate actions against British policies; the Second Continental Congress (1775–1789) conducted the war and adopted the Declaration of Independence and the Articles of Confederation.

Convict leasing System developed in the post–Civil War South that generated income for the states and satisfied planters' need for cheap labor by renting prisoners out; the convicts were often treated poorly.

Copperheads Republican term for northerners opposed to the Civil War; it derived from the name of a poisonous snake.

Coral Sea, Battle of the Fought on May 7–8, 1942, near the eastern coast of Australia, it was the first U.S. naval victory over Japan in World War II.

Cotton gin Invented by Eli Whitney in 1793, the machine separated cotton seed from cotton fiber, speeding cotton processing and making profitable the cultivation of the more hardy, but difficult to clean, short-staple cotton; led directly to the dramatic nineteenth-century expansion of slavery in the South.

Counterculture "Hippie" youth culture of the 1960s, which rejected the values of the dominant culture in favor of illicit drugs, communes, free sex, and rock music.

Court-packing plan President Franklin D. Roosevelt's failed 1937 attempt to increase the number of U.S. Supreme Court justices from nine to fifteen in order to save his Second New Deal programs from constitutional challenges.

Coverture Principle in English and American law that a married woman lost her legal identity, which became "covered" by that of her husband, who therefore controlled her person and the family's economic resources.

Crédit Mobilier scandal Millions of dollars in overcharges for building the Union Pacific Railroad were exposed; high officials of the Ulysses S. Grant administration were implicated but never charged.

Creoles (*Criollos* in Spanish) Persons born in the New World of European ancestry.

Cuban missile crisis Caused when the United States discovered Soviet offensive missile sites in Cuba in October 1962; the U.S.-Soviet confrontation was the Cold War's closest brush with nuclear war.

Cult of domesticity The nineteenth-century ideology of "virtue" and "modesty" as the qualities that were essential to proper womanhood.

Crop-lien system Merchants extended credit to tenants based on their future crops, but high interest rates and the uncertainties of farming often led to inescapable debts.

D-Day June 6, 1944, when an Allied amphibious assault landed on the Normandy coast and established a foothold in Europe, leading to the liberation of France from German occupation.

***Dartmouth College v. Woodward* (1819)** U.S. Supreme Court upheld the original charter of the college against New Hampshire's attempt to alter the board of trustees; set precedent of support of contracts against state interference.

Dawes Act Law passed in 1887 meant to encourage adoption of white norms among Indians; broke up tribal holdings into small farms for Indian families, with the remainder sold to white purchasers.

Declaration of Independence Document adopted on July 4, 1776, that made the break with Britain official; drafted by a committee of the Second Continental Congress, including principal writer Thomas Jefferson.

Deindustrialization Term describing decline of manufacturing in old industrial areas in the late twentieth century as companies shifted production to low-wage centers in the South and West or in other countries.

Deism Enlightenment thought applied to religion; emphasized reason, morality, and natural law.

Democratic Party Established in 1828 and led by Andrew Jackson and Martin Van Buren, the party was a major opponent of the Whig Party until the Civil War; unlike the Whigs, Democrats believed government should adopt a hands-off approach toward the economy.

Democratic-Republican Societies Organizations created in the mid-1790s by opponents of the policies of the Washington administration and supporters of the French Revolution.

Department of Homeland Security Created to coordinate federal antiterrorist activity following the 2001 terrorist attacks on the World Trade Center and Pentagon.

Depression Period in which economic output declines sharply and unemployment rises; it applied especially to the Great Depression of the 1930s.

Depression of 1893 Worst depression of the nineteenth century, set off by a railroad failure, too much speculation on Wall Street, and low agricultural prices.

Disenfranchise To deprive of the right to vote; in the United States, exclusionary policies were used to deny groups, especially African-Americans and women, their voting rights.

Division of Powers The division of political power between the state and federal governments under the U.S. Constitution (also known as federalism).

Dixiecrats Deep South delegates who walked out of the 1948 Democratic National Convention in protest of the party's support for civil rights legislation and later formed the States' Rights Democratic (Dixiecrat) Party, which nominated Strom Thurmond of South Carolina for president.

Dollar Diplomacy A foreign policy initiative under President William Howard Taft that promoted the spread of American influence through loans and economic investments from American banks.

Dominion of New England Consolidation into a single colony of the New England colonies—and later New York and New Jersey—by royal governor Edmund Andros in 1686; dominion reverted to individual colonial governments three years later.

Dred Scott v. Sandford (1857) U.S. Supreme Court decision in which Chief Justice Roger B. Taney ruled that Congress could not prohibit slavery in the territories, on the grounds that such a prohibition would violate the Fifth Amendment rights of slaveholders, and that no black person could be a citizen of the United States.

Due-process clause Clause in the Fifth and the Fourteenth Amendments to the U.S. Constitution guaranteeing that states could not "deprive any person of life, liberty, or property, without due process of law."

Dust Bowl Great Plains counties where millions of tons of topsoil were blown away from parched farmland in the 1930s; massive migration of farm families followed.

Eighteenth Amendment (1919) Prohibition amendment that made illegal the manufacture, sale, or transportation of alcoholic beverages; repealed in 1933.

Ellis Island Reception center in New York Harbor through which most European immigrants to America were processed from 1892 to 1954.

Emancipation Proclamation (1863) President Abraham Lincoln issued a preliminary proclamation on September 22, 1862, freeing the slaves in areas under Confederate control as of January 1, 1863, the date of the final proclamation, which also authorized the enrollment of black soldiers into the Union army.

Embargo Act of 1807 Attempt to exert economic pressure by prohibiting all exports from the United States, instead of waging war in reaction to continued British impressment of American sailors; smugglers easily circumvented the embargo, and it was repealed two years later.

Emergency Banking Relief Act (1933) First New Deal measure that provided for reopening the banks under strict conditions and took the United States off the gold standard.

Emergency Immigration Act of 1921 Limited U.S. immigration to 3 percent of each foreign-born nationality in the 1910 census; three years later, Congress restricted immigration even further.

Encomienda System under which officers of the Spanish conquistadores gained ownership of Indian land.

Enlightenment Revolution in thought in the eighteenth century that emphasized reason and science over the authority of traditional religion.

Environmental Protection Agency (EPA) Created in 1970 during the first administration of President Richard M. Nixon to oversee federal pollution control efforts.

Equal Rights Amendment Amendment to guarantee equal rights for women, introduced in 1923 but not passed by Congress until 1972; it failed to be ratified by the states.

Era of Good Feelings Contemporary characterization of the administration of popular Republican president James Monroe, 1817–1825.

Erie Canal Most important and profitable of the canals of the 1820s and 1830s; stretched from Buffalo to Albany, New York, connecting the Great Lakes to the East Coast and making New York City the nation's largest port.

Espionage and Sedition Acts (1917–1918) Limited criticism of government leaders and policies by imposing fines and prison terms on those who opposed American participation in the First World War.

Eugenics "Science" of improving the human race by regulating who can bear children; flourished in early twentieth century and led to laws for involuntary sterilization of the "feeble-minded."

Fair Deal Domestic reform proposals of the Truman administration; included civil rights legislation, national health insurance, and repeal of the Taft-Hartley Act, but only extensions of some New Deal programs were enacted.

Fair Employment Practices Commission Created in 1941 by executive order, the FEPC sought to eliminate racial discrimination in jobs; it possessed little power but represented a step toward civil rights for African-Americans.

Family wage Idea that male workers should earn a wage sufficient to enable them to support their entire family without their wives having to work outside the home.

Federalism A system of government in which power is divided between the central government and the states.

Federal Trade Commission Act (1914) Established the Federal Trade Commission to enforce existing antitrust laws that prohibited business combinations in restraint of trade.

The Federalist Collection of eighty-five essays that appeared in the New York press in 1787–1788 in support of the Constitution; written by Alexander Hamilton, James Madison, and John Jay and published under the pseudonym "Publius."

Federalist Party One of the two first national political parties; led by George Washington, John Adams, and Alexander Hamilton, it favored a strong central government.

Feminism Term that entered the lexicon in the early twentieth century to describe the movement for full equality for women, in political, social, and personal life.

Fifteenth Amendment Constitutional Amendment ratified in 1870, which prohibited states from discriminating in voting privileges on the basis of race.

"Fifty-four forty or fight" Democratic campaign slogan in the presidential election of 1844, urging that the northern border of Oregon be fixed at 54°409 north latitude.

Filibuster In the nineteenth century, invasions of Central American countries launched privately by groups of Americans seeking to establish personal rule and spread slavery; in the twentieth century, term for the practice of members of the U.S. Senate delivering interminable speeches in order to prevent voting on legislation.

***Fletcher v. Peck* (1810)** U.S. Supreme Court decision in which Chief Justice John Marshall upheld the initial fraudulent sale contracts in the Yazoo Fraud cases; it upheld the principle of sanctity of a contract.

Fordism Early twentieth-century term describing the economic system pioneered by Ford Motor Company based on high wages and mass consumption.

Fort McHenry Fort in Baltimore Harbor unsuccessfully bombarded by the British in September 1814; Francis Scott Key, a witness to the battle, was moved to write the words to "The Star-Spangled Banner."

Fort Sumter First battle of the Civil War, in which the federal fort in Charleston (South Carolina) Harbor was captured by the Confederates on April 14, 1861, after two days of shelling.

Four Freedoms Freedom of speech, freedom of worship, freedom from want, and freedom from fear.

Fourteen Points President Woodrow Wilson's 1918 plan for peace after World War I; at the Versailles peace conference, however, he failed to incorporate all of the points into the treaty.

Fourteenth Amendment (1868) Guaranteed rights of citizenship to former slaves, in words similar to those of the Civil Rights Act of 1866.

Franchise The right to vote.

"Free person of color" Negro or mulatto person not held in slavery; immediately before the Civil War, there were nearly a half million in the United States, split almost evenly between North and South.

Free Soil Party Formed in 1848 to oppose slavery in the territory acquired in the Mexican War; nominated Martin Van Buren for president in 1848. By 1854 most of the party's members had joined the Republican Party.

Free Speech Movement Founded in 1964 at the University of California at Berkeley by student radicals protesting restrictions on their right to distribute political publications.

Freedmen's Bureau Reconstruction agency established in 1865 to protect the legal rights of former slaves and to assist with their education, jobs, health care, and landowning.

Freedom Rides Bus journeys challenging racial segregation in the South in 1961.

French and Indian War Known in Europe as the Seven Years' War, the last (1755–1763) of four colonial wars fought between England and France for control of North America east of the Mississippi River.

Fugitive Slave Act of 1850 Gave federal government authority in cases involving runaway slaves; aroused considerable opposition in the North.

Fundamentalism Anti-modernist Protestant movement started in the early twentieth century that proclaimed the literal truth of the Bible; the name came from The Fundamentals, published by conservative leaders.

Gadsden Purchase (1853) Thirty thousand square miles in present-day Arizona and New Mexico bought by Congress from Mexico primarily for the Southern Pacific Railroad's transcontinental route.

Gag Rule Rule adopted by House of Representatives in 1836 prohibiting consideration of abolitionist petitions; opposition, led by former president John Quincy Adams, succeeded in having it repealed in 1844.

Geneva Accords (1954) A document that had promised elections to unify Vietnam and established the 17th Parallel demarcation line which divided North and South Vietnam.

Gentlemen's Agreement (1907) The United States would not exclude Japanese immigrants if Japan would voluntarily limit the number of immigrants coming to the United States.

Gettysburg, Battle of Fought in southern Pennsylvania, July 1–3, 1863; the Confederate defeat and the simultaneous loss at Vicksburg marked the military turning point of the Civil War.

***Gibbons v. Ogden* (1824)** U.S. Supreme Court decision reinforcing the "commerce clause" (the federal government's right to regulate interstate commerce) of the Constitution; Chief Justice John Marshall ruled against the State of New York's granting of steamboat monopolies.

GI Bill of Rights (1944) The legislation that provided money for education and other benefits to military personnel returning from World War II.

***Gideon v. Wainwright* (1963)** U.S. Supreme Court decision guaranteeing legal counsel for indigent felony defendants.

The Gilded Age Mark Twain and Charles Dudley Warner's 1873 novel, the title of which became the popular name for the period from the end of the Civil War to the turn of the century.

Glass-Steagall Act (Banking Act of 1933) Established the Federal Deposit Insurance Corporation and included banking reforms, some designed to control speculation. Repealed in 1999, opening the door to scandals involving banks and stock investment companies.

Globalization Term that became prominent in the 1990s to describe the rapid acceleration of international flows of commerce, financial resources, labor, and cultural products.

Glorious Revolution A coup in 1688 engineered by a small group of aristocrats that led to William of Orange taking the British throne in place of James II.

Gold standard Policy at various points in American history by which the value of a dollar is set at a fixed price in terms of gold (in the post–World War II era, for example, $35 per ounce of gold).

Good Neighbor Policy Proclaimed by President Franklin D. Roosevelt in his first inaugural address in 1933, it sought improved diplomatic relations between the United States and its Latin American neighbors.

Gospel of Wealth The idea proposed by Andrew Carnegie in 1889 that those who are wealthy have an obligation to use their resources to improve society.

Grandfather clause Loophole created by southern disfranchising legislatures of the 1890s for illiterate white males whose grandfathers had been eligible to vote in 1867.

Granger movement Political movement that grew out of the Patrons of Husbandry, an educational and social organization for farmers founded in 1867; the Grange had its greatest success in the Midwest of the 1870s, lobbying for government control of railroad and grain elevator rates and establishing farmers' cooperatives.

Great Awakening Fervent religious revival movement in the 1720s through the 1740s that was spread throughout the colonies by ministers like New England Congregationalist Jonathan Edwards and English revivalist George Whitefield.

Great Compromise (Connecticut Compromise) Settled the differences between the New Jersey and Virginia delegations to the Constitutional Convention by providing for a bicameral legislature, the upper house of which would have equal representation for each state and the lower house of which would be apportioned by population.

Great Depression Worst economic depression in American history; it was spurred by the stock market crash of 1929 and lasted until World War II.

Great Migration Large-scale migration of southern blacks during and after World War I to the North, where jobs had become available during the labor shortage of the war years.

Great Society Term coined by President Lyndon B. Johnson in his 1965 State of the Union address, in which he proposed legislation to address problems of voting rights, poverty, diseases, education, immigration, and the environment.

Greenback-Labor Party Formed in 1876 in reaction to economic depression, the party favored issuance of unsecured paper money to help farmers repay debts; the movement for free coinage of silver took the place of the greenback movement by the 1880s.

***Griswold v. Connecticut* (1965)** Supreme Court decision that, in overturning Connecticut law prohibiting the use of contraceptives, established a constitutional right to privacy.

Gulf of Tonkin resolution (1964) A resolution passed by Congress authorizing the president to take "all necessary measures to repel armed attack" in Vietnam.

Gulf War Military action in 1991 in which an international coalition led by the United States drove Iraq from Kuwait, which it had occupied the previous year.

Habeas corpus, Writ of An essential component of English common law and of the U.S. Constitution that guarantees that citizens may not be imprisoned without due process of law; literally means, "you may have the body"; suspended by President Lincoln during the Civil War and limited by President Bush after the attacks of September 11, 2001.

Hacienda Large-scale farm in the Spanish New World empire worked by Indian laborers.

Harlem Renaissance African-American literary and artistic movement of the 1920s centered in New York City's Harlem neighborhood; writers Langston Hughes, Jean Toomer, Zora Neale Hurston, and Countee Cullen were among those active in the movement.

Harpers Ferry, Virginia Site of abolitionist John Brown's failed raid on the federal arsenal, October 16–17, 1859; Brown became a martyr to his cause after his capture and execution.

Hart-Celler Act (1965) Eliminated the national origins quota system for immigration established by laws in 1921 and 1924; led to radical change in the origins of immigrants to the United States, with Asians and Latin Americans outnumbering Europeans.

Hartford Convention Meeting of New England Federalists on December 15, 1814, to protest the War of 1812; proposed seven constitutional amendments (limiting embargoes and changing requirements for officeholding, declaration of war, and admission of new states), but the war ended before Congress could respond.

Hawley-Smoot Tariff Act (1930) Raised tariffs to an unprecedented level and worsened the Great Depression by raising prices and discouraging foreign trade.

Haymarket affair Violence during an anarchist protest at Haymarket Square in Chicago on May 4, 1886; the deaths of eight, including seven policemen, led to the trial of eight anarchist leaders for conspiracy to commit murder.

Hessians German soldiers, most from Hesse-Cassel principality (hence, the name), paid to fight for the British in the Revolutionary War.

Holding company Investment company that holds controlling interest in the securities of other companies.

Homestead Act (1862) Authorized Congress to grant 160 acres of public land to a western settler, who had to live on the land for five years to establish title.

Homestead Strike Violent strike at the Carnegie Steel Company near Pittsburgh in 1892 that culminated in the defeat of the Amalgamated Association of Iron and Steel Workers, the first steelworkers' union.

House Un-American Activities Committee (HUAC) Formed in 1938 to investigate subversives in the government and holders of radical ideas more generally; best-known investigations were of Hollywood notables and of former State Department official Alger Hiss, who was accused in 1948 of espionage and Communist Party membership. Abolished in 1975.

Hundred Days Extraordinarily productive first three months of President Franklin D. Roosevelt's administration in which a special session of Congress enacted fifteen of his New Deal proposals.

Impeachment Bringing charges against a public official; for example, the House of Representatives can impeach a president for "treason, bribery, or other high crimes and misdemeanors" by majority vote, and after the trial the Senate can remove the president by a vote of two-thirds. Two presidents, Andrew Johnson and Bill Clinton, have been impeached and tried before the Senate; neither was convicted.

Implied powers Federal powers beyond those specifically enumerated in the U.S. Constitution; based on the "elastic clause" of Article I, Section 8, of the Constitution that allows Congress to enact laws that promote the "general welfare."

"In God We Trust" Phrase placed on all new U.S. currency as of 1954.

Indentured servant Settler who signed on for a temporary period of servitude to a master in exchange for passage to the New World; Virginia and Pennsylvania were largely peopled in the seventeenth and eighteenth centuries by English and German indentured servants.

Indian Removal Act (1830) Signed by President Andrew Jackson, the law permitted the negotiation of treaties to obtain the Indians' lands in exchange for their relocation to what would become Oklahoma.

Individualism Term that entered the language in the 1820s to describe the increasing emphasis on the pursuit of personal advancement and private fulfillment free of outside interference.

Industrial Workers of the World Radical union organized in Chicago in 1905 and nicknamed the Wobblies; its opposition to World War I led to its destruction by the federal government under the Espionage Act.

Inflation An economic condition in which prices rise continuously.

Insular Cases Series of cases between 1901 and 1904 in which the Supreme Court ruled that constitutional protection of individual rights did not fully apply to residents of "insular" territories acquired by the United States in the Spanish-American War, such as Puerto Rico and the Philippines.

Interstate Commerce Commission Reacting to the U.S. Supreme Court's ruling in Wabash Railroad v. Illinois (1886), Congress established the ICC to curb abuses in the railroad industry by regulating rates.

Iran-Contra affair Scandal of the second Reagan administration involving sales of arms to Iran in partial exchange for release of hostages in Lebanon and use of the arms money to aid the Contras in Nicaragua, which had been expressly forbidden by Congress.

Iraq War Military campaign in 2003 in which the United States, unable to gain approval by the United Nations, unilaterally occupied Iraq and removed dictator Saddam Hussein from power.

Iron Curtain Term coined by Winston Churchill to describe the Cold War divide between western Europe and the Soviet Union's eastern European satellites.

Isolationism The desire to avoid foreign entanglements that dominated the United States Congress in the 1930s; beginning in 1935, lawmakers passed a series of Neutrality Acts that banned travel on belligerents' ships and the sale of arms to countries at war.

Jamestown, Virginia Site in 1607 of the first permanent English settlement in the New World.

Japanese-American internment Policy adopted by the Roosevelt administration in 1942 under which 110,000 persons of Japanese descent, most of them American citizens, were removed from the West Coast and forced to spend most of World War II in internment camps; it was the largest violation of American civil liberties in the twentieth century.

Jay's Treaty Treaty with Britain negotiated in 1794 by Chief Justice John Jay; Britain agreed to vacate forts in the Northwest Territories, and festering disagreements (border with Canada, prewar debts, shipping claims) would be settled by commission.

Jim Crow Minstrel show character whose name became synonymous with racial segregation.

Kansas Exodus A migration in 1879 and 1880 by some 40,000–60,000 blacks to Kansas to escape the oppressive environment of the New South.

Kansas-Nebraska Act (1854) Law sponsored by Illinois senator Stephen A. Douglas to allow settlers in newly organized territories north of the Missouri border to decide the slavery issue for themselves; fury over the resulting repeal of the Missouri Compromise of 1820 led to violence in Kansas and to the formation of the Republican Party.

Kellogg-Briand Pact Representatives of sixty-two nations in 1928 signed the pact (also called the Pact of Paris) to outlaw war.

Keynesianism Economic theory derived from the writings of British economist John Maynard Keynes, which rejected the laissez-faire approach in favor of public spending to stimulate economic growth, even at the cost of federal deficits; dominated economic policies of administrations from the 1940s to the mid-1970s.

"King Cotton diplomacy" An attempt during the Civil War by the South to encourage British intervention by banning cotton exports.

King Philip's War Began in 1675 with an Indian uprising against white colonists. A multi-year conflict, the end result was broadened freedoms for white New Englanders and the dispossession of the region's Indians.

Knights of Labor Founded in 1869, the first national union lasted, under the leadership of Terence V. Powderly, only into the 1890s; supplanted by the American Federation of Labor.

Know-Nothing (American) Party Nativist, anti-Catholic third party organized in 1854 in reaction to large-scale German and Irish immigration; the party's only presidential candidate was Millard Fillmore in 1856.

Korean War Conflict touched off in 1950 when Communist North Korea invaded South Korea; fighting, largely by U.S. forces, continued until 1953.

Ku Klux Klan Organized in Pulaski, Tennessee, in 1866 to terrorize former slaves who voted and held political offices during Reconstruction; a revived organization in the 1910s and 1920s stressed white, Anglo-Saxon, fundamentalist Protestant supremacy; the Klan revived a third time to fight the civil rights movement of the 1950s and 1960s in the South.

Kyoto Protocol (1997) An international agreement that sought to combat global warming. To great controversy, the Bush administration announced in 2001 that it would not abide by the Kyoto Protocol.

Laissez-faire Term adopted from French, meaning "let people do as they choose," describing opposition to government action to regulate economic or personal behavior.

Land Ordinance of 1785 Directed surveying of the Northwest Territory into townships of thirty-six sections (square miles) each, the sale of the sixteenth section of which was to be used to finance public education.

League of Nations Organization of nations to mediate disputes and avoid war established after World War I as part of the Treaty of Versailles; President Woodrow Wilson's "Fourteen Points" speech to Congress in 1918 proposed the formation of the league, which the United States never joined.

Lend-Lease Act (1941) Permitted the United States to lend or lease arms and other supplies to the Allies, signifying increasing likelihood of American involvement in World War II.

Levittown Low-cost, mass-produced developments of suburban tract housing built by William Levitt after World War II on Long Island and elsewhere.

Lexington and Concord, Battle of The first shots fired in the Revolutionary War, on April 19, 1775, near Boston; approximately 100 minutemen and 250 British soldiers were killed.

Leyte Gulf, Battle of Largest sea battle in history, fought on October 25, 1944, and won by the United States off the Philippine island of Leyte; Japanese losses were so great that they could not rebound.

Liberalism Originally, political philosophy that emphasized the protection of liberty by limiting the power of government to interfere with the natural rights of citizens; in the twentieth century, belief in an activist government promoting greater social and economic equality.

Liberty Party Abolitionist political party that nominated James G. Birney for president in 1840 and 1844; merged with the Free Soil Party in 1848.

Lincoln-Douglas debates Series of senatorial campaign debates in 1858 focusing on the issue of slavery in the territories; held in Illinois between Republican Abraham Lincoln, who made a national reputation for himself, and incumbent Democratic senator Stephen A. Douglas, who managed to hold onto his seat.

Little Bighorn, Battle of Most famous battle of the Great Sioux War took place in 1876 in the Montana

Territory; combined Sioux and Cheyenne warriors massacred a vastly outnumbered U.S. Cavalry commanded by Lieutenant Colonel George Armstrong Custer.

***Lochner v. New York* (1905)** Decision by Supreme Court overturning a New York law establishing a limit on the number of hours per week bakers could be compelled to work; "Lochnerism" became a way of describing the liberty of contract jurisprudence, which opposed all governmental intervention in the economy.

Long Telegram A telegram by American diplomat George Kennan in 1946 outlining his views of the Soviet Union that eventually inspired the policy of containment.

Louisiana Purchase President Thomas Jefferson's 1803 purchase from France of the important port of New Orleans and 828,000 square miles west of the Mississippi River to the Rocky Mountains; it more than doubled the territory of the United States at a cost of only $15 million.

Loyalists Colonists who remained loyal to Great Britain during the War of Independence.

Lusitania British passenger liner sunk by a German U-boat, May 7, 1915, creating a diplomatic crisis and public outrage at the loss of 128 Americans (roughly 10 percent of the total aboard); Germany agreed to pay reparations, and the United States waited two more years to enter World War I.

Lyceum movement Founded in 1826, the movement promoted adult public education through lectures and performances.

Lynching Practice, particularly widespread in the South between 1890 and 1940, in which persons (usually black) accused of a crime were murdered by mobs before standing trial. Lynchings often took place before large crowds, with law enforcement authorities not intervening.

Manhattan Project Secret American program during World War II to develop an atomic bomb; J. Robert Oppenheimer led the team of physicists at Los Alamos, New Mexico.

Manifest Destiny Phrase first used in 1845 to urge annexation of Texas; used thereafter to encourage American settlement of European colonial and Indian lands in the Great Plains and the West and, more generally, as a justification for American empire.

***Marbury v. Madison* (1803)** First U.S. Supreme Court decision to declare a federal law—the Judiciary Act of 1801—unconstitutional.

March on Washington Civil rights demonstration on August 28, 1963, where the Reverend Martin Luther King Jr., gave his "I Have a Dream" speech on the steps of the Lincoln Memorial.

Marshall Plan U.S. program for the reconstruction of post–World War II Europe through massive aid to former enemy nations as well as allies; proposed by General George C. Marshall in 1947.

Massive resistance In reaction to the Brown decision of 1954, effort by southern states to defy federally mandated school integration.

Maya Pre-Columbian society in Mesoamerica before about A.D. 900.

Mayflower Compact Signed in 1620 aboard the Mayflower before the Pilgrims landed at Plymouth, the document committed the group to majority-rule government.

McCarran Internal Security Act (1950) Passed over President Harry S. Truman's veto, the law required registration of American Communist Party members, denied them passports, and allowed them to be detained as suspected subversives.

McCarthyism Post–World War II Red Scare focused on the fear of Communists in U.S. government positions; peaked during the Korean War; most closely associated with Joseph McCarthy, a major instigator of the hysteria.

McCulloch v. Maryland (1819) U.S. Supreme Court decision in which Chief Justice John Marshall, holding that Maryland could not tax the Second Bank of the United States, supported the authority of the federal government versus the states.

McNary-Haugen bill Vetoed by President Calvin Coolidge in 1927 and 1928, the bill to aid farmers would have artificially raised agricultural prices by selling surpluses overseas for low prices and selling the reduced supply in the United States for higher prices.

Meat Inspection Act (1906) Passed largely in reaction to Upton Sinclair's The Jungle, the law set strict standards of cleanliness in the meatpacking industry.

Medicaid Great Society program established in 1965 that provided free medical care to the poor.

Medicare Key component of Great Society of Lyndon B. Johnson; government program created in 1965 to pay medical costs of elderly and disabled Americans.

Mercantilism Policy of Great Britain and other imperial powers of regulating the economies of colonies to benefit the mother country.

Mestizo Spanish word for person of mixed Native American and European ancestry.

Mexican War Controversial war with Mexico for control of California and New Mexico, 1846–1848; the Treaty of Guadalupe Hidalgo fixed the border at the Rio Grande and extended the United States to the Pacific coast, annexing more than a half-million square miles of Mexican territory.

Midway, Battle of Decisive American victory near Midway Island in the South Pacific on June 4, 1942; the Japanese navy never recovered its superiority over the U.S. navy.

Military-industrial complex The concept of "an immense military establishment" combined with a "permanent arms industry," which President Eisenhower warned against in his 1961 Farewell Address.

Mill girls Women who worked at textile mills during the Industrial Revolution who enjoyed new freedoms and independence not seen before.

Minstrel show Blackface vaudeville entertainment popular in the decades surrounding the Civil War.

Miranda v. Arizona (1966) U.S. Supreme Court decision required police to advise persons in custody of their rights to legal counsel and against self-incrimination.

Missouri Compromise Deal proposed by Kentucky senator Henry Clay in 1820 to resolve the slave/free imbalance in Congress that would result from Missouri's admission as a slave state; Maine's admission as a free state offset Missouri, and slavery was prohibited in the remainder of the Louisiana Territory north of the southern border of Missouri.

Molly Maguires Secret organization of Irish coal miners that used violence to intimidate mine officials in the 1870s.

Monitor and Merrimac, Battle of the First engagement between ironclad ships; fought at Hampton Roads, Virginia, on March 9, 1862.

Monroe Doctrine President James Monroe's declaration to Congress on December 2, 1823, that the American continents would be thenceforth closed to European colonization, and that the United States would not interfere in European affairs.

Montgomery bus boycott Sparked by Rosa Parks's arrest on December 1, 1955, for refusing to surrender her seat to a white passenger, a successful year-long boycott protesting segregation on city buses; led by the Reverend Martin Luther King Jr.

Moral Majority Televangelist Jerry Falwell's political lobbying organization, the name of which became synonymous with the Religious Right—conservative evangelical Protestants who helped ensure President Ronald Reagan's 1980 victory.

Mormons Founded in 1830 by Joseph Smith, the sect (officially, the Church of Jesus Christ of Latter-day

Saints) was a product of the intense revivalism of the "burned-over district" of New York; Smith's successor Brigham Young led 15,000 followers to Utah in 1847 to escape persecution.

Muckrakers Writers who exposed corruption and abuses in politics, business, meatpacking, child labor, and more, primarily in the first decade of the twentieth century; their popular books and magazine articles spurred public interest in reform.

Mugwumps Reform wing of the Republican Party that supported Democrat Grover Cleveland for president in 1884 over Republican James G. Blaine, whose influence peddling had been revealed in the Mulligan letters of 1876.

Multiculturalism Term that became prominent in the 1990s to describe a growing emphasis on group racial and ethnic identity and demands that jobs, education, and politics reflect the increasingly diverse nature of American society.

***Munn v. Illinois* (1877)** U.S. Supreme Court ruling that upheld a Granger law allowing the state to regulate grain elevators.

NAFTA Approved in 1993, the North American Free Trade Agreement with Canada and Mexico allowed goods to travel across their borders free of tariffs; critics argued that American workers would lose their jobs to cheaper Mexican labor.

Nat Turner Rebellion Most important slave uprising in nineteenth-century America, led by a slave preacher who, with his followers, killed about sixty white persons in Southampton County, Virginia, in 1831.

National Association for the Advancement of Colored People (NAACP) Founded in 1910, this civil rights organization brought lawsuits against discriminatory practices and published The Crisis, a journal edited by African-American scholar W. E. B. Du Bois.

National Defense Education Act (1958) Passed in reaction to America's perceived inferiority in the space race; encouraged education in science and modern languages through student loans, university research grants, and aid to public schools.

National Industrial Recovery Act (1933) Passed on the last of the Hundred Days, it created public-works jobs through the Federal Emergency Relief Administration and established a system of self-regulation for industry through the National Recovery Administration, which was ruled unconstitutional in 1935.

National Organization for Women Founded in 1966 by writer Betty Friedan and other feminists, NOW pushed for abortion rights, nondiscrimination in the workplace, and other forms of equality for women.

National Road First federal interstate road, built between 1811 and 1838 and stretching from Cumberland, Maryland, to Vandalia, Illinois.

National Security Act (1947) Authorized the reorganization of government to coordinate military branches and security agencies; created the National Security Council, the Central Intelligence Agency, and the National Military Establishment (later renamed the Department of Defense).

National Youth Administration Created in 1935 as part of the Works Progress Administration, it employed millions of youths who had left school.

Nativism Anti-immigrant and anti-Catholic feeling especially prominent in the 1830s through the 1850s; the largest group was New York's Order of the Star-Spangled Banner, which expanded into the American (Know-Nothing) Party in 1854.

Naval stores Tar, pitch, and turpentine made from pine resin and used in shipbuilding; an important industry in the southern colonies, especially North Carolina.

Navigation Acts Passed by the English Parliament to control colonial trade and bolster the mercantile system, 1650–1775; enforcement of the acts led to growing resentment by colonists.

Neutrality Acts Series of laws passed between 1935 and 1939 to keep the United States from becoming involved in war by prohibiting American trade and travel to warring nations.

New Deal Franklin D. Roosevelt's campaign promise, in his speech to the Democratic National Convention of 1932, to combat the Great Depression with a "new deal for the American people"; the phrase became a catchword for his ambitious plan of economic programs.

New Freedom Democrat Woodrow Wilson's political slogan in the presidential campaign of 1912; Wilson wanted to improve the banking system, lower tariffs, and, by breaking up monopolies, give small businesses freedom to compete.

New Frontier John F. Kennedy's program, stymied by a Republican Congress and his abbreviated term; his successor Lyndon B. Johnson had greater success with many of the same concepts.

New Harmony Founded in Indiana by British industrialist Robert Owen in 1825, the short-lived New Harmony Community of Equality was one of the few nineteenth-century communal experiments not based on religious ideology.

New Left Radical youth protest movement of the 1960s, named by leader Tom Hayden to distinguish it from the Old (Marxist-Leninist) Left of the 1930s.

New Nationalism Platform of the Progressive Party and slogan of former president Theodore Roosevelt in the presidential campaign of 1912; stressed government activism, including regulation of trusts, conservation, and recall of state court decisions that had nullified progressive programs.

New Orleans, Battle of Last battle of the War of 1812, fought on January 8, 1815, weeks after the peace treaty was signed but prior to the news reaching America; General Andrew Jackson led the victorious American troops.

New South Atlanta Constitution editor Henry W. Grady's 1886 term for the prosperous post–Civil War South he envisioned: democratic, industrial, urban, and free of nostalgia for the defeated plantation South.

Nineteenth Amendment (1920) Granted women the right to vote.

Ninety-Five Theses The list of moral grievances against the Catholic Church by Martin Luther, a German priest, in 1517.

Nisei Japanese-Americans; literally, "second generation."

Normalcy Word coined by future president Warren G. Harding as part of a 1920 campaign speech—"not nostrums, but normalcy"—signifying public weariness with Woodrow Wilson's internationalism and domestic reforms.

North Atlantic Treaty Organization (NATO) Alliance founded in 1949 by ten western European nations, the United States, and Canada to deter Soviet expansion in Europe.

Northwest Ordinance of 1787 Created the Northwest Territory (area north of the Ohio River and west of Pennsylvania), established conditions for self-government and statehood, included a Bill of Rights, and permanently prohibited slavery.

Nullification Concept of invalidation of a federal law within the borders of a state; first expounded in Thomas Jefferson's draft of Kentucky resolution against Alien and Sedition Acts (1798); cited by South Carolina in its Ordinance of Nullification (1832) of the Tariff of Abominations, used by southern states to explain their secession from the Union (1861), and cited again by southern states to oppose the Brown v. Board of Education decision (1954).

Occupy Wall Street A grassroots movement in 2011 against growing economic inequality, declining opportunity, and the depredations of Wall Street banks.

Office of Price Administration Created in 1941 to control wartime inflation and price fixing resulting from shortages of many consumer goods, the OPA imposed wage and price freezes and administered a rationing system.

Okies Displaced farm families from the Oklahoma dust bowl who migrated to California during the 1930s in search of jobs.

Oneida Community Utopian community founded in 1848; the Perfectionist religious group practiced "complex marriage" under leader John Humphrey Noyes.

OPEC Organization of Petroleum Exporting Countries.

Open Door Policy In hopes of protecting the Chinese market for U.S. exports, Secretary of State John Hay demanded in 1899 that Chinese trade be open to all nations.

Open shop Situation in which union membership is not a condition of employment in a factory or other business.

Operation Dixie CIO's largely ineffective post–World War II campaign to unionize southern workers.

Oregon Trail Route of wagon trains bearing settlers from Independence, Missouri, to the Oregon Country in the 1840s through the 1860s.

Ostend Manifesto Memorandum written in 1854 from Ostend, Belgium, by the U.S. ministers to England, France, and Spain recommending purchase or seizure of Cuba in order to increase the United States' slaveholding territory.

Panic of 1819 Financial collapse brought on by sharply falling cotton prices, declining demand for American exports, and reckless western land speculation.

Panic of 1837 Beginning of major economic depression lasting about six years; touched off by a British financial crisis and made worse by falling cotton prices, credit and currency problems, and speculation in land, canals, and railroads.

Panic of 1857 Beginning of economic depression lasting about two years and brought on by falling grain prices and a weak financial system; the South was largely protected by international demand for its cotton.

Panic of 1873 Onset of severe six-year depression marked by bank failures and railroad and insurance bankruptcies.

Peace of Paris Signed on September 3, 1783, the treaty ending the Revolutionary War and recognizing American independence from Britain also established the border between Canada and the United States, fixed the western border at the Mississippi River, and ceded Florida to Spain.

Pendleton Civil Service Act (1883) Established the Civil Service Commission and marked the end of the spoils system.

Pentagon Papers Informal name for the Defense Department's secret history of the Vietnam conflict; leaked to the press by former official Daniel Ellsberg and published in the New York Times in 1971.

Pequot War An armed conflict in 1637 that led to the destruction of one of New England's most powerful Indian groups.

"Perfectionism" The idea that social ills once considered incurable could in fact be eliminated, popularized by the religious revivalism of the nineteenth century.

"Pet banks" Local banks that received deposits while the charter of the Bank of the United States was about to expire in 1836. The choice of these banks was influenced by political and personal connections.

Philippine War American military campaign that suppressed the movement for Philippine independence after the Spanish-American War; America's death toll was over 4,000 and the Philippines' was far higher.

Pilgrims Puritan Separatists who broke completely with the Church of England and sailed to the New World aboard the Mayflower, founding Plymouth Colony on Cape Cod in 1620.

Pinckney's Treaty Treaty with Spain negotiated by Thomas Pinckney in 1795; established United States boundaries at the Mississippi River and the thirty-first parallel and allowed open transportation on the Mississippi.

Plantation An early word for a colony, a settlement "planted" from abroad among an alien population in Ireland or the New World. Later, a large agricultural enterprise that used unfree labor to produce a crop for the world market.

Planter In the antebellum South, the owner of a large farm worked by twenty or more slaves.

Platt Amendment (1901) Amendment to Cuban constitution that reserved the United States' right to intervene in Cuban affairs and forced newly independent Cuba to host American naval bases on the island.

***Plessy v. Ferguson* (1896)** U.S. Supreme Court decision supporting the legality of Jim Crow laws that permitted or required "separate but equal" facilities for blacks and whites.

Poll tax Tax that must be paid in order to be eligible to vote; used as an effective means of disenfranchising black citizens after Reconstruction, since they often could not afford even a modest fee.

Popular Front A period during the mid-1930s when the Communist Party sought to ally itself with socialists and New Dealers in movements for social change, urging reform of the capitalist system rather than revolution.

Popular sovereignty Allowed settlers in a disputed territory to decide the slavery issue for themselves; program most closely associated with Senator Stephen A. Douglas of Illinois.

Populist Party Founded in 1892, it advocated a variety of reform issues, including free coinage of silver, income tax, postal savings, regulation of railroads, and direct election of U.S. senators.

Port Huron Statement (1962) A manifesto by Students for a Democratic Society that criticized institutions ranging from political parties to corporations, unions, and the military-industrial complex, while offering a new vision of social change.

Potsdam Conference Last meeting of the major Allied powers, the conference took place outside Berlin from July 17 to August 2, 1945; United States president Harry Truman, Soviet dictator Joseph Stalin, and British prime minister Clement Attlee finalized plans begun at Yalta.

Proclamation of Amnesty and Reconstruction President Lincoln's proposal for reconstruction, issued in 1863, allowed southern states to rejoin the Union if 10 percent of the 1860 electorate signed loyalty pledges, accepted emancipation, and had received presidential pardons.

Proclamation of 1763 Royal directive issued after the French and Indian War prohibiting settlement, surveys, and land grants west of the Appalachian Mountains; caused considerable resentment among colonists hoping to move west.

Progressive Party Created when former president Theodore Roosevelt broke away from the Republican Party to run for president again in 1912; the party supported progressive reforms similar to the Democrats but stopped short of seeking to eliminate trusts. Also the name of party backing Robert La Follette for president in 1924.

Progressivism Broad-based reform movement, 1900–1917, that sought governmental action in solving problems in many areas of American life, including education, public health, the economy, the environment, labor, transportation, and politics.

Proposition 13 Measure approved by California voters in 1978 prohibiting future increases in property taxes; marked beginning of "tax revolt" as major political impulse.

Public sphere The world of political organization and debate in private associations and publications outside the control of government.

Pueblo Revolt Uprising in 1680 in which Pueblo Indians temporarily drove Spanish colonists out of modern-day New Mexico.

Pullman Strike Strike against the Pullman Palace Car Company in the company town of Pullman, Illinois, on May 11, 1894, by the American Railway Union under Eugene V. Debs; the strike was crushed by court injunctions and federal troops two months later.

Pure Food and Drug Act (1906) First law to regulate manufacturing of food and medicines; prohibited dangerous additives and inaccurate labeling.

Puritans English religious group that sought to purify the Church of England; founded the Massachusetts Bay Colony under John Winthrop in 1630.

Quakers (Society of Friends) Religious group in England and America whose members believed all persons possessed the "inner light" or spirit of God; they were early proponents of abolition of slavery and equal rights for women.

Radical Republicans Group within the Republican Party in the 1850s and 1860s that advocated strong resistance to the expansion of slavery, opposition to compromise with the South in the secession crisis of 1860–1861, emancipation and arming of black soldiers during the Civil War, and equal civil and political rights for blacks during Reconstruction.

Railroad Strike of 1877 Interstate strike, crushed by federal troops, which resulted in extensive property damage and many deaths.

Reaganomics Popular name for President Ronald Reagan's philosophy of "supply side" economics, which combined tax cuts with an unregulated marketplace.

Reconquista The "reconquest" of Spain from the Moors completed by King Ferdinand and Queen Isabella in 1492.

Reconstruction Act (1867) Established temporary military governments in ten Confederate states—excepting Tennessee—and required that the states ratify the Fourteenth Amendment and permit freedmen to vote.

Reconstruction Finance Corporation Federal program established in 1932 under President Herbert Hoover to loan money to banks and other institutions to help them avert bankruptcy.

Red Scare Fear among many Americans after World War I of Communists in particular and noncitizens in general, a reaction to the Russian Revolution, mail bombs, strikes, and riots.

Redeemers Conservative white Democrats, many of them planters or businessmen, who reclaimed control of the South following the end of Reconstruction.

Regulators Groups of backcountry Carolina settlers who protested colonial policies.

Republican motherhood The ideology that emerged as a result of American independence where women played an indispensible role by training future citizens.

Republican Party Organized in 1854 by antislavery Whigs, Democrats, and Free Soilers in response to the passage of the Kansas-Nebraska Act; nominated John C. Frémont for president in 1856 and Abraham Lincoln in 1860; also the name of the party formed by Thomas Jefferson and James Madison in the 1790s.

Republicanism Political theory in eighteenth-century England and America that celebrated active participation in public life by economically independent citizens as central to freedom.

Revolution of 1800 First time that an American political party surrendered power to the opposition party; Jefferson, a Republican, had defeated incumbent Adams, a Federalist, for president.

Right-to-work State laws enacted to prevent imposition of the closed shop; any worker, whether or not a union member, could be hired.

***Roe v. Wade* (1973)** U.S. Supreme Court decision requiring states to permit first-trimester abortions.

Roosevelt Corollary (1904) President Theodore Roosevelt announced in what was essentially a corollary to the Monroe Doctrine that the United States could intervene militarily to prevent interference from European powers in the Western Hemisphere.

Rough Riders The first U.S. Volunteer Cavalry, led in battle in the Spanish-American War by Theodore Roosevelt; they were victorious in their only battle near Santiago, Cuba, and Roosevelt used the notoriety to aid his political career.

Sacco-Vanzetti case A case held during the 1920s in which two Italian-American anarchists were found guilty and executed for a crime in which there was very little evidence linking them to the particular crime.

Salem witch trials A crisis of trials and executions in Salem, Massachusetts, in 1692 that resulted from anxiety over witchcraft.

Santa Fe Trail Beginning in the 1820s, a major trade route from St. Louis, Missouri, to Santa Fe, New Mexico Territory.

Saratoga, Battle of Major defeat of British general John Burgoyne and more than 5,000 British troops at Saratoga, New York, on October 17, 1777.

Scalawags Southern white Republicans—some former Unionists—who supported Reconstruction governments.

***Schenck v. U.S.* (1919)** U.S. Supreme Court decision upholding the wartime Espionage and Sedition Acts; in the opinion he wrote for the case, Justice Oliver Wendell Holmes set the now-familiar "clear and present danger" standard.

Scientific management Management campaign to improve worker efficiency using measurements like "time and motion" studies to achieve greater productivity; introduced by Frederick Winslow Taylor in 1911.

Scopes trial (1925) Trial of John Scopes, Tennessee teacher accused of violating state law prohibiting teaching of the theory of evolution; it became a nationally celebrated confrontation between religious fundamentalism and civil liberties.

Scottsboro case (1931) In overturning verdicts against nine black youths accused of raping two white women, the U.S. Supreme Court established precedents in Powell v. Alabama (1932), that adequate counsel must be appointed in capital cases, and in Norris v. Alabama (1935), that African-Americans cannot be excluded from juries.

Second American Revolution The transformation of American government and society brought about by the Civil War.

Second Great Awakening Religious revival movement of the early decades of the nineteenth century, in reaction to the growth of secularism and rationalist religion; began the predominance of the Baptist and Methodist churches.

Second Great Migration The movement of black migrants from the rural South to the cities of the North and West, which occurred from 1941 through World War II, that dwarfed the Great Migration of World War I.

Segregation Policy of separating persons on the basis of race in schools, transportation, and other public facilities; de facto segregation refers to social customs that accomplish this, de jure segregation to laws requiring it.

Seneca Falls Convention First women's rights meeting and the genesis of the women's suffrage movement; held in July 1848 in a church in Seneca Falls, New York, organized by Elizabeth Cady Stanton and Lucretia Coffin Mott.

"Separate but equal" Principle underlying legal racial segregation, upheld in Plessy v. Ferguson (1896) and struck down in Brown v. Board of Education (1954).

Separation of Powers Feature of the U.S. Constitution, sometimes called "checks and balances," in which power is divided between executive, legislative, and judicial branches of the national government so that no one can dominate the other two and endanger citizens' liberties.

Servicemen's Readjustment Act (1944) The "GI Bill of Rights" provided money for education and other benefits to military personnel returning from World War II.

Settlement houses Late-nineteenth-century movement to offer a broad array of social services in urban immigrant neighborhoods; Chicago's Hull House was one of hundreds of settlement houses that operated by the early twentieth century.

Seventeenth Amendment (1913) Progressive reform that required U.S. senators to be elected directly by voters; previously, senators were chosen by state legislatures.

Shakers Founded by Mother Ann Lee in England, the United Society of Believers in Christ's Second Appearing settled in Watervliet, New York, in 1774 and subsequently established eighteen additional communes in the Northeast, Indiana, and Kentucky.

Sharecropping Type of farm tenancy that developed after the Civil War in which landless workers—often former slaves—farmed land in exchange for farm supplies and a share of the crop.

Shays's Rebellion (1787) Massachusetts farmer Daniel Shays and 1,200 compatriots, seeking debt relief through issuance of paper currency and lower taxes, attempted to prevent courts from seizing property from indebted farmers.

Sherman Antitrust Act (1890) First law to restrict monopolistic trusts and business combinations; extended by the Clayton Antitrust Act of 1914.

Sherman Silver Purchase Act (1890) In replacing and extending the provisions of the Bland-Allison Act of 1878, it increased the amount of silver periodically bought for coinage.

Single tax Concept of taxing only landowners as a remedy for poverty, promulgated by Henry George in Progress and Poverty (1879).

Sit-down strikes Tactic adopted by labor unions in the mid- and late 1930s, whereby striking workers refused to leave factories, making production impossible; proved highly effective in the organizing drive of the Congress of Industrial Organizations.

Sit-ins Tactic adopted by young civil rights activists, beginning in 1960, of demanding service at lunch counters or public accommodations and refusing to leave if denied access; marked the beginning of the most militant phase of the civil rights struggle.

Sixteenth Amendment (1913) Legalized the federal income tax.

***Smith v. Allwright* (1944)** U.S. Supreme Court decision that outlawed all-white Democratic Party primaries in Texas.

"Social contract" In leading industries, labor and management hammered out what has been called a new "social contract." Unions signed long-term agreements that left decisions regarding capital investment, plant location, and output in management's hands, and they agreed to try to prevent unauthorized "wildcat" strikes.

Social Darwinism Application of Charles Darwin's theory of natural selection to society; used the concept of the "survival of the fittest" to justify class distinctions and to explain poverty.

Social Gospel Preached by liberal Protestant clergymen in the late nineteenth and early twentieth centuries; advocated the application of Christian principles to social problems generated by industrialization.

Social Security Act (1935) Created the Social Security system with provisions for a retirement pension, unemployment insurance, disability insurance, and public assistance (welfare).

Socialist Party Political party demanding public ownership of major economic enterprises in the United States as well as reforms like recognition of labor unions and women's suffrage; reached peak of influence in 1912 when presidential candidate Eugene V. Debs received over 900,000 votes.

Sons of Liberty Organizations formed by Samuel Adams, John Hancock, and other radicals in response to the Stamp Act.

South Carolina Exposition and Protest Written in 1828 by Vice-President John C. Calhoun of South Carolina to protest the so-called Tariff of Abominations, which seemed to favor northern industry; introduced the concept of state interposition and became the basis for South Carolina's Nullification Doctrine of 1833.

Southeast Asia Treaty Organization (SEATO) Pact among mostly Western nations signed in 1954; designed to deter Communist expansion and cited as a justification for U.S. involvement in Vietnam.

Southern Christian Leadership Conference (SCLC) Civil rights organization founded in 1957 by the Reverend Martin Luther King Jr., and other civil rights leaders.

"Southern Manifesto" (1956) A document that repudiated the Supreme Court decision in *Brown v. Board of Education* and supported the campaign against racial integration in public places.

Spoils system The term—meaning the filling of federal government jobs with persons loyal to the party of the president—originated in Andrew Jackson's first term.

Sputnik First artificial satellite to orbit the earth; launched October 4, 1957, by the Soviet Union.

Stagflation A combination of stagnant economic growth and high inflation present during the 1970s.

Stalwarts Conservative Republican Party faction during the presidency of Rutherford B. Hayes, 1877–1881; led by Senator Roscoe B. Conkling of New York, Stalwarts opposed civil service reform and favored a third term for President Ulysses S. Grant.

Stamp Act (1765) Parliament required that revenue stamps be affixed to all colonial printed matter, documents, and playing cards; the Stamp Act Congress met to formulate a response, and the act was repealed the following year.

Standard Oil Company Founded in 1870 by John D. Rockefeller in Cleveland, Ohio, it soon grew into the nation's first industry-dominating trust; the Sherman Antitrust Act (1890) was enacted in part to combat abuses by Standard Oil.

Staple crop Important cash crop, for example, cotton or tobacco.

Steamboats Paddlewheelers that could travel both up- and down-river in deep or shallow waters; they became commercially viable early in the nineteenth century and soon developed into America's first inland freight and passenger service network.

Stono Rebellion A slave uprising in 1739 in South Carolina that led to a severe tightening of the slave code and the temporary imposition of a prohibitive tax on imported slaves.

Strategic Defense Initiative ("Star Wars") Defense Department's plan during the Reagan administration to build a system to destroy incoming missiles in space.

Student Nonviolent Coordinating Committee (SNCC) Founded in 1960 to coordinate civil rights sit-ins and other forms of grassroots protest.

Students for a Democratic Society (SDS) Major organization of the New Left, founded at the University of Michigan in 1960 by Tom Hayden and Al Haber.

Sugar Act (Revenue Act of 1764) Parliament's tax on refined sugar and many other colonial products.

Taft-Hartley Act (1947) Passed over President Harry Truman's veto, the law contained a number of provisions to weaken labor unions, including the banning of closed shops.

Tariff Federal tax on imported goods.

Tariff of Abominations (Tariff of 1828) Taxed imported goods at a very high rate; aroused strong opposition in the South.

Tariff of 1816 First true protective tariff, intended to protect certain American goods against foreign competition.

Tax Reform Act (1986) Lowered federal income tax rates to 1920s levels and eliminated many loopholes.

Tea Party A grassroots Republican movement, named for the Boston Tea Party of the 1770s and developed in 2009, that opposed the Obama administration's sweeping legislative enactments and advocated for a more stringent immigration policy.

Teapot Dome Harding administration scandal in which Secretary of the Interior Albert B. Fall profited from secret leasing to private oil companies of government oil reserves at Teapot Dome, Wyoming, and Elk Hills, California.

Tennessee Valley Authority Created in 1933 to control flooding in the Tennessee River valley, provide work for the region's unemployed, and produce inexpensive electric power for the region.

Tenure of Office Act (1867) Required the president to obtain Senate approval to remove any official whose appointment had also required Senate approval; President Andrew Johnson's violation of the law by firing Secretary of War Edwin Stanton led to Johnson's impeachment.

Tet Offensive Surprise attack by the Viet Cong and North Vietnamese during the Vietnamese New Year of 1968; turned American public opinion strongly against the war in Vietnam.

Thirteenth Amendment Constitutional amendment adopted in 1865 that irrevocably abolished slavery throughout the United States.

Three-fifths clause A provision signed into the Constitution in 1787 that three-fifths of the slave population would be counted in determining each state's representation in the House of Representatives and its electoral votes for president.

Three Mile Island Nuclear power plant near Harrisburg, Pennsylvania, site of 1979 accident that released radioactive steam into the air; public reaction ended the nuclear power industry's expansion.

Title IX Part of the Educational Amendments Act of 1972 that banned gender discrimination in higher education.

Tonkin Gulf Resolution (1964) Passed by Congress in reaction to supposedly unprovoked attacks on American warships off the coast of North Vietnam; it gave the president unlimited authority to defend U.S. forces and members of SEATO.

Totalitarianism The term which described aggressive, ideologically driven states that sought to subdue all of civil society to their control, thus leaving no room for individual rights or alternative values.

Townshend Acts (1767) Parliamentary measures (named for the chancellor of the Exchequer) that taxed tea and other commodities, and established a Board of Customs Commissioners and colonial vice-admiralty courts.

Trail of Tears Cherokees' own term for their forced removal, 1838–1839, from the Southeast to Indian lands (later Oklahoma); of 15,000 forced to march, 4,000 died on the way.

Transcendentalism Philosophy of a small group of mid-nineteenth-century New England writers and thinkers, including Ralph Waldo Emerson, Henry David Thoreau, and Margaret Fuller; they stressed personal and intellectual self-reliance.

Transcontinental railroad First line across the continent from Omaha, Nebraska, to Sacramento, California, established in 1869 with the linkage of the Union Pacific and Central Pacific railroads at Promontory, Utah.

Truman Doctrine President Harry S. Truman's program announced in 1947 of aid to European countries—particularly Greece and Turkey—threatened by communism.

Trust Companies combined to limit competition.

Twenty-first Amendment (1933) Repealed the prohibition of the manufacture, sale, and transportation of alcoholic beverages, effectively nullifying the Eighteenth Amendment.

Twenty-second Amendment (1951) Limited presidents to two full terms of office or two terms plus two years of an assumed term; passed in reaction to President Franklin D. Roosevelt's unprecedented four elected terms.

Twenty-sixth Amendment (1971) Lowered the voting age from twenty-one to eighteen.

U.S.S. Maine Battleship that exploded in Havana Harbor on February 15, 1898, resulting in 266 deaths; the American public, assuming that the Spanish had mined the ship, clamored for war, and the Spanish-American War was declared two months later.

Uncle Tom's Cabin Harriet Beecher Stowe's 1852 antislavery novel popularized the abolitionist position.

Underground Railroad Operating in the decades before the Civil War, the "railroad" was a clandestine system of routes and safehouses through which slaves were led to freedom in the North.

Understanding clause Added to southern state constitutions in the late nineteenth century, it allowed illiterate whites to circumvent literacy tests for voting by demonstrating that they understood a passage in the Constitution; black citizens would be judged by white registrars to have failed.

Unitarianism Late-eighteenth-century liberal offshoot of the New England Congregationalist Church; rejecting the Trinity, Unitarianism professed the oneness of God and the goodness of rational man.

United Farm Workers Union for the predominantly Mexican-American migrant laborers of the Southwest, organized by César Chavez in 1962.

United Nations Organization of nations to maintain world peace, established in 1945 and headquartered in New York.

Universal Negro Improvement Association Black nationalist movement active in the United States from 1916 to 1923, led by Marcus Garvey.

USA Patriot Act (2001) A mammoth bill that conferred unprecedented powers on law-enforcement agencies charged with preventing domestic terrorism, including the power to wiretap, read private messages, and spy on citizens.

V-E Day May 8, 1945, the day World War II officially ended in Europe.

Versailles Treaty The treaty signed at the Versailles peace conference after World War I which established President Woodrow Wilson's vision of an international regulating body, redrew parts of Europe and the Middle East, and assigned economically-crippling war reparations to Germany, but failed to incorporate all of Wilson's fourteen points.

Vertical integration Company's avoidance of middlemen by producing its own supplies and providing for distribution of its product.

Veto President's constitutional power to reject legislation passed by Congress; a two-thirds vote in both houses of Congress can override a veto.

Vicksburg, Battle of The fall of Vicksburg, Mississippi, to General Ulysses S. Grant's army on July 4, 1863, after two months of siege was a turning point in the war because it gave the Union control of the Mississippi River.

Vietnam War Longest war in which the United States has been involved; began with giving American financial assistance to France, who sought to maintain control over Vietnam colony; moved to dispatching advisers to bolster the government of South Vietnam; and finally sent over 500,000 American soldiers by the mid-1960s; resulted in massive antiwar movement, eventual American withdrawal, and communist victory in 1975; only war the United States has lost.

Virginia and Kentucky Resolutions (1798–1799) Passed by the Virginia and the Kentucky legislatures; written by James Madison and Thomas Jefferson in response to the Alien and Sedition Acts, the resolutions advanced the state-compact theory of the Constitution. Virginia's resolution called on the federal courts to protect free speech. Jefferson's draft for Kentucky stated that a state could nullify federal law, but this was deleted.

Virginia and New Jersey Plans Differing opinions of delegations to the Constitutional Convention: New Jersey wanted one legislative body with equal representation for each state; Virginia's plan called for a strong central government and a two-house legislature apportioned by population.

Volstead Act (1919) Enforced the Prohibition amendment, beginning January 1920.

Voting Rights Act of 1965 Passed in the wake of Martin Luther King Jr.'s, Selma to Montgomery March, it authorized federal protection of the right to vote and permitted federal enforcement of minority voting rights in individual counties, mostly in the South.

***Wabash Railroad v. Illinois* (1886)** Reversing the U.S. Supreme Court's ruling in Munn v. Illinois, the decision disallowed state regulation of interstate commerce.

Wade-Davis bill (1864) Radical Republicans' plan for reconstruction that required loyalty oaths, abolition of slavery, repudiation of war debts, and denial of political rights to high-ranking Confederate officials; President Lincoln refused to sign the bill.

Wagner Act (National Labor Relations Act of 1935) Established the National Labor Relations Board and facilitated unionization by regulating employment and bargaining practices.

War Industries Board Run by financier Bernard Baruch, the board planned production and allocation of war materiel, supervised purchasing, and fixed prices, 1917–1919.

War of 1812 Fought with Britain, 1812–1814, over issues that included impressment of American sailors, interference with shipping, and collusion with Northwest Territory Indians; settled by the Treaty of Ghent in 1814.

War on Poverty Announced by President Lyndon B. Johnson in his 1964 State of the Union address; under the Economic Opportunity Bill signed later that year, Head Start, VISTA, and the Jobs Corps were created, and programs were created for students, farmers, and businesses in efforts to eliminate poverty.

War Powers Act Law passed in 1973, reflecting growing opposition to American involvement in Vietnam War; required congressional approval before president sent troops abroad.

War Production Board Created in 1942 to coordinate industrial efforts in World War II; similar to the War Industries Board in World War I.

Warren Court The U.S. Supreme Court under Chief Justice Earl Warren, 1953–1969, decided such landmark cases as Brown v. Board of Education (school desegregation), Baker v. Carr (legislative redistricting), and Gideon v. Wainwright and Miranda v. Arizona (rights of criminal defendants).

Washington Armaments Conference Leaders of nine world powers met in 1921–1922 to discuss the naval race; resulting treaties limited to a specific ratio the carrier and battleship tonnage of each nation (Five-Power Naval Treaty), formally ratified the Open Door to China (Nine-Power Treaty), and agreed to respect each other's Pacific territories (Four-Power Treaty).

Watergate Washington office and apartment complex that lent its name to the 1972–1974 scandal of the Nixon administration; when his knowledge of the break-in at the Watergate and subsequent coverup was revealed, Nixon resigned the presidency under threat of impeachment.

Webster-Hayne debate U.S. Senate debate of January 1830 between Daniel Webster of Massachusetts and Robert Hayne of South Carolina over nullification and states' rights.

Welfare state A term that originated in Britain during World War II to refer to a system of income assistance, health coverage, and social services for all citizens.

Whig Party Founded in 1834 to unite factions opposed to President Andrew Jackson, the party favored federal responsibility for internal improvements; the party ceased to exist by the late 1850s, when party members divided over the slavery issue.

Whiskey Rebellion Violent protest by western Pennsylvania farmers against the federal excise tax on whiskey, 1794.

Wilmot Proviso Proposal to prohibit slavery in any land acquired in the Mexican War, but southern senators, led by John C. Calhoun of South Carolina, defeated the measure in 1846 and 1847.

Women's Christian Temperance Union Largest female reform society of the late nineteenth century; it moved from opposing sale of liquor to demanding the right to vote for women.

Works Progress Administration (WPA) Part of the Second New Deal, it provided jobs for millions of the unemployed on construction and arts projects.

Wounded Knee, Battle of Last incident of the Indian Wars took place in 1890 in the Dakota Territory, where the U.S. Cavalry killed over 200 Sioux men, women, and children.

Writs of assistance One of the colonies' main complaints against Britain, the writs allowed unlimited search warrants without cause to look for evidence of smuggling.

XYZ affair French foreign minister Tallyrand's three anonymous agents demanded payments to stop French plundering of American ships in 1797; refusal to pay the bribe was followed by two years of undeclared sea war with France (1798–1800).

Yalta conference Meeting of Franklin D. Roosevelt, Winston Churchill, and Joseph Stalin at a Crimean resort to discuss the postwar world on February 4–11, 1945; Joseph Stalin claimed large areas in eastern Europe for Soviet domination.

Yellow journalism Sensationalism in newspaper publishing that reached a peak in the circulation war between Joseph Pulitzer's New York World and William Randolph Hearst's New York Journal in the 1890s; the papers' accounts of events in Havana Harbor in 1898 led directly to the Spanish-American War.

Yeoman farmers Small landowners (the majority of white families in the Old South) who farmed their own land and usually did not own slaves.

Yick Wo v. Hopkins Supreme Court decision in 1886 overturning San Francisco law that, as enforced, discriminated against Chinese-owned laundries; established principle that equal protection of the law embodied in Fourteenth Amendment applied to all Americans, not just former slaves.

Yorktown, Battle of Last battle of the Revolutionary War; General Lord Charles Cornwallis along with over 7,000 British troops surrendered at Yorktown, Virginia, on October 17, 1781.

Young Americans for Freedom Organization of conservative students founded in 1960; played major role in 1964 presidential campaign of Barry Goldwater and in rebirth of conservatism in the 1960s.

Zimmermann Telegram From the German foreign secretary to the German minister in Mexico, February 1917, instructing him to offer to recover Texas, New Mexico, and Arizona for Mexico if it would fight the United States to divert attention from Germany in the event that the United States joined the war.

CREDITS

PHOTOS

1 Collection du monastère des Ursulines de Québec, Musée des Ursulines de Québec (1997.1017); **5** Photo Courtesy of Edward E. Ayer Collection, The Newberry Library, Chicago; **7** National Park Service, Chaco Culture National Historic Park, Chaco Archive neg. no. 25462; **9** Bridgeman Art Library; **10** Library of Congress; **11** Courtesy Lilly Library, Indiana University, Bloomington, IN; **16** Granger Collection; **19** Granger Collection; **20** The Art Archive at Art Resource, NY; **22** Museo de la Basilica de Guadalupe, Mexico City; **23** Library of Congress; **30** National Museum of American History, Smithsonian Institution, Behring Center; **33** Bettmann/Corbis; **35** GLCO3582 Novi Belgi Novaeque Angliae (New Netherland and New England) by Nicholas Visscher, 1682/ Courtesy of The Gilder Lehrman Institute of American History; **36** Museum of the City of New York; **38** Woburn Abbey, Bedfordshire, UK/The Bridgeman Art Library; **42** The John Carter Brown Library at Brown University; **43** Granger Collection; **46** The London Art Archive/Alamy; **47** Museum of Art, Rhode Island School of Design. Gift of Robert Winthrop. Photography by Erik Gould; **49 (top)** Granger Collection; **(bottom)** National Portrait Gallery, Smithsonian Institution/Art Resource, NY; **50** George Arents Collection, New York Public Library. Art Resource, NY; **51** Corbis; **54** American Antiquarian Society; **55** Courtesy of the Massachusetts Archives; **56** Worcester Art Museum, Worcester, Massachusetts, Gift of William A. Savage; **57** Massachusetts Historical Society; **60** The New York Public Library/Art Resource, NY; **64** Annenberg Rare Book and Manuscript Library, Van Pelt-Dietrich Library Center, U Penn; **65** Library of Congress; **66** Mrs. Elizabeth Freake and Baby Mary, unknown artist, 1963.134, Worcester Art Museum, Worcester, Massachusetts; **68** Private Collection/Bridgeman Art Library; **69** By permission of the British Library/Art Resource; **72** Art Resource; **86** The John Carter Brown

Library at Brown University; **77** Library of Congress; **79** Unidentified artist, British, 18th century or first quarter 19th century; *Quaker Meeting*; Oil on canvas; 64.1 x 76.2cm (25 1/4 x 30in.); Museum of Fine Arts, Boston; Bequest of Maxim Karolik; 64.456. Photograph (c) 2013 Museum of Fine Arts, Boston; **82** © British Library Board. All Rights Reserved/ The Bridgeman Art Library; **84** National Maritime Museum, London; **89** Rare Books Dividsion, The New York Public Library, Astor, Lenox and Tilden Foundations. Art Resource, NY; **95** Benjamin West, Pennsylvania Academy of the Fine Arts; Joseph and Sarah Harrison Collection; **97** Winterthur Museum; **99** Photograph (c) 2013 Museum of Fine Arts, Boston; **101** Gift of Edgar William and Bernice Chrysler Garbisch, Image © 2006 Board of Trustees, National Gallery of Art, Washington; **111** Granger Collection; **106** Library of Congress; **109** © Musée d'histoire de Nantes – Château des ducs de Bretagne/ Alain Guillard; **104** Abby Aldrich Rockefeller Folk Art Museum, Colonial Williamsburg Foundation, Williamsburg, VA; **114** Charleston Library Society; **117** Chicago Historical Society; **118** Library of Congress; **120** The Library Company of Philadelphia; **123** Library of Congress; **124** Portrait of Benjamin Franklin, Mason Chamberlin, Oil on canvas, 1762, Philadelphia Museum of Art: Gift of Mr. and Mrs Wharton Sinkler, 1956; **126** National Portrait Gallery, London; **129** Benard de la Harpe, "Carte Nouvelle de la Partie de l'Ouest de la Province de la Louisiane" [map], 1720, Louisiana Research Collection, Tulane University; **131** Library of Congress; **139** *George Washington's War in Caricature and Print*. Kenneth Baker, Grub Street Publishing; **141** Library of Congress; **143** The Colonial Williamsburg Foundation; **144** Kunhardt/Picture History; **147** Library of Congress; **148** Michael Nicholson/Corbis; **149** Library of Congress; **151** Chicago Historical Society; **153** American Philosophical Society; **154** American Antiquarian Society; **155** Sid Lapidus Collection. Rare Books Division. Department of Rare Books and Special Col-

lections. Princeton University Library; **165** Library of Congress; **159** Anne S.K. Brown Military Collection, Brown University; **167** Library Company of Philadelphia. Gift of the artist, 1792; **169** National Gallery of Art, Washington, Gift of Mrs. Robert Homans; **170** Historical Society of Pennsylvania; **172** Courtesy of the New-York Historical Society; **173** York County Historical Society, America, USA/The Bridgeman Art Library; **175** American Antiquarian Society; **177** Bettmann/ Corbis; **178** Reproduced by permission of the Huntington Library, San Marino, California; **179** Library of Congress; **182** Corbis; **185** Library of Congress; **188** Collection of The New-York Historical Society; **184** Bequest of Miss Lucy T. Aldrich 39.002 Museum of Art, Rhode Island School of Design, Providence; **189** Southern Historical Collection, Wilson Library, The University of North Carolina at Chapel Hill; **190** Charles Wilson Peale, Portrait of John and Elizabeth Lloyd Cadwalader, and their daughter Anne, Philadelphia Museum of Art: Purchased from the Cadwalader Collection with funds contributed by the Myrin Trust and the gift of an anonymous donor; **191** Library of Congress; **193** Collection of the New-York Historical Society/Bridgeman Art Library; **200** Print Collection, Miriam and Ira D. Wallach Division of Art, Prints, and Photographs, The New York Public Library; Astor, Lenox, and Tilden Foundations. Art Resource, NY; **201 (top)** Library of Congress; **(bottom)** Independence National Historical Park; **202** Library of Congress; **205** The Library of Virginia; **206** MPI/Getty Images; **207** Library of Congress; **209** Granger Collection; **214** Library of Congress; **216** Chicago Historical Society; **218** Granger Collection; **219**; Virginia Historical Society, Richmond/Bridgeman Art Library; **221** Photography by Erik Arneson (c) Nicholas S. West; **223** Fenimore Art Museum, Cooperstown, New York. Photo by Richard Walker; **224** Library of Congress; **227** Courtesy, Winterthur Museum, Bequest of Henry F. DuPont; **230** Print Collection, Miriam and Ira D. Wallach Division of Art, Prints, and

Society; **443** Library of Congress; **444 (top)** Library of Congress; **(bottom)** Photographic History Collection, Division of Information Technology and Communications, National Museum of American History, Smithsonian Institution; **445** Granger Collection; **447** Smithsonian American Art Museum, Washington, DC/Art Resource, NY; **448** Library of Congress; **449** Cook Collection, Valentine Richmond History Center; **453 (top)** Library of Congress; **(bottom)** Kemper Leila Williams Foundation /The Historic New Orleans Collection; **455** Library of Congress; **456** Library of Congress; **457** Ed Sullivan Collection, Special Collections, University of Hartford; **459** Library of Congress; **460** Library of Congress; **462** Library of Congress; **463** (both) Library of Congress; **464** Granger Collection; **466** Clements Library Collection, University of Michigan; **467** Granger Collection; **469** (both) Library of Congress; **473** Library of Congress; **475** © The Metropolitan Museum of Art. Image source: Art Resource, NY; **480 (top left)** Chicago History Museum/Getty Images; **(top right)** Granger Collection; **(bottom)** Granger Collection; **481** Library of Congress; **483** Library of Congress; **484** Museum of the City of New York, The Jacob Riis Collection (#108); **485** Private Collection/The Bridgeman Art Library; **486** Solomon Butcher Collection. Nebraska State Historical Society; **487** Granger Collection; **488** Image copyright © The Metropolitan Museum of Art/Art Resource, NY; **489** Library of Congress; **490 (top)** Private Collection, Photograph by courtesy of David A. Schorsch and Eileen M. Smiles and The American Folk Art Museum; **(bottom)** Photography Collection. Miriam and Ira D. Wallach Division of Art, Prints and Photographs, The New York Public Library, Astor, Lenox and Tilden Foundations; **494** (both) Library of Congress; **495** Library of Congress; **497** The Ohio State University Billy Ireland Cartoon Library & Museum; **498** Museum of the City of New York/The Art Archive at Art Resource, NY; **502** Bettmann/Corbis; **503** Bettmann/Corbis; **506** Wisconsin Historical Society, WHS-47662; **508** Hawai'i State Archives. Honolulu, Hawai'i. Kahn Collection [37/36]; **509** Library of Congress; **511** Kansas State Historical Society; **514** Picture History; **515** Library of Congress; **517** Florida State Archives; **518** Library of Congress; **519** Library of Congress; **522** (both) Library of Congress; **523** Library of Congress; **524** Courtesy of the Tennessee State Museum; **526 (top)** The Denver Public Library, Western

History Collection, X-21518; **(bottom)** University of Washington Libraries, Special Collections, #UW1678; **527** Library of Congress; **529** Library of Congress; **531** Courtesy of the Bernice Pauahi Bishop Museum Archives; **533** Frederic Remington Art Museum; **535 (top)** Granger Collection; **(bottom)** National Archives; **538** Library of Congress; **539** North Wind Picture Archives/Alamy; **540** David J. & Janice L. Frent Collection/Corbis; **543** © 2013 Delaware Art Museum/Artists Rights Society (ARS), New York/The Philadelphia Museum of Art; **546** Bettmann/Corbis; **549 (top)** Library of Congress; **(bottom)** Courtesy of author; **550** Library of Congress; **551** Image Courtesy of The Advertising Archives; **552** Corbis; **557** Brown Brothers; **558 (top)** Library of Congress; **(bottom)** Bettmann/Corbis; **560** Museum of the City of New York, The Byron Collection; **562** University of Illinois at Chicago, the University Library, Jane Addams Memorial Collection; **563** Nebraska State Historical Society; **566** Hulton Archive/Getty Images; **567 (top)** provided courtesy (c) HarpWeek LLC; **(bottom)** Purchase, Jim and Carol Kautz, class of 1955, in honor of Richard and Ronay Menschel/Francis Lehman Loeb Art Center, Vassar College; **568** Library of Congress; **569** Courtesy of Debs Collection, Cunningham Memorial Library, Indiana State University; **574** Library of Congress; **578** Library of Congress; **580** Albin Egger-Lienz, Nordfrankreich, 1917/Photo by Ji-Elle. 2012 http://creativecommons.org/licenses/by-sa/3.0/deed.en; **581** Private Collection/Chris Deakes/The Art Archive. Art Resource, NY; **582** Bettmann/Corbis; **585 (top)** Library of Congress; **(bottom)** Eileen Tweedy/The Art Archive at Art Resource, NY; **586** Library of Congress; **587** Cover of Union Signal, Jan 27, 1916, Frances E. Willard Memorial Library and Archives; **590** National Archives; **595** St Louis Post-Dispatch, 17 April 1906; **596** Library of Congress; **598 (top)** Tulsa Historical Society; **(bottom)** Library of Congress; **600** Bettmann/Corbis; **601** National Archives; **608** The Metropolitan Museum of Art, Gift of AXA Equitable, 2012 (2012.478a-j) Image © The Metropolitan Museum of Art/Art Resource; **609** Library of Congress; **610** Library of Congress; **613** Minnesota Historical Society; **614** Charles Sheeler (1883-1965) *River Rouge Plant*, 1932, oil on canvas, 20x24 1/8 in. (50.8x61.28 cm) Whitney Museum of American Art, New York; Purchase 32.43. Photography copyright © 1996 Whitney Museum; **615** Honolulu Academy of Arts: Gift of Philip H.

Roach, Jr., 2001; **616** (left) Legacy Tobacco Documents Library, University of California, San Francisco; (right) Procter & Gamble; **617** The Art Archive/Culver Pictures. Art Resource, NY; **618** Granger Collection; **622 (top)** San Diego Museum of Art; **(bottom)** The Denver Public Library, Western History Collection, Rh-1158; **623** Smithsonian Institutions Archives; **624** Washington State Historical Society; **625** Los Angeles Public Library Photo Collection; **627** Library of Congress; **630** Photographs and Prints Division, Schomburg Center for Research in Black Culture, The New York Public Library, Astor, Lenox, and Tilden Foundations/Art Resource, NY; **631** Collection of David J. And Janice L. Frent/Corbis; **632** Library of Congress; **633** Courtesy of author; **634 (top)** National Archives; **(bottom)** Museum of History & Industry/Corbis; **635** Robert F. Wagner Labor Archives, New York University, Charles Rivers Collection, photograph by Charles Rivers; **636** AP Photo; **639** Smithsonian American Art Museum/Art Resource; **642** Granger Collection; **643** Bettmann/Corbis; **644** National Archives; **645** David Rumsey Map Collection; **647** Kansas State Historical Society; **648** Punch Limited; **650** Bettmann/Corbis; **651** (both) Library of Congress; **652** Billy Graham Center Archives, Wheaton College, Wheaton, IL; **653 (top)** Library of Congress; **(bottom)** National Archives; **654** Library of Congress; **655** Franklin D. Roosevelt Library; **658** Franklin D. Roosevelt Library; **660** Bettmann/Corbis; **663** Photograph © Morgan and Marvin Smith; **664** HOLC Residential Security Map, Federal Home Loan Bank Board, Records of the City Survey Program," RG 195, 450/68/03/02, National Archives II, College Park, MD; **666** Franklin D. Roosevelt Presidential Library; **667 (top)** Library of Congress; **(bottom)** Brown Brothers; **672** Library of Congress; **674** Library of Congress; **675** Washington Star; **676** Andreas Feninger/George Eastman House/Getty Images; **678** National Archives; **680 (top)** Used with permission of Joshua Brown; **(bottom)** Bettmann/Corbis; **682** AP Photo; **683** Library of Congress; **685** (both) Library of Congress; **686 (top)** Library of Congress; **(bottom)** McCall's Magazine Collection, California Lutheran University; **687** National Archives; **689** Courtesy Northwestern University Library; **690** Detroit Free Press; **692** National Archives; **694** AP Photo; **695** National Archives; **696** Library of Congress; **697** National Archives; **702** Unidentified Photographer, (Interior damage to steel frame of Honkawa Grammar School Auditorium, Hiroshima), November 8, 1945 International Center Of Photography, Purchase, with funds provided by the ICP Acquisitions Committee, 2006; **703** Library of Congress; **707** Cover to the propaganda comic book, Catechetical Guild "Is This Tomorrow" http://en.wikipedia.org/wiki/Public_domain; **709** The Lincoln Highway National Museum & Archives; **710** Bettmann/Corbis; **712** Bettmann/Corbis; **717** AP Photo; **721** Michael Barson Collection; **723** Bettmann /Corbis; **724** Library of Congress, Visual Materials from the NAACP Records, LC-USZ62-84483; **725** Hy Peskin's SL & WH, www.HyPeskin.com; **726** Bettmann/Corbis; **727** Vintage Vegas; **729** Bettmann/Corbis; **730** Office of the Historian of the U.S. Senate; **731** © 1949 Herbert Block; **736** Courtesy of Hagley Museum and Library; **737** Howard Sochurek/Time Life Pictures/Getty Images; **741** Hulton Archive/Getty Images; **743 (top)** Bettmann/Corbis; **(bottom)** Advertising Archive; **744** American Economic Foundation, "Man's Belief in God is Personal," CU Libraries Exhibitions, accessed February 22, 2013, https://exhibitions.cul.columbia.edu/items/show/2829; **746** Dwight D. Eisenhower Presidential Library; **749** Bettmann/Corbis; **751** AP Photo; **752** Dan Weiner/Time Life Pictures/Getty Images; **753 (top)** Bruce Davidson/Magnum Photos; **(bottom)** Frank Driggs Collection; **754** Cal Bernstein/LOOK Magazine; **756** Ed Clark/Time Life Pictures/Getty Images; **757** Carl/Wasaki/Time Life Pictures/Getty Images; **758** AP Photo; **760** Collection of Civil Rights Archive, CADVC-UMBC, Baltimore, MD, 2005.183. On Center for Art, Design and Visual Culture, University of MD Baltimore County website. http://www.umbc.edu/cadvc/foralltheworld/section3/context.php; **761** Bettmann /Corbis; **764** Time & Life Pictures /Getty Images; **765** Bettmann/Corbis; **768** National Archives; **769** Image courtesy of the Raleigh City Museum; **770** (c) Cecil Williams; **771 (top)** Ed Jones/The Birmingham News/Landov; **(bottom)** Bettmann/Corbis; **772** © Walter P. Reuther Library, Wayne State University; **775 (top)** Ed Meek/University of Mississippi; **(bottom)** Photo by Carl Mydans/Time Life Pictures/Getty Images; **777** AP Photo; **779** Bettmann /Corbis; **781** LBJ Library photo by Cecil Stoughton; **783** Bettmann/Corbis; **785** Scurlock Studio Records, Archives Center, National Museum of American History, Smithsonian Institution; **786** Photo by

C. Clark Kissinger; **787** Lon Wilson/UC Berkeley, University Archives; **790** Photograph by Yoichi Okamoto, courtesy of the Lyndon Baines Johnson Library ; **792 (top)** Library of Congress; **(bottom)** Photograph by Gene Anthony. © Wolfgang's Vault, all rights reserved; **793** Getty Images; **794 (top)** Courtesy Wheaton College Archives and Special Collections; **(bottom)** Ralph Crane/Time Life Pictures/Getty Images; **796** Boston Globe via Getty Images; **797** JP Laffont/Sygma/Corbis; **798** AP Photo; **799** Billy Ireland Cartoon Library & Museum, The Ohio State University; **801 (top)** © Grey Villet; **(bottom)** © 1963 Herbert Block; **802** Copyrighted photo by Richard Copley; **803** Frederick Douglass mural on the 'Solidarity Wall', Falls Road, Belfast; http://en.wikipedia.org/wiki/GNU_Free_Documentation_License; **806** Courtesy Ronald Reagan Library; **808** National Archives; **811** © Co Rentmeester; **812** Photo by Ollie Atkins/Time Life Pictures/Getty Images; **813** May 4 Collection. Kent State University Libraries. Special Collections and Archives; **814** David Fenton/Getty Images; **818 (top)** Bob Kreisel/Alamy; **(bottom)** AP Photo; **819** Courtesy Gerald R. Ford Library; **821** Fox Photos/Getty Images; **822** AP Photo; **823** Bettmann/Corbis; **827** © 1982 Doug Marlette; **828 (top)** Mark Meyer/Time & Life Pictures/Getty Images; **(bottom)** Bettmann/Corbis; **830** University of Southern California; **831** Time Life Pictures/Getty Images **833 (top)** Library of Congress; **(bottom)** © Mary Ellen Mark; **834 (top)** Ronald Reagan Presidential Library; **(bottom)** Photofest; **836** AP Photo; **840** Peter Turnley/Corbis; **841** Patrick Hagerty/Corbis Sygma; **843** AP Photo; **845** AP Photo; **847** Courtesy of Edward Sorel, published as the cover of The New Yorker; **850** Erik Freeland/Corbis; **852** Peter Turnley/Corbis; **853** Photo by Joi Ito; http://creativecommons.org/licenses/by/2.0/deed.en; **854** © 2004 Bob Sacha; **855** Reprinted with permission of David Jacobson; **857** Hans Haacke/Artists Rights Society [ARS], New York/VG Bild-Kunst, Bonn; **858** Gilles Mingasson/Getty Images; **859** Catherine Karnow/Corbis; **860** Takaaki Iwabu KRT/Newscom; **863 (top)** AP Photo; **(bottom)** Reuters/Corbis; **864** Courtesy The Aldrich Contemporary Art Museum; **867** Ralf-Finn Hestoft/Corbis; **868** © 1998 Herbert Block; **869** Reuters/Corbis; **870** A. Ramey/Woodfin Camp and Associates; **872** © Renee Cox; **874** Ralf-Finn Hestoft/Corbis; **876** Steve Ludlum/The New York Times/Redux; **877** Lionel

Hahn/Abaca; **878 (top)** Serge J-F. Levy **(bottom)** Steve Benson/Creators Syndicate; **880** Mario Tama/Getty Images; **881 (top)** AP Photo; **(bottom)** Joe Raedle/Getty Images; **883** Hank Walker/Getty Images; **884** Michael Ramirez/Creators Syndicate; **887** AP Photo; **888** AP Photo; **892** Joshua Lott/The New York Times/Redux; **894** AUTH © 2009 The Philadelphia Inquirer. Reprinted with permission of UNIVERSAL UCLICK. All rights reserved; **896** © Tribune Media Services, Inc. All Rights Reserved. Reprinted with permission; **897** AP Photo; **900** AP Photo; **901** AP Photo/Port Authority of NY & NJ, Durst Organization; **903** Monique Jacques/Corbis; **905** Spencer Platt/Getty Images; **907** Eli Reed/Magnum Photos.

TEXT, TABLES, AND FIGURES

28 Bartolomé de las Casas: *History of the Indies*, translated and edited by Andrée Collard (New York: Harper & Row, 1971), pp. 82, 112–115. Copyright © 1971 by Andrée M. Collard, renewed © 1999 by Joyce J. Contrucci. Reprinted by permission of Joyce J. Contrucci; **62** Thomas Hutchinson: "The Examination of Mrs. Anne Hutchinson at the Court of Newtown." Reprinted by permission of the publisher from *The History of the Colony and Province of Massachusetts Bay, Vol. II* by Thomas Hutchinson, edited by Lawrence Shaw Mayo, pp. 366–391, Cambridge, Mass.: Harvard University Press, Copyright © 1963 by the President and Fellows of Harvard College. Copyright © renewed 1964 by Lawrence Shaw Mayo; **91** (Table 3.1) Aaron S. Fogleman, "From Slaves, Convicts, and Servants to Free Passengers: The Transformation of Immigration in the Era of the American Revolution," Journal of American History 85 (June 1998) 43–76; **93** Johannes Hanner: Letter by an Immigrant to Pennsylvania, 1769, *Unpublished Documents on Emigration from the Archives of Switzerland*, Albert B. Faust, *Deutsch-Amerikanische Geschichtsblätter*, Vol. 18–19, pp. 37–39. Translation by Volker Berghahn. Reprinted by permission of Volker Berghahn; **112** (Table 4.1) Ira Berlin, *Many Thousands Gone: The First Two Centuries of Slavery in North America* (Cambridge, Mass.: Harvard University Press, 1998) 369–70; **186** Abigail Adams: "Abigail Adams to John Adams, 31 March 1776." Reprinted by permission of the publisher from *The Adams Papers: Adams Family Correspondence, Volume I: December 1761–May*

INDEX

Page numbers in *italics* refer to illustrations.

READING YESTERDAY, WRITING TODAY

*A Guide to the Study of History
at Oklahoma State University*

READING YESTERDAY, WRITING TODAY: A GUIDE TO THE STUDY OF HISTORY AT OKLAHOMA STATE UNIVERSITY; A STUDENT GUIDE

PREPARED BY THE OSU
DEPARTMENT OF HISTORY

OSU Department of History. Reading Yesterday, Writing Today: A Guide to the Study of History at Oklahoma State University; A Student Guide.

TABLE OF CONTENTS

INTRODUCTION

This pamphlet has its origins in the perception of the History Department faculty, that students at Oklahoma State University are confused about the purposes of the discipline of history and the appropriate means to study it. We can attribute this lack of understanding to many causes but largely we believe that in popular culture and the secondary school system history is treated as an agglomeration of unrelated facts whose major reason for existence is memorization. Nothing could be further from the truth, especially at the college level. Studying history is one means, although certainly not the only means, of probing the human being and understanding the structures of humanity's existence, the choices societies make, the institutions people create, and the motivations that drive individuals to take certain actions. While history requires memorization of certain events, people, and dates—all disciplines require some memorization—the goal is not memorization itself but rather the use of recorded information to derive conclusions about human existence.

This guide not only intends to make the purposes of the study of history clear to college students, from freshmen to seniors, but also to introduce them to the ways history is created—the use of primary sources from which historians write the histories that are offered to the public. On a more practical note, it hopes to make clear to students the procedures of the classroom, the knowledge students should be absorbing, the goal of generalization that students should be engaging in on the basis of the information they have received, and the skills they should be learning and honing.

Many of the topics covered in these few pages have been dealt in much greater length elsewhere. We are not engaging in such overkill here. This pamphlet is meant to be a first step. Your classroom professors will be making refinements and extensions of the ideas in these pages with greater clarity in the classes you take. We have to give one admonition to students, however. No matter how often we write or speak or give explanations of what we are doing and the procedures involved in learning history, the only way the student can really learn history is by engaging in the study of it—reading the material with earnestness, taking notes in class, thinking about various subjects, writing outlines, and composing essays and papers. The student must be an active participant in learning; passivity will yield no understanding and no knowledge.

CHAPTER I

THE PURPOSES OF HISTORY

I. What History Teaches Us

To engage in the study of a discipline, one must understand first its essential purposes. This is the rock on which many student ships flounder. It is hardly any wonder that many students have difficulty with the subject when they do not comprehend its reason for existence.

We start first with the illegitimate reasons for studying history, and they are many. First, history is not a memorization contest. All disciplines, to be worthy of the name, seek an understanding of their subject matter; all use facts to derive conclusions. No discipline seeks merely to accumulate facts. Facts exist for the purpose of locating patterns. History is no different from other disciplines in this quest.

Within popular culture, there are other reasons for studying history, most of which to some degree or another exhibit a political or domineering purpose. Various people want to use history to say some sort of version of "History proves . . ." and then go on to say whatever political program they have in mind is justified by the past. In some cases it is to prove that one group of people have a quality that merits special respect; in some cases it is to prove that some people have been subjected to injustice and tyranny; in some cases it is to show why certain people or individuals have unusual greatness and must be blindly followed. None of these are legitimate purposes of history, for they are guided by a purposeful intention to make history serve an existing political agenda. The study of history may or may not disprove such propositions, but the effort to force the history into a preconceived conclusion is a violation of the canons of truthful inquiry.

Reputable historians have a number of legitimate purposes in mind for their explorations of the past. Here are four of them:

1. *History is a way of exploring the human condition and responses of people to differing circumstances; it is an assessment of the capabilities and the limitations of the human animal and the societies people create.*

Let us for a moment consider the source of other disciplines that investigate human beings. Political Science looks at political structures; Sociology and Anthropology consider the rules of group behavior; Economics looks at how humans allocate scarce resources and attempt a higher standard of living; English and the Fine Arts probe the capacity of people to express their awareness of existence and to capture the emotional side of life; Psychology hopes to unravel individual human motivation and thought processes. These are all obvious and reasonable approaches to understanding the human animal.

What makes history unique is the dimension of time. The other disciplines usually have a "presentist" point of view—they deal with conditions within the lifespans of people now living. Thus their investigations of people are inherently limited by the conditions of the present. History uncovers how people have responded to their environments, how they have created their societies, how they generated understandings of the world, how they have interpreted themselves and nature under the vastly different conditions of the past. Such evaluations of past societies tell us something about the capacity of people to act and think when conditions vary. In short, history rounds out our understanding of human beings by letting us view them under enormously different circumstances.

History's purpose in this sense is somewhat artistic. It teaches a general understanding about human beings in the way that novels or paintings or sculptures teach us about the aspirations and follies of human societies.

2. History is the Experience of Human Beings Over Time.

Another way to understand the purpose of the discipline of history is to consider the word "experience." Consider the related word "experiment" and what it means to the physical sciences. Physicists and chemists conduct "experiments" to find out if their calculations are correct or to discover new properties of nature. Human beings have exhibited a wide display of behaviors, beliefs, and idea systems over time; their "experience" has given people in the present a fund of information to understand the capabilities and limitations of humans. So we can use this fund of experience to come to some conclusions about what people can do and not do. In a sense, history is a record of "experiments" of trying to produce appropriate institutions and belief systems to guide them through existence. As physical scientists learn from experiments, so humanists and social scientists can learn from the record of the human past—from the "experience" of past peoples and societies.

However, what we learn from experience in the human realm is considerably different from what is learned in the physical realm. Scientists can control their experiments and direct their focus to exactly the variables they are interested in. Human experience does not have a tight structuring that permits an isolation of influences, does not have a complete record that provides all the knowledge that is necessary to make a firm conclusion, and produces results that are less precise than mathematical formulae. (History nonetheless demands rigor and precision in thinking and producing logical arguments.) In the physical sciences, the lessons learned from experiments become exact and formalized in mathematical expressions; in history, the lessons learned from experience are inexact, verbal, and differ from historian to historian. Moreover, the lessons of historians in one time period may be overthrown entirely by historians who come later because of the discovery of new information, the application of new research techniques, and the acknowledgment that certain social problems that had previously been trivialized are actually of a more substantial nature.

In a nutshell, physical sciences yield formulae that enable people to predict the results of specific physical processes in nature. History, in contrast, teaches understanding. This is the record of human struggle, achievement, and perhaps failure over time; the experience of humans over time gives us a general understanding of the capabilities of human beings but does not give us a mathematical formula. But history provides a depth of understanding about the human being that no other discipline affords, and the reason is because historians deal with the varied experience of humans over time. The accumulation of that knowledge, and the interpretation of that knowledge into understanding, we call, among our best practitioners, wisdom.

3. History as Science: Patterns of the Past.

History as art and history as experience are general, inexact methods of coming to grips with the nature of human beings because the conclusions derived are ambiguous and broad. But in one specific sense, history has a scientific side. Historians are concerned with long range patterns of human society: economic, social, psychological, political, and ideological. One of the bywords of the profession is that historians are concerned with "change over time." One cannot measure change without establishing a pattern to show that change. Thus historians are interested in detecting continuity (patterns that repeat) so that they can assess change when it occurs (when the pattern takes a new direction).

Analysis of patterns consumes much of the attention of historians in two ways. First, the repetition of patterns has to be explained. What are the general "forces" or conditions that permit repetition of existing patterns? Second, what alteration in the environment or within the human population forces a change in the patterns? The latter means historians attempt to explain why change comes to human civilization.

4. History and the Present.

The study of history has a direct relation to events and social movements occurring in the present—and for the student to understand adequately the history being taught in colleges and universities, it is vital for the student to keep abreast of current events. There are some complex reasons why this is so. First, many problems of the present have deep roots in time. Tackling these problems requires an understanding of the history involved in these problems. Without taking the history into account, one easily can misjudge the forces at work and the strength of those forces; a presentist attitude has something of a superficial quality. Second, difficulties in the present may signal a deficiency in histories written several decades ago. History is written by people, and historians are heavily influenced by the times in which they live and the troubles they personally see in the world about them. Their investigations mirror those concerns. Thus, they can easily leave out of their histories the story of forces and problems not of interest to them.

More subtle but more pervasive is the simple fact that historians also imbibe the ideological perspective of the world they live in or of some political program.

That inevitably means historians are blinded to some circumstances or handle them in awkward and inadequate ways. Historians in later years may have more of a grasp of the bias of earlier historians and try to correct them. This is called "revisionism." It is almost an inescapable dilemma for the historian. One is always part of a society; one almost invariably imbibes the "spirit of the age" one is born into or learns an ideology from one source or another; one always confronts a set of problems peculiar to the time period in which one lives; and, therefore, one always writes a history that is limited by the human condition of being part of a peculiar society in a specific time period. This is why "revision" of past histories always has taken place and always will take place.

Yet there are some limits to this revisionism. First, revisionism is restricted to *interpretation* of events and information. The events and information themselves have an independent existence and will always exist; understanding of those events and information change over time. Second, essential patterns of political, economic, and social life are not likely to change greatly unless new information is found. Once again, however, interpretation of the patterns may change.

Historians are probably today much more aware of their capacity to find "truth" than were historians of, say, fifty or one hundred years ago. That still does not invalidate the purpose of history in explaining the present. We use history to flesh out the forces acting on the present and to determine the strength of those forces. In that sense, the present does guide historical inquiry.

II. Basic Intellectual Frameworks and Skills

Before we plunge into the types of courses offered at Oklahoma State and the assignments given, we should detail some of the basic tools/concepts used in historical analysis.

1. CONTEXT

Perhaps no construct of historians is more vital to the discipline than the idea of *context.* By context we mean that certain societies have over certain periods of time created a pattern of living that emphasizes certain ways of life and thinking, but precludes other ways of life and thinking. A context for a society (group of people, nation-state, city, etc.) is the collection of political institutions, social practices, economic relationships, technological level, and belief/ideological systems in operation. So, for example, people in medieval Europe adhered to an ordered society in which individualism was frowned upon; this is in opposition to the United States of the nineteenth century in which individualism was the social goal and social ordering was regarded as retrograde. Much of what historians do is to establish the context for a society. They establish context by intensive research among material artifacts and through written records. But students are given the context either in lectures or in their reading assignments. Students rarely go through the process of determining context by reference to the mountain of documents by which context is determined.

2. SIGNIFICANCE.

A second analytical construct basic to the endeavor of all historians is *significance*. The easy way to understand significance is to ask the question of an event or a historical figure: so what? What effects did the person or event have? How is the person or event connected to the larger processes at work in the society or to monumental changes for the society? Historians in their research sort out the power of people or events by the consequences they produce. Thus, some events and people have more significance than others; that is, some information is used in the creation of history while other information is discarded. This sorting out the important information from the unimportant is not simple. Major battles among historians rage over what gets to be called significant.

For the student, however, significance has another application altogether, and it is one that is heavily used in grading techniques. It is the ability of the student to know how a person or event figures into a society's pattern of continuity or change, how evidence fits into the context. Let us be more specific so the difference between how history is written and how the student studies history can be made appreciated. Historians write history by accumulating evidence and making interpretations; then the interpretations are given to the public with the appropriate factual information that substantiates the interpretation. Students travel the road in reverse. They are tested by being given a term or fact and then asked to match it to the appropriate generalization and then explain the connection.

Significance is vital to the study of history, and anyone taking a history course must be aware of it and what is being asked. Why are people and events important? What are the consequences? How are terms connected to interpretations? Answering these questions successfully will take the student a long way into doing well in history classes.

CHAPTER II

THE INTRODUCTORY COURSES: THE SURVEY CLASSES

I. Content of the Survey Courses.

The History Department offers a variety of survey courses; a one-semester United States survey class, a two-semester United States survey class (restricted to secondary education majors), a two-semester Western Civilization survey class, and a one-semester Eastern Civilization survey class. These classes cover huge stretches of time and often a variety of cultures and nations. They are introductions to the histories of these portions of the globe.

II. The Value of Survey Courses

Most historians enjoy intense scrutiny of a limited time period of one or two cultures. This enables the historians to dissect features of the society in great detail to understand what was happening or to detail vital decisions the society undertook that determined its future course in time. Surveys do not usually offer such intense scrutiny unless the instructor decides to approach the material by looking at a few vital episodes, allowing the student to glean more general information from a textbook.

Surveys usually give the student basic patterns of a society or civilization, explain the continuities, and then examine the moments of great change. Thus in a survey course, you should be aware that the presentation will likely focus on the basic context of a society/civilization for long periods of time and the forces that generate change. Thus, the student should expect that the testing procedure will be how well the students understand the basic patterns of the civilization, the forces that sustain the patterns, and the forces that alter the patterns. It will be asked as well that the student be able to identify events, people, or processes that reveal the existence of these patterns.

III. Methods of Presentation

THE LECTURE

There are various ways your instructor may give you the history of the survey course. The usual means is lecture. For the length of the class time, the instructor will give explanations about the history of the civilization being dealt with. Lectures have a format that is actually prevalent in almost everything historians do.

UNDERSTANDING THE LECTURE

To understand what you should get out of the lecture, and how to use the information in a test, you have to understand the format. Instructors will begin by giving a general proposition for a time period, a problem, or some special subject matter for the civilization being investigated. This general proposition represents a *thesis* statement; it is an interpretation. The interpretation is then broken down into several component parts. These are sub-interpretations that are connected to the basic interpretation or thesis. Finally, the instructor will interject facts, dates, personalities, and other specific information into each of the sub-interpretations to show that these sub-interpretations are logical and fit with what actually occurrred. This is the format of virtually all lectures: major thesis/interpretation, sub-theses/interpretations, factual material/evidence. It is vital you understand this structure.

OTHER FORMS OF PRESENTATION—DISCUSSION

Your instructor has other ways to introduce you to historical material, the most prominent being discussion. Usually discussions are centered around assigned readings (a textbook, a book of readings, or a book on a specific topic). From the reading you are expected to detect the interpretation the author is giving and the evidence that supports it. (See Chapter 5.) At the same time, discussions are often used to point out alternative interpretations or different ways the information can be looked at or assembled to come to a different conclusion. Sometimes, it will be asked how to take the information from one source (say, lectures) and apply it to information from another source (say the readings). You should prepare for discussions by reading the material and answering the questions the instructor has given, and you should contribute to the discussion by participation.

OTHER FORMS OF PRESENTATION—VIDEO AND OTHER MEDIA

Instructors are increasingly turning to other materials to give to students. Some instructors use video or films in their classes; some use material acquired from the internet; others use slides showing architecture or material conditions in the past. Understand that these presentations are not for entertainment value. You are expected to draw information from them and general interpretations about the civilization you are studying.

IV. Duties of Students

NOTE-TAKING

Understanding the structure of the lecture and the purpose of discussion and video presentations should greatly assist you in note-taking. *Of course you should take notes!* Why? Two reasons: first, the act of writing down important information and ideas is a good way to inscribe them in your mind. The act of writing gives the student a memory boost; it will make you more familiar with the ideas and data so that later on it will be easier to use them for papers and tests Second, a lot of information and ideas are presented to you that are easily capable of being forgotten; taking notes will give you a record to refer to. Do not expect instructors to repeat their lectures for your private benefit!

Note-Taking and Lecture Format

How you take notes is crucial, and here understanding the approach of historians to the way they present their information will assist you greatly. Above all, write down the basic interpretations and sub-interpretations the instructor gives; these are, in fact, the "meat" of the lectures. Next, understand where the factual material fits into the sub-arguments. If you can master this way of taking notes, you have nearly solved from the start the problem students have with significance. Simply by starting from the given event or person and working up to the sub-theme and then to the major theme will give the significance.

READING

The Textbook

Understand that a textbook is a basic narrative, usually not particularly exciting, and generally over-laden with information that few people will master in their lifetimes. So what should you be doing with it?

- First, the textbook will define the basic time-periods into which the civilization you are studying is usually divided into (that is, the movement over time from one context to another).
- Second, it will introduce you to the basic themes or interpretations for each time-period. These themes and interpretations can be easily found, so do not be overwhelmed by the amount of detail usually given in a textbook. A good look at the chapter headings and the division of each chapter into its compenent parts usually gives the basic interpretations and the sub-interpretations for the civilization's time period. And if the interpretation and sub-interpretation are not immediately recognizable, then read carefully the introduction to the chapter and the introduction to each sub-division of the chapter—there the interpretations are almost always made explicit. The bulk of the chapter divisions then lays out the information that the author(s) believe substantiates the interpretations given.

Non-textbook Reading

Additional reading assignments usually offer much more focused interpretations than the textbook. Such reading may be in the form of articles or books devoted to a time period or a specific event or process. In reading these works, you need to do two tasks: understand the basic argument being given, and then figure out the prominent factual material used to support the argument. Readings of this kind tend to be more conducive for discussion. Usually the authors are giving arguments in favor of a specific interpretation. That means other interpretations exist. When reading short pieces or books devoted to specific topics, you should be thinking about what other ways exist to explain the same phenomena. What other materials might be used to do the research? What other motivations may have been in effect when societies determined to act in a certain way? It is because authors in articles or monographs (as we call books devoted to a specific topic) offer an argument favoring one particular interpretation that we can discuss alternatives.

What applies to articles and monographs, also applies to video presentations or slides yielding aspects of material life and geography: what are the arguments being presented, how well does the information match those arguments, what interpretive alternatives may exist?

In the case of collateral readings and presentations, you should remember to take notes, determine the basic interpretations or arguments, and jot down the essential information used to make interpretations.

V. A Word of Advice About Interpretations

Freshmen in particular need to understand one thing about history and historical inquiry. *There is no orthodoxy, no truth beyond question, no dogma to be learned. History is a discipline always subject to criticism and scrutiny, to revision and alteration, to refinement and change. There is never One Truth that lasts for all time. History is a constant quest for wisdom and understanding.* Historians may come to conclusions and believe in them vehemently, aggressively, and passionately; but those conclusions are never permitted to become sacrosanct and above question. Criticism and reevaluation is a way of life for historians because new evidence and new perspectives are always being found; and though historians may come to the same conclusions over and over again about the way people act and why human experience has taken the course it has, the historian is never permitted to say an eternal truth has been found. Constant reassessment and reevaluation is the lot of doing history and the quest for finding wisdom.

VI. Skill Development: Writing

Evaulation of students takes various forms, but the members of the Department of History of Oklahoma State University most often employ three basic forms: identifications, the essay test, and the paper assignment. We will briefly take each one in turn.

THE IN-CLASS EXAMINATION

For freshmen, a quarterly or tri-semester test is a standard method of evaluation. It is often composed of two parts: identification terms and the writing of an essay. Instructors have various ways they prepare you for exams, and you must rely on them for details. In general however, tests take a certain form and ask for certain types of responses.

- The *identification* portion of an examination wants you to identify a term (an event, process, person, etc.) by giving the appropriate dates, identifying the term (the details about it), and then giving its significance. Most of the identification material and the date can be gleaned easily from your textbook.
- Most instructors are keen on insuring students understand the *significance* of the person, event, or process. This asks you for the consequences of the term and how it fits into the historical context or how it illustrates an ongoing process or how it exhibits a portion of an important sequence of events that leads to an important result. In figuring out signficance, the earlier parts of this handbook are vital, especially Chapter I, part 2. Knowing the way information is presented to you, both in lectures and in readings, will easily lead you to significance. More is developed on significance in Chapter II on test taking.
- The essay portion of the exam usually has a standard approach as well. The instructor wants you to explain the evolution of a civilization or how a civilization handled a certain difficulty. In the broadest sense, the instructor is handing you a problem in understanding a civilization's past; you are to construct an answer using the information in lectures, readings, and visual presentations. You answer the question by collecting the pertinent information, coming to a conclusion, organizing the information into an intelligent response that operates with a basic thesis statement (interpretation) and divided into logical supporting sub-theses (sub-interpretations), and using evidence (facts) to substantiate your sub-theses. In essence, you are writing your own little lecture the way your instructor would. More is given on writing essays in Chapter VI.

QUALITY OF WRITING IN IN-CLASS TESTS

For freshmen, we offer a few words of comfort. History is a discipline that uses writing for communication, and therefore good writing is prized. However, we do not hold students to exacting standards when in-class tests are employed, nor do we demand a near-perfect essay form. For in-class tests, we want students to strive to adhere to the form as best they can. You are graded on the substance of your answer, not on your spelling, grammar, or organization (although bad organization will count against you).

WHAT HISTORY TESTS ARE *NOT*

One thing you must understand about tests. *Examinations in history classes are not memory dumps. Examinations in history classes are not unrelated strings of information spewed mindlessly on paper. Examinations in history ask students to explain an evolution of a society or to offer an answer to a problem. Mere lists of facts that have no explanation and no relevance to a question are failing answers. Good grades are awarded to students who answer questions with good information, good organization, and intelligent interpretations. Bad grades go to people who cannot use information to answer questions, have little organization of information but merely give lists, and have no central interpretations. History is not memorizing lists; it is about coming to conclusions about the nature of the evolution of societies.*

If the preceding paragraph seems intimidating, remember that at the freshmen level, the questions asked are very broad, the amount of factual information limited, and the level of generalization basic. More advanced courses will require more refinement and subtlety. The reality of most survey courses is that subtlety is thrown out the window and brute generalization is the best we can hope to achieve.

OTHER ASSIGNMENTS

Many instructors add an additional component to their survey classes: a short paper written on a film, a book, or an article. The paper may vary in length from three to ten typed pages. The instructor may ask you to write on a specific question he or she has composed, may ask you to criticize the interpretation an author has given, ask how the material fits in with interpretations given in lectures, or simply wants a description of the presentation's argument and evidence. In any event, the rules governing the writing of a paper are no different from the rules writing an essay. Collect the information pertinent to the task, decide upon a thesis, determine the sub-arguments behind your thesis, and use facts to substantiate your sub-arguments. Consult Chapter VI for the appropriate form.

Instructors may have other assignments for you. Some may ask you to work from workbooks; some may have have specific assignments asking you to answer questions; some may want you to keep a diary of your thoughts and questions during the course of the semester. We offer this advice: *Take the assignments you are given seriously!* Most of these assignments will help you in understanding the purposes of history better, and most of them will boost your grade.

VII. A Final Word About Tests and Grading

If you do your assignments, understand the purposes of the survey course, and pay attention to the way history is done, you should be able to pass these courses without great difficulty. But you need to do the work. Most things in life are learned not by contemplating action, but doing the action itself. You do not learn history not by being disengaged, by not taking notes, by being inattentive in class, by doing as little writing and thinking as possible. Simply put: little work, lousy grade. If you put forth the effort, you should not have difficulty with the survey class.

CHAPTER III

UPPER-DIVISION CLASSES

I. Purposes of Upper-Division History Classes

UPPER-DIVISION CLASSES

Upper-division classes in history (the 3000 and 4000 numbered courses) engage in a much more intensive scrutiny of the past than do the surveys. Surveys, by their nature, look at basic patterns over time and can only involve generalized understandings of human actors and the forces acting on them. Upper-division courses are more restricted chronologically and/or geographically. That enables the instructor to delve more into the patterns governing the society at that moment, and perhaps some of the complexities the patterns can take. The usual case is that the upper-division courses allow for more investigation into social, political, or economic developments—a closer elaboration of the forces at work, the choices people made (or could have made), the ambiguities involved, and the unexpected as well as expected results of the developments. Frequently, instructors will invoke other disciplines to help explain the historical path of the society under investigation.

HISTORIOGRAPHY

In the 3000 and 4000 level courses, the undergraduate student will probably be introduced to some of the basic *historiography* of the subject. Historiography is the body of historians' writing on the subject matter: the schools of thought that have evolved, the kinds of interpretations that have been offered, the debates over what sets of information are most important. Students in upper-division courses discover the continuous controversy that is the hallmark of modern historical writing. Historians disagree over why human societies have acted the way they have in the past and the results of their decisions, and this disagreement is virtually impossible to eradicate.

REQUIREMENTS IN UPPER-DIVISION CLASSES

In terms of intellectual requirements for students, the upper-division courses are much more demanding than the surveys. Students must come to conclusions of their own based on the information given them in their reading and lectures. The student will first collect the information and then make an informed assessment of the likely forces at work. Key assumptions need to be spelled out. For instance, what motivates people? Religious values? Material wants? Primal desires? Most upper-division courses present a variety of available explanations: students must then exercise their mental faculties to determine which explanation works best and to give specific reasons for that.

Likewise, students are expected to engage in critical assessment of explanations—to be able to engage in critiques of books, articles, and theories.

Critiquing is the mental exercise of determining why a theory or an explanation is strong or weak; what information is excluded; what points of view are excluded; what novel information is used. It is not enough to say that a particular author is very good or very bad; one has to explain why the author's explanation is satisfactory or not. Being dull or difficult to follow is not the same as being incorrect or illogical.

In upper-division courses, both the reading requirements and the writing requirements increase. It is not uncommon for students to read four to ten books and to write in total about 30 to 60 typed pages. History is a discipline that uses the written word; in order to engage in it, one has to read (a lot!) and one has to write. These end up being the basic, important skills that history teaches: how to extract information from a written text, how to understand and evaluate it, how to communicate ideas to other in direct, clearly written English. These skills, of course, are not unique to history; however, students should be emphatically aware that if the reading and writing load is light, they are not deriving the maximum benefit they should be receiving by taking history courses.

II. Evaluation in Upper-division Courses

TESTING

Testing procedures in these courses are fairly similar to those of the survey. There may be in-class examinations including identification tests and/or essays. Frequently, essay tests are given as take-home examinations.

IDENTIFICATIONS

Structurally there is little difference in the format of the identification test and the essay test when given in the survey class versus upper-division classes. An identification requires date, description, and significance; an exam essay should include a thesis statement and then an argument divided logically into sub-theses substantiated by reference to ideas, facts, and information. The content, however, differs greatly between the two levels of course. In the survey course, bare descriptions of terms is about all that can be reasonably asked for; the upper-division course will demand much more detail and will expect much more sophistication in understanding significance—the consequences or relations attached to the term.

ESSAY EXAMS

Likewise, the essay tests will expect much better performance from students than the survey course, and in a couple of distinct areas. First, organization should be much better, much tighter, and more easily followed. Instructors expect these essays to make sense, to flow logically, to use information correctly. Non sequi-turs, for instance, should be minimized. A non sequitur is a statement that is supposed to be justified by second statement (or fact, evidence, or demonstration) but actually has no relation to the first statement. For example, one might argue that the Civil War introduced the United States to modernizing tendencies, and then talk about the Security Exchange Commission established by the New Deal. There is no relationship between the Civil War and the SEC. A common error among students is to place information in a category (a sub-thesis) that has no obvious relation to the topic sentence.

Moreover, in the upper-division courses professors expect students to start handling complexity and ambiguity in understanding the past. In the survey course, the desire is to make the student aware of basic patterns of human activity over time. But in the upper-division course, students should begin to understand that simple rules sometimes fail and that many counter-currents are at work in a society. In terms of writing an essay, a student may argue strongly (and correctly) for a certain interpretation about a society's development; at the same time, the student needs to show the limitations of the argument, the places where the argu-ment fails, and the existence of other explanations that may have merit as well. The student's interpretation becomes filled with the complexity of historical situ-ations and thus the student acknowledges the difficulty of interpretation.

OTHER METHODS OF EVALUATION

Instructors in upper-division classes may use a variety of methods besides the identification test and the essay test for evaluating the work of students. These may include geography tests; quizzes; short writing assignments; or interpreta-tions of films, material culture, architecture, or television shows. As well, stu-dents may be assigned a new task—the research paper (see chapter IX).

CHAPTER IV

BEYOND THE UNDERGRADUATE WORLD

This chapter is less a chapter than an afterword. Most students leave Oklahoma State University and plunge into the world to make their fortunes (or at least a respectable living). What from the field of history should you have taken?

HISTORY AND OCCUPATIONS

There are occupations directly related to the field of history, so majors may select them as their steps into the "real" world. Secondary school teachers, law school, business school (MBA), diplomatic service and government agency work, university employment, and public history are traditional fields for history majors and minors. However, this is not the expectation that history faculty have for students taking their courses. History is a field that develops general skills and abilities that may be learned in other fields as well; but their application to all areas of human endeavor is vast.

ACQUIRED SKILLS

Among the skills you should develop by taking history courses are communication skills. This especially includes:

- clear, concise, expository writing.
- the location of information.
- the capability to discern vital information from less crucial information.
- the ability to organize and order information.
- a developed critical faculty that enables you to sort out good explanations from feeble ones.
- an enhanced capacity for logical thought; good courses in history force students to make decisions while understanding the complexities and ambiguities that suffuse all human life.

Good history courses make you think; the more you are required to think, the better the quality of your thinking becomes. Unlike many people who believe history is largely a matter of memorizing lists, faculty at Oklahoma State University believe it to be a highly creative discipline in which answers are found by intense thinking and reflection, that solutions are not simply given by the "facts" themselves. In activities outside an academic setting, the abilities to communicate, find and organize information, derive intelligent generalizations and explanations from the information, separate strong explanations from weak ones, and thinking creatively are important abilities. Your history instruction should be inculcating them in you.

A final comment. Some students will decide to continue the study of history in graduate school and earn a Doctor of Philosophy degree (Ph.D.) and obtain employment at a college or university. A worthy goal, and this faculty encourage all who have this desire. Be aware, however, of the change of pace that occurs when one leaves undergraduate study for graduate study. Graduate study places students at the edge of historical knowledge and nudges them further to find new information, generate new ideas, and uncover new problems that historians had not found previously. More specifically, the purpose of graduate school is to advance students to the point where they can discover and write about subjects that teach existing historians new things. The acid test, therefore, is to write histories that other historians will want to read and that will teach them new perspectives and give them new ways of understanding the patterns of the past. The quality of intellectual thought becomes much more demanding in graduate study than it is in undergraduate study. The transition from undergraduate to graduate activity is a significant leap.

CHAPTER V

READING CRITICALLY

I. Reading and History

Reading is essential to the study of history. In general, people read for different reasons: enjoyment, information, inspiration, analysis. As a result, there is more than one way to read almost anything, including history. That is so basically for two reasons. One has to do with how you read, the other with what you read.

Begin with the issue of what you read. Reading materials divide into several types. For history, the two most important types are labeled primary and secondary.

II. Primary and Secondary Materials

Primary and secondary materials are defined by three characteristics. One is who wrote the material. The second is when it was written. The third is the author's relationship to the events being recounted. If posed in the form of questions, the three characteristics translate into who, when, and what?

1. What are primary materials?

For primary materials—often called primary sources—the questions who, when, and what could be answered as follows.

- In the case of who, the person who wrote the material participated in or saw the events in question or received his information from a participant or observer. Hence, the information is first-hand or primary.
- In the case of when, the material was written approximately at the time of the event in question, although this can involve considerable flexibility for ancient times.
- In the case of what, primary sources are documents or materials (including art and artifacts) that come from the time and place of the original event or that were provided by someone who received information from that time and place.

So, primary materials are not primary because they are necessarily most important, although they may be. They are primary in that they are closely related in time to the events in question. Hence, they are the sources that appear relatively soon after the events or first (primary).

2. What are secondary materials?

In the case of secondary materials—often called secondary works—the answers to the same three questions of who, when, and what are as follows.

- In the case of who, the author does not have first-hand knowledge of the events and did not participate in them but learned about them second-hand.

- In the case of when, the material describes events that occurred some time in the past.
- In the case of what, secondary works are accounts of events that are not closely related in time to the events and that rely on descriptions provided by primary sources and by historians offering interpretations in other secondary works.

So, history divides primarily into two kinds of materials—primary sources and secondary works. If the secondary work is a book dedicated to a single topic, as most history books are (other than text books and readers), then the book is called a monograph. A monograph invariably presents an interpretation of the events in question. So, both primary sources and secondary works must be placed in context and their authors' intentions identified.

III. How to Read

Reading history is also affected by how you read it. When reading anything, including history, you should read on at least two levels at once. On one level, read for content; on the other, read for the author's purpose.

Reading for content is fairly straight forward. The reader seeks to understand and absorb the information being provided. To do this effectively, the reader needs to focus on the material and, even better, interact with it. That means you must think about what is being presented.

IV. Basic Questions You Should Ask

A) When reading for content, you should first orient yourself so that the material makes sense. Obtain a sense of the subject to be covered and—in history—the course of events. Ask yourself the following questions:
   i)   what are the major events,
   ii)   what is going to happen,
   iii) how do these events fit together—is there causation or merely a confluence of events?

B) Several steps can help identify the major events and what the author intends to cover.
   i)   First, look over the table of contents.
   ii)   Second, note the chapter headings.
   iii) Third, read the preface.
   iv)   Fourth, read the conclusion.

These steps should give you a mental map of where the author will lead you including some idea of the main points the author intends to make and his interpretation of the events.

V. Reading Critically

More important than orienting yourself is reading critically. This involves first, reading both for content and for the author's purpose and second, asking questions of the material being read.

1. READING FOR CONTENT

To read most effectively for content, you need to take an interest in the narrative, in the author's argument. Treat the process of reading as if it were a conversation—the author on one side, you on the other. So, while reading the material, respond to the author and what he or she is saying. This can be done by:

- Jotting down your thoughts,
- Making comments,
- Asking questions.

After finishing the chapter, article, or book, go back over it and take notes. As part of this process, identify:

- The main points in each chapter,
- The specific information worth remembering,
- Your conclusions or assessment.

For history, you should also be thinking about such things as the time frame (what period of time is involved?), sequencing (in what order do the events occur?), causation (does one event bring about a subsequent event?).

2. READING FOR INTERPRETATION

A. Author's Purpose

Just as important as reading for content, is reading to identify the author's purpose. The author has written this account or commentary for some reason. What is it? What is the author's thesis—the proposition that the author intends to prove? He or she should state the thesis in the first or second paragraph of an essay and perhaps in the introduction to a book. But the argument may continue to develop throughout the work. So, to identify the author's purpose and thesis, you must read critically. Ask questions, and actively engage the material.

There are at least two reasons for trying to identify the author's purpose.

1) One is to understand the content better.
2) The other is to critique the author's argument.

B. Interpretations

Why do historians write interpretations? History can be described as both an account of what happened in the past and as a series of interim reports, reports that reveal both a changing knowledge of the past and a changing understanding of the past.

- Changing knowledge can come from newly discovered information.
- Changing understanding can come from new experiences.

Each generation, if not each individual, has a different understanding of the past because each has a different set of experiences. Each sees previous events in a new light and therefore asks new questions which lead to new answers, new insights, and new ways of explaining what has happened. Each history, therefore, is a slightly different interpretation although historians can be identified as belonging to schools of thought. Therefore, one of the principal goals of reading critically is to identify the author's interpretation.

C. Identifying Interpretations

There are several steps you can take to identify the author's interpretation and make the most of an article or book.

- Summarize the author's argument in a few sentences.
- Think about how the author's ideas diverge from, parallel, or converge with the ideas in other sources.
- Consider the relationship between the author's approach to the material and the conclusions drawn.
- Decide why the author has written the material (e.g., propaganda, historical record, nostalgia, personal advancement, etc.).
- Ask yourself if essential information is missing from the account and if so, why?
- Consider what new ideas you gained.
- Ask why the reading was assigned.
- Determine its significance.

D. Critiquing Material

The next step in reading critically is to critique the author's argument. A critique analyzes the merits of an argument. A critique is not a summary of the book or a record of your "feelings." Instead, it explains why a work is strong or weak. To critique secondary works of historians:

- Examine the author's argument. Determine if the argument is logical. Does it cover all elements of the problem? Does it omit any essential information?
- Test the author's ideas. Take the opposite point of view. Consider other interpretations and explanations. Check whether the importance of certain individuals, institutions, customs, or beliefs has been exaggerated.
- Check the evidence given. Does it support the author's generalization? Are quotations accurate and used wisely? Are dates and numbers correct?
- Look for inconsistencies. Are some actions or ideas given more weight for no apparent reason? Does the author exhibit unexplained biases?
- Consider other explanations. Would another explanation of the events make more sense? Are there other interpretations offering more insight?
- Note the ideology of the author. Does the author have a particular outlook? Is there evidence of actual bias? Such a bias could take many forms: Marxist, free market, religious, regional, political.
- Be aware of novelty. Are new research techniques being used? Does it include new theories about society, politics, economics, and culture? Does it express new insights based on the use of material objects?

3. READING PRIMARY SOURCES

Primary sources should also be read critically. Use the following guidelines.

- Identify the source. Answer such questions as where is it from, who wrote it, when was it written, and what type of document is it?
- Analyze the source. Identify its subject and note any biases that it might express. You also want to know who was it written for and why was it written? What does it state or imply about the practices and institutions of the society in question? What does it reveal about the society's political structure, religious beliefs, social structure, and economy? Finally, does the source provide any unique information or a unique perspective?
- Consider any omissions. Is there something that the source does not mention? What are its limitations? What is its focus? What information cannot be drawn from it?

If writing about the source, explain what the source can tell the reader and how it applies to the topic at hand.

In summary, reading critically offers you, the reader, several advantages. You will be able to comprehend the content and organization of the book or article more quickly and thoroughly. In addition, you should be able to understand the author's argument and thesis more easily. That should also lead to a clearer understanding of how the events or developments fit together and their significance. Moreover, you should be able to gain insights into the subject and begin to develop an interpretation of your own.

CHAPTER VI

TEST TAKING

I. Identifications

Tests in the History Department generally consist of two parts: identifications and essays. Identifications assess the student's knowledge of the important factual material. In the study of history, factual material is often referred to as "significant terms" or "significant events and people." These significant terms, events, and people are the "facts" students use to build essays and understandings of processes over time. From these very general considerations, the reader should understand exactly what history is not: it is not the compilation of a list of events, or reminiscences, or mountains of detail, or dates memorized for their own sake. The mastery of factual information is a necessary but not a sufficient step toward an understanding of the past. Just because one knows all of the elements of the periodic table does not make one a chemist. A chemist is one who knows how to use those elements for creating and understanding larger compounds. The same relationship exists between historical data and historical understanding.

In most cases, identifications are short answers that have three distinct parts. The first consists of knowledge of dates, either specific in some instances or general (when dealing with a broad movement or an age). Remembering dates is brute memorization, but it is vital because dating enables one to see the sequencing of actions in the past. Actions in the past occur over time, and often there is a reasonable pattern to those actions. Understanding the flow of history is revealed when one shows an understanding of the chronology of events. In the case of the United States, one cannot have the Constitution until independence of the colonies was achieved. Students who place the Constitution prior to the Declaration of Independence obviously have no idea of the basic movements necessary for the Constitution to have been written in the first place. So the dating is important and students should learn at least the general dating of events and actions.

The second aspect of an identification is simple description. Who was involved, where, and what happened, are the major questions to be answered. The third aspect of an identification is *significance*. This is the term historians use to describe the connection between an event, action, person, or other thing and a generalization. Usually the generalization involves the unfolding of some process going on in society, some feature of the population, or helps to explain a sequence of events leading to a major development for the society. In other words, the significance of a fact is why the term is worth remembering and what it shows about the past in question.

II. Essays

History is a written form of communication, and its foundation is the expository essay. Historians research the records of the past, interpret their results, and offer their conclusions in writing. Essay writing thus becomes one of the most essential skills associated with the profession of history.

For beginning college students, essay writing is considerably shortened from that of the historian, and the usual tasks assigned to pupils are either the writing of essays on tests or in short papers (three to ten pages). These writing assignments have the student answer a question as to how some major event or crisis originated, or provide an explanation for the sequencing of events. In doing these tasks, students should understand how they are duplicating the general practices of historians. Like the historian, the student has to determine the essential outline of events associated with the development or crisis. To give an answer as to why a development or crisis occurred or took the shape it did, the historian (or student) has to ask of the material a number of questions involving specifics, origins, and power of different forces. In short, an answer does not automatically leap out from basic facts but has to be teased out of them. Students are fairly well restricted to the material provided in lectures and class readings. When an historian presents his or her conclusions about the phenomenon, he or she does so by organizing the answer in a logical manner so that the reader may grasp the reasons underlying the general answer. In their test answers, students must do likewise as well.

BASIC STEPS

There are some basic steps that a student should take to answer an essay question. First, one should read it thoroughly twice in order to fully grasp the question, as well as the limits of time and subject. Do not answer some other question, do not make up one of your own, and make sure you get information that pertains to the question asked. Second, collect information (facts and ideas) from lectures, books, and any other assigned material. Third, separate out the information most vital to answering the question. You do not have unlimited time and unlimited space to provide an answer; therefore, you have to assess what information is more useful and what information is less useful. Part of the testing process is to assess your ability to determine the most vital information. Fourth, think about and create an answer. If you have to diagram out possible solutions, do so; if you need to put ideas on note cards and then shuffle them around, do so. If you have to wear headphones and listen to acid rock, do so. But spend time thinking about your answer beforehand. The truth is that absolutely correct answers in history are rare creatures, the unicorns of the profession. Dispute rages over every serious question about the way societies form and evolve over time; there are always a multitude of answers. You need to choose an answer that seems best suited to the information you have at hand, but you can only understand the available choices if you do the thinking and decide matters before you ever put pen to paper. Fifth, write an outline. An outline organizes an answer by collecting the information into common categories (called paragraphs), and then the student shows the instructor how each paragraph justifies the answer given. Within the paragraphs are the facts that justify the common category, or idea.

STRUCTURE OF THE ESSAY ANSWER

The answer the student devises is called the thesis, and the first paragraph of the essay is called the thesis paragraph. This is where the student repeats the problem asked by the instructor and then gives an answer to the problem. The rest of the body of the essay explains how the student justifies his/her thesis by grouping the information by ideas (categories) and using facts to prove the accuracy of their ideas. Schematically, an essay looks like this:

- Thesis Paragraph
  ○ Restate the question/problem.
  ○ Provide your answer to the question/problem.

- Paragraph 1. Idea 1 (category 1)
  ○ Topic sentence: introduces idea and ties it to the thesis
  ○ Facts, evidence, explanation

- Paragraph 2. Idea 2 (category 2)
  ○ Topic sentence: introduces idea and ties it to the thesis
  ○ Facts, evidence, explanation

- Paragraph 3. Idea 3 (category 3)
  ○ Topic sentence: introduces idea and ties it to the thesis
  ○ Facts, evidence, explanation

- [Continues until the student exhausts the pertinent ideas & evidence]

- Conclusion
  ○ Restate the problem and the thesis.

AN EXAMPLE

Let us consider an explicit example, one that derives from the first part of the HIST 1103 class. Suppose this was the question: "The world in which the British colonies were formed was one of kings and ruling dynasties. By 1776, the Americans announced they would create a government that had no kings or dynasties, but would run on republican principles—the people would elect their rulers, and the rulers would be subject to constant reelection to insure that they conformed to the wishes of the majority of the population. How did such a system come to the American colonies? Provide an answer up to 1765, and do not plunge into the quarrel that erupted between England and the colonies after 1764."

After some consideration, rereading the question, collecting the information, deciding upon a solution, this could be one of the ways an outline might be arranged.

- Thesis Paragraph
  - Restatement: Where did American self-government come from, seeing that the world at the time was ruled by Kings.
  - Thesis Statement: Self-government in the colonies came from 3 sources: British political institutions and ideals, the existence of vast amount of unoccupied land (except for the Indians), and the failure of the British to govern the colonies directly and forcefully.

- Paragraph 1. (Idea/Category: British institutions)
  - Topic Sentence: American self-government had its roots in the British system of government, especially the example of the House of Commons in the Parliament.
  - Evidence: British system of monarchy, but idea of representation existed; land in order to vote and hold office; belief in English liberties; limitations on the King; other countries more monarchical so England somewhat unique

- Paragraph 2. (Idea/Category: Transference of British customs to North America)
  - Topic Sentence: British established systems of self-govt in the initial settling process, thus setting the groundwork for self-govt.
  - Evidence: Virginia allows House of Burgesses to attract settlers; Massachusetts Puritans want self government to make sure evil-doers get punished; Pennsylvania uses self-government to attract settlers; places that try aristocratic forms (New York, Carolina) are tardy in setting up self-government and they lag behind other colonies.

- Paragraph 3. (Idea/Category: Effect of Land)
  - Topic Sentence: The land laws of England came to North America and inadvertently permitted the rise of wider participation in politics than was true in England
  - Evidence: To attract settlers, need an easy land policy, example of Pennsylvania; because English law permitted the owner of 40 acres to vote and hold office, more people could participate in colonial politics than English politics; in England, land monopolized by aristocracy; in North America, no land monopoly and owning land much less difficult. Probably some 60% of white adult males could vote; in England, less than

20%. Structurally, this permitted a much more open political system, although the habits of deference did not allow it.

- Paragraph 4. (Idea/Category: Lack of British Presence)
  - Topic Sentence: The land worked on creating an idea of participation because the British failed to create their own institutions in North America and force the Americans into aristocratic ways, thus enabling the practice of self govt to take root.
  - Evidence: British did not establish an aristocracy, did not create land monopoly, failed to send over a standing army or an active bureaucracy; they only tried to tighten up control of the empire during the 1670s (Dominion of New England) but that was undone by the Glorious Revolution; decision by 1720 was policy of benign neglect, let colonies run themselves because colonial trade so profitable for English merchants; they did so until the 1750s, up to 1763—got used to self-government without an aristocracy.

- Paragraph 5. (Idea/Category: Rise of Assemblies)
  - Topic Sentence: The creation of self-government in colonies due to land and lack of British oversight signalled by the near omnipotence of the colonial assemblies.
  - Evidence: Assemblies took over power in the colonies; they viewed themselves as little Houses of Commons; no taxation without their consent; they determined pay of governors; they sought control of colonial bureaucracy; they refused to pay church leaders effectively; they contested laws of trade; governors were third rate and transitory and could not offer much opposition; England's attention was elsewhere. So the Assemblies became dominant and carried for the population as a whole the example and practice of self-government.

- Paragraph 6. (Idea/Category: Other explanations lacking)
  - Topic Sentence: There are other explanations for the rise of self-government in North America by 1765, but they are not as robust.
  - Evidence; idea of Protestant radicalism/individualism; was there but not enough; Great Awakening not sufficient on its own; not ideological but more based on customs of colonies for some 60 years at least; not just a reaction to events in 1760s and 1770s because then might have created own aristocracy.

- Paragraph 7. Conclusion.
  - In a world of kings and aristocrats and various forms of despotism, the United States in 1776 was unique because it did not have kings and aristocrats. But a special evolution was responsible for this circumstance.

North American got the benefit of English institutions (the House of Commons) but was spared British governance. The British failed to guide and even coerce the Americans into proper aristocratic government forms and practices. In addition, because the abundant amount of land permitted most white male American colonists to vote, Americans grew accustomed to running their own governments and setting their own policies without much Kingly interference. The existence of available land for small farmers, the voting laws of England, and England's failure to govern directly produced American self-government, or at least the practice of it. When policy battles erupted in the 1760s and 1770s, the Americans would find self-government an easy answer to the problem of the form of government they should adopt.

It would behoove students to look closely at this outline and how it is arranged, ideas formulated, and facts brought in. Most of the questions asked in history courses are of this form and are susceptible to this method of preparation.

III. Test Preparation–A Checklist

Here are some tips for essay examination writing.

A. GENERAL POINTS

1. In an essay the goal is to examine a question in an organized, systematic manner.
2. An essay should have an introduction, in which one makes a thesis statement or argument; a body, in which one marshals the evidence for one's argument; and a conclusion, in which the findings of the essay are summarized.

B. PREPARATION BEFORE EXAM

1. Review lecture notes and reading assignments. Learn to summarize information and to note the most important and relevant facts. Taking good class notes is essential to success in most classes; fortunately, it is mostly a matter of practice. It is not necessary to write down every word that an instructor says. The most important thing is to record in your own words the essence of the most essential points and factual information.
2. Read the essay questions on the review sheet very carefully if there is one. *Your grade will depend on how well you answer the specific question.*
3. Ask yourself how the readings and lectures relate to the questions. *Essay questions seldom focus solely on one lecture or reading assignment.*

4. In making the connections between readings and lecture on the one hand and the question on the other you might want to make an outline of your answer. This will help you to pull the information together while keeping an eye on answering the question.

5. Address evidence potentially contradictory to your argument.

6. Support your general points with specific examples.

7. Take advantage of instructor's office hours. If you have made an effort to prepare, the instructor will spend whatever time necessary with you. Do not, however, expect help from your instructor if you have not already tried to help yourself.

8. Study and prepare. None of the points above apply if you don't know the material.

C. WHILE TAKING THE EXAM

1. A proven way for writing a good essay is to spend a few minutes before the essay to think about you want to say and then organize those thoughts in an outline. The outline guides the writing process and the instructor may look at it if the exam taker runs out of time.

2. Remember to give some chronological context by using dates in connection with events.

3. WRITE SOMETHING. One page is not an essay. Neither is spending ten minutes writing an answer. If you spend only half of the allotted time on an exam, you might get half the grade you want.

CHAPTER VII

WRITING STYLE

History is a discipline that uses narrative, analytical, expository writing to communicate its findings to an audience. It is therefore essential that students write clearly and logically so that their conclusions may be understood. Clear writing is a skill that is learned; the study of history should assist you in becoming a better writer, one who avoids the common pitfalls that lead to poor writing which only confuses readers instead of enlightening them. There are many good works on writing. Two much used by historians are:

> Joseph M. Williams, Style: Ten Lessons in Clarity and Grace. 5th ed.
> William Strunk, Jr., and E. B. White, The Elements of Style, 3d ed.

I. General Tips About Writing

- Your goal is to communicate your conclusions to another person and to explain how you derived your conclusion. Good writing serves the purpose of making your thinking clear to others.
- To write clearly, you need to know your subject well. Poor writing first starts from a confused writer who is not sure of his/her facts or conclusions. Before you write a word on paper, first make all your decisions about conclusions, important facts, and logical conclusions.
- Write an outline for your paper or essay. Order your arguments and check to make sure they follow logically. Make sure your information is placed in the correct categories.
- Avoid polysyllables and ten-dollar words. You are writing for clarity, not for social climbing. You want people to understand you, not to be confused by you.
- Before you hand in a paper or any take-home assignment, read it over and revise it. Check for spelling, punctuation, and grammatical errors. Do this even after you have printed off your last copy—make pen and ink changes if necessary. Your instructors welcome such changes because it means you are checking your work and trying to correct it. There is nothing worse, in an instructor's mind, than a paper that looks clean but is loaded with silly mistakes that any ten-year old could have caught by reading it over.
- Your paper will be returned to you with general comments about how you performed. There probably also will be numerous marks indicating problems with the writing. DO NOT IGNORE THOSE CORRECTIONS! Take the time to understand the areas of weakness in your writing and then resolve to correct them in future writing assignments. It does you no good to repeat mindlessly the same mistakes in writing for four years of your college career. You can improve if you take these corrections seriously and try to adjust your writing style.

Europe; European

existence

government

great

Great Britain

hierarchy

independent

necessary

possess; possession

Protestants

receive

redeem

secede, secession

separate

similar

sovereignty

their

transcendentalism; transcendentalist

truly

were

VOCABULARY

Many instructors also have lists of terms they use in class. If you do not know their meaning, then ask the instructor or consult a dictionary. The following are terms you may well see.

Political Terms

annexation	expansion	monarchy
armistice	faction	municipality
Authoritarian	fascism	oligarchy
autocrat	feudalism	parliament
autonomy	franchise	plebiscite
bicameral	guerrilla	Populist
capitalist	hegemony	proletariat
centrist	impeach	propaganda
coalition	imperialist	regent
communism	imperium	regime
conservatism	indemnity	republicanism
de facto	insurrection	rightist
decentralize	interregnum	socialist
demobilization	isolationism	sovereignty
democracy	leftist	subjugation
dictatorship	libertarian	suffrage
dissension	mandate	suzerainty
dynasty	Marxism-Leninism	totalitarianism
emancipation	Marxist	vassal

Economic Terms

bullion	monetary	protectionism
depopulation	monopoly	revenue
embargo	nationalization	subsidy
fiscal	productivity	tariff

Social Terms

anti-clerical	encyclical	papacy
clergy	excommunication	peasant
conscription	famine	plebeian
demography	hereditary	privilege rural
dialect	heresy	serfdom
anti-clerical	hierarchy	tenancy
ecclesiastical	literacy	urban
elite	migration	urbanization

General Vocabulary

abdicate	controversial	multifarious
acquiescence	expulsion	ordinance
antithesis	extirpate	paternalism
aspiration	grievance	pauperism
auspices	homogeneous	phenomenon
capitulate	impunity	polemic
cataclysmic	indigenous	promulgate
compensation	inherent	provocation
concession	innovation	stalemate
confiscate	medieval	ubiquitous
conspiracy	militarism	usurp

CHAPTER VIII

WRITING ASSIGNMENTS

I. Overview

There are many different types of writing assignments that history instructors may give. The general purpose of all such assignments is to ensure that students have read and understood the pertinent material, and that they can communicate their knowledge effectively. Survey courses in history typically require somewhere between eight and twenty total typed pages of writing over the duration of the semester. Upper-division courses may require more than twice as much writing. This section of the handbook will explain some of the common types of paper assignments; bear in mind that professors will probably have particular instructions or expectations for the papers for their course. The research paper, which is usually only assigned in upper-division classes, is covered in chapter IX.

II. Worksheets

Worksheets (or workbooks or assignment sheets) for the survey classes, when used, are self-explanatory. They ask students to put down basic information that they should be learning from the textbook readings and lectures.

III. Response Papers

Response papers are also fairly self-explanatory. For these, students should have read the assigned material (or watched the film, or observed the object). They then respond with their own reactions and observations. A response paper may incorporate questions about the reading; make connections between the reading and the student's life; make connections between the reading and other readings; or in some other way show an understanding of the reading or other source material. These papers are usually quite short, perhaps only half a page to a page in length, and instructors may not mind a more informal style than they would expect in other types of writing assignments.

IV. Short Papers

A short paper of 3–4 pages is likely to be an analysis of a longer text (or work in another medium, such as a film). These are formally written and the instructor may require the use of footnotes or endnotes to indicate where specific information can be found in the source. The assignment may include questions that students should consider and answer in the course of the paper. Generally speaking there are seven points to think about and include when writing a short analytical paper based on a primary source:

- What kind of a document is it?
- Who wrote it?
- Why was it written?
- Who was it written for?
- What does the source talk about?
- What does the source *not* talk about?
- What makes this source valuable?

In short, the paper should answer the question: What does this source tell us about the place and time in which it was written?

V. Book Reviews

This type of paper may be assigned in an upper-division course as a way of getting students to begin to understand the historiography of a topic. Reviews are not simply summaries of the book in question. While a good review does indicate the contents of the book, it also evaluates how effectively the author has presented the information and whether, in the reviewer's judgment, both the facts and the author's analysis and interpretations are reliable. Even if a student does not know a great deal about the topic it is possible to write a strong and critical review by thinking about whether the arguments in the book hold together and whether the student is aware of any contradictory evidence that the author has not taken into account.

Book reviews are usually fairly short in length, between 2–4 pages. There are two reasons for this. First, a long review may more easily become a summary of the book's factual contents rather than an evaluation of the author's arguments. Second, professional reviews are usually limited in length; journals only have so much space and if one review is too long, another book might not be reviewed at all. Learning to discipline the length of one's writing and to include only the most important points is a valuable skill, and writing short reviews can help students learn this skill.

CHAPTER IX

CREATING HISTORY: THE RESEARCH PAPER

I. The Research Paper

To bring students to a fuller appreciation of the complexity involved in the study of human societies over time, instructors often assign research papers. These papers may vary in length between about 8 to 25 pages, depending on the instructor and on the student's drive and verbosity. Instructors will discuss their specific requirements for the paper, but a few general observations and rules can be given in advance.

PRIMARY SOURCES

History is written from sources that have survived time. Many of these records are written. These written documents take a number of forms: diaries, books, reminiscences, government scrolls, government publications, census reports, court decisions, letters, tablets with inscriptions upon them, and many others. All these forms of contemporary communication and recording are called *primary sources*. They are materials that were written by participants in the society's activity at the time. The primary sources also include many material objects: pictures, French postcards, vases, spear heads, cloth, architectural ruins—and now, television programs, radio programs, movies, and similar non-written media. When historians write their histories, they are largely based on these primary sources.

SECONDARY SOURCES

When investigating the past, historians (including history students) need to acknowledge what others have written and especially to note the interpretations offered by others. In articles and books (monographs as well as textbooks), historians obtain a framework for understanding the past written by others and may find references to some factual information that these authors have unearthed. Such books and articles are called *secondary sources*—they are writings done by nonparticipants in the past, interpretations foisted upon the history by observers removed in time. Secondary sources are invaluable for several reasons. In terms of scholarship, it is absolutely vital that the researcher know what has already been written on a subject, what the basic interpretations have been, and what areas have not been covered. When one writes a history, one either modifies old interpretations, offers new interpretations, or confirms the ones already in existence. This is the way that historical scholarship becomes cumulative; the various ways of approaching a problem in the past are mapped out and made available to other readers. The other reason for paying attention to secondary sources is less exalted but no less important: authors let researchers know what materials are available, what materials may not exist, and, by implication, what other materials ought to be consulted. Secondary sources are a good way to make a list of the primary sources one can use in one's own investigation.

II. Writing a Research Paper

CHOOSING A TOPIC

One of the first problems confronting a student who has to write a paper is topic selection. The following are only general guidelines; instructors may provide more specific instructions. First, research what interests you. You have chosen a course; you have selected it as a matter of your personal interest. Keep following that interest. The second rule is to refine your interest to a manageable question. You will not be writing a 200-page Master's thesis in an upper-division course. Therefore, think of a topic that is limited in time and subject matter. Third, select a topic that the library at Oklahoma State University can support. The library's holdings are stronger on United States subjects than on foreign countries, and are stronger on the United States since 1815 than before 1815. There simply are certain limitations on what you can choose.

At the beginning of the semester, if a research paper is being assigned and you are searching for a topic, the best thing to do is to thumb through your textbook, look at the topics covered, and see if one of them interests you. That is a starting point. Use your textbook to guide you to secondary sources on the topic. Textbooks often include bibliographies of such works. By reading the introduction and preface of these books, you can begin to get an idea of the records available for consultation and the basic historiography of the subject.

Most of the time, however, you will have to be assisted by your instructors. Sometimes they will prepare lists of questions for you; sometimes they will guide you to specific topics; sometimes they will tell you what the available sources are and then let you decide how to use them. You should consult with your instructor about research papers to find out what the expectations are.

FINDING SOURCES

Your instructor should give you guidance on pertinent secondary and primary sources for the course, and from it you should choose material that is most germane to your topic. If you have trouble finding information, *ask a reference librarian*. Then you can commence the research. When you begin to do the research, you write down important ideas, arguments, quotations: whatever material is presented to you that informs your topic. When you do that, make sure that in your notes you know precisely where you found each piece of information. The discipline of history requires that people must be able to check your work and the accuracy of your depictions or quotations—to make sure you have used sources correctly. You are not permitted to make up artifacts or documents; rather, the "proof" of your argument is the material you have found, and for it to have substance, other people must be able to find the material and ensure you have read it correctly and interpreted the information appropriately.

What are the sources available to undergraduates at Oklahoma State University? To some degree it depends on the topic, the country, and the time period. Consult your instructor for guides to the important sources for your subject. Most secondary literature in history is on the fourth floor of the library and is contained in the 900s (Dewey Decimal System). Much primary information in the form of government documents is on the fifth floor. There the reports of the various branches of the United States government, the congressional debates, and congressional documents are held. The staff on the fifth floor will assist you in finding material for your topic; there are many finding guides. Moreover, the fifth floor also houses documents from other countries. For example, the British Parliamentary Session papers (parliamentary debates) are held there; reports of the Organization for the European Community Development (OECD) are shelved there.

Likewise, there are interesting holdings in the Nonbook Room of the library on the first floor. The Nonbook room holds basically microfilm reels and microcard collections. Many newspapers are on microfilm; tribal records of the Oklahoma Tribes are on microfilm; and several large manuscript collections are on microfilm. The Nonbook Room also contains a large microdot collection of Early American Imprints (that is, tracts and printed material).

If you want to know the appropriate government documents to consult, if you want to know the right search question to ask the computer, if you need help finding guides to research, if you need assistance with microfilms, microcards, and finding guides: *ask a librarian*. This cannot be stressed too much. The reference librarians are there to help you find the information you need; they cannot tell you how to write your paper, but if you go in knowing your topic, they are happy to make sure that you can locate all the available information.

A service that is used by faculty and graduate students, but is less likely to be useful to undergraduates, is interlibrary loan. Simply speaking, at the undergraduate level, professors will not ask students to obtain information for research papers that is not available at our library. Graduate students and faculty have to travel to other repositories to get suitable information; undergraduates do not unless they are on very special projects for very special reasons.

What is available is the internet. The internet now has web sites that contain many primary documents, and some that give good representations of material culture. For example, the Library of Congress now has an extensive web site (www.loc.gov) that is loaded with early American documents, congressional debates, and government publications. It also contains photographs and paintings of early American life. Other nations have central libraries or archives that have also put much material on their web site. This information is certainly suitable for research papers; if you use such sites, however, make sure you take down the web site information accurately so people can access the same material you claim to have looked at. Always be careful and critical in choosing to use material from the internet. Official government sites are generally reliable; organizations' and individuals' sites may not be. When in deoubt, ask your professor for his/her opinions as to whether a webite's material is suitable for use in your paper.

Finding the secondary literature covering a topic is fairly simple. The easiest way is to begin with a textbook and then follow the textbook author's suggestion about additional readings. Those additional readings will then list articles and books pertaining to the topic in their bibliographies and their introductions may well detail the historiography of the subject. In addition, one can consult historical journals to see if new works have appeared or if summary articles have been published. In some cases, reference books have been published on the available literature on topics (such as the *Harvard Guide to American History*.)

The Oklahoma State University Library does have its limitations from the research historian's viewpoint, but it also has its strengths. Many books have been written by the faculty primarily from the information available at Edmon Low Library. So, do not discount the quality of the information at your disposal, nor believe that you cannot do a good job of investigating a subject while a student at this school.

DOCUMENTING YOUR WORK

This brings us to the documentation aspect of writing research papers—or articles in professional journals or historical monographs. You have to prove to an audience that you have done the research necessary to sustain your arguments, that you have considered the arguments of others, that you have been faithful in your use of primary sources. The means by which you communicate this knowledge is through footnotes (or endnotes) and a bibliography. The current publication standard in the profession is endnotes rather than footnotes, but your instructor will tell you which he/she prefers. The purpose of either type of note is to tell the reader where you have obtained an idea, an interpretation, or a piece of factual information; it serves as a guide for the interested reader to check your accuracy. It also tells the reader how much work you have done and the quality of your research. In a real sense, you are putting your work ethic on the line so others may assess how much validity they will give to your ideas—if very incomplete work, then very little validity. The bibliography is a formal summation at the end listing the primary sources and the secondary sources (usually divided in that fashion) that you have consulted. It represents a quick means for reviewers to assess your research effort and to see if there was a body of evidence you missed. Examples of proper footnote style and bibliographic entries are given in chapter X.

Beginning students often have trouble determining when they should note their sources. Follow these general rules. One: whenever you quote, you have to acknowledge the source in a footnote or an endnote. Two: whenever you are referring specifically to an interpretation not your own, you must acknowledge the source in a note. Three: whenever you are using evidence from primary sources—

the actions, words, material evidence of historical actors—you may use notes at the end of the paragraph; this is to say, do not put a note at the end of every sentence. It is not necessary and is a positive nuisance and distraction to your reader. Rather, cite all the sources used in the construction of a paragraph together at the end of the paragraph, especially when you are just giving factual information derived from primary sources. Fourth, do not footnote generally known information—that is, information that has been put into survey textbooks that does not count as quotes, interpretations, or details of events. For example, do not footnote the name of the British kings at the time of the American Revolution, the founding date of Massachusetts Bay Colony, the date of the French Revolution, etc. These are basic facts easily accessible from a standard textbook and represent information that any modestly motivated person could find on his or her own.

PULLING IT TOGETHER

Now, you are interested in a topic; perhaps you have found a problem involving an aspect of a civilization you want to find more information about, or you have been outraged by someone's interpretation of an historic event. You conduct your research, take your notes, and carefully record the publication data necessary for endnotes and bibliography. So how do you write your paper? Actually, pretty much the way you write an essay exam with one or two refinements. To begin with, you need to establish within the first two pages of your research paper three points: first, the historical problem you are dealing with and why it is important; second, what other historians have written about it (the historiography); and, third, the interpretation that you are offering—whether you agree with an existing interpretation, offer a modification, or have created an entirely new way of looking at the phenomena. Then comes the body of the paper in which you present the history. Your narrative here is guided by the sub-sections that pertain to the problem you are investigating. Over the course of the paper you present your argument, your narrative, your analysis in a logical fashion (and make sure you use strong topic sentences, see chapter VII). At the end is your conclusion when you represent your argument in all its glory.

CHAPTER X

STANDARD FORMS FOR ENDNOTES, FOOTNOTES, AND BIBLIOGRAPHIC ENTRIES

First, understand that it is your duty to acknowledge where you obtained your information. If you are working with the ideas of another person, you must acknowledge that person as the source of the idea. To do otherwise is to commit plagiarism. The Department has this standard definition of plagiarism:

> "Plagiarism may be defined as the act of using another's words or ideas as one's own and may include any of the following practices: 1) direct copying from any source without citation; 2) direct copying from any source without quotation marks (even if footnotes are used); 3) paraphrasing (putting into your own words) the argument of another author or student without citation; 4) presenting purchased or down-loaded work as one's own."

Most footnotes or endnotes can now be added easily due to the advances of computers and word processing programs. The following forms should be sufficient for most undergraduate papers. Number footnotes or endnotes consecutively throughout the paper (don't start new numbering on each page). After the first full citation, a shortened form with the author's surname, a short form of the title, and the page number(s) may be used for later references to the same work.

Historians usually follow the format widely referred to as Chicago. Two good general guides for format of bibliography entries (and notes as well) are *The Chicago Manual of Style*, 15th edition (in the reference section of the library, 655.25 C532m 2003,) and *A Manual for Writers of Term Papers, Theses, and Dissertations*, 6th edition, by Kate Turabian (in the reference section, 808.02 T929m 1996; there are also several copies that circulate.) In case of doubt, or to cite sources that do not fit under one of the general schemes below, consult one of these guides for more specific examples.

I. Note Format Examples

The format of note citations is the same whether they are footnotes at the bottom of the page or endnotes at the end of the page. If you wish to use internal citation, as many of the social sciences do, consult your professor as to suitability and style.

A scholarly book (monograph):

[1]Hilda L. Smith, *Reason's Disciples: Seventeenth-Century English Feminists* (Urbana: University of Illinois Press, 1982), 59.

General short form: [Short forms may be applied to any of the following types of notes as well.]

[2]Smith, *Reason's Disciples*, 11.

A scholarly book in a series: [This example is an edited work; for an ordinary monograph simply omit the "ed." notation.]

[3]Thomas Austin, ed., *Two Fifteenth-Century Cookery-Books*, Early English Text Society, Original Series, no. 91 (London: N. Trübner, 1888), xii-xxiii.

A book with two authors:

[4]Thomas Woodcock and John Martin Robinson, *The Oxford Guide to Heraldry* (Oxford: Oxford University Press, 1988), 89.

An article in a book:

[5]Natalie Zemon Davis, "Gender and Genre: Women as Historical Writers, 1400-1820," in *Beyond Their Sex: Learned Women of the European Past*, ed. Patricia H. Labalme (New York: New York University Press, 1980), 166.

An article in a professional journal:

[6]Frances Harris, "Accounts of the Conduct of Sarah, Duchess of Marlborough, 1704-1742," *British Library Journal* 8 (Spring 1982): 30.

An article in another periodical such as a magazine:

[7]John F. Ross, "Unmasking George Washington," *Smithsonian*, October 2005, 41.

A newspaper article: [Normally specific articles are not listed separately in a bibliography; instead only the information for the issue is given. Include the city name in parentheses if it is not included in the name of the paper]

[8]Jennifer Weiss, "Future of Tree With a Long Past Is in Doubt," *New York Times*, 20 August 2006, 14(NJ).

Government documents: [There are a wide variety of published governmental documents from the U.S. federal, state, and local governments. For correct citation forms, you should refer to *The Chicago Manual of Style*.]

A contemporary (historical) printed source lacking some information: [Here the missing information is the year, indicated by "n.d." for "no date." If the place or publisher is unknown, use "n.p." in the appropriate location.]

[9]Giovanni Boccaccio, *The pleasant and sweet history of patient Grissell Shewing how she from a poore mans daughter, came to be a great lady in France, being a petterne*

for all vertuous vvomen. Translated out of Italian (London: Printed by E. P. for Iohn Wright, n.d.), 22.

An edited/translated primary source such as a diary: [A translated text is formatted in the same way, substituting the word "trans." for "ed."]

[10]Lady Mary Wortley Montagu, *The Nonsense of Common-Sense, 1737–1738*, ed. Robert Halsband (Evanston, Ill.: Northwestern University, 1947), 4.

An edited/translated source that is part of a multi-volume work:

[11]Lady Mary Wortley Montagu, *The Complete Letters of Lady Mary Wortley Montagu*, 3 vols., ed. Robert Halsband (Oxford: Clarendon Press, 1965–67), 1:70-1.

An edited collection of works:

[12]A. R. Myers, ed., *English Historical Documents, 1327–1485* (New York: Oxford University Press, 1969), 694.

A single document from an edited collection:

[13]Anonymous, "Carmina Burana," in *Wine Women and Song: Medieval Latin Students' Songs*, ed. John Addington Symonds (New York: Cooper Square Publishers, 1966), 174.

Manuscripts: [Like government documents, manuscript citations are extremely variable. Normally you will provide the author's name and as much additional information as is available, but refer to *The Chicago Manual of Style* for more specifics.]

Internet sources: [It is important to include the date of access in parentheses as the last item since sometimes URLs disappear. Note that this item has no author, but the page editor's name is included.]

[14]"Charter of Privileges to the Butchers of Paris, 1182," *Internet Medieval Sourcebook*, ed. Paul Halsall, September 1998, <http://www.fordham.edu/halsall /source/1182butchers-paris.html> (10 March 2005).

II. Bibliography Format Examples

The following are the same examples as above, but arranged as they would be in a bibliography: divided into primary and secondary sources, and then alphabetized by author's surname within each section. Note that bibliography entries are single-spaced, with a blank line between each, and are formatted with a hanging indent to facilitate the identification of the author.

PRIMARY SOURCES

Anonymous. "Carmina Burana." In *Wine Women and Song: Medieval Latin Students' Songs*, edited by John Addington Symonds. New York: Cooper Square Publishers, 1966.

Austin, Thomas, editor. *Two Fifteenth-Century Cookery-Books*. Early English Text Society, Original Series, no. 91. London: N. Trübner, 1888.

Boccaccio, Giovanni. *The pleasant and sweet history of patient Grissell Shewing how she from a poore mans daughter, came to be a great lady in France, being a petterne for all vertuous vvomen. Translated out of Italian*. London: Printed by E. P. for Iohn Wright, n.d.

"Charter of Privileges to the Butchers of Paris, 1182." In the *Internet Medieval Sourcebook*, ed. Paul Halsall. September 1998. <http://www.fordham.edu/halsall/source/1182butchers-paris.html> Accessed 10 March 2005.

Montagu, Lady Mary Wortley. *The Nonsense of Common-Sense, 1737–1738*. Edited by Robert Halsband. Evanston, Ill.: Northwestern University, 1947.

———. *The Complete Letters of Lady Mary Wortley Montagu*. 3 vols. Edited by Robert Halsband. Oxford: Clarendon Press, 1965–67.

Myers, A. R. Myers, editor. *English Historical Documents, 1327-1485*. New York: Oxford University Press, 1969.

SECONDARY SOURCES

Davis, Natalie Zemon. "Gender and Genre: Women as Historical Writers, 1400-1820." In *Beyond Their Sex: Learned Women of the European Past*, edited by Patricia H. Labalme. New York: New York University Press, 1980.

Harris, Frances. "Accounts of the Conduct of Sarah, Duchess of Marlborough, 1704–1742." *British Library Journal* 8 (Spring 1982): 7–35.

Ross, John F. "Unmasking George Washington." *Smithsonian*, October 2005, 40–42.

Smith, Hilda L. *Reason's Disciples: Seventeenth-Century English Feminists*. Urbana: University of Illinois Press, 1982.

Weiss, Jennifer. "Future of Tree With a Long Past Is in Doubt." *New York Times*, 20 August 2006, 14(NJ).

Woodcock, Thomas, and John Martin Robinson. *The Oxford Guide to Heraldry*. Oxford: Oxford University Press, 1988.

READINGS FROM
THE NORTON MIX:
HISTORY

The Starving Time in Jamestown (1624)

Captain John Smith (1580–1631) was one of the original 104 English colonists who founded Jamestown, the first permanent English settlement in Virginia, in 1607. Jamestown's earliest period was extremely difficult; more than half of the settlers died of disease and poor nutrition. With the colony near collapse by 1608 as a result of mismanagement and lack of necessary skills such as farming, Smith gained control and instituted policies that brought discipline and order to the colony, including his famous proclamation that "He that will not work shall not eat." Badly injured in an accidental explosion of gunpowder, Smith returned to England for treatment in October 1609. He never returned to the colony.

Meanwhile shiploads of ill-prepared settlers continued to arrive at Jamestown, now without Smith's able leadership. The subsequent winter of 1609–10, a time of terrible hardship during which all but 60 of the 500 colonists died, became known as the "starving time." More than a decade later, when Smith wrote A General Historie of Virginia to memorialize those who had been at Jamestown, he had few reliable records to draw upon. As you read the following selection, consider why the Jamestown colony struggled initially. What fundamental mistakes do the colonists appear to have made?

I t might well be thought, a Countrie so faire (as Virginia is) and a people so tractable, would long ere this have beene quietly possessed, to the satisfaction of the adventurers, & the eternizing of the memory of those that effected it. But because all the world doe see a defailement;[1] this following Treatise shall give satisfaction to all indifferent Readers, how the businesse hath bin carried: where no doubt they will easily understand and answer to their question, how it came to passe there was no better speed and successe in those proceedings.

* * *

The day before Captaine Smith returned for England with the ships, Captaine Davis arrived in a small Pinace,[2] with some sixteene proper men more. . . . For the Salvages[3] no sooner understood Smith was gone, but they all revolted, and did

---

1. Failure.
2. Small boat.
3. Savages; that is, the Native Americans.

spoile and murther all they incountered. Now wee were all constrained to live onely on that Smith had onely for his owne Companie, for the rest had consumed their proportions. . . . Sickelmore upon the confidence of Powhatan,[4] with about thirtie others as carelesse as himselfe, were all slaine, onely Jeffrey Shortridge escaped, and Pokahontas the Kings daughter saved a boy called Henry Spilman, that lived many yeeres after, by her meanes, amongst the Patawomekes. . . . Now we all found the losse of Captaine Smith, yea his greatest maligners could now curse his losse: as for corne, provision and contribution from the Salvages, we had nothing but mortall wounds, with clubs and arrowes; as for our Hogs, Hens, Goats, Sheepe, Horse, or what lived, our commanders, officers & Salvages daily consumed them, some small proportions sometimes we tasted, till all was devoured; then swords, armes, pieces, or any thing, wee traded with the Salvages, whose cruell fingers were so oft imbrewed in our blouds, that what by their crueltie, our Governours indiscretion, and the losse of our ships, of five hundred within six moneths after Captaine Smiths departure, there remained not past sixtie men, women and children, most miserable and poore creatures; and those were preserved for the most part, by roots, herbes, acornes, walnuts, berries, now and then a little fish: they that had startch[5] in these extremities, made no small use of it; yea, even the very skinnes of our horses. Nay, so great was our famine, that a Salvage we slew, and buried, the poorer sort tooke him up againe and eat him, and so did divers one another boyled and stewed with roots and herbs: And one amongst the rest did kill his wife, powdered her, and had eaten part of her before it was knowne, for which hee was executed, as hee well deserved; now whether shee was better roasted, boyled or carbonado'd,[6] I know not, but of such a dish as powdered wife I never heard of. This was that time, which still to this day we called the starving time; it were too vile to say, and scarce to be beleeved, what we endured.

Study Questions

1. What reasons does Smith give for the hardships the colonists suffered? Does he offer any solutions?

2. What do you think they could have done to prevent starvation?

3. Why do you think Smith refers to himself in the third person in this excerpt?

4. The document was written in 1624, 15 years after Smith left Jamestown. How do you think Smith's account was affected by the passage of time, and especially by the facts that Smith was absent during the worst of the colony's hardships and that, by 1624, the colony was prospering?

4. Smith's name for the chief of the Powhattan Indians.
5. Plant starch, a tasteless powder normally used to stiffen fabric.
6. Scored with a knife and then grilled.

OTTOBAH CUGOANO

Narrative of the Enslavement
of a Native of Africa (1787)

*From the fifteenth century through the nineteenth, Europeans—most signifi-
cantly the Dutch and the English—carried an estimated 10 to 12 million Africans across the Atlantic Ocean in the largest forced migration in world history.
The harrowing experience aboard the slave ships was referred to as the "Middle
Passage," so called because it was the second of a three-part journey: ships would
carry gold and European manufactured goods to trade to Africans for slaves;
then, laden with men, women, and children, the ships headed westward across
the Atlantic; having deposited their "cargo" in the Americas, the ships would
return to Europe carrying American agricultural products such as sugar, rice,
and tobacco.*

*Of the millions of people forced to endure the experience of enslavement and
the Middle Passage, only a very few left behind firsthand accounts. One of them
was Ottobah Cugoano (ca. 1757–?), an African born in present-day Ghana who
was captured and enslaved at the age of thirteen. Surviving the Middle Passage,
Cugoano experienced the brutal working conditions on a sugar plantation on the
Caribbean island of Grenada. Taken to England by his master in 1772, Cugoano
taught himself to read and write, converted to Christianity, and took the name
John Stuart. After his emancipation, he spent much of the next two decades fighting for the abolition of slavery. His story, published as* Thoughts and Sentiments on the Evil and Wicked Traffic of the Slavery and Commerce of the
Human Species, *first appeared in 1787. Four years later, in 1791, Cugoano published another edition of his work. After this, Cugoano, like most of the untold
millions of other Africans ensnared in the international slave trade, disappears
from the historical record.*

From *The Negro's Memorial, or, Abolitionist's Catechism* (London: Hatchard
and Co., and J. and A. Arch, 1825), 120–27 of appendix.

I was early snatched away from my native country, with about eighteen or
twenty more boys and girls, as we were playing in a field. We lived but a few
days' journey from the coast where we were kidnapped, and as we were
decoyed and drove along, we were soon conducted to a factory, and from thence,
in the fashionable way of traffic, consigned to Grenada. Perhaps it may not be

amiss to give a few remarks, as some account of myself, in this transposition of captivity.

I was born in the city of Agimaque, on the coast of Fantyn:[1] my father was a companion to the chief in that part of the country of Fantee, and when the old king died I was left in his house with his family; soon after I was sent for by his nephew, Ambro Accasa, who succeeded the old king in the chiefdom of that part of Fantee, known by the name of Agimaque and Assinee. I lived with his children, enjoying peace and tranquillity, about twenty moons, which, according to their way of reckoning time, is two years. I was sent for to visit an uncle, who lived at a considerable distance from Agimaque. The first day after we set out we arrived at Assinee, and the third day at my uncle's habitation, where I lived about three months, and was then thinking of returning to my father and young companion at Agimaque; but by this time I had got well acquainted with some of the children of my uncle's hundreds of relations, and we were some days too venturesome in going into the woods to gather fruit and catch birds and such amusements as pleased us. One day . . . we went into the woods, as usual but we had not been above two hours, before our troubles began, when several great ruffians came upon us suddenly, and said we had committed a fault against their lord, and we must go and answer for it ourselves before him.

Some of us attempted, in vain, to run away, but pistols and cutlasses were soon introduced, threatening, that if we offered to stir, we should all lie dead on the spot. One of them pretended to be more friendly than the rest, and said that he would speak to their lord to get us clear, and desired that we should follow him; we were then immediately divided into different parties, and drove after him.

* * *

I soon became very uneasy, not knowing what to do, and refused to eat or drink, for whole days together, till the man of the house told me that he would do all in his power to get me back to my uncle; then I eat a little fruit with him, and had some thoughts that I should be sought after, as I would be then missing at home about five or six days. I inquired every day if the men had come back, and for the rest of my companions, but could get no answer of any satisfaction. I was kept about six days at this man's house, and in the evening there was another man came, and talked with him a good while and I heard the one say to the other he must go, and the other said, the sooner the better; that man came out and told me that he knew my relations at Agimaque, and that we must set out to-morrow morning, and he would convey me there. Accordingly we set out next day, and travelled till dark, when we came to a place where we had some supper and slept. He carried a large bag, with some gold dust, which he said he had to buy some goods at the sea-side to take with him to Agimaque. Next day we travelled on, and

1. Present-day Ghana.

in the evening came to a town, where I saw several white people, which made me afraid that they would eat me, according to our notion, as children, in the inland parts of the country. This made me rest very uneasy all the night, and next morning I had some victuals brought, desiring me to eat and make haste, as my guide and kidnapper told me that he had to go to the castle with some company that were going there, as he had told me before, to get some goods. After I was ordered out, the horrors I soon saw and felt, cannot be well described; I saw many of my miserable countrymen chained two and two, some handcuffed, and some with their hands tied behind. We were conducted along by a guard, and when we arrived at the castle, I asked my guide what I was brought there for, he told me to learn the ways of the *browfow*, that is, the white-faced people. I saw him take a gun, a piece of cloth, and some lead for me, and then he told me that he must now leave me there, and went off. This made me cry bitterly, but I was soon conducted to a prison, for three days, where I heard the groans and cries of many, and saw some of my fellow-captives. But when a vessel arrived to conduct us away to the ship, it was a most horrible scene; there was nothing to be heard but the rattling of chains, smacking of whips, and the groans and cries of our fellow-men. Some would not stir from the ground, when they were lashed and beat in the most horrible manner. I have forgot the name of this infernal fort; but we were taken in the ship that came for us, to another that was ready to sail from Cape Coast.[2] When we were put into the ship, we saw several black merchants coming on board, but we were all drove into our holes, and not suffered to speak to any of them. In this situation we continued several days in sight of our native land; but I could find no good person to give any information of my situation to Accasa at Agimaque. And when we found ourselves at last taken away, death was more preferable than life; and a plan was concerted amongst us, that we might burn and blowup the ship, and to perish all together in the flames: but we were betrayed by one of our own countrywomen, who slept with some of the headmen of the ship, for it was common for the dirty filthy sailors to take the African women and lie upon their bodies; but the men were chained and pent up in holes. It was the women and boys which were to burn the ship, with the approbation and groans of the rest; though that was prevented, the discovery was likewise a cruel bloody scene.

But it would be needless to give a description of all the horrible scenes which we saw, and the base treatment which we met with in this dreadful captive situation, as the similar cases of thousands, which suffer by this infernal traffic, are well known. Let it suffice to say that I was thus lost to my dear indulgent parents and relations, and they to me. All my help was cries and tears, and these could not avail, nor suffered long, till one succeeding woe and dread swelled up another. Brought from a state of innocence and freedom, and, in a barbarous and cruel manner, conveyed to a state of horror and slavery, this abandoned situation may

2. A port city in present-day Ghana.

be easier conceived than described. From the time that I was kidnapped, and conducted to a factory,[3] and from thence in the brutish, base, but fashionable way of traffic, consigned to Grenada, the grievous thoughts which I then felt, still pant in my heart; though my fears and tears have long since subsided. And yet it is still grievous to think that thousands more have suffered in similar and greater distress, under the hands of barbarous robbers, and merciless task-masters; and that many, even now, are suffering in all the extreme bitterness of grief and woe, that no language can describe . . . Being in this dreadful captivity and horrible slavery, without any hope of deliverance, for about eight or nine months, beholding the most dreadful scenes of misery and cruelty, and seeing my miserable companions often cruelly lashed, and, as it were, cut to pieces, for the most trifling faults; this made me often tremble and weep, but I escaped better than many of them. For eating a piece of sugar-cane, some were cruelly lashed, or struck over the face, to knock their teeth out. Some of the stouter ones, I suppose, often reproved, and grown hardened and stupid with many cruel beatings and lashings, or perhaps faint and pressed with hunger and hard labour, were often committing trespasses of this kind, and when detected, they met with exemplary punishment. Some told me they had their teeth pulled out, to deter others, and to prevent them from eating any cane in future. Thus seeing my miserable companions and countrymen in this pitiful, distressed, and horrible situation, with all the brutish baseness and barbarity attending it, could not but fill my little mind horror and Indignation. But I must own, to the shame of my own countrymen, that I was first kidnapped and betrayed by some of my own complexion, who were the first cause of my exile, and slavery; but if there were no buyers there would be no sellers. So far as I can remember, some of the Africans in my country keep slaves, which they take in war, or for debt; but those which they keep are well fed, and good care taken of them, and treated well; and as to their clothing, they differ according to the custom of the country. But I may safely say, that all the poverty and misery that any of the inhabitants of Africa meet with among themselves, is far inferior to those inhospitable regions of misery which they meet with in the West-Indies, where their hard-hearted overseers have neither Regard to the laws of God, nor the life of their fellow-men.

Thanks be to God, I was delivered from Grenada, and that horrid brutal slavery. A gentleman coming to England took me for his servant, and brought me away, where I soon found my situation become more agreeable. After coming to England, and seeing others write and read, I had a strong desire to learn, and getting what assistance I could, I applied myself to learn reading and writing, which soon became my recreation, pleasure, and delight; and when my master perceived that I could write some, he sent me to a proper school for that purpose to learn. Since, I have endeavoured to improve my mind in reading, and have sought to get

---

3. An establishment for traders carrying on business in a foreign country.

all the intelligence I could, in my situation of life, towards the state of my brethren and countrymen in complexion, and of the miserable situation of those who are barbarously sold into captivity, and unlawfully held in slavery.

Study Questions

1. How was Cugoano enslaved?

2. What was Cugoano's reaction to the first sight of Europeans? What did Cugoano experience aboard the slave ship?

3. What became of Cugoano when he landed in the New World? How was his fate different from that of the millions of other Africans who were forced into slavery?

4. What distinctions does Cugoano make between slavery as practiced in Africa and slavery in the West Indies?

5. What does Cugoano's writing reveal about the nature of his eventual education? about his intended audience?

Slave Laws in Virginia

(1661, 1691, and 1705)

Slavery evolved over time in the American colonies. In the first half of the seventeenth century, indentured servants (laborers working to repay the cost of their passage to America) in the Chesapeake colonies could reasonably hope for their freedom, but as economic conditions changed and more labor was needed for the farming of tobacco, indentured servitude gave way to race-based slavery. Over the first century of settlement, the authorities began to codify increasingly severe new slave laws that limited the rights of African slaves and cut off legal paths to freedom. The laws and customs governing slavery in Virginia became the model for the other colonies.

The following documents demonstrate this progression of legal codes, from legislation regarding runaway indentured servants, through laws to deal with anxiety over miscegenation and the possible presence of free blacks, to an excerpt from the 1705 slave code that pieced together laws passed over the previous century, ruling definitively that slaves were property for life. Take note of the terms used to describe slaves and servants and their races, and how these terms changed over the course of the forty-year span of time represented by these documents.

MARCH 1661

Whereas there are diverse loytering runaways in this country who very often absent themselves from their masters service and sometimes in a long time cannot be found, that losse of the time and the charge in the seeking them often exceeding the value of their labor: Bee it therefore enacted that all runaways that shall absent themselves from their said masters service shall be lyable to make satisfaction by service after the times by custome or indenture is expired (vizt.)[1] double their times of service soe neglected, and if the time of their running away was in the crop[2] or the charge of recovering them extraordinary the court shall lymitt a longer time of service proportionable to the damage the master shall make appeare he hath susteyned, . . . it is enacted that the master of any runaway that intends to take the benefit of this act, shall as soone as he hath recovered him carry him to the next commissioner and there

---

1. Abbreviation of *videlicet* (Latin), "namely."
2. That is, during harvest time.

declare and prove the time of his absence, . . . and the court on that certificate passe judgment for the time he shall serve for his absence; and in case any English servant shall run away in company of any negroes who are incapable of making satisfaction by addition of a time, it is enacted that the English soe running away in the company with them shall at the time of service to their owne masters expired, serve the masters of the said negroes for their absence soe long as they should have done by this act if they had not beene slaves, every christian in company serving his proportion; and if the negroes be lost or dye in such time of their being run away, the christian servants in company with them shall by proportion among them, either pay fower thousand five hundred pounds of tobacco and caske or fower yeares service for every negroe soe lost or dead.

APRIL 1691

. . . And for prevention of that abominable mixture and spurious issue which here-after may encrease in this dominion, as well by negroes, mulattoes, and Indians intermarrying with English, or other white women, as by their unlawfull accompanying with one another, Be it enacted . . . that for the time to come, . . . whatso-ever English or other white man or woman being free shall intermarry with a negroe, mulatto, or Indian man or woman bond or free shall within three months after such marriage be banished and removed from this dominion forever, . . .

. . . and be it further enacted . . . That if any English woman being free shall have a bastard child by any negro or mulatto, she pay the sume of fifteen pounds sterling,[3] within one moneth after such bastard child be born, to the Church war-dens of the parish . . . , and in default of such payment she shall be taken into the possession of the said Church wardens and disposed of for five yeares, and the said fine of fifteen pounds, or whatever the woman shall be disposed of for, shall be paid, one third part to their majesties for and towards the support of the gov-ernment . . . , and one other third part to the use of the parish where the offence is committed, and the other third part to the informer, and that such bastard child be bound out as a servant by the said Church wardens untill he or she shall attaine the age of thirty yeares, and in case such English woman that shall have such bastard child be a servant, she shall be sold by the said church wardens, (after her time is expired that she ought by law to serve her master) for five yeares, and the money she shall be sold for divided as is before appointed, and the child to serve as aforesaid.

. . . Be it enacted . . . That no negro or mulatto be . . . set free by any person or persons whatsoever, unless such person or persons, their heires, executors or administrators pay for the transportation of such negro or negroes out of the coun-trey within six moneths after such setting them free, upon penalty of paying of

---

3. Nearly $4,000 in today's U.S. currency.

tenn pounds sterling[4] to the Church wardens of the parish where such person shall dwell with, which money, or so much thereof as shall be necessary, the said Church wardens are to cause the said negro or mulatto to be transported out of the countrey, and the remainder of the said money to imploy to the use of the poor of the parish.

OCTOBER 1705

. . . be it enacted . . . That all servants imported and brought into this country, by sea or land, who were not Christians in their native country, (except Turks and Moors in amity with her majesty, and others that can make due proof of their being free in England, or any other Christian country, before they were shipped, in order to transportation hither) shall be accounted and be slaves, and as such be here bought and sold notwithstanding a conversion to Christianity afterwards.

Study Questions

1. What would happen to the child of an English woman and an African American father? Why do you think the law was created that based a slave's condition upon that of the mother, not the father?

2. What issues of sex and religion are addressed by the laws? What incentives do you see in the documents to report others who commit these infractions?

3. Why do you think it was important to colonial Virginians to emphasize that conversion to Christianity would not exempt a slave from bondage?

4. Considering them together, why do you think these laws were enacted? Evaluate the changes you see in attitudes toward servants and slaves, and connect them to what you know about the evolving economy of the Chesapeake colonies.

---

4. Nearly $2,600 in today's U.S. currency.

THOMAS JEFFERSON

On Race (1785)

FROM *Notes on the State of Virginia*

Despite Thomas Jefferson's voluminous writings, he authored only one book, Notes on the State of Virginia, *which he had privately published in 1785. In the course of discussing Virginia's climate, geography, population, and history, Jefferson also commented on education, agriculture, and slavery. By far the most controversial portion of the* Notes on the State of Virginia *was Jefferson's thoughts on race.*

Jefferson, like many of his contemporaries, was both uneasy with the practice of slavery and dependent on its survival. Although in the Notes *Jefferson vaguely hoped for a "total emancipation," it was slave labor that created Jefferson's fortune and sustained his family, and it was slavery that allowed him the leisure to read and write, to participate in public affairs, and, most ironically, to contemplate human rights. Jefferson understood the contradiction, but throughout his career, his opposition to slavery in principle never translated into actual practice. One crucial reason for this inactivity was Jefferson's belief that peoples of African ancestry were naturally inferior to people of European ancestry, as the following excerpt makes abundantly clear.*

From Thomas Jefferson, *Notes on the State of Virginia* (Boston: Lilly and Wait, 1832), 144–150.

The first difference which strikes us is that of colour. Whether the black of the negro resides in the reticular membrane between the skin and scarf-skin,[1] or in the scarf-skin itself; whether it proceeds from the colour of the blood, the colour of the bile, or from that of some other secretion, the difference is fixed in nature, and is as real as if its seat and cause were better known to us. And is this difference of no importance? Is it not the foundation of a greater or less share of beauty in the two races? Are not the fine mixtures of red and white, the expressions of every passion by greater or less suffusions of colour in the one, preferable to that eternal monotony, which reigns in the countenances, that immovable veil of black which covers all the emotions of the other race? Add to these, flowing

1. The epidermis, the outermost layer of the skin.

hair, a more elegant symmetry of form, their own judgment in favour of the whites, declared by their preference of them, as uniformly as is the preference of the Oranootan[2] for the black women over those of his own species. The circumstance of superior beauty, is thought worthy attention in the propagation of our horses, dogs, and other domestic animals; why not in that of man? Besides those of colour, figure, and hair, there are other physical distinctions proving a difference of race. They have less hair on the face and body. They secrete less by the kidnies, and more by the glands of the skin, which gives them a very strong and disagreeable odour. This greater degree of transpiration[3] renders them more tolerant of heat, and less so of cold than the whites. Perhaps too a difference of structure in the pulmonary apparatus, which a late ingenious experimentalist[4] has discovered to be the principal regulator of animal heat, may have disabled them from extricating, in the act of inspiration, so much of that fluid from the outer air, or obliged them in expiration, to part with more of it. They seem to require less sleep. A black after hard labour through the day, will be induced by the slightest amusements to sit up till midnight, or later, though knowing he must be out with the first dawn of the morning. They are at least as brave, and more adventuresome. But this may perhaps proceed from a want of forethought, which prevents their seeing a danger till it be present. When present, they do not go through it with more coolness or steadiness than the whites. They are more ardent after their female: but love seems with them to be more an eager desire, than a tender delicate mixture of sentiment and sensation. Their griefs are transient. Those numberless afflictions, which render it doubtful whether heaven has given life to us in mercy or in wrath, are less felt, and sooner forgotten with them. In general, their existence appears to participate more of sensation than reflection. To this must be ascribed their disposition to sleep when abstracted from their diversions, and unemployed in labour. An animal whose body is at rest, and who does not reflect, must be disposed to sleep of course. Comparing them by their faculties of memory, reason, and imagination, it appears to me, that in memory they are equal to the whites; in reason much inferior, as I think one could scarcely be found capable of tracing and comprehending the investigations of Euclid; and that in imagination they are dull, tasteless, and anomalous. It would be unfair to follow them to Africa for this investigation. We will consider them here, on the same stage with the whites, and where the facts are not apocryphal on which a judgment is to be formed. It will be right to make great allowances for the difference of condition, of education, of conversation, of the sphere in which they move. Many millions of them have been brought to, and

---

2. Orangutan.

3. Perspiration.

4. Dr. Adair Crawford (1748–95), a physician and a professor of chemistry at Royal Military Academy, Woolwich, whose *Experiments and Observations on Animal Heat, and the Inflammation of Combustible Bodies* (1779) studied the nature and effects of human respiration.

born in America. Most of them indeed have been confined to tillage, to their own homes, and their own society: yet many have been so situated, that they might have availed themselves of the conversation of their masters; many have been brought up to the handicraft arts, and from that circumstance have always been associated with the whites. Some have been liberally educated, and all have lived in countries where the arts and sciences are cultivated to a considerable degree, and have had before their eyes samples of the best works from abroad. The Indians, with no advantages of this kind, will often carve figures on their pipes not destitute of design and merit. They will crayon out an animal, a plant, or a country, so as to prove the existence of a germ in their minds which only wants cultivation. They astonish you with strokes of the most sublime oratory; such as prove their reason and sentiment strong, their imagination glowing and elevated. But never yet could I find that a black had uttered a thought above the level of plain narration; never see even an elementary trait of painting or sculpture. In music they are more generally gifted than the whites with accurate ears for tune and time, and they have been found capable of imagining a small catch.[5] Whether they will be equal to the composition of a more extensive run of melody, or of complicated harmony, is yet to be proved. Misery is often the parent of the most affecting touches in poetry.—Among the blacks is misery enough, God knows, but no poetry. Love is the peculiar cestrum[6] of the poet. Their love is ardent, but it kindles the senses only, not the imagination. Religion indeed has produced a Phyllis Whately;[7] but it could not produce a poet. . . . The heroes of the Dunciad are to her, as Hercules to the author of that poem.[8] Ignatius Sancho[9] has approached nearer to merit in composition; yet his letters do more honour to the heart than the head. They breathe the purest effusions of friendship and general philanthropy, and shew how great a degree of the latter may be compounded with strong religious zeal. He is often happy in the turn of his compliments, and his stile is easy and familiar, except when he affects a Shandean[1] fabrication of words. But his imagination is wild and

5. A round for three or more unaccompanied voices.

6. A fragrant tropical flower such as night jasmine.

7. Phillis Wheatley (c. 1753–84), an African American poet and ardent Christian born in Gambia, whose *Poems on Various Subjects, Religious and Moral* (1773) was widely acclaimed and put forth as proof that persons of African descent were the intellectual and artistic equals of whites.

8. The Dunciad was an epic poem by Alexander Pope (1688–1744) that satirized a number of British authors he thought to be dull and unimaginative. Pope himself was hunchbacked and only four and a half feet tall. Thus, Jefferson is saying that the difference between the second-rate poets Pope lampooned and Wheatley is equivalent to the physical difference between the god Hercules and the disfigured and diminutive Pope.

9. (Charles) Ignatius Sancho (c. 1729–80); born on a slave ship headed for the West Indies, Sancho was taken to England, where he was educated. H is posthumously published *Letters of the Late Ignatius Sancho, an African* (1782) was hailed as further proof of the intellectual capabilities of Africans.

1. A reference to the protagonist of Laurence Sterne's comic novel *The Life and Opinions of Tristram Shandy, Gentleman* (1759–66); Sancho was known for writing in a style closely derived from Sterne's work.

extravagant, escapes incessantly from every restraint of reason and taste, and, in the course of its vagaries, leaves a tract of thought as incoherent and eccentric, as is the course of a meteor through the sky. His subjects should often have led him to a process of sober reasoning: yet we find him always substituting sentiment for demonstration. Upon the whole, though we admit him to the first place among those of his own colour who have presented themselves to the public judgment, yet when we compare him with the writers of the race among whom he lived, and particularly with the epistolary class, in which he has taken his own stand, we are compelled to enroll him at the bottom of the column. This criticism supposes the letters published under his name to be genuine, and to have received amendment from no other hand; points which would not be of easy investigation. The improvement of the blacks in body and mind, in the first instance of their mixture with the whites, has been observed by every one, and proves that their inferiority is not the effect merely of their condition of life.

* * *

The opinion, that they are inferior in the faculties of reason and imagination, must be hazarded with great diffidence. To justify a general conclusion, requires many observations, even where the subject may be submitted to the anatomical knife, to optical glasses, to analysis by fire, or by solvents. How much more then where it is a faculty, not a substance, we are examining; where it eludes the research of all the senses; where the conditions of its existence are various and variously combined; where the effects of those which are present or absent bid defiance to calculation; let me add too, as a circumstance of great tenderness, where our conclusion would degrade a whole race of men from the rank in the scale of beings which their Creator may perhaps have given them. To our reproach it must be said, that though for a century and a half we have had under our eyes the races of black and of red men, they have never yet been viewed by us as subjects of natural history, I advance it therefore as a suspicion only, that the blacks, whether originally a distinct race, or made distinct by time and circumstances, are inferior to the whites in the endowments both of body and mind.

Study Questions

1. How and why, according to Jefferson, are people of African origin distinct from people of European origin?

2. At several points, Jefferson ascribes social and cultural characteristics to genetic origins. What are some examples?

3. A decade before the publication of *Notes on the State of Virginia*, Jefferson wrote in the Declaration of Independence that "All men are created equal." Is it possible to reconcile these two documents? How do you think Jefferson would answer such a question?

4. How would you characterize the tone of Jefferson's writing in *Notes on the State of Virginia*? Who are his intended readers?

JONATHAN EDWARDS

Sinners in the Hands of an Angry God (1741)

The First Great Awakening—a series of fervent religious revivals that emphasized the sinfulness of mankind and the power of faith to initiate a spiritual rebirth—swept the American colonies for two decades beginning in the 1730s. Many Americans, who came to be known as "New Lights," were thrilled with the new religious style and its emphasis on sudden and powerful conversion. However, many other Americans—"Old Lights"—were appalled by what they saw as ecstatic, frenzied forms of worship. Often the two groups were members of the same congregation, and conflict between them convulsed churches throughout the thirteen colonies.

Jonathan Edwards (1703–1758), the Congregationalist minister at Northampton, Massachusetts, tirelessly promoted the revivals, and is today considered colonial America's most brilliant theologian. In the summer of 1741, Peter Reynolds, the minister at Enfield, Connecticut, offered his pulpit to Edwards, hoping that he would be able to rouse his apathetic congregation and convince them that their spiritual indifference had placed their souls in mortal jeopardy. And so on July 8, the thirty-seven-year-old Edwards delivered the following sermon in a measured, quiet tone. It had an electrifying effect on the congregation. According to one eyewitness, "before the sermon was done there was a great moaning and crying went out through the whole House. . . . 'What shall I do to be saved,' 'Oh, I am going to Hell,' 'Oh, what shall I do for Christ,' and so forth. So yet the minister was obliged to desist, the shrieks and cry were piercing and amazing." Although it was not typical of Edwards's preaching—he was more likely to stress God's love rather than His wrath—"Sinners in the Hands of an Angry God" has become the most famous sermon in American history.

From *The Works of President Edwards* (New York: Leavitt & Allen, 1852), 4:313–18, 321.

There is nothing that keeps wicked men at any one moment out of hell, but the mere pleasure of God. . . .

The truth of this observation may appear by the following considerations.

1. There is no want[1] of power in God to cast wicked men into hell at any moment. Men's hands cannot be strong when God rises up: the strongest have no power to resist him, nor can any deliver out of his hands.

---

1. Lack.

He is not only able to cast wicked men into hell, but he can most easily do it. Sometimes an earthly prince meets with a great deal of difficulty to subdue a rebel, that has found means to fortify himself, and has made himself strong by the number of his followers. But it is not so with God. There is no fortress that is any defence against the power of God. Though hand join in hand, and vast multitudes of God's enemies combine and associate themselves, they are easily broken in pieces: they are as great heaps of light chaff before the whirlwind; or large quantities of dry stubble before devouring flames. We find it easy to tread on and crush a worm that we see crawling on the earth; so it is easy for us to cut or singe a slender thread that any thing hangs by; thus easy is it for God, when he pleases, to cast his enemies down to hell. What are we, that we should think to stand before him, at whose rebuke the earth trembles, and before whom the rocks are thrown down!

2. They deserve to be cast into hell; so that divine justice never stands in the way, it makes no objection against God's using his power at any moment to destroy them. Yea, on the contrary, justice calls aloud for an infinite punishment of their sins. Divine justice says of the tree that brings forth such grapes of Sodom, "Cut it down, why cumbereth it the ground?" Luke xiii. 7. The sword of divine justice is every moment brandished over their heads, and it is nothing but the hand of arbitrary mercy, and God's mere will, that holds it back.

3. They are already under a sentence of condemnation to hell. They do not only justly deserve to be cast down thither, but the sentence of the law of God, that eternal and immutable rule of righteousness that God has fixed between him and mankind, is gone out against them; and stands against them; so that they are bound over already to hell: John iii. 18. "He that believeth not is condemned already. . . ."

4. They are now the objects of that very same anger and wrath of God, that is expressed in the torments of hell: and the reason why they do not go down to hell at each moment, is not because God, in whose power they are, is not then very angry with them; as angry, as he is with many of those miserable creatures that he is now tormenting in hell, and do there feel and bear the fierceness of his wrath. Yea, God is a great deal more angry with great numbers that are now on earth; yea, doubtless, with many that are now in this congregation, that, it may be, are at ease and quiet, than he is with many of those that are now in the flames of hell.

So that it is not because God is unmindful of their wickedness, and does not resent it, that he does not let loose his hand and cut them off. God is not altogether such a one as themselves, though they may imagine him to be so. The wrath of God burns against them; their damnation does not slumber; the pit is prepared; the fire is made ready; the furnace is now hot; ready to receive them; the flames do now rage and glow. The glittering sword is whet, and held over them, and the pit hath opened her mouth under them.

5. The devil stands ready to fall upon them, and seize them as his own, at what moment God shall permit him. They belong to him; he has their souls in his possession, and under his dominion.

* * *

6. There are in the souls of wicked men those hellish principles reigning, that would presently kindle and flame out into hell-fire, if it were not for God's restraints.

* * *

7. It is no security to wicked men for one moment, that there are no visible means of death at hand. It is no security to a natural man, that he is now in health, and that he does not see which way he should now immediately go out of the world by any accident, and that there is no visible danger in any respect in his circumstances. The manifold and continual experience of the world in all ages, shows that this is no evidence that a man is not on the very brink of eternity, and that the next step will not be into another world. The unseen, unthought of ways and means of persons' going suddenly out of the world are innumerable and inconceivable. Unconverted, men walk over the pit of hell on a rotten covering, and there are innumerable places in this covering so weak that they will not bear their weight, and these places are not seen. The arrows of death fly unseen at noonday; the sharpest sight cannot discern them. God has so many different, unsearchable ways of taking wicked men out of the world and sending them to hell, that there is nothing to make it appear, that God had need to be at the expense of a miracle, or go out of the ordinary course of his providence, to destroy any wicked man, at any moment. . . .

8. Natural men's prudence and care to preserve their own lives, or the care of others to preserve them, do not secure them a moment. This, divine providence and universal experience do also bear testimony to. There is this clear evidence that men's own wisdom is no security to them from death; that if it were otherwise we should see some difference between the wise and politic men of the world, and others, with regard to their liableness to early and unexpected death; but how is it in fact? Eccles. ii. 16, "How dieth the wise man? As the fool."

9. All wicked men's pains and contrivance they use to escape hell, while they continue to reject Christ, and so remain wicked men, do not secure them from hell one moment. Almost every natural man that hears of hell, flatters himself that he shall escape it. . . .

* * *

But the foolish children of men do miserably delude themselves in their own schemes, and in their confidence in their own strength and wisdom, they trust to nothing but a shadow. The bigger part of those that heretofore have lived under the same means of grace, and are now dead, are undoubtedly gone to hell; and it was not because they were not as wise as those that are now alive; it was not because they did not lay out matters as well for themselves to secure their own escape.

* * *

10. God has laid himself under no obligation, by any promise, to keep any natural man out of hell one moment: God certainly has made no promises either of eternal life, or of any deliverance or preservation from eternal death, but what are contained in the covenant of grace,[2] the promises that are given in Christ, in whom all the promises are yea and amen.[3] But surely they have no interest in the promises of the covenant of grace that are not the children of the covenant, and that do not believe in any of the promises of the covenant, and have no interest in the Mediator of the covenant.

So that, whatever some have imagined and pretended about promises made to natural men's earnest seeking and knocking, it is plain and manifest, that whatever pains a natural man takes in religion, whatever prayers he makes, till he believes in Christ, God is under no manner of obligation to keep him a moment from eternal destruction.

So that thus it is, that natural men are held in the hand of God over the pit of hell; they have deserved the fiery pit, and are already sentenced to it; and God is dreadfully provoked, his anger is as great towards them as to those that are actually suffering the executions of the fierceness of his wrath in hell, and they have done nothing in the least, to appease or abate that anger, neither is God in the least bound by any promise to hold them up one moment; the devil is waiting for them, hell is gaping for them, the flames gather and flash about them, and would fain lay hold on them and swallow them up; the fire pent up in their own hearts is struggling to break out; and they have no interest in any Mediator, there are no means within reach that can be any security to them. In short, they have no refuge, nothing to take hold of; all that preserves them every momont is the mere arbitrary will, and uncovenanted, unobliged forbearance of an incensed God.

APPLICATION.

The use may be of awakening to unconverted persons in this congregation. This that you have heard is the case of every one of you that are out of Christ. That world of misery, that lake of burning brimstone, is extended abroad under you. There is the dreadful pit of the glowing flames of the wrath of God; there is hell's wide gaping mouth open; and you have nothing to stand upon, nor any thing to take hold of. There is nothing between you and hell but the air; it is only the power and mere pleasure of God that holds you up.

---

2. The idea that God saves humans because of their faith alone, not for their good works.

3. Corinthians 1:20: "For all the promises of God in him are yea, and in him Amen, unto the glory of God by us." That is, all God's promises will be fulfilled.

You probably are not sensible[4] of this; you find you are kept out of hell, but do not see the hand of God in it; but look at other things, as the good state of your bodily constitution, your care of your own life, and the means you use for your own preservation. But indeed these things are nothing; if God should withdraw his hand, they would avail no more to keep you from falling, than the thin air to hold up a person that is suspended in it.

Your wickedness makes you as it were heavy as lead, and to tend downwards with great weight and pressure towards hell; and if God should let you go, you would immediately sink and swiftly descend and plunge into the bottomless gulf, and your healthy constitution, and your own care and prudence, and best contrivance, and all your righteousness, would have no more influence to uphold you and keep you out of hell, than a spider's web would have to stop a falling rock. Were it not that so is the sovereign pleasure of God, the earth would not bear you one moment; for you are a burden to it; the creation groans with you.

* * *

There are the black clouds of God's wrath now hanging directly over your heads, full of the dreadful storm, and big with thunder; and were it not for the restraining hand of God, it would immediately burst forth upon you. The sovereign pleasure of God, for the present, stays his rough wind; otherwise it would come with fury, and your destruction would come like a whirlwind, and you would be like the chaff of the summer threshing floor.

* * *

The God that holds you over the pit of hell, much as one holds a spider, or some loathsome insect, over the fire, abhors you, and is dreadfully provoked; his wrath towards you burns like fire; he looks upon you as worthy of nothing else, but to be cast into the fire; he is of purer eyes than to bear to have you in his sight; you are ten thousand times so abominable in his eyes, as the most hateful and venomous serpent is in ours. You have offended him infinitely more than ever a stubborn rebel did his prince: and yet it is nothing but his hand that holds you from falling into the fire every moment: it is ascribed to nothing else, that you did not go to hell the last night; that you was suffered to awake again in this world, after you closed your eyes to sleep; and there is no other reason to be given, why you have not dropped into hell since you arose in the morning, but that God's hand has held you up: there is no other reason to be given why you have not gone to hell, since you have sat here in the house of God, provoking his pure eyes by your sinful wicked manner of attending his solemn worship: yea, there is nothing else that is to be given as a reason why you do not this very moment drop down into hell.

4. Conscious, aware.

O sinner! consider the fearful danger you are in: it is a great furnace of wrath, a wide and bottomless pit, full of the fire of wrath, that you are held over in the hand of that God, whose wrath is provoked and incensed as much against you, as against many of the damned in hell: you hang by a slender thread, with the flames of divine wrath flashing about it, and ready every moment to singe it, and burn it asunder; and you have no interest in any Mediator, and nothing to lay hold of to save yourself, nothing to keep off the flames of wrath, nothing of your own, nothing that you ever have done, nothing that you can do, to induce God to spare you one moment.

* * *

How dreadful is the state of those that are daily and hourly in danger of this great wrath and infinite misery! But this is the dismal case of every soul in this congregation that has not been born again, however moral and strict, sober and religious, they may otherwise be. Oh that you would consider it, whether you be young or old! There is reason to think, that there are many in this congregation now hearing this discourse, that will actually be the subjects of this very misery to all eternity. We know not who they are, or in what seats they sit, or what thoughts they now have. It may be they are now at ease, and hear all these things without much disturbance, and are now flattering themselves that they are not the persons; promising themselves that they shall escape. If we knew that there was one person, and but one, in the whole congregation, that was to be the subject of this misery, what an awful thing it would be to think of! If we knew who it was, what an awful sight would it be to see such a person! How might all the rest of the congregation lift up a lamentable and bitter cry over him! But alas! Instead of one, how many is it likely will remember should not be in hell in a very short time, before this year is out. And it would be no wonder if some persons, that now sit here in some seats of this meeting-house in health, and quiet and secure, should be there before to-morrow morning.

Study Questions

1. In the opinion of Edwards, how does God look upon mankind? What is the character, according to Edwards, of "natural man"?

2. Why do you think the sermon so upset Edwards's listeners? Do you think it retains its power today? Why or why not?

3. How does Edwards's tone in "Sinners in the Hands of an Angry God" characterize—or contradict—the tone of the broader Awakening movement?

4. What do you think of Edwards's beliefs about humans' relationship with God and the nature of salvation?

BENJAMIN FRANKLIN

Albany Plan of Union (1754)

In 1754, amid worsening relations with French settlers and their Indian allies beyond the Appalachian Mountains, Americans colonists were instructed by British authorities to develop a plan for the improvement of frontier defenses. Accordingly, representatives from seven colonies gathered at a conference in Albany, New York. Benjamin Franklin (1706–1790), a delegate from Pennsylvania, was easily the most famous participant, and it was he who put forth the so-called Albany Plan of Union. The proposal was warmly supported by, among others, Thomas Hutchinson (1711–1780), a delegate from Massachusetts, who would later become a mortal enemy of Franklin's during the American Revolution.

After three weeks of discussion and debate, the delegates managed to put together an outline of intercolonial cooperation. Its most important component was a "Grand Council" to be composed of representatives from all the colonies, which would meet once a year to oversee relations with Native Americans and govern western territories. The Albany Plan, however, came to nothing. Colonial leaders were highly suspicious of one another—the conference itself was beset by intrigue and convoluted webs of mutual suspicion—and delegates were unwilling to cede even partial authority to a central government. English authorities, meanwhile, rejected the plan out of fear that a more unified colonial America would be more difficult to control. Nonetheless, the Albany Plan remains as the first proposal for cooperation among the British North American colonies.

From Benjamin Franklin, "Albany Plan of Union," (The Avalon Project of Yale Law School, 2008), www.avalon.law.yale.edu.

It is proposed that humble application be made for an act of Parliament of Great Britain, by virtue of which one general government may be formed in America, including all the said colonies, within and under which government each colony may retain its present constitution, except in the particulars wherein a change may be directed by the said act, as hereafter follows.

1. That the said general government be administered by a President-General, to be appointed and supported by the crown; and a Grand Council, to be chosen by the representatives of the people of the several Colonies met in their respective assemblies.

2. That within——months after the passing such act, the House of Representatives that happen to be sitting within that time, or that shall especially for that purpose convened, may and shall choose members for the Grand Council, in the following proportion, that is to say,

Massachusetts Bay	7
New Hampshire	2
Connecticut	5
Rhode Island	2
New York	4
New Jersey	3
Pennsylvania	6
Maryland	4
Virginia	7
North Carolina	4
South Carolina	4
	48

3. —— who shall meet for the first time at the city of Philadelphia, being called by the President-General as soon as conveniently may be after his appointment.

4. That there shall be a new election of the members of the Grand Council every three years; and, on the death or resignation of any member, his place should be supplied by a new choice at the next sitting of the Assembly of the Colony he represented.

5. That after the first three years, when the proportion of money arising out of each Colony to the general treasury can be known, the number of members to be chosen for each Colony shall, from time to time, in all ensuing elections, be regulated by that proportion, yet so as that the number to be chosen by any one Province be not more than seven, nor less than two.

6. That the Grand Council shall meet once in every year, and oftener if occasion require, at such time and place as they shall adjourn to at the last preceding meeting, or as they shall be called to meet at by the President-General on any emergency; he having first obtained in writing the consent of seven of the members to such call, and sent duly and timely notice to the whole.

7. That the Grand Council have power to choose their speaker; and shall neither be dissolved, prorogued, nor continued sitting longer than six weeks at one time, without their own consent or the special command of the crown.

8. That the members of the Grand Council shall be allowed for their service ten shillings sterling[1] per diem, during their session and journey to and from the place of meeting; twenty miles to be reckoned a day's journey.

9. That the assent of the President-General be requisite to all acts of the Grand Council, and that it be his office and duty to cause them to be carried into execution.

10. That the President-General, with the advice of the Grand Council, hold or direct all Indian treaties, in which the general interest of the Colonies may be concerned; and make peace or declare war with Indian nations.

11. That they make such laws as they judge necessary for regulating all Indian trade.

12. That they make all purchases from Indians, for the crown, of lands not now within the bounds of particular Colonies, or that shall not be within their bounds when some of them are reduced to more convenient dimensions.

13. That they make new settlements on such purchases, by granting lands in the King's name, reserving a quitrent to the crown for the use of the general treasury.

14. That they make laws for regulating and governing such new settlements, till the crown shall think fit to form them into particular governments.

15. That they raise and pay soldiers and build forts for the defence of any of the Colonies, and equip vessels of force to guard the coasts and protect the trade on the ocean, lakes, or great rivers; but they shall not impress[2] men in any Colony, without the consent of the Legislature.

16. That for these purposes they have power to make laws, and lay and levy such general duties, imposts, or taxes, as to them shall appear most equal and just (considering the ability and other circumstances of the inhabitants in the several Colonies), and such as may be collected with the least inconvenience to the people; rather discouraging luxury, than loading industry with unnecessary burdens.

17. That they may appoint a General Treasurer and Particular Treasurer in each government when necessary; and, from time to time, may order the sums in the treasuries of each government into the general treasury; or draw on them for special payments, as they find most convenient.

18. Yet no money to issue but by joint orders of the President-General and Grand Council; except where sums have been appropriated to particular purposes, and the President-General is previously empowered by an act to draw such sums.

19. That the general accounts shall be yearly settled and reported to the several Assemblies.

---

1. Roughly equivalent to $100 in today's value.
2. To force into public service; conscript.

20. That a quorum of the Grand Council, empowered to act with the President-General, do consist of twenty-five members; among whom there shall be one or more from a majority of the Colonies.

21. That the laws made by them for the purposes aforesaid shall not be repugnant, but, as near as may be, agreeable to the laws of England, and shall be transmitted to the King in Council for approbation, as soon as may be after their passing; and if not disapproved within three years after presentation, to remain in force.

22. That, in case of the death of the President-General, the Speaker of the Grand Council for the time being shall succeed, and be vested with the same powers and authorities, to continue till the King's pleasure be known.

23. That all military commission officers, whether for land or sea service, to act under this general constitution, shall be nominated by the President-General; but the approbation of the Grand Council is to be obtained, before they receive their commissions. And all civil officers are to be nominated by the Grand Council, and to receive the President-General's approbation before they officiate.

24. But, in case of vacancy by death or removal of any officer, civil or military, under this constitution, the Governor of the Province in which such vacancy happens may appoint, till the pleasure of the President-General and Grand Council can be known.

25. That the particular military as well as civil establishments in each Colony remain in their present state, the general constitution notwithstanding; and that on sudden emergencies any Colony may defend itself, and lay the accounts of expense thence arising before the President-General and General Council, who may allow and order payment of the same, as far as they judge such accounts just and reasonable.

Study Questions

1. What sort of intercolonial government did Franklin envision for the colonies? In particular, what authority would the proposed Grand Council possess?

2. Do you see any aspects of the plan that, had it been enacted, might have created conflict between the colonies?

3. What does the failure of the Albany Plan to be enacted say about colonists' anxieties concerning government, economics, and the military?

4. Based on your reading of the document, would a delegate or observer of the Albany Conference have been optimistic about the chances of the colonies working together to protest policies of the mother country?

The Declaration of Independence (1776)

On June 7, 1776, Richard Henry Lee, Virginia delegate to the Second Continental Congress, introduced a resolution declaring that "these United Colonies are, and of right ought to be, free and independent States." The Congress then appointed a committee—including Thomas Jefferson, Benjamin Franklin, and John Adams—to draft a statement explaining America's position. Jefferson, a relatively obscure thirty-three-year-old planter from Virginia, drafted the bulk of the resultant document, the Declaration of Independence. Although his fellow congressmen made important changes to the document, most notably in excising Jefferson's highly questionable charge that the king had forced the slave trade upon the colonies, the Declaration of Independence is essentially Jefferson's work.

The Declaration's purpose was to explain to the world why America was cutting ties with Great Britain, and ideally to secure the assistance of other countries—most obviously England's long-time enemy, France. The Declaration could have been a more or less dispassionate document, simply arguing the justice of the American position. But Jefferson made the Declaration far more. Drawing upon the work of a number of natural rights theorists, most notably John Locke, Jefferson appealed to the fundamental, inborn rights of all mankind—and not just the "rights of Englishmen," as so many other patriots had. In doing so, Jefferson announced the birth of the United States in a language that has continued to inspire people across the world for well over two centuries.

From "The Declaration of Independence," (U.S. National Archives), 1–4.

July 4, 1776

In Congress, The unanimous Declaration of the thirteen united States of America.

When in the course of human events, it becomes necessary for one people to dissolve the political bands which have connected them with another, and to assume among the powers of the earth, the separate and equal station to which the laws of nature and of nature's God entitle them, a decent respect to the opinions of mankind requires that they should declare the causes which impel them to the separation.

We hold these truths to be self-evident:

That all men are created equal; that they are endowed by their Creator with certain unalienable rights; that among these are life, liberty, and the pursuit of happiness; that, to secure these rights, governments are instituted among men, deriving their just powers from the consent of the governed; that whenever any form of government becomes destructive of these ends, it is the right of the people to alter or to abolish it, and to institute new government, laying its foundation on such principles, and organizing its powers in such form, as to them shall seem most likely to effect their safety and happiness. Prudence, indeed, will dictate that governments long established should not be changed for light and transient causes; and accordingly all experience hath shown that mankind are more disposed to suffer, while evils are sufferable than to right themselves by abolishing the forms to which they are accustomed. But when a long train of abuses and usurpations, pursuing invariably the same object, evinces a design to reduce them under absolute despotism, it is their right, it is their duty, to throw off such government, and to provide new guards for their future security. Such has been the patient sufferance of these colonies; and such is now the necessity which constrains them to alter their former systems of government. The history of the present King of Great Britain is a history of repeated injuries and usurpations, all having in direct object the establishment of an absolute tyranny over these states. To prove this, let facts be submitted to a candid world.

He has refused his assent to laws, the most wholesome and necessary for the public good.

He has forbidden his governors to pass laws of immediate and pressing importance, unless suspended in their operation till his assent should be obtained; and, when so suspended, he has utterly neglected to attend to them.

He has refused to pass other laws for the accommodation of large districts of people, unless those people would relinquish the right of representation in the legislature, a right inestimable to them, and formidable to tyrants only.

He has called together legislative bodies at places unusual, uncomfortable, and distant from the depository of their public records, for the sole purpose of fatiguing them into compliance with his measures.[1]

He has dissolved representative houses repeatedly, for opposing, with manly firmness, his invasions on the rights of the people.[2]

He has refused for a long time, after such dissolutions, to cause others to be elected; whereby the legislative powers, incapable of annihilation, have returned to the people at large for their exercise; the state remaining, in the mean time, exposed to all the dangers of invasions from without and convulsions within.

He has endeavored to prevent the population of these states; for that purpose obstructing the laws for naturalization of foreigners; refusing to pass others to

---

1. In 1768 and 1774, Massachusetts governors had summarily changed the meeting place of the Massachusetts House of Representatives (known as the "General Court").

2. In 1768 and 1769, assemblies in New York, Massachusetts, Maryland, South Carolina, Georgia, and Virginia were dissolved by royal governors for defiance of imperial authority.

encourage their migration hither, and raising the conditions of new appropriations of lands.[3]

He has obstructed the administration of justice, by refusing his assent to laws for establishing judiciary powers.

He has made judges dependent on his will alone, for the tenure of their offices, and the amount and payment of their salaries.[4]

He has erected a multitude of new offices, and sent hither swarms of officers to harass our people and eat out their substance.[5]

He has kept among us, in times of peace, standing armies, without the consent of our legislatures.[6]

He has affected to render the military independent of, and superior to, the civil power.

He has combined with others to subject us to a jurisdiction[7] foreign to our Constitution and unacknowledged by our laws, giving his assent to their acts of pretended legislation:

For quartering large bodies of armed troops among us;[8]

For protecting them, by a mock trial, from punishment for any murders which they should commit on the inhabitants of these states;[9]

For cutting off our trade with all parts of the world;[1]

For imposing taxes on us without our consent;

For depriving us, in many cases, of the benefits of trial by jury;[2]

For transporting us beyond seas, to be tried for pretended offenses;

For abolishing the free system of English laws in a neighboring province, establishing therein an arbitrary government, and enlarging its boundaries, so as to

---

3. The British government, alarmed that almost a quarter of a million English, Scottish, and Irish had moved to the colonies after 1760, discussed limiting migration. No such act, however, was ever passed.

4. Colonial judges were appointed and removed by the British crown.

5. A reference to the Board of Customs Commissioners, an agency set up in 1767 to enforce the Townshend Duties. They were given power to inspect and seize materials they claimed to have been illegally imported.

6. Colonists as well as English people had long feared "standing armies," that is, the maintenance of armed forces in times of peace. Thus colonists were outraged when the British ministry ordered troops into New York City and Boston.

7. Parliament's jurisdiction. The following section lists the acts of Parliament that the colonists found most objectionable.

8. The Quartering Acts of 1765 and 1774 required colonists to provide shelter and provisions for troops stationed in America.

9. The Administration of Justice Act (1774), one of the notorious Intolerable Acts passed by Parliament to punish Massachusetts for the Boston Tea Party, provided that any British soldier accused of a crime against an American would be tried in England.

1. The Prohibitory Act of 1775, enacted after the onset of hostilities between America and Britain, sought to shut down American commerce by means of a naval blockade.

2. A reference to the despised vice-admiralty courts. When colonists were accused of avoiding payment of taxes, they were brought before this juryless military venue. The military judges, if they found against the accused colonist, would be given a percentage of the seized property.

render it at once an example and fit instrument for introducing the same absolute rule into these colonies;[3]

For taking away our charters, abolishing our most valuable laws, and altering fundamentally the forms of our governments;[4]

For suspending our own legislatures, and declaring themselves invested with power to legislate for us in all cases whatsoever.[5]

He has abdicated government here, by declaring us out of his protection and waging war against us.

He has plundered our seas, ravaged our coasts, burned our towns, and destroyed the lives of our people.[6]

He is at this time transporting large armies of foreign mercenaries to complete the works of death, desolation, and tyranny already begun with circumstances of cruelty and perfidy scarcely paralleled in the most barbarous ages, and totally unworthy the head of a civilized nation.[7]

He has constrained our fellow-citizens, taken captive on the high seas, to bear arms against their country, to become the executioners of their friends and brethren, or to fall themselves by their hands.[8]

He has excited domestic insurrection among us, and has endeavored to bring on the inhabitants of our frontiers the merciless Indian savages, whose known rule of warfare is an undistinguished destruction of all ages, sexes, and conditions.[9]

In every stage of these oppressions we have petitioned for redress in the most humble terms; our repeated petitions have been answered only by repeated injury.

---

3. A reference to the Quebec Act of 1774, which extended the Canadian province of Quebec into the Ohio Valley, where a number of colonies and colonial land speculators claimed millions of acres of land.

4. The Massachusetts Governing Act, another of the hated Intolerable Acts, altered Massachusetts' colonial charter so that the governor's council would be appointed and the actions of town meetings would be severely restricted.

5. In 1768 and 1769, assemblies in New York, Massachusetts, Maryland, South Carolina, Georgia, and Virginia were dissolved by royal governors for defiance of imperial authority. The phrase "in all cases whatsoever" referenced the American Colonies Act of 1766 (better known as the Declaratory Act), which proclaimed Parliament's absolute authority over the American colonies.

6. On October 18, 1775, a British fleet under the command of Captain Henry Mowat bombarded the town of Falmouth, Massachusetts (present-day Portland, Maine) with incendiary cannonballs and then sent troops to set fire to any structure that remained standing. On January 1, 1776, British naval forces under the command of Commodore Henry Pellow bombarded Norfolk, Virginia, completely destroying the town.

7. Because of manpower shortages in England, George III bought the services of approximately 30,000 German mercenaries to fight the Americans during the Revolutionary War. The largest source of the soldiers was the principality of Hesse, and thus the Americans referred to the mercenaries as "Hessians."

8. A reference to impressment—the practice of forcing men to serve in the British navy. Thousands of American sailors were forced into service aboard British ships.

9. "He has excited Domestic Insurrections" refers to the proclamation of Lord Dunmore, the last royal governor of Virginia, who, in 1775 issued a proclamation promising freedom to slaves of rebel masters if they would take up arms against the rebellion. Although Native Americans fought on both sides of the Revolutionary War, far more fought on the side of Great Britain, perceiving that Americans under British rule would be less likely to encroach upon their territories.

A prince, whose character is thus marked by every act which may define a tyrant, is unfit to be the ruler of a free people.

Nor have we been wanting in our attentions to our British brethren. We have warned them, from time to time, of attempts by their legislature to extend an unwarrantable jurisdiction over us. We have reminded them of the circumstances of our emigration and settlement here. We have appealed to their native justice and magnanimity; and we have conjured them, by the ties of our common kindred, to disavow these usurpations which would inevitably interrupt our connections and correspondence. They too have been deaf to the voice of justice and of consanguinity. We must, therefore, acquiesce in the necessity which denounces our separation, and hold them as we hold the rest of mankind, enemies in war, in peace friends.

We, therefore, the representatives of the United States of America, in General Congress assembled, appealing to the Supreme Judge of the world for the rectitude of our intentions, do, in the name and by the authority of the good people of these colonies, solemnly publish and declare, That these United Colonies are, and of right ought to be, FREE AND INDEPENDENT STATES; that they are absolved from all allegiance to the British crown, and that all political connection between them and the state of Great Britain is, and ought to be, totally dissolved; and that, as free and independent states, they have full power to levy war, conclude peace, contract alliances, establish commerce, and do all other acts and things which independent states may of right do. And for the support of this declaration, with a firm reliance on the protection of Divine Providence, we mutually pledge to each other our lives, our fortunes, and our sacred honor.

[Signed by]
JOHN HANCOCK [President]

New Hampshire:
Josiah Bartlett
Wm. Whipple
Matthew Thornton

Massachusetts Bay:
Saml. Adams
John Adams
Robt. Treat Paine,
Elbridge Gerry

Rhode Island:
Step. Hopkins
William Ellery

Connecticut:
Roger Sherman
Sam'el Huntington
Wm. Williams
Oliver Wolcott

New York:
Wm. Floyd
Phil. Livingston
Frans. Lewis
Lewis Morris

New Jersey:
Richd. Stockton
Jno. Witherspoon
Fras. Hopkinson
John Hart
Abra. Clark

Pennsylvania:
Robt. Morris
Benjamin Rush
Benja. Franklin
John Morton
Geo. Clymer
Jas. Smith
Geo. Taylor
James Wilson
Geo. Ross

Delaware:
Cæsar Rodney
Geo. Read
Tho. M'kean

Maryland:
Samuel Chase
Wm. Paca
Thos. Stone
Charles Carroll of Carrollton

Virginia:
George Wythe
Richard Henry Lee
Th. Jefferson
Benja. Harrison
Ths. Nelson, Jr.
Francis Lightfoot Lee
Carter Braxton

North Carolina:
Wm. Hooper
Joseph Hewes,
John Penn

South Carolina:
Edward Rutledge.
Thos. Hayward, Junr.
Thomas Lynch, Junr.
Arthur Middleton

Georgia:
Button Gwinnett
Lyman Hall
Geo. Walton.

Study Questions

1. What specifically, according to Jefferson, gave Americans the right to revolt against British rule?

2. What specific complaints against King George III does the Declaration mention?

3. Of these allegations, taxation is not mentioned until the seventeenth complaint. Why do you think this was the case?

4. Do you believe that America since the Revolution has held true to the ideals of the Declaration of Independence? Do you think America today adheres to these "self-evident truths"?

Slaves' Petitions for Freedom During the American Revolution (1773, 1774)

After 1763, even as white colonists protested British policies by appealing to concepts of liberty and equality, and decrying their metaphorical "enslavement" to British authorities, approximately 500,000 actual slaves in British North America endured the day-to-day torments of bondage. Yet this is precisely why slaves immediately embraced the rhetoric of the American Revolution—to them, the denial of freedom and equality was not an abstraction, but a lived reality.

The following documents—petitions from slaves in Massachusetts asking for their freedom in 1773 and 1774—represent but two examples of a continent-wide questioning of slavery precipitated by the coming of the American Revolution. And it was not just the slaves themselves who recognized the hypocrisy of slavery in a land rising up to demand freedom. White Americans, including a great number of slaveholders, increasingly understood that the implications of their ideas might very well undermine the legitimacy of slavery.

Of the petitioners, we know very little. We do know that despite the upswell of hostility toward slavery, the Massachusetts assembly and two successive governors, Thomas Hutchinson and Thomas Gage, ignored their pleas.

Boston, April 20th, 1773.

Sir,

The efforts made by the legislature of this province in their last sessions to free themselves from slavery, gave us, who are in that deplorable state, a high degree of satisfaction.[1] We expect great things from men who have made such a noble stand against the designs of their *fellow-men* to enslave them. We cannot but wish and hope Sir, that you will have the same grand object, we mean civil and religious liberty, in view in your next session. The divine spirit of *freedom*, seems to fire every humane breast on this continent, except such as are bribed to assist in executing the execrable plan.

We are very sensible that it would be highly detrimental to our present masters, if we were allowed to demand all that of *right* belongs to us for

---

1. In 1767 the colonial assembly, the Massachusetts General Court, debated but did not pass a bill that would have abolished slavery in Massachusetts. Four years later, however, that body did prohibit any further importation of slaves from Africa.

past services; this we disclaim. Even the *Spaniards*, who have not those sublime ideas of freedom that English men have, are conscious that they have no right to all services of their fellowmen, we mean the *Africans*, whom they have purchased with their money; therefore they allow them one day in a week to work for themselve, to enable them to earn money to purchase the residue of their time, which they have a right to demand in such portions as they are able to pay for (a due appraizment of their services being first made, which always stands at the purchase money.) We do not pretend to dictate to you Sir, or to the honorable Assembly,[2] of which you are a member : We acknowledge our obligations to you for what you have already done, but as the people of this province seem to be actuated by the principles of equity and justice, we cannot but expect your house will again take our deplorable case into serious consideration, and give us that ample relief which, *as men*, we have a natural right to.

But since the wise and righteous governor of the universe, has permitted our fellow men to make us slaves, we bow in submission to him, and determine to behave in such a manner, as that we may have reason to expect the divine approbation of, and assistance in, our peaceable and lawful attempts to gain our freedom.

We are willing to submit to such regulations and laws, as may be made relative to us, until we leave the province, which we determine to do as soon as we can from our joynt labours procure money to transport ourselves to some part of the coast of *Africa*, where we propose a settlement. We are very desirous that you should have instructions relative to us, from your town, therefore we pray you to communicate this letter to them, and ask this favor for us.

In behalf of our fellow slaves in this province,
And by order of their Committee.

> *Peter Bestes,*
> *Sambo Freeman,*
> *Felix Holbrook,*
> *Chester Joie.*

For the Representative of the town of Taunton.

To his Excellency Thomas Gage Esq[3] Captain General and Governor in Chief in and over This Province

2. The General Court, the legislative assembly of the Massachusetts Bay Colony.

3. General Thomas Gage (1719–1787) had recently become the governor of Massachusetts; military rule was one of the means by which Great Britain had punished the colony for the Boston Tea Party.

To the Honourable his Majestys Council and the Honourable House of Representatives in General Court assembled may 25 1774

The Petition of a Grate Number of Blackes of this Province who by divine permission are held in a state of Slavery within the bowels of a free and Christian Country Humbly Shewing That your Petitioners apprehend we have in common With all other men a naturel right to our freedoms without Being depriv'd of them by our fellow men as we are a freeborn Pepel and have never forfeited this Blessing by aney [any] compact or agreement whatever. But we were unjustly dragged by the cruel hand of power from our dearest frinds [friends] and others sum [some] of us stolen from the bosoms of our tender Parents and from a Populous Pleasant and plentiful country and Brought hither to be made slaves for Life in a Christian land Thus are we deprived of every thing that hath a tendency to make life even tolerable, the endearing ties of husband and wife we are strangers to for we are no longer man and wife then our masters or Mestreses [Mistresses] thinkes proper marred [married] or onmarred [unmarried]. Our Children are also taken from us by force and sent maney [many] miles from us wear [where] we seldom or ever see them again there to be made slaves of fore [for] Life which sumtimes is verey [very] short by Reson [reason] of Being dragged from their mothers Breest [Breast] Thus our Lives are imbittered to us on these accounts by our deplorable situation we are rendered incapable of shewing our obedience to Almighty God how can a Slave perform the duties of a husband to a wife or parent to his child How can a husband leave master and work and Cleave to his wife How can the wife submit [theres ?] [there?] themselves to there [their] Husbands in all things. How can the child obey thear [their] parents in all things. There is a grat [great] number of us Member Sencear [Sincere] thou [though] once members of Christs Church the Church of Christ how can the master and the Slave be said to fullfil that command Live in love let Brotherly Love contuner [continue] and abound Beare [Bear] yea onenothers [one another's] Bordenes [Burdens] How can the master be said to Beare my Borden [Burden] when he Beares [Bears] me down, whith the Have chanes [chains] of slavery and operson [oppression] aganst my will and How can we fullfill our parte [parte] of duty to him whilst in this Condition and as we cannot searve [serve] our god as we ought whilst in this situation Nither [Neither] can we reap an equal benefet [benefit] from the laws of the Land which doth not justifi [justify] but condemes [condemns] Slavery or if there had bin [been] aney [any] Law to hold us in Bondege [Bondage] we are Humbely of the opinion ther never was aney [any] to inslave our children for life when Born in a free Countrey. We therfor [therefore] Bage [Beg] your Excellency and Honours will give this it its deu [due] weight and consideration and that you will accordingly cause an act of the legislative to be pessed [passed] that we may obtain our Natural right our freedoms and our Children be set at lebety [liberty] at the yeare of Twenty one for whoues [whose] sekes [sakes] more Petequeley [Particularly] your Petitioners is is in Duty ever to Proy [Pray].

Study Questions

1. What do the petitioners specifically complain of?

2. On what grounds do these petitions condemn slavery? What roles do religion, natural rights, and nationality play in their arguments?

3. How would you characterize the overall tone of the petitions? Why do you think the petitioners offered to move to Africa?

GEORGE WASHINGTON

On Shays's Rebellion (1786)

In the fall of 1786, several thousand farmers in western and central Massachusetts, overburdened by taxation and debt, took up arms and forcibly shut down courts in several townships to prevent any more judge-mandated forced sales of property. In January 1787, the revolt culminated in a battle outside the federal arsenal at Springfield, Massachusetts, where an armed throng of Massachusetts farmers had attempted to seize weapons. The rebels were defeated by the forces of the state government.

The doomed revolt quickly became known as "Shays's Rebellion"—named after one of its leaders, a Revolutionary War veteran named Daniel Shays (ca. 1747–1825). Historians today, however, have more accurately referred to the episode not as a revolt led by one man (in fact, Shays was only one leader among many) but as a popular "regulation," an eighteenth-century term describing popular actions designed to remedy perceived instances of governmental abuse or neglect.

The so-called Massachusetts Regulation horrified many Americans who believed it to be a sign that their experiment in republican government was failing. The weak national government established by the Articles of Confederation, America's first national constitution, increasingly seemed inadequate—foreign countries bullied America, and to some, the states seemed to be out of control. The Massachusetts Regulation only heightened this sense of crisis, and within four months of the end of the revolt, fifty-five delegates met in Philadelphia intent on strengthening the federal government.

As the following letters make clear, George Washington (1732–1799) was among those who were convinced that the events in New England demonstrated the need for constitutional reform. It was the Massachusetts Regulation, in fact, that convinced him to attend the Constitutional Convention—where he would be elected president of the proceedings. The American people held Washington in such high esteem that his mere presence guaranteed that whatever the gathering produced, it would be given serious consideration.

From John C. Fitzpatrick, ed., *The Writings of George Washington*, vol. 29 (Washington, D.C.: U.S. Government Printing Office, 1939), 50–52, 121–24.

TO DAVID HUMPHREYS[1]

Mount Vernon, October 22, 1786.

* * *

I am pleased with the choice of Delegates which was made at your State meeting; and wish the Representatives of all the State societies may appear at the Genl. Meeting, with as good dispositions as I believe they will. It gives me pleasure also to hear that so many Officers are sent to your Assembly: I am persuaded they will carry with them more liberality of sentiments, than is to be found among any other class of Citizens. The speech of our friend Cobb[2] was noble, worthy of a patriot and himself; as was the conduct of Genl. Sullivan.[3] But for God's sake tell me what is the cause of all these commotions: do they proceed from licentiousness, British-influence disseminated by the tories,[4] or real grievances which admit of redress? If the latter, why were they delayed 'till the public mind had become so much agitated? If the former why are not the powers of Government tried at once? It is as well to be without, as not to live under their exercise. Commotions of this sort, like snow-balls, gather strength as they roll, if there is no opposition in the way to divide and crumble them. Do write me fully, I beseech you, on these matters; not only with respect to facts, but as to opinions of their tendency and issue. I am mortified beyond expression that in the moment of our acknowledged independence we should by our conduct verify the predictions of our transatlantic foe,[5] and render ourselves ridiculous and contemptible in the eyes of all Europe. My health (I thank you for the enquiry) is restored to me; and all under this roof join me in most affectionate regards, and in regretting that your letter has held out no idea of visiting it again this winter, as you gave us hope of doing when you left us. To all the gentn. of my acquaintance who may happen to be in your circle, I beg to be remembered with sincere regard.

---

1. David Humphreys (1752–1818), a colonel in the Continental Army and a member of Washington's staff during the Revolutionary War; Humphreys assumed command of the Connecticut state militia that fought against the "regulators."
2. David Cobb (1748–1830), a militia general and judge in Taunton, Massachusetts, who, in September 1786, faced down a group of insurgents threatening to prevent the court from convening; he reportedly declared, "Away with your whining. I will hold this court if I hold it in blood; I will sit as judge or die as a general!"
3. John Sullivan (1740–95), a general in the Continental Army; on September 20, 1786, in Exeter, New Hampshire, Sullivan, then the governor of New Hampshire, helped disperse 200 armed insurgents who had surrounded the building where the state legislature was in session.
4. Americans who remained loyal to Great Britain during the American Revolution.
5. Great Britain.

To assure you of the sincerity of my friendship for you, would be unnecessary; as you must I think be perfectly satisfied of the high esteem and affection with which, I am, etc.

* * *

TO HENRY LEE III[6]

Mount Vernon, October 31, 1786

My Dr. Sir:

I am indebted to you for your several favors of the 1st. 11th. and 17th. of this instt: and shall reply to them in the order of their dates; but first let me thank you for the interesting communications imparted by them.

The picture which you have exhibited, and the accounts which are published of the commotions, and temper of numerous bodies in the Eastern States,[7] are equally to be lamented and deprecated. They exhibit a melancholy proof of what our trans-Atlantic foe has predicted; and of another thing perhaps, which is still more to be regretted, and is yet more unaccountable, that mankind when left to themselves are unfit for their own Government. I am mortified beyond expression when I view the clouds that have spread over the brightest morn that ever dawned upon any Country. In a word, I am lost in amazement when I behold what intrigue, the interested views of desperate characters, ignorance and jealousy of the minor part, are capable of effecting, as a scourge on the major part of our fellow Citizens of the Union; for it is hardly to be supposed that the great body of the people, tho' they will not act, can be so shortsighted, or enveloped in darkness, as not to see rays of a distant sun thro' all this mist of intoxication and folly.

You talk, my good Sir, of employing influence to appease the present tumults in Massachusetts. I know not where that influence is to be found; and if attainable, that it would be a proper remedy for the disorders. Influence is no Government. Let us have one by which our lives, liberties and properties will be secured; or let us know the worst at once. Under these impressions, my humble opinion is, that there is a call for decision. Know precisely what the insurgents aim at. If they have *real* grievances, redress them if possible; or acknowledge the justice of them, and your inability to do it in the present moment. If they have not,

6. Henry "Light-Horse Harry" Lee III (1756–1818), a cavalry officer under Washington in the Revolutionary War; his son was Confederate general Robert E. Lee
7. Generally, the region of New England.

employ the force of government against them at once. If this is inadequate, *all* will be convinced that the superstructure is bad, or wants support. To be more exposed in the eyes of the world, and more contemptible than we already are, is hardly possible. To delay one or the other of these, is to exasperate on the one hand, or to give confidence on the other, and will add to their numbers; for, like snow-balls, such bodies increase by every movement, unless there is something in the way to obstruct and crumble them before the weight is too great and irresistible.

These are my sentiments. Precedents are dangerous things; let the reins of government then be braced and held with a steady hand, and every violation of the Constitution[8] be reprehended: if defective, let it be amended, but not suffered to be trampled upon whilst it has an existence.

* * *

The China came to hand without much damage; and I thank you for your attention in procuring and forwarding of it to me. Mrs. Washington joins me in best wishes for Mrs. Lee and yourself and I am &c.

TO HENRY KNOX[9]

Mount Vernon, December 26, 1786

My dear Sir:

. . . Lamentable as the conduct of the Insurgents of Massachusetts is, I am exceedingly obliged to you for the advices respecting them; and pray you, most ardently, to continue the acct. of their proceedings; because I can depend upon them from you without having my mind bewildered with those vague and contradictory reports which are handed to us in Newspapers, and which please one hour, only to make the moments of the next more bitter. I feel, my dear Genl. Knox, infinitely more than I can express to you, for the disorders which have arisen in these States. Good God! who besides a tory could have foreseen, or a Briton predicted them! were these people wiser than others, or did they judge of us from the corruption, and depravity of their own hearts? The latter I am persuaded was the case, and that notwithstanding the boasted virtue of America, we are far gone in every thing ignoble and bad.

I do assure you, that even at this moment, when I reflect on the present posture of our affairs, it seems to me to be like the vision of a dream. My

8. The Articles of Confederation.
9. Henry Knox (1750–1806), an officer in the Continental Army and a close friend of Washington's; he would later serve as the secretary of war in Washington's administration.

mind does not know how to realize it, as a thing in actual existence, so strange, so wonderful does it appear to me! In this, as in most other matter, we are too slow. When this spirit first dawned, probably it might easily have been checked; but it is scarcely within the reach of human ken, at this moment, to say when, where, or how it will end. There are combustibles in every State, which a spark might set fire to. In this State, a perfect calm prevails at present, and a prompt disposition to support, and give energy to the foederal System is discovered, if the unlucky stirring of the dispute respecting the navigation of the Mississippi[1] does not become a leaven that will ferment, and sour the mind of it.

The resolutions of the prest. Session respecting a paper emission, military certificates, &ca., have stamped justice and liberality on the proceedings of the Assembly, and By a late act, *it* seems very desirous of a General Convention to revise and amend the foederal Constitution.[2] Apropos, what prevented the Eastern States from attending the September meeting at Annapolis? Of all the States in the Union it should have seemed to me, that a measure of this sort (distracted as they were with internal commotions, and experiencing the want of energy in the government) would have been most pleasing to them. What are the prevailing sentiments of the one now proposed to be held at Philadelphia, in May next? and how will it be attended? You are at the fountain of intelligence, and where the wisdom of the Nation, it is to be presumed, has concentered; consequently better able (as I have had abundant experience of your intelligence, confidence, and candour to solve these questions.

The Maryland Assembly has been violently agitated by the question for a paper emission. It has been carried in the House of Delegates, but what has, or will be done with the Bill in the Senate I have not yet heard. The partisans in favor of the measure in the lower House, threaten, it is said, a secession if it is rejected by that Branch of the Legislature. Thus are we advancing. . . .

In both your letters you intimate, that the men of reflection, principle and property in New England, feeling the inefficacy of their present government, are contemplating a change; but you are not explicit with respect to the nature of it. It has been supposed, that, the Constitution of the State of Massachusetts was amongst the most energetic in the Union; May not these disorders then be ascribed to an endulgent exercise of the powers of Administration? If your laws authorized, and your powers were adequate

---

1. In 1784 Spain closed the port of New Orleans to western farmers, thus denying them an outlet for their goods.
2. The United States Constitution in effect in 1786, that is, the Articles of Confederation.

to the suppression of these tumults, in the first appearances of them, delay and temporizing expedients were, in my opinion improper; these are rarely well applied, and the same causes would produce similar effects in any form of government, if the powers of it are not enforced. I ask this question for information, I know nothing of the facts.

That G. B[3] will be an unconcerned Spectator of the present insurrections (if they continue) is not to be expected. That she is at this moment sowing the Seeds of jealousy and discontent among the various tribes of Indians on our frontier admits of no doubt, in my mind. And that she will improve every opportunity to foment the spirit of turbulence within the bowels of the United States, with a view of distracting our governments, and promoting divisions, is, with me, not less certain. Her first Manoeuvres will, no doubt, be covert, and may remain so till the period shall arrive when a decided line of conduct may avail her. Charges of violating the treaty, and other pretexts, will not then be wanting to colour overt acts, tending to effect the grt. objects of which she has long been in labour. A Man is now at the head of their American Affairs well calculated to conduct measures of this kind, and more than probably was selected for the purpose. We ought not therefore to sleep nor to slumber. Vigilance in watching, and vigour in acting, is, in my opinion, become indispensably necessary. If the powers are inadequate amend or alter them, but do not let us sink into the lowest state of humiliation and contempt, and become a byword in all the earth. I think with you that the Spring will unfold important and distressing Scenes, unless much wisdom and good management is displayed in the interim. Adieu; be assured no man has a higher esteem and regard for you than I have; none more sincerely your friend, and more Affecte. etc.

Study Questions

1. What did Washington believe was the cause of Shays's Rebellion?

2. How should the rebels be dealt with, according to Washington?

3. Why do you think Washington was so concerned about European perceptions of America?

4. Washington wrote that the Massachusetts Regulation was "proof . . . that mankind left to themselves are unfit for their own government." What does this suggest about Washington's attitude toward democracy?

3. Great Britain.

WILLIAM LLOYD GARRISON

Inaugural Editorial in *The Liberator* (1831)

William Lloyd Garrison (1805–1879) was born in Newburyport, Massachusetts, where he began an apprenticeship with a local newspaper in 1818. This and subsequent jobs in journalism gave him his schooling as a writer and the confidence to express himself on political matters. In April 1829, Garrison became co-editor of an anti-slavery paper published in Baltimore by the Quaker activist Benjamin Lundy. Garrison's own growing anti-slavery convictions were deepened by this opportunity to witness the evils of the institution directly in the Upper South. He soon became the publisher and editor of the abolitionist paper, The Liberator, which he launched in Boston at the beginning of 1831. This publication was the focus of Garrison's activism until its final issue appeared on December 29, 1865, shortly after the ratification of the Thirteenth Amendment abolished slavery. His had been one of the loudest and most principled voices in the abolition movement that culminated in this constitutional and moral victory.

Garrison hailed from New England, a region whose strongly anti-slavery leanings reflected the moral principles of its Puritan heritage. Like many early abolitionists, Garrison was initially drawn to colonization, the notion that the compensated emancipation of slaves would be followed by their resettlement outside the United States. By 1830, however, Garrison had rejected this strategy for its impracticality and implicit racism. As you read his opening editorial in the Liberator, *consider the degree to which Garrison believed this paper would be the beginning of a new direction for the anti-slavery movement.*

From *Selections from the Writings and Speeches of William Lloyd Garrison* (Boston: R. F. Wallcutt, 1852), 62–64.

During my recent tour for the purpose of exciting the minds of the people by a series of discourses on the subject of slavery, every place that I visited gave fresh evidence of the fact, that a greater revolution in public sentiment was to be effected in the free States—and particularly in New England—than at the South. I found contempt more bitter, opposition more active, detraction more relentless, prejudice more stubborn, and apathy more frozen, than among slave owners themselves. Of course, there were individual exceptions to the contrary. This state of things afflicted, but did not dishearten me. I determined, at every hazard, to lift up the standard of emancipation in the eyes of the nation, within sight of Bunker Hill, and in the birth-place of liberty. That standard is now unfurled; and long may it float, unhurt by the spoliations of time or the missiles of a desperate foe; yea, till every chain be broken, and every bondman set free! Let Southern oppressors tremble; let their secret abettors tremble; let their Northern apologists tremble; let all the enemies of the persecuted blacks tremble.

I deem the publication of my original Prospectus unnecessary, as it has obtained a wide circulation. The principles therein inculcated will be steadily pursued in this paper, excepting that I shall not array myself as the political partisan of any man. In defending the great cause of human rights, I wish to derive the assistance of all religions and of all parties.

Assenting to the 'self-evident truths' maintained in the American Declaration of Independence, 'that all men are created equal, and endowed by their Creator with certain inalienable rights—among which are life, liberty, and the pursuit of happiness,' I shall strenuously contend for the immediate enfranchisement of our slave population. In Park Street Church, on the Fourth of July, 1829, in an address on slavery, I unreflectingly assented to the popular but pernicious doctrine of gradual abolition. I seize this opportunity to make a full and unequivocal recantation, and thus publicly to ask pardon of my God, of my country, and of my brethren, the poor slaves, for having uttered a sentiment so full of timidity, injustice and absurdity. A similar recantation, from my pen, was published in the 'Genius of Universal Emancipation,'[1] at Baltimore, in September, 1829. My conscience is now satisfied.

I am aware, that many object to the severity of my language; but is there not cause for severity? I will be as harsh as truth, and as uncompromising as justice. On this subject, I do not wish to think, or speak, or write, with moderation. No! no! Tell a man, whose house is on fire, to give a moderate alarm; tell him to moderately rescue his wife from the hands of the ravisher; tell the mother to gradually extricate her babe from the fire into which it has fallen; but urge me not to use moderation in a cause like the present! I am in earnest. I will not equivocate—I will not excuse—I will not retreat a single inch—AND I WILL BE HEARD. The apathy of the people is enough to make every statue leap from its pedestal, and to hasten the resurrection of the dead.

It is pretended, that I am retarding the cause of emancipation by the coarseness of my invective, and the precipitancy of my measures. The charge is not true. On this question, my influence, humble as it is, is felt at this moment to a considerable extent, and shall be felt in coming years—not perniciously, but beneficially—not as a curse, but as a blessing; and POSTERITY WILL BEAR TESTIMONY THAT I WAS RIGHT. I desire to thank God, that he enables me to disregard 'the fear of man which bringeth a snare,' and to speak his truth in its simplicity and power. And here I close with this fresh dedication:—

---

1. The abolitionist paper published in Baltimore by Benjamin Lundy.

'Oppression! I have seen thee, face to face,
And met thy cruel eye and cloudy brow;
But thy soul-withering glance I fear not now—
For dread to prouder feelings doth give place,
Of deep abhorrence! Scorning the disgrace
Of slavish knees that at thy footstool bow,
I also kneel—but with far other vow
Do hail thee and thy herd of hirelings base:—
I swear, while life-blood warms my throbbing veins,
Still to oppose and thwart, with heart and hand,
Thy brutalizing sway—till Afric's chains
Are burst, and Freedom rules the rescued land,
Trampling Oppression and his iron rod:—
Such is the vow I take—so help me, God!'

Boston, January 1, 1831.

Study Questions

1. Why does Garrison decide to base *The Liberator* in Boston rather than in other parts of the country? What is the paper's ultimate goal? Why might some anti-slavery activists find this objectionable?

2. What insight does this editorial give regarding Garrison's religious views? Would his faith be of greater or lesser advantage in his work as an abolitionist? Explain.

3. What is most distinctive about Garrison's tone and writing style? What is his attitude toward moderation? Evaluate the merits of Garrison's journalistic approach.

4. In your view, who was *The Liberator's* primary audience? How might Garrison believe such a publication could hasten the demise of slavery?

ANDREW JACKSON

Presidential Message on Indian Removal (1829)

Andrew Jackson is commonly described as the first "popular" president. Indeed, he nearly became president in 1824, when he won a plurality of electoral votes but lost the election in the House of Representatives to John Quincy Adams, because, Jackson charged, Adams had made a "corrupt bargain" with his soon-to-be secretary of state, Henry Clay. A vicious and lengthy campaign for the 1828 election ensued, resulting in a landslide victory for Jackson. One reason for his massive popularity is that he shared many of the prejudices rampant in his era, including favoring the forcible removal of native populations from states of the union. Indeed, by the 1820s much of his national renown stemmed from his having commanded troops against such tribes as the Creeks and the Seminoles.

By the time Jackson became president in 1829, popular pressure was building to take action against the Indians who still lived east of the Mississippi, in particular the Five Civilized Tribes—Cherokees, Creeks, Choctaws, Chickasaws, and Seminoles—who populated the southeast. Jackson articulated his policy recommendations in his first annual message to Congress on December 8, 1829. The end result was the passage of the Indian Removal Act of 1830, one of the hallmarks (for better or for worse) of Jackson's presidency. As you read Jackson's address, consider what it reveals about his true feelings toward Native Americans and their ultimate place in American society.

From James D. Richardson, *A Compilation of the Messages and Papers of the Presidents*, vol. 2 (Bureau of National Literature, 1897), 1019–1022.

The condition and ulterior destiny of the Indian tribes within the limits of some of our States have become objects of much interest and importance. It has long been the policy of Government to introduce among them the arts of civilization, in the hope of gradually reclaiming them from a wandering life. This policy has, however, been coupled with another wholly incompatible with its success. Professing a desire to civilize and settle them, we have at the same time lost no opportunity to purchase their lands and thrust them farther into the wilderness. By this means they have not only been kept in a wandering state, but been led to look upon us as unjust and indifferent to their fate. Thus, though lavish in its expenditures upon the subject, Government has constantly defeated its own policy, and the Indians in general, receding farther and farther to the west, have retained their savage habits. A portion, however, of the Southern tribes, having mingled much with the whites and made some progress in the arts of civilized life, have lately attempted to erect an independent government within the limits of Georgia and Alabama.[1] These States, claiming to be the only sovereigns within their territories, extended their laws over the Indians, which induced the latter to call upon the United States for protection.

Under these circumstances the question presented was whether the General Government had a right to sustain those people in their pretensions. The Constitution declares that "no new State shall be formed or erected within the jurisdiction of any other State" without the consent of its legislature. If the General Government is not permitted to tolerate the erection of a confederate State within the territory of one of the members of this Union against her consent, much less could it allow a foreign and independent government to establish itself there. Georgia became a member of the Confederacy which eventuated in our Federal Union as a sovereign State, always asserting her claim to certain limits, which, having been originally defined in her colonial charter and subsequently recognized in the treaty of peace, she has ever since continued to enjoy. . . . Alabama was admitted into the Union on the same footing with the original States, with boundaries which were prescribed by Congress. There is no constitutional, conventional, or legal provision which allows them less power over the Indians within their borders than is possessed by Maine or New York.

* * *

If the principle involved . . . be abandoned, it will follow that the objects of this Government are reversed, and that it has become a part of its duty to aid in destroying the States which it was established to protect.

Actuated by this view of the subject, I informed the Indians inhabiting parts of Georgia and Alabama that their attempt to establish an independent government would not be countenanced by the Executive of the United States, and advised them to emigrate beyond the Mississippi or submit to the laws of those States.

Our conduct toward these people is deeply interesting to our national character. Their present condition, contrasted with what they once were, makes a most powerful appeal to our sympathies. Our ancestors found them the uncontrolled possessors of these vast regions. By persuasion and force they have been made to retire from river to river and from mountain to mountain, until some of the tribes have become extinct and others have left but remnants to preserve for awhile

---

1. In 1827 the Cherokee Nation East adopted a constitution modeled largely on the U.S. Constitution, establishing a three-branch goverment with a bicameral legislature and an independent judiciary.

their once terrible names. Surrounded by the whites with their arts of civilization, which by destroying the resources of the savage doom him to weakness and decay, the fate of the Mohegan, the Narragansett, and the Delaware is fast overtaking the Choctaw, the Cherokee, and the Creek. That this fate surely awaits them if they remain within the limits of the States does not admit of a doubt. Humanity and national honor demand that every effort should be made to avert so great a calamity. It is too late to inquire whether it was just in the United States to include them and their territory within the bounds of new States, whose limits they could control. That step can not be retraced. A State can not be dismembered by Congress or restricted in the exercise of her constitutional power. But the people of those States and of every State, actuated by feelings of justice and a regard for our national honor, submit to you the interesting question whether something can not be done, consistently with the rights of the States, to preserve this much-injured race.

As a means of effecting this end I suggest for your consideration the propriety of setting apart an ample district west of the Mississippi, and without the limits of any State or Territory now formed, to be guaranteed to the Indian tribes as long as they shall occupy it, each tribe having a distinct control over the portion designated for its use. There they may be secured in the enjoyment of governments of their own choice, subject to no other control from the United States than such as may be necessary to preserve peace on the frontier and between the several tribes. There the benevolent may endeavor to teach them the arts of civilization, and, by promoting union and harmony among them, to raise up an interesting commonwealth, destined to perpetuate the race and to attest the humanity and justice of this Government.

This emigration should be voluntary, for it would be as cruel as unjust to compel the aborigines to abandon the graves of their fathers and seek a home in a distant land. But they should be distinctly informed that if they remain within the limits of the States they must be subject to their laws. In return for their obedience as individuals they will without doubt be protected in the enjoyment of those possessions which they have improved by their industry. . . . Submitting to the laws of the States, and receiving, like other citizens, protection in their persons and property, they will ere long become merged in the mass of our population.

Study Questions

1. What is the immediate problem in Indian relations that Jackson is addressing? How does he propose to solve it? What choices does he give Indians in regard to their future?

2. In what sense would Jackson view Indians as being "savage"? In his mind, how had certain tribes in Alabama and Georgia become more "civilized"? To what degree would this earn more favorable treatment from the federal and state governments?

3. How might Jackson's outlook be seen as sympathetic toward Indians? Was it so in reality? Would relocation west of the Mississippi ultimately be beneficial to the Indians in the way Jackson suggests? Why or why not?

4. Recent presidential ranking surveys indicate that current-day Americans (including historians) are less admiring of Jackson than those of prior generations. To what degree do you think his Indian policy is responsible? What other factors might account for Jackson's diminished standing? How permissible is it to judge him by standards of the present?

Appeal of the Cherokee Nation (1830)

One of the ugliest aspects of Andrew Jackson's presidency was his willingness to appeal to the racism and land hunger of many of the common white men who supported him. Jackson's experience as an Indian fighter and expansionist make unsurprising his strongly held view that the Indian tribes which continued to occupy lands east of the Mississippi should be compelled to relocate west of the river. The state of Georgia, emboldened by Jackson's election to the presidency in 1828, announced soon afterward that it was extending its authority over the Cherokees within its borders, a move which would strip the Indians of rights and lands guaranteed by federal treaty. The Cherokees had made great advances in prior years as they practiced extensive agriculture, established permanent towns, adopted a written constitution, and created a distinctive written language. None of this would save them. Congress passed the Indian Removal Act, which President Jackson signed on May 28, 1830. Despite a favorable Supreme Court ruling in 1832, the Cherokees were forced to yield to relentless state and federal pressure and relocate to Oklahoma in 1838–1839. Thousands died en route along the notorious Trail of Tears.

The following document is an appeal to Congress authored primarily by Cherokee principal chief John Ross (1790–1866), a man of mixed Scottish and Cherokee descent. As you read it, consider its effect upon Congress and the broader public audience. At the time of its writing, Ross remained hopeful the Cherokees might be allowed to remain on their ancestral lands. In 1838, with all options now exhausted, Ross accompanied his people on the long and dreadful march to their new domicile in the West.

From Lewis Ross et al., "Address of the Committee and Council of the Cherokee Nation," in *General Council convened, to the people of the United States* (July 17, 1803).

Soon after the war of the revolution, as we have learned from our fathers, the Cherokees looked upon the promises of the whites with great distrust and suspicion; but the frank and magnanimous conduct of General Washington did much to allay these feelings. The perseverance of successive presidents, and especially of Mr. Jefferson, in the same course of policy, and in the constant assurance that our country should remain inviolate, except so far as we voluntarily ceded it, nearly banished anxiety in regard to encroachments from the whites. To this result the aid which we received from the United States in the attempts of our people to become civilized, and the kind efforts of benevolent societies, have greatly contributed. Of late years, however, much solicitude was occasioned among our people by the claims of Georgia. This solicitude arose from the apprehension, that by extreme importunity, threats, and other undue influence, a treaty would be made, which should cede the territory, and thus compel the inhabitants to remove. But it never occurred to us for a moment that without any new treaty, without any assent of our rulers and people, without even a pretended compact, and against our vehement and unanimous protestations, we should be delivered over to the discretion of those, who had declared by a legislative act, that they wanted the Cherokee lands and would have them.

Finding that relief could not be obtained from the chief magistrate, and not doubting that our claim to protection was just, we made our application to congress. During four long months our delegation waited, at the doors of the national legislature of the United States, and the people at home, in the most painful suspense, to learn in what manner our application would be answered; and, now that congress has adjourned, on the very day before the date fixed by Georgia for the extension of her oppressive laws over the greater part of our country, the distressing intelligence has been received that we have received no answer at all; and no department of the government has assured us, that we are to receive the desired protection. But just at the close of the session, an act was passed, by which an half a million of dollars was appropriated towards effecting a removal of Indians; and we have great reason to fear that the influence of this act will be brought to bear most injuriously upon us. The passage of this act was certainly understood by the representatives of Georgia as abandoning us to the oppressive and cruel measures of the state, and as sanctioning the opinion that treaties with Indians do not restrain state legislation. We are informed by those, who are competent to judge, that the recent act does not admit of such construction; but that the passage of it, under the actual circumstances of the controversy, will be considered as sanctioning the pretensions of Georgia, there is too much reason to fear.

Thus have we realized, with heavy hearts, that our supplication has not been heard; that the protection heretofore experienced is now to be withheld; that the guaranty, in consequence of which our fathers laid aside their arms and ceded the best portions of their country, means nothing; and that we must either emigrate to an unknown region and leave the pleasant land to which we have the strongest attachment, or submit to the legislation of a state, which has already made our people outlaws, and enacted that any Cherokee, who shall endeavor to prevent the selling of his country, shall be imprisoned in the penitentiary of Georgia not less than four years. To our countrymen this has been melancholy intelligence, and with the most bitter disappointment has it been received.

But in the midst of our sorrows, we do not forget our obligations to our friends and benefactors. It was with sensations of inexpressible joy that we have learned that the voice of thousands, in many parts of the United States, has been raised in our behalf, and numerous memorials offered in our favor, in both houses of congress. To those numerous friends, who have thus sympathized with us in our low estate, we tender our grateful acknowledgements. In pleading our cause, they have pleaded the cause of the poor and defenceless throughout the world. Our special thanks are due, however, to those honorable men, who so ably and eloquently asserted our rights, in both branches of the national legislature. Their efforts will be appreciated wherever the merits of this question shall be known; and we cannot but think, that they have secured for themselves a permanent reputation among the disinterested advocates of humanity, equal rights, justice, and good faith. We even cherish the hope, that these efforts, seconded and followed by others of a similar character, will yet be available, so far as to mitigate our sufferings, if not to effect our entire deliverance.

* * *

We are aware, that some persons suppose it will be for our advantage to remove beyond the Mississippi. We think otherwise. Our people universally think otherwise. Thinking that it would be fatal to their interests, they have almost to a man sent their memorial to congress deprecating the necessity of a removal. This question was distinctly before their minds when they signed their memorial. Not an adult person can be found, who has not an opinion on the subject, and if the people were to understand distinctly, that they could be protected against the laws of the neighboring states, there is probably not an adult person in the nation, who would think it best to remove; though possibly a few might emigrate individually. There are doubtless many, who would flee to an unknown country, however beset with dangers, privations and sufferings, rather than be sentenced to spend six years in a Georgia prison for advising one of their neighbors not to betray his country. And there are others who could not think of living as outlaws in their native land, exposed to numberless vexations, and excluded from being parties or witnesses in a court of justice. It is incredible that Georgia should ever have enacted the oppressive laws to which reference is here made, unless she had supposed that something extremely terrific in its character was necessary in order to make the Cherokees willing to remove. We are not willing to remove; and if we could be brought to this extremity, it would be not by argument, not because our judgment was satisfied, not because our condition will be improved; but only because we cannot endure to be deprived of our national and individual rights and subjected to a process of intolerable oppression.

We wish to remain on the land of our fathers. We have a perfect and original right to remain without interruption or molestation. The treaties with us, and laws of the United States made in pursuance of treaties, guaranty our residence and our privileges, and secure us against intruders. Our only request is, that these treaties may be fulfilled, and these laws executed.

But if we are compelled to leave our country, we see nothing but ruin before us. The country west of the Arkansas territory[1] is unknown to us. From what we can learn of it, we have no prepossessions in its favor. All the inviting parts of it, as we believe, are preoccupied by various Indian nations, to which it has been assigned. They would regard us as intruders, and look upon us with an evil eye. The far greater part of that region is, beyond all controversy, badly supplied with wood and water; and no Indian tribe can live as agriculturists without these articles. All our neighbors, in case of our removal, though crowded into our near vicinity; would speak a language totally different from ours, and practice different customs. The original possessors of that region are now wandering savages lurking for prey in the neighborhood. They have always been at war, and would be easily tempted to turn their arms against peaceful emigrants. Were the country to which we are urged much better than it is represented to be, and were it free from the objections which we have made to it, still it is not the land of our birth, nor of our affections. It contains neither the scenes of our childhood, nor the graves of our fathers.

The removal of families to a new country, even under the most favorable auspices, and when the spirits are sustained by pleasing visions of the future, is attended with much depression of mind and sinking of heart. This is the case, when the removal is a matter of decided preference, and when the persons concerned are in early youth or vigorous manhood. Judge, then, what must be the circumstances of a removal, when a whole community, embracing persons of all classes and every description, from the infant to the man of extreme old age, the sick, the blind, the lame, the improvident, the reckless, the desperate, as well as the prudent, the considerate, the industrious, are compelled to remove by odious and intolerable vexations and persecutions, brought upon them in the forms of law, when all will agree only in this, that they have been cruelly robbed of their country, in violation of the most solemn compacts, which it is possible for communities to form with each other; and that, if they should make themselves comfortable in their new residence, they have nothing to expect hereafter but to be the victims of a future legalized robbery!

Such we deem, and are absolutely certain, will be the feelings of the whole Cherokee people, if they are forcibly compelled, by the laws of Georgia, to remove; and with these feelings, how is it possible that we should pursue our present course of improvement, or avoid sinking into utter despondency? We have been called a poor, ignorant, and degraded people. We certainly are not rich; nor have we ever boasted of our knowledge, or our moral or intellectual elevation. But there is not a man within our limits so ignorant as not to know that he has the right to live on the land of his fathers, in the possession of his immemorial privileges, and that this right has been acknowledged and guaranteed by the United

---

1. The capital of the Cherokee Nation today is located just west of Arkansas in Tahlequah, Oklahoma.

States; nor is there a man so degraded as not to feel a keen sense of injury, on being deprived of this right and driven into exile.

* * *

We entreat those to whom the foregoing paragraphs are addressed, to remember the great law of love. "Do to others as ye would that others should do to you"— Let them remember that of all nations on the earth, they are under the greatest obligation to obey this law. We pray them to remember that, for the sake of principle, their forefathers were compelled to leave, therefore driven from the old world, and that the winds of persecution wafted them over the great waters and landed them on the shores of the new world, when the Indian was the sole lord and proprietor of these extensive domains—Let them remember in what way they were received by the savage of America, when power was in his hand, and his ferocity could not be restrained by any human arm. We urge them to bear in mind, that those who would now ask of them a cup of cold water, and a spot of earth, a portion of their own patrimonial possessions, on which to live and die in peace, are the descendants of those, whose origin, as inhabitants of North America, history and tradition are alike insufficient to reveal. Let them bring to remembrance all these facts, and they cannot, and we are sure, they will not fail to remember, and sympathize with us in these our trials and sufferings.

Study Questions

1. Why do the Cherokees object to the actions taken by Georgia? Upon what rights do they insist? What are their primary arguments against removal?

2. The Cherokee appeal refers to "our friends and benefactors." Who might these have been? What sections of the United States might have contained the greatest number of Indian sympathizers?

3. What does this document reveal of Cherokee relations with other Indians? What might have caused them to have tense relations with other tribes? Who were the "wandering savages" that lived west of the Mississippi and why were they especially to be feared?

4. Evaluate the appeal made by the Cherokees in the final paragraph of this document. Why was it ultimately ineffective at preventing their expulsion? What does this document predict or imply about the future well-being of the Cherokee people?

JOHN BROWN

Aftermath of the Raid on Harpers Ferry: Final Speech and Prison Communications (1859)

John Brown's September 1859 raid on the federal armory in Harpers Ferry, Virginia, polarized North and South at the end of a tumultuous decade of contention over the future of slavery. Brown (1800–1859), a native of Connecticut and lifelong abolitionist, intended to seize weapons that he would then distribute to local slaves. Brown and his small army then planned to retreat into the surrounding mountains and wage guerilla warfare against slavery. The incursion into Harpers Ferry resulted in military calamity, however, as almost all of his force of twenty-two men were killed or taken prisoner by federal soldiers.

Brown himself was taken alive and soon tried in a Virginia court for treason, murder, and inciting slave insurrection. Upon being convicted and sentenced to hang, Brown made a last address to the court on November 2. His remarks profoundly affected many readers who read them in the northern press. The documents that follow are the text of that speech, a final letter written to his family, and a note he handed to a jailer just before he departed for the gallows. As you read them, consider how they would have influenced northern and southern readers (Brown's prison correspondence was aimed at a wide public audience) and why John Brown's Raid thereby became one of the key events that led to civil war.

From F. B. Sanborn, ed., *The Life and Letters of John Brown* (Boston: Roberts Brothers, 1891), 584–585, 613–615, 620.

FINAL SPEECH

I have, may it please the Court, a few words to say.

"In the first place, I deny everything but what I have all along admitted,—the design on my part to free the slaves. I intended certainly to have made a clean thing of that matter, as I did last winter, when I went into Missouri and there took slaves without the snapping of a gun on either side, moved them through the country, and finally left them in Canada.[1] I designed to have done the same thing again, on a larger scale. That was all I intended. I never did intend murder, or treason, or the destruction of property, or to excite or incite slaves to rebellion, or to make insurrection.

"I have another objection: and that is, it is unjust that I should suffer such a penalty. Had I interfered in the manner which I admit, and which I admit has been fairly proved (for I admire the truthfulness and candor of the greater portion of the witnesses who have testified in this case),—had I so interfered in behalf of the rich, the powerful, the intelligent, the so-called great, or in behalf of any of their friends,—either father, mother, brother, sister, wife, or children, or any of that class,—and suffered and sacrificed what I have in this interference, it would have been all right; and every man in this court would have deemed it an act worthy of reward rather than punishment.

"This court acknowledges, as I suppose, the validity of the law of God. I see a book kissed here which I suppose to be the Bible, or at least the New Testament. That teaches me that all things whatsoever I would that men should do to me, I should do even so to them. It teaches me, further, to 'remember them that are in bonds, as bound with them.' I endeavored to act up to that instruction. I say, I am yet too young to understand that God is any respecter of persons. I believe that to have interfered as I have done—as I have always freely admitted I have done—in behalf of His despised poor, was not wrong, but right. Now, if it is deemed necessary that I should forfeit my life for the furtherance of the ends of justice, and mingle my blood further with the blood of my children[2] and with the blood of millions in this slave country whose rights are disregarded by wicked, cruel, and unjust enactments,—I submit; so let it be done!

"Let me say one word further.

"I feel entirely satisfied with the treatment I have received on my trial. Considering all the circumstances, it has been more generous than I expected. But I feel no consciousness of guilt. I have stated from the first what was my intention, and what was not. I never had any design against the life of any person, nor any disposition to commit treason, or excite slaves to rebel, or make any general insurrection. I never encouraged any man to do so, but always discouraged any idea of that kind.

"Let me say, also, a word in regard to the statements made by some of those connected with me. I hear it has been stated by some of them that I have induced them to join me. But the contrary is true. I do not say this to injure them, but as regretting their weakness. There is not one of them but joined me of his own accord, and the greater part of them at their own expense. A number of them I never saw, and

---

1. In December 1858, Brown led a raiding party of twenty men into Missouri, where he took eleven slaves from their plantations and accompanied them to freedom in Canada. Contrary to what Brown says, one slaveowner was shot and killed in the process.

2. Brown's sons Watson and Oliver were killed in the raid on Harpers Ferry. Brown had already lost his son Frederick during a battle with pro-slavery men at Osawatomie, Kansas in August 1856.

never had a word of conversation with, till the day they came to me; and that was for the purpose I have stated.

"Now I have done."

LAST LETTERS

Charlestown Prison, Jefferson County, Va.,
Nov. 30, 1859.

My DEARLY BELOVED WIFE, SONS, AND DAUGHTERS, EVERY ONE,—As I now begin probably what is the last letter I shall ever write to any of yon, I conclude to write to all at the same time. I will mention some little matters particularly applicable to little property concerns in another place.

I recently received a letter from my wife, from near Philadelphia, dated November 22, by which it would seem that she was about giving up the idea of seeing me again. I had written her to come on if she felt equal to the undertaking, but I do not know that she will get my letter in time. It was on her own account, chiefly, that I asked her to stay back. At first I had a most strong desire to see her again, but there appeared to be very serious objections; and should we never meet in this life, I trust that she will in the end be satisfied it was for the best at least, if not most for her comfort.

I am waiting the hour of my public murder with great composure of mind and cheerfulness; feeling the strong assurance that in no other possible way could I be used to so much advantage to the cause of God and of humanity, and that nothing that either I or all my family have sacrificed or suffered will he lost. The reflection that a wise and merciful as well as just and holy God rules not only the affairs of this world but of all worlds, is a rock to set our feet upon under all circumstances,—even those more severely trying ones in which our own feelings and wrongs have placed us. I have now no doubt but that our seeming disaster will ultimately result in the most glorious success. So, my dear shattered and broken family, be of good cheer, and believe and trust in God with all your heart and with all your soul; for He doeth all things well. Do not feel ashamed on my account, nor for one moment despair of the cause or grow weary of well-doing. I bless God I never felt stronger confidence in the certain and near approach of a bright morning and glorious day than I have felt, and do now feel, since my confinement here. I am endeavoring to return, like a poor prodigal as I am, to my Father, against whom I have always sinned, in the hope that he may kindly and forgivingly meet me, though a very great way off.

Oh, my dear wife and children, would to God you could know how I have been travailing in birth for you all, that no one of you may fail of the grace of God through Jesus Christ; that no one of you may be blind to the truth and glorious light of his Word, in which life and immortality are brought to light. I beseech you, every one, to make the Bible your daily and nightly study, with a child-like, honest, candid, teachable spirit of love and respect for your husband and father. And I beseech the God of my fathers to open all your eyes to the discovery of the truth. You cannot imagine how much you may soon need the consolations of the Christian religion.

* * *

I mention this as a reason for endeavoring to leave a valuable copy of the Bible, to be carefully preserved in remembrance of me, to so many of my posterity, instead of some other book at equal cost.

I beseech you all to live in habitual contentment with moderate circumstances and gains of worldly store, and earnestly to teach this to your children and children's children after you, by example as well as precept. Be determined to know by experience, as soon as may be, whether Bible instruction is of divine origin or not. Be sure to owe no man anything, but to love one another. John Rogers[3] wrote to his children: "Abhor that arrant whore of Rome." John Brown writes to his children to abhor, with undying hatred also, that sum of all villanies,— slavery. Remember, "he that is slow to anger is better than the mighty," and "he that ruleth his spirit than he that taketh a city." Remember also that "they being wise shall shine, and they that turn many to righteousness, as the stars for ever and ever."

And now, dearly beloved family, to God and the work of his grace I commend you all.

Your affectionate husband and father,
John Brown.

---

3. English clergyman (c. 1500–55), translator of the Bible into English and first English martyr for Protestantism during the reign of Mary I.

NOTE BEFORE THE GALLOWS

Charlestown, Va., Dec, 2, 1859.

I, John Brown, am now quite *certain* that the crimes of this *guilty land* will never be purged away but with *blood*. I had, as I now think vainly, flattered myself that without very much bloodshed it might be done.

Study Questions

1. In his words to the court, what does John Brown proclaim to have been his objective at Harpers Ferry? Why did he "feel no consciousness of guilt" for what he had done? What are his most important final instructions to his family?

2. Why in his courtroom speech does John Brown specifically reference the New Testament? How might his anti-slavery activities have been influenced by the Old Testament example of Moses as well? Where would John Brown most likely fit on the American religious landscape today?

3. Brown predicted that his "seeming disaster would ultimately result in the most glorious success." What did he mean by this? What, if anything, did he accomplish in the last weeks of his life?

4. What does Brown's final note prophesy about the coming civil war? Was he right? Did this make his violent resistance to slavery at Harpers Ferry and elsewhere more or less defensible? Explain fully.

FREDERICK DOUGLASS

Fourth of July Speech (1852)

Frederick Douglass (1818–1895) was one of the most remarkable Americans ever to live, and certainly the most prominent leader among African Americans through the second half of the nineteenth century. Douglass was born a slave on a large Maryland plantation in 1818, suspected to be the son of his master. He learned to read at an early age and later testified that his literacy had given him an absolute determination to be free. After becoming a skilled shipyard worker in Baltimore, Douglass escaped to the North in 1838. Douglass met prominent white abolitionists such as William Lloyd Garrison and Wendell Phillips and, by the early 1840s, was drawing large audiences across the Northeast as an antislavery speaker. His autobiography, published in Boston in 1843, secured his fame and remains one of the classic narratives of the slave experience.

The following speech was delivered on Independence Day of 1852 before an antislavery audience of 600 in Rochester, New York. As you read this excerpt, evaluate Douglass's oratorical skill and imagine his credibility, as a former slave, in the minds of his listeners. Douglass went on to serve the Union cause during the Civil War as a military recruiter and a principled critic of Lincoln's war leadership, continually pushing the president for bolder policies in regard to emancipation and black equality. After the war, Douglass served in a number of diplomatic and government positions and ceaselessly advocated for the rights and uplift of African Americans.

From Frederick Douglass, *Oration, Delivered in Corinthian Hall* (Rochester: Lee, Mann & Co., 1852), 3–4, 14–21.

He who could address this audience without a quailing sensation, has stronger nerves than I have. I do not remember ever to have appeared as a speaker before any assembly more shrinkingly, nor with greater distrust of my ability, than I do this day. A feeling has crept over me, quite unfavorable to the exercise of my limited powers of speech. The task before me is one which requires much previous thought and study for its proper performance. I know that apologies of this sort are generally considered flat and unmeaning. I trust, however, that mine will not be so considered. Should I seem at ease, my appearance would much misrepresent me. The little experience I have had in addressing public meetings, in country school houses, avails me nothing on the present occasion.

The papers and placards say, that I am to deliver a 4th July oration. This certainly, sounds large, and out of the common way, for me. It is true that I have often had the privilege to speak in this beautiful Hall, and to address many who now honor me with their presence. But neither their familiar faces, nor the perfect gage I think I have of Corinthian Hall, seems to free me from embarrassment.

The fact is, ladies and gentlemen, the distance between this platform and the slave plantation, from which I escaped, is considerable—and the difficulties to be overcome in getting from the latter to the former, are by no means slight. That I am here to-day, is, to me, a matter of astonishment as well as of gratitude. You will not, therefore, be surprised, if in what I have to say, I evince no elaborate preparation, nor grace my speech with any high sounding exordium. With little experience and with less learning, I have been able to throw my thoughts hastily and imperfectly together; and trusting to your patient and generous indulgence, I will proceed to lay them before you.

* * *

Fellow-citizens, pardon me, allow me to ask, why am I called upon to speak here to-day? What have I, or those I represent, to do with your national independence? Are the great principles of political freedom and of natural justice, embodied in that Declaration of Independence, extended to us? and am I, therefore, called upon to bring our humble offering to the national altar, and to confess the benefits and express devout gratitude for the blessings resulting from your independence to us?

Would to God, both for your sakes and ours, that an affirmative answer could be truthfully returned to these questions! Then would my task be light, and my burden easy and delightful. For *who* is there so cold, that a nation's sympathy could not warm him? Who so obdurate and dead to the claims of gratitude, that would not thankfully acknowledge such priceless benefits? Who so stolid and selfish, that would not give his voice to swell the hallelujahs of a nation's jubilee, when the chains of servitude had been torn from his limbs? I am not that man. In a case like that, the dumb might eloquently speak, and the "lame man leap as an hart."[1]

But, such is not the state of the case. I say it with a sad sense of the disparity between us. I am not included within the pale[2] of this glorious anniversary! Your high independence only reveals the immeasurable distance between us. The blessings in which you, this day, rejoice, are not enjoyed in common. The rich

---

1. "Then shall the lame man leap as an hart, and the tongue of the dumb sing" (Isaiah 35:6).
2. Douglass here employs "pale" in the sense of an area enclosed by a fence or a boundary.

inheritance of justice, liberty, prosperity and independence, bequeathed by your fathers, is shared by you, not by me. The sunlight that brought life and healing to you, has brought stripes and death to me. This Fourth July is *yours*, not *mine*. *You* may rejoice, *I* must mourn. To drag a man in fetters into the grand illuminated temple of liberty, and call upon him to join you in joyous anthems, were inhuman mockery and sacrilegious irony. Do you mean, citizens, to mock me, by asking me to speak to-day? If so, there is a parallel to your conduct. And let me warn you that it is dangerous to copy the example of a nation whose crimes, towering up to heaven, were thrown down by the breath of the Almighty, burying that nation in irrecoverable ruin! I can to-day take up the plaintive lament of a peeled and woe-smitten people!

"By the rivers of Babylon, there we sat down. Yea! we wept when we remembered Zion. We hanged our harps upon the willows in the midst thereof. For there, they that carried us away captive, required of us a song; and they who wasted us required of us mirth, saying, Sing us one of the songs of Zion. How can we sing the Lord's song in a strange land? If I forget thee, O Jerusalem, let my right hand forget her cunning. If I do not remember thee, let my tongue cleave to the roof of my mouth."[3]

Fellow-citizens; above your national, tumultuous joy, I hear the mournful wail of millions! whose chains, heavy and grievous yesterday, are, to-day, rendered more intolerable by the jubilee shouts[4] that reach them. If I do forget, if I do not faithfully remember those bleeding children of sorrow this day, "may my right hand forget her cunning, and may my tongue cleave to the roof of my mouth!" To forget them, to pass lightly over their wrongs, and to chime in with the popular theme, would be treason most scandalous and shocking, and would make me a reproach before God and the world. My subject, then, fellow-citizens, is AMERICAN SLAVERY. I shall see, this day, and its popular characteristics, from the slave's point of view. Standing, there, identified with the American bondman, making his wrongs mine, I do not hesitate to declare, with all my soul, that the character and conduct of this nation never looked blacker to me than on this 4th of July! Whether we turn to the declarations of the past, or to the professions of the present, the conduct of the nation seems equally hideous and revolting. America is false to the past, false to the present, and solemnly binds herself to be false to the future. Standing with God and the crushed and bleeding slave on this occasion, I will, in the name of humanity which is outraged, in the name of liberty which is fettered, in the name of the constitution and the Bible, which are disregarded and trampled upon, dare to call in question and to denounce, with all the emphasis I can command, everything that serves to perpetuate slavery—the great sin and

---

3. Psalm 137:1–6.

4. In ancient Hebrew law, Jubilee was the year every fifty years when all slaves were freed.

shame of America! "I will not equivocate; I will not excuse;"[5] I will use the severest language I can command; and yet not one word, shall escape me that any man, whose judgment is not blinded by prejudice, or who is not at heart a slaveholder, shall not confess to be right and just.

But I fancy I hear some one of my audience say, it is just in this circumstance that you and your brother abolitionists fail to make a favorable impression on the public mind. Would you argue more, and denounce less, would you persuade more, and rebuke less, your cause would be much more likely to succeed. But, I submit, where all is plain there is nothing to be argued. What point in the anti-slavery creed would you have me argue? On what branch of the subject do the people of this country need light? Must I undertake to prove that the slave is a man? That point is conceded already. Nobody doubts it. The slaveholders themselves acknowledge it in the enactment of laws for their government. They acknowledge it when they punish disobedience on the part of the slave. There are seventy-two crimes in the State of Virginia, which, if committed by a black man, (no matter how ignorant he be,) subject him to the punishment of death; while only two of the same crimes will subject a white man to the like punishment.—What is this but the acknowledgement that the slave is a moral, intellectual and responsible being. The manhood of the slave is conceded. It is admitted in the fact that Southern statute books are covered with enactments forbidding, under severe fines and penalties, the teaching of the slave to read or to write.—When you can point to any such laws, in reference to the beasts of the field, then I may consent to argue the manhood of the slave. When the dogs in your streets, when the fowls of the air, when the cattle on your hills, when the fish of the sea, and the reptiles that crawl, shall be unable to distinguish the slave from a brute, *then* will I argue with you that the slave is a man!

For the present, it is enough to affirm the equal manhood of the negro race. Is it not astonishing that, while we are ploughing, planting and reaping, using all kinds of mechanical tools; erecting houses, constructing bridges, building ships, working in metals of brass, iron, copper, silver and gold; that, while we are reading, writing and cyphering, acting as clerks, merchants and secretaries, having among us lawyers, doctors, ministers, poets, authors, editors, orators and teachers; that, while we are engaged in all manner of enterprises common to other men, digging gold in California, capturing the whale in the Pacific, feeding sheep and cattle on the hill-side, living, moving, acting, thinking, planning, living in families as husbands, wives and children, and, above all, confessing and worshipping the Christian's God, and looking hopefully for life and immortality beyond the grave, we are called upon to prove that we are men!

<hr>

5. William Lloyd Garrison's words from the first issue of his abolitionist paper, *The Liberator*, upon its appearance in 1831; Douglass became an avid subscriber in New Bedford, Massachusetts, soon after his escape from slavery.

Would you have me argue that man is entitled to liberty? that he is the rightful owner of his own body? You have already declared it. Must I argue the wrongfulness of slavery? Is that a question for republicans? Is it to be settled by the rules of logic and argumentation, as a matter beset with great difficulty, involving a doubtful application of the principle of justice, hard to be understood? How should I look to-day, in the presence of Americans, dividing, and subdividing a discourse, to show that men have a natural right to freedom? speaking of it relatively, and positively, negatively, and affirmatively. To do so, would be to make myself ridiculous, and to offer an insult to your understanding.—There is not a man beneath the canopy of heaven, that does not know that slavery is wrong *for him.*

What, am I to argue that it is wrong to make men brutes, to rob them of their liberty, to work them without wages, to keep them ignorant of their relations to their fellow men, to beat them with stick, to flay their flesh with the lash, to load their limbs with irons, to hunt them with dogs, to sell them at auction, to sunder their families, to knock out their teeth, to burn their flesh, to starve them into obedience and submission to their masters? Must I argue that a system thus marked with blood, and stained with pollution, is *wrong?* No I will not. I have better employment for my time and strength, than such arguments would imply.

What, then, remains to be argued? Is it that slavery is not divine; that God did not establish it; that our doctors of divinity are mistaken? There is blasphemy in the thought. That which is inhuman, cannot be divine! *Who* can reason on such a proposition? They that can, may; I cannot. The time for such argument is past.

At a time like this, scorching irony, not convincing argument, is needed. O! had I the ability, and could I reach the nation's ear, I would, to-day, pour out a fiery stream of biting ridicule, blasting reproach, withering sarcasm, and stern rebuke. For it is not light that is needed, but fire; it is not the gentle shower, but thunder. We need the storm, the whirlwind, and the earthquake. The feeling of the nation must be quickened; the conscience of the nation must be roused; the propriety of the nation must be startled; the hypocrisy of the nation must be exposed; and its crimes against God and man must be proclaimed and denounced.

What, to the American slave, is your 4th of July? I answer; a day that reveals to him, more than all other days in the year, the gross injustice and cruelty to which he is the constant victim. To him, your celebration is a sham; your boasted liberty, an unholy license; your national greatness, swelling vanity; your sounds of rejoicing are empty and heartless; your denunciations of tyrants, brass fronted impudence; your shouts of liberty and equality, hollow mockery; your prayers and hymns, your sermons and thanksgivings, with all your religious parade, and solemnity, are, to him, mere bombast, fraud, deception, impiety, and hypocrisy—a thin veil to cover up crimes which would disgrace a nation of savages. There is not a nation on the earth guilty of practices, more shocking and bloody, than are the people of these United States, at this very hour.

Go where you may, search where you will, roam through all the monarchies and despotisms of the old world, travel through South America, search out every abuse, and when you have found the last, lay your facts by the side of the every day practices of this nation, and you will say with me, that, for revolting barbarity and shameless hypocrisy, America reigns without a rival.

Study Questions

1. What tone did Douglass employ at the very beginning of his speech? In what way was this part of a conscious oratorical strategy? Which parts of the speech might have been most uncomfortable or even offensive to his audience?

2. What were Douglass's feelings toward the Declaration of Independence? To what degree was he or was he not an American patriot?

3. Fully explain why Douglass cites the scriptural passage on the "rivers of Babylon." What was his criticism of American Christians in the 1850s? What can you surmise about his own religious beliefs?

4. Analyze this speech in terms of its literary quality. How did a former slave develop such power and eloquence as a writer? What can you imagine of Frederick Douglass's ability as a public speaker?

GEORGE FITZHUGH

A Defense of Slavery (1854)

In the 1830s abolitionists increasingly began to assault slavery on moral grounds, an approach that naturally put slave owners on the defensive. The South's reaction in many cases was to defend—with varying degrees of sophistication—that region's "peculiar institution." Slavery's apologists employed biblical justifications (the Old Testament includes numerous rules governing the treatment of Jewish and non-Jewish slaves), "scientific racism" (allegedly scientific evidence "proved" black inferiority), and history (after all, slavery dated from ancient times and so must be legitimate) in their published writings. A number of southern politicians and intellectuals began to make the case that slavery was not a necessary evil necessitated by their region's labor needs, as they had previously argued, but that the institution was in reality a "positive good," beneficial to slaves as well as masters, given the paternalistic instincts of benevolent white slave owners.

One of slavery's most interesting and notorious defenders was George Fitzhugh (1806–1881), an attorney with close ties to his native Virginia's planter elite. Fitzhugh lived most of his life in Port Royal, Caroline County, Virginia, an area where the population was composed mostly of slaves. His close observations of his own slaves, combined with his voracious and wide-ranging reading, were the basis for the contents of his book Sociology for the South, *published in 1854. Most notably, Fitzhugh defended slavery by attacking the free society of the North. In the excerpts that follow, consider the role that Fitzhugh's writings, along with famous abolitionist works like* Uncle Tom's Cabin, *might have played in elevating sectional tensions and pushing the nation closer to civil war.*

From George Fitzhugh, *Sociology for the South, or the Failure of Free Society*, (Richmond, Va.: A. Morris, 1854), 82–85, 88, 92, 94–95.

We have already stated that we should not attempt to introduce any new theories of government and of society, but merely try to justify old ones, so far as we could deduce such theories from ancient and almost universal practices. Now it has been the practice in all countries and in all ages, in some degree, to accommodate the amount and character of government control to the wants, intelligence, and moral capacities of the nations or individuals to be governed. A highly moral and intellectual people, like the free citizens of ancient Athens, are best governed by a democracy. For a less moral and intellectual one, a limited and constitutional monarchy will answer. For a people either very ignorant or very wicked, nothing short of military despotism will suffice. So among individuals, the most moral and well-informed members of society require no other government than law. They are capable of reading and understanding the law, and have sufficient self-control and virtuous disposition to obey it. Children cannot be governed by more law; first, because they do not understand it, and secondly, because they are so much under the influence of impulse, passion and appetite, that they want sufficient self-control to be deterred or governed by the distant and doubtful penalties of the law. They must be constantly controlled by parents or guardians, whose will and orders shall stand in the place of law for them. Very wicked men must be put into penitentiaries; lunatics into asylums, and the most wild of them into straight jackets, just as the most wicked of the sane are manacled with irons; and idiots must have committees to govern and take care of them. Now, it is clear the Athenian democracy would not suit a negro nation, nor will the government of mere law suffice for the individual negro. He is but a grown up child, and must be governed as a child, not as a lunatic or criminal. The master occupies towards him the place of parent or guardian. We shall not dwell on this view, for no one will differ with us who thinks as we do of the negro's capacity, and we might argue till dooms-day, in vain, with those who have a high opinion of the negro's moral and intellectual capacity.

Secondly. The negro is improvident; will not lay up in summer for the wants of winter; will not accumulate in youth for the exigencies of age. He would become an insufferable burden to society. Society has the right to prevent this, and can only do so by subjecting him to domestic slavery.

In the last place, the negro race is inferior to the white race, and living in their midst, they would be far outstripped or outwitted in the chase of free competition. Gradual but certain extermination would be their fate. We presume the maddest abolitionist does not think the negro's providence of habits and money-making capacity at all to compare to those of the whites. This defect of character would alone justify enslaving him, if he is to remain here. In Africa or the West Indies, he would become idolatrous, savage and cannibal, or be devoured by savages and cannibals. At the North he would freeze or starve.

We would remind those who deprecate and sympathize with negro slavery, that his slavery hero relieves him from a far more cruel slavery in Africa, or from idolatry and cannibalism, and every brutal vice and crime that can disgrace humanity; and that it christianizes, protects, supports and civilizes him; that it governs him far better than free laborers at the North are governed. There, wife-murder has become a mere holiday pastime; and where so many wives are murdered, almost all must be brutally treated. Nay, more: men who kill their wives or treat them brutally, must be ready for all kinds of crime, and the calendar of crime at the North proves the inference to be correct. Negroes never kill their wives. If it be objected that legally they have no wives, then we reply, that in an experience of more than forty years, we never yet heard of a negro man killing a negro woman. Our negroes are not only better off as to physical comfort than free laborers, but their moral condition is better.

* * *

Would the abolitionists approve of a system of society that set white children free, and remitted them at the age of fourteen, males and females, to all the rights, both as to person and property, which belong to adults? Would it be criminal or praiseworthy to do so? Criminal, of course. Now, are the average of negroes equal in information, in native intelligence, in prudence or providence, to well-informed white children of fourteen? We who have lived with them for forty years, think not. The competition of the world would be too much for the children. They would be cheated out of their property and debased in their morals. Yet they would meet every where with sympathizing friends of their own color, ready to aid, advise and assist them. The negro would be exposed to the same competition and greater temptations, with no greater ability to contend with them, with these additional difficulties. He would be welcome nowhere; meet with thousands of enemies and no friends. If he went North, the white laborers would kick him and cuff him, and drive him out of employment. If he went to Africa, the savages would cook him and eat him. If he went to the West Indies, they would not let him in, or if they did, they would soon make of him a savage and idolater.

* * *

But far the worst feature of modern civilization, which is the civilization of free society, remains to be exposed. Whilst labor-saving processes have probably lessened by one half, in the last century, the amount of work needed for comfortable support, the free laborer is compelled by capital and competition to work more than he ever did before, and is less comfortable. The organization of society cheats him of his earnings, and those earnings go to swell the vulgar pomp and pageantry of the ignorant millionaires, who are the only great of the present day. These reflections might seem, at first view, to have little connexion with negro slavery; but it is well for us of the South not to be deceived by the tinsel glare and glitter of free society, and to employ ourselves in doing our duty at home, and studying the past, rather than in insidious rivalry of the expensive pleasures and pursuits of men whose sentiments and whose aims are low, sensual and grovelling.

* * *

We deem this peculiar question of negro slavery of very little importance. The issue is made throughout the world on the general subject of slavery in the abstract. The argument has commenced. One set of ideas will govern and control after awhile the civilized world. Slavery will every where be abolished, or every where be re-instituted. We think the opponents of practical, existing slavery, are estopped by their own admission; nay, that unconsciously, as socialists, they are the defenders and propagandists of slavery, and have furnished the only sound arguments on which its defence and justification can he rested. We have introduced the subject of negro slavery to afford us a better opportunity to disclaim the purpose of reducing the white man any where to the condition of negro slaves here. It would be very unwise and unscientific to govern white men as you would negroes. Every shade and variety of slavery has existed in the world. In some cases there has been much of legal regulation, much restraint of the master's authority; in others, none at all. The character of slavery necessary to protect the whites in Europe should be much milder than negro slavery, for slavery is only needed to protect the white man, whilst it is more necessary for the government of the negro even than for his protection. But even negro slavery should not be outlawed. We might and should have laws in Virginia, as in Louisiana, to make the master subject to presentment by the grand jury and to punishment, for any inhuman or improper treatment or neglect of his slave.

We abhor the doctrine of the "Types of Mankind;"[1] first, because it is at war with scripture, which teaches us that the whole human race is descended from a common parentage; and, secondly, because it encourages and incites brutal masters to treat negroes, not as weak, ignorant and dependent brethren, but as wicked beasts, without the pale of humanity.[2] The Southerner is the negro's friend, his only friend. Let no intermeddling abolitionist, no refined philosophy, dissolve this friendship.

Study Questions

1. According to Fitzhugh, what are the chief benefits of slavery to the slaves? In what fundamental ways did George Fitzhugh hold racist views toward blacks?

2. What did Fitzhugh see as the major problems confronting free northern laborers in the 1850s? Is his analysis valid? To what extent did Fitzhugh criticize capitalism itself?

3. Fitzhugh claims that "slavery will everywhere be abolished, or everywhere be reinstituted." How would readers outside of the South likely have responded to this statement? How does Fitzhugh anticipate or even help provoke the Civil War?

4. Fitzhugh says in closing, "The Southerner is the negro's friend, his only friend." Fully evaluate this statement. To what degree did Fitzhugh hold sympathetic views toward African Americans? To what extent would African Americans welcome his sympathy?

1. The then-widespread theory of polygenism, positing that the races of humankind have separate, unrelated origins, as opposed to monogenism, positing a single origin for all of humankind (as espoused in the Bible's account of Adam and Eve, or in Charles Darwin's single-origin hypothesis described in *The Descent of Man*).
2. That is, outside the bounds of humanity.

SENECA FALLS CONVENTION

Declaration of Sentiments (1848)

The American women's rights movement arguably began in 1848 when a hand-ful of activists called a convention to assemble in a Methodist church in Seneca Falls, New York. Lucretia Mott (1793–1880), a Quaker minister, and Elizabeth Cady Stanton (1815–1902), an abolitionist, were the foremost leaders in this effort. Both were representative of educated, middle-class women who had been prepared in church and the antislavery movement to take leading roles in additional antebellum reform causes. Women from such backgrounds were increasingly likely to push against the constraints imposed upon them in a male-dominated society.

About three hundred people showed up for the two-day conference that opened on July 19; since men were present, in deference to established tradition Lucretia Mott's husband chaired the proceedings. Delegates debated and approved a dozen women's rights resolutions. At the conference's conclusion, sixty-eight women and thirty-two men signed the Declaration of Sentiments, which was authored primar-ily by Elizabeth Cady Stanton. As you read this document, ponder the wisdom and effectiveness of Stanton's modeling it on Thomas Jefferson's Declaration of Inde-pendence. The Seneca Falls meeting enjoyed national press coverage and inspired subsequent feminist efforts. Not until 1920 would one of its major demands—full voting equality for women—reach fruition with the adoption of the Nineteenth Amendment.

From Elizabeth Cady Stanton, Susan B. Anthony, and Matilda Joslyn Gage, eds., "Seneca Falls Declaration of Sentiments," in *History of Woman Suffrage* (New York: Fowler & Wells, 1881).

When, in the course of human events, it becomes necessary for one por-tion of the family of man to assume among the people of the earth a position different from that which they have hitherto occupied, but one to which the laws of nature and of nature's God entitle them, a decent respect to the opinions of mankind requires that they should declare the causes that impel them to such a course.

We hold these truths to be self-evident: that all men and women are created equal; that they are endowed by their Creator with certain inalienable rights; that among these are life, liberty, and the pursuit of happiness; that to secure these rights governments are instituted, deriving their just powers from the consent of the governed. Whenever any form of government becomes destructive of these ends, it is the right of those who suffer from it to refuse allegiance to it, and to insist upon the institution of a new government, laying its foundation on such principles, and organizing its powers in such form, as to them shall seem most likely to effect their safety and happiness. Prudence indeed, will dictate that governments long established should not be changed for light and transient causes; and accordingly all experience hath shown that mankind are more disposed to suffer, while evils are sufferable, than to right themselves by abolishing the forms to which they were accustomed. But when a long train of abuses and usurpations, pursuing invariably the same object evinces a design to reduce them under absolute despotism, it is their duty to throw off such government, and to provide new guards for their future security. Such has been the patient sufferance of the women under this government, and such is now the necessity which constrains them to demand the equal station to which they are entitled.

The history of mankind is a history of repeated injuries and usurpations on the part of man toward woman, having in direct object the establishment of an absolute tyranny over her. To prove this, let facts be submitted to a candid world.

He has never permitted her to exercise her inalienable right to the elective franchise.

He has compelled her to submit to laws, in the formation of which she had no voice.

He has withheld from her rights which are given to the most ignorant and degraded men—both natives and foreigners.

Having deprived her of this first right of a citizen, the elective franchise, thereby leaving her without representation in the halls of legislation, he has oppressed her on all sides.

He has made her, if married, in the eye of the law, civilly dead.

He has taken from her all right in property, even to the wages she earns.

He has made her, morally, an irresponsible being, as she can commit many crimes with impunity, provided they can be done in the presence of her husband. In the covenant of marriage, she is compelled to promise obedience to her husband, he becoming, to all intents and purposes, her master—the law giving him power to deprive her of her liberty and to administer chastisement.

He has so framed the laws of divorce, as to what shall be the proper causes, and in case of separation, to whom the guardianship of the children shall be given, as to be wholly regardless of the happiness of women—the law, in all cases, going upon a false supposition of the supremacy of man, giving all power into his hands.

After depriving her of all rights as a married woman, if single, and the owner of property, he has taxed her to support a government which recognizes her only when her property can be made profitable to it.

He has monopolized nearly all the profitable employments, and from those she is permitted to follow, she receives but a scanty remuneration. He closes against her all the avenues to wealth and distinction which he considers most honorable to himself. As a teacher of theology, medicine, or law, she is not known.

He has denied her the facilities for obtaining a thorough education, all colleges being closed against her.

He allows her in Church, as well as State, but a subordinate position, claiming Apostolic authority[1] for her exclusion from the ministry, and, with some exceptions, from any public participation in the affairs of the Church.

He has created a false public sentiment by giving to the world a different code of morals for men and women, by which moral delinquencies which exclude women from society, are not only tolerated, but deemed of little account in man.

He has usurped the prerogative of Jehovah himself, claiming it as his right to assign for her a sphere of action, when that belongs to her conscience and to her God.

He has endeavored, in every way that he could, to destroy her confidence in her own powers, to lessen her self-respect, and to make her willing to lead a dependent and abject life.

Now, in view of this entire disfranchisement of one-half the people of this country, their social and religious degradation—in view of the unjust laws above mentioned, and because women do feel themselves aggrieved, oppressed, and fraudulently deprived of their most sacred rights, we insist that they have immediate admission to all the rights and privileges which belong to them as citizens of the United States.

In entering upon the great work before us, we anticipate no small amount of misconception, misrepresentation, and ridicule; but we shall use every instrumentality within our power to effect our object. We shall employ agents, circulate tracts, petition the State and National legislatures, and endeavor to enlist the pulpit and the press in our behalf. We hope this Convention will be followed by a series of Conventions embracing every part of the county.

———————

Whereas, The great precept of nature is conceded to be, that "man shall pursue his own true and substantial happiness." Blackstone in his Commentaries[2] remarks, that this law of Nature being coeval with mankind, and dictated by God himself, is of course superior in obligation to any other. It is binding over all the globe, in all countries and at all times; no human laws are of any validity if contrary

1. Authority derived from that of the original twelve apostles of Jesus.
2. Sir William Blackstone published his seminal commentaries on English common law between 1765 and 1769.

to this, and such of them as are valid, derive all their force, and all their validity, and all their authority, mediately and immediately, from this original; therefore,

Resolved, That such laws as conflict, in any way, with the true and substantial happiness of woman, are contrary to the great precept of nature and of no validity, for this is "superior in obligation to any other."

Resolved, That all laws which prevent woman from occupying such a station in society as her conscience shall dictate, or which place her in a position inferior to that of man, are contrary to the great precept of nature, and therefore of no force or authority.

Resolved, That woman is man's equal—was intended to be so by the Creator, and the highest good of the race demands that she should be recognized as such.

Resolved, That the women of this country ought to be enlightened in regard to the laws under which they live, that they may no longer publish their degradation by declaring themselves satisfied with their present position, nor their ignorance, by asserting that they have all the rights they want.

Resolved, That inasmuch as man, while claiming for himself intellectual superiority, does accord to woman moral superiority, it is pre-eminently his duty to encourage her to speak and teach, as she has an opportunity, in all religious assemblies.

Resolved, That the same amount of virtue, delicacy, and refinement of behavior that is required of woman in the social state, should also be required of man, and the same transgressions should be visited with equal severity on both man and woman.

Resolved, That the objection of indelicacy and impropriety, which is so often brought against woman when she addresses a public audience, comes with a very ill-grace from those who encourage, by their attendance, her appearance on the stage, in the concert, or in feats of the circus.

Resolved, That woman has too long rested satisfied in the circumscribed limits which corrupt customs and a perverted application of the Scriptures have marked out for her, and that it is time she should move in the enlarged sphere which her great Creator has assigned her.

Resolved, That it is the duty of the women of this country to secure to themselves their sacred right to the elective franchise.

Resolved, That the equality of human rights results necessarily from the fact of the identity of the race in capabilities and responsibilities.

Resolved, therefore, That, being invested by the Creator with the same capabilities, and the same consciousness of responsibility for their exercise, it is demonstrably the right and duty of woman, equally with man, to promote every righteous cause by every righteous means; and especially in regard to the great subjects of morals and religion, it is self-evidently her right to participate with her brother in teaching them, both in private and in public, by writing and by speaking, by any instrumentalities proper to be used, and in any assemblies proper to be held; and this being a self-evident truth growing out of the divinely implanted principles of human nature, any custom or authority adverse to it, whether modern or wearing the hoary sanction of antiquity, is to be regarded as a self-evident falsehood, and at war with mankind.

———————

R *esolved*, That the speedy success of our cause depends upon the zealous and untiring efforts of both men and women, for the overthrow of the monopoly of the pulpit, and for the securing to woman an equal participation with men in the various trades, professions, and commerce.

Study Questions

1. What are the most significant departures from the Declaration of Independence in the opening sections of this document? While Jefferson's document contains a whole series of sentences in which "he" refers to King George III, who is the "he" whose offenses are cited in the Declaration of Sentiments? How much difference does it make?

2. What is the evidence in this document that many of women's grievances in this era were church-related? How might churchgoing women have encountered discrimination in religious settings?

3. Why does this Declaration place so much emphasis on the right to vote? Who could or could not vote in 1848? What other forms of equality were women demanding?

4. Analyze the use of the term "sentiments" in the title of the statement. How would you imagine the Declaration of Sentiments was received by the press and general public upon its adoption?

SOJOURNER TRUTH

Ar'n't I[1] a Woman? (1851)

Isabella Baumfree (ca. 1797–1883) was born a slave in upstate New York. By the time she was freed in 1827, she had been sold a number of times, married, and had five children. Soon after her emancipation, Isabella converted to Methodism and joined a number of unorthodox charismatic religious groups. In 1843, at the age of forty-five or so, she began calling herself Sojourner Truth—a name she chose as she embarked upon a journey around the Northeast proclaiming that the Second Coming was near.

During this time, Truth became involved in both the women's rights and the antislavery movements, befriending leading abolitionists such as Frederick Douglass, William Lloyd Garrison, and Harriet Beecher Stowe. In May 1851, Truth traveled to Akron, Ohio, to attend the Ohio Women's Rights Convention. On the second day of the convention, a number of conservative ministers disrupted the proceedings, arguing that the teachings of the Bible and the "superior intellect" of men necessitated women's subordination. As the disapproval of these authority figures deeply unsettled some of the attendees, Truth rose from her seat and walked to the stage. According to Frances Dana Gage, the presiding officer of the convention, when Truth took the podium "the tumult subsided at once, and every eye was fixed on this almost Amazon form, which stood nearly six feet high, head erect, and eyes piercing the upper air like one in a dream. At her first word there was a profound hush." Truth's presentation, according to one eyewitness, was "one of the most unique and interesting speeches of the Convention," adding that "it is impossible to transfer it to paper, or convey any adequate idea of the effect it produced upon the audience." Although it can be difficult to appreciate in the written text, Truth used humor to soften the fact that she was directly challenging the authority of these ministers. In fact, according to one reporter, "the power and wit of this remarkable woman convulsed the audience with laughter."

No exact transcription of the speech exists; Truth herself gave the speech extemporaneously and no one bothered to take down exactly what she said. The version reprinted here—as recalled and written by Gage twelve years later—should be considered an approximation of the speech.

---

1. Most likely, Truth used the word "ain't."

Well, chilern, whar dar is so much racket dar must be something out o'kilter. I tink dat 'twixt de niggers of de Souf and de women at de Norf[2] all a talkin' 'bout rights, de white men will be in a fix pretty soon. But what's all dis here talkin' 'bout? Dat man ober dar say dat women needs to be helped into carriages, and lifted ober ditches, and to have de best place every whar. Nobody eber help me into carriages, or ober mud puddles, or gives me any best place, and ar'n't I a woman? Look at me! Look at my arm! I have plowed, and planted, and gathered into barns, and no man could head me—and ar'n't I a woman? I could work as much and eat as much as a man (when I could get it), and bear de lash as well—and ar'n't I a woman? I have borne thirteen chilern and seen 'em mos' all sold off into slavery, and when I cried out with a mother's grief, none but Jesus heard—and ar'n't I a woman? Den dey talks 'bout dis ting in de head—what dis dey call it? ["Intellect," whispered some one near.] Dat's it honey. What's dat got to do with women's rights or niggers' rights? If my cup won't hold but a pint and yourn holds a quart, would n't ye be mean not to let me have my little half-measure full?

Den dat little man in black dar,[3] he say women can't have as much rights as man, cause Christ wa'n't a woman. Whar did your Christ come from? From God and a woman. Man had nothing to do with him. . . . If de fust woman God ever made was strong enough to turn the world upside down, all 'lone, dese togedder ought to be able to turn it back and get it right side up again, and now dey is asking to do it, de men better let em. 'Bleeged to ye for hearin' on me, and now ole Sojourner ha'n't got nothing more to say.

Study Questions

1. What connection does Truth draw between northern women and southern slaves?

2. To what sources of moral authority does Truth appeal?

3. How do you think Truth tailored her message to her audience?

---

2. "Souf" is South and "Norf" is North; this transcription of Truth's dialect was made by the president of the convention, Frances D. Gage; what she renders as "ar'n't," contemporary writers would probably spell "ain't."
3. One of the ministers who opposed women's rights.

Mississippi Black Code (1865) and the Fourteenth Amendment (1868)

Before the end of 1865, slavery was abolished entirely by the ratification of the Thirteenth Amendment to the U.S. Constitution. During the earliest phase of Reconstruction, southern state governments moved as quickly as possible to codify the status of roughly four million former slaves. Under President Andrew Johnson's Reconstruction plan, black men were denied the right to vote. As a result, the governments elected in the former Confederate states were dominated by planters— the very same social elite that had wielded political power in the antebellum era and through the war. Unsurprisingly, southern legislatures controlled by the planters and their allies enacted so-called Black Codes designed to regulate the activities of the former slaves.

Mississippi, which had a majority black population, took the lead. Its Black Code, enacted on November 25, 1865, would later be judged one of the harshest in terms of its treatment of the freedmen. As you read it, consider its underlying motives. The Black Codes sparked a fierce reaction in the North, ultimately leading to the victory of the Radical Republicans in the 1866 congressional elections and to the subsequent enactment of the Fourteenth Amendment. As you read the amendment's crucial first section, consider its implications for true racial change in the South.

From Walter L. Fleming, ed., "Mississippi Black Codes," in *Documentary History of Reconstruction*, vol. 1 (Cleveland: Arthur H. Clark Company, 1960), 282-290. From "Fourteenth Amendment" (Cornell University, Legal Information Institute), www.law.cornell.edu.

Mississippi Black Code

CIVIL RIGHTS OF FREEDMEN IN MISSISSIPPI

Laws of Mississippi, 1865, p. 82. Mississippi, South Carolina, and Tennessee gave fewer civil rights to the blacks than the other Southern states gave.

[November 25, 1865]

Sec. 1. *Be it enacted*, . . That all freedmen, free negroes, and mulattoes may sue and be sued, implead and be impleaded, in all the courts of law and equity of this State, and may acquire personal property, and choses in action,[1] by descent or purchase, and may dispose of the same in the same manner and to the same extent that white persons may: *Provided*, That the provisions of this section shall not be so construed as to allow any freedman, free negro, or mulatto to rent or lease any lands or tenements except in incorporated cities or towns, in which places the corporate authorities shall control the same.

Sec. 2. . . . All freedmen, free negroes, and mulattoes may intermarry with each other, in the same manner and under the same regulations that are provided by law for white persons: *Provided*, That the clerk of probate shall keep separate records of the same.

Sec. 3. . . . All freedmen, free negroes, or mulattoes who do now and have herebefore lived and cohabited together as husband and wife shall be taken and held in law as legally married, and the issue shall be taken and held as legitimate for all purposes; that it shall not be lawful for any freedman, free negro, or mulatto to intermarry with any white person; nor for any white person to intermarry with any freedman, free negro, or mulatto; and any person who shall so intermarry, shall be deemed guilty of felony, and on conviction thereof shall be confined in the State penitentiary for life; and those shall be deemed freedmen, free negroes, and mulattoes who are of pure negro blood, and those descended from a negro to the third generation, inclusive, though one ancestor in each generation may have been a white person.

Sec. 4. . . . In addition to cases in which freedmen, free negroes, and mulattoes are now by law competent witnesses, freedmen, free negroes, or mulattoes shall be competent in civil cases, when a party or parties to the suit, either plaintiff or plaintiffs, defendant or defendants; also in cases where freedmen, free negroes, and mulattoes is or are either plaintiff or plaintiffs, defendant or defendants, and a white person or white persons, is or are the opposing party or parties, plaintiff or plaintiffs, defendant or defendants. They shall also be competent witnesses in all criminal prosecutions where the crime charged is alleged to have been com-

---

1. That is, property rights in intangible things, enforceable by court or legal action.

mitted by a white person upon or against the person or property of a freedman, free negro, or mulatto: *Provided*, that in all cases said witnesses shall be examined in open court, on the stand; except, however, they may be examined before the grand jury, and shall in all cases be subject to the rules and tests of the common law as to competency and credibility.

* * *

Sec. 6. . . . All contracts for labor made with freedmen, free negroes, and mulattoes for a longer period than one month shall be in writing, and in duplicate, attested and read to said freedman, free negro, or mulatto by a beat, city or county officer, or two disinterested white persons of the county in which the labor is to be performed, of which each party shall have one; and said contracts shall be taken and held as entire contracts, and if the laborer shall quit the service of the employer before the expiration of his term of service, without good cause, he shall forfeit his wages for that year up to the time of quitting.

Sec. 7. . . . Every civil officer shall, and every person may, arrest and carry back to his or her legal employer any freedman, free negro, or mulatto who shall have quit the service of his or her employer before the expiration of his or her term of service without good cause; and said officer and person shall be entitled to receive for arresting and carrying back every deserting employe aforesaid the sum of five dollars, and ten cents per mile from the place of arrest to the place of delivery; and the same shall be paid by the employer, and held as a set-off for so much against the wages of said deserting employe: *Provided*, that said arrested party, after being so returned, may appeal to the justice of the peace or member of the board of police of the county, who, on notice to the alleged employer, shall try summarily whether said appellant is legally employed by the alleged employer, and has good cause to quit said employer; either party shall have the right of appeal to the county court, pending which the alleged deserter shall be remanded to the alleged employer or otherwise disposed of, as shall be right and just; and the decision of the county court shall be final.

* * *

MISSISSIPPI APPRENTICE LAW

> *Laws of Mississippi, 1865*, p. 86. Alabama had a similar law; other states, except South Carolina, had practically the same laws for both races. Alabama and Mississippi had distinct laws for the whites.

> [November 22, 1865]

Sec. 1. . . . It shall be the duty of all sheriffs, justices of the peace, and other civil officers of the several counties in this State, to report to the probate courts of their respective counties semi-annually, at the January and July terms of said courts, all freedmen, free negroes, and mulattoes, under the age of eighteen, in their respective counties, beats, or districts, who are orphans, or whose parent or parents have not the means or who refuse to provide for and support said minors; and thereupon it shall be the duty of said probate court to order the clerk of said court to apprentice said minors to some competent and suitable person, on such terms as the court may direct, having a particular care to the interest of said minor: *Provided*, that the former owner of said minors shall have the preference when, in the opinion of the court, he or she shall be a suitable person for that purpose.

Sec. 2. . . . The said court shall be fully satisfied that the person or persons to whom said minor shall be apprenticed shall be a suitable person to have the charge and care of said minor, and fully to protect the interest of said minor. The said court shall require the said master or mistress to execute bond and security, payable to the State of Mississippi, conditioned that he or she shall furnish said minor with sufficient food and clothing; to treat said minor humanely; furnish medical attention in case of sickness; teach, or cause to be taught, him or her to read and write, if under fifteen years old, and will conform to any law that may be hereafter passed for the regulation of the duties and relation of master and apprentice. . .

Sec. 3. . . . in the management and control of said apprentices, said master or mistress shall have the power to inflict such moderate corporal chastisement as a father or guardian is allowed to inflict on his or her child or ward at common law: *Provided*, that in no case shall cruel or inhuman punishment be inflicted.

Sec. 4. . . . if any apprentice shall leave the employment of his or her master or mistress, without his or her consent, said master or mistress may pursue and recapture said apprentice, and bring him or her before any justice of the peace of the county, whose duty it shall be to remand said apprentice to the service of his or her master or mistress; and in the event of a refusal on the part of said apprentice so to return, then said justice shall commit said apprentice to the jail of said county, on failure to give bond, to the next term of the county court; and it shall be the duty of said court at the first term thereafter to investigate said case, and if the court shall be of opinion that said apprentice left the employment of his or her master or mistress without good cause, to order him or her to be punished, as provided for the punishment of hired freedmen, as may be from time to time provided for by law for desertion, until he or she shall agree to return to the service of his or her master or mistress: . . if the court shall believe that said apprentice had good cause to quit his said master or mistress, the court shall discharge said apprentice from said indenture, and also enter a judgment against the master or mistress for not more than one hundred dollars, for the use and benefit of said apprentice. . .

* * *

MISSISSIPPI VAGRANT LAW

Laws of Mississippi, 1865, p. 90. Applies to both races. There were similar laws in the other Southern states.

[November 24, 1865]

Sec. 1. *Be it enacted*, etc., . . That all rogues and vagabonds, idle and dissipated persons, beggars, jugglers, or persons practicing unlawful games or plays, runaways, common drunkards, common night-walkers, pilferers, lewd, wanton, or lascivious persons, in speech or behavior, common railers and brawlers, persons who neglect their calling or employment, misspend what they earn, or do not provide for the support of themselves or their families, or dependants, and all other idle and disorderly persons, including all who neglect all lawful business, habitually misspend their time by frequenting houses of ill-fame, gaming-houses, or tippling shops, shall be deemed and considered vagrants, under the provisions of this act, and upon conviction thereof shall be fined not exceeding one hundred dollars, with all accruing costs, and be imprisoned, at the discretion of the court, not exceeding ten days.

Sec. 2. . . . . All freedmen, free negroes and mulattoes in this State, over the age of eighteen years, found on the second Monday in January, 1866, or thereafter, with no lawful employment or business, or found unlawfully assembling themselves together, either in the day or night time, and all white persons so assembling themselves with freedmen, free negroes or mulattoes, or usually associating with freedmen, free negroes or mulattoes, on terms of equality, or living in adultery or fornication with a freed woman, free negro or mulatto, shall be deemed vagrants, and on conviction thereof shall be fined in a sum not exceeding, in the case of a freedman, free negro, or mulatto, fifty dollars, and a white man two hundred dollars, and imprisoned at the discretion of the court, the free negro not exceeding ten days, and the white man not exceeding six months.

* * *

Sec. 7. . . . . If any freedman, free negro, or mulatto shall fail or refuse to pay any tax levied according to the provisions of . . . this act, it shall be *prima facie* evidence of vagrancy, and it shall be the duty of the sheriff to arrest such freedman, free negro, or mulatto or such person refusing or neglecting to pay such tax, and proceed at once to hire for the shortest time such delinquent tax-payer to any one who will pay the said tax, with accruing costs, giving preference to the employer, if there be one.

CERTAIN OFFENSES OF FREEDMEN (MISSISSIPPI)

Laws of Mississippi, 1865, p. 195.

[November 29, 1865]

Sec. 1. *Be it enacted*, . . That no freedman, free negro or mulatto, not in the military service of the United States government, and not licensed so to do by the board of police of his or her county, shall keep or carry fire-arms of any kind, or any ammunition, dirk or bowie knife, and on conviction thereof in the county court shall be punished by fine, not exceeding ten dollars, and pay the costs of such proceedings, and all such arms or ammunition shall be forfeited to the informer; and it shall be the duty of every civil and military officer to arrest any freedman, free negro, or mulatto found with any such arms or ammunition, and cause him or her to be committed to trial in default of bail.

Sec. 2 . . . Any freedman, free negro, or mulatto committing riots, routs, affrays, trespasses, malicious mischief, cruel treatment to animals, seditious speeches, insulting gestures, language, or acts, or assaults on any person, disturbance of the peace, exercising the function of a minister of the Gospel without a license from some regularly organized church, vending spirituous or intoxicating liquors, or committing any other misdemeanor, the punishment of which is not specifically provided for by law, shall, upon conviction thereof in the county court, be fined not less than ten dollars, and not more than one hundred dollars, and may be imprisoned at the discretion of the court, not exceeding thirty days.

Sec. 3 . . . If any white person shall sell, lend, or give to any freedman, free negro, or mulatto any fire-arms, dirk or bowie knife, or ammunition, or any spirituous or intoxicating liquors, such person or persons so offending, upon conviction thereof in the county court of his or her county, shall be fined not exceeding fifty dollars, and may be imprisoned, at the discretion of the court, not exceeding thirty days . . .

Sec. 5 . . . If any freedman, free negro, or mulatto, convicted of any of the misdemeanors provided against in this act, shall fail or refuse for the space of five days, after conviction, to pay the fine and costs imposed, such person shall be hired out by the sheriff or other officer, at public outcry, to any white person who will pay said fine and all costs, and take said convict for the shortest time.

Amendment XIV

SECTION 1.

All persons born or naturalized in the United States, and subject to the jurisdiction thereof, are citizens of the United States and of the state wherein they reside.

No state shall make or enforce any law which shall abridge the privileges or immunities of citizens of the United States; nor shall any state deprive any person of life, liberty, or property, without due process of law; nor deny to any person within its jurisdiction the equal protection of the laws.

Study Questions

1. Under the Mississippi Black Code, what rights would blacks have that they had been denied as slaves? Which rights would they still be denied?

2. What is the major purpose of the apprentice and vagrancy sections of the Code? Who would most directly benefit from the application of these laws? Was slavery really abolished in Mississippi by 1865?

3. What parts of the Black Code are designed to control the behavior of whites? How can this be explained?

4. Imagine yourself a Union veteran from Ohio reading news of the passage of the Black Codes in the South. What would your response be? What effect would the Fourteenth Amendment have upon the Black Code of Mississippi?

HORACE GREELEY AND ABRAHAM LINCOLN

Exchange on Emancipation (1862)

Horace Greeley (1811–1872) founded the New York Tribune in 1841 and served as its editor for the next three decades, becoming one of the most influential journalists in the United States. In his writings and activities Greeley championed practically every major reform movement in the antebellum period, including women's rights, utopian socialism, temperance, and abolition. His strong anti-slavery views led him to oppose the Mexican-American War and the Kansas-Nebraska Act and made him one of the earliest champions of the new Republican party, which emerged when the Whig party fatally split over the issue of slavery's further spread. The Republicans fielded their first presidential candidate—John C. Frémont—in 1856 and captured the White House with Abraham Lincoln's candidacy four years later.

With Lincoln's victory and the coming of the Civil War, Greeley took a hard-line stand against the slaveholders he deemed to be the instigators of the rebellion. His editorial of August 19, 1862, "The Prayer of Twenty Millions," took the form of an open letter to the president, berating Lincoln for his timidity with regard to emancipation. Three days later Lincoln elaborated his own views on the subject of the Union's war objectives in a written response to Greeley that the president intended for full public consumption. What Greeley remained unaware of—and what Lincoln did not reveal—was that the president had recently drafted a preliminary proclamation to emancipate the slaves. Lincoln would wait to make it public until the favorable outcome of the Battle of Antietam, a month later. As you read this exchange, consider the political constraints under which Lincoln had to operate, and judge the extent to which he succeeded in clarifying his views on slavery and the war.

From Frank Moore, ed., "Correspondence between Horace Greeley and President Lincoln," in *The Rebellion Record* (New York: D. Van Nostrand, 1871), 480, 482–83.

THE PRAYER OF TWENTY MILLIONS.[1]

To Abraham Lincoln, President of the United States:

DEAR SIR: I do not intrude to tell you—for you must know already—that a great proportion of those who triumphed in your election, and of all who desire the unqualified suppression of the rebellion now desolating our country, are sorely disappointed and deeply pained by the policy you seem to be pursuing with regard to the slaves of rebels. I write only to set succinctly and unmistakably before you what we require, what we think we have a right to expect, and of what we complain.

* * *

II. We think you are strangely and disastrously remiss in the discharge of your official and imperative duty with regard to the emancipating provisions of the new Confiscation Act.[2] Those provisions were designed to fight Slavery with Liberty. They prescribe that men loyal to the Union, and willing to shed their blood in her behalf, shall no longer be held, with the nation's consent, in bondage to persistent, malignant traitors, who for twenty years have been plotting and for sixteen months have been fighting to divide and destroy our country. Why these traitors should be treated with tenderness by you, to the prejudice of the dearest rights of loyal men, we cannot conceive.

* * *

VIII. On the face of this wide earth, Mr. President, there is not one disinterested, determined, intelligent champion of the Union cause who does not feel that all attempts to put down the rebellion and at the same time uphold its inciting cause are preposterous and futile—that the rebellion, if crushed out to-morrow, would be renewed within a year if Slavery were left in full vigor—that army officers who remain to this day devoted to Slavery can at best be but half-way loyal to the Union—and that every hour of deference to Slavery is an hour of added and deepened peril to the Union. I appeal to the testimony of your Embassadors in Europe. It is freely at your service, not at mine. Ask them to tell you candidly whether the seeming subserviency of your policy to the slaveholding, slavery-upholding interest, is not the perplexity, the despair of statesmen of all parties, and be admonished by the general answer!

---

1. The approximate population of the free states.
2. The Second Confiscation Act had been passed by Congress on July 17, 1862.

IX. I close as I began with the statement that what an immense majority of the loyal millions of your countrymen require of you is a frank, declared, unqualified, ungrudging execution of the laws of the land, more especially of the Confiscation Act. That act gives freedom to the slaves of rebels coming within our lines, or whom those lines may at any time inclose—we ask you to render it due obedience by publicly requiring all your subordinates to recognise and obey it. The rebels are everywhere using the late anti-negro riots in the North, as they have long used your officers' treatment of negroes in the South, to convince the slaves that they have nothing to hope from a Union success—that we mean in that case to sell them into a bitter bondage to defray the cost of the war. Let them impress this as a truth on the great mass of their ignorant and credulous bondmen, and the Union will never be restored—never. We cannot conquer ten millions of people united in solid phalanx against us, powerfully aided by Northern sympathizers and European allies. We must have scouts, guides, spies, cooks, teamsters, diggers, and choppers from the blacks of the South, whether we allow them to fight for us or not, or we shall be baffled and repelled. As one of the millions who would gladly have avoided this struggle at any sacrifice but that of principle and honor, but who now feel that the triumph of the Union is indispensable not only to the existence of our country but to the well-being of mankind, I entreat you to render a hearty and unequivocal obedience to the law of the land.

> *Yours,*
> Horace Greeley.
> New-York, *August 19, 1869.*

PRESIDENT LINCOLN'S LETTER.

> Executive Mansion,
> Washington, August 22, 1869.

Hon. Horace Greeley:

Dear Sir: I have just read yours of the nineteenth, addressed to myself through the New-York *Tribune.* If there be in it any statements or assumptions of fact which I may know to be erroneous, I do not now and here controvert them. If there be in it any inferences which I may believe to be falsely drawn. I do not now and here argue against them. If there be perceptible in it an impatient and dictatorial tone, I waive it in deference to an old friend, whose heart I have always supposed to be right.

As to the policy I "seem to be pursuing," as you say, I have not meant to leave any one in doubt.

I would save the Union. I would save it the shortest way under the Constitution. The sooner the National authority can be restored, the nearer the Union will be "the Union as it was." If there be those who would not save the Union unless they could at the same time *save* Slavery, I do not agree with them. If there be those who would not save the Union unless they could at the same time *destroy* Slavery, I do not agree with them. My paramount object in this struggle *is* to save the Union, and is *not* either to save or destroy Slavery. If I could save the Union without freeing *any* slave. I would do it; and if I could save it by freeing *all* the slaves, I would do it; and if I could do it by freeing some and leaving others alone, I would also do that. What I do about Slavery and the colored race, I do because I believe it helps to save this Union; and what I forbear, I forbear because I do *not* believe it would help to save the Union. I shall do *less* whenever I shall believe what I am doing hurts the cause, and I shall do *more* whenever I shall believe doing more will help the cause. I shall try to correct errors when shown to be errors; and I shall adopt new views so fast as they shall appear to be true views. I have here stated my purpose according to my view of *official* duty, and I intend no modification of my oft-expressed *personal* wish that all men, everywhere, could be free.

Yours,
A. LINCOLN.

Study Questions

1. What is Greeley's major frustration with Lincoln's performance as war leader? How will emancipation, in Greeley's mind, advance the war effort?

2. To what extent do Greeley and Lincoln differ in their views on slavery and the Union? How might one read Lincoln's letter as an indication of his lack of concern about slavery? Would this be an accurate interpretation?

3. Why do you think Lincoln felt compelled to answer Greeley's editorial? Evaluate the truthfulness and effectiveness of the president's reply.

4. Lincoln states his willingness to "correct errors . . . and adopt new views." Is such willingness an important trait in a president or does it reveal a lack of belief and commitment to principle? Elaborate fully.

Declaration of Causes
of Secession (1860)

With the election of Abraham Lincoln in November 1860, for the first time in American history a man who had publicly proclaimed his moral opposition to slavery was poised to assume the presidency. After a decade of escalating sectional tension over the potential expansion of slavery, this result immediately triggered a national crisis. Nowhere was the crisis more palpable than in South Carolina. That state had revealed its radical leanings during Andrew Jackson's first term, when it had challenged the federal government over protective tariffs and threatened secession if its ability to nullify the Tariff of 1832 were not acknowledged. South Carolina's plantation-dominated economy always made it vulnerable to duties on imports, which would raise the prices its consumers paid for manufactured goods—hence its resistance to this kind of federal policy. Nothing had changed in the succeeding three decades in terms of South Carolina's basic interests. The 1860 census registered South Carolina's slave population at 57 percent, the highest of all fifteen slave-holding states. Not surprisingly, South Carolina felt most threatened by Lincoln's victory, whatever his reassurances that slavery would remain unhindered in the states where it was currently legal.

As it had done during the Nullification Crisis of 1832, South Carolina thereby took the lead in expressing its defiance of federal authority. A special state convention met and adopted an Ordinance of Secession on December 20, 1860. Six other slave states—all located in the Lower South—followed suit in the months leading up to Lincoln's inauguration on March 4, 1861. These seven states formed the Confederacy with its initial capital in Montgomery, Alabama. As you read the Declaration of Causes adopted by the secession convention, consider whether it made an effective case to justify South Carolina's departure from the federal union.

From Howard W. Preston, ed., *Documents Illustrative of American History, 1606–1863* (New York: G. P. Putnam's Sons, 1886), 305–12.

CONFEDERATE STATES OF AMERICA - DECLARATION OF THE IMMEDIATE CAUSES WHICH INDUCE AND JUSTIFY THE SECESSION OF SOUTH CAROLINA FROM THE FEDERAL UNION

The people of the State of South Carolina, in Convention assembled, on the 26th day of April, A.D., 1852, declared that the frequent violations of the Constitution of the United States, by the Federal Government, and its encroachments upon the reserved rights of the States, fully justified this State in then withdrawing from the Federal Union; but in deference to the opinions and wishes of the other slaveholding States, she forbore at that time to exercise this right. Since that time, these encroachments have continued to increase, and further forbearance ceases to be a virtue.

And now the State of South Carolina having resumed her separate and equal place among nations, deems it due to herself, to the remaining United States of America, and to the nations of the world, that she should declare the immediate causes which have led to this act.

* * *

In 1787, Deputies were appointed by the States to revise the Articles or Confederation, and on 17th September, 1787, these Deputies recommended for the adoption of the States, the Articles of Union, known as the Constitution of the United States.

* * *

By this Constitution, certain duties were imposed upon the several States, and the exercise of certain of their powers was restrained, which necessarily implied their continued existence as sovereign States. But to remove all doubt, an amendment[1] was added, which declared that the powers not delegated to the United States by the Constitution, nor prohibited by it to the States, are reserved to the States, respectively, or to the people. On the 23d May, 1788, South Carolina, by a Convention of her People, passed an Ordinance assenting to this Constitution, and afterwards altered her own Constitution, to conform herself to the obligations she had undertaken.

Thus was established, by compact between the States, a Government with definite objects and powers, limited to the express words of the grant. . . .

We hold that the Government thus established is subject to the two great principles asserted in the Declaration of Independence;[2] and we hold further, that the mode of its formation subjects it to a third fundamental principle, namely: the law of compact. We maintain that in every compact between two or more

---

1. That is, the 10th amendment.
2. These two principles are defined in the 1860 document as: "the right of a State to govern itself; and the right of a people to abolish a Government when it becomes destructive of the ends for which it was instituted."

parties, the obligation is mutual; that the failure of one of the contracting parties to perform a material part of the agreement, entirely releases the obligation of the other; and that where no arbiter is provided, each party is remitted to his own judgment to determine the fact of failure, with all its consequences.

In the present case, that fact is established with certainty. We assert that fourteen of the States have deliberately refused, for years past, to fulfill their constitutional obligations, and we refer to their own Statutes for the proof.

The Constitution of the United States, in its fourth Article, provides as follows: "No person held to service or labor in one State, under the laws thereof, escaping into another, shall, in consequence of any law or regulation therein, be discharged from such service or labor, but shall be delivered up, on claim of the party to whom such service or labor may be due."[3]

This stipulation was so material to the compact, that without it that compact would not have been made. The greater number of the contracting parties held slaves, and they had previously evinced their estimate of the value of such a stipulation by making it a condition in the Ordinance[4] for the government of the territory ceded by Virginia. . . .

The laws of the General Government have ceased to effect the objects of the Constitution. The States of Maine, New Hampshire, Vermont, Massachusetts, Connecticut, Rhode Island, New York, Pennsylvania, Illinois, Indiana, Michigan, Wisconsin and Iowa, have enacted laws which either nullify the Acts of Congress or render useless any attempt to execute them.

* * *

Thus the constituted compact has been deliberately broken and disregarded by the non-slaveholding States, and the consequence follows that South Carolina is released from her obligation.

* * *

We affirm that these ends for which this Government was instituted have been defeated, and the Government itself has been made destructive of them by the action of the non-slaveholding States. Those States have assumed the right of deciding upon the propriety of our domestic institutions; and have denied the rights of property established in fifteen of the States and recognized by the Constitution; they have denounced as sinful the institution of slavery; they have permitted open establishment among them of societies, whose avowed object is to disturb the peace and to eloign the property of the citizens of other States.

---

3. This clause in the Constitution became the basis of the first Fugitive Slave Act, passed by Congress in 1793. Nowhere in the original Constitution do the words "slave" or "slavery" actually appear.

4. That is, the Northwest Ordinance of 1787, which established the Ohio River as the border between free states and slave states as the nation expanded westward.

They have encouraged and assisted thousands of our slaves to leave their homes; and those who remain, have been incited by emissaries, books and pictures to servile insurrection.

For twenty-five years this agitation has been steadily increasing, until it has now secured to its aid the power of the common Government. Observing the *forms* of the Constitution, a sectional party has found within that Article establishing the Executive Department, the means of subverting the Constitution itself. A geographical line has been drawn across the Union, and all the States north of that line have united in the election of a man to the high office of President of the United States, whose opinions and purposes are hostile to slavery. He is to be entrusted with the administration of the common Government, because he has declared that that "Government cannot endure permanently half slave, half free," and that the public mind must rest in the belief that slavery is in the course of ultimate extinction.

This sectional combination for the submersion of the Constitution, has been aided in some of the States by elevating to citizenship, persons who, by the supreme law of the land, are incapable of becoming citizens; and their votes have been used to inaugurate a new policy, hostile to the South, and destructive of its beliefs and safety.

On the 4th day of March next, this party will take possession of the Government. It has announced that the South shall be excluded from the common territory, that the judicial tribunals shall be made sectional, and that a war must be waged against slavery until it shall cease throughout the United States.

The guaranties of the Constitution will then no longer exist; the equal rights of the States will be lost. The slaveholding States will no longer have the power of self-government, or self-protection, and the Federal Government will have become their enemy.

Sectional interest and animosity will deepen the irritation, and all hope of remedy is rendered vain, by the fact that public opinion at the North has invested a great political error with the sanction of more erroneous religious belief.

We, therefore, the People of South Carolina, by our delegates in Convention assembled, appealing to the Supreme Judge of the world for the rectitude of our intentions, have solemnly declared that the Union heretofore existing between this State and the other States of North America, is dissolved, and that the State of South Carolina has resumed her position among the nations of the world, as a separate and independent State; with full power to levy war, conclude peace, contract alliances, establish commerce, and to do all other acts and things which independent States may of right do.

Adopted December 24, 1860

Study Questions

1. According to this document, what are the major reasons that justified or compelled South Carolina to secede from the United States? Why was the recent election a triggering cause behind this decision? What "equal rights" was South Carolina fearful of losing?

2. In what ways does this document mirror the Declaration of Independence? Are its contents and underlying views more in line with those of the Declaration or in contradiction to them? Fully explain.

3. Did South Carolina view the United States as a unified nation or as something very different? Consider the meaning of the terms "States," "Federal," "Confederation," and "compact" in arriving at an answer.

4. Why did the secession of South Carolina and other slave states ultimately lead to civil war? What alternatives to war might there have been? Would options other than war have been acceptable? Why or why not?

IGNATIUS DONNELLY

Populist Party Platform (1892)

The rise of industry in the Gilded Age corresponded to deepening agrarian distress as farmers struggled to survive amidst booming crop yields and declining commodity prices. Farmers naturally cast bankers and railroads in the role of villains, accusing them of charging extortionate interest and freight rates. And farmers naturally turned to the political arena for redress, beginning with the founding of the Grange in the late 1860s and later with the proliferation of the Farmers Alliance through the South and the West in the 1880s. Grangers and Alliance men often worked within the established major parties to promote their reform agendas, but when this tactic yielded little, Alliance men launched the People's or Populist party in 1892.

Populists gathered in Omaha that summer to nominate a presidential ticket headed by James B. Weaver of Iowa and to adopt a platform. That document's arresting preamble was written by a Minnesota firebrand named Ignatius Donnelly (1831–1901), a former Republican member of Congress and author of a well-known book on the supposed lost continent of Atlantis. Read this document for its description of what ailed the country and its detailed prescriptions for a solution. The Populists would do respectably in 1892 but saw their efforts come undone in the 1896 election when they pursued a fusion strategy with the Democrats. Nevertheless, later reform movements would bring to fruition many of their proposals.

From "The Omaha Platform: Launching the Populist Party," in *The World Almanac*, 1893 (New York: 1893), 83–85.

PREAMBLE

The conditions which surround us best justify our co-operation; we meet in the midst of a nation brought to the verge of moral, political, and material ruin. Corruption dominates the ballot-box, the Legislatures, the Congress, and touches even the ermine of the bench.[1] The people are demoralized; most of the States have been compelled to isolate the voters at the polling places to prevent universal intimidation and bribery. The newspapers are largely subsidized or muzzled, public opinion silenced, business prostrated, homes covered with mortgages, labor impoverished, and the land concentrating in the hands of

---

1. Refers to the fur which once adorned the robes of judges.

capitalists. The urban workmen are denied the right to organize for self-protection, imported pauperized labor beats down their wages, a hireling standing army, unrecognized by our laws, is established to shoot them down,[2] and they are rapidly degenerating into European conditions. The fruits of the toil of millions are boldly stolen to build up colossal fortunes for a few, unprecedented in the history of mankind; and the possessors of those, in turn, despise the republic and endanger liberty. From the same prolific womb of governmental injustice we breed the two great classes—tramps and millionaires.

* * *

We have witnessed for more than a quarter of a century the struggles of the two great political parties for power and plunder, while grievous wrongs have been inflicted upon the suffering people. We charge that the controlling influences dominating both these parties have permitted the existing dreadful conditions to develop without serious effort to prevent or restrain them. Neither do they now promise us any substantial reform. They have agreed together to ignore, in the coming campaign, every issue but one. They propose to drown the outcries of a plundered people with the uproar of a sham battle over the tariff, so that capitalists, corporations, national banks, rings, trusts, watered stock, the demonetization of silver and the oppressions of the usurers may all be lost sight of. They propose to sacrifice our homes, lives, and children on the altar of mammon,[3] to destroy the multitude in order to secure corruption funds from the millionaires.

Assembled on the anniversary of the birthday of the nation, and filled with the spirit of the grand general and chief who established our independence, we seek to restore the government of the Republic to the hands of "the plain people," with which class it originated. We assert our purposes to be identical with the purposes of the National Constitution; to form a more perfect union and establish justice, insure domestic tranquillity, provide for the common defence, promote the general welfare, and secure the blessings of liberty for ourselves and our posterity.

We declare that this Republic can only endure as a free government while built upon the love of the whole people for each other and for the nation; that it cannot be pinned together by bayonets; that the civil war is over, and that every passion and resentment which grew out of it must die with it, and that we must be in fact, as we are in name, one united brotherhood of free men.

Our country finds itself confronted by conditions for which there is no precedent in the history of the world; our annual agricultural productions amount

2. The Pinkerton Detective Agency, frequently hired by management to provide security during strikes.
3. Material riches; see Matthew 6:24, King James version.

to billions of dollars in value, which must, within a few weeks or months, be exchanged for billions of dollars' worth of commodities consumed in their production; the existing currency supply is wholly inadequate to make this exchange; the results are falling prices, the formation of combines and rings, the impoverishment of the producing class. We pledge ourselves that if given power we will labor to correct these evils by wise and reasonable legislation, in accordance with the terms of our platform.

We believe that the power of government—in other words, of the people—should be expanded (as in the case of the postal service) as rapidly and as far as the good sense of an intelligent people and the teachings of experience shall justify, to the end that oppression, injustice, and poverty shall eventually cease in the land.

While our sympathies as a party of reform are naturally upon the side of every proposition which will tend to make men intelligent, virtuous, and temperate,[4] we nevertheless regard these questions, important as they are, as secondary to the great issues now pressing for solution, and upon which not only our individual prosperity but the very existence of free institutions depend; and we ask all men to first help us to determine whether we are to have a republic to administer before we differ as to the conditions upon which it is to be administered, believing that the forces of reform this day organized will never cease to move forward until every wrong is remedied and equal rights and equal privileges securely established for all the men and women of this country.

PLATFORM

We declare, therefore—

First.—That the union of the labor forces of the United States this day consummated shall be permanent and perpetual; may its spirit enter into all hearts for the salvation of the Republic and the uplifting of mankind.

Second.—Wealth belongs to him who creates it, and every dollar taken from industry without an equivalent is robbery. "If any will not work, neither shall he eat."[5] The interests of rural and civic labor are the same; their enemies are identical.

Third.—We believe that the time has come when the railroad corporations will either own the people or the people must own the railroads, and should the government enter upon the work of owning and managing all railroads, we should favor an amendment to the Constitution by which all persons engaged in the

---

4. A reference to the anti-alcohol campaign that would eventually result in prohibition in 1919.
5. II Thessalonians 3:10. Captain John Smith famously pronounced this policy during his tenure as leader of Jamestown.

government service shall be placed under a civil-service regulation of the most rigid character, so as to prevent the increase of the power of the national administration by the use of such additional government employes.

FINANCE.—We demand a national currency, safe, sound, and flexible, issued by the general government only, a full legal tender for all debts, public and private, and that without the use of banking corporations, a just, equitable, and efficient means of distribution direct to the people, at a tax not to exceed 2 per cent per annum, to be provided as set forth in the sub-treasury plan of the Farmers' Alliance, or a better system; also by payments in discharge of its obligations for public improvements.

1. We demand free and unlimited coinage of silver and gold at the present legal ratio of 16 to 1.
2. We demand that the amount of circulating medium be speedily increased to not less than $50 per capita.
3. We demand a graduated income tax.

* * *

TRANSPORTATION—Transportation being a means of exchange and a public necessity, the government should own and operate the railroads in the interest of the people. The telegraph, telephone, like the post-office system, being a necessity for the transmission of news, should be owned and operated by the government in the interest of the people.

LAND.—The land, including all the natural sources of wealth, is the heritage of the people, and should not be monopolized for speculative purposes, and alien ownership of land should be prohibited. All land now held by railroads and other corporations in excess of their actual needs, and all lands now owned by aliens should be reclaimed by the government and held for actual settlers only.

EXPRESSION OF SENTIMENTS

Your Committee on Platform and Resolutions beg leave unanimously to report the following:

Whereas, Other questions have been presented for our consideration, we hereby submit the following, not as a part of the Platform of the People's Party, but as resolutions expressive of the sentiment of this Convention.

1. RESOLVED, That we demand a free ballot and a fair count in all elections and pledge ourselves to secure it to every legal voter without Federal Intervention, through the adoption by the States of the unperverted Australian or secret ballot system.

2. RESOLVED, That the revenue derived from a graduated income tax should be applied to the reduction of the burden of taxation now levied upon the domestic industries of this country.

3. RESOLVED, That we pledge our support to fair and liberal pensions to ex-Union soldiers and sailors.

4. RESOLVED, That we condemn the fallacy of protecting American labor under the present system, which opens our ports to the pauper and criminal classes of the world and crowds out our wage-earners; and we denounce the present ineffective laws against contract labor,[6] and demand the further restriction of undesirable emigration.

5. RESOLVED, That we cordially sympathize with the efforts of organized workingmen to shorten the hours of labor, and demand a rigid enforcement of the existing eight-hour law on Government work, and ask that a penalty clause be added to the said law.

6. RESOLVED, That we regard the maintenance of a large standing army of mercenaries, known as the Pinkerton system, as a menace to our liberties, and we demand its abolition. . . .

7. RESOLVED, That we commend to the favorable consideration of the people and the reform press the legislative system known as the initiative and referendum.

8. RESOLVED, That we favor a constitutional provision limiting the office of President and Vice-President to one term, and providing for the election of Senators of the United States by a direct vote of the people.

9. RESOLVED, That we oppose any subsidy or national aid to any private corporation for any purpose.

10. RESOLVED, That this convention sympathizes with the Knights of Labor and their righteous contest with the tyrannical combine of clothing manufacturers of Rochester, and declare it to be a duty of all who hate tyranny and oppression to refuse to purchase the goods made by the said manufacturers, or to patronize any merchants who sell such goods.

---

6. The practice of employers signing up low-wage workers in Europe before they had even emigrated to the United States.

Study Questions

1. According to the Populists, what is fundamentally wrong with the country? How do they propose to fix it? How is their view of the role of government a departure for a party dominated by farmers?

2. Which of the Populist proposals strike you as being most radical? Why? Which seem most moderate? Where would the Populists fit on the political spectrum today?

3. What parts of the Populist platform would most appeal to industrial workers? Why would the Populists adopt a strategy of appealing to urban as well as rural voters?

4. Was Populism's ultimate failure primarily due to its underlying ideas, or were other factors more responsible? Explain. What does the experience of the People's party teach about third parties in American history?

ANDREW CARNEGIE

Wealth (1889)

Andrew Carnegie (1835–1919) is by any measure one of the most important figures in the business and cultural history of the United States. Carnegie, son of a poor Scottish weaver, migrated from Scotland to Pittsburgh with his family at age twelve. Displaying an astonishing drive and work ethic, Carnegie worked in textiles, telegraphy, and the railroad industry. After a successful tenure as an executive with the Pennsylvania Railroad, Carnegie went into the steel business in the early 1870s. By introducing the new Bessemer process, an inexpensive method for manufacturing steel that had been patented in England in 1855, Carnegie transformed steelmaking in the United States. By the time he sold his firm, Carnegie Steel, to the Wall Street financial titan J. P. Morgan in 1901 (thereby enabling the creation of U.S. Steel), Carnegie had amassed a fortune that, adjusted to contemporary dollars, made him the second-richest American—behind only John D. Rockefeller—who ever lived.

Carnegie used the last years of his life to engage in extensive philanthropy, essentially giving his fortune away by the time of his death in 1919. His well-thought-out philosophy justifying this activity was articulated in a widely read article, "Wealth," published in the North American Review, *a prestigious literary magazine, in June 1889. As you read it, consider Carnegie's views on the social responsibilities of the wealthy and how he distinguished himself from many elite Americans of the period. Carnegie's perspective would soon become known as the "Gospel of Wealth" due to the wording he employed in the last sentence of this essay. That phrase would come to embody the dominant values of the Gilded Age.*

From Andrew Carnegie, *North American Review*, 148 no. 391 (June 1889), 656–664.

The problem of our age is the proper administration of wealth, so that the ties of brotherhood may still bind together the rich and poor in harmonious relationship. The conditions of human life have not only been changed, but revolutionized, within the past few hundred years. In former days there was little difference between the dwelling, dress, food, and environment of the chief and those of his retainers. The Indians are to-day where civilized man then was. When visiting the Sioux, I was led to the wigwam of the chief. It was just like the others in external appearance, and even within the difference was trifling between it and those of the poorest of his braves. The contrast between the palace of the millionaire and the cottage of the laborer with us to-day measures the change which has come with civilization.

This change, however, is not to be deplored, but welcomed as highly beneficial. It is well, nay, essential for the progress of the race, that the houses of some should be homes for all that is highest and best in literature and the arts, and for all the refinements of civilization, rather than that none should be so. Much better this great irregularity than universal squalor. Without wealth there can be no Maecenas.[1] The "good old times" were not good old times. Neither master nor servant was as well situated then as to-day. A relapse to old conditions would be disastrous to both—not the least so to him who serves—and would sweep away civilization with it. But whether the change be for good or ill, it is upon us, beyond our power to alter, and therefore to be accepted and made the best of. It is a waste of time to criticise the inevitable.

It is easy to see how the change has come. One illustration will serve for almost every phase of the cause. In the manufacture of products we have the whole story. It applies to all combinations of human industry, as stimulated and enlarged by the inventions of this scientific age. Formerly articles were manufactured at the domestic hearth or in small shops which formed part of the household. The master and his apprentices worked side by side, the latter living with the master, and therefore subject to the same conditions. When these apprentices rose to be masters, there was little or no change in their mode of life, and they, in turn, educated in the same routine succeeding apprentices. There was, substantially, social equality, and even political equality, for those engaged in industrial pursuits had then little or no political voice in the State.

But the inevitable result of such a mode of manufacture was crude articles at high prices. To-day the world obtains commodities of excellent quality at prices which even the generation preceding this would have deemed incredible. In the commercial world similar causes have produced similar results, and the race is benefited thereby. The poor enjoy what the rich could not before afford. What were the luxuries have become the necessaries of life. The laborer has now more comforts than the farmer had a few generations ago. The farmer has more luxuries than the landlord had, and is more richly clad and better housed. The landlord has books and pictures rarer, and appointments more artistic, than the King could then obtain.

The price we pay for this salutary change is, no doubt, great. We assemble thousands of operatives in the factory, in the mine, and in the counting-house, of whom the employer can know little or nothing, and to whom the employer is little better than a myth. All intercourse between them is at an end. Rigid Castes are formed, and, as usual, mutual ignorance breeds mutual distrust. Each Caste is without

1. Wealthy Roman famed as a friend of emperors and a patron of poets.

sympathy for the other, and ready to credit anything disparaging in regard to it. Under the law of competition, the employer of thousands is forced into the strictest economies, among which the rates paid to labor figure prominently, and often there is friction between the employer and the employed, between capital and labor, between rich and poor. Human society loses homogeneity.

The price which society pays for the law of competition, like the price it pays for cheap comforts and luxuries, is also great; but the advantages of this law are also greater still, for it is to this law that we owe our wonderful material development, which brings improved conditions in its train. But, whether the law be benign or not, we must say of it, as we say of the change in the conditions of men to which we have referred: It is here; we cannot evade it; no substitutes for it have been found; and while the law may be sometimes hard for the individual, it is best for the race, because it insures the survival of the fittest in every department. We accept and welcome, therefore, as conditions to which we must accommodate ourselves, great inequality of environment, the concentration of business, industrial and commercial, in the hands of a few, and the law of competition between these, as being not only beneficial, but essential for the future progress of the race. Having accepted these, it follows that there must be great scope for the exercise of special ability in the merchant and in the manufacturer who has to conduct affairs upon a great scale. That this talent for organization and management is rare among men is proved by the fact that it invariably secures for its possessor enormous rewards, no matter where or under what laws or conditions. The experienced in affairs always rate the man whose services can be obtained as a partner as not only the first consideration, but such as to render the question of his capital scarcely worth considering, for such men soon create capital; while, without the special talent required, capital soon takes wings. Such men become interested in firms or corporations using millions; and estimating only simple interest to be made upon the capital invested, it is inevitable that their income must exceed their expenditures, and that they must accumulate wealth. Nor is there any middle ground which such men can occupy, because the great manufacturing or commercial concern which does not earn at least interest upon its capital soon becomes bankrupt. It must either go forward or fall behind; to stand still is impossible. It is a condition essential for its successful operation that it should be thus far profitable, and even that, in addition to interest on capital, it should make profit. It is a law, as certain as any of the others named, that men possessed of this peculiar talent for affairs, under the free play of economic forces, must, of necessity, soon be in receipt of more revenue than can be judiciously expended upon themselves; and this law is as beneficial for the race as the others.

Objections to the foundations upon which society is based are not in order, because the condition of the race is better with these than it has been with any others which have been tried. Of the effect of any new substitutes proposed we cannot be sure. The Socialist or Anarchist who seeks to overturn present conditions is to be regarded as attacking the foundation upon which civilization itself rests, for civilization took its start from the day that the capable, industrious workman said to his incompetent and lazy fellow," If thou dost not sow, thou shalt not reap,"[2] and thus ended primitive Communism by separating the drones from the bees. One who studies this subject will soon be brought face to face with the conclusion that upon the sacredness of property civilization itself depends—the right of the laborer to his hundred dollars in the savings bank, and equally the legal right of the millionaire to his millions. To those who propose to substitute Communism for this intense Individualism the answer, therefore, is: The race has tried that. All progress from that barbarous day to the present time has resulted from its displacement. Not evil, but good, has come to the race from the accumulation of wealth by those who have the ability and energy that produce it. But even if we admit for a moment that it might be better for the race to discard its present foundation, Individualism—that it is a nobler ideal that man should labor, not for himself alone, but in and for a brotherhood of his fellows, and share with them all in common, realizing Swedenborg's[3] idea of Heaven, where, as he says, the angels derive their happiness, not from laboring for self, but for each other—even admit all this, and a sufficient answer is, This is not evolution, but revolution. It necessitates the changing of human nature itself—a work of eons, even if it were good to change it, which we cannot know.

It is not practicable in our day or in our age. Even if desirable theoretically, it belongs to another and long-succeeding sociological stratum. Our duty is with what is practicable now; with the next step possible in our day and generation. It is criminal to waste our energies in endeavoring to uproot, when all we can profitably or possibly accomplish is to bend the universal tree of humanity a little in the direction most favorable to the production of good fruit under existing circumstances. We might as well urge the destruction of the highest existing type of man because he failed to reach our ideal as to favor the destruction of Individualism, Private Property, the Law of Accumulation of Wealth, and the Law of Competition; for these are the highest results of human experience, the soil in which society so far has produced the best fruit. Unequally or unjustly, perhaps, as these laws sometimes operate, and imperfect as they appear to the Idealist, they are, nevertheless, like the highest type of man, the best and most valuable of all that humanity has yet accomplished.

We start, then, with a condition of affairs under which the best interests of the race are promoted, but which inevitably gives wealth to the few. Thus far, accepting conditions as they exist, the situation can be surveyed and pronounced good. The question then arises—and, if the foregoing be correct, it is the only question

2. Carnegie's adaptation of Micah 6:15 from the Bible: "Thou shalt sow, but thou shall not reap."
3. Emanuel Swedenborg (1688–1722), Swedish scientist and Christian theologian whose teachings emphasized the importance of good works as well as faith.

with which we have to deal—What is the proper mode of administering wealth after the laws upon which civilization is founded have thrown it into the hands of the few? And it is of this great question that I believe I offer the true solution. It will be understood that fortunes are here spoken of, not moderate sums saved by many years of effort, the returns from which are required for the comfortable maintenance and education of families. This is not wealth, but only competence, which it should be the aim of all to acquire.

There are but three modes in which surplus wealth can be disposed of. It can be left to the families of the decedents; or it can be bequeathed for public purposes; or, finally, it can be administered during their lives by its possessors. Under the first and second modes most of the wealth of the world that has reached the few has hitherto been applied. Let us in turn consider each of these modes. The first is the most injudicious. In monarchical countries, the estates and the greatest portion of the wealth are left to the first son,[4] that the vanity of the parent may be gratified by the thought that his name and title are to descend to succeeding generations unimpaired. The condition of this class in Europe to-day teaches the futility of such hopes or ambitions. The successors have become impoverished through their follies or from the fall in the value of land. Even in Great Britain the strict law of entail[5] has been found inadequate to maintain the status of an hereditary class. Its soil is rapidly passing into the hands of the stranger. Under republican institutions the division of property among the children is much fairer, but the question which forces itself upon thoughtful men in all lands is: Why should men leave great fortunes to their children? If this is done from affection, is it not misguided affection? Observation teaches that, generally speaking, it is not well for the children that they should be so burdened. Neither is it well for the state. Beyond providing for the wife and daughters moderate sources of income, and very moderate allowances indeed, if any, for the sons, men may well hesitate, for it is no longer questionable that great sums bequeathed oftener work more for the injury than for the good of the recipients. Wise men will soon conclude that, for the best interests of the members of their families and of the state, such bequests are an improper use of their means.

It is not suggested that men who have failed to educate their sons to earn a livelihood shall cast them adrift in poverty. If any man has seen fit to rear his sons with a view to their living idle lives, or, what is highly commendable, has instilled in them the sentiment that they are in a position to labor for public ends without reference to pecuniary considerations, then, of course, the duty of the parent is to see that such are provided for in moderation. There are instances of millionaires' sons unspoiled by wealth, who, being rich, still perform great services in the community. Such are the very salt of the earth, as valuable as, unfortunately, they are

4. The practice known as primogeniture.
5. Entail requires that a man's estate during his lifetime be kept intact.

rare; still it is not the exception, but the rule, that men must regard, and, looking at the usual result of enormous sums conferred upon legatees, the thoughtful man must shortly say, "I would as soon leave to my son a curse as the almighty dollar," and admit to himself that it is not the welfare of the children, but family pride, which inspires these enormous legacies.

As to the second mode, that of leaving wealth at death for public uses, it may be said that this is only a means for the disposal of wealth, provided a man is content to wait until he is dead before it becomes of much good in the world. Knowledge of the results of legacies bequeathed is not calculated to inspire the brightest hopes of much posthumous good being accomplished. The cases are not few in which the real object sought by the testator is not attained, nor are they few in which his real wishes are thwarted. In many cases the bequests are so used as to become only monuments of his folly. It is well to remember that it requires the exercise of not less ability than that which acquired the wealth to use it so as to be really beneficial to the community. Besides this, it may fairly be said that no man is to be extolled for doing what he cannot help doing, nor is he to be thanked by the community to which he only leaves wealth at death. Men who leave vast sums in this way may fairly be thought men who would not have left it at all, had they been able to take it with them. The memories of such cannot be held in grateful remembrance, for there is no grace in their gifts. It is not to be wondered at that such bequests seem so generally to lack the blessing.

The growing disposition to tax more and more heavily large estates left at death is a cheering indication of the growth of a salutary change in public opinion. The State of Pennsylvania now takes—subject to some exceptions—one-tenth of the property left by its citizens. The budget presented in the British Parliament the other day proposes to increase the death-duties; and, most significant of all, the new tax is to be a graduated one. Of all forms of taxation, this seems the wisest. Men who continue hoarding great sums all their lives, the proper use of which for public ends would work good to the community, should be made to feel that the community, in the form of the state, cannot thus be deprived of its proper share. By taxing estates heavily at death the state marks its condemnation of the selfish millionaire's unworthy life.

It is desirable that nations should go much further in this direction. Indeed, it is difficult to set bounds to the share of a rich man's estate which should go at his death to the public through the agency of the state, and by all means such taxes should be graduated, beginning at nothing upon moderate sums to dependents, and increasing rapidly as the amounts swell, until of the millionaire's hoard, as of Shylock's, at least

> The other half
> Comes to the privy coffer of the state.[6]

6. Lines spoken by Portia about the fortune amassed by Shylock, the villainous moneylender, in Shakespeare's *The Merchant of Venice* (4.1.351–2).

This policy would work powerfully to induce the rich man to attend to the administration of wealth during his life, which is the end that society should always have in view, as being that by far most fruitful for the people. Nor need it be feared that this policy would sap the root of enterprise and render men less anxious to accumulate, for to the class whose ambition it is to leave great fortunes and be talked about after their death, it will attract even more attention, and, indeed, be a somewhat nobler ambition to have enormous sums paid over to the state from their fortunes.

There remains, then, only one mode of using great fortunes; but in this we have the true antidote for the temporary unequal distribution of wealth, the reconciliation of the rich and the poor a reign of harmony—another ideal, differing, indeed, from that of the Communist in requiring only the further evolution of existing conditions, not the total overthrow of our civilization. It is founded upon the present most intense individualism, and the race is prepared to put it in practice by degrees whenever it pleases. Under its sway we shall have an ideal state, in which the surplus wealth of the few will become, in the best sense, the property of the many, because administered for the common good, and this wealth, passing through the hands of the few, can be made a much more potent force for the elevation of our race than if it had been distributed in small sums to the people themselves. Even the poorest can be made to see this, and to agree that great sums gathered by some of their fellow-citizens and spent for public purposes, from which the masses reap the principal benefit, are more valuable to them than if scattered among them through the course of many years in trifling amounts.

If we consider what results flow from the Cooper Institute, for instance, to the best portion of the race in New York not possessed of means, and compare these with those which would have arisen for the good of the masses from an equal sum distributed by Mr. Cooper[7] in his lifetime in the form of wages, which is the highest form of distribution, being for work done and not for charity, we can form some estimate of the possibilities for the improvement of the race which lie embedded in the present law of the accumulation of wealth. Much of this sum, if distributed in small quantities among the people, would have been wasted in the indulgence of appetite, some of it in excess, and it may be doubted whether even the part put to the best use, that of adding to the comforts of the home, would have yielded results for the race, as a race, at all comparable to those which are flowing and are to flow from the Cooper Institute from generation to generation. Let the advocate of violent or radical change ponder well this thought.

We might even go so far as to take another instance, that of Mr. Tilden's[8] bequest of five millions of dollars for a free library in the city of New York, but in

---

7. Peter Cooper (1791–1883), wealthy industrialist and founder of the Cooper Union, a free college for the working class of New York City.
8. Samuel J. Tilden (1814–86), governor of New York, Democratic presidential candidate, and a founding benefactor of the New York Public Library.

referring to this one cannot help saying involuntarily, How much better if Mr. Tilden had devoted the last years of his own life to the proper administration of this immense sum; in which case neither legal contest nor any other cause of delay could have interfered with his aims. But let us assume that Mr. Tilden's millions finally become the means of giving to this city a noble public library, where the treasures of the world contained in books will be open to all forever, without money and without price. Considering the good of that part of the race which congregates in and around Manhattan Island, would its permanent benefit have been better promoted had these millions been allowed to circulate in small sums through the hands of the masses? Even the most strenuous advocate of Communism must entertain a doubt upon this subject. Most of those who think will probably entertain no doubt whatever.

Poor and restricted are our opportunities in this life; narrow our horizon; our best work most imperfect; but rich men should be thankful for one inestimable boon. They have it in their power during their lives to busy themselves in organizing benefactions from which the masses of their fellows will derive lasting advantage, and thus dignify their own lives. The highest life is probably to be reached, not by such imitation of the life of Christ as Count Tolstoy[9] gives us, but, while animated by Christ's spirit, by recognizing the changed conditions of this age, and adopting modes of expressing this spirit suitable to the changed conditions under which we live; still laboring for the good of our fellows, which was the essence of his life and teaching, but laboring in a different manner.

This, then, is held to be the duty of the man of Wealth: First, to set an example of modest, unostentatious living, shunning display or extravagance; to provide moderately for the legitimate wants of those dependent upon him; and after doing so to consider all surplus revenues which come to him simply as trust funds, which he is called upon to administer, and strictly bound as a matter of duty to administer in the manner which, in his judgment, is best calculated to produce the most beneficial results for the community—the man of wealth thus becoming the mere agent and trustee for his poorer brethren, bringing to their service his superior wisdom, experience, and ability to administer, doing for them better than they would or could do for themselves.

We are met here with the difficulty of determining what are moderate sums to leave to members of the family; what is modest, unostentatious living; what is the test of extravagance. There must be different standards for different conditions. The answer is that it is as impossible to name exact amounts or actions as it is to define good manners, good taste, or the rules of propriety; but, nevertheless, these are verities, well known although undefinable. Public sentiment is quick to know

9. That is, Leo Tolstoy (1828–1910), Russian aristocrat famed for his novels *War and Peace* and *Anna Karenina* and to his ardent devotion to an ascetic life inspired by Jesus Christ.

and to feel what offends these. So in the case of wealth. The rule in regard to good taste in the dress of men or women applies here. Whatever makes one conspicuous offends the canon. If any family be chiefly known for display, for extravagance in home, table, equipage, for enormous sums ostentatiously spent in any form upon itself—if these be its chief distinctions, we have no difficulty in estimating its nature or culture. So likewise in regard to the use or abuse of its surplus wealth, or to generous, freehanded co-operation in good public uses, or to unabated efforts to accumulate and hoard to the last, whether they administer or bequeath. The verdict rests with the best and most enlightened public sentiment. The community will surely judge, and its judgments will not often be wrong.

The best uses to which surplus wealth can be put have already been indicated. Those who would administer wisely must, indeed, be wise, for one of the serious obstacles to the improvement of our race is indiscriminate charity. It were better for mankind that the millions of the rich were thrown into the sea than so spent as to encourage the slothful, the drunken, the unworthy. Of every thousand dollars spent in so called charity to-day, it is probable that $950 is unwisely spent; so spent, indeed, as to produce the very evils which it proposes to mitigate or cure. A well-known writer of philosophic books admitted the other day that he had given a quarter of a dollar to a man who approached him as he was coming to visit the house of his friend, He knew nothing of the habits of this beggar; knew not the use that would be made of this money, although he had every reason to suspect that it would be spent improperly. This man professed to be a disciple of Herbert Spencer;[1] yet the quarter-dollar given that night will probably work more injury than all the money which its thoughtless donor will ever be able to give in true charity will do good. He only gratified his own feelings, saved himself from annoyance—and this was probably one of the most selfish and very worst actions of his life, for in all respects he is most worthy.

In bestowing charity, the main consideration should be to help those who will help themselves; to provide part of the means by which those who desire to improve may do so; to give those who desire to rise the aids by which they may rise; to assist, but rarely or never to do all. Neither the individual nor the race is improved by alms-giving. Those worthy of assistance, except in rare cases, seldom require assistance. The really valuable men of the race never do, except in cases of accident or sudden change. Every one has, of course, cases of individuals brought to his own knowledge where temporary assistance can do genuine good, and these he will not overlook. But the amount which can be wisely given by the individual for individuals is necessarily limited by his lack of knowledge of the circumstances connected with each. He is the only true reformer who is as careful

1. Spencer (1820–1903) was the English biologist and philosopher who popularized the notion that Charles Darwin's principles of natural selection applied to human society as well as the plant and animal kingdom.

and as anxious not to aid the unworthy as he is to aid the worthy, and, perhaps, even more so, for in alms-giving more injury is probably done by rewarding vice than by relieving virtue.

The rich man is thus almost restricted to following the examples of Peter Cooper, Enoch Pratt of Baltimore,[2] Mr. Pratt of Brooklyn,[3] Senator Stanford,[4] and others, who know that the best means of benefiting the community is to place within its reach the ladders upon which the aspiring can rise—free libraries, parks, and means of recreation, by which men are helped in body and mind; works of art, certain to give pleasure and improve the public taste, and public institutions of various kinds, which will improve the general condition of the people; in this manner returning their surplus wealth to the mass of their fellows in the forms best calculated to do them lasting good.

Thus is the problem of Rich and Poor to be solved. The laws of accumulation will be left free; the laws of distribution free. Individualism will continue, but the millionaire will be but a trustee for the poor; intrusted for a season with a great part of the increased wealth of the community, but administering it for the community far better than it could or would have done for itself. The best minds will thus have reached a stage in the development of the race in which it is clearly seen that there is no mode of disposing of surplus wealth creditable to thoughtful and earnest men into whose hands it flows save by using it year by year for the general good. This day already dawns. Men may die without incurring the pity of their fellows, still sharers in great business enterprises from which their capital cannot be or has not been withdrawn, and is left chiefly at death for public uses, yet the day is not far distant when the man who dies leaving behind him millions of available wealth, which was his to administer during life, will pass away "unwept, unhonored, and unsung,"[5] no matter to what uses he leaves the dross which he cannot take with him. Of such as these the public verdict will then be: The man who dies thus rich dies disgraced.

Such, in my opinion, is the true Gospel concerning Wealth, obedience to which is destined some day to solve the problem of the Rich and the Poor, and to bring "Peace on earth, among men Good-Will."[6]

---

2. Businessman and philanthropist (1808–96), founder of a still-functioning public library system in Baltimore.

3. Oil millionaire Charles Pratt, (1830–91) founder of an industrial college in Brooklyn, the Pratt Institute, in 1887.

4. Railroad tycoon Leland Stanford (1824–93), who served as U.S. senator from California and established the elite university in Palo Alto, California, that bears his name.

5. From the poem "Breathes There the Man" by Scottish novelist Sir Walter Scott (1771–1832).

6. From the Christmas story, Luke 2:14.

Study Questions

1. How does Carnegie believe that industrial capitalism has "revolutionized" American life? What are the benefits and shortcomings of this change? How does he feel about doctrines like socialism that address the ills of industrial society?

2. Analyze Carnegie's claim that the American economic system "inevitably gives wealth to the few." Why would he advise rich men to practice "unostentatious living"? How would they likely respond?

3. According to Carnegie, what are the three methods of disposing of surplus wealth? Which does he favor and why? On what grounds does he reject the other approaches?

4. How does Carnegie think wealthy philanthropists can best benefit society? What are his thoughts on charitable contributions to the poor?

5. At the time of Carnegie's writing, Social Darwinist ideas of survival of the fittest were commonplace among men of his class. To what degree is Carnegie's "gospel of wealth" compatible with Social Darwinist thinking? Fully explain.

6. Why did Carnegie oppose aristocracy of the type that existed in Europe? Do American aristocrats exist today? If so, what might Carnegie advocate to correct the situation?

JACOB RIIS

FROM *How the Other Half Lives* (1890)

Following the Civil War, a massive economic boom spurred explosive urban growth as foreign immigrants and rural Americans poured into great industrial cities to fulfill a growing demand for factory labor. Jacob Riis (1849–1914) was a New York City journalist who documented the poverty and exploitation that so often resulted. Riis, a native of Denmark who emigrated to America in 1870, experienced years of hardship and even homelessness until landing a position as a police reporter for the New York Tribune, *one of the city's largest-circulation daily newspapers, in 1877. For the next two decades, Riis was based in an office on Mulberry Street on Manhattan's Lower East Side, in proximity to some of the city's worst slums. In the late 1880s Riis trained himself in new flash photographic methods that allowed him to capture images in dark alleys and tenement-house interiors. This greatly enhanced his reportage of urban pathologies and helped bring him to the attention of municipal reformers like Theodore Roosevelt.*

In 1890 Riis published How the Other Half Lives, *his best-known book. In its exposure of social problems and its advocacy for reform, the book exemplifies the journalism of emerging progressivism. What follows are two short chapters and two photos that are representative of Riis's work. Examine them for what they reveal about the underside of America's spectacular growth in the Gilded Age.*

From Jacob A. Riis, *How the Other Half Lives: Studies Among the Tenements of New York* (New York: Charles Scribner's Sons, 1890), 48–54, 263–67.

THE ITALIAN IN NEW YORK.

Certainly a picturesque, if not very tidy, element has been added to the population in the "assisted" Italian immigrant who claims so large a share of public attention, partly because he keeps coming at such a tremendous rate, but chiefly because he elects to stay in New York, or near enough for it to serve as his base of operations, and here promptly reproduces conditions of destitution and disorder which, set in the frame-work of Mediterranean exuberance, are the delight of the artist, but in a matter-of-fact American community become its danger and reproach. The reproduction is made easier in New York because he finds the material ready to hand in the worst of the slum tenements; but even

Tenement life in New York City. Riis photographed these lodgers in a Bayard Street tenement in 1889. *Museum of the City of New York / Bridgeman Art Library.*

where it is not he soon reduces what he does find to his own level, if allowed to follow his natural bent.[1] The Italian comes in at the bottom, and in the generation that came over the sea he stays there. In the slums he is welcomed as a tenant who "makes less trouble" than the contentious Irishman or the order-loving German, that is to say: is content to live in a pig-sty and submits to robbery at the hands of the rent-collector without murmur. Yet this very tractability makes of him in good hands, when firmly and intelligently managed, a really desirable tenant. But it is not his good fortune often to fall in with other hospitality upon his coming than that which brought him here for its own profit, and has no idea of letting go its grip upon him as long as there is a cent to be made out of him.

Recent Congressional inquiries have shown the nature of the "assistance" he receives from greedy steamship agents and "bankers," who persuade him by false promises to mortgage his home, his few belongings, and his wages for months to

---

1. The process can be observed in the Italian tenements in Harlem (Little Italy), which, since their occupation by these people, have been gradually sinking to the slum level. [Unless otherwise indicated, footnotes are those of the author.]

come for a ticket to the land where plenty of work is to be had at princely wages. The padrone—the "banker" is nothing else—having made his ten per cent. out of him en route, receives him at the landing and turns him to double account as a wage-earner and a rent-payer. In each of these rôles he is made to yield a profit to his unscrupulous countryman, whom he trusts implicitly with the instinct of utter helplessness. The man is so ignorant that, as one of the sharpers who prey upon him put it once, it "would be downright sinful not to take him in." His ignorance and unconquerable suspicion of strangers dig the pit into which he falls. He not only knows no word of English, but he does not know enough to learn. Rarely only can he write his own language. Unlike the German, who begins learning English the day he lands as a matter of duty, or the Polish Jew, who takes it up as soon as he is able as an investment, the Italian learns slowly, if at all. Even his boy, born here, often speaks his native tongue indifferently. He is forced, therefore, to have constant recourse to the middle-man, who makes him pay handsomely at every turn. He hires him out to the railroad contractor, receiving a commission from the employer as well as from the laborer, and repeats the performance monthly, or as often as he can have him dismissed. In the city he contracts for his lodging, subletting to him space in the vilest tenements at extortionate rents, and sets an example that does not lack imitators. The "princely wages" have vanished with his coming, and in their place hardships and a dollar a day, beheft[2] with the padrone's merciless mortgage, confront him. Bred to even worse fare, he takes both as a matter of course, and, applying the maxim that it is not what one makes but what he saves that makes him rich, manages to turn the very dirt of the streets into a hoard of gold, with which he either returns to his Southern home,[3] or brings over his family to join in his work and in his fortunes the next season.

The discovery was made by earlier explorers that there is money in New York's ash-barrel,[4] but it was left to the genius of the padrone to develop the full resources of the mine that has become the exclusive preserve of the Italian immigrant. Only a few years ago, when rag-picking was carried on in a desultory and irresponsible sort of way, the city hired gangs of men to trim the ash-scows before they were sent out to sea. The trimming consisted in levelling out the dirt as it was dumped from the carts, so that the scow might be evenly loaded. The men were paid a dollar and a half a day, kept what they found that was worth having, and allowed the swarms of Italians who hung about the dumps to do the heavy work for them, letting them have their pick of the loads for their trouble. To-day Italians contract for the work, paying large sums to be permitted to do it. The city received not less than $80,000 last year for the sale of this privilege to the contractors, who in addition have to pay gangs of their countrymen for sorting out the bones, rags, tin cans

2. Burdened. [Ed.]
3. Most Italian immigrants hailed from Southern Italian locales such as Naples, Calabria, or Sicily. [Ed.]
4. Garbage can. [Ed.]

Bandits' Roost. An alley at 59 Mulberry Street in New York City photographed by Riis in 1887.
Granger Collection.

and other waste that are found in the ashes and form the staples of their trade and their sources of revenue. The effect has been vastly to increase the power of the padrone, or his ally, the contractor, by giving him exclusive control of the one industry in which the Italian was formerly an independent "dealer," and reducing him literally to the plane of the dump. Whenever the back of the sanitary police is turned, he will make his home in the filthy burrows where he works by day, sleeping and eating his meals under the dump, on the edge of slimy depths and amid surroundings full of unutterable horror. The city did not bargain to house, though it is content to board, him so long as he can make the ash-barrels yield the food to keep him alive, and a vigorous campaign is carried on at intervals against these unlicensed dump settlements; but the temptation of having to pay no rent is too strong, and they are driven from one dump only to find lodgement under another a few blocks farther up or down the river. The fiercest warfare is waged over the patronage of the dumps by rival factions represented by opposing contractors, and it has happened that the defeated party has endeavored to capture by strategy what he failed to carry by assault. It augurs unsuspected adaptability in the Italian to our system of self-government that these rivalries have more than once been suspected of being behind the sharpening of city ordinances, that were apparently made in good faith to prevent meddling with the refuse in the ash-barrels or in transit.

Did the Italian always adapt himself as readily to the operation of the civil law as to the manipulation of political "pull" on occasion, he would save himself a good deal of unnecessary trouble. Ordinarily he is easily enough governed by authority—always excepting Sunday, when he settles down to a game of cards and lets loose all his bad passions. Like the Chinese, the Italian is a born gambler. His soul is in the game from the moment the cards are on the table, and very frequently his knife is in it too before the game is ended. No Sunday has passed in New York since "the Bend"[5] became a suburb of Naples without one or more of these murderous affrays coming to the notice of the police. As a rule that happens only when the man the game went against is either dead or so badly wounded as to require instant surgical help. As to the other, unless he be caught red-handed, the chances that the police will ever get him are slim indeed. The wounded man can seldom be persuaded to betray him. He wards off all inquiries with a wicked "I fix him myself," and there the matter rests until he either dies or recovers. If the latter, the community hears after a while of another Italian affray, a man stabbed in a quarrel, dead or dying, and the police know that "he" has been fixed, and the account squared.

With all his conspicuous faults, the swarthy Italian immigrant has his redeeming traits. He is as honest as he is hot-headed. There are no Italian burglars in the Rogues' Gallery;[6] the ex-brigand toils peacefully with pickaxe and shovel on American ground. His boy occasionally shows, as a pick-pocket, the results of his training with the toughs of the Sixth Ward slums. The only criminal business to which the father occasionally lends his hand, outside of murder, is a bunco game, of which his confiding countrymen, returning with their hoard to their native land, are the victims. The women are faithful wives and devoted mothers. Their vivid and picturesque costumes lend a tinge of color to the otherwise dull monotony of the slums they inhabit. The Italian is gay, lighthearted and, if his fur is not stroked the wrong way, inoffensive as a child. His worst offence is that he keeps the stale-beer dives. Where his headquarters is, in the Mulberry Street Bend, these vile dens flourish and gather about them all the wrecks, the utterly wretched, the hopelessly lost, on the lowest slope of depraved humanity. And out of their misery he makes a profit.

THE MAN WITH THE KNIFE.

A MAN stood at the corner of Fifth Avenue and Fourteenth Street the other day, looking gloomily at the carriages that rolled by, carrying the wealth and fashion

5. A section of Mulberry Street, once dominated by the Irish, which by 1890 had become largely Italian. [Ed.]
6. Police collection of photographs of criminals, used for identification. [Ed.]

of the avenues to and from the big stores down town. He was poor, and hungry, and ragged. This thought was in his mind: "They behind their well-fed teams have no thought for the morrow; they know hunger only by name, and ride down to spend in an hour's shopping what would keep me and my little ones from want a whole year." There rose up before him the picture of those little ones crying for bread around the cold and cheerless hearth—then he sprang into the throng and slashed about him with a knife, blindly seeking to kill, to revenge.

The man was arrested, of course, and locked up. Today he is probably in a madhouse, forgotten. And the carriages roll by to and from the big stores with their gay throng of shoppers. The world forgets easily, too easily, what it does not like to remember.

Nevertheless the man and his knife had a mission. They spoke in their ignorant, impatient way the warning one of the most conservative, dispassionate of public bodies had sounded only a little while before: "Our only fear is that reform may come in a burst of public indignation destructive to property and to good morals."[7] They represented one solution of the problem of ignorant poverty *versus* ignorant wealth that has come down to us unsolved, the danger-cry of which we have lately heard in the shout that never should have been raised on American soil—the shout of "the masses against the classes"—the solution of violence.

There is another solution, that of justice. The choice is between the two. Which shall it be?

"Well!" say some well-meaning people; "we don't see the need of putting it in that way. We have been down among the tenements, looked them over. There are a good many people there; they are not comfortable, perhaps. What would you have? They are poor. And their houses are not such hovels as we have seen and read of in the slums of the Old World. They are decent in comparison. Why, some of them have brown-stone fronts. You will own at least that they make a decent show."

Yes! that is true. The worst tenements in New York do not, as a rule, *look bad*. Neither Hell's Kitchen, nor Murderers' Row bears its true character stamped on the front. They are not quite old enough, perhaps. The same is true of their tenants. The New York tough may be ready to kill where his London brother would do little more than scowl; yet, as a general thing he is less repulsively brutal in looks. Here again the reason may be the same: the breed is not so old. A few generations more in the slums, and all that will be changed. To get at the pregnant facts of tenement-house life one must look beneath the surface. Many an apple has a fair skin and a rotten core. There is a much better argument for the tenements in the assurance of the Registrar of Vital Statistics that the death-rate of these houses has of late been brought below the general death-rate of the city, and that it is lowest in the biggest houses. This means two things: one, that the almost

---

7. Forty-fourth Annual Report of the Association for Improving the Condition of the Poor. 1887.

exclusive attention given to the tenements by the sanitary authorities in twenty years has borne some fruit, and that the newer tenements are better than the old—there is some hope in that; the other, that the whole strain of tenement-house dwellers has been bred down to the conditions under which it exists, that the struggle with corruption has begotten the power to resist it. This is a familiar law of nature, necessary to its first and strongest impulse of self-preservation. To a certain extent, we are all creatures of the conditions that surround us, physically and morally. But is the knowledge reassuring? In the light of what we have seen, does not the question arise: what sort of creature, then, this of the tenement? I tried to draw his likeness from observation in telling the story of the "tough." Has it nothing to suggest the man with the knife?

I will go further. I am not willing even to admit it to be an unqualified advantage that our New York tenements have less of the slum look than those of older cities. It helps to delay the recognition of their true character on the part of the well-meaning, but uninstructed, who are always in the majority.

The "dangerous classes" of New York long ago compelled recognition. They are dangerous less because of their own crimes than because of the criminal ignorance of those who are not of their kind. The danger to society comes not from the poverty of the tenements, but from the ill-spent wealth that reared them, that it might earn a usurious interest from a class from which "nothing else was expected." That was the broad foundation laid down, and the edifice built upon it corresponds to the groundwork. That this is well understood on the "unsafe" side of the line that separates the rich from the poor, much better than by those who have all the advantages of discriminating education, is good cause for disquietude. In it a keen foresight may again dimly discern the shadow of the man with the knife.

Two years ago a great meeting was held at Chickering Hall—I have spoken of it before—a meeting that discussed for days and nights the question how to banish this spectre; how to lay hold with good influences of this enormous mass of more than a million people, who were drifting away faster and faster from the safe moorings of the old faith. Clergymen and laymen from all the Protestant denominations took part in the discussion; nor was a good word forgotten for the brethren of the other great Christian fold[8] who labor among the poor. Much was said that was good and true, and ways were found of reaching the spiritual needs of the tenement population that promise success. But at no time throughout the conference was the real key-note of the situation so boldly struck as has been done by a few far-seeing business men, who had listened to the cry of that Christian builder: "How shall the love of God be understood by those who have been nurtured in sight only of the greed of man?" Their practical programme of "Philanthropy and five per cent." has set examples in tenement building that show,

---

8. Roman Catholics. [Ed.]

though they are yet few and scattered, what may in time be accomplished even with such poor opportunities as New York offers to-day of undoing the old wrong. This is the gospel of justice, the solution that must be sought as the one alternative to the man with the knife.

"Are you not looking too much to the material condition of these people," said a good minister to me after a lecture in a Harlem church last winter, "and forgetting the inner man?" I told him, "No! for you cannot expect to find an inner man to appeal to in the worst tenement-house surroundings. Yon must first put the man where he can respect himself. To reverse the argument of the apple: you cannot expect to find a sound core in a rotten fruit."

Study Questions

1. In the first photograph, what is most significant about the living conditions depicted? What would you guess to be the occupations or the ethnicity of the men pictured?

2. What are the most revealing details of urban life captured in the second photo? What seems to be the attitude of the people photographed toward the picture taker?

3. What warning did "the man with the knife" (the subject of one of the last chapters in Riis's book) represent to New York society? Why did Riis note that his offense occurred on Fifth Avenue? What does Riis put forward as solutions to the dangerous conditions growing in the city?

4. What ethnic stereotypes does Riis employ in describing Italians and other immigrant New Yorkers? How might Riis's own ethnic identity be a source of his bias toward Italians especially? In what ways does he view them sympathetically?

5. Compare and contrast the social and economic divisions of Jacob Riis's era to those of the United States in the twenty-first century. What has or has not fundamentally changed?

6. In your judgment, is it Riis's photos or his writings that most effectively promote his objective of urban reform? To what degree did he bring different or similar skills to both these areas of his work?

WILLIAM GRAHAM SUMNER

On Social Darwinism (1894)

FROM "The Absurd Effort to Make the World Over"

Charles Darwin's publication of On the Origin of Species *in 1859 provoked a firestorm of controversy on religious grounds due to the way his theory of evolutionary progress through natural selection challenged the Genesis creation story. Further contention resulted when the English biologist and philosopher Herbert Spencer (1820–1903) extended the notion of natural selection from the plant and animal world and used it as a metaphor for societal progress, contending that the "survival of the fittest" marked human relations as well. Those who rose to the top of the socio-economic ladder, Spencer reasoned, deserved to do so. Spencer and his disciples thereby celebrated free-market capitalism for its inherent competition and argued that government efforts to interfere with resulting inequalities were ill advised and doomed to failure. This philosophy, which naturally appealed to business elites in the late nineteenth century, became known as Social Darwinism.*

The foremost American proponent of Social Darwinism was Yale sociology professor William Graham Sumner (1840–1910). His seminal essay "The Absurd Effort to Make the World Over" was published in Forum *magazine in 1894. Sumner wrote at a time of economic distress and political ferment following the Panic of 1893. Socialists and anarchists were demanding the overthrow of industrial capitalism, and the surging Populist movement was issuing detailed economic reforms that involved a dramatically expanded role for government. As you read Sumner's article, consider its merits as a defense of the Gilded Age's economic status quo.*

From Albert Galloway Keller, ed., "The Absurd Effort to Make the World Over," in *War and Other Essays* (New Haven: Yale University Press, 1911), 199–206, 208–10.

If it is said that there are some persons in our time who have become rapidly and in a great degree rich, it is true; if it is said that large aggregations of wealth in the control of individuals is a social danger, it is not true.

The movement of the industrial organization has brought out a great demand for men capable of managing great enterprises. Such have been called "captains of industry." The analogy with military leaders suggested by this name is not misleading. The great leaders in the development of the industrial organization need those talents of executive and administrative skill, power to command, courage, and fortitude, which were formerly called for in military affairs and scarcely anywhere else. The industrial army is also as dependent on its captains as a military body is on its generals. One of the worst features of the existing system is that the employees have a constant risk in their employer. If he is not competent to manage the business with success, they suffer with him. Capital also is dependent on the skill of the captain of industry for the certainty and magnitude of its profits. Under these circumstances there has been a great demand for men having the requisite ability for this function. As the organization has advanced, with more impersonal bonds of coherence and wider scope of operations, the value of this functionary has rapidly increased. The possession of the requisite ability is a natural monopoly. Consequently, all the conditions have concurred to give to those who possessed this monopoly excessive and constantly advancing rates of remuneration.

Another social function of the first importance in an intense organization is the solution of those crises in the operation of it which are called the conjuncture of the market. It is through the market that the lines of relation run which preserve the system in harmonious and rhythmical operation. The conjuncture is the momentary sharper misadjustment of supply and demand which indicates that a redistribution of productive effort is called for. The industrial organization needs to be insured against these conjunctures, which, if neglected, produce a crisis and catastrophe; and it needs that they shall be anticipated and guarded against as far as skill and foresight can do it. The rewards of this function for the bankers and capitalists who perform it are very great. The captains of industry and the capitalists who operate on the conjuncture, therefore, if they are successful, win, in these days, great fortunes in a short time. There are no earnings which are more legitimate or for which greater services are rendered to the whole industrial body.

* * *

But it is repeated until it has become a commonplace which people are afraid to question, that there is some social danger in the possession of large amounts of wealth by individuals. I ask, Why? I heard a lecture two years ago by a man who holds perhaps the first chair of political economy in the world. He said, among other things, that there was great danger in our day from great accumulations; that this danger ought to be met by taxation, and he referred to the fortune of the Rothschilds[1] and to the great fortunes made in America to prove his point. He omitted, however, to state in what the danger consisted or to specify what harm

1. Wealthy European banking family.

has ever been done by the Rothschild fortunes or by the great fortunes accumulated in America. It seemed to me that the assertions he was making, and the measures he was recommending, ex-cathedra, were very serious to be thrown out so recklessly. It is hardly to be expected that novelists, popular magazinists, amateur economists, and politicians will be more responsible. It would be easy, however, to show what good is done by accumulations of capital in a few hands—that is, under close and direct management, permitting prompt and accurate application; also to tell what harm is done by loose and unfounded denunciations of any social component or any social group. In the recent debates on the income tax the assumption that great accumulations of wealth are socially harmful and ought to be broken down by taxation was treated as an axiom, and we had direct proof how dangerous it is to fit out the average politician with such unverified and unverifiable dogmas as his warrant for his modes of handling the direful tool of taxation.

Great figures are set out as to the magnitude of certain fortunes and the proportionate amount of the national wealth held by a fraction of the population, and eloquent exclamation-points are set against them. If the figures were beyond criticism, what would they prove? Where is the rich man who is oppressing anybody? If there was one, the newspapers would ring with it. The facts about the accumulation of wealth do not constitute a plutocracy, as I will show below. Wealth, in itself considered, is only power, like steam, or electricity, or knowledge. The question of its good or ill turns on the question how it will be used. To prove any harm in aggregations of wealth it must be shown that great wealth is, as a rule, in the ordinary course of social affairs, put to a mischievous use. This cannot be shown beyond the very slightest degree, if at all.

* * *

Democracy is, of course, a word to conjure with. We have a democratic-republican political system, and we like it so well that we are prone to take any new step which can be recommended as "democratic" or which will round out some "principle" of democracy to a fuller fulfillment. Everything connected with this domain of political thought is crusted over with false historical traditions, cheap philosophy, and undefined terms, but it is useless to try to criticize it. The whole drift of the world for five hundred years has been toward democracy. That drift, produced by great discoveries and inventions, and by the discovery of a new continent, has raised the middle class out of the servile class. In alliance with the crown they crushed the feudal classes. They made the crown absolute in order to do it. Then they turned against the crown and, with the aid of the handicraftsmen and peasants, conquered it. Now the next conflict which must inevitably come is that between the middle capitalist class and the proletariat, as the word has come to be used. If a certain construction is put on this conflict, it may be called that between democracy and plutocracy, for it seems that industrialism must be developed into plutocracy by the conflict itself. That is the conflict which stands before civilized society to-day. All the signs of the times indicate its commencement, and it is big with fate to mankind and to civilization.

Although we cannot criticise democracy profitably, it may be said of it, with reference to our present subject, that up to this time democracy never has done anything, either in politics, social affairs, or industry, to prove its power to bless mankind. If we confine our attention to the United States, there are three difficulties with regard to its alleged achievements, and they all have the most serious bearing on the proposed democratization of industry.

1. The time during which democracy has been tried in the United States is too short to warrant any inferences. A century or two is a very short time in the life of political institutions, and if the circumstances change rapidly during the period the experiment is vitiated.

2. The greatest question of all about American democracy is whether it is a cause or a consequence. It is popularly assumed to be a cause, and we ascribe to its beneficent action all the political vitality, all the easiness of social relations, all the industrial activity and enterprise which we experience and which we value and enjoy. I submit, however, that, on a more thorough examination of the matter, we shall find that democracy is a consequence. There are economic and sociological causes for our political vitality and vigor, for the ease and elasticity of our social relations, and for our industrial power and success. Those causes have also produced democracy, given it success, and have made its faults and errors innocuous.

* * *

3. It is by no means certain that democracy in the United States has not, up to this time, been living on a capital inherited from aristocracy and industrialism. We have no pure democracy. Our democracy is limited at every turn by institutions which were developed in England in connection with industrialism and aristocracy, and these institutions are of the essence of our system. While our people are passionately democratic in temper and will not tolerate a doctrine that one man is not as good as another, they have common sense enough to know that he is not. . . .

* * *

We must not drop the subject of democracy without one word more. The Greeks already had occasion to notice a most serious distinction between two principles of democracy which lie at its roots. Plutarch says that Solon[2] got the archonship in part by promising equality, which some understood of esteem and dignity, others

---

2. Plutarch (c. 46–120 CE), the notable historian of ancient Greece and Rome, recounted the story of the Greek lawmaker Solon, who was archon (chief magistrate) of Athens in the sixth century BCE.

of measure and number. There is one democratic principle which means that each man should be esteemed for his merit and worth, for just what he is, without regard to birth, wealth, rank, or other adventitious circumstances. The other principle is that each one of us ought to be equal to all the others in what he gets and enjoys. The first principle is only partially realizable, but, so far as it goes, it is elevating and socially progressive and profitable. The second is not capable of an intelligible statement. The first is a principle of industrialism. It proceeds from and is intelligible only in a society built on the industrial virtues, free endeavor, security of property, and repression of the baser vices; that is, in a society whose industrial system is built on labor and exchange. The other is only a rule of division for robbers who have to divide plunder or monks who have to divide gifts. If, therefore, we want to democratize industry in the sense of the first principle, we need only perfect what we have now, especially on its political side. If we try to democratize it in the sense of the other principle, we corrupt politics at one stroke; we enter upon an industrial enterprise which will waste capital and bring us all to poverty, and we set loose greed and envy as ruling social passions.

* * *

Everyone of us is a child of his age and cannot get out of it. He is in the stream and is swept along with it. All his sciences and philosophy come to him out of it. Therefore the tide will not be changed by us. It will swallow up both us and our experiments. It will absorb the efforts at change and take them into itself as new but trivial components, and the great movement of tradition and work will go on unchanged by our fads and schemes. The things which will change it are the great discoveries and inventions, the new reactions inside the social organism, and the changes in the earth itself on account of changes in the cosmical forces. These causes will make of it just what, in fidelity to them, it ought to be. The men will be carried along with it and be made by it. The utmost they can do by their cleverness will be to note and record their course as they are carried along, which is what we do now, and is that which leads us to the vain fancy that we can make or guide the movement. That is why it is the greatest folly of which a man can be capable, to sit down with a slate and pencil to plan out a new social world.

Study Questions

1. According to Sumner, what explains and legitimates the vast fortunes of some American businessmen? How does he view the income tax?

2. Comment upon Sumner's statement that "democracy never has done any-thing . . . to prove its power to bless mankind." Why would Sumner be fearful of a society that was excessively democratic?

3. To what degree is Sumner's writing influenced by science and Darwinist ideas? What does he think of each individual's capacity to promote social change?

4. Imagine yourself a business tycoon in the 1890s. What would you think of Sumner's ideas? What might you do to promote them?

Plessy v. Ferguson (1896)

*By the 1880s, southern states had begun to pass laws mandating racial segrega-
tion. Modes of transportation such as streetcars and passenger trains were obvious candidates for such so-called Jim Crow statutes due to the way they inherently
fostered a mingling of blacks and whites. Louisiana enacted such a law in 1890
requiring "equal but separate accommodations" for both races on all passenger
trains operating within the state. In reaction, a group of New Orleans activists
organized to challenge this measure through the courts.*

*A shoemaker named Homer Plessy (1862–1925) agreed to violate the law so
that its constitutionality could be tested. Born free into a New Orleans Creole family, Plessy was only one-eighth black and was so light-skinned that he could readily
pass for white. In 1892, he bought a first-class ticket and sat in a whites-only compartment. By prior arrangement, the railroad company (which disliked the extra
expense of providing separate cars, and thus had its own motive for participating)
had a private detective arrest him. Plessy was convicted in a Louisiana court presided over by Judge John Howard Ferguson, but his appeal eventually came before
the U.S. Supreme Court. Albion Tourgée, a notable white lawyer from New York,
argued on behalf of Plessy that his rights under the Thirteenth and Fourteenth
Amendments had been violated. The more solid claim rested upon the Fourteenth
Amendment given its guarantee to all citizens (including African Americans, who
were now deemed such by virtue of this same amendment) of "the equal protection of the laws." Surely, Plessy's attorney argued, a segregation law such as Louisiana's, which separated out and stigmatized its black citizens, violated this equal
protection clause. What follows is from Justice Henry Brown's majority opinion of
May 18, 1896. As you read, think of the implications for American race relations
for the next half century during which this ruling remained in force.*

From *Plessy v. Ferguson*, 163 U.S. 537, 1896.

M r. Justice BROWN, after stating the facts delivered the opinion of the
court.

This case turns upon the constitutionality of an act of the general assembly of the
state of Louisiana, passed in 1890, providing for separate railway carriages for
the white and colored races.

The first section of the statute enacts "that all railway companies carrying passengers in their coaches in this state, shall provide equal but separate accommodations for the white, and colored races, by providing two or more passenger coaches for each passenger train, or by dividing the passenger coaches by a partition so as to secure separate accommodations: provided, that this section shall not be construed to apply to street railroads. No person or persons shall be permitted to occupy seats in coaches, other than the ones assigned to them, on account of the race they belong to."

By the second section it was enacted "that the officers of such passenger trains shall have power and are hereby required to assign each passenger to the coach or compartment used for the race to which such passenger belongs; any passenger insisting on going into a coach or compartment to which by race he does not belong, shall be liable to a fine of twenty-five dollars, or in lieu thereof to imprisonment for a period of not more than twenty days in the parish[1] prison, and any officer of any railroad insisting on assigning a passenger to a coach or compartment other than the one set aside for the race to which said passenger belongs, shall be liable to a fine of twenty-five dollars, or in lieu thereof to imprisonment for a period of not more than twenty days in the parish prison; and should any passenger refuse to occupy the coach or compartment to which he or she is assigned by the officer of such railway, said officer shall have power to refuse to carry such passenger on his train, and for such refusal neither he nor the railway company which he represents shall be liable for damages in any of the courts of this state."

The third section provides penalties for the refusal or neglect of the officers, directors, conductors, and employees of railway companies to comply with the act, with a proviso that "nothing in this act shall be construed as applying to nurses attending children of the other race." The fourth section is immaterial.

The information filed in the criminal district court charged, in substance, that Plessy, being a passenger between two stations within the state of Louisiana, was assigned by officers of the company to the coach used for the race to which he belonged, but he insisted upon going into a coach used by the race to which he did not belong. Neither in the information nor plea was his particular race or color averred.

The petition for the writ of prohibition averred that petitioner was seven-eights Caucasian and one-eighth African blood; that the mixture of colored blood was not discernible in him; and that he was entitled to every right, privilege, and immunity secured to citizens of the United States of the white race; and that, upon such theory, he took possession of a vacant seat in a coach where passengers of the white race were accommodated, and was ordered by the conductor to

---

1. In Louisiana, parishes are the equivalents of counties.

vacate said coach, and take a seat in another, assigned to persons of the colored race, and, having refused to comply with such demand, he was forcibly ejected, with the aid of a police officer, and imprisoned in the parish jail to answer a charge of having violated the above act.

The constitutionality of this act is attacked upon the ground that it conflicts both with the thirteenth amendment of the constitution, abolishing slavery, and the fourteenth amendment, which prohibits certain restrictive legislation on the part of the states.

1. That it does not conflict with the thirteenth amendment, which abolished slavery and involuntary servitude, except a punishment for crime, is too clear for argument. Slavery implies involuntary servitude—a state of bondage; the ownership of mankind as a chattel, or, at least, the control of the labor and services of one man for the benefit of another, and the absence of a legal right to the disposal of his own person, property, and services.

* * *

A statute which implies merely a legal distinction between the white and colored races—a distinction which is founded in the color of the two races, and which must always exist so long as white men are distinguished from the other race by color—has no tendency to destroy the legal equality of the two races, or re-establish a state of involuntary servitude. Indeed, we do not understand that the thirteenth amendment is strenuously relied upon by the plaintiff in error in this connection.

2. By the fourteenth amendment, all persons born or naturalized in the United States, and subject to the jurisdiction thereof, are made citizens of the United States and of the state wherein they reside; and the states are forbidden from making or enforcing any law which shall abridge the privileges or immunities of citizens of the United States, or shall deprive any person of life, liberty, or property without due process of law, or deny to any person within their jurisdiction the equal protection of the laws.

* * *

The object of the amendment was undoubtedly to enforce the absolute equality of the two races before the law, but, in the nature of things, it could not have been intended to abolish distinctions based upon color, or to enforce social, as distinguished from political, equality, or a commingling of the two races upon terms unsatisfactory to either. Laws permitting, and even requiring, their separation, in places where they are liable to be brought into contact, do not necessarily imply the inferiority of either race to the other, and have been generally, if not universally, recognized as within the competency of the state legislatures in the exercise of their police power. The most common instance of this is connected with the establishment of separate schools for white and colored children, which have been held to be a valid exercise of the legislative power even by courts of states where the political rights of the colored race have been longest and most earnestly enforced.

* * *

Laws forbidding the intermarriage of the two races may be said in a technical sense to interfere with the freedom of contract, and yet have been universally recognized as within the police power of the state.

* * *

It is claimed by the plaintiff in error that, in an mixed community, the reputation of belonging to the dominant race, in this instance the white race, is "property," in the same sense that a right of action or of inheritance is property. Conceding this to be so, for the purposes of this case, we are unable to see how this statute deprives him of, or in any way affects his right to, such property. If he be a white man, and assigned to a colored coach, he may have his action for damages against the company for being deprived of his so-called "property." Upon the other hand, if he be a colored man, and be so assigned, he has been deprived of no property, since he is not lawfully entitled to the reputation of being a white man.

In this connection, it is also suggested by the learned counsel for the plaintiff in error that the same argument that will justify the state legislature in requiring railways to provide separate accommodations for the two races will also authorize them to require separate cars to be provided for people whose hair is of a certain color, or who are aliens, or who belong to certain nationalities, or to enact laws requiring colored people to walk upon one side of the street, and white people upon the other, or requiring white men's houses to be painted white, and colored men's black, or their vehicles or business signs to be of different colors, upon the theory that one side of the street is as good as the other, or that a house or vehicle of one color is as good as one of another color. The reply to all this is that every exercise of the police power must be reasonable, and extend only to such laws as are enacted in good faith for the promotion of the public good, and not for the annoyance or oppression of a particular class.

* * *

So far, then, as a conflict with the fourteenth amendment is concerned, the case reduces itself to the question whether the statute of Louisiana is a reasonable regulation, and with respect to this there must necessarily be a large discretion on the part of the legislature. In determining the question of reasonableness, it is at liberty to act with reference to the established usages, customs, and traditions of the people, and with a view to the promotion of their comfort, and the preservation of the public peace and good order. Gauged by this standard, we cannot say that a law which authorizes or even requires the separation of the two races in public conveyances is unreasonable, or more obnoxious to the fourteenth amendment than the acts of congress requiring separate schools for colored children in the District of Columbia, the constitutionality of which does not seem to have been questioned, or the corresponding acts of state legislatures.

We consider the underlying fallacy of the plaintiff's argument to consist in the assumption that the enforced separation of the two races stamps the colored race with a badge of inferiority. If this be so, it is not by reason of anything found in the act, but solely because the colored race chooses to put that construction upon it. The argument necessarily assumes that if, as has been more than once the case, and is not unlikely to be so again, the colored race should become the dominant power in the state legislature,[2] and should enact a law in precisely similar terms, it would thereby relegate the white race to an inferior position. We imagine that the white race, at least, would not acquiesce in this assumption. The argument also assumes that social prejudices may be overcome by legislation, and that equal rights cannot be secured to the negro except by an enforced commingling of the two races. We cannot accept this proposition. If the two races are to meet upon terms of social equality, it must be the result of natural affinities, a mutual appreciation of each other's merits, and a voluntary consent of individuals. As was said by the court of appeals of New York in People v. Gallagher: "This end can neither be accomplished nor promoted by laws which conflict with the general sentiment of the community upon whom they are designed to operate. When the government, therefore, has secured to each of its citizens equal rights before the law, and equal opportunities for improvement and progress, it has accomplished the end for which it was organized, and performed all of the functions respecting social advantages with which it is endowed." Legislation is powerless to eradicate racial instincts, or to abolish distinctions based upon physical differences, and the attempt to do so can only result in accentuating the difficulties of the present situation. If the civil and political rights of both races be equal, one cannot be inferior to the other civilly or politically. If one race be inferior to the other socially, the constitution of the United States cannot put them upon the same plane.

* * *

The judgment of the court below is therefore affirmed.[3]

---

2. A reference to the fact that during Reconstruction, Republicans—supported by the black vote—had controlled legislatures in most Southern states. Louisiana itself had three African American lieutenant governors between 1868 and 1876.

3. The court's vote on its Plessy ruling was seven to one, with one justice not participating.

Study Questions

1. Why did the Court quickly reject the argument that the Thirteenth Amendment applied in this case? On what grounds did Plessy's attorney argue that his client's Fourteenth Amendment rights had been violated? What did the Court rule in regard to this?

2. What did the majority opinion conclude about combating racial prejudice through legislation? In regard to this, what if any effect did the civil rights laws of the 1960s have on the intensity of racism in the United States?

3. Assess the Court's claim that segregation laws did not imply the inferiority of one race to another. What distinction did it make between social and political equality?

4. Who were the ultimate winners and losers in the *Plessy* decision? Was the Court's ruling true to or in violation of the spirit of the equal protection clause of the Fourteenth Amendment? Elaborate fully.

JANE ADDAMS

FROM *Twenty Years at Hull-House* (1911)

During the first two decades of the twentieth century, diverse American reformers grappled with the notion of "progress" and particularly with the rapid social changes wrought by industrialization, urbanization, and immigration. The result was an explosion of reform movements that historians refer to collectively as Progressivism. While some Progressives fought to regulate business, conserve national resources, or restrict immigration, others pushed for women's suffrage, the reform of city governments, and prohibition.

Perhaps no Progressive reformer was better known than Jane Addams (1860– 1935), the founder of a Chicago settlement house known as Hull House. Located in crowded immigrant neighborhoods of industrial cities, settlement houses aided the poor by providing educational programs and a variety of other services. The houses were staffed by middle-class women and men known as "residents." Residents both helped their poor neighbors directly and also campaigned nationally on behalf of child labor laws, women's rights, better sanitation, and other social reforms. Addams and a friend got the idea for Hull House when they visited a pioneering social settlement in London in 1887. Returning to Chicago, they founded Hull House in 1889. Eventually the settlement encompassed thirteen buildings and a playground, and included a gymnasium, a community kitchen, a boarding house for working women, and a kindergarten. Hull House residents offered their neighbors lessons in English and cooking, as well as courses in civics, music, art, and crafts. Hull House quickly became a model; by 1900 there were some 100 settlement houses in cities across the United States. As you read this excerpt from Addams' memoir Twenty Years at Hull-House, *think about whom she believes these institutions benefited.*

From Jane Addams, *Twenty Years at Hull-House* (Chautauqua, NY: The Chautauqua Press, 1911), 113–37.

SUBJECTIVE NECESSITY FOR SOCIAL SETTLEMENTS

The Ethical Culture Societies[1] held a summer school at Plymouth, Massachusetts, in 1892, to which they invited several people representing the then new Settlement movement, that they might discuss with others the general theme of Philanthropy and Social Progress.

I venture to produce here parts of a lecture I delivered in Plymouth, both because I have found it impossible to formulate with the same freshness those early motives and strivings, and because, when published with other papers given that summer, it was received by the Settlement people themselves as a satisfactory statement.

* * *

This paper is an attempt to analyze the motives which underlie a movement based, not only upon conviction, but upon genuine emotion, wherever educated young people are seeking an outlet for that sentiment of universal brotherhood, which the best spirit of our times is forcing from an emotion into a motive. These young people accomplish little toward the solution of this social problem, and bear the brunt of being cultivated into unnourished, oversensitive lives. They have been shut off from the common labor by which they live which is a great source of moral and physical health. They feel a fatal want of harmony between their theory and their lives, a lack of coordination between thought and action. I think it is hard for us to realize how seriously many of them are taking to the notion of human brotherhood, how eagerly they long to give tangible expression to the democratic ideal. These young men and women, longing to socialize their democracy, are animated by certain hopes which may be thus loosely formulated; that if in a democratic country nothing can be permanently achieved save through the masses of the people, it will be impossible to establish a higher political life than the people themselves crave; that it is difficult to see how the notion of a higher civic life can be fostered save through common intercourse; that the blessings which we associate with a life of refinement and cultivation can be made universal and must be made universal if they are to be permanent; that the good we secure for ourselves is precarious and uncertain, is floating in mid-air, until it is secured for all of us and incorporated into our common life. It is easier to state these hopes than to formulate the line of motives, which I believe to constitute the trend of the subjective pressure toward the Settlement. There is something primordial about these motives, but I am perhaps overbold in designating them as a great desire to share the race[2] life.

* * *

1. Movement founded in 1877 by Felix Adler (1851–1933) to foster humanism, democracy, education, and philanthropy; Ethical Culture Societies were established in many U. S. and British cities and continue to flourish today.
2. The term "race" in this context refers to "human race" and is used likewise throughout the essay.

"It is true that there is nothing after disease, indigence and a sense of guilt, so fatal to health and to life itself as the want of a proper outlet for active faculties." I have seen young girls suffer and grow sensibly lowered in vitality in the first years after they leave school. In our attempt then to give a girl pleasure and freedom from care we succeed, for the most part, in making her pitifully miserable. She finds "life" so different from what she expected it to be. She is besotted with innocent little ambitions, and does not understand this apparent waste of herself, this elaborate preparation, if no work is provided for her. There is a heritage of noble obligation which young people accept and long to perpetuate. The desire for action, the wish to right wrong and alleviate suffering haunts them daily. Society smiles at it indulgently instead of making it of value to itself.

* * *

Parents are often inconsistent: they deliberately expose their daughters to knowledge of the distress in the world; they send them to hear missionary addresses on famines in India and China; they accompany them to lectures on the suffering in Siberia; they agitate together over the forgotten region of East London. In addition to this, from babyhood the altruistic tendencies of these daughters are persistently cultivated. They are taught to be self-forgetting and self-sacrificing, to consider the good of the whole before the good of the ego. But when all this information and culture show results, when the daughter comes back from college and begins to recognize her social claim to the "submerged tenth,"[3] and to evince a disposition to fulfill it, the family claim is strenuously asserted; she is told that she is unjustified, ill-advised in her efforts. If she persists, the family too often are injured and unhappy unless the efforts are called missionary and the religious zeal of the family carry them over their sense of abuse. When this zeal does not exist, the result is perplexing. It is a curious violation of what we would fain believe a fundamental law—that the final return of the deed is upon the head of the doer. The deed is that of exclusiveness and caution, but the return, instead of falling upon the head of the exclusive and cautious, falls upon a young head full of generous and unselfish plans. The girl loses something vital out of her life to which she is entitled. She is restricted and unhappy; her elders, meanwhile, are unconscious of the situation and we have all the elements of a tragedy.

We have in America a fast-growing number of cultivated young people who have no recognized outlet for their active faculties. They hear constantly of the great social maladjustment, but no way is provided for them to change it, and their uselessness hangs about them heavily.

* * *

---

3. A phrase coined by W.E.B. Du Bois in the early 1890s to describe the black American underclass (in contrast to the "talented tenth"); in 1893 journalist Elizabeth Jordan titled her book about New York tenement life *The Submerged Tenth*.

This young life, so sincere in its emotion and good phrases and yet so undirected, seems to me as pitiful as the other great mass of destitute lives. One is supplementary to the other, and some method of communication can surely be devised. Mr. Barnett, who urged the first Settlement,—Toynbee Hall, in East London,[4]—recognized this need of outlet for the young men of Oxford and Cambridge, and hoped that the Settlement would supply the communication. It is easy to see why the Settlement movement originated in England, where the years of education are more constrained and definite than they are here, where class distinctions are more rigid. The necessity of it was greater there, but we are fast feeling the pressure of the need and meeting the necessity for Settlements in America. Our young people feel nervously the need of putting theory into action, and respond quickly to the Settlement form of activity.

Other motives which I believe make toward the Settlement are the result of a certain renaissance going forward in Christianity. The impulse to share the lives of the poor, the desire to make social service, irrespective of propaganda, express the spirit of Christ, is as old as Christianity itself.

* * *

The early Christians were preeminently nonresistant. They believed in love as a cosmic force. There was no iconoclasm during the minor peace of the Church.[5] They did not yet denounce nor tear down temples, nor preach the end of the world. They grew to a mighty number, but it never occurred to them, either in their weakness or in their strength, to regard other men for an instant as their foes or as aliens. The spectacle of the Christians loving all men was the most astounding Rome had ever seen. They were eager to sacrifice themselves for the weak, for children, and for the aged; they identified themselves with slaves and did not avoid the plague; they longed to share the common lot that they might receive the constant revelation. It was a new treasure which the early Christians added to the sum of all treasures, a joy hitherto unknown in the world—the joy of finding the Christ which lieth in each man, but which no man can unfold save in fellowship. A happiness ranging from the heroic to the pastoral enveloped them. They were to possess a revelation as long as life had new meaning to unfold, new action to propose.

I believe that there is a distinct turning among many young men and women toward this simple acceptance of Christ's message. They resent the assumption that Christianity is a set of ideas which belong to the religious consciousness, whatever that may be. They insist that it cannot be proclaimed and instituted apart from the social life of the community and that it must seek a simple and natural expression

---

4. Samuel Augustus Barnett (1844–1913) was an Anglican clergyman who, together with his wife, established a pioneering social settlement named Toynbee Hall in London's impoverished East End.

5. An idealized view of the early communitarian Christian church of the second century C.E.

in the social organism itself. The Settlement movement is only one manifestation of that wider humanitarian movement which throughout Christendom, but pre-eminently in England, is endeavoring to embody itself, not in a sect, but in society itself.

* * *

It is quite impossible for me to say in what proportion or degree the subjective necessity which led to the opening of Hull-House combined the three trends: first, the desire to interpret democracy in social terms; secondly, the impulse beating at the very source of our lives, urging us to aid in the race progress; and, thirdly, the Christian movement toward humanitarianism. It is difficult to analyze a living thing; the analysis is at best imperfect. Many more motives may blend with the three trends; possibly the desire for a new form of social success due to the nicety of imagination, which refuses worldly pleasures unmixed with the joys of self-sacrifice; possibly a love of approbation, so vast that it is not content with the treble clapping of delicate hands, but wishes also to hear the bass notes from toughened palms, may mingle with these.

The Settlement, then, is an experimental effort to aid in the solution of the social and industrial problems which are engendered by the modern conditions of life in a great city. It insists that these problems are not confined to any one por-tion of a city. It is an attempt to relieve, at the same time, the overaccumulation at one end of society and the destitution at the other; but it assumes that this overac-cumulation and destitution is most sorely felt in the things that pertain to social and educational advantages. From its very nature it can stand for no political or social propaganda. It must, in a sense, give the warm welcome of an inn to all such propaganda, if perchance one of them be found an angel. The one thing to be dreaded in the Settlement is that it lose its flexibility, its power of quick adapta-tion, its readiness to change its methods as its environment may demand. It must be open to conviction and must have a deep and abiding sense of tolerance. It must be hospitable and ready for experiment. It should demand from its residents a scientific patience in the accumulation of facts and the steady holding of their sympathies as one of the best instruments for that accumulation. It must be grounded in a philosophy whose foundation is on the solidarity of the human race, a philosophy which will not waver when the race happens to be represented by a drunken woman or an idiot boy. Its residents must be emptied of all conceit of opinion and all self-assertion, and ready to arouse and interpret the public opinion of their neighborhood. They must be content to live quietly side by side with their neighbors, until they grow into a sense of relationship and mutual interests. Their neighbors are held apart by differences of race and language which the residents can more easily overcome. They are bound to see the needs of their neighborhood as a whole, to furnish data for legislation, and to use their influence to secure it. In short, residents are pledged to devote themselves to the duties of good citizenship and to the arousing of the social energies which too largely lie dormant in every neighborhood given over to industrialism. They are bound to regard the entire life of their city as organic, to make an effort to unify it, and to protest against its over-differentiation.

* * *

SOME EARLY UNDERTAKINGS AT HULL-HOUSE

If the early American Settlements stood for a more exigent standard in philanthropic activities, insisting that each new undertaking should be preceded by carefully ascertained facts, then certainly Hull-House held to this standard in the opening of our new coffee-house first started as a public kitchen. An investigation of the sweatshops had disclosed the fact, that sewing women during the busy season paid little attention to the feeding of their families, for it was only by working steadily through the long day that the scanty pay of five, seven, or nine cents for finishing a dozen pairs of trousers could be made into a day's wage; and they bought from the nearest grocery the canned goods that could be most quickly heated, or gave a few pennies to the children with which they might secure a lunch from a neighboring candy shop.

One of the residents made an investigation, at the instance of the United States Department of Agriculture, into the food values of the dietaries of the various immigrants, and this was followed by an investigation made by another resident, for the United States Department of Labor, into the foods of the Italian colony, on the supposition that the constant use of imported products bore a distinct relation to the cost of living. I recall an Italian who, coming into Hull-House one day as we were sitting at the dinner table, expressed great surprise that Americans ate a variety of food, because he believed that they partook only of potatoes and beer. A little inquiry showed that this conclusion was drawn from the fact that he lived next to an Irish saloon and had never seen anything but potatoes going in and beer coming out.

At that time the New England kitchen was comparatively new in Boston, and Mrs. Richards[6] who was largely responsible for its foundation, hoped that cheaper cuts of meat and simpler vegetables, if they were subjected to slow and thorough processes of cooking, might be made attractive and their nutritive value secured for the people who so sadly needed more nutritious food. It was felt that this could be best accomplished in public kitchens, where the advantage of scientific training and careful supervision could be secured. One of the residents went to Boston for a training under Mrs. Richards, and when the Hull-House kitchen was fitted under her guidance and direction, our hopes ran high for some modifica-

---

6. Ellen Swallow Richards (1842–1911), educated at MIT and Vassar College in Chemistry, pioneered the study of food science and home economics.

tion of the food of the neighborhood. We did not reckon, however, with the wide diversity in nationality and inherited tastes, and while we sold a certain amount of the carefully prepared soups and stews in the neighboring factories—a sale which has steadily increased throughout the years—and were also patronized by a few households, perhaps the neighborhood estimate was best summed up by the woman who frankly confessed, that the food was certainly nutritious, but that she didn't like to eat what was nutritious, that she liked to eat "what she'd ruther."

If the dietetics were appreciated but slowly, the social value of the coffee-house and the gymnasium, which were in the same building, were quickly demonstrated. At that time the saloon halls were the only places in the neighborhood where the immigrant could hold his social gatherings, and where he could celebrate such innocent and legitimate occasions as weddings and christenings.

These halls were rented very cheaply with the understanding that various sums of money should be "passed across the bar," and it was considered a mean host or guest who failed to live up to this implied bargain.[7] The consequence was that many a reputable party ended with a certain amount of disorder, due solely to the fact that the social instinct was traded upon and used as a basis for money making by an adroit host. From the beginning the young people's clubs had asked for dancing, and nothing was more popular than the increased space for parties offered by the gymnasium, with the chance to serve refreshments in the room below. We tried experiments with every known "soft drink," from those extracted from an expensive soda water fountain to slender glasses of grape juice, but so far as drinks were concerned we never became a rival to the saloon, nor indeed did any one imagine that we were trying to do so. I remember one man who looked about the cozy little room and said, "This would be a nice place to sit in all day if one could only have beer." But the coffee-house gradually performed a mission of its own and became something of a social center to the neighborhood as well as a real convenience. Business men from the adjacent factories and school teachers from the nearest public schools, used it increasingly. The Hull-House students and club members supped together in little groups or held their reunions and social banquets, as, to a certain extent, did organizations from all parts of the town. The experience of the coffee-house taught us not to hold to preconceived ideas of what the neighborhood ought to have, but to keep ourselves in readiness to modify and adapt our undertakings as we discovered those things which the neighborhood was ready to accept.

Better food was doubtless needed, but more attractive and safer places for social gatherings were also needed, and the neighborhood was ready for one and not for the other.

---

7. In other words, the use of saloons for social gatherings led to alcohol consumption. Progressives, including Adams, often aligned with the temperance movement.

* * *

Of course there was always present the harrowing consciousness of the difference in economic condition between ourselves and our neighbors. Even if we had gone to live in the most wretched tenement, there would have always been an essential difference between them and ourselves, for we should have had a sense of security in regard to illness and old age and the lack of these two securities are the specters which most persistently haunt the poor. Could we, in spite of this, make their individual efforts more effective through organization and possibly complement them by small efforts of our own?

Some such vague hope was in our minds when we started the Hull-House Coöperative Coal Association, which led a vigorous life for three years, and developed a large membership under the skillful advice of its one paid officer, an English workingman who had had experience in coöperative societies at "'ome." Some of the meetings of the association, in which people met to consider together their basic dependence upon fire and warmth, had a curious challenge of life about them. Because the coöperators[8] knew what it meant to bring forth children in the midst of privation and to see the tiny creatures struggle for life, their recitals cut a cross section, as it were, in that world-old effort—the "dying to live" which so inevitably triumphs over poverty and suffering. And yet their very familiarity with hardship may have been responsible for that sentiment which traditionally ruins business, for a vote of the coöperators that the basket buyers be given one basket free out of every six, that the presentation of five purchase tickets should entitle the holders to a profit in coal instead of stock "because it would be a shame to keep them waiting for the dividend," was always pointed to by the conservative quarter-of-a-ton buyers as the beginning of the end. At any rate, at the close of the third winter, although the Association occupied an imposing coal yard on the southeast corner of the Hull-House block and its gross receipts were between three and four hundred dollars a day, it became evident that the concern could not remain solvent if it continued its philanthropic policy, and the experiment was terminated by the coöperators taking up their stock in the remaining coal.

Our next coöperative experiment was much more successful, perhaps because it was much more spontaneous.

At a meeting of working girls held at Hull-House during a strike in a large shoe factory, the discussions made it clear that the strikers who had been most easily frightened, and therefore first to capitulate, were naturally those girls who were paying board and were afraid of being put out if they fell too far behind. After a recital of a case of peculiar hardship one of them exclaimed: "Wouldn't it be fine if we had a boarding club of our own, and then we could stand by each other in a

8. That is, members of co-operative associations, or "co-ops."

time like this?" After that events moved quickly. We read aloud together Beatrice Potter's[9] little book on "Coöperation," and discussed all the difficulties and fascinations of such an undertaking, and on the first of May, 1891, two comfortable apartments near Hull-House were rented and furnished. The Settlement was responsible for the furniture and paid the first month's rent, but beyond that the members managed the club themselves. The undertaking "marched," as the French say, from the very first, and always on its own feet. Although there were difficulties, none of them proved insurmountable, which was a matter for great satisfaction in the face of a statement made by the head of the United States Department of Labor who, on a visit to the club when it was but two years old, said that his department had investigated many coöperative undertakings, and that none founded and managed by women had ever succeeded. At the end of the third year the club occupied all of the six apartments which the original building contained, and numbered fifty members.

Study Questions

1. According to Jane Addams, what motivated settlement house workers? Why were women particularly likely to become "residents" of these institutions?

2. What approaches did Addams and other "residents" use to help the poor/immigrants? Which were most successful?

3. Why did Addams believe that flexibility and tolerance were the most important qualities for a settlement house to have?

4. Whom was Addams hoping to reach with this book? How did this affect her writing?

---

9. English sociologist and social reformer (1858–1943), best known for coining the term "collective bargaining" and for cofounding the London School of Economics.

The Scopes Trial (1925)

The decade after World War I was a period of intense cultural struggle in America between those who welcomed the forces of modernism and those who embraced more traditional values. In 1925, a trial in the small town of Dayton, Tennessee, highlighted this clash in values. Earlier that year the Tennessee General Assembly had passed a statute banning the teaching of evolution in the state's public schools and universities. The newly formed American Civil Liberties Union recruited a young high school biology teacher, John Scopes (1900–1970), to test the law. He taught evolution and was duly indicted. Clarence Darrow (1857–1938), America's top criminal lawyer, defended Scopes. William Jennings Bryan (1860–1925), a three-time Democratic presidential candidate renowned for his populist oratory, aided the prosecution.

The excerpts below are taken from a book called The World's Most Famous Court Trial, *published within months of the trial, which purported to offer a "complete stenographic report" of the proceedings. The first excerpt is a portion of the statute that launched the case. The defense had hoped to call a series of experts on evolution, but—as seen in the second excerpt—the trial judge banned them from testifying. The third excerpt is a prayer used to open the seventh day of the proceedings. The remaining excerpts are all taken from Darrow's famous cross-examination of Bryan near the end of the trial. Since his own experts had been deemed irrelevant, Darrow called Bryan to the stand as an expert on the Bible. Darrow's two-hour interrogation of Bryan provided the most sensational moment of what had become a media circus. As you read these excerpts, think about both why the trial might have attracted such intense nationwide interest and also what that suggests about American culture at the time.*

This act in part reads as follows:

Section 1. Be it enacted by the general assembly of the state of Tennessee, that it shall be unlawful for any teacher in any of the universities, normals[1] and all other public schools of the state, which are supported in whole or in part by the public school funds of the state, to teach any theory that denies the story of the Divine creation of man as taught in the Bible, and to teach instead that man has descended from a lower order of animals.

* * *

---

1. That is, normal schools, usually two-year colleges for the training of elementary school teachers.

In the final analysis this court, after a most earnest and careful consideration, has reached the conclusions that under the provisions of the act involved in this case, it is made unlawful thereby to teach in the public schools of the state of Tennessee the theory that man descended from a lower order of animals. If the court is correct in this, then the evidence of experts would shed no light on the issues.

Therefore, the court is content to sustain the motion of the attorney-general to exclude the expert testimony.

* * *

SEVENTH DAY OF DAYTON EVOLUTION TRIAL—MONDAY, JULY 20, 1925.

. . . Prayer by Rev. Standefer:

Almighty God, our Father in Heaven, we thank Thee for all the kindly influences Thou hast surrounded our lives with. Thou hast been constantly seeking to invite us to contemplate higher and better and richer creations of Thine, and sometimes we have been stupid enough to match our human minds with revelations of the infinite and eternal. May we, as a nation, have Thy guiding and directing presence with us in all ultimate things, and wilt Thou this morning be the directing presence that supplements human limitations and enables each individual in his respective position to meet the full requirements of this position. Do Thou grant to all of us Thy presence and Thy direction in all things, we ask for Christ's sake. Amen.

* * *

Q—But when you read that Jonah[2] swallowed the whale—or that the whale swallowed Jonah—excuse me please—how do you literally interpret that?

A—When I read that a big fish swallowed Jonah—it does not say whale.

Q—Doesn't it? Are you sure?

A—That is my recollection of it. A big fish, and I believe it, and I believe in a God who can make a whale and can make a man and make both do what He pleases.

* * *

Q—Now, you say, the big fish swallowed Jonah, and he there remained how long—three days—and then he spewed him upon the land. You believe that the big fish was made to swallow Jonah?

A—I am not prepared to say that; the Bible merely says it was done.

---

2. Ancient Israelite prophet (c. eighth century BCE) whose evangelizing journey is recounted in the Hebrew Bible and the Qu'ran.

Q—You don't know whether it was the ordinary run of fish, or made for that purpose?

A—You may guess; you evolutionists guess.

* * *

Mr. Darrow—You do know that there are thousands of people who profess to be Christians who believe the earth is much more ancient and that the human race is much more ancient?

A—I think there may be.

Q—And you never have investigated to find out how long man has been on the earth?

A—I have never found it necessary.

* * *

Q—You don't care how old the earth is, how old man is and how long the animals have been here?

A—I am not so much interested in that.

Q—You have never made any investigation to find out?

A—No, sir, I have never.

* * *

Gen. Stewart[3]—I want to interpose another objection. What is the purpose of this examination?

Mr. Bryan—The purpose is to cast ridicule on everybody who believes in the Bible, and I am perfectly willing that the world shall know that these gentlemen have no other purpose than ridiculing every Christian who believes in the Bible.

Mr. Darrow—We have the purpose of preventing bigots and ignoramuses from controlling the education of the United States and you know it, and that is all.

* * *

Mr. Bryan—I am simply trying to protect the word of God against the greatest atheist or agnostic in the United States. (Prolonged applause.)

* * *

Mr. Bryan—I think it would be just as easy for the kind of God we believe in to make the earth in six days as in six years or in 6,000,000 years or in 600,000,000 years. I do not think it important whether we believe one or the other.

Q—Do you think those were literal days?

---

3. A. Thomas Stewart (1892–1972), the chief prosecutor at the Scopes Trial.

A—My impression is they were periods, but I would not attempt to argue as against anybody who wanted to believe in literal days.

Q—Have you any idea of the length of the periods?

A—No; I don't.

Q—Do you think the sun was made on the fourth day?

A—Yes.

Q—And they had evening and morning without the sun?

A—I am simply saying it is a period.

Q—They had evening and morning for four periods without the sun, do you think?

A—I believe in creation as there told, and if I am not able to explain it I will accept it. Then you can explain it to suit yourself.

Study Questions

1. How does Darrow characterize Bryan and his allies in this exchange? How does Bryan characterize Darrow?

2. Judging by the applause, with whom did the courtroom audience side? Why? What were they intending to communicate, and to whom?

3. Why do you think the prosecuting attorney objected to Darrow's interrogation of Bryan? What was at issue in this case? Why might the prosecutor have seen Darrow's questions as irrelevant?

4. What do you think Darrow hoped to achieve by cross-examining Bryan? Whom do you think he saw as his audience? Was he most concerned about the Tennessee locals in the courtroom? The members of the jury? The national audience following the trial through the press?

NEW YORK WORLD

The Triangle Shirtwaist Fire
(March 26, 1911)

America's industrial economy grew at an astonishing rate in the late nineteenth and early twentieth centuries. For workers, however, industrial growth often meant long hours, low pay, and grueling, dangerous working conditions. Nothing did more to focus national attention on the plight of American workers than the fire that broke out in the Triangle Waist Company (often called the Triangle Shirtwaist Company) on March 25, 1911. The factory, which occupied the top floors of a building in New York's Greenwich Village district, employed some 500 workers at very low wages to sew women's blouses. Most were young Jewish and Italian immigrant women, and some were as young as 14. Two years earlier, attempts to unionize Triangle employees had sparked a massive strike by 20,000 garment workers. The factory's owners responded by locking exits to keep organizers out. Most fire escapes were also broken, so when the blaze erupted many workers found themselves trapped.

The resulting horror, unfolding in broad daylight in the midst of the nation's largest city, was witnessed by scores of passersby and reporters. News of the tragedy appeared in newspapers around the nation, stirring public outrage and prompting New York State to pass the most sweeping set of workplace-safety and labor-reform laws enacted to that point. The following account appeared in the New York World, a paper owned by Joseph Pulitzer (1847–1911), which was known for its use of sensationalist coverage to boost readership. As you read this story, think about both turn-of-the-century working conditions and the relationship between the press and progressive reform.

At 4:35 o'clock yesterday afternoon fire springing from a source that may never be positively identified was discovered in the rear of the eighth floor of the ten-story building at the northwest corner of Washington Place and Greene Street, the first of three floors occupied as a factory of the Triangle Shirtwaist Company.

At 11:30 o'clock Chief Croker made this statement: "Everybody has been removed. The number taken out, which includes those who jumped from windows, is 141 . . .

At 2 o'clock this morning Chief Croker estimated the total dead as one hundred and fifty-four. He said further, "I expect something of this kind to happen in these so-called fire-proof buildings, which are without adequate protection as far as fire-escapes are concerned."

More than a third of those who lost their lives did so in jumping from windows. The firemen who answered the first of the four alarms turned in found 30 bodies on the pavements of Washington Place and Greene Street. Almost all of these were girls, as were the great majority of them all. . . .

Inspection by Acting Superintendent of Buildings Ludwig will be made the basis for charges of criminal negligence on the ground that the fire-proof doors leading to one of the inclosed tower stairways were locked. . . .

It was the most appalling horror since the Slocum disaster and the Iroquois Theater fire in Chicago.[1] Every available ambulance in Manhattan was called upon to cart the dead to the morgue—bodies charred to unrecognizable blackness or reddened to a sickly hue—as was to be seen by shoulders or limbs protruding through flame-eaten clothing. Men and women, boys and girls were of the dead that littered the street; that is actually the condition—the streets were littered.

The fire began in the eighth story. The flames licked and shot their way up through the other two stories. All three floors were occupied by the Triangle Waist Company. The estimate of the number of employees at work is made by Chief Croker at about 1,000. The proprietors of the company say 700 men and girls were in their place. . . .

Before smoke or flame gave signs from the windows, the loss of life was fully under way. The first signs that persons in the street knew that these three top stories had turned into red furnaces in which human creatures were being caught and incinerated was when screaming men and women and boys and girls crowded out on the many window ledges and threw themselves into the streets far below.

They jumped with their clothing ablaze. The hair of some of the girls streamed up aflame as they leaped. Thud after thud sounded on the pavements. It is a ghastly fact that on both the Greene Street and Washington Place sides of the building there grew mounds of the dead and dying.

And the worst horror of all was that in this heap of the dead now and then there stirred a limb or sounded a moan.

Within the three flaming floors it was as frightful. There flames enveloped many so that they died instantly. When Fire Chief Croker could make his way into these three floors, he found sights that utterly staggered him, that sent him, a man used to viewing horrors, back and down into the street with quivering lips.

---

1. On June 15, 1904, the *General Slocum*, a passenger steamboat, caught fire and sank in New York City's East River, killing 1,021 people. On December 30, 1903, a fire broke out in the Iroquois Theatre in Chicago, killing at least 605 people.

The floors were black with smoke. And then he saw as the smoke drifted away bodies burned to bare bones. There were skeletons bending over sewing machines. The elevator boys saved hundreds. They each made twenty trips from the time of the alarm until twenty minutes later when they could do no more. Fire was streaming into the shaft, flames biting at the cables. They fled for their own lives.

Some, about seventy, chose a successful avenue of escape. They clambered up a ladder to the roof. A few remembered the fire escape. Many may have thought of it but only as they uttered cries of dismay.

Wretchedly inadequate was this fire escape—a lone ladder running down to a rear narrow court, which was smoke filled as the fire raged, one narrow door giving access to the ladder. By the score they fought and struggled and breathed fire and died trying to make that needle-eye road to self-preservation. . . .

Shivering at the chasm below them, scorched by the fire behind, there were some that still held positions on the window sills when the first squad of firemen arrived.

The nets were spread below with all promptness. Citizens were commandeered into service, as the firemen necessarily gave their attention to the one engine and hose of the force that first arrived.

The catapult force that the bodies gathered in the long plunges made the nets utterly without avail. Screaming girls and men, as they fell, tore the nets from the grasp of the holders, and the bodies struck the sidewalks and lay just as they fell. Some of the bodies ripped big holes through the life-nets. . . .

Concentrated, the fire burned within. The flames caught all the flimsy lace stuff and linens that go into the making of spring and summer shirtwaists[2] and fed eagerly upon the rolls of silk.

The cutting room was laden with the stuff on long tables. The employees were toiling over such material at the rows and rows of machines. Sinisterly the spring day gave aid to the fire. Many of the window panes facing south and east were drawn down. Draughts had full play.

The experts say that the three floors must each have become a whirlpool of fire. Whichever way the entrapped creatures fled they met a curving sweep of flame. Many swooned and died. Others fought their way to the windows or the elevator or fell fighting for a chance at the fire escape, the single fire escape leading into the blind court that was to be reached from the upper floors by clambering over a window sill!

On all of the three floors, at a narrow window, a crowd met death trying to get out to that one slender fire escape ladder.

---

2. A shirtwaist was a button-down blouse that could be tucked into the waistband of a skirt and worn without a jacket. During the late nineteenth and early twentieth centuries, this garment was very popular among independent working woman.

It was a fireproof building in which this enormous tragedy occurred. Save for the three stories of blackened windows at the top, you would scarcely have been able to tell where the fire had happened. The walls stood firmly. A thin tongue of flame now and then licked around a window sash. . . .

Study Questions

1. According to the newspaper, why did the fire spread so quickly? Why did so few workers escape the flames?

2. How does the newspaper describe the fire's victims? Who were they? How did they die?

3. The article begins and ends by noting that the building in which the fire occurred was "fireproof." Why do you think the author makes this point? What does it suggest about the relative importance of material possessions like buildings and workers' lives?

4. The Triangle Fire was hardly the worst workplace disaster of the era. Between 1907 and 1909, more than 1,000 men and boys died in coal mining disasters, with 362 perishing in a single West Virginia accident. Yet Progressive efforts to improve working conditions for miners met with little success. What made the Triangle Fire different? Do you think the outrage would have been as great if most of the victims had been grown men?

FRANKLIN DELANO ROOSEVELT

Annual Address to Congress: The "Four Freedoms" (1941)

In November 1940, with much of the world already embroiled in World War II, Franklin Delano Roosevelt (1882–1945) was elected to an unprecedented third term as president. During the previous spring Nazi troops had swept across Europe, conquering Denmark, Norway, Belgium, the Netherlands, Luxembourg, and France in a matter of weeks. During the summer and fall, the Germans waged an intense air campaign against the United Kingdom. Despite the danger that Britain too might fall, many Americans continued to believe that the United States should remain neutral and stay out of the conflict.

It was in this context of war and uncertainty that Roosevelt delivered his annual message to Congress on January 6, 1941. In the speech, Roosevelt warned Americans of the "unprecedented" risk they faced "from without," he urged them to take action, and he sketched out a vision for the future. As you read Roosevelt's speech, think about the way he brings American history to bear on current events. Consider also how he mixes practical recommendations with an articulation of lofty ideals.

From Franklin D. Roosevelt, "Annual Message to Congress," Records of the United States Senate, Sen. 77A–H1, January 6, 1941.

*M*r. President, Mr. Speaker, Members of the Seventy-Seventh Congress:
I address you, the members of the Seventy-Seventh Congress, at a moment unprecedented in the history of the Union. I use the word "unprecedented," because at no previous time has American security been as seriously threatened from without as it is today.

Since the permanent formation of our government under the Constitution, in 1789, most of the periods of crisis in our history have related to our domestic affairs. Fortunately, only one of these—the four-year War between the States—ever threatened our national unity. Today, thank God, one hundred and thirty million Americans, in forty-eight sates, have forgotten points of the compass in our national unity.

It is true that prior to 1914 the United States often had been disturbed by events in other continents. We had even engaged in two wars with European nations and in a number of undeclared wars in the West Indies, in the Mediterranean, and in the Pacific for the maintenance of American rights and for the principles of peaceful commerce. But in no case had a serious threat been raised against our national safety or our continued independence.

What I seek to convey is the historic truth that the United States as a nation has at all times maintained clear, definite opposition, to any attempt to lock us in behind an ancient Chinese wall while the procession of civilization went past. Today, thinking of our children and of their children, we oppose enforced isolation for ourselves or for any other part of the Americas.

That determination of ours, extending over all these years, was proved, for example, during the quarter century of wars following the French Revolution.

While the Napoleonic struggles did threaten interests of the United States because of the French foothold in the West Indies and in Louisiana, and while we engaged in the War of 1812 to vindicate our right to peaceful trade, it is nevertheless clear that neither France nor Great Britain, nor any other nation, was aiming at domination of the whole world.

In like fashion from 1815 to 1914—ninety-nine years—no single war in Europe or in Asia constituted a real threat against our future or against the future of any other American nation.

Except in the Maximilian interlude in Mexico,[1] no foreign power sought to establish itself in this hemisphere; and the strength of the British fleet in the Atlantic has been a friendly strength. It is still a friendly strength.

Even when the World War broke out in 1914, it seemed to contain only small threat of danger to our own American future. But, as time went on, the American people began to visualize what the downfall of democratic nations might mean to our own democracy.

We need not overemphasize imperfections in the Peace of Versailles.[2] We need not harp on failure of the democracies to deal with problems of world reconstruction. We should remember that the Peace of 1919 was far less unjust than the kind of "pacification" which began even before Munich,[3] and which is being carried on under the new order of tyranny that seeks to spread over every continent today. The American people have unalterably set their faces against that tyranny.

Every realist knows that the democratic way of life is at this moment being directly assailed in every part of the world—assailed either by arms, or by secret spreading of poisonous propaganda by those who seek to destroy unity and promote discord in nations that are still at peace.

---

1. In 1864, following the French invasion of Mexico, an Austrian nobleman named Ferdinand Maximilian (1832–67) was installed as emperor of the country. In 1867 he was overthrown by liberal forces and executed.

2. The 1919 peace treaty ending World War I was signed in Versailles, France.

3. In an effort to appease Adolf Hitler (1889–1945) and avert war, France and the United Kingdom signed the Munich Agreement in September 1938. The accord allowed Nazi Germany to annex Czechoslovakia's Sudetenland, an area primarily inhabited by ethnic Germans.

During sixteen long months this assault has blotted out the whole pattern of democratic life in an appalling number of independent nations, great and small. The assailants are still on the march, threatening other nations, great and small.

Therefore, as your president, performing my constitutional duty to "give to the Congress information of the state of the Union," I find it, unhappily, necessary to report that the future and the safety of our country and of our democracy are overwhelmingly involved in events far beyond our borders.

Armed defense of democratic existence is now being gallantly waged in four continents. If that defense fails, all the population and all the resources of Europe, Asia, Africa, and Australasia will be dominated by the conquerors. Let us remember that the total of those populations and their resources in those four continents greatly exceeds the sum total of the population and the resources of the whole of the Western Hemisphere—many times over.

In times like these, it is immature—and incidentally, untrue—for anybody to brag that an unprepared America, single-handed, and with one hand tied behind its back, can hold off the whole world.

No realistic American can expect from a dictator's peace international generosity, or return of true independence, or world disarmament, or freedom of expression, or freedom of religion—or even good business.

Such a peace would bring no security for us or for our neighbors. "Those who would give up essential liberty to purchase a little temporary safety, deserve neither liberty nor safety."[4]

As a nation, we may take pride in the fact that we are softhearted; but we cannot afford to be soft-headed.

We must always be wary of those who with sounding brass and a tinkling cymbal preach the "ism" of appeasement.

We must especially beware of that small group of selfish men who would clip the wings of the American eagle in order to feather their own nests.

I have recently pointed out how quickly the tempo of modern warfare could bring into our very midst the physical attack which we must eventually expect if the dictator nations win this war.

There is much loose talk of our immunity from immediate and direct invasion from across the seas. Obviously, as long as the British navy retains its power, no such danger exists. Even if there were no British navy, it is not probable that any enemy would be stupid enough to attack us by landing troops in the United States from across thousands of miles of ocean, until it had acquired strategic bases from which to operate.

But we learn much from the lessons of the past years in Europe—particularly the lesson of Norway, whose essential seaports were captured by treachery and surprise built up over a series of years.

4. Attributed to Benjamin Franklin.

The first phase of the invasion of this hemisphere would not be the landing of regular troops. The necessary strategic points would be occupied by secret agents and their dupes—and great numbers of them are already here, and in Latin America.

As long as the aggressor nations maintain the offensive, they—not we—will choose the time and the place and the method of their attack.

That is why the future of all the American republics is today in serious danger.

That is why this annual message to the Congress is unique in our history.

That is why every member of the executive branch of the government and every member of the Congress faces great responsibility and great accountability.

The need of the moment is that our actions and our policy should be devoted primarily—almost exclusively—to meeting this foreign peril. For all our domestic problems are now a part of the great emergency.

Just as our national policy in internal affairs has been based upon a decent respect for the rights and the dignity of all our fellow men within our gates, so our national policy in foreign affairs has been based on a decent respect for the rights and dignity of all nations, large and small. And the justice of morality must and will win in the end.

Our national policy is this:

First, by an impressive expression of the public will and without regard to partisanship, we are committed to all-inclusive national defense.

Second, by an impressive expression of the public will and without regard to partisanship, we are committed to full support of all those resolute peoples, everywhere, who are resisting aggression and are thereby keeping war away from our hemisphere. By this support, we express our determination that the democratic cause shall prevail; and we strengthen the defense and the security of our own nation.

Third, by an impressive expression of the public will and without regard to partisanship, we are committed to the proposition that principles of morality and considerations for our own security will never permit us to acquiesce in a peace dictated by aggressors and sponsored by appeasers. We know that enduring peace cannot be bought at the cost of other people's freedom.

In the recent national election there was no substantial difference between the two great parties in respect to that national policy. No issue was fought out on this line before the American electorate. Today it is abundantly evident that American citizens everywhere are demanding and supporting speedy and complete action in recognition of obvious danger.

Therefore, the immediate need is a swift and driving increase in our armament production.

Leaders of industry and labor have responded to our summons. Goals of speed have been set. In some cases these goals are being reached ahead of time; in some cases we are on schedule; in other cases there are slight but not serious delays;

and in some cases—and I am sorry to say very important cases—we are all concerned by the slowness of the accomplishment of our plans.

The army and navy, however, have made substantial progress during the past year. Actual experience is improving and speeding up our methods of production with every passing day. And today's best is not good enough for tomorrow.

I am not satisfied with the progress thus far made. The men in charge of the program represent the best in training, in ability, and in patriotism. They are not satisfied with the progress thus far made. None of us will be satisfied until the job is done.

No matter whether the original goal was set too high or too low, our objective is quicker and better results. To give you two illustrations:

We are behind schedule in turning out finished airplanes; we are working day and night to solve the innumerable problems and to catch up.
We are ahead of schedule in building warships but we are working to get even further ahead of that schedule.

To change a whole nation from a basis of peacetime production of implements of peace to a basis of wartime production of implements of war is no small task. And the greatest difficulty comes at the beginning of the program, when new tools, new plant facilities, new assembly lines, and new shipways must first be constructed before the actual material begins to flow steadily and speedily from them.

The Congress, of course, must rightly keep itself informed at all times of the progress of the program. However, there is certain information, as the Congress itself will readily recognize, which, in the interests of our own security and those of the nations that we are supporting, must of needs be kept in confidence.

New circumstances are constantly begetting new needs for our safety. I shall ask this Congress for greatly increased new appropriations and authorizations to carry on what we have begun.

I also ask this Congress for authority and for funds sufficient to manufacture additional munitions and war supplies of many kinds, to be turned over to those nations which are now in actual war with aggressor nations.

Our most useful and immediate role is to act as an arsenal for them as well as for ourselves. They do not need manpower, but they do need billions of dollars' worth of the weapons of defense.

The time is near when they will not be able to pay for them all in ready cash. We cannot, and we will not, tell them that they must surrender, merely because of present inability to pay for the weapons which we know they must have.

I do not recommend that we make them a loan of dollars with which to pay for these weapons—a loan to be repaid in dollars.

I recommend that we make it possible for those nations to continue to obtain war materials in the United States, fitting their orders into our own program.[5] Nearly all their material would, if the time ever came, be useful for our own defense.

Taking counsel of expert military and naval authorities, considering what is best for our own security, we are free to decide how much should be kept here and how much should be sent abroad to our friends who by their determined and heroic resistance are giving us time in which to make ready our own defense.

For what we send abroad, we shall be repaid within a reasonable time following the close of hostilities, in similar materials, or, at our option, in other goods of many kinds, which they can produce and which we need.

Let us say to the democracies: "We Americans are vitally concerned in your defense of freedom. We are putting forth our energies, our resources and our organizing powers to give you the strength to regain and maintain a free world. We shall send you, in ever-increasing numbers, ships, planes, tanks, guns. This is our purpose and our pledge."

In fulfillment of this purpose we will not be intimidated by the threats of dictators that they will regard as a breach of international law or as an act of war our aid to the democracies which dare to resist their aggression. Such aid is not an act of war, even if a dictator should unilaterally proclaim it so to be.

When the dictators, if the dictators, are ready to make war upon us, they will not wait for an act of war on our part. They did not wait for Norway or Belgium or the Netherlands to commit an act of war.

Their only interest is in a new one-way international law, which lacks mutuality in its observance, and, therefore, becomes an instrument of oppression.

The happiness of future generations of Americans may well depend upon how effective and how immediate we can make our aid felt. No one can tell the exact character of the emergency situations that we may be called upon to meet. The nation's hands must not be tied when the nation's life is in danger.

We must all prepare to make the sacrifices that the emergency—almost as serious as war itself—demands. Whatever stands in the way of speed and efficiency in defense preparations must give way to the national need.

A free nation has the right to expect full cooperation from all groups. A free nation has the right to look to the leaders of business, of labor, and of agriculture to take the lead in stimulating effort, not among other groups but within their own groups.

The best way of dealing with the few slackers or troublemakers in our midst is, first, to shame them by patriotic example, and, if that fails, to use the sovereignty of government to save government.

---

5. Having described the United States as the "Arsenal of Democracy" in 1940, Roosevelt was pressing hard for the Lend-Lease program which, upon being passed by Congress and signed into law just two months after this speech, would result in more than $50 billion in war material being shipped to Britain, the Soviet Union, France, and China during World War II.

As men do not live by bread alone, they do not fight by armaments alone. Those who man our defenses, and those behind them who build our defenses, must have the stamina and the courage which come from unshakable belief in the manner of life which they are defending. The mighty action that we are calling for cannot be based on a disregard of all things worth fighting for.

The nation takes great satisfaction and much strength from the things which have been done to make its people conscious of their individual stake in the preservation of democratic life in America. Those things have toughened the fiber of our people, have renewed their faith and strengthened their devotion to the institutions we make ready to protect.

Certainly this is no time for any of us to stop thinking about the social and economic problems which are the root cause of the social revolution which is today a supreme factor in the world.

For there is nothing mysterious about the foundations of a healthy and strong democracy. The basic things expected by our people of their political and economic systems are simple. They are:

Equality of opportunity for youth and for others.
Jobs for those who can work.
Security for those who need it.
The ending of special privilege for the few.
The preservation of civil liberties for all.
The enjoyment of the fruits of scientific progress in a wider and constantly rising standard of living.

These are the simple, basic things that must never be lost sight of in the turmoil and unbelievable complexity of our modern world. The inner and abiding strength of our economic and political systems is dependent upon the degree to which they fulfill these expectations.

Many subjects connected with our social economy call for immediate improvement. As examples:

We should bring more citizens under the coverage of old-age pensions and unemployment insurance.
We should widen the opportunities for adequate medical care.
We should plan a better system by which persons deserving or needing gainful employment may obtain it.

I have called for personal sacrifice. I am assured of the willingness of almost all Americans to respond to that call.

A part of the sacrifice means the payment of more money in taxes. In my budget message I shall recommend that a greater portion of this great defense program be paid for from taxation than we are paying today. No person should try, or be allowed, to get rich out of this program; and the principle of tax payments in accordance with ability to pay should be constantly before our eyes to guide our legislation.

If the Congress maintains these principles, the voters, putting patriotism ahead of pocketbooks, will give you their applause.

In the future days, which we seek to make secure, we look forward to a world founded upon four essential human freedoms.

The first is freedom of speech and expression—everywhere in the world.

The second is freedom of every person to worship God in his own way—everywhere in the world.

The third is freedom from want—which, translated into world terms, means economic understandings which will secure to every nation a healthy peacetime life for its inhabitants—everywhere in the world.

The fourth is freedom from fear—which, translated into world terms, means a worldwide reduction of armaments to such a point and in such a thorough fashion that no nation will be in a position to commit an act of physical aggression against any neighbor—anywhere in the world.

That is no vision of a distant millennium. It is a definite basis for a kind of world attainable in our own time and generation. That kind of world is the very antithesis of the so-called new order of tyranny which the dictators seek to create with the crash of a bomb.

To that new order we oppose the greater conception—the moral order. A good society is able to face schemes of world domination and foreign revolutions alike without fear.

Since the beginning of our American history, we have been engaged in change—in a perpetual peaceful revolution—a revolution which goes on steadily, quietly adjusting itself to changing conditions—without the concentration camp or the quicklime in the ditch.[6] The world order which we seek is the cooperation of free countries, working together in a friendly, civilized society.

This nation has placed its destiny in the hands and heads and hearts of its millions of free men and women; and its faith in freedom under the guidance of God. Freedom means the supremacy of human rights everywhere. Our support goes to those who struggle to gain those rights or keep them. Our strength is our unity of purpose. To that high concept there can be no end save victory.

---

6. A reference to the hasty disposal of bodies in mass graves during wartime.

Study Questions

1. According to Roosevelt, why was American security threatened by a war being waged in a different hemisphere? What must Americans do to avert the danger they faced? What kinds of sacrifices did Roosevelt urge Americans to make?

2. What adjective did Roosevelt repeatedly use to describe those nations battling the Axis Powers? Do you think this term was always justified?

3. Review what you've learned about the New Deal. Do you see any connection between the goals and policies of the New Deal and the "Four Freedoms" that Roosevelt articulated at the end of the speech?

4. What was Roosevelt trying to achieve with this speech, particularly with his opening discussion of American history from 1789 through the end of World War I? Can you think of another way to tell this history?

Brown v. Board of Education (1954)

On May 17, 1954, the U.S. Supreme Court issued a landmark ruling in Brown v. Board of Education, *a case challenging state-sanctioned racial segregation in public schools. The case originated in Topeka, Kansas, where the father of a third-grader challenged a school district board-sanctioned policy that required his daughter to walk to a distant "black" elementary school even though a "white" school was nearby. Such legal segregation might appear to violate the "equal protection" clause of the Fourteenth Amendment; but in* Plessy v. Ferguson *(1896), the Supreme Court had held that separate facilities were legal as long as they were equal in quality, a ruling that opened the door to widespread segregation of schools and other public facilities for more than half a century. After World War II, the National Association for the Advancement of Colored People filed a series of lawsuits challenging the "separate but equal" doctrine in various arenas. The Supreme Court sided with the N.A.A.C.P. in some of these challenges, but not until the* Brown *decision did it explicitly overturn its earlier ruling and declare that segregated public schools were inherently unequal. The unanimous decision, drafted by Chief Justice Earl Warren (1891–1974), marked a legal turning point and helped launch the best-known phase of the civil rights movement.*

As you read this decision, think carefully about the reasons the Court offers for rejecting the "separate but equal" doctrine in 1954. What had changed since 1896?

From *Brown v. Board of Education,* 347 US 483 (1954).

M R. CHIEF JUSTICE WARREN delivered the opinion of the Court.
These cases come to us from the States of Kansas, South Carolina, Virginia, and Delaware.[1] They are premised on different facts and different local conditions, but a common legal question justifies their consideration together in this consolidated opinion.

In each of the cases, minors of the Negro race, through their legal representatives, seek the aid of the courts in obtaining admission to the public schools of

---

1. The Court consolidated the lead case, which originated in Topeka, Kansas, with school desegregation cases from South Carolina, Virginia, and Delaware.

their community on a nonsegregated basis. In each instance, they had been denied admission to schools attended by white children under laws requiring or permitting segregation according to race. This segregation was alleged to deprive the plaintiffs of the equal protection of the laws under the Fourteenth Amendment. In each of the cases other than the Delaware case, a three-judge federal district court denied relief to the plaintiffs on the so-called "separate but equal" doctrine announced by this Court in *Plessy v. Ferguson.* Under that doctrine, equality of treatment is accorded when the races are provided substantially equal facilities, even though these facilities be separate. In the Delaware case, the Supreme Court of Delaware adhered to that doctrine, but ordered that the plaintiffs be admitted to the white schools because of their superiority to the Negro schools.

The plaintiffs contend that segregated public schools are not "equal" and cannot be made "equal," and that hence they are deprived of the equal protection of the laws. Because of the obvious importance of the question presented, the Court took jurisdiction. Argument was heard in the 1952 Term, and reargument was heard this Term on certain question propounded by the Court.

Reargument was largely devoted to the circumstances surrounding the adoption of the Fourteenth Amendment in 1868. It covered exhaustively consideration of the Amendment in Congress, ratification by the states, then-existing practices in racial segregation, and the views of proponents and opponents of the Amendment. This discussion and our own investigation convince us that, although these sources cast some light, it is not enough to resolve the problem with which we are faced. At best, they are inconclusive. The most avid proponents of the post-War Amendments[2] undoubtedly intended them to remove all legal distinctions among "all persons born or naturalized in the United States." Their opponents, just as certainly, were antagonistic to both the letter and the spirit of the Amendments and wished them to have the most limited effect. What others in Congress and the state legislatures had in mind cannot be determined with any degree of certainty.

An additional reason for the inconclusive nature of the Amendment's history with respect to segregated schools is the status of public education at that time. In the South, the movement toward free common schools, supported by general taxation, had not yet taken hold. Education of white children was largely in the hands of private groups. Education of Negroes was almost nonexistent, and practically all of the race were illiterate. In fact, any education of Negroes was forbidden by law in some states. Today, in contrast, many Negroes have achieved outstand-

---

2. The Thirteenth, Fourteenth, and Fifteenth Amendments, which were passed immediately after the Civil War. The Thirteenth Amendment abolished slavery. The Fourteenth Amendment granted citizenship to all persons born in the United States and guaranteed all citizens "due process" and "equal protection" before the law. The Fifteenth Amendment barred both the federal and state governments from denying any citizen the right to vote because of race.

ing success in the arts and sciences, as well as in the business and professional world. It is true that public school education at the time of the Amendment had advanced further in the North, but the effect of the Amendment on Northern States was generally ignored in the congressional debates. Even in the North, the conditions of public education did not approximate those existing today. The curriculum was usually rudimentary; ungraded schools were common in rural areas; the school term was but three months a year in many states, and compulsory school attendance was virtually unknown. As a consequence, it is not surprising that there should be so little in the history of the Fourteenth Amendment relating to its intended effect on public education.

In the first cases in this Court construing the Fourteenth Amendment, decided shortly after its adoption, the Court interpreted it as proscribing all state-imposed discriminations against the Negro race. The doctrine of "separate but equal" did not make its appearance in this Court until 1896 in the case of *Plessy v. Ferguson*, involving not education but transportation. American courts have since labored with the doctrine for over half a century.

* * *

There are findings below that the Negro and white schools involved have been equalized, or are being equalized, with respect to buildings, curricula, qualifications and salaries of teachers, and other "tangible" factors. Our decision, therefore, cannot turn on merely a comparison of these tangible factors in the Negro and white schools involved in each of the cases. We must look instead to the effect of segregation itself on public education.

In approaching this problem, we cannot turn the clock back to 1868, when the Amendment was adopted, or even to 1896, when *Plessy v. Ferguson* was written. We must consider public education in the light of its full development and its present place in American life throughout the Nation. Only in this way can it be determined if segregation in public schools deprives these plaintiffs of the equal protection of the laws.

Today, education is perhaps the most important function of state and local governments. Compulsory school attendance laws and the great expenditures for education both demonstrate our recognition of the importance of education to our democratic society. It is required in the performance of our most basic public responsibilities, even service in the armed forces. It is the very foundation of good citizenship. Today it is the principal instrument in awakening the child to cultural values, in preparing him for later professional training, and in helping him to adjust normally to his environment. In these days, it is doubtful that any child may reasonably be expected to succeed in life if he is denied the opportunity of an education. Such an opportunity, where the state has undertaken to provide it, is a right which must be made available to all on equal terms.

We come then to the question presented: Does segregation of children in public schools solely on the basis of race, even though the physical facilities and other "tangible" factors may be equal, deprive the children of the minority group of equal educational opportunities? We believe that it does.

In *Sweatt v. Painter*[3] in finding that a segregated law school for Negroes could not provide them equal educational opportunities, this Court relied in large part on "those qualities which are incapable of objective measurement but which make for greatness in a law school." In *McLaurin v. Oklahoma State Regents*,[4] the Court, in requiring that a Negro admitted to a white graduate school be treated like all other students, again resorted to intangible considerations: ". . . his ability to study, to engage in discussions and exchange views with other students, and, in general, to learn his profession." Such considerations apply with added force to children in grade and high schools. To separate them from others of similar age and qualifications solely because of their race generates a feeling of inferiority as to their status in the community that may affect their hearts and minds in a way unlikely ever to be undone. The effect of this separation on their educational opportunities was well stated by a finding in the Kansas case by a court which nevertheless felt compelled to rule against the Negro plaintiffs:

> Segregation of white and colored children in public schools has a detrimental effect upon the colored children. The impact is greater when it has the sanction of the law, for the policy of separating the races is usually interpreted as denoting the inferiority of the negro group. A sense of inferiority affects the motivation of a child to learn. Segregation with the sanction of law, therefore, has a tendency to [retard] the educational and mental development of negro children and to deprive them of some of the benefits they would receive in a racial[ly] integrated school system.

Whatever may have been the extent of psychological knowledge at the time of *Plessy v. Ferguson*, this finding is amply supported by modern authority. Any language in *Plessy v. Ferguson* contrary to this finding is rejected.

We conclude that, in the field of public education, the doctrine of "separate but equal" has no place. Separate educational facilities are inherently unequal. Therefore, we hold that the plaintiffs and others similarly situated for whom the actions have been brought are, by reason of the segregation complained of, deprived of the equal protection of the laws guaranteed by the Fourteenth Amendment. . . .

---

3. A 1950 case in which the Supreme Court ruled that the University of Texas could not deny an African American man admission to law school simply because of his race.

4. A 1950 case in which the Supreme Court ruled that the University of Oklahoma could not deny an African American man admission to a Ph.D. program in education simply because of his race.

Study Questions

1. According to the *Brown* decision, why do the circumstances surrounding the adoption of the Fourteenth Amendment have limited bearing on this case?

2. Why does the Supreme Court reject its own precedent in *Plessy v. Ferguson*? On what kind of evidence or logic does its argument rest?

3. In 1954 the United States was in the midst of a cold war and less than ten years removed from World War II. How might this have affected the Court's judgment about the role of education in American society?

4. Chief Justice Warren thought it essential that the Court issue a unanimous decision in *Brown*. (He considered this so critical, in fact, that he agreed to postpone a ruling on the decision's implementation and eventually accepted vague language on this point.) Why do you think Warren considered unanimity in this case so crucial?

AMERICAN GIs AND NURSES

FROM *Dear America, Letters Home from Vietnam* (1966–1969)

Preceded by military advisors and over $1 billion in aid between 1955 and 1961, U.S. combat soldiers entered Vietnam in large numbers in 1964 following the passage of the Gulf of Tonkin Resolution in Congress. Until the United States withdrew its forces in 1975, the military draft was employed to send hundreds of thousands of young men to Vietnam, and of these, approximately 58,000 were killed and 300,000 wounded. Women also served voluntarily, many as nurses. American involvement in Vietnam was part of a "containment" policy dedicated to preventing the spread of communism in Europe and Southeast Asia. Policy makers insisted on a "domino theory" that one country after another, unless stopped, would "fall to the Communists"—that is, join forces with America's Cold War rival, the Soviet Union. As the war in Vietnam dragged on, though, more and more Americans began to question this rationale. The war gradually became a polarizing issue that brought an end to post–World War II consensus and gave rise to the counterculture of the late nineteen-sixties and -seventies.

For U.S. soldiers and nurses sent to Vietnam, letters were the only practical means of communicating with friends and family, who could see the war almost daily on television. The media's coverage of the war became increasingly critical over time. As you read, consider how letters home might reflect the soldiers' awareness of how the war was being portrayed on the evening news, and ponder the impact of critical coverage on troop morale. Also consider the points of view in the three letters and how the tone of letters home may have changed between 1964 and 1975.

From "Letter dated July 24, 1969" from *Home Before Morning: The Story of an Army Nurse in Vietnam* by Lynda Van Devanter. Copyright © 1983. Reprinted by permission of the Estate of Lynda Van Devanter.

Dec. 23, 1966

Dear Mom and Dad,

Everything is just fine—in fact it's better than I thought it would be. They have us in a big base camp. We're going to be staying here for a month. This area is perfectly safe. While we're in base camp, we aren't allowed to carry ammo or even keep it in our tents. . . .

Besides the platoon leader, I'm the next most important man in the platoon. All the talk I hear from the guys who have been here awhile make it sound pretty easy over here. We eat three hot meals a day. I heard when we go to the field, they fly hot meals to us in the morning and night, and for lunch you eat C-rations, and you're allowed two canteens of water a day. When you're in home base you drink all you want, plus while you're in the field you get a beer and soda free every other day.

Last night I had a little trouble falling asleep because of the artillery rounds going off. It's a 175 [mm gun], and it has a range of miles, but when it goes off it sounds like a firecracker going off in your ear. All in all things look pretty good. They have PX's[1] where you can buy whatever you want or need, which is doing me no good because I'm broke. Don't send me money because it's no good here. We use scrip for money which looks like a Sweepstakes ticket, and besides I'll be getting paid in a few days. You should be receiving a $150 in about a week. If you need it, you can use it, but if you don't, then put it in a bank, OK?

The people live like pigs. They don't know how to use soap. When they have to go to the bathroom, they go wherever they're standing, they don't care who is looking. Kids not even six [years old] run up to you and ask for a cig. The houses they live in are like rundown shacks. You can see everything—they have no doors, curtains. I'm real glad I have what I have. It seems poor to you maybe, and you want new things because you think our house doesn't look good, but after seeing the way these people live, there's no comparison. We are more than millionaires to these people—they have nothing. I can't see how people can live like this. It seems funny, in one of your letters you write about the TV going on the blink. At the same time, I almost had to laugh. These people don't even have the slightest idea what a TV is even.

Right now our big guns are going off and it sounds good knowing it's yours and they don't have any. . . .

It takes me a day to write one letter, and every chance I have I'd rather write to you than anyone else. Tell Susan I'm sorry, but I just don't have the time to write as much as I would like to. . . . Mom, the least of my problems now are girls. That's one of the things I don't have time to worry about.

One thing I don't do is worry—it doesn't pay. If I worried about everything over here that there is to worry about, I'd have a nervous breakdown. I'm very fortunate, because I have a cool head. Things that make other guys scared or shaky don't seem to bother me. Also I'm

---

1. Post Exchange, or base commissary.

fortunate because my platoon leader, Lt. Sanderson, also keeps a cool head. This man is really sharp when it comes to this stuff. I have already learned a lot about human nature from this man. He's only 23 years old, but his knowledge is really something. A person can't go wrong following his example.

Well, it's about time. I thought you would never send those onions. I can't wait for them to arrive. . . .

For sure, now, I'm going to close this short novel.

With all my love,
Your grateful son,
Johnny

On 2 February 1967, less than two months after he arrived in country, PFC John Dabonka was killed in action near the Mekong Delta town of My Tho. He was 20 years old.

———

27 March, 1968

Dear Mom and Dad,

Would you believe I am now officially assigned to a unit? It's taken so long that it's quite a relief. I have a new address that should be permanent. It is:

Company A, 4th Battalion, 3rd Infantry

11th Light Infantry Brigade, APO San Francisco 96217

I don't know if you've sent me any mail yet, but if so it hasn't gotten to me and I doubt that it ever will. But with this address everything should reach me, so no sweat. . . .

I am told that our AO is quite a good one. There is almost no contact with Charlie,[2] and what little there is rarely turns into much of a fight because he runs away. The principal danger here is from mines and booby traps.

From the people I've talked to I've come up with some new ideas on the war. For the most part nobody is particularly wild with patriotic feeling. There are, of course, those who just get a real charge out of killing people. One lieutenant I talked to said what a kick it had been to roll a gook[3] 100 yards down the beach with his machine gun. But most people generate their enthusiasm for two reasons: one is self-preservation—if I don't shoot him, he'll eventually shoot me—and the other is revenge. It's apparently quite something to see a good

---

2. GI slang for enemy guerrillas, the Viet Cong. *AO*: area of operations.
3. Contemptuous GI slang for a Vietnamese soldier or civilian.

friend blown apart by a VC booby trap, and you want to retaliate in kind.

While I am able to read *Stars and Stripes* and listen to AFVN[4] radio newscasts, I still feel very cut off from the world outside of Vietnam. I would love it dearly if you would subscribe to *Newsweek* for me. Also, what do you think of Bobby [Kennedy] for president? What about [General William] Westmoreland's new job? What does everything mean?

I now have one last editorial comment about the war and then I'll sign off. I am extremely impressed by almost every report I've heard about the enemy I am about to go and fight. He is a master of guerrilla warfare and is holding his own rather nicely with what should be the strongest military power in the world. But it is mostly his perseverance that amazes me. He works so hard and has been doing so for so long. You've heard of his tunnelling capability? A captured VC said that in coming from North Vietnam down to Saigon, he walked over 200 miles completely underground. Anyone who would dig a 200-mile tunnel and who would still do it after being at war for some 30 years must be right!

All love,
Mike

2Lt. Robert C. ("Mike") Ransom, Jr., raised in Bronxville, New York, arrived in Vietnam in March 1968. He was a platoon commander with Company A, 4th Battalion, 3rd Infantry, 11th Light Infantry Brigade, Americal Division, operating out of Chu Lai. He died after two months in country, eight days after he was wounded by shrapnel from a mine. He was 23 years old.

———————

24 July, 1969

Dear Family,

Things go fairly well here. Monsoon is very heavy right now—haven't seen the sun in a couple of weeks. But this makes the sky that much prettier at night when flares go off. There's a continual mist in the air which makes the flares hazy. At times they look like falling stars; then sometimes they seem to shine like crosses.

At 4:16 A.M. our time the other day, two of our fellow Americans landed on the moon. At that precise moment, Pleiku Air Force Base, in the sheer joy and wonder of it, sent up a whole skyful of flares—

———————

4. American Forces Vietnam Network, which operated radio and television stations in Vietnam, also by authority of the Department of Defense. *Stars and Stripes:* newspaper published by the Department of Defense.

white, red, and green. It was as if they were daring the surrounding North Vietnamese Army to try and tackle such a great nation. As we watched it from the emergency room door, we couldn't speak at all. The pride in our country filled us to the point that many had tears in their eyes.

It hurts so much sometimes to see the paper full of demonstrators, especially people burning the flag. Fight fire with fire, we ask here. Display the flag, Mom and Dad, please, every day. And tell your friends to do the same. It means so much to us to know we're supported, to know not everyone feels we're making a mistake being here.

Every day we see more and more why we're here. When a whole Montagnard[5] village comes in after being bombed and terrorized by Charlie, you know. These are helpless people dying every day. The worst of it is the children. Little baby-sans being brutally maimed and killed. They never hurt anyone. Papa-san comes in with his three babies—one dead and two covered with frag wounds.[6] You try to tell him the boy is dead—"fini"—but he keeps talking to the baby as if that will make him live again. It's enough to break your heart. And through it all, you feel something's missing. There! You put your finger on it. There's not a sound from them. The children don't cry from pain; the parents don't cry from sorrow; they're stoic.

You have to grin sometimes at the primitiveness of these Montagnards. Here in the emergency room, doctors and nurses hustle about fixing up a little girl. There stands her shy little (and I mean little—like four feet tall) papa-san, face looking down at the floor, in his loin cloth, smoking his long marijuana pipe. He has probably never seen an electric light before, and the ride here in that great noisy bird (helicopter) was too much for him to comprehend. They're such characters. One comes to the hospital and the whole family camps out in the hall or on the ramp and watches over the patient. No, nobody can tell me we don't belong here. . . .

Love,
Lynda

1Lt. Lynda Van Devanter, 71st Evac. Hosp., Pleiku, and 67th Evac. Hosp., Qui Nhon, 1969–1970.

---

5. Mountain people (French), the people of the Central Highlands of Vietnam.
6. Wounds caused by the fragments of a grenade.

Study Questions

1. What do these letters tell you about the experience of soldiers and nurses in the war?

2. How do the letters differ in describing a view of the war and of the combat experience?

3. Compare the various depictions of Vietnamese people in the different letters. What is similar and different about the authors' views of the Vietnamese people?

4. These letter writers were corresponding with their parents. Do you think they would have said the same things to friends or sweethearts? Do you see a difference between the letters dated earlier in the war and the letters dated late in the war? How do these letters compare with news accounts and textbook accounts of the war?

NATIONAL ORGANIZATION FOR WOMEN

Statement of Purpose (1966)

A series of developments in the early 1960s helped to reinvigorate the feminist movement. In 1961 President John F. Kennedy (1917–1963) established a Presidential Commission on the Status of Women; although the commission's recommendations were limited, it raised expectations and fostered a national network of those concerned about women's equality. Two years later Betty Friedan (1921–2006) published The Feminine Mystique, *a landmark book whose reception revealed the deep sense of frustration shared by many middle-class women. Feminists also drew inspiration—and some practical support—from the African American freedom struggle. The 1964 Civil Rights Act was primarily designed to address racial inequality; however, one provision of the act (Title VII) outlawed employment discrimination on the basis of race, creed, or sex. The act also established a commission to implement Title VII, but some women soon became frustrated with what they saw as its failure to take sex discrimination seriously. In 1966 these women (and a few men) gathered in Washington, D.C., and established the National Organization for Women. At the organizing conference, members debated and adopted a statement of purpose drafted by Betty Friedan.*

The founding members of NOW were mostly middle-class professional women who had long been active in the political arena. As you read this document, think about how that background might have shaped their agenda.

From The National Organization for Women Statement of Purpose (1966), reprinted with permission. This is a historical document and may not reflect the current language or priorities of the organization.

We, men and women who hereby constitute ourselves as the National Organization for Women, believe that the time has come for a new movement toward true equality for all women in America, and toward a fully equal partnership of the sexes, as part of the world-wide revolution of human rights now taking place within and beyond our national borders.

The purpose of NOW is to take action to bring women into full participation in the mainstream of American society now, exercising all the privileges and responsibilities thereof in truly equal partnership with men.

We believe the time has come to move beyond the abstract argument, discussion and symposia over the status and special nature of women which has raged in

America in recent years; the time has come to confront, with concrete action, the conditions that now prevent women from enjoying the equality of opportunity and freedom of choice which is their right, as individual Americans, and as human beings.

NOW is dedicated to the proposition that women, first and foremost, are human beings, who, like all other people in our society, must have the chance to develop their fullest human potential. We believe that women can achieve such equality only by accepting to the full the challenges and responsibilities they share with all other people in our society, as part of the decision-making mainstream of American political, economic and social life.

We organize to initiate or support action, nationally, or in any part of this nation, by individuals or organizations, to break through the silken curtain of prejudice and discrimination against women in government, industry, the professions, the churches, the political parties, the judiciary, the labor unions, in education, science, medicine, law, religion and every other field of importance in American society.

Enormous changes taking place in our society make it both possible and urgently necessary to advance the unfinished revolution of women toward true equality, now. With a life span lengthened to nearly 75 years it is no longer either necessary or possible for women to devote the greater part of their lives to child-rearing; yet childbearing and rearing which continues to be a most important part of most women's lives—still is used to justify barring women from equal professional and economic participation and advance.

Today's technology has reduced most of the productive chores which women once performed in the home and in mass-production industries based upon routine unskilled labor. This same technology has virtually eliminated the quality of muscular strength as a criterion for filling most jobs, while intensifying American industry's need for creative intelligence. In view of this new industrial revolution created by automation in the mid-twentieth century, women can and must participate in old and new fields of society in full equality—or become permanent outsiders.

Despite all the talk about the status of American women in recent years, the actual position of women in the United States has declined, and is declining, to an alarming degree throughout the 1950's and 60's. Although 46.4% of all American women between the ages of 18 and 65 now work outside the home, the overwhelming majority—75%—are in routine clerical, sales, or factory jobs, or they are household workers, cleaning women, hospital attendants. About two-thirds of Negro women workers are in the lowest paid service occupations. Working women are becoming increasingly—not less—concentrated on the bottom of the job ladder. As a consequence full-time women workers today earn on the average only 60%

of what men earn, and that wage gap has been increasing over the past twenty-five years in every major industry group. In 1964, of all women with a yearly income, 89% earned under $5,000 a year; half of all full-time year round women workers earned less than $3,690; only 1.4% of full-time year round women workers had an annual income of $10,000 or more.

Further, with higher education increasingly essential in today's society, too few women are entering and finishing college or going on to graduate or professional school. Today, women earn only one in three of the B.A.'s and M.A.'s granted, and one in ten of the Ph.D.'s.

In all the professions considered of importance to society, and in the executive ranks of industry and government, women are losing ground. Where they are present it is only a token handful. Women comprise less than 1% of federal judges; less than 4% of all lawyers; 7% of doctors. Yet women represent 51% of the U.S. population. And, increasingly, men are replacing women in the top positions in secondary and elementary schools, in social work, and in libraries—once thought to be women's fields.

Official pronouncements of the advance in the status of women hide not only the reality of this dangerous decline, but the fact that nothing is being done to stop it. The excellent reports of the President's Commission on the Status of Women and of the State Commissions[1] have not been fully implemented. Such Commissions have power only to advise. They have no power to enforce their recommendation; nor have they the freedom to organize American women and men to press for action on them. The reports of these commissions have, however, created a basis upon which it is now possible to build. Discrimination in employment on the basis of sex is now prohibited by federal law, in Title VII of the Civil Rights Act of 1964. But although nearly one-third of the cases brought before the Equal Employment Opportunity Commission[2] during the first year dealt with sex discrimination and the proportion is increasing dramatically, the Commission has not made clear its intention to enforce the law with the same seriousness on behalf of women as of other victims of discrimination. Many of these cases were Negro women, who are the victims of double discrimination of race and sex. Until now, too few women's organizations and official spokesmen have been willing to speak out against these dangers facing women. Too many women have been restrained by the fear of being called "feminist." There is no civil rights movement to speak for women, as there has been for Negroes and other victims of discrimination. The National Organization for Women must therefore begin to speak.

---

1. Commissions established by states at the recommendation of the President's Commission on the Status of Women to continue research and advocacy on behalf of women's equality.
2. Commission established by the Civil Rights Act of 1964 to implement Title VII.

WE BELIEVE that the power of American law, and the protection guaranteed by the U.S. Constitution to the civil rights of all individuals, must be effectively applied and enforced to isolate and remove patterns of sex discrimination, to ensure equality of opportunity in employment and education, and equality of civil and political rights and responsibilities on behalf of women, as well as for Negroes and other deprived groups.

We realize that women's problems are linked to many broader questions of social justice; their solution will require concerted action by many groups. Therefore, convinced that human rights for all are indivisible, we expect to give active support to the common cause of equal rights for all those who suffer discrimination and deprivation, and we call upon other organizations committed to such goals to support our efforts toward equality for women.

WE DO NOT ACCEPT the token appointment of a few women to high-level positions in government and industry as a substitute for serious continuing effort to recruit and advance women according to their individual abilities. To this end, we urge American government and industry to mobilize the same resources of ingenuity and command with which they have solved problems of far greater difficulty than those now impeding the progress of women.

WE BELIEVE that this nation has a capacity at least as great as other nations, to innovate new social institutions which will enable women to enjoy the true equality of opportunity and responsibility in society, without conflict with their responsibilities as mothers and homemakers. In such innovations, America does not lead the Western world, but lags by decades behind many European countries. We do not accept the traditional assumption that a woman has to choose between marriage and motherhood, on the one hand, and serious participation in industry or the professions on the other. We question the present expectation that all normal women will retire from job or profession for 10 or 15 years, to devote their full time to raising children, only to reenter the job market at a relatively minor level. This, in itself, is a deterrent to the aspirations of women, to their acceptance into management or professional training courses, and to the very possibility of equality of opportunity or real choice, for all but a few women. Above all, we reject the assumption that these problems are the unique responsibility of each individual woman, rather than a basic social dilemma which society must solve. True equality of opportunity and freedom of choice for women requires such practical, and possible innovations as a nationwide network of child-care centers, which will make it unnecessary for women to retire completely from society until their children are grown, and national programs to provide retraining for women who have chosen to care for their children full-time.

WE BELIEVE that it is as essential for every girl to be educated to her full potential of human ability as it is for every boy—with the knowledge that such education is the key to effective participation in today's economy and that, for a girl as for a boy, education can only be serious where there is expectation that it will be used in society. We believe that American educators are capable of devising means of imparting such expectations to girl students. Moreover, we consider the decline in the proportion of women receiving higher and professional education to be evidence of discrimination. This discrimination may take the form of quotas against the admission of women to colleges, and professional schools; lack of encouragement by parents, counselors and educators; denial of loans or fellowships; or the traditional or arbitrary procedures in graduate and professional training geared in terms of men, which inadvertently discriminate against women. We believe that the same serious attention must be given to high school dropouts who are girls as to boys.

WE REJECT the current assumptions that a man must carry the sole burden of supporting himself, his wife, and family, and that a woman is automatically entitled to lifelong support by a man upon her marriage, or that marriage, home and family are primarily woman's world and responsibility—hers, to dominate—his to support. We believe that a true partnership between the sexes demands a different concept of marriage, an equitable sharing of the responsibilities of home and children and of the economic burdens of their support. We believe that proper recognition should be given to the economic and social value of homemaking and child-care. To these ends, we will seek to open a reexamination of laws and mores governing marriage and divorce, for we believe that the current state of "half-equity" between the sexes discriminates against both men and women, and is the cause of much unnecessary hostility between the sexes.

WE BELIEVE that women must now exercise their political rights and responsibilities as American citizens. They must refuse to be segregated on the basis of sex into separate-and-not-equal ladies' auxiliaries in the political parties, and they must demand representation according to their numbers in the regularly constituted party committees—at local, state, and national levels—and in the informal power structure, participating fully in the selection of candidates and political decision-making, and running for office themselves.

IN THE INTERESTS OF THE HUMAN DIGNITY OF WOMEN, we will protest, and endeavor to change, the false image of women now prevalent in the mass media, and in the texts, ceremonies, laws, and practices of our major social institutions. Such images perpetuate contempt for women by society and by women for themselves. We are similarly opposed to all policies and practices—in church, state, college, factory, or office—which, in the guise of protectiveness, not only deny opportunities but also foster in women self-denigration, dependence, and evasion of responsibility, undermine their confidence in their own abilities and foster contempt for women.

NOW WILL HOLD ITSELF INDEPENDENT OF ANY POLITICAL PARTY in order to mobilize the political power of all women and men intent on our goals. We will strive to ensure that no party, candidate, president, senator, governor, congressman, or any public official who betrays or ignores the principle of full equality between the sexes is elected or appointed to office. If it is necessary to mobilize the votes of men and women who believe in our cause, in order to win for women the final right to be fully free and equal human beings, we so commit ourselves.

WE BELIEVE THAT women will do most to create a new image of women by acting now, and by speaking out in behalf of their own equality, freedom, and human dignity—not in pleas for special privilege, nor in enmity toward men, who are also victims of the current, half-equality between the sexes—but in an active, self-respecting partnership with men. By so doing, women will develop confidence in their own ability to determine actively, in partnership with men, the conditions of their life, their choices, their future and their society.

Study Questions

1. What kinds of changes did those who approved NOW's Statement of Purpose hope to achieve? Do they seem more concerned about women's opportunities in the public arena or with personal issues and private life?

2. According to this document, what social, demographic, or technological changes made 1966 a ripe moment "to advance the unfinished revolution of women toward true equality"? What kind of language do the NOW members use to justify their argument for women's rights?

3. What do the authors of this document mean by "the silken curtain" of prejudice against women? What relationship with men do they hope to achieve?

4. How does this document reflect the particular views and concerns of the middle-class professionals who adopted it? How do you think poor or working-class women would respond to this document?

U.S. SUPREME COURT

Roe v. Wade (1973)

In 1973 the Supreme Court handed down a decision that turned out to be one of its most controversial ever. In their landmark Roe v. Wade ruling, seven of the Court's nine justices disallowed a Texas law that banned abortion except to save the life of a mother. The decision, which rested on a legal doctrine known as the "right of privacy," effectively disallowed many efforts on the state and federal levels to restrict abortion. When Roe v. Wade came before the Court, most states had laws that severely restricted or banned abortion; however, anti-abortion laws were increasingly coming under attack as a result of the sexual revolution of the 1960s and the revitalized feminist movement. Indeed, feminists had made women's right to control their own bodies a central tenet of their movement. Between 1967 and 1972, approximately one-third of the states liberalized or repealed their criminal abortion laws in response to the Roe v. Wade decision.

Justice Harry Blackmun (1908–1999) wrote the opinion for the court majority. An appointee of President Richard Nixon (1913–1994), Blackmun had worked from 1950 to 1959 as the first in-house counsel to the Mayo Clinic, a prestigious medical practice and research group based in Rochester, Minnesota; he returned to the clinic in 1973 to conduct research for his opinion. As you read this decision, think about the relative weight the Court gave to medical, philosophical, theological, and feminist reasoning.

From *Roe v. Wade*, 410 US 113 (1973).

Mr. Justice Blackmun delivered the opinion of the Court.

* * *

We forthwith acknowledge our awareness of the sensitive and emotional nature of the abortion controversy, of the vigorous opposing views, even among physicians, and of the deep and seemingly absolute convictions that the subject inspires. One's philosophy, one's experiences, one's exposure to the raw edges of human existence, one's religious training, one's attitudes toward life and family and their values, and the moral standards one establishes and seeks to observe, are all likely to influence and to color one's thinking and conclusions about abortion.

In addition, population growth, pollution, poverty, and racial overtones tend to complicate and not to simplify the problem.

Our task, of course, is to resolve the issue by constitutional measurement, free of emotion and of predilection. We seek earnestly to do this, and, because we do, we have inquired into, and in this opinion place some emphasis upon, medical and medical-legal history and what that history reveals about man's attitudes toward the abortion procedure over the centuries. We bear in mind, too, Mr. Justice Holmes' admonition in his now-vindicated dissent in *Lochner v. New York* (1905).[1]

> [The Constitution] is made for people of fundamentally differing views, and the accident of our finding certain opinions natural and familiar or novel and even shocking ought not to conclude our judgment upon the question whether statutes embodying them conflict with the Constitution of the United States.

I

The Texas statutes that concern us here are Arts. 1191–1194 and 1196 of the State's Penal Code. These make it a crime to "procure an abortion," as therein defined, or to attempt one, except with respect to "an abortion procured or attempted by medical advice for the purpose of saving the life of the mother." Similar statutes are in existence in a majority of the States.

* * *

II

Jane Roe[2] a single woman who was residing in Dallas County, Texas, instituted this federal action in March 1970 against the District Attorney of the county.[3] She sought a declaratory judgment that the Texas criminal abortion statutes were unconstitutional on their face, and an injunction restraining the defendant from enforcing the statutes.

---

1. A controversial decision in which the Supreme Court struck down a New York law limiting the number of hours a baker could work. A slim court majority ruled that "liberty of contract" was implicit in the due process clause of the Fourteenth Amendment, and declared that the New York law violated this liberty.

2. A pseudonym used in court filings to protect the real identity of a female plaintiff. In this case, "Jane Roe" was an unwed 21-year-old who became pregnant in 1969 and wanted to terminate her pregnancy because of both economic hardship and the social stigma associated with bearing an illegitimate child. (She couldn't afford to travel out of state for an abortion.) She was later identified as Norma McCorvey (b. 1947). The case continued under her alias, even though—by the time the court ruled—she had delivered her baby and given the child up for adoption. Her attorneys amended the case to a class-action suit so that "Jane Roe" would represent all pregnant women.

3. The defendant was the district attorney in Dallas County, Texas, Henry B. Wade.

Roe alleged that she was unmarried and pregnant; that she wished to terminate her pregnancy by an abortion "performed by a competent, licensed physician, under safe, clinical conditions"; that she was unable to get a "legal" abortion in Texas because her life did not appear to be threatened by the continuation of her pregnancy; and that she could not afford to travel to another jurisdiction in order to secure a legal abortion under safe conditions. She claimed that the Texas statutes were unconstitutionally vague and that they abridged her right of personal privacy, protected by the First, Fourth, Fifth, Ninth, and Fourteenth Amendments. By an amendment to her complaint, Roe purported to sue "on behalf of herself and all other women" similarly situated.

* * *

V

The principal thrust of appellant's attack on the Texas statutes is that they improperly invade a right, said to be possessed by the pregnant woman, to choose to terminate her pregnancy. Appellant would discover this right in the concept of personal "liberty" embodied in the Fourteenth Amendment's Due Process Clause; or in personal, marital, familial, and sexual privacy said to be protected by the Bill of Rights or its penumbras, *see Griswold v. Connecticut*,[4] (1965); *Eisenstadt v. Baird* (1972); or among those rights reserved to the people by the Ninth Amendment. Before addressing this claim, we feel it desirable briefly to survey, in several aspects, the history of abortion, for such insight as that history may afford us, and then to examine the state purposes and interests behind the criminal abortion laws.

VI

It perhaps is not generally appreciated that the restrictive criminal abortion laws in effect in a majority of States today are of relatively recent vintage. Those laws, generally proscribing abortion or its attempt at any time during pregnancy except when necessary to preserve the pregnant woman's life, are not of ancient or even of common law origin. Instead, they derive from statutory changes effected, for the most part, in the latter half of the 19th century.

* * *

. . . It is undisputed that, at common law, abortion performed before "quickening"— the first recognizable movement of the fetus *in utero*, appearing usually from the 16th

---

4. In *Griswold v. Connecticut*, the Supreme Court invalidated a Connecticut law that banned the use of contraceptives on the grounds that the law violated the "right to marital privacy." In the *Eisenstadt* case, the Court upheld the right of unmarried people to possess contraceptives.

to the 18th week of pregnancy—was not an indictable offense. The absence of a common law crime for pre-quickening abortion appears to have developed from a confluence of earlier philosophical, theological, and civil and canon law concepts of when life begins. These disciplines variously approached the question in terms of the point at which the embryo or fetus became "formed" or recognizably human, or in terms of when a "person" came into being, that is, infused with a "soul" or "animated." A loose consensus evolved in early English law that these events occurred at some point between conception and live birth.

* * *

In this country, the law in effect in all but a few States until mid-19th century was the preexisting English common law. Connecticut, the first State to enact abortion legislation, adopted in 1821 that part of Lord Ellenborough's Act that related to a woman "quick with child." The death penalty was not imposed. Abortion before quickening was made a crime in that State only in 1860. In 1828, New York enacted legislation that in two respects, was to serve as a model for early anti-abortion statutes. First, while barring destruction of an unquickened fetus as well as a quick fetus, it made the former only a misdemeanor, but the latter second degree manslaughter. Second it incorporated a concept of therapeutic abortion by providing that an abortion was excused if it

> shall have been necessary to preserve the life of such mother, or shall have been advised by two physicians to be necessary for such purpose.

. . . Gradually, in the middle and late 19th century, the quickening distinction disappeared from the statutory law of most States and the degree of the offense and the penalties were increased. By the end of the 1950s, a large majority of the jurisdictions banned abortion, however and whenever performed, unless done to save or preserve the life of the mother. The exceptions, Alabama and the District of Columbia, permitted abortion to preserve the mother's health. Three States permitted abortions that were not "unlawfully" performed or that were not "without lawful justification," leaving interpretation of those standards to the courts. In the past several years, however, a trend toward liberalization of abortion statutes has resulted in adoption, by about one-third of the States, of less stringent laws, . . .

It is thus apparent that, at common law, at the time of the adoption of our Constitution, and throughout the major portion of the 19th century, abortion was viewed with less disfavor than under most American statutes currently in effect. Phrasing it another way, a woman enjoyed a substantially broader right to terminate a pregnancy than she does in most States today. At least with respect to the early stage of pregnancy, and very possibly without such a limitation, the opportunity to make this choice was present in this country well into the 19th century. Even later, the law continued for some time to treat less punitively an abortion procured in early pregnancy.

* * *

VII

Three reasons have been advanced to explain historically the enactment of criminal abortion laws in the 19th century and to justify their continued existence.

It has been argued occasionally that these laws were the product of a Victorian social concern to discourage illicit sexual conduct. Texas, however, does not advance this justification in the present case, and it appears that no court or commentator has taken the argument seriously. The appellants and *amici*[5] contend, moreover, that this is not a proper state purpose, at all and suggest that, if it were, the Texas statutes are overbroad in protecting it, since the law falls to distinguish between married and unwed mothers.

A second reason is concerned with abortion as a medical procedure. When most criminal abortion laws were first enacted, the procedure was a hazardous one for the woman. This was particularly true prior to the development of antisepsis. Antiseptic techniques, of course, were based on discoveries by Lister, Pasteur,[6] and others first announced in 1867, but were not generally accepted and employed until about the turn of the century. Abortion mortality was high. Even after 1900, and perhaps until as late as the development of antibiotics in the 1940s, standard modern techniques such as dilation and curettage were not nearly so safe as they are today. Thus, it has been argued that a State's real concern in enacting a criminal abortion law was to protect the pregnant woman, that is, to restrain her from submitting to a procedure that placed her life in serious jeopardy.

Modern medical techniques have altered this situation. Appellants and various *amici* refer to medical data indicating that abortion in early pregnancy, that is, prior to the end of the first trimester, although not without its risk, is now relatively safe. Mortality rates for women undergoing early abortions, where the procedure is legal, appear to be as low as or lower than the rates for normal childbirth. Consequently,

---

5. Shortened form of *amici curiae*, meaning "friends of the court" (Latin). The term refers to those who offer to provide information to assist a court in deciding a case, even though they are not party to the case.

6. Joseph Lister (1827–1912) was a British surgeon and pioneer of antiseptic surgery. Lister's work was based on that of Louis Pasteur (1822–95), a French chemist and microbiologist who helped to show that germs cause disease.

any interest of the State in protecting the woman from an inherently hazardous procedure, except when it would be equally dangerous for her to forgo it, has largely disappeared. Of course, important state interests in the areas of health and medical standards do remain. The State has a legitimate interest in seeing to it that abortion, like any other medical procedure, is performed under circumstances that insure maximum safety for the patient. This interest obviously extends at least to the performing physician and his staff, to the facilities involved, to the availability of after-care, and to adequate provision for any complication or emergency that might arise. The prevalence of high mortality rates at illegal "abortion mills" strengthens, rather than weakens, the State's interest in regulating the conditions under which abortions are performed. Moreover, the risk to the woman increases as her pregnancy continues. Thus, the State retains a definite interest in protecting the woman's own health and safety when an abortion is proposed at a late stage of pregnancy.

The third reason is the State's interest—some phrase it in terms of duty—in protecting prenatal life. Some of the argument for this justification rests on the theory that a new human life is present from the moment of conception. The State's interest and general obligation to protect life then extends, it is argued, to prenatal life. Only when the life of the pregnant mother herself is at stake, balanced against the life she carries within her, should the interest of the embryo or fetus not prevail. Logically, of course, a legitimate state interest in this area need not stand or fall on acceptance of the belief that life begins at conception or at some other point prior to live birth. In assessing the State's interest, recognition may be given to the less rigid claim that as long as at least potential life is involved, the State may assert interests beyond the protection of the pregnant woman alone.

Parties challenging state abortion laws have sharply disputed in some courts the contention that a purpose of these laws, when enacted, was to protect prenatal life. Pointing to the absence of legislative history to support the contention, they claim that most state laws were designed solely to protect the woman. Because medical advances have lessened this concern, at least with respect to abortion in early pregnancy, they argue that with respect to such abortions the laws can no longer be justified by any state interest. There is some scholarly support for this view of original purpose. The few state courts called upon to interpret their laws in the late 19th and early 20th centuries did focus on the State's interest in protecting the woman's health, rather than in preserving the embryo and fetus. Proponents of this view point out that in many States, including Texas, by statute or judicial interpretation, the pregnant woman herself could not be prosecuted for self-abortion or for cooperating in an abortion performed upon her by another. They claim that adoption of the "quickening" distinction through received common law and state statutes tacitly recognizes the greater health hazards inherent in late abortion and impliedly repudiates the theory that life begins at conception.

VIII

The Constitution does not explicitly mention any right of privacy. In a line of decisions, however, going back perhaps as far as *Union Pacific R. Co. v. Botsford*,[7] (1891), the Court has recognized that a right of personal privacy, or a guarantee of certain areas or zones of privacy, does exist under the Constitution.

* * *

This right of privacy, whether it be founded in the Fourteenth Amendment's concept of personal liberty and restrictions upon state action, as we feel it is, or, as the District Court determined, in the Ninth Amendment's reservation of rights to the people, is broad enough to encompass a woman's decision whether or not to terminate her pregnancy. The detriment that the State would impose upon the pregnant woman by denying this choice altogether is apparent. Specific and direct harm medically diagnosable even in early pregnancy may be involved. Maternity, or additional offspring, may force upon the woman a distressful life and future. Psychological harm may be imminent. Mental and physical health may be taxed by child care. There is also the distress, for all concerned, associated with the unwanted child, and there is the problem of bringing a child into a family already unable, psychologically and otherwise, to care for it. In other cases, as in this one, the additional difficulties and continuing stigma of unwed motherhood may be involved. All these are factors the woman and her responsible physician necessarily will consider in consultation.

On the basis of elements such as these, appellant and some *amici* argue that the woman's right is absolute and that she is entitled to terminate her pregnancy at whatever time, in whatever way, and for whatever reason she alone chooses. With this we do not agree. Appellant's arguments that Texas either has no valid interest at all in regulating the abortion decision, or no interest strong enough to support any limitation upon the woman's sole determination, are unpersuasive. The Court's decisions recognizing a right of privacy also acknowledge that some state regulation in areas protected by that right is appropriate. As noted above, a State may properly assert important interests in safeguarding health, in maintaining medical standards, and in protecting potential life. At some point in pregnancy, these respective interests become sufficiently compelling to sustain regulation of the factors that govern the abortion decision. The privacy right involved, therefore, cannot be said to be absolute.

* * *

---

7. This case stemmed from a suit filed against the Union Pacific Railway Co. by a female passenger who sustained serious injuries after the upper berth in a sleeping car collapsed on her. The railroad wanted to force the plaintiff to submit to a surgical exam before the trial, but the Supreme Court ruled that no trial court could order such an examination.

IX

The appellee and certain *amici* argue that the fetus is a "person" within the language and meaning of the Fourteenth Amendment. In support of this, they outline at length and in detail the well known facts of fetal development. If this suggestion of personhood is established, the appellant's case, of course, collapses, for the fetus' right to life would then be guaranteed specifically by the Amendment. The appellant conceded as much on reargument. On the other hand, the appellee conceded on reargument that no case could be cited that holds that a fetus is a person within the meaning of the Fourteenth Amendment.

The Constitution does not define "person" in so many words. Section 1 of the Fourteenth Amendment contains three references to "person." The first, in defining "citizens," speaks of "persons born or naturalized in the United States." The word also appears both in the Due Process Clause and in the Equal Protection Clause. "Person" is used in other places in the Constitution.

* * *

But in nearly all these instances, the use of the word is such that it has application only post-natally. None indicates, with any assurance, that it has any possible pre-natal application.

All this, together with our observation, *supra*,[8] that, throughout the major portion of the 19th century, prevailing legal abortion practices were far freer than they are today, persuades us that the word "person," as used in the Fourteenth Amendment, does not include the unborn.

* * *

Texas urges that, apart from the Fourteenth Amendment, life begins at conception and is present throughout pregnancy, and that, therefore, the State has a compelling interest in protecting that life from and after conception. We need not resolve the difficult question of when life begins. When those trained in the respective disciplines of medicine, philosophy, and theology are unable to arrive at any consensus, the judiciary, at this point in the development of man's knowledge, is not in a position to speculate as to the answer.

It should be sufficient to note briefly the wide divergence of thinking on this most sensitive and difficult question. There has always been strong support for the view that life does not begin until live birth. This was the belief of the Stoics.[9]

8. Above (Latin).
9. A school of Greek philosophers.

It appears to be the predominant, though not the unanimous, attitude of the Jewish faith. It may be taken to represent also the position of a large segment of the Protestant community, insofar as that can be ascertained; organized groups that have taken a formal position on the abortion issue have generally regarded abortion as a matter for the conscience of the individual and her family. As we have noted, the common law found greater significance in quickening. Physician and their scientific colleagues have regarded that event with less interest and have tended to focus either upon conception, upon live birth, or upon the interim point at which the fetus becomes "viable," that is, potentially able to live outside the mother's womb, albeit with artificial aid. Viability is usually placed at about seven months (28 weeks) but may occur earlier, even at 24 weeks. The Aristotelian theory of "mediate animation,"[1] that held sway throughout the Middle Ages and the Renaissance in Europe, continued to be official Roman Catholic dogma until the 19th century, despite opposition to this "ensoulment" theory from those in the Church who would recognize the existence of life from the moment of conception. The latter is now, of course, the official belief of the Catholic Church. As one brief *amicus* discloses, this is a view strongly held by many non-Catholics as well, and by many physicians. Substantial problems for precise definition of this view are posed, however, by new embryological data that purport to indicate that conception is a "process" over time, rather than an event, and by new medical techniques such as menstrual extraction, the "morning-after" pill, implantation of embryos, artificial insemination, and even artificial wombs.

In areas other than criminal abortion, the law has been reluctant to endorse any theory that life, as we recognize it, begins before live birth, or to accord legal rights to the unborn except in narrowly defined situations and except when the rights are contingent upon live birth.

X

In view of all this, we do not agree that, by adopting one theory of life, Texas may override the rights of the pregnant woman that are at stake. We repeat, however, that the State does have an important and legitimate interest in preserving and protecting the health of the pregnant woman, whether she be a resident of the State or a nonresident who seeks medical consultation and treatment there, and that it has still *another* important and legitimate interest in protecting the potentiality of human life. These interests are separate and distinct. Each grows in substantiality as the woman approaches term and, at a point during pregnancy, each becomes "compelling."

---

1. The belief that the soul enters the embryo or fetus at some point between conception and birth.

With respect to the State's important and legitimate interest in the health of the mother, the "compelling" point, in the light of present medical knowledge, is at approximately the end of the first trimester. This is so because of the now-established medical fact that, until the end of the first trimester mortality in abortion may be less than mortality in normal childbirth. It follows that, from and after this point, a State may regulate the abortion procedure to the extent that the regulation reasonably relates to the preservation and protection of maternal health. Examples of permissible state regulation in this area are requirements as to the qualifications of the person who is to perform the abortion; as to the licensure of that person; as to the facility in which the procedure is to be performed, that is, whether it must be a hospital or may be a clinic or some other place of less-than-hospital status; as to the licensing of the facility; and the like.

This means, on the other hand, that, for the period of pregnancy prior to this "compelling" point, the attending physician, in consultation with his patient, is free to determine, without regulation by the State, that, in his medical judgment, the patient's pregnancy should be terminated. If that decision is reached, the judgment may be effectuated by an abortion free of interference by the State.

With respect to the State's important and legitimate interest in potential life, the "compelling" point is at viability. This is so because the fetus then presumably has the capability of meaningful life outside the mother's womb. State regulation protective of fetal life after viability thus has both logical and biological justifications. If the State is interested in protecting fetal life after viability, It may go so far as to proscribe abortion during that period, except when it is necessary to preserve the life or health of the mother.

Measured against these standards, Art. 1196 of the Texas Penal Code, in restricting legal abortions to those "procured or attempted by medical advice for the purpose of saving the life of the mother," sweeps too broadly. The statute makes no distinction between abortions performed early in pregnancy and those performed later, and it limits to a single reason, "saving" the mother's life, the legal justification for the procedure. The statute, therefore, cannot survive the constitutional attack made upon it here. . . .

XI

To summarize and to repeat:

1. A state criminal abortion statute of the current Texas type, that excepts from criminality only a lifesaving procedure on behalf of the mother, without regard to pregnancy stage and without recognition of the other interests involved, is violative of the Due Process Clause of the Fourteenth Amendment.

(a) For the stage prior to approximately the end of the first trimester, the abortion decision and its effectuation must be left to the medical judgment of the pregnant woman's attending physician.

(b) For the stage subsequent to approximately the end of the first trimester, the State, in promoting its interest in the health of the mother, may, if it chooses, regulate the abortion procedure in ways that are reasonably related to maternal health.

(c) For the stage subsequent to viability, the State in promoting its interest in the potentiality of human life may, if it chooses, regulate, and even proscribe, abortion except where it is necessary, in appropriate medical judgment, for the preservation of the life or health of the mother.

* * *

This holding, we feel, is consistent with the relative weights of the respective interests involved, with the lessons and examples of medical and legal history, with the lenity of the common law, and with the demands of the profound problems of the present day. The decision leaves the State free to place increasing restrictions on abortion as the period of pregnancy lengthens, so long as those restrictions are tailored to the recognized state interests. The decision vindicates the right of the physician to administer medical treatment according to his professional judgment up to the points where important state interests provide compelling justifications for intervention. Up to those points, the abortion decision in all its aspects is inherently, and primarily, a medical decision, and basic responsibility for it must rest with the physician. If an individual practitioner abuses the privilege of exercising proper medical judgment, the usual remedies, judicial and intra-professional, are available.

Study Questions

1. As the decision notes, the Constitution never explicitly mentions a "right of privacy." Where in the Constitution does the Court find support for this right?

2. According to the Court, what are the state's interests in regulating abortion? At what point do these interests take priority over a woman's "right of privacy"?

3. Does this decision rely more heavily on medical or on feminist reasoning? Does the Court seem more concerned with the right of physicians to make decisions about their patients or the right of women to control their own bodies?

4. How does the Court justify its reluctance to rule on the question of when life begins? Would reactions to the decision have been more or less heated if the court had ruled on that question?

Controversy Over the USA PATRIOT ACT (2001, 2005)

The United States has always had a strong commitment to civil liberties, but during times of war this commitment has often clashed with the perceived demands of national security. During the Civil War, President Abraham Lincoln suspended the writ of habeas corpus and ordered the arrest of anyone deemed "guilty of any disloyal practice." During World War I, Congress passed the Sedition Act, which made it a crime for anyone to publicly criticize the government or interfere with the war effort. The internment of more than 110,000 West Coast residents of Japanese descent during World War II drew sharp criticism from many civil libertarians. So too did an array of state and federal policies that targeted those suspected of Communist sympathies during the early decades of the cold war.

This tension emerged again in the United States in the months following the terrorist attacks of September 11, 2001. On that day, Islamic militants hijacked four jetliners, crashing two into the World Trade Center in New York City, one into the Pentagon in Washington, D.C., and a fourth into a field in Pennsylvania. All told, some three thousand people died in the September 11 attacks. Over the next several weeks, someone mailed letters containing spores of the deadly disease anthrax to U.S. Senate offices and several news outlets. The spore-laden letters killed five people and sickened seventeen others. In this context, the administration of President George W. Bush (b. 1946) declared a "war on terrorism." In late October, with little debate, Congress passed the USA PATRIOT ACT, which greatly expanded the government's powers in anti-terrorism investigations.

When Bush signed the Act, he went to great lengths to note that it took "an essential step in defeating terrorism, while protecting the constitutional rights of all Americans." Many critics, however, objected that the Patriot Act allowed egregious and unnecessary violations of civil liberties. This was the argument that counterterrorism expert Suzanne Spaulding made when she testified before the Senate Judiciary Committee in May 2005 about extending portions of the Act that were set to expire. Despite the concerns of critics like Spaulding, though, Congress has repeatedly extended the Patriot Act's controversial provisions. What questions do these selections raise about the proper balance between civil liberties and national security?

From George W. Bush, "Remarks on Signing the USA PATRIOT ACT of 2001, October 26, 2001," online by Gerhard Peters and John T. Woolley (The American Presidency Project), www.presidency.ucsb.edu; and "Testimony of Suzanne E. Spaulding" (United States Senate Committee on the Judiciary), www.judiciary.senate.gov.

REMARKS OF GEORGE W. BUSH ON SIGNING
THE USA PATRIOT ACT (OCTOBER 26, 2001)

Good morning and welcome to the White House. Today we take an essential step in defeating terrorism, while protecting the constitutional rights of all Americans. With my signature, this law will give intelligence and law enforcement officials important new tools to fight a present danger.

* * *

The changes, effective today, will help counter a threat like no other our Nation has ever faced. We've seen the enemy and the murder of thousands of innocent, unsuspecting people. They recognize no barrier of morality. They have no conscience. The terrorists cannot be reasoned with. Witness the recent anthrax attacks through our Postal Service.

Our country is grateful for the courage the Postal Service has shown during these difficult times. We mourn the loss of the lives of Thomas Morris and Joseph Curseen, postal workers who died in the line of duty. And our prayers go to their loved ones.

I want to assure postal workers that our Government is testing more than 200 postal facilities along the entire eastern corridor that may have been impacted. And we will move quickly to treat and protect workers where positive exposures are found.

But one thing is for certain: These terrorists must be pursued; they must be defeated; and they must be brought to justice. And that is the purpose of this legislation. Since the 11th of September, the men and women of our intelligence and law enforcement agencies have been relentless in their response to new and sudden challenges.

We have seen the horrors terrorists can inflict. We may never know what horrors our country was spared by the diligent and determined work of our police forces, the FBI, ATF agents, Federal marshals, customs officers, Secret Service, intelligence professionals, and local law enforcement officials. Under the most trying conditions, they are serving this country with excellence and often with bravery.

They deserve our full support and every means of help that we can provide. We're dealing with terrorists who operate by highly sophisticated methods and technologies, some of which were not even available when our existing laws were written. The bill before me takes account of the new realities and dangers posed by modern terrorists. It will help law enforcement to identify, to dismantle, to disrupt, and to punish terrorists before they strike.

For example, this legislation gives law enforcement officials better tools to put an end to financial counterfeiting, smuggling, and money laundering. Secondly, it gives intelligence operations and criminal operations the chance to operate not on separate tracks but to share vital information so necessary to disrupt a terrorist attack before it occurs.

As of today, we're changing the laws governing information sharing. And as importantly, we're changing the culture of our various agencies that fight terrorism. Countering and investigating terrorist activity is the number-one priority for both law enforcement and intelligence agencies. Surveillance of communications is another essential tool to pursue and stop terrorists. The existing law was written in the era of rotary telephones. This new law that I sign today will allow surveillance of all communications used by terrorists, including e-mails, the Internet, and cell phones. As of today, we'll be able to better meet the technological challenges posed by this proliferation of communications technology.

Investigations are often slowed by limit on the reach of Federal search warrants. Law enforcement agencies have to get a new warrant for each new district they investigate, even when they're after the same suspect. Under this new law, warrants are valid across all districts and across all States.

And finally, the new legislation greatly enhances the penalties that will fall on terrorists or anyone who helps them. Current statutes deal more severely with drug traffickers than with terrorists. That changes today. We are enacting new and harsh penalties for possession of biological weapons. We're making it easier to seize the assets of groups and individuals involved in terrorism. The Government will have wider latitude in deporting known terrorists and their supporters. The statute of limitations on terrorist acts will be lengthened, as will prison sentences for terrorists.

This bill was carefully drafted and considered. Led by the Members of Congress on this stage and those seated in the audience, it was crafted with skill and care, determination and a spirit of bipartisanship for which the entire Nation is grateful. This bill met with an overwhelming—overwhelming—agreement in Congress because it upholds and respects the civil liberties guaranteed by our Constitution.

This legislation is essential not only to pursuing and punishing terrorists but also preventing more atrocities in the hands of the evil ones. This Government will enforce this law with all the urgency of a nation at war. The elected branches of our Government and both political parties are united in our resolve to find and stop and punish those who would do harm to the American people.

It is now my honor to sign into law the USA PATRIOT ACT of 2001.

TESTIMONY OF SUZANNE E. SPAULDING BEFORE THE U.S. SENATE COMMITTEE ON THE JUDICIARY (MAY 10, 2005)

Let me begin by emphasizing that I have spent over twenty years working on efforts to combat terrorism, starting in 1984 when I had the privilege to serve as Senior Counsel to then Committee member and now Committee Chairman,

Senator Arlen Specter, who, as many of you know, in 1986 introduced and guided to enactment the first law to provide extraterritorial jurisdiction over terrorist attacks against Americans abroad.

Over the succeeding two decades, in my work at the Central Intelligence Agency, at both Senate and House intelligence oversight committees, and as Executive Director of two different commissions on terrorism and weapons of mass destruction, I have seen how the terrorist threat changed from one aptly characterized in the mid-80s by Brian Jenkin's[1] remark that "terrorists want a lot of people watching, not a lot of people dead," to one that is now better described by former DCI Jim Woolsey's[2] observation that "the terrorists of today don't want a seat at the table, they want to destroy the table and everyone sitting at it."

There is no question that today we face a determined set of adversaries bent on destroying American lives and our way of life. The counterterrorism imperative is to deny the terrorists both of these objectives. Evaluating how well the USA PATRIOT ACT, as enacted and as implemented, satisfies this counterterrorism imperative is the fundamental task for this committee, for the Congress as a whole, and for the American public.

One of my greatest concerns about the USA PATRIOT ACT and other changes in the law over the last several years is the migration of intrusive criminal investigative powers into the careful legal framework we had established for domestic intelligence collection, which is largely governed by the Foreign Intelligence Surveillance Act (FISA), and a reverse migration of the kind of secrecy and nondisclosure that characterizes intelligence operations into the criminal context of Title 18.[3] Tearing down the wall that hampered the sharing of information between intelligence and law enforcement was essential and I supported it. Nevertheless, there are significant differences in the way that information is collected by intelligence operations as opposed to criminal law enforcement investigations, differences that require particularly careful oversight of any new powers granted in the intelligence context.

Intelligence operations, by necessity, are often wide-ranging rather than specifically focused—creating a greater likelihood that they will include information about ordinary, law-abiding citizens; they are conducted in secret, which means abuses and mistakes may never be uncovered; and they lack safeguards against abuse that are present in the criminal context where inappropriate behavior by the government could jeopardize a prosecution. These differences between intelligence and law enforcement help explain this nation's long-standing discomfort with the idea of a domestic intelligence agency.

---

1. Brian Michael Jenkins (b. 1942), an expert on terrorism and transportation security.
2. R. James Woolsey (b. 1941), director of Central Intelligence Agency from 1993 to 1995.
3. The portion of the federal legal code that deals with federal crimes and criminal procedures.

Because the safeguards against overreaching or abuse are weaker in intelligence operations than they are in criminal investigations, powers granted for intelligence investigations should be no broader or more inclusive than is absolutely necessary to meet the national security imperative and should be accompanied by rigorous oversight by Congress and, where appropriate, the courts.

Unfortunately, this essential caution was often ignored in the FISA amendments contained in the Patriot Act. The authority actually became broader as it moved into the intelligence context and oversight was not accordingly enhanced.

Changes to FISA were often justified on the grounds that this authority is already available in the criminal context and "if it's good enough for use against drug dealers, we certainly should be able to use it against international terrorists." But in the FISA amendments in sections 214 and 215 of the Patriot Act,[4] for example, we moved from the criminal requirement that information demanded by the government is "relevant to a criminal investigation" to requiring only that information is "relevant to an investigation to protect against international terrorism." Consider this term. It does not say "an investigation into international terrorism activities"—which would at least mean there was some specific international terrorism activity being investigated. Instead, it says "an investigation to protect against international terrorism." Imagine if the FBI was engaged in an investigation to protect against bank robbery. What does that mean? Just how broad is that scope? Whose records could not be demanded under such a broad standard?

We often say that democracy is our strength. A key source of that strength stems from the unique relationship between the government and the governed, one based on transparency and trust. Intelligence collection imperatives challenge those democratic foundations and demand rigorous oversight.

---

4. One of the most controversial portions of the Patriot Act, Section 215, allows the FBI to demand that a person or entity turn over "tangible things" like books, papers, and records sought in connection with a terror investigation without first obtaining a warrant and showing probable cause. The person or entity served with a Section 215 order is prohibited from disclosing that fact. Civil libertarians have argued that Section 215 violates the Constitution and expands the government's power to secretly spy on ordinary people living in the United States. They have also argued that it can be used to investigate people based on their exercise of First Amendment rights. Section 214 expands the government's power to use "trap and trace" surveillance to gather information on the source of telephone conversations, personal letters, e-mail, and other electronic communications.

Study Questions

1. How does President Bush describe terrorists? Why does he think they represent "a threat like no other our Nation has ever faced"? Does Spaulding agree with him? How does she think the terrorist threat has changed?

2. Why does Bush argue that new legislation is necessary to combat the terrorist threat? What specifically does the Patriot Act do?

3. According to Spaulding, how do intelligence operations differ from criminal investigations? Why is this distinction important?

4. Although traditional wars have a defined enemy, the War on Terror is defined by a tactic and thus is open-ended. Why might this matter to a discussion about the proper balance between national security and civil liberties?

BARACK OBAMA

A More Perfect Union (2008)

In 2008 a young Democratic Senator from Illinois, Barack Obama (b. 1961), became the first African American to be elected president. The son of a Kenyan father and a white mother from Kansas, Obama was a relative newcomer on the national political scene. He was born and mostly raised in Honolulu, Hawaii; graduated from Columbia University and Harvard Law School; and worked as a community organizer and civil rights attorney in Chicago before entering the Illinois State Senate. Elected to the U.S. Senate in 2004, he rose to national prominence that same year when he delivered the keynote address at the Democratic National Convention. In that speech, Obama argued that Americans had more in common than politicians and pundits often suggested: "There's not a liberal and conservative America," he declared. "There's the United States of America."

Obama brought this same emphasis on common ground to his campaign for the presidency four years later. He tried to downplay racial issues during the Democratic primaries, and to cast himself as someone who could unify Americans and attract religious voters back into the Democratic Party. In March 2008, however, videos surfaced showing his longtime pastor, the Reverend Jeremiah Wright (b. 1941), giving sermons that were widely seen as racially incendiary. Obama denounced Wright's statements, but soon decided that he needed to address the race issue head-on. As you read the address that he delivered on March 18, 2008, in Philadelphia, think about how Obama meets the complex challenge of acknowledging racial anger while offering a vision of unity and hope.

From "Remarks of Senator Barack Obama: A More Perfect Union," March 18, 2008, Philadelphia (www.barackobama.com).

"We the people, in order to form a more perfect union."[1]

Two hundred and twenty-one years ago, in a hall that still stands across the street,[2] a group of men gathered and, with these simple words, launched America's improbable experiment in democracy. Farmers and scholars; statesmen and patriots who had traveled across an ocean to

1. The opening words of the Preamble to the Constitution of the United States (1787).
2. Independence Hall, site of the Constitutional Convention of 1787.

escape tyranny and persecution finally made real their declaration of independence at a Philadelphia convention that lasted through the spring of 1787.

The document they produced was eventually signed but ultimately unfinished. It was stained by this nation's original sin of slavery, a question that divided the colonies and brought the convention to a stalemate until the founders chose to allow the slave trade to continue for at least twenty more years, and to leave any final resolution to future generations.

Of course, the answer to the slavery question was already embedded within our Constitution—a Constitution that had at its very core the ideal of equal citizenship under the law; a Constitution that promised its people liberty, and justice, and a union that could be and should be perfected over time.

And yet words on a parchment would not be enough to deliver slaves from bondage, or provide men and women of every color and creed their full rights and obligations as citizens of the United States. What would be needed were Americans in successive generations who were willing to do their part—through protests and struggle, on the streets and in the courts, through a civil war and civil disobedience, and always at great risk—to narrow that gap between the promise of our ideals and the reality of their time.

This was one of the tasks we set forth at the beginning of this campaign—to continue the long march of those who came before us, a march for a more just, more equal, more free, more caring, and more prosperous America. I chose to run for the presidency at this moment in history because I believe deeply that we cannot solve the challenges of our time unless we solve them together—unless we perfect our union by understanding that we may have different stories, but we hold common hopes; that we may not look the same and we may not have come from the same place, but we all want to move in the same direction—towards a better future for our children and our grandchildren.

This belief comes from my unyielding faith in the decency and generosity of the American people. But it also comes from my own American story.

I am the son of a black man from Kenya and a white woman from Kansas. I was raised with the help of a white grandfather who survived a depression to serve in Patton's army during World War II and a white grandmother who worked on a bomber assembly line at Fort Leavenworth while he was overseas. I've gone to some of the best schools in America and lived in one of the world's poorest nations.[3] I am married to a black American who carries within her the blood of slaves and slaveowners—an inheritance we pass on to our two precious daughters. I have brothers, sisters, nieces, nephews, uncles, and cousins, of every race and every hue, scattered across three continents, and for as long as I live, I will never forget that in no other country on Earth is my story even possible.

---

3. Between the ages of six and ten, Obama lived in Indonesia.

It's a story that hasn't made me the most conventional candidate. But it is a story that has seared into my genetic makeup the idea that this nation is more than the sum of its parts—that out of many, we are truly one.

Throughout the first year of this campaign, against all predictions to the contrary, we saw how hungry the American people were for this message of unity. Despite the temptation to view my candidacy through a purely racial lens, we won commanding victories in states with some of the whitest populations in the country. In South Carolina, where the Confederate flag still flies, we built a powerful coalition of African Americans and white Americans.

This is not to say that race has not been an issue in the campaign. At various stages in the campaign, some commentators have deemed me either "too black" or "not black enough." We saw racial tensions bubble to the surface during the week before the South Carolina primary. The press has scoured every exit poll for the latest evidence of racial polarization, not just in terms of white and black, but black and brown as well.

And yet, it has only been in the last couple of weeks that the discussion of race in this campaign has taken a particularly divisive turn.

On one end of the spectrum, we've heard the implication that my candidacy is somehow an exercise in affirmative action; that it's based solely on the desire of wide-eyed liberals to purchase racial reconciliation on the cheap. On the other end, we've heard my former pastor, Reverend Jeremiah Wright, use incendiary language to express views that have the potential not only to widen the racial divide, but views that denigrate both the greatness and the goodness of our nation; that rightly offend white and black alike.

I have already condemned, in unequivocal terms, the statements of Reverend Wright that have caused such controversy. For some, nagging questions remain. Did I know him to be an occasionally fierce critic of American domestic and foreign policy? Of course. Did I ever hear him make remarks that could be considered controversial while I sat in church? Yes. Did I strongly disagree with many of his political views? Absolutely—just as I'm sure many of you have heard remarks from your pastors, priests, or rabbis with which you strongly disagreed.

But the remarks that have caused this recent firestorm weren't simply controversial. They weren't simply a religious leader's effort to speak out against perceived injustice. Instead, they expressed a profoundly distorted view of this country—a view that sees white racism as endemic, and that elevates what is wrong with America above all that we know is right with America; a view that sees the conflicts in the Middle East as rooted primarily in the actions of stalwart allies like Israel, instead of emanating from the perverse and hateful ideologies of radical Islam.

As such, Reverend Wright's comments were not only wrong but divisive, divisive at a time when we need unity; racially charged at a time when we need to come together to solve a set of monumental problems—two wars, a terrorist threat, a falling economy, a chronic health-care crisis, and potentially devastating climate change; problems that are neither black or white or Latino or Asian, but rather problems that confront us all.

Given my background, my politics, and my professed values and ideals, there will no doubt be those for whom my statements of condemnation are not enough. Why associate myself with Reverend Wright in the first place, they may ask? Why not join another church? And I confess that if all that I knew of Reverend Wright were the snippets of those sermons that have run in an endless loop on the television and YouTube, or if Trinity United Church of Christ conformed to the caricatures being peddled by some commentators, there is no doubt that I would react in much the same way.

But the truth is, that isn't all that I know of the man. The man I met more than twenty years ago is a man who helped introduce me to my Christian faith, a man who spoke to me about our obligations to love one another; to care for the sick and lift up the poor. He is a man who served his country as a U.S. Marine; who has studied and lectured at some of the finest universities and seminaries in the country, and who for over thirty years led a church that serves the community by doing God's work here on Earth—by housing the homeless, ministering to the needy, providing day care services and scholarships and prison ministries, and reaching out to those suffering from HIV/AIDS.

In my first book, *Dreams From My Father*, I described the experience of my first service at Trinity:

> People began to shout, to rise from their seats and clap and cry out, a forceful wind carrying the reverend's voice up into the rafters. . . . And in that single note—hope!—I heard something else; at the foot of that cross, inside the thousands of churches across the city, I imagined the stories of ordinary black people merging with the stories of David and Goliath, Moses and Pharaoh, the Christians in the lion's den. Ezekiel's field of dry bones. Those stories—of survival, and freedom, and hope—became our story, my story; the blood that had spilled was our blood, the tears our tears; until this black church, on this bright day, seemed once more a vessel carrying the story of a people into future generations and into a larger world. Our trials and triumphs became at once unique and universal, black and more than black; in chronicling our journey, the stories and songs gave us a means to reclaim memories that we didn't need to feel shame about . . . memories that all people might study and cherish—and with which we could start to rebuild.

That has been my experience at Trinity. Like other predominantly black churches across the country, Trinity embodies the black community in its entirety—the doctor and the welfare mom, the model student and the former gang-banger. Like other black churches, Trinity's services are full of raucous laughter and sometimes humor. They are full of dancing, clapping, screaming, and shouting that may se jarring to the untrained ear. The church contains in full the kindness and cruelty, the fierce intelligence and the shocking ignorance, the struggles and successes, the love and, yes, the bitterness and bias that make up the black experience in America.

And this helps explain, perhaps, my relationship with Reverend Wright. As imperfect as he may be, he has been like family to me. He strengthened my faith, officiated my wedding, and baptized my children. Not once in my conversations with him have I heard him talk about any ethnic group in derogatory terms, or treat whites with whom he interacted with anything but courtesy and respect. He contains within him the contradictions—the good and the bad—of the community that he has served diligently for so many years.

I can no more disown him than I can disown the black community. I can no more disown him than I can my white grandmother—a woman who helped raise me, a woman who sacrificed again and again for me, a woman who loves me as much as she loves anything in this world, but a woman who once confessed her fear of black men who passed by her on the street, and who on more than one occasion has uttered racial or ethnic stereotypes that made me cringe.

These people are a part of me. And they are a part of America, this country that I love.

Some will see this as an attempt to justify or excuse comments that are simply inexcusable. I can assure you it is not. I suppose the politically safe thing would be to move on from this episode and just hope that it fades into the woodwork. We can dismiss Reverend Wright as a crank or a demagogue, just as some have dismissed Geraldine Ferraro, in the aftermath of her recent statements, as harboring some deep-seated racial bias.[4]

But race is an issue that I believe this nation cannot afford to ignore right now. We would be making the same mistake that Reverend Wright made in his offending sermons about America—to simplify and stereotype and amplify the negative to the point that it distorts reality.

The fact is that the comments that have been made and the issues that have surfaced over the last few weeks reflect the complexities of race in this country that we've never really worked through—a part of our union that we have yet to perfect. And if we walk away now, if we simply retreat into our respective corners, we will never be able to come together and solve challenges like health care, or education, or the need to find good jobs for every American.

---

4. Geraldine Ferraro (1935–2011), longtime member of the U.S. House of Representatives and the 1984 Democratic Party vice-presidential nominee. In the 2008 primary campaign, Ferraro created a furor when, as a staunch supporter of Senator Hillary Clinton, she told a California newspaper that "if [Obama] was a white man, he would not be in this position. And if he was a woman (of any color), he would not be in this position."

this reality requires a reminder of how we arrived at this point.
...er[5] once wrote, "The past isn't dead and buried. In fact, it isn't
... not need to recite here the history of racial injustice in this
... need to remind ourselves that so many of the disparities that
... American community today can be directly traced to inequal-
... an earlier generation that suffered under the brutal legacy of
...[6]

...gated schools were, and are, inferior schools; we still haven't fixed them, fifty years after *Brown v. Board of Education*,[7] and the inferior education they provided, then and now, helps explain the pervasive achievement gap between today's black and white students.

Legalized discrimination—where blacks were prevented, often through violence, from owning property, or loans were not granted to African-American business owners, or black homeowners could not access FHA[8] mortgages, or blacks were excluded from unions, or the police force, or fire departments—meant that black families could not amass any meaningful wealth to bequeath to future generations. That history helps explain the wealth and income gap between black and white, and the concentrated pockets of poverty that persist in so many of today's urban and rural communities.

A lack of economic opportunity among black men, and the shame and frustration that came from not being able to provide for one's family, contributed to the erosion of black families—a problem that welfare policies for many years may have worsened. And the lack of basic services in so many urban black neighborhoods—parks for kids to play in, police walking the beat, regular garbage pick-up, and building code enforcement—all helped create a cycle of violence, blight, and neglect that continue to haunt us.

This is the reality in which Reverend Wright and other African-Americans of his generation grew up. They came of age in the late fifties and early sixties, a time when segregation was still the law of the land and opportunity was systematically constricted. What's remarkable is not how many failed in the face of discrimination, but rather how many men and women overcame the odds; how many were able to make a way out of no way for those like me who would come after them.

But for all those who scratched and clawed their way to get a piece of the American Dream, there were many who didn't make it—those who were ultimately defeated, in one way or another, by discrimination. That legacy of defeat was passed on to future generations—those young men and, increasingly, young women who

5. American novelist (1897–1962), winner of the Nobel Prize for Literature in 1949.
6. The system of laws and customs that enforced racial segregation and discrimination against African Americans for nearly a century following the Civil War.
7. American legal case (1954) that resulted in a landmark decision by the U.S. Supreme Court declaring that racial segregation in education is unconstitutional.
8. The Federal Housing Administration, an agency of the U.S. government.

we see standing on street corners or languishing in our prisons, w
prospects for the future. Even for those blacks who did make it, ques
and racism, continue to define their worldview in fundamental ways. F
and women of Reverend Wright's generation, the memories of humilia
doubt and fear have not gone away; nor has the anger and the bitterness o
years. That anger may not get expressed in public, in front of white co-worke
white friends. But it does find voice in the barbershop or around the kitchen tal
At times, that anger is exploited by politicians, to gin up votes along racial line
or to make up for a politician's own failings.

And occasionally it finds voice in the church on Sunday morning, in the pulpit
and in the pews. The fact that so many people are surprised to hear that anger in
some of Reverend Wright's sermons simply reminds us of the old truism that the
most segregated hour in American life occurs on Sunday morning. That anger is
not always productive; indeed, all too often it distracts attention from solving real
problems; it keeps us from squarely facing our own complicity in our condition,
and prevents the African-American community from forging the alliances it
needs to bring about real change. But the anger is real; it is powerful; and to simply wish it away, to condemn it without understanding its roots, only serves to
widen the chasm of misunderstanding that exists between the races.

In fact, a similar anger exists within segments of the white community. Most
working- and middle-class white Americans don't feel that they have been particularly privileged by their race. Their experience is the immigrant experience—as far
as they're concerned, no one's handed them anything, they've built it from scratch.
They've worked hard all their lives, many times only to see their jobs shipped overseas or their pensions dumped after a lifetime of labor. They are anxious about
their futures, and feel their dreams slipping away; in an era of stagnant wages and
global competition, opportunity comes to be seen as a zero-sum game, in which
your dreams come at my expense. So when they are told to bus their children to a
school across town; when they hear that an African American is getting an advantage in landing a good job or a spot in a good college because of an injustice that
they themselves never committed; when they're told that their fears about crime in
urban neighborhoods are somehow prejudiced, resentment builds over time.

Like the anger within the black community, these resentments aren't always
expressed in polite company. But they have helped shape the political landscape
for at least a generation. Anger over welfare and affirmative action helped forge the
Reagan Coalition.[9] Politicians routinely exploited fears of crime for their own electoral ends. Talk show hosts and conservative commentators built entire careers
unmasking bogus claims of racism while dismissing legitimate discussions of racial
injustice and inequality as mere political correctness or reverse racism.

9. Ronald Reagan was able to win decisively in the presidential elections of 1980 and 1984 by attracting substantial numbers of working-class Democrats to his base of conservative Republican voters.

proved counterproductive, so have these white resent-
⁀om the real culprits of the middle-class squeeze—a
ide dealing, questionable accounting practices, and
n dominated by lobbyists and special interests;
few over the many. And yet, to wish away the
⁀ label them as misguided or even racist, within legitimate concerns—this too widens the
nderstanding.

.v. It's a racial stalemate we've been stuck in for
⁀ns of some of my critics, black and white, I have never
⁀elieve that we can get beyond our racial divisions in a single
., or with a single candidacy—particularly a candidacy as imperfect
⁀wn.

But I have asserted a firm conviction—a conviction rooted in my faith in God
and my faith in the American people—that working together we can move beyond
some of our old racial wounds, and that in fact we have no choice if we are to
continue on the path of a more perfect union.

For the African-American community, that path means embracing the burdens of our past without becoming victims of our past. It means continuing to
insist on a full measure of justice in every aspect of American life. But it also
means binding our particular grievances—for better health care, and better
schools, and better jobs—to the larger aspirations of all Americans: the white
woman struggling to break the glass ceiling, the white man who's been laid off,
the immigrant trying to feed his family. And it means taking full responsibility
for our own lives—by demanding more from our fathers, and spending more
time with our children, and reading to them, and teaching them that while they
may face challenges and discrimination in their own lives, they must never succumb to despair or cynicism; they must always believe that they can write their
own destiny.

Ironically, this quintessentially American—and yes, conservative—notion of
self-help found frequent expression in Reverend Wright's sermons. But what my
former pastor too often failed to understand is that embarking on a program of
self-help also requires a belief that society can change.

The profound mistake of Reverend Wright's sermons is not that he spoke
about racism in our society. It's that he spoke as if our society was static; as if no
progress has been made; as if this country—a country that has made it possible
for one of his own members to run for the highest office in the land and build a
coalition of white and black, Latino and Asian, rich and poor, young and old—
is still irrevocably bound to a tragic past. But what we know—what we have seen—
is that America can change. That is true genius of this nation. What we have
already achieved gives us hope—the audacity to hope—for what we can and must
achieve tomorrow.

In the white community, the path to a more perfect union ~~~ing that what ails the African-American community does not ~~~minds of black people; that the legacy of discrimination, and curren~~~discrimination, while less overt than in the past, are real and must be a~~~Not just with words, but with deeds—by investing in our schools and ou~~~munities; by enforcing our civil rights laws and ensuring fairness in our crimi~~~justice system; by providing this generation with ladders of opportunity that were unavailable for previous generations. It requires all Americans to realize that your dreams do not have to come at the expense of my dreams; that investing in the health, welfare, and education of black and brown and white children will ultimately help all of America prosper.

In the end, then, what is called for is nothing more, and nothing less, than what all the world's great religions demand—that we do unto others as we would have them do unto us. Let us be our brother's keeper, Scripture tells us.[1] Let us be our sister's keeper. Let us find that common stake we all have in one another, and let our politics reflect that spirit as well.

For we have a choice in this country. We can accept a politics that breeds division, and conflict, and cynicism. We can tackle race only as spectacle—as we did in the O.J. trial[2]—or in the wake of tragedy, as we did in the aftermath of Katrina[3]—or as fodder for the nightly news. We can play Reverend Wright's sermons on every channel, every day and talk about them from now until the election, and make the only question in this campaign whether or not the American people think that I somehow believe or sympathize with his most offensive words. We can pounce on some gaffe by a Hillary[4] supporter as evidence that she's playing the race card, or we can speculate on whether white men will all flock to John McCain[5] in the general election regardless of his policies.

We can do that.

But if we do, I can tell you that in the next election, we'll be talking about some other distraction. And then another one. And then another one. And nothing will change.

That is one option. Or, at this moment, in this election, we can come together and say, "Not this time." This time we want to talk about the crumbling schools

---

1. "Then the Lord said to Cain, 'Where is your brother Abel?' 'I don't know,' he replied. 'Am I my brother's keeper?'" (Genesis 4:9).

2. That is, the 1995 trial of former professional football player O.J. Simpson, charged with murdering his ex-wife, Nicole Simpson, and her companion, Ron Goldman. The racially polarizing proceedings were a national obsession; Simpson was found not guilty in his criminal trial, but was held liable for the murders in a subsequent civil trial.

3. That is, Hurricane Katrina, which devastated New Orleans in 2005.

4. Senator Hillary Clinton, wife of former president Bill Clinton and Obama's chief rival for the Democratic Party presidential nomination in 2008.

5. Arizona senator John McCain (b. 1936) was the presumptive Republican Party nominee for the presidency at the time of Obama's speech.

lack children and white children and Asian children
ative American children. This time we want to reject
these kids can't learn; that those kids who don't look
problem. The children of America are not those kids,
ll not let them fall behind in a twenty-first-century

about how the lines in the emergency room are filled
Hispanics who do not have health care; who don't
to overcome the special interests in Washington, but
do it together.

alk about the shuttered mills that once provided a
decent life for men of every race, and the homes for sale that once
belonged to Americans from every religion, every region, every walk of life. This
time we want to talk about the fact that the real problem is not that someone who
doesn't look like you might take your job; it's that the corporation you work for
will ship it overseas for nothing more than a profit.

This time we want to talk about the men and women of every color and creed
who serve together, and fight together, and bleed together under the same proud
flag. We want to talk about how to bring them home from a war that never should've
been authorized and never should've been waged,[6] and we want to talk about how
we'll show our patriotism by caring for them, and their families, and giving them
the benefits they have earned.

I would not be running for president if I didn't believe with all my heart that
this is what the vast majority of Americans want for this country. This union may
never be perfect, but generation after generation has shown that it can always be
perfected. And today, whenever I find myself feeling doubtful or cynical about
this possibility, what gives me the most hope is the next generation—the young
people whose attitudes and beliefs and openness to change have already made
history in this election.

There is one story in particular that I'd like to leave you with today—a story
I told when I had the great honor of speaking on Dr. King's birthday[7] at his home
church, Ebenezer Baptist, in Atlanta.

There is a young, twenty-three year old white woman named Ashley Baia who
organized for our campaign in Florence, South Carolina. She had been working
to organize a mostly African-American community since the beginning of this
campaign, and one day she was at a round-table discussion where everyone went
around telling their story and why they were there.

6. The 2003 invasion of Iraq was ordered by President George W. Bush in order to rid Iraq of weapons of mass
destruction; following the invasion no such weapons were found. Obama was an early and consistent critic of
President Bush's policies toward Iraq.
7. Beginning in 1986, the third Monday in January has been observed as Martin Luther King Jr. Day by the
federal government; King's actual birth date is January 15, 1929.

And Ashley said that when she was nine years old, her mo[...] because she had to miss days of work, she was let go and lost her h[...] had to file for bankruptcy, and that's when Ashley decided that s[...] something to help her mom.

She knew that food was one of their most expensive costs, and so Ashle[...] vinced her mother that what she really liked and really wanted to eat more th[...] anything else was mustard and relish sandwiches. Because that was the cheapest way to eat.

She did this for a year until her mom got better, and she told everyone at the roundtable that the reason she joined our campaign was so that she could help the millions of other children in the country who want and need to help their parents too.

Now, Ashley might have made a different choice. Perhaps somebody told her along the way that the source of her mother's problems were blacks who were on welfare and too lazy to work, or Hispanics who were coming into the country illegally. But she didn't. She sought out allies in her fight against injustice.

Anyway, Ashley finishes her story and then goes around the room and asks everyone else why they're supporting the campaign. They all have different stories and reasons. Many bring up a specific issue. And finally they come to this elderly black man who's been sitting there quietly the entire time. And Ashley asks him why he's there. And he does not bring up a specific issue. He does not say health care or the economy. He does not say education or the war. He does not say that he was there because of Barack Obama. He simply says to everyone in the room, "I am here because of Ashley."

"I'm here because of Ashley." By itself, that single moment of recognition between that young white girl and that old black man is not enough. It is not enough to give health care to the sick, or jobs to the jobless, or education to our children.

But it is where we start. It is where our union grows stronger. And as so many generations have come to realize over the course of the two-hundred and twenty-one years since a band of patriots signed that document in Philadelphia, that is where the perfection begins.

 her got cancer. And
ealth care. They
e had to do
con-

ha, what was the "profound mistake" that Reverend
s?

lieve race plays in American life? Which Americans
d frustrated, and why?

ha titled this speech "A More Perfect Union"? What
derscore? How does Obama use the story of his own
hemes?

praised by both liberal and conservative commentators. Some have argued that it propelled Obama to victory in both the nomination fight and the general election. Why do you think this speech resonated with so many diverse Americans?